# Pocket Thesaurus

# Pocket Thesaurus

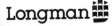
Longman

LONGMAN GROUP LIMITED
Longman House, Burnt Mill, Harlow,
Essex CM20 2JE, England
and Associated Companies throughout the World.

First published 1982
Fifth impression 1985
ISBN 0 582 55545 0

Produced by Longman Group (FE) Ltd
Printed in Hong Kong

# Foreword

This pocket thesaurus has the same format as the famous original Roget's thesaurus and is just as easy to use. To find a synonym or alternative phrase, simply look up the original word in the index. There you will find a number referring to a paragraph in the main text in which common alternatives are listed. Words in **bold** appear in the index and head paragraphs of their own elsewhere in the book. This handy treasure house of words and phrases is the perfect constant companion to ensure that you need never again struggle to find the word you want.

## 1 Existence

**N. existence**, being, entity; absolute being; a being, an entity, essence; Platonic idea, universal; **life**; survival, eternity, **perpetuity**; **priority**; this life, **present time**; **presence**; becoming, evolution; creation, **production**; potentiality, **possibility**; metaphysics; realism, materialism, idealism, existentialism, **philosophy**.

**reality**, actuality; actual existence; **speciality**; positiveness; **truth**; fact, fact of life; **event**; real thing; basics, bedrock, **important matter**.

**essence**, nature, **substance**; inner being, **essential part**; prime constituent, soul, heart, core, centre.

**Adj. existing**, existent; existential; essential, **intrinsic**; absolute, given; being, living, **alive**; prior; **present**; undying, immortal, eternal, **perpetual**; extant, standing, indestructible; rife, prevalent, afloat, afoot, **ubiquitous**; metaphysical.

**real**, essential, **substantial**; actual, positive, factual, **true**; natural, of nature, physical, **material**; concrete, solid, tangible, **dense**.

**Vb. be**, exist, have being; **be true**; **be intrinsic**; **be before**; coexist, coincide, subsist, **be now**; abide, continue; endure, **last**; vegetate; be alive, breathe, live, move, draw breath, **live**; be found, be met with, stand, lie, **be situated**; be here, be there, meet one, **be present**; obtain, prevail, reign, **be rife**, **pervade**; take place, come about, occur, **happen**; hold, hold good, **be true**; represent, **be identical**.

**become**, come to be, take flesh, **be born**; arise, **begin**; unfold, develop, grow, take form, take shape, **evolve**.

**Adv. actually**, really; essentially, substantially, inherently; virtually; **possibly**; positively, **truly**.

## 2 Nonexistence

**N. nonexistence**, non-entity, nothingness; **absence**; blank, vacuum; nothing, nil, **zero**; a nothing, nonentity, **insubstantial thing**; **nobody**; nihilism.

**extinction**, oblivion, nirvana; **death**; decay; nihilism, **destruction**; abeyance, suspension; amnesty, **oblivion**; cancellation, erasure, clean slate.

**Adj. nonexistent**, without being; null, minus; nowhere, missing, **absent**.

**unreal**, without reality, baseless, groundless, unfounded, false, **erroneous**; fictitious, fabulous, visionary, **imaginary**; without substance, intangible, **insubstantial**; undeveloped, **immature**; potential, only possible, **possible**; only supposed.

**unborn**, yet to come, **future**.

**extinct**; defunct, **dead**; obsolescent, **dying**; obsolete; finished, **past**.

**Vb. not be**; lack reality; never happen; be yet unborn.

**pass away**, cease to exist, become extinct; **die**; **perish**; come to nothing, **miscarry**; go, vanish; **disappear**; evaporate; melt, dissolve, **liquefy**.

**nullify**, reduce to nothing, annihilate, extinguish, suspend, **abrogate**; negative, **negate**; cancel, obliterate; abolish, **destroy**.

**Adv. negatively**.

## 3 Substantiality

**N. substantiality**, reality; personality, personal existence; visibility, solidity; weight, **gravity**; stuff, material, **matter**; totality of existence, world, world of nature, **universe**.

**substance**; core, **essential part**; entity, thing, something, somebody, **object**; person, creature; body, living matter, **life**; solid, **solid body**; pith, marrow, meat; gist, **meaning**.

**Adj.** substantial, personal, **intrinsic**, real, objective, natural, phenomenal, physical, **material**; concrete, solid, tangible, palpable, **dense**; considerable, **important**; bulky, **large**; heavy, **weighty**; pithy, meaty, full of substance.

**Adv.** substantially, bodily, physically; personally; really, **actually**; essentially; largely, mainly, **greatly**.

## 4 Insubstantiality

**N.** **insubstantiality**, nothingness; naught, nothing, nothing at all, **zero**; **nobody**; abstraction; lack of substance; **rarity**; lack of depth; vacancy, void; vanity; hallucination; **deception**; fantasy.

**insubstantial thing**, emblem, token, symbol; mind, soul, **spirit**; abstraction; shadow without substance, shadow, shade, ghost, phantom, vision, dream, mirage; **visual fallacy**; air, wind, breath, vapour, mist; bubble, gossamer, snowflake, snowman, **weak thing**; wisp, straw, **trifle**; vain thing, bauble; vanity, **folly**; flight of fancy, pipe dream, **fantasy**; all talk, moonshine; hot air, idle talk, gossip, rumour, **empty talk**; tall talk, **exaggeration**; cry of wolf, **false alarm**; mockery, pretence, **ostentation**; figment, courtesy title; figurehead, man of straw, **nonentity**; pompous ass, **vain person**; fictitious person; pseudonym.

**Adj.** **insubstantial**, abstract, metaphysical, ideal; inessential; **immaterial**; bloodless; lightweight; airy, **light**; thin, tenuous, gossamer, **transparent**; pale, **colourless**; misty; fragile, delicate, brittle, unsound, **flimsy**; **spooky**; fleeting, shadowy, vague, **dim**; vacuous, vacant, hollow, void, **empty**; vain, inane; honorary, nominal,

paper, fictitious; token; without substance, groundless, unfounded; visionary, dreamy, chimerical, **imaginary**; pointless, senseless, **meaningless**; blank, characterless, featureless, null; without depth, superficial, **shallow**.

**Vb.** not be, **nullify**.

**Adv.** unsubstantially.

## 5 Intrinsicality

**N.** **intrinsicality**; potentiality, **ability**; autism; ego, personality, **self**.

**essential part**, important part; prime ingredient, prime constituent, **essence**; principle, property, mark, attribute; virtue, capacity; quintessence, flower; stuff, **substance**; incarnation, embodiment; life, sap; artery; heart, soul, inner man, **spirit**; backbone, marrow, pith, fibre; core, kernel, **centre**; focus, gist, nub, nucleus, **chief thing**.

**character**, nature, quality; make-up, personality, type, make, stamp, breed, **sort**; constitution; cast, colour, hue, complexion; features; diagnosis.

**temperament**, temper, humour, disposition, mood, spirit; grain, vein, streak, strain, trait, **tendency**; foible, habit, peculiarity, **speciality**.

**heredity**; DNA, chromosome, gene; inborn capacity **or** tendency, original sin; ancestry, **genealogy**; **recurrence**; genetics, **biology**.

**Adj.** **intrinsic**, deep-seated, deep-rooted, ingrained; inherent, integral, **component**; inward, internal, **interior**; implicit; indispensable, inseparable, **identical**; subjective, reflexive, introverted; characteristic, personal; indigenous, native; natural; basic, radical, central, organic, **fundamental**; original, primary, elemental, cardinal, normal; essential, constitu-

tional; virtual, potential, capable.
**genetic**, hereditary, heritable; native, inborn, innate, congenital; inbred.
**characteristic**, **special**; qualitative; proper; ineradicable, incurable, invariable; constant.
**Vb. be intrinsic**, belong; be born like it; inherit, take after; be marked with; involve, mean, **imply**.
**Adv. intrinsically**, at bottom, fundamentally, essentially, substantially, virtually; per se.

**6 Extrinsicality**
**N. extrinsicality**; outer space; projection; accidence; accident, contingency, **chance**; accessory, **adjunct**.
**Adj. extrinsic**, alien, foreign, **extraneous**; transcendent, **superior**; outward, external, extramural, **exterior**; inbred, accessory, adventitious; **additional**; incidental, accidental, contingent, fortuitous, **casual**; inessential; subsidiary, subordinate, **inferior**.
**Vb. be extrinsic**, lie without; transcend, **be superior**; supervene, **accrue**.
**make extrinsic**, project; body forth, **represent**.
**Adv. extrinsically**, outwardly.

**7 State: absolute condition**
**N. state**, modal existence, state of being, condition; estate, lot, walk, walk of life; case, way, plight, pickle, **circumstance**; position, category, status, footing, standing, rank; habit, disposition, complexion, **temperament**; attitude, frame of mind, vein, temper, mood; state of mind, spirits, morale; state of health, physical condition; trim, fettle, fig.
**modality**, mode, manner, fashion, style; stamp, set, fit, mould, **form**; shape, frame, fabric, **structure**; aspect,

phase, light, complexion, character, guise, **appearance**; tenor, tone, **tendency**.
**Adj. such**; modal, conditional, formal, **formative**; organic.
**Vb. be in a state of**, be such, be so; stand, lie; do, fare.
**Adv. conditionally**, it being so.

**8 Circumstance: relative condition**
**N. circumstance**, situation, circumstances, conditions; total situation, personal world, life space; environment, milieu, **surroundings**; context, **relation**; how things stand; set-up, **state**; posture, attitude; aspect, look of things, appearances, **appearance**; **situation**; sphere, background, footing, standing, status, relative position, **serial place**; awkward situation, plight, pickle, pass, pinch, corner, hole, jam, dilemma, **predicament**.
**juncture**, stage, point, **event**; contingency, eventuality; crossroads, turning point, match point; moment, hour, right time, opportunity, **occasion**; critical moment, hour of decision, emergency, exigency, **crisis**.
**Adj. circumstantial**, given, modal, **such**; situated, placed; provisional, temporary, **transient**; variable; relative, contingent, incidental, adventitious, **eventual**; emergent, critical, crucial; auspicious, favourable, **opportune**; suitable, seemly; appropriate, convenient, **advisable**.
**Adv. thus**, so; like this.
**accordingly**.
**if**, if so be, should it so happen, should it be that; provided that; taking it that; unless, except, without.

## 9 Relation

N. **relation**, rapport, reference, respect, regard; bearing, direction; concern, interest, import; implication; **attraction**; relationship, affinity; kinship, **consanguinity**; classification, **arrangement**; affiliation, alliance, **association**; relations, friendly terms, **friendship**; link, tie-up, **bond**; commercial relations, **business**; common reference, common source, common denominator; ecology; context, milieu, environment, **circumstance**; import, intention, **meaning**.

**relativeness**, relativity, mutual relation; same relation, **identity**, **equality**; similar relation, analogy, **similarity**; **comparison**; close relation, apposition, approximation, **approach**, **accompaniment**; parallel relation, **symmetry**; perspective, proportion, ratio; scale; causal relation, **cause**; dependence; **effect**; **influence**; subordinate relation; relative position, stage, status, rank, **degree**; serial order, **sequence**.

**relevance**, **reasoning**; chain of reasoning; just relation, due proportion; point, application, propriety, **fitness**; good example, **example**.

**referral**, making reference, reference, application, allusion, mention; citation, quotation; frame of reference, object of reference; referee.

Adj. **relative**, **circumstantial**; respective; related; concerning; of concern, of interest, of import, **important**; mutual, reciprocal, corresponding; serial, consecutive; congenial, cognate, kindred, **akin**; like, **similar**; comparative, comparable; **near**; collateral, **parallel**; proportional, proportionate, to scale; commensurate.

**relevant**, apposite, pertinent, applicable; pointed, **rational**; proper, appropriate, suitable, fitting, **apt**; quotable.

Vb. **be related**, have a relationship; have reference to, regard, respect, have to do with; be a factor, **influence**; touch, concern, deal with, interest, affect; be a relation, **be akin**; belong; approximate to, **approach**; answer to, correspond, reciprocate; be congruent, **accord**; be proportionate; be relevant, have some point, support an analogy.

**relate**; connect with, gear to, gear with; apply; link, connect, bracket together, entwine, **tie**; provide a background; compare; proportion, parallel; balance; draw a parallel, find an example, **reason**; make a reference to, mention; index, **indicate**.

Adv. **relatively**; comparatively; to scale.

**concerning**, regarding; with regard to, with respect to; relative to, with reference to, about, re; apropos; whereas; concerning which.

## 10 Unrelatedness: absence of relation

N. **unrelatedness**; **freedom**; **separation**; individuality, **speciality**; **disorder**; wrong association, **error**; disproportion; disparity, **inequality**; diversity, **difference**; **nonconformity**; **misfit**; exotic, alien element.

**irrelevance**; bad example; parenthesis, **interjection**; red herring, **deviation**; episode, incidental **event**; inessential.

Adj. **unrelated**, absolute; independent; **original**; regardless, unilateral, arbitrary; unidentified; rootless; adrift, wandering, astray; insular, **alone**; unconcerned, **indifferent**; detached, without context, disconnected; incidental, **discontinuous**; separate, singular, individual, **special**; private, without interest, nothing to do with; inessential, **extrinsic**; exotic, foreign, alien, strange, outlandish, **extraneous**; intrusive, untimely, **ill-timed**; inappropriate, incompatible; incommensurable, disparate, **unequal**; disproportionate; irreconcilable, **contrary**; heterogeneous; multifarious, **multiform**.

irrelevant, illogical; inapplicable, pointless; impertinent, inept; **erroneous**; peripheral; rambling, wandering, **diffuse**; adrift, neither here nor there; trivial, inessential; inconsequential; incidental, **casual**; remote, far-fetched, forced, strained; academic, impractical, immaterial.

**Vb. be unrelated**; owe nothing to, disown; be irrelevant, draw a red herring; force, strain; ramble, wander, **be diffuse**.

**Adv. unrelatedly**, regardless; without regard, without respect, without reference, without relation to; incidentally.

## 11 Consanguinity: relations of kindred

**N. consanguinity**, kinship, kindred, blood, **parentage**; affiliation, relationship, affinity, propinquity; blood relationship; ancestry, lineage, descent, **genealogy**; alliance, family; tribalism, nationality; nation; nepotism; **heredity**.

kinsman, kin, kindred, kinsfolk, relations; near relative, next of kin; distant relation; father, mother, **parentage**; offspring, issue, **posterity**; cognate, collateral; twin, sibling; sister, brother, brother or sister german, stepbrother; cousin, cousin german; uncle, aunt; nephew, niece; clansman, tribesman, compatriot.

family, matriarchy, patriarchy; motherhood, fatherhood, brotherhood; fraternity; foster child, godchild, step-

child, in-laws; family circle; household, **home**; nuclear family, tribe, horde.

race, stock, stem, breed, strain, line, side, house, tribe, clan; ethnic group; nation, people; nationalism, racialism, **prejudice**; inbreeding.

**Adj. akin**, kindred, kin; matrilineal; patrilineal; maternal, paternal; sibling, fraternal, sisterly; avuncular; related, family, collateral, allied; cognate, german; near, related, **relative**; step-.

ethnic, clannish **national**; interracial; inbred, **mixed**.

**Vb. be akin**; **be related; wed**; father, sire, **generate**; be brother or sister to, brother, sister; affiliate, adopt, foster.

## 12 Correlation: double or reciprocal relation

**N. correlation**, mutual relation, **relation**; proportion, **symmetry**; texture, design, pattern, **arrangement**; grid, **network; similarity**; opposite number, **identity**; mutual dependence; interplay, mutual influence; seesaw; **interchange**; each, each other, one another; **compromise**; exchange, change, **barter**.

**Adj. correlative**, reciprocal, functional, **relative**; corresponding, opposite, parallel, **similar**; proportional, proportionate; complementary, interdependent; mutual; alternate, seesaw; **equivalent**; woven; interchangeable; interracial, international; two-way, bilateral.

**Vb. correlate**, interrelate, interlock, interplay, interact; be a function of; proportion; correspond, answer to, reflect, **resemble**; react, recoil; alternate, **oscillate; interchange**; reciprocate, **retaliate**; exchange, barter, trade; balance; **compensate**.

**Adv. correlatively**, each to each, each other, one another; **equally**; contrariwise; between.

## 13 Identity

**N. identity**, sameness, **unity**; it, absolutely it; ditto, tautology, **repetition**; other self, alter ego, ba, genius, double; identification, coincidence, **agreement**; absorption, **reception**; **equality**; distinction without a difference, indistinguishability; **meaning**; same kind; invariant, constant, **fixture**; counterpart, duplicate, **copy**; fellow, pair, match, twin, **analogue**; synonym, **word**.

**Adj. identical**, same, self, selfsame, of that ilk; **one**; indistinguishable, interchangeable, unisex, convertible, equivalent, **equal**; coincident, congruent; invariable, invariant, constant; monotonous, **tedious**; homogeneous, monolithic, **uniform**.

**Vb. be identical**, ditto, **repeat**; coincide, coalesce, merge, be one with; be congruent, register, **accord**; phase.

**identify**, unify; equate; assimilate, match, pair.

**Adv. identically**, without distinction; ibidem; ditto; same here.

## 14 Contrariety

**N. contrariety**, absolute difference, **difference**; antipathy, repugnance, hostility, **hatred**; antagonism, **opposition**; antidote; conflict, clash, **collision**; discord; contrast, relief, variation, undertone, counterpoint; antonym, **meaning**; paradox; antithesis, direct opposite, antipodes, opposite pole; other extreme; other side; reverse, wrong side, **rear**; inverse; converse, reverse image, mirror, mirror symmetry, **reflection**; opposite direction, headwind, undertow.

**polarity**.

**Adj. contrary**, anything but, **different**; incompatible; inconsistent; ambivalent, bittersweet; **negative**; diametrically opposite, **opposite**; reverse, converse, inverse, inimical, hostile; adverse, untoward; counter-.

**Vb. be contrary**, **differ**; contrast, **disagree**; clash, conflict with; run counter to, **be opposite**; **be equivocal**; contravene, **oppose**, **disobey**; exclude, deny, contradict, negate; **counteract**; **invert**.

**Adv. contrarily**, contrariwise; topsyturvy; otherwise.

## 15 Difference

**N. difference**; disparity, odds, **inequality**; margin, differential, minus, plus, **remainder**; wide margin, **distance**; narrow margin; variety, diversity; **deviation**; discrepancy; antipathy, **dislike**; disharmony, discord, **dissension**; contrast; opposite, antithesis, variation, alteration, **change**.

**differentiation**, **discrimination**; specification, **speciality**; distinction, nuance, nicety, shade of difference, fine shade of meaning, **meaning**; distinction without a difference, **identity**; conjugation, declension, **grammar**.

**variant**, different thing, something else; this; quite another matter, different kettle of fish; another story, another version, horse of another colour; special case, **speciality**; freak, sport, **nonconformist**; new version, new edition, **edition**.

**Adj. different**, unlike, **dissimilar**; original, fresh, **new**; various, variform, diverse, heterogeneous; multifarious, **multiform**; assorted, all manner of, divers, **mixed**; distinct, distinguished, **separate**; odd, **unusual**; incongruous;

disparate, **unequal**; wide apart, anything but, **contrary**; other, another, peculiar, **special**; **superior**, **inferior**; somehow different.

**distinctive**, **characteristic**; comparative, superlative.

**Vb. differ**, show variety; **deviate**; contrast, clash, jar, conflict, **disagree**; **quarrel**; modify, vary, **change**.

**differentiate**, distinguish, **discriminate**; shade, refine, make a distinction, **specify**; **set apart**.

**Adv. differently**, variously, after alteration; otherwise, some other way, with a difference.

## 16 Uniformity

**N. uniformity**, consistency, constancy, **stability**; **continuity**; order, method, **order**; **similarity**; monolithic quality; unity, unison, accordance, **agreement**; **symmetry**, sameness, **identity**; even tenor; same old story; even pace, jog trot, rhythm; **round**, routine, drill, treadmill, **habit**; monotone; drone, sing-song, monologue; monolith; pattern, mould; **type**, stereotype, **copy**; stamp, same mint; set, assortment; suit, flush; standard dress, **uniform**; mass production, **conformity**; **repetition**; closed shop, **compulsion**.

**uniformist**, sergeant major; equalitarian, egalitarian.

**Adj. uniform**, all of a piece, one-piece; same all through, solid, monolithic; of one kind; homogeneous, of a piece, of a pattern, **similar**; same, consistent, constant, steady, stable, **fixed**; invariable, **permanent**; equable; measured, **smooth**; unrelieved, **plain**; without contrast, lacking variety; characterless, featureless, faceless, blank; monotonous, sing-song, monotone; monochrome, drab, grey; running through; standard, normal, **typical**; unisex;

assorted; **orderly**, regular; straight, even, flush, level, **flat**.

**Vb. be uniform**, follow routine, **be wont**; chorus, **accord**; typify, **conform**; dress; wear uniform.

**make uniform**, stamp, run through, **mark**; level; assimilate; size, grade; drill; regiment; stereotype, pattern; mass-produce; **make conform**.

**Adv. uniformly**, like clockwork; without exception.

## 17 Nonuniformity

**N. nonuniformity**, variability; **caprice**; irregularity, **disorder**; roughness; **difference**; contrast; **deviation**; diversity, variety; mixed bag, lucky dip, **medley**; patchwork, motley, crazy paving, mosaic; exception, special case, sport, mutation, **nonconformity**; lone wolf, rogue elephant; individuality, **speciality**.

**Adj. nonuniform**, variable, changeable; spasmodic, sporadic, **fitful**; inconstant, inconsistent, **capricious**; temperamental, **excitable**; patchy, **unequal**; random, irregular; **amorphous**; uneven, bumpy, lumpy, choppy, jerky, **rough**; erratic; **contrary**; heterogeneous, various, diverse, **different**, **dissimilar**; multifarious, miscellaneous, **multiform**; aberrant, atypical; exceptional, unusual, **abnormal**; unique, lone, **special**; individual, hand-made.

**Adv. nonuniformly**; all anyhow; here, there and everywhere.

## 18 Similarity

**N. similarity**, resemblance, likeness; semblance, seeming, look, **appearance**; fashion, style, **form**; common feature, point of resemblance, **relation**; **agreement**; affinity, kinship, **consanguinity**; analogy, parity, **equal-**

ity; **symmetry**; **identity**; general resemblance, family likeness; close resemblance, good likeness, striking likeness, **representation**; approximation; partial likeness, faint resemblance; suggestion, hint; fair comparison, sufficient resemblance.

**assimilation**, **comparison**; reduction to, identification, **identity**; simulation, camouflage, mimicry; parable, allegory; **description**; **picture**; alliteration, assonance, rhyme, **prosody**; pun.

**analogue**, suchlike; type, good example, **example**; simile, parallel, metaphor; equivalent, **substitute**; brother, sister, twin; match, fellow, mate, companion; complement, counterpart, other half; alter ego, other self, genius, ba; fetch; double; likeness, reflection, shadow, **image**; another edition of, dead spit of, living image; couple, pair; two of a kind; reproduction, copy, clone, **duplicate**.

**Adj. similar**, like, alike, twin, matching; much of a muchness, nothing to choose between, **identical**; of a piece, **uniform**; parallel, **equivalent**, corresponding; homogeneous, **akin**; close, approximate, **near**; typical, representative; something like; **equivocal**.

**lifelike**, realistic, exact, faithful, natural, typical; good of one, true to life, true to nature, true to type; graphic, vivid, **visible**.

**simulating**; seeming, deceptive, mock, **spurious**; making a show of; synthetic, artificial, ersatz.

**Vb. resemble**, be similar to, bear a resemblance; mirror, reflect, **imitate**; seem, seem like; look like, take after; savour of, smack of; compare with, approximate to, come near to, **approach**; match, correspond to, answer to, **accord**; rhyme; typify, represent.

**liken**, assimilate to, approximate, **compare**; reduce to, **identify**; pair, twin, bracket with; use a simile; portray, **imitate**; rhyme, **repeat**; pun, be **equivocal**.

**Adv. similarly**, like, so to speak; likewise, so; like father like son.

# 19 Dissimilarity

**N. dissimilarity**; disparity, **inequality**; diversity, **difference**; variation, variety; contrast; novelty; camouflage, make-up, **disguise**; caricature, bad likeness; foreign body, alien element; **misfit**.

**Adj. dissimilar**, unlike, distinct, diverse, **different**; various, **multiform**; disparate, **unequal**; far above, **superior**; far below, **inferior**; unmatched; unique, peerless, original, **inimitable**; atypical, exotic; unprecedented, novel, **new**; **distant**

**Vb. be unlike**, differ; be superior, be **inferior**.

**make unlike**, discriminate, distinguish, **differentiate**; innovate, modify, modulate, **change**, **convert**; caricature, **misrepresent**, **distort**; dissemble, **deceive**; disguise, **conceal**; camouflage, **fake**.

**Adv. dissimilarly**, variously.

# 20 Imitation

**N. imitation**; **conformity**; following; **affectation**; **representation**; reflection, mirror, echo, shadow; paraphrase, translation; **interpretation**; literary theft; forgery, counterfeit, fake, **falsehood**; tracing, **copy**; multiplication, **reproduction**, **photography**.

**mimicry**, **representation**; onomatopoeia; mime, pantomime, sign language, **gesture**; ventriloquism, **speech**; **painting**, **description**; realism; mockery, caricature, parody, spoof, burlesque, **satire**; travesty; **repetition, affectation**; simulator, simulation exercise, **teaching**; simulation, semblance, disguise, protective colouring, camouflage, **similarity**; pretence, mockery, pale shadow, **sham**.

**imitator**, copycat, ape, monkey; mockingbird, parrot, echo; sheep, **follower**; yes-man; **humorist**; mime, mimic, drag artiste, illusionist, **entertainer**; actor, **artist**; printer; naturalist; simulator, hypocrite, **impostor**; forger; duplicator, copier, stencil.

**Adj. imitative**, mimetic; apish; following; **affected**; mock, mimic; sham, counterfeit, **false**; ersatz, synthetic; hackneyed, **usual**; derivative, secondhand; conventional; slavish, literal; burlesque; easy to copy.

**Vb. imitate**, ape, parrot, flatter, echo, mirror, reflect, **resemble**; make a show of, pose, **be affected**; pretend, masquerade, make-believe; act, mimic, mime, portray, paint, **represent**; parody, caricature, burlesque, travesty, **ridicule**; sham, simulate, feign, **dissemble**; disguise, camouflage, **conceal**; **deceive**.

**copy**, draw, trace; copy faithfully, catch; **print**; reprint, duplicate, photocopy; reduplicate, multiply, **reproduce**; transcribe, transliterate, type; paraphrase, translate, **interpret**; crib, borrow, **steal**; counterfeit, forge, **fake**.

**do likewise**; follow, follow suit, follow my leader, **follow**; echo, ditto, chorus, **repeat**; follow precedent, **conform**; emulate, rival, **contend**.

**Adv. imitatively**; verbatim, **truly**.

## 21 Originality

**N. originality, imagination**; creation, invention, all my own work, **production**; **priority**; **unity**; defiance of precedent, **freedom**; precedent, example, **prototype**; **beginning**; something new, novelty, innovation; individuality, **nonconformity**.

**no imitation**; real thing; it, absolutely it, **identity, self**; autograph, manuscript, usual signature.

**Adj. original**, creative, inventive, **imaginative**; primordial, primary; first, first-hand, **prior**; unprecedented, fresh, novel, **new**; individual, personal, **special**; independent, **free**; eccentric.

**inimitable**, transcendent, unmatched, incomparable, **superior**; atypical, **different**; unique, **one**; authentic, real, true, **genuine**; natural, **intrinsic**; sincere, unadulterated.

## 22 Copy

**N. copy**, clone, **reproduction**; replica, facsimile, tracing; fair copy, transcript, counterpart, **analogue**; cast, death mask; stamp, seal, impress, impression, imprint; mechanical copy, stereotype, lithograph, print, offprint, **engraving**; photocopy, photograph, positive, negative, contact print, **photography**; microfilm, **record**; dummy, pastiche; forgery, counterfeit, fake, **sham**; crib; a likeness, resemblance, semblance, **similarity**; study, portrait, drawing, **picture**; image, **representation**; model, effigy, statue, **sculpture**; faithful copy, reflex, echo, mirror, **repetition, reflection**; bad copy, mockery of; malicious copy, caricature, cartoon, travesty, parody, **ridicule**; hint, shadow; silhouette, outline, sketch, diagram, first copy, draft; paraphrase, **translation**.

**duplicate**, flimsy, carbon copy, carbon; stencil, master copy; transfer, rubbing; photograph, **photography**;

reprint, **edition**; model, specimen, **example**.

**23 Prototype**

**N. prototype**, archetype; type, common type, norm, **average**; primitive form, protoplasm, **organism**; original, **origin**; first occurrence, precedent, test case, **priority**; guide, rule, maxim, **precept**; standard, criterion, touchstone, standard of comparison, frame of reference; ideal, **perfection**; cynosure, **paragon**; keynote, metronome, **gauge**; module, unit; specimen, sample, **example**; model, subject; pattern; dummy, mock-up; copybook, copy, text, manuscript; blueprint, design, master plan, scheme, **plan**; rough plan, outline, draft, sketch.

**living model**, model, poser, sitter, subject; fashion model, mannequin; stroke, pacemaker; conductor, drum major, **leader**.

**mould**, matrix, mint; plate, shell; stencil, negative; frame, **form**; wax figure; last; die, stamp, punch, seal, intaglio, **printing**.

**Adj. prototypal**, exemplary, model, standard, classic, copybook.

**Vb. be an example**, model, pose.

**24 Agreement**

**N. agreement**; consent; **assent**; accord, accordance, chorus, unison; harmony, **melody**; consonance, concordance; concert, understanding, mutual understanding, entente; concordat, convention, pact, **compact**; unity, solidarity, **consensus**; consortium; union, **combination**; peace, **concord**.

**conformance, conformity**; coincidence, **identity**; consistency; coherence, consequence, logic, **reasoning**; similarity.

**fitness**, qualification, capability, apti-

tude; propriety, **good policy**; perfect candidate, **identity**; good example; proportion, **relation**; right moment, fit occasion, **occasion**.

**adaptation**, matching; reconciliation; accommodation, **compromise**; **arrangement**; fitting, good fit.

**Adj. agreeing**, right; corresponding, correspondent; proportional, proportionate, commensurate; coincident, congruent, **equal**; of a piece with, consistent, **uniform**; consonant; matching, **similar**; becoming, **tasteful**; natural, congenial, **sympathetic**; compatible; agreeable, acquiescent; concurrent, at one, unanimous; united, concerted; of like mind, bipartisan; **contractual**.

**apt**, applicable, admissible, germane, appropriate, pertinent, pointed, **relevant**; pat, apropos; right, happy, felicitous, idiomatic, **elegant**; at home; seasonable, opportune, **timely**.

**fit**, fitting, seemly, decorous; adaptable; capable, qualified, **skilful**; suitable, **advisable**; meet, proper, **right**.

**adjusted, orderly, accurate**; strung, **musical**; balanced, **equal**; fitting, tight; made to measure, tailor-made, snug, comfortable.

**Vb. accord**, agree, concur, **assent, consent**; respond, echo, chorus, ditto, **repeat**; coincide, square with, dovetail, **join**; fit, fit like a glove; tally, correspond, match, **resemble**; go with; come naturally to; take to like a duck to water; belong, feel at home; answer, do, meet, suit, **be expedient**; fall pat, come apropos, prove timely; befit; keep together; be consistent, hang together, **be reasonable**; seek accord, treat, negotiate, come to terms, **make terms; befriend**; be natural, behave naturally, be oneself.

**adjust, rectify**; readjust, repair, **restore**;

fit, suit, adapt, accommodate, conform; tune, pitch, string; modulate; regulate, **order**; graduate, proportion; dress, **arrange**; balance; cut, trim, **compensate**; tailor, make to measure; concert; focus.

Adv. pertinently, apropos of.

## 25 Disagreement

N. disagreement; failure to agree, agreement to disagree, **dissent**; conflict of opinion, controversy, **argument**; wrangle, **quarrel**; disunity, faction, **dissension**; schism; clash, **collision**; challenge, defiance, rupture, breach, **war**; discrepancy, **difference**; variety; opposition, conflict; dissonance, disharmony, **discord**; disparity, **inequality**; disproportion; hostility, **enmity**. inaptitude; **bad taste**; **nonconformity**.

misfit, bad fit; bad match, misalliance; **marriage**; paradox; false note, jar, **discord**; outsider, foreigner, foreign body; dissident, dissenter, **nonconformist**; joker, freak, sport; eccentric, oddity, **laughingstock**; **fool**; **sham**.

Adj. disagreeing; challenging, **defiant**; at odds; at loggerheads, at war; hostile, **inimical**; **contrary**; unnatural, inconsistent; incompatible; odd, foreign, **extraneous**; incommensurable; disproportionate; inharmonious, grating; ill-assorted **different**; incongruous, **absurd**.

unapt, incapable, incompetent; inept, maladjusted, **clumsy**; wrong, unfortunate, improper, undue, inappropriate, **inexpedient**; impracticable, **impossible**; ineligible; intrusive, ill-timed, **inopportune**; malapropos, inapplicable, inadmissible, **irrelevant**; **inelegant**.

Vb. disagree, **dissent**; differ, dispute, argue; quarrel; bicker; clash, conflict, collide, contradict, be **contrary**; vary,

diverge, **differ**; be **obstructive**; have nothing to do with; come amiss, interfere, intrude; be incongruous, strike a false note, jar.

mismatch, misfit, fit badly; miscast, misplace, mistime.

Adv. in defiance of, despite.

## 26 Quantity

N. quantity, amount, sum, **addition**; total, **whole**; magnitude, amplitude, extent, **measurement**; mass, substance, body, bulk, **size**; dimension, dimensions, longitude, **length**; width, thickness, **breadth**; altitude, **height**; depth; area, volume, extension, **space**; weight, **gravity**; strength, force, flow, potential, pressure, tension, stress, strain, torque, **energy**; numbers, **multitude**; quotient, fraction, multiple, function, vector, **number**, **mathematics**, **fraction**, zero, **infinity**; mean, median, **average**.

finite quantity, matter of, limited amount, definite figure; lower limit, ceiling, **limit**; definite amount, quantum, quota, quorum; measured quantity, measure, dose, **measurement**; avoirdupois; ration, whack, **portion**; pittance, driblet, spoonful; bagful; whole amount, lot, batch; load, **contents**; lock, **whole**; large amount, masses, **great quantity**; small amount, bit, **small quantity**; greater amount, more, most, majority, **increase**, **greater number**; less, **decrease**; stint, piece, task, **labour**.

Adj. quantitative, some, certain, any, more or less; so many, so much; measured.

Vb. quantify; allot, rate, ration, **apportion**.

Adv. to the amount of; to such an extent.

**27 Degree: relative quantity**

N. **degree**, relative quantity, proportion, ratio, scale, **comparison**; ration, stint, **portion**, **part**; amplitude, extent, frequency, magnitude, size, **quantity**; level, pitch, altitude, **height**, **depth**; key, register, **musical note**; reach, compass, scope, **range**; rate, tenor, way, speed, **motion**; gradation, graduation; differential, shade, nuance; grade, remove, stepping-stone; step, rung, tread, stair, **ascent**; point, stage, milestone, turning point, crisis, **juncture**; mark, peg, notch, score, **indicator**; bar, line, interval, **notation**; value, **measurement**; ranking, **classification**; class, kind, **sort**; standard, rank, grade, **serial place**; military rank, majority; **church office**; hierarchy, **authority**; sphere, station, status, standing, footing, **circumstance**.

Adj. **gradational**, scalar; gradual.

**comparative**, relative, proportional, **relative**; **limited**.

Vb. **graduate**, rate, class, rank, **grade**; scale, calibrate; compare, measure.

**shade off**, taper, dissolve, fade; augment; **abate**; pare, trim, **shorten**.

Adv. **by degrees**; to some extent, just a bit; however little, however much.


**28 Equality: sameness of quantity or degree**

N. **equality**, same quantity, same degree; parity, coincidence, **agreement**; symmetry, balance, poise; level; **justice**.

**equivalence**, likeness, similarity; sameness, **identity**; equation; **interchange**; synonym; exchange, **barter**; par, quits; equivalent, value, just price; **price**; level bet, even money.

**equilibrium**, equipoise, stable equilibrium, balance, poise; even keel; state of equilibrium, balance of forces, balance of nature, balance of power, balance of trade; deadlock, stalemate, **stop**; stable state; **stability**; seat; fin, aileron; balance; **acrobat**, **athlete**.

**equalization**, equation; coordination, **restoration**; equal division, going halves; **interchange**; **offset**; equator; return match, second chance.

**draw**, drawn game, drawn battle; tie, dead heat; stalemate, deadlock; photo finish; love all, deuce; near thing, narrow margin, **short distance**.

**compeer**, peer, equal, match, mate, twin; fellow, brother, **analogue**; equivalent, parallel, opposite number, counterpart, shadow; rival, competitor, **contender**.

Adj. **equal**; same, identical; like, **similar**; neither more nor less, coordinate, coincident, congruent; equidistant; balanced, poised; steady, stable, **fixed**; even, level, round, square, flush, **smooth**; equilateral, regular, uniform, equable, monotonous; rival; dingdong, Greek meeting Greek, drawn; parallel, running level, abreast; fifty-fifty; impartial, democratic, equitable, **just**; par, quits.

**equivalent**, comparable, parallel, interchangeable, virtual, convertible; corresponding, reciprocal; tantamount, indistinguishable; all one, **similar**; worth

Vb. **be equal**, equal, compensate; add nothing, coincide with, **accord**; be equal to, reach, touch; cope with, **be able**; pass muster, **suffice**; run abreast, be level; parallel, **be parallel**; match, twin, **resemble**; tie, draw; break even; make it all square; go halves, go shares, **participate**.

**equalize**, equate; bracket; match; parallel, **compare**; balance, poise; trim, dress, square, make flush, level, smooth, **make uniform**; fit, accommodate, readjust, **adjust**; give points to, handicap, **compensate**; restore to equilibrium; right oneself.

Adv. **equally**.

## 29 Inequality: difference of quantity or degree

N. **inequality**, difference of degree; irregularity, variability; **roughness**; disproportion; disparity, **difference**; unstable equilibrium, imbalance, unbalance; overweight, **gravity**; underweight, short weight; defect, shortcoming; odds, **difference**; offset; bonus, **extra**; casting vote; partiality, discrimination, **bias**, **injustice**.

Adj. **unequal**, disparate, **different**, **dissimilar**; unique, unequalled, at an advantage, **superior**, **excellent**; at a disadvantage, below par, **inferior**; disproportionate; irregular, scalene, lopsided; askew, awry, **oblique**; odd, uneven; variable, patchy, **variegated**; deficient, inadequate, **insufficient**; underweight, **light**; overweight, **weighty**; swinging, **unstable**; topheavy, unwieldy, **clumsy**, leaning, **oblique**; dizzy; partial.

Vb. **be unequal**, disagree; leave a remainder, **differ**; fall short, **be inferior**; preponderate, give points to, outclass, **be superior**; outstrip, **outdo**; be deficient; overweight, **weigh**; be underweight, **be light**; unbalance; overbalance, capsize; list, tilt, lean, **be oblique**; rock, swing, sway, **fluctuate**, vary, **change**.

Adv. **unevenly**.

## 30 Mean

N. **average**, medium, mean, median; middle term, **serial place**; balance; happy medium, golden mean, **moderation**; standard product, **generality**; ruck, ordinary run; norm, par; **habit**.

**middle point**, middle distance, half way, **middle**; middle years, **middle age**; middle class; midway, middle course, **middle way**; **compromise**; central position, **centre**.

**common man**, **commoner**; typical individual, average specimen.

Adj. **median**, mean, average, medial, **middle**, **central**; neither hot nor cold, lukewarm; intermediate, grey; normal, standard, par, ordinary, commonplace, run-of-the-mill, mediocre, **middling**; moderate, **neutral**; middle class, middle brow.

Vb. **average out**, average; go halfway, **compromise**; strike a balance.

Adv. **on an average**, **generally**; taking one thing with another, taking all things together.

## 31 Compensation

N. **compensation**, weighting; rectification, **amendment**; reaction; commutation, **interchange**; redemption, recovery; **acquisition**; reparation, redress, **restitution**, **restoration**; amends; recompense, **reward**, **revenge**.

**offset**, allowance, balance, weighting, ballast; indemnity, reparations, damages, **restitution**; refund; amends, penance; equivalent, **substitute**; **interchange**; cover, collateral, hostage, **security**; **requirement**; **defence**; **attraction**; concession, **compromise**; bribe, hush money, tribute, **payment**, **reward**.

Adj. **compensatory**, **equivalent**.

Vb. **compensate**, make amends, do penance, **atone**; indemnify, restore, pay back; make good, do instead, **substitute**; ballast; pay, repay, **restitute**; bribe, square, **reward**; reimburse, pay overtime, **pay**; redeem, outweigh.

**set off**, offset; balance; cancel, nullify, **counteract**; cover, hedge, **be cautious**;

concede, cede, **compromise**.

**recoup**, recover, **retrieve**; indemnify oneself, take back, get back, **take**; make a comeback.

**Adv. in return**; though, although; nevertheless, regardless of; despite, notwithstanding; but, still, even so; after all; taking one thing with another; at least, at any rate.

## 32 Greatness

**N. greatness**, girth, **size**: large scale, generous proportions, outsize dimensions; muchness, abundance, **plenty**; amplitude, maximum; superabundance, more than enough; excess, **exaggeration**; enormity, **infinity**; **multitude**; dimensions, magnitude, **quantity**, degree; extension, extent, **length**, **breadth**, **height**, **depth**; expanse, area, volume, capacity, **space**; **room**; might, strength, **power**, **influence**; magnification, multiplication; **increase**; significance; eminence, grandeur, **nobility**, **pride**; majesty, **authority**; fame, renown, **repute**, **prestige**; noise, din.

**great quantity**, muchness, galore, **plenty**; crop, harvest, profusion, abundance, productivity; superabundance, shower, flood, spate, torrent; **stream**; expanse, sheet, lake, sea, ocean, world, universe, sight of, world of, power of; much, lot, whole, fat, deal; too much; stock, mint, mine, **store**; quantity, peck, bushel; lump, heap, mass, stack, mountain, **accumulation**; packet of, pack of, load of, cargo, **contents**; lashings, oodles, bags; masses; volumes; numbers, masses, **multitude**; all, entirety, **whole**.

**main part**, almost all, principal part, **chief part**; greater part, majority, **greater number**; body, bulk, mass, substance; soul, **essence**.

**Adj. great**, greater, main, most, major, **superior**; maximum, **supreme**; grand, big, **large**; pretty big; substantial, considerable, respectable; of size, bulky, massive, heavy, **weighty**; prolonged, lengthy, **long**; wide, thick, **broad**; swollen; ample, generous, voluminous, capacious, **spacious**; profound, **deep**; tall, lofty, **high**; Herculean, **strong**, mighty, **powerful**; intense, violent, **vigorous**; noisy, **loud**; at its height, **topmost**; abundant; **redundant**; many, teeming, **multitudinous**; antique, ancient, venerable, immemorial, **olden**; imperial, august, precious, of value, **valuable**, **noble**; sublime, exalted, **impressive**; glorious, famous, grave, solemn, serious, **important**; excellent, **best**.

**extensive**, far-flung, **spacious**; widespread, prevalent, epidemic; worldwide, universal, cosmic; mass, indiscriminate, wholesale, full-scale, sweeping, comprehensive, **inclusive**.

**enormous**, immense, vast, colossal, giant, gigantic, monumental, **huge**; towering, sky-high, **high**; record.

**prodigious**, marvellous, amazing, **wonderful**; fantastic, fabulous, incredible, unbelievable, passing belief, **improbable**, **impossible**; stupendous, tremendous, **terrific**; dreadful, frightful, breathtaking, **impressive**.

**remarkable**, signal, noticeable, **noteworthy**; outstanding, extraordinary, exceptional, **unusual**; eminent, distinguished, marked, of mark, **notable**.

**whopping**, whacking, thumping, thundering, howling; hefty, husky, hulking, strapping, overgrown, clumsy, **unwieldy**.

**flagrant**, glaring, stark, staring; signal, shocking, **discreditable**.

**unspeakable**, unutterable, indescribable, ineffable; beyond expression, **inex-**

**pressible**.

**exorbitant**, extortionate, harsh, stringent, severe; **excessive**, passing, extreme, utmost; monstrous, outrageous, swingeing, unconscionable, unbearable, **intolerable**; inordinate, unwarranted, preposterous, extravagant, astronomical; going too far.

**consummate**, **complete**; finished, **perfect**; entire, sound, **whole**; thorough, thoroughgoing; utter, total, arch, crass, gross, arrant, rank, regular, downright, desperate, unmitigated; far gone.

**absolute**; essential, positive, unequivocal; stark, pure, sheer, mere; **infinite**, unabated.

**Vb. be great**; bulk, bulk large, loom; stretch, **extend**; tower, soar, mount, **ascend**; scale, transcend, **be superior**; clear; exceed, **overstep**; enlarge, **augment, expand**; swamp, overwhelm, **fill**.

**Adv. positively**, verily, actually, indeed, **truly**; **certainly**; absolutely, definitely, finally; directly, specifically; essentially, fundamentally; **downright**, plumb.

**greatly**, much, well; very, right, so; very much, mighty, ever so; fully, quite, without reservation, **wholly**; wholesale; **generally**; largely, mainly, mostly, to a large extent; something, fairly, pretty, pretty well; a sight, a deal, ever so much; substantially; more than ever, doubly; specially; dearly, vitally, vastly, hugely, enormously; mightily; narrowly, hotly; enough; preeminently, superlatively; rarely.

**extremely**; beyond measure, beyond all bounds; beyond comparison, beyond compare; overly, unduly, to a fault; with a vengeance; madly; exceedingly; beastly; hellishly; terribly, dreadfully,

awfully; finally; mortally.

**remarkably**; notably, signally; preeminently, **eminently**; singularly, peculiarly, uncommonly.

**painfully**; badly, hard; sorely; miserably; mortally.

## 33 Smallness

**N. smallness**, small size; brevity; **rarity**; scarcity, **shortfall**; moderation; intermediate technology, small means, **poverty**; **average**; abbreviation, **contraction**; **decrease**; nothingness, zero.

**small quantity**, fraction, modicum, minimum, **finite quantity**; trivia; peanuts, **trifle**; detail, petty detail; nutshell, **compendium**; trifling amount; spoonful, mouthful; trickle, dribble, sprinkling, sprinkle, dash, splash, squirt, squeeze; tinge, tincture, trace, spice, smack, lick, smell, breath, whisper, suspicion, vestige, thought, suggestion, nuance, shade, shadow, touch, cast; vein, strain, streak; spark, gleam, flash, flicker, ray; pinch, snatch, handful; snack, sip, bite, mite, scrap, morsel, sop; dole, pittance, iron ration; fragment, **piece**; whit, bit, mite; iota, jot; ounce, scruple, minim; inch, micron, millimetre, **short distance**; second, moment, **instant**; next to nothing, hardly anything; **insubstantial thing**.

**small thing**, **miniature**; particle, atom; dot, point, pinpoint; dab, spot, fleck, speck, mote, smut; grain, granule, seed, crumb, **powder**; drop, droplet, driblet; thread, wisp, shred, rag, tatter, fragment, **piece**; smithereens, confetti; flake, snip, snippet, small slice, finger; confetti; splinter, chip, clipping, shiver, sliver, slip; snick, prick, nick; hair, **filament**.

**small coin**, groat, farthing, halfpenny,

mite, cent, nickel, dime; sou, centime, bean, small change, **coinage**.

**small animal**, amoeba, **microorganism**; gnat, flea, ant; minnow, shrimp, sprat; sparrow, wren; mouse, shrew, bantam, toy dog; midget, **dwarf**.

**Adj. small**, exiguous, moderate, modest, minimal, infinitesimal; microscopic, **invisible**; tiny, wee, minute, diminutive, miniature, **little**; **lesser**; least, minimum; undersized; slim, slender, lean, meagre, thin, **narrow**; slight, feeble, puny, frail, **weak**; delicate, dainty, fragile, **brittle**; flimsy, weightless, **light**; fine, subtle, rarefied, **rare**; quiet, soft, low, faint; squat, **low**; brief, **short**; cut, compact, compendious; scanty, scant, scarce, **deficient**; **insufficient**; limited, **restrained**; at low ebb, less.

**inconsiderable**, minor, lightweight, trifling, trivial, petty, paltry, insignificant; **few**; imperceptible, **invisible**; shadowy, tenuous, evanescent, **transient**; marginal, negligible, remote, slight; superficial, cursory, **insubstantial**; skin-deep, **shallow**; average, middling, fair, so-so, **median**; moderate, modest, humble, tolerable, passable, **middling**; second-rate, **inferior**; just, only, mere, bare; plain, simple.

**Vb. be small**, stay small, **be little**; be low; be light; **sound faint**; be less, **fall short**; get less, **decrease**; shrink, **become small**.

**Adv. slightly**, to a small degree, little; lightly; fairly, tolerably, quite; comparatively, relatively, rather, enough, poorly, badly, miserably; hardly, scarcely, barely, only just; narrowly; hardly at all; only, merely, purely, simply; at least.

**partially**, to some degree, to a certain extent; somehow, after a fashion, sort of; some, somewhat, a little, a bit, just

a bit, ever so little; within bounds; partly.

**almost**, all but, within an ace of, within an inch of, within sight of, **near**; **nearly**; pretty near, just short of, virtually.

**about**, somewhere, somewhere about, thereabouts; more or less; near enough, a little more, a little less; at a guess, say.

**in no way**.

## 34 Superiority

**N. superiority**, superior elevation, higher position; altitude, **height**; top, **summit**; quality, **goodness**; **perfection**; **choice**; primacy, pride of place, **precedence**, **priority**; eminence, **prestige**; higher rank, higher degree, **degree**, **nobility**, **aristocracy**; supremacy, sovereignty, majesty, **authority**; domination, hegemony, **influence**; leadership, **management**; **inequality**; win, championship, **victory**; prominence; one-upmanship, **cunning**, **success**; excess, surplus; climax, zenith, culmination; maximum, top, peak, pinnacle, crest; record, high, **summit**.

**advantage**, privilege, prerogative, handicap, favour, **benefit**; head start, lead, inside track; odds, points, pull, edge; command, upper hand; trump card; majority, **greater number**; scope, **room**.

**superior**, superior person; superman, **prodigy**; better man or woman, first choice, **favourite**; select few, **elite**; top people, **bigwig**; nobility, aristocracy, **upper class**; lord, sovereign, **master**; commander, chief, prophet, guide, **leader**; boss, foreman, **manager**; primate, president, prime minister, **director**; model, **paragon**; star, virtuoso, **proficient person**; specialist, expert; mastermind, **sage**; winner, champion, **victor**; first lady, head boy or girl; firstborn, elder, senior.

**Adj. superior**, more so; comparative, superlative; major, greater, **great**; upper, higher, senior, over, super; supernormal, above average, **different**; better, a cut above, **excellent**; ahead, **preceding**; prior, preferable, favourite, **chosen**; record; victorious, outstanding, marked, distinguished, **noteworthy**; rare, **unusual**; high-powered, **important**; commanding, **ruling**.

**supreme**, arch-, **great**; uppermost, **topmost**; first, chief, foremost, **preceding**; main, principal, leading, overriding, cardinal, capital, **important**; excellent, classic, superlative, super, champion, tip-top, top-notch, first-rate, first-class, A1, 5-star, **best**; second to none, none such; dominant, paramount, preeminent, sovereign, royal, every inch a king or queen; **incomparable**, unrivalled, matchless, peerless, unparalleled, unequalled, **inimitable**; ultimate; without comparison, beyond compare, beyond criticism, **perfect**; transcendent, transcendental.

**crowning**, climactic, maximal, maximum; record, best ever, **best**.

**Vb. be superior**, transcend, rise above, surmount, overlook, command, **be high**; go beyond, **overstep**; exceed; pass, surpass, reach a new high; better, cap, trump; show quality, shine, excel, **be good**; eclipse, overshadow; **ridicule**; best, outclass, **outdo**; outplay, outpoint, outmanoeuvre, outwit; overtake, leave behind, lap, **outstrip**; worst, beat, beat hollow, **defeat**.

**predominate**, preponderate, overbalance, **be unequal**; override, **prevail**; lead.

**come first, come before**; take precedence, play first fiddle, **be important**; lead, star; head, captain, **direct**.

**culminate**, come to a head; cap, crown all, **crown**; rise to a peak; set a new record, reach a new high, **climax**.

**Adv. beyond**, more; above par; upwards of; at its height, at an advantage.

**eminently**, preeminently, superlatively; above all, of all things; to crown it all, to cap it all; especially, peculiarly; even more, still more, ever more, **extremely**.

## 35 Inferiority

**N. inferiority**, minority, inferior numbers; dependence; second fiddle; **humility**; second rank, back seat; disadvantage, handicap, **hindrance**; blemish, defect, deficiency, **shortfall**; failure, **defeat**; poor quality, second best; vulgarity, **bad taste**; **poverty**; decline; record low, low, minimum, nadir, **base**; depression, trough; level, plain.

**inferior**, subordinate, sub, underling, assistant, subsidiary, **auxiliary**; agent, **deputy**, **substitute**; tool, pawn, **instrument**; follower, retainer, **dependant**; menial, hireling, **servant**; poor relation, small fry, **nonentity**; subject, underdog, **slave**; private, other ranks; second, second best, second string, second fiddle; bad second, also-ran; failure, reject, dregs, lesser creation, beast, worm; junior, minor.

**Adj. lesser**, less, minor, small-time, one-horse; small, **inconsiderable**; diminished; least, minimal, minimum; minus, **deficient**.

**inferior**, lower, junior, sub-; subordinate, **serving**; dependent, **subject**; secondary, tributary, ancillary, subsidiary, auxiliary; second, second-class, second-rate, mediocre; third-rate;

humble, lowly, low-level, menial; subnormal, substandard; slight, underweight, **deficient**; shop-soiled;
unsound, patchy, unequal, **imperfect**;
failing, **insufficient**; shoddy, crummy,
**bad**, **cheap**, **vulgar**; low, common,
**plebeian**; scratch, makeshift; temporary, provisional, **ephemeral**; feeble,
**weak**; worsted, beaten; nothing
special, nothing to shout about,
nothing to write home about.

**Vb.** **be inferior**, come short of, fall
below, **fall short**; lag, fall behind;
trail, **follow**; want, lack; **fail**; bow to,
**obey**; yield, cede, hand it to, **submit**;
play second fiddle, **serve**; take a back
seat; lose face, lose caste, **lose repute**;
get worse, **deteriorate**; slump, sink,
sink low, touch rock bottom, **descend**,
**plunge**.

**Adv.** less, minus, short of; beneath;
below average, below par; at low ebb;
poorly.

## 36 Increase

**N.** **increase**, increment, crescendo;
advance, progress, **progression**;
growth, growth area, boom town;
development, **production**; beginning;
extension; spread, inflation; **abundance**; multiplication; **numerical
operation**; **addition**; enlargement,
magnification; excess, **exaggeration**;
appreciation, **elevation**; concentration, **condensation**; acceleration,
speeding, **spurt**; **heating**; advancement, boost; rise, spiral, upward
curve, upward trend, upswing,
**ascent**; upsurge, flood, tide, swell,
surge, **wave**; cumulative effect, snowball, **accumulation**; **series**.

**increment**, bulge; accretion, accession,
**addition**; supplement, pay rise, **extra**;
padding, stuffing; percentage, commission, rake-off, **earnings**; interest,

profit, **gain**; plunder, prey, **booty**;
prize, **reward**; produce, harvest, **product**; takings, receipts, proceeds,
**receiving**.

**Adj.** **increasing**, progressive; greater
than ever, **great**; filling, crescent; supplementary, **additional**; cumulative,
**continuous**; intensive; productive,
fruitful, **prolific**; swollen, bloated.

**Vb.** **grow**, increase, gain, develop, escalate; dilate, swell, bulge, wax, fill,
**expand**; fatten, thicken, **be broad**;
**weigh**; sprout, bud, burgeon, flower,
blossom, **reproduce itself**; breed,
spread, swarm, proliferate, mushroom, multiply, **be many**, **be fruitful**;
**mature**; **be high**; spiral, climb, mount,
rise, rocket, **ascend**; **be hot**, **shine**;
gain strength, **be strong**; improve, **get
better**; flourish, thrive, prosper; gain
ground, advance, snowball, accumulate, **progress**; earn interest; appreciate, **be dear**; boom, surge, exceed,
overflow, **be great**; rise to a maximum.

**augment**, increase, double, triple, **treble**,
**quadruple**; redouble, square, cube;
duplicate, **repeat**; multiply, **reproduce**; grow, breed, raise, rear, **breed
stock**, cultivate, mature; enlarge,
magnify, distend, inflate, **expand**;
amplify, develop, **make complete**;
condense, concentrate, **be dense**; supplement, enrich, repay with interest;
bring to, contribute to; accrue, **add**;
extend, prolong, stretch, **lengthen**;
broaden, widen, thicken, deepen;
heighten, enhance, **make higher**;
raise, exalt, **elevate**; advance, promote; aim higher; **accelerate**; intensify, redouble, stimulate, **invigorate**;
recruit, reinforce, boost, **refresh**;
**restore**, **strengthen**; glorify, **exaggerate**, **overrate**; stoke, exacerbate,
**aggravate**; bring to a head, **climax**.

**Adv.** crescendo, more so, with a vengeance.

## 37 Decrease: no increase

**N.** decrease; wane, **contraction**; ebb, retreat; ebb tide; **series**; subsidence, decline, declension, downward curve, downward trend, fall, drop, plunge, **descent**, **ruin**; deflation, recession, slump; loss of value; loss of reputation, **disrepute**; **weakness**; **poverty**; shortage, **scarcity**; exhaustion; shrinkage, erosion, attrition, decay; leakage, wastage, damage, loss; consumption, **waste**; anticlimax; forfeit, levy, **penalty**, **loss**.

diminution, making less; exception, **exclusion**; reduction, restraint; cut, **economy**; cutting back, pruning, shaving, clipping, abbreviation, **shortening**; squeeze, **contraction**; abrasion, erosion, **friction**; melting, dissolution; moderation.

**Adj.** decreasing; melting; ruinous, dilapidated.

**Vb.** abate, make less, diminish, decrease, lessen; deduct, **subtract**; except, **exclude**; reduce, attenuate, whittle, pare, scrape, **make thin**; clip, trim, slash, **cut**; shrink, abridge, abbreviate, **shorten**; squeeze, compress, contract; limit, curtail, **restrain**; cut back, retrench; reduce speed, decelerate, **retard**; depress, **lower**; mitigate, extenuate, **moderate**; allay, alleviate, **relieve**; deflate, puncture; disparage, decry, belittle, depreciate, **underestimate**, **cheapen**; dwarf, overshadow, **be superior**; obscure; degrade, demote, **humiliate**; loosen, ease, relax, **disencumber**; remit, pardon, **forgive**; unload, throw overboard, **lighten**; drain, exhaust, **empty**; consume, **waste**; let escape, let evaporate; **liquefy**; grind, crumble; abrade, file,

rub; gnaw, nibble at, **eat**; erode, rust, **impair**; strip, peel, denude, **uncover**; pillage, plunder, dispossess, **impoverish**; emasculate, **disable**; dilute, **weaken**, **mix**; thin, depopulate, **render few**; eliminate, expel, **eject**; decimate, slaughter, **destroy**, **kill**; reduce to nothing, annihilate, **nullify**; hush, quiet, **silence**, **make mute**; cool, **extinguish**; quell, subdue, tame, **subjugate**.

decrease, grow less, lessen; suffer loss; abate, slacken, ease, moderate, subside; dwindle, shrink, contract, **become small**; wane, waste, decay, degenerate, **deteriorate**; fade, grow dim, **be dim**; retreat, withdraw, ebb, **regress**, recede; run low, fail; **be narrow**, **converge**; subside, sink, **plunge**; decline, fall, drop, spiral, slump, collapse, **descend**; lag, **decelerate**; **disappear**; evaporate; thin, become scarce, **be few**, **disperse**; become extinct; lose weight, reduce, **be light**, starve; be mute; lose, shed; **doff**; forfeit, sacrifice, **lose**.

**Adv.** diminuendo; at low ebb.

## 38 Addition

**N.** addition, fixture, agglutination, **union**; **location**; **precedence**; **sequence**; **aid**; load; accession, accretion; interjection; reinforcement, **increase**; increment, supplement, addendum, appendage, appendix, **adjunct**; extra time, overtime; **accompaniment**; summation, total, toll.

**Adj.** additional, additive; adventitious, occasional, **extraneous**, **extrinsic**; supplementary; subsidiary, auxiliary, contributory; another, further, more; extra, spare, **superfluous**; preceding.

**Vb.** add, sum, total, **transfer**; add to, annex, append; attach, pin to, clip to; hitch to, yoke to, unite to, **join**, **tie**;

preface, prefix, affix, suffix; introduce, **put between**; interpose, interject; engraft, **insert**; bring to, contribute to, **augment**; swell, extend, expand, **enlarge**; supplement, crown, **make complete**; impose, saddle with, **stow**, **hinder**; superimpose, **bring together**; ornament, add frills, embellish, **decorate**; plaster, coat; mix with, **mix**; take to oneself, annex, **take**; encompass, **number with**; absorb, include, receive, **admit**.

accrue; supervene, **arrive**, **be present**; adhere, join, **join a party**; mix with, **combine**; make an extra, make an addition to, make one more; reinforce, recruit, **strengthen**.

Adv. **in addition**, more, plus, extra; with interest, with a vengeance; too, also, item, furthermore, further; likewise, to boot; else, besides; moreover, inclusive of, with, let alone; together with; even with, despite.

## 39 Subtraction

N. **subtraction**, **numerical operation**; **decrease**; abstraction, removal, **taking**; expulsion, clearance; **displacement**, **extraction**; precipitation, sedimentation, abrasion, erosion, **friction**; **shortening**; severance; **numerical element**; discount.

Adj. **subtracted**; headless; minus, without, **deficient**.

Vb. **subtract**, deduct; diminish, decrease, abate; cut, **discount**; allow; except, **exclude**; expel, **eject**; abstract, **take**, **steal**; withdraw, remove; unload, unpack, **displace**; shift, **transfer**; **empty**; abrade, erode, **rub**; eradicate, uproot, **extract**; pick, **select**; delete, censor, **obliterate**; expurgate, garble, mutilate, **impair**; sever, separate, amputate, excise; shear, clip, **cut**; retrench, cut back, lop, prune, pare,

decapitate, behead, dock, curtail, abridge, abbreviate, **shorten**; geld, castrate, spay, emasculate; peel, skin, strip, denude, **uncover**.

Adv. **in deduction**, at a discount; less; short of; minus, without, except, barring, bar, save, exclusive of.

## 40 Adjunct: thing added

N. **adjunct**, **addition**; addendum, carryover; supplement, annex; attachment, fixture; affix, suffix, prefix; adjective, adverb, **part of speech**; ticket, tab, tag, **label**; appendage, tail, train, following, **sequel**; wake, trail, **sequence**; appendix, postscript, coda, ending, **extremity**; codicil, rider, **qualification**; corollary, complement; accessory; companion piece, fellow, **analogue**; extension, second part; wing (of a house) offices, outhouse, **edifice**; **branch**; arm, extremity, **limb**; accretion; increment, **increase**; patch, reinforcement, **repair**; padding, stuffing, **lining**; interlude, intermezzo; gusset, gore, **garment**; flap, lapel; admixture, ingredient, **component**; fringe, border, frill, edging, **edge**; embroidery; garnish, seasoning, **sauce**; frills, trappings, **dressing**, **covering**; equipment, **provision**.

extra, additive, addendum, increment, by-product; percentage, interest, **gain**; bonus, tip, perquisite, **reward**; free gift, gratuity, golden handshake, **gift**; windfall, find, allowance, **offset**; oddment, item, extra; **provision**; extra help, reinforcement, **auxiliary**; surplus; extra time, overtime.

## 41 Remainder: thing remaining

N. **remainder**, residue; residual, result, resultant, **effect**, **product**; margin, **difference**; outstanding, balance, **offset**; surplus, carry-over, **increment**;

excess; relic, rest, remnant; rump, stump, stub, scrag end, **extremity**; torso, trunk, **piece**; fossil, skeleton, **corpse**; husk, shell; wreck, wreckage, debris, **ruin**; **powder**; track, fingerprint, **record**, **trace**; wake, afterglow, **sequel**; all that is left, **remembrance**; survival; vestige, remains.

**leavings**; precipitate, deposit, sediment; alluvium, silt, **soil**; drift, loess, moraine, detritus; grounds, lees, dregs; scum, dross, slag, sludge; bilge; scrapings, filings, sawdust, **powder**; bran, chaff, stubble; peel, peelings; skin, slough, scurf; scraps, lumber, **rubbish**; **derelict**; waste, sewage, **excrement**; refuse, litter, **dirt**.

**survivor**; heir, successor, **beneficiary**; widower, widow; orphan, **derelict**; descendant, **posterity**.

**Adj. remaining**, left, resultant; residual; left behind, sedimentary; odd; net, surplus; outstanding; spare, superfluous, **redundant**; cast-off, outcast; orphan, widowed.

**Vb. be left**, remain, rest, result, survive.

**leave over, exclude**; leave, leave behind, discard, abandon, **reject**.

**42 Decrement: thing deducted**

**N. decrement**, cut; allowance; remission; tare, drawback, rebate, **discount**; refund, shortage, defect, **shortfall**; loss, sacrifice, forfeit, **penalty**; leak, leakage, escape; shrinkage, **shortening**; wastage, consumption, **waste**; rake-off, **taking**; toll, **tax**.

**43 Mixture**

**N. mixture**, stirring; admixture, **addition**; **union**; **crossing**; **combination**; merger, **association**; fusion, infusion; contamination, infection; **marriage**; crucible, melting pot; mixer, beater, shaker, blender; churn.

**tincture**, admixture; ingredient, **component**; strain, streak; sprinkling, infusion; tinge, touch, drop, dash, **small quantity**; smack, hint, flavour, **taste**; seasoning, spice, **condiment**; colour, dye, **hue**; stain, blot, **blemish**.

a **mixture**; blend, harmony, **concord**; composition, **structure**; amalgam, fusion, compound, confection, **combination**; pastiche; alloy, bronze, brass, pewter, steel; magma, paste; soup, stew, hash, ragout, **dish**; cocktail, brew, solution, infusion; medicinal compound, **remedy**.

**medley**, variety; motley, patchwork, mosaic; **assortment**, miscellany, mixed bag, job lot, ragbag, lucky dip; farrago, hotchpotch, mishmash, potpourri; jumble, hash, mess; conglomeration, **accumulation**; tangle, entanglement, imbroglio, **confusion**; phantasmagoria, kaleidoscope; clatter, **discord**; motley crew, **crowd**; menagerie, circus, **zoo**; variety show, **stage show**; paraphernalia.

**hybrid**, cross, cross-breed, mongrel; mule; half-breed; Eurasian, Cape Coloured, Creole, mulatto.

**Adj. mixed**; eclectic; fused; qualified; sophisticated; composite, fifty-fifty; complex, complicated, involved, **intricate**; heterogeneous, **multiform**; patchy, dappled, motley, **variegated**; shot, **iridescent**; miscellaneous, random, **indiscriminate**; soluble; pervasive, **infectious**; hybrid, mongrel; of mixed blood; multiracial.

**Vb. mix**, make a mixture, stir, shake; shuffle, scramble, **jumble**; knead, pound together, mash; brew, compound, **compose**; fuse, alloy, merge, amalgamate, **join**; blend, **combine**; mingle, intermingle, intersperse;

interleave, **insert**; intertwine, interlace, interweave, **weave**; tinge, dye, **colour**; instil, impregnate, **infuse**; dash, sprinkle, **moisten**; water, adulterate, **weaken**; temper, doctor, **modify**; season, spice, fortify, lace, spike; cross, cross-breed, **generate**.

**be mixed**, be involved; pervade, permeate, run through, **infiltrate**; infect, contaminate; stain, colour; intermarry, interbreed, cross with, **reproduce itself**.

**Adv. among**, amid, with.

## 44 Simpleness: freedom from mixture

**N. simpleness**; purity; **unity**; bedrock, **essence**; lack of complication, simplicity; **absence**.

**simplification**; reduction; **identity**.

**elimination**; riddance, clearance; expulsion, **exclusion**.

**Adj. simple**, homogeneous, monolithic, all of a piece, **uniform**; sheer, mere, utter, nothing but; asexual; single, **one**; elemental, indivisible, entire, **whole**; primary, irreducible, fundamental, basic, **intrinsic**; elementary, **intelligible**; direct, **straight**; unsophisticated, homespun, **plain**, artless; single-minded, whole-hearted, sincere, downright, unaffected, **veracious**, **honourable**; bare, naked.

**unmixed**, without alloy; clear, pure, **clean**; thoroughbred, **noble**; excluding; **perfect**; unalloyed; unadulterated, neat, **strong**; unqualified; **tasteless**; **white**.

**Vb. simplify**, render simple, **make uniform**; reduce, reduce to its elements, **decompose**; disentangle, unscramble, **unravel**; unify, make one, unite.

**eliminate**, sift, **class**; winnow, sieve, pan; purge, **purify**; clear, clarify, cleanse, distil; **exclude**; expel, **eject**.

**Adv. simply**; only, merely.

## 45 Union

**N. union**, junction, coming together, meeting, conjunction; clash, **collision**; contact, **touch**; congress, reunion, **assembly**; confluence, **focus**; fusion, merger, **mixture**; **combination**; cohesion, agglutination, **coherence**; **condensation**; coalition, alliance, symbiosis, **association**; tie-up, **bond**; wedlock, **marriage**; **crossing**; communication, **passage**; intercommunication, intercourse; trade, traffic, exchange, **interchange**, **trade**; **relation**; arrival, latecomer; partner; **companion**.

**joining together, assemblage; combination**; composition, **structure**; suture, knitting, sewing, **crossing**; drawing together, contraction, **closure**; tying, binding; fastening; attachment, **addition**; injection; fixture, **coherence**; coupling, matching, **comparison**; **punctuation**; joiner; go-between, **intermediary**, **matchmaker**.

**coition**, coitus, sexual intercourse, sex, carnal knowledge; generation; coupling; union, **marriage**; **rape**.

**joint**, juncture, crease, fold; suture, seam, **bond**; English bond, weld; splice; mitre, mitre joint; dovetail; hasp, latch, catch, **pivot**; finger, wrist, ankle, knuckle, knee, elbow; node; junction, intersection, crossroads; **crossing**; figure X, **cross**.

**Adj. joined**; equal; joint, allied, incorporated, **corporate**; wedded, **married**; intimate, involved, **intrinsic**; adhesive; composite; put together.

**conjunctive**, adhesive; astringent; coincident, **concurrent**; venereal.

**firm**, close, fast, secure, sound, **fixed**; solid, set, **dense**; put, pat; rooted; ingrown, impacted; crowded, tight, stuck; **inextricable**, inseparable, immovable; packed, **full**.

**tied**, bound; tight, taut, tense, fast, secure; intricate, involved, inextricable.

**Vb. join**, couple, yoke, harness together; pair, match, **compare**, **marry**; bracket; put together, assemble, unite, **combine**; collect, gather, mass, **bring together**; add to, amass, accumulate, **add**, **store**; associate, ally, (twin town); merge, **mix**; incorporate, consolidate, make one, unify, **be one**, **make uniform**; lump together; include, embrace, **comprise**; grip, **retain**; make a joint, hinge, articulate, dovetail, mortise, mitre; fit, set, interlock, engage, gear to; wedge, jam, **insert**; weld, solder, fuse, cement; draw together, lace, knit, sew, stitch; pin, buckle; fasten, **close**; lock, latch; close a gap; darn, patch, mend, **repair**.

**connect**, attach, annex; staple, clip, pin together; contact, **touch**; make contact, earth, **juxtapose**; link, bridge, span, straddle, bestride, **pass**; communicate, intercommunicate, establish communication; put through to; **relate**; entwine.

**affix**, attach, fix, fasten; yoke, leash, harness, saddle, bridle; moor, anchor; tie to, tether, picket; suffix, prefix, **add**; splice, engraft, implant, **insert**; impact, set, frame, **enclose**; **strike**; wedge, jam; screw, nail, rivet, bolt, clamp, clinch; thread, pass through.

**tie**, knot, hitch, lash, belay; knit, sew, stitch, suture; tack, baste; braid, plait, crochet; twine, twist, intertwine, lace, interlace, interweave, **weave**; truss, string, rope, strap; tether, picket, moor; pinion, manacle, handcuff; hobble, shackle, **fetter**; bind, splice, gird, girdle; bandage, swathe, swaddle, wrap; enfold, embrace, grip, **enclose**, **retain**.

**tighten**, jam, impact; constrict, compress, narrow; fasten, make firm, make fast, secure; draw tight, brace.

**unite with**, join, meet, **converge**; fit tight, adhere, hang together, **cohere**; mesh, interlock, engage, grip, clinch; embrace, entwine; partner, **be sociable**; league together, **join a party**; marry, **wed**; live with, cohabit; go to bed with, lie with, make love, have intercourse, have carnal knowledge; consummate a marriage or a union; know, enjoy, possess, have, do; lay, bed, tumble; deflower, rape, ravish, violate, **debauch**; copulate, couple, mate, pair, **generate**; mount, cover, serve; cross with.

**Adv. conjointly**, with; all together.
**inseparably**; fast, tight.

## 46 Disunion

**N. disunion**; break; breakup, dissolution, decay; abstraction; **resignation**; surrender, sacrifice, **decrease**; moving apart, **deviation**; split, schism (see **separation**); detachment; quarantine, segregation, zone, compartment, box, cage, **prison**; lack of unity, **dissension**; **speciality**; isolationism, separatism; distance apart; dichotomy, **difference**; interval, space, opening, hole, breach, break, rent, rift, tear, split; fissure, crack, cleft, chasm; cleavage, slit, slot, cut, **gap**.

**separation**, severance, parting; **divorce**; undoing; **liberation**; setting apart, segregation, apartheid; exception, **exclusion**; boycott; expulsion; selection, **choice**; storage; conservation, **preservation**; abstraction, deprivation, **taking**; detachment, removal, transfer, **displacement**; dissolution, resolution; analysis, breakdown; fragmentation, **destruction**; splitting, fission; rupture, fracture; caesura; wall, hedge, **partition**; curtain, **screen**; boundary, **limit**.

scission, section, cleavage, cutting; division, dichotomy; partition; **shortening**; cutting open, opening, **surgery**; nipping.

Adj. **disunited**; disconnected, unstuck; broken, **discontinuous**; bipartite; cut; torn, rent, cleft, cloven; scattered, fugitive; loose, free, **liberated**.

separate, apart, asunder; adrift, lost; distinct, discrete, separable, distinguishable, **different**; exempt; abstracted; alien, foreign, **extraneous**; external, **extrinsic**, **exterior**; insular, self-sufficient, lonely, **alone**, **friendless**; cast-off; set apart, **chosen**; left; hostile, **inimical**, **contrary**, **opposite**; selective, **distinctive**.

severable, separable; divisible; biodegradable; distinguishable.

Vb. **separate**, stand apart, **avoid**; go, **depart**; go apart, go different ways, radiate, **diverge**; go another way, **deviate**; part, part company, cut adrift, cut loose, divorce; get free, get loose, disengage free oneself, **achieve liberty**; let go; leave, quit, **relinquish**; scatter, **disperse**; spring apart, **recoil**; come apart, break, disintegrate, **decompose**; come undone, unravel, ladder, run; **come unstuck**; split, crack, **open**.

disunite, dissociate, divorce; part, separate, sunder, sever; uncouple, disconnect; disengage; dislocate, wrench; detach, unseat, dismount; remove, deduct, **subtract**, **transfer**; skin, denude, strip, flay, peel, pluck, **uncover**; undo, unzip, unlock, **open**; untie, disentangle, **unravel**; unpick; loosen, relax, slacken, **moderate**; loose, free, release, **liberate**; expel, **eject**; dispel, scatter, disband, **disperse**; disintegrate, **decompose**,

destroy.

set apart, put aside, **store**; conserve, **preserve**; distinguish, **differentiate**, **discriminate**; **select**; except, exempt, **exclude**; boycott, send to Coventry, **avoid**; taboo, black, blacklist, **prohibit**; insulate, isolate, **enclose**; zone, **circumscribe**; segregate, quarantine, maroon, **seclude**; keep apart, drive a wedge between, estrange, alienate, set against, **excite hate**.

sunder (see disunite); divide, keep apart, flow between, subdivide, fragment, segment; reduce, analyse; dissect, **decompose**; halve, **bisect**; split, partition, **apportion**; dismember, quarter, carve (see **cut**); behead, decapitate, curtail, dock, amputate, **shorten**; take apart, dismantle, dismount; force open, force apart, **open**; slit, split; cleave, **pierce**. See break.

cut, hew, hack, slash, gash, **wound**; prick, stab, knife, **pierce**; cut through, cleave, saw, chop; cut open, slit, **open**; incise, **engrave**; cut deep, carve, slice; cut round, pare, whittle, chisel, chip, trim, bevel, skive; clip, snick, snip; cut short, shave, **shorten**; fell, scythe, mow; lop, prune, dock, curtail (see **sunder**); quarter, dismember; dice, shred, mince, make mincemeat of; bite, bite through, **chew**; scratch, scarify, score, plough, groove, nick, **notch**.

rend, tear, scratch, claw; gnaw, fret, fray, make ragged; rip, slash, slit (see **cut**); lacerate, dismember; tear to tatters, **destroy**; mince, grind, crunch, scrunch, **chew**; explode, burst.

break, fracture, rupture, bust; split, burst, explode; smash, shatter, splinter, shiver, **demolish**; fragment, crumble, grind; disintegrate, **decompose**; dismantle (see **sunder**); chip, crack, damage, **impair**; bend, buckle, warp, **distort**; snap; cleave, force apart, **open**.

**Adv. separately**, severally, singly, piecemeal.

**apart**, open, asunder, adrift; to tatters.

**47 Bond: connecting medium**

**N. bond**, chain, shackle, fetter, tie, band, hoop, yoke; bond of union, sympathy, fellow feeling, **pity**; obligation, **duty**; nexus, link, **relation**; junction, hinge, **joint**; ramification, **branch**; copula; hyphen, dash, bracket, **punctuation**; cement (see **adhesive**); binder; stretcher, girder, **beam**; strut, stay, **prop**; intercommunication, channel, passage, corridor, **access**; steppingstone, causeway, **bridge**; span, arch; isthmus, neck; col, ridge; stair, ladder, **ascent**; lifeline.

**cable**, line, guy, hawser, painter, moorings; ripcord, lanyard, communication cord; rope, cord, whipcord, string, tape, twine, **fibre**; chain, wire, earth.

**tackling**, tackle; rig, rigging, shroud; guy, stay; garnet, bowline, lanyard, harness.

**ligature**, ligament, tendon, muscle; tendril, osier, bass, raffia, **fibre**; lashing, binding; string, cord, thread, tape, band, fillet, ribbon; bandage, roller, tourniquet, **compressor**; drawstring, thong, lace, tag; braid, plait, **network**; tie, stock, cravat; knot, hitch, clinch, bend; half hitch.

**fastening**, fastener, press-stud, popper, zip fastener, zip; drawstring, ripcord; stitch; button, buttonhole, eyelet, loop, frog; stud; garter, suspender; braces; brooch; clip, grip, slide; hairpin, hatpin; skewer, spit; pin, peg, dowel, nail, tack, **sharp point**; staple, clamp, brace, batten, cramp, **nippers**; nut, bolt, screw, rivet; buckle, clasp;

hasp, hinge, **joint**; catch, pawl, click; latch, bolt; lock, **closure**; combination lock, padlock, handcuffs, **fetter**; key; hold, bar, post, pile, pale, stake, bollard.

**coupling**, yoke; hook, claw; anchor, **safeguard**.

**girdle**, band, strap, **belt**; waistband, girth, cinch; sash, shoulder belt; collar; fillet.

**halter**, collar, noose; tether, lead, leash, jess; lasso, **loop**; shackle, **fetter**.

**adhesive**, glue, fish glue, lime, gum; fixative, hair lacquer, hair spray, grease; solder; paste, size, clay, cement, putty, mortar, stucco, plaster, **facing**; wafer; sticker, stamp, adhesive tape, flypaper, **trap**; **coherence**.

**48 Coherence**

**N. coherence**, **continuity**; chain, **series**; holding together, cohesion; adherence, adhesion; agglutination, **union**; conglomeration, set, **condensation**; union, **unity**; phalanx, serried ranks; monolith, agglomerate, concrete, **solid body**; leech, limpet, barnacle, parasite, clinging vine; gum, plaster, **adhesive**.

**Adj. cohesive**, coherent, adhesive, adherent; clinging, tenacious; indigestible, **tough**; sticky, tacky, gummy, viscous; compact, well-knit, solid, concrete, frozen, **dense**; shoulder to shoulder, serried; monolithic, **uniform**; united, indivisible, inseparable, inextricable; close, tight, skintight, clinging, moulding.

**Vb. cohere**, hang together, grow together, **combine**; hold, stick close, hold fast; bunch, stand shoulder to shoulder, rally, **congregate**; grip, take hold of, **retain**; hug, clasp, embrace, twine round; close with, clinch; fit, fit tight; adhere, cling, stick; stick to, cleave to; stick like a leech, stick like a limpet, cling like a shadow, cling like ivy; cake, coagulate, agglomerate, conglomerate, solidify, consolidate, freeze, **be dense**.

**agglutinate**, glue, gum, paste, lute, cement, weld, **join**; stick to, affix, **add**.

**Adv. cohesively**.

## 49 Noncoherence

**N. noncoherence**; chaos; relaxation, freedom, **separation**; rope of sand; lone wolf, **nonconformist**.

**Adj. nonadhesive**, slippery, **smooth**; dry; detached, semidetached, **separate**; incoherent, loose; free, at large, **liberated**; lax, slack, baggy, floppy, flying; watery, liquid, runny, **fluid**; pendulous, **hanging**; **extraneous**; aloof.

**Vb. unstick**; detach; free, loosen, loose, slacken, **disunite**; unseat, dismount; shed, slough, **doff**.

**come unstuck**, melt, thaw, run, **liquefy**; totter, slip, **tumble**; dangle, flap, **hang**, rattle, shake, flap.

## 50 Combination

**N. combination**, composition; **union**; fusion, **mixture**; merger, digestion, absorption, **reception**; **unity**; embodiment; marriage, union, league, alliance, federation, **association**; conspiracy, cabal, **plot**; chord, counterpoint, **music**; chorus, **agreement**; harmony, **concord**; aggregation, assembly, **assemblage**; synopsis, **compendium**; mosaic, jigsaw, collage.

**compound**, alloy, amalgam, blend, composite, **a mixture**; portmanteau word; make-up, **composition**.

**Adj. combined**, united, **one**; incorporate, inbred, ingrained, **intrinsic**; fused, **mixed**; conjugate, allied; **concurrent**.

**Vb. combine**, put together, **compose**;

intertwine, interweave, **weave**; **accord**; bind, tie, **join**; unite, unify; incorporate, embody, integrate, absorb, assimilate; merge, amalgamate, pool; blend, fuse, compound, **mix**; impregnate, instil, inoculate, **infuse**; lump together, **add**; group, regroup, rally, **bring together**; band together, brigade, associate; ally, league with; partner; **be friendly**; cement a union, marry, **wed**; mate, couple, **pair**; conspire, **plot**; coalesce, grow together, have an affinity, combine with; combine with water, hydrate, **add water**.

## 51 Decomposition

**N. decomposition**; division, partition, **separation**; analysis, breakdown; **grammar**; resolution, electrolysis, hydrolysis, dissolution; fission; devolution, delegation; collapse, breakup, entropy, **destruction**; chaos.

**decay**; erosion; **death**; corruption, putrefaction, gangrene, caries; rot, rust, mould, **blight**; carrion, **corpse**.

**Adj. decomposed**, chaotic, **dilapidated**; putrid, rotten, bad, high, rancid, sour.

**decomposable**, disposable, biodegradable.

**Vb. decompose**, unscramble; resolve, reduce, **simplify**; separate, parse, dissect; analyse, **sunder**; split, fission, **disunite**; **demolish**; disband, disperse, **apportion**; unsettle, disorder, disturb, cause chaos, **derange**; dissolve, melt, **liquefy**; erode, **abate**; rot, rust, moulder, decay, consume, crumble, wear, perish, **deteriorate**; corrupt, putrefy, mortify, gangrene, **be unclean**; disintegrate.

**Adv. analytically**.

## 52 Whole. Principal part

**N. whole**; integrity, **unity**; a whole, whole number, integer, entity, **unit**; entirety, ensemble, complex; totality, summation, sum, **addition**; **generality**; system, world, cosmos, **universe**; life space, total situation, **state**; grand view, panorama, synopsis, **view**; whole course, round, circuit.

**all**, everybody; **crowd**; total, aggregate, gross amount, sum, sum total; ensemble; lock, stock and barrel; hook, line and sinker unit, family; set, **series**; outfit, pack, kit; complete list, inventory, **list**; lot, whole.

**chief part**, best part, **chief thing**; bulk, mass, substance; heap, lump, **great quantity**; tissue, staple, stuff; body, torso, trunk, bole, stem, stalk; hull, hulk, skeleton; gist; almost all, nearly all; all but a few, majority, **greater number**.

**Adj. whole**, total, universal; integral, pure, unadulterated; entire, sound, **perfect**; grand, gross, full, **complete**; individual, single, **one**.

**intact**, unaffected; virgin, **new**; undivided; still there; without a scratch; uncut, unabridged.

**indivisible**; inseparable; monolithic, **uniform**.

**comprehensive**, omnibus, full-length, **inclusive**; wholesale, sweeping, **extensive**; widespread, epidemic, **general**; international, world, world-wide, cosmic, **universal**, **ubiquitous**.

**Adv. wholly**, fully, every inch; one hundred per cent.

**on the whole**, altogether, all things considered; substantially, essentially; virtually; mainly, **greatly**; almost, all but, **nearly**.

**collectively**, all together; bodily.

## 53 Part

**N. part**, portion; proportion, majority, **main part**, **greater number**; minority, **small quantity**; fraction, half, quarter, tithe, percentage; factor, **number**; balance, surplus, **remainder**; quota, contingent; dividend, share, whack, **portion**; item, particular, detail; sentence, paragraph, **phrase**; ingredient, member, constituent, element, **component**; dissident element, schism, faction, **party**; leg, lap, round, **period**; side; group, detachment; attachment, fixture, wing, **adjunct**; page, leaf, sheet, **book**; excerpt, extract, passage, quotation, **choice**; text; segment, sector, section; arc, **curve**; hemisphere, **sphere**; part payment, instalment, advance, deposit, earnest, **payment**; sample, foretaste, **example**; fragment (see **piece**).

**limb**, member, organ, appendage; hind limb, **leg**; **wing**; flipper, fin, **propeller**; arm, forearm, hand, **feeler**; elbow, funny bone.

**subdivision**, segment, sector, section; division, compartment; group, species, family, **group**; classification, **arrangement**; ward, parish, department, **district**; chapter, paragraph, clause, subordinate clause, phrase; verse; part, number, issue, instalment, volume, **edition**, **reading matter**; canto, **poem**.

**branch**, ramification, **adjunct**; bough, limb, spur, twig, tendril, leaf, leaflet; switch, shoot, scion, sucker, slip, sprig, spray, **foliage**.

**piece**, torso, trunk, stump, **remainder**; limb, segment, section (see **part**); patch, **adjunct**; length, roll, textile; strip, swatch; fragment; bit, scrap, shred, wisp, rag, **small thing**; morsel, bite, crust, crumb, **small quantity**; splinter, sliver, chip, snip, snippet;

cut, wedge, finger, slice, rasher; cutlet, chop, steak; hunk, chunk, wad, slab, lump, mass, **bulk**; clod, turf, divot, sod, **soil**; sherd, shard, potsherd, flake, scale; dollop, dose, **portion; medley**; brash, rubble, scree, detritus, moraine, debris, **rubbish**; tatters, **poverty**; piece of land, parcel, plot, allotment.

**Adj.** fragmentary, broken, crumbly, **brittle; imperfect**; partial, bitty, scrappy, **insufficient**; fractional, half; sectional; **separate; small**.

**Vb. part**, divide, partition, segment; **sunder; apportion;** fragment, **disunite**.

**Adv. partly**, partially.

**piecemeal;** a little at a time.

## 54 Completeness

**N. completeness**, nothing lacking, nothing to add, **whole; unity**; solidity, solidarity; harmony, balance, **concord; sufficiency**; entirety, totality, **all; generality; perfection;** limit; peak, culmination, crown, **summit;** finish, **end;** last touch; fulfilment, **finality**; whole hog; nothing less than, **extremity**.

**plenitude**, amplitude, capacity, maximum, saturation, **sufficiency**; saturation point; filling, refill; full house, complement, full crew, full load; full measure, bumper; bellyful; full size, full length, full extent, full volume; complement, supplement.

**Adj. complete**, plenary, full; utter, total; integral, **whole;** entire, with nothing missing, with supplement, **intact, perfect;** full-blown; undivided, solid, **dense;** self-contained, self-sufficient, **sufficient;** comprehensive, full-scale, **inclusive;** exhaustive, circumstantial, **diffuse;** absolute, extreme, radical; thorough, thoroughgoing, sweeping,

wholesale, regular, **consummate;** unmitigated, downright, plumb, plain; supplementary, complementary, **additional;** unqualified, **unconditional.**

**full,** replete; level with, flush; **redundant;** fit to burst; chock-full, chock-a-block; packed, tight, **firm;** laden, fraught, fully charged; standing room only; overrun, full of; dripping with; inexhaustible.

**Vb. be complete,** make a whole; reach or touch perfection, have everything; come to a head, **climax;** reach an end, come to a close, **end;** be self-sufficient, **have enough;** want nothing, **be content;** become complete, attain full growth, reach maturity, **mature;** fill, brim, overflow; gorge, **get drunk.**

**make complete,** complete, complement, integrate, **join;** make whole, **restore;** piece together, **compose;** supplement, supply, fill a gap, **add;** make good, **compensate;** leave nothing to add, **carry through;** be superfluous; **terminate.**

**fill,** brim, top; soak, saturate, **drench;** swamp, drown, overwhelm; replenish, **provide;** satisfy, **suffice, content,** sate; fill to capacity, cram, pack, stuff, line, **insert;** load, charge; freight, **stow;** fill space, occupy, **cover;** reach to, extend to, **extend;** overrun, **pervade;** fit tight, be chock-a-block, **tighten;** enter, **add.**

**Adv. completely,** fully, wholly, extremely, greatly; all told; virtually, quite, all of, altogether; outright, downright; clean, stark, hollow; hook, line and sinker; with a vengeance; every whit, every inch; at full length; to capacity.

**throughout,** all round.

## 55 Incompleteness

**N. incompleteness**; sketch, outline, first draft, **plan**; torso, trunk, **piece**; deficiency, **shortfall**; **discontent**; break, gap, missing link, **interval**; half, quarter; instalment, part payment, **part**.

**deficit**, part wanting, screw loose, missing link, **defect**; shortfall, **loss**; default; want, lack, need, **requirement**.

**Adj. incomplete**, inadequate, **deficient**; short, scant, **insufficient**; **useless**; wanting, lacking, **demanding**; short of, shy of; lame; without, -less; **short**; **imperfect**; half, partial, **fragmentary**; undeveloped, **immature**; raw, crude, rough-hewn, **amorphous**; sketchy, scrappy, bitty, hollow; superficial, meagre, thin, poor, **insubstantial**; perfunctory, half-hearted, undone; left hanging; missing, lost, **absent**; **discontinuous**.

**unfinished**; begun, **beginning**.

**Vb. be incomplete**, miss, lack, need, **require**, **fall short**; be wanting, be **absent**; default, leave undone, **neglect**; omit, **exclude**; interrupt, **discontinue**; leave hanging.

**Adv. incompletely**, partially.

## 56 Composition

**N. composition**, constitution, setup, make-up; make, formation, build, **structure**; **arrangement**; temper, habit, nature, character, condition; **temperament**; embodiment; compound, **mixture**, **combination**, **organism**; syntax, sentence, period, **phrase**; artistic composition, **music**, **art**, **painting**, **sculpture**; architecture, **edifice**; authorship, **writing**, **poetry**; dramatic art, **drama**; printing, typography, **print**; compilation, **assemblage**; work, **production**; choreography, ballet; instrumentation, score, **musical piece**; work of art, picture, sculpture, model; literary work, **book**, **poem**, **dissertation**, **anthology**; play, **stage play**; ballet, **dance**; pattern, design.

**Adj. composing**, making; made of; **inclusive**.

**Vb. constitute**, compose, form, make; belong to, **be one of**.

**contain**, include, **comprise**; hold, have, absorb, **admit**; comprehend, embrace, embody, **enclose**; involve, imply, **be intrinsic**; hide, **conceal**.

**compose**, compound, **mix**, **combine**; **arrange**; put together, **join**; compile, assemble, **bring together**; compose, **print**; draft, **write**; orchestrate, score, **compose music**; draw, **paint**; construct, build, make, fabricate, **produce**; knit, interweave, **weave**; pattern, design.

## 57 Exclusion

**N. exclusion**, preoccupation, preemption; **hindrance**; monopoly, closed shop; an exception, special case; dispensation, **liberation**; blackball; closed door, lockout; picket line; embargo, ban, bar, taboo, **prohibition**; boycott; segregation, quarantine, caste system, colour bar, apartheid; repression, **prejudice**; expulsion; suspension; exile, removal, **displacement**; cancellation; dam, wall, barricade, screen, partition, pale, curtain, **barrier**; great wall of China, **defence**; customs' barrier, tariff, tariff wall, **tax**; place of exile, place of segregation, ghetto.

**Adj. excluding**, exclusive; restrictive, **sectional**; preventive, prohibitive; preemptive; silent about, **taciturn**.

**excluded**, barred, extra-; peripheral; outcast; inadmissible, **impossible**; foreign, **extraneous**.

Vb. **be excluded**, stay outside; suffer
exile, **depart**, **be absent**.

**exclude**, preclude, **make impossible**;
preempt, forestall, **come before**;
**restrain**; blackball, deny entry, spurn,
**reject**; bar, ban, taboo, black, **prohibit**; cold-shoulder, boycott, send to
Coventry, **avoid**; exempt, dispense,
excuse, **liberate**; except, make an
exception, **make unlike**; omit, disregard, **neglect**; lay aside, relegate, **set
apart**; cancel, **obliterate**; disbar,
remove, disqualify, **displace**, **punish**;
quarantine, **circumscribe**, **enclose**;
excommunicate, segregate, **seclude**;
dismiss, deport, extradite, exile, banish, outlaw, expatriate; weed, sift,
**eliminate**; eradicate, uproot, **eject**;
expurgate, censor, **purify**; deny,
**refuse**; abandon.

Adv. **exclusive of**, barring, bar, except,
save; outside of, short of; let alone;
outside of, extra-.

## 58 Component

N. **component**, component part,
element, item; piece, bit, segment;
link, stitch; word, letter; constituent,
**part**; factor, leaven, **influence**; additive, feature, **adjunct**; one of, member,
one of us; staff, crew, men, company,
complement, **personnel**; ingredient,
**contents**, **tincture**; works, interior;
machinery, **machine**; spare part,
**extra**; set, outfit, **unit**.

Adj. **component**, constituent, ingredient;
proper, native, inherent, **intrinsic**;
made a member, part of, one of;
involved, **mixed**.

Vb. **be one of**, make part of, belong, **be
intrinsic**; **constitute**; become involved
with, share, **participate**; **be mixed**;
belong to, **be related**.

## 59 Extraneousness

N. **extraneousness**; foreign body,
foreign substance, accretion, **addition**;
alien element, **nonconformity**.

**foreigner**, **traveller**; alien, stranger;
Southerner, Northerner; Martian,
little green men; Celtic fringe; limey;
Yank, Yankee, Aussie, Kiwi; paleface; colonial, Creole, **settler**; resident
alien, expatriate; migrant, migrant
worker, emigrant, exile; refugee, **wanderer**; diaspora.

**intruder**, interloper, squatter; outsider,
**upstart**; arrival, new face, newcomer,
new boy, tenderfoot.

Adj. **extraneous**, of external origin,
ulterior, outside, **exterior**, **extrinsic**;
**distant**; foreign, alien, unearthly;
strange, outlandish, barbarian; overseas, ultramarine, transatlantic; extraterrestrial; exotic, hothouse; nomad,
wandering; **separate**; **incoming**;
intrusive; exceptional, **unusual**; **different**; unnatural, supernatural, **magical**;
inadmissible.

Adv. **abroad**; overseas.

## 60 Order

N. **order**, state of order; proportion,
**symmetry**; peace, quiet, **quietude**;
harmony, **concord**; good order,
economy, system, method,
methodology; fixed order, pattern,
rule; custom, routine, **habit**, **ritual**; strict order, discipline; due order,
hierarchy, gradation, rank, place,
position, **serial place**; course, even
tenor, progression, series, **continuity**;
**sequence**; disposition, array, **arrangement**, **composition**.

Adj. **orderly**, decorous, **well-bred**,
**obedient**; **regular**; ordered, classified,
schematic, methodical, systematic,
businesslike; strict, invariable, **uniform**; routine, steady, **habitual**; cor-

rect, shipshape, trim, neat, tidy; spruce, dapper, well-groomed, **clean**; unruffled, **smooth**, direct, **straight**; clear, lucid, **intelligible**.

**Vb. order**, reduce to order, dispose, **arrange**; schematize; regulate, **adjust**; **make uniform**; keep order, call to order, police, control, govern, **rule**, **command**.

**be in order**, accord; range oneself; station oneself; **place oneself**; rally, rally round, **congregate**; follow routine, **be wont**.

**Adv. in order**, just so, **to rule**; orderly; all correct.

## 61 Disorder

**N. disorder**, random order; muddle, chaotic state, chaos, mayhem, **anarchy**; irregularity, anomaly; disharmony, **discord**; violent behaviour, outbreak (see **turmoil**); nihilism, **sedition**; neglect; disarray; dissolution; upheaval, **revolution**; destruction, **havoc**.

**confusion** (see **disorder**); welter, jumble, shambles, hugger-mugger, medley, imbroglio, **mixture**; wilderness, jungle; chaos; swarm, scramble, **crowd**; muddle, litter, clutter, lumber, **rubbish**; farrago, mess, mishmash, hash, hotchpotch, jumble sale, lucky dip, **medley**; Babel, bedlam, madhouse (see **turmoil**).

**complexity**, complication, snarl-up, **difficulty**, **hindrance**; implication, imbroglio, kink, **convolution**; maze, labyrinth, warren; web, **network**; coil, tangle, twist, snarl, ravel; knot; clockwork, machinery; puzzle; awkward situation, pretty kettle of fish, pickle, **predicament**.

**turmoil**, turbulence, tumult, frenzy, ferment, storm, **violence**; pandemonium, inferno; hullabaloo, hubbub, racket,

row, riot, uproar; affray, fracas, dustup, brawl, **fight**; hurly-burly, to-do, rumpus, pother, trouble, disturbance, **commotion**; whirlwind, tornado, hurricane, **gale**; shambles, madhouse, Bedlam; roughhouse, all hell broken loose; gang warfare, **quarrel**; devil to pay.

**slut**, sloven, slattern, **dirty person**; ragamuffin, **poor person**.

**anarchist**, nihilist; lord of misrule, **rioter**.

**Adj. orderless**, **useless**; **sick**; askew, awry; topsy-turvy; wandering; random, **amorphous**; incoherent, rambling; irregular, anomalous; desultory, aimless, casual; chaotic, messy, all anyhow, haywire; unkempt, dishevelled, windswept; bedraggled, messy, **dirty**; sloppy, slipshod, slack, careless.

**complex**, intricate, involved, elaborate, sophisticated, complicated; inextricable.

**disorderly**, unruly; rumbustious, **riotous**; frantic; **drunken**; rough, tempestuous, turbulent, **violent**; lawless, wild, harum-scarum, boisterous.

**Vb. be disordered**, scatter, **disperse**; lose cohesion, **come unstuck**; riot, **disobey**; **come before**; disorder, **derange**.

**rampage**, storm, **be violent**; rush, mob; roister, riot, **revolt**; romp, **amuse oneself**; **be absurd**; fete, give a riotous welcome, **celebrate**.

**Adv. confusedly**, without order, anyhow; without rhyme or reason; pell-mell, higgledy-piggledy, helter-skelter, harum-scarum; topsy-turvy.

## 62 Arrangement: reduction to order

**N. arrangement**, reduction to order; disposal, disposition, **location**; grouping, **assemblage**; division, allotment; method; **coherence**; **management**;

**preparation**; taxonomy, classification, **nomenclature**; analysis; digestion; syntax, conjugation, **grammar**; gradation, graduation, **measurement**, **series**; **continuity**; timing; **composition**; result of arrangement, array, system, form, **order**; cosmos, **universe**; organic creature, **organism**; score, **music**; layout, pattern, architecture, **structure**; weave, **crossing**; choreography, **dance**; collection, assortment, **accumulation**; schematic arrangement; computer program; register, file, **record**; inventory, catalogue, table, **list**; code, digest, synopsis, **compendium**; treatise, essay, article, **dissertation**, book; atlas, **map**; scheme, **plan**; composition, **compromise**, **compact**, **conditions**; class, group, **classification**.

**sorting**; reference system, cross-reference; file, folder, card index, pigeonhole, slot; sieve, strainer.

**Adj. arranged**, disposed, ordered, schematic; methodical, systematic; precise, definite; classified, assorted; **regular**; **orderly**.

**Vb. arrange**, set, dispose; formulate, form, orchestrate, score, **compose**; range, rank; position, **place**; marshal, array; bring back to order, rally, **bring together**; grade, size, group, space; thread together, **connect**; settle, fix, determine, define; allot, allocate, assign, distribute, deal, **apportion**; rearrange, trim, tidy, **prepare**, **plan**, **manage**.

**regularize**, reduce to order, put to rights, **rectify**, **adjust**; regulate, coordinate, phase; schematize; **make uniform**.

**class**, classify, group; specify, **name**; process; analyse, divide; dissect, **decompose**; rate, rank, grade, evaluate, **estimate**; sort, sift, seed; **eliminate**;

docket, label, **mark**; file, pigeonhole; index, reference, tabulate; catalogue, inventory, **list**; register, **record**; codify, program, digest.

**unravel**, untangle, disentangle, disembroil, ravel, card, **evolve**; iron, press, **smooth**; **make better**; unscramble; **clean**; remove misunderstanding, explain, **interpret**.

## 63 Derangement

**N. derangement**; interchange; displacement; sabotage, **hindrance**; **separation**; disturbance; timestop; **fold**; madness; **violence**; state of disorder, **disorder**.

**Adj. disarranged**; demented, **insane**.

**Vb. derange**, disorder; disturb, touch, **move**; meddle, interfere, **hinder**; mislay, lose, **misplace**; muddle, confound, confuse, convulse, make havoc, scramble; spoil, mar, damage, sabotage, **impair**; strain, bend, twist, **force**; unhinge, dislocate, sprain, rick, **displace**; unseat, dislodge, derail; unbalance, upset, overturn, capsize, **invert**; shake, jiggle, toss, **agitate**; trouble, perturb, unsettle, discompose, disconcert, ruffle, rattle, flurry, fluster, **distract**; interrupt, mistime; misdirect, disorientate, **mislead**, pervert; unhinge, drive mad, **make mad**, **enrage**.

**jumble**, shuffle, interchange, **transpose**; **mix**; toss, tumble, **agitate**; ruffle, tousle; rumple, crumple, crease, crush, **fold**; mess; muddle, litter, clutter; scatter, fling about, **disperse**; play havoc with, play merry hell with, **hinder**.

**bedevil**, confuse, make a hash of; confound, complicate, perplex, involve, ravel, entangle, tangle, embroil; turn topsy-turvy, **invert**; send haywire.

## 64 Precedence

**N. precedence**, antecedence, going before, **preceding**; **priority**; front position, prosthesis, **front**; higher position, pride of place; preference, **choice**; leadership, hegemony, **authority**; leading; precedent, **precursor**; past history, **past time**.

**Adj. preceding**, precedent, antecedent, foregoing, outgoing; anterior, former, previous, **prior**; aforesaid, said; anticipatory; leading, avant-garde; preliminary, preparatory; **frontal**; first come.

**Vb. come before**, be first to arrive, **precede**; go first, run ahead; lead, guide, conduct, **indicate**; pioneer, **discover**; head; have precedence, **be superior**; **influence**; open, **begin**; preamble, prelude, **preface**; introduce; get ahead, **be before**; antedate, **be past**.

**put in front**, lead with, advance, send ahead, station before, **place**; prefix, **add**; front, face, tip, top; presuppose, **suppose**; preface, prelude, **initiate**.

**Adv. before**, ahead; preparatory to; above.

## 65 Sequence

**N. sequence**, coming after, descent, line, lineage; going after, **following**; reasoning, **addition**; succession, **transfer**; rota; series, **continuity**; pursuance, **pursuit**; **success**; second place; last place, **rear**; consequence, **sequel**, **effect**; end.

**Adj. sequential**, following; incoming; proximate, next, **near**; posterior, latter, **subsequent**; another, second, third, **additional**; successive, consecutive, **continuous**; alternate, every second, every other, **back**; consequent.

**Vb. come after**, come next, ensue, **follow**; follow close, **be near**; succeed,

inherit, supplant, **substitute**; alternate, **be periodic**; relieve.

**place after**, suffix, append; subscribe, **add**.

**Adv. after**, following; afterwards, **rearward**; **consequently**; **finally**; next; below.

## 66 Precursor

**N. precursor**, predecessor, ancestor, forbear, patriarch, **parentage**; early man, **humankind**; **antiquity**; eldest, firstborn; pioneer, pathfinder, **traveller**; guide, pilot, **leader**; scout; vanguard, avant-garde; forerunner, outrider; herald, harbinger, **messenger**; dawn, foretaste, prognostic, preview, premonition, **warning**, **omen**; trailer; precedent, **example**; antecedent, prefix, preposition, **adjunct**; eve, vigil, day before, **priority**.

**prelude**, preliminary, preamble, preface, prologue, foreword; opening, introduction, **beginning**; lead, " heading, frontispiece, **front**; groundwork, foundation, **basis**, **preparation**; aperitif, appetizer; overture, voluntary, **musical piece**; premises, **supposition**.

**Adj. precursory**, preliminary, exploratory, **preparatory**; **beginning**; precedent, **preceding**.

## 67 Sequel

**N. sequel**, consequence, result, aftermath, by-product, spin-off, **effect**; **end**; aftereffect; hangover, morning after; aftertaste; afterglow, fallout; afterbirth, placenta, **obstetrics**; legacy, surprise, **lack of expectation**; afterthought; double take, second try; epilogue, postscript; peroration, last words; follow-through, follow-up; sequel, **hook**; tag, coda, **rear**; appendage, appendix, codicil, supplement, **adjunct**; suffix, affix, **grammar**; tail;

queue, pigtail, ponytail, **hair**; afters, dessert, **dish**; survival, afterlife, hereafter, **future state**.

**retinue**, following, **follower**; queue, **series**; suite, train, **procession**; tail, tailback, wake; trailer, **vehicle**.

**successor**, descendant, **posterity**; heir, **beneficiary**; replacement, **substitute**; fresh blood, new broom, **upstart**; latecomer, newcomer; satellite, hanger-on, **dependant**; finalist, **survivor**.

**68 Beginning**

**N. beginning**, birth, rise (see **origin**); infancy, babyhood, **youth**; onset, **arrival**; **appearance**; inception, institution, constitution, foundation, establishment; invention; creation, **production**; innovation; initiative; introduction, **prelude**; alpha, first letter, initial; head, heading, headline, caption, **label**; title page; van, front, forefront, **front**; dawn, **morning**; first blush, first glance, first sight, first impression, first lap, first round, first stage; primer, outline; rudiments, elements, first principles, alphabet, ABC; **approach**; outbreak, onset, **attack**; debutante, starter, **beginner**; precedent, **precursor**; **preparation**.

**debut**, presentation, initiation; opening; first night, first appearance, first offence; first step, first move, move, gambit; maiden voyage, maiden speech; baptism of fire.

**start**, outset; zero hour, D-day; send-off; house-warming, honeymoon; fresh start, new beginning, **reversion**; precedent; standing start, starter.

**origin**, conception, genesis, birth, nativity; ancestry, **parentage**; rise, **source**; nest, womb, seedbed; bud, germ, seed; egg, protoplasm, **organism**; cradle, **home**.

**entrance**; inlet, **gulf**; mouth, opening,

orifice; threshold, **access**; porch, **lobby**; gateway, **doorway**; frontier, border, **limit**; outskirts, environs, suburbs, **surroundings**; pass, corridor, **approach**, **passage**.

**Adj. beginning**, initiative; elemental, **fundamental**; aboriginal, primordial, **primal**; rudimentary, elementary, crude, **immature**; germinal, nascent, budding, incipient, inchoate, raw, begun; early, infant, **new**; just begun.

**first**, initial, primary, maiden, natal; **original**; unprecedented, **new**; foremost, front, **frontal**; leading, principal, head, chief, **supreme**.

**Vb. begin**, make a beginning, commence, inchoate; open; dawn, burst forth; arise, emerge, appear; rise; sprout, germinate; **be born**; start; start work; **prepare**; resume, begin again, go back to square one, make a fresh start; start afresh, reshuffle, resume; set to, set about, set to work; attack, tackle, face, address oneself; go to it, **undertake**.

**initiate**, found, launch; originate, invent, think of, **discover**; **generate**; introduce; start; prompt, promote, set going; raise; put to work, **employ**; lead, pioneer, break new ground, **come before**; broach, open, ventilate, air; open fire.

**auspicate**, inaugurate, open; institute, install, **commission**; found, establish, **cause**; be a founder member; christen, launch, **name**; initiate, blood, flesh; **prepare**.

**Adv. initially**, originally; first, firstly; primarily, first of all, before everything.

**69 End**

**N. end**, close; payoff, result, **effect**; expiration, lapse; determination, closure, guillotine; death blow, quietus; knockout, clincher, **knock**; catastrophe, denouement; ending, finish, curtain; term, period, stop, halt, **cessation**; final stage, latter end, **evening**; peroration, last words, swansong, coda, **sequel**; last stage, last round, last lap, home stretch; last ball; last breath, last gasp, extremities, **decease**; final examination.

extremity, final point, omega; ultimate point, extreme, pole, antipodes; extreme case; farthest point; fringe, verge, brink, **edge**; frontier, boundary, **limit**; terminal point, terminus, terminal, **goal, objective**; dregs, foot, toe, bottom, nadir, **base**; bottom dollar, last penny, **poverty**; tip, cusp, point, **sharp point**; vertex, peak, head, top, **summit**; tail, tail end, **sequel**; arm, stump, **limb**; shirt-tail, **hanging object**; end, butt end, **rear**; tag, epilogue, postscript, appendix, **adjunct**; suffix, **grammar**.

finality; bitter end; time, deadline; breakup, **cessation**; dissolution, **destruction**; last things, doom, destiny, **fate**; last trump, crack of doom; resurrection day, end of time, end of all things, **future state**.

Adj. ending, final, terminal, last, ultimate, supreme, extreme, polar; definitive, conclusive; at an end; settled, decided, set at rest; finished; penultimate, last but one; last but two; hindmost, rear, **back**.

Vb. end, come to an end, expire, **elapse**, close, finish, conclude; become extinct, **die**; come to a close, have run its course; stop, go home, **cease**.

terminate, conclude, close, determine, decide, settle; bring to an end, put an end to, put a term to, put a stop to, make an end of, put paid to; discontinue, drop; finish, achieve, consummate, get through, **carry through**; call it a day; stop, **halt**.

Adv. **finally**; at last, at long last; never again, nevermore.

## 70 Middle

N. middle, midst; mean, **average**; medium, middle term; thick, thick of things; heart, body, kernel, nave, hub, navel, **centre**; nucleus; midweek, half tide; **middle way**; equator; midriff, diaphragm, **partition**; half distance, halfway house; mixed economy, **mixture**.

Adj. middle, medial, mean, mezzo, mid, **median**; mediate, **central**; intermediate; equidistant; mediterranean.

Adv. **midway**; halfway.

## 71 Continuity: uninterrupted sequence

N. continuity; overlap; immediacy; succession; line, lineage, descent, dynasty; one thing after another, **sequence**; natural sequence; continuous time, continuum, **perpetuity**; continuous motion, assembly line; endless band, **rotation**; recurrence, cycle, **repetition, frequency**; snowball, **increase**; course, run, career, flow, trend, **tendency; progression**; circuit, round; daily round, routine, practice, custom, **habit**; track, trail, wake, **sequel**; chain, chain reaction, domino theory; circle.

series, gradation, **degree**; succession, run, rally, break; progression, **increase; decrease**; pedigree, family tree, lineage, **genealogy**; chain, line, string, thread; line of battle, line ahead, line abreast; rank, file, echelon; array, **arrangement**; row; range, ridge; portico; ladder, steps, stairs, staircase, **ascent**; range, tier, storey, **layer**; keyboard, manual; set, suite, suit (of cards); assortment, **classification**; spectrum, rainbow; gamut, scale, **musical note**; **bridge**; hierarchy, pyramid.

**procession**; crocodile, queue, traffic jam; tail, train, suite, **retinue**; caravan, file, funeral procession; triumph, **celebration**; cavalcade, **pageant**.

**Adj. continuous**; consecutive, running, successive; serial; progressive, gradual; solid, smooth, circular; direct, immediate; continual, incessant, ceaseless, unremitting, nonstop, constant, **perpetual**; **periodic**; recurrent, monotonous, **uniform**; linear, rectilinear, **straight**.

**Vb. run on**, continue; succeed, overlap, **come after**; file, defile; circle, **circuit**.

**continue**, extend, prolong, **lengthen**; thread, string, **connect**; size, grade, **graduate**; file, tabulate, **list**; maintain continuity, **persevere**; provide an heir.

**Adv. continuously**; one after another; at a stretch, together, running; nose to tail.

## 72 Discontinuity: interrupted sequence

**N. discontinuity**, lack of continuity; **cessation**; interval, hiatus, pause, time lag, **lull**; **disorder**, **roughness**; broken ranks; ladder, run; parenthesis, episode, **interjection**; caesura, division, **separation**, **punctuation**; break, fracture, flaw, fault, split, crack, cut, **gap**; missing link; broken thread; **sophistry**; patchwork, crazy paving; purple patch, **misfit**; irregularity, ragged volley.

**Adj. discontinuous**; broken; disconnected; discrete, **separate**; **infrequent**; patchy, bitty, **variegated**; desultory, irregular, intermittent, **fitful**; alternate, stop-go, **periodical**; spasmodic, jerky, bumpy, uneven, **rough**; incoherent, **illogical**; **extraneous**.

**Vb. be discontinuous**, halt, rest, **pause**; alternate.

**discontinue**, suspend, desist; interrupt, intervene, break, **interfere**; interpose, interject, punctuate, **put between**; disconnect, **disunite**.

**Adv. discontinuously**.

## 73 Term: serial position

**N. serial place**, term, order, remove, **degree**; rank, ranking, grade, gradation; station, place, position, slot; status, standing, footing; point, mark, pitch, level, storey; step, tread, round, rung; stage, milestone, climacteric, climax, **summit**; bottom rung, nadir, base.

**Vb. grade**, rank, rate, place; stagger, **space**, **graduate**.

**have rank**, hold a place, occupy a position, **be situated**; find a niche, **place oneself**.

## 74 Assemblage

**N. assemblage**, collection, **combination**, **arrangement**; compilation, anthology, **composition**; gathering, harvest, vintage, **agriculture**, **acquisition**; harvest home, **storage**, **celebration**; concentration; **focus**; muster, levy, call-up; review, parade, **pageant**; march, rally; roundup; **animal husbandry**; collective, **compulsion**, **farm**; conspiracy, caucus, **party**; collective noun, syntax, **grammar**.

**assembly**, mutual attraction, **attraction**; congregation; gathering, meeting, meet; coven; business meeting, convention, convocation, **synod**; shire moot, **council**; eisteddfod, festival, **celebration**; reunion, get-together, **social gathering**; company, at home, party; circle; encounter group, **therapy**; symposium, **conference**.

**group**, constellation, galaxy, cluster, **star**; troop, bevy, swarm, flock, herd; drove, team; pack, kennel; stable, string; nest; brood, hatch, litter, gaggle, flight, skein, shoal, school; unit, brigade, **formation**; batch, lot, clutch; brace, pair, span; leash; set, class, genus, species, **sort**; breed, tribe, clan, household, **family**; brotherhood, fellowship, guild, union, **association**; club, **society**; sphere, quarter, circle; **elite**; social group, **nobility**; they, self; age group, stream, **class**; hand (at cards); set, **series**.

**band**, company, troupe; cast, **actor**; brass band, pop group, **orchestra**; team, string, fifteen, eleven, eight; knot, bunch; set, clique, ring; gang, squad, party, crew, complement; manpower, staff, **personnel**; following, **retinue**; squadron, troop, platoon; unit, regiment, corps, **formation**; squad, posse; force, body, host, **armed force**, **multitude**; **society**; merry men, **friendship**; committee, commission, **consignee**; panel, **list**; establishment, cadre, **structure**.

**crowd**, throng, **multitude**; huddle, cluster, swarm, colony; small crowd, knot, bunch; mass, mob, ruck, **rabble**; full house; press, squash, squeeze, jam, scrum, rush, crush; rush hour, **haste**; flood, spate, deluge, stream, **great quantity**; volley, shower, hail, storm; **increase**; invasion; herd instinct, crowd psychology, mass hysteria, **feeling**.

**bunch**, assortment, lot, **medley**; clump, tuft, wisp, handful; fan; bag, **receptacle**; hand (tobacco); bundle, packet, wad; batch, pack, package, parcel; portfolio, file, dossier, **record**; bale, roll, bolt; load, pack, **contents**; faggot;

tussock, shock, sheaf, truss, heap; swathe, rick, stack, **storage**; thicket, **wood**; bouquet, nosegay, posy, spray; skein, hank.

**accumulation**; conglomeration, aggregation; concentration; pileup, **collision**; masonry, mass, pile, pyramid, **edifice**, **high structure**; heap; drift, snowdrift; snowball, **increment**; debris, detritus; dump, **rubbish**; cumulus, storm cloud, **cloud**; store, storage, **provision**, **treasury**; magazine, battery, armoury, quiver, **arsenal**; bus garage, car park; set, lot, **series**; mixed lot, mixed bag, **medley**; kit, stock; range, selection, assortment, **merchandise**; shop window, display, **exhibit**; museum, **collection**; menagerie, aquarium, **zoo**; literary collection, **library**; miscellany, compilation, **composition**; symposium, **dissertation**.

**accumulator**, squirrel, miser, **niggard**, **treasurer**; connoisseur, **collector**; harvester, picker, **farmer**; assembler; whip; shepherd, sheep dog, **herdsman**.

**Adj. assembled**, met; crowded, packed, serried, **dense**; tight; lousy with, stiff with, **full**; populous, teeming, **multitudinous**.

**Vb. congregate**, meet, rendezvous; assemble, rejoin; associate, come together, make a crowd, gather, gather round, collect, troop, rally; resort to, **converge**; band together; mass, concentrate; conglomerate, huddle, cluster, bunch, **crowd**; throng, swarm, seethe, mill around; surge, stream, flood, **grow**; infest, invade.

**bring together**, assemble, put together, **join**; draw, **attract**; gather, collect, rally, muster; concentrate, consolidate; lump together, group, brigade, unite; compile, **compose**; focus, centre; convene, convoke, summon; hold a meeting; herd, shepherd, corral, **enclose**; mass, aggregate; accumulate, conglomerate, heap, pile, amass; catch, take, net, **acquire**; scrape together, **store**; truss, bundle, parcel, package; bunch, bind, **tie**; pack, cram, stuff, **fill**; stack, **elevate**.

**Adv.together**; all together.

## 75 Nonassembly. Dispersion
**N.dispersion**, breakup, **separation**; spread, scatter, radiation; sprawl, suburbia, delegation; **waste**; circulation; sprinkling; going home; sea drift, driftwood; diaspora.

**Adj.unassembled**, scattered, sporadic, sparse, **infrequent**; broadcast; widespread, far-flung, **spacious**; epidemic, **universal**; spread, **separate**; dishevelled; centrifugal; adrift, astray; wandering.

**Vb.be dispersed**, disperse, scatter, spread, **rarefy**; spread fast, spread like wildfire, flood; radiate, branch, **diverge**; break ranks, **separate**; lose coherence, **come unstuck**; go each their own ways, **wander**; drift apart; straggle, trail, fall behind, **stray**; cover, litter; explode, burst, fly apart, **be violent**; evaporate, melt, **liquefy**; disintegrate, dissolve, decay, **decompose**.

**disperse**, scatter, diffract; splay, **diverge**; separate, **sunder**; disseminate, diffuse, broadcast, sow, strew, bestrew, spread; dissipate, dispel, disintegrate, **decompose**; **waste**; dispense, deal, allot, **apportion**; disband, dismiss, send home, **disunite**; draft, detach, **send**; sprinkle, splash, spray, spatter, **moisten**; circulate; disorder, **derange**; rout, **defeat**.

**Adv.sporadically**; everywhere.

## 76 Focus: place of meeting
**N.focus**, junction, town centre, **centre**; crossroads; switchboard, exchange, nerve centre; hub, nub, core, heart, kernel, **middle**; hall, civic centre, village hall, village green; campus, quad; market place, **market**; resort, retreat, haunt; club, pub, local, **tavern**; headquarters, depot; standard; venue, rendezvous, **meeting place**; nest, home ground, **home**; fireside; cynosure, centre of attraction, **attraction**; place of pilgrimage, Mecca, **goal**, **objective**.

**Vb.focus**, **converge**; concentrate; bring to a point, point to.

## 77 Class
**N.classification**, arrangement; taxonomy; diagnosis, specification; category, class, bracket; set; head, heading, section; division, branch, department, faculty; pocket, pigeonhole, **compartment**; tier, rank, caste, status, standing, **degree**; province, domain, sphere, range; sex, gender; blood group, stream, **group**; clique, **band**; persuasion, school of thought, denomination, **sect**.

**sort**, order, type, version, variety, kind, species; manner, genre, style; nature, quality, grade, calibre, **character**; mark, brand, **label**; ilk, stripe, kidney, feather, colour; stamp, mould, shape, frame, make, **form**; assortment, kit, set, suit, lot, **series**.

**breed**, strain, blood, family, kin, tribe, clan, caste, line, **race**, **genealogy**; kingdom, phylum, class, order, genus, species.

**Adj.generic**, typical; sexual, masculine, feminine, neuter.

**classificatory**; sectional, **sectarian**.

**78 Inclusion**

N. inclusion; embodiment; comprehension, admission, **reception**; membership; coverage, **generality**; skill; set, complement, package, **whole**; package deal, **compact**; constitution, **composition**; capacity, volume, measure, **space**, **measurement**; accommodation, **room**.

Adj. **inclusive**; holding; all-in; accommodating; overall, **comprehensive**; wholesale, blanket, sweeping, **extensive**; without exception, total, global, worldwide, universal, whole; expansive, general.

included; admissible, eligible; constituent; inherent, **component**, **intrinsic**; pertinent, **relative**; classified with, **similar**; **akin**; additional; inner, **interior**.

Vb. **be included**, make one of, **be one of**; enlist, join, obtain membership, **join a party**; **be one of**; **be mixed**; **be related**; **enter**; constitute, **compose**; overlap, belong, **be intrinsic**.

comprise, include, involve, imply, hold, have, count, boast, **contain**; take, measure, **be equal**; receive, **admit**; accommodate; comprehend, encapsulate, cover; embody, incorporate, encompass, embrace, encircle, envelop, **enclose**; have everything, **be complete**.

number with, reckon among, enumerate with; **class**.

Adv. **including**.

**79 Generality**

N. **generality**; universal; macrocosm, **universe**; panorama, synopsis, **whole**; open house, dragnet; currency, custom, **habit**, **fashion**; **presence**; pandemic, epidemic, **disease**; open letter, circular, **publicity**; ruck, run, **average**; internationalism, **philanthropy**; classification.

everyman; little man; common type, **common man**; everybody, every one, each one, every man Jack, **all**; all sorts, anyone, whosoever, N or M; anything, what have you, what you will.

Adj. **general**, generic, typical, representative, standard; collective, pan-, blanket, **comprehensive**; broad, sweeping; current, prevalent, **ubiquitous**; usual, normal, customary, **habitual**; vague, loose, indefinite, **inexact**; impersonal; common, ordinary, average, **median**; commonplace, **typical**; popular, mass, vulgar, plebeian.

universal, catholic; national, international, cosmopolitan, global, worldwide, widespread, **extensive**; pervasive, penetrating, besetting, prevalent, epidemic, pandemic, **ubiquitous**; every, each, any, all, all without exception, **whole**.

Vb. **be general**, **comprise**; prevail, obtain, have currency, **be wont**; penetrate, pervade.

generalize, broaden, widen; spread, broadcast, diffuse, **disperse**.

Adv. **generally**, without exception, mainly, **wholly**; to a man, always.

**80 Speciality**

N. **speciality**, specific quality, personality; **unity**; individuality; personality, make-up, **character**; characteristic; idiosyncrasy, peculiarity, distinctive feature, trademark, mannerism, quirk, foible; trait, mark, feature, attribute; **accompaniment**; distinction, point of difference, **difference**; idiom, jargon, brogue, patois, **dialect**; technical language, **language**; variant reading, version, **variant**; exception, special case, **nonconformity**; special skill, special study, **skill**.

**particulars**, special points, specification; circumstances.

**particularism**, chosen race, chosen few; caste; chauvinism, nationality, nationalism, individualism, egoism.

**self**, ego, id, identity, personality; psyche, soul, **spirit**; I, myself, number one; we, ourselves; yourself, himself, herself, itself, themselves; us, **group**; real self, a person, a character, individual, being, **person**.

**Adj. special**, specific, respective, particular; peculiar, singular, unique, **one**; individual, characteristic, idiomatic, original, **inimitable**; native, proper, personal, private; appropriate, apt; typical, **characteristic**; distinctive, marked, noteworthy, **unusual**; several, **different**.

**definite**, definitive; distinct, concrete, express, explicit, clear-cut; certain, exact, precise, **accurate**; circumstantial; bespoke, made to order, made to measure.

**private**, intimate, esoteric, personal, exclusive; secret, **latent**.

**Vb. specify**, be specific, enumerate, quantify, **number**; detail, **list**; cite, mention, **name**; be diffuse; define, determine, **limit**, discriminate; pinpoint, locate, **place**; explain, interpret; signify, denote, **mean**; designate, **indicate**; substantiate, cause; **differentiate**; be attentive, **study**.

**Adv. specially**, especially; personally; specifically, to order; with respect to.

**severally**, each, apiece; respectively.

**namely**, that is to say, to wit.

## 81 Rule

**N. rule**, norm, formula, canon, code; maxim, principle, **precept**; law, law of nature, universal principle; firm principle; strict law; statute, **law**; regulation, order, party line; guide, precedent, model, pattern, **prototype**; form, standard, keynote, **example**.

**regularity**, consistency, constancy; **order**; normal state, natural condition; form, routine, drill, practice, custom, **habit**; fixed ways, rut, groove; method, system, **arrangement**; convention, **conformity**.

**Adj. regular**, constant, steady, **periodical**; even, **smooth**; circular, square; **uniform**, methodical, systematic, **orderly**; normal, **typical**; customary, **usual**; conventional.

**Adv. to rule**; regularly.

## 82 Multiformity

**N. multiformity**, multiplicity; variety, diversity; schizophrenia, split personality; metamorphosis; variability; **caprice**; kaleidoscope.

**Adj. multiform**, multifarious; multiple, multiplex, manifold, many-sided; versatile, all-round; variform, heterogeneous, diverse; motley, mosaic, **mixed**; indiscriminate, irregular, **variegated**; divers, sundry; all manner of, of every description, **different**; variable, changeable, whimsical, **capricious**.

## 83 Conformity

**N. conformity**; **observance**; accommodation, reconciliation, **agreement**, **adaptation**; submission; similarity; bourgeois ethic, **etiquette**; convention, form, **fashion**, **practice**; affectation; repetition, flattery; generality.

**example**, type, pattern, model, **prototype**; stock example; case, instance, illustration, object lesson; sample, cross-section; representative, specimen, specimen page, representative selection; trailer, foretaste, **precursor**;

precedent.

**conformist**; Philistine; pedant; copycat, yes-man, **imitator**; follower, loyalist.

**Adj. conformable**, adaptable, consistent with; malleable, **flexible**; agreeable, complaisant, accommodating; following, faithful, loyal, true-blue; conventional, **orthodox**; slavish, servile.

**typical**, normal, natural, of daily occurrence, everyday, ordinary, common, common or garden, **general**; average, **median, middling**; true to type; commonplace, prosaic; conventional; heterosexual, straight; habitual, **usual**; representative, stock, standard; exemplary; **relevant**.

**regulated**, regular; shipshape, copybook, **orderly**; correct, sound, proper, **orthodox**; precise, scrupulous, meticulous, **formal**; rigid, strict, unbending, uncompromising, **severe**.

**Vb. conform**, correspond, conform to, **accord**; adapt oneself; pass, pass muster, **suffice**; bend, yield, **soften**; **submit**; comply with, **observe**; tally with, **accord**; rubberstamp, echo, **repeat**; follow precedent, **obey**; emulate, follow suit, **imitate, copy**; **be irresolute**; **be wont**.

**make conform**, conform, assimilate; acclimatize; drill, **make uniform**; shape, press, **form**; stamp, imprint, **mark**; train, lead, **direct**; bend, twist, force, **compel**; accommodate, fit, square, trim, **adjust**; **smooth**.

**exemplify**, illustrate, cite, quote, instance; produce an example, give an instance.

**Adj. conformably**, to rule; of course.

## 84 Nonconformity

**N. nonconformity**; contrast, oasis; **dissent**; irregularity, **deviation**; oddity; rarity; infraction; breach of practice, defiance of custom; wonder, miracle,

**prodigy**; anomaly, exception, **exclusion**; escape clause; special case, **speciality**; individuality, idiosyncrasy, quirk, kink, peculiarity, mannerism.

**abnormality**, aberration, **deviation**; mutation, **variant**; abortion, monstrous birth, monstrosity, monster; sadism, masochism; **male; female.**

**nonconformist**, dissident, dissenter, maverick, **heretic, sectarian**; blackleg, scab, **cad**; Bohemian, dropout; rebel, angry young man, punk, handful, recalcitrant, fanatic, **crank**; outsider, outlaw, criminal; pariah, **outcast**; hermit, loner, **solitary**; nomad, tramp, **wanderer**; joker, ugly duckling; **misfit**; deviant, odd type, albino, sport, freak; oddity, original, character, card, caution, odd customer, oddball, **crank**; queer fish, **laughing stock**; curiosity, rarity, rare example; neither fish, flesh, fowl nor good red herring; hermaphrodite, **eunuch**; invert, homosexual, lesbian, gay; pansy, fairy, queen, queer; transvestite, **transformation**; pervert; mongrel, half-breed, **hybrid**.

**rara avis**, unicorn, phoenix; sphinx, centaur, Minotaur; dragon, salamander, hydra; sea serpent, leviathan, Lock Ness monster; mermaid, siren; gorgon, cyclops; **fantasy**.

**Adj. unconformable**; **contrary**; stiff, **rigid, obstinate**; recalcitrant, **defiant**; crotchety, prickly, awkward, eccentric, whimsical, **capricious, sullen**; arbitrary, a law to oneself, **independent**; freakish, outlandish; original, unique, **special**; solitary, standoffish, **unsociable**; dissident, nonconformist, **sectarian**; unorthodox; offbeat, Bohemian, informal; irregular; lawless, criminal, **illegal**; aberrant, astray; incongruous; alien, exotic, **extraneous**;

hard to place, nondescript, nameless, **unknown**; stray, wandering; amphibious, ambiguous, **equivocal**; exempt.

**unusual**; **unknown**; newfangled, **new**; exotic, **extraneous**; extraordinary, way-out; phenomenal; unparalleled; singular, unique, **special**, **infrequent**; rare, choice, **excellent**; strange, bizarre, curious, odd, queer, rum; funny, peculiar, fantastic, grotesque, **ridiculous**; noteworthy, remarkable, surprising, miraculous, **wonderful**; mysterious, inexplicable, unaccountable, **occult**; incredible, **impossible**, **improbable**; monstrous; unnatural, preternatural, supernatural; outsize, **enormous**; shocking; indescribable, **inexpressible**.

**abnormal**, unnatural, supernatural, preternatural see (**unusual**); aberrant, freakish; atypical, exceptional; anomalous; deviant; homosexual, lesbian, gay, bent, queer; bisexual; mongrel, hybrid, **mixed**; irregular; nonstandard, substandard, subnormal; **great**; amorphous.

**Vb. be unconformable**; infringe a law, infringe usage, infringe custom; break a law, break a habit, break with custom; violate a law, violate custom; **be free**; **be early**; **look back**; get round; stretch a point; baffle all description.

**Adv. unconformably**, except, unless, save, barring, beside, without, let alone; however, yet, but.

## 85 Number

**N. number**, real number, prime number, integer; numeral, digit, figure, character; decimal system, quantity, X, symbol, constant; mapping; operator, sign; function, variable, argument; vector, matrix; surd; expression; formula, series.

**numerical element**; coefficient, multiple, dividend, divisor; quotient, factor, fraction, mixed number; numerator, denominator; decimal; common factor, common denominator; reciprocal, complement; parameter; power, root, exponent, index, logarithm, antilogarithm; differential, derivative, integral, determinant.

**ratio**, proportion; progression, sine, tangent; cosine, cotangent; percentage, per cent.

**numerical result**, answer, product, equation; sum, total, aggregate, **whole**; difference, residual, **remainder**; bill, score, tally, **addition**.

**Adj. numerical**, numeral; cardinal, ordinal; round, whole; even, odd; prime; positive, negative, surd, radical; divisible; multiple; reciprocal, complementary; fractional, decimal; incommensurable; proportional; exponential, differential, integral; transcendental; rational, irrational.

## 86 Numeration

**N. numeration**, census, reckoning, sum, tally, score, runs, points; count, recount; summation, calculation, computation, **measurement**; algorithm, decimal system; accountancy; poll.

**numerical operation**, notation; addition, multiplication, division, proportion, rule of three, practice, analysis; extraction of roots, reduction, **evolution**, convolution, approximation; permutation, combination, variation.

**mathematics**, arithmetic, algebra; set theory; differential calculus; topology; geometry, trigonometry; algorithm, operational research, critical path analysis; **policy**; **reasoning**.

**statistics**, figures; mode, mean, **average**; significance, deviation, standard error; skew; poll, **vote**; census; roll call, muster, muster roll, account, **list**; demography, birth rate, vital statistics; price index, cost of living, **price**; bar graph, histogram, scatter diagram, pie chart, **plan**; **map**.

**data processing**, computation; computer technology, cybernetics, **mechanics**; software, program, input, output, throughput, feedback; storage; timesharing; machine code, computer language, BASIC, Fortran, Cobol; card punch, keyboard; data, bit, byte; processor, word processor; data bank, memory, **store**; visual display unit, **appearance**; hard copy, printout; **information**.

**counting instrument**, abacus; multiplication table; tape measure, yardstick, **gauge**; calculating machine, calculator, cash register, tote; computer microprocessor, **microelectronics**.

**enumerator**, computer; calculator, counter, teller; wrangler; programmer; actuary, **accountant**; **surveyor**.

**Adj. numerable**; calculable, measurable, mensurable, **metrical**; commensurate, **equal**; proportionate, **relative**; incommensurate, incommensurate, **unequal**; eligible, admissible.

**statistical**; geometrical; quartile.

**computerized**; automatic; analogue, binary.

**Vb. number**, cast, count, tell; score, keep a count; affix numbers; enumerate, poll; take a poll, take a census; muster, take roll call; take stock, inventory, **list**; recount, **repeat**; check, audit, balance, **account**; aggregate, amount to, total, come to.

**do sums**, add; **subtract**; multiply, **augment**; divide, **sunder**; square, cube, extract roots; integrate, differentiate; figure; reduce; map; compute, calculate, reckon, **measure**; estimate,

appraise.

**computerize**, automate, **empower**; program, process; compute, **operate**.

## 87 List

**N. list**; inventory, stock list; chart, table, catalogue; portfolio, **security**; statement, schedule, manifest; invoice; numerical list; score; price list, tariff, bill, account, **price**; registry; file, register, **record**; ticket, docket, tally, **label**; ledger, books, **account book**; table of contents, index; bill of fare, menu, calorie table; programme, prospectus, synopsis, syllabus, **compendium**; roll, electorate; muster roll, payroll; Army List, **personnel**; census; book list, bibliography, **reading matter**; rota, roster, panel; family tree, pedigree, **genealogy**; scroll, roll of honour, honours' board; blacklist, **accused person, censure**; sick list, **sick person**; calendar, engagement book; question paper, questionnaire; alphabet, **order, letter**; repertory, repertoire.

**word list**, vocabulary, glossary, lexicon, thesaurus, **dictionary**.

**directory**, gazetteer, atlas; almanac, calendar, timetable, **chronology**; ABC; Army List, Who's Who, **reference book**.

**Adj. listed**.

**Vb. list**, enumerate; inventory, catalogue, calendar, index, tabulate; file, docket, schedule, enter, book, post, **register**; enlist, matriculate, inscribe; score, keep count, **number**.

## 88 Unity

**N. unity**; **identity**; **whole**; individuality, **speciality**; monotheism; singleness; solitude; **separation**; union, solidarity, coherence, association; **combination**.

**unit**, integer, one, ace, item, piece; individual, atom, entity, **person**; single piece, monolith; nonce word; none else, naught beside; single instance, only exception; solo, monologue; single person, bachelor, **celibate**; single parent, **divorce**; hermit, **solitary**; set, outfit, package; package deal.

**Adj. one**, singular, sole, single, solitary; unique, only, lone; **identical**; without a second; once only; a, an, a certain, **anonymous**; individual, **special**; absolute, universal, **general**; unilateral; mono-; all of a piece, monolithic **uniform**; compact, solid; **dense**; indivisible.

**alone**, lonely, **friendless**; lonesome, solitary, lone, **unsociable**; insular, **distant**; single-handed; unaccompanied; celibate.

**Vb. be one**, stand alone; unite, **combine**; isolate, **set apart**.

**Adv. singly**, one at a time; once, once only; just this once, never again, only, simply; alone, per se.

## 89 Accompaniment

**N. accompaniment, continuity, union**; permanent attribute, **society**; companionship, togetherness, **friendship**; **association**; coincidence; attendance, company; parallel course.

**concomitant**, attribute, **essential part**; complement; accessory, appendage, fixture, **adjunct**; by-product, corollary; symptom; coincidence, **chance**; context, circumstance, **state**; background; accompaniment, obbligato; accompanist, **musician**; entourage, court, **retainer**; attendant, following, suite, **retinue**; convoy, escort, guide, **leader**; bodyguard, **protector**, keeper; suitor, **lover**; **hunter**; inseparable, shadow, **follower**; consort, **spouse**; comrade, companion, **friend**; stable companion, mate, partner, associate, **colleague**; accomplice; twin, fellow, **analogue**; satellite, parasite, hanger-on, **dependant**.

**Adj. accompanying**, with, attendant, background; always with, inseparable; **concurrent**; obbligato; accessory, **component**; satellite, **subject**; parallel, collateral; incidental, **casual**; contemporaneous, contemporary, simultaneous.

**Vb. accompany**, be found with, coexist; cohabit, live with, string along with; attend, come to heel, **follow**; bear one company, squire, protect, **safeguard**; convoy, escort, guide, conduct, lead, usher, **come before**; track, dog, shadow, **pursue**; associate with, partner; **befriend**; coincide, keep time with, **concur**; imply, **be intrinsic**; carry with, **cause**; be inseparable, depend; belong, go with, go together, **be related**.

**Adv. with**, herewith; together with; all together.

## 90 Duality

**N. duality**; double life, dual personality; **polarity**; double, deuce, duo, twain; couple, brace, pair; Gemini, **analogue**; yoke, span, double file; couplet; double harness, twosome; duel; duet; tandem; biped; bivalve.

**Adj. dual**; binary, binomial; bilateral; twin; double-barrelled, **double**; conjugate; two abreast; both; bipartisan; amphibious; ambidextrous; **double**; two-faced.

**Vb. pair**, couple, match, bracket, yoke; mate.

## 91 Duplication

**N. duplication**, fold; encore, repeat, repeat performance; echo, **repetition**; **restoration**; copy, photocopy, **dupli-**

cate; double exposure; living image, **analogue**.

**Adj. double**, twice; two-edged; amphibious, ambidextrous; two-way; of double meaning, **equivocal**; bisexual, hermaphrodite; twin, duplicate; second; **dual**.

**Vb. double**, redouble, square; encore, echo, second, **repeat**; renew, **restore**; duplicate, twin; reduplicate, stencil, **copy**.

**Adv. twice**, two times, once more; **again**; again; doubly.

**92 Bisection**
**N. bisection**, dichotomy; half, fifty per cent, **part**; hemisphere, **sphere**.

**bifurcation**; fork, prong, **cross**.

**dividing line**, diameter, diagonal, equator; parting, seam; date line; party wall, **partition**.

**Adj. bisected**, bipartite; forked; split, cloven, cleft.

**Vb. bisect**; divide, split, cleave, **sunder**; share, go halves, go fifty-fifty, **apportion**; halve.

**bifurcate**, separate, fork; ramify, **diverge**.

**93 Triality**
**N. triality**, trinity.

**three**; Fates, Graces; Faith; triumvirate, leash; triplet, trio, tern; trefoil, shamrock, triangle, trident, tripod, trivet; tricycle, triptych, trilogy; third power, cube; third person, gooseberry.

**Adj. three**; tripartite, tricolour; three-dimensional; triangular, trilateral, three-cornered; quarterly.

**Adv. in threes**; three times, thrice.

**94 Triplication**
**N. triplication**; hat trick.

**Adj. treble**, triple, triplex, triplicate;

third, tertiary; trilateral.

**Vb. treble**, triple, triplicate, cube.

**Adv. trebly**; three times, thrice.

**95 Quaternity**
**N. quaternity**, four; square, quadrilateral, quad; tetrahedron; quarter; swastika, **cross**; quatrain; quadruplet, quad; quadruped.

**Adj. four**; square, quadrilateral, four-square.

**96 Five and over**
**N. five**, quintuplet, quin; pentagon, pentagram; pentathlon; cinquefoil; five senses.

**over five**, six, sextet; hexagon, hexagram; seven, week, sabbatical year; septet; eight, octave, octet; octagon; nine, three times three; ten, tenner, decade; eleven; twelve, dozen; thirteen, double figures, teens.

**twenty and over**, twenty, a score; two dozen; pony; forty, two score; fifty, half a hundred, jubilee; sixty, three score; sexagenarian; seventy, septuagenarian; eighty, four score, octogenarian; ninety, nonagenarian.

**hundred**, century, centenary; hundredweight; centurion; centenarian; centipede; hundred per cent; treble figures.

**over one hundred**, a gross; thousand, grand; millennium; ten thousand, myriad; hundred thousand; million; ten million; thousand million; billion; million million, trillion; millionaire.

**Adj. fifth and over**, five, fifth; ninth; decimal, denary, tenth; twelfth; duodecimal, centennial, centenary, centenarian; secular; bicentenary.

**97 Plurality**
**N. plurality**; multiplicity, **multitude**; polygon, polyhedron; polytheism; a

number, a certain number; some, one or two, two or three; a few, several; majority, **greater number**.

**Adj. plural**; composite, multiple; multiform; many-sided; multilateral; poly-; more than one, some, certain; upwards of, more, **many**.

**Adv. et cetera**.

## 98 Fraction: less than one

**N. fraction, numerical element**; fractional part, fragment, **part, portion**; shred, **small quantity**.

**Adj. fractional**, partial, **fragmentary, small**.

## 99 Zero

**N. zero**, nil, nothing, next to nothing; naught, nought; love, duck; blank; figure nought; nothingness; none, nobody, **absence**; zero level, nadir.

**Adj. not one**; zero; invisible, null, **insubstantial**.

## 100 Multitude

**N. multitude**, multiplicity; large number, million; a quantity, **great quantity**; numbers; a sea of, a world of, a sight of; forest, thicket; host, array, fleet, **army**; throng, mob, high turn-out, **crowd**; tribe, horde.

**certain quantity**, peck, bushel, pinch; galaxy, bevy, cloud, flock, flight; shoal, school; flock, herd, drove; swarm, hive, colony, **group**; nest, clutch, litter, brood, **young creature**.

**greater number**, weight of numbers, majority, mass, bulk, mainstream, **main part**; multiplication, multiple.

**Adj. many**, myriad, several, sundry, divers, various; quite a few, considerable, numerous, very many, a good many, many more, umpteen, n; untold, unnumbered, **infinite**; multifarious, manifold, **multiform**; fre-

quent; much, ample, multiple; profuse, abundant, generous, lavish, galore, **great**.

**multitudinous**, crowded, **full**; populous, **dense**; teeming, lousy with, alive with, **prolific**; thick; **frequent**; incalculable, innumerable, inexhaustible, countless, endless, **infinite**.

**Vb. be many**, swarm with, **fill**; multiply, **be fruitful**; clutter, crowd, throng, swarm, mass, flock, troop, **congregate**; flood, overflow, swamp, overwhelm; infest, overrun; **augment**; make a majority, **be great**.

## 101 Fewness

**N. fewness**; rarity; **scarcity**; a few, a handful; tuft; thin audience, low turn-out; small number, trickle, **small quantity**; almost none; limited number, too few; minority, one or two, two or three, half a dozen; remnant, sole survivor, **remainder**.

**Adj. few**, precious few, scant, scanty, light, little, **scarce**; thin, sparse, rare, scattered, **infrequent**; hardly any; too few, without a quorum.

**Vb. be few**, straggle; seldom occur.

**render few**, reduce, diminish, pare; decimate; eliminate, weed, thin, **eject**; defect, desert.

**Adv. here and there**; rarely.

## 102 Repetition

**N. repetition**, doing again; ditto; recital, practice, rehearsal; beginning again, reprise, **beginning**; saying again, **ornament**; tautology; **speech defect**; a repetition, repeat, repeat performance, encore; second helping, playback, replay, return match, revenge; chorus, refrain, **vocal music**; echo, repercussion; quotation; citation; hardy annual (**see recurrence**); old story, chestnut, **tedium**; gramophone record; new edition, reprint, **edition**; remake, rehash, revival, **restoration**; repeater, cuckoo, parrot; creature of habit.

**recurrence, frequency**; cycle, round, return, rebirth, reincarnation, **regular return**; succession, run, series, serial, **continuity**; throwback, **heredity**; curtain call; rhythm; alliteration, assonance, rhyme, **prosody**; stale repetition, **tedium**; same old round, routine, **habit**.

**Adj. repeated**; recurrent, **periodical**; haunting; repetitious; stale, **feeble**; **similar**; monotonous, singsong, dingdong, **uniform**, **tedious**; incessant, habitual, **frequent**; said before; aforesaid.

**Vb. repeat**, do again; duplicate, reduplicate, redouble, **double**; multiply, **reproduce**; reiterate, say again, recapitulate; restate, reword; always say; recite, say after; echo, ditto, parrot; **copy, flatter**; quote, cite, **remember**; practise, rehearse; play back, rerun; recycle; begin again, resume, **begin**; replay, give an encore; reprint; rehash, remake, renew, revive, **restore**.

**repeat oneself**, give an encore; reverberate, **resound**; chant, chorus, **be uniform**; quote oneself, **be diffuse**; stutter, **stammer**; plug, labour; hammer at; recur to, return to, **remember**; go back, **regress**; be a creature of habit, **be wont**.

**reoccur**, recur, return, happen again; reappear; haunt, obsess.

**Adv. repeatedly, often**; parrot fashion; times without number; time after time, day after day, year after year; morning.

**again**, afresh, anew, once more; ditto; encore; re-.

**103 Infinity**

**N. infinity**; infinite space, **space**; eternity, **perpetuity**.

**Adj. infinite**, indefinite; immense, measureless; eternal, **perpetual**; numberless, countless, innumerable, immeasurable, illimitable, interminable; incalculable, unfathomable, incomprehensible, beyond reckoning, beyond comprehension; inexhaustible, without number, without limit, without end; without measure, limitless, endless, boundless; untold, unnumbered, **many**; unmeasured, unbounded.

**Adv. infinitely**, to infinity; without end; **greatly**.

**104 Time**

**N. time**, tide; tense, **grammar**; duration, extent, **long duration**; limited time, season, term, semester, tenancy, tenure; tour, shift, spell, stint; span, space, **period**; a bit, a while; life, lifetime; eternity, **perpetuity**; passage of time, lapse, course, **course of time**; years; Time, Father Time, Time's scythe, Time's hourglass; fourth dimension; indefinite time; past time, past tense, retrospective time, **past time**, priority; prospective time, **futurity**; **present time**; recent time; antiquity, distant time.

**interim**, intermediate time, meantime, while; interval, interlude, break, pause, **lull**; vacation, **leisure**; interregnum, interlude, episode; close season, respite, **delay**; midweek, **middle**.

**date**, day, age, reign, era; vintage, year, time of life, **chronology**; birthday, **anniversary**; calends, ides; time of day, **clock time**; moment, **instant**; target date, zero hour, D-day; term, fixed day, quarter day, payday.

**Adj. continuing**, permanent, **perpetual**;

pending; recurrent; temporal, **period-ical**.

**intermediate**; midweek.

**dated**; prior; **subsequent**.

**Vb. continue**, endure, **last**; intervene, pass, **elapse**; take time, **extend**; live through, sustain; stay, remain, abide, outlive, survive, **outlast**; take its time, wait, **be pending**.

**pass time**, vegetate, breathe, subsist, **live**; age, **grow old**; spend time, **be busy**; summer, winter, weekend, **have leisure**; waste time; mark time, **wait**; seize an opportunity; enjoy a spell of.

**fix the time**, calendar, date, put a date to, **time**.

**Adv. while**, during, pending; **all along**; meantime, meanwhile; hourly, **often**; till, until, yet; always; all along, **throughout**.

**when**, what time; one day, one fine morning.

**anno domini**, AD; before Christ, BC.

## 105 Neverness

**N. neverness**, Greek Calends; blue moon; jam tomorrow; eternity, **perpetuity**.

**Adv. never**; nevermore, never again; never before; without date, sine die.

## 106 Period

**N. period**, matter of time; long period, long run, **long duration**; short period, short run; season; close season, **lull**; time of day, morning, evening; time of year, spring, summer, autumn, winter, **morning, evening**; term; notice, warning, ultimatum, **conditions**, **finality**; measured time, spell, tour, stint, shift, span, stretch, sentence; innings, turn; round, bout, lap; vigil, watch; length of time, second, minute, hour; particular time, rush hour;

pause, interval, **interim**; day, weekday, working day; week; fortnight, month, moon; quarter; half year, semester; twelve month, year, Olympiad; decade; golden wedding, jubilee, **anniversary**; century, millennium; life, lifetime, life sentence.

**era**, time, period, generation; age; epoch; cycle, Platonic year, Great Year; Ice Age; **antiquity**; Renaissance, Age of Enlightenment; modern times, Machine Age.

**Adj. periodic, seasonal**; hourly; annual, biennial, centennial; period, **olden**.

**secular**; neolithic, **primal**.

**Adv. man and boy**, in a lifetime; periodically, seasonally.

## 107 Course: indefinite duration

**N. course of time**, stream of time, duration, **time**; continuous tense, **grammar**; indefinite time, **long duration**.

**Adj. elapsing**, wearing, passing, rolling, **progressive**; **transient**.

**Vb. elapse**, pass, lapse, flow, run, roll, proceed, advance, **progress**; crawl; flit, fly, slip, slide, glide, **move fast**; run its course, expire, **end**; be past; spend time, **pass time**.

**Adv. in time**.

## 108 Long Duration

**N. long duration**, length of time, years; a lifetime, life sentence; a century, an age, **perpetuity**; longevity, **old age**; distance of time, antiquity, **past time**.

**durability**, endurance, defiance of time; stamina, **strength**; survival; **stability**; long standing, good age; long run, long innings.

**protraction**, extension; **hindrance**, **resistance**; wait, long haul, **delay**; extra time, overtime, **addition**.

**Adj. lasting**, abiding; secular, lifelong,

livelong; longstanding, inveterate, deep-seated, deep-rooted; of long duration, long-term, marathon, **long**; too long, unconscionable; durable, **strong**; **immemorial**; evergreen, fresh, new; eternal, perennial, **perpetual**; persistent, chronic, **obstinate**; constant, stable, permanent.

protracted, prolonged; **slow**; **late**; interminable, longwinded.

Vb. **last**, endure, stand, stay, remain, abide, continue; defy time, never end, **be eternal**; **grow old**; wear, wear well, **be strong**.

**outlast**, outlive, outstay; survive; remain, **be left**; live to fight another day; have nine lives.

**spin out**, protract, prolong, **lengthen**; gain time, procrastinate; filibuster, **obstruct**.

**drag on**, be interminable, never end; inch, creep, linger, dawdle; tarry, delay, waste time, wait, **be late**.

Adv. **for a long time**, long, many a long day.

**all along**, all day, all day long; ever since.

**long ago**, long since, long long ago; **formerly**.

**at last**, at long last.

## 109 Transience

N. **transience**; ephemerality, impermanence; evanescence; mortality, **death**; frailty, **weakness**; **caprice**; temporary arrangement, makeshift, **substitute**; interregnum, **interim**.

**brief span**, short space of time, short while; brevity; mortal span; summer lightning, meteor; bubble, mayfly; April shower, summer cloud, **insubstantial thing**; bird of passage; brief encounter; short run, **period**, **spurt**; spasm, moment, **instant**.

Adj. **transient**, temporal, impermanent, passing, **insubstantial**; fair-weather, summer; cursory, flying, fleeting, fugitive, **speedy**; precarious, volatile; evanescent; unsettled, rootless, mutable, changeable; fickle, flighty, **capricious**.

**ephemeral**, of a day, short-lived; throwaway, disposable, biodegradable; perishable, mortal, **dying**; annual, deciduous, frail, **weak**, **brittle**; impermanent, temporary, acting, provisional.

**brief**, short-term, **short**; summary, **concise**; quick, fleet, brisk, **speedy**; sudden, momentary, meteoric, like a flash; hurried, **hasty**; at short notice, extemporaneous, offhand, **spontaneous**.

Vb. **be transient**; flit, fleet, fly, gallop, **move fast**; fade, flicker, vanish, melt, evaporate, **disappear**; fade like a dream, flit like a shadow, pass like a summer cloud, burst like a bubble.

Adv. **transiently**, briefly, temporarily; awhile; easy come, easy go.

## 110 Perpetuity: endless duration

N. **perpetuity**, endless time, infinite duration, **infinity**; eternity; **long duration**; endurance, **continuity**.

Adj. **perpetual**, perennial, durable; **immemorial**; nonstop, constant, continual, ceaseless, incessant; flowing, **continuous**; ageless, immutable, **permanent**; evergreen, everlasting, incorruptible; imperishable, undying, deathless, immortal; interminable; endless, without end, timeless, eternal.

Vb. **perpetuate**, make permanent, establish.

**be eternal**, never cease.

Adv. **for ever**; evermore; time without end; till doomsday; to infinity; nonstop.

## 111 Instantaneity: point of time

**N.** instantaneity, immediacy; **present time; lack of expectation;** precise time.

instant, moment, point, point of time; second, tick, trice, jiffy, breath; burst, crack; stroke, coup; flash, twinkle, twinkling; two shakes.

**Adj.** instantaneous, simultaneous, immediate, instant, sudden, abrupt, snap; like a flash, **speedy;** punctual, early.

**Adv.** instantaneously, at once, immediately, directly; without delay, forthwith; soon; readily, presto, pronto; without warning, without notice; overnight, all at once, all of a sudden; plump, slap, slap-bang; at a stroke, at one jump, at one fell swoop; extempore, impromptu; before you could say knife; like a flash, like a shot.

## 112 Chronometry

**N.** chronometry, horology; timing; **time.**

clock time, right time, date, date line; time of day, time of night; summer time, daylight saving.

timekeeper, chronometer, timepiece; clock, dial, face; hand; bob, pendulum; electric clock; watch, ticker; turnip, hunter, repeater; wristwatch, sundial; hourglass, sand-glass, egg timer; time signal, pip, siren, hooter; gong, bell; timer, stopwatch; traffic light, **traffic control;** time fuse, time switch, time bomb; metronome, conductor.

chronology; date, age, epoch, style, **era;** old style, new style, almanac, calendar, astronomical almanac; chronicle, annals, diary, journal, log-book, **record;** date list, **list;** timetable, **directory.**

chronologist; diarist, **recorder.**

**Adj.** chronological; **recording;** temporal; **timely.**

**Vb.** time, clock; timetable; match times; phase, **adjust; be early; be late; make ready;** calendar, chronicle, **record;** date, be dated, bear a date; measure time; **begin; cease; initiate; terminate.**

**Adv.** o'clock.

## 113 Anachronism

**N.** anachronism; wrong date, wrong day; disregard of time; neglect of time, **oblivion;** wrong moment.

**Adj.** anachronistic; previous, before time, too early, **early; late;** overdue, behind time; slow; fast; old-fashioned, **antiquated.**

**Vb.** misdate, mistime; antedate, anticipate, **be early; be** overdue, be behind time, postdate, **be late;** be fast, gain; be slow, lose.

## 114 Priority

**N.** priority, antecedence; birthright; eldest, firstborn; flying start, **precedence;** leading, **preceding;** yesterday, **past time;** eve, vigil, day before; precedent, antecedent; foretaste, preview; premonition, presentiment, **foresight;** herald, **precursor.**

**Adj.** prior, fore; earliest, first, precedent, **preceding;** previous, anterior, antecedent; antediluvian, prehistoric; BC; antenatal; elder, eldest, firstborn; former, onetime, sometime, retired; foregoing; aforesaid, said; preliminary; given, **supposed.**

**Vb.** be before, be early; come before, **precede;** foreshadow.

do before, presuppose, **suppose;** prefabricate, prearrange, preempt, prejudge, preview; be previous, anticipate, forestall, be beforehand with; **outstrip;** lead, **precede, come before.**

**Adv. before**, prior to, beforehand; just before; formerly; ere; ere now, ere then, already, yet; until now.

## 115 Posteriority

**N. posteriority**; succession, **sequence**, **following**; **futurity**; line, lineage, descent, successor, descendant, **posterity**; cadet; latecomer, new arrival; remainder; aftermath, **sequel**.

**Adj. subsequent**, post-, posterior, following, next, after; junior, cadet, **young**; designate, to be, **future**; posthumous; after Christ, AD.

**Vb. ensue**, supervene, follow after, **come after**; go after, **follow**, **result**; succeed, **inherit**.

**Adv. subsequently**; after, afterwards; next, next time; thereafter; since; after a while, after a time; soon after; next month.

## 116 The Present Time

**N. present time**, contemporaneousness, **modernism**; time being, present time, present day, present moment; this hour, this moment, this instant; juncture, opportunity, crisis, **occasion**; this time; today, nowadays; this date, present generation, **contemporary**.

**Adj. present**, actual, instant, current, extant; of this date, topical, contemporary, contemporaneous; present-day, latest, **modern**; occasional.

**Vb. be now**, exist, **be**; be modern.

**Adv. at present**, now, right now, at this time, at this moment; live; contemporaneously; today, nowadays; at this time of day, even now; already, but now, just now; this time; extempore; now or never.

**until now**, to this day, to date; through; **all along**.

## 117 Different Time

**N. different time**, other times, **futurity**, **past time**; another time, any time but this; jam yesterday, but never jam today; **anachronism**.

**Adj. not contemporary**; **antiquated**

**Adv. not now**, ago, then; sometimes; once; one day, one fine morning; someday, sometime, some time or other; any time, any time now; soon; whenever you will.

## 118 Synchronism

**N. synchronism**; coincidence, **accompaniment**; same time; contemporaneousness, same date, same day, **present time**; same age, twin birth, **equality**; level time, dead heat, **draw**.

**contemporary**, twin; age group, class, year, **group**.

**Adj. synchronous**; contemporary, contemporaneous, **present**, **modern**; simultaneous, coincident; level, **equal**; twin; punctual.

**Vb. synchronize**; concur, coexist, **accompany**; encounter, coincide, **meet**; keep time; say together, chorus; tune, phase, **adjust**; run a dead heat, be equal; pace.

**Adv. synchronously**, along with; with one voice; while, **with**.

## 119 Futurity: prospective time

**N. futurity**, future tense; womb of time, time to come; morrow; future, time ahead, prospect, outlook, **expectation**; fate, **event**, **destiny**; near future, tomorrow, next week, next year, **present time**; advent, **approach**; long run, distant future, **distance**; heritage, **posterity**; shadow cabinet, **sequence**, **preparation**.

**future state, destiny, fate**; doomsday, crack of doom, **finality**; afterlife, life to come, hereafter, kingdom come, **heaven**; damnation, **hell**; good time coming, millennium; rebirth, reincarnation, **repetition**.

looking ahead, **preparation**; delay; prospect, prospects, outlook, **expectation**; expectancy, **hope**; horoscope, forecast, **prediction**.

Adj. **future**, to be, to come; coming, nigh, close at hand, **near**; due, destined, fated, imminent, **impending**; ahead, yet to come, **eventual; preparatory**; prospective, designate, **chosen; probable**; predictable, sure, **certain**; ready to, rising; potential, promising, **possible**; ulterior, posterior, **subsequent**.

Vb. be to come, lie ahead; be destined, threaten, overhang; near, draw nigh, **approach**; be imminent, cast its shadow before, **be near**; shall, will.

look ahead, look forward, see it coming, await, **expect, hope**; foresee, **predict**; anticipate, forestall, **be early; prepare oneself**.

Adv. **prospectively**, eventually, ultimately; tomorrow, soon, some day; hereafter; about to.

henceforth.

**120 Past Time: retrospective time**

N. past time, **priority**; retrospection, **remembrance**; past tense, perfect, pluperfect, **grammar**; only yesterday; distant past, history, antiquity; old story, matter of history; past times, yesterday, former times; Victorian Age, Renaissance, **era**.

antiquity; creation, time immemorial, distance of time; prehistory, ancient world; Stone Age, **era**; relics, **remainder, archaism**; ruin, ancient monument, megalith, **monument, earthwork**; dig; museum, **collection**; ancient lineage, **genealogy**.

fossil, trilobite, ammonite; trace fossil, fossil footprint, **record**; coal forest, **fuel**; sponge, coral, **organism**; dinosaur, **animal**.

palaeology; **humankind**; archaeology; industrial archaeology.

antiquarian; antiquary, **scholar**; historian; **linguist**.

Adj. **past**; ancient, prehistoric, olden; early, primitive, **primal; new**; wholly past, gone, bygone, lost, irrecoverable; **extinct, dead**; passé, has-been, obsolete, **antiquated; hard**; done, behind one; lapsed, finished, **ending**.

**former**, late, sometime, **prior**; retired, outgoing; ancient, prehistoric, **immemorial**.

preterite; simple past, past continuous, perfect, imperfect, pluperfect.

foregoing, last, latter, **preceding**; recent, overnight, **new**.

retrospective; retroactive, going back; with hindsight.

Vb. **be past**; have run its course, have had its day; pass, elapse, **end**; be a dead letter.

look back, trace back, exhume; hark back, **retrospect**.

Adv. **formerly**, of old, of yore; time was, ago; long ago, long since; a long while, a long time ago; years ago; lately, some time ago, some time back; yesterday; last year, last season, last month.

retrospectively; before now, hitherto; already, yet; till now, **until now**.

**121 Newness**

N. **newness**; recent date, recent occurrence, recent past, **past time, present time**; innovation; novelty; **youth**; restoration, resurrection, **revival**; new leaf, new broom.

modernism; **present time**; latest fashion; new look, contemporary style, fashion.

**modernist**; avant-garde; bright young thing, trendy; modern generation.

**upstart**, vulgarian.

**Adj. new**, recent, of recent date, of recent occurrence, overnight; upstart, mushroom; novel, unprecedented, unheard of, **original**; brand-new, like new, **clean**; green, evergreen, juicy, **vernal**; fresh; maiden, virgin, virginal; newborn, **young**; raw, **immature**; unused, first-hand; **unknown**; budding, **beginning**.

**modern**, late; contemporary, topical, **present**; with it; à la mode; trendy, **fashionable**; modernistic, advanced, avant-garde, futuristic, revolutionary; newfangled.

**modernized**; given a new look; **clean**.

**Vb. modernize**; update; go modern, go contemporary, get with it; **progress**.

**Adv. newly**, freshly, afresh, anew, like new; fresh-, new-; overnight, just now, only yesterday; lately, latterly, of late.

## 122 Oldness

**N. oldness, beginning**; olden times, **era**; age; ruins, **antiquity**; maturity, **autumn**; decline, rust, decay; **old age**.

**archaism, antiquity**; museum piece, antique, heirloom, bygone; dodo, dinosaur, **fossil**; old fossil, fuddy-duddy; square, old-timer, has-been, back number.

**tradition**, lore, folklore, mythology; custom, prescription, immemorial usage, **habit**; common law; ancient wisdom; word of mouth, **speech**.

**Adj. olden**, old, ancient, antique, antiquarian; veteran, vintage; venerable, patriarchal; archaic; ancient; prehistoric, mythological, heroic, classic, Hellenic, feudal, medieval, Saxon,

Norman, Romanesque, Gothic, Elizabethan, Jacobean, Georgian, Regency, Victorian; **past**.

**primal**, prime, primitive, primordial, aboriginal, **beginning**; fossil, neolithic; early, dawn-; antediluvian.

**immemorial**, time-honoured, **habitual**; venerable; inveterate, rooted, long-standing, **fixed**.

**antiquated**, of other times, archaic; **prior**; **retrospective**; static, **permanent**; dated, antediluvian; conservative, Victorian, old-fashioned, square; outdated, outmoded; passé, old hat; **past**; **dilapidated**; rusty, moth-eaten, fusty, stale, secondhand; obsolete, obsolescent; old.

**Vb. be old**, have had its day, **end**; age, **grow old**; fade, wither, **deteriorate**; moulder, rot, rust, decay, **decompose**.

**Adv. anciently, formerly**.

## 123 Morning. Spring. Summer

**N. morning**, morn, forenoon; matins, prime; dawn, morning twilight, cock-crow, dawn chorus, **precursor**; sunrise, daybreak, **light**; peep of day, first blush of day; daylight; full day; Aurora; orb of day, **sun**.

**noon**, high noon, meridian, midday; twelve o'clock.

**spring**, vernal season; first cuckoo; vernal equinox, first point of Aries.

**summer, heat**; midsummer, summer solstice, high summer; Indian summer.

**Adj. matinal**, morning; diurnal; fresh, **early**; noon, meridian.

**vernal**, spring; juicy, flowering, **young**.

**summery**, summer, **warm**.

**Adv. at sunrise**, at dawn of day, at first light, at crack of dawn; past midnight.

**124 Evening. Autumn. Winter**

N. **evening**, even, eve, evensong, vespers, afternoon; afternoon tea, five o'clock; sunset, sundown, setting sun; evening star, Hesperus; dusk, twilight; candle-light; **moon**; close of day, nightfall, dark; **sleep**; curfew, last post, **finality**.

**midnight**, dead of night.

**autumn**, fall; harvest; harvest moon, Michaelmas; Indian summer.

**winter**; yuletide, Christmas; winter solstice.

Adj. **vespertine**, afternoon; evening; dusky, crepuscular, **dark**, **dim**; nightly, nocturnal; benighted, late.

autumnal.

**wintry**, winter, snowbound, **cold**; stark, bleak.

Adv. **post meridiem**, late, late at night; at night.

**125 Youth**

N. **youth**; young blood; babyhood, infancy, childhood, childish years, tender age, **beginning**; puppy fat; girlhood; teenage, addlescence, pubescence, age of puberty, awkward age; young idea, **youngster**; minor, ward.

**nonage**, tender age, minority, infancy, leading strings; cradle, nursery, kindergarten.

**salad days**, school days; heyday; prime of life, bloom.

Adj. **young**, girlish; virginal, maidenly; adolescent; teenage, juvenile; budding, blooming, flowering, **vernal**; green, callow, awkward, raw, **immature**; minor, infant, pre-school; minor, junior, cadet; childish; young at heart, evergreen, ageless.

**126 Age**

N. **age**, time of life, years, **long duration**.

**middle age**, middle years, middle life; years of discretion; maturity, prime of life; a certain age, climacteric, change of life, menopause.

**old age**; advanced years, **old person**; vale of years, autumn or winter of life; **weakness**; second childhood, dotage; longevity, green old age, ripe old age.

**seniority**, **precedence**; **priority**; higher rank; doyen; presbytery, senate, **council**.

**gerontology**, geriatrics, **therapy**.

Adj. **ageing**, aged, old, elderly, matronly; ripe, mature, mellow; over-blown, run to seed; of a certain age; going grey; hoary; senescent, moribund, **dying**; wizened, decrepit, rickety; **foolish**; senile, failing; full of years; **healthy**; venerable, patriarchal; so many years old, rising; too old, past it; retired, **leisurely**; passé **antiquated**.

**older**, major; elder, senior, **superior**; firstborn, eldest, **prior**; eldest.

Vb. **grow old**, age; go grey, turn white.

**127 Young person. Young animal. Young plant**

N. **child**, small fry; babe, baby, bundle of joy; infant, suckling; bairn, little one, tiny tot, little chap, mite, moppet, toddler; brat, kid; papoose; little darling, little angel, little monkey, little imp, imp of mischief; cherub, young innocent; changeling. See **young creature**.

**youngster**, juvenile, young person, young adult, young hopeful; young people, **youth**; boy, schoolboy, stripling, adolescent; youth, young man, lad, sonny; urchin, nipper, cub, young shaver, whippersnapper; rocker, punk; girl, young woman; lass, wench, maid, maiden, virgin; chit, slip, chick, miss; teenager; tomboy, hoyden; little minx, baggage; colleen, mademoiselle, damsel, nymph.

**young creature**, young animal, yearling, lamb, kid, calf, heifer; piglet; fawn, colt, foal, filly; kitten; puppy, pup, whelp, cub; chick, chicken, pullet; duckling, gosling, cygnet, **animal**, bird; fledgling, nestling; fry, litter, farrow, clutch, spawn, brood; larva, pupa, nymph; caterpillar, grub; chrysalis, cocoon; tadpole; embryo, foetus, **source**.

**young plant**, seedling, set; sucker, shoot, sprout, slip; twig, sprig, scion, sapling, **plant**.

**Adj. infantine**, baby, infantile, babyish, childish, childlike; juvenile, girlish, **young**; coltish; newborn, **new**; small, **little**.

## 128 Old person

**N. old person**, pensioner, senior citizen; old dear, old body; sexagenarian, septuagenarian, octogenarian, nonagenarian, centenarian; Methuselah.

**old man**, old gentleman, patriarch, elder statesman, Nestor, **sage**; grandfather, **paternity**; veteran, old soldier, old hand, old-timer, **expert**; old boy, gaffer; old geezer; fossil, **archaism**.

**old woman**, old lady, dowager; grandmother, gran; old girl, old trout; old dutch, **spouse**; crone, hag, witch.

**old couple**.

## 129 Adultness

**N. adultness**, development, **preparedness**; years of discretion; legal age, majority, full age; manhood, womanhood, **male**, **female**; badge of manhood, beard; maturity, prime, prime of life, **middle age**; bloom; meridian of life.

**adult**, grown-up, big boy, big girl; man, **male**; woman, matron, **female**; youth, stripling.

**Adj. grown-up**, adult; major, of age, responsible; mature; nubile, **marriageable**; virile, **male**; matronly, **female**; blooming, full-blown; **young**.

**Vb. come of age**, mature, **grow**; have a vote; grow a beard; leave home.

## 130 Earliness

**N. earliness**, early hour, prime, **morning**; early stage, **beginning**; early riser, early bird; first arrival, **precursor**; primitive, aborigine, earliest inhabitant, **native**.

**punctuality, occasion, activity**; immediacy.

**anticipation, foresight, preparation**; early maturity; **precedence**.

**Adj. early**; previous, **prior**; timely, punctual, prompt; forward, advance; advanced, precocious, ahead of its time, **new**; summary, sudden, immediate; forthcoming, ready, **prepared**; impending, imminent, at hand, **near**; too early, premature, **immature**.

**Vb. be early**, anticipate; forestall; get there first, **come before**; **outdo**; engage, book, preempt, reserve; secure, order, bespeak; expedite, **accelerate**; **hasten**; be precocious, ripen early; start too soon; gain time, gain, go fast.

**Adv. betimes**, early, soon, anon; before long; first thing; with time to spare; time enough.

**beforehand**; too soon.

**suddenly**, without notice; without delay; forthwith, shortly, directly; at short notice.

**131 Lateness**

**N. lateness,** late hour, **midnight;** high time, last minute; slow development; lagging; afterthought, **sequel;** latecomer, last arrival; late developer; slow starter, late riser, **slowcoach.**

**delay,** Fabian policy, **caution;** filibuster, **hindrance;** check; detention, holdup, **restraint;** remand, pause, truce, time lag, jet lag, **lull;** moratorium, respite; suspension, stay, stay of execution; suspension of penalty, reprieve; red tape; shelving, cold storage.

**Adj. late,** deathbed; too late; overdue, belated, benighted; behindhand, lagging, after time, behind schedule; sluggish, tardy; backward, **slow;** Fabian, **cautious;** dilatory; posthumous, **subsequent.**

**Vb. be late,** rise late; lag, lag behind, **follow;** stay, tarry, be long about it, linger, dawdle, saunter, loiter; hang about, hang around, hang back; dally, dilly-dally; miss a chance, lose an opportunity, oversleep, **lose a chance;** be behindhand; **look back;** lose, stop (clock).

**wait, await;** bide, stay, **pause;** stand about.

**be pending,** drag; hang fire, **be uncertain;** stand, stay put, **be quiescent.**

**put off,** defer, postpone, adjourn; keep, reserve; keep pending, file, pigeonhole; table, shelve; remand, send back; suspend; grant respite, reprieve, **forgive;** procrastinate, protract, delay, retard, set back, gain time, filibuster, stall, withhold; **refuse.**

**Adv. late,** after time, at sunset, last thing; at length, at last, ultimately; too late.

**tardily,** leisurely.

**132 Occasion: timeliness**

**N. occasion,** happy chance, **event;** juncture; readiness; **fitness, good policy;** right time, suitable season; auspicious hour, moment, well-timed initiative; high time.

**opportunity,** given time, **offer;** favourable opportunity, **possibility;** break, lucky moment, piece of luck, **chance;** best chance, **choice;** only chance, opening, look-in, room, field, **scope;** liberty, freedom of choice, **freedom;** convenience, spare time, **leisure;** clear field, clear stage, **fair chance;** handle, lever, instrument, **tool, means;** stepping-stone, **bridge.**

**crisis,** critical time, key point, key moment; turning point, psychological moment, emergency, extremity, pressure, pinch, push, **predicament;** last minute.

**Adj. timely;** punctual, **early;** seasonable, welcome, well-timed.

**opportune,** favourable, providential, heaven-sent, auspicious, propitious; fortunate, lucky, happy, **prosperous;** fitting, **apt, advisable;** occasional, **infrequent.**

**crucial,** critical, key, momentous, decisive, **important.**

**Vb. profit by;** make an opening; exploit, turn to good account, **use.**

**Adv. opportunely;** now or never.

**incidentally;** apropos.

**133 Untimeliness**

**N. untimeliness,** wrong time; mishap; evil hour, **misfortune;** disturbance; anachronism.

**Adj. ill-timed,** ill-advised; untimely, untoward; intrusive; malapropos, inconvenient, **inexpedient;** late; premature, **early.**

**inopportune,** untoward, inauspicious, unfavourable, unhappy, **adverse.**

**Vb. mistime**, time it badly, **misjudge**; intrude, disturb, find engaged.

**be engaged**, be too busy; be otherwise engaged, have other fish to fry, **be busy**.

**lose a chance**, waste time, **fail**; drop a sitter, bungle; oversleep, **be late**; allow to lapse, **neglect**; spoil a good chance.

**Adv. inopportunely**, amiss.

## 134 Frequency

**N. frequency**, rapid succession, rapid fire, **continuity**; **repetition**; haunting, assiduous attendance.

**Adj. frequent**, recurrent; common, of common occurrence, **many**; **multitudinous**; incessant, perpetual, continual, nonstop, constant, steady; regular, hourly, **periodical**; haunting, assiduous, **habitual**.

**Vb. recur**; do nothing but; keep, **repeat oneself**; frequent, haunt, **visit**; obsess; plague, pester, **trouble**.

**Adv. often**, oft, many a time; commonly, generally; regularly, daily, hourly, every hour, every minute.

**perpetually**; at all times, day after day, morning.

**sometimes**, every so often; at times; often enough.

## 135 Infrequency

**N. infrequency**, rarity; phoenix.

**Adj. infrequent**, sporadic, occasional; intermittent, **discontinuous**; scarce, rare, **few**; like gold dust, **of price**; almost unheard of, unprecedented, **unusual**; single, **one**.

**Adv. seldom**, little; rarely, scarcely, hardly, only sometimes; scarcely ever; once, just this once, once only.

## 136 Periodicity: regularity of recurrence

**N. periodicity**, rhythm; timing, **continuity**; tidal flow, wave movement; shuttle service; pulse, tick, beat, throb, rhythm, swing; chorus, refrain, **recurrence**; roll; tide, **wave**; frequency, turn, round, circuit, lap; shift, relay, **period**.

**regular return**, rota, cycle, circuit, revolution, life cycle, wheel of life, **rotation**; menstrual cycle, menses; yearly cycle, **morning**, **evening**; fixed interval, **period**; routine, daily round, **order**, **habit**; leap year.

**anniversary**, birthday, jubilee, silver wedding, centenary, bicentenary; **holy day**; Fourth of July, **special day**.

**Adj. periodical**, periodic, cyclic, **rotary**; tidal; measured, steady, even, regular, constant, punctual, like clockwork, **regular**; breathing; beating; recurrent, intermittent, remittent; reciprocal, alternate; serial, successive, **continuous**.

**seasonal**, anniversary; paschal; hourly, daily, nightly, diurnal, biweekly, weekly, fortnightly, monthly; menstrual; yearly, annual, biennial, triennial; centennial, secular.

**Vb. be periodic**, recur; **come after**; turn, revolve, circle, **rotate**; return, come round again; take its turn, alternate; be intermittent; reciprocate, fluctuate, undulate, **oscillate**; beat, pulse, throb; heave, pant, **breathe**; swing, sway, **hang**; ply, commute, **be wont**.

**Adv. periodically**, regularly; hourly, daily, weekly, monthly, yearly; every so often.

**by turns**, every other day.

**137 Fitfulness: irregularity of recurrence**

N. **fitfulness**, irregularity, **disorder**; **spasm**; remission; variability, **change**; April weather, **caprice**; staggering.

Adj. **fitful**, periodic, remittent, intermittent, stop-go, **discontinuous**; irregular; uneven, **unequal**; occasional, **infrequent**; inconstant, uncertain; variable; spasmodic, jerky; halting, desultory; erratic, eccentric, moody, **capricious**.

Adv. fitfully.

**138 Change: difference at different times**

N. **change**, alteration, variation, **difference**; mutation, permutation, declension; frequent change, variability; partial change, process, treatment, **qualification**; total change; sudden change, **revolution**; break, innovation; reformation; change of direction, shift, turn, **deviation**; change of position, transition, **passage**; translation, **interchange**; overthrow; change of mind.

**transformation**, transfiguration; metamorphosis; metabolism; transubstantiation; reincarnation; version, adaptation, translation, **interpretation**.

**alterer**; converter, transformer; catalyst, enzyme, ferment, leaven; editor; censor; chemist; decorator; magician, **sorcerer**; kaleidoscope; weathercock, renegade; new broom; bad influence, bad apple.

Adj. **changeable**, variable, mutable; fickle, **capricious**; affected, newfangled, **new**; provisional; alternative; **variegated**.

Vb. **change**, alter, **vary**; **grow**, **decrease**; change colour, change countenance, **lose colour**; vacillate, wobble, **be uncertain**; be **capricious**; turn, shift,

veer, change course, **deviate**; make a transition, pass to, **pass**; take a turn; **get better**; submit to change, **conform**.

**modify**, alter, vary, modulate, diversify; superimpose, **add**; make a change, innovate; subvert, **invert**; reverse, turn back; rearrange, **arrange**; adapt, **adjust**; conform, **make conform**; remould, **form**; process, treat; revise, edit, correct, **rectify**; reform, **make better**; revamp, patch, darn, **restore**; **pervert**; mar, spoil, **impair**; warp, bend, strain, twist, deform, **distort**; stain, dye, discolour, **colour**; adulterate, doctor, qualify, **mix**, **weaken**; cover, mask, disguise, **conceal**; change round, **interchange**, **transpose**; try a change, **experiment**; effect a change, leaven, **cause**; affect, **influence**; transform, transfigure, transmute, transubstantiate, **convert**; digest; conjure, juggle, **deceive**.

Adv. mutatis mutandis.

**139 Permanence: absence of change**

N. **permanence**, **stability**; endurance, duration, **perpetuity**; fixity, fixity of purpose; rock, bedrock, foundation, solidity, **density**; sustenance, maintenance, conservation, **preservation**; law, rule; fixed law, entrenched clause, **fixture**; standing; tradition, custom, practice, **habit**; fixed attitude, conservatism; routine, **order**; static condition; conservative, reactionary, true blue, stick-in-the-mud, die-hard, **obstinate person**.

Adj. **permanent**, durable; persistent, unfailing, **perpetual**; inveterate, long-standing, **immemorial**; standing, entrenched, fixed, immutable; intact; living; conservative, reactionary, die-hard, **obstinate**; stationary, static, immobile, **quiescent**; unaffected, identical.

**Vb. stay**, come to stay, **be stable**; abide, endure, subsist, outlive, survive, outlast, **last**; persist, hold, hold good; hold it, maintain, sustain; rest, remain, tarry, live, **dwell**; stand fast, **persevere**; stand pat, **stand firm**; stand still, resist change, **be quiescent**; grow moss, **be old**; allow to stand, let be, let alone, **permit**.

**Adv. as before**; at a standstill.

**140 Cessation: change from action to rest**

**N. cessation**; arrest, **restraint**; **resignation**.

stop, halt, dead stop; standstill, deadlock, stalemate, **draw**; checkmate, **defeat**; breakdown, **failure**; stoppage, stall; shutdown, **end**; hitch, check, **hindrance**; blockage, **closure**; walkout, **dissension**; closure of debate, guillotine, **silence**.

strike, **resistance**; general strike, 'national holiday'; work to rule; stoppage, walkout, sit-down strike, unofficial strike, mutiny; lockout, **exclusion**.

lull, interval, pause, remission; break, breather, rest, **refreshment**; holiday, **leisure**; interlude, breathing space, **interim**; abeyance, suspension; close season, respite, moratorium, truce, armistice, **cease-fire**, standstill, **delay**.

stopping place, port of call, port, harbour; stop, halt, pull-up, station; bus stop, terminus, terminal, **air travel**; dead end, blind alley, cul-de-sac; billet, destination, **goal**.

**Vb. cease**, stay, desist, refrain, hold; stop, halt; stand, rest, **repose**; have done with, end, finish, **terminate**; interrupt, **discontinue**; **be mute**; cease work, strike, **resist**; **exclude**; **be silent**;

come to an end; **disappear**; end its run; collapse, **fail**; **be past**; withdraw, retire, **resign**; leave; **relinquish**; close; cease fire, **make peace**; call it a day, **be quiescent**, **sleep**.

halt, stop, put a stop to; arrest, check, stem, **obstruct**; cut short, call a halt, interrupt, **restrain**; cause a stoppage, stage a strike; bring to a standstill, freeze; checkmate, stalemate, thwart, **hinder**; check oneself, stop short, stop dead; grind to a halt, seize, stall, jam, stick, catch; brake, **retard**.

pause; hold back, hang fire; hesitate; wait awhile, suspend, adjourn, remit, **wait**; rest, **repose**.

**Int.** halt! hold! stop! enough! whoa! belay there! refrain! leave off! shut up! give over! cut it out! chuck it! drop it! knock it off! come off it! stow it!

**141 Continuance in action**

**N. continuance**, **continuity**; flow, **tendency**; extension; maintenance, **perpetuity**; progress, **progression**; break, run, rally, **series**; recurrence, **repetition**.

**Adj. unceasing**, continual, steady; nonstop, unremitting, incessant, **continuous**; **regular**; standing, **fixed**; undying, **perpetual**; unfailing, inexhaustible; invariable; persistent; haunting, recurrent.

**Vb. go on**, wag; keep going, proceed, advance, **progress**; never end, **be eternal**; pursue its course, trend, tend; endure, stick, hold, abide, rest, remain, linger, **stay**; obsess, haunt, frequent, **recur**; keep at it, persist, **persevere**; wait, **carry through**; **end**.

**sustain**, maintain, uphold, **support**; follow through, **continue**; keep alive, **preserve**; **repeat**; prolong, protract, **perpetuate**; let be, let alone, let things take their course, **give scope**, **be lax**.

**Int.** carry on! drive on! never say die! not out!

## 142 Conversion: change to something different

**N. conversion, production;** reduction, resolution; fermentation, ferment, leaven; chemistry, alchemy; mutation, transfiguration, **transformation; sorcery; progress, progression, growth;** course, lapse, flux, **course of time;** development, **increase; evolution, biology;** perversion; reformation; rebirth, **restoration; loss of right; influence; teaching, inducement; possibility.**

**transition,** transit, **passage;** movement, shift, translation, transfer; alteration, **change;** life cycle.

**crucible,** melting pot, retort, test tube; laboratory, foundry, **workshop.**

**changed person,** new man or woman; convert, neophyte, proselyte; renegade, turncoat; pervert, degenerate, **bad person.**

**Adj. converted,** affected; reborn, regenerate; becoming; **different;** convertible, impressionable, **changeable.**

**Vb. be turned to,** become, get; come to, turn to, ferment, **evolve; pass;** be mixed; mellow, **mature;** wax, **grow;** degenerate, **deteriorate;** suffer a sea change, **change;** enter a phase, enter a stage.

**convert,** reduce, process, ferment, leaven; reduce to, enchant, **bewitch;** transmute; render, make, mould, shape, **form;** brainwash **influence; teach; convince;** regenerate, **revive; pervert.**

**transform,** transfigure; landscape, **decorate;** camouflage, disguise, **conceal;** render, **translate;** traduce, **misinterpret;** deform, **distort; modify;** reform, make something of, **make better;** remodel, redress, **restore;** assimilate; **exclude.**

**Adv. convertibly.**

## 143 Reversion

**N. reversion,** going back, return, regress, retreat, ebb; tracing back, **source; archaism;** throwback, **heredity;** retrospection, **remembrance;** retrospective action; reaction; repercussion, backlash, backfire, **recoil;** revulsion, revulsion of feeling, **regret;** counter-revolution, **revolution; relapse; restoration; curvature;** replacement, **restitution;** recovery, **acquisition;** taking back, **taking;** reply, feedback, **answer;** retort; turn, turning point, **crisis;** swing, **recurrence;** round trip; return journey, return ticket; **start.**

**Adj. reverted,** recessive, reflexive; reactive; reactionary, retroactive, **retrospective; genetic.**

**Vb. revert,** go back, turn, return, retrace, **regress;** reverse, face about, **invert;** ebb, retreat, withdraw, **recede;** kick back, rebound, **recoil;** slip back, backslide, **relapse;** retract, **recant;** hark back; start again, undo, **begin;** revive, **restore; liberate;** disenchant, **dissuade;** take back, recover, **retrieve;** resume, **acquire; retaliate;** give back, make restitution, reinstate, replace.

**Adv. reversibly.**

## 144 Revolution: sudden or violent change

**N. revolution,** full circle, circuit, **rotation;** radical change, clean slate, clean sweep; sudden change, catastrophe, surprise, **lack of expectation;** leap, plunge, jerk, start, **spasm;** shift, swing, switch, landslide; violent change, upset, overthrow; upheaval, eruption, explosion, cataclysm, **out-**

break; avalanche, crash, debacle, **descent**, **havoc**; revulsion, rebellion, counter-revolution, **reversion**, **revolt**; total change, abolition.

**revolutionist**, radical, revolutionary, Red; **agitator**; **destroyer**; idealist.

Adj. **revolutionary**, **new**; radical, thoroughgoing, **complete**; seismic, violent; subversive, red, **disobedient**; **destructive**.

Vb. **revolutionize**, subvert, overturn, **invert**; uproot, eradicate, make a clean sweep, **obliterate**, **demolish**; remodel; change beyond recognition, **transform**.

## 145 Substitution: change of one thing for another.

N. **substitution**; by-election, **vote**; commutation, exchange, switch, shuffle, **interchange**; replacement, transfer; self-sacrifice.

**substitute**, sub, proxy, alternate, agent, representative, **deputy**; dual representative; understudy, stand-in, **actor**; ghost, **author**; locum, **doctor**; reserve, twelfth man, **auxiliary**; supply, replacement, remount; relief, **successor**; double, changeling, **impostor**; mother figure, foster parent; synonym, doublet, **word**; metaphor, symbol, **representation**; prosthesis, artificial limb, pacemaker; transplant; alternative, second best, ersatz; scapegoat, sacrifice; makeshift, stopgap; **moderator**; expedient, **compromise**, **good policy**.

**quid pro quo**, equivalent; consideration; purchase money; value, worth, **price**; redemption, **offset**; replacement; change, **money**.

Adj. **substituted**; vicarious, **disinterested**; interchangeable, **equivalent**; dummy, plastic, mock, ersatz, counterfeit, **spurious**; makeshift, stopgap,

provisional, acting, temporary, **ephemeral**.

Vb. **substitute**, commute; exchange, switch, **interchange**; compound, **compromise**; **deceive**; make do with, replace with; replace, succeed, **come after**; supersede, supplant, displace, oust, **eject**; replace.

Adv. **instead**.

## 146 Interchange: double or mutual change

N. **interchange**; exchange, **barter**; commutation, permutation, anagram; mutual transfer; all change, general post; shuffle; interplay, two-way traffic; rally (tennis); retort, repartee, rejoinder.

Adj. **interchanged**; mutual, two-way; reciprocal; intercontinental; interchangeable, convertible, **equivalent**.

Vb. **interchange**, exchange; change money, convert; barter, **trade**; permute, commute; switch, shuffle, castle (chess); **transpose**; **compromise**; reciprocate; requite, **retaliate**; bandy words, answer back, rejoin, **answer**.

Adv. **in exchange**.

## 147 Changeableness

N. **changeableness**, change; variability, variety; irregularity; instability, imbalance, unstable equilibrium, **inequality**; weak foundation; inquietude, disquiet; turning; flicker, flash; caprice; **inattention**; aptitude.

**changeable thing**, moon, chameleon; kaleidoscope; wax, clay; mercury, quicksilver, **fluid**; wind, weathercock; eddy; wheel, mobile, **motion**; fortune, wheel of Fortune; luck, **chance**; variable, variable quantity, **numerical element**; play of expression, mobile features, **appearance**; grasshopper mind, **inattention**; floating voter.

Adj. **changeful**, mutable, **changeable**; variant, variable; **iridescent**; **multiform**; quick-change, versatile, **skilful**; uncertain, **irresolute**; unaccountable; volatile, **different**; wayward, fickle, whimsical, **capricious**; giddy, dizzy, flighty, wanton, irresponsible; shifty, inconstant, unfaithful, disloyal.

**unstable**, unsound; rocky, rolling, mobile, restless, fidgety, desultory, spasmodic, **fitful; transient**; turning; gusty, **windy**; unsettled, loose, floating; erratic, rootless, **extraneous**, vagrant, rambling, wandering; tidal, **periodical**, yielding, impressionable, malleable, plastic, **soft**; flowing, running, melting, **fluid**.

Vb. **vary**, show variety; **change**; dodge, double, **avoid**; shuffle, be shifty, **be equivocal**; writhe, **wriggle**, dart, flit; leap, dance, flicker, gutter, **shine**; twinkle, flash; wave, flutter, flap, **hang**; shake, tremble; wobble, stagger, rock, reel, sway, swing, vibrate, **oscillate**; alternate, **fluctuate**; veer, tack, yaw, **deviate**, **navigate**; puff, blow; vacillate, waver, hesitate, float, drift, **be irresolute**; hover; be inconstant, **be capricious**.

Adv. **changeably**; now this now that.

## 148 Stability

N. **stability**; constancy; fixity; rest; steady state, stable equilibrium, balance, **equality**; nerve, aplomb, **resolution**; **hardness**; solidarity, solidity, density; stiffening.

**fixture**, establishment, firm foundation; foundations, rock, bedrock, pillar, tower, pyramid; invariant, constant; fast colour, indelible ink; law, written constitution, entrenched clause.

**stabilizer**, fin, centreboard, keel; ballast, **offset**; buttress, **prop**.

Adj. **unchangeable**; stiff, inflexible, **obstinate**; **resolute**; predictable, reliable, **certain**; immutable; irreducible; changeless, irreversible, invariable, constant, **uniform**; steady, **regular**; durable, **permanent**; undying, perennial, evergreen, **perpetual**; imperishable, indestructible, inextinguishable, **invulnerable**. See fixed.

**established**, entrenched, settled; inveterate; irrevocable, irreversible; incontrovertible, of right; valid, confirmed.

**fixed**, steadfast, firm, secure, immovable; steady, stable, balanced; fast, ingrained, indelible; ineradicable, rooted, deep-seated, foursquare, well-founded; standing, pat; at rest, at anchor, run aground, stuck fast, stranded; immobile, frozen, like a statue, **still**.

Vb. **be stable**, stand, stick fast, hold, **stand firm**; show aplomb, show self-assurance; **outlast**; come to stay, **stay**; settle, **dwell**; strike root, strike deep, have long roots.

**stabilize**, root, found, establish, **perpetuate**; erect, **support**; float, set afloat; fix, set, stereotype; make valid, confirm, ratify, **endorse**; retain, stet; bind, make sure, make fast, **tie**; keep steady, retain equilibrium, balance.

## 149 Present Events

N. **event**, phenomenon, fact, **reality**; case, circumstance, **state**; occurrence, eventuality, incidence, happening; incident, episode, adventure, **occasion**; milestone, **juncture**; fortune, accident, casualty, contingency, **chance**; misadventure, mishap, **misfortune**; emergency, pass, **crisis**; coincidence; advent, **approach**; encounter, meeting; proceeding, **action**; result, product, consequence, issue, outcome, upshot, **effect**; denouement, solution, **evolution**; catastrophe, **end**.

**affairs**, doings, **deed**; agenda; concern, interests, **business**; world, life, situation, **circumstance**; **course of time**; vicissitudes, **adversity**.

**Adj. eventual**, consequential, resultant; circumstantial, contingent.

**happening**, incidental, accidental, occasional; doing, current, afloat.

**eventful**, stirring, busy, full of incident, **active**; momentous, critical, **important**.

**Vb. happen**, become, **be born**; **succeed**; take place, occur, come about, come to pass; befall, betide, **chance**; arise, **arrive**; present itself, **be present**; supervene, **follow**; issue, transpire, **result**; take its course, advance, **progress**; continue; **be past**; be so, prove, prove to be; bring about, occasion, **cause**.

**meet with**, incur, encounter, **meet**; find, **discover**; experience, pass through, have been through, **know**, feel; endure, undergo, **suffer**.

**Adv. eventually**, ultimately.

## 150 Destiny: future events

**N. destiny**, fate; horoscope, forecast, **prediction**; prospect, outlook, **expectation**; **futurity**, **intention**; danger, **threat**; proximity, **approach**; future existence, hereafter, **future state**; next world, world to come, **heaven**; predestination, **necessity**, **certainty**.

**Adj. impending**, imminent; **preparatory**; destined, **fated**; forthcoming, forecast; inescapable, inevitable, going to be, bound to happen, **certain**; due, **necessary**; **probable**; **visible**; to come, **future**; at hand, close, **near**; instant, immediate, about to be; pregnant with; ready, **prepared**; **beginning**.

**Vb. impend**, **be to come**; hover, lour, loom, **threaten**; draw nigh, **approach**; front, face; **be near**; ripen, **mature**.

**predestine**, doom, preordain, foreordain, **necessitate**; foreshadow, presage, **predict**; have ready, **make ready**; plan, intend, **predetermine**.

**Adv. in the future**; **eventually**; whatever may happen; **probably**; soon, at any moment.

## 151 Cause: constant antecedent

**N. causation**; authorship; creation; invention; inspiration, **influence**; generation, provocation, **production**; impulsion, **motive**; cultivation, **agriculture**; temptation, **inducement**; opportunity, **occasion**.

**cause**, God; **existence**; creator, maker, **producer**; father, **parentage**; author, founder; agent, leaven; stimulus, **stimulant**; contributor, factor, moment, determinant; mainspring; **influence**; **destiny**; fate, **necessity**, force, **compulsion**.

**source**, fountain, **origin**; spring, fountainhead; mine, quarry, **store**; home; genesis, ancestry, lineage, descent, **parentage**; parent, ancestor, progenitor; loins; element, principle, first thing; nucleus, germ, seed, sperm, spore; egg, foetus, embryo; chrysalis, cocoon, **young creature**; bud, stem, stock; taproot, root, bulb, **plant**; radical, etymology, **linguistics**; foundation, bedrock, **base**; groundwork, spadework, **beginning**; raw material, ore.

**seedbed**, hotbed, **nest**; cradle, nursery, **origin**; breeding place, incubator, womb, fertile soil; hothouse, conservatory, **garden**.

**causal means**, appliance, **means**; pivot, hinge, lever, instrument, **tool**; dynamo, generator, battery, spark, energy; motor, engine, turbine, **machine**.

**reason why**, reason, cause; explanation, key, **answer**, **interpretation**; excuse, **pretext**; ground, basis, motive, idea, occasion.

**Adj. causal**, formative, effective, effectual; determinant, decisive, final, **ending**; seminal, germinal, **productive**; **beginning**; suggestive; answerable, responsible; original; explanatory; creative, inventive, **inimitable**.

**fundamental**, primary, elemental, ultimate; radical, basic, **intrinsic**; crucial, central, **important**; original, aboriginal, **first**; primitive, primordial, **primal**.

**Vb. cause**, originate, create, make, **produce**; beget, **generate**; invent, **discover**; underlie; be answerable, be responsible, be to blame; institute, found, inaugurate; erect, **elevate**; launch, set afloat, set afoot, set going, **begin**; open, broach, **initiate**; seed, sow, plant, water, **cultivate**; contrive, effect, effectuate, bring about, bring to pass, **succeed**; procure, **find means**; stage-manage, engineer, **plan**; induce, precipitate, **hasten**; evoke, elicit, **attract**; provoke, arouse, **excite**; stimulate, **invigorate**; kindle, inspire, incite, tempt, **induce**; occasion, **motivate**; have an effect, show its result, make or mar, **influence**; **do**; determine, decide, **judge**; **prevail**, **predominate**.

**conduce**, tend to, **tend**; lead to, **come before**; contribute to, operate to, **be instrumental**; involve, imply, be **intrinsic**; entail, give rise to, **initiate**; promote, advance, encourage, foster, foment, abet, **aid**.

**Adv. causally**, because.

## 152 Effect: constant sequel

**N. effect**, consequent, consequence, corollary, **sequence**; result; derivative, precipitate, **remainder**; upshot, outcome, issue, denouement, **event**; final result; visible effect, mark, print, impress, **trace**; by-product, spin-off; aftermath, legacy, backwash, wake, repercussion, **sequel**; resultant action, response, **answer**; performance, **deed**; reaction, backlash; offspring, **posterity**; handiwork, **product**; karma, **fate**; moral effect, **influence**.

**growth**, development, **increase**; bud, blossom, fruit; ear, spike; produce, crop, harvest; profit, **gain**.

**Adj. caused**, due to; consequential; contingent, **subject**; resultant, derivative, descended; secondary; emergent, born of; **eventual**; done.

**inherited**, heritable, hereditary, Mendelian, **genetic**.

**Vb. result**, come of; accrue, **follow**; be due to; owe everything to, **borrow**; have a common origin, **be related**; take its source; issue, proceed, **emerge**; develop, unfold, **evolve**; bud, sprout, germinate, **grow**; show a trace, show an effect, receive an impression, **be plain**; **meet with**; **happen**; **produce**.

**depend**, be subject.

**Adv. consequently**; because of; of course, naturally, necessarily; **hence**.

## 153 Attribution: assignment of cause

**N. attribution**, assignment of cause; reference to, imputation, theory, hypothesis, model, assumption, conjecture, **supposition**; explanation, **interpretation**; enquiry; reason why; affiliation, **parentage**, **source**; attribute; credit, credit title.

**Adj. attributed**; **relative**; putative, **supposed**.

**Vb. attribute**; say of, assert of, predicate, **affirm**; accord, grant, allow, **give**; assign to, point to, trace to, connect with, **relate**; affiliate, charge with; make responsible, scapegoat, **accuse**; bring home to, **demonstrate**; credit, credit with, acknowledge.

**account for**, explain, **interpret**; assume, **suppose**.

**Adv. hence**, thence, therefore; whence, wherefore; since, because, thanks to, ergo, thus, so.

**why**! wherefore! whence! how! how come! cui bono!

**somehow**; somehow or other.

**154 Chance: no assignable cause**

**N. chance**; lot, fortune, **fate**; potluck; good fortune, luck; bad luck, **misfortune**; hap, hazard, accident, casualty, contingency, coincidence, **event**; chance hit, lucky shot, fluke; rare chance; chance meeting, chance encounter, **lack of expectation**; serendipity.

**equal chance**, fifty-fifty, **equality**; tossup; lucky dip, random sample; lottery, raffle, tombola, sweepstake, premium bond; **divination**.

**fair chance**, possibility; half a chance; good chance, **opportunity**; long odds, odds, **advantage**; small risk, safe bet, **probability**.

**calculation of chance**, doctrine of chance; assurance, insurance, **undertaking**; **experiment**.

**Adj. casual**, fortuitous, chance, haphazard, random, stray; adventitious, accidental, incidental, contingent, **happening**; chancy, dicey, incalculable, **uncertain**.

**causeless**, groundless, indeterminate, **uncertain**; unaccountable, inexplicable.

**Vb. chance**, hap, so happen, **happen**; meet with, **discover**; risk it, chance it, leave it to chance, **gamble**; have small chance, **be unlikely**.

**Adv. by chance**; **at random**; perchance, perhaps; **possibly**.

**155 Power**

**N. power**; **authority**; control, sway; moral power, **influence**; spiritual power, charisma, witchcraft, sorcery; endurance, **stability**; driving force, **motive**; physical power, might, muscle, right arm, right hand, **strength**; dint, effort, endeavour; force, **compulsion**; stress, strain, shear; weight, **gravity**; weight of numbers, **greater number**; manpower, **personnel**; position of power, **advantage**; **truth**; emphasis; extra power, overdrive.

**ability**, capability, potentiality, **possibility**; competence, efficacy, **skill**; capacity, faculty, virtue, property; qualification, **fitness**; attribute; gift, **aptitude**; compass, reach, grasp, **range**; trend, **tendency**; **permission**.

**energy**, vigour, drive; internal energy, work, binding energy, mechanical energy, pedal power, engine power, horsepower; inertia; resistance, **friction**; force, **science of forces**; force of gravity, **gravity**; spring; pressure, head, charge, steam; full pressure; tension, motive **power**; **traction**; thrust, jet, jet propulsion, **propulsion**; momentum, impetus, **impulse**; **attraction**; **repulsion**; suction, **reception**; expulsion; potential function, potential; unit of work, erg, joule; calorie.

**sources of energy**, coal, gas, oil, **fuel**; wind power, solar energy; power station, hydroelectric station, **waterfall**; tidal barrage, tide mill; windmill; solar panel, solar battery, **heater**; generator, turbine, motor, **machine**.

electricity; lightning; induction, inductance, capacitance; resistance, conduction; frequency; electric charge, pulse, shock; electric current, circuit, electrode, anode, cathode; positive, negative; conductor, semiconductor, nonconductor, insulator; lightning conductor, earth, **safeguard**; live wire, **danger**.

**electronics**, electron physics, optics, **optics**; **radiation**; microprocessor, **microelectronics**; computer electronics; automation, **machine**; telegraph, telephone, television, radio, **telecommunication**; electrical engineering, electricity supply; power line, lead, flex, **cable**; distributor; pylon, grid, generator, magneto, dynamo; oscillator, alternator; transformer, commutator, power pack; battery, accumulator; cell, valve, tube, transistor; voltage, volt, watt, kilowatt; ohm; amp.

**nucleonics**, nuclear physics; fission, fusion, thermonuclear reaction; particle accelerator; Jet; atomic pile, nuclear reactor; moderator, coolant; radioactivity, fallout, **radiation**; **poison**; atomic bomb, **bomb**.

**Adj. powerful**, potent, **strong**; mighty, **great**; rising; prevalent, prevailing; almighty, omnipotent, irresistible; **supreme**; plenipotentiary, **authoritative**; virtual, potential, **possible**; competent, capable, able, adequate, equal to, **sufficient**; with resources, **rich**; **expert**; efficacious, effectual, effective; of power, of might, operative, workable; valid; cogent, compulsive, forcible, **violent**; bellicose, **warlike**.

**dynamic**, energetic, **vigorous**; high-tension, supercharged; **drawing**; locomotive, kinetic, **moving**; **mechanical**; electric, electrical, electronic; solid-state; live, charged; atomic, nuclear, thermonuclear; hydroelectric.

**Vb. be able**, can; be capable of; compass, manage, **do**; **suffice**; have power, control, **dominate**; force, **compel**; gain power, **prevail**.

**empower**, enable, endow; endow with power, arm, **strengthen**; electrify, charge; automate; power, drive.

**Adv. powerfully**.

## 156 Impotence

**N. impotence**, lack of power, power vacuum; **weakness**; inability; **failure**; **inaptitude**; decrepitude; disqualification; sterility, sterilization.

**helplessness**, **restraint**; impotent fury, **anger**; exhaustion, **fatigue**; collapse, breakdown, **failure**; faint, swoon, coma; **insensibility**; stroke, apoplexy, paraplegia, **disease**; torpor, **inaction**; atrophy; old age, **age**; loss of control; mental decay; mental weakness; minority; babyhood, infancy, **youth**; invalid, **sick person**, **weakling**.

**eunuch**; gelding, capon, bullock, steer, neuter; hermaphrodite.

**ineffectuality**; vanity; dead letter, scrap of paper; figurehead, dummy, man of straw, broken reed, **insubstantial thing**; bluster, **empty talk**.

**Adj. powerless**, impotent, unable; without authority; nominal, figurehead, constitutional, **insubstantial**; nugatory, invalid; **illegal**; **weak**; inoperative, unemployed; withdrawn; obsolete, kaput; unqualified, inept; dud, **useless**; inadequate, **insufficient**; ineffective, ineffectual, feeble; incapable, incompetent, inefficient.

**defenceless**, helpless, without resource; bereaved, bereft; orphan, **friendless**; weak, harmless, **innocent**; unarmed; indefensible, untenable, **vulnerable**.

**impotent**, powerless, feeble, **weak**; unsexed; sexless, neuter; sterile, barren, infertile; effete; senile; paralytic, stiff, **rigid**; unconscious, comatose, **insensible**; without self-control, incontinent; **supine**; nerveless, spineless, **irresolute**; **nervous**; helpless, waterlogged.

Vb. **be impotent**, be unable, cannot; **be useless**; avail nothing, **fail**; **fall short**; **be subject**; **submit**; feel helpless, shrug; **regret**; do nothing, **watch**; have a hopeless case; **disappear**; faint, swoon, **be insensible**; drop, collapse, **be weak**.

**disable**, incapacitate, **make useless**; disqualify; invalidate, **abrogate**; disarm, **weaken**; **counteract**; undermine, sap, **make concave**; exhaust, consume, **waste**; wind, prostrate, **strike**; paralyse; sprain, rick, wrench, twist, dislocate; cripple, lame, maim, hobble, nobble, hamstring, **hinder**, **impair**; stifle, throttle, suffocate, strangle, garrotte, **kill**; muzzle, deaden, **silence**; sabotage; deflate; unhinge, **disunite**.

**unman**, unnerve, enervate, paralyse, **frighten**; **weaken**; emasculate, castrate, neuter, spay, geld, **make sterile**.

## 157 Strength

N. **strength**, might, horsepower, HP, **power**; energy; force, **brute force**; spring; tone, temper; tensile strength; iron, steel, **hardness**; oak, heart of oak; endurance, grit, **stamina**.

**vitality**, **health**; vim, vigour, **life**; animal spirits; guts, nerve, backbone, **resolution**; physique, muscle, biceps; brawn, **size**; grip.

**athletics**, **sport**, **contest**; gymnastics, acrobatics, **exercise**; stadium, gymnasium, **arena**.

**athlete**, gymnast, tumbler, acrobat, contortionist, trapeze artist, circus rider, stunt man, **entertainer**; Blue, con-

tender; heavyweight; strong man; champion; he-man, muscle man, **male**; strongarm man, bully, bruiser, tough guy, **desperado**; bouncer; amazon, virago, **woman**; matador, picador, toreador; Atlas, Titan, **giant**; tower of strength, **auxiliary**.

**strengthening**, reinforcement, **aid**; stiffening; tonic effect; **refreshment**; revival, **restoration**; emphasis, stress.

**science of forces**, dynamics, statics; thermodynamics; triangle of forces.

Adj. **strong**, lusty, vigorous, **young**; mighty, potent, armed, **powerful**; high-powered, high-tension; omnipotent, **superior**; incontestable, irresistible, victorious; sovereign, supreme, **ruling**; valid; **great**; **healthy**; heavy, **weighty**; strongarm, forceful, forcible, **severe**; urgent, pressing, compulsive; **assertive**; steely, **hard**; **tough**; deep-rooted, **firm**; solid, substantial, stable, **fixed**; stout, heady, alcoholic; neat, **whole**; entrenched, inviolable, **invulnerable**.

**unyielding**, staunch, **resolute**; stubborn, **obstinate**; persistent; **rigid**; solid, **dense**; impregnable, **invulnerable**; of iron nerve, indomitable, invincible; inextinguishable; unflagging, tireless, **industrious**; indestructible, proof, sound; waterproof, weatherproof, impermeable; fireproof, bulletproof.

**stalwart**, stout, sturdy, hardy, rugged, robust, doughty, **vigorous**; of good physique, able-bodied, muscular, brawny; sinewy, wiry, **active**; strapping, well-knit, well set-up, thickset, stocky, burly, beefy, husky, hefty, **large**; gigantic, colossal, Herculean, **huge**.

**athletic**, fit, **healthy**.

**manly**, masculine, **male**; virile, red-blooded, manful, **courageous**; grown-up.

Vb. **be strong**; pack a punch; **prepare**; overpower, overwhelm, **overmaster**; rally, recover, revive; blow hard, **blow**.

**strengthen**, confirm, give strength to, lend force to, **augment**; underline, stress; reinforce, fortify; stuff, pad, **line**; buttress, prop, sustain, **support**; nerve, brace, steel; **give courage**; stiffen, toughen, temper, **harden**; act like a tonic, **invigorate**; animate, enliven, quicken, **excite**; **revive**; **refresh**; **cure**; **elevate**; **tighten**; power, engine, motor, **empower**.

Adv. **strongly**.

## 158 Weakness

N. **weakness**, lack of strength; delicacy, **sensibility**; **inequality**; weak foundation, instability; moral weakness, frailty; bodily weakness, **old age**; delicate health, **ill health**; **bulk**; weak state; anaemia; loss of strength, languor, torpor; exhaustion, collapse, **fatigue**; swoon, **insensibility**; decline, declension; **moderation**; relaxation; **mixture**; effect of weakness, crack, fault, **gap**; flaw, **blemish**; strain, sprain; weak point, **defect**.

**weakling**, effeminate, pansy; lightweight, **nonentity**; mollycoddle; old woman, invalid, **sick person**; lame dog, lame duck; infant, kitten, **young creature**; baby, **coward**; **favourite**; doormat, jellyfish, drip, weed, wet; victim, **sufferer**; gull, **dupe**.

**weak thing**, flimsy article, reed, thread, rope of sand; sandcastle, mud pie, house of cards, cobweb, gossamer, **insubstantial thing**; matchwood, eggshell, paper, glass, china; water, thin gruel.

Adj. **weak**, powerless, **impotent**; without force, invalid, **powerless**; helpless;

harmless, **innocent**; babyish; effeminate, pansy, womanish, **female**; poor, feeble, slight, puny, **small**; lightweight, **light**; of poor physique, **little**; thin, **lean**; imbecile, **foolish**; sheepish, gutless, half-hearted, **irresolute**; nerveless, **nervous**; spineless, weak-kneed, submissive, yielding; **insubstantial**; **dry**; bloodless, anaemic, pale, **colourless**; limp, flaccid, flabby, floppy, **soft**; **hanging**; unstrung, slack, loose, **lax**; watery, wishy-washy, insipid, **tasteless**; low, quiet, faint; decrepit, old; too weak, past it; **capricious**; rickety, shaky, **unstable**; torpid, **quiescent**; only beginning, infant, **beginning**, new, **young**. See **flimsy**.

**weakened**, diminished, dissipated, spent, effete, **used**; laid low; bare; failing, weary; strained; weatherbeaten, worn, broken, tumbledown, **dilapidated**; rotten; **inert**.

**weakly**, infirm, delicate, sickly, **unhealthy**; groggy, rocky; seedy, poorly; underweight, skinny, **lean**; languid, listless; faint; sallow, wan, lacklustre, **colourless**.

**crippled**, impotent; halt, lame, game; knock-kneed; rheumatic; **imperfect**.

**flimsy**, gossamer, sleazy, tenuous, **insubstantial**; delicate, dainty, frail, fragile, **brittle**; shoddy, **useless**; rickety, ramshackle, shaky, wonky, crazy, tumbledown, **dilapidated**.

Vb. **be weak**, weaken; sicken, be ill; faint, fail, languish, flag; drop, fall, **tumble**; dwindle, **decrease**; decline, **deteriorate**; droop, wilt, fade, **grow old**; wear thin, crumble; yield, give way, sag, **soften**; split, **open**; dodder, totter, teeter, sway, reel, **oscillate**; tremble, shake; halt, limp, go lame; **be old**.

**weaken**, enfeeble, debilitate, enervate; unnerve, rattle, **frighten**; relax, slacken, loosen, **disunite**; shake, **soften**; strain, sprain, cripple, lame, **disable**; hurt, injure, **wound**; cramp, **obstruct**; effeminate; disarm, cushion, **blunt**; starve, rob; reduce, extenuate, thin, lessen, **abate**; dilute, water, adulterate, **mix**; eviscerate; **counteract**; decimate, **render few**; muffle, **mute**; invalidate, **abrogate**; damage, spoil, **impair**; sap, undermine; dismantle, **demolish**.

## 159 Production

**N. production**, creation; mental creation, **thought**; invention, original work; creative urge, productivity; effort, endeavour, **attempt**, **undertaking**; artistic effort, composition, authorship, **art**, **painting**, **sculpture**, **writing**; musical skill; doing, performance, output, throughput, turnout, **action**; execution, accomplishment, achievement; **preparation**; workmanship, **formation**; design, **plan**; **structure**, **arrangement**; tectonics, engineering, building, architecture; establishment, erection, **elevation**; making, manufacture, industry, **business**; process; assembly; assembly line, **continuity**, **machine**; factory, **workshop**; technology; mass production, automation; productivity deal; development, growth, **increase**, **abundance**; **scarcity**; farming, factory farming, **agriculture**; breeding, **animal husbandry**.

**product**, creature, creation, result, **effect**; output, turnout; printout; waste, slag; extract, essence; confection, compound, **a mixture**; handiwork; manufacture, article, thing, **object**; goods, wares, **merchandise**; gross national product; earthenware, **pottery**; stoneware, hardware; fabric, cloth, **textile**; production, work, opus,

piece, **composition**; **masterpiece**; fruit, flower, blossom, berry; produce, yield, harvest, crop, vintage, **growth**; interest, increase, return, **gain**; mental product, brainchild, conception, **idea**; figment, fiction; offspring, young, egg, spawn, seed, **young creature**.

**edifice**, piece of architecture, building, structure, erection, pile, dome, tower, skyscraper, **high structure**; pyramid, **monument**; church, **temple**; mausoleum, **tomb**; habitation, mansion, hall, **house**; college, **school**; fortress, **fort**; stonework, brickwork, **building material**.

**producer**, creator, maker, Nature; founder, **cause**; **parentage**; creative worker, writer, **author**; composer, **musician**; painter, sculptor, **artist**; developer, architect, engineer; industrialist, **agent**; executive, **doer**; labourer, **worker**; artificer, **artisan**; grower, planter, cultivator, **farmer**; stock farmer, sheep farmer; miner; **stage manager**.

**Adj. productive**, creative, inventive, **imaginative**; constructive; industrial, **formative**; fruitful, **prolific**; **generative**.

**produced**, made; artificial, man-made, synthetic, cultivated; handmade, homemade, homespun; ready-made; begotten, **born**; grown; thought of.

**Vb. produce**, create, originate, make; invent, **discover**; conceive, **imagine**; write, design, **compose**; operate, **do**; frame, fashion, shape, **form**; knit, spin, **weave**; sew, tie; forge, chisel, carve, sculpture, cast; coin, **mint**; manufacture, fabricate, prefabricate, process, mill, machine; mass-produce, multiply, **reproduce**; construct, build, raise, rear, erect, **elevate**; put together, assemble, compose, cobble together, **join**; blend, **combine**; mine, quarry, **extract**; establish, found, constitute, institute, **initiate**; **arrange**; develop, exploit; automate; engineer, contrive, **plan**; perform, implement, execute, achieve, accomplish; bring about, effect, **cause**; unfold, develop, **evolve**; breed, hatch, rear, **breed stock**; sow, grow, farm, **cultivate**; bear young, **reproduce itself**; educate, **train**.

## 160 Destruction

**N.** **destruction**, undoing, **reversion**; **extinction**; abolition; **silence**; **revolution**; precipitation, overthrow; dissolution; **separation**; **burning**; mass murder, massacre, genocide, **slaughter**; hatchet job; mischief, vandalism, **violence**, sabotage, **hindrance**; fireraising, arson.

**havoc**, scene of destruction, disaster area, chaos, **confusion**, turmoil; wilderness, **desert**; carnage, shambles, **slaughterhouse**; upheaval, cataclysm, storm, **outbreak**; ravages; depredation, raid, **spoliation**; blitz, explosion, nuclear blast, **bombardment**; holocaust, hecatomb.

**ruin**, downfall, ruination, perdition; **adversity**; catastrophe, disaster, act of God, **misfortune**; collapse, landslide, **revolution**; breakdown, break-up, **failure**; crash, smash, smash-up, **collision**; wreck, shipwreck, wreckage, wrack; loss, Waterloo, **defeat**; knockout blow, KO, **knock**; slippery slope, road to ruin; apocalypse, doom, crack of doom, knell, end, **finality**; ruins.

**Adj.** **destructive**, internecine, **complete**; ruinous, **wasteful**; costly, **dear**; apocalyptic, **violent**; **furious**; merciless, **pitiless**; mortal, suicidal, cut-throat, **deadly**; subversive, **revolutionary**; incendiary, mischievous, pernicious, poisonous, **toxic**.

**destroyed**, undone, fallen; ground; lost, sunk, sunk without trace; had it, kaput; **dilapidated**; ending.

**Vb.** **destroy**, undo; abolish, annihilate, liquidate, exterminate, axe, **nullify**; devour, consume, **waste**; engulf, **absorb**; swamp, overwhelm, drown, **drench**; incinerate, gut, **burn**; wreck, shipwreck, sink (see **suppress**); end, put an end to, **terminate**; **kill**; poison, **murder**; decimate, **render few**; exterminate, spare none, **slaughter**, **be pitiless**; remove, extirpate, eradicate, uproot, **eject**; expunge, efface, erase, delete, cancel, **obliterate**; annul, revoke, **abrogate**; dispel, scatter, dissipate, **disperse**; dissolve, **liquefy**; evaporate; mutilate, deface, **deform**; make short work of; trounce, **defeat**; dish, sabotage, **obstruct**; play hell with, **bedevil**, **waste**; ruin.

**demolish**, dismantle, **disunite**; level, raze, **flatten**; steamroller, bulldoze, fell; **slaughter**; subvert, overthrow, overturn, upset, **invert**; sap, **weaken**; undermine, mine, dynamite, explode, blow sky-high; bombard, bomb, blitz, **fire at**; wreck, smash, shatter, shiver, smash to smithereens, **break**; pulp, crush, grind; make mincemeat of; rend, **sunder**; **agitate**; batter, ram, **strike**; gut, strip bare, **uncover**.

**suppress**, quench, **extinguish**; cut short, abort, **discontinue**; quell, **oppress**; squelch, squash, **flatten**; quash, revoke, **abrogate**; blanket, stifle, smother, suffocate, strangle, **disable**; repress, **subjugate**; cover, **conceal**; drown, submerge, sink, scuttle, scupper, torpedo, sink without trace, **plunge**, **lower**.

**lay waste**, desolate, devastate, depopulate, **empty**; raid, ransack, **rob**; damage, spoil, mar, ruin, **impair**; ravage, deal destruction, run amok, make havoc, make a shambles, **be violent**; **waste**; **abase**; **burn**; defoliate, **make sterile**.

**consume**, devour; engulf, **absorb**; squander, run through, **waste**; cast before swine, **misuse**.

**be destroyed**, go west, be lost, **perish**; sink, **plunge**; have had it, **end**; fall, **tumble**; split; crumble, crumble to dust, **deteriorate**; succumb; go to pot, go to hell, go to blazes.

**Adv. destructively**, with a sledge hammer.

## 161 Reproduction

**N. reproduction**; **production**; **repetition**; mass production; multiplication, printing, **print**; **restoration**; **revival**; resurrection, resurgence; **recurrence**; **heredity**; reincarnation, **future state**; new edition, reprint, **edition**; copy, **duplicate**; Phoenix.

**Adj. reproduced**; **generative**.

**Vb. reproduce**, remake, reconstruct; rebuild; duplicate, clone, **copy**, **repeat**; take after, inherit, **resemble**; renovate, renew, **restore**; regenerate, resuscitate, reanimate, **revive**; reappear; resurrect; mass-produce, multiply; **print**; breed, **reproduce itself**, **be many**.

## 162 Propagation

**N. propagation**, **reproduction**; fertility; multiplication, **increase**; breeding, hatching, incubation, **animal husbandry**; eugenics, **biology**; sex; generation, genesis, **source**; parthenogenesis, virgin birth; spontaneous generation; AID; fertility drug, **fertilizer**; conception, pregnancy, gestation (see **obstetrics**); birth, nativity, happy event, **origin**; **failure**; birth rate; development, **growth**; fruition, flowering; puberty, maternity, paternity, **parentage**; donor; fertilizer; cultivator.

**obstetrics**; parturition, birth, childbirth, confinement; **anaesthetic**; labour, labour pains; delivery, breech delivery; waters, caul; placenta, afterbirth; maternity specialist, midwife, **nurse**; stork, gooseberry bush.

**genitalia**, loins, womb, **source**; genitals; male member, penis; scrotum; prostate; vulva, clitoris, vagina, uterus, ovary; ovum, egg; semen, seminal fluid, sperm, spermatozoa; seed, pollen.

**Adj. generative**, potent, virile; productive; fertile, fecund, **prolific**; germinal, seminal, genetic, **fundamental**; sexual, bisexual.

**fertilized**; breeding, broody, pregnant; heavy with, big with; with child; fallen; brought to bed of; **medical**; puerperal, maternity; antenatal; viviparous.

**Vb. reproduce itself**, yield, give increase, **be fruitful**; hatch, breed, spawn, multiply, teem, **be many**; germinate, sprout, burgeon, **grow**; bloom, flower, fruit, bear fruit, **mature**; seed, seed itself; conceive, get pregnant, fall; carry, bear; be brought to bed of, bring forth, give birth, have a baby; abort, **miscarry**; have young, have offspring, have progeny; drop, farrow, lamb, foal, calve, cub, pup, whelp, kitten, litter; **be born**.

**generate**, evolve, **produce**; give life to; beget, get, engender, spawn, father, sire; copulate, **unite with**; impregnate, inseminate, pollinate; procreate, propagate; breed, hatch, incubate, raise, rear, **breed stock**; bud, graft, layer, **cultivate**.

## 163 Destroyer

N. **destroyer**; wrecker, vandal; raider; extinguisher; hatchet man, assassin; executioner; barbarian, Vandal, Hun; time, time's scythe, **course of time**; angel of death, **death**; destructive agency, locust, **glutton**; moth, woodworm, rust, erosion, **decay**; acid, mildew, blight, poison, **bane**; earthquake, fire, flood, **havoc**; **war**; instrument of destruction, sword, **weapon**; gunpowder, dynamite, **explosive**; blockbuster, **bomb**; juggernaut, bulldozer.

## 164 Parentage

N. **parentage**, paternity, maternity; fatherhood, motherhood; loins, womb, **source**; kinship, **family**; adoption, **protection**; parent, **humankind**; single parent, **divorce**; godparent, guardian, **protection**

**genealogy**, family tree, lineage, kin, **consanguinity**; race history, pedigree, heredity; line, blood, strain; blue blood, **nobility**; stock, stem, tribe, house, clan, **race**; descent, extraction, birth, ancestry, **origin**.

**paternity**, fatherhood; dad, pop, papa, pater, governor; grandfather, **old man**; ancestor, progenitor, forefather, forbear, patriarch, predecessor, **precursor**; father figure; adoptive father, father-in-law.

**maternity**, motherhood; maternal instinct, **love**; expectant mother, mother-to-be; mother, dam; mummy, mum; grandmother, gran; matron; **old woman**; mother substitute; mother-in-law; Mother Church, mother country.

Adj. **parental**, paternal; maternal, matronly; fatherly; motherly; family, patrilineal, matrilineal; hereditary, **genetic**; patriarchal, **immemorial**; ethnic.

## 165 Posterity

N. **posterity**, progeny, issue, offspring, young, **child**; breed, **race**; brood, seed, litter, farrow, spawn, **young creature**; **family**; succession, heritage; rising generation, **youth**.

**descendant**, son, daughter; infant, **child**; scion, shoot, sprout, **young plant**; heir, **beneficiary**; love child; branch, ramification, colony; graft, offset.

**sonship**, line, lineage, descent, **consanguinity**; indirect descent, ramification; irregular descent; succession, heredity; **priority**.

Adj. **filial**; descended; collateral; **prior**; adoptive; step-; hereditary, Mendelian, **genetic**.

## 166 Productiveness

N. **productiveness**, productivity, mass production, **production**; boom; superabundance, glut; fertility, Green Revolution, **plenty**; high birthrate, baby boom, population explosion; productive capacity; multiplication; **imagination**.

**fertilizer**, manure, dung, guano, compost; potash, lime; mulch, **agriculture**; semen, sperm, seed; fertility drug; fertility cult, **phallus**; Earth Mother.

**abundance**, wealth, riot, profusion, harvest, **great quantity**; teeming womb, mother earth, rich soil; hotbed, nursery, **seedbed**; cornucopia, horn of plenty; second crop, aftermath, **sequel**; rabbit warren, ant heap, **multitude**.

Adj. **prolific**, fertile, fecund; teeming, **generative**; fruitful; pregnant, heavy with; exuberant, lush, leafy, verdant, luxuriant, rich, fat; copious; creative, inventive, resourceful.

Vb. **make fruitful**; plant, water, irrigate, manure, compost, top-dress, culti-

vate; impregnate, inseminate; procreate, produce, propagate, **generate**.

be **fruitful**, flourish; burgeon, bloom,
blossom; germinate; conceive, bear,
give birth, **reproduce itself**; teem, proliferate, swarm, multiply, mushroom,
**be many**, **augment**; populate.

## 167 Unproductiveness

N. **unproductiveness**, dearth, famine,
**scarcity**; erosion; dying race, zero
population growth, **decrease**; change
of life, menopause; poor return, **loss**;
waste of time, **lost labour**; slump,
slack market.

**contraception**, birth control, family
planning; contraceptive, pill, coil,
loop, diaphragm, Dutch cap, French
letter, condom, sheath; rhythm
method, chastity, **restraint**; vasectomy.

**desert**; waste, lunar landscape; heath,
moor, bush, wild, wilderness; dust-
bowl, **waste**; salt flat, **marsh**; **ice**;
waste of waters, **ocean**.

Adj. **unproductive**; sparse, scarce, **insufficient**; waste, desert, desolate; bleak,
gaunt, bare, **empty**; poor, stony, shallow; unprolific, barren, infertile, sour,
sterile; rootless, arid, **dry**; fallow;
impotent; without issue; celibate;
fruitless, inoperative, **impotent**; ineffective; abortive.

Vb. **be unproductive**, - unprolific etc.
adj. rust, stagnate, lie fallow; cease
work, **cease**; hang fire, come to
nothing, come to naught, **fail**; abort,
**miscarry**; practise birth control.

**make sterile**, **waste**; castrate, geld; **lay
waste**; addle, **decompose**; disinfect,
purify.

## 168 Agency

N. **agency**, operation, work, working,
doing, **action**; job, office, **function**;
exercise, **use**; force, strain, stress,
play, swing, **power**; influence; **management**; service; effectiveness; maintenance, support, **aid**; execution; process, treatment.

Adj. **operative**, effectual, efficient,
efficacious; drastic, **severe**; executive,
operational, functional; acting, work-
ing, at work, **doing**, **used**; **active**; live,
potent, **dynamic**, **vigorous**; practical,
workable, applicable, **advisable**; serviceable, **useful**.

Vb. **operate**, play; act, work, go, run, **do**;
idle; serve, execute, perform, **function**; do its job; take effect, **cause**; have
effect, **influence**; take action, strike,
**be active**; maintain, sustain, **support**;
crew, man; make operate; power,
drive, **move**; process, treat; manipulate, handle, wield, **touch**, **use**; stimulate, excite, **invigorate**.

## 169 Vigour: physical energy

N. **vigorousness**, energy, vigour, life,
**activity**; physical energy, pressure,
force, impetus, **energy**; high pressure,
**strength**; dash, **haste**; effort, **labour**;
fervour, enthusiasm, **vigour**; gusto,
relish, zest, **joy**; spirit, vim, zip; fire,
mettle, blood, **courage**; ginger, fizz,
verve, snap, pep, drive, go; enterprise,
initiative, **undertaking**; **violence**;
oomph, thrust, push, kick, punch,
**attack**; grip, bite, teeth, backbone,
spunk, **resolution**; guts, grit, **stamina**,
**vitality**; live wire, spark, dynamo,
dynamite, quicksilver; rocket, jet; display of energy, **spurt**; show of force.

**stimulation**, tonic effect; boost, **increase**;
excitement; stir, bustle, **activity**; ferment, fermentation; ebullience, **commotion**; froth, **bubble**; steam, **heat-**

ing.

**keenness**, acrimony; point, edge; zeal.

**stimulant**, booster; yeast, leaven, catalyst; stimulus, fillip, shot; spur, prick, prod, goad, lash, **incentive**; restorative, tonic, pep pill, **tonic**; aperitif, appetizer; seasoning, spice, **sauce**; liquor, alcohol, **alcoholic drink**; aphrodisiac, philtre, Spanish fly; pep talk, rousing cheer.

**Adj. vigorous**, energetic, **active**; **deadly**; forcible, forceful, vehement, **violent**; vivid, vibrant, **dynamic**; highpressure, intense, strenuous, **industrious**; enterprising, go-ahead, **progressive**; aggressive, keen, **willing**; doubleedged, potent, **powerful**; hearty, virile, full-blooded, **strong**; full of punch, full of pep, lusty, mettlesome, **lively**; blooming, bouncing, **healthy**; brisk, nippy, snappy, heady, racy; tonic, bracing, rousing, **exciting**; drastic, stringent, harsh, punishing, **severe**; **powerful**; lush, **prolific**.

**keen**, acute, sharp, incisive, trenchant, **forceful**; mordant, biting, poignant, pointed; virulent, caustic, **pungent**; acrid, acid, **sour**.

**Vb. be vigorous**, thrive, have zest, enjoy life, **be healthy**; burst with energy, **be strong**; show energy, **be active**; **exert oneself**; exert energy, drive, push, **impel**; bang, slam, wrench, cut right through, **force**; **accelerate**; be thorough, strike home, **carry through**; strike hard, hammer, dint, dent, **strike**; make an impression, **influence**, **impress**; **meddle**; show fight, **attack**.

**invigorate**, activate; electrify, intensify, double, redouble, boost, **strengthen**; rouse, kindle, inflame, stimulate, enliven, quicken, **excite**; act like a tonic, hearten, animate, **cheer**; intoxicate, **inebriate**; revive, **refresh**; give an edge to, **sharpen**; irrigate, **cultivate**.

**Adv. vigorously**, forcibly, hard, with telling effect; with a will; at full tilt, full steam ahead.

## 170 Inertness

**N. inertness**, inertia, **inaction**; languor, torpor, **insensibility**; rest, vegetation, passivity; apathy, sloth; passive resistance; vegetable, cabbage; extinct volcano.

**Adj. inert**, passive, dead; lifeless, languid, torpid, numb, **insensible**; heavy, sluggish, **slow**; **sleepy**; quiet, stagnant, **quiescent**; fallow; slack, lax; limp, flaccid, **weak**; apathetic, neutral, **indifferent**, **impassive**; pacific, **peaceful**; **powerless**; dormant, **latent**.

**Vb. be inert**, slumber, sleep; hang fire; smoulder, **lurk**; lie, stagnate, vegetate, **be quiescent**; just sit there.

**Adv. inactively**, at rest.

## 171 Violence

**N. violence**, frenzy, ferment; vandalism, **destruction**; turbulence, **commotion**; bluster, uproar, riot, row, roughhouse, rumpus, furore, **turmoil**; roughness; force, high hand, strongarm tactics; terrorism, **brute force**; atrocity, outrage, torture, **cruel act**; barbarity, blood lust, **inhumanity**; ferocity; rage, hysterics, **excitable state**; fit, throes, paroxysm, **spasm**; shock, clash, **collision**; wrench, twist.

**outbreak**, outburst; flood, tidal wave, **wave**; cataclysm, earthquake, quake, tremor, **revolution**; eruption, volcano, **furnace**; explosion, blow-up, burst, blast, **destruction**; rush, onrush, assault, sortie, **attack**; gush, spurt, jet, torrent, **stream**.

**storm**, turmoil, turbulence; weather; squall, tempest, typhoon, hurricane, cyclone, **gale**; thunder; cloudburst, **rain**; blizzard; sandstorm, **gale**.

**violent creature**, brute, beast, dragon, tiger, wolf, mad dog; demon, devil, **monster**; savage, barbarian, vandal, iconoclast, **destroyer**; he-man, **male**; man of blood, assassin, executioner, butcher; homicidal maniac, **madman**; rough, tough, rowdy, thug, **ruffian**; hooligan, bully, bully boy, terror, **tyrant**; bravo; firebrand, incendiary, **agitator**; revolutionary; madcap, **desperado**; virago, termagant, Amazon, fury, scold, **shrew**.

**Adj. violent**, vehement, forcible, **strong**; acute, **sharp**; unmitigated; excessive, outrageous, extravagant, **exorbitant**; rude, abrupt, brusque, bluff, **discourteous**; extreme, severe, heavy-handed; primitive, barbarous, savage, brutal, bloody, **cruel**; hot-blooded, **irascible**; aggressive, bellicose, **warlike**; rampant; thrashing about, **disorderly**; rough, wild, furious, blustery, tempestuous, stormy, gale force, **windy**; **rainy**; uproarious, obstreperous, **loud**; rowdy, turbulent, tumultuous, boisterous, **riotous**; incendiary, **revolutionary**; intemperate, immoderate, unbridled, unrestrained; ungovernable, unruly, **disobedient**; irrepressible, inextinguishable, **vigorous**; hot, red-hot, inflamed, **heated**; inflammatory, flaming, **fiery**; volcanic, seismic, **destructive**; explosive; spasmodic; full of violence, disturbed.

furious, towering; mad, **angry**; impetuous, rampant; roaring, howling; headstrong, **hasty**; desperate, **rash**; savage, wild; vicious, fierce, ferocious, **cruel**; blood-thirsty, rabid, berserk, **murderous**; waspish, tigerish, frantic, hysterical.

**Vb. be violent**, break bounds, run wild, run riot, run amok, **lay waste**; tear, rush, dash, hurtle, hurl oneself, **move fast**; surge forward, stampede, mob, charge; raise a storm, riot, roughhouse, **rampage**; resort to violence, take to arms, **go to war**, revolt; see red, go berserk, **be angry**; storm, rage, roar, bluster, **blow**; ferment, foam, fume, run high, **effervesce**; flood, overwhelm, **flow**; explode, detonate, burst, fly, flash, flare; let fly, fulminate; erupt, struggle, strain, scratch, bite, kick, **resist**; savage, maul, **wound**; ride roughshod, **oppress**.

**force**, smash, **break**; tear, rend, **sunder**; bruise, crush; **demolish**; strain, wrench, pull, dislocate, sprain; twist, warp, deform, **distort**; force open, **open**; blow open, shock, shake, **agitate**; do violence to, abuse, **misuse**; violate, ravish, rape, **debauch**; torture, **ill-treat**.

**make violent**, stir, quicken, stimulate, **excite**; urge, goad, lash, whip, **incite**; inflame, kindle, **heat**; foment, exacerbate, exasperate, **aggravate**; whet, **sharpen**; irritate, infuriate, **enrage**; madden, **make mad**.

**Adv. violently**, forcibly, bodily; at one fell swoop; with a vengeance, like mad; slap bang, wham; head foremost, head first; like a bull at a gate.

## 172 Moderation

**N. moderation**, nonviolence; measure, golden mean; restraint, self-control, **temperance**; **sobriety**; **middle way**; mutual concession, **compromise**; **relief**; relaxation, remission; appeasement; quiet, calm, **quietude**; control, check, **restraint**.

**moderator**, **remedy**; **balm**; rose water, milk; sedative, lullaby; nightcap, barbiturate, **soporific**; opiate, opium, **anaesthetic**; dummy, **stopper**; wet blanket, damper; cold water, cold shower, **extinguisher**; brake, restraint; neutralizer; **antidote**; cushion; third force, peacemaker, mediator; rein.

**Adj. moderate**, reasonable, judicious, **just**; tame, gentle, harmless, mild, lenient; innocuous, **innocent, weak**; measured, limited, low-key, **restrained**; subdued, **temperate**, sober; cool, calm; still, quiet, **tranquil**; peaceable, pacific, **peaceful**; pink, **neutral, indifferent**.

lenitive, **remedial**; sedative, narcotic, **soporific**; smooth, **soft**; bland; emollient; **refreshing**.

**Vb. be moderate, be halfway**; go easy, keep within bounds, keep within reason, **be temperate**; settle, **be quiescent**; disarm, **be at peace**; remit, relent, **show mercy**; show consideration, **be lenient**; **decelerate**.

moderate, mitigate, temper, correct, adjust; tame, check, curb, control, chasten, govern, limit, **restrain**; lessen, diminish, slacken, **abate**; palliate, extenuate, qualify, **weaken, blunt**; cushion, **support**; soft-pedal, moderate language, **purify**; sober, dampen, damp, cool, chill, **refrigerate**, dissuade; blanket, smother, subdue, quell, **extinguish**.

assuage, ease, pour balm, mollify, soften; alleviate, lighten, **relieve**; counteract; allay, dull, deaden, **render insensible**; soothe, calm, comfort, still, quiet, hush, lull, rock, cradle, rock to sleep, **bring to rest**; sweeten; disarm, appease, **pacify**; slake, **drink**.

**Adv. moderately**, within bounds, within compass, within reason; at half speed, gingerly.

## 173 Influence

**N. influence**, capability, power, potentiality, **ability**; magnitude; upper hand, casting vote; footing, hold, grip; play, **scope**; purchase, **pivot**; clout, weight, pressure; pull, drag, **attraction; repulsion**; thrust, drive, **propulsion**; impact, **impulse**; leaven, contagion, infection; atmosphere, climate, **circumstance**; **heredity**; occult influence, magic, spell, **sorcery**; destiny, **fate**; fascination, hypnotism; malign influence, curse, ruin, **bane**; emotion, impulse, impression, feeling, persuasion, suggestion, impulsion, inspiration, **motive**; personality, charisma, leadership, credit, repute, **prestige**; hegemony, domination, tyranny, **authority**; sway, control, dominance, reign; sphere of influence, orbit; factor, vital role, leading part, **cause**; indirect influence, patronage, interest, favour, pull, friend at court, **aid**; strings, lever, **tool**; secret influence, Grey Eminence; force; lobby, pressure group, **inducement**; person of influence, uncrowned king or queen, big noise, big shot, **bigwig**; **government**.

**Adj. influential**, dominant, prevalent, prevailing, **supreme**; ruling, regnant, commanding; with authority, **authoritative**; rising; strong, potent, mighty, **great**, **powerful**; leading; busy, **active**; effective, **causal**; weighty, key, momentous, decisive, earth-shaking, **important**; telling, moving, emotional, **impressive**; appealing, attractive; gripping; irresistible; persuasive, suggestive; instructive, **educational**; catching, contagious, **infectious**; pervasive, **ubiquitous**.

**Vb. influence**, have a pull, carry weight, cut ice, **be important**; be well-connected; **command**; dominate, bestride; **be superior**; exert influence, make oneself felt, assert oneself;

lobby, pull strings, **motivate**; gain a hearing, **attract notice**; have a voice; affect, tell; **impress**; **flatter**; urge, prompt, tempt, incite, inspire, dispose, persuade, convince, carry with one, **induce**; force, **compel**; sway; predispose, brainwash, prejudice, **bias**; appeal, allure, fascinate, **attract**; disgust, **repel**; **counteract**; make, **make better**; make or mar, change, **transform**; infect, leaven, colour, **modify**; contaminate, mar, **impair**; work, **operate**; play a part, guide, **direct**; **be an example**.

**prevail**, outweigh, override, **predominate**; overawe, overcome, subdue, subjugate; gain full play, master, **overmaster**; control, rule, **dominate**; hold, **retain**; gain a footing, take root, take hold, settle, **stay**; permeate, run through, colour, **pervade**; spread, rage, be rife, spread like wildfire.

Adv. **influentially**, to good effect.

### 174 Tendency

N. **tendency**, trend, tenor; tempo, rhythm, set, drift, **direction**; course, stream, main current, main stream; climate, **influence**; gravitation, affinity, **attraction**; polarity; **fitness**; gift, **aptitude**; proclivity, propensity, readiness, penchant, predilection, leaning, bias, prejudice; weakness; cast, bent, turn, grain; a strain of **tincture**; vein, humour, mood; tone, quality, nature, characteristic, **temperament**; special gift, idiosyncrasy, **speciality**.

Adj. **tending**, conducive, leading to; working towards; **probable**; centrifugal; subservient, **liable**; apt to, prone to; ready to, about to, **prepared**.

Vb. **tend**, trend, verge, lean, incline; set, set towards, **approach**; affect, dispose, carry, bias, bend to, warp, turn, influ-

ence; point to, lead to; bid fair to, **be likely**; contribute to, **promote**.

### 175 Liability

N. **liability**, weakness, **tendency**; exposure; **sensibility**; potentiality, **possibility**; likelihood, **probability**; obligation, responsibility, **duty**.

Adj. **liable**, apt to; subject to, prey to, **subject**; open to, **vulnerable**; contingent; incident to, incidental; possible; susceptible; answerable, responsible, amenable, accountable.

Vb. **be liable**, be responsible, **incur a duty**; incur, lay oneself open to; stand to gain, stand to lose; **be subject**; open a door to.

### 176 Concurrence: combination of causes

N. **concurrence**, joint effort; coincidence, **conformity**; concord, harmony, **agreement**; compliance, **consent**; concurrent opinion, consensus, **assent**; **submission**; concert, conspiracy, **plot**; league, alliance, **association**; conjunction, **union**.

Adj. **concurrent**, coincident, parallel; **corporate**; of one mind, at one with; joint; involved.

Vb. **concur**, acquiesce, **assent**; collude, connive, conspire, **plot**; agree, **accord**; hang together; contribute, help, aid, abet, serve, **minister to**; promote; go with, keep abreast of, run parallel to, **accompany**; unite, stand together, **cohere**.

Adv. **concurrently**, with one consent, with one accord.

### 177 Counteraction

N. **counteraction**; polarity; antagonism, antipathy, clash, conflict, **collision**; return action, reaction, repercussion, backfire, backlash, **recoil**; resistance, opposition; inertia, friction, drag, check, **hindrance**; interference, repression, **restraint**; **moderation**; cancellation, **destruction**; crosscurrent, headwind, **obstacle**; neutralizer, **antidote**; **offset**; **tactics**; deterrent, **defence**; preventive, **prohibition**.

**Adj. counteracting**, counter; **contrary**; hostile, **inimical**; recalcitrant; reactionary, reactive; preventive, contraceptive; **remedial**.

**Vb. counteract**, counter, cross, traverse, work against, **hinder**; react, **recoil**; agitate against, persecute, **be inimical**; resist, withstand, defend oneself, **oppose**; antagonize, conflict with, **be contrary**; clash, **collide**; interfere, **meddle**; repress, **suppress**; undo, cancel, **abrogate**; find a remedy, cure, **remedy**; recover, retrieve, obviate, prevent, inhibit, **prohibit**.

**Adv. although**, despite, notwithstanding; against, contrary to.

## 178 Space: indefinite space

**N. space**, expanse; extension, extent, surface, area; volume, cubic content; continuum, stretch, **continuity**; time; empty space; depth of space, abyss, **depth**; **infinity**; sky, outer space; world; terrain, open space, open country; lung, green belt, **plain**; prairie, steppe, **grassland**; outback, hinterland, **region**; wild, wilderness, waste, **desert**; everywhere, **presence**.

**measure**, proportions, dimension, **length**, **breadth**, **height**, **depth**; **area**, square measure, acreage; square inch, square yard, square metre, hide; volume, cubic content, **size**.

**range**, reach, carry, compass, coverage; stretch, grasp, span; radius, latitude, amplitude; sweep, spread, ramification; play, swing, **scope**; sphere, field, arena, **region**; prospect, **view**; per-

spective, **distance**; telescopic range; **optics**.

**room**, space, accommodation; capacity, stowage, storage space, **storage**; seating capacity, seating; standing room; margin, clearance; room to spare, elbowroom, room to swing a cat; room overhead, headroom, headway; sea room, seaway, leeway; opening, way, **open space**; living space.

**Adj. spatial**, space; cubic, three-dimensional; flat, superficial.

**spacious**, **extensive**; expansive, roomy, commodious; ample, vast, cavernous, capacious, broad, deep, wide; voluminous, baggy, **large**; **general**; far-flung, widespread, worldwide, global, world, **whole**; boundless, **infinite**; trackless.

**Vb. extend**, spread, range, cover; span, straddle, bestride; extend to, reach to, **be contiguous**; branch, ramify.

**Adv. widely**, everywhere, wherever; **throughout**; at every turn, here, there and everywhere.

## 179 Region: definite space

**N. region**, locality, **place**; sphere, orb, hemisphere; zone, belt; latitude, parallel, meridian; climate; tract, terrain, country, ground, soil, **land**; island, peninsula, continent; sea, **ocean**; Old World; Third World; compass, circumference, circle, circuit, **outline**; bounds, shore, confines, **limit**; pale, precincts, close, enclave, salient; corridor, **access**; area, field, theatre, **arena**; exclusive area.

**territory**, sphere, zone; beat, pitch, ground; lot, holding, claim; grounds, park, **estate**; domain, territorial waters; airspace, defensible space; possession, dependency, protectorate, dominion; colony, settlement; homeland, **home**; commonwealth, republic, kingdom, realm, state, empire.

**district**, purlieus, haunt, **locality**; quarter, division; state, province, county, shire, riding, lathe, hundred, rape; diocese, bishopric; parish, ward, constituency; borough, township, municipality; county, district; department, commune; hamlet, village, town, **abode**; **housing**; garden city, new town; suburb, suburbia, subtopia, dormitory suburb, stockbroker belt; green belt, **space**; golden circle; provinces, back of beyond; Wild West; outback, backwoods, bush, brush; countryside, **land**; hinterland.

**city**, metropolis, conurbation; West End, East End, City, Wall Street.

**Adj. regional**, territorial, insular; national, state; local, municipal, parochial, redbrick, **provincial**; suburban, urban, rural, up-country; district, town, country.

## 180 Place: limited space

**N. place**, site, location, position, **situation**; station, substation; quarter, locality, **district**; pitch, beat, billet, socket, groove; centre, meeting place, **focus**; dwelling place, fireside, **home**; place of residence, address, habitat, **locality**, **quarters**; premises, building, mansion, **house**; spot, plot; point, dot, pinpoint; niche, nook, corner, hole, pigeonhole, pocket, **compartment**; confines, bounds, baseline, crease (cricket); **limit**; prison, coffin, grave; precinct, bailey, paddock, compound, pen; close, quad, square; yard, area, courtyard, court, **open space**; farmyard, field, **farm**; stock farm.

**Adv. somewhere**, some place, wherever it may be; locally, **near**.

## 181 Situation

**N. situation**, position, setting; scene; location, address, whereabouts; point, stage, milestone, **degree**; site, seat, base, **place**; habitat, range, **region**; post, station; standpoint, standing, ground, footing, **state**; side, aspect, attitude, posture; frontage; geography, topography; chart, **map**.

**bearings**, compass direction, declination, right ascension; **direction**; **location**.

**Adj. situated**, living at, to be found at; settled, set; local, topical.

**Vb. be situated**; be found at; be, lie, stand; live, live at, **dwell**; touch, **be near**.

**Adv. in place**, here, there; hereabouts, thereabouts; whereabouts.

## 182 Location

**N. location**, placement, disposition; radar; population; settlement, establishment, fixation, installation; deposition, **arrangement**; stowage, **storage**.

**locality**, quarters, environs, environment, surroundings, milieu, neighbourhood, **district**; vicinity, **near place**; address, street, place of residence, habitat, **abode**; seat, site, **place**; meeting place, venue, haunt, **focus**; genius loci, spirit of place.

**station**, seat, site, position, **situation**; depot, base, colony, settlement; anchorage, **shelter**; lines, camp, temporary abode; hostel, **abode**; halting place, lay-by.

**Adj. located**, situated; rooted, settled, **fixed**; at anchor, **quiescent**; possessed.

**Vb. place**, assign a place, **arrange**; position, site, locate; base, centre; pinpoint; place right, aim well, hit, **aim**; put, lay, set, seat; station, post, park;

install, ensconce, establish, fix; root, plant, implant, embed, graft, **insert**; bed, put to bed, cradle; accommodate, lodge, house, quarter, billet; impose; moor, tether, picket, anchor, **tie**; dock, berth, **bring to rest**; deposit, stand, erect, **elevate**; place with, transfer, bestow, invest, **assign**; array, deploy.

**replace**, put back, sheathe, bring back, reinstate, **restore**; repatriate, resettle, **transpose**.

**stow**, pocket, pouch, pack, bale, store, freight, **load**; **fill**.

**place oneself**, stand, anchor, **come to rest**; settle, strike root, gain a footing, **stay**; perch, alight, sit, squat, park; encamp, camp; stop at, lodge; hive, burrow; ensconce oneself, locate oneself, find a home; settle, populate, people, **dwell**; become a citizen.

## 183 Displacement

**N. displacement**; wrong place; shift, move, **motion**; red shift; aberration, **deviation**; transfer, mutual transfer, **interchange**; relief, replacement; removal, **extraction**; expulsion; exile; refugee, **wanderer**; **misfit**; docker, stevedore, removal man.

**Adj. displaced**; aberrant; unplaced; rootless, unsettled, roofless.

**misplaced**, **abnormal**; inappropriate, **irrelevant**; lost, missing, **absent**.

**Vb. displace**, disturb, disorientate, derail, dislocate; dislodge, unseat, **disunite**; dispel, scatter, send flying, **disperse**; shift, remove, **move**; transport, **transfer**; change round; transpose, **interchange**; post, **send**; relegate, banish, exile, **dismiss**; set aside, supersede, **substitute**, depose; evict, **eject**; eradicate, uproot, **destroy**; discharge, unload, off-load; rake, sweep, **clean**; lift, raise, uplift, **elevate**; draw,

extract.

**misplace**, mislay, lose, lose touch with, lose track of.

## 184 Presence

**N. presence**, being there, existence; whereabouts, **situation**; being somewhere; being everywhere; physical presence, attendance, residence, occupation, sit-in, **possession**; visit, descent, stay; present moment, **present time**; spectator, bystander.

**Adj. on the spot**, present, existent; resident; attendant; still there; ready, available, **prepared**; at home, at hand, within reach; **obvious**.

**ubiquitous**, omnipresent, pervasive, universal.

**Vb. be present**, exist, be; occupy; inhabit, **dwell**; hold, **possess**; stand, lie, be situated; witness, **watch**; resort to, frequent, haunt, meet one at every turn; occur, **happen**; stay, sojourn, summer, winter, **visit**; attend, assist at; take part, make one at, make one of; present oneself, **arrive**; face, confront, **defy**.

**pervade**, permeate, fill, **make complete**; impregnate, soak, run through; overrun, spread, meet one at every turn, **infiltrate**; **influence**.

**Adv. here**, there, where, everywhere; aboard, at home; on the spot; before; personally.

## 185 Absence

**N. absence**, lack, **scarcity**; deprivation, loss; being nowhere, Utopia, **fantasy**; being elsewhere, alibi; leave of absence, furlough; absenteeism, French leave; absentee, truant; absentee landlord; postal voter.

**emptiness**, empty space, void, vacancy; blank, **gap**; nothing inside, shell; vacuum, air pocket; blank cartridge,

blank paper, clean sheet; virgin territory; waste, **desert**; vacant lot, bomb
site, **room**.

**nobody**, nobody present.

**Adj. absent**; gone, flown; lacking, wanting, missing; absent without leave;
truant, absentee; lost, nowhere to be
found.

**empty**, vacant, vacuous, inane; void,
devoid, bare; blank, clean; characterless, featureless; without content, hollow; vacant; desert; unsettled; godforsaken, lonely; bleak, desolate;
uninhabitable.

**Vb. be absent**; absent oneself, cut, skip,
take French leave, **avoid**; leave a gap;
leave empty, evacuate, vacate;
exhaust, **empty**.

**go away**, withdraw, leave, **depart**; make
oneself scarce, retreat, **decamp**,
**escape**; vanish, **disappear**; make
room, vacate.

**Adv. without**, minus, sans.

**not here**; neither here nor there; elsewhere, somewhere else; nowhere.

## 186 Inhabitant

**N. dweller**, inhabitant, denizen; transient, visitant; migrant, expatriate,
**foreigner**; insular, islander; water
gipsy; highlander; commuter; provincial; peasant, **farmer**; bedouin; troglodyte; **poor person**. See **native**.

**resident**, householder; housewife,
housekeeper; crofter; addressee,
occupier, incumbent, **possessor**; **substitute**; tenant, lessee; inmate, in-
patient; house surgeon, **doctor**; garrison, crew, **personnel**; lodger, boarder,
guest, visitor; cuckoo, squatter; parasite, **bane**.

**native**, aboriginal, **precursor**; people,
tribe, **nation**; local, local inhabitant;
parishioner, city person, city slicker;
cockney; yokel, rustic; fellow coun-

tryman or -woman, fellow citizen;
national, patrial, citizen, burgess,
voter; Briton; North Briton; Paddy;
Northerner, Southerner; New
Yorker, Parisian, **foreigner**; terrestrial; Martian.

**settler**, pioneer, **precursor**; colonist, colonial, creole; planter, **farmer**; resident
alien, **foreigner**.

**inhabitants**, population, townspeople,
country folk; populace, people, people
at large, citizenry, yeomanry; suburbia, **housing**; household, **family**;
settlement, stronghold; colony, commune, community.

**Adj. native**, vernacular, popular,
national, ethnic; indigenous, aboriginal; earthbound, terrestrial; home,
home-made; domestic, domiciliary;
settled; resident.

**occupied**; manned.

## 187 Abode: place of habitation or resort

**N. abode**, habitat, haunt, station, **situation**; place of residence, **locality**;
habitation, street, house, home,
address, house number, number;
domicile, residence; town, city, **district**; headquarters, base, seat, **focus**;
temporary abode, camp, pad; week-
end cottage, country seat, holiday
home, seaside resort, hill station,
**pleasure ground**; spa, sanatorium,
**hospital**; lines, **station**; camp, caravan
park.

**quarters**, accommodation, lodging, billet, berth, squat; barrack; rooms,
chambers, digs; residential hotel,
guest house, pension; boarding
school, hostel, dormitory; hall of residence; convent, **monastery**.

**dwelling**, roof; prehistoric dwelling;
tower, keep; cave, hut, kraal, igloo;
wigwam, tepee, tent, **canopy**; lair,

den, hole, form, burrow, warren, earth, **shelter**.

**nest**; branch, **tree**; perch, roost; covert, rookery, hatchery, aviary, apiary; anthill.

**home**, hearth, fireside, chimney corner, inglenook, roof; homestead, household; cradle, 'house where I was born', **origin**; native land, homeland, God's own country; native soil, native sod, native ground, native heath, home ground, home town; haunt; familiar territory, second home; household gods.

**house**, building, **edifice**; house of God, **temple**; home, residence, dwelling, dwelling house; country house, villa, detached house; prefab; ranch house, chalet, bungalow, seat, place, mansion, hall, stately home; palace, dome; castle, keep, tower, peel; manor house, manor, grange, lodge, priory, abbey; vicarage, **parsonage**; farmhouse, croft, hacienda, **farm**; official residence, Mansion House, White House, embassy, consulate.

**small house**, chalet, lodge, cottage, cot; cabin, hut, shanty; hovel, dump, hole, slum dwelling; box; shed, shack, lean-to, outhouse, outbuilding; shelter, tent, **canopy**; kiosk, booth, stall; houseboat, **boat**; mobile home, caravan, trailer, **vehicle**. See flat.

**housing**, **building material**; urban sprawl; asphalt jungle, urban blight; conurbation; town, burgh, suburb, **city**; housing estate, residential area, **district**; suburbia, subtopia, crescent, close, terrace, circus, square, avenue, street, **road**; block, court, row; inner city, ghetto, slum; shanty town; hamlet, village; scattered settlement.

**flat**, flatlet, penthouse; apartment, suite, chambers; bed-sitter, **chamber**; apartment block, mews.

**stable**, byre, cowshed; kennel, doghouse; sty, fold; dovecote, pigeon loft; stall, cage, coop, hutch, battery; stabling, mews, garage, carport, hangar; boathouse, marina, dock, basin, wharf, port, **shelter**; berth, quay, jetty, pier.

**inn**, hotel, hostelry, roadhouse, motel, bed and breakfast; doss-house, kip; hospice, night shelter; youth hostel; caravanserai, khan; rest house.

**tavern**, boozer; public house, pub, local; free house, gin palace, saloon; speakeasy, dive, joint; wine cellar, wine bar; beer cellar, beer hall, beer garden; bar.

**café**, restaurant, cafeteria; bistro, grill room, rotisserie; coffee bar, soda fountain; lunch counter, snack bar, sandwich bar; teahouse, tearoom; refreshment room, buffet, canteen, Naafi; take-away; coffee stall, pull-in.

**meeting place**, meeting house, **church**; day centre, village hall; assembly rooms, club, night club, holiday camp, **place of amusement**; football ground, racecourse, dog track, **arena**; theatre, concert hall, stadium, stand; sports centre, gymnasium, drill hall, parade ground; quad, campus, village green, **focus**; **market**.

**pleasance**, park, grounds, green; walk, mall, avenue, parade, promenade, boulevard; national park, chase, **pleasure ground**.

**pavilion**, kiosk, bandstand, rotunda, folly, bower, grotto, **arbour**; arcade; tent, marquee, **canopy**.

**retreat**, sanctuary, refuge, asylum, ark, **shelter**; cubbyhole, den, sanctum, study, **chamber**; cell, hermitage; cloister, **monastery**; almshouse, workhouse, poorhouse; orphanage, home, hospice, halfway house, sheltered housing.

**Adj. residing**, abiding, dwelling, living; at home; residential.

**urban**, cosmopolitan, suburban.

**provincial**, parochial, local, domestic, vernacular; up-country, countrified, rural, rustic.

**architectural**; Gothic; classical, olden; brick, concrete, cob, half-timbered; modest, substantial, palatial, grand; detached; multistorey, high-rise.

**Vb. dwell**, inhabit, populate, people, **be present**; settle, **appropriate**; frequent, haunt, **visit**; reside, remain, abide, sojourn, live, **be situated**; take rooms, stay, keep, lodge, lie, sleep at; have an address; tenant, occupy, squat, **possess**; nestle, perch, roost, nest, hive, burrow, stable; camp, encamp, **place oneself**; tent, shelter, **seek refuge**; berth, dock, anchor, **come to rest**.

**urbanize**, develop.

**188 Contents: things contained**

**N. contents, component**; inventory, **list**; furnishings, equipment, **provision**; load, payload, cargo, freight, shipment; inside, stuffing, filling, wadding, **lining**; handful, **small quantity, great quantity**.

**Vb. load**, freight, charge, burden, **stow**; ship; **weigh**; pack, **insert**; pack tight, cram, stuff, **fill**; pad, wad, line; hide, conceal, **cover**.

**189 Receptacle**

**N. receptacle**, container, holder; frame, **prop**; hutch, cage, **prison**; folder, wrapper, envelope, cover, file; net, **network**; sheath, chrysalis, cocoon; **wrapping**; capsule, ampoule; pod, calyx, boll; mould, **form**; socket, mortise, **cavity**; groove, slot, **furrow**; hole, cave, cavity, **opening**; bosom, lap, **fold**; pin cushion; trap; well, reservoir,

hold, repository, **store**; drain, cesspit, sump, **sink**; crockery, glassware, **pottery**.

**bladder**, airbladder; inner tube; football; balloon; sac, cyst, vesicle, blister, bubble, **swelling**; udder, teat, **bosom**.

**maw**, stomach, tummy; abdomen, belly, pot belly, paunch, **swelling**; gizzard, gullet, crop, jaws, mouth, **orifice**.

**compartment**, cell, follicle, ventricle; tray, cage, iron lung; cubicle, booth, stall; sentry box; box, **theatre**; pew, **church interior**; niche, nook, cranny, recess, bay; pigeonhole, cubbyhole; drawer, locker; shelving, rack, **shelf**; storey, floor, deck, **layer**.

**cabinet**, closet, commode, wardrobe, press, chest of drawers, tallboy; cupboard, unit; whatnot, dresser, china cabinet; buffet, sideboard, **stand**; freezer, **refrigerator**; cocktail cabinet, dumbwaiter; bureau, desk, console; bookcase.

**basket**; hamper, picnic basket; pannier; trug, punnet, rush basket, frail; crib, cradle, bassinet; laundry basket; workbasket; wickerwork; framework, crate, **frame**; **fortification**.

**box**, chest, ark; coffer, locker; case, canteen; safe, till, **treasury**; coffin, sarcophagus, **tomb**; tea chest; attaché case; suitcase, trunk, portmanteau; sea chest; hat box; ammunition chest, canister, caisson, **ammunition**; luggage, baggage; boot, luggage van.

**small box**; cardboard box, carton, packet; plastic box, airtight container; metal box, can, tin, canister; casket, **ritual object**; salt cellar, pepper mill; castor.

**bag**, sack, poke; handbag, vanity case, reticule, clutch bag, cornet, twist; survival bag; holdall, grip; haversack, rucksack; ditty bag, pouch, sling; pannier, saddlebag, nosebag; school bag, satchel, bundle, swag.

**case,** housewife; wallet, pocket book; spectacle case, compact; briefcase, portfolio; file, scabbard, sheath; pistol case, holster; arrow case, quiver, **store.**

**pocket,** fob, pouch; purse, sporran.

**vat,** butt, cask, barrel, tun, tub, keg, breaker; drum, **cylinder;** wine cask, pipe, hogshead, firkin; hopper, cistern, tank, **store.**

**vessel,** vase, urn, jar, amphora, crock, pot, pitcher, ewer, jug; **plant;** carafe, bottle; leather bottle; wine bottle, demijohn, magnum, jeroboam; flask, flagon, phial; crucible, retort, pipette, test tube; chamber pot, bedpan, **latrine;** pail, bucket, churn, can, flowerpot; bin, dustbin, **sink;** scuttle, hod; skip; bath, tub.

**cauldron, heater;** boiler, copper, kettle, skillet, pan, saucepan, steamer; girdle; casserole, Dutch oven; mess tin; tea urn, teapot, samovar, coffeepot, percolator; vacuum flask.

**cup,** eggcup, coffee cup, teacup, breakfast cup; tea service, tea set; chalice, goblet, beaker; horn, tankard, can, mug, stein, noggin, schooner; tumbler, glass, wineglass, brandy balloon, pony.

**bowl,** basin, pudding basin, punch bowl; porringer; manger, trough; colander, vegetable dish, tureen, gravy boat; rose bowl, vase.

**plate,** salver, tray; platter, charger, dish; palette; saucer; pan, scale; pallet, mortarboard, hod.

**ladle,** dipper, scoop; spoon, tablespoon, dessertspoon; teaspoon; spade, trowel, spatula, slice, shovel.

**chamber,** room, apartment, **flat;** cockpit, cubicle, cab; cabin, stateroom; audience chamber, throne room; cabinet, closet, study, den, sanctum,

**retreat;** library, studio, office, **workshop;** nursery; reception room, drawing room, lounge, parlour, salon, boudoir; bedroom, dormitory; dressing room, bathroom, washroom; mess, hall, refectory, canteen; smoking room, bar, snug, **tavern;** galley, kitchen; scullery, pantry, larder; dairy, laundry, utility room, offices, outhouse; garage, **stable;** storeroom, box room, glory hole, **storage;** cloakroom, lavatory, **latrine.** See **compartment.**

**lobby,** vestibule, foyer; corridor, passage, hall; gallery, patio, balcony, portico, porch; **doorway;** extension, lean-to.

**cellar,** vault, crypt, basement, **base;** coalhole, bunker, **storage;** hold, dungeon, **prison.**

**attic,** loft; penthouse, garret, **summit.**

**arbour,** alcove, bower, grotto, summerhouse, gazebo, folly, pergola, **pavilion;** sun lounge, conservatory, greenhouse, glasshouse, **garden.**

**Adj. recipient,** capacious, voluminous, **spacious;** hiding; baggy.

**cellular,** honeycombed, **concave;** marsupial; ventral, **convex.**

**capsular;** vascular.

## 190 Size

**N. size,** magnitude, proportions, dimensions, **measure;** extent, expanse, area, **space;** extension, **length, height, depth;** width, amplitude, **breadth;** volume; girth, circumference; **outline;** bulk, mass, weight, **gravity;** capacity, intake, tonnage; measured size, calibre, **measurement;** real size, true dimensions; maximum; full size, life size; large size, magnum, **chief part;** excessive size.

**hugeness;** enormity; towering proportions, monstrosity, **height.**

**bulk**, mass, weight, avoirdupois, **gravity**; lump, block, clod, boulder, **solid body**; hunk, chunk, **piece**; mound, heap, **great quantity**; mountain, pyramid, **high structure**; double chin, rotund figure, spare tyre, **swelling**; muscle man, **athlete**; fat person, tub, dumpling, mound of flesh, tub of lard, hulk.

**giant**, colossus, **tall creature**; mountain of a man or woman, young giant; ogre, monster; leviathan; whale, hippopotamus, elephant, jumbo; mammoth, dinosaur; Titan, Cyclops.

**whopper**, whacker, humdinger; a mountain of a.**l** .**l** .

**Adj. large**, of size, big, **great**; large size, jumbo; pretty large, considerable; bulky, massive, **weighty**; ample, capacious, voluminous, baggy; comprehensive, **broad**; vast, extensive, **spacious**; monumental, towering, mountainous, **tall**; fine, magnificent, thumping, thundering, whacking, **whopping**; elephantine; megalithic; lusty, healthy, **strong**; so big, of that order.

**huge**, immense, enormous, vast, mighty, grandiose, stupendous, monstrous, **prodigious**; record size; colossal, mammoth, gigantic, giant, mountainous; Herculean, gargantuan; megalithic; outsize, **exorbitant**; limitless, **infinite**.

**fleshy**, meaty, fat, stout, obese, overweight; plump, ample, chubby, podgy, **thick**; squat, square, dumpy, chunky, stocky, **broad**; tubby, portly, corpulent, pot-bellied, **convex**; puffy, bloated, bosomy; round, rotund, roly-poly, full, buxom, jolly; strapping, lusty, burly, beefy, brawny, **stalwart**.

**unwieldy**, cumbersome, hulking, gangling; lumpy; too big, elephantine,

overweight; awkward, muscle-bound, **clumsy**.

**Vb. be large**, become large, **expand**; have size, loom large, bulk, fill space, **extend**; tower, soar, **be high**.

## 191 Littleness

**N. littleness**, small size, miniature quality; lack of height.

**minuteness**, point, pinpoint, pinhead; crystal; atom, molecule, particle, electron, neutron, proton, quark; nucleus, cell; corpuscle; drop, droplet, dust, grain; seed, **small thing**; bubble, button, molehill, **trifle**.

**miniature**, picture; microfilm, **photography**; pocket edition, **edition**; epitome, **compendium**; model, microcosm; bubble car, **automobile**.

**dwarf**, midget, pigmy; little people; elf; chit, slip; mite, tot, tiddler, **child**; bantam, **small animal**; pipsqueak, squirt, **nonentity**; doll, puppet; shrimp, runt, miserable specimen.

**microorganism**, protozoan, plankton, amoeba; bacteria, microbe, germ, virus; algae, **plant**.

**microscopy**, microscope, micrometer.

**microelectronics**, **electronics**; chip, microprocessor.

**Adj. little**, **small**; petite, dainty, dolly; diminutive, pigmy; wee, tiny; toy, baby, pocket, mini-; miniature, model; portable, handy, compact; snug, cosy, poky, cramped, **narrow**; puny, **weak**; petty, **inconsiderable**; one-horse.

**dwarfish**, dwarf, pigmy, undersized, wizened; squat, dumpy, **short**.

**exiguous**, minimal, slight, scant, scanty, **small**; thin, skinny, scraggy, **lean**; rudimentary, **beginning**; bitty, **fragmentary**.

**minute**, microscopic, infinitesimal; atomic; **powdery**; imperceptible, intangible, impalpable, **invisible**.

**Vb.** **be little**, contract, **become small**; dwindle, **decrease**; require little space.

**Adv.** **in small compass**, in a nutshell; on a small scale.

## 192 Expansion

**N.** **expansion**, increase of size, crescendo; enlargement, **increase**; reinforcement, **addition**; hyperbole, **exaggeration**; extension, spread; ribbon development, urban sprawl, **housing**; increment, accretion, **adjunct**; development, **growth**.

**dilation**; inflation, reflation, puff; dropsy, tumour, **swelling**.

**Adj.** **expanded**; widespread; expansive, **spacious**; flared, **broad**; wide open, **open**; tumescent, budding, flowering; full-blown; overblown, overgrown; obese, puffy, pot-bellied, bloated, fat; swollen, turgid; tight; varicose, **convex**.

**Vb.** **expand**, wax, increase, snowball, **grow**, widen, broaden, flare, splay, **be broad**; spread, extend, sprawl, deploy, take open order; spread like wildfire, overrun, mantle, straddle, **cover**; rise, gather, swell, distend, dilate; mushroom, balloon, belly, **be convex**; get fat, gain flesh; bud, burgeon, shoot, sprout, open, put forth, blossom, flower, blow, bloom, **be fruitful**.

**enlarge**; expand; leaven, **elevate**; bore, ream; widen, broaden, open; stretch, extend, **lengthen**; intensify, heighten, deepen; amplify, supplement, reinforce, **add**; double, redouble; develop, **augment**; distend, inflate, reflate, puff, **blow**; bulk, thicken, stuff, pad, **line**; cram, **fill**; fatten, **feed**; enlarge, **photograph**; magnify, **exaggerate**.

## 193 Contraction

**N.** **contraction**, reduction, deflation; decrease, shrinkage, diminuendo; abbreviation, **shortening**; **condensation**; **closure**; labour pains, **obstetrics**; consumption, atrophy; decline, retreat, recession, slump; neck, isthmus, bottleneck, hourglass; epitome, **compendium**.

**compression**, pressure, squeeze, strangulation.

**compressor**, mangle, roller; astringent; bandage, binder, tourniquet, **surgical dressing**; belt, band, garter, **girdle**; whalebone, stays, corset, **underwear**; straitjacket, iron boot, thumbscrew, **instrument of torture**; bear, python.

**Adj.** **contracted**, **small**; dense, compact; drawn tight, **narrow**, **closed**; contractile; wizened; consumptive.

**compressive**, astringent, binding.

**Vb.** **become small**, grow less, lessen, dwindle, wane, ebb, **decrease**; shrivel, wither, **decompose**; lose weight, lose flesh, **be light**; contract, shrink, narrow, taper, **be narrow**; condense, **be dense**; evaporate; draw together, **close**; pucker, purse, corrugate, wrinkle, **fold**.

**make smaller**, lessen, reduce, abate; contract, shrink, abridge, dwarf, stunt, **shorten**; diet, slim, **lighten**; taper, narrow, attenuate, thin, emaciate, **make thin**; puncture, deflate, rarefy, exhaust, drain, **empty**; evaporate; dehydrate, **dry**; cramp, constrict, pinch, nip, squeeze, bind, bandage, corset; draw tight, strain, **tighten**; draw together, clench, **close**, **join**; hug, crush, strangle; compress, compact, constipate, condense; **be dense**; huddle, crowd together; pack tight, cram, jam, **fill**; squash, **flatten**; cramp, restrict, **restrain**; limit, **circumscribe**; shave, shear, clip, trim, prune, pollard, **cut**; scrape, file, grind; crumple, **fold**; roll, press, flatten, **smooth**.

## 194 Distance

**N. distance**, light years, depths of space, **space**; measured distance, mileage, footage, **length**; elongation, aphelion, apogee; far distance, horizon, skyline, offing; background, **rear**; periphery, circumference, **outline**; drift, **deviation**; reach, grasp, compass, span, stride, **range**; far cry, long way, tidy step, long long trail, marathon.

**farness**, far distance; removal, **separation**; antipodes, pole; back of beyond; Far West, Far East; outpost; purlieus, outskirts; outer edge, frontier, **limit**; **absence**.

**Adj. distant**, distal, peripheral, terminal; far, farther; ulterior; ultimate, farthest, furthest, furthermost; long-range; yonder; outlying, peripheral, remote, aloof, far-flung, godforsaken; telescopic; lost to sight, lost to view, **invisible**; **wide**.

**removed**, inaccessible; beyond; overseas, transatlantic.

**Vb. be distant**, stretch to, reach to, extend to, spread to, go to, get to, carry to, **extend**; carry, range; outdistance, **outdo**; keep clear of, stand aloof, stand clear of, keep a safe distance, give a wide berth, **avoid**.

**Adv. afar**, far, far afield, way behind; yonder; at a distance; asunder, apart, abroad, afield; at arm's length.

**beyond**, further, farther; ahead; clear of, wide of.

**too far**, out of reach, out of range, out of bounds.

## 195 Nearness

**N. nearness**, proximity, propinquity, near distance, foreground, **front**; vicinity, neighbourhood, **surroundings**; brink, verge, **edge**; collision course; approximation, **approach**; **location**.

**short distance**, beeline, short cut; step, striking distance, close quarters; close range, earshot, gunshot; short span, inch, millimetre, **gap**; close-up, near approach, perigee, perihelion; close finish, near thing, **contest**.

**near place**, vicinity, neighbourhood, environs, suburbs, confines, **locality**; next door; second place, **sequence**.

**Adj. near**, proximate, proximal; very near, approximate; warm; about to meet; nearby, wayside, roadside, **accessible**; inshore; near at hand, at hand, handy, present; **shallow**; home, local; close to, next to, neighbouring, adjacent, **contiguous**; facing, **frontal**; close, intimate, inseparable; at close quarters; with nothing between; level; related, **akin**.

**Vb. be near**, be around, be about, **be present**; hang around, hang about; approximate, draw near, get warm, **approach**; meet, **converge**; neighbour, stand next to, adjoin, border, **be contiguous**; encroach; come close, skirt, graze, shave, brush, skim, hedge-hop; jostle, buzz, **obstruct**; follow close, shadow; come to heel, **follow**; clasp, cling to, hug, cuddle, **caress**; huddle, crowd, congregate.

**bring near**, approach, approximate, **juxtapose**.

**Adv. near**, locally; nigh, close to, at close range, at close quarters; close behind, within call, within hearing, within earshot, only a step; within reach, close at hand; face to face, eyeball to eyeball; next door, beside, alongside.

**nearly**, practically, almost, all but; more or less, near enough, roughly, around, somewhere around; about, hereabouts, thereabouts, circa; well-nigh; within an ace of, just about to.

## 196 Interval

**N. interval**, distance between, space; narrow interval, **short distance**; daylight, head, length; clearance, margin, freeboard, **room**; interval of time, **interim**; pause, break, truce, **lull**; hiatus; jump, leap; musical interval, tone, semitone, third, fourth, fifth, **musical note**.

**gap**, interstice, mesh, **network**; cavity, hole, **orifice**; pass, defile, **passage**; firebreak, **safeguard**; ditch, trench, **drain**, water jump, ha-ha, sunk fence, **partition**; ravine, gorge, chimney, crevasse, canyon, **valley**; cleft, crevice, chink, crack, rift, cut, gash, tear, rent, slit; flaw, fault, breach, break, split; fracture, rupture, fissure, chap, **separation**; slot, groove, **furrow**; indentation, **notch**; seam, join, **joint**; leak, **outlet**; abyss, chasm, **depth**; void; inlet, creek, **gulf**.

**Adj. spaced**, with an interval; split, cloven, cleft, cracked; **open**; far between.

**Vb. space**, interval, **set apart**; crack, split, start, gape, **open**; clear, show daylight between; lattice, mesh.

**Adv. at intervals**; now and again, every so often, off and on; with an interval.

## 197 Contiguity

**N. contiguity**, apposition, proximity; **touch**, **continuity**; contact; intercommunication, osculation; meeting, encounter; **union**; close contact, adhesion, cohesion, **coherence**; coincidence, **accompaniment**; tangent; border, fringe, edge; borderland, frontier, **limit**; buffer state.

**Adj. contiguous**; intercommunicating;

tangential, end to end; adjacent, **continuous**; close, to, **near**.

**Vb. be contiguous**, overlap, brush, rub, skim, scrape, graze, kiss; join, meet, **converge**; stick, adhere, **cohere**; lie end to end; adjoin, reach to, extend to, **extend**; sit next to, crowd, jostle, **be near**; border with, skirt, **hem**; coexist, coincide, **accompany**; intercommunicate, **connect**; contact.

**juxtapose**, range together.

**Adv. contiguously**; next, close; end to end.

## 198 Length

**N. length**, longitude; extent, extension; reach, long arm; full length, stretch, span, mileage, footage, **distance**; perspective, **depth**.

**lengthening**, extension, production; tension.

**line**, bar, rule, tape, strip, stripe, streak; spoke, radius; single file, line ahead, crocodile, queue, **sequence**; straight line; bent line, **curvature**.

**long measure**, measurement of length, **measurement**; unit of length, finger, hand, palm, span, cubit; arm's length, fathom; head, length; pace, step; inch, foot, yard; rod, pole, perch; chain, furlong; mile, knot, league; millimetre, centimetre, metre, kilometre; degree of latitude, degree of longitude; micron, wavelength; astronomical unit, light year, parsec.

**Adj. long**, lengthy, extensive, a mile long; lank, lean, lanky, **tall**; interminable, **tedious**; **diffuse**, unabridged, full-length, **complete**.

**longitudinal**, oblong, linear.

**Vb. be long**, stretch; make a long arm; reach, stretch to, **extend**; drag, trail, drag its slow length along.

**lengthen**, stretch, elongate, **make thin**;

spreadeagle, **expand**; sprawl, **be horizontal**; deploy, **disperse**; extend, unroll, unfold, **evolve**; produce, continue; prolong, protract; drawl, **stammer**.

**look along**; have a clear view, **scan**.

**Adv. longwise**; along; at full length, end to end, overall; head to foot, head to tail, stem to stern, top to toe.

## 199 Shortness

**N. shortness**, brevity; **brief span**; inch, centimetre, **short distance**; low stature; shrinkage; short hair, bob, crew cut; shorts.

**shortening**, abbreviation; **compendium**; cutback, cut, reduction; contraction.

**shortener**, cutter.

**Adj. short**, brief, **transient**; **little**; squat, dumpy, stumpy, stocky, thickset, stubby, **thick**; **low**; snub, blunt; scanty, **insufficient**; cut, topless, headless; shorn; sparing of words, terse, **concise**; potted, compact, **compendious**.

**Vb. be short**, **fall short**.

**shorten**, abridge, abbreviate; pot, **abstract**; recapitulate, **be concise**; compress, contract, telescope; reduce, diminish, **abate**; foreshorten, **distort**; kilt; behead, guillotine, axe, **sunder**; cut short, dock, curtail, truncate; cut back, slash, lop, prune; shear, shave, trim, crop, clip, bob, shingle, **cut**; mow, scythe; stunt, **retard**; scrimp, skimp, **make insufficient**.

**Adv. shortly**.

## 200 Breadth. Thickness

**N. breadth**, width, latitude; width across, span, wingspan; diameter, radius; gauge, bore, calibre; expanse, superficial extent, amplitude, **range**.

**thickness**, bulk.

**Adj. broad**, wide, expansive, **spacious**; full, flared, ample, baggy; wide-awake (hat); wide-angle (lens), **open**; **stalwart**; **general**.

**thick**, stout, dumpy, squat, **short**; thickset, tubby, stubby; thick-skinned; **strong**; **dense**; lumpy, to be cut with a knife.

**Vb. be broad**, get broad, broaden, widen, fatten, thicken; flare, splay, **expand**; straddle, bestride, span.

**Adv. broadways**; **sideways**.

## 201 Narrowness. Thinness

**N. narrowness**, narrow interval, tight squeeze, crack, chink, **short distance**; lack of breadth, line, strip, stripe, streak; vein, capillary, **filament**; knife-edge, tightrope, wire; narrow gauge; bottleneck, strait, **gulf**; ridge, col, saddle, **high land**; ravine, **valley**; pass, defile, **passage**; neck, isthmus, **bridge**.

**thinness**, rarity; consumption; scrag, skeleton; miserable specimen, scarecrow, rake, broomstick, shadow; lantern jaws, hatchet face; thread, paper, tissue, **transparency**; shaving, splinter, **small thing**; slip, wisp, **filament**.

**narrowing**, **contraction**; taper; neck, isthmus, stricture; waistline, waist, hourglass.

**Adj. narrow**, single track; strait, tight, close; fine, thin, **transparent**; spun, **long**; capillary, **fibrous**; slight, delicate, **weak**; attenuate, slender, slim, svelte; willowy; lanky, gangling.

**lean**, thin, spare, wiry; meagre, skinny, bony; cadaverous, haggard, gaunt, drawn, lantern-jawed; spindly, spidery; undersized, weedy, scrawny, scrubby, scraggy, **exiguous**; consumptive, wizened, peaky, **sick**; starveling; worn to a shadow, without an ounce of flesh to spare.

**Vb. be narrow**, narrow, taper, **converge**;

**become small**.

**make thin**, contract, compress, pinch, nip; make oneself thin, starve, reduce, lose weight; slim; draw, spin, spin fine, **lengthen**; attenuate, **rarefy**.

## 202 Layer

**N. layer**, stratum, underlay, floor, **base**; outcrop, basset, **projection**; bed, course, range, row; zone, vein, seam, lode; thickness, ply; storey, tier, floor, landing; stage, planking, platform, **frame**; deck, quarterdeck, bridge, **ship**; film; bloom, dross, scum; patina, coating, coat, veneer, top layer; **covering**; scale, scab, membrane, peel, sheathe, bark, **skin**; level, water table; atmospheric layer, **atmosphere**.

**lamina**, sheet, slab, foil, strip; plate glass, plate, tinplate, sheet iron, sheet steel; plank, board, weatherboard, fascia; laminate, plywood; slat, lath, leaf; tablet, plaque, panel, pane; slab, flag, flagstone, slate; shingle, tile; slide, wafer, shaving, flake, slice, rasher; cardboard, sheet of paper, **paper**; card, platter, disc, **circle**.

**stratification**, bedding; overlap; Russian doll; onion skin; layer cake, sandwich, double-decker.

**Adj. layered**, flaky; slaty; scaly; filmy.

**Vb. laminate**, lay, deck, layer, shingle, overlap; zone, stratify, sandwich; plate, veneer, **coat**; split; whittle, skive, pare, peel, strip, **uncover**; shave, slice, **make thin**.

## 203 Filament

**N. filament**, flagellum, lash, eyelash, beard, **hair**; barb, **plumage**; flock, lock, shred of wool, lock of hair, wisp, curl; fringe, **edging**; stalk, tendril, **plant**; whisker, antenna, **feeler**; gossamer, cobweb, web, **network**; capillary, vein, **conduit**; ramification, branch;

wire, element, wick, **torch**.

**fibre**, hair, Angora, mohair, cashmere; llama hair, alpaca; wool, merino; shoddy; silk, wild silk, floss; vegetable fibre, cotton, cotton wool, silk cotton, kapok; linen, flax; hemp; jute, sisal, coir; tow, oakum; raffia; worsted, yarn; spun yarn, thread, twine, twist, strand, cord, string, line, rope, **cable**; artificial fibre, rayon, nylon, **textile**; staple, denier, **texture**.

**strip**, fascia, band, bandage; braid, tape, strap, ribbon; fillet, **girdle**; lath, slat, batten, stave; shaving, wafer; splinter, shiver, shred, **piece**; streak, **line**.

**Adj. fibrous**; woolly, silky; downy, fleecy; **hairy**; wiry; capillary; **narrow**; stringy, **thick**.

## 204 Height

**N. height**, perpendicular length, vertical range, long way to fall; altitude, elevation, ceiling, pitch, **summit**; dizzy height; stature; eminence; sky, stratosphere, **atmosphere**.

**high land**, height, wold, moor, downs, rolling country; rising ground, rise, bank, slope, climb, **incline**; hill, eminence, mount, mountain; fell, scar, tor; mountain range, chain, sierra, cordillera; ridge, col, saddle, spur, headland, foothill, **projection**; crest, peak, pike, **summit**; precipice, cliff, crag, scar, bluff, steep, escarpment; gorge, canyon, ravine, **valley**; summit level; plateau, tableland.

**small hill**, hillock, hump, dune, moraine; barrow, **tomb**; mound, heap, **earthwork**; cairn, tell, **monument**; anthill, molehill, tussock, **swelling**.

**high structure**, column, pillar, turret, tower; pile, skyscraper, **edifice**; steeple, spire, belfry, **church exterior**; minaret, obelisk; dome, cupola, **roof**; colossus, **sculpture**; mausoleum, pyramid, **tomb**; pagoda, **temple**; ziggurat, Tower of Babel; mast, topmast; flagstaff; pole, maypole; lamppost, standard; pylon, radio mast; masthead, **summit**; watchtower, lookout, **view**; column of smoke, mushroom cloud.

**tall** creature, giraffe, elephant, mammoth, lamppost, grenadier, colossus, **giant**; poplar, pine, sequoia, **tree**.

**high** water, high tide, **current**; billow, tidal wave, **wave**; cataract, **waterfall**; flood, flood level.

altimetry, altimeter, **meter**, **gauge**.

**Adj. high**, sky-high; eminent, exalted, lofty, sublime, **elevated**; **topmost**; aerial, airborne, flying; towering; steep, dizzy.

**tall**, lanky, **narrow**; statuesque, Junoesque; colossal, gigantic, monumental, **huge**.

**alpine**; mountainous, hilly, highland; rolling.

**overhanging**; incumbent; aloft; prominent.

**Vb. be high**, tower, soar; surmount, clear, overlook, dominate, command, **be superior**; overhang, overshadow, **cover**; beetle; hover, hang; **climax**; mount, bestride; rise, **ascend**; **lift oneself**.

**make higher**, heighten, raise, hold aloft; **elevate**.

**Adv. aloft**; atop; above, overhead; above stairs, upstairs; upwards; breast high; **throughout**.

## 205 Lowness

**N. lowness**; sea level; **marsh**; steppe, **plain**; low elevation, molehill, pimple; gentle slope, slight gradient, **incline**; lower level, foothill; bottom, hollow, depression, **valley**; **ocean**; depths, cellar, well, mine, **depth**; floor, foot, **base**; nadir; low water, low ebb, low

tide, **current**; low ball.

**Adj. low**, squat, **short**; oblique; recumbent, laid low, prostrate, **supine**; flat, at sea level, **flat**; low-level; lower, nether, **inferior**; sunken, **concave**; blunt; subterranean, underground, submarine, **latent**, **deep**; underfoot.

**Vb. be low**, lie low, lie flat, **be horizontal**; be beneath, underlie, lurk; slouch, crouch, **stoop**; crawl, wallow, grovel; depress, **lower**.

**Adv. under**, beneath, underneath; below; downwards; underfoot, underground, downstairs, below stairs; at a low ebb; below par.

## 206 Depth

**N. depth**, drop, fall; perspective, **length**; vertical range, profundity, nadir; deep water, **ocean**; unknown depths, **pitfall**; depression, bottom, **valley**; hollow, pit, shaft, mine, well, **cavity**; abyss, chasm, **gap**; vault, crypt, dungeon, **cellar**; cave, catacomb; potholing, **descent**; underworld, bottomless pit, **hell**; soundings, sound, probe, plummet, lead, lead line; sonar; bathyscaphe; submarine, submariner, frogman, **diver**; draught, displacement; **measurement**.

**Adj. deep**, steep, profound; abysmal, cavernous; deep-seated, deep-rooted, **fixed**; bottomless, fathomless; unfathomed, unfathomable; subterranean, underground; underwater, submarine, sunk; navigable; infernal.

**Vb. be deep**, gape, yawn; deepen, hollow, dig, **make concave**; fathom, sound, take soundings, plumb; drop, lower, **let fall**; go deep, touch bottom, plunge, **founder**.

**Adv. deeply**, profoundly.

## 207 Shallowness

**N.** shallowness; thin surface; veneer, thin coat, **skin**; surface injury; scratch, graze, **trifle**; shoal water, shallows; ford, **passage**; pond, puddle, lake; ripple, **wave**; light soil, stony ground, **soil**.

**Adj. shallow**, slight, superficial, **insubstantial**; surface, skin-deep; shoal; light, thin, **narrow**.

## 208 Summit

**N. summit**, sky, heaven, pole, top, peak, crest, apex, pinnacle, crown; maximum height, pitch; zenith, meridian, high noon, culmination, apogee; acme, **perfection**; **limit**; climax, turning point, **crisis**; divide, watershed, Great Divide, **partition**; coping, keystone; lintel, architrave; tympanum, capital, cornice; battlements, parapet, **fortification**.

**vertex**, apex, crown, cap, brow, head; tip, cusp, spike, nib, end, **extremity**; spire, **church exterior**; landing, **ascent**; **fort**; summit level, plateau, tableland, **high land**; gable; ceiling, **roof**; upper chamber, garret, **attic**; top storey; topside, upper deck, quarter-deck, hurricane deck, bridge, **ship**; topmast; masthead, **high structure**.

**head**, headpiece, pate, poll; nob, nut, noggin, conk, crumpet, bean, block, chump; upper storey, belfry; brow, dome, temple, forehead; loaf, brain, grey matter, **intelligence**; scalp, crown, skull, cranium, **cavity**; phrenology.

**Adj. topmost**, top, **high**; uppermost, **supreme**; polar; capital, head; meridian; tiptop, super, **best**.

**Vb. crown**, cap, head, top, tip, surmount, crest, **be high**; consummate, **climax**; take top place, **be superior**; **make complete**.

**Adv. atop**, on top, at the top; tiptoe.

## 209 Base

**N. base**, foot, toe, skirt; bottom, root; rock bottom, nadir, low water; footing, foundation, **basis**; fundamental, **origin**; groundwork, substructure, infrastructure, chassis, **frame**; pedestal, **stand**; floor, bed, bedrock; subsoil; ground, earth, foundations; footing, sill; damp course; basement, ground floor, **cellar**; flooring, pavement, hard standing, **paving**; carpet, wainscot, dado; keel; hold, bilge; sump, drain, **sink**.

**foot**, pedal extremities; sole, heel, instep, arch; toe, toenail, big toe; trotter, hoof, paw, pad; claw, talon, **nippers**; ankle, fetlock, pastern.

**Adj. undermost**, nethermost, bottom, **low**; basic, fundamental.

**footed**, pedal; shod.

**Adv. in the trough**; basically, fundamentally.

## 210 Verticality

**N. verticality**, upright carriage; **height**; right angle, square; elevation, azimuth circle; vertical line, plummet; vertical structure, hoist, upright, pole, stalagmite, **pillar**; sheer face, precipice, cliff, bluff, scarp, steep, **high land**; perpendicular drop, vertical height, rise.

**Adj. vertical**, upright, erect, standing; perpendicular; sheer, abrupt, steep, precipitous, **high**; straight, plumb; upstanding; bolt upright, unbowed; rampant.

**Vb. be vertical**, bristle; stand erect, stand upright, hold oneself straight; rise, stand, ramp, rear; keep standing.

**make vertical**, erect, rear, raise, pitch, elevate; up-end; stand.

Adv. **vertically**, upright; standing, all standing; at right angles; plumb.

## 211 Horizontality

N. **horizontality**; horizontal angle, azimuth; horizontal line, ruler, rule; horizontal course, strike; level, plane, dead level, dead flat, level plane; sea level, water table; stratum; slab, tablet, table, **layer**; level stretch, steppe, **plain**; **marsh**; platform, ledge, **projection**; terrace, esplanade; plateau, tableland, **high land**; bowling green, cricket ground, croquet lawn, **arena**; platter, **plate**; spirit level, **gauge**; horizon, horizon line, **limit**.

**recumbency**; lying down; prostration, proneness.

**flattener**, iron, mangle, press, rolling pin, roller, steamroller; bulldozer, juggernaut, **destroyer**.

Adj. **flat**, horizontal, level, plane, even, flush, **smooth**, trodden, trodden flat; smooth, calm.

**supine**; prone, prostrate; recumbent.

Vb. **be horizontal**, lie, lie flat, lie prostrate; recline, couch, sprawl, loll; grovel, **stoop**; become horizontal.

**flatten**, spread; lay flat, squash; make flush, level, even, grade, plane; iron, **smooth**; smooth down, prostrate, floor, ground, **fell**.

Adv. **horizontally**, flat; at full length.

## 212 Pendency

N. **pendency**; suspension, hanging, dangle; set, hang, drape.

**hanging object**, hanging ornament, drop, earring; tassel, tag, **trimming**; hangings, curtains, tapestry, **covering**; train, skirt; flap; pigtail, tail, **sequel**; **hair**; dewlap, lobe, appendix, **adjunct**; pendulum, bob, swing, hammock; chandelier, **lamp**, icicle, stalactite.

**hanger**, curtain rod, curtain ring, runner, rack; hook, peg, knob, nail, **prop**; suspender, braces, suspender belt, **underwear**; **cable**; clotheshorse, **frame**; davit, crane; spar, mast, pillar; gallows, gibbet, **pillory**.

Adj. **hanging**, pendent, pendulous; dependent, weeping; open-ended, loose; baggy, flowing.

Vb. **hang**, be pendent, drape, set; trail, flow; swing, sway, dangle, bob; nod, weep, loll, droop, sag, swag; stream, wave, float, ripple, flap; hover; overhang, lour; suspend, sling, hitch, fasten to, append, **join**; curtain, **cover**.

## 213 Support

N. **support**, aid; footing, ground; hold, foothold; life jacket, **safeguard**.

**prop**, support, bearing; carriage, carrier, chassis; buttress; bulwark, embankment, wall, shore, jack; flagstaff, stanchion, rod, bar, transom, brace, strut; stay, mainstay, guy, rigging; boom, spar, mast, yard, yardarm, **projection**; trunk, stem, stalk, **plant**; arch, **curve**; keystone, cornerstone; cantilever; pier (see **pillar**); bandage, jockstrap, truss, splint; stiffener, whalebone; corset, **underwear**; yoke, **hanger**; rest, headrest, stirrup; handrail (see **handle**); skid, chock, wedge, **obstacle**; staff, baton, stick, cane, crutch, crook; leg support, irons; bracket (see **shelf**); trivet, hob (see **stand**); arm, back, shoulder; shoulder blade, clavicle, collarbone, backbone (see **pillar**); Atlas; supporter, patron, **auxiliary**.

**handle**, holder, **receptacle**; hold, grip, hilt, pommel, haft; knob; lug, ear, loop; railing, handrail, rail, taffrail; balustrade; shaft, loom; tiller; crank; lever, trigger, **tool**.

**basis**, foundation, deck; raft, pallet, sleeper; **layer**; ground, groundwork, floor, bed, bedrock, rock bottom,

**base**; flooring, pavement, **paving**, **land**; perch, footing, foothold.

**stand**, tripod, trivet, hob; table mat, coaster; anvil, block, bench; trolley; table, board; sideboard, dresser, **cabinet**; work table, desk, counter; pedestal; platform, gantry; footplate; landing, landing stage, pier; dais, pulpit, stage, **rostrum**; doorstep, threshold; altar step, **altar**; step, stair, tread, rung, round, **ascent**; stilt; shank, leg.

**seat**, throne, woolsack; bank, bench, form, settle; bucket seat, dicky; pew, **church interior**; stall, **theatre**; chair, armchair, easy chair, sofa, settee, divan, couch, ottoman, chesterfield, sociable; stool, footstool; saddle, pillion, pad, howdah; stocks, **pillory**; electric chair, hot seat; lap; mat.

**bed**, cot, crib, cradle, bassinet; marriage bed, bunk; couch; four-poster; pallet, airbed, shakedown; hammock, **hanging object**; sick bed, litter, hurdle, stretcher, **hospital**; bier, **funeral**; bedding, **coverlet**; bedstead, divan.

**cushion**, pillow; bolster, Dutch wife; mattress.

**beam**, joist, girder, rafter, tie beam, truss, **bond**; summer; **roof**; transom, crossbar, traverse; architrave, lintel.

**pillar**, shaft, pier, pile, pole, stake, stud, **structure**; post, king post, jamb; stanchion; banister; mullion; pilaster, column, caryatid; spinal column, spine, backbone; neck, cervix.

**pivot**, fulcrum, lever, purchase; hinge, **joint**; pole, axis; axle, swivel, spindle; bearing, gudgeon; rowlock; centre-board, keel.

**shelf**, ledge, offset, **projection**, corbel, bracket, console; niche, **compartment**; sill, windowsill; mantelpiece, rack, dresser, **cabinet**; counter, plank, board, table, leaf, slab.

**frame**, skeleton; framework, scaffolding, **structure**; trellis; chassis, fuselage, body (of a car); undercarriage; trestle; easel, clotheshorse; housing; picture frame, sash, **outline**.

**Adj. supporting**; fundamental; spinal; holding.

**Vb. support**, sustain, bear, carry, hold, shoulder; uphold; prop, underpin, **elevate**; buttress, bolster, cushion; reinforce, **strengthen**; bandage, brace, truss, **tighten**; steady, stay; cradle, pillow, cup; maintain, **provide**; give support, **aid**; frame, set, mount, **enclose**; give foundations, bottom, ground, found, base, embed; stand, endure, **suffice**.

**be supported**; press; command support, have behind one.

**Adv. astride**, piggyback.

## 214 Parallelism

**N. parallelism**; parallel, **equality**; parallel lines, lines of latitude; rails, railway lines; parallelogram.

**Adj. parallel**, collateral, concurrent, concentric; equidistant, **equal**; corresponding, correspondent, **similar**.

**Vb. be parallel**, run together, run abreast, lie parallel; correspond, concur; parallel.

**Adv. in parallel**, alongside; abreast.

## 215 Obliquity

**N. obliquity**; oblique line, diagonal; oblique figure, rhomboid, **angular figure**; oblique angle; squint; curvature, camber, bend, humpback, **curve**; zigzag, chevron; switchback; oblique motion, swerve, lurch, stagger, **deviation**; splay, bias, twist, warp; leaning, list, tip, cant; slope, slant, tilt, pitch, rake; batter; bevel; inclined plane, ramp, chute, slide; leaning tower; **angular measure**.

incline, rise, ascent; ramp, gradient; hill, rising ground, **small hill**; fall, dip, downhill, **descent**; easy ascent, easy descent, gentle slope, escarpment, cliff, precipice; scarp, **fortification**; bank, scree, landslide.

**Adj. oblique**, inclined, bevel; tipsy; askew, skew, slant, aslant; leaning; recumbent; **angular**; wry, awry, wonky, crooked, cock-eyed, knock-kneed; diagonal, transverse; athwart, across; indirect, zigzag, herringbone, bent.

**sloping**, uphill, rising; downhill; steep, abrupt, sheer, precipitous, breakneck, **vertical**; easy, gentle, shelving.

**Vb. be oblique**, incline, lean, tilt; pitch, slope, slant, shelve, dip, decline, **descend**; rise, climb, **ascend**; cut, cut across, **cross**; lean, list, tip, bank, heel, cant; bend, sag, give; **stoop**; walk sideways, edge, sidle, sidestep; look sideways, squint; zigzag; dodge, swerve, diverge, converge.

**make oblique**, incline, lean, slant, slope, cant, tilt, tip, rake; splay, **deviate**; bend, crook, twist, warp, skew, **distort**; bevel; sway, bias, divert, **deflect**; curve, camber.

**Adv. obliquely, across**; askew; aslant; askance; crabwise, sidelong, sideways; at an angle.

## 216 Inversion

**N. inversion**, turning back to front; palindrome; turning inward, **reversion**; turning inward; return; **interchange**; spoonerism.

**overturning**, upset, spill; somersault, cartwheel; **revolution**.

**Adj. inverted**, inverse; keel upwards; topheavy; topsy-turvy; flat, prone, **supine**; reverse, **contrary**; **opposite**.

**Vb. be inverted**, turn round, turn about, right about turn, **turn back**; capsize,

turn turtle; **be oblique**; **tumble**; reverse, back, go backwards, **regress**.

**invert**, transpose, **interchange**; reverse; turn back; **fold**; introvert; upend; upturn, overturn, spill, upset, capsize; turn topsy-turvy.

**Adv. inversely**; contrariwise, other way round; back to front; topsy-turvy; face downwards.

## 217 Crossing: intertexture

**N. crossing**; crisscross, intersection; arabesque, **pattern**; braid, wreath, plait, **convolution**; entanglement, skein; crossroads, intersection, road junction, **road**; level crossing, **railway**; viaduct, flyover, **bridge**, **traffic control**.

**cross**, crux, crucifix, **ritual object**; pectoral; **heraldry**; swastika; flag; crossbar, transom, beam; scissors, **nippers**.

**network**, reticulation, netting, chicken wire; webbing, matting, wickerwork, trellis, wattle; honeycomb, lattice, grating, grid, grille; tracery, fretwork, filigree; lace, crochet, knitting, tatting, **needlework**; web, cobweb; net, drag-net, trawl; mesh.

**textile**, weave, web, loom; woven stuff, piece goods, bolt, roll, length, piece, cloth, stuff, material; broadcloth, fabric, tissue; batik; jute, hessian, canvas, duck; ticking, crash, towelling, candlewick; chintz, damask, brocade, rep, tapestry, **covering**; mohair, cashmere; alpaca, angora, **fibre**; wool, worsted; frieze, felt, baize; homespun, tweed, serge; flannel, swansdown; paisley, **pattern**; jersey, flannelette, winceyette; velvet, velveteen; corduroy; cotton, denim, drill, khaki; fustian; poplin, calico, gingham, seersucker; organdie; cheesecloth, muslin, mull, voile; cambric, lawn; linen; silk;

georgette, chiffon; satin, taffeta, moire; shantung; tulle, net, gauze; lace; rayon, nylon, polyester, fibreglass, **fibre**.

**weaving**, texture; web, warp, weft, woof; nap, pile, **hair**; frame, loom, shuttle; weaver; knitting machine, distaff, whorl; spinner, spider.

**Adj. crossed**, crossing, cross, crisscross; diagonal, transverse, cross-eyed, **oblique**; crucial, forked, **angular**; **complex**; textile, woven; twill, herringbone; honeycombed, barred; striped, **variegated**.

**reticular**, webbed; micromesh.

**Vb. cross**, **pass**; intersect, cut, be **oblique**; splice, dovetail, link, **join**; mesh, net, knot; fork, **make angular**.

**weave**, loom; plait, braid; felt, twill, knit, crochet; spin.

**enlace**, interlace, interlink, interlock, intertwine, interweave, enmesh, engage gear; twine, entwine, wattle, twist, wreathe; mat, ravel, snarl, tangle, entangle, **derange**.

**Adv. across**, athwart; crosswise.

## 218 Exteriority

**N. exteriority**; **surroundings**; periphery, circumference, **outline**; exterior, outward appearance, **appearance**; surface, crust, cortex, shell, **skin**; outer side, face, facet, facade, **front**; other side; outside, open air; outer space, **distance**, **exclusion**; **nonconformity**; outsider, **nonconformist**.

**Adj. exterior**, outward, extra-; external; roundabout, peripheral; outer, outermost, outlying, extraterrestrial, **distant**; outside; outdoor, extramural; foreign, **extraneous**, **excluding**; **extrinsic**; centrifugal; eccentric; surface, superficial; skin-deep, **shallow**; facial, **frontal**.

**Vb. be exterior**, lie beyond, frame,

enclose, **surround**; look outward, be **extrinsic**.

**externalize**, body forth, **make extrinsic**; project, extrapolate; expel, **eject**.

**Adv. externally**, outwardly, outwards; outside.

## 219 Interiority

**N. interiority**, interior, inside, indoors; inner surface; **skin**; sapwood, heartwood, **wood**; inmost being, soul; heart, centre, breast, bosom; inland, Midlands, hinterland, up-country; pith, marrow, **substance**; subsoil, base; **presence**; **interval**; cave, pit, **depth**; **marriage**; self-absorption, egoism, egotism; introvert; inmate; internee, **prisoner**.

**insides**, **contents**; inner man, interior man; viscera, vitals; heart, ticker; lights; liver, spleen; offal, **meat**; bowels, entrails, innards, guts, pluck; tripe; colon, rectum; abdomen, belly, paunch; womb, uterus; stomach, tummy; chest; gland; endocrine; cell, **organism**.

**Adj. interior**, internal, inward, **intrinsic**; inside, inner, **central**; inland, upcountry; domestic, home, vernacular; intimate, familiar, **known**; indoor, intramural; inboard; endemic; deepseated, ingrown, **fixed**; intravenous, subcutaneous; introvert; **intrinsic**.

**Vb. be inside**, lie within, lie beneath; show through, **be visible**.

**hold within**, hold, **comprise**; place within, embed, **insert**; keep inside, intern, **imprison**; enfold, **enclose**; absorb.

**Adv. inside**, within; at heart; indoors, at home.

## 220 Centrality

**N. centrality**; concentration, **condensation**; central position; midriff, waistline, parting, **partition**.

**centre**, centre of mass, centre of gravity, centre of pressure, centre of percussion; nerve centre, ganglion; centre of activity, **focus**; epicentre; storm centre, hotbed; heart, core, kernel, **essential part**; nub, hub; nucleus; navel; spine, backbone; marrow, pith; pole, axis, fulcrum, centreboard, **pivot**; centre point, **middle**; **heraldry**; eye, pupil; bull's-eye, target, **objective**.

**Adj. central**; nuclear; **middle**; concentric; geocentric; spinal; centripetal; chief, head, **supreme**.

**Vb. centralize**, centre, focus; concentrate, consolidate, **be dense**.

**Adv. centrally**, at heart, at the core, middle, midst.

## 221 Covering

**N. covering**; overlap; coating, **layer**; top layer, top dressing, mulch, topsoil, **soil**; topping, icing, frosting; cover, lid; gravestone, ledger, **tomb**; hatch, trapdoor; flap, shutter; film; glass, glass front, watch glass, crystal, **transparency**; cap, top, plug, bung, cork, **stopper**; plaster, **surgical dressing**; carapace, shell, tortoiseshell, **hardness**; mail, plate, **armour**; shield, cowl, cowling, bonnet, hood (of a car); scab; crust, fur, **dirt**; capsule, ferrule, sheath, envelope, **receptacle**; pillowcase; table cloth, chair cover, antimacassar; soft furnishings; hangings, curtains, **hanging object**; wallpaper, **lining**; mask, domino, **disguise**.

**roof**, cupola, **dome**; **vertex**; pantile, shingle, thatch, **building material**; eaves, **edge**; ceiling, deck; vault, **beam**.

**canopy**; tilt, awning, sunblind; **screen**; marquee, pavilion, big top; tent, bell tent, tepee, **dwelling**; canvas, tarpaulin, fly sheet; mosquito net, **network**.

**shade**, hood, eyelid, eyelash; blind; curtain, veil; umbrella, gamp, brolly; parasol, sunshade; sun hat, sun helmet; visor, eye shade, **screen**; peak (of a cap); dark glasses.

**wrapping**, wrapper, paper, cellophane, polythene; polystyrene, **lining**; blister pack, **receptacle**; bandage, roller, **girdle**; plaster cast, **surgical dressing**; book cover, binding, boards, dust jacket or cover; tunic, coat, **jacket**; mantle, **cloak**; scarf; life belt, life jacket, **safeguard**; lagging; cocoon, chrysalis; shroud, **grave clothes**.

**skin**; outer skin, epidermis, cuticle; true skin; peel, bark, crust, rind, coat, cortex; husk, hull, shell, pod, jacket; membrane, film; scalp, **head**; scale; pelt, fleece, fell, fur; leather, hide, rawhide; shagreen; patent leather; crocodile, alligator; pigskin, morocco, calf, kid, chamois, buff, buckskin; sheepskin, lamb, astrakhan; mink, sable, ermine, chinchilla, **fibre**; **plumage**.

**paving**, flooring, floor, parquet; deck, duckboards; pavement; paving stone, crazy paving; cobble, cobblestone; gravel, asphalt, tarmac, **road**.

**coverlet**, bedspread, counterpane, bedding, bedclothes, bed linen; sheet, quilt, eiderdown, duvet; blanket, rug; trappings; pall.

**floor-cover**, carpet, broadloom, pile carpet, mat, doormat, bath mat; rug; linoleum, vinyl; matting, red carpet, **formality**.

**facing**, veneer, coating, varnish, japan, lacquer, enamel, glaze; incrustation, roughcast, pebbledash; **building material**; stucco, plaster, rendering; wash, whitewash, distemper, emulsion, paint; stain, polish; coat of paint, **pigment**.

**Adj. overlying**, overlaying; overlapping.

**covered**, vaulted; **safe**; hooded; snow-capped; plastered.

**dermal**, cutaneous; scaly.

**Vb. cover**, superimpose; roof, cap, tip; ice, frost, decorate (a cake); spread, lay (a table), smother; insulate, lag, **line**; lap, enfold, envelope, **enclose**; blanket, shroud, mantle, muffle; hood, veil, **conceal**; case, bind, cover (books), box, pack; wrap, bandage, swathe, wrap round, dress, **doctor**; sheathe, encapsulate, encase, **insert**, garage.

**overlie**, overhang, overlap; overshadow; span, bestride, straddle, **be broad**; flood, inundate, **drench**; crust, scab.

**overlay**, pave, floor, cement; roof, dome, vault, deck; tile, thatch; paper, wall-paper, **line**; topdress, mulch; spread, smear; butter, anoint; powder, dust, sand; gravel, tarmac, metal.

**coat**, face, front; roughcast, encrust, shingle; stucco, plaster, render, **decorate**; veneer, varnish, lacquer, japan, enamel, glaze, size; paint, whitewash, distemper, emulsion, stain, **colour**; creosote; tar, pitch, pay; daub, bedaub, grease; gild, plate, silver; electroplate; waterproof, fireproof, **safeguard**.

## 222 Lining

**N. lining**, liner; coating, stuffing, wadding, padding; kapok, foam; lagging, insulation; backing, facing; upholstery; wallpaper, panelling, wainscot; metal lining, bush; brake lining; **wrapping**; filling, washer.

**Vb. line**, encrust, **coat**; insulate, **cover**; inlay, back, face, paper, wallpaper; upholster, cushion; stuff, pad, wad;

fill, pack; bush, **insert**.

## 223 Dressing

**N. dressing**, investment, investiture; clothing, covering, toilet; **fashion**; dress, garb, attire, rig; panoply, array; trim, harness, housing, trappings; paraphernalia; rig-out, turn-out.

**clothing**, wear, apparel, raiment, linen; clothes, togs, gear, kit, clobber; outfit, wardrobe, trousseau; maternity wear; baby clothes, old clothes, tatters; working clothes; leisure wear, casual clothes; fine raiment; Sunday best; party dress, frippery, **finery**; fancy dress, masquerade; motley; colours; national costume.

**garment**, article of clothing; neck (see **neckline**); top, bodice, bosom; bib; waistline (see **belt**); bustle, train; crutch, codpiece; arms (see **sleeve**); fly, **opening**; patch pocket, **pocket**; gusset, gore, pleat, kick pleat; lapel, turn-up, **fold**; cuff, hemline, **edging**.

**formal dress, formality**; evening dress; morning dress; academic dress; mourning, black.

**uniform**, regimentals, **livery**; dress uniform, undress, mess kit; khaki; school uniform; clerical dress. **dress**, un0DFC (6) . **\*\*--0000 . LONGMAN** . . . . . .

**informal dress**, undress, mufti; casual clothes, slacks, jeans; dishabille; dressing gown, bathrobe, wrapper, housecoat; smoking jacket.

**robe**, gown, drapery; sari; kimono; toga; cassock; shroud, **grave clothes**.

**dress**, frock, gown; creation, number; cocktail dress; chemise, shift, sack; shirtwaister, pinafore dress, gymslip.

**suit**, outfit, ensemble; coordinates; lounge suit, costume, tweeds; leotard, body stocking; overalls, boiler suit, tracksuit; spacesuit.

**jacket**, coat, tail coat, dinner jacket, tuxedo; monkey jacket, blazer, reefer, sports jacket, riding habit, hunting pink; donkey jacket, parka, windcheater, anorak; bomber jacket; jerkin, tunic, tabard, waistcoat; bolero, matinee jacket.

**jersey**, pullover, woolly, jumper, sweater, polo neck, Fair Isle, cardigan, tank top, twin set.

**trousers**, trews; cords, flannels; bellbottoms; slacks, bags, plus fours; breeches, jodhpurs, knickerbockers; chaps, dungarees, denims, jeans, shorts; bloomers, pantaloons, rompers.

**skirt**; dirndl, kilt, kirtle; sarong; straight skirt, culottes; ballet skirt, tutu; crinoline, hoop.

**loincloth**, dhoti, sarong; fig leaf, G-string, jockstrap; nappy or diaper.

**apron**, bib, pinafore, pinny, overall.

**shirt**, smock, angel top; polo neck, tee shirt, sweatshirt; blouse, camisole, top, sun top.

**underwear**, underclothes, undies, linen; lingerie, smalls; underpants, pants, boxer shorts; briefs, panties, French knickers, camiknickers, knickers, bloomers, drawers; combinations, thermal underwear; singlet, vest, chemise, slip, petticoat; foundation garment, corset, stays, girdle; brassiere, bra; suspender belt, braces.

**nightwear**, nightclothes; nightdress, negligee; nightshirt, pyjamas; bed jacket, nightcap.

**beachwear**, bikini; swimming costume, bathing suit, trunks.

**overcoat**, coat (see **jacket**); fur coat, **skin**; topcoat, greatcoat, frock coat; raglan; car coat, waterproof; mac, mackintosh, raincoat; trench coat; light coat, duster.

**cloak**, mantle; cape; domino, **disguise**;

djellaba, shawl, plaid, poncho, Afghan.

**neckwear**, scarf; stole, boa; muffler; neckerchief, stock, cravat, tie, necklace; ruff, collar.

**headgear**; hat, cap, lid; headdress, mantilla; **finery**; coronet, tiara, **regalia**; fillet, snood; kerchief, headband, sweatband; turban; hood, cowl, wimple; veil, yashmak, **screen**; fez; busby, bearskin, helmet, **armour**; tin hat, crash helmet, skid lid, **safeguard**; woolly hat, sou'wester; cap, beret, tam-o'-shanter; deerstalker; Homburg, trilby, beaver, bowler, derby; slouch hat, stetson, sombrero, shovel hat, boater, panama, coolie hat, pith helmet, **shade**; bonnet, mob cap, cloche, pillbox; top hat, topper, silk hat, mortarboard.

**wig**; false hair, hairpiece, toupee; coiffure, **hair**.

**neckline**, boat neck, crewneck, cowlneck, poloneck, halterneck.

**belt**, waistband; cummerbund, sash; armband; **girdle**.

**sleeve**, arm, armhole; wristband, cuff.

**glove**, gauntlet; mitten, mitt, muff.

**legwear**, hosiery; nylons, tights; trunks, hose; leggings; **armour**; garter, suspender, **fastening**.

**footwear**; sock; slipper, mule; clog, sabot; creepers; brothel creepers; shoe, high heels, stiletto heels; slingbacks, lace-ups; boots, cowboy boots, wellingtons, wellies, gumboots.

**clothier**; tailor; **fashion**; seamstress; shoemaker; cobbler, **artisan**; hosier, hatter, milliner, draper, haberdasher; boutique; valet, **domestic**; dresser.

**Adj. dressed**, clad; shod.

**tailored**, tailor-made, bespoke, made-to-measure; single-breasted, one-piece, unisex; classic; skintight; bouffant, **broad**; sartorial.

**Vb.dress**, clothe, array, apparel, garment, garb, attire; robe, drape, sheet, mantle; invest, uniform, equip, harness, **make ready**; deck; envelop, wrap, lap, enfold, swaddle, swathe, shroud, sheathe, **cover**.

**wear**, assume, don, clothe oneself; **tie**; change; carry, sport.

## 224 Uncovering

**N.uncovering**, exposure, **disclosure**; nudism, naturism; striptease, **stage show**; undress, dishabille, **informal dress**; moult; shaving; **havoc**.

**bareness**, decollete, bare neck, plunging neckline; nudity, nakedness; the altogether, state of nature, birthday suit; baldness, alopecia.

**stripper**, striptease artiste; flasher, streaker; furrier, peeler; depilatory; nude figure, nude.

**Adj.uncovered**; showing, **manifest**; undressed; topless; unshod; hatless; bare, naked, nude, raw; mother naked; stark, stark naked, starkers; threadbare, ragged, **poor**; drawn.

**hairless**, bald, smooth; threadbare; mangy; thin.

**Vb.uncover**, unveil, undress; strip, skin, scalp, flay; pluck, peel, bark, excoriate; hull, pod, shell, stone; bone, fillet, **empty**; denude, **lay waste**; expose, bare, lay open, **disclose**; draw (a sword); **extract**; unfold, unpack; **open**; abrade, **rub**.

**doff**, uncover; drop; change; shed, cast, cast a clout; moult, slough, cast its skin; scale; undress, disrobe, peel, strip; undo, untie, **disunite**.

## 225 Surroundings

**N.surroundings**; ambience, atmosphere, aura; medium, matrix; compass, circuit, circumference, periphery, perimeter, **outline**; milieu, environment,

entourage; background, setting, scene, **situation**; neighbourhood, vicinity, **near place**; outskirts, environs, suburbs; green belt; purlieus, precincts, **housing**; outpost, border, **limit**; wall, fortification, **fence**; cordon, **girdle**.

**Adj.circumjacent**; atmospheric; peripheral; roundabout, **circuitous**; suburban, **near**.

**Vb.surround**, lie around, compass, encompass, lap; encircle, **circle**; girdle, **enclose**; wreathe around, embrace, hug, **caress**; contain, cloister, **circumscribe**; invest, blockade, besiege.

**Adv.around**, about, round about, all round; without, outside.

## 226 Interjacency

**N.interjacency**, **presence**; **crossing**; union; middle position, **middle**.

**partition**, curtain, **screen**; Great Wall of China; **exclusion**; wall, bulkhead, **fence**; divide, watershed, parting, **separation**; division, panel; septum, diaphragm, midriff, **centre**; field boundary, hedge, ditch, **gap**; common frontier, **limit**.

**intermediary**, medium, link, **bond**; go-between, broker, **mediator**; marriage broker, **matchmaker**; **agent**, **deputy**; middleman, retailer, **merchant**; advocate, **patron**; buffer, bumper, fender, cushion, **safeguard**; air lock, buffer state, halfway house, **middle**.

**interjection**; embolism, closure; interference, **hindrance**; episode, parenthesis, **adjunct**; insert, fly leaf; wedge, washer, **lining**.

**interjector**; interloper.

**Adj.interjacent**; intermediary; intrusive, **extraneous**; interplanetary, interstellar; intermediate; median, medium, mean, mediterranean, **middle**.

**Vb.** lie between, intervene, be halfway; permeate, **pervade**.

**introduce, admit**; sheathe; **insert; infuse**; splice, dovetail, mortise, **join**; insinuate, **infiltrate**.

**put between**, sandwich; cushion, **line**; interpose, interject; interpolate, intercalate; interleave, intersperse; interweave; bracket.

**interfere**, come between, intercept, **hinder**; intervene, intercede, **mediate**; interrupt; obtrude, **intrude**; invade, trespass, **encroach; meddle**.

**Adv.** between, 'twixt; among, amid, mid, midst; **while**.

## 227 Circumscription

**N. circumscription**; drawing round, circle, balloon; investment, siege, blockade, **attack**; confinement; ring, **fence**.

**Adj. circumscribed**;                 landlocked; **restrained**; limited, finite.

**Vb. circumscribe**, describe a circle, ring round, encircle, encompass; envelop, invest, blockade, picket, **besiege**; corral; enclose; box, cage, immure, cloister, **imprison**; frame, **surround**; encase, enfold, enshrine; edge, border, **limit**; clasp, hug, embrace, **caress**.

## 228 Outline

**N. outline**, circumference, perimeter, periphery; surround, frame, rim, **edge**; compass, circuit, **circle**; lines, features, **feature**; profile, relief; silhouette, skyline, **picture**; sketch, **plan**; figure, diagram; trace, tracing; skeleton, framework, **structure**; contour, contour line, shape, **form**; coastline, bounds, limit; circlet, band, loop; balloon, circle; ring, cordon, **barrier**.

**Adj. outlined**, framed; peripheral.

**Vb. outline**, describe a circle, construct a figure, **circumscribe**; frame, **sur-**

round; delineate, draw, silhouette, profile, trace, **represent**; etch, **engrave**; map, sketch.

## 229 Edge

**N. edge**, verge, brim; outer edge, fly (of a flag); tip, brink, skirt, fringe, margin, **extremity**; inner edge, hoist (of a flag); confines, bounds, boundary, frontier, border, limit; littoral, coast, coastline, beach, strand, seaside, seashore, waterline, water's edge, front, waterfront, **shore**; wharf, quay, dock, **stable**; sideline, side, brim, kerb, wayside, roadside, bank; hedge, railing, **fence**; tyre, **wheel**; lip, ledge, cornice, rim, welt, flange, **projection**; horizon, skyline.

**threshold**, sill, doorstep, door, portal, porch, **doorway**; mouth, jaws, chaps.

**edging**, frame, **outline**; thrum, list; hem, hemline, border; **pattern**; binding, piping; fringe, frill, ruffle, flounce, valance, **trimming**; **notch**; wavy edge, purl, **coil**.

**Adj. marginal**, border; roadside, wayside.

**Vb. hem**, edge, border, trim, fringe, purl; mill, **notch**; bound, confine, **limit**.

## 230 Enclosure

**N. enclosure**, envelope, case, **receptacle**; wrapper, **wrapping**; girdle, ring, perimeter, circumference, periphery, **outline**; surround, frame, precinct, close; cloister, courtyard, **place**; reserve, lot, holding, claim, **territory**; fold, pen, sty, cattle pen; stockyard, croft, **farm**; park, **garden**; compound, yard, pound, paddock, field; car park, **stable**; corral, kraal, stockade, lines; net, trawl, **network**; lobster pot, **trap**; cell, box, cage, **prison**.

**fence, network**; hurdle, wooden fence,

ha-ha, hedge, hedgerow; rails, balustrade, railing, taffrail; pale, wall, moat, ditch, trench, curtain wall.

**barrier**, wall, **partition**; **protection**; barricade, cordon, pale; balustrade, parapet; turnstile, **obstacle**; palisade, stockade, **fort**; portcullis, gate, door, bolt, bar, **closure**.

**Vb. enclose**, cordon, surround, wall; pen, hem, ring, **circumscribe**; cloister, immure, cage, **imprison**; wrap, lap, enfold, **fold**; hug, embrace, **caress**; frame, set, mount, box.

## 231 Limit

**N. limit, qualification**; definition; upper limit, ceiling, **summit**; lower limit, threshold, **base**; legal limit, Plimsoll line; saturation point; utmost, extreme, furthest point, farthest reach, pole, **extremity**; terminus, terminal, **end**; goal, target, touch, touchline, home, base, **objective**; turning point, **crisis**; Rubicon, **resolution**; limit of endurance, tolerance, capacity; physical limit, outside edge, perimeter, periphery, circumference, **outline**; tidemark, sea line, **shore**; landmark, boundary stone; milestone, **degree**; kerb, **road**; boundary, verge; frontier, border, **edge**; national frontier, state boundary; line, divide, parting, **partition**; horizon, equator; deadline, time limit, term, **period**; ultimatum, **threat**; speed limit; sound barrier.

**Adj. limited**, definite, finite; terminal; frontier, border, borderline, boundary.

**Vb. limit**, bound, border, edge, hem; top, **crown**; define, confine, condition, **qualify**; restrict, stint, **restrain**; encompass, **circumscribe**; demarcate; **mark**.

**Adv. thus far**, so far; on the border-

line.

## 232 Front

**N. front**, fore, forefront, **precedence**; forepart; prefix, **frontispiece**; forelock, **hair**; forecourt, entrance, **doorway**; foreground, proscenium; **priority**; front rank, first line, forward line, centre forward; avant-garde, vanguard, van, advance guard; spearhead, bridgehead; outpost, scout; forerunner, pioneer, **precursor**.

**face**, frontage; face of a coin, obverse, head; right side; front view, front elevation; **head**; brow, forehead; chin, features, visage, countenance, mug, mush, kisser, dial, clock, **feature**; prominent feature, nose, snout, conk, **protuberance**.

**prow**, nose, beak, rostrum, figurehead; bow; bowsprit; jib, forecastle, fo'c'sle, **ship**.

**Adj. frontal**, fore, forward, front, obverse; full frontal, head-on, oncoming, facing, **opposite**; anterior, **preceding**.

**Vb. be in front**, front, confront, face, be opposite; breast, stem, brave; **be oblique**; forge ahead, head, **precede**.

**Adv. in front**, before; ahead, **beyond**; far ahead, landward; face to face; head first, head foremost.

## 233 Rear

**N. rear**, rearward, back end, tail end, stern, **extremity**; heel; coda, **musical piece**; tail, brush, scut, pigtail, **sequel**; wake, train, **retinue**; last place, rear rank, back seat; rearguard, **successor**; background, backdrop, **stage set**; hinterland, depths, far corner, **distance**; behind, backstage, back side; reverse side; reverse, other side, flip side; back door, back entrance, postern, **doorway**; backbone, spine, **prop**; nape, scruff; **head**.

**buttocks**, backside, behind, posterior; bottom, seat; bum, arse, ass, fanny; rear, stern, tail; hindquarters, croup; hunkers; rump, loin; dorsal region, lower back; anus.

**poop**, stern, quarter, counter, rudder, mizzenmast, **ship**.

**Adj. back**, rear, postern; posterior, after, hind, hinder, rearmost; bent back, **convex**; reverse, **opposite**; placed last, **inferior**; spinal, dorsal, lumbar; anal.

**Vb. be behind**, back; **aid**; follow, **come after**; lag, trail, drop behind, fall astern; tail, shadow, dog, **pursue**; follow at heel, **follow**; bend backwards, be oblique.

**Adv. rearward**, behind, back of; after; aft, astern; backward; above; overleaf; close behind; back to back.

### 234 Laterality
**N. laterality**; side movement; sidestep, **deviation**; sideline, side, bank, **edge**; coast, **shore**; siding, side entrance, side door; gable; broadside; beam; quarter, **poop**; flank, wing, fin, hand; cheek, jowl, chaps; side whiskers, **hair**; profile, side elevation; lee, lee side, leeward; windward, **direction**; east, Orient; west, Occident, **compass point**.

**Adj. lateral**; side, **marginal**; sidelong, glancing; manysided, multilateral, bilateral, trilateral, quadrilateral; collateral, **parallel**; moving sideways, edging; eastern, eastward, easterly, orient; west, western, westerly, westward.

**Vb. flank**, side, edge, skirt, border, **hem**; coast, move sideways, passage, sidle; sideslip, sidestep, **deviate**; extend sideways, deploy, outflank, **overstep**.

**Adv. sideways**, crabwise; askance; side-

long; abreast, alongside; aside, beside; **near**; to windward, to leeward.

### 235 Contraposition
**N. contraposition**, antithesis, opposition, antipodes; frontage, **direction**; opposite side, reverse, back, **rear**; polarity; crosscurrent, headwind, **opposition**; inverse.

**Adj. opposite**, reverse, inverse, **contrary**; facing, oncoming, **frontal**; diametrically opposite; polar; antarctic, arctic, northern, southern.

**Vb. be opposite**, stand opposite, subtend; face, confront; run counter, **counteract**; oppose.

**Adv. against**; facing, face to face; back to back; overleaf; contrariwise.

### 236 Dextrality
**N. dextrality**, right hand; right, offside, starboard; right-hand page, recto; right wing.

**Adj. dextral**; right-hand, starboard, offside; right-handed, ambidextrous, **skilful**.

**Adv. dextrally**, on the right; to the right, dextrad.

### 237 Sinistrality
**N. sinistrality**, left hand; left, near side, port; left wing; southpaw.

**Adj. sinistral**, sinister, left, left-handed; onside, nearside.

**Adv. sinistrally**, on the left; offside; sinistrad.

### 238 Form
**N. form**, idea; **whole**; essence, **substance**; significant form, **character**; art form, **art**, verse form; word form, **linguistics**; shape, turn, lines, architecture; formation, configuration, fashion, style, design, **structure**; contour, silhouette, relief, profile, frame, outline;

figure, cut, set, trim, build, **feature**; **face**; look, expression, appearance, **mien**; posture, attitude, stance; get-up, turnout, rig; type, kind, pattern, stamp, cast, mould, blank, **prototype**; format, typeface, typography, **print**.

**formation**, creation, **production**; expression, **arrangement**; designing; knitting, **network**; **needlework**; **pottery**; moulding, **sculpture**; turning, joinery, **skill**; etymology, **linguistics**.

**Adj.** **formed**, receiving form, plastic; shaped; ready-made; ready, **prepared**; solid, concrete, **dense**.

**formative**, formal; plastic.

**Vb.** **form**, create, make; **produce**; shape, fashion, figure, pattern; blow (glass); turn, round, square; cut, tailor; silhouette, **outline**; sketch, draw, **represent**; model, carve, whittle, chisel; hew, **cut**; mould, cast; stamp, coin, mint; carpenter, mason; forge, smith; knead, work; construct, build, frame, **elevate**; express, formulate.

### 239 Amorphism: absence of form

**N.** **amorphism**, absence of form; prime matter; confusion, chaos, **disorder**; lack of shape; lack of definition; raw material; rough diamond; deformity.

**Adj.** **amorphous**, formless, inchoate; liquid, **fluid**; featureless, characterless; messy, chaotic; lacking definition, indistinct, nebulous, vague, fuzzy, shadowy; **beginning**; raw, **immature**; **incomplete**; rude, uncouth, barbaric, **artless**; rugged, **rough**; **unsightly**; malformed, misshapen, gnarled.

**Vb.** **deform**, **destroy**; dissolve, melt, **liquefy**; batter, **break**; grind, pulp; warp, twist, **distort**; deface, disfigure, **make ugly**; mutilate, truncate, **impair**; jumble, disorder, **derange**.

### 240 Symmetry: regularity of form

**N.** **symmetry**, proportion; balance, **equilibrium**; ramification; regular features, **beauty**; harmony, **agreement**; rhythm; finish, **perfection**.

**Adj.** **symmetrical**, balanced, **equal**; congruent; corresponding, **parallel**; similar; smooth, even, **uniform**; round, equilateral, **regular**; crystalline; formal, classic, comely, **shapely**; well set-up, **straight**; finished, **complete**.

### 241 Distortion: irregularity of form

**N.** **distortion**, disproportion, disproportionateness, want of symmetry; imbalance, **inequality**; projection, **map**; thrust, stress, strain, shear; bias, warp; buckle, bend, screw, twist, **convolution**; grimace, snarl, **gesture**.

**deformity**, monstrosity, abortion; **curvature**; clubfoot, rickets, **blemish**; eyesore.

**Adj.** **distorted**, irregular, asymmetric, scalene, disproportionate; weighted; grotesque; **amorphous**; gnarled, wry, awry, askew, crazy, crooked, cockeyed, **oblique**.

**deformed**, ugly, **unsightly**; **imperfect**; misshapen, misbegotten; bandy, bow-legged, knock-kneed; round-shouldered; stumpy, **short**; haggard, gaunt, **lean**; bloated.

**Vb.** **distort**, disproportion, weight, bias; contort, screw, twist, knot, **twine**; bend, warp, **crinkle**; spring, buckle, crumple; strain, sprain, skew, wrest, torture, rack, **derange**; botch, **deform**; mangle, batter, **impair**; pervert, **misrepresent**; misconstrue, **misinterpret**; writhe, **wriggle**; wince, grimace, gesticulate; snarl, scowl, frown, **be sullen**.

## 242 Angularity

**N. angularity,** crotchet, bracket, crook, hook; bend, scythe, sickle, scimitar, **curvature;** chevron, zigzag; elbow, knee; shoulder blade, withers, **camber; knuckle,** ankle, groin, **joint;** crutch, crotch, fluke, **cross;** fork, **crossing;** corner, nook, niche, recess, **compartment;** nose, **protuberance;** wedge, arrowhead, **sharp point;** broad arrow, cusp; **fold,** indentation, **notch.**

**angle.**

**angular measure,** trigonometry; angular elevation, angular distance, angular velocity; zenith distance; second, degree, minute; altimeter; level, theodolite; transit circle; sextant, quadrant; protractor, set square.

**angular figure,** triangle; parallelogram, rectangle; square; quadrilateral, lozenge, diamond; rhombus, rhomboid; trapezium, trapezoid; polygon, pentagon, hexagon, octagon; cube, pyramid, wedge; prism.

**Adj. angular,** hooked, aquiline; crooked, zigzag, **oblique;** jagged, serrated; akimbo, knock-kneed; forked.

**angulated,** triangular, trilateral, cuneiform; square, foursquare, quadrilateral; trapezoid; multilateral.

**Vb. make angular,** angle, corner, hook, crook, bend; wrinkle, fold, **crinkle;** zigzag, **be oblique;** fork, branch, ramify, **diverge; deviate.**

## 243 Curvature

**N. curvature;** inward curve; outward curve; **fold;** sweep; **obeisance;** swerve, detour, **deviation;** downward bend, **descent;** curling, **convolution; deformity.**

**curve,** camber; elbow; turn, bend, U-turn; horseshoe; bay, **gulf;** figure of eight, **loop;** tracery, curl, **convolution;**
festoon, swag, **pattern;** bow, rainbow, **arc;** arch, arcade, vault, **dome;** sickle, scimitar, crescent, meniscus, lens; trajectory, parabola, hyperbola; caustic; instep; swan neck.

**Adj. curved,** bent, **oblique;** bosomy, wavy; aquiline, **angular;** bent back; circumflex; vaulted; bow-legged; hooked; **round;** crescent, lunar.

**Vb. be curved,** curve, swerve, bend, loop, camber, arch, sweep, sag, swag, give, **hang; twine; leap.**

**make curved,** bend, crook, **make angular;** turn, round, **make round;** inflect; bend back, **invert;** bow, incline, **stoop; fold; deflect;** arch; coil, **twine;** loop, curl, wave, **crinkle;** make figures of eight.

## 244 Straightness

**N. straightness; hardness;** chord, radius, line; straight line, beeline; Roman road; straight stretch, straight, reach; short cut, **short distance.**

**Adj. straight,** direct, even, right, true; linear; rectilinear; perpendicular, **vertical;** stiff, inflexible, **rigid;** dead straight, unswerving.

**Vb. be straight,** steer straight; go straight, turn neither right nor left.

**straighten,** make straight; **flatten;** unbend (a bow); **smooth;** stretch tight; **unravel;** unroll, unfold, **evolve.**

**Adv. straight on,** directly, **towards;** straight, plumb.

## 245 Circularity: simple circularity

**N. circularity,** roundness, **rotundity.**

**circle,** circumference, **outline;** great circle, equator; orb; roundel; plate, saucer; round, disc, discus; coin, button, sequin; washer, hoop, ring; eye, iris; eyelet, loophole, **orifice;** circular course, circuit, circus, roundabout; zodiac; fairy ring; smoke ring.

loop, figure of eight, **convolution**; bow, knot; ringlet, curl, **hair**; circlet, bracelet, torque, **finery**; crown, coronet, **regalia**; corona, halo; wreath, garland; collar, necklace; band, cordon, sash, girdle, **belt**; **girdle**; lasso, **halter**.

**wheel**, pulley, castor; hub, tyre; rubber tyre, inner tube, roller.

**arc**, semicircle; crescent, rainbow, **curve**; sector, quadrant, sextant; ellipse, oval, ovule.

**orbit**, cycle, circuit, ecliptic; circulation.

**Adj. round**, circular, cyclic; annular, oval, elliptic, ovoid; spherical, **rotund**.

**Vb. make round**, round, turn.

**go round**, girdle, encircle, **surround**; describe a circle, **outline**; move round, circulate, orbit, **circle**.

### 246 Convolution: complex circularity

**N. convolution**; torsion; reticulation, **network**; twine, twist; fibre; ripple, **wave**; wrinkle, **fold**; indentation, ragged edge, **notch**; undulation, **curve**.

**coil**, roll, twist; turban; spiral, helix; screw, worm, corkscrew; spring, whorl, ammonite; whirlpool, eddy, **vortex**; tendril, **plant**; scollop, **edging**; kink, curl; ringlet, **hair**; scroll, flourish, twirl, squiggle.

**meandering**, meander; **deviation**; labyrinth, maze; switchback, zigzag.

**serpent**, snake, eel, worm, **reptile**.

**Adj. convoluted**; cranky; sinuous, tortuous; ragged.

**labyrinthine**, serpentine; turning, **circuitous**.

**snaky**, serpentine, vermiform.

**undulatory**, rolling; switchback; wavy, curly, frizzy; ragged; flamboyant.

**coiled**, spiral; wound.

intricate, involved, complicated, **complex**.

**Vb. twine**, twist, twirl, roll, coil, corkscrew, spiral, **rotate**; wreathe, entwine; bend.

**crinkle**, crimp, frizz, crisp, curl; wave, undulate, ripple; wrinkle, corrugate, **fold**; indent, scollop, **notch**; crumple, **distort**.

**meander**, loop, snake, zigzag, corkscrew. See **twine**.

**wriggle**, writhe, squirm, shake; worm.

**Adv. in and out**, round about.

### 247 Rotundity

**N. rotundity**, roundness; **circularity**.

**sphere**, globe, spheroid; hollow sphere, bladder; balloon; **airship**; soap bubble, **bubble**; ball, football, wood (bowls), marble, alley; cannonball, bullet, shot, pellet; bead, pill, pea, boll, puffball, globule; drop, droplet; blot; vesicle, bulb, onion, knob, pommel, **swelling**; boulder, rolling stone; hemisphere, hump, mushroom, **dome**; round head.

**cylinder**, roll, rolypoly; roller, rolling pin; round, rung; round tower, column; bole, trunk, stalk; pipe, drainpipe, **tube**; funnel, chimneypot; round box, pillbox; drum, barrel.

**cone**, shadow cone, penumbra; **dome**; cornet, horn, **cup**; top, pear shape.

**Adj. rotund, round**; spherical, globular, global; beady; ovoid; cylindrical, conical; **convex**; pot-bellied.

**Vb. round**, make spherical; sphere, globe, ball, bead; balloon, **be convex**; roll, **rotate**.

### 248 Convexity

**N. convexity**; **curvature**; bulge, bump; projection, protuberance, **prominence**; swelling; **bulk**; lens.

**swelling**, bump, lump, bulge, growth,

excrescence, gall, knot, node, nodule; knuckle; emphysema; tumour; bunion, corn, wart, verruca; boil, carbuncle, pimple, blister, vesicle; polyp, adenoids, piles; proud flesh, weal, welt; cauliflower ear; drop, **sphere**; air bubble, **bubble**; boss, knob, nub; bulb, button, bud; belly, potbelly, corporation, paunch, **bulk**; billow, swell, **wave**.

**bosom**, bust, breast; boobs, bristols, knockers; nipple, pap, dug, teat, udder; thorax, chest; cuirass, breastplate.

**dome**, cupola, vault, **roof**; brow, forehead, **face**; skull, cranium, bald head, **head**; hemisphere, arch of heaven; mound; hillock, **small hill**; molehill, mushroom, umbrella.

**earthwork**, tumulus; tell, **monument**; barrow, hill fort; embankment.

**camber**, gentle curve, **curve**; arch, bow, rainbow; hump, humpback, hunchback, **deformity**; calf, elbow.

Adj. **convex**, **rotund**; lumpy, bosomy; ballooning, bouffant; swelling, swollen; bloated, potbellied; turgid, tumescent; **rough**.

**arched**, cambered, **curved**.

Vb. **be convex**, camber, arch, bow; swell, belly, bulge, bag, balloon; make convex, emboss, chase.

**249 Prominence**

N. **prominence**, eminence, **high land**; **visibility**; solar prominence, solar flare, tongue, tongue of flame.

**projection**, salient, salient angle, **angle**; forefinger, bowsprit, outrigger; tongue of land, spit, point, mull; promontory, headland, ness, land; peninsula, **island**; spur, foothill, jetty, mole, breakwater, pier, **shelter**; outwork, **fortification**; pilaster, buttress, **prop**; shelf, sill, ledge, balcony; eaves,

roof; overhang, rake; flange, lip, **edge**; nozzle, spout; tang, tongue; tenon, **joint**; snag, stump, outcrop; landmark, **high structure**.

**protuberance**, bump, **swelling**; prominent feature; nose, snout, conk; bill, beak, rostrum; muzzle, proboscis, trunk; antenna, **feeler**; chin, jaw, brow, beetle brow, **face**; figurehead, **prow**; horn, antler, **sharp point**.

**relievo**, relief, low relief; cameo, **sculpture**.

Adj. **projecting**, prominent, salient, bold; protuberant, pop-eyed; toothy; **rough**.

Vb. **jut**, project, protrude, pout, pop, **be visible**; **roughen**; **expand**; overhang, **hang**.

**250 Concavity**

N. **concavity**, **curvature**; depression, dint, dent; impression, stamp, imprint, footprint, **trace**; intaglio, **engraving**, **furrow**; indentation, notch; gap, **interval**.

**cavity**, hollow, niche, nook, cranny, recess, corner, **compartment**; hole, den, burrow, warren; chasm, abyss, **depth**; cave, cavern; grotto, alcove, **arbour**; bowl, cup, saucer, basin, trough, **vessel**; sump, **sink**; cell, follicle, pore, **orifice**; dimple, pockmark; saltcellar, armpit; honeycomb, sponge; funnel, tunnel, **tube**; groove, mortise, socket, pocket, **furrow**; sinus; bay, cove, creek, inlet, **gulf**; channel, riverbed, ditch, moat, canal, **conduit**; dip, depression, pothole, crater, pit.

**valley**, vale, dell, cwm, corrie, cirque, river valley; glen, dip, depression; ravine, gill, gorge, canyon, **gap**.

**excavation**, dugout, grave, **tomb**; opencast mining; shaft, well, mine, pit, colliery, quarry, **store**; gallery, sap, trench, burrow, warren; underground railway, tube, **tunnel**; dig; cutting, cut.

**excavator**, miner; dredger; sapper.

**Adj. concave,** hollow, cavernous; vaulted; sunk, sunken; cellular; honeycombed; spongy, porous.

**Vb. be concave,** retreat, retire; cup.

**make concave,** depress, stamp, impress; buckle, dent, dint; crush; excavate, hollow, dig, spade, delve, scrape, scratch, scrabble, trench, **groove**; mine, sap, undermine, burrow, tunnel, bore; honeycomb, perforate, **pierce**; **eject**; hole, pit, pockmark; indent, **notch**; sink a shaft, make a hole.

## 251 Sharpness

**N. sharpness,** acuity, sting; prickliness; suddenness.

**sharp point,** sting, prick, point, cusp, **vertex**; nail, tack, staple, **fastening**; nib, tag, pin, needle, stylus, bodkin, skewer, spit, broach; awl, gimlet, drill, auger; arrow, shaft, bolt, quarrel, arrowhead; barb, fluke, rapier, lance, pike, **spear**; fishing spear, gaff, harpoon; dagger, dirk, stiletto, **side arms**; spike, barbed wire; spur; goad, **incentive**; fork, prong, tine, pick, horn, antler; claw, talon, **nippers**; spire, steeple; peak, crag, **summit**.

**prickle**, thorn, bramble, thistle, nettle, cactus; bristle, **hair**; beard; porcupine, hedgehog; spine, needle, quill.

**tooth**, tusk, fang; first teeth; eyetooth, incisor, molar, premolar teeth; front teeth, set of teeth, denture, false teeth, plate, bridge; comb, saw; cog, ratchet, sprocket, **notch**.

**sharp edge,** edge tool; jagged edge, broken glass; cutlery, steel, razor; blade, razor blade; share, ploughshare, **farm tool**; spade, mattock, trowel, shovel; scythe, sickle, hook,

billhook; cutter, lawn mower; scissors, shears, clippers, secateurs; surgical knife, scalpel; chisel, plane, spokeshave, scraper; knife, carving knife; penknife, machete; chopper, cleaver, wedge; hatchet, axe, adze; battleaxe, axe; sword, broadsword, cutlass, scimitar, **side arms**.

**sharpener**, whetstone, grindstone; hone, steel, file, strop; emery, emery paper, sandpaper.

**Adj. sharp,** keen, acute; cutting; pointed; barbed; spiny, thorny; prickly, bristly, bearded, **hairy**; craggy, jagged, **rough**.

**toothed**; toothy; dental; serrated.

**tapering**, conical; horned.

**Vb. be sharp,** have a point, prick, sting; bristle with; have an edge, bite, **cut**; taper, come to a point, converge.

**sharpen**, edge, whet, hone, grind, file, strop; barb, spur, point, stud.

## 252 Bluntness

**N. bluntness,** lack of bite; blunt instrument, foil; blunt edge, blade, flat.

**Adj. unsharpened;** blunt, obtuse, rusty, dull; pointless; lacking bite; stubby, snub, square; round; flat, bluff.

**Vb. blunt,** make blunt, turn; dull, rust; be blunt, pull, scrape, tear.

## 253 Smoothness

**N. smoothness,** smooth texture; silk, satin, velvet; swansdown; smooth hair; smooth surface, mahogany, marble, glass, ice; dance floor, ice rink; lawn, plumb wicket, bowling green; tarmac, asphalt, **paving**; polish, varnish, gloss, glaze, shine, finish; slipway, slide; smooth water, calm.

**smoother**, roller, steamroller; bulldozer; rolling pin; iron; mangle, wringer; press, plane, spokeshave, draw knife, **sharp edge**; rake, harrow, comb, brush, hairbrush; sandpaper, emery board; file; polish, varnish, enamel, **facing**; grease, oil, grease gun, **lubricant**.

Adj. **smooth**; **uniform**; slippery; greasy, buttery; shiny; soft, suave, bland; silky, silken, satiny; downy, woolly, **fleecy**; marble, glassy; bald, cleanshaven; sleek, slick, unruffled; plane, even, level, flush, **flat**; glassy, quiet, calm, **still**; blunt.

Vb. **smooth**, remove friction, streamline; oil, grease, butter, **lubricate**; plane, even, level; rake, comb; file, **rub**; roll, calender, press, iron, **flatten**; mow, shave, cut, **shorten**; **unravel**; starch, launder, **clean**; shine, burnish, **make bright**; buff, polish, glaze, wax, varnish, **coat**; pave, tarmac.

go smoothly, glide, float, roll, bowl along; slip, slide, skid; skate, ski; coast.

## 254 Roughness

N. **roughness**, asperity; broken ground; rough water, **wave**; rough air, turbulence, **wind**; broken glass, **sharp edge**; saw edge, **notch**; sierra, **high land**; rough going, dirt road; ripple, ripple mark, **fold**; rut, **furrow**; coarse grain; rough surface, washboard, grater, file, sandpaper, emery paper; rough texture, tweed, homespun, **textile**; gooseflesh; rough skin, chap, crack; undergrowth, **wood**; stubble, burr, bristle, **prickle**.

hair, **filament**; thatch, fuzz; wool; crop, mop, mane, fleece; bristle, stubble, five o'clock shadow; locks, tresses, ringlet, tight curl; kiss curl; strand, plait, braid; pigtail, ponytail; topknot, forelock, dread locks; fringe, quiff, roll, French pleat, bun, chignon; false hair, hairpiece, switch, wig, toupee; thin hair, wisp; beard, beaver, goatee,

imperial, Van Dyke; whiskers, face fungus, sideboards; moustache, toothbrush, handlebars; cilia; wool, fur, **skin**; tuft, flock; mohair, cashmere, Angora, **fibre**; pile, nap; velvet, plush; floss, fluff, fuzz, thistledown; **lining**.

**plumage**, pinion, **wing**; quill, barb, web; ruff, frill, plume, panache, crest; **finery**.

Adj. **rough**, uneven, broken; choppy; bumpy; chunky, crisp, roughcast; lumpy, stony, nodular; gnarled, crossgrained, coarse; cracked; craggy, jagged; scabrous, scaly; unkempt.

**hairy**; woolly, fleecy, furry; hirsute, shaggy, shagged, shock-headed; bristly, **sharp**; bearded, curly, frizzy, fuzzy, woolly.

**downy**; **smooth**; feathery, fledged.

fleecy, woolly.

Vb. **be rough**, bristle; creep (of flesh); scratch, catch; jolt, bump, jerk.

**roughen**, roughcast; mill, indent, **notch**; stud, boss; crisp, corrugate, wrinkle, ripple, **crinkle**; disorder, ruffle, tousle, **derange**; rumple, crumple, **fold**.

Adv. **on edge**.

## 255 Notch

N. **notch**, saw edge; indentation; nick, snip, cut, gash; **gap**; indent, dent, dimple; scallop, **pattern**; sprocket, cog, ratchet, cogwheel, saw, hacksaw, circular saw, **tooth**.

Adj. **notched**, jagged, **sharp**; serrated.

Vb. **notch**, tooth, cog; nick, blaze, score, scratch, scotch, scarify, bite, slice, **cut**; indent; jag, pink, slash; dent, mill, **roughen**; pinch, snip, crimp, **fold**.

## 256 Fold

N. **fold**; facing, revers, hem; lapel, cuff, turnup, dog's ear; plait, ply, pleat, tuck, gather, pucker, ruffle, flounce, frill; crumple, rumple, crease;

wrinkle, ruck; frown, lines, **age**; crinkle; joint, elbow.

**Adj. folded**; dog-eared; turn-over.

**Vb.** fold, double, roll; crease, pleat; corrugate, furrow, wrinkle, **groove**; rumple, crumple, **derange**; curl, frizzle, frizz, **crinkle**; pucker, purse; ruffle, gather, frill, ruck, smock; tuck, kilt; hem, cuff; enfold, wrap, swathe, **enclose**; furl, reef.

### 257 Furrow

**N.** furrow, groove, chase, slot, slit, mortise; crack, chink, cranny, **gap**; trough, hollow, **cavity**; flute, fluting; gash, slash, scratch, score; streak, **stripe**; wake, rut, **trace**; gutter, runnel, ditch, trench, dugout, moat, channel, **conduit**; ravine, **valley**; corduroy, washboard; ripple, **wave**.

**Adj. furrowed**; striated; wavy, **flowing**.

**Vb. groove**, slot, flute, rifle; chase; gash, scratch, score, incise, **cut**; claw, tear, **wound**; streak; grave, carve, etch, **engrave**; furrow, plough, channel, rut, wrinkle, line; corrugate, **fold**.

### 258 Opening

**N. opening**, yawn; splitting, hiatus, space, interval, **gap**; aperture, split, crack, leak; hole, potato, hollow, **cavity**; pocket.

**perforation**, piercing, puncture, acupuncture; bore, calibre; eyelet.

**porosity**, sponge; sieve, sifter, riddle; screen; strainer, colander; grater, honeycomb.

**orifice**, aperture, slot; oral cavity, mouth, gob, trap, jaws, muzzle; throat, gullet; sucker; mouthpiece, flue pipe, **air pipe**; nozzle, spout, vent, **outlet**; blower, blowhole; nasal cavity, nostril; inlet, outlet; small orifice; pore; hole, crater, pothole, **cavity**; manhole, armhole, buttonhole; punch

hole, pigeonhole, **compartment**; eye, eye of a needle, eyelet; ring, **loop**.

**window**; shop window, glass front; loophole, **fortification**; lattice, grille; rose window, **church interior**; light, fanlight, skylight, sunshine roof; companion, cabin window, port, porthole; peephole; squint; car window, windscreen, windshield; window frame, sash, mullion, transom; window pane, **transparency**.

**doorway**, archway; doorstep, threshold, **entrance**; approach, drive, drive-in, entry; exit; passage, corridor, gangway, drawbridge, **access**; gate; portal, porch; door, lychgate; back door, postern, **rear**; small door, wicket, scuttle, hatch; trapdoor, companionway; stairwell; door jamb, gatepost, lintel; **doorkeeper**.

**open space**, space; yard, court, **place**; opening, clearing, glade; panorama, vista, **view**; rolling downs, landscape, open country, **plain**; alley, aisle, gangway, thoroughfare, **passage**; estuary, gulf.

**tunnel**; subway, underpass, underground railway, tube; Channel Tunnel; mine, shaft, pit, gallery; cave, **cavity**; bolthole, rabbit hole, **dwelling**; funnel, cone; sewer, drain.

**tube**, pipe, duct, **conduit**; pipette; tubing, piping, pipeline, hose; artery, vein, capillary; colon, gut; funnel, fistula.

**chimney**, chimneypot, chimney stack, smokestack, funnel; flue; volcano, **furnace**.

**opener**, key; handle; corkscrew, tin opener, **purgative**; password, open sesame; passport, safe conduct; pass, ticket, **permit**.

**perforator**; gimlet, corkscrew, auger, drill, burr, bit; probe; bodkin, needle, awl, bradawl, **sharp point**; pin, nail, **fastening**; skewer, spit, broach, stiletto, **weapon**; punch, stapler; dibble; pickaxe, pick.

**Adj. open**, patent, **manifest**; ajar; **accessible**; agape; opening; blooming.

**perforated**, perforate; honeycombed; shot through.

**porous**, spongy, leaky.

**tubular**; cylindrical, **rotund**; vascular, capillary.

**Vb. open**, unfold, unpack, undo; unlock, **admit**; uncover, bare, **doff**; unstop, uncork; unrip, **disunite**; lay open, **show**; force open, **force**; cut open, enlarge a hole, ream; fly open, split, gape, yawn; burst, explode; start, leak; **space**; deploy; separate, part, hold apart; bloom.

**pierce**, transfix, impale; gore, run through, stick, pink, lance, bayonet, spear, **wound**; spike, skewer, spit; prick, puncture, tattoo; probe, stab, poke; inject; perforate, hole, riddle, pepper, honeycomb; nail, drive, **strike**; punch; hull (a ship), scuttle; tap, drain, **extract**; bore, drill; burrow, tunnel, mine, **make concave**; cut through, penetrate, **enter**.

**Adv. openly**, patently.

### 259 Closure

**N. closure**; stoppage; contraction, strangulation; blockade; embolism; constipation; dead end, cul-de-sac, impasse, blank wall, road block, **obstacle**; blind gut.

**stopper**, cork, plug, bung, peg, spill, spigot; ramrod, piston; valve, wedge, wad, tampon; wadding, padding, stuffing, **lining**; dummy, gag, muzzle, **fetter**; shutter; screen; tight bandage, tourniquet, **compressor**; damper, choke, cut-out; tap, stopcock; top, lid, cap, cover, seal, **covering**; lock, key, bolt, bar, **fastening**; door, gate, **doorway**; cordon, **fence**.

**doorkeeper**, doorman, porter, janitor; commissionaire; sentry, night watchman, **protector**; warden, guard, keeper; jailer, turnkey.

**Adj. closed**; barred; impervious, impermeable, **dense**; impenetrable, impassable, **impracticable**; **secluded**; blank; drawn tight, drawn together.

**sealed off**; close, stuffy, muggy, fusty, **insalubrious**; staunch, tight, airtight, watertight, proof, waterproof, **invulnerable**.

**Vb. close**, shut, seal; clinch, fix, bind, make tight, **tighten**; **cover**; make all tight; clap to, slam, bang (a door); lock, fasten, snap, snap to; plug, caulk, cork, stopper; button, **join**; knit; clench (fist); block, dam, staunch, choke, throttle, strangle, smother, asphyxiate, **obstruct**; blockade, **besiege**; enclose, surround, **circumscribe**; trap, bolt, bar, **imprison**.

### 260 Motion: successive change of place

**N. motion**, change of position, **change**; movement, going, move, march; speed rate, speed, pace, tempo; locomotion; kinetic energy, motive power; forward motion, advance, progress, headway, **progression**; backward motion, **recession**; motion towards, **approach**; shift, **deviation**; egress; upward motion, rising, **ascent**; downward motion, **descent**, plunge; motion round; **rotation**, **evolution**; irregular motion; stir, bustle, unrest, **activity**; rapid motion, **velocity**; slow motion; regular motion, **continuity**; rhythm; **preceding**; motion after, **following**, **pursuit**; conduction; current, flow, flux, drift, **stream**; course, career, run; traffic, traffic movement, flow of traffic, **passing along**; transit, **passage**; transportation, **transport**; running, walking; riding; travel, **land travel**, **water travel**, **air travel**; gliding, rolling; manoeuvre, footwork; bodily movement, exercise, **athletics**; **gesture**; cinematography, motion picture, **cinema**; kinetics, dynamics.

**gait**, walk, port, carriage, **conduct**; tread, tramp, footfall, stamp; pace, step, stride; run, lope, jog; jog trot, dance step, hop, skip, jump, **leap**; skid, slide, waddle, shuffle; swagger, proud step, stalk, strut, goosestep, **formality**; march, double; trot, amble, canter, gallop.

**Adj. moving**; motive, motor; mobile; progressive; locomotive, **passing**; restless, **active**; erratic, runaway; kinetic.

**Vb. be in motion**, move, go, hie, gang, wend, trail; gather way, **navigate**; budge, stir; flutter, wave, flap, **hang**; march, tramp, **walk**; tread; trip, dance, **leap**; shuffle, waddle, toddle, patter; run, **move fast**; roll, taxi; stream, drift, **flow**; paddle, row; skitter, slide, slither, skate, ski, toboggan, glide; fly, frisk, flit, dart, hover; climb, **ascend**; sink, plunge, **descend**; cruise, steam, chug, keep going, proceed; **progress**; pass through, **pass**; make a move, shift, dodge, duck, shift about, tack, manoeuvre, **deviate**; twist, wriggle; creep, crawl; hover about, **wait**; move house; **interchange**; make room; travel, stray, **wander**.

**move**, impart motion, set going, power; **operate**; stir, jerk, pluck, twitch, agitate; budge, shift, manhandle, trundle, roll, wheel, **displace**; push, shove, **impel**; drive, hustle, **hasten**; tug, pull, **draw**; fling, throw, **propel**; convey, transport, **transfer**; **send**; **bring together**; scatter, disperse; raise, uplift, **elevate**; drop, **let fall**; motion, gesture, **gesticulate**; transpose, inter-

change.

**Adv. on the move**, underway.

**261 Quiescence**

**N. quiescence**; subsidence, **cessation**; rest; pause, truce, standstill, **lull**; stand, stoppage, halt, fix, deadlock, lock; full stop, **stop**; embargo, freeze, **prohibition**; fixity, **hardness**; equilibrium, **stability**; trance, faint, **insensibility**.

**quietude**, quiet, hush, **silence**; peace; rest, **repose**; eternal rest, **death**; slumber, **sleep**; calm; dead quiet; armchair travel; composure; passivity; **pacifist**; **moderator**.

**resting place**, **quarters**; roof, home, inn; shelter, haven, **refuge**; place of rest, pillow, **bed**; **goal**; last rest, grave, tomb.

**Adj. quiescent**, quiet, still; asleep, sleepy; at rest, becalmed; at anchor; at a stand, at a standstill, idle; unemployed, **unused**; dormant, dying, **dead**; standing, stagnant, static, stationary, **inert**; sitting, sedentary; **supine**; housebound, **restrained**; settled, stay-at-home, **content**; cautious; unmoved, **indifferent**.

**tranquil**, secluded; peaceful, restful; easy-going, **leisurely**; uneventful, without incident, **uniform**; calm, airless, glassy, **smooth**; sunny, halcyon, palmy; at ease, comfortable, unruffled, serene.

**still**; flat, **tasteless**; immobile, motionless; expressionless, deadpan, **impassive**; steady; standing still, rooted, **fixed**; immovable, unable to move, stuck; stiff, frozen, **rigid**; benumbed, numb, **insensible**; quiet, **silent**; stockstill.

**Vb. be quiescent**, subside, decrease; be silent; stand still, keep quiet; stagnate, vegetate, **be inert**; stand, mark time,

wait; stay put, sit tight, stand pat,
remain, abide, **stay**; stand to, lie to,
ride at anchor; tarry, **pause**; rest, take
breath, **repose**; retire, go to bed, **sleep**;
settle, **place oneself**; stay at home, **be
unsociable**; ground, stick fast; catch,
jam, lodge; stand fast, stand firm; be
at a standstill, **cease**.

**come to rest**, stop, hold, stop short,
freeze, **halt**; **decelerate**; anchor,
alight, **land**; relax, rest, pause,
**repose**.

**bring to rest**, quiet, quieten, quell, hush,
**silence**; lull, soothe, **assuage**; lull to
sleep, cradle, rock; let alone, let well
alone, **avoid**; bring to a standstill,
bring to, lay to, heave to; brake,
**retard**; stay.

**Adv. at a stand**, at a halt.

**Int.** stop! stay! halt! whoa! hold! hold
hard! hold on! hold it! don't move!

## 262  Land travel

**N. land travel**, travel; tourism; walking,
riding, driving, motoring; journey,
voyage, peregrination, odyssey;
course, passage, sweep; pilgrimage;
quest, expedition, safari, trek; field
trip; reconnaissance; visit, trip, tour,
circuit, turn, round, patrol; round
trip; jaunt, hop, spin; ride, drive, lift,
excursion, outing, airing; ramble,
constitutional.

**wandering**, wanderlust; vagrancy; rambling, walkabout; migration, **egress**;
transmigration, **passage**.

**pedestrianism**, walking, footing it; walkabout; walk, promenade, constitutional; stroll, saunter, amble, ramble;
hike, tramp, march, walking tour;
run, cross-country run, jog, trot, lope,
**gait**; paddle; foot race, marathon, **racing**; stalk, **chase**; somnambulism.

**marching**, campaign; advance, retreat;
march, quick march, march past,

parade, cavalcade, procession, **formality**; column, file, train, caravan.

**equitation**, manège, dressage, **skill**;
point-to-point racing, **contest**; horse
racing; riding, **athletics**; gait.

**conveyance**, lift, escalator; foot; horse-
back, mount, **horse**; bicycle, car, bus,
train, coach, taxi, ambulance, **vehicle**;
traffic, **passing along**.

**leg**, limb; shank, shin, calf; thigh, ham;
knee, kneecap; **prop**; stump, wooden
leg, **substitute**.

**itinerary**, route, **way**; march, course,
**direction**; route map, plan, chart,
**map**; guide, timetable; milestone,
**signpost**; halt, stop, stopover, terminus.

**Adj. travelling**, vagrant; dusty, **dirty**;
travelled; passing through, visiting,
**passing**; nomad, floating, unsettled,
restless, rootless, **extraneous**; footloose, errant, rambling, wandering;
peripatetic; vagabond; walking, pedestrian; locomotive, **moving**.

**legged**, bow-legged; leggy, **tall**; spindly,
**lean**.

**Vb. travel**, fare, journey; tour, visit,
explore, **discover**; get around, knock
about; pilgrimage; make a journey,
trek; hike; fare forth, take wing,
**depart**; migrate, emigrate, immigrate,
settle, **place oneself**; shuttle, commute; go to, hie to, repair to, resort to,
**arrive, visit**; go; wend, tread a path,
plough through; **sustain**; course, race,
post, **move fast**; proceed, advance,
**progress**; coast, glide, slide, skate, ski,
skim, roll along.

**traverse**, cross, range, pass through,
**pass**; go round, **circle**; patrol; scout,
reconnoitre, **scan**; scour, sweep,
sweep through.

**wander**, migrate, rove, roam, bum
around; ramble, amble, stroll, saunter, potter, dawdle, walk about, trail

around; gallivant, hover, flit about; prowl, skulk, **lurk**; straggle, trail; **stray**.

**walk**, step, tread, pace, stride; **move fast**; strut, stalk, prance, mince, **be proud**; tread lightly, tiptoe, trip, skip, dance, **leap**; lumber, clump, stamp, tramp, goosestep; toddle, patter, pad; totter, stagger, lurch, reel, stumble, **oscillate**; limp, hobble, waddle, shuffle, shamble, dawdle; paddle, wade; foot it, hoof it, hike, footslog; plod, stump, trudge, jog; go, perambulate; **march**, quick march, slow march, troop; file, file past, defile, **come after**; walk past, **follow**; **precede**.

**ride**, mount, take horse, hack; trot, amble, canter, gallop; prance, caper, passage; cycle, bicycle, bike, motorcycle; drive, motor; **fly**; take a lift, hitchhike.

**Adv. on foot**; en route; by road, by rail.

**Int. come along! move along there! get along! get going! get out! git! go away! be off! buzz off! hop it! skedaddle! scram!**

### 263 Traveller

**N. traveller**; adventurer, **mariner**; air traveller; pioneer, pathfinder, **precursor**; mountaineer, **climber**; pilgrim, globe-trotter, tourist, **spectator**; tripper; holidaymaker, visitor, roundsman, **pedlar**; commercial traveller, **seller**; messenger, **courier**; daily traveller, commuter.

**wanderer**, migrant, bird of passage, visitant, **bird**; floating population, nomad, bedouin, Romany, Bohemian; ranger; wandering minstrel, **entertainer**; rolling stone, drifter, vagrant, vagabond, tramp; hobo, bum, bummer; beachcomber; emigrant, refugee, deportee, exile,

foreigner; runaway, fugitive; **solitary**; waif, stray, destitute, street beggar, **poor person**; Wandering Jew.

**pedestrian**, foot passenger; runner, **contender**; toddler; wader; **infantry**; sleepwalker.

**rider**; horseman, equestrian; **courier**; cavalier, knight, knight errant, **cavalry**; hunt, huntsman, **hunter**; jockey, show jumper, **contender**; breaker; cowboy; circus rider, trick rider, **athlete**; motor-cyclist, moped rider; passenger.

**driver**, drover, muleteer; coachman, whip; carter; car driver, chauffeur; joy rider; **beginner**; taxi driver; bus driver; train driver, stoker, fireman, guard, conductor, ticket collector; pilot.

### 264 Water travel

**N. water travel**; seafaring, nautical life; sailing; voyage, cruise, sail; course, run, passage, crossing; sea trip, breath of sea air, **refreshment**; way, headway, steerage way, seaway, **motion**; leeway, **deviation**; wake, track, wash, backwash, **eddy**; ocean track, steamer route, sea lane, **route**; boat, sailing ship, **ship**; sailor, **mariner**.

**navigation**; plane sailing, compass reading, dead reckoning, **measurement**; **skill**; nautical experience, weather eye; naval tactics, **tactics**.

**aquatics**, sailing, yacht racing, **racing**; surf riding, **sport**; swimming, floating; stroke, crawl, butterfly; **plunge**.

**sailing aid**, sextant, quadrant, **angular measure**; chronometer; log, line; lead, plummet, **depth**; anchor, **safeguard**; compass, needle, card; binnacle; radar; helm, wheel, tiller, rudder; sea mark, buoy, lighthouse, lightship, **signpost**; chart, **map**; nautical almanac.

propeller, screw, twin screw, blade, rotor; paddle wheel; oar, sweep, paddle, scull; pole, fin, flipper, **limb**; canvas, **sail**.

**Adj. seafaring**, sea, salty; nautical, naval, **marine**; sailing; at sea, afloat, waterborne, seaborne, rolling; seasick, green; seaworthy, tight, snug; navigable, deep.

**swimming**, floating, sailing; afloat; aquatic, like a fish; amphibian.

**Vb. go to sea**; become a sailor; live afloat; go sailing, boat, yacht; launch, launch a ship.

**voyage**, sail; take ship, book a passage, embark, put to sea, set sail; **traverse**; disembark, land, **arrive**; cruise; navigate, steam, ply, run, tramp, ferry; coast; roll, pitch, toss, tumble, wallow, **oscillate**.

**navigate**, man a ship, crew; put to sea, set sail; launch; weigh anchor; raise steam, hoist sail, spread canvas; carry sail; set a course; **orientate**, pilot, steer, captain, **direct**; stroke, cox; square; change course, veer, yaw, **deviate**; put about, wear ship, **turn round**; scud, **move fast**; fall to leeward; luff; beat to windward, tack, weather; round, double a point, circumnavigate, **circle**; be caught amidships; list, **be oblique**; turn turtle, capsize, overturn, **invert**; keep afloat, **escape**; seek refuge; lie to, lay to, heave to, **bring to rest**; take soundings, **measure**; **await**; tow, haul, warp, **draw**; ground, run aground, wreck, **destroy**; sight land, make a landfall, **approach**; make port; cast anchor, moor, dock, disembark; **land**; outmanoeuvre, **obstruct**, foul, collide; back, go astern, regress; surface, break water, **emerge**; dive, **plunge**; shoot, shoot a bridge, **pass**.

**row**; pull, stroke, scull; feather; catch a crab; punt; paddle, canoe; boat.

**swim**, float, sail, ride; scud, skim, skitter; surf, aquaplane; tread water; dive, **plunge**; bathe, dip, duck; wade, paddle, splash about, get wet, **be wet**.

**Adv. under way**, all aboard.

**Int. ship ahoy! avast! belay there! all aboard! man overboard! yo-heave-ho! hard aport! hard astarboard! steady as she goes! land ahoy!**

## 265 Mariner

**N. mariner**, sailor, seaman, seafaring man; salt; tar, Jack Tar, limey; landlubber; skipper, master mariner, master, mate, bosun; able seaman, **expert**; deckhand; cabin boy, **servant**; crew, complement, men, watch, **personnel**; trawler, whaler; privateer, buccaneer, sea king, Viking, pirate; sea scout, sea cadet; Ancient Mariner; Neptune, **sea god**.

**navigator**, pilot, sailing master, helmsman, steersman, quartermaster, cox, **leader**; lookout man; reefer; compass, binnacle, **sailing aid**.

**nautical personnel**, marine, submariner, naval cadet, rating, **naval man**; petty officer, midshipman, lieutenant, commander, captain, commodore, admiral, **naval officer**; Admiralty, Sea Lord; Trinity House, lighthouse keeper, coastguard, **protector**; river police, naval patrol.

**boatman**, waterman, wet bob; galley slave; oar, oarsman; gondolier; bargee; stevedore, docker, longshoreman; lock keeper.

**Adj. seamanlike**, like a sailor, **expert**; nautical, naval, **marine**.

## 266 Aeronautics

**N. aeronautics**, aerodynamics; ballooning; aerospace; rocketry, **rocket**;

flight, **velocity**; aviation, flying; gliding, skydiving, free fall; flypast, formation flying, aerobatics, **ostentation**; vapour trail; spin, roll, side slip; nose dive; crash dive, crash, **descent**; pancake, landing, **arrival**; takeoff.

**air travel**, air transport, airlift, **transport**; air service, airline; airlane, airway, air route; flight path, line of flight, **direction**; air space, **territory**; takeoff, landing, landing field, airbase; airstrip, runway, tarmac, airfield, aerodrome, airport, heliport; terminal, **goal**; hangar, **stable**; fear of flying.

**space travel**, space flight, **spaceship**; liftoff; orbit; space walk; reentry, soft landing.

**aeronaut**, glider, sky diver; **soldier**; aviator; astronaut, cosmonaut, space traveller; air traveller, air passenger, jet set, **traveller**; air hostess, **servant**; pilot, copilot; automatic pilot; navigator, air crew; pilot officer, **air officer**; aircraftman, **air force**; air personnel, ground crew, **personnel**; Mercury.

**wing**, pinion, wing feather, wing spread, **plumage**; aileron.

**Adj. flying**, **moving**; pinnate, aerial, airy; airworthy, airborne, airsick; aerospace.

**Vb. fly**, wing; soar, rise, **ascend**; hover, **hang**; flutter, flit; taxi, clear, climb, circle, **depart**; be airborne, take off; glide, plane; float, drift, drift like thistledown, **be light**; stunt, spin, roll, side-slip; hedgehop, buzz, **be near**; stall, dive, spiral, **plunge**; crash, crashland, pancake, ditch, **tumble**; **land**; jump, parachute, eject; orbit, **circle**.

**Adv. in flight**, on the wing.

## 267 Transference

**N. transference**, change of place, transfer; shift, drift, **deviation**; interchange;

removal, expulsion; **displacement**; export, **trade**; mutual transfer, **barter**; importation, import, **reception**; logistics, **provision**; remittance; recall, **extraction**; recovery, **acquisition**; delivery; takeover, **purchase**; conveyance, transfer of property, **transfer**; committal, trust, **commission**; gaol delivery, release, **liberation**; transition; ferry, **passage**; transmigration, **transformation**; transmission, throughput; conduction, convection; communication, contact, **touch**; contagion, infection, **influence**; **translation**.

**transport**, transportation; conveyance, carriage, shipping, shipment; portage, porterage, haulage, draught, **traction**; cartage, air freight, airlift; means of transport, rail, road, **vehicle**; sea, canal, **ship**; pipeline.

**thing transferred**, jetsam, driftwood, drift, alluvium, detritus, scree, moraine, sediment, deposit; pledge, hostage, trust, **security**; legacy, **gift**; lease, **property**; cargo, load, payload, freight; black ivory, **slave**; shipment, **contents**; goods, luggage, baggage; container; passenger, rider, commuter, **traveller**.

**transferrer**, testator; sender; shipper, shipping agent, transporter; **merchant**; haulier, removal man, **carrier**; post office, post, **postal communications**; transmitter; vector, carrier (of a disease), **sick person**.

**Adj. transferable**, negotiable; portable; roadworthy, airworthy, seaworthy; conductive; communicable; contagious, **infectious**.

**Vb. transfer**, deliver, assign; devise, leave, **bequeath**; commit, **commission**; transmit; hand to, pass to; export, transport, convey, ship, airlift, fly, ferry, **carry**; infect, contaminate, influence; conduct; **add**; transfer itself to, adhere, stick, **cohere**.

**transpose**, shift, move, **displace**; transfer, switch, shunt, shuffle, castle (chess), **interchange**; detach, detail; draft; relegate, deport, expel, **eject**; drag, pull, **draw**; push, shove, **impel**; **load**; funnel, transfuse, decant, **empty**; unload, remove, **displace**; shovel, ladle, excavate, **make concave**; transliterate, **translate**.

**send**, remit, transmit; direct, consign, address; post, mail; readdress, forward; order, **require**; detach, detail; send flying, **propel**.

**Adv. in transit.**

## 268 Carrier

**N. carrier**, haulier, carter; shipper, transporter; lorry driver, **driver**; delivery van, lorry, truck, cart, goods train, **vehicle**; barge, cargo vessel, freighter, tramp, **ship**; chassis, undercarriage, **prop**; pallet, container; carrier bag, **bag**; escalator.

**bearer, retainer**, porter, coolie, stevedore; letter carrier, carrier pigeon, postman or -woman, special messenger, **courier**.

**beast of burden**, pack train; ass, donkey; ox, bullock, **cattle**; sledge dog, husky; camel, dromedary; elephant, **mammal**.

**horse**, equine species, quadruped; dobbin, gee-gee; nag; mount, steed; stallion, gelding, mare, colt, filly, foal; stud horse, brood mare, stud, stable; circus horse, roan, grey, bay, chestnut, sorrel, black, piebald, skewbald, dun, palomino.

**thoroughbred**; Arab, Barb; trotter; racehorse, stayer; fencer, jumper, hunter.

**draught horse**, punch, pit pony.

**warhorse**, remount; charger, steed, **cav-**

alry.

**saddle horse**, cow pony; mount, hack; jade, screw, nag; pad; mustang, bronco.

**pony**, cob.

**Adj. bearing**, carrier, loaded.

**equine**, horsy; roan, asinine; mulish.

**Vb. carry**, bear, **support**; hump, heave, tote; shoulder; fetch, bring, reach; transport, cart, truck, rail, railway; ship, waft, raft; lift, fly, **transfer**; carry through, carry across, ferry; convey, conduct, convoy, escort, **accompany**; have a rider; be loaded with, be fraught, **be complete**.

## 269 Vehicle

**N. vehicle**, conveyance, public service vehicle, transport, vehicular traffic, pedal driver; litter, stretcher, hurdle, crate; ambulance, fire engine; hearse; snowplough, weasel; tractor, bulldozer; amphibian, moon buggy; switchback; time machine.

**sled**, sledge, sleigh; bobsleigh, toboggan, coaster, ice yacht; surfboard; skate, skateboard; runner.

**bicycle**, cycle, bike, wheel, crate; velocipede, hobbyhorse, penny-farthing, Ordinary, Safety; sports model, tourist; tandem; tricycle, trike; moped; scooter, motorcycle, motorbike, trail bike; motorcycle combination, sidecar; invalid carriage.

**pushcart**, perambulator, pram, baby buggy, pushchair; bath chair, wheelchair; barrow, wheelbarrow, handcart, go cart; trolley, truck, float.

**cart**, dray, milk float; farm cart; prairie schooner; caravan, trailer, horse-box, dustcart.

**carriage**, equipage, turnout, rig; chariot, coach; landau, phaeton, buggy; chaise; racing chariot; drag, brake; whisky; trap, gig, dogcart, governess cart.

**war chariot,** gun carriage, caisson; tank, armoured car, **cavalry;** jeep, staff car.

**stagecoach,** stage, mail coach; post chaise, omnibus. See **bus.**

**cab,** hackney carriage, hansom, fly; taxi.

**bus;** omnibus, double-decker; motor coach, coach, minibus.

**tram,** trolley.

**automobile,** car, motor car; motor; limousine; saloon, buggy; convertible; coupé, sports car; racing car; hatchback, estate car; jeep; police car, veteran car, vintage car; banger, bus, jalopy, old crock; beetle, bubble car; invalid car; minibus.

**lorry,** truck, refuse lorry, dustcart; container lorry, juggernaut; tanker; car transporter; van; electric van, float.

**train;** express train, APT; slow train, goods train, freightliner; milk train, night mail; rolling stock, multiple unit; coach, carriage, compartment, smoker, nonsmoker; Pullman, sleeper; restaurant car; truck, trolley; steam train, live rail; cable railway, **railway;** Golden Arrow, Orient Express.

**locomotive,** iron horse; steam engine, shunter, cab, tender; Rocket; traction engine, steam roller.

**conveyor;** escalator, moving staircase, moving pavement; shovel, hod, **ladle;** fork, trowel, **farm tool;** crane.

**Adj. vehicular;** automobile, locomotive; non-stop, express, through; local.

## 270 Ship

**N. ship,** vessel, boat, craft; bark, barque; great ship, little ship, cockleshell; bottom, keel, sail; hooker, tub, hull; hulk; Golden Hind; steamer, motor vessel; paddle steamer; passenger ship, liner; ocean greyhound, floating palace; channel steamer, ferry; hovercraft, hydrofoil; rotor ship; packet, dredger, hopper; transport; tender, escort vessel; pilot vessel; tug, launch; lightship, weather ship; underwater craft, submarine, U-boat, **warship.**

**galley;** pirate ship, privateer, corsair; Viking ship, longship; trireme.

**merchant ship,** merchantman; cog, galleon; banana boat, tea clipper; slave ship, slaver; cargo boat, freighter, tramp; coaster; lugger; collier, tanker.

**fishing boat,** fishing smack, hooker; drifter, trawler; factory ship; whaler.

**sailing ship,** sailing boat; windjammer, clipper, tall ship; barque; brig, brigantine, schooner; frigate, corvette, **warship;** cutter, sloop, ketch, yawl; wherry; yacht, sailing dinghy, smack; dhow, junk, sampan.

**rig,** square rig.

**sail,** canvas; square sail, lug; course, mainsail, foresail, royal; jib, spinnaker, balloon sail, ripping; mast, mainmast, mizzenmast, **prop.**

**boat,** skiff, lifeboat; tender, dinghy, pram; longboat, jolly boat; cutter, gig; surf boat, barge, lighter, pontoon; ferry; houseboat; tugboat, tug; powerboat, motorboat, motor launch; cabin cruiser.

**rowing boat,** galley; eight, shell; skiff, dinghy, rubber dinghy; coracle; punt, gondola; canoe, outrigger, dugout; kayak.

**raft,** balsa, catamaran, trimaran; float, pontoon.

**shipping,** craft; fleet, flotilla, squadron, **navy;** marine, mercantile marine, merchant navy, shipping line; flag of convenience, **flag.**

**Adj. marine**, maritime, naval, nautical, **seafaring**; sea-worthy; snug, tight, shipshape.

**Adv. afloat**, aboard.

## 271 Aircraft

**N. aircraft, aeronautics**; flying machine; aeroplane, airplane, crate; plane, monoplane, biplane; amphibian; hydroplane, flying boat; airliner, airbus, transport, freighter; fighter, bomber, **air force**; jet plane, jet, turbojet, turboprop; VTOL; helicopter, chopper; hovercraft, **ship**; glider; joystick, rudder; fin, tail; aileron, **wing**; prop, **propeller**; cockpit, flight deck; undercarriage, landing gear; parachute; test bed, wind tunnel; flight simulator; aerodrome, **air travel**.

**airship**, balloon, captive balloon; dirigible, Zeppelin; kite, parachute, chute; hang glider; magic carpet; nacelle, car, gondola.

**rocket**, rocketry; step rocket, booster; nose cone, warhead; **missile weapon**.

**spaceship**, spacecraft, space probe, space capsule, space shuttle; lunar module; space station, **satellite**; flying saucer, UFO, unidentified flying object.

**Adj. aviational**, aerospace; airworthy, **flying**; supersonic; vertical take-off.

## 272 Velocity

**N. velocity**, celerity, speed, alacrity; speed of thought; expedition; speed, tempo, rate, pace, bat, **motion**; mach number; speed of light, speed of sound, supersonic speed; great speed, maximum speed, full steam; utmost speed, press of sail, precipitation; hurry, flurry, **haste**; reckless speed; streak, streak of lightning, flash, flight, gale, hurricane, tempest, torrent; electricity, telegraph, lightning,

speed measurement, speedometer, **gauge**; wind gauge; log; speed trap, **trap**.

**spurt**, acceleration; burst, burst of speed, burst of energy; thrust, drive, impetus, **impulse**; jump, spring, bound, pounce, **leap**; swoop, zip; dive, flying start, rush, dash, scamper, run, sprint, gallop.

**speeding**, driving, racing; bowling along, course, race, career, full speed, full lick; pace, fair clip; quick march, double, forced march, **haste**; quick retreat, **escape**; race course, speed track, **racing**.

**speeder**, speed merchant, speed maniac, scorcher, racing driver, **driver**; runner, harrier; racehorse, **thoroughbred**; greyhound, cheetah, hare, deer, doe, gazelle, antelope; ostrich, eagle, swallow; arrow, bullet, cannonball, **missile**; jet, rocket; clipper, **ship**; express, express train; express messenger, Mercury, **courier**; magic carpet.

**Adj. speedy**, swift, fast, quick, rapid, nimble; dashing, lively, brisk, smart, snappy, nifty, zippy, **vigorous**; expeditious, **hasty**; double-quick; prompt, **early**; immediate; speeding, racing, ton-up; running, runaway; flying; tempestuous; breakneck, precipitate, **rash**; fleet, fleet of foot; agile, nimble, slippery, evasive; like quicksilver; like a bird; like an arrow; like a flash; meteoric, electric, telegraphic, supersonic.

**Vb. move fast**, move, shift, travel, speed; drive, pelt, streak, flash, shoot; scorch; scud; skim, nip, cut; bowl along; sweep along, tear, rip, zip, rush, dash; fly, wing; hurtle, dive; dash forward; plunge, lunge, swoop; run, trot, double, lope, spank, gallop; bolt, hotfoot it, leg it, scoot, skedaddle, scamper, scurry, scuttle;

hare, run like mad; start, dart, flit; frisk, whisk; spring, bound, leap, jump, pounce; ride hard; hie, hurry, post, haste, **hasten**; chase, charge, stampede, career, go full tilt, go full pelt, go full lick, go full bat, go full steam.

**accelerate**, gather momentum, spurt, sprint, let it rip; quicken, give one his head, drive, spur, urge forward; lend wings to, expedite, **hasten**.

**outstrip**, overtake, overhaul; lap, outrun, **outdo**; distance, outdistance, leave behind, leave standing; lose; romp home, **be superior**.

**Adv. swiftly**, apace, posthaste, with speed, at full tilt; helter-skelter; presto, pronto, like a shot; full speed ahead; like wildfire.

**273 Slowness**

**N. slowness**, languor; inertia; refusal to be hurried, deliberation; **caution**; reluctance; working to rule, **strike**; drag, **friction**; brake, curb, **restraint**; time to spare, leisurely progress, **leisure**; slow motion, low gear; slow march, slow time, andante; slow pace, crawl, creep, dawdle; walk, amble, jog trot, **gait**; standing start, lagging, lag, time lag, **delay**.

**slowcoach**, snail, slug, tortoise; funeral procession; slow starter, late developer; sleepyhead; **slacker**; drone.

**Adj. slow**; dripping; **clumsy**; halting; tardy, dilatory, lagging, **late**; long about it, **leisurely**, sedate, **formal**; deliberate, **patient**; painstaking, **careful**; Fabian, **cautious**; tentative; languid, slack, sluggish, **lazy**; apathetic, phlegmatic, **insensible**; gradual, imperceptible, invisible.

**Vb. move slowly**, go slow, amble, crawl, creep, inch, inch along, ooze, drip, trickle, dribble, **flow**; drift, **deviate**; hover; shamble, slouch, shuffle, scuff; toddle, waddle, take short steps, mince; plod, trudge, tramp, lumber, stump, stump along; wobble, totter, stagger, lurch; struggle, toil, labour, chug, jolt, bump, creak; limp, hobble, go lame; flag, falter; trail, lag, fall behind, **follow**; hang fire, drag o.e-self; tarry, be long about it, **be late**; laze, maunder, idle; take it easy, linger, stroll, saunter, dawdle, **walk**; barely move, hardly beat; grope, **be tentative**; soft-pedal, hesitate, **be cautious**; drawl, **stammer**.

**decelerate**, lose momentum; reduce speed; relax, slacken, **pause**; lose ground, flag, falter.

**retard**, check, curb, **moderate**; reef, shorten sail, strike sail, **navigate**; brake, **restrain**; regress, back-water, reverse, **regress**; handicap, **hinder**.

**Adv. slowly**, leisurely; at half speed, with leaden step; gingerly; adagio, largo.

**gradatim**, one at a time.

**274 Impulse**

**N. impulse**, impulsion, pressure; impetus, momentum; boost, **stimulant**; **incentive**; thrust, push, shove, heave; stroke, throw, fling, **propulsion**; lunge, kick, **attack**; percussion, beating; beat, **roll**; thud; butt (see **collision**); shock, impact, slam, bang; flick, clip, tap, **touch**; shake, rattle, jolt, jerk, wrench; pulse, **spasm**; science of forces, mechanics, dynamics.

**knock**, dint, dent; rap, tap, clap; dab, pat, fillip, flip, flick; nudge, dig, **gesture**; smack, slap, cuff, clout, clump, buffet; blow; lash, stroke, hit, crack; cut, drive (cricket); thump, biff, bang; punch, left, right, straight left, uppercut, jab, hook; body blow, swipe; knock-out blow, stamp, kick; whop, swat; flogging, thrashing, beating; hiding, **corporal punishment**; assault, **attack**; fisticuffs, **turmoil**.

**collision**, encounter, meeting; head-on collision, bird strike; graze, scrape, **friction**; clash; cannon; impact, bump, shock, crash, smash, smashup, accident; brunt, charge, force, **attack**; collision course; multiple collision, pileup, **accumulation**.

**hammer**; punch; beetle, maul, mallet; flail; bat, hockey stick, golf club; knocker, cosh, knuckle-duster; cudgel, club, mace, bicycle chain, sandbag, **weapon**; boxing glove; pestle, anvil; beater.

**ram**, bulldozer; monkey; ramrod; cue, pusher.

**Adj. impelling**; dynamic.

**Vb. impel**, fling, heave, throw, **propel**; give an impetus, impart momentum; slam, bang, **close**; press; push, thrust, shove; tamp; pole, punt; hustle, prod, urge, spur, **accelerate**; fillip, flip, flick; jerk, shake, rattle, shock, jog, jolt, jostle, **agitate**; shoulder, elbow, push around, **deflect**; expel, eject; frogmarch; drive forward, goad, **incite**, drive, start, run, set going, set moving, **operate**; raise, **elevate**; plunge, dip, **lower**.

**collide**, make impact, **touch**, **encroach**; **converge**; meet, encounter, clash; fence, **strike at**; ram, butt, batter, dint, dent; batter at, bulldoze, **demolish**; bump against; graze, graze against, **rub**; butt against; clash with, foul, fall foul of; run against, **charge**; clash against; trip, **tumble**; knock together.

**strike**, smite, hit, land a blow, aim a blow; lunge, lunge at, poke at, strike at; let fly; swing, flail; strike hard,

slam, bang, knock; send flying; floor, **fell**; pat, patter; flip, fillip, tickle; tap, rap, clap; slap, smack; clump, clout, clobber; box, spar, **fight**; buffet, punch, thump, whack, wham, pummel, trounce, belabour, sock it to, let one have it; give one a black eye or a bloody nose; pound, batter, bludgeon; biff, bash, dash, slosh, sock, slog, slug, cosh, cudgel, club, mug; sandbag, crown; concuss, stun, leave senseless; spank, wallop, thrash, lash, beat, whip, cane, **flog**; leather, strap, belt, give a hiding, **punish**; thresh, flail; hammer, drum; flap, squash, swat, **flatten**; paw, stroke, **caress**; scratch, maul, **wound**; run through, bayonet, pink, **pierce**; tear, **cut**; stone, pelt, snowball; head (a football); bat, strike a ball, swipe, drive, turn, glance, cut, crack, lift, lob, smash, volley, **propel**.

**kick**, spurn, boot, knee; trample; ride roughshod; spur; heel, dribble, shoot (a football).

## 275 Recoil

**N. recoil**, revulsion, reaction, **reversion**; repercussion, echo; reflex, **reflection**; kick, kickback, backlash; ricochet, cannon; rebound, bounce, spring, springboard, trampoline; volley, return (at tennis), boomerang; rebuff, repulse, **repulsion**; riposte, return fire.

**Adj. recoiling**, reactive; retroactive.

**Vb. recoil**, react, **counteract**; shrink, wince, flinch, jib, shy, **avoid**; kick back, ricochet, cannon; spring back, rebound; return, swing back; reverberate, echo, **resound**; reflect, **shine**; boomerang, **retaliate**.

## 276 Direction

**N. direction**, bearing, compass reading, **bearings**; **situation**; set, drift, **current**; tenor, trend, **tendency**; aim; course, beam; beeline, straight shot, line of sight; course, tack; line, line of march, track, way, path, road, **route**; steerage; aim, target, **goal**; compass, **sailing aid**; gauge; direction finder, gauge; cross-country race, point-to-point.

**compass point**, cardinal points, half points, quarter points; quarter, North, East, South, West; azimuth.

**Adj. directed**; **parallel**; diagonal, **oblique**; sideways, **lateral**; facing, **opposite**; direct, unswerving, straightforward, one-way, **straight**; northbound, southbound; northern, northerly, southerly; western; eastern; directive.

**Vb. orientate**, orientate oneself, **navigate**; take a direction, bear; direct oneself; signpost, direct, **indicate**; pinpoint, locate, **place**; **be straight**; face, front, **be opposite**.

**steer for**, steer, make towards, go to, go towards; **be straight**.

**point to**, point, point towards, signpost, **indicate**; trend, trend towards, verge, dip, bend, **tend**.

**aim**, level, point; take aim, aim at; level at; cover; aim well, land, plant, **place**.

**Adv. towards**, versus, facing; through, via; straight, direct; point blank; directly, full tilt at; upstream, downstream; downwind; seaward, landward, homeward; cross-country; hither, thither; clockwise, anticlockwise, counterclockwise; whither, which way!

## 277 Deviation

**N. deviation**, wrong course, wrong turning; aberration, deflection; shift, veer, slew, swing; declension; swerve, bend, **curvature**; detour, long way round, **circuit**; vagrancy, **wandering**; fall, lapse, **error**; wandering mind; drift, leeway; oblique motion, sidestep, sideslip; break, (googly cricket); yaw, tack; zigzag, slalom course.

**Adj. deviating**, aberrant, nonconformist, abnormal, deviant; eccentric; errant, wandering, rambling, vagrant, loose, footloose; random, erratic, **inexact**; desultory, **discontinuous**; abstracted; discursive, **irrelevant**; lost, stray, astray; wide; devious, roundabout, **circuitous**; indirect, crooked, zigzag, **oblique**.

**Vb. deviate**, digress, make a detour, **diverge**; turn, filter, turn a corner, turn aside, swerve, slew; step aside; alter course, change direction, yaw, tack; veer, (back wind); trend, bend, curve; zigzag, twine, twist, **meander**; swing, wobble, **oscillate**; steer clear of; sidle, passage; slide, skid, sideslip; break (cricket); glance, **be oblique**; shy, jib, sidestep, **avoid**.

**turn round**, turn about, about turn, wheel, wheel about; reverse, reverse direction, return; go back, **turn back**.

**stray**, err, ramble, rove, drift, straggle, **wander**; go astray, go adrift, get lost; **blunder**; lose track of.

**deflect**, bend, crook, **make oblique**; warp, skew; misdirect, **mislead**; avert, **parry**; divert; sidetrack, draw aside; bias, slice, pull, hook, glance, bowl a break, bowl (wide cricket); shuffle, shift, switch, shunt, **interchange**; wear ship, **navigate**.

**Adv. astray**, adrift; right about; round about; all manner of ways; at a tangent, sideways; crabwise.

## 278 Preceding: going before

**N.** preceding, **priority**, **precedence**; going before, leading, heading, flying start; preemption; pride of place, lead, leading role; pioneer, **precursor**, van, vanguard, avant-garde, **front**.

**Adj.** foremost, first.

**Vb.** precede, go before, herald; introduce; head, spearhead, lead; guide, conduct, **direct**; have a head start; preempt; get ahead of, lap, **outstrip**; be beforehand, **be early**; have right of way, **come before**.

**Adv.** ahead, before, foremost; primarily, first of all; age before beauty.

## 279 Following: going after

**N.** following, sequence; run, suit, **series**; pursuit, pursuance, **chase**; succession, reversion, **transfer**; last place, **rear**.

follower, attendant, hanger-on, camp follower, **dependant**; train, tail, wake, suite, **retinue**; following, party, adherent, supporter; satellite, moon, artificial satellite, space station, **spaceship**; trailer, caravan, **cart**; tender, **ship**.

**Adj.** following, subsequent.

**Vb.** follow, come behind, succeed, follow after, come to heel, tag after; stick like a shadow, tag after; attend, **serve**; tag along, **accompany**; dog, shadow, trail, tail, track, **pursue**; drop behind, lag, trail, dawdle; **be behind**.

**Adv.** behind, rearward; **after**; one after another.

## 280 Progression: motion forwards

**N.** progression, going forward; procession, march, way, course, career; march of time, **course of time**; progress, forward march, **motion**; sudden progress, stride, leap, jump, **spurt**;

irresistible progress, flood, tide, **current**; gain, advance, headway; **preceding**; next step, development, evolution, **ascent**, **continuity**; mystic progress, **piety**, **worship**; furtherance, promotion, advancement; rise, raise, lift, **elevation**; enterprise, **undertaking**; achievement, **success**; economic progress, **progressive**; gogetter, coming man or woman, upstart, **prosperous person**.

**Adj.** progressive, enterprising, forward-looking; **moving**, irreversible; advanced, **modern**.

**Vb.** progress, proceed; advance, go forward, take a step forward, develop, **evolve**; show promise, **get better**; do well, **prosper**; maintain progress, never look back; push forward, press onwards, **hasten**; make a good start, make initial progress; gain, gain ground, make headway, **move fast**; get ahead; distance, outdistance, leave behind, **outstrip**; gain height, rise, rise higher, **climb**; reach towards; recover lost ground, **recoup**; gain time.

promote, further, contribute to, advance, **aid**; prefer, upgrade, raise, lift, **elevate**; bring forward, push, force, develop, **invigorate**; **accelerate**; put ahead, put forward; favour, **cause**.

**Adv.** forward, onward, forth, ahead.

**Int.** Forward! Forrard! En avant! Excelsior!

## 281 Regression: motion backwards

**N.** regression, regress; reverse direction, backward step, **reversion**; retreat, recession; backing; decline, drop, fall, slump.

return, homeward journey; homecoming, **arrival**; reentry; going back, ebb, **current**; backing; relapse; U-turn, volte-face, about turn, **reversion**;

turn, turning point, **crisis**; reflex, **recoil**.

**Adj. regressive**; reflex; backward; reactionary, **retrospective**; retroactive; backing, anticlockwise, counterclockwise; reverse; resilient, **elastic**; homing, homeward bound.

**Vb. regress**, recede, retrogress; retreat, retire, withdraw, fall back, turn tail; disengage, **resign**; backtrack, backpedal; give way, give ground, **disappear**; fall behind, fall astern; reverse, back, back water, go backwards; run back, flow back, regurgitate; slip back; ebb, slump, fall, drop, decline, **descend**; bounce back, **recoil**.

**turn back**; go back, go home, return; look back, hark back, **retrospect**; veer round, about face, execute a volteface; double, double back; start back, jib, shrink, **avoid**; come back, come back again, come home.

**Adv. backwards**, back, astern.

**Int. back! hard astern! hands off!**

## 282 Propulsion

**N. propulsion**, drive; impulsion, push, **impulse**; projection; precipitation; cast, throw, chuck, toss, fling, sling, shy; pot shot, pot, shot, discharge, volley, **bombardment**; bowling, throw-in, full toss, yorker, lob (cricket); kick, punt, dribble (football); stroke, drive, swipe, **knock**; pull, slice (golf); rally, volley, smash (tennis); ballistics; **skill**; gunshot, **distance**.

**missile**, projectile, shell, rocket, cannonball, ball, bullet, shot, pellet, brickbat, stone, snowball; arrow, dart, **missile weapon**; ball, football, rugby ball; bowl, wood, jack, puck, curling stone; discus, javelin; hammer, caber.

**propellant**, thrust, driving force, jet,

steam, **energy**; spray, aerosol; pusher, **ram**; tail wind, **wind**; lever, treadle, pedal, oar, sweep, paddle; screw, blade, **propeller**; coal, petrol, **fuel**; gunpowder, dynamite, **explosive**; shotgun, rifle, **firearm**; revolver, **pistol**; airgun, pop gun, water pistol; blowpipe, pea-shooter; catapult, sling, bow, **missile weapon**.

**shooter**, gunman, rifleman, musketeer; gunner; archer, bowman; marksman, sharpshooter, shot, **proficient person**.

**thrower**; bowler, pitcher, curler.

**Adj. propulsive**, explosive, projectile, missile.

**Vb. propel**, launch, project; flight, throw, cast, deliver, heave, pitch, toss, cant, chuck, shy, bung; bowl, lob, york; hurl, fling, sling, catapult; dart, flick; pelt, stone, shower, snowball; precipitate, send flying; expel, pitchfork, **eject**; explode; serve, return, volley, smash, kill (tennis); bat, slam, slog, wham; sky, loft; drive, cut, pull, hook, glance (cricket); slice, **strike**; kick, dribble, punt (football); putt, push, shove, shoulder, ease along, **impel**; wheel, pedal, roll, bowl, trundle, **rotate**; drive, hustle, **move**; sweep, sweep before one, drive like leaves; put to flight, **defeat**.

**shoot**, fire, open fire; volley, discharge, explode; let fly; cannonade, bombard, **fire at**; snipe, pot, pot at; pepper, **pierce**.

## 283 Traction

**N. traction**; **attraction**; haulage; draught, pull, haul; tug, tow; rake, harrow; trawl, dragnet; drawer, tower, haulier; square sail, **sail**; windlass; tug, tugboat, **ship**; tractor, traction engine, **locomotive**; loadstone, **magnet**; strain, tug of war, **contest**;

thing drawn, trailer, **cart**.

**Adj. drawing**; retractile; attractive; ductile; drawn.

**Vb. draw**, pull, haul, hale; trice, warp, **navigate**; tug, tow; lug, drag, train, trail, trawl; rake, harrow; winch, lift, heave, **elevate**; **lower**; **absorb**; pluck, **extract**; wrench, **distort**; yank, jerk, twitch, tweak, pluck at, snatch at, **agitate**; pull towards, **attract**; pull back, retract.

**Int.** yo-heave-ho!

## 284 Approach: motion towards

**N. approach**, coming towards, advance, **progression**; near approach, approximation; flowing towards, **stream**; meeting, **confluence**; access, accession, advent, coming, **arrival**, **presence**; **pursuit**; onset, **attack**; advances, overture; **offer**; means of approach, **access**.

**Adj. approaching**, close, **near**; meeting; **affluent**, tributary; **imminent**, **impending**; coming, oncoming.

**accessible**, approachable, get-at-able; within reach, **possible**; available; wayside, roadside, nearby, **near**; inviting, **sociable**.

**Vb. approach**, draw near, **be near**; approximate, **bring near**; come within range, **arrive**; be visible; be drawn; come to close quarters, meet, **converge**; **collide**; near, move near; **congregate**, **enter**; accede, adhere, join, **accrue**; waylay, buttonhole; accost, **greet**; make overtures, meet, nestle, **caress**; lean towards, incline, trend; move towards, advance, **progress**; attack; close, **circumscribe**; hover; overtake, **outstrip**; follow hard, run one close; make a landfall, **land**, **navigate**.

**Int.** this way! come closer! roll up! land ahoy!

## 285 Recession: motion from

**N. recession**, retreat; leak; resignation; flight, **escape**; revulsion, **recoil**.

**Adj. receding**, retreating.

**Vb. recede**, retire, withdraw, fall back, retreat, **regress**; ebb, subside, shrink, decline, **decrease**; **disappear**; go, leave, evacuate, emigrate, **depart**; go outside, **emerge**; leak; move further, put space between, **be distant**; stand aside, make way, **deviate**; **stray**; flinch, **avoid**; flee; **escape**; go back, **turn back**; jump back, **recoil**; come unstuck, **separate**.

## 286 Attraction

**N. attraction**, pull, drag, draw, tug; drawing to; gravity, itch, **desire**; affinity, sympathy; allure, appeal, allurement, seduction, temptation, lure, bait, decoy, charm, siren song, **inducement**; siren; centre of attraction, cynosure, **favourite**.

**magnet**, coil magnet, solenoid; lodestar, **guide**.

**Adj. attracting**, attractive; siren, seductive; centripetal.

**Vb. attract**, pull, drag, tug, **draw**; exercise a pull, draw towards, appeal, charm, move, **impress**; lure, allure, bait, **tempt**; decoy, **ensnare**.

## 287 Repulsion

**N. repulsion**, repellent quality; reflection, **recoil**; **defence**; repulse, rebuff, snub, refusal.

**Adj. repellent**, off-putting; centrifugal.

**Vb. repel**, excite nausea, **cause dislike**; butt, head, **impel**; repulse, block, **parry**; dispel, **disperse**; reflect, **deflect**; be deaf to **refuse**; rebuff, snub, **reject**; cold-shoulder, keep at arm's length, make one keep his distance; send one about his business; sack, **dismiss**.

**Int.** be off! away with you! scram! hop it! get lost!

## 288 Convergence

**N.** convergence, mutual approach, **approach**; collision course, **collision**; confluence, meeting, **union**; congress, concentration, resort, assembly, **assemblage**; pincer movement; **focus**; coming to a point, taper; tangent; perspective, **view**.

**Adj.** convergent; centripetal; concurrent; tangential; pointed, conical; knock-kneed.

**Vb.** converge; come together, **meet**; unite, gather together, **congregate**; **enter**; close with, intercept, **circumscribe**; pinch, nip; concentrate, focus; centre; taper, come to a point, **be narrow**.

## 289 Divergence

**N.** divergence, difference; going apart; moving apart, parting, **separation**; aberration, declination, **deviation**; spread; fork, crossroads, points, **crossing**; radiation, ramification; star.

**Adj.** divergent; radiant; centrifugal, centrifuge; aberrant.

**Vb.** diverge, differ; radiate; ramify; fork; part, part ways, part company, **separate**; change direction, switch; **deviate**; deploy, spread, scatter; straddle, spread-eagle; splay, splay apart.

## 290 Arrival

**N.** arrival, advent, accession, appearance, entrance, **approach, presence**; onset, **beginning**; coming, making; landfall, landing; meeting, encounter, **event**; greeting, handshake, **courteous act**; homecoming, **return**; reception, welcome, **celebration**; guest, visitor, visitant, new arrival, homing pigeon;

finish, **contest**; last lap, home stretch.

**goal, objective**; native land, **home**; final point, terminus, **extremity**; stop, stopover, stage, halt; billet, landing stage, pier; port, harbour, haven, anchorage, **shelter**; dock, berth, **stable**; aerodrome, airport, heliport, terminal, **air travel**; terminus, railway station, depot, rendezvous, **meeting place**.

**Adj.** arriving, homing; terminal; **impending**.

**Vb.** arrive, come, reach, get there, **be present**; make land, sight, raise; make a landfall, make port; dock, berth, moor, drop anchor, **come to rest** (see **land**); park; home, **regress**; hit, make, win to, gain, attain; **carry through**; **enter**; make an entrance; appear, **visit**; stop at, stop, **pause**; **be early**; arrive at, find, **discover**; **prosper**; be brought, come to hand.

**land**, unload, discharge, **displace**; beach, ground, run aground, make a landing; step ashore, disembark, **emerge**; alight, perch, **descend**; dismount, set foot to ground.

**meet**, join, rejoin, see again; receive, greet, welcome, **be sociable**; go to meet; keep a date, rendezvous; encounter, hit, collide with, **collide**; gather, assemble, **congregate**.

**Int.** welcome! welcome home! greetings! hullo! hi! pleased to meet you! aloha! shalom! salaam!

## 291 Departure

**N.** departure, parting, removal; walkout, exit, **egress, recession**; going back, **return**; migration, exodus, hop, flight, flit, getaway, **escape**; outset, **start**; takeoff, **ascent**; zero hour.

**valediction**, funeral oration, epitaph, obituary; last handshake, **courteous act**; send-off, farewell address; last post, last words, parting shot; stirrup cup, nightcap.

**Adj. departing,** farewell; parting, outward bound.

**Vb. depart,** quit, leave, abandon, **relinquish**; retire, withdraw, **turn back**; remove, move house, leave home, emigrate, expatriate oneself; take wing; be going; bid farewell, say good night, part, part company; leave work, **cease**; go home, **emerge**; exit, **resign**; depart this life, **die**.

**decamp,** break camp; evacuate; make oneself scarce; take wing, **fly**; vamoose, skedaddle, beat it, hop it, scram, bolt, scuttle, skip, **move fast**; flee, take flight; flit, **disappear**; elope, abscond, **escape**.

**start out,** get going, **begin**; set forth, **emerge**; gird oneself, be ready to start, **make ready**; take ship, embark, **enter**; weigh anchor, set sail, **navigate**; mount, bit, bridle, harness, saddle, **ride**; emplane; catch a train, catch a plane, catch a bus.

**Int. goodbye! farewell! adieu! au revoir! auf Wiedersehen! a rivederci! be seeing you! cheerio! ciao! bye-bye! ta-ta! so long! pleasant journey! bon voyage! God be with you!**

## 292 Ingress: motion into

**N. ingress,** incoming, entry, entrance; reentry, **return**; influx, flood, **stream**; trespass, invasion, forced entry, inroad, raid, irruption, incursion, **attack**; osmosis, intake, **reception**; import, importation; right of entry, admission, admittance, access, **permission**; free trade, free market, **trade**, scope; ticket, pass, **permit**; **opener**.

**way in,** way, path, **access**; entrance, entry, door, **doorway**; mouth, opening, **orifice**; intake, inlet, **gulf**; channel, **conduit**; open door, free port, market.

**incomer,** newcomer; new arrival, new member, new face; new boy; **beginner**; visitant, visitor, caller, **sociable person**; migrant, colonist, settler, **foreigner**; raider; house-breaker, thief; entrant, competitor, **contender**; ticket holder, audience, house, gate.

**Adj. incoming,** inward, inward bound, homing; intrusive; penetrating.

**Vb. enter; come after; open;** gain admittance; call, **visit**; board, get aboard; insinuate oneself; **pierce; notch;** tumble; **plunge**; join, be one of; immigrate, **place oneself; admit; insert;** enter oneself, **contend**.

**infiltrate,** percolate, seep, soak through, penetrate, permeate, **mix**; taint, infect, **impair**.

**burst in, force;** flood, overflow, **flow**; congregate; invade, raid, break through, board, storm, **attack**.

**intrude,** trespass, gatecrash; interrupt, **derange**; burgle, **steal**.

## 293 Egress: motion out of

**N. egress,** exit; walkout, exodus; exile; issue; eruption, outburst, **outbreak**; sortie, **escape**; export; migrant, emigrant, **foreigner**; expatriate, colonist, settler; exile, remittance man.

**outflow,** effusion; emission; issue; weeping; bleeding, **haemorrhage**; perspiration, sweat; leak, escape, leakage, **waste**; drain, running sore, **loss**; discharge, drainage; overflow, spill, flood, **waterfall**; jet, fountain, spring, **source**; gush, squirt, **stream**; geyser; runny nose.

**outlet,** vent, chute; spout, nozzle, tap; pore, blowhole, **orifice, respiration**; sluice, floodgate, **conduit**; exhaust, exhaust pipe; spout, drainpipe, gargoyle; exit, path, **access; doorway**; escape, loophole, **means of escape.**

**Adj. outgoing**, outward bound; emergent; runny, leaky; running, bleeding; explosive, volcanic; spent.

**Vb. emerge**, project; be visible; surface, break water, **ascend**; transpire; egress; issue, debouch, sally, make a sortie; issue forth, **walk**; **leap**; evacuate, **decamp**; emigrate, **travel**; exit, **depart**; erupt, break through, **escape**.

**flow out**, **flow**; gush, spout, jet, **emit**; run, drip, dribble, trickle, ooze; rise, surge, overflow, spill, escape, leak, vent itself, debouch; bleed, weep; flood, inundate, **drench**.

**exude**, perspire, sweat, steam, be hot; ooze, seep, seep through, percolate, strain, filter, distil; run, dribble, drip, drop, drivel, drool, slaver, slobber, salivate, **be wet**; transpire, exhale, breathe.

## 294 Reception

**N. reception**, admission, admittance, access; invitation, **offer**; acceptance, open arms, welcome, **celebration**; initiation, baptism, **debut**; asylum, sanctuary, shelter, **protection**; introduction; importation, import; radio receiver, **telecommunication**; **respiration**; suction; digestion, absorption; fluid intake; intake, consumption, **waste**; infusion; interjection.

**Adj. admitting**, receptive; inviting, **accessible**; receivable, admissible, acceptable; absorbent, hygroscopic; digestive.

**Vb. admit**, receive, accept; grant asylum, afford sanctuary, shelter, **safeguard**; welcome; invite, **offer**; enlist, **employ**; give entrance or admittance to, allow access, give a ticket to; throw open, **open**; import, land, **transfer**; introduce, **come before**; **send**; initiate, **teach**; infiltrate, **insert**; take, be given, get, **receive**.

**absorb**, incorporate, engross, assimilate, digest; suck; sponge, blot, **dry**; ingest, imbibe; swallow, engulf, gulp, gobble, devour, **eat**, drink; inhale, **breathe**; sniff, snuff, **smell**; taste.

## 295 Ejection

**N. ejection**, expulsion; precipitation, **propulsion**; disqualification, **exclusion**; discharge, sack, boot, push; exile; **displacement**; deprivation; jettison; clean sweep, **destruction**; emission, effusion; libation; secretion; radioactivity, **radiation**; deportee, refugee, **outcast**.

**ejector**, bailiff, **substitute**; bouncer; emetic, **purgative**; **explosive**; volcano, **furnace**; radiator, radio transmitter, **telecommunication**; **aircraft**.

**voidance**, clearance, drainage, aspiration; eruption, **outbreak**; nausea, vomit, puke; gas, wind, burp, belch.

**Adj. expulsive**, explosive; sickening, emetic.

**vomiting**, sick, green; seasick, airsick.

**Vb. eject**, expel, **punish**; disbar, excommunicate, **exclude**; export, **transfer**; deport, expatriate, repatriate, resettle; exile, banish, transport, **seclude**; extrude, wash ashore; bounce, **propel**; precipitate, **propel**; **extract**; unearth, uproot, eradicate, **destroy**; obliterate; get shot of; dispossess, expropriate; oust, evict, dislodge, turn adrift, **displace**; **hunt**; jettison, discard, throw overboard; blackball, **reject**; cut, cut dead, send to Coventry; supplant, supersede, replace, **substitute**.

**dismiss**, discharge, make redundant, drop; axe, sack, fire; send one about his business, **repel**; **frighten**; tell to go, **prohibit**.

**empty**, drain, void; evacuate, eliminate, **excrete**; vent, disgorge, discharge;

decant, **transpose**; **drink**; aspirate; **open**; tap, broach, **pierce**; milk, bleed, let blood, **extract**; clear, make a clean sweep of, **clean**; unload, unpack, **displace**; disembowel, eviscerate, gut, clean, bone, fillet, **uncover**; **purify**; desolate, depopulate, **render few**.

emit, give vent to; **send**; **radiate**; emit a smell, exhale, perfume, scent, **smell**; vapour, fume, smoke, steam, puff; spit, spatter, splutter; pour, spill, shed, sprinkle, spray; spurt, squirt, jet, gush, **moisten**; bleed; drip, drop, ooze; dribble, drool, slobber, **exude**; sweat, perspire, **be hot**; secrete, **store**; pass, **excrete**; drop (a foal); lay (an egg); **generate**.

vomit, be sick, disgorge, retch, gag; spew, puke, cat, honk, poop; be seasick; feel nausea, heave.

eruct, belch, burp; break wind; cough, hawk, expectorate, spit, gob.

## 296 Food: eating and drinking

N. **eating**, taking food; nutrition; consumption; biting; digestion; table, diet; lack of appetite, anorexia; **bulk**; appetite, voracity, **hunger**; table manners, **practice**; vegetarianism; food chain, food web.

**feasting**; orgy, feast; reception, wedding breakfast, annual dinner, do, **celebration**; harvest supper; Christmas dinner, blowout, spread (see **meal**); loaded table; **plenty**; refectory.

**dieting**, dietetics, **therapy**; diet; regimen, regime, course, diet sheet; meagre diet, poor table; malnutrition, **disease**; vitamin pill; nutrition expert.

**gastronomy**; good living; dainty palate, **discrimination**; epicure, gourmet.

**cookery**, cuisine, food preparation; dressing; domestic science, home economics, **provision**; baker, cook, chef; bakery, rotisserie, restaurant; kitchen;

galley; oven, **furnace**; butter, margarine, **oil**; dripping, lard, **fat**; yeast, **leaven**; recipe, cookery book, **textbook**.

**eater**, feeder, consumer, picker, pecker; boarder; dainty feeder, connoisseur, gourmet, epicure, gourmand, **glutton**; carnivore; man-eater, cannibal; vegetarian, vegan, herbivore; omnivore, hearty eater, wolf, vulture, locust; teeth, jaws, **tooth**; mouth, pecker, gullet, stomach, belly, paunch.

**provisions**, stores, commissariat; foodstuff, groceries, keep, board, entertainment, sustenance, **provision**; home-grown food; commons, helping, **portion**; buttery, pantry, larder, cellar, **storage**; hay box, meat safe; freezer, fridge, **refrigerator**.

**provender**, animal food, fodder, feed, pasture, pasturage, forage; corn, oats, barley, grain, hay, grass, clover, lucerne, silage; dry feed, chicken feed, pigswill, cattle cake; saltlick.

**food**, meat, bread, staff of life; nutriment, nutrition; nurture, sustenance, pap; manna; daily bread, staple food; wheat, maize, rice; eats, victuals; grub, tuck, nosh, scoff; tack, biscuit, salt pork; heavy food, stodge; bad food, carrion, offal; health food; cheer, good food, good table; delicatessen; garnish, flavouring, sauce, **condiment**.

**food content**; roughage, bulk, fibre; calcium, iron; protein; fat, oil, cholesterol; starch; sugar, glucose, sucrose, lactose, **sweet thing**; additive, preservative, artificial flavouring.

**mouthful**, bite, nibble, morsel, **small quantity**; sop, sip, swallow; slice, titbit; sandwich, snack, crust; chocolate, sweet, popcorn; cud, quid, something to chew; tablet, pill, **drug**.

**meal**, refreshment, fare; light meal,

snack, bite to eat; piece, sandwich, hamburger, hot dog; packed lunch, square meal, heavy meal; sit-down meal, repast, spread, feed, blowout, junket, **festivity**; picnic, barbecue; chance meal, potluck; breakfast, elevenses, lunch, brunch, tiffin; tea, five o'clock, high tea; dinner, supper; menu, bill of fare, diet sheet, **list**; cover, table, place; help, helping, **portion**; serving; self-service.

dish, course; main dish; salad; dessert, savoury; speciality; casserole, stew, hotpot, ragout, **a mixture**; goulash, curry; pilau, paella, risotto; pasta, ravioli, macaroni, spaghetti; pancake, pizza, pasty, pie, flan, quiche; fricassee; fry-up, mixed grill; egg dish; rehash.

hors-d'oeuvres, smorgasbord; starter; soup, broth, brew; stock, bouillon, bisque, chowder, puree; mulligatawny, minestrone; salami, pâté, galantine; salad, coleslaw; mayonnaise, **sauce**.

fish food, fish, fish pie, kedgeree; white fish, freshwater fish, trout, salmon, eel; cod, coley, rock salmon, dogfish; whiting, plaice, sole, skate, hake, halibut, haddock, turbot, mullet, mackerel, herring, whitebait; sardine, pilchard, tuna, tunny; seafood, shellfish, oyster, lobster, crayfish, crab, shrimp, prawn, scampi; cockle, winkle, mussel, whelk, jellied eel; roe.

meat, flesh; human flesh, long pig; red meat, beef, mutton, lamb, veal, pork, venison, game; pheasant, chicken, **table bird, poultry**; meat substitute; roast meat, Sunday roast; haggis, black pudding; mince; sausage, banger, frankfurter; Cornish pasty; cut, joint, leg; baron of beef, sirloin; shoulder, hand of pork, skirt, scrag end, breast, brisket; shin, loin, flank,

topside, silverside; cutlet, chop, escalope; steak, pork pie, ham, bacon, bacon rasher, gammon; tongue, knuckle, Bath chap, brawn, oxtail, tripe; offal, kidney, liver; suet, dripping, crackling; forcemeat, stuffing.

dessert, pudding, sweet; milk pudding, semolina, tapioca; rolypoly; jam tart, crumble, charlotte; stewed fruit, fool; fresh fruit, fruit salad; sorbet, mousse, sundae, trifle, blancmange, jelly, custard, **sweet thing**; cheese board.

sweets, confectionery; candy, chocolate, caramel, Turkish delight; acid drops, barley sugar, butterscotch, nougat; aniseed ball, lolly, lollipop, **sweet thing**; sweetmeat, bonbon; candy floss.

fruit, soft fruit, berry, gooseberry, strawberry, raspberry, loganberry, blackberry, bilberry, mulberry; currant, redcurrant, blackcurrant; stone fruit, apricot, peach, nectarine, plum, greengage, damson, cherry; apple, russet, pear; orange, grapefruit, lemon, lime, tangerine, mandarin; banana, pineapple, grape; rhubarb; date, fig; dried fruit, currant, raisin, sultana, prune; pomegranate, passion fruit, guava; mango, avocado; melon, honeydew; pawpaw; nut, coconut, pecan, peanut, groundnut, monkey nut; almond, walnut, chestnut, hazel nut; **sweet thing**.

vegetable, greens, **plant**; root vegetable, tuber, turnip, swede, parsnip, carrot; potato, yam; spud; green vegetable, cabbage, cauliflower, broccoli; spring greens, sorrel, spinach, asparagus, globe artichoke; leek, onion, marrow, courgette, pumpkin, squash; aubergine, eggplant, capsicum, pepper, chilli; lettuce, chicory; spring onion, radish, celery, beetroot; tomato; cucumber; cress, watercress; edible fungus, mushroom, truffle; edible seaweed; sauerkraut, ratatouille.

**potherb**, herb; marjoram, rosemary, sage, mint, parsley, thyme, basil, savory, tarragon, dill, fennel; coriander, caraway; caper; horse radish, **condiment**; borage.

**cereals**, wheat, buckwheat, oats, rye, maize, corn; rice, millet; breakfast cereal, cornflakes, muesli, oatmeal, porridge, gruel; flour, meal, wholemeal, wheat germ, bran; batter, dough; bread, crust, crumb; white bread, pumpernickel, toast, rusk; loaf, tin, farmhouse, bloomer, French stick; roll, croissant, crumpet, muffin, scone, teacake, oatcake, bannock; tortilla, waffle, wafer, cracker.

**pastries**, confectionery, pasty, turnover, dumpling; tart, flan, puff, pie; pastry, patisserie, gateau, cake, cheesecake; meringue, eclair, macaroon; bun, doughnut, flapjack, gingerbread, shortbread.

**dairy product** (see **milk**); cream, whey, junket; cheese, Cheddar, Caerphilly, Wensleydale, sage Derby; Gouda, Edam; Camembert, Brie; Parmesan; ripe cheese, Roquefort, Gorgonzola, Stilton, Danish blue.

**drinking**, fluid intake; potation; libation; drinker; **drunkard**.

**draught**, drink, beverage, dram; gulp, sip, sup; bottle, bowl, glass, **cup**; cuppa; bumper; swig, nip, noggin, tot, slug; peg, double peg, snifter, chaser; long drink; short drink, short; quick one, snort; nightcap; loving cup; health, toast; mixed drink, cocktail, **mixture**; potion, infusion, **medicine**; divine drink, nectar.

**soft drink**; water, spring water, fountain; soda water, soda, soda fountain; table water, squash; milk, milk shake; ginger beer, ginger ale, fizz, pop, lemonade, orangeade; cordial, fruit juice; coconut milk; tea, char, pekoe, maté, **tonic**; coffee, black coffee, espresso; cocoa (see **milk**); sherbet, syrup, julep.

**alcoholic drink**, booze, wallop, tipple, poison; brew, alcohol, malt liquor, beer; draught beer, strong beer; ale, real ale; barley wine; stout, lager, bitter, porter, mild, home brew; shandy; scrumpy; perry, mead; wheat wine, rice beer, toddy, sake, tequila; spirits, firewater, hooch, moonshine, mountain dew, rotgut, hard stuff; brandy, cognac; gin, schnapps, blue ruin; whisky, Scotch whisky, scotch; rye, bourbon; poteen; vodka; rum, demon rum, grog, punch, egg flip; cordial; cup, mixed drink, pink gin; cocktail; aperitif; liqueur.

**wine**, red wine; vermouth; vino, plonk; table wine, sack, sherry, port, madeira; champagne, fizz, bubbly; claret, burgundy, Beaujolais; hock, Moselle, Bordeaux; retsina, chianti.

**milk**; cream; buttermilk, plant milk; milk drink, cocoa, chocolate; junket. See **dairy product**.

**Adj. feeding**; insectivorous; vegetarian, vegan; omnivorous; teetotal, **temperate**; **drunken**.

**edible**, eatable; kosher; drinkable; milky; palatable, succulent, dainty, delicious, **tasty**, **savoury**; cereal, wheaten; alcoholic, hard; soft.

**nourishing**, nutritious; rich, calorific; wholesome, **salubrious**.

**culinary**; done to a turn, well-done; underdone, red, rare, raw; burnt.

**Vb. eat**, feed, fare, board, mess; partake, **taste**; take a meal, have a feed, break bread; breakfast, lunch, have tea, dine, sup; feast, banquet, carouse, **revel**; eat well, have a good appetite, do justice to; drool, raven, **be hungry**;

fall to, set to; stuff oneself, **sate**; guzzle; **expand**; take every course, leave a clean plate; **consume**; swallow, devour, bolt, wolf, make short work of; nibble, peck, lick, have a poor appetite; nibble at, peck at, sniff at; ingest, digest, **absorb**.

**chew**, masticate, champ, munch, crunch, scrunch; mumble, mouth, worry, gnaw, grind; bite, tear, rend, **cut**.

**graze**, browse, pasture, crop, feed; ruminate.

**drink**, imbibe, suck, **absorb**; quaff, drink like a fish, lap, sip; crack a bottle; booze, swill, swig, tipple, **get drunk**; knock it back; pledge, **toast**; have another; **replenish**; give to drink, wine, water; **provide**.

**feed**, nourish, nurture, sustain, **board**; give to eat, cater, purvey, **provide**; nurse, breast-feed, give suck; pasture, graze; fatten, **enlarge**; dine, feast, banquet, have to dinner, **be hospitable**.

**cook**, prepare a meal; bake, brown; roast, braise; broil, grill, barbecue, griddle, devil, curry; fry, scramble, poach; boil, parboil, coddle, seethe, simmer, steam; casserole, stew; baste, lard, bard; whip, whisk, beat, blend, liquidize, stir; draw, gut, bone, fillet, stuff, dress, garnish; dice, shred, mince, grate; sauce, flavour, spice, **season**.

**Int.**bon appétit! here's health! here's mud in your eye! bottoms up! down the hatch! prosit! skol! cheers!

## 297 Excretion

**N.excretion**, discharge, secretion; effusion; **egress**; **respiration**; **infection**; cold, catarrh, hay fever; cough; waterworks.

**haemorrhage**, bleeding, haemophilia, **blood**; menses, period, curse.

**defecation**, clearance; motion; constipation.

**excrement**, waste matter; faeces, stool, excreta, ordure, night soil; dung, cowpat, manure, muck; droppings, guano; urine, water; sweat, lather; spittle, spit, sputum; saliva, slaver, slobber, froth, foam; phlegm; catarrh, mucus, snot; matter, pus; afterbirth; slough, cast, pellet; **dirt**.

**Adj.excretory**; purgative, laxative; diuretic; menstrual; anal, urinary; watery; mucous; cast-off.

**Vb.excrete**, secrete; pass, move; defecate; relieve oneself; urinate, piddle, pee; have a pee, take a leak; make water, spend a penny; wet oneself; sweat, perspire, steam, glow, **be hot**; salivate, slobber, snivel; cough, spit; weep, **exude**; **be hungry**; **be angry**; cast, slough, **doff**.

## 298 Insertion: forcible ingress

**N.insertion**, parenthesis, **interjection**; **addition**; introduction; injection, shot, **perforation**; infusion, enema; insert, inset; stuffing, **lining**.

**immersion**, dip, bath, **plunge**; baptism, **Christian rite**; burial, burial at sea.

**Adj.inserted**, additional; intermediate.

**Vb.insert**, introduce, intrude; transfix, run through, **pierce**; load; pocket, stow; impel; inlay, inset, **line**; mount, frame, **circumscribe**; **add**; interpose, **put between**; let fall; putt; pot, hole; bury; sheathe, encapsulate, encase, **cover**.

**infuse**, instil, **mix**; impregnate, **infiltrate**; transfuse, decant, **transpose**; inject, **pierce**.

**implant**, plant, transplant; graft, engraft, bud; inoculate, vaccinate; embed, bury; impact, dovetail, **join**.

**immerse**, bathe, steep, souse, marinate, soak, **drench**; duck, dip, **lower**; submerge, flood; immerse oneself, **plunge**.

**299 Extraction: forcible egress**

N. extraction, removal, **displacement**; abortion; **destruction**; liberation; **deliverance**; forceps delivery; expression; suction, aspiration; pull, tug, wrench, **traction**; mining; fishery; essence, extract.

extractor; miner; wrench, forceps, pincers, pliers, tweezers, **nippers**; mangle; corkscrew, screwdriver, **opener**; lever, **pivot**; scoop, spoon, shovel; pick, pickaxe; rake; toothpick; vacuum cleaner; excavator, dredge, dredger; syringe; suction pump.

Adj. **extracted**.

Vb. **extract**, remove, pull, **draw**; elicit, educe; unfold, **evolve**; pluck; withdraw, excise, excavate, mine, quarry, unearth; dredge; expel, **eject**; extort; express, milk, tap; aspirate, suck, void, pump; eliminate, uproot, eradicate, extirpate, **destroy**; prune, **render few**; distil; extricate, unravel, free, **liberate**; unpack, unload, **displace**; eviscerate, gut, **empty**; **uncover**; **select**.

**300 Passage: motion through**

N. **passage**, transmission; transportation, **transport**; passing, passing through; **transition**; trespass; transit, traverse, crossing, journey, patrol, land travel; osmosis, egress; right of way, **access**; stepping-stone, flyover, underpass, **bridge**; track, route, orbit, **path**; intersection, junction, **crossing**; channel, **conduit**.

passing along, passage, thoroughfare; traffic, road traffic, traffic movement, flow of traffic, circulation; walking, crossing, driving; traffic load, traffic density; traffic jam, procession, queue; **pedestrian, driver**; passerby.

**traffic control**, traffic engineering; highway code, **precept**; traffic lane, oneway street, dual carriageway, clearway, **road**; alternative route, **deviation**; white lines; street furniture, traffic lights, roundabout; pedestrian crossing, bollard, refuge, island; car park; lay-by; point duty, road patrol, speed trap; traffic police, traffic cop; traffic engineer; traffic warden, meter maid; lollipop man or lady.

Adj. **passing**.

Vb. **pass**, skirt, coast, **be near**; **move fast**, **be transient**; go past; pass along, circulate, weave; pass through, transit, traverse; shoot through, shoot a bridge, **navigate**; **emerge**; go through, percolate, permeate, **pervade**; patrol, beat, scour; penetrate, infiltrate, **enter**; bore, perforate, **pierce**; thread, thread through, string, **connect**; rake; open a way, force a passage; squeeze through, **progress**; cross, go across, make a crossing, **arrive**; wade across, ford; get through, get past, negotiate, pass beyond, **overstep**; **turn back**; cut across, **obstruct**; straddle, bestride; bridge, **cover**; carry across, transmit, **send**; pass to, hand, reach, **transfer**.

Adv. **en passant**, by the way.

**301 Overstepping: motion beyond**

N. **overstepping**, going beyond, **passage**; excursion, **deviation**; trespass, **guilty act**; infraction; **desire**; ribbon development; **exaggeration**.

Adj. **surpassing, superior**; too strong; excessive, exorbitant.

Vb. **overstep**, overpass; pass, leave behind; go beyond, go too far; exceed; overrun, override, overshoot, aim too high; overlap; surmount, **leap**; cross, **pass; fill**; overdo, **exaggerate**; strain, stretch, stretch a point; overestimate, **overrate**; **be intemperate**; oversleep, be late.

**encroach,** invade, **attack;** infringe, transgress, trespass, **be illegal;** poach, **steal;** squat, usurp, **appropriate; intrude;** overlap; erode, **impair;** infest, overrun; overflow, flood, **drench.**

**outdo,** exceed, surpass, outclass; transcend, rise above, **be superior;** go one better, outbid; outwit, overreach, **deceive;** outmanoeuvre, outflank; **move fast;** outrun, outdistance, distance; overhaul, overtake, shoot ahead; lap, leave standing, **outstrip;** leave behind, race, beat, beat hollow, **defeat.**

## 302 Shortfall

**N. shortfall;** a minus, deficit, short measure, shortage, loss; leeway, drift, **deviation;** default; **lost labour; failure;** fault, defect, shortcoming, **blemish;** something missing, want, lack, need, **requirement.**

**Adj. deficient,** short, short of, minus, wanting, lacking, missing; substandard; undermanned, understaffed, below establishment; perfunctory, **incomplete;** inadequate, **insufficient;** failing, running short, **scarce;** below par, **imperfect.**

**Vb. fall short;** lack, want, be without, **require;** miss; lag, **be late;** stop short; fall behind, lose ground, slip back; slump, collapse, **regress;** fall through, come to nothing, fail, **miscarry; waste effort; disappoint.**

**Adv. behindhand,** in arrears; not enough; far from it; in vain.

## 303 Ascent: motion upwards

**N. ascent,** ascension, lift, upward motion; defiance of gravity; takeoff, lift-off; spiral; **aeronautics;** culmination, **summit;** rising, uprising, rise, upturn; upsurge, crescendo, **increase;** rising air, rising current, thermal; sunrise, dawn, **morning;** mountaineering; **attack;** jump, vault, pole jump, leap; bounce, **recoil;** rising ground, hill, **high land;** gradient, slope, ramp, **incline;** rising pitch, **musical note;** means of ascent, stairs, steps, stile, flight of stairs, staircase, landing; ladder, companionway; rope ladder; stair, step, tread, rung; lift, escalator; fire escape, **means of escape.**

**climber,** mountaineer; steeplejack; rocket, lark, skylark; geyser, fountain, **stream.**

**Adj. ascending;** rampant; floating, **light;** airborne; uphill, steep, **vertical.**

**Vb. ascend,** rise; defy gravity; become airborne, **fly;** gain height, mount, soar, spiral, climb; surface, break water; spring, vault, leap; bounce, **recoil; grow;** curl upwards; tower, aspire, spire, **be high;** gush, spout, jet, play; rear, ramp, **be vertical; lift oneself;** trend upwards, steepen, **be oblique.**

**climb;** mount; mountaineer; clamber, scramble, climb like a monkey; surmount, top, breast, conquer, scale, **be high;** attack; go upstairs, climb a ladder; mount (a horse).

**Adv. up,** uphill, upstairs; upwards, **aloft;** ever higher.

## 304 Descent

**N. descent,** declension, declination, **deviation;** cadence; landing; downward trend, spiral, decline, drop, slump, **decrease;** sunset; comedown; downfall, collapse, **fall;** trip, stumble; lurch, capsize; tumble, crash, spill, fall; cropper, swoop, stoop, pounce; dive, header, **plunge;** nosedive, **aeronautics;** landing; **arrival;** subsidence, landslide, avalanche; **wind;** downpour, shower, **rain;** cascade, **water-**

fall; slope, tilt, dip, **incline**; chute, slide, helter-skelter; precipice, sheer drop; mining; pot-holing; tumbler; plunger, **diver**; miner, sapper, **excavator; soldier**.

**Adj. descending**; tumbledown; submersible.

**Vb. descend**, decline, abate, ebb, **decrease**; reach a lower level, slump, fall, drop, sink; sink like a lead balloon, **weigh**; **infiltrate**; touch bottom, **be low; be inferior**; precipitate, settle, set; collapse; subside, slip, give way; droop, sag, swag, **hang**; draw, have draught; submerge, dive, **plunge; drown, founder; go underground**; burrow, bore, tunnel, mine, sap; undermine, **make concave**; parachute; swoop, stoop, **pounce**; lose height, swing low; alight, light, perch, **land**; lower oneself; dismount; toboggan; fall like rain, shower, cascade, drip, **rain**; take a lower place, **regress**; dip, duck, **stoop**; flop, plop.

**tumble**, fall; topple, overbalance, capsize; slip, trip, stumble, stagger, totter, lurch, tilt, droop, **be oblique**; pitch, toss, roll; take a header, dive, **plunge**; take a running jump, precipitate oneself, **leap**; take a fall, come a cropper, fall prostrate; plop, plump; slump, sprawl; spiral, nosedive, crash.

**Adv. down**, downwards; downhill, downstairs, downstream.

## 305 Elevation

**N. elevation**, erection, uplift, upheaval; lift; hoist, boost; **aid**; exaltation, assumption; uprising, upswing, **ascent**; an elevation, eminence, **high land, prominence**; height above sea level, **height**.

**lifter**; yeast, **leaven**; lever, jack, **pivot**; dredger; crane, derrick, hoist, wind-

lass; winch, capstan; forklift, elevator, dumb waiter, escalator, lift, cable railway; hot air, gas, hydrogen, helium; spring, springboard, trampoline; scaffolding, platform, **stand**.

**Adj. elevated**, exalted; erectile; upright, erect, upstanding, rampant, **vertical**; lofty, sublime, **high**.

**Vb. elevate**, heighten, **make higher**; swell, leaven, **enlarge**; raise, erect, build; lift; uplift, prop, **support; make vertical**; raise aloft, wave; hoist, trice; weigh, trip (anchor); **extract**; chair, shoulder; exalt, **honour**; mount, **crown; promote**; give a lift, **aid**; sky, loft, lob, **propel**; bristle, **be vertical**.

**lift oneself**, arise, rise, **ascend; be vertical**.

**Adv. on**, on tip toe; on the back of.

**Int. upsy-daisy!**

## 306 Lowering

**N. lowering**, depression, **impulse; plunge**; reduction; **revolution**; overthrow; overturn, upset; precipitation, **propulsion**; a depression, dent, dip, hollow, **cavity**; low pressure, **weather**.

**obeisance**, reverence, bow, salaam, kowtow, **courtesy**; bob, duck, nod, **courteous act; respect**.

**Adj. lowered**, at a low ebb, **low**; prostrate, **supine; sedentary**, sitting, sitdown; submersible.

**Vb. lower**, depress, impel; close; **suppress**; lower, lower a flag, dip, halfmast, strike; deflate, puncture, flatten, squash, crush; let drop (see **let fall**); sink, scuttle, drown, **descend**; duck, souse, dip, **plunge; weigh**; capsize, tip, tilt, **invert**; crush, dent, hollow, **make concave**.

**let fall**, drop, shed; let go; pour, decant, **empty**; spill, slop, **moisten**; sprinkle, shower, scatter, dust, dredge; sow, broadcast, **disperse**; pitch or chuck overboard; precipitate, **propel**.

**fell**; trip, topple, tumble, overthrow; prostrate, spread-eagle, lay low, **flatten**; skittle, floor, drop, **impel**; raze, level, **demolish**; axe, **cut**; **blow**; undermine; wing, **shoot**.

**abase**, debase; demote, cashier, **depose**; humble, deflate, puncture, **humiliate**; crush, squash, **suppress**.

**sit down**, sit, squat; subside, sink, lower oneself; kneel, recline, **be horizontal**; roost, nest, **repose**; take a seat, seat oneself, park oneself; perch, alight, **descend**.

**stoop**, bend, bend forward, bend backward; lean forward; cringe, crouch, cower; slouch; bow, scrape, duck, bob; nod, make obeisance, salaam, prostrate oneself, kowtow, **show respect**; kneel, kneel to, genuflect.

**307 Leap**

**N. leap**; jump, hop, skip; spring, bound, vault; high jump, hop, skip and a jump; caper, gambol, frolic; kick, jeté; prance; springy step, light tread, **gait**; dance step; dance, reel, jig, Highland fling.

**jumper**; skipper, hopper; twister, rock 'n roller, **dance**; **entertainer**; kangaroo, goat, chamois, springbok; frog, grasshopper, flea; Jack-in-the-box, **plaything**.

**Adj. leaping**; skittish, frisky, fresh, **lively**; bouncing.

**Vb. leap**, jump, spring, bound, vault, hurdle, steeplechase; skip, hop, leapfrog, bob, bounce, rebound, buck, **oscillate**; trip, foot it, tread a measure, stamp, **dance**; caper, gambol, frisk, romp; prance, ramp, rear, plunge; cavort; start, give a jump; pounce; **ascend**; clear, flounce, flounder, jerk, writhe, **wriggle**.

**Adv. by leaps and bounds**; at a single bound.

**308 Plunge**

**N. plunge**, swoop, pounce, stoop, **descent**; nosedive, power dive, **aeronautics**; dive, header, swallow dive, dip; crash dive.

**diver**, frogman; dipper, **bird**; submariner; submarine; plunger, lead, plummet.

**Vb. plunge**, dip, duck, bathe, **be wet**; plump, plop; dive, make a plunge, take a header, go headfirst; welter, wallow; souse, immerse, drown; submerge, **descend**; sink, scuttle, **lower**; sound, fathom, **measure**.

**founder**, descend; drown, be deep; plummet, sink, sink like lead, **weigh**.

**309 Circuition: curvilinear motion**

**N. circuition**, circulation, wheeling, spiral, **rotation**; turning, turn, U-turn, **return**; orbit; lap; circuit, tour, round trip, full circle; figure of eight, loop; helix, **coil**; roundabout way, **circuit**.

**circler**; mariner; roundsman; **sailor**, patrolman or -woman; moon, satellite, **planet**.

**Adj. circuitous**, ecliptic; peripatetic; circumflex; devious, **roundabout**.

**Vb. circle**, circulate; compass, circuit, lap; tour; go round, skirt; circumnavigate; turn, round, double a point, round a corner, corner, revolve, orbit; wheel, spiral, come full circle, **rotate**; turn round, put about, **turn back**; draw a circle, describe a circle, **circumscribe**; curve, wind, twist, **meander**; make a detour, **circuit**.

**310 Rotation: motion in a continued circle**

**N. rotation**; revolution, full circle; circulation; spin; rolling, **progression**;

spiral, roll, spin, turn, twirl, pirouette, waltz, **dance**; whirl, whirr; dizzy round, rat race; vertigo.

**vortex**, whirl; whirlwind, tornado, cyclone, **gale**; whirlpool, swirl, **eddy**; maelstrom, Charybdis; smoke ring, **loop**.

**rotator**, rotor, spinner; top, roundabout, merry-go-round; churn, whisk; lathe, circular saw; flywheel, wheel of Fortune, **wheel**; gyroscope, turntable; gramophone record, disc; wind pump, windmill, fan, sail; propeller, prop, screw; turbine, capstan; swivel, hinge; spit, jack; spindle, axle, axis, shaft, **pivot**; reel, roller, **cylinder**; rolling stone, planet, satellite, **wanderer**.

**Adj. rotary**, cyclic; dizzy.

**Vb. rotate**, revolve, orbit, **circle**; turn right round; spin, spin like a top, twirl, pirouette; corkscrew, **twine**; gyrate, waltz, wheel; whirl, whirr, hum, **resound**; mill around, swirl, eddy, **flow**; bowl, trundle; set rolling, roll, roll along; twirl, twiddle; churn, whisk, **mix**; turn, crank, wind, reel, spool, spin; slew, slew round, swing round, furl, **fold**; scroll.

**Adv. round and round**, clockwise, anti-clockwise, counterclockwise.

**311 Evolution: motion in a reverse circle**

**N. evolution**, unrolling, unfolding; dénouement; development, **growth**.

**Adj. evolving**.

**Vb. evolve**, unfold, unroll, unwind, explicate, disentangle, **unravel**; develop, **become**; roll back, **open**.

**312 Oscillation: reciprocating motion**

**N. oscillation**; harmonic motion; vibration, tremor; rhythm; pulse, beat, throb; flutter; breathing, **respiration**; undulation, wave motion, frequency, frequency band, wavelength, **radiation**; sound wave, **wave**; seismic disturbance, earthquake, tremor, **violence**; seismology, seismograph; oscillator; pendulum, bob, yoyo.

**fluctuation**; shuttle service; rolling; roll, pitch, lurch, stagger, reel; shake, nod, wag, dance; springboard; swing, seesaw; rocker; shuttlecock, shuttle.

**Adj. oscillating**, vibrant; earth-shaking, seismic; pendulous, groggy; rhythmic, **periodical**.

**Vb. oscillate**; **radiate**; wave, undulate; vibrate, pulsate, pulse, beat, drum; tick, throb, palpitate; respire, pant, heave, **breathe**; play, sway, nod; swing, dangle, **hang**; seesaw, rock; lurch, reel, stagger, totter, teeter, waddle, wobble, wiggle, waggle, wag; bob, bounce, dance, **leap**; toss, roll, pitch, tumble, wallow; rattle, chatter, shake; flutter, quiver, shiver; flicker, **shine**; echo, **resound**.

**fluctuate**, alternate, reciprocate; shuttle; slosh about.

**brandish**, wave, wag, waggle, shake, flourish; pump; flutter, **agitate**.

**Adv. to and fro**; side to side; zigzag, seesaw; like a yoyo.

**313 Agitation: irregular motion**

**N. agitation**, irregular motion; broken water, rolling, **roughness**; flicker, twinkle, **flash**; sudden motion, start, jump, **lack of expectation**; hop, **leap**; shake, jig, jiggle; toss, **propulsion**; shock, jar, jolt, jerk, judder, bounce, bump, **impulse**; nudge, dig, jog, **gesture**; vibration, thrill, throb, pulse, flutter; shudder, shiver; quiver, quaver, tremor; fever; turning; rock 'n roll, **activity**; itch; twitch, grimace; disquiet, **worry**, trepidation, twitter, flap; shivers, jitters; aspen, aspen leaf.

spasm; twitch, tic; lockjaw, tetanus; cramp; **pang**; paroxysm, access, orgasm, **frenzy**; fit, epilepsy; pulse, throb; attack, seizure, stroke.

**commotion**, turbulence, tumult, **turmoil**; hurly-burly, hubbub; fever, flurry, rush, bustle, **haste**; furore, **frenzy**; fuss, bother, kerfuffle; racket, din; stir, ferment, fermentation, **bubble**; ground swell, heavy sea, **wave**; squall, tempest, thunderstorm, **storm**; whirlpool, **vortex**; whirlwind, **gale**; disturbance, atmospherics.

**Adj. agitated**, **active**; feverish, fevered, restless; scratchy, jumpy, all of a twitter, **nervous**; breathless; itchy; spasmodic, spastic; skittish **lively**; flighty; shaky, tremulous.

**Vb. be agitated**, ripple, boil, **bubble**; stir, move, dash; shake, tremble, quiver, quaver, shiver; have a fever, throw a fit; writhe, squirm, twitch, **wriggle**; toss, turn, toss about, kick, plunge, rear, **be violent**; flounder, flop, wallow, roll, reel, pitch, **fluctuate**; sway, **be oblique**; pulse, beat, thrill, vibrate, judder, shudder; wag, waggle, wobble, stagger, lurch, dodder, totter, teeter, dither, **oscillate**; whirr, whirl, **rotate**; jig around, jump about, hop, bob, bounce, dance, **leap**; flicker, twinkle, gutter, sputter, **shine**; flap, flutter, twitter, start, jump; throb, pant, palpitate, miss a beat, **be excited**; bustle, rush, mill around, **rampage**; ramp, roar, **be angry**.

**agitate**, disturb, rumple, ruffle, **derange**; discompose, perturb, worry, **trouble**; ripple, puddle, muddy; stir, **mix**; whisk, whip, beat, churn, **rotate**; shake; wag, waggle, wave, flourish, **brandish**; flutter, fly (a flag), jog, jiggle, jolt, nudge, dig; jerk, pluck, twitch.

**effervesce**, froth, spume, foam, **bubble**;

boil, seethe, simmer, sizzle, spit, **be hot**; ferment, work.

**Adv. jerkily**; by fits and starts with a hop, skip and a jump; spasmodically.

## 314 Materiality

**N. materiality**, empirical world, world of experience; material existence, world of nature; physical being, physical condition, **existence**; **world**; solidity, **density**; weight, **gravity**; personality, individuality, **speciality**; embodiment, incarnation, reincarnation; materialism, sensuality.

**matter**, stuff; prime matter; mass, material, fabric, body, frame, **structure**; substance; organic matter, flesh, plasma, protoplasm, **organism**; real world of nature, Nature.

**object**, inanimate object, still life; physical presence, body, real person, **person**; thing, gadget, something, commodity, article, item; **mineral**; raw material.

**element**, elementary unit; principle, **origin**; earth, air, fire, water; unit of being; factor, ingredient, **component**; chemical element, basic substance; isotope; physical element, atom, molecule; elementary particle, electron, neutron, proton, quark; nucleus; quantum; ion.

**physics**, physical science, science of matter; natural history, **biology**; chemistry, mechanics, theory of relativity; thermodynamics; atomic physics, nuclear physics; applied physics, technology, **skill**; natural philosophy, **science**; chemist, physicist.

**Adj. material**; real, natural, solid, concrete, palpable, tangible, sensible, weighty; physical; objective, impersonal, neuter; **substantial**; incarnate; corporal, bodily, carnal; worldly, sensual.

**Vb. materialize**, substantiate; make real, body forth; embody, incarnate, personify.

## 315 Immateriality

**N. immateriality**; idealism; spirituality; animism; spiritualism; other world, world of spirits, eternity, **perpetuity**; idealist, **philosopher**; **ghost**.

**subjectivity**, personality, myself, me, yours truly, **self**; ego, id; Conscious, Unconscious; psyche, higher self, **spirit**.

**Adj. immaterial**, without mass; incorporate; abstract, **mental**; shadowy, **insubstantial**; imponderable, intangible; disembodied; unearthly, transcendent; psychic; spiritual, otherworldly, **religious**; personal, subjective; illusory, **imaginary**.

**Vb. disembody**, spiritualize, dematerialize.

## 316 Universe

**N. universe, whole**; world, creation, sum of things, **matter**; cosmos, macrocosm, microcosm; outer space, void; big bang theory, **start**.

**world**; home of man; earth; middle earth, globe, sphere; biosphere; terrestrial surface, crust; plate tectonics, **land**; **ocean**; atlas, **map**; Old World, New World, **region**; geocentric system, personal world, **circumstance**.

**heavens**, sky, welkin, ether, hemisphere; firmament, vault of heaven; night sky, northern lights; **glow**.

**star**, heavenly body; sidereal sphere, host of heaven; constellation, Great Bear, Plough, Big Dipper, Orion, Southern Cross; starlight; main sequence; blue star, red star; double star, binary; multiple star; variable star; giant, red giant; dwarf, X-ray

star, **radiation**; quasar, pulsar, neutron star, black hole; nova, supernova; Pole Star, North Star; Dog star; Milky Way, Galaxy; star cluster, galaxy, island universe; stellar motion, radial velocity.

**nebula**; cosmic dust, interstellar matter.

**zodiac**, ecliptic; house, mansion.

**planet**, asteroid; Mercury; Venus, morning star, Hesperus; Mars, red planet; Earth, Jupiter, Saturn, Uranus, Neptune, Pluto; comet, wandering star; **rotation**.

**meteor**, fireball; meteorite; meteoroid; meteor shower; radiant point.

**sun**, orb of day, eye of heaven; midnight sun; mock sun; sunlight; granule, sun spot, prominence, solar flare, corona; solar wind; Sol; solar system.

**moon**, satellite; new moon, mock moon; crater, mare; parish lantern; moonlight, moonshine.

**satellite**, moon; earth satellite, weather satellite; space station; space shuttle, **spaceship**; astronaut.

**astronomy**, star lore, stargazing; astrophysics; astrology, horoscope, **divination**; observatory, planetarium; **telescope**; astronomical telescope; transit instrument; radio telescope, dish; **photography**; celestial globe, astrolabe; astronomer, astrophysicist; stargazer.

**uranometry**; right ascension, declination, hour; hour circle, ecliptic; celestial pole, celestial equator; equinox, first point of Aries; solstice, galactic latitude or longitude; node; precession.

**cosmography**, cosmology.

**earth sciences**, geography, oceanography; geology.

**Adj. cosmic**, universal; interstellar, interplanetary; galactic.

celestial, heavenly; sidereal; stellar; solar; lunar; nebulous; geocentric; meteoric.

telluric, terrestrial; polar; worldwide, world, global, international, universal, spacious; worldly, earthly.

astronomic, astronomical, stargazing; telescopic.

geographic, geographical, oceanographic; geological; geodetic.

Adv. under the sun, here below.

## 317 Gravity

N. gravity, gravitation, force of gravity; gravity feed; weight, bulk; specific gravity; pressure; displacement, draught; load, freight; burden; ballast, offset; mass, lump, solid body; lump of, weight of, mass of; plummet, diver; weight, bob, lead, stone, millstone; statics.

weighing; equipoise; avoirdupois weight, grain, carat, scruple; ounce, pound, stone, quarter, hundredweight, ton; kilogram; megaton; axle load, laden weight.

scales; balance, pan, scale, weight; platform scale, weighbridge.

Adj. weighty, heavy, ponderous; leaden; cumbersome, unwieldy; massive, dense; pressing, incumbent; with a weight of; weighted, loaded, laden, charged; top-heavy, unequal.

Vb. weigh, have weight, balance, be equal; compensate; outweigh, overbalance, predominate; wallow, sink, settle, founder, descend; weigh heavy, press, hang like a millstone, lower; load, hinder; measure; weigh oneself.

make heavy, weight; charge, burden, overweight, overload, load; gain weight, be large.

Adv. weightily, heavily; like a lead balloon.

## 318 Lightness

N. lightness; air, ether, rarity; defiance of gravity, ascent; feather, thistledown, cobweb, gossamer; fluff, dust, straw, insubstantial thing; cork, buoy; balloon, bubble; hot air, helium.

leaven; ferment, enzyme, yeast.

Adj. light, underweight, deficient; lightweight, featherweight; portable, handy, little; weightless, without weight, lighter than air; imponderable; sublime, airy, volatile, rare; doughy, barmy, yeasty; floating; feathery.

Vb. be light, defy gravity, surface, float, swim; drift, waft, glide, be airborne, fly; soar, hover, ascend.

lighten, make light, make lighter, reduce weight, case, disencumber; lighten ship, throw overboard, jettison, empty; gasify, aerate; leaven, work; raise, elevate.

## 319 Density

N. density, solidity, consistency; thickness, concentration; hardness; cohesion, coherence; relative density, specific gravity.

condensation, concentration; constipation; thrombosis; sedimentation; precipitation; condenser, compressor, gelatine, rennet, pepsin.

solid body, solid; block, mass, matter; knot, nugget, lump; condensation, nucleus, hard core; aggregate, conglomerate; concrete, cement; stone, crystal, rock; precipitate, deposit, sediment, silt, clay, cake, clod, clump; bone; gristle, cartilage; curd, clot, solid mass, phalanx, serried ranks; forest, thicket; wall, obstacle.

Adj. dense, thick, crass; close, heavy, stuffy (air); foggy, murky, to be cut with a knife; lumpy; consistent, monolithic; firm, knotty, gnarled;

substantial, massive, **weighty**; concrete, solid, frozen, crystalline; compact, **full**; thickset, thick, bushy, luxuriant; serried, **rigid**; impenetrable, impermeable, impervious; indivisible, **strong**.

**indissoluble**, insoluble; sedimentary.

**solidifying**, binding; styptic, astringent.

Vb. **be dense**, become solid, solidify, consolidate; conglomerate, cement, **cohere**; condense, form a core or kernel; thicken; precipitate, deposit; freeze, **be cold**; set, jell; congeal, coagulate, clot, curdle; cake, crust; petrify, ossify, **harden**; compact, compress, contract, squeeze; pack, cram, load; mass, crowd, **bring together**; bind, constipate; precipitate, deposit.

## 320 Rarity

N. **rarity**, low pressure, vacuum; lack of substance; ether, gas, **air**; pressure reduction.

Adj. **rare**, tenuous, thin, fine, subtle; flimsy, slight, **insubstantial**; spongy, **elastic**; rarefied; void, hollow, **empty**; **light**; **immaterial**; straggly.

Vb. **rarefy**, expand, dilate; make a vacuum, exhaust, **empty**; attenuate, refine, thin; dilute, adulterate, **weaken**; gasify.

## 321 Hardness

N. **hardness**, resistance; rigour; temper; grit, stone, pebble; flint, silica, quartz, granite, marble, diamond, **rock**; adamant, metal; steel, iron, hardware, stoneware; cement, concrete, brick; block, board, heartwood; hardwood, teak, oak, **wood**; bone, gristle, cartilage; callus, corn; horn, ivory; crust, shell, hard core, hard centre; brick wall; stiffener, starch, wax; whalebone, corset, splint, **prop**.

**hardening**; stiffening, backing; sclerosis.

Adj. **hard**; **strong**; armoured; proof; iron, steel, steely; sun-baked; stony, rocky, flinty; gravelly, pebbly; crystalline, vitreous, glassy; horny, callous; bony; **tough**; icy, frozen, frozen solid.

**rigid**, stubborn, intractable; firm, inflexible, unbending; starchy; musclebound, **clumsy**; tense, taut, tight, set, solid; crisp, **brittle**; stiff, stark.

Vb. **harden**, steel, **strengthen**; temper, toughen; crisp, bake, **heat**; petrify, ossify; calcify, **be dense**; freeze, **refrigerate**; stiffen, back, bone, starch, wax (a moustache), **tighten**.

## 322 Softness

N. **softness**; compliance; suspension; **marsh**; butter, grease, oil, wax, putty, paste, clay, dough, soap, plastic; padding, wadding, pad, **lining**; cushion, pillow, armchair, feather bed, **euphoria**; velvet, plush, fluff, fleece, hair; **plumage**; snow, snowflake.

Adj. **soft**, tender, **edible**; melting, **fluid**; yielding; springy, sprung, **elastic**; pneumatic, podgy; waxy, doughy; spongy, soggy, mushy, **marshy**; pithy; squashy, juicy; fleecy, **downy**; grassy; silky, **smooth**; limp; flaccid, flabby, floppy; unstrung, slack, loose; emollient.

**flexible**, whippy; pliable; ductile, malleable, tractable, plastic; **elastic**; lithe, willowy, supple, double-jointed; **athletic**.

Vb. **soften**, render soft; mellow, **mature**; oil, grease, **lubricate**; knead, massage, mash, pulp, squash; macerate, steep, **drench**; melt, thaw, **liquefy**; cushion, pillow; relax, **disunite**; yield, give, give way, relax, bend, unbend, **be elastic**.

**323 Elasticity**

N. **elasticity**, give, stretch; spring; suspension; bounce, recoil; rubber; guttapercha; whalebone; elastic; rubber band, rubber ball; gum.

Adj. **elastic**, stretchy, tensile; rubbery, springy, resilient; sprung, ductile, **soft**.

Vb. **be elastic** - tensile etc. adj. bounce, spring, spring back, **recoil**; stretch, give.

**324 Toughness**

N. **toughness**, strength; cohesion, **coherence**; leather, gristle, cartilage, **hardness**.

Adj. **tough**, durable, **strong**; tenacious, clinging, sticky; shockproof; weatherbeaten; hardboiled, overdone; stringy, sinewy, woody, fibrous; rubbery, leathery, indigestible, inedible; stubborn, **rigid**.

Vb. **be tough**, resist fracture; toughen, tan; temper, anneal, **strengthen**.

**325 Brittleness**

N. **brittleness**; frailty, **weakness**; bubble, eggshell, pie crust, matchwood, shale, slate; glass, porcelain, **pottery**; glasshouse, house of cards, sandcastle, **weak thing**.

Adj. **brittle**, rigid; fragile; papery, like parchment; shivery; crumbly, **powdery**; crisp, short, flaky; splitting; frail, delicate, flimsy, eggshell, **weak**; crazy, **insubstantial**; tumbledown, **dilapidated**; ready to break, ready to burst, explosive.

Vb. **be brittle**, fracture, **break**; crack, snap; star, craze; chip, split, shatter, shiver, fragment; splinter; burst, fly, explode; give way, crash, **tumble**; deteriorate; wear thin; crumble.

Int. fragile! with care!

**326 Structure. Texture**

N. **structure**, pattern, plan; complex, syndrome, **whole**; mould, shape, build, **form**; constitution, make-up, set-up, content, substance, **composition**; make, works, workings; architecture, tectonics; fabric, work, brickwork, stonework, woodwork; substructure, superstructure, **edifice**; scaffold, framework, chassis, shell, **frame**; cleavage; body, person, physique, anatomy, **organism**; bony structure, skeleton, bone, horn; science of structure, physiology, histology, **biology**.

texture, network, **crossing**; tissue, fabric, stuff, **textile**; staple, denier, **fibre**; web, weave; nap, pile, **hair**; grain, grit; **roughness**, surface; feel, **touch**.

Adj. **structural**, organic.

textural, textile, woven; silky, satiny, smooth; **rough**; fine, delicate, filmy; coarse, homespun, **hairy**.

**327 Powderiness**

N. **powderiness**; dirt; attrition, erosion; abrasion, **friction**; fragmentation, frosting.

powder, talc, chalk; pollen, spore; dust, soot, ash, **dirt**; flour; grist, meal, bran; sawdust, filings; powdery deposit; scurf, dandruff; debris, detritus; sand, grit, gravel, shingle; grain, seed, crumb, **piece**; granule, grain of powder, **small thing**; flake, snowflake; smut, smoke, smoke cloud, fog, smog, **cloud**; dust storm, dust devil, fen blow, **storm**.

pulverizer, miller; roller; mill, millstone; pestle; hand mill, grater, grindstone; file; abrasive, sandpaper, emery paper; molar, **tooth**; chopper, **sharp edge**; sledgehammer, **hammer**; bulldozer, **ram**.

Adj. **powdery**; dusty, smoky, **dirty**;

sandy, **dry**; farinaceous, mealy; gravelly; flaky; ground; crumbly, **brittle**.

**Vb. pulverize**, powder, granulate; crush, mash, smash, shatter, fragment, disintegrate, **break**; grind, mill, mince, beat, bruise, pound, bray; knead; crumble, crumb, crunch, scrunch, **chew**; chip, flake, grate, scrape, rasp, file, abrade, **rub**; weather, rust, erode, **decompose**.

## 328 Friction

**N. friction**, drag; attrition, rubbing against, rubbing together, **collision**; erasure; abrasion; erosion, **destruction**; scrape, graze, scratch; rub; polish, elbow grease; shampoo, massage, facial; pumice stone; rubber; whetstone; masseur, **beautician**.

**Adj. rubbing**, grating; abrasive.

**Vb. rub**, rub against, strike (a match); gnash, grind; fret, fray, chafe, gall; graze, scratch, bark, **wound**; abrade; skin, flay; scuff, scrape, scrub, scour, burnish; brush, towel, curry, **clean**; polish, buff, **smooth**; erase, **obliterate**; gnaw, erode, **consume**; rasp, file, grind; knead, shampoo, massage; anoint, **lubricate**; wax, grate, be rusty, catch, stick, snag; stroke, **caress**; iron, **smooth**.

## 329 Lubrication

**N. lubrication**; an ointment, unction, oiling.

**lubricant**, graphite, black lead; wax, grease, **oil**; soap, lather, **cleanser**; saliva, spit, spittle; ointment, salve, **balm**; emollient, **unguent**.

**Adj. lubricated**; smooth-running, well-oiled; silent.

**Vb. lubricate**, oil, grease, wax, soap, lather; butter, **grease**; anoint, pour balm.

## 330 Fluidity

**N. fluidity**, liquidity; **water**; haemophilia; viscosity; hydraulics; fluid mechanics.

**fluid, gas**; liquid; water, water; drink, **draught**; milk, whey; juice, sap, latex; humour, mucus, saliva, **excrement**; serum, lymph, plasma; pus, matter; gore (see **blood**); dropsy, **disease**.

**blood**, claret; **life**; bloodstream, circulation; red blood, **vitality**; blue blood, **nobility**; gore; clot, **solid body**; corpuscle; lymph, plasma, serum, haemoglobin; blood group, Rhesus factor; blood count.

**Adj. fluid, amorphous**; liquid; clear; soluble, melting; viscous; fluent, running, **flowing**; runny, **watery**; succulent, juicy, squashy; pussy, **toxic**.

**sanguineous**; bloody, gory, bleeding.

## 331 Gaseousness

**N. gaseousness**, flatulence, **wind**; volatility; aerodynamics.

**gas**, vapour, elastic fluid; ether, **air**; miasma, **egress**; **wind**; fumes, reek, smoke; steam, water vapour, **cloud**; methane, **fuel**; marsh gas, **poison**; damp, **bladder**; balloon, **airship**; gasworks; gas plant, **workshop**; gasholder, **storage**; neon light, **lamp**; gas stove, **furnace**; gas meter, **meter**.

**Adj. gaseous**; volatile; aerial, airy, **airy**; carbonated, **bubbly**; gassy, windy; pneumatic.

**Vb. gasify**, vapour, steam, emit vapour, **emit**; aerate.

## 332 Liquefaction

**N. liquefaction**; fusion, **mixture**; dissolution; thaw, melting, **heating**; solvent, flux; liquidizer.

**solution**, infusion; suspension; flux.

**Adj. liquefied**, molten; runny; solvent; soluble, **fluid**.

**Vb. liquefy**, liquidize, render liquid, clarify, **make flow**; dissolve, run, **flow**; thaw, melt, smelt, **heat**; fuse, render, clarify; leach; cast, found.

## 333 Vaporization

**N. vaporization**, atomization; exhalation, **cloud**; evaporation, distillation; steaming, volatility.
**vaporizer**; spray, aerosol; retort, still, distillery.
**Adj. vaporific**; gassy, smoky; volatile.
**Vb. vaporize**, evaporate; **gasify**; distil, sublime, sublimate, exhale, transpire, emit vapour, **emit**; smoke, fume, reek, steam; fumigate, spray; **make a spray**.

## 334 Water

**N. water**, HR2O; heavy water DR2O; **hard water**; **drinking water**, **tap water**, **mineral water**, **soft water**; water vapour, steam, **cloud**; rain water, **rain**; spring water, **stream**; holy water, **ritual object**; weeping, sweat, saliva, **fluid**; high water, high tide, low water, **wave**; standing water, **lake**; sea water, brine, **ocean**; water cure, **therapy**; bath water, bath, shower, douche, splash, **ablutions**; lotion, lavender water, **cosmetic**; damp, wet; jug, ewer, **vessel**; tap, standpipe, hydrant, **conduit**; hose; water supply, waterworks; well, **store**.
**Adj. watery**, aqueous, aquatic, **fluid**; **weak**; still; wet, moist, **humid**.
**Vb. add water**, water, adulterate, dilute, **weaken**; steep, soak, liquor; irrigate, drench, **moisten**; combine with water, hydrate; slake, **decompose**.

## 335 Air

**N. air**, gas; thin air, ether, **rarity**; cushion of air, air pocket; blast, **wind**; common air, oxygen, nitrogen, argon;

welkin, blue, blue sky, **cloud**; open air, open, exposure, **space**; sea air, ozone; fresh air; **airing**; air-conditioning; ventilator, blower, fan, **refrigerator**; air-filter, **cleanser**; humidifier.
**atmosphere**, stratosphere, ionosphere; radiation layer; aerospace; greenhouse effect, **heating**.
**weather**; fair weather; dry spell, heat wave, **heat**; doldrums; atmospheric pressure, anticyclone, high pressure; cyclone, depression, low pressure; rough weather, **storm**, **gale**; bad weather, **rain**; cold weather; changeable weather; meteorology; weather forecast, **prediction**; isobar, millibar; glass, mercury, barometer; vane, weathercock; weather ship, weather station, rain gauge; climate; climatology.
**pneumatics**, aerodynamics; barometer.
**Adj. airy**, **insubstantial**; aerial; pneumatic; inflated; breezy, **windy**; fresh; atmospheric; high-pressure, **dense**; **rare**; climatic.
**Vb. aerate**; air, expose, **dry**; ventilate, **clean**; fan, winnow, make a draught, **blow**; breathe.
**Adv. alfresco** out of doors, in the open.

## 336 Moisture

**N. moisture**, humidity, sap, juice, **fluid**; dew point; condensation, rising damp; saturation, saturation point; rainfall, wet weather, **rain**; damp, wet; spray, froth, foam, **bubble**; mist, fog, fog bank, **cloud**; Scotch mist, drizzle, drip, dew, drop, raindrop, teardrop; wet eyes; saliva, slobber, spit, spittle, **excrement**; ooze, slime, mud, squelch, fen, **marsh**; sop.
**moistening**, saturation, deluge, **rain**; sprinkling, sprinkle, aspersion; overflow, flood, **waterfall**; wash, bath,

ablutions; baptism, **Christian rite**.

**irrigator**, sprinkler; spray, rose; hose, syringe, squirt; pump, fire engine; swipe; water butt, dam, reservoir, **store**; sluice, water pipe, **conduit**.

**hygrometry**; rain gauge, **gauge**.

**Adj. humid**, wet, **watery**; **rainy**; damp, moist, dripping; dank, muggy, foggy, misty, **cloudy**; muddy, slimy, sloppy, squashy, **marshy**; fresh; juicy, **fluid**; gory, bloody.

**drenched**; sopping, soggy, sodden; wet through, sopping wet; waterlogged, awash.

**Vb. be wet**, be soggy, squelch, suck; slobber, salivate, sweat, perspire, **exude**; steam, reek, **emit**; percolate, seep, **infiltrate**; weep, bleed, stream; ooze, drip, leak; trickle, drizzle, rain, pour, **rain**; get wet; dip, duck, dive, **plunge**; bathe, wash; wallow; paddle, wade, ford.

**moisten**, wet, dampen; dilute, hydrate, **add water**; lick, lap, wash; splash, splatter; spill, slop; flood, spray, shower, spatter, sprinkle, syringe; dabble; baste, **infuse**.

**drench**, saturate; soak, deluge, wet through, make run with; leach; wash, bathe; sluice, slosh, rinse, **clean**; baptize, **perform ritual**; plunge, dip, duck, submerge, drown, **immerse**; swamp, flood, inundate; dunk, souse, steep; macerate, marinate; pickle, brine, **preserve**.

**irrigate**, water, hose, pump; inundate, flood, overflow, submerge; percolate, **infiltrate**; squirt, inject.

## 337 Dryness

**N. dryness**; thirst, **hunger**; drought, low rainfall, desert conditions; **desert**; dry climate, dry season; sun, **heat**.

**desiccation**; airing; drainage; **heating**; searing.

**dryer**; silica gel, sand, blotter; absorbent, absorbent material; mop, swab, sponge, towel, towelling; wringer, mangle; **hanger**; airing cupboard.

**Adj. dry**, thirsty, **hungry**; arid; sandy, dusty, **powdery**; bare, brown; desert; **colourless**; burnt, **hot**; sunny, fine, fair; waterproof; watertight, tight, snug, proof; dry-shod.

**Vb. be dry**, keep dry, wear waterproof clothing; keep watertight; evaporate; become dry.

**dry**, desiccate, freeze-dry; dehydrate; ditch, drain, suck dry, **empty**; mangle; spin-dry, air, evaporate; sun, expose to sunlight, sun-dry; smoke, kipper, cure; parch, scorch, bake, burn, **heat**; shrivel, bleach; mummify, **preserve**; **staunch**; blot, mop, sponge, **absorb**; swab, wipe, wipe dry.

## 338 Ocean

**N. ocean**, sea, blue, salt water, brine; waters, tide, **wave**; main, deep, deep sea; great waters; trackless deep, watery waste; herring pond, drink; sea lane, shipping lane; ocean floor, sea bed, sea bottom, ooze; Antarctic Ocean, Red Sea, Mediterranean, North Sea.

**sea god**, Neptune, Triton, Tethys; old man of the sea.

**sea nymph**, Nereid, siren; Calypso; mermaid; bathing beauty; water sprite, **fairy**.

**oceanography**; sea survey, Admiralty chart; bathyscaphe.

**Adj. oceanic**, pelagic; sea, marine, maritime; seaworthy, **seafaring**; submarine, underwater; **deep**.

**Adv. at sea**; afloat.

## 339 Land

**N. land**; earth, ground, crust, **world**; continent, mainland; hinterland; midland, inland, interior; delta, promontory, tongue of land, **projection**; isthmus, neck of land; terrain, **high land**; polder; **steppe**, **plain**; wilderness, **desert**; oasis, Fertile Crescent; isle, **island**; zone; country, district, tract, **region**; territory, estate; physical features, landscape, scenery; topography, geography, geology; landlubber, islander.

shore, coastline, **outline**; coast, **edge**; strand, beach, shingle; seaboard, seashore, seaside; sea cliff, sea wall; lido; bank, river bank, lea, water meadow.

soil, arable land, **farm**; pasture, **grassland**; deposit, moraine, loess, silt, alluvium; topsoil, sand, dust, subsoil; mould, humus; loam, clay, bole, marl; china clay, kaolin, **pottery**; flinty soil, gravel; stone, pebble, flint; turf, sod, clod, **piece**.

rock, cliff, scar, crag; stone, boulder; reef; stack; dyke, sill; igneous rock, granite, basalt; volcanic glass; magma, lava; sedimentary rock, sandstone, shale, limestone, chalk, conglomerate; schist, marble; massive rock, ore, **mineralogy**; precious stone, gem.

Adj. **territorial**, terrestrial, farming, **agrarian**; earthy, sandy; flinty, pebbly, gravelly, stony, rocky; marble, slaty; **seasonal**.

**coastal**, littoral, seaside; shore.

**inland**, midland, mainland, interior, central.

Adv. **on land**, overland, ashore.

## 340 Gulf: inlet

N. gulf, bay, cove, creek, reach, lagoon; natural harbour, road; inlet, outlet, fleet; sea loch; mouth, estuary; sound, strait, belt, gut, channel.

## 341 Lake.

N. **lake**, lagoon, land-locked water; loch, lough; fresh-water lake, inland sea, Dead Sea; broad; sheet of water, backwater; mud flat, wash, **marsh**; pool, tarn, mere, pond; stew; swimming pool, swimming bath; millpond; artificial lake, dam, reservoir, **storage**; well, **water**; basin, tank, cistern, sump, **sink**; ditch, **drain**; waterhole, puddle, splash, wallow.

Adj. lacustrine, land-locked.

## 342 Marsh

N. marsh, morass; flat, salt marsh, fen; moor; moss, bog, quagmire, quicksand; saltpan; wallow, slough, mire, mud; ooze; swamp, mangrove swamp.

Adj. marshy; moorish; boggy; squashy, spongy, **soft**; muddy, **dirty**; waterlogged.

## 343 Plain

N. **plain**; flood plain; river basin, **valley**; marsh; delta; waste, **desert**; tundra; ice plain, ice field, ice floe, **ice**; steppe, prairie, pampas; heath, common, wold, downs, moor, fell; plateau, tableland, **high land**; bush, range, open country, **space**; green belt, national park, **open space**.

grassland, pasture, pasturage, **animal husbandry**; field, meadow, mead, lea; chase, park, grounds; green, lawn, turf.

Adj. campestral, rural; flat, open, rolling.

## 344 Island

N. **island**, isle, islet; river island; lagoon island, atoll, reef, key; sandbank, bar; floating island, iceberg; peninsula; island continent; island universe, galaxy, **star**; archipelago; islander.

**Adj. insular,** sea-girt; isolated, marooned.

**345 Stream: water in motion**

**N. stream,** running water, watercourse, river, navigable river; tributary, branch, feeder; brook, burn, beck, gill, runnel; torrent, force; spring, fountain, fountainhead; **source;** jet, spout, gush; geyser, hot spring, well, **store.**

**current,** flow, set, flux, **progression;** egress; confluence; undercurrent, undertow, crosscurrent, rip tide; tide, tidal flow, tidal current; bore; race, millrace; tap, standpipe, hydrant, **conduit;** bloodstream, circulation.

**eddy,** whirlpool, swirl, maelstrom, vortex; surge, **recession;** wash, backwash, wake, **sequel.**

**waterfall,** falls, cataract; cascade, force, shoot, weir; water power; flush, chute, spillway, sluice; overflow, spill; fresh; flood, spate, deluge, cataclysm.

**wave,** wash, backwash; ripple, **furrow,** swell, billow, roller, breaker, surf, spume; tidal wave; bore; rip; broken water, **roughness;** sea, angry sea; undulation.

**rain,** rainfall, **moisture;** precipitation; drizzle, Scotch mist; sleet, hail; shower, downpour, deluge, cloudburst, thunderstorm, **storm;** flurry, **gale;** wet spell, foul weather; rainy season, monsoon; patter; rain gauge.

**Adj. flowing,** runny, fluid; fluent, affluent; tidal; making, running, coursing, racing; rolling; choppy, **rough;** sluggish, **slow;** sheeting, lashing, driving, dripping; **outgoing; incoming.**

**rainy,** showery, drizzly; wet, **humid.**

**Vb. flow,** run, course, pour; ebb, regurgitate, **regress;** swirl, eddy, **rotate;** surge, break, dash, ripple, wrinkle; roll, swell; buck, bounce, **leap;** gush, rush, spout, spew, jet, play, squirt, splutter; well, issue, **emerge;** pour, stream; trickle, dribble, **exude;** drip, drop, **descend;** lap, wash, slosh, splash, **moisten;** purl, trill, murmur, babble, bubble, burble, gurgle, glide, slide; overflow, cascade, flood, inundate, deluge, **drench; enter;** discharge itself; flow through, leak, ooze, percolate, **pass;** ooze, wind, **meander.**

**rain,** shower, stream, pour, pelt; snow, sleet, hail; fall, rain hard, pour with rain; sheet; patter, drizzle, drip, drop, spit, sprinkle; be wet.

**make flow, emit;** make or pass water, **excrete;** broach, tap, **open;** pour, spill, **let fall;** transfuse, decant, **transpose;** empty; water, **irrigate;** clear, clarify, melt, **liquefy.**

**staunch, dry;** apply a tourniquet; stop a leak, plug, **close;** stem, dam, **obstruct.**

**346 Conduit**

**N. conduit,** water channel, riverbed; trough, basin, canyon, ravine, gorge, **valley;** canal system; canal, channel, watercourse; ditch; trench, moat, runnel; Irish bridge; gutter, mill race; duct, aqueduct; plumbing, water pipe; main, pipe, hose; standpipe, hydrant, tap, spout, funnel, **tube;** valve, sluice, weir, lock, floodgate, spillway; chute, **waterfall;** pipeline; gullet, throat; neck (of a bottle); blood vessel, vein, artery, aorta, carotid; capillary.

**drain,** gutter, gargoyle; scupper, overflow, drainpipe; **outlet;** culvert; open drain, ditch, sewer, **sink;** intestine, colon; catheter.

**347 Wind: air in motion**

**N. wind, air;** draught, thermal; weather; blast, blow (see **breeze, gale**); air stream, current, crosswind, headwind; tailwind, following wind; air flow, slip stream; air pocket; calm air, **quietude**; cold draught, cold wind, icy blast; hot wind, sirocco; seasonal wind, monsoon; regular wind; north wind; south wind; east wind; west wind, westerly, Zephyr; wind god.

**anemometry**, aerodynamics; wind rose; wind gauge, weathercock, windsock.

**breeze**, zephyr; breath, breath of air, waft, whiff, puff, gust; light breeze, sea breeze.

**gale**, strong wind, blow, blast, gust, flurry, flaw; squall, sou'wester, hurricane, whirlwind, cyclone, tornado, twister, typhoon, **vortex**; thunderstorm, dust storm, dust devil, blizzard, **storm**; weather, gale force.

**blowing**, inflation; pump, bellows, windbag; woodwind, brass, **musical instrument**; blowpipe; exhaust pipe, exhaust, **outlet**.

**ventilation**, airing, **air**; draught; ventilator, **air pipe**; blower, fan, **refrigerator**.

**respiration**, breathing, expiration, inspiration; stomach wind, flatulence, belch; bellows; respirator, iron lung, oxygen tent; windpipe, **air pipe**; cough, croup, **respiratory disease**; sigh, sob, gulp, yawn; hard breathing; wheeze, rattle.

**Adj. windy**, airy, draughty, breezy, blowy; fresh; gusty, blustery, dirty, foul, stormy, tempestuous, boisterous, **violent**, windswept; stormbound; gassy.

**puffing**; stertorous; breathless; pulmonary; chesty.

**Vb. blow**, puff, blast; blow hard, blow a hurricane, rage, storm, **be violent**; wail, howl, roar; screech, scream, whistle, pipe, **shrill**; hum, moan, mutter, sigh, **sound faint**; wave, flap,

shake, flutter, **agitate**; draw, make a draught, ventilate, fan, **refrigerate**; blow along, waft, **propel**; veer, back, **deviate**; drop, abate.

**breathe**, respire, inhale; draw a deep breath; exhale; aspirate, puff, huff, whiff; sniff, sniffle, snuffle, snort; breathe hard, gasp, pant, heave; wheeze, sneeze, cough, **rasp**; sigh, sob, gulp, yawn; belch, burp.

**blow up**, inflate, dilate, **enlarge**; exhaust, **empty**.

## 348 Air pipe

**N. air pipe**, airway, air shaft, air well; wind tunnel, smoke tunnel; blowpipe, peashooter; windpipe, trachea, larynx; throat, gullet; nose, nostril, blowhole, nozzle, vent, mouthpiece, **orifice**; flue pipe, mouth organ, **organ**; gas main, gas pipe; tobacco pipe, briar, hookah, **tobacco**; funnel, flue, exhaust pipe, **chimney**; airbrick, air duct, ventilator, grating, louvre, air hole, **window**.

## 349 Semiliquidity

**N. semiliquidity**; thickness; emulsion, gore, albumen, mucus, phlegm, clot, **solid body**; pus, matter; juice, sap; soup, slop, gruel, cream; molten lava; oil slick; mud, slush, sludge, thaw, ooze, slime; silt, **marsh**.

**thickening**, **condensation**; starch, flour; gelatine, pectin.

**viscidity**, viscosity, **coherence**; glue, gluten, gum, **adhesive**; emulsion; size, paste, glaze, slip; gel, jelly; treacle, jam, syrup, honey, goo; wax, mastic, **resin**.

**Adj. semiliquid**, stodgy, starchy, thick, lumpy, **dense**; jellied, juicy, milky; mushy, sloppy, waterlogged, muddy, squashy, squidgy, **marshy**.

**viscid**, viscous, gummy, gooey; slimy,

clammy, sticky, tacky; jammy; treacly; mucous.

**Vb. thicken,** congeal, **be dense;** coagulate, **cohere;** emulsify; gel, jelly, jell; starch, **harden;** curdle, clot; churn, mash, pulp; muddy, puddle, **make unclean.**

## 350 Bubble. Cloud: air and water mixed

**N. bubble,** suds, soapsuds, lather, foam, froth; head, top; sea foam, spume, surf, spray, **moisture;** mousse, meringue, candyfloss; yeast, **leaven;** scum, **dirt;** fermentation, fizz.

**cloud,** scud, rack; cloudbank; rain cloud, cumulus, cirrus; mackerel sky; vapour, steam; haze, mist, fog, smog; film; **nebula.**

**Adj. bubbly;** effervescent, frizzy; foaming; frothy, soapy; yeasty, **light;** scummy, **dirty.**

**cloudy,** overcast; nebulous; thick, foggy, hazy, misty, **dim.**

**Vb. bubble,** spume, foam, froth, cream, form a head; mantle, scum; boil, simmer, fizzle, gurgle, **effervesce;** work, ferment, fizz, sparkle; aerate; steam.

**cloud,** overcast; be cloudy, **be dim.**

## 351 Pulpiness

**N. pulpiness;** poultice, pulp, pith, paste, putty, porridge, pap, puree; mush, mash, squash; dough, batter, sponge; soft fruit, jam; mousse, **bubble;** ooze, slush; wood pulp.

**Adj. pulpy;** mushy, **soft;** succulent, juicy, squashy, ripe; flabby, doughy, pasty; soggy, spongy, **marshy.**

## 352 Unctuousness

**N. unctuousness,** oiliness, greasiness, soapiness, **lubrication.**

**oil,** animal oil, vegetable oil, mineral oil, petroleum; refined oil, fuel oil, paraf-

fin, kerosene, petrol, gas, **fuel; lubricant.**

**fat,** grease; blubber, tallow; wax, beeswax; suet, lard, dripping, bacon fat, **cookery;** margarine, butter; cream; buttermilk; soap, **cleanser.**

**unguent,** salve, ointment; liniment, embrocation, lanolin; cream, cold cream, **cosmetic.**

**resin,** gum, gum arabic, myrrh, frankincense, camphor; amber, ambergris; pitch, tar, bitumen, asphalt; varnish, mastic, shellac, lacquer, japan; synthetic resin.

**Adj. fatty,** fat, adipose; sebaceous, waxy, waxen; buttery, milky, rich, **savoury.**

**unctuous,** greasy, oleaginous; dripping with oil; slippery.

**resinous;** tarry; gummy.

**Vb. grease,** oil, anoint, **lubricate;** baste; butter; resin.

## 353 Organisms: living matter

**N. organism,** organic matter; ecosystem; living matter, **life;** microscopic life, **microorganism;** cell, protoplasm; cytoplasm; nucleus; RNA, DNA; chromosome, gene, **heredity;** albumen, protein; enzyme; organic remains, **fossil.**

**biology,** microbiology; natural history, nature study; biochemistry, developmental biology, cytology; histology; anatomy, physiology, **structure; botany;** ecology; marine biology; genetics, eugenics, genetic engineering; evolution, natural selection; mechanism; naturalist.

**Adj. organic;** cellular.

**biological;** biogenetic; physiological, zoological.

## 354 Mineral: inorganic matter

**N. mineral**, mineral world, mineral kingdom; **inorganic matter**, **rock**; ore, metal, alloy, **a mixture**.

mineralogy, geology, petrology; metallurgy.

**Adj. inorganic**; inanimate; mineral; metallic.

## 355 Life

**N. life**, living, being alive, animate existence, being, **existence**; living being, being, soul, spirit; plant life, **vegetable life**; animal life; human life, **humankind**; gift of life, birth, nativity, **origin**; new birth, **revival**; life to come, **future state**; immortal life, **heaven**; animation; vitality, vital force, vital principle, life force; soul, **spirit**; beating heart, strong pulse; survival, longevity, **long duration**; animal spirits, animation, **moral sensibility**; wind, breath, breathing, **respiration**; vital air, breath of life; **essential part**; vital spark, vital flame; seat of life, heart, artery; vital necessity, staff of life, **food**; motherhood, fatherhood; sex, sexual activity; living matter, protoplasm, tissue; cell, **organism**; symbiosis, **association**; lifetime; life expectancy, life span, life cycle; viability, **possibility**.

**Adj. alive**, living, quick, live; breathing; **lively**; incarnate; above ground; tenacious of life; capable of life, viable; vital.

**born**, born alive; begotten; out of, by, **akin**; laid.

**Vb. live**, be alive, have life; respire, draw breath, **breathe**; exist, subsist, **be**; come to life, quicken, revive; survive, **be left**; cheat death, have nine lives; **dwell**.

**be born, begin**; fetch breath, be begotten.

vitalize, give birth to, beget, conceive, support life, **generate**; enliven, bring to life, **invigorate**; reanimate, **revive**; support life, provide a living; keep alive, **feed**.

## 356 Death

**N. death**, extinction; process of death, dying (see **decease**); Dance of Death, mortality; sentence of death, doom, knell, execution, martyrdom; deathblow, quietus, **killing**; decay; rest, long sleep, **quietude**; **heaven**; tomb; hand of death, nether regions, Hades, **hell**; Death; Angel of Death; Pluto; autopsy, **inquest**; mortuary, morgue, **cemetery**.

**decease**, clinical death, end of life, extinction, exit, demise, curtains, **end**; passing; natural death, quiet end, euthanasia, **euphoria**; release, welcome end; loss of life, fatality, fatal casualty; sudden death, untimely end; watery grave; fatal disease, mortal illness, **disease**; dying day, last hour; deathbed, deathwatch, death scene; last agony, last gasp, last breath, swan song, death rattle, **finality**; passing bell.

**the dead**, forefathers, **precursor**; **saint**; ghost; dead body, **corpse**; next world, **future state**; world of spirits, underworld; Hades, Stygian shore; happy hunting grounds.

**death roll**, mortality, fatality, death toll, death rate; bill of mortality, casualty list; death register, **list**; death certificate, **record**; obituary, death notice.

**Adj. dying**, mortal, ephemeral, perishable, **transient**; moribund; had it; going; sick unto death, **sick**; fated to die, fey.

**dead**; gone, gone before; long gone; born dead, stillborn; lifeless, breathless; still; extinct, inanimate, bereft of life;

stone dead, cold, stiff; kaput; beyond mortal ken; gone to Elysium; defunct, late, sainted, of sainted memory.

**Vb. die (see perish);** be dead, be gone, cease to be, cease to live; die young; die a natural death; decease; succumb, expire, stop breathing; fall asleep; pass; depart this life, **depart;** go to glory, reach a better world, awake to life immortal; croak, snuff it; cop it, have bought it; go west.

**perish,** become extinct; wilt, wither, come to dust, **decompose;** die hard; fall, be lost; become a martyr; die untimely; meet a sticky end, die a violent death; bleed to death; drown, **founder;** be put to death, suffer execution; commit suicide, **kill oneself.**

**Adv. post-obit,** post mortem.

**357 Killing: destruction of life**

**N. killing, destruction;** destruction of life; taking life, dealing death; blood sports, hunting, **chase;** blood-letting; selective killing, cull; mercy killing, euthanasia; murder, strangulation, hanging; ritual killing, sacrifice; martyrdom; crucifixion, execution, **capital punishment;** judicial murder, burning alive; deathblow, final stroke, quietus; violent death, fatal accident, fatal casualty, car crash, plane crash.

**homicide,** manslaughter; murder; regicide, parricide, patricide, matricide, fratricide; infanticide; genocide (see **slaughter**).

**suicide;** suttee, hara-kiri; mass suicide.

**slaughter,** bloodshed, carnage; wholesale murder, bloodbath, massacre, fusillade, holocaust; pogrom, purge, **destruction;** genocide, Final Solution; war, battle, **warfare;** Roman holiday, duel.

**slaughterhouse,** abattoir, shambles;

bullring, **arena;** field of battle; battlefield; field of blood; gas chamber.

**killer, man of blood;** soldier, **combatant;** butcher, knacker, huntsman, **hunter;** trapper, rodent officer; toreador, picador, matador, **athlete;** executioner, hangman; lynch mob; homicidal maniac, psychopath; headhunter, cannibal; beast of prey, maneater; block, gibbet, axe, guillotine, scaffold, **means of execution;** insecticide, fungicide, pesticide, poison, **bane.**

**murderer,** homicide; assassin; thug; hatchet man, gangster, gunman; bravo, desperado, cutthroat, **ruffian;** parricide, regicide; suicide.

**Adj. deadly,** killing, lethal; fell, mortal, fatal; capital; malignant, poisonous, **toxic;** unhealthy, **insalubrious,** inoperable, incurable.

**murderous,** homicidal; suicidal; internecine, trigger-happy; ensanguined, bloody, gory, red-handed; bloodthirsty, **cruel.**

**Vb. kill,** slay, take life, **destroy;** put to sleep; hang, behead, guillotine, electrocute, **execute;** stone, stone to death; lynch; send one to his account; deal a deathblow, give one his quietus; shed blood, knife, sabre, spear, lance, bayonet, stab, run through, **pierce;** pistol, **shoot;** strangle, garrotte, choke, suffocate, smother, stifle, drown; bury alive; smite, brain, poleaxe, sandbag, **strike;** burn alive, **burn;** immolate, sacrifice; martyr; condemn to death, **condemn.**

**slaughter,** butcher, poleaxe; massacre; decimate, scupper; spare none, **be pitiless;** annihilate, exterminate, liquidate, purge, commit genocide, **destroy.**

**murder,** assassinate, fix, settle; smother, suffocate, strangle, poison, gas.

kill oneself, commit suicide; suicide;
commit hara-kiri, commit suttee;
hang oneself; die Roman fashion; gas
oneself; take poison, take an overdose;
jump overboard, drown oneself; have
a fatal accident, perish.

Adv. in at the death, in at the kill.

Int. no quarter! cry havoc!

## 358 Corpse

N. corpse, dead body, body; dead man
or woman, victim; defunct, goner,
stiff; cadaver, skeleton, death's-head,
skull; mummy; mortal remains, relics;
clay, dust, earth; tenement of clay;
carrion; long pig, meat; organic
remains, fossil; shade, ghost.

Adj. cadaverous; stiff, carrion.

## 359 Interment

N. interment, burial; urn burial; burial
customs; myrrh; coffin, shell, casket,
urn, sarcophagus; pyre, funeral pile,
crematorium, mortuary, morgue;
funeral parlour; sexton; undertaker,
funeral director.

obsequies; mourning, wake; burial service; funeral solemnity, funeral procession; knell, passing bell; dead
march, last post; memorial service,
requiem, dirge, lament; inscription, epitaph, obituary; sepulchral
monument, tombstone, gravestone,
ledger; brass; cross, war memorial;
cenotaph, monument; monumental
mason.

funeral, hearse, bier, pall, coffin;
mourner; mute, pallbearer.

grave clothes, shroud, mummy wrapping.

cemetery, burial place; churchyard,
graveyard, God's Acre; tower of
silence; garden of remembrance.

tomb, vault, crypt; burial chamber,

pyramid; mausoleum, sepulchre; pantheon; grave, narrow house, long
home; common grave, mass grave,
plague pit; grave pit, barrow, earthwork; dolmen, monument; shrine,
memorial, cenotaph.

inquest, enquiry; autopsy, post-
mortem.

Adj. buried, laid to rest, below ground,
dead.

funereal, funerary; sombre, sad, black;
mourning; mortuary, sepulchral;
obituary; lapidary.

Vb. inter, bury; embalm, mummify; coffin; urn, entomb; consign to earth, lay
to rest, put to bed with a shovel;
cremate, incinerate, burn; go to a
funeral; mourn, keen, hold a wake,
lament.

exhume, disinter; unearth.

Adv. in memoriam, post-mortem; RIP.

## 360 Animality. Animal

N. animality, animal life, wild life; animal kingdom, fauna, brute creation;
physique, flesh.

animal, living thing; creature, brute,
beast, dumb animal; protozoon;
microorganism; mammal, amphibian,
fish, bird, reptile; worm, mollusc;
crustacean, insect, arachnid; invertebrate, vertebrate; biped, quadruped;
carnivore, herbivore, omnivore, ruminant, man-eater; wild animal, game,
big game; prey, beast of prey; pack,
flock, herd, group; stock, livestock,
stock farm; tame animal, household
pet, goldfish, hamster, guinea pig, tortoise; young animal, young creature;
draught animal, horse, beast of burden; blue whale, onyx; extinct animal,
dodo, auk; prehistoric animal, ptero-
dactyl, dinosaur, brontosaurus, tyran-
nosaurus rex, mammoth, mastodon;
fabulous beast, unicorn.

**mammal**, viviparous animal; man, **humankind**; primate, ape, anthropoid ape, gorilla, chimpanzee, gibbon, baboon, mandrill, monkey; marmoset, lemur; marsupial, kangaroo, wallaby, wombat, koala bear, opossum; rodent, rat, mouse, dormouse, shrew, vole, porcupine, mongoose, chipmunk, skunk, polecat, squirrel; insectivorous mammal, ant-eater, mole; nocturnal mammal, bat, bush baby, badger, hedgehog, stoat, weasel, ferret; fox, vixen; jackal, lion (see **cat**); hare, rabbit, bunny; aquatic mammal, otter, beaver, water rat, water vole; marine mammal, mammal, walrus, seal, sea lion; cetacean, dolphin, porpoise, whale, pachyderm, elephant, rhinoceros, hippopotamus; bear; giant panda; giraffe, zebra (see **cattle**); deer, stag, hart, buck, doe, fawn; red deer; reindeer, caribou; elk, moose; gazelle, antelope, chamois, springbok, wildebeest, gnu; horse, donkey, camel, **beast of burden**.

**bird**, fowl; fledgling, **young creature**; canary, budgerigar; parrot, macaw; songbird, songster, warbler, nightingale, lark, thrush, blackbird, linnet; curlew, plover, lapwing, peewit; dove, pigeon, woodpecker, jay, magpie, pie; jackdaw, rook, raven, crow; finch, goldfinch, chaffinch, tit, wren, robin, sparrow, wagtail, exotic bird; golden oriole; bird of passage, summer visitor, migrant, cuckoo, swallow, swift, martin; winter visitor, redwing, snow bunting; flightless bird, emu, ostrich, rhea, kiwi, penguin; owl; vulture, carrion crow; bird of prey, eagle; kite, kestrel, harrier, osprey, buzzard, hawk, falcon, hobby, shrike; fishing bird, pelican, kingfisher, gannet, cormorant, skua, gull, kittiwake, tern, oystercatcher, puffin, guillemot;

ocean bird, albatross, petrel; marsh bird, wader, stork, crane, avocet, heron, bittern; ibis, flamingo; water bird, swan, cob, pen, cygnet; duck, drake, duckling; goose, gander, gosling; teal, mallard, widgeon; moorhen, coot, diver, dipper, grebe, dabchick.

**table bird**, woodcock, wood pigeon; peacock; grouse, ptarmigan, pheasant, partridge, quail; goose, duck, snipe; turkey; guinea fowl.

**poultry**, fowl, hen; cock, cockerel, rooster, Chanticleer; chicken, pullet; spring chicken, boiler, capon; bantam.

**cattle**, livestock, **stock farm**; bull, cow, calf, heifer, yearling; bullock, steer; beef cattle; dairy cattle, Jersey; ox; buffalo, bison; yak, musk ox; goat.

**sheep**, ram, ewe, lamb; Merino; mountain sheep.

**pig**, swine, boar, warthog; hog, sow, piglet, porker; Large White.

**dog**, canine; bitch, whelp, pup, puppy; cur, hound, mutt; mongrel, pariah dog, guide dog, bloodhound, mastiff; sheepdog, collie; bull terrier; bulldog, boxer; borzoi, Afghan hound, Dalmatian; greyhound, whippet; foxhound, beagle; basset, dachshund; gun dog, retriever, pointer, setter, terrier; spaniel, show dog, chihuahua; lap dog, pug; Welsh corgi; poodle, husky, sledge dog; wild dog, dingo; wolf, coyote.

**cat**, feline; puss, pussy, kitten, kit; tabby; mouser; big cat, lion; tiger, leopard, cheetah, panther, puma, jaguar, cougar, ocelot; wildcat, lynx.

**amphibian**, frog, bullfrog, tree frog; frogspawn, tadpole, paddock, toad; newt; salamander.

**reptile**, serpent, snake, viper, adder; cobra; puff adder, mamba, rattle-

snake; anaconda, python; crocodile,
alligator; lizard, slowworm; chameleon, iguana, monitor, gecko;
turtle, tortoise, terrapin.

**marine life**; cetacean (see **mammal**); sea
urchin, sea horse, sea anemone, coral,
coral reef, jellyfish, Portuguese man
of war, starfish; shellfish, mollusc,
bivalve, clam, oyster, mussel, cockle;
whelk, winkle, limpet; cuttlefish,
squid, octopus; crustacean, crab, lobster, crayfish, shrimp; barnacle.

**fish**, swordfish, dogfish, shark; piranha,
barracuda; stingray, electric ray;
tunny, turbot, bass, **fish food**;
coelacanth; pike, roach, perch,
bream, carp; trout; salmon; eel, elver,
lamprey; minnow, gudgeon, stickle-
back.

**insect**, larva, pupa; fly, bluebottle; mayfly; gnat, midge, mosquito; greenfly,
aphid; ladybird; firefly, glow-worm;
dragonfly, crane fly; butterfly, moth,
bee, bumble bee, drone; wasp, hornet;
beetle, cockroach; vermin, bug, bed
bug, flea, louse, nit, mite, tick; woodworm, weevil, cockchafer, deathwatch beetle, **blight**; ant, termite;
stick insect; locust, grasshopper,
cicada, cricket.

**creepy-crawly**; grub, maggot, caterpillar; worm, earthworm, lugworm,
wireworm, tapeworm, fluke; centipede; slug, snail; earwig, woodlouse;
spider, tarantula; scorpion, **noxious
animal**.

**Adj.animal**; beastly, bestial; feral, domestic; human, subhuman; vertebrate,
invertebrate; warm-blooded; anthropoid; equine, asinine, mulish; bovine,
ruminant; sheepish; elephantine;
canine; feline, tigerish; foxy; aquiline;
cold-blooded; fishy; amphibian,
amphibious; saurian, serpentine.

**361 Vegetable life**

**N.vegetable life**, vegetable kingdom;
flora, vegetation; biomass; flowering,
blooming; **plenty, abundance**; Flora,
Pan; faun, dryad, wood nymph,
**nymph**.

**wood**, timber, lumber, softwood, hardwood, heartwood, sapwood; forest,
jungle; bush, heath, scrub; woodland,
coppice, spinney; thicket, brake, covert; park, chase, game preserve; plantation, arboretum; orchard, **garden**;
grove, clump; clearing, glade; undergrowth; shrubbery, windbreak,
hedge, hedgerow.

**forestry**, conservation; forester; lumber-
jack.

**tree**, shrub, bush, sapling, scion, stock;
pollard; shoot, sucker, trunk, bole;
limb, branch, bough, twig; conifer,
fruit tree, mahogany, ebony, teak,
walnut, oak, elm, ash, beech, syca-
more, maple, plane, lime, linden;
horse chestnut, copper beech; red-
wood, larch, fir, spruce, pine, poplar,
aspen, alder, sallow, willow, birch,
rowan, mountain ash; crab apple,
sweet chestnut; hazel, elder, spindle,
hawthorn, may, blackthorn, sloe;
privet, yew, holly, ivy, box, bay,
laurel; rhododendron, camellia, aza-
lea; magnolia, laburnum, lilac; wist-
eria; palm, mangrove; gum tree, euca-
lyptus, rubber tree, **agriculture**.

**foliage**; greenery; umbrage; limb,
branch, bough, twig, shoot; spray,
sprig; leaf, frond, flag, blade; leaflet;
pine needle; cotyledon; petiole, node,
stalk, stem; tendril, prickle, thorn.

**plant**, herb, weed; root, tuber, rhizome,
bulb, corm, **source**; cutting, **young
plant**; culinary herb, medicinal herb,
**remedy**; food plant, fodder, **vegetable,
fruit**; national plant, rose, leek, daffodil, thistle, shamrock; garden plant,

pansy, carnation, lily; lavender, honeysuckle; wild plant, daisy, dandelion, buttercup; water plant, water lily, flag; desert plant, cactus, succulent; prickly plant, bramble, gorse, insectivorous plant, sundew; deadly nightshade, **poisonous plant**; creeper, climber, vine; parasite, mistletoe; fern, bracken; moss; lichen, fungus, mushroom, puffball; mould, penicillin; seaweed, wrack; algae, **microorganism**.

**flower**, blossom, bloom, bud, burgeon; head, spike, catkin; petal, sepal; corolla, calyx; ovary, ovule, receptacle; pistil, style, stigma, stamen, anther, pollen; fruit, berry, nut; seed vessel, pod, capsule, cone; pip, spore, seed, **source**; annual, biennial, perennial; house plant, exotic; garden flower, wild flower; flowerbed, seedbed; horticulture, **garden**.

**grass**, hay; pasture, pasturage, **grassland**; turf, sod, lawn; meadow grass; sedge, rush, bulrush, reed, papyrus; Pampas grass, bamboo, sugar cane; grain plant, wheat, oats, barley, rye, millet, rice; grain, husk, chaff, stubble, straw.

**Adj. vegetal**, vegetable, botanical; evergreen; deciduous; hardy; floral, flowery, blooming; rank, lush, overgrown; weedy; leafy, verdant, **green**; grassy, herbaceous, herbal; composite; pinnate; fungous.

**arboreal**; timbered; woodland, woody, wooded; wild, scrubby, bushy.

**wooden**, wood, woody.

**Vb. vegetate**, germinate, sprout, shoot, **grow**; plant, garden, **cultivate**; forest, afforest.

## 362 Zoology: the science of animals

**N. zoology**; animal physiology, **structure**; **biology**; anatomy; **anthropology**;
ornithology, bird lore; entomology; taxidermy.

**zoologist**.

**Adj. zoological**.

## 363 Botany: the science of plants

**N. botany**; taxonomy; plant physiology, plant pathology; plant ecology; **forestry**; mycology; botanical garden, **garden**; herbal; herbalist.

**Adj. botanical**.

**Vb. botanize**.

## 364 Animal husbandry

**N. animal husbandry**, animal management; training, manège; breeding; veterinary science; dairy farming, **cattle**; sheep farming, poultry farming; veterinary surgeon, vet, horse doctor, **doctor**; ostler, groom, stable boy, **servant**; farrier, blacksmith; keeper, gamekeeper; game warden.

**stock farm**, stud; dairy farm, ranch; fish farm, hatchery; fish pond, fish tank; duck pond; pig farm; hive, apiary; pasture, **grassland**; poultry farm, chicken run, free range; battery, deep litter; factory farm.

**cattle pen**, byre, **stable**; hutch, coop; cowshed, pigsty; bird cage, aviary.

**zoo**, menagerie, circus; aviary, vivarium, aquarium; reptile house, monkey temple; bear pit; wildlife park, game park, game reserve.

**breeder**; cattle farmer; fancier.

**herdsman**; stockman, cowboy; shepherd; milkmaid; kennel maid.

**Adj. tamed**, broken; gentle, docile; domestic; thoroughbred.

**Vb. break in**, tame, domesticate, acclimatize; train, **teach**; back, mount, whip, spur, **ride**; yoke, harness, hitch, bridle, saddle; herd, corral, cage, **enclose**.

**breed stock**, breed, rear, raise, grow,

hatch, culture, incubate, nurture, fatten; ranch, farm, **cultivate**.

**groom**, stable; tend, herd, shepherd; shear, fleece; milk; drench, water, fodder, **feed**.

## 365 Agriculture

**N. agriculture**, rural economy; cultivation; growth, harvest, produce, crop, vintage, **store**; cash crop, husbandry, farming; cattle farming, **animal husbandry**; cereal farming, hydroponics, tray agriculture, tank farming; tillage, spadework; horticulture; **forestry**; landscape architecture; water, dung, manure, **fertilizer**; fodder, winter feed; silage, **storage**.

**farm**, grange; arable farm, **stock farm**; ranch, hacienda; model farm; farmhouse; farmyard, barnyard; state farm, kibbutz; arable land, fallow, **soil**; rice paddy; pasturage, pasture, **grassland**; demesne, manor farm, estate, holding, smallholding, croft, allotment, kitchen garden; market garden, nursery, garden centre; vineyard; fruit farm, orchard; tea garden, tea estate, sugar plantation.

**garden**, vegetable garden, cabbage patch, kitchen garden, allotment; fruit garden, orchard; arboretum, **wood**; patch, plot, grass, lawn, park; shrubbery, border, bed, flowerbed; seedbed, frame; cloche, conservatory, hothouse, greenhouse, glasshouse; flowerpot.

**farmer**, farm manager, bailiff; cultivator, planter; peasant; serf; villein; sharecropper, tenant farmer; gentleman farmer, yeoman; crofter; fruit grower, fruit farmer; farm hand, farm labourer; land girl; tractor driver, harvester; thresher; picker; farming community, peasantry; rustic.

**gardener**, flower grower; nurseryman or

-woman; **forestry**; planter.

**farm tool**, plough, ploughshare; harrow, spade, fork, hoe, rake, trowel; dibble; drill; pitchfork; scythe, sickle, shears, secateurs, **sharp edge**; flail; winepress; thresher, binder, combine harvester; tractor; haystack; elevator, barn, silo, **storage**.

**Adj. agrarian**, peasant, farming; bucolic, pastoral, rural, rustic; collective; arable, cultivable; dug.

**horticultural**, garden, topiary; herbal; cultured, forced, hothouse, exotic.

**Vb. cultivate, make fruitful**; farm, ranch, garden, grow; till, dig, delve, spade, dibble; seed, sow, broadcast, set, plant, transplant, plough, harrow, rake, hoe; weed, prune, **shorten**; graft, engraft, **implant**; layer; force, topdress, mulch, dung, manure, **invigorate**; sod; leave fallow; harvest, **store**; glean, reap, mow, cut, scythe, cut a swathe; bind, bale, sheaf; flail, thresh, winnow, sift, bolt, **separate**; crop, pluck, pick, gather; fence, **enclose**; ditch, drain, reclaim; water, **irrigate**.

## 366 Humankind

**N. humankind**, mankind, womankind; humanity, human nature; flesh, mortality; everybody, ourselves; human race, human species; man; human being, Eve, lords of creation; political animal; primitive humanity; early humanity; Australopithecus; bionic person, android; ethnic type, **race**.

**anthropology**; ethnology, ethnography, folklore, mythology; social anthropology, demography; social science, humanitarianism, **sociology**; humanism; anthropomorphism, pathetic fallacy.

**person**, individual, human being; creature, mortal, body, bod; a being, soul,

God's image; one, somebody, such a one; party, customer, character, type, element; chap, fellow, **male**; girl, female, **woman**; personage, figure, person of note, VIP, **bigwig**; celebrity, star, **favourite**; **personnel**; unit, head, hand, nose.

**social group**, society, community, **group**; kinship group, **family**; primitive society, tribalism; community at large, people, folk; public, **generality**; population, populace, citizenry; **upper class, aristocracy**.

**nation**, nationality, nationalism; chauvinism, jingoism, imperialism, colonialism; civil society, body politic, people; state, realm, commonwealth; democracy, republic, **government**.

**Adj. human**, mortal; anthropoid; subhuman, **inferior**; **ethnic**; personal, individual.

**national**, state, civic, civil, public, general, communal, social; cosmopolitan, international.

**367 Male**

**N. male**, male sex, man, he, him; masculinity, manhood; male chauvinism; patriarchy; gentleman, sir, master; lord, his lordship; mister, monsieur, Herr, señor, don, signor, sahib; comrade; squire; Mac; mate, buddy, pal, **chum**; swain; gaffer, buffer, **old man**; fellow, guy, scout, bloke, chap, johnny; codger, card, cove, joker; blade, rake, gay dog; he-man, caveman; **weakling**; homosexual, **nonconformist**; eunuch; escort, beau, boy friend; bachelor, widower; bridegroom; married man, husband, **spouse**; family man, patriarch; father, **paternity**; uncle, brother, nephew; lad, boy, **youngster**; son; stag party, menfolk.

**male animal**, jack, cock, cockerel, rooster; drake, gander, cob; buck, stag, hart; horse, stallion, entire horse, colt; bull, bullock, ox, steer; boar, hog; ram; dog, dog fox; gelding, capon, **eunuch**.

**Adj. male**, masculine, chivalrous; virile; mannish, butch.

**368 Female**

**N. female**, feminine gender, she, her; womanhood; feminism; matriarchy; effeminacy, **weakness**; gynaecology; obstetrics.

**womankind**, second sex; hen party; seraglio, harem.

**woman**, Eve, she; girl, **youngster**; virgin, maiden; nun, old maid, **spinster**; bachelor girl, career woman; sister; suffragette; bride, married woman, wife, squaw, widow, matron, **spouse**; dowager, **old woman**; mother, grandmother, **maternity**; working wife or mother, housewife; aunt, niece, sister, daughter; wench, lass, nymph; colleen, damsel; petticoat, skirt, doll, chick, bird; honey, baby; brunette, redhead; girl friend, sweetheart, moll, crumpet, bit of fluff; broad, courtesan, **loose woman**; lesbian, **nonconformist**; minx, hussy, baggage, jade; shrew, virago, Amazon; Venus.

**lady**, dame; her ladyship; madam, ma'am, mistress, Mrs, Ms, miss, madame, mademoiselle, Frau, Fraulein; signora, signorina, señora, señorita.

**female animal**, hen, pen, bitch; mare, filly; cow, heifer; sow, gilt; ewe; nanny goat; hind, doe; vixen, tigress.

**Adj. female**, she, feminine, petticoat, girlish, ladylike, maidenly, matronly; child-bearing, **generative**; lesbian; womanish, effeminate, pansy.

## 369 Physical sensibility

N. **sensibility**, sensitiveness, tenderness; soreness, sensitivity, touchiness; awareness, consciousness, **moral sensibility**; allergy; funny bone; aesthetics; aesthete, **people of taste**; touchy person, sensitive plant, thin skin.

**sense**; sensory apparatus, sense organ, nerve system; five senses; touch, hearing, taste, smell, sight; sensation, impression, **feeling**; effect, response, reaction, reflex; ESP; telepathy.

Adj. **sentient**, perceptive, sensitive; sensible, susceptible, sensory; sensuous, aesthetic, **feeling**; percipient, aware, conscious, **knowing**; acute, sharp, keen, **painful**; ticklish, itchy; tender, raw, sore; impressionable, alive, alive to, warm, responsive; hypersensitive.

**striking**, keen, sharp, poignant, acute, vivid, clear, lively; **exciting**; sudden, sensational, **impressive**.

Vb. **have feeling**, sense, become aware; perceive, **know**; be sensible of, **feel**; react, tingle, **be sensitive**; hear, see, touch, taste, smell; be alert.

**cause feeling**, stir, disturb, **agitate**; arouse, excite, make or produce an impression, **impress**; arrest, astonish, cause a sensation, **surprise**; sharpen, cultivate, **invigorate**; refine; hurt, **give pain**.

Adv. to the quick.

## 370 Physical insensibility

N. **insensibility**; mental insensibility; anaesthesia; analgesia; hypnosis, hypnotism; apoplexy, palsy; stupor, coma, faint, swoon, blackout; narcolepsy, **disease**; twilight sleep; sleep; Rip van Winkle.

**anaesthetic**, dope, **drug**; local anaesthetic, ether, chloroform, morphine, cocaine; gas, nitrous oxide; narcotic, knockout drops, draught, **soporific**;

opium; painkiller, analgesic, **moderator**; acupuncture.

Adj. **insensible**, insensitive; obtuse, dull; oblivious; **deaf**; unseeing, **blind**; senseless, unconscious; inert; inanimate, dead, **quiescent**; numb, benumbed, frozen; paralytic; stoned, **dead drunk**; punch-drunk; comatose; anaesthetic, analgesic; **soporific**.

**unfeeling**, cold, callous, thick-skinned; stony, proof, shockproof, **impassive**.

Vb. **be insensible**; have a thick skin, **be insensitive**; harden oneself, cease to feel; become insensible, faint, swoon.

**render insensible**, make insensible; blunt, deaden; paralyse; freeze, **refrigerate**; put to sleep, send to sleep; gas, chloroform; drug, dope; dull, stupefy; stun, concuss, brain, render unconscious, **strike**; pall, cloy, **sate**.

## 371 Physical pleasure

N. **pleasure**; thrill; sensuality; self-indulgence, hedonism; round of pleasure, rest, **refreshment**; treat, entertainment, **amusement**; feast; relish, **taste**; gusto, zest, keen appreciation; mental or spiritual pleasure, delight, ecstasy, **joy**.

**euphoria**, well-being, **content**; physical well-being, **health**; ease, convenience, comfort; luxury; lap of luxury, **wealth**; feather bed, velvet, cushion, pillow; peace, quiet, rest, **repose**; sleep; painlessness, euthanasia.

Adj. **pleasant**, pleasing, delightful; welcome, grateful, **refreshing**; genial, congenial, cordial, heart-warming; nice, agreeable, enjoyable; palatable, delicious, tasty; sugary, **sweet**; fragrant; **melodious**; lovely, **beautiful**.

**comfortable**, homely, snug, cosy, warm, restful; painless, peaceful, **tranquil**; convenient, easy, cushy; downy, **soft**;

luxurious; happy, **content**; relieved.

**sensuous**, bodily, physical, **material**; voluptuous, **sensual**.

**Vb. enjoy**, relish, like, feel pleasure, **be pleased**; thrill to, **be excited**; **taste**; prosper; give pleasure, **please**.

**Adv. in comfort**; in clover, on a bed of roses.

## 372 Physical pain

**N. pain**, discomfort, malaise, inconvenience; distress, thin time, hell, **adversity**; exhaustion, strain, **fatigue**; hurt, bruise, sprain; cut, gash, **wound**; heartache, anguish, agony, **suffering**; slow death, torment, torture; crucifixion, martyrdom; rack, wheel, thumbscrew, **instrument of torture**; painful aftermath, hangover.

**pang**, thrill, throes; stab, twinge, nip, pinch; stitch, crick, cramp, **spasm**; smart, sting, sharp pain, ache, headache, splitting head, migraine; toothache, earache, stomachache, bellyache, gripes, colic, collywobbles; neuralgia; arthritis, rheumatism; sciatica, lumbago, backache, **ill health**.

**Adj. painful**, excruciating, exquisite; harrowing; poignant; burning, biting, stabbing; sore, raw, tender; bitter, bittersweet, **sour**; disagreeable, uncomfortable, inconvenient, **unpleasant**.

**pained**, hurt, suffering.

**Vb. give pain**, ache, hurt, pain, sting; put to torture, lacerate, torment, **torture**; flog, crucify, martyr, **punish**; vivisect, tear, lacerate, **cut**; prick, stab, **pierce**; gripe, nip, pinch, tweak, twinge, shoot, throb, devour, bite, gnaw; grind, grate, jar; fret, chafe, gall, **rub**; irritate, **aggravate**; **discord**; inconvenience, annoy, distress, **trouble**.

**feel pain**, **suffer**; ache, smart, chafe; twitch, wince, flinch, writhe, squirm, creep, shiver, quiver, tingle; have a thin time, be a martyr, go through it, **have trouble**; shriek, yell, scream, howl, groan, **cry**; weep, **lament**.

## 373 Touch: sensation of touch

**N. touch**, feeling; massage, squeeze, pressure, **friction**; graze, contact; light touch; stroke, pat, caress; flick, flip, tap, **knock**; sense of touch, precision; delicacy, artistry, **skill**.

**formication**, gooseflesh; tingle; itch; rash, prickly heat, **skin disease**.

**feeler**, organ of touch, antenna, whisker, tentacle; proboscis, tongue; digit, forefinger, thumb (see **finger**); hand, paw, palm, flipper, mitt.

**finger**, forefinger, index, middle finger; thumb; big toe, **foot**; bunch of fives, bone sandwich; hand, fist, **nippers**; fingernail, talon, claw.

**Adj. tactual**, tactile; prehensile; tangible, palpable, **material**; light of touch, **clumsy**.

**handed**; right-handed; left-handed; manual.

**Vb. touch**, make contact, graze, scrape, shave, brush, glance; kiss, **be contiguous**; overlap; hit, meet, **collide**; feel; finger, thumb, pinch, nip, massage, **rub**; palm, stroke, **smooth**; wipe, sweep, **clean**; touch lightly, tap, pat, dab, flick, flip, tickle, scratch; lip, lap, lick, tongue; nuzzle; paw, fondle, **caress**; handle, twiddle, fiddle with; manipulate, wield, ply, manhandle, **operate**; touch roughly, bruise, crush, **give pain**; fumble, grope, scrabble; **be tentative**.

**itch**, tickle, tingle, creep, crawl, have gooseflesh; prick, prickle, titillate; scratch; thrill, excite, irritate, inflame, **cause feeling**.

## 374 Heat

**N.** heat; radiant heat; emission of heat; flame, glow, flush, blush; warmth, fervour, ardour; specific heat, sweat, swelter; fever heat, fever, hectic, **disease**; high temperature, white heat; torrid heat, high summer, flaming June; heat haze, **summer**; heat wave, scorcher; hot wind, sirocco; geyser, hot water, steam; tropics, torrid zone; sun, sunshine, solar heat, **heating**.

**fire;** bonfire, bale fire, **glow;** death fire, pyre; coal fire, **furnace;** Greek fire, **bomb;** conflagration, holocaust; heath fire, forest fire; fireball, blaze, flame, spark, flicker, arc, **flash;** flare, **torch;** eruption, volcano; pyrotechnics; arson; fire worship, **worship;** salamander, phoenix.

**thermometry,** heat measurement, thermometer, thermostat; calorimeter; thermal unit, British Thermal Unit, therm, calorie; solar constant; thermodynamics.

**Adj. hot,** heated; inflamed, fervent, fervid; flaming, glowing, red-hot, like an oven; piping hot, **pungent;** feverish, febrile, fevered; sweltering, smoking; running with sweat, scalding; tropical, torrid, searing, **heated;** thirsty, burning, **dry;** running a temperature.

**fiery,** ardent, burning, flaming; smoking; ablaze, afire; incandescent, molten, glowing, aglow, **red;** igneous; lit, alight; volcanic.

**warm,** tepid, lukewarm; temperate, mild, genial, balmy; fair, sunny; summery; tropical; torrid, sultry; stuffy, close, muggy; **insalubrious;** snug, **comfortable;** at room temperature, at blood heat; calorific; thermal.

**Vb. be hot,** be warm; burn; kindle, catch fire, draw; blaze, flare, flame; glow,

flush; smoke, smoulder, reek, fume; steam, **emit;** boil, seethe, **effervesce;** toast, grill, roast, sizzle, crackle, frizzle, fry, bake, **burn;** get burnt, scorch, boil dry; bask, sun oneself, sunbathe; get sunburnt, tan; swelter, sweat, perspire, glow; melt, thaw, **liquefy;** thirst, parch, **be dry;** stifle, pant; be feverish, have a fever, run a temperature; keep warm.

## 375 Cold

**N. coldness,** low temperature, cool; cold, zero temperature, zero; frigidity; sensation of cold, rigour, hypothermia, shivers, gooseflesh, frostbite; chill, catching cold; cold climate, Frigid Zone, North Pole, Arctic; snowline, permafrost; glacial epoch, Ice Age; polar bear, Eskimo.

**wintriness,** winter, cold snap; cold weather, cold front; arctic conditions, polar temperature; blizzard; frost, Jack Frost, rime, hoarfrost; white frost, sleet, hail, hailstone; silver thaw, black ice, freeze.

**snow,** snowfall, snowflake, snow crystal; avalanche, snow slip, snowdrift; flurry of snow; snowball, snowman; snowplough, snowshoe; winter sports, **sport.**

**ice,** ice cube; hailstone, icicle; ice cap, ice field, ice sheet, ice shelf, floe, iceberg, ice front, glacier; shelf ice, frozen sea; ice yacht; ice house, **refrigerator;** ice action.

**Adj. cold,** without heat, impervious to heat; cool, temperate, shady, chill, chilly, parky, nippy; fresh, raw, keen, bitter, nipping, biting, piercing; below zero; frigid, frosty, frostbound, snowy, icy; glacial; polar, arctic.

**chilly,** feeling cold; shivery; blue, blue with cold; perishing, frozen, frostbitten; like ice.

**Vb. be cold**, grow cold, lose heat; feel cold, chatter, shiver, tremble, shake, quake, quiver, shudder; freeze, starve, perish with cold; catch cold, get a chill; chill, **refrigerate**.

**Adv. frostily**, bitterly, coldly.

## 376 Heating

**N. heating**, increase of temperature; calorific value; keeping warm; space heating; district heating system, **heater**; melting; **cookery**; antifreeze mixture.

**burning**, combustion; kindling, ignition; conflagration, **fire**; roasting; suttee, **suicide**; holocaust; burner, **furnace**; caustic; hot iron, brand; match, **lighter**; stoker, fireman; burn mark, burn, brand, singe, scald, sunburn, tan.

**incendiarism**, arson, fire-raising, pyromania; incendiary, fire-bug; fire-brand, revolutionary, **agitator**.

**warm clothes**, woollens, red flannel, thermal underwear; parka, wrap, muffler, muff; winter coat, **overcoat**; blanket, **coverlet**; padding, wadding, lining.

**ash**, volcanic ash, lava; carbon, soot, smut, lamp-black, smoke; product of combustion, clinker, charcoal, ember, cinder, char, slag, dross, oxide.

**pottery**, ceramics; earthenware, stoneware, faience, porcelain; crockery, china, delft, willow pattern, terracotta; tile, brick, adobe; pot, urn, **vessel**.

**Adj. heated**, **hot**; lit; burnt; fused, molten; smoky; sunburnt.

**heating**, calorific, caustic, burning; oil-fired; incendiary, inflammatory; inflammable, **combustible**; antifreeze.

**Vb. heat**, warm; provide heating; thaw; inflame, foment, poultice; stew, stifle,

suffocate; sun, parch, shrivel, sear, **dry**; toast, bake, grill, fry, roast, **cook**; melt, defrost, de-ice, **liquefy**; smelt; fuse, weld, cast, found.

**kindle**, ignite, light, set fire to, **fire**; fuel, stoke, rub two sticks together.

**burn**, gut; make a bonfire of; fire, set fire to; cremate, incinerate; boil dry, **dry**; corrode; coal, char, singe, scorch, tan; brand; scald.

## 377 Refrigeration

**N. refrigeration**, reduction of temperature; **ice**; **condensation**; exposure; air-conditioning; cold storage, **refrigerator**.

**incombustibility**, fire resistance; asbestos.

**extinguisher**, foam, water, hose, sprinkler, hydrant, standpipe; fire engine, fire brigade, fire station; fireman.

**Adj. cooled**; frozen; with ice, **cold**.

**incombustible**, fireproof.

**Vb. refrigerate**, cool, fan, **refresh**; ventilate, air, **aerate**; shade, shadow, **screen**; frost, freeze, congeal; freeze-dry; make ice, ice; chill, starve, nip, pinch, bite, pierce; frost-bite.

**extinguish**, quench, snuff, choke, stifle, smother, **suppress**; damp, stop burning.

## 378 Furnace

**N. furnace**; the stake, **means of execution**; volcano; gun barrel; forge, blast furnace, kiln; incinerator; crematorium; brazier, stove, oven, range; cooker, gas ring, burner, blowlamp, oxyacetylene lamp; fire, **fire**; brand, **lighter**; fireplace, grate, hearth; firedog; poker, tongs, shovel; hob, trivet, fireguard, fender, flue, **chimney**.

**heater**, radiator, solar panel; geyser, boiler, copper, kettle; hotplate; electric blanket; still, retort, crucible; blowpipe, bellows, damper; hot baths, Turkish bath, sauna, **ablutions**; hotbed, hothouse, conservatory, **garden**; sun trap, solarium; kitchen, galley; grill, saucepan; toaster, iron, curling tongs; heating agent, flame, sunlight, **heating**; gas, electricity, solar energy; steam, hot air; wood, coal, **fuel**.

## 379 Refrigerator

**N. refrigerator**; ventilator, fan; fridge, ice bucket; coolant, snow, ice; ice pack; rocks; cold storage, freezer.

## 380 Fuel

**N. fuel**, inflammable material, combustible; kindling; wood, faggot, log, biomass, **vegetable life**; turf, peat; cow dung, lignite, brown coal, charcoal; fossil fuel, coal, natural gas, petroleum, **oil**, gas; nuclear fuel, uranium, plutonium; petrol, four-star, juice; derv; paraffin, kerosene; alcohol, spirit, North Sea gas, acetylene, propane, butane, methane.

**coal**, black diamond, sea coal, anthracite; coal dust, slack; coal seam, coal deposit, coal measure, coalfield, **store**; cinders, **ash**; coke.

**lighter**, light, taper, spill, candle, **torch**; coal, ember, brand, firebrand; fire ship, incendiary bomb, **bomb**; wick, fuse, match, percussion cap, detonator; safety match; flint, steel, tinder, punk, spunk; tinderbox.

**fumigator**, incense, sulphur, brimstone.

**Adj. combustible**, inflammable, incendiary, explosive; carboniferous.

**Vb. fire**, stoke, feed, fuel, coal; put a match to, **kindle**.

## 381 Taste

**N. taste**, savour; flavour, flavouring; smack, tang, twang, aftertaste; relish, gusto, zest, appetite; palate, tongue; tooth, stomach.

**Adj. tasty**, palatable, full of flavour, mouth-watering, appetizing, **savoury**; salty, peppery, **pungent**; spicy, racy, rich, strong, fruity, generous, mellow, vintage.

**Vb. taste**, find palatable, **enjoy**; savour, sample, try; sip, lick, sup, nibble, **eat**; have a taste, taste of, smack of, savour of, **resemble**; taste good, **make appetizing**.

## 382 Insipidity

**N. insipidity**, flatness, staleness, tastelessness; milk and water, water, pap.

**Adj. tasteless**, without taste, devoid of taste; vapid, insipid, watery; mild; with water, wishy-washy, sloppy; **unsavoury**; flat, stale.

## 383 Pungency

**N. pungency**, sting, kick, bite, edge; burning taste; hot taste; sharp taste, acerbity, acidity; roughness; strong taste, strength, tang, twang; bad taste; salt, brine, pepper, pickle, spice, **condiment**; revival; cordial, **stimulant**; dram, nip, tot, **draught**; hemp, **drug**.

**tobacco**, baccy, snout, nicotine; tobacco leaf; blend, smoking mixture; snuff; plug of tobacco, plug, quid; twist; flake; cigar, cheroot, Havana, corona; smoke, cigarette, fag; reefer, joint; filter tip, cork tip; butt, stub; tobacco pipe, churchwarden; briar, corncob; hookah; pipe of peace; bowl, stem; tobacco juice; snuffer; smoker, tobacconist, cigarette machine; snuff box, cigarette case, cigarette box, cigar box; pipe rack; pipe cleaner; tobacco pouch, tobacco jar; smoker, smoking compartment.

**Adj. pungent**, penetrating, strong; mordant, biting, **sharp**; caustic, burning, smoky; harsh, **rough**; bitter, acrid, tart, astringent, **sour**; heady; nutty, **tasty**; high; spicy; hot, peppery; piquant, **savoury**.

salty, salt, brackish, saline.

**Vb. be pungent**, sting, set the teeth on edge, make the eyes water.

**season**, salt, brine, marinade, souse, pickle; flavour, sauce; spice, pepper, devil, curry; smoke, kipper, **preserve**.

**smoke**, use tobacco, indulge, smoke a pipe, pull, draw, suck, inhale; take a drag; puff; smoke like a chimney; chew a quid; snuff, take snuff, take a pinch.

### 384 Condiment

**N. condiment**, seasoning, flavouring, dressing, relish, garnish; aspic; salt, mustard, pepper, paprika, chilli, caper; black pepper, peppercorn; curry powder, turmeric; onion, garlic; spice, allspice, mace, cinnamon, ginger, nutmeg, clove, caraway seed, vanilla pod.

**sauce**, roux; gravy, stock; brown sauce; parsley sauce; apple sauce, **sweet thing**; tomato sauce, ketchup; chilli sauce, chutney, piccalilli; salad dressing, mayonnaise, vinaigrette.

**Vb. spice**, season.

### 385 Savouriness

**N. savouriness**, right taste; fine flavour; body, bouquet; savoury, relish, appetizer; delicacy, dainty, titbit, **mouthful**; game, venison, turtle; ambrosia, nectar.

**Adj. savoury**, nice, good, good to eat; spicy, **tasty**; done to a turn; appetiz-

ing, piquant, **pungent**; palatable, sweet; dainty, delicate; delectable, delicious, exquisite, choice; scrumptious; fresh, crisp; ripe, mellow, luscious, juicy, succulent; rich; racy, high; vintage.

**Vb. make appetizing**, spice, ginger, **season**; be savoury, smell good, taste good, taste sweet, **sweeten**; like, relish, savour, **taste**.

**Int.** yum-yum! mmm!

### 386 Unsavouriness

**N. unsavouriness**, nasty taste; roughness; acerbity; prison fare; rue; bitter pill; emetic, **poison**.

**Adj. unsavoury**, flat, **tasteless**; coarse, raw, undressed; overdone, burnt; inedible; stale, hard, leathery; **tough**; soggy, **soft**; rough, **pungent**; bitter, acrid, acid, **sour**; rank, rancid, putrid, rotten, high, stinking, **fetid**; nasty, foul, revolting, loathsome, **unpleasant**; sickly, mawkish, sickening, emetic, nauseous; poisonous, **toxic**.

**Vb. be unpalatable**, taste horrid; disgust, repel, sicken, nauseate, **cause dislike**; poison; lose its savour, pall.

**Int.** Ugh! yuk!

### 387 Sweetness

**N. sweetness**, sweetening; sweet tooth.

**sweet thing**, sweetening, honey, honeycomb, honeydew; honeysuckle; saccharin, sucrose, glucose, dextrose, lactose; sugar; molasses, syrup, treacle; sweet sauce, custard; sweet drink, julep, nectar, mead; conserve, preserve; candied peel; jam, marmalade, jelly; marzipan, icing, sugar coating; fudge, candy; lozenge, pastille; lollipop, ice cream, candyfloss, rock; confectionery, confection, cake, **dessert**.

**Adj. sweet**, honeyed, candied, sugary,

saccharine; luscious, delicious, pleasant; savoury.

**Vb. sweeten**, sugar, candy, ice; sweeten wine, mull.

## 388 Sourness

**N. sourness**, acerbity; acidity; acid, tartar; lemon, vinegar; sloe, crab apple; alum; gall.

**Adj. sour**, acid; crabbed, tart; bitter; sharp, astringent, **pungent**; **unsavoury**; green, hard, rough, **immature**; dry.

**Vb. be sour**, sour, turn, turn sour; acidify; ferment.

## 389 Odour

**N. odour**, smell, aroma, bouquet, nose; sweet smell, perfume, essence; bad smell, stink, **stench**; smoke, fume, reek; breath, whiff, waft; strong smell; tang, scent, trail, **trace**; sense of smell; nostril, nose, **protuberance**; good nose, flair.

**Adj. odorous; fragrant**; strong, heady, heavy, **pungent**; smelly, redolent; malodorous, **fetid**; smell; olfactory.

**Vb. smell**, have an odour; smell of, breathe of, reek of; reek; exhale; scent, nose, wind, get wind of, **detect**; get a whiff of; snuff, sniff, inhale, **breathe**; cause to smell, scent, perfume, incense, fumigate.

## 390 Inodorousness

**N. inodorousness**; absence of smell, inability to smell; lack of flair; deodorant, fumes, incense, pastille.

**Adj. odourless**, without smell; without sense of smell, without flair.

**Vb. have no smell**; ventilate, **purify**.

## 391 Fragrance

**N. fragrance**, sweet smell, sweet savour; aroma, bouquet, **odour**; violet, rose;

flower garden, **garden**; buttonhole, nosegay.

**scent**, perfume; balm, myrrh, incense, frankincense; **condiment**; musk, ambergris, camphor, sandalwood, patchouli; essential oil, attar; lavender, thyme, spearmint, vanilla; frangipani; honeysuckle; toilet water; hair oil; face powder, **cosmetic**; mothball, lavender bag, sachet; pomander, potpourri, scent bottle, vinaigrette.

**Adj. fragrant**, redolent, **pleasant**; balmy; spicy, fruity.

**Vb. be fragrant**, smell sweet, smell like a rose, have a perfume, scent, perfume, fumigate; embalm.

## 392 Stench

**N. stench**; bad smell, bad odour; body odour; foul breath, halitosis; stink, pong; reek; noxious stench; fumes, miasma, **gas**; smell of death, taint, corruption, putrefaction, **decay**; **dirt**; stale air, fug; fungus, garlic; hydrogen sulphide, ammonia; skunk, polecat; stink bomb, bad egg; dung, **excrement**; latrine, sewer, **sink**.

**Adj. fetid**, heavy, strong; malodorous; smelly; stinking, rank, foxy; fruity; high; bad, rancid; putrid; stale, airless, musty, fusty, smoky, stuffy; foul, noisome, noxious, **toxic**; acrid, burning, **pungent**; nasty, disagreeable, offensive, **unpleasant**.

**Vb. stink**, smell, reek, pong, hum; make a smell; have a bad smell, smell strong, smell offensive; smell bad, **decompose**; stink to high heaven; smell like a bad egg, smell like a drain; stink like a goat, stink like a polecat; overpower with stink.

## 393 Sound

**N. sound**, auditory effect; reception, **hearing**; audio, mono, monophonic sound, stereo; electronic sound, sound effect; sound track; noise, loud sound; low sound; quality of sound, tone, pitch, level, cadence; accent, intonation, twang, timbre, voice; tune, strain, melody, music; bang, roll, cry, discord; transmission of sound, telephone, radio, telecommunication; high fidelity, hi-fi; gramophone; loudspeaker, hearing aid; unit of sound, decibel; sonic barrier.

acoustics, phonics; phonetics; sound engineer.

speech sound, phone, syllable, polysyllable; consonant, liquid, sibilant; dental, nasal, guttural; aspiration, inspiration, expiration; rough breathing, stop, click; mute, aspirate, surd; glide, glide sound; vowel; diphthong, voice; rising diphthong; vowel gradation; umlaut; word; sound symbol, international phonetic alphabet, IPA, script.

Adj. sounding; sonic; supersonic; plain, audible, distinct; resounding, sonorous, resonant; stentorian, loud; auditory, acoustic; monophonic, mono; stereo, high fidelity, hi-fi; audio, audiovisual; phonetic; vocal; surd, voiceless.

Vb. sound; make a noise, be loud, resound; voice.

## 394 Silence

N. silence; hush, lull, rest, peace, quiet; solemn silence.

Adj. silent, still; calm, peaceful, quiet, quiescent; soft, faint; inaudible; soundproof; speechless, mute, voiceless; solemn, awful.

Vb. be silent, be taciturn; be mute; be still; become silent, be quiet.

silence, still, lull, hush, quiet, quieten, make silent; soft-pedal; stifle, muffle, gag, stop, muzzle, put to silence,

make mute; drown.

Int. hush! sh! silence! quiet! peace! soft! whist! hold your tongue! keep your mouth shut! shut up! keep your trap shut! dry up! cut the cackle! stow it! mum's the word!

## 395 Loudness

N. loudness, sound; noise, high volume; broken silence, knock; burst of sound, report, sonic boom, slam, clap, thunderclap, burst, explosion, bang; siren, alarm, honk, toot, danger signal; prolonged noise, boom, rattle, roll; thunder, storm; dashing; fire, gunfire, artillery, blitz, bombardment; blast, blare, bray, fanfare, flourish; trumpet blast, clarion call, call; clang; peal, campanology; swell, crescendo, fortissimo, full blast, full chorus; clamour, outcry, roaring, shouting, whoop, shout, howl, shriek, scream, roar, cry; loud laughter, laughter; loud breathing, respiration; din, row, racket, crash, clash, clatter, hubbub, hullabaloo, ballyhoo, uproar, tumult, bedlam, pandemonium, all hell let loose, turmoil.

megaphone, amplifier, loud pedal; public address system, loudhailer, loudspeaker, speaker, microphone, mike; ear trumpet, hearing aid; loud instrument, whistle, siren, hooter, horn, klaxon, gong; rattle; buzzer, bell, alarm, door knocker; trumpet, brass; stentorian voice, iron throat.

Adj. loud, distinct, audible; at full volume; noisy, full of noise, uproarious, rowdy, rumbustious, disorderly; clamorous, shouting, crying; sonorous, deep, full, powerful; lusty, full-throated, stentorian; piercing; thundering, thunderous, 'crashing'; shrill, strident; brassy; resounding, resonant; swelling, crescendo; fortissimo.

**Vb. be loud;** give tongue, call, catcall, caterwaul; scream, whistle, **shrill;** vociferate, shout, **cry; laugh;** clap, stamp; roar, bellow, howl; din, sound, boom, reverberate, **resound;** rattle, thunder, fulminate, storm, clash; ring, peal, clang, crash; bray, blare; slam, **bang;** burst, explode, detonate; knock, knock hard, hammer, drill; deafen, stun; swell; **rampage.**

**Adv. loudly;** aloud; full blast, full chorus; fortissimo, crescendo.

**396 Faintness**

**N. faintness;** less sound, low volume, reduction of sound; dull sound, thud, thump, bump; whisper; breath; undertone, undercurrent of sound; murmur, hum, drone, **roll;** sigh, moan; scratch, squeak, creak, pop; tick, click; tinkle, clink, chink; buzz, whirr; purr, purl, swish; burble, gurgle, rustle; patter; soft footfall, pad; soft voice, quiet tone, conversation level.

**silencer,** mute, damper, muffler, soft pedal, **mute;** cork; grease, oil, **lubricant.**

**Adj. muted,** distant, faint, inaudible, barely audible, just caught; weak, feeble; soft, low, gentle; piano, subdued; dull, dead; bated, **hoarse.**

**Vb. sound faint,** whisper, breathe, murmur, mutter, **speak low;** sing low, hum, croon, purr; buzz, drone; purl, babble, ripple, lap, gurgle, **flow;** tinkle, chime; moan, sigh, **blow;** rustle, swish; tremble, melt; squeak, creak; plop, pop; tick, click; clink, chink; thud, thump, **sound dead.**

**mute,** soften, dull, deaden, dampen, soft-pedal; hush, muffle, stifle, **silence.**

**Adv. faintly,** with bated breath; aside; piano, pianissimo.

**397 Bang: sudden and violent noise**

**N. bang,** report, explosion, blast, blow-out, backfire, sonic boom; peal, thunderclap, crash; crackling, crackle; smack, crack, snap; slap, clap, tap, rap; knock, slam; pop, plop; burst, burst of fire; volley, round, salvo; shot, cracker, banger, squib; bomb, grenade; gun, rifle, shot gun, **firearm.**

**Adj. rapping;** banging, crashing, popping.

**Vb. crackle;** sizzle, fizzle, spit, **effervesce;** crack, split; click, rattle; snap, clap, rap, tap, slap, smack; plop, plonk.

**bang,** slam, wham, clash, crash, boom; explode, blast, detonate; pop, backfire; burst, **be loud.**

**398 Roll: repeated and protracted sounds**

**N. roll,** rumbling, grumbling; mutter, murmur, rhubarb rhubarb; din, rattle, racket, clack, clatter, chatter, clutter; clang, ping; tattoo, peal, carillon, **campanology;** dingdong, cuckoo, **repetition;** trill, tremolo, vibrato, **musical note;** quaver; hum, whirr, buzz, drone; singing; barrage, cannonade, machine gun.

**Adj. rolling,** resonant; dingdong, monotonous.

**Vb. roll,** drum, tattoo, tap, thrum; chug; boom, roar; grumble, rumble, drone, hum, whirr; trill, chime, peal, toll; tick, beat, **oscillate;** rattle, chatter, clatter, clack; reverberate, clang, ping, ring, sing; quaver, shake, tremble, vibrate; patter, **sound faint.**

**399 Resonance**

**N. resonance;** vibration; reflection; echo, **recurrence;** twang; singing; peal, carillon; boom; clang; brass;

peal, blare, bray, flourish; tinkle, jingle; chink, clink; ping, ring, chime; low note, **musical note**; low voice, bass, baritone, contralto.

**Adj. resonant**, vibrant; fruity, **loud**; sonorous; hollow, sepulchral.

**Vb. resound**, vibrate, reverberate, echo, **roll**; whirr, buzz; hum, sing; ring, jingle, jangle, chink, clink, clank; tinkle; twang, thrum; gong, chime; tootle, toot, trumpet, blare, bray, **be loud**.

## 400 Nonresonance

**N. nonresonance**, dead sound, thud, thump, bump; plump, plop, plonk; cracked bell, **discord**; mute, damper, silencer.

**Adj. nonresonant**; dead, dull, heavy; cracked, **hoarse**; soundproof, **silent**.

**Vb. sound dead**; click, flap; thump, thud, bump, pound; soft-pedal, muffle, damp, stop, soften, deaden, stifle, silence, **mute**.

## 401 Sibilation: hissing sound

**N. sibilation**, hiss; sigma, sibilant; sputter, splutter; splash; rustle, squelch; swish, escape of air; goose, serpent.

**Adj. sibilant**.

**Vb. hiss**; snort, wheeze, snuffle, whistle; buzz, fizz, fizzle, sizzle, sputter, splutter, spit; splash, **effervesce**; swish; squelch, suck; rustle, **rasp**.

## 402 Stridor: harsh sound

**N. stridor**, cacophony, **discord**; roughness; harsh sound, aspirate, guttural; **friction**; scrape, scratch, creak, squeak; shriek, screech, squawk, yelp; high pitch, piping; wolf whistle; bleep; piercing note, **musical note**; high voice, soprano, treble, falsetto, tenor, countertenor; twang, drone; brass, blare; pipe, fife, piccolo, penny

whistle, **flute**.

**Adj. strident**; grating, rusty, harsh, brassy, brazen, metallic; high, acute, shrill, piping; penetrating, piercing, tinny, **loud**; dry, reedy, squeaky, scratchy; cracked; sharp, flat, inharmonious.

**hoarse**, husky, throaty, guttural, raucous, rough, gruff; hollow, deep, sepulchral; stertorous.

**Vb. rasp**, stridulate, grate, crunch, scrunch, grind, saw, scrape, scratch, squeak; snore, snort; cough, hawk, choke, gasp, sob; bray, croak, caw, screech; grunt, burr, aspirate; crack, jar, clash, jangle, twang, clank, clink, **discord**.

**shrill**, stridulate, bleep; drone; trumpet, blare, **be loud**; pipe, flute, **play music**; whistle, catcall, caterwaul, **cry**; scream, squeal, yelp, screech, squawk; buzz, hum, whine; go right through one, strain.

## 403 Human cry

**N. cry**, animal cry; human cry, exclamation, **voice**; **speech**; talk, chat, conversation; shouting, outcry, clamour, hullabaloo; yodel, song, chant, chorus, **vocal music**; shout, yell, whoop, bawl; howl, scream, shriek, **pain**; hail, **call**; tallyho, **chase**; cheer; laugh, giggle, **laughter**; hoot, boo, **disapprobation**; plaint, complaint; sob, sigh; caterwaul, squeal, wail, whine, boohoo; grunt, gasp, **respiration**; barker.

**Adj. crying**, clamorous; loud, vocal, vociferous; stentorian, full-throated, lusty; rousing, cheering.

**Vb. cry**, exclaim, ejaculate, **speak**; call, hail, **greet**; raise a cry, whoop, hoot, boo, whistle, **disapprove**; cheer, scream, screech, yowl, howl, groan, **feel pain**; snigger, giggle, **laugh**; caterwaul, squall, boohoo, whine, whimper, wail, fret, pule, **weep**; moan, sob, sigh, **lament**; mutter, grumble, **sound faint**: gasp, grunt, snort, snore, **breathe**; squeak, squawk, yap, bark.

**vociferate**, clamour, start shouting, shout, bawl, yell, holler; chant, chorus, **sing**; cheer, give three cheers, exult, **rejoice**; hiss, hoot, boo, **disapprove**; roar, bellow; yell, make oneself hoarse, **be loud**.

### 404 Ululation: animal sounds

**N. ululation**, animal noise, howling; drone; warble, call, cry, note; squeak, cheep, twitter; buzz, hum; croak, caw, coo, hiss, quack, cluck, squawk, screech; baa, moo, neigh, whinny; cock-a-doodle-doo, cuckoo; miaow, bark, yelp, yap, snap, snarl.

**Adj. ululant**; full-throated, **loud**; roaring.

**Vb. ululate**, cry, call, give tongue; squawk, screech; caterwaul, yowl, howl, wail; roar, bellow, bell; hum, drone, buzz; spit, **hiss**; woof, bark, bay; yelp, yap; snap, snarl, growl, whine; trumpet, bell; bray, neigh, whinny; bleat, baa; low, moo; miaow, purr; quack, cackle, gaggle, gobble, gabble, cluck, clack; grunt, snort, squeal; pipe, pule; chatter, sing, chirp, cheep, peep, tweet, twitter, chuckle, whirr, coo; caw, croak; hoot, honk, boom; grate, stridulate, squeak, **rasp**; sing like a bird, warble, carol, whistle, **sing**.

### 405 Melody: concord

**N. melody**, music; musical quality, tonality, euphony; chime, harmony, concord, concert, **agreement**; consonance, assonance; unison; resolution (of a discord); cadence, counterpoint, polyphony; thorough bass, figured

bass, part, second, chorus; instrumentation; tone, tone colour; **musical skill**; phrase, passage, theme, coda; movement, **musical piece**.

**musical note**, note, keyboard, manual, pedal point; sharp, flat, double sharp, accidental, natural, tone, semitone; keynote, fundamental note; tonic, dominant, leading note; interval, second, third, fourth, fifth, octave, ninth; gamut, scale (see **key**); chord, arpeggio; grace note, grace, ornament, crush note, acciaccatura, mordent, turn, shake, trill, tremolo, vibrato, cadenza; tone, tonality, register, pitch, high note; low note; undertone, harmonic, upper partial; monotone, drone; phrase, flourish, **tune**; bugle call, **call**.

**notation**, tonic solfa; written music, score; signature, clef, bar, stave, staff; line, space, brace; rest, pause, interval; breve, semibreve, minim, crotchet, quaver, semiquaver.

**tempo**, time, beat; rhythm, prosody; measure, timing; upbeat, downbeat; suspension, long note; rallentando, andante, adagio.

**key**, signature, clef, major key, scale, gamut, major scale, series, tone row; mode; Indian mode, raga.

**Adj. melodious**, musical, catchy; low, soft; sweet, velvet, mellifluous; clear; silvery; **resonant**; euphonious, true.

**harmonious**, consonant, matching, **similar**; monophonic; monotonous.

**harmonic**, chromatic; tonal, atonal, sharp, flat; modal, minor, major.

**Vb. harmonize**, concert, blend, chime, **accord**; chorus, **sing**; tune, pitch, string, **adjust**; compose, put to music, orchestrate, **compose music**; modulate, transpose; resolve a discord, restore harmony.

**406 Discord**

**N.** **discord**, dissonance, disharmony; tone row; imperfect cadence; preparation (of a discord); cacophony; Babel; row, din, noise, pandemonium, bedlam, tumult, racket, **turmoil**; atmospherics, wow, flutter.

**Adj.** **discordant**; **contrary**; grating, harsh, raucous, **strident**; inharmonious; cracked; sharp, flat; atonal, toneless, singsong.

**Vb.** discord, lack harmony, **disagree**; jangle, jar, grate, clash, crash; saw, scrape, **rasp**; be harsh; play sharp, play flat; thrum, drone, whine; prepare a discord.

**407 Music**

**N.** **music**, harmony; sweet music, **melody**; **musical skill**; writing music, composition; instrumental music, counterpoint, contrapuntal music; classical music, light music, pop; musical wallpaper, disco music; hot music, jazz, blue note, blues, mainstream jazz, trad, Dixieland, ragtime, swing, bop, stride piano; jive, rock 'n roll, rock music, heavy metal, new wave, punk; reggae; rhythm 'n blues, blue grass, folk; written music, score, performance, concert, prom; singsong; music festival, eisteddfod; school of music; Tin Pan Alley.

**campanology**; carillon, chime, peal; touch; hunting, making place; hunt, hunt forward, hunt backward, dodge; round; method, Plain Bob, Treble Bob; doubles; minor, major, royal; bell; treble bell, **gong**; church bell, **call**.

**tune**, melody, strain; theme song, signature tune; descant; reprise, refrain; air, aria, solo; peal, chime, carillon; flourish; phrase, passage, measure.

**musical piece**, piece, composition, opus,

work, piece of music; tape, recording, **gramophone**; instrumentation; arrangement, adaptation, setting; accompaniment, obbligato; voluntary, prelude, overture, intermezzo; incidental music, romance, rhapsody, extravaganza, impromptu, fantasia, caprice, divertimento, raga; medley, potpourri; study; suite, fugue, canon, toccata; sonata, concerto, symphony; pastorale, scherzo, rondo, jig, reel; gavotte, minuet, tarantella, mazurka, polonaise, polka, waltz, **dance**; march, dirge; nocturne, serenade; statement, exposition, development, variation; theme, motive; movement; passage, phrase; chord, **musical note**; cadenza, coda.

**vocal music**, singing, lyricism; scat singing; part, opera, operetta, light opera, musical comedy, musical, **stage play**; oratorio, cantata, chorale; descant; chant, plainsong; recitative; coloratura; singing practice, solfa; anthem, psalm, **hymn**; song, lay, roundelay, carol, lyric, lilt; lieder, ballad; folk song, top twenty, hit parade; ditty, shanty, calypso; spiritual, blues; part song, glee, madrigal, round, catch, canon; chorus, refrain, burden; choral hymn; boat song, barcarole; lullaby, cradle song; serenade; love song, amorous ditty; song, bird call, dawn chorus; requiem, dirge, threnody, **lament**; recitative; words to be sung, libretto; psalter.

**duet**, duo, trio, sextet, septet, octet; concerto, solo; ensemble.

**Adj.** **musical**, **melodious**; philharmonic; vocal; recitative; lyric; choral; contrapuntal; set, set to music; instrumental; blue, cool; hot, jazzy, swinging, swung.

**Adv.** **adagio**, lento, largo, andante, moderato; allegro, allegretto; vivace, presto, prestissimo; piano, pianissimo, forte, fortissimo, sforzando; glissando, legato; staccato; crescendo, diminuendo, rallentando; tremolo, pizzicato, vibrato.

## 408 Musician

N. **musician**, artiste, virtuoso, soloist; **proficient person**; player; performer, concert artist; bard, minstrel, troubadour; street musician; composer; scorer; swinger, cat; music writer, librettist, song writer, psalmist; music teacher, music master, conductor (see **orchestra**); Pan; music lover, music critic.

**instrumentalist**, player, pianist, accompanist; keyboard performer, organist, concertina player; scraper; lyre player; piper, piccolo player, flautist; horn player; drummer, drummer boy, drum major; percussionist; hurdygurdy man.

**orchestra**; ensemble, strings, brass, woodwind, percussion; band, skiffle group, steel band; conductor, maestro; leader, first violin; orchestra player, bandsman.

**vocalist**, songster, warbler; Siren, mermaid; troubadour, minstrel; coloratura; treble, soprano, contralto, alto, tenor, countertenor, baritone, bass; songbird, nightingale, lark, thrush, blackbird, **bird**.

**choir**, chorus, waits, glee club; choir festival, eisteddfod; chorister, choirboy; cantor.

**musical skill**, musical ability, musical appreciation; performance, execution, fingering, touch, expression; **skill**.

Adj. **musicianly**, fond of music, knowing music, musical; minstrel; vocal, coloratura, lyric, choral; plain-song, **melodious**; instrumental, contrapuntal.

Vb. **be musical**, learn music, sight-read; have a good ear, have perfect pitch.

**compose music**, compose, write music, put to music, score, arrange, transpose, orchestrate, improvise.

**play music**, play, perform, execute, render, interpret; conduct, beat time; syncopate; accompany; pedal, vamp, strum; harp, pluck; thrum, twang; fiddle, bow, scrape, saw; wind, blow, bugle, sound, trumpet, toot, tootle; pipe, flute, whistle; drum, tattoo, beat, tap, ruffle, **roll**; ring, ring a change; toll, knell; tune, string, set to concert pitch; practise, improvise, play a voluntary, prelude; give an encore.

**sing**, chant, hymn; intone, descant; warble, carol, lilt, trill, croon, hum; whistle; yodel; solfa; sing seconds; chorus, choir; sing to, serenade; minstrel; chirp, twitter, pipe; purr, **sound faint**.

## 409 Musical instruments

N. **musical instrument**, band, music, concert, orchestra; strings, brass, wind, woodwind, percussion; diaphragm, sound box.

**harp**; lyre, lute, sitar; zither, guitar, mandolin, ukulele, banjo, balalaika, zither; plectrum, fret.

**viol**, violin, fiddle, kit; crowd; viola or tenor violin, cello or violoncello; musical saw; bow; string, catgut; bridge; resin.

**piano**, grand piano, concert grand, upright piano, dulcimer, harpsichord, spinet, clavichord; player piano, pianola; keyboard, manual; loud pedal, damper.

**organ**; reed organ, harmonium, American organ; mouth organ, harmonica; comb; accordion, concertina; barrel organ, hurdy-gurdy; great organ,

organ pipe, organ stop, manual, key-board.

**flute**, fife, piccolo, flageolet, recorder; woodwind, reed instrument, clarinet, basset horn; saxophone, oboe; bassoon, ocarina; pipe, reed, straw; bagpipes; pan pipes; nose flute; whistle; mouthpiece.

**horn**, brass; bugle horn, bugle, trumpet, clarion; alpenhorn, French horn, sousaphone; euphonium, serpent; cornet, trombone, sackbut, tuba, bass tuba; conch, shell.

**gong**, bell; treble bell, church bell, alarm bell, **danger signal**; peal, carillon; rattle, clappers, castanets; xylophone, marimba; vibraphone; musical glasses, harmonica; glockenspiel; triangle; percussion instrument.

**drum**, timpani; war drum, tomtom; tabor, tambourine.

**gramophone**, record player, radiogram; tape recorder, hi-fi, stereo set, music centre; playback; recording, tape, cassette; gramophone record, disc, platter, LP, album, single, track, **registration**; musical box, jukebox; head, needle, stylus, pickup, cartridge; deck, turntable; amplifier, speaker, tweeter, woofer.

**mute**, damper, pedal, **silencer**.

## 410 Hearing

**N. hearing**, audition, **acoustics**; sense of hearing, good ear; reception, earshot, range, reach; something to hear, earful.

**listening**, **attention**; aural examination, **enquiry**; **interpretation**; sound recording, **record**; audition, **experiment**; interview, audience, hearing, **conference**; legal hearing, **legal trial**.

**listener**, hearer, audience, auditorium; stalls, pit, gallery, **spectator**; radio ham; disciple; monitor; little pitcher, **inquisitive person**.

**ear**, auditory apparatus, auditory nerve, acoustic organ; lug, lobe, auricle; aural cavity, cochlea, eardrum, tympanum; auditory canal, labyrinth; hearing specialist.

**hearing aid**, deaf-aid, ear trumpet; hearing instrument, stethoscope; loudspeaker, loudhailer, tannoy, public address system, **publication**; microphone, mike, amplifier, **megaphone**; telephone, phone, blower; receiver, earpiece; walkie-talkie, **telecommunication**; sound recorder, sonar, **recording instrument**; radiogram, **gramophone**.

**Adj. auditory**, hearing, aural; audiovisual; acoustic; **attentive**; within earshot, audible.

**Vb. hear**, catch; list, listen; lip-read, **interpret**; prepare to hear; overhear, eavesdrop; intercept, bug, tap; hearken, give ear, give audience, interview, grant an interview, **interrogate**; hear confession, **confess**; be attentive; catch a sound; be told, hear it said, **be informed**.

**be heard**, become audible, **sound; be loud**; gain a hearing, have an audience; be broadcast.

**Adv. in earshot**, in one's hearing.

## 411 Deafness

**N. deafness**, hardness of hearing; inaudibility, **silence**.

**Adj. deaf**, dull of ear, hard of hearing; unable to hear; deaf to; deaf to music, tone-deaf; hard to hear; inaudible, **silent**.

**Vb. be deaf**, hear nothing, fail to catch; refuse to hear, **disregard**; turn a deaf ear to, **refuse**; use a hearing aid, lip-read, **translate**.

**deafen**, make deaf, stun, **be loud**.

**412 Light**

N. light, daylight, light of day, noon, broad day, **morning**; sunbeam, sunlight, sun; starlight, moonlight, moonshine; twilight; artificial light, candlelight, firelight, **lighting**; splendour; candle power, magnitude; sheen, shine, gloss, lustre (see **reflection**); blaze, blaze of light, glare, dazzle; flare, flame, **fire**; halo, nimbus, glory, corona; variegated light, spectrum, rainbow; coloration, riot of colour, **colour**; white.

flash; lightning, lightning flash; beam, stream, shaft, bar, ray, pencil; streak, meteor flash; sparkle, spark, glint, glitter, play, play of light; blink, twinkle, twinkling, flicker, glimmer, gleam, shimmer; spangle, tinsel; searchlight, **lamp**; firefly, **glowworm**.

glow, flush, sunset glow, afterglow, dawn, sunset; steady flame, steady beam; aurora; northern lights; radiance, incandescence, **heat**; phosphorescence; will-o'-the-wisp, **glowworm**.

radiation, emission, absorption; radioactivity; radioisotope; particle counter, fallout, mushroom cloud, **poison**; radiation belt, **atmosphere**; radio wave, **sound**; sky wave; wavelength; high frequency, VHF, UHF; interference, static, **electricity**; microwave; infrared radiation, radiant heat or energy; visible light; ultraviolet radiation; X-ray, cosmic radiation, cosmic noise; photoelectric cell; roentgen.

reflection, interference, polish, gloss, sheen, shine, lustre; glare, dazzle, blink, reflector, **mirror**; mirror image, **image**.

light contrast, tonality, chiaroscuro; value, half-tone, mezzotint.

optics, fibre optics; **photography**; radiology; magnification.

Adj. luminous, lucid; light, lit; bright, gay, resplendent, splendid, brilliant, flamboyant, vivid; colourful, coloured; radiant, refulgent; glaring, lurid, garish; incandescent, flaming, aflame, aglow, ablaze, **fiery**; glowing, red; fluorescent; soft; lustrous, shiny, glossy.

undimmed, clear, bright, fair, unclouded; sunny; starlit; glassy; lucid, pellucid, diaphanous, translucent, **transparent**.

radiating, radiant; cosmic; hot; reflective.

Vb. shine, be bright, burn, blaze, flame, flare, be hot; glow; shine full, glare, dazzle, blind; play, dance; flash, coruscate; glisten, blink; glimmer, flicker, twinkle; glitter, shimmer, glance; scintillate, sparkle, spark; shine again, reflect; take a shine, gleam, glint.

radiate, beam, shoot, **emit**; reflect, refract; bombard; X-ray.

make bright, lighten, dawn, rise, wax (moon); clear, lift, brighten; light, ignite, **kindle**; show a light, shed lustre; flood with light, irradiate, illuminate; shine within, shine through, be visible; pass light through; polish, burnish, **clean**.

**413 Darkness**

N. darkness, dark; black; night, nightfall; dead of night, **midnight**; Stygian gloom; murk, gloom, dusk; shade, shadow, umbra, penumbra; silhouette, negative, radiograph, **photography**; dark place, darkroom; cavern, mine, dungeon, depths.

obscuration, blackout, shade; eclipse; extinction of light; sunset, sundown, **evening**; shading, hatching, chiaroscuro; dark lantern; snuffer, dip switch.

**Adj. dark**, sombre, swarthy, **black**; obscure, inky; cavernous; Stygian; murky; funereal, dreary, dismal, sombre; lurid, **dim**, shady, **shadowy**; all black; benighted; nocturnal; secret, **occult**.

**unlit**; overcast; cloudy, **opaque**.

**Vb. be dark**; lour; gather; **be dim**; **lurk**; look black, gloom.

**darken**, black, brown; occult, eclipse, mantle, **cover**; curtain, shutter, veil, **screen**; obscure, obfuscate; dim; overcast, overshadow, spread gloom; spread a shade, cast a shadow; silhouette, **represent**; shade, hatch; **blur**; **blacken**.

**snuff out**, extinguish, quench, dip.

**Adv. darkling**; at night.

## 414 Dimness

**N. dimness**, blur, soft focus; loom; grey; lacklustre, lack of sparkle; matt finish; poor visibility; murk, gloom; fog, mist, **cloud**; shadow, shade, shadow of a shade; spectre, **visual fallacy**.

**half-light**, bad light; **evening**; twilight, dusk; daybreak, break of day, grey dawn; penumbra, partial eclipse.

**glimmer**, flicker, **flash**; 'ineffectual fire', firefly, **glow-worm**; side lights; candlelight, firelight, **light**; ember, hot coal; smoky light, tallow candle, dip; dark lantern, **lamp**; moonbeam, moonlight, starlight.

**Adj. dim**; dusky, dusk, twilight, crepuscular; wan, dun, grey, pale, **colourless**; faint; indistinct, bleary; glassy, dull, lacklustre, leaden; flat, matt; filmy, hazy, foggy, fogbound, misty, nebulous, **cloudy**; thick, smoky, muddy, **opaque**; dingy, rusty, **dirty**.

**shadowy**, shady, overcast; vague, indistinct, obscure, fuzzy; deceptive; with-

drawn, **invisible**; dreamlike, **insubstantial**.

**Vb. be dim**, be indistinct, loom; grow grey, fade, wane, pale, **lose colour**; lour, gloom; glimmer, flicker, gutter, sputter; **lurk**.

**bedim**, dim, dip; obscure, **blur**; smirch, smear, besmirch, sully; rust, mildew, muddy, dirty, **make unclean**; smoke, fog, mist, **make opaque**; overshadow, overcast; shade, shadow, veil, **cover**; hatch, **darken**.

**Adv. dimly**, vaguely, indistinctly.

## 415 Luminary: source of light

**N. luminary**, **light**; naked light, flame, **fire**; flare, source of light, orb of day, **sun**; orb of night, **moon**; starlight, **star**; bright star; evening star, Hesperus, Venus; morning star; fireball, **meteor**; galaxy, Milky Way, northern lights; lightning, lightning flash; spark, sparkle, **flash**.

**glow-worm**, **glow**; firefly; will-o'-the-wisp, Jack-o'-lantern; fireball; fiery dragon.

**torch**, brand, coal, ember; torchlight, link, match, **lighter**; candle, tallow candle, taper, spill, wick, dip, rushlight, nightlight, naked light, flare, gas jet, burner.

**lamp**; lantern, bull's-eye; safety lamp, oil lamp, gas lamp, gas mantle, mantle; electric lamp, flash gun, torch, flashlight, searchlight, arc light, floodlight; headlight, side light; tail light, reflector; bulb, flashbulb, electric bulb, filament; vapour light, mercury vapour lamp, Chinese lantern, fairy lights; magic lantern, projector; light fitting, chandelier, lustre; standard lamp, lamppost, standard; socket, bracket; candle holder, candlestick.

**lighting**, **light**; artificial lighting, indirect lighting; gas lighting, limelight, spotlight.

**signal light, danger signal;** traffic light, winker; Very light, rocket, flare, star shell, parachute flare, flare, flare path, beacon, beacon fire, **signal;** lighthouse, lightship.

**fireworks,** illuminations, firework display, pyrotechnics; sky rocket, Roman candle, sparkler; banger, **explosive.**

**Adj. luminescent,** luminous, incandescent; fluorescent, neon; radiant; colourful, **coloured;** bright, gay.

**Vb. illuminate,** light, shine, **make bright.**

## 416 Screen

**N. screen,** shield, **protection;** covert, **shelter;** bower, **arbour;** shady nook; sunshade, parasol; sun hat, **shade;** awning, **canopy;** visor; lampshade; blinkers; eyelid, **eye;** dark glasses; partition; wall, hedge, **fence;** filter, **exclusion;** mask, **disguise;** hood, veil, mantle, **cloak.**

**curtain, shade;** window curtain, shade, blind, sunblind; shutter.

**obfuscation,** smoke screen; fog, mist, **moisture;** pall, cloud, dust, film, scale.

**Adj. screened,** sheltered; cool, **cold;** shady, **shadowy;** hooded, **blind;** impervious, impermeable.

**Vb. screen,** shield, shelter, **safeguard;** protect, **defend;** parry; blanket, **exclude;** veil, hood, **cover;** mask, hide, shroud, **conceal;** intercept, **obstruct;** blindfold, **blind;** shade, shadow, darken; curtain, canopy; **close;** cloud, fog, mist; smoke, frost, glaze, film, **make opaque.**

## 417 Transparency

**N. transparency,** transmission of light; clarity; transparent medium, water,

ice, crystal, perspex, cellophane, glass, lens, eyepiece; pane, sheer silk, gossamer, gauze, lace, chiffon, **insubstantial thing.**

**Adj. transparent,** diaphanous, sheer, see-through; thin, fine, filmy, pellucid; translucent; liquid, limpid; crystal, crystalline, vitreous, glassy; clear, serene, lucid.

**Vb. be transparent,** transmit light, show through; shine through, pass light through, **make bright;** render transparent, clarify.

## 418 Opacity

**N. opacity;** thickness, solidity, **density;** frost; **dirt;** fog, mist, dense fog, smog, **cloud;** film, scale, **screen;** smoke screen

**Adj. opaque,** thick, impervious to light, blank; cloudy, milky, filmy, turbid, muddy; foggy, hazy, misty, murky, smoky, **dim; dirty.**

**Vb. make opaque;** cloud, thicken; frost, film, smoke; obfuscate; **coat;** be opaque, **screen.**

## 419 Semitransparency

**N. semitransparency;** dark glasses; gauze, muslin, net; pearl, opal; horn, mica; tissue, tissue paper.

**Adj. semitransparent,** filmy; translucent, opalescent, milky, pearly; matt, misty, **dim,** cloudy.

## 420 Colour

**N. colour,** complementary colour, chromatic aberration; range of colour, chromatic scale; prism, spectrum, rainbow; mixture of colours, harmony, discord; colour scheme, palette; coloration, **painting;** colour photography, riot of colour, splash; tincture, metal, fur, **heraldry.**

**chromatics,** science of colour, spectrum

analysis; prism.

**hue**, colour quality, saturation, tone, value; warmth; coloration, livery; pigmentation, colouring, complexion, natural colour; hue of health, flush, blush, glow; sickly hue, pallor; tint, shade, nuance, cast, dye; tinge, patina; half-tone, mezzotint.

**pigment**, colouring matter, rouge, **cosmetic**; dye, madder, cochineal, **red pigment**; indigo; woad; artificial dye, stain, fixative, mordant; wash, whitewash, distemper; paint, **art equipment**.

**Adj. coloured**, fast, constant; colourful, chromatic; **uniform**; prismatic; **variegated**.

**florid**, colourful; ruddy, **red**; intense, deep, strong; vivid, brilliant, **luminous**; warm, glowing, rich, gorgeous; gay, bright; gaudy, garish, showy, flashy; glaring, spectacular; harsh, stark, raw, crude; lurid, loud.

**soft-hued**, soft, quiet, tender, delicate, refined; pearly; light, pale, pastel; dull, flat, matt, dead; simple, sober, sad, **plain**; sombre, dark, **black**; drab, dingy; mellow; matching.

**Vb. colour**, crayon, daub, paint; rouge, **redden**; pigment, tattoo; dye, dip; woad, **blue**; tint; shade, shadow, **blacken**; tincture, tinge; wash, distemper, lacquer, **coat**; stain, run, discolour; tan, weather, mellow; illuminate, emblazon; whitewash, silver, **whiten**; yellow, **gild**; enamel.

## 421 Achromatism: absence of colour

**N. achromatism**; **photography**; pallor; anaemia; pigment deficiency; neutral tint; monochrome; albino, blond.

**bleacher**, peroxide, bleach, lime.

**Adj. colourless**, toneless, neutral; faint; albino, fair, blond, **yellow**; mousy; bloodless, anaemic; without colour;

pale, pallid, **white**; ashy, ashen, livid, pasty, doughy, mealy, sallow, sickly, **unhealthy**; dingy, dull, leaden, grey; blank, glassy, lacklustre; lurid, ghastly, wan, **dim**; cadaverous, **dead**.

**Vb. lose colour**, be dim; pale, fade, bleach, blanch, turn pale, change countenance, **whiten**; run.

**decolorize**, fade, etiolate; blanch, bleach, peroxide; **whiten**; deaden, weaken; pale, dim; dull, tarnish, discolour, **make unclean**.

## 422 Whiteness

**N. whiteness**; lack of pigment; white light, **light**; white heat; white man, white woman, white, paleface; albino.

**white thing**, alabaster, marble; snow, chalk, paper, milk, flour, salt, ivory, lily, swan; albino; silver, white metal, white gold, pewter, platinum; pearl, teeth; white patch, blaze.

**whiting**, white lead; whitewash, white paint, Chinese white.

**Adj. white**, candid, pure; light, bright, **luminous**; silvery, silver; alabaster, marble; snowy, snow-capped; frosty; white hot, **hot**; white like ivory; pure white; lacking pigment; **clean**.

**whitish**, pearly, milky; ivory, waxen, sallow, pale, **colourless**; off-white, mushroom, magnolia; ecru, **brown**; hoary, grizzled, **grey**; pepper-and-salt, **mottled**; blond, fair, Nordic; dusty, white with dust.

**Vb. whiten**, white, whitewash, wash, **clean**; blanch, bleach; pale, fade; frost, silver, grizzle.

## 423 Blackness

**N. blackness**; black, sable; pigmentation, pigment, dark colouring; colour; depth, deep tone; chiaroscuro, **chequer**; black man, black woman, black, Negro, Negress; coloured man or woman, coloured; blackamoor.

**black thing**, coal, charcoal, soot, pitch, tar; ebony, jet, ink, smut; bruise, black eye; blackberry, sloe; crow, raven, blackbird; black clothes, mourning.

**black pigment**, blacking, lampblack; ivory black; ink, japan; burnt cork.

**Adj. black**, sable; jetty, inky, **dark**, smoky, smutty, **dirty**; dark, brunette; coloured; sombre, mourning, **funereal**; deep; nocturnal.

**blackish**, rather black; swarthy, dusky, dark, coloured; livid; **dim**.

**Vb. blacken**, black, japan, ink; dirty, blot, smudge, smirch, **make unclean**; deepen, **darken**; singe, char, **burn**.

### 424 Greyness

**N. greyness**, neutral tint; hoary head; pewter, silver; gunmetal, slate; grey, oyster.

**Adj. grey**, neutral, dull, sombre, leaden, livid; cool, quiet; grizzled, hoary; silvery, pearly; mousy, dun, drab; steely, ashen, ashy, smoky; dapple-grey.

### 425 Brownness

**N. brownness**, brown, bronze, copper, amber; tobacco leaf, autumn colours; cinnamon, coffee, chocolate; butterscotch, caramel, burnt almond; walnut, mahogany; dark skin or complexion, suntan; brunette.

**brown pigment**, ochre, sepia, raw sienna, raw umber.

**Adj. brown**, bronze; sunburnt; dark, brunette; hazel; light brown, ecru, oatmeal, beige, buff, fawn, biscuit, mushroom; dun, drab; khaki; tawny, tan, foxy; bay, roan, sorrel, chestnut, auburn; russet, maroon; puce; dark brown, mocha, chocolate.

**Vb. embrown**, brown, bronze, tan, sunburn; singe, char, toast, **burn**.

### 426 Redness

**N. redness**, blush, flush, sunset, dawn, **glow**; warmth; bloom; high colour; red colour, crimson, scarlet, carnation, rose, geranium, poppy; cherry, tomato; burgundy, port, claret; gore, **blood**; ruby, garnet, cornelian; flame, **fire**; red ink, rubric; red planet, Mars; redskin, Red Indian; redhead.

**red pigment**, red dye, cochineal, carmine; vermilion, madder, crimson lake; red ochre, red lead; rouge, lipstick, **cosmetic**.

**Adj. red**, ruddy, sanguine, florid; warm, hot, fiery, glowing, red-hot, **hot**; fevered; bright red; carroty, sandy, auburn, russet, rusty, **brown**; pink, rosy, coral, carnation, damask; crimson, cerise, carmine; fuchsia, magenta, maroon, **purple**; sanguine; scarlet, vermilion, pillarbox red.

**bloodstained**, bloodshot; sanguine; ensanguined, bloody, gory.

**Vb. redden**, rouge; dye red, stain with blood; flush, blush, glow; mantle, colour, crimson, go red.

### 427 Orange

**N. orange**, gold, old gold; or, **heraldry**; copper, amber; sunflower, marigold; apricot, tangerine; marmalade; ochre, Mars orange, henna.

**Adj. orange**, ginger, tan; brassy.

### 428 Yellowness

**N. Yellowness**, yellow, brass, gold, old gold, topaz, amber, old ivory; sulphur, brimstone; buttercup, daffodil, primrose, dandelion; lemon, honey; saffron, mustard; jaundice, yellow fever; sallow skin, fair hair; blond.

**yellow pigment**, gamboge, cadmium yellow; yellow ochre, weld.

**Adj. yellow**, gold, tawny, sandy; fallow; pale yellow, jasmine, champagne;

canary yellow, gilt, gilded; deep
yellow; sallow, jaundiced.

**gild,** yellow.

## 429 Greenness

**N. greenness,** greenery; grass, moss,
turf, green leaf, **foliage;** lime, greengage; jade, emerald, beryl, aquamarine; verdigris, patina.

**green pigment,** vindian, bice; chloro-
phyll.

**Adj. green,** verdant; grassy, leafy; emerald, **blue;** avocado, olive.

## 430 Blueness

**N. blueness,** blue, azure; blue sky, blue
sea; sapphire, aquamarine, turquoise;
bluebell, cornflower, forget-me-not.

**blue pigment,** blue dye, indigo, woad;
ultramarine, cobalt, cobalt blue.

**Adj. blue,** azure; cerulean; turquoise;
light blue, pale blue, sapphire,
aquamarine, ultramarine, deep blue,
navy; indigo; livid; cold, steely, blue
with cold.

**Vb. blue,** turn blue; dye blue, woad.

## 431 Purpleness

**N. purpleness,** purple; imperial purple;
amethyst; lavender, violet, heliotrope,
heather, foxglove; plum, damson,
aubergine; gentian violet; lilac,
mauve.

**Adj. purple,** violet, mauve, lavender,
lilac, fuchsia, magenta, puce; heliotrope; dark purple, mulberry; livid,
purple with rage; **blue.**

**Vb. empurple,** purple.

## 432 Variegation

**N. variegation,** variety, diversity, **difference;** glancing, **light;** play of colour,
shot colours, opal, mother-of-pearl;
shot silk, moire; tricolour; **colour;**
peacock, peacock butterfly, tortoise-

shell, chameleon; motley, harlequin,
patchwork; mixture of colour;
kaleidoscope; rainbow, rainbow
effect, band of colour; spectrum,
prism.

**chequer,** check, pepper-and-salt; plaid,
tartan; marquetry, inlay, inlaid work;
mosaic, crazy paving, **medley.**

**stripe,** line, streak, band, bar; agate;
zebra, tiger; mackerel sky; crack,
craze, crackle; reticulation, **network.**

**maculation;** patch, speck, speckle,
freckle, **blemish;** fleck, dot, blotch,
splash; leopard, Dalmatian.

**Adj. variegated;** colourful, **florid;** tricolour; motley, random, crazy, of all
colours; **multiform;** plaid, tartan;
rainbow; prismatic; mosaic, tessel-
lated, parquet.

**iridescent,** chameleon; mother-of-pearl;
opalescent, pearly; shot, shot through
with.

**pied,** pepper-and-salt, grizzled, piebald,
skewbald, roan, check, dappled,
patchy.

**mottled,** marbled; spotted, spotty,
patchy; streaky, striated, barred,
striped; brindled, tabby; cloudy, powdered, dusty.

**Vb. variegate,** diversify, fret, pattern;
punctuate; chequer, check; patch;
**repair;** embroider, work, **decorate;**
braid, quilt; inlay, tile; stud, pepper,
dot with, speckle, freckle, spangle,
spot; sprinkle, powder, dust; tattoo,
stipple; streak, stripe; craze, crack, **be
brittle;** marble, vein, cloud, **make
opaque;** stain, blot, discolour, **make
unclean;** make iridescent; interchange
colour, play.

## 433 Vision

**N. vision,** sight; eyesight; **imagination;**
perception, recognition; acuity (of
vision); good sight, short sight, **dim**

sight; second sight; type of vision, double vision, magnification; tired vision, blinking; oculist, optician, optics; dream, **visual fallacy**.

**eye**, visual organ, organ of vision, eyeball, iris, pupil, white, cornea, retina, optic nerve; optics; saucer eyes, eyelid, **screen**; naked eye, clear eye, weak eyes, **dim sight**; dull eye; evil eye, **sorcery**; hawk, eagle, cat, lynx; Gorgon.

**look**, regard, glance, squint; glint, blink, flash; penetrating glance, gaze, watch; stare, glad eye, ogle, leer; wink, hint; grimace, dirty look, scowl, evil eye; peep, peek, glimpse, half an eye.

**inspection**, **visibility**; examination, autopsy, **enquiry**; view, preview, **manifestation**; oversight, **management**; survey, sweep, reconnaissance, reconnoitre; sight-seeing; look, once-over, rapid survey, rapid glance; second glance, double take; review; catching sight, view, first sight; espionage.

**view**; vista, prospect, outlook, perspective; aspect, **appearance**; panorama, horizon, line of sight, line of vision; range of view, ken; field of view, amphitheatre; scene, setting, stage, **theatre**; angle of vision, slant, point of view, viewpoint, standpoint; lookout, watchtower, **high structure**; gazebo; observatory; stand, grandstand, stall; loophole, peephole, **window**.

**Adj.** seeing, visual, perceptible, **visible**; ocular; binocular; perspicacious, clear-sighted, vigilant, all eyes; visionary, **imaginative**.

**Vb.** see, behold; see truly; perceive, discern, distinguish, ken, **know**; see at a glance, **be wise**; descry, discover, **detect**; sight, espy, spy, spot, observe, notice; catch sight of, sight land; catch a glimpse of, glimpse; view,

command a view of; witness, be a spectator, **watch**; dream, see things, **imagine**; have second sight, **foresee**; become visible, **be visible**.

**gaze**, regard, quiz, gaze at, look, look at; eye, stare, peer; stare at, stare hard, goggle, gape, gawk, gawp; focus; glare, glower, look black, **be angry**; glance, glance at; squint, look askance; wink, blink, **hint**; make eyes at, ogle, leer, **court**; gloat, **be pleased**; steal a glance, peep, peek, take a peep; notice, **be attentive**; look round; look ahead, **be cautious**; **be blind**; look at each other, make eye contact.

**scan**, inspect, examine, take stock of; contemplate, pore, **study**; look through, have or take a look at, take a gander or a squint at; take a make a pilgrimage, go to see, **visit**; view, survey, sweep, reconnoitre; scout; peep, peek, **be curious**; spy, pry, snoop; observe, watch, **invigilate**; **await**; keep watch; peer; squint at; crane.

**Adv. at sight**, at first sight; **visibly**.

**Int.** look! view halloo! land ahoy!

**434 Blindness**

**N.** blindness, lack of vision; lack of light; darkness, **ignorance**; eye disease, cataract; **dim sight**; blind side, blind spot; tunnel vision, blind eye, **inattention**; dyslexia; glass eye, blind man or woman; **sleep**; Braille; white stick, guide dog.

**Adj.** blind, sightless, dark; unseeing; blindfold; benighted.

**Vb. be blind**; go blind; lose sight of; **be tentative**; wear blinkers; be blind to; ignore, have a blind spot; **disregard**; blink, wink, squint.

**blind**; dazzle, daze; darken, obscure; eclipse; blindfold, bandage, **screen**; hoodwink, bluff, **mislead**.

**435 Dim-sightedness: imperfect vision**

N. dim sight; weak eyes, eyestrain; myopia; long sight, double sight, double vision, cataract, film; swimming; conjunctivitis, pink eye; cast; squint; wink, blink; veil, curtain, **screen**; blind side, blind spot.

visual fallacy; refraction, **reflection**; aberration of light, **deviation**; false light; illusion, trick of light, phantasmagoria, mirage, **deception**, **ghost**; will-o'-the-wisp, **glow-worm**; phantom, spectre, wraith, apparition, **ghost**; vision, dream, **fantasy**; magic lantern.

Adj. dim-sighted, dark; short-sighted, long-sighted; colour-blind; cross-eyed; boss-eyed; blinking; **blind**; swimming, dizzy.

Vb. be dim-sighted, need spectacles, grope, peer, squint; blink; wink; see double, dazzle, swim; dim, fail.

blur, render indistinct, confuse; glare, dazzle, daze, **shine**; darken, dim, mist, fog, smoke, smudge; be indistinct, loom, **be dim**.

**436 Spectator**

N. spectator; seer, mystic, **visionary**; viewer, inspector, **manager**; waiter, attendant, **servant**; witness, eyewitness; passerby, bystander, onlooker; tourist, globetrotter, **traveller**; stargazer; train spotter, lookout; watchman, watch, sentry; patrolman, patrol; scout, spy, snoop, **detective**; **cinema**; viewer, TV addict; captive audience.

onlookers, audience, auditorium; box office, gate; house, gallery, gods, circle, pit, stalls; grandstand; crowd, **patron**.

Vb. watch, look at, view, see; witness, **be present**; follow, observe, attend, **be attentive**; eye, ogle, quiz; gape, gawk, stare; spy, scout, **scan**.

**437 Optical instrument**

N. optical device; glass, crystal, **transparency**; optic, lens, meniscus, eyepiece, ocular, objective; burning glass; **optics**; prism; kaleidoscope; stereoscope; light meter; visual display unit; projector, magic lantern, **cinema**; microfilm reader, slide viewer, **photography**.

eyeglass, spectacles, goggles; glasses; pince-nez, sunglasses, dark glasses, bifocals; thick glasses, contact lens; lorgnette, monocle; hand lens; oculist, optician.

telescope, reflector; terrestrial telescope, **astronomy**; sight, finder, viewfinder; periscope; spyglass, night glass; binoculars, field glasses.

microscope, electron microscope; microscopy, microphotography.

mirror, reflector; metal mirror; glass, full-length mirror.

camera; box camera, single-lens reflex camera, slr; cine camera, television camera; electric eye; shutter, aperture, stop; flashgun, **lamp**; film, **photography**.

**438 Visibility**

N. visibility; **appearance**; sight, exposure, clarity, definition, prominence; eyewitness, ocular proof, visible evidence, object lesson, **manifestation**; visual aid, **teaching**; scene, field of view, **view**; atmospheric visibility, high visibility, limit of visibility, ceiling, horizon, visible distance, **range**; landmark, signpost.

Adj. visible; perceptible; noticeable, remarkable; unmistakable, palpable; apparent; evident, showing, **manifest**; . open, naked, sighted; telescopic, just visible.

obvious, showing, **shown**; plain, clear, clear-cut; definite; distinct; unclouded; spectacular, conspicuous, pointed, prominent, salient; striking, **luminous**; glaring, staring, pronounced; vivid; plain to see.

**Vb.** be visible, become visible, be seen, show, show through, **be transparent**; attract attention, **attract notice**; hit, strike; come to light; loom, show its face, **appear**; show up, **arrive**; arise, **begin**; surface, **ascend**; emanate, come out, **emerge**; project; show, develop; manifest itself, **be plain**; **enter**; come forward, advance; dazzle, glare; shine forth, **shine**; remain visible; make visible, expose, **manifest**.

**Adv.** visibly; on show, on view.

### 439 Invisibility

**N.** invisibility, **absence**; poor visibility; distance; privacy; hiding; mystery, **secrecy**; smoke screen, mist, fog, veil, curtain; blind spot, blind eye; blind corner, **pitfall**; **danger**; blank wall; black light, **radiation**.

**Adj.** invisible, imperceptible, indiscernible; indistinguishable; unseen; sightless; remote, **distant**; **secluded**; **latent**; shadowy, dark, secret, mysterious; dark.

**indistinct**, indefinite, indistinct, **dim**; faint, inconspicuous, microscopic, **minute**; vague; fuzzy, misty, hazy.

**Vb.** be unseen, hide, go to earth, **lurk**; escape notice, blush unseen, **be humble**; become invisible, pale, fade, die, **be dim**; be lost to view, vanish, **disappear**; make invisible, submerge, **conceal**; veil, **screen**; darken, eclipse.

**Adv.** invisibly.

### 440 Appearance

**N.** appearance, phenomenon; **visibility**; first appearance, rise, **beginning**; becoming, embodiment, presence, **existence**; showing, exhibition, display, view, preview, **manifestation**; **prediction**, **probability**; revelation; outside; appearances, look of things; visual impact, face value, first blush; impression, effect; image, pose, front, public face, **duplicity**; veneer, show, seeming, semblance; side, aspect, facet; phase, guise, garb, **dressing**; colour, light, outline, shape, dimension, **form**; set, hang, look; respect, light, angle, slant, point or angle of view, **view**; a manifestation; vision, **fantasy**; false appearance, mirage, hallucination, illusion, **visual fallacy**; apparition, spectre, **ghost**; reflection, image, **similarity**; mental image, likeness, **representation**; visual, **image**.

**spectacle**, effectiveness, impression, effect; vision, sight, scene; scenery, landscape; panorama, **view**; display, pageantry, pageant, parade, review, **ostentation**; revue, extravaganza, pantomime, floor show, **stage show**; television, video; illuminations; pyrotechnics; presentation, show, exhibition, exposition, **exhibit**; art exhibition, **picture**; visual entertainment, peep show, home movies; phantasmagoria, kaleidoscope; panorama, cyclorama; tableau, transformation scene; set, decor, setting, backcloth, background, **stage set**.

**cinema**, cinematography; big screen, Hollywood, film industry; film studio, film production, **photography**; direction, continuity, cutting, montage, projection; screenplay, scenario, script; special effects, animation; sound effects, soundtrack; projector; picture house, picture palace, circuit cinema, flea pit, **theatre**; film director, film star, **actor**.

**film**, pictures, movies, flicks, celluloid; 3-D, silent film, talkie; X certificate, big picture, short, newsreel, trailer; cartoon, travelogue, documentary, feature film; art film, new wave; epic, blockbuster, extravaganza, musical, box-office movie, thriller, cliffhanger, war film, blue movie; Western, horse opera, remake; rush, preview; general release.

**mien**, look, face; play of feature, expression; brow, countenance, looks; complexion, colour, cast; air, demeanour, carriage, bearing, deportment, poise, presence; gesture, posture, behaviour, **conduct**.

**feature**, trait, mark; lines, cut, shape, fashion, figure, **form**; outline, contour, relief, elevation, profile, silhouette; visage, **face**.

**Adj. appearing**, apparent, phenomenal; seeming, specious, ostensible; deceptive; outward, external, superficial; **exterior**; salient, showing, **visible**; visual, video-; open to view, hung, **shown**; impressive, effective, spectacular, **showy**; decorative, meretricious; showing itself, **manifest**; visionary, dreamlike, **imaginary**.

**Vb. appear**, show, show through, be visible; seem, look so, **resemble**; display oneself, cut a figure; **manifest**, start, rise, arise, dawn, break, **begin**; **happen**; **arrive**; walk, haunt.

**Adv. apparently**, **visibly**; seemingly, to all appearances, at first sight, at first blush.

## 441 Disappearance

**N. disappearance**, loss; flight, **escape**; exit; dissolution; extinction; eclipse; thin air.

**Adj. disappearing**; evanescent, **transient**; dissipated; missing, **absent**; lost, lost to sight, lost to view, **invisible**; gone to earth; **gone, extinct**.

**Vb. disappear**; vanish; evaporate; dissolve, melt, **liquefy**; dwindle, **decrease**; fade, pale, **lose colour**; **be transient**; suffer an eclipse, **be dim**; disperse, dissipate, diffuse, scatter; absent oneself, fail to appear, play truant, **be absent**; go, be gone, depart, **decamp**; **escape**; hide, lie low, **lurk**; **conceal**; be lost to sight, **be unseen**; seclude oneself, **seclude**; become extinct; make disappear, erase, dispel, **obliterate**.

## 442 Intellect

**N. intellect**, mind, psyche, mentality; affect; **will**; conception; thinking principle, intellectual faculty; reasoning power; reason, **reasoning**; philosophy, **thought**; sense, **attention**; cognition, perception, insight; instinct, **intuition**; flair, **discrimination**; mental capacity, brains, senses, sense, grey matter, **intelligence**; great intellect, genius; mental evolution; seat of thought, brain, cerebellum, cortex, **head**; electroencephalograph; healthy mind.

**spirit**, soul, mind, inner sense; heart, breast, bosom, inner man, **essential part**; double, ba, genius, **self**; psyche, id, ego, self; personality; spiritualism.

**psychology**, science of mind; abnormal psychology; Freudian psychology, configuration theory; behaviourism; crowd psychology; psychiatry, psychotherapy, psychoanalysis, **therapy**; psychosurgery, **surgery**.

**psychologist**, psychiatrist, **doctor**; shrink.

**Adj. mental**, thinking, reasoning,

**rational**; cerebral, intellectual, abstract; theoretical; **immaterial**; percipient, perceptive; cognizant, **knowing**; conscious, subjective.

**psychic**, psychological; psychosomatic; subconscious, subliminal; spiritual, otherworldly, **immaterial**.

**Vb. cognize**, perceive, know; sense, become aware of, become conscious of; note, **see**; advert, mark, **notice**; **reason**; understand, **be wise**; think; conceive, invent, **discover**; imagine; appreciate, **estimate**.

### 443 Absence of intellect

**N. absence of intellect**; brute creation; vegetation, **vegetable life**; inanimate nature; instinct, **intuition**; **absence of thought**; brain damage, unsound mind.

**Adj. mindless**; animal, vegetable; mineral, inanimate, **inorganic**; unreasoning, **unthinking**; brute; brainless, empty-headed, **foolish**; moronic, wanting, **insane**.

### 444 Thought

**N. thought**, mental process, thinking; mental act; intellectual exercise, mental action, **intellect**; intellectual exercise, mental action, **intellect**; hard thinking, hard thought, concentration, **attention**; deep thought, profundity, **wisdom**; abstract thought, **idea**; conception; current of thought, reason, **reasoning**; brown study, reverie; invention, **imagination**; afterthought, **sequel**; retrospection, hindsight, **memory**; mature thought, **preparation**; forethought, **foresight**; telepathy.

**meditation**, enquiry; lateral thinking; reflection, consideration; absorption; introspection; retreat, mysticism, **piety**; deliberation, taking counsel, **advice**; examination, close study, con-

centration, application, **study**.

**philosophy**, metaphysics, ethics; philosophical thought, scientific thought, science, natural philosophy; philosophical doctrine, philosophical system, philosophical theory, **supposition**; school of philosophy, **opinion**; idealism; realism, **reasoning**; existentialism; determinism, mechanism; humanism, hedonism; utilitarianism, materialism; pragmatism; relativity; scepticism, **doubt**; nihilism, fatalism, **fate**; Scepticism; Marxism; Hinduism, Buddhism, Yoga, Zen; **religion**.

**philosopher**, man or woman of thought, **intellectual**; Academy, Garden, Porch; **ascetic**.

**Adj. thoughtful**; full of thought, pensive, ruminant, ruminative, reflective; introspective; dreamy, **abstracted**; concentrated, **attentive**; studious; considerate; prudent.

**philosophic**, metaphysical, speculative, abstract, systematic, rational.

**Vb. think**, suppose; conceive, fancy, **imagine**; think about, cogitate (see **meditate**); concentrate, **be attentive**; mull, **study**; think hard, worry at; think through, **reason**; invent, **discover**; devise, **plan**; entertain a notion, have an idea; **believe**; be mindful, **remember**.

**meditate**, ruminate, digest; wonder about, debate, **enquire**; reflect, contemplate, study; speculate; think about, consider; take stock of, ponder, weigh, **estimate**; revolve; reconsider, review, think better of; take counsel, advise with, **consult**; commune with oneself; brood, muse.

**dawn upon**, occur to, strike one; suggest itself.

**cause thought**, make one think, make an impression, **impress**; penetrate, obsess, **bias**.

**engross**, absorb, preoccupy; haunt, obsess, **bias**; fascinate, **bewitch**.

**Adv. in mind**; all things considered; after due thought; come to think of it.

## 445 Absence of thought

**N. absence of thought**, inability to think, **absence of intellect**; blank mind, **ignorance**; vacancy, abstraction; empty head; want of thought, **inattention**; gut reaction; instinct, **intuition**.

**Adj. unthinking**, **mindless**; incapable of thought; automatic; blank, vacant, empty-headed, **empty**; thoughtless, inconsiderate, **selfish**; irrational, **illogical**; stolid, stupid, wanting; inanimate, animal, vegetable, mineral.

**unthought**, inconceivable, unconsidered, impossible.

**Vb. not think**; be blank, be vacant; **disregard**; dream; **misjudge**.

## 446 Idea

**N. idea**, notion, abstraction, a thought; object of thought, abstract idea, concept; mere idea, theory, **supposition**; image, Platonic idea, archetype, **prototype**; conception, perception, apprehension, **intellect**; reflection, **thought**; impression, conceit, fancy, **imagination**; product of imagination, figment, fiction; complex; invention, brain-child; brain wave, happy thought; wheeze, wrinkle, device; view, slant, attitude, **opinion**; principle, leading idea, main idea; one idea.

**Adj. ideational**, **thoughtful**; theoretical; notional, ideal, **imaginary**.

## 447 Topic

**N. topic**, subject of thought; gossip, rumour, **news**; subject matter, subject; contents, chapter, section, head; what it is about, argument, plot, theme, message; text, commonplace, burden, motif; musical topic, statement, **musical piece**; concern, interest, matter, affair, situation, **circumstance**; shop, **business**; agenda, order paper, **policy**; motion, **request**; resolution; problem, headache, **question**; gist, pith; theorem, proposition, **supposition**; thesis, case, point, **argument**; issue, moot point, point at issue; field, field of enquiry, field of study, **study**.

**Adj. topical**; challenging; **uncertain**; thought about.

**Adv. in question**, in the mind, on-the brain; on the agenda; before the house, under consideration, under discussion.

## 448 Curiosity: desire for knowledge

**N. curiosity**, **study**; interest, itch; zeal; wanting to know; **question**; sightseeing, **land travel**; morbid curiosity.

**inquisitive person**; busybody, gossip; gossip columnist; **news reporter**; globetrotter, **spectator**; snoop, spy, **detective**; interceptor.

**Adj. inquisitive**, curious, interested; searching, **studious**; ghoulish, prurient; agog, **attentive**; wanting to know, burning with curiosity; officious.

**Vb. be curious**, want to know, only want to know; seek, **search**; test, research, **experiment**; feel a concern, be interested, take an interest; show interest, show curiosity, **be attentive**; peep, peek, spy, **scan**; snoop, pry, **enquire**; eavesdrop, intercept, bug, listen, **hear**; interfere, **meddle**; quiz, question, **interrogate**; look, stare, gape, gawk, **gaze**.

**Int.** well! what news! what's going on! who! what! where! when! how! why! why on earth!

**449 Incuriosity**

N. **incuriosity**, lack of interest, mental inertia; insouciance; apathy, **moral insensibility**.

Adj. **incurious**, **unthinking**; without interest, uninterested; aloof, distant; unconcerned, **indifferent**; listless, inert, apathetic, **impassive**.

Vb. **be incurious**; **be indifferent**; **be insensitive**; see nothing, **disregard**.

**450 Attention**

N. **attention**, notice, regard, **look**; consideration, **thought**; heed, readiness, solicitude, observance; watch, guard, **surveillance**, **caution**; introspection; **resolution**; undivided attention, whole mind, concentration, application, close study, **study**; examination, scrutiny, checkup, review; close attention, attention to detail, pedantry; diligent attention, pains, trouble; exclusive attention; absorption, preoccupation, brown study, **inattention**; interest, inquisitive attention, **curiosity**; fixation, obsession, monomania, **mania**.

Adj. **attentive**, intent, diligent, assiduous, **industrious**; considerate, thoughtful, **courteous**; mindful, regardful, **careful**; alert, ready, with it; open-eyed, waking, wakeful, awake, awake to, alive to, **sensitive**; aware, conscious, thinking, **thoughtful**; observing, watchful, **vigilant**; rapt, missing nothing; all eyes; all attention; serious, earnest; eager to learn, **studious**; close, minute, nice, meticulous, particular, punctilious, **accurate**, **fastidious**; on the look-out, **expectant**.

**obsessed**, interested **inquisitive**; singleminded, possessed; rapt; **crazy**.

Vb. **be attentive**, attend, give attention, look to, heed, mind, **be careful**; trouble oneself, care, take trouble, take pains, bother, **exert oneself**; listen; take seriously, **make important**; **think**; think of nothing else; concentrate, miss nothing; watch, be all eyes, **gaze**; **hear**; examine, inspect, vet, review, **scan**; overhaul, revise, **make better**; pore, mull, read, digest, **study**; pay some attention, glance at, flip through.

**be mindful**, be thinking of, **remember**; think of, regard, **see**; lend an ear to, **hear**, take care of, see to, **look after**; have regard to, have an eye to, **intend**; keep track of, **pursue**.

**notice**, note, register, mark, spot; review, reconsider, **meditate**; take account of, consider, weigh, **judge**; talk about, **converse**; mention, hint; recall, hark back, **repeat**; think worthy of attention, deign to notice; acknowledge, salute, **greet**.

**attract notice**, cut a figure; arouse notice, interest, **impress**; excite attention, **be visible**; make one see, **show**; bring forward, call attention to, advertise, **publish**; point to, **indicate**; stress, underline; occupy, **tempt**; fascinate, haunt, obsess, **engross**; alert, warn; call to attention, **command**.

Int. see! mark! lo! ecce! behold! lo and behold! look! look here! look out! look alive! look to it! hark! oyez! hey! mind out! nota bene! take notice! warning! cave! take care! watch your step!

**451 Inattention**

N. **inattention**, oblivion; oversight, aberration; lapse, **error**; lack of interest; detachment; disregard; want of thought; **deviation**; levity, caprice; unseeing eyes, blind spot, blind side; distraction, red herring, **inducement**; **absence of thought**; stargazer; scatterbrain, grasshopper mind, butterfly.

abstractedness, abstraction, wandering attention, absence of mind; stargazing; fit of abstraction, reverie, brown study; distraction, preoccupation.

Adj. **inattentive**, careless, **negligent**; unseeing, **blind**; **deaf**; inadvertent, **unthinking**; half asleep, only half awake; uninterested, **indifferent**; apathetic, **impassive**, oblivious, **forgetful**; inconsiderate, thoughtless, without consideration, regardless, **rash**; cavalier, offhand, cursory, superficial, **shallow**.

**abstracted**, absent-minded, absent; lost, rapt, stargazing; bemused, pensive, dreamy; **sleepy**.

**distracted**; otherwise engaged; **nervous**.

**light-minded**, wandering, desultory, trifling; frivolous, flippant; airy, volatile, flighty, giddy, dizzy, scatty, harebrained, featherbrained; wild, harumscarum; **crazy**; inconstant, to one thing constant never, **capricious**.

Vb. **be inattentive**, hear nothing, **be blind**; **be deaf**; overlook, commit an oversight, **blunder**; let slip, catch oneself doing; lose track of, lose sight of, **forget**; dream, drowse, nod, **sleep**; trifle, play at; be abstracted, wander, **imagine**; muse, moon; idle, doodle, digress, **stray**; be rattled, be **nervous**; **hinder** (see **distract**); disregard, ignore, **neglect**; think nothing of, think little of, **hold cheap**.

**distract**, divert; make forget; entice, **tempt**; confuse, muddle, **derange**; disturb, interrupt, **discontinue**; disconcert, upset, perplex, discompose, fluster, bother, flurry, rattle, **agitate**; put one off his stroke, **obstruct**; daze, dazzle, **blind**; bewilder, flummox, **puzzle**; fuddle, addle, **make mad**.

**escape notice**, escape attention, blush unseen, **lurk**; meet a blind spot.

Adv. **inadvertently**; rashly, giddily.

## 452 Carefulness

N. **carefulness**, pains; heed, care, **attention**; anxiety, solicitude, **worry**; loving care, **benevolence**; **order**; attention to detail; nicety; pedantry; conscience, **probity**, **readiness**; preparedness; **caution**; forethought, **foresight**.
**surveillance**, **protection**; lookout, weather eye; vigil, watch, deathwatch; guard; **eye**; duenna, sentry, **protection**, keeper.

Adj. **careful**, thoughtful, considerate, considered, mindful, regardful, **attentive**; taking care, painstaking; solicitous, anxious; cautious, afraid to touch; loving, tender; conscientious, scrupulous, honest, **honourable**; diligent, assiduous, **industrious**; thorough, thorough-going; meticulous, minute, particular, circumstantial; nice, exact, **accurate**; perfectionist, **fastidious**; tidy, neat, clean, **orderly**; thrifty, **parsimonious**.

**vigilant**, alert, ready, **prepared**; watchful, wakeful, wide-awake; all eyes, open-eyed; prudent, provident, far-sighted; surefooted; circumspect, guarded, wary, **cautious**.

Vb. **be careful**, mind, heed, beware, **be attentive**; think twice, check, **be cautious**; keep a lookout, look right then left, **be tentative**; tidy, **arrange**; take pains, do with care, be meticulous; try, **exert oneself**.

**look after**, look to, see to, take care of, **manage**; take charge of; mind, tend, keep, **safeguard**; baby-sit; nurse, foster, cherish, **pet**; **respect**; keep an eye, monitor; escort, play gooseberry; serve, **minister to**.

**invigilate**, stay awake; keep vigil, watch; keep watch; keep a sharp lookout; mount guard, set watch, stand to, safeguard.

Adv. **carefully**; with care, gingerly.

## 453 Negligence

N. **negligence**, **inattention**; forgetfulness, **oblivion**; neglect, oversight; default; unguarded hour or minute; disregard; insouciance; **delay**; untidiness, **disorder**; trifling; botched job, loose ends, **failure**; trifler, slacker, waster; sloven, **slut**.

Adj. **negligent**, neglectful, careless; remiss, thoughtless, **unthinking**; oblivious, **forgetful**; **indifferent**; regardless, reckless, **rash**; casual, offhand, happy-go-lucky, **lax**; sloppy, slipshod, slaphappy, slapdash, perfunctory, superficial; hurried, **hasty**; inaccurate, **inexact**; slack, supine, lazy; **late**; untidy, **dirty**; unguarded; improvident; lapsed, **irreligious**.

**neglected**, unkempt; **dirty**; unguarded; unattended, left alone; lost sight of; unconsidered; **invisible**; put aside, **late**; unstudied; undone, perfunctory, **unused**.

Vb. **neglect**, omit; lose sight of, overlook; leave undone; botch, bungle, **be clumsy**; slur, skimp, scamp, **shorten**; skip, skim, jump, skim through, **conceal**; play with, trifle, **amuse oneself**.

**disregard**, ignore, dodge, shirk, blink, **avoid**; allow to pass, let pass, wink at, connive at, **be lax**; refuse to see, turn a blind eye to, dismiss, **be blind**; forbear, forget it, excuse, overlook, **forgive**; discount, **underestimate**; **deviate**; slight, cold-shoulder, cut, cut dead, **be rude**; turn a deaf ear to, be **deaf**; take lightly, **be indifferent**; pooh-pooh, **hold cheap**; **exclude**; desert, abandon, **relinquish**.

**be neglectful**, doze, drowse, nod, **sleep**; oversleep; drift, procrastinate, let slide, let slip; take it easy, let things go; shelve, pigeonhole, lay aside, push aside; make neglectful, lull, **surprise**.

Adv. **negligently**; anyhow; any old how.

## 454 Enquiry

N. **enquiry**, challenge (see **question**); taking information, **information**; close enquiry, witch-hunt, spy mania (see **search**); inquisition, examination, visitation; checkup, medical; inquest, autopsy, audit, trial, **legal trial**; public enquiry, commission of enquiry; census, survey, market research; poll, **vote**; probe, test, check, trial run, **experiment**; review, scrutiny; introspection, self-examination; research, **study**; analysis; reconnaissance, reconnoitre, survey; airing, soundings, **conference**; philosophical enquiry, **philosophy**; **curiosity**.

**interrogation**, forensic examination; leading question, cross-question; quiz, brains trust; interrogatory; catechism; inquisition, third degree; dialogue; question time.

**question**, question mark, **punctuation**; query, questionnaire, **list**; question sheet, question paper, interrogatory; challenge, fair question, catch, cross-question, indirect question, feeler; leading question, moot point, point at issue, **topic**; crucial question, controversy, **argument**; problem, poser, headache.

**exam**, examination; interview, audition, **hearing**; practical examination, test, battery; intelligence test, IQ test; eleven-plus, entrance examination, common entrance; Certificate of Secondary Education, CSE, sixteen-plus, General Certificate of Education, GCE, O' level, A' level; tripos, finals; degree level, **respondent**; entrant, sitter.

**search**, probe, enquiry; quest, hunt, **pursuit**; domiciliary visit, house-to-house search; dig; potholing; search party; searchlight; search warrant.

**police enquiry**, detection; detective work; third degree; CID, FBI, Interpol; secret police, Gestapo.

**secret service**, espionage, intelligence; MI5, SIS, CIA; informer, spy, undercover agent, cloak-and-dagger man; double agent, mole; spy ring.

**detective**; plain-clothes man; enquiry agent, private detective, private eye; hotel detective, amateur detective; Federal agent, CID man; sleuth, bloodhound, nose, spy, **informer**; handwriting expert.

**enquirer**; **news reporter**; student, **philosopher**; search party; talent scout; scout, spy, surveyor; inspector, visitor; scrutineer, censor; test pilot, research worker, analyst; sampler; **traveller**.

**questioner**; **inquisitive person**; question or quiz master; confessor, **clergy**.

**Adj. enquiring**, curious, **inquisitive**; quizzical; interrogatory, interrogative; searching, exploratory, empirical, tentative.

**moot**, questionable; problematic, doubtful, **uncertain**; knotty, **difficult**; undecided, left open.

**Vb. enquire**, ask, want to know, seek an answer; demand, **request**; agitate, air, ventilate, discuss, query, subject to examination, **argue**; seek (see **search**); **pursue**; probe, sound, take a look at, investigate, throw open to enquiry, hold or conduct an enquiry; try, hear, **try a case**; review, overhaul, audit, monitor, screen; analyse, dissect, parse, sift, winnow; research, **study**; consider, examine, meditate; check; take soundings; fathom, X-ray, **scan**;

peer, peep, snook, snoop, spy, pry, nose around, **be curious**; survey, reconnoitre, case; explore, **be tentative**; test, try, sample, taste, **experiment**.

**interrogate**, question; cross-question, cross-examine; badger, challenge, heckle; interview; examine, probe, quiz, grill; **torture**; pump, suck one dry; pose, propose a question, moot.

**search**, seek; conduct a search, rummage, ransack, comb; scrabble, forage, root about; scour, rake through; explore every inch; overhaul, frisk, fish, go fishing; explore every avenue, **exert oneself**; cast about, seek a clue, **pursue**; probe, explore, **be tentative**; dig, excavate; prospect, dowse.

**be questionable**, be open to question, arouse suspicion, challenge an answer, demand or require an explanation; be subject to examination, be open to enquiry.

**Adv. on trial**, under investigation.

**in search of**, on the track of.

## 455 Answer

**N. answer**, reply, response; reaction; return; official reply; returns, **record**; feedback, **information**; echo, respond, **repetition**; password, countersign, **identification**; open sesame; backchat, repartee; retort, riposte; dialogue; last word, final answer; clue, key, right answer, explanation, **interpretation**; solution, **remedy**; enigmatic answer, oracle, Delphic Oracle.

**rejoinder**, reply; defence, reply; refutation.

**respondent**, defendant; correspondent; candidate, applicant, entrant, sitter, **contender**.

**Adj. answering**, respondent, responsive; counter; corresponding; corresponding to; **negative**; conclusive, final.

Vb. **answer**, reply, write back, acknowledge, respond, be responsive, echo, **repeat**; react, answer back, flash back, come back at, retort, riposte, **retaliate**; rejoin, rebut, counter; field; parry, refuse to answer, **avoid**; contradict, **negate**; be respondent; defend; **be expedient**; **interpret**; settle, decide, **judge**; **be expedient**; answer to, correspond to.
Adv. in reply.

## 456 Experiment

N. **experiment**; probe; analysis, examination, **enquiry**; object lesson, proof; assay, **estimate**; check, test, test case; probation; practical test, trial, trial run, test flight, **attempt**; audition, voice test; ordeal, **legal trial**; pilot scheme, rough sketch, first draft; first steps, **debut**.

**empiricism**, guesswork, **conjecture**; tentative method; experience, practice, rule of thumb, trial; random shot, gamble; instinct, light of nature, **intuition**; random sample, straw vote; feeler, **question**; trial balloon.

**experimenter**, research worker, analyst; chemist; test driver, test pilot; adventurer.

**testing agent**, criterion, touchstone; standard, yardstick, **gauge**; breathalyser; control; reagent, litmus paper, retort, test tube, **crucible**; wind tunnel; simulator, test track; laboratory.

**testee**, **respondent**; probationer, **beginner**; candidate, entrant, sitter, **contender**; subject of experiment, subject, patient; laboratory animal, guinea pig, rat, monkey.

Adj. **experimental**; provisional, tentative, **speculative**; trial, exploratory; empirical; venturesome; **uncertain**.

Vb. **experiment**; check, verify; prove; assay, analyse; research; dabble; vivisect, make a guinea pig of; test, **enquire**; try, try a thing once; give a trial to, **attempt**; give one a try; sample, **taste**; take a random sample, take a straw vote; put to the vote, **vote**; rehearse, practise, **train**; undergo a test.

**be tentative**, be empirical, seek experience; feel, **touch**; probe, grope, fumble; **learn**; fly a kite; fish, trawl; see how far one can go; speculate, **gamble**, venture, explore, prospect, **undertake**; probe, sound, **enquire**.

Adv. **experimentally**, on trial, on approval; by trial and error; on spec.

## 457 Comparison

N. **comparison**; check, **enquiry**; points of comparison, analogy, parallel, likeness, **similarity**; identification, **identity**; antithesis; contrast; simile, allegory, **metaphor**; standard of comparison, criterion, pattern, model, check list, control, **prototype**.

Adj. **compared**, set against; comparative, comparable; relative; **figurative**.

Vb. **compare**, collate, confront; bring together, **juxtapose**; draw a comparison, **identify**; parallel; contrast, **differentiate**; **discriminate**; match, pair, balance; view together, check with; institute a comparison, draw a parallel; compare to, compare with.

Adv. **comparatively**; relatively.

## 458 Discrimination

N. **discrimination**, distinction; discretion; insight, perception, flair, **intelligence**; appreciation, critique, critical appraisal, **estimate**; sensibility, **moral sensibility**; tact, delicacy, refinement, **good taste**; timing, sense of occasion; nicety; fine palate, **taste**; hair-splitting, **reasoning**; separation; selection, **choice**; nice difference, nuance, fine shade, **difference**.

Adj. discriminating, selective, judicious, discerning, discreet; sensitive, **accurate**; fine, delicate, nice, particular, **fastidious**; thoughtful, **imaginative**; critical, **judicial**; **distinctive**.

Vb. discriminate, distinguish, **differentiate**; **compare**; sort, sieve, sift; separate, **set apart**; select; exercise discretion, make a distinction, make an exception, **qualify**; refine, **reason**; appraise, taste, **estimate**; weigh, consider, **judge**; discern, have insight; **know**; give weight to, **make important**; attribute just value to, **be just**.

**459 Indiscrimination**

N. indiscrimination, lack of discrimination, **generality**; simplicity; want of consideration; insensibility; **moral insensibility**; lack of refinement, vulgarity, **bad taste**; loose terms.

Adj. indiscriminate; undistinguished, **uniform**; random; unmeasured, **uncertain**; promiscuous, haphazard, wholesale, blanket, **general**.

indiscriminating, uncritical; obtuse; insensitive, **impassive**; coarse, **vulgar**; indiscreet, **rash**; tone-deaf, **deaf**; colour-blind, **blind**; inaccurate, **inexact**.

Vb. not discriminate, be indiscriminate, avoid precision, **be neutral**; be foolish; swallow whole; lump everything together, **bring together**; jumble, muddle, confuse, confound, **derange**; average.

**460 Measurement**

N. measurement; mensuration; dose, **finite quantity**; rating; appraisal, appreciation, estimation, **estimate**; calculation, computation, reckoning;

dead reckoning; check; reading; **long measure**; trigonometry; second, degree, minute, quadrant, **angular measure**.

geometry; solid geometry; Euclidean geometry.

metrology, dimensions, length, breadth, height, depth, thickness, **size**; metric system, unit of measurement; axle load; linear measure, **long measure**; measure of capacity, volume, cubic contents, **measure**; liquid measure, gill, pint, quart, gallon, barrel, pipe, hogshead, **vessel**; litre; minim, dram; dry measure, peck, bushel, quarter; unit of energy, ohm, watt, **electricity**; horse power, **energy**; candlepower, **light**; decibel, **sound**.

coordinate, polar coordinates; grid reference.

gauge, measure, scale, time scale; balance; micrometer; yardstick, metre bar; yard measure, metal rule; chain, link, pole, perch, rod; lead, log; ruler, slide rule; T-square, set square, dividers, callipers, compass, protractor; sextant, quadrant, **sailing aid**; theodolite; astrolabe, **astronomy**; index, Plimsoll line, Plimsoll mark; tidemark, water line, **limit**; axis, coordinate; standard, criterion, **prototype**; milestone, signpost.

meter; altimeter; **depth**; thermometer; barometer; speed gauge, speedometer, **velocity**; **land travel**; time gauge, metronome, time switch; micrometer; seismograph.

surveyor, topographer.

appraiser, valuer, assessor, surveyor.

Adj. metrical; imperial, metric; cubic, linear.

measured; mensurable, measurable, calculable.

Vb. measure, survey; compute, calculate, count, reckon, **number**; quantify;

tape, span; probe, sound, fathom, plumb, **plunge**; take soundings; pace, **time**; balance, **weigh**.

**gauge**, meter, take a reading, read; set a standard, **make uniform**; grade, calibrate, **graduate**; reduce to scale, map, **represent**.

**appraise**, gauge, value, cost, rate, **price**; evaluate, estimate, appreciate, assess, **estimate**; form an opinion, **judge**; tape.

**mete out**, weigh, divide, share, **participate**, apportion.

## 461 Evidence

**N. evidence**, data, case history; grounds; premises; hearsay, hearsay evidence, **report**; indirect evidence, circumstantial evidence, **circumstance**; constructive evidence, **supposition**; proof; corroboration; **certainty**; one-sided evidence, piece of evidence, fact, document, exhibit, **record**; clue, **hint**; sign; reference, quotation, citation; line of evidence; authority.

**testimony**, witness; statement, **information**; admission, confession, **disclosure**; plea, **pretext**; word, assertion; Bible evidence; sworn evidence, deposition, affidavit, **oath**; word of mouth, oral evidence, documentary evidence, evidence to character; case record, dossier, **record**; written contract, compact; deed, testament, **security**.

**credential**, testimonial, chit, character, recommendation; seal, signature, docket; voucher, warranty, warrant, certificate, diploma, **security**; ticket, passport, visa, **permit**; authority, scripture.

**witness**, spectator; ear witness; indicator, telltale, **informer**; signatory; witness to character, referee; sponsor, **patron**.

**Adj. evidential**, offering evidence;

suggestive, significant, **meaningful**; showing, indicative; indirect, secondary, circumstantial; firsthand, direct, seen; **probable**, constructive; cumulative; telling, damning; reliable, **certain**; demonstrative, conclusive, decisive, final; factual, documentary, **positive**; authentic, well-grounded, well-founded, **true**; weighty, authoritative; **orthodox**; spoken to, sworn to.

**Vb. evidence**, show, evince, furnish evidence; **give hope**; bespeak, **represent**; breathe of, tell of, declare witness to, **manifest**; lend colour to, **make likely**; tell its own tale, speak volumes; have weight, **influence**; suggest, **indicate**; argue, involve, **imply**.

**testify**, witness, swear, be sworn, **affirm**; bear witness, give evidence, speak to, depose, swear to; authenticate, certify, **make certain**; attest, subscribe, countersign, endorse, sign; plead, **argue**; admit, avow, acknowledge, **confess**; give a character reference.

**corroborate**, support, buttress, strengthen; sustain, **vindicate**; verify; confirm, ratify, establish, make good, **make certain**; lead evidence, document; collect evidence, concoct evidence, **fake**.

## 462 Counterevidence

**N. counterevidence**; evidence against, defence, **answer**; refutation; denial; oath against oath, one word against another; mitigating evidence, **qualification**; hostile witness, hostile evidence.

**Adj. countervailing**; cutting both ways, ambiguous, **equivocal**; converse, opposite, **contrary**; **negative**; telling against.

**unattested**; lacking proof, **uncertain**; **false**.

**Vb. tell against**; weigh against; contravene, traverse, run counter, contradict; rebut; oppose, **be contrary**; **counteract**; cut both ways, **be equivocal**; prove a negative, **negate**; fail to confirm, tell another story; weaken, damage, spoil; undermine, subvert, **destroy**; convict of perjury; contradict oneself, turn hostile.

Adv. conversely, on the other hand.

### 463 Qualification

N. **qualification**, specification, **speciality**; prerequisite, **requirement**; assumption, **supposition**; leaven, colouring, tinge; **change**; **moderation**; condition, **conditions**; proviso, reservation; exception, salvo, saving clause; demur, but, **opposition**; consideration, concession, allowance; redeeming feature, **offset**.

Adj. **qualifying**; colouring; contingent, provisional, **conditional**; saving; qualified; exceptional, exempt.

Vb. **qualify**, condition, limit, restrict, **restrain**; colour, shade; leaven, alter, **modify**; temper, season, palliate, mitigate, **moderate**; adulterate, weaken; excuse, **extenuate**; grant, concede, lessen, **abate**; **exempt**; introduce new conditions; **require**; relax, **be lax**; take exception, object, demur, **deprecate**.

Adv. **provided**, provided always, subject to; with a pinch of salt; unless, **if**; though, although, even if.

**nevertheless**, even so, after all; despite; but, yet, still; whether.

### 464 Possibility

N. **possibility**, potentiality; capacity, **ability**; what is possible, **sufficiency**; what may be, **futurity**; what might be, **past time**; what one can do, best one can do; contingency, eventuality, a possibility, chance, **fair chance**; good chance, **opportunity**; bare possibility, ghost of a chance; likelihood, **probability**; credibility, **belief**; **good policy**; feasibility, **facility**; compatibility, **agreement**; risk of.

Adj. **possible**, potential, hypothetical; able, capable, viable; arguable, reasonable; feasible, practicable, negotiable, **easy**; workable, operable; approachable, accessible; available, still open; conceivable, thinkable, credible, imaginable; practical, **advisable**; allowable, permissible, legal; contingent, **future**; **probable**; only possible; liable.

Vb. **be possible**, may, might, maybe, might be; might have been, admit of, allow, **permit**; bear, be open to; be a possibility, depend, be contingent; stand a chance, **be likely**.

**make possible**, enable, **empower**; allow, **permit**; facilitate.

Adv. **possibly**; perhaps, perchance; within reach; peradventure, haply; may be, could be; if possible, if so be; God willing.

### 465 Impossibility

N. **impossibility**; what cannot be, what can never be; impasse, deadlock, **obstacle**; **prohibition**; impossible task, **hard task**.

Adj. **impossible**; hopeless; unnatural, against nature; unreasonable, contrary to reason, self-contradictory, **illogical**; **erroneous**; too improbable, incredible, inconceivable, unthinkable, unheard of; miraculous, **wonderful**; visionary, **imaginary**, irrevocable, beyond recall.

**impracticable**; insoluble, inextricable, too hard, beyond one, **difficult**; incurable, inoperable; insuperable, insurmountable, impassable; impenetrable; inaccessible; elusive.

Vb. **be impossible**, exceed possibility,

defy nature.

**make impossible,** exclude, **prohibit;** set an impossible task; eat one's hat if, **negate.**

**attempt the impossible, waste effort;** weave a rope of sand, skin a flint.

**Adv. impossibly,** nohow, no way.

## 466 Probability

**N. probability,** likelihood, **chance;** good chance, **possibility;** prospect, **prediction;** fair expectation, **expectation; well-grounded hope, hope; safe bet, certainty;** real risk, real danger, **danger;** natural course, **tendency;** presumption, **evidence;** likely belief, **belief;** good reason; colour, show of, semblance, **appearance;** theory of probability.

**Adj. probable,** likely, **liable;** natural; presumable; reliable, **certain;** hopeful, promising; **impending; vulnerable;** highly possible, **possible.**

**plausible,** specious; apparent, ostensible; reasonable, **rational;** convincing, persuasive, easy to believe, **credible;** well-grounded, well-founded, **true; apt.**

**Vb. be likely,** have a chance, stand a chance, **be possible;** bid fair to, **tend;** promise, **give hope.**

**make likely,** make probable; involve, **imply;** entail; promote, **aid;** lend colour to, point to, **evidence.**

**assume,** presume, flatter oneself, **believe;** conjecture, guess, dare say, **suppose;** think likely, **expect;** see ahead, **foresee; be certain;** gather, deduce, infer, **reason.**

**Adv. probably,** very likely, ten to one; seemingly, apparently, to all appearances; like enough.

## 467 Improbability

**N. improbability,** doubt; little chance, long shot; scarcely any chance; long odds, bare possibility; forlorn hope, poor prospect, **lack of expectation;** rare occurrence, rarity; implausibility, **falsehood.**

**Adj. improbable,** unlikely, more than doubtful, dubious, **uncertain;** unforeseen; hard to believe, fishy; rare, **infrequent;** unheard of, inconceivable; incredible; too good to be true.

**Vb. be unlikely,** have a bare chance, show little hope, offer small chance; be hard to believe, **cause doubt;** think unlikely.

**Int.** not likely! no fear! not on your life! not a hope! some hopes!

## 468 Certainty

**N. certainty,** certitude, certain knowledge, **knowledge;** certain issue, necessity, **fate;** reliability, **truth;** certainty of meaning; proof; **testimony;** making sure, check, enquiry; dead certainty, cert; sure thing, safe bet, cinch; **fact;** matter of fact, **event;** settled decision; gospel, Bible, **oracle;** dogma; dictum, axiom, **maxim;** court of final appeal, **tribunal;** last word, ultimatum, **conditions.**

**positiveness,** subjective certainty, assurance, confidence, conviction, persuasion, **belief; opinion;** fixity, obsession, bias; self-confidence.

**doctrinaire;** self-opinionated person, **obstinate person;** bigot, fanatic, zealot; oracle, Sir Oracle, knowall.

**Adj. certain,** sure, solid, well-founded, well-grounded, **substantial;** reliable, **trustworthy;** authoritative, official, **genuine;** factual, **true;** tried, foolproof, **safe;** infallible, unerring, **veracious;** self-evident, evident, apparent; unequivocal; unmistakable, clear, **obvious;** inevitable, irrevocable, inexorable, **fated;** bound, bound to be;

inviolable, **invulnerable**; demonstrable.

**positive**, confident, assured, sure; opinionated; pontifical, **assertive**; doctrinaire, **orthodox**; set, fixed; clean-cut, definite, unequivocal, **intelligible**; convincing, **credible**; classified; affirmative, categorical, absolute, unqualified, unreserved, final, ultimate, conclusive, settled, without appeal.

**undisputed**, beyond doubt, without a shadow of doubt; undoubted, indubitable, unquestionable, incontrovertible, incontestable, unimpeachable, undeniable, irrefutable.

**Vb. be certain**, stand to reason, **be reasonable**; be positive, be assured, satisfy oneself, feel sure, **believe**; understand, **know**; dismiss all doubt.

**dogmatize**, pontificate, **affirm**.

**make certain**, certify, authenticate, ratify, seal, sign, **endorse**; guarantee, warrant, assure; settle, decide, **judge**; remove doubt, persuade, **convince**; classify, **arrange**; make sure, ascertain, check, double-check, verify, confirm, clinch, **corroborate**; reassure oneself, take a second look, do a double take; insure against, **safeguard**; **be cautious**; ensure, make inevitable, **necessitate**.

**Adv. certainly**, definitely, to be sure, doubtless, of course; without fail, sink or swim, rain or shine, come hell or high water, come what may.

## 469 Uncertainty

**N. uncertainty**; mist, haze, fog; borderline case; query, question mark, **question**; open question; guesswork, **conjecture**; contingency, doubtful event, **chance**; gamble, toss-up, wager; bow at a venture, blind date; something or other, this or that.

**dubiety**, doubt; state of doubt, open mind, open verdict; suspense, **expectation**; doubt, indecision, hesitancy; seesaw, floating vote; embarrassment, perplexity, nonplus, quandary; dilemma, cleft stick.

**unreliability**, error; insecurity, touch and go, **danger**; variability; unpredictability, **lack of expectation**; Fickleness, **caprice**; lack of security, bare word, scrap of paper.

**Adj. uncertain**, doubtful, dubious; insecure, chancy; subject to chance; occasional, sporadic, **infrequent**; temporary, provisional, **transient**; fluid, **unstable**; contingent, **conditional**; indeterminate; random; indecisive, undecided, open; open to question, questionable, **moot**; arguable, disputable; suspicious, **improbable**; hypothetical, speculative; borderline; ambiguous, **equivocal**, **illogical**; enigmatic, cryptic, obscure; vague, hazy, misty, cloudy, **shadowy**; mysterious, **occult**; **complex**.

**unreliable**; treacherous, **dishonest**; unstable, variable, changeable; fickle, **capricious**; fallible, open to error, **erroneous**; precarious, ticklish.

**doubting**, doubtful, dubious, full of doubt; agnostic, sceptical; mistrustful, **cautious**; uncertain, diffident; hesitant, undecided, **irresolute**; unable to say, afraid to say; perplexed, distraught; brought to a standstill; lost, abroad, all at sea, adrift, astray, at a loss, at fault, clueless, **ignorant**.

**uncertified**, unchecked; unwarranted; unofficial, apocryphal; untold.

**Vb. be uncertain**, be contingent; **depend**; be open to question, be ambiguous, **be equivocal**; **doubt**; **await**; have a suspicion, suspect, wonder, wonder whether; dither, hover, float, sway,

seesaw, waver, teeter, vacillate, shilly-
shally, falter, pause, hesitate, **be
irresolute**; avoid a decision, boggle,
demur; flounder, drift, be at sea;
grope, fumble, cast about, experiment, **be tentative**; get lost, **stray**;
come to a standstill; be at a loss; could
be wrong.

**puzzle**, perplex, confuse, maze, daze,
bewilder, baffle, nonplus, flummox,
stump, floor, **defeat**; mystify; bamboozle; fog, fox, **mislead; cause doubt**;
make one think, demand reflection.

**Adv. in suspense.**

**470 Reasoning**

**N. reasoning**, force of argument; reason,
lateral thinking, **intuition**; sweet
reason; art of reasoning, logic; distinction, **discrimination**, induction,
inductive reasoning, **philosophy**; set
theory; **mathematics**; plain reason,
simple arithmetic.

**premise**, postulate, basis of reasoning;
principle, assumption, **supposition**;
axiom, self-evident truth, **maxim**;
data; hypothesis, provisional hypothesis.

**argumentation**, critical examination,
analysis, **enquiry**; dialogue; formal
logic; proposition, statement, thesis,
theorem, problem; predicate; corollary; dilemma; QED; paradox.

**argument**, symposium, dialogue; controversy, debate, **dissent**; appeal to
reason, set or formal argument, plea,
thesis, case; submission; defensive
argument, defence; aggressive argument, polemics; **peace offering**; war of
words, paper war, **quarrel**; propaganda, **teaching**; hair-splitting; **dissension**; bad argument, sophistry;
legal argument; parity of reasoning;
same to you.

**reasons**, basis of argument, grounds;

cause; **pretext**; case, case to answer;
sound argument; point, clincher.

**reasoner**, **philosopher**; rationalist; dis-
putant; **proponent**, **lawyer**; wrangler;
argumentative person, sea lawyer,
pedant; scholastic, **intellectual**.

**Adj. rational**, clear-headed, reasoning,
reasonable; cogent, acceptable,
admissible, pointed, well-grounded,
**relevant**; sensible, fair, **just**; synthetic;
consistent, systematic; discursive,
inductive, universal; **certain**; **possible**.

**arguing**, appealing to reason; apologetic;
argumentative; disputable, arguable,
**uncertain**.

**Vb. be reasonable**, be likely; stand to
reason, follow, hang together; hold
water; appeal to reason, listen to
reason, admit, concede, grant, allow,
**assent**; have a case.

**reason**, **think**; apply reason, bring
reason to bear; infer, deduce; explain,
**interpret**.

**argue**; hold an argument, hold a symposium; discuss, **confer**, debate, dispute; quibble, chop logic; stress,
strain, work an argument to death;
plead; pamphleteer, **teach**; defend;
attack; join issue, demur, cavil, **dissent**; analyse; overwhelm with argument, bludgeon; **demonstrate**; have
words, wrangle, **bicker**; answer back,
make a rejoinder, **answer**; start an
argument; propose, moot.

**premise**, postulate, stipulate, assume,
**suppose**.

**Adv. reasonably**, fairly; much less;
consequently.

**471 Intuition: absence of reason**

**N. intuition**, instinct, association, automatic reaction, **absence of thought**;
light of nature; telepathy; insight,
second sight, clairvoyance; id, sub-

conscious, **spirit**; direct apprehension; divination; inspiration, presentiment, impulse, **feeling**; feminine logic; rule of thumb; hunch, impression, sense, guesswork; **bias**.

**Adj. intuitive**, impulsive; devoid of logic, **illogical**; impressionistic, subjective; involuntary, **spontaneous**; subconscious, **psychic**; above reason, independent of reason, unknown to logic, inspired, direct.

**Vb. intuit**; sense, have a funny feeling, have a hunch; somehow feel; dispense with reason, use feminine logic; guess, use guesswork.

**Adv. intuitively**, instinctively.

## 472 Sophistry: false reasoning

**N. sophistry**; feminine logic, **intuition**; double think; mental reservation; word fencing; subtlety; hair-splitting; claptrap, mere words, **empty talk**; quibble; chicanery, subterfuge, shuffle, dodge, evasion, pretext.

**sophism**, a sophistry, specious argument, exploded argument, fallacy; bad logic, loose thinking, solecism, flaw; circular reasoning; weak case.

**sophist**; devil's advocate.

**Adj. sophistical**, specious, plausible; evasive, insincere; hollow, empty; deceptive, illusory; pettifogging, sophisticated, tortuous.

**illogical**, contrary to reason, irrational, unreasonable; arbitrary; fallacious, fallible; inconsistent, incongruous; unwarranted, invalid, untenable, unsound; unfounded, groundless; inconsequential; incorrect, false, **erroneous**.

**poorly reasoned**, inconclusive; weak, feeble; frivolous, airy, flimsy; loose, woolly.

**Vb. reason badly**; talk at random, babble, burble, **mean nothing**.

**sophisticate**, mislead; mystify; quibble, cavil, **argue**; equivocate, **be equivocal**; dodge, shuffle, fence, **parry**; be diffuse; evade, **elude**; varnish, whitewash, cant; colour, **misrepresent**; pervert, misapply, **misuse**; pervert reason, torture logic; prove that white is black.

## 473 Demonstration

**N. demonstration, evidence**; proven fact, **truth**; proof, establishment, conclusive proof, **certainty**; **experiment**; argument, **reasoning**; exposition, **manifestation**; burden of proof, onus.

**Adj. demonstrating**, demonstrative; consequential, following, **relevant**; **affirmative**; convincing, conclusive, categorical, decisive, crucial; **educational**.

**demonstrated**, evident; undeniable, irrefutable, irresistible, incontrovertible, **certain**; capable of proof, demonstrable.

**Vb. demonstrate**, prove; show, evince, **manifest**; justify, **vindicate**; corroborate; document, substantiate, establish, verify, **evidence**; infer, deduce, draw, **reason**; satisfy, **make certain**; clinch an argument, **convince**.

**be proved**, prove to be true, emerge, follow, follow of course, stand to reason, **be reasonable**; stand, hold water, hold good, **be true**.

**Adv. of course**; QED.

## 474 Confutation

**N. confutation**, refutation; exposure; conviction; rejoinder, complete answer, **answer**; clincher, knockdown argument, retort, repartee, **witticism**; **ridicule**; denial, denunciation; exploded argument.

**Adj. confuted**; refutable.

**Vb. confute,** refute, disprove, invalidate, rebut, retort, have an answer; negative, deny, contradict, **negate**; force to withdraw; confound, silence, floor, gravel, nonplus; expose; convict, **condemn**; blow sky-high, puncture, riddle, destroy, explode, **demolish**; have; overthrow, squash, crush, overwhelm, **defeat**; parry; stand; dismiss, override, sweep aside, **affirm**.

**be confuted;** have nothing left to say.

**Adv. in rebuttal;** on the other hand.

## 475 Judgment: conclusion

**N. judgment,** discretion, discrimination; lack of discretion; **authority**; verdict, finding; sentence, **punishment**; pronouncement; decision, award; order, ruling; **decree**; decree nisi; decree absolute; irrevocable decision; settled decision; result, upshot; moral, **maxim; intuition**; corollary, **reasoning; wisdom**; unclouded eye, **justice**; referendum, plebiscite, poll, **vote**.

**estimate,** estimation, view, opinion; **philosophy**; calculation, **measurement**; consideration, **comparison**; appreciation, appraisal, **interpretation**; criticism, **aid**; destructive criticism, **hindrance**; critique, review, notice, comment, **article**; survey; **report**; favourable report, **approbation**; unfavourable report, censure, **disapprobation**; legal opinion, **advice**.

**estimator,** judge; umpire, referee; surveyor, valuer; inspector, reporter, ombudsman; counsellor, **adviser**; censor, critic, reviewer; commentator; juror, assessor, **jury**; voter, elector, **electorate**.

**Adj. judicial,** judicious, shrewd, **wise**; dispassionate, **just**; juridical; conclusive; moralistic, sententious; expressive of opinion; censorious, critical, appreciative; advisory.

**Vb. judge;** arbitrate, referee; hear, try, **hold court**; rule, pronounce; find, find against; decree, award, adjudicate; decide, settle, conclude; confirm, make absolute; sentence, doom, **condemn**; **vote**; judge well, see straight; deduce, infer, **reason**; gather, collect; recapitulate; **teach**.

**estimate,** measure, calculate, make, **gauge**; value, evaluate, appraise; rate, rank; conjecture, guess, **suppose**; take stock, **account**; consider, weigh, ponder, **meditate**, examine, investigate, vet, **enquire**; express an opinion; commentate, comment, review; survey; scan; censor, censure, **disapprove**.

**Adv. sub judice,** under trial, under sentence.

## 476 Misjudgment. Prejudice

**N. misjudgment,** wrong impression, error; loose thinking, misconstruction; wrong verdict, miscarriage of justice, **injustice; deception; fantasy**; false dawn.

**prejudgment;** preconceived idea; hangup, fixation, monomania, **mania**.

**prejudice,** prepossession, predilection; partiality, favouritism, **injustice**; bias, jaundiced eye; blind spot, blind side; party spirit, **party**; sectionalism; chauvinism, my country right or wrong; class war, class prejudice; sexism, sex prejudice; racialism; colour prejudice; colour bar, apartheid, segregation, discrimination, **exclusion**; anti-Semitism; **hatred**.

**narrow mind,** narrow sympathies; closed mind; pedantry; **positiveness**; pedant, stickler, **perfectionist; crank**; zealot, bigot, fanatic, **doctrinaire**.

**bias,** unbalance, **inequality**; warp, bent, slant, **tendency**; angle, point of view, private opinion, **opinion**; obsession;

fad, craze, **whim**.

**Adj. misjudging, mistaken;** fallible, gullible, **foolish;** wrong, wrong-headed; unseeing, **blind;** short-sighted; subjective, visionary, impractical; whimsical, **crazy;** besotted, infatuated, **enamoured**.

**narrow-minded,** narrow, cramped, hidebound; parochial, provincial, insular; donnish, **severe;** literal, matter-of-fact; hypercritical, fussy, **fastidious;** stiff, unbending, **obstinate; positive;** opinionated; **proud**.

**biased;** jaundiced; prejudiced, closed; clannish, **sectional;** one-sided, **sectarian;** prepossessed, preconceived; unreasoning, unreasonable, **illogical;** discriminatory; illiberal, intolerant; fanatic, **obstinate; blind.**

**Vb. misjudge,** miscalculate, miscount; **blunder;** reckon without; **underestimate;** overestimate, **overrate;** guess wrong, misconceive, **misinterpret;** overreach oneself; **be foolish; reason badly.**

**prejudge,** judge beforehand, **predetermine;** presuppose, presume; **be rash.**

**bias,** warp, twist, bend; jaundice, prejudice, predispose, **influence;** haunt, obsess, **engross.**

**be biased,** be one-sided, see one side only, show favouritism, favour one side, **do wrong;** lean, favour, hold it against one, discriminate against, **oppress;** pontificate; blind oneself to, have a blind side, have a blind spot, **be blind.**

### 477 Overestimation

**N. overestimation,** overestimate; **exaggeration; boast;** ballyhoo, **publicity;** panegyric, gush, hot air, **empty talk;** much ado about nothing; megalomania, vanity, **pride;** egotism; optimism; unnecessary pessimism, defeat-

ism; **hope;** prophet of doom, Jonah; barker.

**Adj. optimistic,** upbeat, sanguine; raving.

**overrated;** overdone.

**Vb. overrate,** overestimate; rave, think too much of; make too much of, **exaggerate;** strain, overdo, inflate, magnify, **enlarge;** boost, puff, **praise;** whitewash.

### 478 Underestimation

**N. underestimation,** underestimate; conservative estimate, modest calculation, **moderation;** understatement, meiosis; euphemism, **prudery;** humility; irony, **affectation;** pessimism; cynic.

**Adj. depreciating,** derogatory, pejorative; conservative, **moderate;** modest, humble; despairing, **hopeless; affected.**

**undervalued,** underrated; slighted, neglected.

**Vb. underestimate,** underrate; discount, **cheapen;** depreciate, disparage; slight, pooh-pooh, **hold cheap;** do less than justice, **misjudge;** understate; softpedal; **disregard;** make little of; deflate, make light of, belittle, think too little of, **despise;** set at naught, scorn, **ridicule.**

### 479 Discovery

**N. discovery,** finding; invention; potholing; **search;** detective instinct, nose, flair, **pursuit;** detection; **location; certainty;** exposure, revelation, **manifestation;** serendipity; an invention, an inspiration; strike, find, treasure trove; eye-opener, **lack of expectation;** solution, explanation, **interpretation;** key, open sesame, **opener.**

**detector,** probe; spy satellite, **spaceship;** sonar; early warning system; radar,

radar trap; finder, **telescope**; sensor; **meter**; spotter, scout; **traveller**.

**Adj. discovering**, exploratory; on the scent, on the track, warm.

**Vb. discover**, invent, explore, find a way, **experiment**; hit it, have it; strike, hit; meet, encounter, **meet with**; tumble to, awake to, **understand**; find, locate, **place**; identify, **know**; verify, ascertain, **make certain**; unearth, uncover, disinter, bring to light, **manifest**; elicit, **search**; get wind of, **be informed**.

**detect**, expose, **show**; find a clue, see daylight; descry, discern, perceive, notice, spot, sight, catch sight of, **see**; sense, trace; smell a rat; nose, scent, wind; follow, trace, **hunt**; trap, **ensnare**.

**Int. eureka! got it!**

## 480 Belief

**N. belief**, suspension of disbelief; credence, credit; state of belief, assurance, conviction, persuasion; strong feeling, firm impression; confidence, reliance, trust, faith; religious belief, **religious faith**; full belief, full assurance; uncritical belief, **credulity**; implicit belief, **certainty**; obsession, blind belief, **prejudice**; **intuition**; subjective belief; expectation, **hope**; folklore; public belief, public opinion; **probability**; **probity**; token of credit, pledge.

**creed**, credo; dogma; principles, articles; catechism, articles of faith; rubric, canon, rule, **maxim**; declaration of faith, professed belief, profession, confession, confession of faith, **disclosure**; doctrine, system, school, **philosophy**; theology.

**opinion**, sentiment, mind, view; point of view, viewpoint, stand, position, attitude, angle, **view**; impression, **feeling**;

conception, concept, thought, **idea**; thinking, way of thinking, way of thought, **philosophy**; assumption, presumption, principle, theory, hypothesis, **supposition**; surmise, guess, **conjecture**.

**Adj. believing**, holding, confident, assured, reliant, secure, **certain**; sure, cocksure, **positive**; possessed; wedded to; confiding, trustful, unquestioning; loyal, pious, **orthodox**; opinionated.

**credible**, plausible, reasonable, **possible**; likely, **probable**; reliable, trustworthy, trusty; worthy of credence, persuasive, convincing, impressive; held; supposed, putative, hypothetical.

**credal**, taught, confessional; orthodox, authoritative; of faith; sacrosanct; undeniable, absolute.

**Vb. believe**, be a believer, **be orthodox**; credit, give faith to; hold, hold to be true; maintain, declare, **affirm**; profess, confess; receive, accept, admit, agree, **assent**; buy, swallow, swallow whole; assume; **be certain**; rest assured, confide, trust, take one at his or her word; be told, understand, know, **be informed**; come to believe; **discover**; grant, allow.

**opine**, think, conceive, fancy; have a hunch, surmise, guess, **suppose**; suspect, **feel**; deem, esteem, apprehend, assume, presume, take it, hold; embrace an opinion, get hold of an idea; have a point of view, account; hold an opinion, express an opinion, **affirm**; **recant**.

**convince**, make believe, assure, persuade, satisfy; bring home to, **demonstrate**; make confident; convert, bring round; propagate a belief, indoctrinate, **teach**; sell an idea to, put across; **influence**; compel belief, obsess, haunt; come round to, convince oneself.

be believed; carry conviction; find credence, pass current, pass for truth.
**Adv.** credibly; faithfully.

## 481 Unbelief. Doubt

**N.** unbelief, disbelief, discredit; disagreement, **dissent**; inability to believe; denial, denial of assent; contrary belief, **opposition**; want of faith, infidelity, **heresy**; scorn, mockery, **ridicule**; change of belief, loss of faith.

doubt; critical attitude; misgiving, distrust, mistrust; scepticism; reserve, reservation, **qualification**, demur, **opposition**; scruple, qualm, suspicion.

unbeliever; heathen, infidel, **heretic**; atheist; sceptic, agnostic; dissenter; lapsed believer; denier; cynic.

**Adj.** unbelieving, incredulous, sceptical; heathen, infidel; unfaithful, lapsed; doubtful, undecided; suspicious, shy, shy of, **nervous**; slow to believe, mistrustful; impervious, hard to convince; hard-boiled.

unbelieved, exploded; incredible, unbelievable, **impossible**; inconceivable, staggering, **wonderful**; hard to believe, hardly credible; untenable; open to suspicion, open to doubt, suspect, suspicious, questionable, disputable, far-fetched; so-called, pretended.

**Vb.** disbelieve, be incredulous, find hard to believe, discredit, refuse credit, greet with scepticism, withhold assent, disagree, **dissent**; mock, scoff at; **ridicule**; deny, deny outright; **negate**; refuse to admit, ignore; retract, lapse, relapse, **recant**.

doubt, be uncertain; demur, object, cavil, question, scruple, boggle, stick at, **qualify**; pause, hesitate, waver, **be irresolute**; treat with reserve, distrust, mistrust, suspect, **be nervous**; be shy of, shy at; be sceptical, take leave to doubt; smell a rat, scent a fallacy; hold back.

cause doubt; render suspect; discredit, **defame**; shake; stagger, startle, **surprise**; pass belief, **be unlikely**; argue against, deter, tempt, **dissuade**; impugn, attack.

**Adv.** incredibly, unbelieveably; in utter disbelief.

doubtfully, with a pinch of salt.

## 482 Credulity

**N.** credulity; simplicity; rash belief, uncritical acceptance, **belief**; will to believe, blind faith, unquestioning belief; dotage; superstition; **conformity**; sucker, mug, **dupe**.

**Adj.** credulous, amenable; **gullible**; simple, unsophisticated, green; childish, silly, soft, stupid, **foolish**; infatuated; confiding, trustful.

**Vb.** be credulous; kid oneself; **reason badly**; believe every word, buy it, believe; accept, **absorb**; swallow, swallow anything, swallow whole, swallow hook; touch wood; **overrate**.

## 483 Assent

**N.** assent, yes, yea, amen; hearty assent; welcome; agreement, **consent**; acceptance; **submission**; recognition; admission, clean breast, plea of guilty; confession, **disclosure**; declaration of faith, profession, sanction, nod, go-ahead, green light, **permission**; approval, **approbation**; concurrent testimony, accordance, corroboration, **evidence**; seal, signature, mark, cross; visa, pass, **permit**; stamp, label; favour, sympathy; support, **aid**; **flattery**.

consensus, same mind, **agreement**; concordance, harmony, unison, **concord**; solid vote, general consent, universal agreement, universal testimony; popular belief, public opinion, general voice; chorus, single voice; thinking alike, same wavelength, mutual sympathy, **similarity**; understanding, bargain, **compact**.

**assenter**, follower; fellow traveller; yesman; willing voter; supporter; **patron**; subscriber, **signatory**; party; professor.

**Adj. assenting**; party to; sympathetic, friendly; unanimous, solid, with one voice; acquiescent, **willing**; **pleased**.

**assented**; unanimous; confirmed; bipartisan.

**Vb. assent**, concur, agree with, **accord**; welcome, hail, cheer, acclaim, **applaud**; be certain, accept, buy it; concede, admit, own, acknowledge, grant, allow, **be reasonable**; plead guilty, avow, **confess**; signify assent, nod, say aye, say yes, agree to, go along with, **consent**; sanction, **permit**; ratify (see **endorse**); see eye to eye; echo, ditto, say amen, say hear hear; chorus; defer to, **respect**; be a yesman, rubber-stamp, **flatter**; reciprocate, **be friendly**; accede, adhere, side with, **join a party**; collaborate, go along with; tolerate (see **acquiesce**); covenant, come to an understanding, have a mutual agreement, **contract**.

**acquiesce**, accept, **obey**; tolerate, suffer, endure, wear it; **submit**; yield, defer to; allow, **permit**; let it happen, **watch**; **conform**.

**endorse**, second, support; subscribe to, attest, **sign**; seal, stamp, rubberstamp, confirm, ratify, sanction, **consent**; authenticate, **make certain**; countersign.

**Adv. consentingly**, willingly; in full agreement, all the way, on all points.

**unanimously**, with one accord, with one voice, with one consent, to a man.

**Int.** amen! amen to that! hear, hear! aye, aye!

## 484 Dissent

**N. dissent**, amicable dissent, agreement to disagree; difference, confirmed opposition, **opposition**; difference of opinion, contrary vote, controversy, **dissension**; party feeling, party spirit, faction, **party**; popular clamour, anger; **discontent**; **disapprobation**; schism; alternative life style, **nonconformity**; walkout, strike; reluctance; denial, lack of consent, **refusal**; **doubt**; cavil, demur, reservation, **qualification**; protest, protestation; **challenge**, **defiance**; passive resistance, **sedition**.

**dissentient**, critic; dissident, dissenter, protestant; **sectarian**; **schismatic**; rebel; dropout, **nonconformist**; **malcontent**; minority; splinter group, cave, faction, **party**; **opposition**; **opponent**; agitator, firebrand, revolutionary.

**Adj. dissenting**, dissident; agnostic, sceptical; schismatic, **sectarian**; nonconformist; malcontent; **deprecatory**; recusant; disinclined, reluctant; obstructive; challenging, **defiant**; intolerant.

**unadmitted**, denied, **negative**.

**Vb. dissent**, differ, disagree; beg to differ, combat an opinion; demur, object, cavil, boggle, scruple, **qualify**; protest, **deprecate**; resist, oppose; challenge, **defy**; show reluctance; withhold assent, **refuse**; **be indifferent**; **prohibit**; negative, contradict, **negate**; repudiate; never intend to, **reject**; look askance at, **disapprove**; secede, withdraw, **relinquish**; recant; retract;

argue, wrangle, bicker, **quarrel**.

**Adv. no**, on the contrary; at issue with; under protest.

**Int.** God forbid! not on your life! not on your nelly! over my dead body! ask me another! tell that to the marines! never again! not likely!

## 485 Knowledge

**N. knowledge**, ken; knowing, cognition, recognition; apprehension, comprehension, perception, understanding, grasp, **intellect**; conscience; insight, **intuition**; precognition, foresight; revelation; lights, enlightenment, **wisdom**; learning, folk wisdom, folklore; occult lore, **sorcery**; education, background; experience, acquaintance, acquaintanceship, familiarity; private knowledge, **information**; public knowledge, notoriety, common knowledge, open secret, **publicity**; complete knowledge, partial knowledge, sidelight, glimpse, inkling, suggestion, **hint**; suspicion, scent; sensory knowledge, impression, **feeling**; introspection; detection, clue; expert knowledge, savvy, know-how, expertise, **skill**; smattering; science of knowledge.

**erudition**, lore, wisdom, scholarship, literature, **learning**; academic knowledge; solid learning, profound learning; smattering; reading; pedantry; information, mine of information, store of knowledge, **library**; department of learning, faculty, **academy**; scholar, **intellectual**.

**culture, literature**; education, instruction, **teaching**; literacy; liberal education; cultivation.

**science**; natural philosophy, scientific knowledge, applied science, technology; tree of knowledge.

**Adj. knowing**, omniscient, **wise**; cognizant, **mental**; conscious, aware, mindful of, **attentive**; alive to, sensible of; experienced, at home with, familiar with; intimate, privy to, wise to, **informed**; fly, canny, shrewd; conversant, practised, proficient, **expert**.

**instructed**, informed of, **informed**; taught; literate; numerate; learned, bookish, literary; erudite, scholarly, **studious**; well-read, well-informed, knowledgeable; donnish, scholastic; highbrow, intellectual, cultured, cultivated, sophisticated, blue-stocking; professional, **expert**.

**known**, seen; **certain**; noted, celebrated, famous; public, notorious, **well-known**; familiar, intimate, dear; too familiar, hackneyed, stale, trite; proverbial, household, commonplace, corny, **usual**; current, prevalent, **general**; **intelligible**.

**Vb. know**, savvy, ken; have knowledge; apprehend, conceive, catch, grasp, twig, click, have, get, **understand**; possess, comprehend, master; come to know; get to know, know again; appreciate; be conscious of, be aware, be cognizant; discern, **discriminate**; perceive, see; examine, study, **scan**; mull, con, **be attentive**; know well, see through, read one like a book; **be certain**; know of, have knowledge of, know something; **be informed**; know backwards, have it pat, be master of, **be expert**; have a little knowledge of; experience, **learn**; be omniscient; **be wise**.

**be known**; be public knowledge.

**Adv. knowingly**, with knowledge.

## 486 Ignorance

**N. ignorance**, unknowing; lack of news; unawareness, unconsciousness, insensibility; incomprehension; obstacle to knowledge; false knowledge, supersti-

tion, **error**; blind ignorance, lack of
knowledge; lack of education; blank
mind; inexperience, lack of experience; simplicity; lack of information,
general ignorance; moral ignorance,
**folly**; Age of Ignorance; imperfect
knowledge, ignorant person, illiterate,
**ignoramus**; layman, amateur; Philistine.

**unknown thing**, obstacle to knowledge;
unknown quantity, matter of ignorance; prehistory, **antiquity**; Greek;
Dark Continent, unknown country,
virgin soil; dark horse, mystery, **secret**; unidentified flying object, UFO;
unidentified body; unknown person.

**sciolism**, smattering, a little learning;
glimpse, **hint**; unreal knowledge,
**error**; affectation of knowledge,
pedantry, bluff, **affectation**.

**Adj. ignorant**, unknowing, blank; unwitting; unconscious, oblivious, **insensible**; unseeing; a stranger to; **uncertain**; clueless, without a clue; **blind**;
tentative; lay, amateurish, unqualified, inexpert; unversed, green; raw;
innocent of (see **innocent**); simple, **artless**;
gauche, awkward; unenlightened,
benighted; savage; pagan; backward,
dull, dense, dumb; empty-headed,
foolish; dark; old-fashioned, **retrospective**, forgetful; regardless; indifferent.

**uninstructed**, uninformed; vague about,
**uncertain**; unschooled; illiterate,
uneducated; lowbrow; Philistine;
simple, dull, dense, dumb (see **ignorant**).

**unknown**, unbeknown, untold, unheard;
unsaid; unseen, never seen, **invisible**;
dark, enigmatic, mysterious, **occult**;
strange, new, unprecedented; **anonymous**; unidentified; unfathomed; virgin, novel, **new**; future; unknown to
fame, unheard of, obscure, humble;

lost, missing, **absent**.

**dabbling**, smattering; unqualified,
quack, **affected**; half-baked, shallow,
superficial, dilettante.

**Vb. not know**, be ignorant, lack information; be innocent of, be green; cannot
say; can only guess, **suppose**; know
nothing of; **be deaf**; **be blind**; be at a
loss, **be uncertain**; have everything to
learn; misunderstand; misconstrue,
**misjudge**; half know, know a little;
half glimpse, guess, suspect, wonder,
**doubt**, forget; lack interest; refuse to
know, ignore, **disregard**; make ignorant; mystify, **keep secret**; profess
ignorance, **be indifferent**; want to
know, ask, **enquire**; grope, fumble, **be
tentative**.

**Adv. ignorantly**, unawares.

## 487 Scholar

**N. scholar**, savant, learned person, man
or woman of learning; don, reader,
professor, pedagogue, **teacher**; doctor, clerk, scribe, pedant, bookworm;
prodigy of learning, mine of information; student, serious student; graduate, qualified person, professional,
specialist, **proficient person**; world of
learning, senior common room.

**intellectual**, academic, scholastic, **philosopher**; brain worker; mastermind,
brain, genius, prodigy, **sage**; know-all;
highbrow, egghead, bluestocking;
man or woman of science; boffin; academician, Immortal; patron of learning.

**collector**, connoisseur, dilettante, **people
of taste**; librarian, curator, **keeper**;
antiquary, **antiquarian**; collector of
words, compiler, **linguist**.

## 488 Ignoramus

**N. ignoramus**, illiterate, lowbrow;
philistine, **vulgarian**; duffer, wooden

spoon, **dunce**; goof, goose, **fool**; greenhorn, novice, raw recruit, **beginner**; babe, innocent, **dupe**; bigot, **narrow mind**.

**sciolist**, pedant; dilettante; quack, charlatan, **impostor**.

## 489 Truth

**N. truth**, verity, intrinsic truth; basic truth; truism, **axiom**; consistency, accordance with fact; honest truth, sober truth, light, light of truth, gospel, Holy Writ, Bible, **revelation**; nature, **world**; **existence**; actuality, **reality**; fact; home truth, candour, **probity**; naked truth; appearance of truth, **probability**.

**authenticity**; it, **identity**.

**accuracy**, attention to fact; realism, local colour; fidelity, precision, **measurement**; mot juste, aptness, **adaptation**; meticulousness, **attention**; pedantry, rigour; **meaning**; true report; statistics, **evidence**.

**Adj. true**, veritable; correct, right, so; real, tangible, **substantial**; actual, factual; well-grounded, well-founded; literal, truthful, **veracious**; true to scale, likely, **probable**; **certain**; unquestionable; consistent, reasonable, **rational**; natural, true to life, true to nature, faithful; realistic, objective; candid, honest.

**genuine**; authentic, veritable, valid, official, pukka; sound, solid, reliable, honest, **trustworthy**; natural, pure, sterling; true-born; rightful, legitimate; unadulterated, unsophisticated, unvarnished.

**accurate**, exact, precise, definite; direct, straight; unerring, constant, regular, **uniform**; punctual, right, correct, true; never wrong, infallible; close, faithful, representative; fine, nice, delicate, sensitive; scientific, electronic; scrupulous, punctilious, meticulous, strict, severe, **attentive**; literal; rigid, just so, **fastidious**.

**Vb. be true**, be so, be just so, happen, exist, **be**; hold, hold true, hold good, hold water, wash, ring true; conform to fact, prove true, hold together, be consistent; have truth, omit nothing, **be truthful**; look true, seem real, come alive, copy nature, **represent**; square, set, trim, **adjust**; substantiate, **corroborate**; prove, **demonstrate**; be right, be correct, **detect**.

**Adv. truly**, verily, really, indeed; **actually**; sic; exactly, precisely, plumb, right, to an inch, to a hair, to a nicety, to a turn, just right.

## 490 Error

**N. error**; untruth; **deviation**; fallacy; superstition, **ignorance**; subjective error; misunderstanding, misconstruction, cross-purposes; bad memory, **oblivion**; **falsehood**; illusion, hallucination, mirage, **visual fallacy**; false light, false dawn; mental error, delusion; dream, **fantasy**; false impression, wrong idea (see **mistake**); prejudice, **bias**.

**inexactness**; systematic error, **generality**; loose thinking, **sophistry**; **anachronism**; misreport; misuse of language, malapropism, **solecism**.

**mistake**, bad idea (see **error**); inappropriate move; **blunder**; wrong impression, mistaken identity, wrong person, wrong address; glaring error, **bloomer**, clanger, howler, gaffe, bull; loose thread, oversight, **inattention**; bosh shot, **failure**; bungle, slip-up, **boob**, goof; fluff, muff; slip, spoonerism, **solecism**; clerical error, misprint, erratum, corrigendum; trip, stumble; bad tactics, wrong step; solecism, **bad taste**; blot, flaw, **blemish**.

Adj. **erroneous**, wrong; **unreal**; aberrant; unsound, self-contradictory, **illogical**; **improbable**; baseless, unfounded; exploded; fallacious; apocryphal; unorthodox; untruthful, lying, **false**; fake, **spurious**; illusory, deceptive; subjective, **imaginary**; wild, crackpot, **absurd**; fallible, liable to error, wrong-headed, perverse, prejudiced; **ignorant**.

**mistaken**; misread; **clumsy**; wandering; wide; at fault, cold, at sea, **uncertain**.

**inexact**, inaccurate; free; broad, **general**; incorrect; erratic, wild, hit or miss; insensitive, clumsy; maladjusted; slow, fast; faulty; misread.

Vb. **err**, commit an error, go wrong, mistake; be mistaken; delude oneself, **misjudge**; receive a wrong impression, be at cross-purposes, misunderstand, misconceive, misapprehend, get it wrong; miscount; **overrate**, **underestimate**; go astray, **stray**; gain, be fast, be **early**; lose, be slow, stop, **be late**.

**blunder**, trip, stumble, miss, fault, be **clumsy**; slip, drop a brick, drop a clanger, boob, goof; betray oneself, **disclose**; blot, flaw; fluff, muff, botch, bungle; blow it, **fail**; miscount, **misjudge**; misread, misquote, misprint, misapprehend, **misinterpret**.

**mislead**, misdirect, **deflect**; misinform, lead astray, pervert, cause to err; beguile, lead one a dance, **deceive**; give a false impression, falsify, garble, **dissemble**; whitewash, **conceal**.

## 491 Maxim

N. **maxim**, gnome, adage, saw, proverb, byword; **aphorism**; dictum, tag, saying, truth; epigram, **witticism**; wise maxim, sage reflection; truism, commonplace, platitude, hackneyed saying, trite remark; motto, watchword, slogan, catchword; formula; text, rule, **precept**; gloss, comment, note, remark, **commentary**; moral, fable, cautionary tale, **narrative**; book of proverbs; folklore.

**axiom**, self-evident truth, truism, tautology; principle, postulate, theorem, formula.

Adj. **aphoristic**, sententious, proverbial, **wise**; piquant, pithy; terse, snappy, **concise**; enigmatic; common, banal, trite, corny, hackneyed, commonplace, **stock**, **usual**.

Adv. **proverbially**, to coin a phrase.

## 492 Absurdity

N. **absurdity**; false logic, **sophistry**; silly season, **folly**; **lost labour**; nonsense verse; rot, rubbish, nonsense, jargon, twaddle, **silly talk**; rhapsody, romance, fustian, bombast, **exaggeration**; Irish bull, malapropism, howler, **mistake**; paradox; **lack of expectation**; spoonerism, joke, **witticism**; pun; riddle; quibble; anticlimax, bathos; sell, catch.

**foolery**, antics, tomfoolery, **revel**; **whim**; extravaganza; escapade, scrape, **predicament**; practical joke, monkey trick, piece of nonsense, drollery; burlesque, parody, caricature, **ridicule**; farce, pretence, **affectation**; ostentation.

Adj. **absurd**, inept; ludicrous, laughable, comical, grotesque, **ridiculous**; rash, silly, asinine, **foolish**; nonsensical, senseless, **meaningless**; preposterous, without rhyme or reason, **illogical**; wild, overdone, extravagant; pretentious, **affected**; frantic, mad, crazy, crackpot, harebrained, **erroneous**; fanciful, fantastic, **imaginative**; futile, fatuous, **useless**; inconsistent, **irrelevant**; punning, **equivocal**.

Vb. **be absurd**, act like a fool, behave like

an idiot, **be foolish**; fool, fool about, lark about, monkey around, **amuse oneself**; be a laughingstock, **be ridiculous**; clown, burlesque, parody, caricature, mimic, guy, **ridicule**; talk like a fool, talk rot, **mean nothing**; rant, rave, **be insane**; romance, **exaggerate**.

### 493 Intelligence. Wisdom

**N. intelligence**, thinking power, **intellect**; brains, brain, grey matter, head, headpiece, loaf, upper storey; wit; lights, understanding, sense, savvy, gumption, knowhow; quick thinking, readiness, ability, capacity, mental grasp; calibre, intelligence quotient, IQ; high IQ; **aptitude**; talent, genius; inspiration, **intuition**; brainwave, bright idea, **idea**.

**sagacity**, discretion, **discrimination**; perception, clear thinking, clear thinking; acumen, acuity; practical mind; balance; forethought, **foresight**; subtlety, craft, **cunning**; worldly wisdom, oneupmanship, **skill**; policy, tact, **tactics**.

**wisdom**, wise understanding; grasp of intellect, profundity of thought, **thought**; depth, depth of mind, experience, ripe knowledge, **knowledge**; tolerance, catholic outlook; mental poise, mental balance, sobriety, enlightenment.

**Adj. intelligent**, brainy, clever, forward, bright; brilliant, of genius, **gifted**; capable, able, practical, **skilful**; apt, ready, quick, receptive; acute, sharp, alive, aware, with it, **attentive**; astute, shrewd, fly, smart, canny, all there; knowing, sophisticated, worldly-wise; clever clever; sagacious, provident, prudent, watchful, **careful**; farsighted, clear-sighted; discerning; penetrating, perspicacious, clear-headed, calculating; subtle, crafty, wily, foxy, artful, **cunning**; politic.

**wise**, sage; thinking, **thoughtful**; reasoning, **rational**; knowledgeable; highbrow, intellectual, profound, deep; sound, sensible, reasonable, **sane**; staid, sober, **serious**; reliable, responsible, **trustworthy**; experienced, cool, collected, unflappable; proof against flattery; balanced, realistic, objective; judicious, impartial, **just**; tolerant, enlightened; unprejudiced; broad, broad-minded; politic, **cunning**; well-advised, **advisable**.

**Vb. be wise**; accumulate experience, have a fund of wisdom, **know**; have brains, sparkle, scintillate, shine, **be good**; see with half an eye, see at a glance; know a thing or two, know how to live, get around; be realistic; show foresight, **foresee**; be prudent, take care, **be cautious**; grasp, fathom, **understand**; discern, see through, penetrate, **see**; distinguish, **discriminate**; have sense, listen to reason, **be reasonable**; plan well, be politic, **plan**; have tact, **be cunning**; repent, **be penitent**.

### 494 Unintelligence. Folly

**N. unintelligence**, lack of intelligence, want of intellect, **absence of intellect**; poverty of intellect; weakness of intellect, lack of brains, low IQ, low mental age; Down's syndrome, mongolism, mental deficiency; mental handicap; idiocy; poor head; simplicity.

**folly**, act of folly, **foolery**; trifling, levity, frivolity, **inattention**; sophistry; **lost labour**; idiocy, lunacy, utter folly; blind side, obsession; second childhood, dotage, **old age**; conceit, vanity.

**Adj. unintelligent**, lowbrow; incompe-

tent, **clumsy**; dull; subnormal; undeveloped, immature; backward,
retarded, moronic, imbecile, **insane**;
deficient, wanting, vacant, a button
short; limited, weak; slow; stupid,
obtuse, dense, thick, crass, gross,
heavy, stolid, bovine; dumb, dim;
cracked, barmy, **crazy**; impenetrable,
impervious; prosaic, literal, matter-
of-fact; wrong-headed.

**foolish**, silly, imbecile, asinine, apish;
nonsensical, senseless, fatuous, futile,
inane, **absurd**; ludicrous, laughable,
**ridiculous**; like a fool, fallible, **gullible**; simple, **artless**; **ignorant**; gauche,
awkward; soft, wet, soppy, goody-
goody, **innocent**; gormless, goofy,
gawky; childish, babyish, puerile,
infantile; senile; besotted, fond; amorous, sentimental, **enamoured**; maudlin, **drunk**; mindless, witless, shallow, superficial, frivolous, feather-
brained; eccentric, unstable, extravagant, wild, madcap; scatty, nutty,
dotty, daft, **crazy**.

**unwise**, unenlightened; unscientific,
**ignorant**; unreasoning, irrational,
**illogical**; indiscreet; injudicious;
unseeing, short-sighted, **blind**;
thoughtless, **unthinking**; impatient,
**hasty**; foolhardy, reckless, **rash**;
prejudiced, intolerant, **narrow-
minded**; inconsistent; unreasonable,
against reason; inept, incongruous,
unseemly, improper, **inexpedient**; ill-
advised, **mistaken**.

**Vb. be foolish**, maunder, drivel, babble,
burble, **mean nothing**; go haywire, **be
insane**; never learn; invite ridicule,
look like a fool, look foolish, **be
ridiculous**; make a fool of oneself, **be
absurd**; misbehave, **amuse oneself**;
**waste effort**; err; miscalculate, **misjudge**.

## 495 Sage

**N.** sage; learned person, **scholar**; wise
man, wise woman; elder statesman or
-woman, counsellor, consultant,
authority, **adviser**; expert, **proficient
person**; genius, master mind; master,
mentor, guide, guru, pundit, **teacher**;
**religious teacher**; seer, prophet,
**oracle**; yogi, **ascetic**; leading light;
master spirit, great soul; doctor, **philosopher**; egghead, boffin, highbrow,
**intellectual**; wizard, witch doctor,
sorcerer, magus, Magi; learned judge;
Nestor; Grand Old Man.

**wiseacre**, wise guy, know-all, **vain person**; brains trust; wise fool.

## 496 Fool

**N.** fool, **madman**; buffoon, clown,
comic, jester, zany, harlequin, **entertainer**; perfect fool, complete idiot,
ass, jackass, donkey, goose, cuckoo;
idiot, born fool, natural; mongol,
cretin, moron, imbecile; half-wit, stupid, silly, stooge, butt, **laughingstock**;
madcap, **desperado**; incompetent,
twit, clot; flibbertigibbet; trifler;
crackpot, eccentric, odd fellow,
**crank**; gaffer; babbler; **old man**.

**ninny**; noodle, nincompoop, muggins,
booby, sap, big stiff, stick, dizzy,
dope, jerk, goof; greenhorn, **beginner**;
wet, weed, drip, mollycoddle, goody-
goody, **weakling**; child, babe, **innocent**; sucker, mug, **dupe**.

**dunce**, dullard; duffer, dolt, dumb cluck,
**ignoramus**; fathead, bonehead, pinhead, dunderhead; nitwit, dimwit;
chump, clot, clod, clodhopper, oaf,
lout, booby, bumpkin; block, stock,
stone.

## 497 Sanity

**N.** sanity; reason; balance, mental equilibrium; sobriety, common sense;

coherence; lucid interval, lucid moment; proper mind, senses; sound mind; mental hygiene, mental health.

**Adj.** sane, normal; of sound mind, all there; rational, reasonable; sober; fully conscious; coherent, **intelligible**; lucid, clear-headed; balanced, cool, calculating, **judicial**; sane enough.

**Vb.** be sane; be of sound mind, become sane, see sense.

make sane, bring to their senses or their right mind; sober, bring round.

**Adv.** sanely; reasonably, like a reasonable human being.

## 498 Insanity

**N.** insanity, lunacy, madness; mental sickness, mental illness; mental instability, intellectual unbalance; abnormal psychology; loss of reason, sick mind, brain damage; mental decay, dotage, **age**; mental deficiency, idiocy, mongolism, Down's syndrome; autism, aberration; **prejudice**; psychiatry, **psychology**; psychotherapy, **therapy**; psychiatrist, **doctor**.

psychopathy, personality disorder; identity crisis; emotional disturbance; neurosis, anxiety neurosis, nerves, nervous disorder; hysteria; attack of nerves, nervous breakdown, brainstorm; shellshock, combat fatigue; obsession, compulsion, claustrophobia, **phobia**; paranoia; split personality, schizophrenia; psychosis; confusion; hypochondria; depression; blues, **melancholy**; manic depression, elation. See **mania**.

mania, megalomania, kleptomania; homicidal mania.

frenzy, furore, frenetic condition; ecstasy, delirium, raving, hysteria; distraction; **alcoholism**; epilepsy, fit, paroxysm, **spasm**; brain fever, sunstroke; vertigo.

eccentricity; strange behaviour; oddity, twist, kink, craze, fad; a screw loose; fixation, hangup, repression; complex, obsession, monomania, ruling passion, fixed idea, **bias**; hobbyhorse, **whim**.

lunatic asylum, mental home, mental hospital, madhouse, Bedlam; nuthouse, funny farm; **hospital**.

**Adj.** insane, mad, lunatic, moon-struck; of unsound mind, demented; certifiable, **mental**; abnormal, sick; maladjusted; psychotic, neurotic, hysterical; paranoid, schizoid; manic; imbecile, moronic, subnormal; raving mad, declared insane.

crazy, wandering, bemused, **abstracted**; demented, infatuated, **possessed**; fond, besotted, **enamoured**; touched, wanting, **foolish**; crackers, cracked, scatty, screwy, nutty, nuts, batty, bats, cuckoo, barmy, bonkers; daft, loony, potty, dotty; cranky, wacky, eccentric, erratic, funny, queer, odd, peculiar, **abnormal**; crotchety, whimsical, **capricious**; dizzy, giddy.

frenzied, rabid, furious, angry; haggard, wild, distraught, **suffering**; possessed, possessed with a devil; frantic, frenetic, demented, like one possessed; beside oneself; berserk, running amok, running wild, **violent**; hysterical, raving, rambling, wandering, incoherent, fevered, **sick**.

**Vb.** be insane, have a screw loose; drivel, be foolish; ramble, wander; babble, rave; see things.

go mad, go crackers, become a lunatic; go berserk, run amok, see red, **get angry**.

make mad, drive insane, madden; craze, derange; **excite**; unhinge, unbalance; infuriate, make one see red, **enrage**; possess, obsess.

## 499 Madman

N. **madman**, lunatic, mental case; nut, nutcase, loony; abnormal character, psychopath, psycho; neurotic; psychotic; schizoid; manic-depressive; raving lunatic, maniac; **drunkard**; dope addict, dope fiend; drug addict; idiot, natural, cretin, moron, **fool**.

**crank**, crackpot, nut; eccentric, oddity, oddball, **laughingstock**; freak, **nonconformist**; fad, fanatic, lunatic fringe; seer, dreamer, **visionary**; knight errant.

**enthusiast**, **busy person**; zealot, **obstinate person**; devotee, aficionado, addict, fiend, nut, freak, bug, buff; fan, supporter, **patron**; connoisseur, fancier, **people of taste**; radio ham, opera buff; **collector**.

## 500 Memory

N. **memory**; tenacious memory, collective memory.

**remembrance**, exercise of memory, recollection, recall; rehearsal, **repetition**; **learning**; reminiscence, reminiscent vein, retrospection, review, retrospect, hindsight; flashback, recurrence; afterthought, **sequel**; nostalgia, regrets, **regret**; memoirs, history, narration, **narrative**; fame, notoriety.

**reminder**, memorial, testimonial, **celebration**; token of remembrance, souvenir, keepsake, relic, memento, autograph; trophy, bust, statue, **monument**; prompter; **witness**; memorandum, memo, chit, note, notebook, diary, album, scrapbook; leading question, prompt, suggestion, cue, **hint**; mnemonic, aid to memory.

**mnemonics**, art of memory; mnemonic device, artificial memory, electronic brain; data bank, **store**.

Adj. **remembered**; green, fresh, of recent memory; of blessed memory; memor-

able, unforgettable; haunting, persistent, undying; deep-rooted, deep-seated, indelible; **known**.

**remembering**, mindful; evocative, memorial; reminiscent; unable to forget; mnemonic.

Vb. **remember**, mind, know again, know; recollect; **retain**; never forget, recall, call to mind, think of; **be mindful**; reminisce; remind oneself, make a note of.

**retrospect**, recollect, recall, recapture; reflect, review, think back, retrace, hark back, bring back to memory, **look back**; recapture old times; make an effort to remember.

**remind**, take one back; drop a hint, prompt, suggest, **hint**; haunt, obsess; **excite**; make one think of, commemorate, raise a memorial, toast, **celebrate**; relate, recount, recapitulate, **repeat**; petition, **request**; write history, narrate, **describe**.

**memorize**, commit to memory, get to know, con, **know**; **learn**; **repeat**.

**be remembered**; recur; ring a bell; haunt; make history, leave a name, **have a reputation**; be eternal.

Adv. **in memory**, lest we forget.

## 501 Oblivion

N. **oblivion**, loss of memory, amnesia, blackout, total blank, mental block; hysterical amnesia, fugue state; insensibility; **ingratitude**; dim memory, hazy recollection; short memory, decay of memory, memory like a sieve; waters of oblivion; good riddance.

**amnesty**; pardon, absolution, **forgiveness**.

Adj. **forgotten**, beyond recall; left; repressed.

**forgetful**, oblivious; insensible; unable to remember; mindless, **negligent**;

absent-minded, inclined to forget, **abstracted**; willing to forget, **forgiving**; **ungrateful**.

Vb. **forget**; consign to oblivion, be oblivious; amnesty, let bygones be bygones, **forgive**; efface, **obliterate**; remember nothing; be forgetful, have a short memory; lose sight of, leave behind, overlook; be absent-minded; dry (up); have a short memory, have a memory like a sieve; almost remember, draw a blank.

be forgotten; escape notice.

## 502 Expectation

N. **expectation**, expectancy, **attention**; **intention**; confident expectation, reliance, confidence, trust, **certainty**; presumption; foretaste; optimism, cheerful expectation; eager expectation, desire; ardent expectation, **hope**; suspense; pessimism, dread, apprehension, **fear**; anxiety, **worry**; **probability**; reckoning, calculation, **estimate**; prospect, lookout, outlook, forecast, **prediction**; contingency, **possibility**; destiny, **fate**; **practice**.

Adj. **expectant**, sure, confident, **certain**; anticipatory; ready, **prepared**; **vigilant**; tense, **excited**; agog; hopeful, sanguine; apprehensive, anxious, **nervous**; **hopeless**; open-eyed, curious, **inquisitive**.

expected; **probable**; prospective, future, **impending**.

Vb. **expect**, face; contemplate, promise oneself, **intend**; reckon, calculate, **estimate**; predict, forecast, **foresee**; see it coming; think likely, presume, dare say, **assume**; be confident, **be certain**; anticipate, forestall, **prepare oneself**; be careful; hang around (see **await**); apprehend, dread, **fear**; look forward to, **hope**, **desire**; flatter oneself, **believe**.

**await**; **wait**; mark time, stand to attention; lead one to expect, **cause desire**.

Adv. **expectantly**, with bated breath.

## 503 Lack of expectation

N. **lack of expectation**; false expectation; resignation; lack of interest, apathy; unforeseen contingency, unusual occurrence; **error**; lack of warning, surprise; surprise packet, Jack-in-the-box; **windfall**, **benefit**; shock, start, jolt, turn; blow, thunderclap, bombshell; revelation, eye-opener; culture shock; paradox; astonishment, **wonder**; anticlimax.

Adj. **unexpected**; unforeseen; **improbable**; unannounced; without warning, surprising; staggering, amazing, **wonderful**; shocking; sudden; like a bombshell; contrary to expectation, **equivocal**; unprecedented, **unusual**; freakish, **abnormal**; whimsical, **capricious**; unaccountable.

**inexpectant**, unguarded; uninformed, **ignorant**; thunderstruck; **hopeless**; apathetic, **indifferent**.

Vb. **not expect**, think unlikely, **be unlikely**; **despair**; get a shock, have a jolt, start, jump; receive a revelation; goggle, stare.

**surprise**; catch, trap, ambush, **ensnare**; catch unawares; startle, jolt, make one jump, give one a turn; stagger, stun; strike one all of a heap; **disappoint**; give one a surprise; astonish, amaze, astound, **be wonderful**; shock, electrify, impress; **derange**; come like a thunderclap.

Adv. **unexpectedly**; all of a sudden, without warning, without notice, unawares.

## 504 Disappointment

**N.** disappointment, regrets, **regret**; false expectation; bad news, **news**; **discontent**; mirage, false dawn; shock, blow, setback, **hitch**; partial success, near failure; bad luck, trick of fortune, **misfortune**; anticlimax, **lack of expectation**; comedown, letdown; damp squib, **failure**.

**Adj.** disappointed; crestfallen; disgruntled; **hopeless**; heartbroken, **dejected**.

disappointing, **insufficient**, abortive, deceptive.

**Vb.** be disappointed, fail; **fall short**; expect otherwise; **regret**; listen to a false prophet; be crestfallen, look blue, look blank; be sick at heart, be without hope, **despair**.

disappoint, **fall short**; disillusion; serve badly, fail one; foil, thwart, frustrate, **hinder**; amaze, **surprise**; disconcert, humble, **humiliate**; betray, play one false, **be dishonest**; play one a trick, jilt; discontent, dissatisfy, sour, **cause discontent**; refuse, deny, **reject**.

**Adv.** disappointingly.

## 505 Foresight

**N.** foresight, prevision; foretaste; precognition, foreknowledge, second sight; premonition, presentiment, foreboding, **omen**; prognosis, **prediction**, **certainty**; programme, prospectus, **plan**; forethought, vision; providence, **caution**; readiness, provision, **preparation**.

**Adj.** foreseeing, prospective, prognostic, prescient, farsighted, sagacious, **wise**; provident, prudent, **cautious**; anticipatory, **expectant**.

**Vb.** foresee, divine, prophesy, forecast, **predict**; forewarn, **warn**; have second sight; have prior information, **be informed**; see ahead, see it coming,

scent; **expect**; be beforehand, anticipate, forestall, **be early**; make provision, **prepare**; surmise, make a good guess, **suppose**; **predetermine**; plan ahead, **plan**; **look ahead**; **be wise**; keep a sharp lookout, **be attentive**; **provide**; provide against, **be cautious**.

## 506 Prediction

**N.** prediction, prophecy; apocalypse, **revelation**; forecast, prognosis; presentiment, foreboding, **foresight**; presage, programme, prospectus, **plan**; announcement, notice, **publication**; warning, warning shot, **danger signal**; prospect, **expectation**; shape of things to come, horoscope, fortune; type, **prototype**.

divination; augury; astrology; necromancy.

omen, portent, presage; prognostic, symptom, sign; augury; caution, **warning**; harbinger, herald, **messenger**; type; **danger**; black cat, **talisman**; portent of bad luck, broken mirror; bird of ill omen, owl, raven.

oracle, consultant, **sage**; calamity prophet, doom merchant; prophet, seer; soothsayer, **sorcerer**; medium; Delphic oracle; Sibyl; cards, dice, lot; tripod, crystal ball, mirror, tea leaves, palm; Bible.

diviner; tipster; fortune-teller, gipsy, palmist; augur.

**Adj.** predicting, apocalyptic; foreboding, **cautionary**.

presageful, significant, ominous, portentous, big with fate, pregnant with doom; auspicious, promising, fortunate, favourable, **prosperous**; inauspicious, sinister, **adverse**.

**Vb.** predict, forecast, make a prediction; prognosticate, make a prognosis; foretell, prophesy, forebode, bode, augur, spell; presage, portend; foreshadow,

shadow forth, herald, be harbinger, **come before**; point to, typify, signify, **indicate**; announce, give notice, notify, **advertise**; forewarn, give warning, **warn**; look black, lour, menace, **threaten**; promise, augur well, bid fair to, **give hope**.

**divine**; cast a horoscope, cast a nativity; **gamble**.

### 507 Supposition

**N. supposition**, notion, **idea**; fancy, conceit; pretence, **affectation**; presumption, assumption, postulate; condition, **conditions**; proposal, proposition, **offer**; submission, **argument**; hypothesis, theory, model, theorem, **topic**; thesis, position, stand, attitude, standpoint, **opinion**; suggestion, **hint**; basis of supposition, clue, data, **evidence**; suspicion, hunch, inkling (see **conjecture**), instinct, **intuition**; **thought**; **possibility**.

**conjecture**, guess, surmise, suspicion; mere notion, bare supposition, vague suspicion, rough guess, crude estimate; shrewd idea, **intuition**; guesswork; gamble, shot.

**theorist**, research worker; academic, critic, armchair detective; **doctrinaire**; **philosopher**; boffin.

**Adj. suppositional**, notional, hypothetical, theoretical, armchair, speculative, academic, of academic interest; gratuitous; suggestive.

**supposed**; **topical**; given; putative; pretended, so-called; **unreal**; imaginable, **imaginary**.

**Vb. suppose**, pretend, fancy, dream, **imagine**; think, conceive, **opine**; divine, have a hunch; surmise, conjecture, guess, suppose so, dare say; persuade oneself, **believe**; presume, assume, presuppose; assert, **affirm**; take, take it, postulate, **reason**; specu-

late, have a theory, **meditate**; sketch, draft, outline, **plan**; **gamble**.

**propound**, propose, **offer**; moot, move, propose a motion, **request**; put a case, submit, **argue**; put forth, make a suggestion, venture to say; put forward a notion, **advise**; suggest, **hint**; urge, **motivate**.

**Adv. supposedly**, seemingly.

### 508 Imagination

**N. imagination**; **skill**; fantasy, understanding, insight, empathy, sympathy, **moral sensibility**; frenzy, ecstasy, inspiration, fancy, imagery; artistry, creative work.

**ideality**, conception, thought; ego ideal; mental image, projection, **appearance**; concept, image, conceit, fancy, notion, **idea**; **whim**; **caprice**; figment, fiction, **falsehood**; work of fiction, story, **novel**; science fiction, fairy tale; imaginative exercise, flight of fancy, romance, fantasy, extravaganza, rhapsody, **exaggeration**; **poetry**; shadow boxing.

**fantasy**; vision, dream, nightmare; phantom, **ghost**; shadow, vapour; mirage, **visual fallacy**; delusion, hallucination, **error**; reverie, brown study; trance, somnambulism, **insensibility**; sick fancy, delirium, **frenzy**; **sophistry**; make-believe, daydream, golden dream, **desire**; romance, stardust; romanticism, escapism, idealism; Utopia; Happy Valley; Shangri-la, Middle Earth; wonderland; cloud-cuckoo-land, dream world; good time coming, millennium, **future state**; idle fancy, myth, **fable**.

**visionary**, seer; dreamer, **inattention**; idealist, Utopian, **philanthropist**; ostrich; romantic; **crank**; creative worker, **artist**.

**Adj. imaginative**, creative, lively, original, inventive, fertile, ingenious; resourceful, **skilful**; romantic; fictional, Utopian; extravagant, grotesque, bizarre, whimsical, preposterous, impractical, **absurd**; visionary, otherworldly, quixotic.

**imaginary**, unreal, **insubstantial**; subjective, notional, chimerical, illusory, **erroneous**; dreamy, visionary, ideal; cloudy, **shadowy**; fictitious, fabulous, mythological; fanciful, hypothetical; pretended, make-believe.

**Vb. imagine, think**; fancy, dream; think of, devise, invent, originate, create, have an inspiration, **improvise**; coin, hatch, concoct, fabricate, **produce**; envisage, **see**; conceive, form an image of; figure to oneself, paint, capture, recapture, **represent**; **exaggerate**; pretend, make-believe, daydream; **understand**.

**Adv. imaginatively**; with imagination.

## 509 Meaning

**N. meaning**, substance, essence, spirit, sum, gist, pith; contents, text, matter, **topic**; deep structure, sense, value, drift, tenor, purport, import, implication, colouring; force, effect; bearing, scope; expression, diction, **style**; semantics, **linguistics**.

**connotation**, significance, reference, application; **interpretation**; context; original meaning, **source**; range of meaning, comprehension; extension; intention, main meaning, leading sense; idiom, **speciality**; usage, acceptance, **practice**; single meaning; double meaning; same meaning, equivalent meaning, convertible terms; synonym, **identity**; opposite meaning, antonym; level of meaning, literal meaning; **metaphor**; esoteric sense, constructive sense.

**Adj. meaningful**, significant, of moment,

**important**; substantial, pithy, meaty, full of meaning, pregnant; indicative; telling, **expressive**; pointed; suggestive, evocative, implicit; express, explicit, **plain**; **affirmative**.

**semantic, linguistic**; literal, verbal, **plain**; **figurative**; **intelligible**; ambiguous, **equivocal**; **identical**; tantamount, equivalent, **similar**; **contrary**; idiomatic, **special**; obscure; clear; constructive, **tacit**; nonsensical, **absurd**; without meaning, **meaningless**.

**Vb. mean**, have a meaning, bear a sense, mean something; convey a meaning, get across, **communicate**; typify, **indicate**; signify, denote, connote, **represent**; import, purport, intend; point to, spell, involve, **imply**; convey, express, declare, assert, **affirm**; bespeak, tell of, speak of, breathe of, speak volumes, **evidence**; mean to say, be driving at, really mean; **be identical**; **repeat**; coincide, **accord**; **disagree**; draw a meaning, infer, **understand**.

**Adv. significantly**, with meaning; so to speak.

## 510 Lack of meaning

**N. lack of meaning**, absence of meaning; truism, platitude, **maxim**; mere words; **sophistry**; dead letter; scribble, script; daub; empty sound, meaningless noise; jargon, rigmarole; abracadabra, hocus-pocus; gabble, double dutch, Greek, Babel; raving, delirium, **frenzy**; double-talk; **flattery**.

**silly talk**, nonsense; stuff, balderdash, rubbish, rot; drivel, twaddle, fiddle-faddle, bosh, tripe, bilge, bull.

**empty talk**, wind, gas, hot air, verbiage; rant, bombast, fustian; eyewash, claptrap, poppycock, **fable**; humbug, **falsehood**; moonshine, bunkum,

bunk, boloney, hooey; flannel,
flummery, blarney, **flattery**; patter,
spiel; talk, chatter, prattle, babble,
gabble, jabber, jabber jabber, yak yak,
rhubarb rhubarb, **chatter**.

**Adj. meaningless**, without meaning;
nonsense, nonsensical, **absurd**; senseless, null; insignificant, inane, empty,
trivial, trite; fatuous, trashy, trumpery; windy; incoherent, raving.

**unmeant**, involuntary; insincere.

**Vb. mean nothing**; scribble, scratch,
daub, strum; talk bunkum, talk like
an idiot, **be absurd**; talk, babble,
prattle, prate, gabble, gibber, jabber,
**be loquacious**; talk double dutch,
doubletalk; rant, **exaggerate**; gush,
rave, drivel, drool, waffle, twaddle;
vapour, talk hot air, gas, **be foolish**;
blarney, **flatter**; make nonsense of,
**misinterpret**; be Greek to, **puzzle**.

**Int.** Rubbish! what rot! nonsense! fiddle-
sticks!

## 511 Intelligibility

**N. intelligibility**; clarity, coherence; precision, **certainty**; simplicity, straightforwardness, plain speech; plain
words, plain English, mother tongue;
paraphrase, **facility**; **interpretation**.

**Adj. intelligible**; coherent, **sane**; audible,
distinguishable, unmistakable,
**known**; explicable; unequivocal,
**meaningful**; explicit, positive, **certain**;
distinct, clear-cut, precise, **definite**;
well-spoken, articulate; downright,
forthright, **plain**; straightforward,
simple, **easy**; obvious, self-
explanatory, easy to understand, easy
to grasp, made easy; popular; clear,
limpid, **transparent**; pellucid, lucid;
readable, legible; luminous, **visible**.

**expressive**, telling, striking, vivid,
graphic, highly coloured, forceful,
strong.

**Vb. be intelligible**, come alive; be readable, read easily; make sense, **be
reasonable**; tell its own tale, **evidence**;
be visible; get across; clarify, elucidate, **interpret**; make easy, simplify,
**facilitate**; recapitulate, **repeat**.

**understand**, comprehend, apprehend,
know; master, **learn**; have, hold,
retain, **remember**; have understanding, **be wise**; see through, penetrate,
fathom, **detect**; spot, descry, discern,
distinguish, see at a glance, see with
half an eye, **see**; grasp, get
hold of, seize, dig; register; be with
one, follow, savvy; collect, get, twig;
get wise to, tumble to, rumble; begin
to understand, see it all; get to know,
be told, **be informed**.

**Adv. intelligibly**, plainly, simply.

## 512 Unintelligibility

**N. unintelligibility**; perplexity, difficulty; **lack of meaning**; double dutch;
jargon, foreign tongue, private language, **dialect**, **slang**; speech defect;
scribble, scrawl, **lettering**; Greek, **secret**; hard saying, paradox, knotty
point, obscure problem, crux, riddle;
mysterious behaviour.

**Adj. unintelligible**, incomprehensible,
inconceivable, inexplicable, unaccountable; **unknown**; unfathomable,
inscrutable, impenetrable, blank,
expressionless, **impassive**; inaudible,
unreadable, illegible, crabbed; **invisible**; **occult**; cryptic, obscure; esoteric,
**private**; enigmatical.

**puzzling**, hard to understand, complex,
**difficult**; hard, beyond one, abstruse,
elusive; enigmatic, mysterious, **occult**;
nebulous, misty, hazy, dim, obscure,
**shadowy**; ambiguous, **equivocal**, of
doubtful meaning; fishy, strange, odd,
**abnormal**; without a solution, insoluble; **uncertain**.

inexpressible, unspeakable; unutterable,
ineffable; incommunicable; profound,
deep; mystic, transcendental.

**puzzled,** unable to understand, perplexed, **uncertain.**

**Vb. be unintelligible,** be hard, be difficult, present a puzzle, **puzzle; be
equivocal;** talk double dutch, **mean
nothing;** speak badly, **stammer;** write
badly, scribble, scrawl; **cause doubt;**
perplex, complicate, entangle, confuse, **bedevil;** require explanation; be
too deep; escape one; pass comprehension, baffle understanding.

**not understand;** make nothing of, make
neither head nor tail of; find too difficult; wonder, be at sea, **be uncertain;**
have a blind spot, **be blind;** misunderstand one another, be at cross-
purposes, **blunder;** get one wrong,
**misjudge.**

### 513 Equivocalness

**N. equivocalness;** double meaning;
doubletalk, weasel word; **lack of
meaning;** conundrum, riddle, oracle;
mental reservation; white lie, **untruth;**
quibble, **sophistry; ornament;** pun,
**witticism;** anagram, acrostic; **analogue.**

**Adj. equivocal,** ambiguous, ambivalent;
double, two-edged; left-handed,
facing both ways; vague, evasive.

**Vb. be equivocal,** cut both ways; pun;
have a second meaning, **mean; be contrary;** fudge, waffle, stall, **avoid;**
equivocate, prevaricate, weasel, **dissemble.**

### 514 Metaphor: figure of speech

**N. metaphor;** allusion, application; allegory; **interpretation;** fable, parable,
**teaching;** symbol; symbolism, imagery, **imagination;** simile, likeness,
**comparison;** personification.

**trope,** figure, figure of speech, flourish;
manner of speech; irony, sarcasm,
**satire; ornament;** hyperbole, **exaggeration;** stress, emphasis; euphuism,
euphemism, **affectation;** contrast,
antithesis, **comparison.**

**Adj. figurative,** tropical; comparative;
**affected;** colloquial, **plain;** hyperbolic;
satirical; flowery, florid, **ornate.**

**Vb. figure,** image, embody, personify;
typify, **represent;** fable; apply; contrast, **compare;** employ metaphor,
**ornament.**

**Adv. metaphorically;** so to speak.

### 515 Interpretation

**N. interpretation,** definition, explanation, exposition; light; illustration,
**example;** resolution, solution, key,
clue, **answer;** amendment; application, particular interpretation, twist,
turn; construe, reading, **meaning;
metaphor;** usual text; alternative
reading, criticism, appreciation, **literature;** critique, review, **estimate;**
critical power; insight, feeling, sympathy, **moral sensibility.**

**commentary,** comment; gloss, footnote;
inscription, caption, legend, **phrase;**
motto, moral, **precept;** exposition,
**dissertation;** critical edition; glossary,
lexicon, **dictionary.**

**translation,** version, rendering, free
translation, loose rendering; faithful
translation, construe; key, crib; paraphrase; epitome, **compendium;** adaptation.

**hermeneutics,** science of interpretation;
**linguistics;** phrenology; prophecy,
**divination.**

**interpreter,** exponent, **teacher, religious
teacher;** rationalist; editor; commentator; critic, reviewer; medium, **spiritualism;** polyglot, **linguist; antiquarian;** spokesman, mouthpiece,

representative, **delegate**; public relations officer; performer, **musician**; player, **actor**; poet, painter, sculptor, **artist**.

**guide**, precedent, **example**; lamp, light, star, courier, **director**; showman, demonstrator.

**Adj. interpretive**, constructive; explanatory; **literary**; definitive; illuminating; exemplary; editorial; polyglot; equivalent, **equal**; literal, strict, **accurate**; faithful; free, **inexact**.

**interpreted**; cracked.

**Vb. interpret**, define, clarify, make clear; explain, unfold, expound, elucidate, **be intelligible**; illustrate, **exemplify**; demonstrate, **show**; show round; edit, annotate, compose a commentary, gloss, read, spell; adopt a reading, accept an interpretation, construe, give a sense to, make sense of, **understand**; illuminate, enlighten, **inform**; deduce, infer, **reason**; be spokesman; typify; simplify, **facilitate**.

**translate**, make a version, make a key, make a crib; render, English; rehash, reword, paraphrase; abridge, amplify, adapt; transliterate, transcribe; encode; lip-read.

**decipher**, crack, decode; read, piece together; solve, resolve, unravel, disentangle.

**Adv. in plain words**, plainly; that is, to wit, namely, to make it plain, to explain.

## 516 Misinterpretation

**N. misinterpretation**, misunderstanding, misconstruction, misapprehension; cross-purposes, **mistake**; wrong explanation; misconstrue; wrong interpretation; twist, turn, perversion; strained sense; false reading; false colouring, dark glasses; **exaggeration**; parody, travesty, **ridicule**; abuse of language, **solecism**.

**Adj. misinterpreted, mistaken**; misread.

**Vb. misinterpret**, misunderstand, misapprehend, misconceive, **misjudge**; get wrong, get one wrong, **blunder**; misread, misspell, **err**; misconstrue; give a twist or turn, pervert, wrench, twist, **distort**; equivocate, weasel, **be equivocal**; add a meaning, **add**; suppress, **subtract**; misquote; falsify, garble, **misrepresent**; travesty, parody, caricature, guy, **ridicule**; **overrate**; **underestimate**; inflate, **exaggerate**; traduce, misrepresent, **defame**.

## 517 Manifestation

**N. manifestation**, revelation, daylight, exposure, **disclosure**; expression; proof, **evidence**; **comparison**; presentation, production, projection, **representation**; sign, token, **signal**; omen; preview, **view**; showing, exhibition; display, **ostentation**; proclamation, **publication**; **publicity**; candour, plain speech, home truth; prominence, **visibility**; apparition, vision, **appearance**; glory; incarnation.

**exhibit**, specimen, sample, **example**; piece of evidence, quotation, citation, **evidence**; model, mock-up, **image**; show piece, antique, curio; display, show, mannequin parade, **spectacle**; scene, **view**; showplace, showroom, showcase, placard, hoarding, **advertisement**; sign, **label**; shop window, museum, gallery, **collection**; retrospective, exhibition, exposition; fair, **market**.

**exhibitor**, publicist; demonstrator; showman; impresario, **stage manager**; peacock, **vain person**; model, mannequin.

**Adj. manifest**, apparent, ostensible; plain, clear, **definite**; **intelligible**; showing, **visible**; conspicuous, noticeable, notable, prominent, pronounced, signal, marked, striking, **obvious**; open, patent, evident; gross, crass, palpable; self-evident, unmistakable, incontestable, **certain**; public, famous, notorious, **well-known**; showy; arrant, glaring, stark staring, flagrant, loud.

**undisguised**, overt, explicit, express, **affirmative**; public; unreserved, open, candid, heart-to-heart, **veracious**; free, frank, downright, forthright, straightforward, outspoken, blunt, **plain**; honest to goodness, honest to God; bold, daring, **defiant**; brazen, shameless, immodest, barefaced, **impure**; bare, naked.

**shown**, declared; showing, **visible**; brought forth; brought face to face; worn.

**Vb. manifest**, reveal, divulge, **disclose**; evince, **evidence**; bring to light, unearth, **discover**; explain, make plain, make obvious, **interpret**; expose, lay bare, unroll, **uncover**; throw open, **open**; elicit, draw forth, **extract**; invent, bring forth, **produce**; shadow forth, incorporate, incarnate, personify; typify, exemplify, **indicate**; accentuate, enhance, develop, **augment**; **illuminate**; highlight, spotlight; express, formulate, **affirm**; bring, mention, cite, quote; **make important**; bring to notice, produce, proclaim, **publish**; solve, elucidate, **decipher**.

**show**, exhibit, display; expose to view, dangle; wave, flourish, **brandish**; sport, **wear**; flaunt, parade; make a show of, affect, **be affected**; present, feature, enact, **represent**; stage, release; televise; stage an exhibition, hang (a picture); demonstrate, **teach**;

show round, draw attention to, bring to notice, **indicate**; confront, bring face to face; reflect, image, mirror, **imitate**; expose, **disclose**.

**be plain**, unveil, **doff**; speak plainly; tell its own story, **be intelligible**; be obvious, stand to reason, go without saying; be conspicuous, **be visible**; be seen, attract notice; loom large, **be near**; rear its head, transpire, come to light, **appear**.

**Adv. manifestly**, plainly, openly; at first blush; honestly, before God, before all.

**518 Latency**

**N. latency**; treachery, **perfidy**; dormant condition, potentiality, **possibility**; mysticism; ambiguous advice, **oracle**; symbolism, allegory, **metaphor**; implication, mystery, **secret**; dark; deceptive appearance; **danger**; dark horse, mystery man; mole, **pitfall**; strings, friend at court, **influence**; Freemasonry; secret influence; something rotten; innuendo, suggestion, **hint**; undercurrent, undertone, aside; secret society, cabal, intrigue, **plot**; ambush; code, invisible writing, cryptography.

**Adj. latent**; dormant; passive, **quiescent**; inert, potential, undeveloped, **possible**; **unknown**; subterranean, **deep**; undercover; unseen, **invisible**; murky, obscure, **dark**; impenetrable, secluded.

**tacit**, unsaid, untold of, unsung; undeclared; implicit; suggestive.

**occult**, mysterious, mystic; **figurative**; cryptic, esoteric; covert, indirect, crooked, **oblique**; clandestine, secret, kept quiet; insidious, treacherous, underhand; hush-hush, top-secret; **private**.

**Vb. lurk**, hide, be latent; burrow, stay

underground; lie low, lie doggo, **be quiescent**; avoid notice, **be unseen**; evade detection, escape recognition; **dissemble**; creep, slink, tiptoe; stage-manage, underlie, **cause**; smoke, smoulder, **be inert**.

imply, insinuate, whisper, murmur, suggest, **hint**; understand, infer; connote, carry a suggestion, involve, spell, **mean**.

**519 Information**

N. **information**, communication of knowledge; data base; tradition, hearsay; enlightenment, instruction, **teaching**; intercommunication; communication; mass media; telling, narration, **narrative**, notification, announcement, annunciation, warning, advice, notice, mention, tip, tip-off (see **hint**); advertisement, circular, **publicity**; common knowledge, general information, gen, info; factual information, background, documentary, **truth**; material, literature, **reading matter**; inside information, dope, lowdown, private source, confidence, **secret**; earliest information, scoop; stock of information, acquaintance, **knowledge**; file, dossier, **record**; piece of information, word, report, intelligence, **news**; a communication, wire, telegram, cable, **message**; flood of information, spate of news; leak, **disclosure**.

report, review, enquiry; paper, Green Paper, account, **narrative**; statement, return, **statistics**; specification, **estimate**; progress report, bulletin, handout, press release, **news**; representation, presentation, case; memorial, petition, **entreaty**; round robin.

hint, whisper, aside; indirect hint; broad hint, signal, nod, wink, look, nudge, kick, **gesture**; prompt, cue; sugges-

tion, lead, leading question; caution, **warning**; tip, tip-off (see **information**); word, verb. sap., **advice**; innuendo, **calumny**; clue, symptom, **interpretation**; sidelight, glimpse, inkling, **glimmer**; suspicion, guess, **conjecture**; good tip, wheeze, dodge, wrinkle.

informant, teller, narrator; **speaker**; mouthpiece, representative, **delegate**; harbinger, herald, **messenger**; **witness**; authority, source; quarter, channel, circle, grapevine; go-between, contact, **intermediary**; information centre; news agency; correspondent, reporter, commentator, columnist, gossip writer, **news reporter**; tipster, **adviser**; guide, topographer; little bird.

informer; spy, snoop, sleuth, **detective**; inside agent, mole; stool pigeon, nark, snitch, sneak, nose, blabber, grass; telltale, talebearer, gossip.

guidebook; travelogue, topography; handbook, manual, ABC; timetable; itinerary, route map, chart, plan, **map**; gazetteer, **reference book**; nautical almanac; telephone directory, phone book; catalogue, **directory**; courier, **guide**.

Adj. **informative**, communicative, chatty; instructive, documentary, **educational**; expressive, **affirmative**; **written**; oral, verbal, spoken; advisory; **cautionary**; explicit, clear, **definite**; candid, **plain**; indiscreet, **loquacious**.

**informed, knowing**; told, genned-up.

Vb. **inform**, certify, advise, intimate, impart, convey (see **communicate**); apprise, have one know, give to understand; brief, instruct, **teach**; let one know; enlighten, fill with information, **educate**; **indicate**; insinuate (see **hint**); confide, get confidential; put one wise, put right, correct, disillusion; be specific, state, name, signify, **specify**; mention, speak of, **speak**; gossip; be indiscreet, talk, **be loquacious**; leak information, reveal, **disclose**; tell, blab, split, grass, snitch, peach, squeal, **confess**; rat, implicate an accomplice; betray one; report against; inform against, lay an information against, shop, denounce, **accuse**.

**communicate**, transmit; **correspond**; report, cover, make a report, report progress, post; get through, get across, contact; convey, bring word, write, **correspond**; flash news, flash, beam; send a message, speak, semaphore, **signal**; wire, telegraph, telex, radio; telephone, phone, call, dial, ring, give one a ring or a tinkle or a buzz; disseminate, broadcast, televise; announce, notify, give notice, **advertise**; carry a report, **publish**; retail, recount, narrate, **describe**; commune, **converse**; exchange information.

**hint**, suggest; prompt, **remind**; caution, **warn**; **advise**; wink; nudge, **gesticulate**; insinuate, breathe, whisper, just mention, let fall, imply, leave one to gather, intimate.

**be informed**, **know**; be told, receive information; get to hear of, overhear, **hear**; get wind of, scent, **discover**; gather, infer, **understand**; come to know, get a report, **learn**; become alive to, **be attentive**; **enquire**; have information, have something to tell; claim to know, **affirm**.

**Adv. reportedly**, as stated, from what one can gather.

## 520 Concealment
**N. concealment**, confinement; hiding; burial; cache; disguise, camouflage, **deception**; masquerade; incognito; smoke screen; **screen**; reserve, discretion; secret thought, mental reservation, ulterior motive; lack of candour, evasion; white lie; subterfuge; D notice; **untruth**; **duplicity**.

**secrecy**, **silence**; mystery, **secret**; seal of secrecy; secret society, Freemasonry; clandestine behaviour; low profile; underhand dealing; conspiracy, **plot**; cryptography, cryptogram, code; invisible ink.

**Adj. concealed**, hiding, lost; **latent**; incommunicado; mysterious; cryptic, **occult**; private, **occluded**, privy, confidential; secret, top secret, hush-hush, inviolable; ex-directory; untold; **anonymous**; covert; hooded; clandestine, undercover, underground, subterranean, **deep**.

**disguised**; incognito, **anonymous**; **unknown**.

**stealthy**, silent, furtive, sneaking, like a thief; clandestine, hugger-mugger, cloak-and-dagger; underhand, surreptitious, **dishonest**.

**reticent**, reserved, withdrawn; noncommittal, cagey, evasive; vague, discreet, silent, **taciturn**; tight-lipped, close, secretive; **unsociable**.

**Vb. conceal**, hide, secrete, ensconce, confine, **seclude**; store; hide underground, bury; whitewash, **cover**; varnish; **obliterate**; slur, disregard; smother, stifle, **suppress**; veil, muffle, mask, disguise, camouflage; shroud, **screen**; shade, obscure, eclipse, **darken**; obfuscate; assume a mask, masquerade, **dissemble**; code, encode.

**keep secret**, keep it dark, keep close; look blank, keep a straight face, keep mum, **be taciturn**; be discreet, neither confirm nor deny; keep back, reserve, withhold; suppress; keep a low profile; blindfold, bamboozle, **deceive**.

**be stealthy**, hugger-mugger, conspire,

plot; snoop, sneak, slink, creep; glide, steal, steal along, steal past; tiptoe, pussyfoot; prowl, skulk, loiter; be anonymous, stay incognito; wear a mask, assume a disguise, **dissemble**; lie doggo, **lurk**; evade, shun, dodge, **avoid**; play hide-and-seek; take cover, go to earth; go underground, vanish, **disappear**; bury oneself, be unsociable; lay an ambush, **ambush**.

**Adv. secretly**, hugger-mugger; with bated breath; between ourselves; aside, to oneself; without beat of drum; incognito.

**stealthily**: underhand.

## 521 Disclosure

**N. disclosure**, revelation, apocalypse; daylight, cold light of day; denouement, catastrophe, **event**; **publication**; exposure, **manifestation**; showdown; communication, leak, **hint**; giveaway; cloven hoof, tell-tale sign, blush; admission, confession; confessional; clean breast, whole truth, **truth**.

**Adj. disclosed, shown**; showing, visible; confessed, avowed; **open**; laid bare.

**disclosing**, opening; apocalyptic; **transparent**; explanatory; communicative, leaky, indiscreet, garrulous, **loquacious**; tell-tale, indicative; confessional, penitent.

**Vb. disclose**, reveal, expose, **manifest**, bare, denude, **doff**; unfold, unroll, unpack; **uncover**; unveil; **open**; lay open, **discover**; detect; **be transparent**; betray; unmask; expose oneself, **blunder**; declare oneself; correct, set right, disillusion, **inform**.

**divulge**, declare, be open about, express, vent, give vent to, **speak**; ventilate, air, **publish**; speak of, talk, must tell; utter, breathe; leak, **communicate**; let drop, let fall, **hint**; **speak plainly**; unbosom oneself, confide; report, tell,

**accuse**; split, peach, squeal, blab, **inform**; rat.

**confess**, admit, avow, acknowledge; concede, grant, allow, own, **assent**; implicate oneself, plead guilty; talk, sing, sing like a canary; come across with, come clean, tell all, admit everything, be **truthful**; make a clean breast of it, go to confession, **be penitent**.

**be disclosed**, break, **appear**; come to light; show its face, show its true colours, **be plain**; transpire, become known, **emerge**; show, **be visible**; show through, **be transparent**.

## 522 Hiding. Disguise

**N. hiding-place**, hide, hideaway, hole, refuge; lair, den, **retreat**; cache, secret place; crypt, vault, **cellar**; closet; secret drawer, safe place, safe, safe deposit, **storage**; recess, corner, nook, cranny, niche, secret passage, cover, underground, **shelter**.

**ambush**; **trap**; catch, **pitfall**; decoy, stool pigeon, **impostor**.

**disguise**, blind, masquerade, **deception**; camouflage, protective colouring; mimicry, dummy, **sham**; veneer, **covering**; mask, visor, veil, domino, **cloak**; fancy dress; cloud, smoke screen, cover, **screen**;

hider; **impostor**.

**Vb. ambush**, lurk; **ensnare**; assume a disguise, wear a mask; obfuscate; waylay.

## 523 Publication

**N. publication, disclosure**; proclamation; edict, ban, **decree**; call-up, summons; cry, bugle call, **call**; beat of drum; press conference, press release, advance publicity (see **advertisement**); notification, public notice, official bulletin; announcement, pronouncement, manifesto, programme, platform; book trade, **book**; **telecommunication**; broadcast, newscast, **news**; **rumour**; circulation, circular, encyclical.

**publicity**, limelight, spotlight, public eye; common knowledge, **knowledge**; **manifestation**; open secret, open scandal; notoriety, fame; currency, circulation, sale, extensive sales; readership, audience; public relations, PR, propaganda; display, showmanship, window dressing, **ostentation**; sensationalism, ballyhoo, **exaggeration**; advertising; medium of publicity, television, radio; public address system, loudspeaker, **hearing aid**; public comment, journalism, coverage, report, **enquiry**; newsreel, newsletter, **news**; open letter; editorial, **article**; pulpit, platform, hustings, soapbox, **rostrum**; printing press, **print**; blaze of publicity.

**advertisement**, notice, advert, ad, personal column; headline, streamer, spread; puff, blurb, ballyhoo; handout, handbill; bill, poster, **exhibit**; billboard, hoarding, placard, sandwich board; advertising copy, slogan, jingle; plug, trailer, commercial; hard sell, subliminal advertising.

**the press**, fourth estate, Fleet Street, newspaper world, news business; newspaper, newssheet, sheet, paper, rag, tabloid, comic; serious press, organ, journal, daily paper, daily, broadsheet, heavy; morning paper, issue, edition, extra; magazine section, supplement, leaflet, handbill, pamphlet, brochure, open letter, newsletter.

**journal**, review, magazine, periodical, daily, weekly, monthly, quarterly, annual; gazette, trade journal, house magazine, trade publication, **reading**

matter.

**publicizer**; herald, trumpet, **messenger**; barker, tout; bill sticker, bill poster; publicist, publicity agent; copywriter, blurb writer, commercial artist, public relations officer, PRO, propagandist, pamphleteer; printer, publisher; reporter, **news reporter**.

**Adj. published**; passing round, current; public, **known**; open; broadcast; mixed media.

**publishing**.

**well-known**, public, celebrated, famous, notorious, crying, flagrant, blatant, glaring, sensational, **manifest**.

**Vb. publish**, make public, carry a report, **communicate**; report, cover; write an open letter, reveal, **divulge**; highlight, spotlight; radio, broadcast, televise, relay, diffuse, **inform**; spread, circulate, distribute, disseminate; ventilate, discuss, **argue**; pamphleteer, propagate, **teach**; **print**; syndicate, edit, sub; issue, release, send forth; bring to public notice, let it be known; spread a rumour, fly a kite; rumour, noise abroad, talk about, retail, pass round, put about, **be loquacious**; voice, broach, talk of, speak of, utter, emit, **speak**.

**proclaim**, announce, herald, promulgate, notify; ban, denounce, **accuse**; pronounce, declare, **affirm**; make a proclamation, issue a pronouncement, publish a manifesto; celebrate, sound, noise, trumpet, blaze abroad, cry, shout, scream, thunder, **be loud**; declaim.

**advertise**; insert a notice, bill, placard, post; headline, splash; spotlight, promote; make much of, feature; sell, boost, puff, extol, **overrate**; din, plug, **repeat**.

**be published**, become public; acquire notoriety; circulate, pass current, pass round, get about, spread abroad, spread like wildfire, fly about, find a publisher; have a circulation, sell well, go like a best-seller, **be sold**.

Adv. **publicly**, openly.

## 524 News

N. **news**, bad news; tidings, gospel, **religion**; intelligence; report, word, advice; piece of information, something to tell, titbit, **information**; bulletin, handout; newspaper report, press notice; news item, news flash, **broadcast**; fresh news, sensation, scoop, exclusive; old news, copy; yarn, story, newscast, newsreel, **publicity**; news value.

**rumour**; flying rumour, fame; hearsay, gossip, talk, tittle-tattle, **chat**; scandal, calumny; whisper, buzz, noise; false report, hoax; grapevine, bush telegraph.

**message**, word of mouth, word, advice, tip, **information**; communication, **signal**; wireless message, radiogram, cable, telegram, wire, **telecommunication**; postcard, **postal communications**; ring, phone call; errand, embassy, **commission**.

**news reporter**, reporter, correspondent, **author**; press representative; gossip; retailer of news; newsagent, newsvendor, newspaper boy or girl.

**messenger**, forerunner, **precursor**; harbinger, **omen**; ambassador, minister, legate, spokesman or -woman, **envoy**; apostle, emissary; herald, trumpet; **law officer**; go-between, contact, contact man, **intermediary**.

**courier**, runner, express; postman, **postal communications**; telegraph boy, page, commissionaire; carrier pigeon, **carrier**; Iris, Mercury.

Adj. **rumoured**; going about, passing round; rife, afloat; full of news,

chatty; newsworthy.

Vb. **rumour**, fly a kite; **correspond**. See **inform**, **disclose**, **publish**.

## 525 Secret

N. **secret**, secret lore, mystery; confidential matter, hush-hush subject, top-secret file, state secret; confidential communication, confidence; sphinx, man or woman of mystery, enigmatic personality; dark horse, unknown quantity; unmentionable thing; unknown country, **unknown thing**.

**enigma**, mystery, puzzle; problem, poser, teaser; hard nut to crack, hard saying, knotty point, crux, **difficulty**; code, cryptogram; anagram, acrostic, crossword; riddle, conundrum, rebus; labyrinth, maze.

## 526 Communications

N. **telecommunication**, telephony; semaphore, **signal**; cable, telegram, wire, **message**; bush telegraph, **rumour**; radar; telex, teleprinter, tape machine, ticker; intercom, walkie-talkie; microphone, **megaphone**; **hearing aid**; telephone; line, telephone exchange, switchboard; wireless operator, radio ham, telephonist.

**postal communications**, Postal Union, GPO; post, mail; surface mail, parcel post, postcode, postage stamp; pillarbox, letterbox; post office, mailbag; postmaster or -mistress, postman or -woman, **messenger**; pigeon post.

**broadcasting**, **publicity**; BBC; ITA; independent radio or television; transmitter, booster, communications satellite; aerial, antenna; AM, FM, **radiation**; radio station, television channel, network; wireless, radio, crystal set; portable, transistor, tranny; television, telly, TV, small screen; colour television; **camera**; videotape, **recording instrument**; autocue; **information**; Open University; viewer, **spectator**.

**broadcast**, transmission, relay, **publication**; recording, repeat, **record**; programme, phone-in, quiz, chat show, music, **amusement**; news, news roundup, **news**; time signal; talk, feature, documentary, **report**; soap opera, **drama**; cartoon, film, **cinema**; commercial, **advertisement**.

**broadcaster**, commentator, newscaster; compere, question master; disc jockey, DJ; media personality, **person of repute**.

## 527 Affirmation

**N. affirmation**; proposition; saying, dictum, **maxim**; statement; submission, thesis, **supposition**; voice, choice, suffrage, ballot, **vote**; expression; written statement, prepared text; declaration, profession; assertion, say-so; admission, confession, **disclosure**; corroboration, assurance, warrant, **testimony**; **vigour**; stress, accent, emphasis; **repetition**; challenge, provocation, **defiance**; protest; appeal, representation, **entreaty**; remark, interjection, **speech**; comment, criticism, **estimate**; self-assertion, push, thrust, drive; **positiveness**.

**oath**, deposition, affidavit, **testimony**; word of a gentleman, word of honour, pledge, promise, warrant, guarantee, **promise**.

**Adj. affirmative**, **positive**; predicative; valid; committed; earnest, meaning; solemn, sworn, formal.

**assertive**, saying, telling; assured, confident, **positive**, trenchant, incisive, pointed, decisive, decided, **forceful**; distinct, **definite**; express, peremp-

tory, categorical, absolute, insistent; vehement, thundering, **violent**; flat, broad, round, blunt, strong, outspoken, **plain**; pontifical, of faith, unquestionable; challenging, provocative, **defiant**.

**Vb. affirm**, state, express, formulate; declare, pronounce, deliver, enunciate, **proclaim**; give expression to, voice, **speak**; remark, comment, observe, say; state with conviction, be bound, dare swear, **opine**; vow, protest; **make a statement**, make an assertion, assert, predicate; maintain, hold, contend, **argue**; **demonstrate**; advance, urge, **propound**; represent, submit; appeal, adjure, claim, **request**; allege, asseverate, aver; bear witness, **testify**; certify, confirm, warrant, guarantee, **corroborate**; commit oneself; pledge, engage, **promise**; **offer**; profess, avow; admit, **confess**; **stand firm**; challenge, **defy**; repudiate, **negate**; say outright, assert roundly, **speak plainly**; be assertive, shout; claim to know, say so, pontificate.

**swear**, be sworn, swear an oath, attest, **corroborate**; negate; **testify**.

**emphasize**, stress, accent, accentuate; underline; shout, thunder, fulminate, **be loud**; be urgent, be earnest, urge, enforce; insist, **command**; say with emphasis, drive home; plug, labour, **repeat**; highlight, enhance, **make important**.

**Adv. affirmatively**, positively.

**Int.** As I stand here! As God is my witness! Cross my heart and hope to die!

## 528 Negation

**N. negation**, negative, nay; denial, **refusal**; refusal of belief, disbelief; **dissent**; contrary assertion, appeal, **rejoinder**; refutation; challenge, defiance; **qualification**; protest; disclaimer; negative attitude, inability to confirm; refusal of consent, **prohibition**; cancellation.

Adj. **negative**; **contrary**; **disobedient**; **deprecatory**; recusant; denied.

Vb. **negate**, negative; contravene, **disobey**; deny, belie, contradict, deny flatly, contradict absolutely; **make impossible**; repudiate, disavow, disclaim, disown, **reject**; refuse to corroborate; **be indifferent**; demur, object, **qualify**; disagree, **dissent**; dissociate oneself, **oppose**; traverse, impugn, question, refute, rebut, disprove; refuse credence, **disbelieve**; protest, appeal against, **deprecate**; challenge, **defy**; thwart, **obstruct**; **refuse**; **prohibit**; revoke, invalidate, **abrogate**; renounce, **relinquish**; abjure, **recant**.

Adv. nay, no.

Int. never! a thousand times no! nothing of the kind! quite the contrary! far from it! anything but! no such thing!

## 529 Teaching

N. **teaching**, pedagogy, private teaching; education, schooling, upbringing; tutelage, leading strings; direction, guidance, instruction, edification; direct method, induction, **reasoning**; tuition, preparation; seminar, teach-in, clinic, workshop, tutorial; initiation, introduction; training, discipline, drill, **exercise**; persuasion, conviction; propaganda, **publicity**.

**education**, culture; classical education, moral education, moral training; technical training, coeducation, progressive education, kindergarten method; elementary education, grounding; day release, sandwich course; physical education, gymnastics.

**curriculum**, course of study, **learning**; core curriculum, common core; ABC, **beginning**; foundation course; set books, **textbook**; set task, project, exercise, homework, prep; liberal arts; grammar, rhetoric, logic; arithmetic, geometry, astronomy, music; night school, **school**.

**lecture**, talk; reading, discourse; sermon, **oration**; lesson, parable; problem play, **stage play**; readership, chair; lecturer, **teacher**.

Adj. **educational**, tutorial; scholastic, scholarly, academic; audiovisual, instructive; didactic, hortative; primary, comprehensive; set; extramural, intramural; extracurricular; redbrick, Oxbridge, Ivy League; humane, scientific; practical, utilitarian.

Vb. **educate**, edify (see **teach**); breed, rear, nurse, nurture, develop, form, mould, shape; put to school, have taught; tutor, teach, school; ground, coach, cram, prime, **prepare**; guide, **direct**; instruct, **inform**; enlighten; stuff with knowledge, indoctrinate, impregnate, infuse, instil, implant, engraft; chasten, sober.

**teach**, be a teacher, take a class; lecture; tutor, impart instruction; dictate; preach, harangue; discourse, hold forth; point a moral; elucidate, expound, **interpret**; indoctrinate, inoculate; pamphleteer; disseminate propaganda, condition, brainwash; **influence**.

**train**, coach, **prepare**; initiate; tame; nurse, foster, cultivate; inure; drill, exercise, practise, make second nature, accustom; make fit, qualify; teach manners, teach how to behave.

### 530 Misteaching

**N. misteaching;** false intelligence; false name; **mistake; ignorance;** false teaching, propaganda, **falsehood;** perversion; false logic, **sophistry.**

**Adj. misteaching,** propagandist; **ignorant; mistaken.**

**Vb. misteach;** misinform, misdirect, misguide, **mislead;** corrupt, **make wicked;** pervert, **distort; misrepresent;** cry wolf, **deceive;** lie, **be false;** suppress knowledge; **brainwash.**

### 531 Learning

**N. learning,** lore, wide reading, scholarship; acquisition of knowledge; intellectual curiosity, **curiosity;** tutelage, apprenticeship, initiation, **preparation;** first steps, **beginning; aptitude;** culture, cultivation, late learning; learned person, **scholar.**

**study;** application; grind; class; homework, prep, **preparation;** further reading, further study; reading, **attention;** research, research work, **enquiry.**

**Adj. studious,** academic; partial to reading, bookish, well-read, scholarly, erudite, learned, scholastic, **knowing;** sedulous, diligent, **industrious;** receptive, docile, **willing; attentive.**

**Vb. learn,** get oneself taught, go to school, attend college, read, take a course; acquire knowledge, gain information, assimilate learning, imbibe, **know;** apprentice oneself, serve an apprenticeship, article oneself, **prepare oneself;** train, practise, exercise, **be wont;** master; graduate.

**study,** apply oneself; do; **enquire;** swot, cram, grind, mug; revise; read, peruse, wade through; thumb, browse, skip; **be studious.**

**Adv. studiously.**

### 532 Teacher

**N. teacher,** mentor, **guide;** minister, **pastor;** guru, **sage;** tutor, coach; governor, governess, **keeper;** educationist, pedagogue; pedant; beak, schoolmarm; master or mistress, school teacher, year tutor; house master or mistress; assistant teacher, deputy head, head teacher, head, headmaster or -mistress, principal; pupil teacher, usher, monitor; prefect; dean, don, fellow; lecturer, demonstrator, exponent; reader, professor; consultant, **adviser;** teaching staff, faculty, senior common room.

**trainer,** coach; disciplinarian.

**preacher,** pastor; orator, **speaker;** evangelist; apostle, missionary, pioneer, **precursor;** seer, prophet, **oracle;** pamphleteer, propagandist.

**Adj. pedagogic, educational.**

### 533 Learner

**N. learner,** disciple, follower; proselyte, convert, initiate; bookworm, **scholar;** pupil, scholar, schoolboy or -girl; day pupil, boarder; classmate, fellow student; gifted child; late developer, remedial pupil; old boy, old girl.

**beginner,** young idea, novice; new boy **or girl,** greenhorn, tenderfoot, neophyte; rabbit, amateur, **lay person;** recruit, rookie; colt, cadet, trainee, apprentice; probationer.

**student;** undergraduate; former student; commoner, pensioner; prize boy; honours student; graduate, fellow; mature student, research worker, specialist.

**class,** form, grade, remove, shell; set, band, stream; age group, vertical grouping, house; lower form, art class, study group, workshop; **conference;** seminar, **teaching.**

**Adj. studentlike, young;** undergraduate, collegiate; scholarly, **studious;** pre-school; rudimentary.

## 534 School

**N.** academy, institute, institution, college, gymnasium; school of music, ballet school, academy of dramatic art; charm school; university, university college, campus; Open University; redbrick university, Oxbridge, varsity; college of further or higher education; polytechnic, poly; school of philosophy, Academy.

**school,** playgroup, kindergarten; infant school, private school, preparatory school; primary school; boarding school; convent school, special school; community home; Borstal; remand home, detention centre; blackboard jungle.

**training school,** nursery, training ground, **arena**; training ship, training college, tech; college of commerce; seminary; law school, medical school, medical college, teaching hospital; military college, staff college; West Point.

**classroom;** study; lecture room, lecture hall, auditorium, amphitheatre; resources area, library; workshop, laboratory, lab, language lab; gymnasium; campus; desk; reader, primer, crib, **textbook**; slate, copybook, workbook, exercise book, **record**; visual aid, blackboard, **spectacle**.

**rostrum,** tribune, dais, forum; platform; stage; hustings, soapbox; chair, **lecture**; pulpit, lectern; microphone; leader page, column, **publicity**.

**Adj.** scholastic, educational.

## 535 Veracity

**N.** veracity; nothing but fact, fidelity, fidelity to fact, realism; candour, **manifestation**; honour bright; love of truth, **probity**; simplicity; plain dealing; plain words, home truth, unvarnished tale, true statement, honest truth, **truth**; clean breast, true confession, unqualified admission, **disclosure**; gate of horn; true prophet.

**Adj.** veracious, truthful, **true**; reliable, **trustworthy**; factual, bald, unvarnished, scrupulous, exact, just, **accurate**; full, particular, circumstantial, **diffuse**; simple, ingenuous, **artless**; meant; unaffected, unpretentious, open, above-board; **candid**, unreserved, forthcoming, blunt, free, downright, forthright, outspoken, straightforward, honest to goodness, honest to God, **plain**; **intelligible**; honest, sincere, **honourable**; truly spoken; infallible.

**Vb.** be truthful, swear true, **swear**; be true; mean it, really mean, **be serious**; keep nothing back, **show**; come clean, make a clean breast of it, **confess**; **disclose**; **predict**; say truly, **demonstrate**.

**Adv.** truthfully, **truly**; without fear or favour; exactly.

## 536 Falsehood

**N.** falsehood; treachery, bad faith, **perfidy**; lying; perjury, **untruth**; fiction, forgery, **deception**; invention, **imagination**; evasion, double-talk, fencing; economy of truth; **sophistry**; **exaggeration**; perversion; false colouring; **ostentation**; humbug, bunkum, boloney, hooey, **empty talk**; cant, eyewash, hogwash (see **duplicity**); euphemism, blarney, soft soap, **flattery**; liar.

**duplicity,** false conduct, double life; guile; front, facade, outside, show, **ostentation**; pretence, bluff, act, fake, counterfeit, **sham**; hypocrisy; acting, simulation, cant; lip service, cupboard love; false piety; show of sympathy; Judas kiss; fraud, legal fiction; cheat, sharp practice; frame-up, **foul play**; **pretension**; low cunning, **cunning**.

**Adj. false**, without truth; untruthful, lying, mendacious; treacherous; artful, **cunning**; disingenuous, dishonest, ambiguous, evasive, **equivocal**; meretricious; overdone; counterfeit, fake, sham, snide, quack, bogus, **spurious**; deceptive, deceitful; packed.

**hypocritical**, hollow, empty, insincere; pretended, seeming; make-believe, acting, double, two-faced, shifty, sly, treacherous, designing, Machiavellian; sanctimonious; plausible, smooth; creepy, goody-goody; mealy-mouthed; **affected**.

**Vb. be false**, perjure oneself, bear false witness, swear that black is white; lie, utter a falsehood; strain, tell a tall story, **exaggerate**; tell a fib, tell a whopper, lie hard; invent, make believe, romance, **imagine**; **misinterpret**; garble, doctor, falsify, **distort**; overstate, understate, **misrepresent**; misreport, misquote, misinform, cry wolf; lull, soothe, **flatter**; play false, play a double game, **be dishonest**; break faith, betray.

**dissemble**, dissimulate, disguise, **conceal**; simulate, counterfeit, **imitate**; assume, affect, play a part, make a show of, **act**; feign, sham, pretend; malinger, **deceive**; lack candour, be less than honest; keep something back, fail to declare; prevaricate, shuffle, dodge, trim, **be equivocal**.

**cant**, be affected; colour, varnish, paint, embroider; act a part.

**fake**, fudge, fabricate, coin, forge, counterfeit, **imitate**; frame; manipulate, fiddle, wangle, rig, pack (a jury); spin, weave, cook, concoct, hatch, invent, **plot**.

**Adv. falsely**.

**537 Deception**

**N. deception**; **credulity**; **folly**; fallacy, **sophistry**; illusion, delusion, hallucination, **error**; false appearance, mockery, mirage, will-o'-the-wisp, **visual fallacy**; show, paint (see **sham**); false reputation; bubble; deceit, lie, pious fraud, **falsehood**; guile, craft, **cunning**; hypocrisy, **duplicity**; treachery, **perfidy**; machination, hanky-panky, jiggery-pokery, **plot**; fraudulence, cheat.

**trickery**, shenanigan; sharp practice, chicanery; swindle, ramp, racket, wangle, fiddle, diddle, swiz, sell, fraud, cheat; **foul play**; trick, confidence trick, fast one, wiles, ruse, shift, dodge, fetch, blind, feint, **stratagem**; wrinkle; bait, gimmick, red herring, tub to a whale; hoax, bluff, spoof; game, sport, joke, rag, **witticism**.

**sleight**, pass, hocus-pocus, illusion, ventriloquism; juggle, googly; magic, **sorcery**.

**trap**, **ambush**; catch; plant, frame-up, foul play; hook, noose, snare, gin, spring gun, man trap; net, web; blind, decoy, decoy duck, bait, lure, sprat to catch a mackerel; flypaper; booby trap, mine, pit, **pitfall**; trapdoor, false bottom, **secret**; fatal gift, Trojan horse.

**sham**, false front, veneer, **duplicity**; lip service; make-believe, pretence, **affectation**; paint, whitewash, varnish, gloss; man of straw, paper tiger; **impostor**; dummy, scarecrow; facsimile, **copy**; film set, **insubstantial thing**; mockery, counterfeit, forgery, fake; masquerade, mask, cloak, disguise, false colours; shoddy, **rubbish**; tinsel, paste; Mosaic gold; German silver.

**Adj. deceiving**, deceitful, lying; deceptive, **latent**; illusory; specious; glib, slick, slippery, **smooth**; treacherous, insidious; **false**; pretended; prestigious; tricky, crafty, wily, artful, **cunning**.

**spurious**, false, fake; sham, counterfeit, **false**; make-believe, mock, ersatz, bogus; so-called; artificial, plastic, paste, cultured; shoddy, **useless**; tinsel, meretricious, flash, catchpenny, **cheap**; cardboard, pasteboard, **brittle**; sophisticated, **mixed**; underweight, **light**.

**Vb. deceive**, delude, dazzle; beguile, give a false impression, belie; **disappoint**; blindfold, **blind**; kid, bluff, bamboozle, hoodwink, hoax, humbug; **mislead**; spoof, mystify; play false, betray, two-time, double-cross, **be dishonest**; intrigue against, **plot**; circumvent, overreach, outwit, outmanoeuvre, **outdo**; forestall, **be early**; pull a fast one, outsmart, **be cunning**; trick, cheat, con, swindle, sell, rook, do; diddle, gyp, fleece, pluck, shortchange, **defraud**; juggle, conjure, force a card, fob; practise chicanery; gerrymander, tinker with, fiddle, wangle; **dissemble**; whitewash, **cant**; counterfeit, **fake**.

**befool**, fool, make a fool of, make an ass of, make one look silly; mock, make fun of, **ridicule**; rag, make an April fool of, **be absurd**; sport with, jilt; have, dupe, gull, outwit; trick, trap, take advantage of; manipulate; kid, spoof, bamboozle, string along (see **deceive**); cajole, get round, lull, soothe, **flatter**; **disappoint**; **mislead**.

**ensnare**, snare, trap, entrap, lime; enmesh, entangle, net; trip, catch, hook; bait, dangle a bait, lure, decoy, entice, **tempt**; waylay, **ambush**; nab, nick, kidnap, shanghai, **steal**.

**Adv. deceptively**.

## 538 Untruth

**N. untruth, falsehood**; understatement; exaggeration; lie, fib, whopper; false statement; broken word, breach of promise, **perfidy**; perjury, false oath; false evidence, frame-up, **evidence**; fiction, invention, false excuse; perversion; gloss, varnish; lie factory, propaganda machine; gate of ivory.

**mental dishonesty**, economy of truth, pious fraud, mental reservation, **qualification**; show, make-believe; pretence, profession, false plea, excuse, **pretext**; evasion, subterfuge, shift, shuffle; irony, backhanded compliment, **affectation**; sham, empty words, **duplicity**; Judas kiss, **perfidy**; mask, disguise.

**fable**, invention, fiction, imaginative exercise; story, tale, **narrative**; tall story, shaggy dog story, **exaggeration**; fairy tale, romance, tale, yarn, story; claptrap, gossip, **rumour**; myth, mythology; moonshine, farce, sell, swiz, hoax, humbug, flummery, **empty talk**.

**Adj. untrue**, lying, mendacious, **false**; nothing less true; mythological, fabulous; unfounded, empty; fictitious, make-believe; artificial, synthetic; bogus, so-called, **spurious**; **boastful**; evasive, surreptitious, **equivocal**; affected; satirical.

**Vb. be untrue**; **be unlikely**; lie, be a liar, **be false**; spin a yarn, **exaggerate**; make-believe, **imagine**; pretend, sham, counterfeit, forge, falsify, **dissemble**.

## 539 Dupe

**N. dupe**, fool, **laughingstock**; **ninny**; gudgeon; easy prey, easy target, sitting duck, soft touch, pushover, cinch; fair game, victim, fall guy, stooge, mug, sucker, gull, pigeon; greenhorn, innocent, **beginner**; puppet, pawn, **instrument**; vulnerable public.

Adj. gullible; had, done, sold a pup; innocent, green, silly, **foolish**.

Vb. be duped, be had, be done; rise, nibble; catch a Tartar.

## 540 Deceiver

N. deceiver; practical joker, Puck, **humorist**; actor, hypocrite, canter, Pharisee; false friend, jilt; turncoat, rat; double agent; traitor, Judas, **knave**; serpent; forger, **imitator**.

liar; story-teller; imaginative person; traveller; **exaggeration**; false witness, **falsehood**.

impostor, adventurer; pretender, charlatan, quack, mountebank; fake, fraud, humbug; front man.

trickster; cheat; cardsharp, rook; shyster; shark; slicker; twister, jobber, rogue, knave; confidence trickster, con man; decoy, stool pigeon; wily bird, fox.

conjuror, illusionist; quick-change artist; magician, **sorcerer**.

## 541 Exaggeration

N. exaggeration, inflation, magnification, enlargement; optimism; stretch, strain; extremism; overkill; excess, violence; **ostentation**; sensationalism, ballyhoo, **publicity**; hyperbole; adulation, **flattery**; colouring, **ornament**; embroidery, **addition**; disproportion; caricature, burlesque, **satire**; big tale; rant, tirade; excessive loyalty, chauvinism, **prejudice**; tall story, yarn, **fable**; flight of fancy, **imagination**; fuss, pother, excitement, much ado about nothing, **commotion**; liar.

Adj. exaggerated; strained, overdone,

inflated; histrionic; melodramatic; swelling, **boastful**; tall, fanciful, steep, egregious, preposterous, outrageous, far-fetched, **absurd**; lofty, extravagant, excessive; violent, immoderate, **exorbitant**; fulsome, inordinate, **superfluous**.

Vb. **exaggerate**, magnify, expand, inflate, **enlarge**; add to, **add**; enhance, heighten, add a flourish, embroider, **decorate**; overdo, overdraw, overcharge, overload, overweight, **make important**; puff, oversell, **overrate**; make much of, make too much of, **flatter**; stretch, strain, **distort**; caricature; protest too much; overact; rant, talk big, **boast**; run riot; go too far, **overstep**; spin a yarn, **be false**; intensify, exacerbate, **aggravate**.

## 542 Indication

N. indication, drawing attention, showing, **manifestation**; meaning; notification, **information**; symbolism; representation; symbol, x, letter; secret symbol, hieroglyph; sacred symbol, cross, crescent; magic symbol, **talisman**; natural symbol, image, type, figure; token, emblem, figurehead (see **badge**); symptom, sign, **evidence**; telltale sign, blush, **disclosure**; nudge, wink, **hint** (see **gesture**); omen; clue, scent, whiff; noise, footfall, **sound**; pointer, finger, forefinger, index finger (see **indicator**); guide, index, **directory**; key, **interpretation**; contour lines; marker, mark; blaze; nick, scratch, **notch**; stamp, print, impression; stigma; prick, tattoo mark, **perforation**; scar, blemish; line, score, stroke; note, catchword (see **punctuation**); legend, caption, **description**; inscription, epitaph; motto, monogram; love token, favour. See badge.

identification, nomenclature, **classification**; means of identification, brand, earmark, trademark, imprint (see label); autograph, signature, hand, **script**; fingerprint, footprint, spoor, track, trail, **trace**; secret sign, password, open sesame, watchword, countersign, shibboleth; colour, colouring; characteristic, trait, outline, form, shape, **feature**; personal characteristic, trick, trick of speech; mole, scar, birthmark, strawberry mark, **blemish**; litmus paper; mark, note.

**symbology**; code, **secrecy**; picture writing, **script**.

**gesture**, sign language; sign, **hint**; pantomime, dumb show, mime; stage business; body language; demeanour, **mien**; motion, move; tic, twitch, **spasm**; shrug; nod, beck, wink, twinkle, glance, ogle, leer, grimace, **look**; smile, laugh, **laughter**; touch, kick, nudge, jog, **knock**; hug; handshake, grip; push, shove, **impulse**; signal, wave; **excitable state**; **resolution**; snap; **defiance**; flag-waving, **celebration**; clap, cheer, **applause**; hiss, boo, catcall, raspberry, **disapprobation**; frown, scowl; pout, **discontent**.

**signal**, **message**; sign, symptom, **manifestation**; flash, rocket, Very light, maroon; railway signal, heliograph, semaphore; telegraph, **telecommunication**; signal lamp, **lamp**; warning light, beacon, beacon fire, **fire**; warning signal, red flag, warning light, green light, all clear, **signal light**; alarm, warning signal, SOS, **danger signal**; whistle, siren, hooter; buzzer, knocker, **gong**; bell, doorbell, alarm bell, angelus, carillon; time signal, pip, minute gun, dinner gong, dinner bell; passing bell, knell.

**indicator**, index, pointer, arrow, needle, arm, finger, hand; Plimsoll line, gauge; traffic indicator, winker; direction finder, radar; white line, **traffic control**; weathercock, wind sock, **weather**.

**signpost**, direction post; milestone; lighthouse, lightship, buoy, **safeguard**; compass, **sailing aid**; lodestar, cynosure, Southern Cross, **star**; landmark; cairn, **earthwork**; monument, memorial; tidemark, **limit**.

**call**, proclamation, ban, **publication**; shout, hail; invitation; call to prayer, church bell, **worship**; summons, word, word of command, **command**; distress call, Mayday; bugle, trumpet, reveille, assemble, charge, advance, rally, retreat; last post; peal, flourish, drum, tattoo, **roll**; call to arms, fiery cross; battle cry, slogan, catchword, watchword, shibboleth; challenge, countersign.

**badge**, token, emblem, symbol, sign, insignia (see **heraldry**); roundel; badge of sovereignty, throne, sceptre, orb, crown, **regalia**; mark of authority, badge of office, Black Rod, mace, **badge of rule**; baton, badge of **rank**; medal, gong, cross, order, star, garter, sash, ribbon; badge of merit, laurels, wreath, fillet, chaplet, garland, **trophy**; colours, blue, cap, oar; badge of loyalty, favour, rosette, love knot; badge of mourning, black, **clothing**.

**livery**, dress, **uniform**; tartan, tie, blazer; chevron, wings; flash, cockade, rosette.

**heraldry**; Roll of Arms; coat of arms; achievement; shield, escutcheon; crest, wreath, helmet, crown, coronet; motto; field, quarter, sinister, chief, base; charge, device, bearing; ordinary, bar, label, pale, bend, bend sinister, chevron, pile, cross; lozenge; quartering; animal charge, lion, unicorn, eagle, falcon; floral charge, cinquefoil, trefoil; badge, rebus, antelope, portcullis; national emblem, rose, thistle, leek, daffodil, shamrock; device, spread eagle, bear; swastika; colour, azure, sable; metal, or; fur, ermine, potent; College of Arms, Earl Marshal, King of Arms, herald, herald extraordinary, Rouge Dragon, Portcullis.

**flag**, ensign, red ensign, Red Duster; jack, flag of convenience; colours, King's Colour, standard, banner; pennon, streamer, pennant, triple tail; bunting; yellow flag; white flag, **submission**; eagle, tricolour; Union Jack; Old Glory; Red Flag; black flag, Jolly Roger; hoist, fly; flagpole, flagstaff.

**label**, mark of identification, tattoo, caste mark (see **identification**); ticket, bill, docket, chit, counterfoil, stub, duplicate; tally, counter, chip; tick, letter, number, check, mark; sticky label, sticker; tab, tag; name tape, fascia; sign, bush, **exhibit**; plate, trade sign, trademark, hallmark, cachet, rebus; earmark, brand, stigma, broad arrow; seal, signet, stamp, impress, impression; masthead, caption, heading, title, superscription; rubric; imprint, watermark; name; card, birth certificate, identification papers, identity card; passport, pass, **permit**; witness, signature, hand, sign manual, autograph, mark, cross, monogram; fingerprint, footprint, **trace**.

**punctuation**, punctuation mark, point, stop, period; comma, colon, semicolon; apostrophe; exclamation mark, question mark; crotchet, crook, brace; hyphen; dash, dot, blank; reference mark, asterisk, star; dagger, squiggle; hand, index; accent, diaeresis, cedilla; vowel point, breve, umlaut, stroke, mark of abbreviation, paragraph; plus sign, decimal point; italics, bold type.

**Adj.indicating**, indicative; expressive, suggestive, **meaningful**; typical, representative, token, nominal; telltale; characteristic, personal, individual, **special**; demonstrative, explanatory, exponential; ominous.

**heraldic**; sinister; azure, sable, or, ermine; rampant.

**marked**; spotted, **mottled**; indelible.

**Vb.indicate**, point, **point to**; exhibit, **show**; blaze, signpost; register, record; name, identify, classify, **specify**; index, reference; guide, **direct**; signify, denote, connote, suggest, imply, involve, spell, bespeak, argue, **mean**; typify, **represent**; declare, **affirm**; highlight; evince, give evidence of, attest, testify, witness to, **evidence**; intimate, smack of, smell of, **hint**; betray, reveal, **disclose**; inform against, **inform**; forebode, presage, **predict**.

**mark**, demarcate, **limit**; label, ticket, docket, tag, tab; earmark, designate; note, annotate, line, score, underline, underscore; number, letter, page; tick; nick, scribe, **notch**; chalk; scratch, scribble, cover, **write**; blot, stain, blacken, **make unclean**; scar, disfigure, **make ugly**; punctuate, dot, dash, cross, asterisk, blaze, brand; prick, tattoo, **pierce**; stamp, seal, punch, impress, emboss; imprint, **print**; etch, **engrave**; emblazon, impale, quarter, difference; marshal, charge.

**sign**, ratify, countersign, **endorse**; autograph; subscribe; initial.

**gesticulate**, pantomime, mime, mimic, **imitate**; wave, wag, waggle, **agitate**; wave to, **greet**; stamp, **applaud**; gesture, motion, sign; point, thumb, beckon, **attract notice**; nod, beck, wink, shrug; jog, nudge, poke, prod; look, look volumes, glance, leer, ogle, **gaze**; twinkle, smile, **laugh**; **disapprove**; **lament**; **be resolute**; **be angry**; snap, bite, **be sullen**; grimace, pout, scowl, frown; **despise**; shuffle; pat, stroke, **caress**.

signal, speak, **communicate**; semaphore, heliograph; thumb; wave through; dip, half-mast, salute; alert, dial 999, **raise the alarm**; fire a warning shot, warn.

Adv.**symbolically.**

### 543 Record

N.**record**, recording; memoir, chronicle, annals, history, **narrative**; case history, **biography**; photograph, portrait, sketch, **representation**; file, dossier; public record, gazette, official journal, Hansard; official publication, blue book, White Paper; minutes; memorandum; returns; **report**; tally, scoreboard; form, **document**; voucher, certificate, diploma, charter; birth certificate, marriage lines, **title deed**; copy, **duplicate**; archives, papers; record, book, roll, register, registry; tablet, table, notebook, logbook, log, diary, journal, commonplace book, scrapbook, album; ledger, **account book**; index, list; card, microfilm, **miniature**; tape, pressing, **gramophone**; inscription, legend, caption, heading; wall writing, graffiti, **script.**

registration, registry; recording, engraving; reservation; entry, book-keeping, accountancy.

monument, memorial; mausoleum, **tomb**; statue, bust, **image**; brass, tablet, slab, inscription; funerary achievement, **heraldry**; pillar, column, memorial arch, obelisk, monolith; ancient monument, dolmen, megalith, **antiquity**; cairn, barrow, tell, **earthwork**; testimonial, cup, ribbon, **trophy.**

trace, vestige, relic, remains; track, footstep, footprint, pug, tread; spoor, slot; scent, smell; wake, wash, trail, furrow, swathe, path; thumb impression; fingerprint, **evidence**; mark, tidemark, stain, scar, scratch, weal, welt, **blemish.**

Adj.**recording**; monumental.

**recorded**; **written**; extant.

Vb.**record**, tape, videotape; film, **photograph**; paint, **represent**; document, docket, file, index, catalogue; inscribe, cut, carve, grave, incise, **engrave**; commit to writing, **write**; **print**; note, mark, make a note of; minute, calendar, chronicle, **describe.**

register, tally, score; tabulate, table, enlist, **list**; enter, post, book, **account**; reserve, inscribe; log, **remember.**

Adv.**on record.**

### 544 Recorder

N.**recorder**, registrar; **notary**; scribe; secretary, receptionist; writer; clerk; record clerk, **accountant**; **engraving**; draughtsman, **artist**; cameraman, **photography**; record room, Record Office; Recording Angel.

**chronicler**, diarist, historian, biographer, **narrator**; **antiquarian**; reporter, columnist, **news reporter**; candid camera.

recording instrument, recorder, tape recorder; record, disc, **gramophone**; teleprinter, tape machine, **telecommunication**; cash register, till, checkout; turnstile; seismograph, speedometer, **gauge**; flight recorder, black box; stopwatch; camera; pen, pencil, **stationery.**

## 545 Obliteration

N. **obliteration**, erasure; blue pencil; cancellation, cancel; burial, oblivion, **amnesty**; blot, stain, **dirt**; clean slate, clean sweep, **revolution**; rubber, duster, sponge; abrasive.

Adj. **obliterated**; intestate.

Vb. **obliterate**, cover, conceal; deface, make illegible; efface, eliminate, erase, abrade, **rub**; expunge, blot, cancel, delete; score through, censor; raze, **demolish**; bury, cover; **forget**; submerge, **lower**; drown, **silence**; dis-appear.

## 546 Representation

N. **representation**, personification, incarnation, embodiment; conventional representation, diagram, **writing**, presentation, **manifestation**; performance, doing, **acting**; therapy; mimicry, dumb show; characterization, **description**; drawing, illustration, **painting**; creation, work of art, **product**; impression, likeness, identikit, **similarity**; exact likeness, double, facsimile, **duplicate**; trace, tracing, **outline**; reflection (see **image**); pictorial equivalent, true picture, striking likeness, realism, **picture**; bad likeness; reproduction, lithograph, **printing**; etching, engraving; design, blueprint, draft, cartoon, sketch, outline, **plan**; projection.

**image**, duplicate; mental image, **idea**; projection, silhouette, **reflection**; visual, visual aid, **spectacle**; idol; cherub; statuary, statue, colossus; statuette, bust, torso, head, **sculpture**; effigy, figure, figurine, figurehead; gargoyle; wax figure; dummy, lay figure; model, doll; marionette, puppet, snowman, gingerbread man; scarecrow, guy; robot, automaton; type, symbol.

**art**, architecture, **formation**; fine arts;

graphic art, **painting**; plastic art, **sculpture**; classical art, Baroque, Rococo; modern art, abstract art; classicism, realism; Surrealism, Expressionism, **school of painting**; op art, kitsch, **bad taste**; functional art; calligraphy, tapestry, embroidery, pottery.

**photography**, radiography; telephotography; cinematography, **cinema**; photograph, photo, picture, snapshot, snap; plate, film, exposure, negative, print, slide, transparency; frame, still; reel, spool, cassette; filmstrip, microfilm, movie, **film**; radiograph, X-ray, **radiation**; photocopy, **copy**; printing; shot, take, close-up, mug shot, pan, cover shot, dissolve, fade; lens, **camera**; cameraman.

**map**, chart, plan, outline, **statistics**; sketch map; Admiralty chart; ground plan; elevation, projection, atlas, globe; **astronomy**; cartography.

Adj. **representing**, representative; pictorial, graphic, vivid; figurative; representational, realistic; primitive, impressionistic; abstract; artistic; photogenic.

**represented**, drawn, fairly drawn; being drawn.

Vb. **represent**, denote, **mean**; type, typify, incarnate, embody, personify; impersonate, **deceive**; pose, model, **be an example**; present, enact, perform, do; project, shadow forth, suggest; reflect, image; mimic, mime, copy, **imitate**; depict, describe; delineate, draw, picture, portray, figure; illustrate, emblazon; **paint**; catch a likeness, catch, capture, register, **record**; make an image, carve, cast; cut, engrave; mould, shape, **form**; design, blueprint, draft, **plan**; diagram, construct a figure, describe a circle, **outline**; sketch, scrawl, doodle, improvise; map, chart, survey, plot.

**photograph**, photo; snapshot, snap, take, shoot, film; X-ray, radiograph; expose, develop, process, print, enlarge, reduce.

## 547 Misrepresentation

**N. misrepresentation**; false light, **falsehood**; bad likeness, **injustice**; travesty, parody, **exaggeration**; caricature, burlesque, guy, **ridicule**; flattery; **art**; bad art; daub, botch, scrawl.

**Adj. misrepresented**; flat, cardboard.

**Vb. misrepresent**; deform, **distort**; give a twist or turn, **flatter**; **exaggerate**; overdraw, caricature, guy, burlesque, parody, travesty; daub, botch, splash; lie, **be false**.

## 548 Painting

**N. painting**, graphic art, colouring; finger painting; washing; drawing, **representation**; artistry, composition, design, technique; line, perspective, golden section; treatment, tone, atmosphere, ambience; highlight, local colour, shading, contrast; monotone, monochrome, **colour**; chiaroscuro.

**art style**, style of painting, grand style, grand manner, **form**; intimate style, genre painting (see **art subject**); pastiche; scene painting, oil painting, watercolour, tempera, gouache; fresco painting.

**school of painting**, Mannerism, Baroque, Rococo, Realism, Romanticism, Impressionism, Symbolism, Cubism, Expressionism, Surrealism, Abstract Expressionism, action painting; minimal art, **art**.

**art subject**, landscape; scene, prospect, panorama, **view**; interior, conversation piece, still life, pastoral, nocturne, nude; crucifixion, nativity.

**picture**, pictorial equivalent, **representation**; tableau, mosaic, tapestry; collage, montage; brass rubbing; painting, pastiche; triptych, panel; fresco, mural, wall painting, poster; canvas, daub; drawing, sketch, outline, cartoon; oil painting, gouache, watercolour, pastel, wash drawing, design, pattern, doodle; cartoon, caricature, silhouette; miniature; old master, masterpiece; study, portrait, head, profile; studio portrait, snap, pin-up; **photography**; reproduction, halftone; woodcut, **engraving**; print, plate; illustration, fashion plate, picture postcard, cigarette card, stamp, transfer, scrap, sticker; picture book, scrapbook, photograph album, **book**.

**art equipment**, palette, palette knife, spatula, paintbrush, paint tube; oils, oil paint, tempera, distemper, gouache, varnish, **facing**; ink, crayon, pastel, chalk, charcoal, heelball; pen, pencil; **paper**; canvas, easel, picture frame, mount; studio, art museum, picture gallery; model, sitter, poser, subject.

**Adj. painted**, graphic, pictorial, scenic, picturesque, decorative; pastel, **coloured**; linear, chiaroscuro; **grey**.

**Vb. paint**, wash, colour; tint, retouch, daub; **coat**; paint a picture, do a portrait, portray, draw, sketch, cartoon, **represent**; illuminate; ink, chalk, crayon, pencil, stencil, shade, stipple.

## 549 Sculpture

**N. sculpture**, plastic art, **representation**; **formation**; carving, stone cutting, wood carving, moulding; rock carving; **school of painting**; mobile; kinetic art; statuary; group; statue, colossus; statuette, figurine, bust, torso, head;

model, cast, death mask, **image**; ceramics, **pottery**; medallion, cameo, intaglio; relief, bas-relief; stone, marble, bronze, clay, wax, plasticine; armature; chisel.

**Adj. glyptic**; statuary, statuesque, marmoreal; plastic.

**Vb. sculpt**, sculpture, **form**; cut, carve, whittle, chisel, chip, chase, engrave, emboss; model, mould, cast.

## 550 Engraving. Printing

**N. engraving**, etching, line engraving; gem cutting; gem engraving; glass engraving; mezzotint; wood engraving, woodcut; steel plate, stone, block, chisel, burr, needle, style.

**printing**, **print**, plate printing, colour printing; fabric printing, batik; stereotype; impression; die, punch, stamp.

**Vb. engrave**, grave, incise, cut, undercut; etch, stipple, scrape; bite; sandblast; impress, stamp; lithograph, **print**; mezzotint.

## 551 Artist

**N. artist**, craftsman or -woman, **artisan**; architect, **producer**; draughtsman or -woman; fashion artist; drawer; illustrator, commercial artist; painter; amateur, Sunday painter; pavement artist; portrait painter, miniaturist; Academician, old master, primitive; Impressionist, action painter, **school of painting**; art historian.

**sculptor**, statuary, monumental mason, moulder.

**engraver**; lapidary, chaser; **printer**.

## 552 Language

**N. language**, tongue, speech, idiom, parlance, talk; parole; spoken language, patter, lingo, **dialect**; personal language; mother tongue, vernacular, common speech, vulgar tongue; colloquial speech, **speech**; correct speech; creole, pidgin, pidgin English; sign language, **gesture**; International Scientific Vocabulary, Basic English; artificial language, Esperanto; official language, Mandarin, Standard English, BBC English; machine language; learned language, Latin, Greek, Sanskrit; polyglot medley, Babel, babble, **confusion**.

**language type**, language group, Indo-European, Celtic, Romance.

**linguistics**, language study, philology, comparative grammar, syntax, **grammar**; phonetics, **pronunciation**; lexicography, **etymology**; semantics, **meaning**; **nomenclature**; linguistic geography; speech community; genius of a language, sense of idiom.

**literature**, written language, creative writing, **reading matter**; classics, arts, humanities; PEN, **author**; literary genre, fiction, nonfiction, **narrative**, **description**; lyricism, poetry, **poem**; **drama**; criticism, **estimate**; literary criticism, **interpretation**; literary style, **metaphor**; literary movement, Classicism, Romanticism, Symbolism, Idealism, Expressionism, Surrealism, Realism; literary history, history of literature; Golden Age, **era**; compendium of literature, **anthology**; digest, reader, **textbook**.

**linguist**, language student, **etymology**; grammarian, **grammar**; **acoustics**; student of literature, **scholar**; classical scholar, **antiquarian**; polyglot, bilingual.

**Adj. linguistic**, grammatical; monosyllabic; tonal; correct, pure; written, literary, standard; spoken, living, idiomatic; vulgar, colloquial, vernacular; local; current, common; bilingual; multilingual, polyglot.

literary, written, polite; classical, romantic, futuristic; learned; formal; critical.

## 553 Letter

**N. letter**; sign, symbol, character, **writing**; alphabet, ABC, criss-cross row; initial teaching alphabet, International Phonetic Alphabet, IPA; **speech sound**; Chinese character, ideogram, cuneiform, hieroglyph, **lettering**; Greek alphabet; lettering, black letter, Gothic; ampersand; big letter, cap; small letter, minuscule; block letter; cursive; type.

**initials**, first letter; monogram; anagram, acrostic, acronym.

**spoken letter**, phone; consonant, vowel, syllable, **voice**, guttural, liquid, **speech sound**.

**spelling**; orthography; spelling game, spelling bee; **translation**.

**Adj. literal**; Cyrillic; cuneiform, **written**; Gothic, roman; large, capital, initial; small, minuscule; phonetic, **vocal**.

**Vb. spell**, read, syllable; transliterate; letter, **write**; initial, **sign**.

**Adv. alphabetically**.

## 554 Word

**N. word**; expression, **phrase**; term, **name**; syllable, **speech sound**; **meaning**; synonym, **identity**; pun, weasel word; antonym; root; folk etymology; derivative, doublet; stem; part of speech, **grammar**; diminutive, pejorative, intensive; contraction, abbreviation, acronym, portmanteau word; catchword, vogue word; **similarity**; swearword, **malediction**; hard word, long word, polysyllable; short word, monosyllable; many words, verbiage.

**dictionary**, lexicon, word list, glossary, vocabulary; thesaurus, **store**; compilation, concordance, index.

**etymology**, philology, **linguistics**; **meaning**; **pronunciation**; terminology, nomenclature; lexicography; compiler.

**Adj. verbal**, literal; titular, nominal; lexical; derivative, conjugate, cognate; wordy, verbose.

**Adv. verbally**; verbatim.

## 555 Neology

**N. neology**, neologism; coinage, new word, catch phrase; loan word, loan translation, **word**; newfangled expression, technical language, jargon, technical term; hybrid, hybrid expression; corruption, telegraphese; baby talk; doubletalk; affected language, archaism, **affectation**; abuse of language, abuse of terms, malapropism, **solecism**; spoonerism, **witticism**; **speech defect**.

**dialect**, idiom, lingo, patois, vernacular, **language**; burr, brogue, accent, **pronunciation**; cockney, Doric; broken English, pidgin; hybrid language; anglicism, Americanism, gallicism; **speech defect**; **linguistics**.

**slang**, vulgarism; jargon, argot, cant; patter; gipsy lingo, Romany; back slang, pig Latin; backchat, **scurrility**; **empty talk**.

**Adj. neological**, newfangled; barbaric, barbarous, hybrid, corrupt, pidgin; foreign, archaic, obsolete; irregular.

**dialectal**, vernacular, Doric, Cockney, broad; guttural, nasal; provincial, local; homely, colloquial; nonstandard, cant; technical, special.

**Vb. neologize**, coin words, invent vocabulary; talk slang, cant; talk cockney, speak with an accent, burr, **voice**.

## 556 Nomenclature

N. **nomenclature**; terminology; description, appellation, denomination; apostrophe; baptism, **Christian rite**.

**name**, first name, forename, Christian name; middle name(s); surname; maiden name, appellation; nickname, pet name, diminutive; epithet, description; handle, style, **title**; heading, caption; signature, **label**; term, trade name; same name, namesake, synonym; pen name, pseudonym, **misnomer**; noun, **part of speech**; place name.

**nomenclator**.

Adj. **named**, titled; alias; so-called; nominal, titular; what one may fairly call.

**naming**.

Vb. **name**, call, give a name, christen, **perform ritual**; give a handle to, surname, nickname, dub; give one his title, sir; title, entitle, style, term, **specify**; distinguish, **discriminate**; define, **mark**; announce; blacklist, **reprobate**.

**be named**; answer to.

Adv. **by name**; namely.

## 557 Misnomer

N. **misnomer**; malapropism, **solecism**; wrong name, pseudonym; nickname, pet name, **name**.

**no name**; anon, certain person, so-and-so; N or M, sir or madam; Miss X; this or that; some, any.

Adj. **misnamed**, self-styled, would-be, so-called.

**anonymous**, unknown, faceless, nameless, without a name; incognito; a certain, certain, such; some, any, this or that.

Vb. **misname**, miscall; nickname, dub; **name**; assume an alias; be anonymous;

dissemble.

## 558 Phrase

N. **phrase**, form of words; clause, sentence, period, paragraph; expression; idiom, mannerism, **speciality**; fixed expression, formula; set phrase, set terms; euphemism, metaphor; catch phrase, slogan; hackneyed expression, well-worn phrase, commonplace, **habit**; saying, motto, moral, epigram, **maxim**; lapidary phrase, epitaph; inscription, legend, caption, **record**; words, compliments, **empty talk**; terminology, **nomenclature**; surface structure, diction, wording, choice of words, choice of expression; roundabout phrase, periphrasis, circumlocution; paraphrase, **translation**; written phrase, **script**.

Adj. **phraseological**, periodic; idiomatic.

Vb. **phrase**, word, articulate, syllable; reword, **translate**; express, formulate, state, **affirm**; put words together, turn a sentence, round a period, **show style**.

Adv. **in terms**.

## 559 Grammar

N. **grammar**, philology, **linguistics**; analysis; accidence, case, declension; conjugation, mood, voice, tense; number, gender, **punctuation**; umlaut, attraction, **etymology**; syntax, word order, ellipsis, apposition; bad grammar, **solecism**; good grammar, correct style, Standard English.

**part of speech**, noun, pronoun; adjective; verb, adverb, preposition; copula, conjunction, interjection; subject, object; article, particle, affix, suffix, prefix; formative; diminutive, intensive.

Adj. **grammatical**, correct; irregular,

anomalous; masculine, feminine, neuter; singular, dual, plural; predicative; verbal; comparative, superlative.

**Vb. parse**, analyse, inflect, conjugate, decline; punctuate; construe, **interpret**.

## 560 Solecism

**N. solecism**, bad grammar; faulty syntax; **ornament**; irregularity, **dialect**; malapropism, bull, slip, **mistake**; **speech defect**.

**Adj. ungrammatical**; irregular, abnormal; faulty, improper, incongruous.

**Vb. be ungrammatical**, violate grammar, commit a solecism; mispronounce, **stammer**; misspell, **blunder**.

## 561 Style

**N. style**, fashion, mode, tone, manner, vein, strain, idiom; idiosyncrasy, mannerism, **speciality**; mode of expression, diction, parlance, **phrase**; choice of words, vocabulary, literary style, command of language or idiom, power, **vigour**; sense of language; literary charm, grace; word magic, **oratory**; weak style; severe style; elaborate style, **ornament**; clumsy style.

**Adj. stylistic**, mannered, literary, elegant, ornate; expressive, eloquent, fluent; racy, idiomatic; plain, forceful.

**Vb. show style**, style, express, **phrase**.

## 562 Perspicuity

**N. perspicuity**, clarity, **transparency**; limpid style; definition.

**Adj. perspicuous**, lucid, limpid, **transparent**; clear, **intelligible**; explicit, clear-cut, **definite**; exact, **accurate**; direct, **plain**.

## 563 Imperspicuity

**N. imperspicuity**; abstraction; involved style, **ornament**; hard words, **difficulty**; profundity, **depth**; ellipsis; cloud of words, verbiage.

**Adj. unclear**, cloudy, **opaque**; cloudy, obscure, **dark**; mysterious, enigmatic; abstruse, profound, **deep**; indirect, **latent**; vague, indefinite, **uncertain**; ambiguous, **equivocal**; tortuous, involved, **complex**; harsh, crabbed, stiff, **inelegant**; hard, full of long words, **difficult**.

## 564 Conciseness

**N. conciseness**, brevity, soul of wit; pithy saying, **maxim**; aphorism, epigram, **witticism**; economy of words, few words; telegraphese; ellipsis, abbreviation, contraction, **shortening**; epitome, outline, brief sketch, **compendium**; portmanteau word; nutshell.

**Adj. concise**, brief, **short**; laconic, monosyllabic, sparing of words, **taciturn**; irreducible, succinct; crisp, brisk; trenchant, incisive; terse, curt, brusque, **ungracious**; compendious, compact, pithy, pregnant, sententious, neat, exact, pointed; elliptic, telegraphic; summary, cut short.

**Vb. be concise**, need few words, cut a long story short; telescope, compress, condense, contract, abridge, abbreviate, **shorten**; outline, sketch; resume, **abstract**; be short with, cut short; be sparing with words, **be taciturn**.

**Adv. concisely**; to cut a long story short.

## 565 Diffuseness

**N. diffuseness**, amplitude; blow-by-blow account; fertility, copiousness, productivity; inspiration, vein, flow; abundance, redundancy; rich vocabulary, wealth of terms, verbiage, flatulence; epic length; **repetition**; **tedium**; gush, rigmarole, waffle, **empty talk**; effusion, tirade, harangue, sermon, **oration**; descant; **dissertation**.

**pleonasm**, redundancy; tautology; circumlocution, periphrasis; padding, expletive, **extra**; episode.

**Adj. diffuse**, verbose, nonstop, **loquacious**; profuse, copious, ample, rich; fertile, abundant, voluminous, **prolific**; inspired, flowing, fluent; exuberant, **redundant**; circumstantial, minute; effusive; windy; turgid; ornate.

**prolix**, of many words, long-winded, wordy, prosy; made to last; **tedious**; lengthy, epic, **long**; discursive; rambling; incoherent; desultory, pointless, **irrelevant**; indirect, roundabout.

**pleonastic**, redundant, excessive, **superfluous**; repetitious.

**Vb. be diffuse**, dilate, amplify, detail, expand; descant, discourse at length; repeat, **repeat oneself**; pad, protract, **lengthen**; gush, **flow**; let oneself go, rant, harangue; use long words; spin a long yarn, **be tedious**; **be loquacious**; wander, waffle, digress, **deviate**; ramble, maunder, drivel, yarn, never end; **be equivocal**.

**Adv. diffusely**, at great length.

## 566 Vigour

**N. vigour**; power, strength, vitality, drive, force, oomph, **energy**; decision; vim, punch, pep, guts; sparkle, verve, panache; spirit, fire, ardour, glow, warmth, fervour, enthusiasm, passion, **feeling**; bite; strong language, stress, emphasis; **repetition**; solemnity, gravity, weight; elevation, grandeur; rhetoric.

**Adj. forceful**, powerful, **strong**; energetic, **vigorous**; racy, idiomatic; bold, dashing, spirited, vivacious, **lively**; warm, glowing, fiery, ardent, impassioned, **fervent**; vehement, insistent, positive, **affirmative**; cutting, incisive, trenchant, **sharp**; pointed, pungent, mordant, salty; grave, sententious, **serious**; heavy, meaty, solid, weighty, forcible, cogent; vivid, graphic, effective; flowing, inspired, **eloquent**; lofty, grand, sublime, **impressive**.

**Adv. forcefully**, with conviction.

## 567 Feebleness

**N. feebleness**, **weakness**; weak style, frigidity; poverty; lack of force, lack of sparkle, lack of conviction; lack of style; anticlimax.

**Adj. feeble**, weak, thin, flat, vapid, insipid, **tasteless**; wishy-washy, watery; sloppy, sentimental; meagre; wan, colourless, bald, **plain**; languid, flaccid, nerveless, tame, conventional; ineffective, cold, frigid, prosaic; monotonous, prosy, pedestrian, dull, dry, **tedious**; hackneyed, stale, pretentious; forced; inane, empty; juvenile, childish; careless, slipshod; lame, **poorly reasoned**; limp, loose, lax, inexact, disconnected, disjointed, rambling; poor, trashy, **vulgar**.

## 568 Plainness

**N. plainness**, simplicity; plain prose, **prose**; plain words, plain English; homespun, household words; rustic flavour, vernacular; common speech, vulgar parlance; idiom; Anglo-Saxon monosyllable.

**Adj. plain**, simple, **artless**; austere, severe; bald, spare, stark, bare; neat, **clean**; pure, unadulterated; unvarnished, **veracious**; unassuming, unpretentious, **modest**; chaste, restrained; unaffected, honest, natural, straightforward; homely, homespun, vernacular; prosaic, sober, **serious**; dry, stodgy, **tedious**; humdrum, workaday, everyday, commonplace, **usual; prosaic**.

Vb. **speak plainly**, call a spade a spade, use plain English, **be intelligible**; say outright, tell it like it is, tell one straight or to his or her face; talk turkey.

Adv. **plainly**, simply; directly, pointblank.

## 569 Ornament

N. **ornament**, colour, embroidery, frills; **phrase**; euphuism; euphemism; rhetoric, purple patch or passage; figure of speech; alliteration, assonance; metaphor, simile, antithesis.

**magniloquence**, high tone; **vigour**; hyperbole, **exaggeration**; flatulence, inflation; affectation, **ostentation**; highfalutin, bombast, rant, fustian, **empty talk**; long words.

**phrasemonger**, fine writer; orator, speaker.

Adj. **ornate**; rich, luxuriant, florid, flowery; precious; pretentious, **affected**; meretricious, flashy, flamboyant, **showy**; brassy, sonorous, **loud**; tropical, **figurative**; stiff, stilted.

**rhetorical**, eloquent; resonant, sonorous, **loud**; orotund; highfalutin; grandiose, stately; pompous, fustian; grandiloquent; inflated, turgid, swollen; **figurative**.

Vb. **ornament**, beautify, grace, adorn, enrich, **decorate**; charge, overload; elaborate, load with ornament.

## 570 Elegance

N. **elegance**, style, grace, **beauty**; refinement, taste, **good taste**; propriety, restraint, distinction, dignity; clarity; purity, simplicity; classicism; harmony, euphony, balance, proportion, **symmetry**; rhythm, ease, flow, readiness, felicity; polish, finish; **ornament**.

**stylist**, stylish writer; classical author, classic, purist.

Adj. **elegant**, stately, **beautiful**; graceful; stylish, polite, refined, **tasteful**; distinguished; chaste, **pure**; good, correct, idiomatic; sensitive, expressive, clear; simple, natural, unaffected, **plain**; ready, easy, smooth, flowing, fluent, tripping, mellifluous, euphonious; balanced; neat, felicitous, happy, right; artistic, wrought, elaborate, artificial; finished; restrained; **perfect**; classic, classical, Attic.

Vb. **be elegant**, show taste, **have taste**; have a good style, write well, have a light touch; elaborate, polish, refine, **perfect**; turn a period, point an antithesis, **show style**.

## 571 Inelegance

N. **inelegance**; roughness; lack of finish; lack of polish; cacophony, **discord**; lack of flow, **hardness**; bad grammar, **solecism**; speech defect; vulgarism, vulgarity, **bad taste**; mannerism, **affectation**; exhibitionism, ostentation; **sham**; lack of restraint, excess.

Adj. **inelegant**, graceless, ugly; faulty, incorrect; crabbed, tortuous; longwinded, **diffuse**; **imperfect**; bald, **plain**; coarse, crude, rude, doggerel, uncouth, barbarous, **artless**; impolite, tasteless, **vulgar**; impure, meretricious; unrestrained, immoderate, excessive; turgid, pompous; forced, artificial, unnatural, mannered, **affected**; ludicrous, grotesque, **ridiculous**; offensive, grating; heavy, ponderous, insensitive; rough, harsh, uneasy, abrupt; halting, cramped; clumsy, awkward, gauche; wooden, stiff, stilted, formal.

## 572 Voice

N. voice, vocal sound, sound; speech; singing voice, vocal music; powerful voice, lung power; tongue, vocal cords; bellows; larynx, voice box; vowel, diphthong, open vowel, syllable, speech sound; delivery, attack; articulate sound, cry; exclamation, gasp; mutter, whisper; tone of voice, timbre, pitch, tone, intonation.

pronunciation, elocution, stress, emphasis; thesis; accent, pure accent, native accent, burr, brogue, drawl, twang, dialect; trill, aspiration, rough breathing, glottal stop; stammer, speech defect; solecism.

Adj. vocal, oral, aloud; phonetic; articulate, distinct, clear; well-spoken, melodious; pronounced, spoken, read aloud; hoarse; tonal; guttural, hoarse; shrill, strident; sibilant.

Vb. voice, pronounce, syllable, speak; mouth, give tongue, give voice, express, utter, enunciate, articulate, inflect, modulate; breathe, aspirate; trill, roll, burr; accent, stress; whisper, exclaim, ejaculate, cry; drone, intone, chant, warble, carol, hum, sing; bellow, shout, vociferate, be loud; mispronounce, lisp, drawl, stammer.

## 573 Voicelessness

N. voicelessness; thick speech; silence; harsh voice; childish treble, falsetto; sob; undertone, low voice, whisper, bated breath; surd; voiceless speech, sign language, gesture; mute.

Adj. voiceless; surd; inaudible; mute, dumb; speechless; inarticulate, tongue-tied; silent, mum, taciturn; dry, hollow, sepulchral, cracked, hoarse; breathless.

Vb. be mute, keep mum, be taciturn; be silent, keep secret; check oneself; be struck dumb; gesticulate; stammer.

make mute, strike dumb, rob one of words; muffle, hush, deaden, mute; muzzle, gag, stifle, suppress; cut one short; still, hush, put to silence, put to sleep, silence.

speak low, whisper, sound faint; hint.

Adv. voicelessly, with bated breath.

## 574 Speech

N. speech, tongue, voice; parlance, language; oral communication, word of mouth, report; spoken word, word; verbal intercourse, discourse, conversation, talk, palaver, prattle, chinwag; address, apostrophe; ready speech; effusion; cultivated speech, elocution, voice production; mode of speech, delivery, pronunciation; ventriloquism; speech without words, sign language, gesture; thing said, speech, dictum, remark, comment, interjection; fine words, empty talk; spiel, patter.

oration, speech, effusion; public speech, discourse, address, talk; celebration; panegyric, eulogy; farewell address, funeral oration; toast, vote of thanks; broadcast, commentary, lecture; recital, reading; set speech, sermon; harangue, earful, mouthful; tirade, diatribe, invective; monologue, soliloquy; written speech, paper, screed, dissertation; preamble, prologue, narration, peroration.

oratory, rhetoric, stump oratory; elocution, rant; vituperation, invective; soapbox, rostrum.

eloquence, eloquent tongue; command of words, style; power of speech, power, vigour; elocution, good delivery, impressive diction, torrent of words, peroration, purple passage.

**speaker;** orator, public speaker, toast-master; soap-box orator, tub-thumper, demagogue, **agitator;** lecturer; prologue, narrator, chorus, **actor;** mouthpiece, spokesman or -woman, **delegate;** advocate, mediator, **intermediary;** patter merchant, **seller.**

**Adj. speaking;** able to speak; bilingual, polyglot; articulate, fluent, out-spoken, talkative, **loquacious;** oral, **vocal;** well-spoken, audible, spoken, verbal; fruity, **resonant.**

**eloquent;** grandiloquent, **forceful;** rousing, **exciting.**

**Vb. speak,** mention, say; utter, articulate, **voice;** pronounce, declare, **affirm;** come clean, **divulge;** whisper, breathe, **hint;** talk, converse; emit, deliver oneself of; break silence; gossip, prattle, chatter, **be loquacious;** patter, jabber, gabble; tell a thing or two, **be diffuse;** recite; read, read aloud, dictate; speak a language; **gesticulate.**

**orate;** declaim, deliver a speech; hold forth, spout; rise to speak; preach, harangue; lecture, address, **teach;** invoke, **speak to;** mouth, rant, rail; speak like an angel, spellbind, be eloquent; talk to oneself; ad-lib, **improvise.**

## 575 Speech defect

**N. speech defect,** loss of speech; stammer, stutter, lisp; drawl, slur; thick speech, cleft palate; burr, brogue, **dialect;** accent, twang, **pronunciation;** affectation; speech therapy.

**Adj. stammering,** nasal; indistinct, thick, inarticulate; tongue-tied; breathless, **voiceless.**

**Vb. stammer,** stutter; drawl, hesitate, falter, quaver; mumble, mutter; lisp;

snuffle, snort, sputter, splutter; drone; gabble, slur; blubber, sob; mis-pronounce.

## 576 Loquacity

**N. loquacity;** runaway tongue, flow of words; spate of words, inexhaustible vocabulary; patter, spiel; garrulous old age, **remembrance.**

**chatter,** gabble, jabber, palaver; clack, quack, cackle, babble, prattle; small talk, gossip, tittle-tattle; waffle, gush, gas, hot air, **empty talk.**

**chatterer,** rapid speaker; chinwag, rattle, chatterbox; gossip, blabber, **news reporter;** magpie, parrot, jay; windbag.

**Adj. loquacious,** talkative, garrulous; communicative, chatty; gassy, windy, verbose, long-winded; nonstop, voluble, fluent, glib, ready, effusive.

**Vb. be loquacious,** have a long tongue, chatter, rattle; gossip, tattle, **converse;** clack, quack, gabble, jabber, **mean nothing;** talk, jaw, yak, prate, prose, gas, waffle, haver, twitter; drone; maunder, drivel; shoot; be glib; talk at length; gush, spout, **be diffuse;** filibuster; talk oneself hoarse; talk shop, bore, **be tedious;** buttonhole.

**Adv. loquaciously.**

**Int. rhubarb rhubarb! blah blah! yak yak!**

## 577 Taciturnity

**N. taciturnity,** silent habit, **silence;** incommunicativeness, reserve, **secrecy;** few words; economy of words; person of few words; clam, oyster, statue; Trappist.

**Adj. taciturn,** mute, mum, **silent;** sparing of words, saying little, monosyllabic, short, curt, laconic, brusque, gruff, **concise;** incommunicative; withdrawn, reserved, guarded, **reti-**

cent; close, tight-lipped; discreet, **cautious**; inarticulate, tongue-tied, **voiceless**; **deaf**.

Vb. **be taciturn**, **be concise**; say nothing, have little to say; observe silence; refuse comment, neither confirm nor deny; **keep secret**; fall silent, **cease**; be **mute**; omit, **disregard**.

Int. hush! shut up! mum's the word! no comment! verb. sap. a word to the wise!

## 578 Allocution

N. **allocution**, apostrophe; address, lecture, talk, speech, pep talk, **oration**; greeting, salutation, hail; appeal, interjection; aside; audience.

Adj. **vocative**.

Vb. **speak to**, speak at; address, talk to, lecture to; turn to; appeal to, pray to, invoke; sir; approach, accost; hail, call to, salute, say good morning, **greet**; parley with, **converse**; take aside, buttonhole.

## 579 Interlocution

N. **interlocution**, parley, converse, conversation, talk; dialogue; exchange, repartee, banter, badinage; **quarrel**; verbal intercourse; commerce, communion, communication, intercommunication, **information**.

**chat**, chinwag, natter; chit-chat, talk, prattle, gossip, **rumour**; tattle, tittle-tattle, **chatter**; fireside chat, cosy chat, heart-to-heart.

**conference**, talks, parley, pow-wow, palaver; debate, forum, symposium, seminar, teach-in; controversy, polemics, **argument**; high-level talks, summit meeting, summit; **treaty**; convention, meeting, gathering, **assembly**; working lunch; reception, party, **social gathering**; audience, interview, audition; huddle, council, **advice**.

**interlocutor**; **respondent**; partner; gossip, **news reporter**.

Adj. **conversing**, chatty, **loquacious**; communicative; advisory.

Vb. **converse**, parley, talk together (see **confer**); buttonhole, bandy words, question, answer; chat, have a chat or a natter or a good talk; have a cosy chat, **speak**; buzz, natter, chinwag, gossip, tattle, **be loquacious**; commune with, get confidential with; whisper together.

**confer**, take counsel, hold a council of war, pow-wow, palaver; discuss, debate, **argue**; parley, negotiate, hold talks; consult with, **consult**.

## 580 Soliloquy

N. **soliloquy**, monologue; interior monologue; apostrophe; aside.

**soliloquist**.

Adj. **soliloquizing**, thinking aloud.

Vb. **soliloquize**, talk to oneself, say to oneself; say aside, think aloud; pray aloud; address an empty house, have an audience of one.

## 581 Writing

N. **writing**, composition, authorship, journalism, itch to write, **description**; literary output, **literature**; script, copy, writings, works, books, **reading matter**; Grub Street; paperwork, **record**; ways of writing, handwriting; longhand; shorthand writing, shorthand, stenography; stereotype; **print**; braille; secret writing, code, **secret**; picture writing; **advertisement**; carving, cutting, **engraving**; study of handwriting.

**lettering**, stroke, down-stroke; line, dot, point; flourish, squiggle, scroll, **convolution**; handwriting, hand, fist; calligraphy, penmanship; fair hand, cursive hand, script, copperplate;

printing; clumsy hand, illegible writing, scribble, scrawl; alphabet, letter; ideogram; hieroglyph; cuneiform, arrowhead.

**script**, written matter; specimen; writing, screed, scrawl, scribble; manuscript, **book**; original, autograph; signature; copy, transcript, fair copy, **duplicate**; typescript, stencil; newsprint; letter, epistle, written reply; inscription, **record**; superscription, caption, heading.

**stationery**; stylus, reed, quill, pen, nib; pencil, crayon, chalk; papyrus, parchment, vellum; foolscap, **paper**; writing paper, notepaper, wove paper, notebook, pad; slate, blackboard; inkstand, inkwell; penknife; blotter; typewriter, ribbon; stencil.

**calligrapher**; scribbler; writer, scribe, clerk, **recorder**; subscriber, signatory; creative writer, **author**; letter writer, **correspondent**; handwriting expert.

**stenographer**, shorthand writer, typist.

**Adj. written**; manuscript, autograph; cursive, copybook, copperplate; cuneiform; Gothic, roman, literal; perpendicular, upright, bold, spidery.

**Vb. write**, be literate; engrave, inscribe; letter, block, print; flourish, scroll; write well, write a clear hand; write badly, scribble, scrawl, blot, erase; commit to paper, note, **record**; transcribe, copy, make a fair copy, engross; type; draft, formulate; compose, concoct; pen, pencil; **correspond**; **sign**; put pen to paper, spill ink; be an author, write books, **describe**; write poetry.

**582 Print**

**N. print**, printing, **writing**; typography, block printing, offset process, web offset; **printing**; **photography**; cold type;
composition, make-up; stereotype; plate, shell.

**letterpress**, print, impression; printout; copy, pull, proof, page proof, revise; imprint, **edition**; dummy, trial copy, offprint.

**print-type**, type, stereotype, plate; matrix; broken type, pie; upper case; face, typeface, boldface, bold, old face, bastard type; roman, Gothic, black letter, **letter**; body, bevel, shoulder, shank, beard; lead, rule, em; space, quad; type bar, slug.

**type size**, type measure, type scale; brilliant, diamond, pearl, ruby, nonpareil, minion, bourgeois, elite, long primer, great primer.

**press**, printing works; rotary press, offset press; galley, chase; roller, web.

**printer**, compositor, type-setter.

**Adj. printed**; set; solid, tight, crowded.

**Vb. print**, stamp; compose; register, justify; make ready, impose, machine; collate; lithograph, offset, stereotype; put to bed; proofread, correct; **publish**.

**583 Correspondence**

**N. correspondence**; communication, **information**; mail, post, postbag, **postal communications**; letter, epistle, missive, bulletin; love letter, Valentine, **endearment**; postcard, card; air letter, air mail, sea mail; business letter, bill, account; open letter, **publicity**; circular, round robin, chain letter; note, line, chit; answer; envelope, cover, stamp, seal; postcode.

**correspondent**, letter writer, poison pen; recipient, addressee; foreign correspondent, contributor, **news reporter**; contact.

**Adj. epistolary**, postal.

**Vb. correspond**, correspond with, **communicate**; write to, send a letter to,

drop a line; report, **inform**; acknowledge, reply, write back, **answer**; **publish**; write again; forward, mail, airmail; stamp, seal, frank, address.
**Adv. by letter.**

## 584 Book

**N. book**, title, volume, tome, roll, scroll, document; manuscript, MS; script, typescript; **publication**, best-seller, potboiler, remainder, **work**, classic; major work, magnum opus; slim volume; booklet; picture book, **picture**; magazine, periodical, rag, **journal**; brochure, pamphlet; bound book, hardback, paperback (see **edition**).

**reading matter, writing**; papers, **record**; script, copy; text, libretto, lyrics, scenario, screenplay, book of words; proof, revise, pull; writings, prose literature, **prose**; poetry; classical literature, **literature**; history, biography, travel, **description**; work of fiction, **novel**; memoirs, **biography**; oration, essay, tract, treatise, **dissertation**; piece, **article**; **poem**; **anthology**; early works; posthumous works, literary remains; complete works; newspaper, magazine, **journal**; issue, number, part, instalment, serial, sequel.

**textbook**, school book, reader, **classroom**; primer, grammar; text; selection, **anthology**; standard text, handbook, manual; pocket book (see **reference book**).

**reference book**, work of reference; lexicon, **dictionary**; gazetteer, yearbook, annual, **directory**; calendar, **chronology**; guide; notebook, diary, album, **record**; bibliography, reading list.

**edition**, impression, issue, run; series, set, collection, library; bound edition, complete works; first edition, reprint;

rehash; adaptation, **compendium**; book production, layout, format; house style; front matter, preface; dedication; title, title page, **label**; table of contents; appendix, supplement, index, bibliography; caption, heading, headline, footnote; guide word, catchword; margin; gutter; page, leaf; sheet, signature, quire; chapter, division, part, section; paragraph, clause, passage, excerpt, inset; plate, print, illustration, halftone, line drawing, **picture**.

**bookbinding**, binding, casing; case, cover, jacket, **wrapping**; boards, **paper**; cloth, linen, leather, pigskin, calf, morocco, vellum, parchment; spine, headband.

**library**, book collection; national library, book club; bookcase; bookstall.

**bookperson**, literary person; reader, bookworm, **scholar**; book lover, book collector; librarian, library assistant; stationer, book dealer; publisher, printer; editor; book reviewer, reviewer.

**author**, writer; literary person; historian, biographer, **narrator**; prose writer, verse writer, **poet**; playwright, librettist, script writer, **dramatist**; freelance; copywriter; **news reporter**; editor, subeditor, copy editor, contributor, correspondent, columnist, gossip writer, diarist; scribbler, hack, potboiler; ghost, ghost writer.

**Adj. bibliographical**; bound, hardback, paperback; loose-leaf; marbled, gilt; antiquarian.

## 585 Description

**N. description**, account, statement, summary, **report**; brief, abstract, inscription, caption, legend, **compendium**; narration, relation, rehearsal, recital, version (see **narrative**); nonfiction, documentary account; specification, characterization, **list**; portrait, sketch, profile, **representation**; psychic profile, case history, **record**; faction, documentary drama; local colour; picture, realism; travelogue; cameo; **poem**; eulogy, **praise**; parody, **satire**; obituary, epitaph, lapidary inscription.

**narrative**, plot, subplot, scenario, **stage play**; episode, **event**; complication; dramatic irony, comic relief; fantasia, **fantasy**; imaginary account, fiction, story, tale, romance, folk tale; tradition, legend, mythology, myth, saga, epic; ballad, **poem**; allegory, parable, cautionary tale; yarn, **fable**; anecdote, reminiscence, **remembrance**; annals, chronicle, history, **record**.

**biography**, human interest; life, life story or history; obituary; personal account, autobiography, memoirs, **remembrance**; diary, **record**.

**novel**, fiction, tale; fictional biography; short story, novelette; light reading, **reading matter**; romance, love story, Western, science fiction; gothic novel, ghost story; novel of low life, picaresque novel; crime story, whodunit; cliffhanger, thriller, penny dreadful, horror comic; paperback, pulp literature; potboiler, trash; popular novel, blockbuster, best-seller, **book**.

**narrator**, reporter; raconteur; storyteller, mythologist; fiction writer, **author**; biographer; memoir writer, diarist; historian, **recorder**; Muse of History.

**Adj. descriptive**, representational; graphic, colourful, vivid; sharp; realistic, convincing; picturesque, striking; impressionistic, suggestive, evocative, emotive; moving, **exciting**; mythological, **figurative**; epic, heroic, romantic, cloak-and-dagger; picaresque; narrative, autobiographical; full, circumstantial, **diffuse**; factual, documentary, nonfiction, **accurate**; fictitious, fictional, imaginative, **imaginary**; **literary**.

**Vb. describe**, delineate, draw, picture, depict, paint, **represent**; evoke, bring to life, make one see; detail, descend to, **specify**; sketch, **outline**; relate, recount, rehearse, recite, report, give an account, **communicate**; write, write about, **record**; narrate, tell, tell a story, yarn, unfold a tale; construct a plot; romance, **imagine**; review, recapitulate, **repeat**; reminisce, **retrospect**.

# 586 Dissertation

**N. dissertation**, treatise, tract; exposition, summary, **compendium**; theme, thesis, **argument**; essay, examination, survey, **enquiry**; discourse, descant; memoir, paper, monograph, study; screed, harangue, sermon, **lecture**; commentary, textbook.

**article**, column; leading article, leader, editorial; essay; literary composition, set piece, comment, review, notice, critique, criticism, write-up, **estimate**.

**dissertator**; pamphleteer, publicist; editor, leader writer, contributor, **author**; reviewer, critic, commentator, pundit.

**Adj. discursive**; critical.

**Vb. dissertate**, treat, handle, write about, deal with, do justice to; descant, **argue**; pursue a theme, develop a thesis; survey; discuss, ventilate; notice; write an essay, do a paper; annotate, commentate, **interpret**.

**587 Compendium**

N. **compendium**, epitome, summary, brief; contents, analysis; abstract, gist; digest; synopsis, survey; review, recap; rundown; draft, minute, note, **record**; sketch, outline, skeleton; blueprint, **plan**; syllabus, prospectus, **list**; abbreviation, **shortening**; contraction.

anthology, treasury, garland; **textbook**; collection, compilation, miscellany; gleanings, leaves, album, scrapbook, notebook, commonplace book.

epitomizer; cutter.

Adj. **compendious**, pithy, **concise**; abstracted, **short**; potted; collected.

Vb. **abstract**, resume; reduce, abbreviate, abridge, **shorten**; encapsulate; docket, **record**; condense, pot, **be concise**; consolidate, compile, **list**; collect, **bring together**; **combine**; excerpt, glean, select; sketch, **outline**.

Adv. **in sum**; at a glance.

**588 Poetry. Prose**

N. **poetry**, song; verse, rhyme, numbers.

poem; lines; narrative verse, heroic poem, epic; dramatic poem, lyric drama, verse drama, Greek tragedy, Greek comedy, trilogy, **drama**; light verse, lyric verse, ode; elegy, dirge; occasional poem; song, hymn, shanty, lay, ballad, **vocal music**; love song; **anthology**; canto, fit; cycle, sequence.

doggerel, lame verse; jingle, ditty, nursery rhyme; nonsense verse; limerick; mock epic, burlesque, satirical verse.

verse form, sonnet, sestet; burden, refrain; couplet; triplet, quatrain; rhyme royal; concrete poetry; verse, stanza, stave; broken line.

prosody, metre, measure, numbers; scansion; rhyme, rhyme scheme; assonance, alliteration; cadence, rhythm, metrical unit, foot; iamb, trochee, spondee; blank verse; heroic couplet, thesis, beat, stress, accent; caesura, diaeresis.

poet, poet laureate; Lake poet; bard, minstrel, troubadour; epic poet, bucolic poet; librettist.

prose, prose rhythm; prose poem; everyday language; prose writer, **author**.

Adj. poetic; heroic, Homeric; lyrical; lyric; bucolic; **literary**; doggerel; metrical, measured.

prosaic, pedestrian; matter-of-fact, plain.

Vb. poetize, sing; scan; rhyme, chime, jingle; versify; compose an epic, write a lyric, write a sonnet; lampoon.

write prose, stick to prose, prose.

**589 Drama. Ballet**

N. drama; West End; silver Screen, Hollywood, **cinema**; show business, dramatic entertainment, straight drama, legitimate theatre; repertory, rep; theatricals; masque, dumb show, tableau; **representation**; tragic mask, sock; Tragic Muse; Comic Muse.

dramaturgy, dramatic form, **narrative**; theatricals, dramatics; good theatre, good cinema; play writing, histrionic art, action, movement, plot, subplot, **narrative**; characterization, **representation**; production, revival; casting; rehearsal, direction, stage management; showmanship; stage directions; dialogue, soliloquy, stage whisper, aside, cue; business; entrance, exit (see **acting**); prologue, chorus; act, scene; curtain, blackout; epilogue; curtain call, encore; interval, intermission, break; performance, preview, first night, first house, road show; sell-out, hit, long run.

stage play, play, drama, work; piece,

show, vehicle; libretto, scenario, script, text, book of words, prompt book; part, lines, **speech**; dramatic representation, **representation**; sketch, skit; double bill; intermezzo; monologue; masque, mystery play, miracle play; Greek drama, trilogy, cycle; melodrama; tragedy, tragicomedy; comedy, comedy of manners, Restoration comedy; black comedy, farce, slapstick, burlesque, extravaganza; pantomime; musical comedy, musical, light opera, grand opera, **vocal music**; radio drama, television play, **broadcast**; screenplay, **cinema**; shadow play, puppet show.

**stage show, spectacle**; ice show, circus, **amusement**; variety, music hall, vaudeville; review, revue, leg show, floor show, cabaret; act, turn; star turn, transformation scene, set piece, tableau.

**ballet**, dance; choreography; classical ballet, modern dance; toe dance, **dance**; solo; arabesque; pirouette, **rotation**; jeté, **leap**.

**stage set**, setting, scenery, scene, **spectacle**; drop curtain, drop, backdrop, backcloth, cyclorama; screen, wings, flat; background, foreground, front stage, upstage, stage, boards; apron, proscenium, proscenium arch; gauze, curtain, trap, prompt box (see **theatre**); costume, make-up, greasepaint.

**theatre**, amphitheatre, stadium, **arena**; circus, hippodrome, fleapit, picture house, **cinema**; Greek theatre, pier, pavilion; big top; playhouse, opera house, music hall, vaudeville theatre, night club, cabaret; stage, boards, proscenium, wings, flies (see **stage set**); dressing room, footlights, spotlight, spot, limelight, floodlight, flood; auditorium, orchestra; seating,

stalls; pit; box, circle, mezzanine; gallery, balcony, gods; front of house, foyer, bar, box office, stage door.

**acting, representation**; interpretation, impression, pantomime, **mimicry**; repertoire; character, personage, role, part, cameo; stock part, heavy father, merry widow, stage villain; principal boy or girl; Harlequin, Columbine, Pierrot, Pantaloon; pantomime dame; chief part, hero, antihero; stage fever; stage fright.

**actor**, actress, mimic, mime, **imitator**; player, trouper, ham; rep player, character actor; star, star actor or actress, film star, starlet, **favourite**; comedian, comedienne, comedy actor or actress; ballerina; protagonist, lead, leading man, leading lady, juvenile lead; understudy, stand-in, **substitute**; **analogue**; super, extra, bit player; chorus; troupe, company, cast; narrator; prologue, **speaker**.

**entertainer**, performer; artiste, artist; impressionist; troubadour, minstrel; street musician; **vocalist**; comic, comedian, comedienne, **humorist**; acrobat, **athlete**; clown, buffoon, **fool**; pierrot, Punch; show girl.

**stagehand**; prop man, stage carpenter, scene painter; electrician, machinist; special effects man, continuity girl; wardrobe mistress, make-up artist; prompter; programme seller, usher, usherette, doorman.

**stage manager**, producer, director; manager, press agent; impresario, showman; backer, sponsor, angel.

**dramatist**; tragic poet, **poet**; playwright, scenario writer, librettist; gag man, **humorist**.

**playgoer**; film fan, opera buff; audience, house, sell-out; stalls, pit, circle, gods, gallery, balcony; **spectator**; dramatic critic, play or film reviewer.

**Adj.dramatic**; scenic, theatrical, stagy; live, legitimate; histrionic, mimetic; tragic; comic; burlesque, knockabout, slapstick, **funny**; melodramatic, sensational, **exciting**; avant-garde; showing, running, **shown**; acting, cast, miscast; stagestruck.

**Vb.dramatize**, be a dramatist; make a play of; do a play, stage, mount, produce, direct, stage-manage; rehearse, cut; cast, typecast, give a part, assign a role; star, feature, bill; present, release, **show**; open.

**act**; perform, enact, play, do a play, **represent**; personify, impersonate; mime, pantomime, **imitate**; create a role, play a part; play opposite, support; star, co-star, upstage; ham, overact, **exaggerate**; rant, roar; underact; understudy, **substitute**; rehearse; fluff, dry; ad-lib, gag.

**Adv.on stage**, upstage, downstage; backstage.

## 590 Will

**N.will**, willing, volition; disposition, mind, preference; act of will; strength of will, willpower, determination, **resolution**; self-control, **temperance**; intent, purpose, **intention**; decision; **command**; desire; self-will, **caprice**; free will, self-determination; free choice, option, discretion, **choice**; unprompted will, **voluntary work**; primacy of will.

**Adj.volitional**, willing; unprompted, spontaneous, original, **voluntary**, optional; minded; wilful, **obstinate**; arbitrary, **authoritarian**; independent, **free**; determined, **resolute**; decided, intentional.

**Vb.will**; **command**; be free; be so minded, see fit, think best, **choose**; purpose, determine, **intend**; wish, **desire**; be independent, **please oneself**;

judge; be obstinate; **be resolute**; volunteer, offer, **be willing**; originate, **cause**.

**Adv.at will**, at pleasure, ad lib.

## 591 Necessity

**N.necessity**; last shift, last resort, **predicament**; what must be, **destiny**; determinism, fatalism; force of circumstances, act of God, fatality, **event**; physical necessity, law of nature; force, **compulsion**; logic, proof; legal necessity, force of law, **law**; moral necessity, obligation, conscience, **duty**; a necessity, a necessary, a must, **requirement**; want, lack, **poverty**; reflex action, reflex, instinct, impulse, **intuition**.

**fate**, lot, cup, portion; weird, karma; doom, predestination, election, **destiny**; book of fate, God's will, will of Allah, will of heaven; fortune, **chance**.

**fatalist**; pawn, tool, automaton, robot, machine.

**Adj.necessary**, indispensable, requisite; demonstrable; imperative, compulsive; overriding, irresistible; **superior**; compulsory, mandatory, binding, **obligatory**; with force of law, **legal**; inevitable, inescapable, inexorable, **certain**.

**involuntary**; unconscious, unthinking, unwitting, blind, impulsive, **spontaneous**; reflex, automatic, mechanical.

**fated**, fatal; appointed, destined; elect, **chosen**; foredoomed; bound, **subject**.

**Vb.be forced, submit**; be fated, bow to fate; needs must; make a virtue of necessity; be unable to help it, be made that way; be subject to impulse, **be subject**.

**necessitate**, dictate, impose, oblige, **compel**; doom, **predestine**; insist;

demand, **require**.

**Adv. necessarily**, of necessity, of course, perforce; willy-nilly.

**592 Willingness**

**N. willingness**; free choice, option, **choice**; disposition, mind; leaning, bent, bias, penchant, propensity, **tendency**; facility, **aptitude**; readiness, right mood, favourable humour, receptive frame of mind; good will, **benevolence**; **assent**; compliance, **consent**; cheerful consent, alacrity, zeal, ardour, enthusiasm; initiative; devotion, dedication, sacrifice; loyalty; **submission**.

**voluntary work**, voluntary service, **philanthropy**; honorary employment, labour of love; gratuitous effort; **gift**.

**volunteer**, willing horse; **busy person**; do-gooder, **philanthropist**.

**Adj. willing**, acquiescent; compliant, agreeable, content; receptive, favourable, inclined, disposed, amenable; gracious, genial, cordial; happy, pleased, glad; ready, **prepared**; prompt, quick, **active**; forward; zealous, eager, dedicated; impatient; dependable, reliable; earnest; helpful, docile, biddable, easy-going; loyal, **obedient**; submissive; obsequious, servile; dying to; would-be; meaning, meaning to.

**voluntary**, unprompted, **spontaneous**; self-imposed; open to choice, optional, **chosen**; **offering**; gratuitous, free, honorary.

**Vb. be willing**, have half a mind to; feel like, have a good mind to, **will**; yearn to, **desire**; mean to, **intend**; agree, acquiesce, **assent**; show willing, comply, **consent**; hearken, lend a willing ear, be found willing, **obey**; try, **attempt**; show zeal; collaborate;

anticipate, meet halfway; swallow, jump at, leap at; can't wait; stomach; choose freely, **choose**; volunteer, sacrifice oneself, **offer oneself**.

**Adv. willingly**, with a will, readily; **at will**; readily, like a shot; with open arms, with a good grace, without demur; with pleasure.

**593 Unwillingness**

**N. unwillingness**, reluctance; **dissent**; demur, **qualification**; protest; **opposition**; **refusal**; **hindrance**; abstention, **absence**; want of alacrity, lack of zeal; **caution**; scruple, qualm of conscience, **doubt**; repugnance, **dislike**; recoil, aversion; grudging service; shelving, **delay**; neglect.

**slacker**; forced labour, **slowcoach**.

**Adj. unwilling**, indisposed, reluctant, averse; adverse, irreconcilable; **deprecatory**; squeamish; full of regrets, with regret; hesitant, **cautious**; shy, bashful, **modest**; half-hearted, lukewarm; backward, **slow**; fractious, restive, recalcitrant, **disobedient**; perfunctory, remiss, **negligent**; grudging, **sullen**; forced.

**Vb. be unwilling**, dislike; disagree, stick, boggle, scruple, **dissent**; object, demur, protest, **deprecate**; resist, **oppose**; reject, refuse; **refuse**; recoil, blench, fight shy, duck, jib, shirk, **avoid**; skimp, scamp, **neglect**; hold back, hang back, hesitate, hang fire, go slow; slack; dissociate oneself, abstain, **obstruct**; grudge, begrudge, grimace, **be sullen**; drag oneself, do with regret, have regrets, **regret**; depart.

**Adv. unwillingly**, with a bad grace; with regret, with a heavy heart.

## 594 Resolution

**N. resolution**, determination, zeal; resolve, decision; drive, vigour; energy, **activity**; fixity of purpose, concentration, iron will, willpower, **will**; strength of character, self-control, self-possession; aplomb, mettle, daring, dash, **attack**; guts, pluck, spunk, grit, backbone, spirit; fortitude, stiff upper lip, moral fibre, **courage**; devotion, dedication; firm principles, reliability, constancy, **stability**; pressure, **compulsion**; **hardness**; iron, steel, rock; bulldog breed, stamina.

**Adj. resolute**, determined, **willing**; desperate; serious, earnest, concentrated; insistent, pressing, urgent, driving, forceful, energetic, heroic, **vigorous**; zealous, thorough, **attentive**; steady, firm, staunch, reliable, constant; strong-minded, decisive, decided, unbending, immovable, inflexible, uncompromising, intransigent, **obstinate**; stern, grim, inexorable, implacable, relentless, ruthless, merciless, **pitiless**; iron, steely, **hard**; undaunted, steadfast, unflinching, game, tenacious; indomitable; armoured, proof; **temperate**; purposeful, single-minded, whole-hearted, devoted, dedicated.

**Vb. be resolute**, steel oneself, take a resolution, will, resolve, determine, purpose, **intend**; decide, fix, seal, conclude, finish with, **terminate**; accept responsibility, **will**; insist, press, urge; cut through, override; mean business, stick at nothing; see it through, **carry through**; face, **face danger**; outface, dare, **defy**; endure, **suffer**; bring to a head; be single-minded, commit oneself, give oneself to; set to, buckle to, go to it, strain, **exert oneself**.

**stand firm**, stay put; never despair, stand fast, **persevere**; endure, **suffer**; die hard, die game.

**Adv. resolutely**; at any price; like a man; come what may, come hell or high water; live or die, neck or nothing.

**Int.** Here goes! Alea jacta est!

## 595 Perseverance

**N. perseverance**; constancy, **resolution**; singleness of purpose, concentration, **attention**; application; hard work; endurance, patience, fortitude, **suffering**; maintenance; **repetition**.

**stamina, strength**; grit, backbone, pluck; bulldog courage, **courage**; hard core, diehard, old guard, **obstinate person**; trier, stayer, willing worker, **worker**.

**Adj. persevering**, persistent, tenacious, stubborn, **obstinate**; game, plucky, patient, dogged, **industrious**; strenuous, **laborious**; steady, unfaltering, unflagging, untiring, indefatigable; sleepless, **vigilant**; unfailing, unremitting, constant; indomitable; undaunted, **resolute**.

**Vb. persevere**, persist, keep at it; never say die, **hope**; endure, **suffer**; try, **attempt**; maintain, **sustain**; plod, slog, work at, **work**; continue, rally, keep going; cling, hold fast, **retain**; stick with it, see it through; survive, **be left**; **be obstinate**; **stand firm**; work till one drops; **exert oneself**; complete, **carry through**.

**Adv. persistently**, never say die; sink or swim.

## 596 Irresolution

**N. irresolution**, loss of nerve; broken resolve, broken promise; indecision, floating vote; **caution**; levity, **caprice**; lack of willpower, lack of drive; passivity; good nature, compromise; apathy; weak will, **weakness**; **submission**.

**waverer**; shuttlecock, butterfly, feather,

**changeable thing**; floating voter; weathercock, chameleon, turncoat.

**Adj. irresolute**, undecided, indecisive; uncertain; squeamish; gutless, timid, tremulous, faint, nerveless; **nervous**; half-hearted, lukewarm, **indifferent**; infirm, infirm of purpose; characterless, featureless, **inert**; weak-kneed, spineless, **weak**; suggestible, flexible, **soft**; easygoing, good-natured, **lax**; inconstant, variable, temperamental; whimsical, **capricious**; emotional, restless, without ballast, **unstable**; uncommitted, irresponsible, giddy, feather-brained, light; fidgety, impatient; superficial, unfaithful.

**Vb. be irresolute**, blink, jib, shy, shirk, **avoid**; shuffle, shilly-shally, **be equivocal**; fluctuate, vacillate, seesaw, wobble, waver, sway, hover, teeter, dither, **oscillate**; **be uncertain**; keep undecided, delay; dally, dilly-dally, **wait**; debate, balance, **argue**; hesitate, **be cautious**; falter, grow weary; **relinquish**; make a compromise, **compromise**; yield, give way, **submit**.

**Adv. irresolutely**; seesaw.

## 597 Obstinacy

**N. obstinacy**; determination, will, **resolution**; self-will; **hardness**; hard line; constancy, fixity, **stability**; stiff neck, **resistance**.

**opinionatedness, positiveness**; ruling passion, obsession, **bias**; blind side; **ignorance**; old school.

**obstinate person**, stubborn fellow, mule; stick-in-the-mud; hard core; fanatic, stickler, pedant, zealot, bigot, **narrow mind**; sticker, stayer, die-hard, **stamina**; **crank**.

**Adj. obstinate**, stubborn; pig-headed, mulish; pertinacious, firm, determined, **resolute**; dogged, tenacious; stiff, wooden, **rigid**; adamant, inflex-

ible, unbending; obdurate, uncompromising, intransigent; unmoved, immovable; inexorable, implacable, merciless, **pitiless**; set, wedded to, hidebound; impervious, blind, deaf; opinionated, **positive**; dour, grim, **sullen**; stiff-necked, **impenitent** (see **wilful**); perverse, incorrigible, bloodyminded, plain cussed, possessive; irreversible; persistent, incurable, chronic.

**wilful**, wayward, arbitrary; headstrong, perverse; unruly, restive, refractory; irrepressible, ungovernable, intractable, **disobedient**; incorrigible; cross-grained, crotchety, **irascible**.

**Vb. be obstinate**, persist, **persevere**; **be impenitent**; stay put, **stand firm**; insist; **please oneself**; cling to custom, **be wont**; **be rash**; become chronic, **last**.

**Adv. obstinately**, like a mule.

## 598 Tergiversation

**N. tergiversation**, change of mind; afterthought, **sequel**; change of allegiance; change of purpose, alteration of plan, new resolve; good resolution; revulsion, **recoil**; **relapse**; change of direction, **deviation**; U-turn, volte-face, **return**; treachery, **perfidy**; **schism**; change of mood, temperament; coquetry, **caprice**.

**recantation**, apology; **oath**; disclaimer; denial; recall.

**tergiversator**, turncoat, rat; weathercock, **changeable thing**; Vicar of Bray; double-dealer, two-faced person; jilt, flirt, coquette, **caprice**; renegade; traitor, **knave**, quisling, fifth columnist; lost leader, quitter; tell-tale, **informer**; strike-breaker, blackleg, scab; **schismatic**; runaway; recidivist; convert, proselyte.

**Adj. tergiversating, equivocal**; slippery,

supple, versatile, treacherous; reactionary, going back; fickle, **capricious**; **irresolute**; renegade; recidivist; false, unfaithful, disloyal.

**Vb. tergiversate**, think again, think better of it, be irresolute; vary; scratch, withdraw, **resign**; crawl; change front, change round, swerve, tack, wheel about; **turn round**; **turn back**; repent, **be penitent**; reform, **get better**; fall back, backslide, **relapse**; trim, shuffle, face both ways, be equivocal; ditch, jilt, desert; forsake, abandon, **relinquish**; turn against, play false.

**apostatize**; switch; desert, defect; blackleg, rat; betray, collaborate, **be dishonest**.

**recant**; eat humble pie; take back, backpedal, backtrack, do a U-turn; withdraw; retract, disavow, disclaim, repudiate, deny, **negate**; renounce, abjure, recall, revoke, rescind, **abrogate**.

## 599 Caprice

**N. caprice**; **bias**; variability, levity.

**whim**, caprice, fancy, fantastic notion, weird idea; passing fancy, impulse; sweet will, humour, mood, fit, crotchet, maggot, quirk, kink, fad, craze, freak; escapade, prank, **foolery**; coquetry, flirtation.

**Adj. capricious**, purposeless; whimsical, fanciful, fantastic, eccentric, temperamental, crotchety, freakish, fitful; hysterical, mad, **crazy**; mischievous, wanton, wayward, perverse; particular, **fastidious**; arbitrary, unreasonable; fretful, moody, contrary, **irascible**; refractory, **wilful**; erratic, uncertain; volatile, skittish, giddy, frivolous; inconsistent, inconstant, variable, **unstable**; irresponsible, fickle, feckless; flirtatious, playful.

**Vb. be capricious**, submit to a whim; be

**fastidious**; vary; be fickle; vacillate, **be irresolute**; **be absurd**; flirt, coquette, amuse oneself.

**Adv. capriciously**, now this, now that.

## 600 Choice

**N. choice**, election, **discrimination**; selection; adoption; appointment, **commission**; right of choice, option; freedom of choice, discretion, pick; deliberate choice, decision; preference, predilection, partiality, leaning, bias, **tendency**; taste; **offer**; range of choice, selection, list, possible choice, alternative; difficult choice, dilemma; limited choice; only choice; blind choice; better choice, greater good, lesser evil, **good policy**; favour, fancy, first choice, top seed; thing chosen, selection, gleanings; literary selection, **anthology**; bad bargain; favouritism, **injustice**.

**vote**, voice, **opinion**; representation, cumulative vote; ballot, open vote, card vote; vote of confidence; division, poll, plebiscite, referendum; suffrage, franchise, right of representation; ballot box; polling; straw vote, election, by-election; indirect election, primary; hustings; candidature; return; suffragette.

**electorate**, elector, electoral college; quorum; electoral roll; constituent, constituency, borough, polling booth, ballot box; slate; ticket, manifesto.

**Adj. choosing**, optional; showing preference, preferential; selective, eclectic; elective, electoral.

**chosen**; preferable, better, **advisable**; select, choice, **excellent**; assorted; elect, designate; special, favourite, fancy, pet; God's own.

**Vb. choose**, have a voice, have free will, **will**; shop around; accept; elect, coopt, adopt, **approve**; would like, favour, fancy, like best; incline, lean, have a bias, **tend**; prefer, have a preference, like better, would rather; might do worse; think fit, think it best to, decide, **judge**; commit oneself; **be resolute**; range oneself, side, back, support, embrace, espouse; **wed**.

**select**, pick, pass, **approve**; nominate, appoint, **commission**; designate, **mark**; earmark, reserve, **set apart**; recommend, propose, **second**; excerpt, cull, **abstract**; glean, winnow, sift, **discriminate**; separate; skim, cream; **be fastidious**.

**vote**, have a voice; poll; cast a vote, divide; elect, return; **reject**; electioneer; accept a candidature, stand, **offer oneself**; take a poll, hold a referendum; hold an election.

**Adv.** optionally, at pleasure; alternatively; rather; à la carte.

## 601 Absence of Choice

**N.** no choice, **necessity**; **compulsion**; any; **justice**; apathy; moral apathy; **equality**; indecision, open mind; floating vote; refusal to vote, abstention; disqualification.

**Adj.** choiceless, without alternative, **necessary**; without a preference, unable to choose, happy either way, **neutral**; open to conviction, undecided, **irresolute**; uninterested, apathetic, **indifferent**; morally neutral, amoral; disinterested; without favouritism, impartial, **just**; without a vote; nothing to offer, featureless, characterless.

**Vb.** be neutral, abstain; waive, stand aside, **relinquish**; stand between, **be halfway**; **be irresolute**; be indifferent.

**have no choice**, take it or leave it, make a virtue of necessity, **be forced**.

**Adv.** neither.

## 602 Rejection

**N.** rejection; **disapprobation**; denial; rebuff, repulse, frozen mitt, cold shoulder, **refusal**; spurn, kick; electoral defeat, lost election, **defeat**; exception, **exclusion**; disuse; discard, reject, wallflower.

**Adj.** rejected, ineligible; sent back; **inexpedient**.

**Vb.** reject, decline, rebuff, repulse, spurn, **refuse**; return, send back, return with thanks, **disapprove**; ignore, **disregard**; vote against, **dissent**; scrap, discard, ditch, junk, throw aside; revoke, **abrogate**; set aside, supersede, **depose**; expel, **eject**; **eliminate**; except, exempt, **exclude**; blackball, cold-shoulder, **be rude**; disclaim, disavow, deny, **negate**; repudiate, **recant**; scout, scorn, disdain, laugh at, mock, deride, **ridicule**; sniff at, **hold cheap**.

## 603 Predetermination

**N.** predetermination, predestination, **necessity**; **destiny**; decree, **will**; resolve, project, **intention**; **preparation**; order paper, agenda, **business**; frame-up, packed jury, **plot**; closed mind, **prejudice**.

**Adj.** predetermined, appointed, **fated**; deliberate, aforethought; with a motive, studied, measured; considered; contrived; packed, **prepared**.

**Vb.** predetermine, appoint, foreordain, **predestine**; premeditate, resolve beforehand, **intend**; agree beforehand; settle, fix; contrive a result, **cause**; contrive, arrange, prearrange, **plan**; frame, pack a jury, **fake**.

## 604 Spontaneity

**N.** spontaneity; impromptu; reflex, impulse, **intuition**; snap decision;

spurt, burst of confidence, **disclosure**; inspiration, sudden thought, hunch, flash, **idea**.

**improviser**; creature of impulse.

**Adj. spontaneous**, offhand, extemporaneous, sudden, snap; makeshift; impromptu; unprompted, unprovoked, **voluntary**; unguarded, **rash**; natural, involuntary, automatic; **artless**; impulsive, emotional, **feeling**.

**Vb. improvise**, vamp, ad-lib; obey an impulse, **be capricious**.

**Adv. extempore**, impromptu, offhand.

## 605 Habit

**N. habit**, disposition, habit of mind, **temperament**; force of habit; familiarity, second nature; study, occupation; addiction, confirmed habit, constitutional; trait, idiosyncrasy; knack, trick, mannerism; instinct, leaning, **tendency**; bad habit; usage, long habit, custom, use, wont; prescription, **long duration**; tradition, law, precedent; way, ways, way of life; beaten track, groove, rut; fixed ways, round, daily grind; run, routine, drill, system, **order**; red tape, conservatism, old school, **conformity**.

**practice**, usual custom, usual policy, matter of course; **conformity**; mores, social usage; institution, ritual, observance, **rite**; religious observance, **cult**; mode, vogue, craze, **fashion**; convention, protocol, done thing; drill; form, **etiquette**; manners; standing order, routine, **conduct**; **order**.

**habituation**, training, **teaching**; seasoning; association, reflex, fixation, complex; drill, **repetition**.

**habitué**, creature of habit, addict, dope fiend; customer, regular, client; devotee, fan.

**Adj. habitual**, customary, familiar,

known; routine, **regular**; conventional, **orthodox**; inveterate, time-honoured, permanent; haunting, besetting, clinging; ingrained, dyed-in-the-wool, **intrinsic**; rooted, deep-seated, **fixed**.

usual, accustomed; natural; household, familiar, well-known, **known**; trodden, beaten, well-worn, hackneyed; banal, commonplace, common, ordinary, **general**; set, stock, **typical**; prevalent, widespread, current, **universal**; monthly, daily, everyday, of everyday occurrence, **frequent**; practised, done; right, settled, professional, official; invariable; **fashionable**.

**habituated**, accustomed to, known to; given to; dedicated, devoted to, wedded to; used to, familiar with, **knowing**; inveterate, confirmed, practised, **prepared**; tame.

**Vb. be wont**, love to, be known to, be used to, use to; be a creature of habit; go daily, haunt, frequent; make a habit of; never vary, observe routine, cling to custom; become a habit, stick; settle, take root; obtain, hold good, **prevail**.

**habituate**, accustom oneself, get used to; take to; catch oneself doing; practise, **repeat**; accustom, inure, season, harden, **train**; domesticate, tame; acclimatize; implant, **teach**; condition, brainwash, **influence**.

**Adv. habitually**, regularly; of course.

## 606 Desuetude

**N. desuetude**, disuse, rust, decay; lost habit, lost skill, lack of practice; **oblivion**; new custom; **nonconformity**; want of habit, inexperience, **ignorance**.

**Adj. unwonted**; unpractised; unnecessary; bad form, non-U, **vulgar**; old-fashioned, defunct, **past**; against custom; unprecedented, **original**.

**unhabituated**, unaccustomed; undomesticated; **immature**; new to, new, raw, fresh, green; rusty.

**Vb. disaccustom**, cure of, **cure**; break a habit, outgrow; slough, shed.

**be unpractised**; try a thing once; offend custom, infringe protocol; lapse, **be old**; rust, **deteriorate**.

## 607 Motive

**N. motive**, cause of action, what is behind it, **cause**; grounds, **reason why**; driving force, impetus, spring, mainspring; intention, **objective**; ideal, principle, lodestar, direction; aspiration, hope; ambition, **desire**; calling, call, **vocation**; conscience, honour, **duty**; shame, **fear**; ulterior motive; impulse, inspiration.

**inducement**, pressure, press; **influence**; indirect influence, side pressure; provocation, inspiration; support, **aid**; invitation, **request**; temptation, allurement, seduction, fascination, charm, sex appeal, **attraction**; flattery; endearment; persuasion, sales talk; pep talk, trumpet call, **call**; **lecture**; advocacy, **advice**; propaganda; advertising, soft sell, **advertisement**; graft, **reward**; honeyed words, siren song.

**persuadability**;    **moral    sensibility**; **credulity**.

**incentive**, inducement; stimulus, fillip, tickle, prod, spur, goad, lash, whip; rod, big stick, **threat**; tonic, provocative, carrot, sop, **stimulant**; charm, **spell**; attraction, **magnet**; will-o'-the-wisp, **visual fallacy**; lure, decoy, decoy duck, bait, **trap**; loss leader, special offer; profit, **gain**; cash, gold, **money**; pay, salary, perks, pay increase, rise, raise, bonus, **payment**; handout, **gift**; gratuity, tip, bribe, hush money, slush fund, **reward**; pork barrel; golden apple, forbidden fruit; offer one cannot refuse, **offer**.

**motivator**, **cause**; manager, **influence**; tactician; prompter; counsellor, **adviser**; vamp, siren; orator, **speaker**; advocate; salesman, propagandist; ringleader, **leader**; firebrand, **agitator**; lobby, pressure group.

**Adj. inducing**, incentive, provocative, persuasive, directive; tonic, challenging, rousing, **exciting**; inviting, attractive; irresistible; **habitual**.

**induced**, inspired; **excited**; receptive, tractable, docile, **willing**.

**Vb. motivate**, motive, move, manipulate, **operate**; **influence**; weigh, count, be a consideration, sway, **prevail**; override, **predominate**; appeal, challenge; infect, inject with, **educate**; interest, intrigue, **impress**; charm, fascinate, captivate, spellbind, **bewitch**; pull, **attract**; push, **impel**; force, enforce, **compel**; bend, incline, dispose; predispose, prejudice, **bias**; predestine, **predetermine**; lead, direct, **manage**; lead astray, **mislead**; give a lead, set an example, **precede**.

**incite**, stimulate, **invigorate**; encourage, **give courage**; inspire, animate, provoke, rouse, rally, **excite**; evoke, call forth, challenge; exhort, invite, urge, insist, press, exert pressure, lobby; nag, needle, goad, prod, jog, jolt; spur, prick, tickle; whip, lash, flog; drive, hurry, **hasten**; instigate, prompt; abet, **aid**; insinuate, suggest, **hint**; advocate, recommend, counsel, **advise**; start, kindle, **initiate**.

**induce**, instigate, bring about, **cause**; persuade, carry with one, **convince**; browbeat (see **motivate**); **compel**; bring round, talk round, **convert**; procure, enlist, engage; cajole, **flatter**;

conciliate, appease, **pacify**; entice, seduce (see **tempt**).

**tempt**, try; entice; tease; allure, lure, **ensnare**; coax, wheedle, **pet**; **facilitate**.

**bribe**, offer an inducement, **offer**; suborn, seduce, corrupt; square; oil; tip, **reward**.

**be induced**, yield, succumb, **submit**; concede, **consent**.

### 608 Dissuasion
**N. dissuasion**, contrary advice; caution, **warning**; setback, **hindrance**; reproof, admonition; rebuff, **resistance**; disincentive; deterrent, **danger signal**; cold water, damper, wet blanket; killjoy, spoilsport.

**Adj. dissuasive**; reluctant; **deprecatory**; warning against, **cautionary**.

**Vb. dissuade**, persuade against; caution, **warn**; remonstrate, castigate, reprove; expostulate, **deprecate**; shake, stagger, give one pause, **cause doubt**; intimidate, **threaten**; deter, daunt, cow, **frighten**; turn one aside, **deflect**; hold one back, keep back, **restrain**; render averse, disenchant, disillusion; set against, repel, disgust, fill with distaste, **cause dislike**; dishearten, discourage, dispirit, **depress**; crush, squelch, dampen, quench, cool, chill; **blunt**; calm, quiet, **moderate**.

### 609 Pretext
**N. pretext**, ostensible motive, statement, profession, **plea**, excuse, defence, apology; loophole, alibi, **means of escape**; **prop**; shallow pretext, thin excuse; quibble; salvo, proviso, **qualification**; subterfuge, **stratagem**; false plea, pretence, previous engagement, **untruth**; blind; smoke screen, cloak, cover, **screen**; makeshift, **substitute**; colour, gloss,

guise, **appearance**; bluff.

**Adj. ostensible**, pretended; specious, plausible; seeming.

**excusing**, apologetic.

**Vb. plead**, allege, claim, profess, **affirm**; pretext, make a plea of, **argue**; offer an excuse, excuse oneself, **justify**; palliate, **extenuate**; find a loophole, **escape**; bluff; varnish, colour; blind; pretend, affect, **dissemble**.

**Adv. ostensibly**.

### 610 Good
**N. good**; supreme good; public weal, common weal, common good; balance of interest, greater good, lesser evil, utilitarianism, **good policy**; weal, well-being, welfare; riches, **wealth**; luck, fortune, happy ending; blessing, world of good (see **benefit**); benediction, **benevolence**.

**benefit**, advantage, interest; service, convenience, behalf, **utility**; crop, harvest, return, **acquisition**; profit, increment, **gain**; edification; boon, **gift**; good turn, **kind act**; favour, blessing; godsend, windfall, piece of luck, treasure trove, find, prize; good thing, desirable object.

**Adj. good**, fine; blessed, beatific, **happy**; gainful; advantageous, heaven-sent, **beneficial**; worthwhile, **valuable**; helpful; praiseworthy; moral, **virtuous**.

**Vb. benefit**, favour, bless; do good, help, serve, avail, be of service, **be useful**; edify, advantage, profit; pay, repay; do one a power of good, **make better**.

**flourish**, thrive, do well; rise, prosper; arrive, **succeed**; improve, **get better**; turn to good account; make a profit, **gain**; make money, **get rich**.

**Adv. well**, aright.

## 611 Evil

**N. evil**, evil conduct, disservice, injury, dirty trick, **foul play**; wrong, injury, outrage, **injustice**; crying evil, shame, abuse; curse, scourge, poison, pest, plague, sore, **bane**; ill; sad world; bale, trouble, **adversity**; affliction, misery, distress, **suffering**; grief, woe, **sorrow**, malaise, discomfort, **worry**; nuisance; hurt, bodily harm, wound, bruise, cut, gash, **pain**; blow, buffet, stroke, **knock**; outrageous fortune, calamity, bad luck, **misfortune**; casualty, accident, **event**; fatality, **death**; catastrophe, **ruin**; tragedy, sad ending; mischief, harm, damage, **loss**; ill effect, bad result; disadvantage; drawback, **defect**; setback, **hitch**; evil plight, **predicament**; **poverty**; sense of injury, grievance, **discontent**; cause of evil.

**Adj. evil**, wicked, **vicious**; black, foul, shameful, **wrong**; bad, too bad; inauspicious, sinister, **adverse**; insidious, prejudicial; **maleficent**; fatal, fell, mortal, **deadly**; ruinous, **destructive**; calamitous, tragic, **unfortunate**; all wrong, awry.

**Adv. amiss**, wrong, all wrong, awry, sour; unfortunately; worse luck!

## 612 Intention

**N. intention**, intent, meaning; calculation, **estimate**; purpose, determination, resolve, **resolution**; mind, **intellect**; criminal intent, **guilt**; **benevolence**; view, prospect; future intention, proposal, constant intention, study, pursuit, occupation, **business**; project, design, **plan**; enterprise, **undertaking**; ambition, **desire**; decision; final decision, ultimatum, **conditions**; bid, **attempt**; engagement, **promise**; solemn threat, **threat**; final intention, destination, **end**; final cause; **reason why**; trend, **tendency**.

**objective**, destination, object, end, aim; axe to grind; mark, butt, target; target area, bull's-eye, **centre**; tape, **goal**; place of pilgrimage, Mecca, **focus**; quarry, game, prey, **chase**; prize, crown, wreath, **trophy**; dream, aspiration, vision.

**Adj. intending**, hell-bent, **resolute**; intentional, deliberate, voluntary; serious; minded, disposed, inclined, **willing**; prospective, would-be, ambitious.

**intended**; deliberate, intentional, studied, purposeful, aforethought.

**Vb. intend**, purpose, propose; have an eye to, contemplate; study, meditate; calculate, **expect**; **foresee**; mean to, really mean, have every intention, be **resolute**; have a purpose, harbour a design; resolve, determine, premeditate, **predetermine**; project, design, **plan**; shoulder, **undertake**; engage, **promise**; threaten to, **threaten**; **predestine**; earmark, **mark**.

**aim at**; go after, drive at, strive after, **pursue**; make a bid, endeavour, **attempt**; be after, promise oneself, propose to oneself, nurse an ambition, aspire to, dream of, think of, talk of, **desire**; take aim, point at, level at, aim high, **aim**.

**Adv. purposely**; designedly, advisedly, knowingly; with malice aforethought; with a view to, with an eye to.

## 613 Nondesign. Gamble

**N. nondesign**, chance; instinct; coincidence, **accompaniment**; accident, fluke, luck, **event**; good luck, windfall; bad luck, **evil**; lottery, **equal chance**; **divination**; lot, wheel of Fortune, **fate**; mascot, amulet, charm, **talisman**.

**gambling**, taking a chance; plunge, risk, hazard, Russian roulette, **danger**;

gamble, potluck, **chance**; venture, flutter, **experiment**; shot, blind bargain; bid, throw; toss of a coin, turn of a card; wager, bet, stake, psychic bet; last throw, desperate bid; dice, die; element of risk, game of chance; bingo; fruit machine; roulette; turf, horse-racing, **racing**; football pool, pools; draw, lottery, raffle, tombola, sweepstake, premium bond; futures.

**gaming-house**, hell; casino, pool room, bingo hall, amusement arcade; racecourse, turf; tote.

**bourse**, exchange, bucket shop.

**gambler**, player; better, layer, backer; turf accountant, bookmaker, tout, tipster; enterprising person; gentleman of fortune, adventurer, undertaker, entrepreneur, **undertaking**; plunger; bear, bull, stag.

**Adj.** **unintentional**, inadvertent, **involuntary**; **spontaneous**; accidental, fortuitous, **casual**.

**designless**, aimless, purposeless; happy-go-lucky; **indiscriminate**; random, haphazard; wandering, footloose.

**speculative**, **uncertain**; hazardous, chancy, dicey; venturesome, adventurous, enterprising.

**Vb.** **gamble**, game, play; throw, dice, bet, stake, wager, lay; play high, offer odds, make a book; back, punt; cover a bet, cover, hedge, **seek safety**; speculate, have a flutter, **experiment**; hazard, risk, tempt Providence; buy blind, **be rash**; venture, chance it, tempt fortune, trust to chance; raffle, draw, spin a coin.

**Adv.** **at random**, incidentally; at a venture.

## 614 Pursuit

**N.** **pursuit**, pursuance, follow-up, **sequence**; hunting, quest, **search**; **following**; witch-hunt; prosecution,

execution; **business**.

**chase**, run; steeplechase, **racing**; hunt, hunting, tally-ho; beat, drive, beating; hunting, **sport**; blood sport, fox hunt; fishing, angling, fly fishing, whaling; coursing; fishing tackle, bait, fly; **firearm**; **trap**; dragnet; game, quarry, prey, victim, **objective**; catch, **acquisition**.

**hunter**, search party; trailer, shadow; huntsman, huntress; whip; beater; sportsman, **player**; gun, shot, marksman or -woman; headhunter; poacher; trapper, rodent officer; falconer; fisherman; trawler, whaler; field, pack, hound, foxhound, bloodhound, **dog**; hawk; **bird**; beast of prey, man-eater, **mammal**; mouser, **cat**.

**Adj.** **pursuing**, sent after; following; hunting; fishing, piscatorial.

**Vb.** **pursue**, seek; **search**; send after; stalk, prowl after, shadow, dog, track, trail, tail, **follow**; **discover**; witch-hunt, harry, persecute, **oppress**; chase, hunt, whoop, hark; rush at, tilt at, ride full tilt at, charge at, **charge**; leap at, jump at, **leap**; snatch at, **take**; **aim at**; run after, woo, **court**; mob; be after, **intend**; busy oneself; persist, **persevere**; **hasten**; **progress**.

**hunt**, go hunting; go fishing, fish, angle; trawl; whale; shrimp; net, catch, **ensnare**; mouse, stalk, fowl, hawk; course; start game, flush, beat, start; poach.

**Adv.** **pursuant to**, after.

**Int.** Halloo! View halloo! Yoicks! Tally-lyho!

## 615 Avoidance

**N.** **avoidance**, **hindrance**; abstinence, abstention, **temperance**; forbearance, **moderation**; refusal; inaction, cop-out; passivity; evasive action, dodge, duck, sidestep; centrifugal force;

retreat; evasion, flight, **escape**; shy, **fear**; wide berth, safe distance, **distance**; revulsion, **recoil**; defence mechanism, defensive reaction, **defence**; repression, **prohibition**; absence; escapism.

avoider; **trickster**; quitter, **coward**; slacker; truant; renegade; runaway, fugitive; refugee; **visionary**; ostrich.

**Adj. avoiding**; evasive, elusive, slippery, hard to catch; wild; shy, **modest**; blinking, **nervous**; backward, reluctant; noncommittal, **taciturn**; passive, inert; uncommitted, **neutral**; centrifugal; fugitive, runaway, fly-by-night; hiding, **latent**.

**avoidable**.

**Vb. avoid**; bypass, circumvent, **deviate**; turn aside, cold-shoulder; hold aloof, stand apart, shun, eschew, leave, let alone, have nothing to do with; give a miss; fight shy, draw back, **recede**; stand aloof, give a wide berth, sup with a long spoon, **be distant**; keep clear; forbear, spare; refrain, abstain, deny oneself, do without, **be temperate**; **moderate**; hold back; shelve, postpone; funk, shirk, **neglect**; shrink, flinch, start aside, jib, refuse, shy, blink, blench, **be nervous**; take evasive action, lead one a dance, play hide-and-seek; sidestep, dodge, duck; deflect, **parry**; get round, obviate, skirt round, fence, hedge, pussyfoot, **be equivocal**; evade, escape, **elude**; skulk, cower, hide, **lurk**; disown, deny, **negate**; repress, suppress, **prohibit**; **plead**; prevent, foil, **hinder**.

**run away**, desert, play truant, jump bail, take French leave; abscond, welsh, flit, elope, **escape**; absent oneself, **be absent**; withdraw, retire, retreat, turn tail, **turn round**; flee, flit, fly, take to flight; bolt, run, beat it, make oneself scarce, scoot, scram, skedaddle, **move fast**; part company, **decamp**; scuttle, do a bunk.

**Int. hands off! keep off! beware! forebear!**

## 616 Relinquishment

**N. relinquishment**; going; dereliction; **schism**; walk-out, **strike**; cop-out; yielding, **transfer**; waiver; **resignation**; disuse; cancellation; world well lost.

**Adj. relinquished**, cast-off, castaway.

**Vb. relinquish**, drop, let go, leave hold of; surrender, resign, yield; waive; **be humble**; cede, transfer, **assign**; forfeit, lose; renounce, recant; forget it, **forget**; wean oneself; deny oneself, abstain, **avoid**; shed, slough, **doff**; drop, discard; lose interest, have other fish to fry, **be indifferent**; abdicate, scratch, withdraw, retire, resign; **submit**; leave, quit, vacate, evacuate, **depart**; forsake, abandon, leave stranded, desert; play truant, **be absent**; strike, **cease**; secede; rat; ditch, jilt, **deceive**; shelve, postpone; annul, cancel, **abrogate**.

## 617 Business

**N. business**, interests; main business, occupation, concern, care; aim, ambition, **intention**; case, agenda; enterprise, venture, undertaking, pursuit, **activity**; routine, round, **practice**; business life, daily work; business world, City; art, technology, industry, commerce, big business; business company, **corporation**; agriculture; cottage industry, industrialism, industrial arts, manufacture, **production**; trade, craft, handicraft, **skill**; guild, union, business association, **association**; employment, work, avocation (see **vocation**); sideline, hobby, pastime, **amusement**.

**vocation**, calling, life work, mission, **commission**; life, walk of life, career, chosen career, labour of love, self-imposed task, **voluntary work**; living, livelihood, daily bread; profession, craft, trade; line, line of country (see **function**); exacting profession, high calling; religious profession, ministry; cloth, veil, habit; military profession, arms, **war**; naval profession, sea; legal profession, **law**; teaching profession, education, **teaching**; medical profession, medicine, practice; business profession, industry, commerce, **trade**; government service, civil service, **management**; public service, public life; social service, **sociology**.

**job**, activity; work, task, set task, exercise, **labour**; duty, charge, commission, mission, errand, quest, **mandate**; employ, service, employment, working day, manhour; occupation, situation, position, berth, incumbency, appointment, post, office; regular employment, full-time job; temporary job; opening, vacancy; labour exchange, employment agency, Job Centre, Department of Employment.

**function**, what one has to do; capacity, office, duty, area, realm, province, orbit, sphere; field, terms of reference, **range**; beat, round; department, line, line of country; role, part; business, job; responsibility, concern, care, look-out, baby, pigeon.

**Adj. businesslike**, efficient, **skilful**; industrious, busy, **active**; vocational, professional, career; industrial, commercial, mercantile; functional; official; routine, systematic, **orderly**; workaday, **habitual**; freelance; **preparatory**.

**Vb. employ**, busy, occupy, keep one engaged; give employment, engage, recruit, hire, enlist, appoint, post, **commission**; **pay**; give a situation to, offer a job to, fill a vacancy, staff with, staff.

**busy oneself**, work, **serve**; have a profession, do a job, earn; earn an honest crust, turn an honest penny, **acquire**; take a situation; be doing, bustle, **be busy**; concern oneself with, **meddle**; work at, ply; turn to; have to do, **incur a duty**; **amuse oneself**.

**function**, work, go, **operate**; fill a role; officiate, act; substitute; hold office, hold a portfolio, hold a place, have a job, serve (see **busy oneself**).

**do business**, transact, negotiate, **make terms**; ply a trade, ply a craft, exercise a profession, follow a calling, work at a job; have a business, drive a trade, keep shop; do business with, **trade**; transact business, be an employer, be an industrialist; open a shop.

**Adv. professionally**.

## 618 Plan

**N. plan**, scheme, design; **order**; programme, project, proposal, **intention**; proposition, suggestion, motion, resolution (see **policy**); master plan, scale drawing, blueprint, **map**; diagram, flow chart, **statistics**; sketch, outline, draft, memorandum; skeleton, roughcast; model, pattern, pilot scheme, **prototype**; proof, revise, proof copy, **copy**; drawing board, back room, headquarters, base.

**policy**, forethought, foresight; **wisdom**; course of action, plan of attack, procedure, strategy, **tactics**; operational research, **enquiry**; address, approach, attack, **way**; steps, **action**; stroke of policy, coup, deed; scenario, forecast, **prediction**; programme, prospectus, platform, plank, ticket, slate; line, formula, **rule**; schedule, agenda, business.

**contrivance**, expedient, resource, recourse, resort, card, **means**; recipe, nostrum, **remedy**; loophole, alternative, answer, **means of escape**; artifice, device, gimmick, dodge, ploy, shift, flag of convenience, **stratagem**; wangle, fiddle, **foul play**; knack, trick, **skill**; stunt, wheeze; inspiration, happy thought, bright idea, **idea**; notion, invention; tool, weapon, contraption, gadget, **instrument**; makeshift, **substitute**; feat; bold move, stroke, masterstroke, **deed**.

**plot**, intrigue; web, web of intrigue; cabal, conspiracy, inside job; scheme, racket, game, **stratagem**; frame-up, machination; **motive**; secret influence; **defence**.

**planner**; projector; founder, author, architect; boffin, **expert**; brains, mastermind; tactician; statesman or -woman, politician, Machiavellian; gogetter, **busy person**; spinner, spider; cabal.

**Adj. planned**, schematic, **prepared**; **orderly**.

**planning**, resourceful, ingenious, **cunning**; purposeful; involved; Machiavellian.

**Vb. plan**, resolve, **intend**; approach, approach a problem, make a plan, design, draft, blueprint; frame, shape, **form**; revise, **rectify**; project, programme; shape a course, schematize, **order**; schedule, phase, adjust; invent, **discover**; conceive a plan, **imagine**; find a way, make shift to; contrive, devise, engineer; hatch, concoct, mature, **prepare**; arrange, prearrange, **predetermine**; calculate, think ahead, **be wise**; have a policy, follow a plan, work to a schedule; do everything with a purpose, have an axe to grind.

**plot**, scheme, have designs; manipulate, pull strings, **influence**; cabal, conspire, intrigue; concoct, brew; hatch a plot, **be cunning**; undermine, **ensnare**; work against, frame, **fake**.

## 619 Way

**N. way**, route, itinerary; manner, wise, fashion, style, **form**; method, guise; mode, line, approach, address, attack; procedure, process, way of, way of doing things, **tactics**; operation, treatment; working arrangement, **compromise**; usual way, routine, **practice**; technique, know-how, **skill**; going, gait, **motion**; way forward, progress, **progression**; royal road, primrose path; way of life, behaviour, **conduct**. See **route**.

**access**, right of way, communications; way to, direct approach, **approach**; entrance, door, **doorway**; drive, gangway; porch, hall, corridor, vestibule, **lobby**; way through, pass, defile, **passage**; intersection, junction, crossing; zebra crossing, **traffic control**; strait, sound, **gulf**; channel, fairway, canal, **conduit**; lock, stile, turnstile, tollgate; stairs, ladder, **ascent**.

**bridge**, brig; footbridge, flyover, aqueduct; suspension bridge, viaduct; span; railway bridge; pontoon bridge, drawbridge; causeway, stepping-stone, gangway, gangplank, catwalk, duckboards; ford, ferry, **passage**; underpass, tunnel; isthmus, neck.

**route**, direction; line, course, march, tack, track, beat; trajectory, orbit; lane, **traffic control**; air lane, sea-lane, seaway, fairway, **conduit**; trade route; short cut, bypass; detour, roundabout way, **circuit**; line of communication, line of retreat, line of advance.

**path**, footpath, pavement; towpath, ride; byway, lane, track, rabbit run, trail, right of way, public footpath; glade, walk, promenade, esplanade, parade, front, avenue, drive, boulevard, mall; pedestrian precinct, arcade, aisle, cloister; racetrack, running track, **arena**; fairway, runway.

**road**, highway; main road, A road, cinder track; switchback; toll road; thoroughfare, through road, artery, bypass, ring road; motorway; clearway; acceleration lane; crossroads, junction, T-junction, turn-off; intersection, roundabout; crossing, **traffic control**; roadway, carriageway, central reservation, crash barrier; cycle track; street, alley; close, avenue, **housing**; pavement, kerb; paving, paving stone; hard shoulder, verge; macadam, tarmac, asphalt, road metal; surface, road building, traffic engineering.

**railway**, railroad, line; permanent way, track, lines, third rail; main line; monorail, cog railway, funicular, ropeway; overhead railway, subway, tube, metro, **train**; light railway, narrow gauge, junction, crossover, level crossing, tunnel, cutting, embankment; siding, turntable; station, halt, stop, platform; signal, gantry, signal box, cabin; rails, points, frog, ballast.

**Adj. communicating, accessible;** through, main, arterial, trunk; tarmac; lit; busy; trodden, beaten.

**Adv. via.**

how.

**620 Middle way**

**N. middle way**, middle course, via media; balance, golden mean, happy medium, **average**; intermediate technology; central position, halfway, halfway house, **middle point**; slack water, half tide; direct course, straight

line, short cut, beeline; short circuit; noncommittal, **moderation**; mutual concession, **compromise**.

**moderate**; neutral, uncommitted person, uncommitted nation.

**Adj. neutral**, impartial, **just**; noncommittal, uncommitted; detached, **indifferent**; moderate, **central**; lukewarm, **irresolute**; grey.

**undeviating**, unswerving, **central**; direct, **straight**; halfway, midway, intermediate.

**Vb. be midstream**, steer a middle course, go straight, look neither to right nor to left.

**be halfway**, go halfway, **compromise**; balance; **be uncertain**.

**621 Circuit**

**N. circuit**, roundabout way, circuitous route, bypass, detour, loop, loop line, **deviation**; **convolution**; circulation, orbit, round, lap; circumference, **circle**; full circle.

**Adj. roundabout**, circuitous, indirect; **diffuse**.

**Vb. circuit**, round, lap, go round, make a circuit, **circle**; make a detour, **deviate**; turn, bypass, short-circuit, **avoid**; lead one a dance; encircle, embrace, encompass, **surround**; skirt, edge round.

**Adv. round about.**

**622 Requirement**

**N. requirement**, essential, a necessary, a must, **necessity**; needs, necessaries; indent, order, requisition; prerequisite, prior conditions, **conditions**; want, lack, need; gap, **absence**; demand, **purchase**; consumption, input, intake; shortage, **shortfall**; balance due, **debt**; claim, **request**; ultimatum, injunction, **command**.

**needfulness**, case of need, occasion;

want, pinch, **poverty**; exigency, emergency, **crisis**; **important matter**; obligation, **duty**; bare minimum.

**Adj. required**, requisite, prerequisite, needful; necessary, essential, vital, indispensable; reserved; lacking, missing, **absent**.

**necessitous**; lacking, deprived of; destitute, **poor**.

**demanding**, crying, imperative, urgent, instant, pressing; compulsory.

**Vb. require**, need, want, lack; be without; miss; need badly, crave, **desire**; claim, **request**; find necessary, find indispensable, be unable to do without, must have; consume, take, **waste**, **use**; create a need, render necessary, necessitate, oblige, **compel**; **demand**; stipulate, **give terms**; order, indent, requisition; reserve, book, earmark.

**Adv. in need**; necessarily; of necessity, at a pinch.

### 623 Instrumentality

**N. instrumentality**, operation, **agency**; occasion, **cause**; result, **effect**; pressure, **influence**; efficacy, **power**; occult power, magic, **sorcery**; help, **aid**; support; interference, **activity**; medium, **means**; use, employment, application, utility; use of machinery, instrumentation, automation, **machine**.

**instrument**, hand, organ, lackey, slave, **servant**; agent, midwife, medium, help, assistant; go-between, **mediator**; catalyst; vehicle; pawn; robot, **machine**; stooge, puppet, creature, **auxiliary**; weapon, implement, appliance, lever, **tool**; magic ring, **spell**; key, skeleton key, passkey, **opener**; open sesame, watchword, password, passport, safeconduct, warrant, **permit**; stepping-stone, **bridge**; channel, high road, highway, **road**; push button, switch; device,

expedient, makeshift, gadget; card, trump.

**Adj. instrumental**, working, **operative**; manual; automatic, push-button, **mechanical**; effective, efficient, efficacious, effectual, **powerful**; telling, weighty; magic, **magical**; conducive, **causal**; practical, applied; serviceable, employable, handy, **useful**; ready, available, **willing**; helpful; functional, subservient; intermediate.

**Vb. be instrumental**, work, act, **operate**; perform, **do**; serve, lend oneself or itself to, **minister to**; help, assist, **aid**; advance, promote; **participate**; **cause**; be useful; intermediate, interpose, intervene, **mediate**; pull strings, **influence**; effect, **cause**; tend; achieve, carry through.

**Adv. through**, per, thanks to.

### 624 Means

**N. means**, wherewithal; power, capacity, **ability**; strong hand; facilities; **tool**; technology, **knowledge**; technique, know-how, **skill**; wherewithal, equipment, supplies, stock, munitions, ammunition, **provision**; resources, raw material; **machine**; labour resources, pool of labour, manpower, **personnel**; **wealth**; liquidity, **money**; capital, **instrument**; stock-in-trade, **property**; investment portfolio; revenue, income, receipts, **receipt**; line of credit, **credit**; stand-by, **safeguard**; freedom of choice, alternative, **choice**; method, steps, **way**; cure, specific, **remedy**; expedient, device, resort, recourse; makeshift, **substitute**; **means of escape**; desperate remedy, last resort, last hope, last throw.

**Vb. find means**, supply, find, furnish, **provide**; equip, **make ready**; finance, promote, float; **be able**; contrive, be

resourceful, find a way, **plan**; beg, borrow or steal, **acquire**.
Adv. **by means of**, with; through.

## 625 Tool

N. **tool**, implement, **instrument**; apparatus, appliance, utensil; weapon, arm, **arms**; device, contraption, gadget; screw, screwdriver, drill; wrench, spanner; pliers, tweezers, **nippers**; chisel, wedge, **sharp edge**; rope, **cable**; peg, nail, **hanger**, **support**; lever, jemmy, crowbar, jack, **pivot**; grip, lug, haft, shaft, tiller, helm, rudder, **handle**; pulley, **wheel**; switch, stopcock; trigger; pedal, pole, **propulsion**; ram, **hammer**; prehistoric tool, flint.

**machine**, mechanical device; machinery, mechanism, works; clockwork; **component**; spring, mainspring, hairspring; automatic gear change; motor, engine, turbine, dynamo; servomechanism, servomotor; robot, automaton; computer.

**mechanics**, engineering; **electronics**; cybernetics; automatic control, automation; mechanical power, mechanical advantage; technology.

**equipment**, furniture; gear, tackle, harness; fixture, **adjunct**; outfit, kit; upholstery; trappings, **dress**; paraphernalia, **property**; wares, stock-in-trade, **merchandise**; plant, **workshop**.

**machinist**, operator, operative; driver, **agent**; engineer, technician, mechanic, fitter; craftsman, **artisan**.

Adj. **mechanical**; automatic, **instrumental**.

## 626 Materials

N. **materials**, resources, **means**; material, stuff, staple, stock, **substance**; raw material, grist; meat, fod-

der, **food**; oil, **fuel**; ore, mineral, metal, ingot; clay, adobe, china clay; gypsum, **soil**; glass, **transparency**; plastic, polythene, polystyrene, latex, celluloid, fibreglass; rope, yarn, wool, **fibre**; leather, hide, **skin**; timber, log, faggot, stick, **wood**; rafter, board, **beam**; plank, planking, plywood, lath, stave; stuffing, **lining**; cloth, fabric, **textile**.

**building material**, building block, brick, **pottery**; cob; **structure**; thatch, slate, tile, shingle, **roof**; stone, marble, flint, masonry; rendering, **facing**; composition, cement, concrete; paving material, flag, cobble, **paving**; hard core, gravel, tarmac, asphalt, **road**.

**paper**, pulp, newsprint; card, cellophane; cardboard, pasteboard, cardboard, hardboard, plasterboard; sheet, foolscap, quire, ream; notepaper, **stationery**.

## 627 Store

N. **store**, mass, heap, load, stack, stockpile, **accumulation**; packet, bundle, bagful, **quantity**; harvest, crop, vintage, mow, **acquisition**; haystack, stock, stock-in-trade, **merchandise**; capital, holding, investment, **property**; fund, backlog; savings, savings account, nest egg; deposit, hoard, treasure; cache; bottom drawer, hope chest, trousseau, **provision**; pool, kitty; common fund, community chest, **joint possession**; quarry, mine, natural resources, natural deposit, coalfield, oilfield; coal mine, colliery, working, shaft; coalface, seam, lode; pipe, pipe vein; vein, bonanza, strike; well; fountain, source; supply, stream; tap, pipeline; treacle well, cornucopia, abundance, **plenty**; repertoire, range (see **collection**).

**storage**, stowage, gathering, **accumu-**

lation; conservation, **preservation**; safe deposit, **protection**; stabling; storage, storage space, space, accommodation, **room**; loft; hold, bunker, **cellar**; supply base, storehouse, storeroom, stockroom; warehouse, goods shed, godown; depository, depot; dock, wharf, garage, **stable**; magazine, arsenal, armoury; treasure house, **treasury**; exchequer, vault, coffer, till, safe, bank; data bank; **memory**; hive, honeycomb; granary, barn, silo; water tower, reservoir, cistern, tank, gasholder; battery, garage, petrol station, petrol pump; dump, sump, drain, sewage farm, **sink**; pantry, larder, buttery, **chamber**; cupboard, shelf, **cabinet**; refrigerator, fridge, deep freeze; portmanteau, holdall, **box**; container, holder, quiver, **receptacle**.

**collection**, set, archives, file, **record**; folder, bundle, portfolio, **accumulation**; museum, **antiquity**; gallery, library, thesaurus, **dictionary**; menagerie, aquarium, **zoo**; waxworks, exhibition, **exhibit**; repertory, repertoire.

**Adj. stored**; held; available; spare.

**Vb. store**, stow, pack, bundle, **load**; dump, garage, stable, warehouse; barn; gather, harvest, reap, mow, pick, glean, **cultivate**; stack, heap, pile, amass, accumulate, **bring together**; panic buy, stockpile, **augment**; fuel, coal, bunker, **provide**; fill, refill, refuel, **replenish**; save, keep, hold, file, **retain**; bottle, pickle, conserve, **preserve**; leave, set aside, keep back, reserve; fund, bank, deposit, invest; hoard, treasure, hive; bury, cache, **conceal**; husband, make a nest egg; equip oneself, **prepare oneself**; pool.

## 628 Provision

**N. provision**, logistics, equipment; service, delivery; self-service; entertainment, maintenance; supply, feed; pipeline; commissariat, supplies, stores, **store**; reinforcement, refill; food, **provisions**; helping, portion, **meal**; produce, **product**; increase, return, **gain**; conservation, resource management, **economy**; budget; possible need, **preparation**.

**provider**, donor; creditor, moneylender; wet nurse, feeder; purser, **treasurer**; steward, butler; quartermaster; victualler; provision merchant, grocer, greengrocer, baker, poulterer, fishmonger, butcher, vintner, wine merchant; retailer, middleman, shopkeeper; pimp.

**caterer**, hotelier, restaurateur; landlord, landlady, mine host, publican; housekeeper, housewife; cook, chef; confectioner.

**Adj. provisioning**; self-service; **sufficient**; provided, all found; well-appointed, three star; available.

**Vb. provide**, afford, offer, lend, **give**; provision, find; equip, furnish, arm, man, **make ready**; supply, maintain supply; yield, **produce**; cater, purvey; procure, pimp; service, service an order, **sell**; deliver; hand round, serve; feed, board, maintain, keep, clothe; stock, budget, make provision, **store**; fuel, coal, bunker; gather food, forage, water, tap, draw, milk, **extract**; export, import, **trade**.

**replenish**, reinforce, make good; refill, **fill**; refuel, reload.

## 629 Waste

**N. waste**, wastage; leakage, ebb; consumption; intake, **requirement**; outlay, expense, **expenditure**; exhaustion, drainage; melting; damage, **loss**; lack of economy, unnecessary expenditure; useless expenditure, **misuse**; vandalism, wilful destruction, sabotage, **destruction**; waste product, refuse, **rubbish**.

Adj. **wasteful**, extravagant, unnecessary, uneconomic, **prodigal**; throwaway, **superfluous**; **destructive**.

**wasted**; gone to waste; fruitless; futile.

Vb. **waste**, consume; swallow, devour, eat; spend, **expend**; take, exhaust, deplete, drain, suck dry, **empty**; dissipate, scatter, **disperse**; abuse, overwork, impoverish, milk dry, **misuse**; erode, damage, misapply; **waste effort**; be extravagant, squander, run through, **be prodigal**; be careless, slop, spill; be destructive, ruin, destroy, sabotage, **lay waste**; suffer loss, **decrease**; leak, run low; melt, **liquefy**; evaporate, gutter, **burn**; run to seed, **deteriorate**; run to waste.

## 630 Sufficiency

N. **sufficiency**, right amount; qualification; right number, quorum; enough; adequate income, competence, living wage; exact requirement; minimum, bare minimum, least one can do; **possibility**; full measure, satisfaction, **content**; fulfilment; bellyful.

**plenty**, cornucopia, **abundance**; flood, spate, **stream**; lashings, galore, **great quantity**; amplitude; riches, **wealth**; luxury, loaded table, feast, banquet; orgy, riot, profusion; fat; fertility, productivity; harvest, bumper crop; rich vein, bonanza, ample store, endless supply, **store**; more than enough, too much, superabundance.

Adj. **sufficient**; self-sufficient **complete**; enough, adequate, competent; enough to go round; equal to, **equal**; satisfactory; measured, commensurate; just

right; barely sufficient, only just enough; makeshift, provisional.

**plenteous**, ample, more than enough, **superfluous**; openhanded, generous, lavish, **liberal**; extravagant, **prodigal**; wholesale, without stint, unsparing, unmeasured, inexhaustible, **great**; luxuriant, riotous, lush, rank, fertile, fat, **prolific**; profuse, abundant, copious, **redundant**; rich, opulent, affluent.

**filled**, flush, **full**; chock-full, replete, ready to burst; **content**; teeming, **multitudinous**.

Vb. **suffice**, be enough, do, answer, **be expedient**; just do, work, serve; qualify, reach; pass, pass muster, wash; do all that is possible; stand, **support**; saturate, **fill**; refill, **replenish**; prove acceptable, satisfy, **content**; more than satisfy, satiate, give one his bellyful, **sate**; make adequate provision, **provide**.

**abound**, proliferate, teem, swarm, bristle with, **be many**; riot, **be fruitful**; flow, shower, snow, pour, stream, sheet, **rain**; brim, overflow; **be rich**.

**have enough**, be content; eat; drink; have had enough; **afford**.

Adv. **enough**, tolerably; ad lib.

## 631 Insufficiency

N. **insufficiency**; **discontent**; little enough, nothing to spare, less than somewhat, **small quantity**; too few; deficiency, **defect**; deficit; failure, weakness, **shortfall**; pittance, dole, mite; **parsimony**; short allowance, short commons, starvation diet; fast day; malnutrition, vitamin deficiency, **disease**.

**scarcity**, dearth, seven lean years; drought, famine, starvation, shortage, **shortfall**; power cut, **decrease**; none to spare, short supply; deprivation, poverty; lack, want, need; ebb, low water.

**Adj. insufficient**; inadequate, too little; scant, scanty, slender; too small, **small**; deficient, lacking, **incomplete**; wanting, poor, **inferior**; incompetent, unequal to; weak, thin, watery, **insubstantial**; stingy, **parsimonious**.

**unprovided**, vacant, bare, **empty**; empty-handed; insatiable; cramped; **poor**; understaffed, undermanned, short-handed; **absent**.

**underfed**; starveling, spare, scurvy, thin, skinny, **lean**.

**scarce**, rare, **infrequent**; sparse, **few**; short, at a premium, hard to get.

**Vb. not suffice**, be insufficient, be imperfect; **restrain**; want, lack, need, require, leave a gap, **require**; fail, disappoint; fall below, **be inferior**; come short, default, **fall short**; tinker.

**be unsatisfied**, come again, take a second helping, still feel hungry, **be hungry**; spurn an offer, reject with contempt, **reject**; miss, want, feel something is missing, **require**; be unable to have enough of.

**make insufficient**, ask too much, expect too much; overwork, impoverish, damage, **impair**; exhaust, deplete, squander, **waste**; grudge, hold back, stint, skimp, ration, **be parsimonious**; disinherit.

**Adv. insufficiently**; failing; at a low ebb.

## 632 Redundance

**N. redundance**, overspill, overflow, flood; abundance, superabundance, riot, profusion, **plenty**; bonanza, **store**; upsurge, **increase**; avalanche, spate, **great quantity**; too many, mob, **crowd**; saturation, saturation point; excess, **waste**; too much, **exaggeration**; overweight; burden, load, over-load, last straw, **gravity**; more than is fair, **main part**; more than enough, bellyful, **sufficiency**; fat; **disease**.

**superfluity**, luxury, frills, luxury article; overkill; bonus, cash crop, spare cash, money to burn, **extra**; margin, overlap, excess, surplus, balance, **remainder**; excrescence, accessory, fifth wheel, parasite; padding, expletive; tautology; redundancy, unemployment; **activity**; too much of a good thing, glut; inflation; surfeit, overdose.

**Adj. redundant**, too many, **many**; overmuch, excessive, immoderate, **exorbitant**; overdone; **full**; **flowing**; **tedious**; replete; bloated.

**superfluous**; needless, unnecessary, **useless**; excessive, **wasteful**; luxury, luxurious; surplus, extra; spare, to spare, **additional**; dispensable, expendable.

**Vb. superabound**, riot, abound; run riot, **be fruitful**; bristle with, meet one at every turn, **be many**; overflow, ooze at every pore, **be complete**; stream, flood, inundate, deluge, overwhelm, **flow**; engulf, absorb; **overstep**; overlap, **extend**; soak, saturate, **drench**; stuff, gorge, cram, **fill**; congest, choke, suffocate; overdose, glut, cloy, satiate, sicken, **sate**; pamper oneself, **be intemperate**; do more than enough, oversell; overstock; overdo, **exaggerate**; overload; overcharge, surcharge; lavish, **be liberal**; be lavish, make a splash, **be prodigal**; crawl with, stink of, **be rich**.

**be superfluous**, be left; duplicate; take a sledgehammer to crack a nut, **waste effort**; **be useless**.

**Adv. redundantly**, too much, overly, beyond measure.

**633 Importance**

N. **importance**, primacy, priority, **precedence**; supremacy; import, consequence, significance, weight, gravity, solemnity; substance, pith, moment; interest, consideration, concern, **business**; mark, prominence, distinction, eminence, **repute**; influence, **prestige**; size, magnitude; rank, high standing, **degree**; value, merit, **goodness**, use, utility; stress, emphasis.

**important matter**, vital concern; turning point, **crisis**; breath of life; grave affair; notable point, memorandum; big news, **news**; great doings, exploit, **deed**; landmark, milestone; **special day**.

**chief thing**, issue, crux, **topic**; bedrock, fact, **reality**; essential, **requirement**; priority, first choice, **choice**; gist, meaning; substance, **essential part**; highlight, main feature; best part, cream, salt, pick, **elite**; keynote, cornerstone, mainstay, kingpin; head, spearhead; heart, core, kernel, nucleus, nub, **centre**; hub, **pivot**; cardinal point, **main part**; chief hope, trump card, main chance.

**bigwig**, personage, notable, personality, heavyweight, somebody, **person of repute**; local worthy; great man or woman, VIP, brass hat; big gun, big shot, big noise, big bug, big wheel, big chief; leading light, master spirit, **sage**; kingpin, key person, **expert**; first fiddle, star, lion, catch, **favourite**; uncrowned king or queen, head, chief, **superior**; superior person, lord of creation; **aristocrat**; magnate, mogul, mandarin; baron, tycoon, **autocrat**; top brass, top people, establishment, **authority**; **influence**.

Adj. **important**, weighty, grave, solemn, serious; pregnant, big; of conse-quence, of consideration, of concern; considerable, worth considering; earth-shaking, momentous, critical, fateful, **timely**; chief, capital, cardinal, staple, major, main, paramount, **supreme**; crucial, essential, material, **relevant**; central; basic, fundamental, bedrock, radical; primary, prime, foremost, leading; overriding, uppermost, **superior**; worthwhile, **valuable**; necessary, vital, indispensable, irreplaceable, key; helpful, **useful**; significant, telling, trenchant, **meaningful**; imperative, urgent; overdue, **late**; high-level, summit, **topmost**; top-secret, **latent**; high, grand, noble, **great**.

**notable**, of mark, egregious, **remarkable**, memorable, signal, unforgettable; first-rate, outstanding, **superior**; ranking, top-flight, **excellent**; conspicuous, prominent, eminent, distinguished, exalted, august, **noteworthy**; imposing, commanding, **impressive**; formidable, powerful; newsworthy, front-page; eventful, stirring, breath-taking, earth-shaking, seismic.

Vb. **be important**, matter, be a consideration, bulk large, **motivate**; weigh, carry, tell, count, cast a long shadow, **influence**; import, signify, **mean**; concern, interest, affect, **be related**; have priority, come first, **predominate**; **come before**; be something, be somebody, **command respect**; deserve notice, make a stir, create a sensation, cut a figure, cut a dash, **attract notice**.

**make important**, give weight to; enhance, highlight; stress, underline, labour; headline, splash, **advertise**; bring to notice, **proclaim**; **celebrate**; magnify, **enlarge**; make much of, **exaggerate**; lionize, honour, glorify, exalt, **show respect**; make a fuss about, make a stir, make much ado; value, esteem, make much of, think everything of, **respect**; overestimate, **overrate**.

Adv. **importantly**, primarily; largely, above all, to crown all.

## 634 Unimportance

N. **unimportance**; lack of substance; nothingness; frivolity; red herring.

**trifle**, inessential, technicality; nothing, parish pump; accessory, secondary matter, side-show; nothing to speak of, nothing to boast of, nothing to worry about; tithe, fraction, **part**; bagatelle, fig, damn, straw, chaff, pin, button, feather, dust; cobweb, gossamer; small item, tuppence, small change, small beer; paltry sum, peanuts, chickenfeed, fleabite; scratch; nothing to it, **easy thing**; jest, joke, farce, **amusement**; peccadillo, venial sin; trivia, detail; whit, jot, trickle, **small quantity**; cent, brass farthing, **small coin**; nonsense, fiddle-faddle, drivel, **empty talk**.

**bauble**, toy, rattle, **plaything**; gewgaw, bric-a-brac; novelty, trinket; tinsel, trumpery, frippery, trash; froth, foam, **bubble**.

**nonentity**, nobody; man of straw, **insubstantial thing**; figurehead; trifler; lightweight, small beer; small fry, small game; banana republic; other ranks, lower orders; second fiddle, **inferior**; underling, **servant**; pawn, stooge, puppet, **instrument**; poor relation, **poor person**; pipsqueak, whippersnapper, squirt, trash, **object of scorn**.

Adj. **unimportant**, immaterial, **insubstantial**; ineffectual, inconsequential; insignificant, **meaningless**; **irrelevant**; inessential, fringe; unnecessary, dispensable, expendable; small, petty, trifling, nugatory, flimsy, paltry, **inconsiderable**; negligible; weak, puny, powerless, **impotent**; measly, miserable, pitiful, pitiable, pathetic; mean, sorry, shabby, **poor**; obscure; beneath notice, beneath contempt; jumped-up, potty; low-level, of second rank, secondary, minor, subsidiary, peripheral, **inferior**.

**trivial**, trifling, fiddling, niggling; pettifogging, nit-picking, technical; footling, frivolous, puerile, childish; **foolish**; windy, airy, **insubstantial**; superficial, **shallow**; slight, small; lightweight, **light**; venial; parishpump, small-time; one-horse, secondrate, potty, grotty, trumpery, trashy, tawdry, catchpenny, shoddy, **bad**; **cheap**; **useless**; toy, token, nominal; mediocre, nondescript, commonplace, ordinary, uneventful, **usual**.

Vb. **be unimportant**, signify little; **disregard**; **hold cheap**; **humiliate**.

Int. no matter! never mind! so what! too bad!

## 635 Utility

N. **utility**, use; efficacy, **ability**; **sufficiency**; good policy; readiness, **presence**; service, avail, help, good stead, **aid**; value, worth, merit, **goodness**, virtue, function, capacity, **power**; advantage, commodity; productivity; profit, mileage, **gain**; convenience, benefit, public utility, common weal, public good, **good**; utilitarianism; employment, **use**.

Adj. **useful**, of use, helpful, of service; sensible, practical, applied, functional; versatile, all-purpose, of all work; practicable, commodious, convenient, expedient, **advisable**; handy, ready, at hand, available; serviceable, disposable, adaptable, applicable;

employable; good, valid, current; subsidiary, subservient, **instrumental**; able, competent, efficacious, effective, effectual, efficient, **powerful**; conducive; adequate, **sufficient**; pragmatic, utilitarian.

**profitable**, remunerative, **gainful**; prolific, fertile, **productive**; beneficial, advantageous, worthwhile, **good**; invaluable, priceless, **valuable**.

**Vb. be useful**, avail, prove helpful, be of value; have some use, perform a function; function, work, **operate**; perform, **do**; serve, answer, suffice; be **expedient**; help, advance, promote, **aid**; do service, **serve**; tend; benefit, profit, advantage, **do good**; bear fruit, **be fruitful**; pay, make a profit.

**find useful**, employ, make use of, **use**; turn to good account; **gain**; **get better**.

**Adv. usefully**.

## 636 Inutility

**N. inutility**; vanity; inability; inconvenience; disservice, mischief, damage, detriment, **loss**.

**lost labour**, failure; waste of breath, waste of time, dead loss; lost trouble; blind alley, **obstacle**.

**rubbish**, good riddance, trash, stuff; waste, refuse, lumber, junk, scrap, litter; wastage, waste paper; chaff, bran; scraps; offal, carrion, dust, muck, debris, slag, clinker, dross, scum, **dirt**; peel, dead wood, stubble, weeds; old clothes; reject; midden, rubbish heap, slag heap, dump.

**Adj. useless**, purposeless, pointless, futile, **absurd**; impracticable; redundant, **superfluous**; expendable, dispensable, unnecessary; inapplicable, **inexpedient**; unqualified, inefficient, incompetent; unable, ineffective, feckless, ineffectual, **impotent**, inoperative, dud; invalid; unserviceable; effete, past work, obsolete, outmoded, **antiquated**; hopeless, vain.

**profitless**; wasteful; vain, abortive; thankless; fruitless, barren, sterile; idle, **lazy**; trashy, **bad**; dear at any price, **dear**.

**Vb. be useless**; **hinder**; **fail**; refuse to work; **be superfluous**.

**make useless**, disqualify, disarm, **disable**; castrate, emasculate; cripple, lame, **impair**; dismantle, sabotage, **obstruct**; undo, **disunite**; deface, **abrogate**; devalue, **cheapen**; pollute, contaminate, lay waste, **make sterile**.

**waste effort**; talk to a brick wall; **be superfluous**; flog a dead horse; tinker; **be absurd**.

**Adv. uselessly**.

## 637 Good policy

**N. good policy**; answer, **utility**; fitness, propriety; high time, opportunity, **occasion**; convenience, pragmatism, utilitarianism, opportunism; profit, advantage, **benefit**; facilities, **means**; an expedient.

**Adj. advisable**; better to, desirable, worthwhile, **beneficial**; acceptable; suitable, **fit**; fitting, seemly, proper, **right**; due; well-timed, auspicious, opportune, **timely**; prudent, politic, judicious, **wise**; expedient; advantageous, **useful**; convenient, workable, practical, pragmatic, practicable, negotiable; qualified; applicable; handy, effective, effectual.

**Vb. be expedient**, befit, help, **aid**; forward, advance, promote, **be useful**; answer; wash, work, do, serve, be better than nothing, **suffice**; **succeed**; fit, **accord**; profit, advantage, benefit, **do good**.

**Adv. expediently, well**.

**638 Inexpedience**

N. **inexpedience**; bad policy, counsel of despair, **error**; **inaptitude**; **wrong**; disqualification, disability, handicap, **obstacle**; inconvenience, disadvantage, detriment; doubtful advantage, mixed blessing; last resort, **necessity**.

Adj. **inexpedient**, undesirable; illadvised, impolitic, imprudent, injudicious; inappropriate, malapropos, unseemly, **undue**; improper, objectionable, **wrong**; ineligible, inadmissible, unhappy, infelicitous, inept; inopportune, untimely, **ill-timed**; **insufficient**; inconvenient; hurtful; unhealthy, **insalubrious**; **useless**; untoward, **adverse**; awkward, **clumsy**; cumbersome, hulking, **unwieldy**.

Vb. **be inexpedient**, come amiss, won't do, won't wash; **be useless**; bother, discommode, incommode, put to inconvenience, **trouble**; disadvantage, hurt, **harm**; work against, **obstruct**; embarrass, **be difficult**.

**639 Goodness**

N. **goodness**, **health**; **skill**; quality, vintage; long suit, good points; merit, desert, title to fame; eminence; virtue, worth, value; **price**; **perfection**; quintessence, **essence**; benevolence; virtuous character, **virtue**.

**elite**, chosen few, chosen people; pick, prime, flower; cream, meritocracy; crack troops; top people, **bigwig**; top drawer, upper crust, aristocracy, **upper class**; choice bit, titbit, prime cut; plum, prize, **trophy**.

**exceller**, nonpareil, nonesuch; prodigy; genius; superman, wonder, **prodigy**; **paragon**; grand fellow, **good person**; treasure, **favourite**; jewel, pearl, ruby, diamond, **gem**; pearl of price, gold, **masterpiece**; best-seller, best ever,

absolute end; winner, humdinger, wow, knockout, hit, **a beauty**; star, idol, **favourite**; best of its kind; top seed; champion, **victor**.

Adj. **excellent**, fine; exemplary; good, **virtuous**; above par, preferable, better, **superior**; very good, first-rate, alpha plus; prime, quality, fine, most desirable; God's own, superlative; rare, vintage, classic, **perfect**; choice, select, exquisite, **chosen**; exclusive, pure; worthy, meritorious; admirable, estimable, praiseworthy, creditable; famous, great; lovely, **beautiful**; glorious, splendid, magnificent, marvellous, wonderful, terrific, sensational, superb.

**super**, fantastic, way-out, fabulous, groovy; spot-on, bang-on; top-notch, top-flight (see **best**); lovely, glorious, gorgeous, heavenly, **prodigious**; smashing, stunning, topping, swell, great, grand, famous, capital, dandy; scrumptious, delicious, juicy, jammy.

**best**, optimum, A1, champion, tiptop, top-notch, nothing like it; first, first-rate, crack; a cut above, second to none, **supreme**; unequalled, unparalleled, unmatched, peerless, matchless, **perfect**; record; capital, cardinal, **important**.

**valuable**, of value, invaluable, inestimable, priceless, above price, costly, rich, **of price**; irreplaceable, unique, rare, precious, golden, worth a king's ransom; sterling, gilt-edged, sound, solid.

**beneficial**, wholesome, healthy, salutary, sound, **salubrious**; refreshing, worthwhile, advantageous, **useful**; favourable, kind, propitious, **prosperous**; harmless, inoffensive, innocuous, **innocent**.

**not bad**, tolerable, passable, respectable,

standard, fair, satisfactory, **sufficient**; nice, decent, pretty good, all right; sound, fresh; unexceptionable; indifferent, middling, mediocre, ordinary, fifty-fifty, average, **median**.

Vb. **be good**, have quality, have merit, deserve well, **deserve**; qualify, pass, pass muster, **suffice**; challenge comparison, vie, rival, **be equal**; excel, transcend, **be superior**.

**do good**, have a good effect, edify; do a world of good, **be salubrious**; make a man of, **make better**; help, **benefit**, favour, **prosper**; do a favour, do a good turn, confer an obligation.

Adv. **aright**, well, rightly, properly, famously.

## 640 Badness

N. **badness**; demerit; low quality, low standard; flaw; poor make; taint, decay, corruption, confusion, **disorder**; **disease**; ill, hurt, harm, injury, detriment, damage, mischief, **evil**; poison, blight, cancer, **bane**; pestilence, sickness, **plague**; centre of infection, plague spot, hotbed, **infection**; affair, scandal, **slur**; abomination, filth; sewer, **sink**; gall; sting, ache, pang, **pain**; anguish, **suffering**; tyranny; cruelty, spite; depravity, vice; sin, **guilt**; bad influence, evil genius; evil spirit, **demon**; ill wind, evil star, **misfortune**; black magic, evil eye, hoodoo, jinx, **sorcery**; curse, **malediction**; bad character.

Adj. **bad**, arrant, vile, base, evil; gross, black; irredeemable; bad of its kind, poor, mean, grotty, measly, execrable, awful, **inferior**; shoddy, tacky, crummy, punk, cancer, **useless**; faulty, **imperfect**; bad at, incompetent, inefficient, unskilled, **clumsy**; badly done; scruffy, **dirty**; foul, noisome, gone bad, rank, unsound,

affected; corrupt; septic; irremediable, incurable; vicious, accursed, **wicked**; heinous, sinful, **guilty**; mean, shabby, **dishonest**; wrongful, **wrong**; sinister; shameful, scandalous, disgraceful, **discreditable**; sad, melancholy, lamentable, pitiable, pitiful, woeful, grievous, sore; **intolerable**; heavy, onerous, burdensome; too bad.

**harmful**, hurtful, prejudicial, **inexpedient**; deleterious, **destructive**; pernicious, fatal, **deadly**; costly, **dear**; ruinous, calamitous, **adverse**; noxious, malign, malignant, unhealthy, noisome, infectious, **insalubrious**; poisonous, **toxic**; sinister, ominous, dire, dreadful, baleful, accursed, **evil**; mischievous, malicious, malevolent; puckish, impish, **unkind**; bloody, bloodthirsty, inhuman, **cruel**; outrageous, rough, furious, **violent**; harsh, intolerant; monstrous, **exorbitant**.

**not nice**, obnoxious, nasty, beastly, horrid, horrible, terrible, gruesome, grim, ghastly, awful, dreadful, scruffy, **disreputable**; foul, rotten, lousy, putrid, stinking, sickening, revolting, nauseous; loathsome, abominable, **hateful**; vulgar, sordid, low, indecent, improper, gross, obscene, **impure**; shocking, reprehensible, monstrous, horrendous; miserable.

**damnable**, confounded, blinking, execrable, accursed, cursed, hellish, infernal, diabolic.

Vb. **harm**, do one a hurt, do one a mischief, **hurt**; cost one dear, **be dear**; disagree with, make one ill; injure, damage, pollute, **impair**; corrupt, **pervert**; play havoc with, **derange**; be useless; worsen, make things worse; do evil, **do wrong**; molest, pain, **torment**; plague, vex, **trouble**; spite, be unkind, **be malevolent.**

**ill-treat,** maltreat, mishandle, abuse, **misuse;** burden; persecute, **oppress;** wrong, **do wrong;** distress, **torment;** outrage, violate, force, **be violent;** savage, maul, bite, scratch, tear, **wound;** stab, **pierce;** batter, bruise, buffet, **strike;** rack, crucify **torture;** spite, **be malevolent;** crush, **destroy.**

Adv. **badly,** amiss, wrong, ill.

### 641 Perfection

N. **perfection,** finish, classic quality; nothing wrong with, mint condition; quintessence, essence; peak, pinnacle, **summit;** height or pitch of perfection, extreme, last word; **masterpiece.**

**paragon,** nonesuch, nonpareil, flower, a beauty, prince of; ideal, saint, classic, pattern, pattern of perfection, standard, norm, model, mirror, **prototype;** phoenix, rarity; superman, demigod, **prodigy.**

Adj. **perfect,** finished, brought to perfection; ripe; just right, ideal, impeccable, infallible; correct, irreproachable; immaculate, spotless, without blemish, without a stain; pure; **innocent;** sound; tight, watertight, seaworthy; whole, entire, one hundred per cent; complete, **intact;** beyond praise, **excellent;** consummate, **supreme;** brilliant, masterly, **skilful;** pattern, standard, model, classic, classical.

**undamaged,** with a whole skin, unscathed; without loss, whole, entire, **intact; healthy.**

Vb. **perfect,** consummate, bring to perfection; ripen, **mature;** correct, **rectify;** crown; complete, **carry through.**

Adv. **perfectly,** to perfection, to a turn.

### 642 Imperfection

N. **imperfection;** possibility of perfection; **error;** bit missing; lack, want, **requirement;** deficiency; failure, failing, weakness, **shortfall;** low standard, pass degree; inferior version, poor relation; second best, makeshift, **substitute;** average; loss of fitness, **fatigue; mixture.**

**defect,** fault, **error;** flaw, rift, leak, loophole, crack, **gap;** deficiency, **shortfall;** kink, foible, screw loose; weak point, soft spot, vulnerable point, tragic flaw; **weakness;** scratch, taint, stain, spot, smudge, **blemish;** drawback, catch, snag, **obstacle.**

Adj. **imperfect,** less than perfect; fallible; uneven, patchy, faulty; cracked; leaky; rickety, **flimsy;** unsound, **vulnerable;** marked; past its best; below par; stale; **unhealthy;** inadequate, deficient, wanting, lacking, **insufficient; incomplete;** partial, broken, **fragmentary;** undermanned, shorthanded, below strength; perfunctory; overwrought, overdone; lame; undeveloped, raw, crude, scratch, **immature;** makeshift, provisional; secondary; second-rate, **inferior;** poor, negative, **bad;** ordinary, much of a muchness, so-so, middling, average, **median;** moderate, nothing to boast of; only passable, tolerable, bearable, better than nothing.

Vb. **be imperfect,** fall short of perfection, have a fault; **fall short;** lie open to criticism, dissatisfy; barely pass, scrape through; fail to gain approval, **incur blame; be weak.**

Adv. **imperfectly,** to a limited extent, barely, almost, all but.

### 643 Cleanness

N. **cleanness,** absence of dust, **purity;** shine, polish; cleanliness.

cleansing, clean, washing; sprinkling; airing; sanitation, drainage, sewerage, plumbing, **hygiene**; water closet, flush, **latrine**.

**ablutions**, washing; hygiene, douche, flush; wash; bathing; bath, tub; hipbath, bidet; washbasin, washstand; hot bath, sauna; shower, bathroom, washroom, public baths; plunge bath, swimming bath, swimming pool; wash, laundry; washboard, dolly; copper, boiler, washing machine, launderette.

**cleanser**; disinfectant, deodorant; soda, detergent, soap; water, shampoo; mouth wash, gargle; lotion, dentifrice; toothpaste; pumice stone; polish, blacking; wax, varnish; whitewash, paint, **whiting**; **black pigment**; **purgative**; sewer, drainpipe, **drain**; waterworks.

**cleaning utensil**, broom, mop, sponge, swab, scourer; duster, whisk; brush, nailbrush, toothbrush, toothpick, dental floss; comb, hair brush, waste bin, dustbin; carpet sweeper, vacuum cleaner; doormat; squeegee; pipe cleaner; screen, sieve, riddle, strainer; filter, blotter; rake, hoe; sprinkler; dishwasher.

**cleaning cloth**, duster, dishcloth, tea towel; leather, chamois, flannel, facecloth, towel, handkerchief, tissue; bib, apron, napkin, serviette, place mat, tablemat, tablecloth; mat; cover, dustsheet; **coverlet**.

**cleaner**, refiner, distiller; dry cleaner, laundress, washerwoman; fuller; scrubber; dish-washer, scullion; charwoman, cleaner, help, home help; sweeper, dustman, refuse collector; lavatory attendant, sanitary engineer; chimneysweep, window cleaner; barber, hairdresser, **beautician**; picker, crow, vulture.

**Adj. clean**; snowy, **white**; clean, bright; cleanly, dainty, nice, **fastidious**; fresh; shorn; spruce, natty, neat, tidy, well groomed, **orderly**; antiseptic, hygienic, sterile, **salubrious**; pure, refined, immaculate, spotless, stainless, **perfect**; blank, kosher, **edible**.

**cleansing**; disinfectant; hygienic, sanitary; purgative, purgatory; detergent.

**Vb. clean**, spring-clean; groom, valet, spruce, trim, **arrange**; wash, wipe, wash clean, dry, wring; sponge, mop, swab; scrub, scour; flush; sandblast, scrape, **rub**; launder, starch, iron; bleach, dry-clean; soap, lather, shampoo; bathe, dip, dunk, rinse, sluice, douche, shower, **drench**; dust, whisk, sweep, beat, vacuum; brush; comb, rake; buff, polish; shine, black, **make bright**; whitewash, **whiten**; erase, **obliterate**; strip, pick, pick clean, clear, make a clean sweep, **eject**.

**purify**, purge; expurgate; sublimate, elevate, **make better**; cleanse; purify oneself; ventilate, fan, fumigate; decontaminate, disinfect, chlorinate; refine, distil, clarify, rack, skim; scum; strain, filter, percolate, leach; sift, sieve, **eliminate**; flush, drain, **make flow**.

**644 Uncleanness**

**N. uncleanness**; **marsh**; squalor, **poverty**; **disorder**; stink, **stench**; pollution; corruption, taint, putrefaction; **infection**; abomination; dirty linen.

**dirt**, filth, stain, patch, blot; muck, mud, sludge, slime; quagmire, bog, **marsh**; night soil, dung, droppings, ordure, faeces, **excrement**; snot, mucus; dust, mote, **powder**; cobweb, grime, smut, smudge, soot, smoke; grounds, dregs, lees; sediment, sedimentation, deposit, precipitate, fur; scum, dross, froth; cinders, clinker, slag, **ash**; drainage, sewerage; cast skin, slough; scurf, dandruff; tartar, plaque; pus, matter; refuse, garbage, litter, **rubbish**; rot, rust, mildew, mould, fungus, **decay**; carrion, offal; vermin, flea, nit, **insect**.

**swill**, hogwash; bilge; sewage, drainage; wallow, slough.

**latrine**, privy, bog, loo; closet, long drop, water closet, WC; cloakroom, powder room, washroom, lavatory, toilet; urinal, public convenience, comfort station; commode, bedpan, chamber pot, potty, jerry.

**sink**, sink of corruption; kitchen sink; cesspit, sump, septic tank; gutter, sewer, main, cloaca, **drain**; midden, rubbish heap, dustbin, **vessel**; coalhole, **cellar**; pigsty, den; slum, tenement, **housing**; shambles, **slaughterhouse**; **infection**; spittoon.

**dirty person**, sloven, slattern, drab, **slut**; litter lout; street arab; beast, pig.

**Adj. unclean**, unholy, **profane**; smutty, obscene, corrupt, **impure**; coarse; septic, poisonous, toxic; **infectious**; sordid, squalid, insanitary, **insalubrious**; foul, offensive, nasty, grotty; abominable; noisome, nauseous, stinking, malodorous, **fetid**; beastly, grubby, scruffy; lousy; high; flyblown, carrion.

**dirty**; dusty, smoky; thick with dust; unkempt, sleazy, bedraggled; black, dingy, greasy; messy, mucky, muddy, slimy, **marshy**; thick, turbid; musty, fusty; mouldy, rotten, **dilapidated**.

**Vb. be unclean**, get dirty, collect dust, clog; rust, mildew, moulder, fester, rot, go bad, addle, **decompose**; grow rank, smell, **stink**; wallow.

**make unclean**, foul; dirty, soil; grime, cover with dust; stain, blot, sully, tarnish; make a mess; daub, smirch,

besmirch, smut, smudge, blur, smoke; spot, patch; streak, smear, grease; cake, clog, muddy, rile; spatter, splash, slobber, slaver, **moisten**; poison, taint, infect, corrupt, pollute, contaminate, **impair**; defile, profane, desecrate.

## 645 Health

**N. health**, good constitution, **vitality**; fitness, condition, pink of condition; bloom, ruddy complexion; well-being, **euphoria**; whole skin; **goodness**; long life, longevity, ripe old age, **age**; hygiene, healthy state, clean bill of health.

**Adj. healthy**, healthful, wholesome, hygienic, sanitary, **salubrious**; fresh, blooming, ruddy, rosy, florid; lusty, bouncing, strapping, hale, hearty, sound, fit, well, fine, bonny, **vigorous**; of good constitution, never ill, robust, hardy, strong, vigorous, **stalwart**; feeling fine, feeling great; A1; a picture of health, feeling good; pretty well.

**Vb. be healthy**, look after oneself; feel fine, bloom, thrive, flourish, enjoy good health; have never felt better; wear well, look young; keep fit, keep well; have a clean bill of health.

**get healthy**, recuperate, be well again, return to health; mend, convalesce, take a fresh lease of life, become a new man or woman, **revive**.

## 646 Ill health. Disease

**N. ill health**, delicacy, weak constitution; **weakness**; loss of condition; chronic complaint, allergy, hay fever, catarrh; chronic ill health, hypochondria; nerves.

**illness**, loss of health; affliction, disability, handicap, **weakness**; sickness, ailment, complaint, complication; condition, history of; bout of sickness, visitation, attack, spasm, stroke, seizure, apoplexy, fit; shock; nausea; vertigo; headache, migraine, **pain**; sign of illness, symptom; temperature, fever, shivers, shakes, **spasm**; hypothermia; delirium, **frenzy**; breakdown, collapse; **insensibility**; coma; terminal disease, fatal illness, **decease**; sickbed, deathbed.

**disease**, malady, distemper, disorder; epidemic disease, infectious disease, alcoholism, drug addiction; deficiency disease, malnutrition, kwashiorkor, pellagra, rickets, scurvy; atrophy; traumatic disease, trauma; organic disease, epilepsy; endocrine disease, diabetes; cancer; respiratory disease; virus disease, febrile disease; dropsy; brain disease.

**plague**, pest, scourge, **bane**; pestilence, infection, contagion; epidemic, pandemic; Black Death.

**infection**, contagion, bug; miasma, pollution, taint; gangrene; sepsis, **poison**; plague spot, hotbed; vector, carrier, host; parasite, worm, **bane**; virus, bacteria, germ; botulism; gastroenteritis, infectious disease, cold, influenza, flu; diphtheria, pneumonia; tuberculosis; measles, German measles, rubella; mumps; smallpox; scarlet fever; fever, malaria (see **tropical disease**); typhus, jail fever; typhoid; polio; meningitis; sleepy sickness; tetanus, lockjaw; rabies, hydrophobia.

**tropical disease**, fever, malaria; cholera, yellow fever; dumdum fever; leprosy; kwashiorkor.

**digestive disorders**, indigestion, dyspepsia; nausea; colic, gripes; stomach ache, guts ache; stomach upset, collywobbles, lurgy; gastroenteritis; dysentery, cholera, typhoid; botulism; flatulence, wind; heartburn; hiatus

hernia; ulcer, enteritis, peritonitis, appendicitis; jaundice, hepatitis, cirrhosis, cystitis, kidney failure; piles; constipation.

**respiratory disease**, cough, cold, sore throat, catarrh; adenoids; laryngitis, croup, bronchitis; emphysema, asthma; pleurisy, pneumonia; pneumoconiosis, silicosis; diphtheria; lung cancer; pulmonary tuberculosis, consumption.

**cardiovascular disease**; gallop rhythm; murmur, valve disease, valvular lesion; heart condition, bad heart, heart trouble; congenital heart disease; rheumatic heart disease, heart failure; coronary thrombosis, coronary; cerebral thrombosis, brain haemorrhage, stroke; blood pressure; low blood pressure; vascular disease; arteriosclerosis; thrombosis, clot, embolism.

**blood disease**, anaemia, leukaemia; haemophilia; bleeding, haemorrhage.

**cancer**, growth; tumour; rodent ulcer.

**skin disease**, skin lesion; mange; leprosy; prickly heat; herpes, shingles; dermatitis, eczema; ringworm; itch; thrush; rash, eruption, acne; pustule, pimple; cyst, blister, wart, verruca, **swelling**; mole, freckle, birthmark, pockmark, **blemish**.

**venereal disease**; syphilis; venereal ulcer.

**ulcer**, gathering; lesion, **wound**; scald, burn, sore, boil, abscess, fistula; cyst; chilblain; corn, **swelling**; gangrene, rot, **decay**; discharge, pus, matter.

**rheumatism**, rheumatics; rheumatic fever; muscular rheumatism; frozen shoulder, tennis elbow; arthritis, gout, **pang**; lumbago, sciatica.

**nervous disorders**, nervous breakdown; brain tumour; brain haemorrhage, stroke, seizure; paraplegia, atrophy, insensibility; palsy; involuntary movements, tremor, tic, **spasm**; epilepsy; polio; multiple sclerosis.

**animal disease**, distemper, swine fever; myxomatosis; anthrax; liver fluke; thrush; fowl pest; hard pad; mange; rabies.

**sick person**, sufferer; patient, case, mental case, **madman**; invalid, martyr to ill health; consumptive; addict, alcoholic; spastic, paralytic; crock, cripple, **weakling**; sick list.

**pathology**, diagnosis, prognosis; bacteriology, **therapy**.

**Adj. unhealthy**, unsound, sickly; infirm, decrepit, **weak**; delicate, of weak constitution, liable to illness, always ill; mangy; peaked; sallow, pale, anaemic, **colourless**; **green**; jaundiced, **yellow**; invalid.

**sick**, ill, unwell, indisposed, below par; queasy; poorly, seedy, squeamish, groggy, grotty, queer; feverish; bedridden; prostrate; **insensible**; critical, serious, comfortable; chronic, incurable, inoperable; mortally ill, moribund, **dying**; peaky.

**diseased**, pathological; affected; rotten; morbid; psychosomatic, **mental**; infectious, contagious; poisonous, purulent, **toxic**; consumptive; anaemic; bloodless; rheumatic, rheumatoid; rickety, paralytic, spastic; venereal; swollen; bronchial, throaty, full of cold; febrile, fevered, feverish; sore, tender; inflamed; spotty; mangy.

**Vb. be ill**, enjoy poor health; ail, suffer, undergo treatment; have a complaint or an affliction, be a chronic invalid; complain of; feel sick, **vomit**; sicken, fall sick, fall ill; catch, catch an infection, catch a bug, contract a disease; be stricken; have a stroke, collapse; languish, pine, peak, droop; fail, flag,

lose strength, get worse, sink, **deteriorate**; grow weak, **be weak**.

**Adv. morbidly**.

**647 Salubrity**

**N. salubrity**, state of health; well-being, **health**; whole food, health food; fresh air, ozone, **air**; sunshine, outdoors; benign climate, health resort.

**hygiene**, sanitation, cleanliness; preventive medicine, prophylaxis, **prophylactic**; quarantine, **protection**; sanatorium, spa, **hospital**; **therapy**; keeping fit, constitutional, **exercise**.

**sanitarian**, sanitary inspector, public health inspector; sanitary engineer; medical officer.

**Adj. salubrious**, healthful, healthy, wholesome; pure, fresh, **clean**; tonic, bracing, refreshing, **restorative**; hygienic, sanitary, sterile, antiseptic; prophylactic, protective, **remedial**; salutary, **beneficial**; nutritious; harmless, benign; innocuous; immune, **invulnerable**.

**Vb. be salubrious**, agree with one; have a good climate; prevent disease; keep fit, **be healthy**.

**sanitate**, disinfect, boil, chlorinate; inoculate, vaccinate; quarantine, isolate, **seclude**; ventilate, aerate; purify; cleanse, **clean**; drain, **dry**; conserve, **preserve**.

**Adv. healthily**.

**648 Insalubrity**

**N. insalubrity**; lack of hygiene, lack of sanitation; unhealthy conditions; slum; bad air, bad climate; smoke haze, smog; sewer, **sink**; infectious person, carrier, **vector**; germ, microbe, **microorganism**; miasma, contagion, **infection**; pollution, radioactivity, fallout; **bane**.

**Adj. insalubrious**, unhealthy; insanitary,

unclean; bad, nasty, noxious; **marshy**; stagnant, foul, inedible; indigestible; unsound, stale, gone bad; airless; stuffy.

**infectious**; contagious, catching, taking, communicable; pestilent; epidemic, pandemic, endemic; sporadic; **dirty**.

**toxic**, poisonous; venomous; gathering, septic, pussy, purulent; lethal, **deadly**.

**Adv.** unwholesomely.

**649 Improvement**

**N.** improvement; uplift; good influence, **influence**; transfiguration, **transformation**; new leaf; revival, recovery, **restoration**; evolution, development; advance, onward march, march of time, progress, **progression**; furtherance, advancement, promotion, kick upstairs, rise, raise, lift, jump, **ascent**; upswing, **elevation**; **increase**.

amendment; repair; **arrangement**; reformation, reform, Borstal, **school**; rectification; red ink, blue pencil; **edition**; revise, proof; review; **sequel**; polish.

**civilization**, culture; black culture; civility, refinement, **good taste**; training, proper upbringing, **education**; cultivation, polish, **culture**; **exercise**.

**reformism**, idealism; socialism, radicalism; extremism, revolution, **sedition**; social engineering, **sociology**.

**reformer**, restorer; editor; progressive; Fabian, **moderate**; liberal, radical, revolutionary, **agitator**; socialist, Red; New Dealer; idealist, Utopian, **visionary**; social worker, **philanthropist**.

**Adj. improved**; **superior**; better; **wise**.

**improving**, reformatory, remedial, **restorative**; progressive, radical; perfectionist, Utopian; perfectionist, **fastidious**.

**Vb. get better**, improve, mend; rally, revive, recover; make progress, make

headway, advance, develop, evolve, **progress**; mellow, ripen, **mature**; bear fruit, **be fruitful**; rise, **ascend**; graduate, **succeed**; better oneself, **prosper**; reform, go straight, **be penitent**; improve oneself, **learn**; take advantage of.

**make better**, better, improve, ameliorate, reform; polish, elaborate, enrich, enhance; do one a power of good, **do good**; transfigure, **transform**; make, have a good influence, leaven, **influence**; uplift, regenerate; refine, elevate, sublimate, **purify**; teach manners; mend, **repair**; restore, **cure**; recruit, revive, **refresh**; soften, mitigate, palliate, **moderate**; forward, advance, upgrade, **promote**; foster, encourage, bring to fruition, **mature**; **use**; develop, reclaim; till, weed, dress, water, **cultivate**; tidy, **arrange**; **clean**; renovate, refurbish, renew, give a face lift; **beautify**; embellish, adorn, ornament, **decorate**.

**rectify**, put right, set right, straighten, **adjust**; mend, patch, **repair**; correct, proof-read; revise, edit, amend, emend; rewrite, remould, remodel, recreate, reform; streamline; review, reconsider; think again, think better of.

**650 Deterioration**

**N.** deterioration; reversion to type, throwback, **heredity**; decline, ebb, **decrease**; twilight; slump, depression, recession; **poverty**; exhaustion, **waste**; corruption, perversion, prostitution, loss of morale, decadence, depravity; downward course, primrose path; **descent**; setback, **relapse**; bad ending, tragedy, **misfortune**.

**dilapidation**, collapse, ruination, **destruction**; lack of maintenance, disrepair; neglect; slum, back street, poverty; ravages of time, erosion, rust, rot, canker, corruption, putrefaction, **decay**; mildew, **blight**; **old age**; atrophy, **disease**; ruin, wreck.

**impairment, misuse**; detriment, damage, waste, **loss**; patina; pollution; **infection**; **mixture**; assault, insult, outrage, **attack**; ruination, **destruction**; injury, mischief, harm, **havoc**; **weakness**; sprain, strain; sabotage.

**wound**, injury, trauma; open wound, bloody nose; sore, **ulcer**; lesion; cut, gash, abrasion, nick, snick, scratch; stab, prick, jab, puncture, **perforation**; bruise, bump, black eye, thick ear, **swelling**; burn, scald; rupture, hernia; broken head, fracture; scar, mark, **blemish**.

**Adj. deteriorated**; hurt, effete, **useless**; stale, gone bad, rotten, **bad**; flat, **tasteless**; tired; worse, far gone; failing, senile, senescent; at low ebb; backward; lapsed, recidivist; degenerate, corrupt, **vicious**; **poor**.

**dilapidated**; broken, cracked; weatherbeaten; decrepit, ruinous, ramshackle, shaky, rickety, tumbledown, rundown; worn, shabby, tatty, dingy; worn to a shadow, **useless**; seedy, **poor**; rusty, rotten, moth-eaten, dogeared.

**Vb. deteriorate**; worsen, get worse; slip, slide, go downhill; **relapse**; slump, decline, wane, ebb, sink, fail, **decrease**; slip back, **regress**; lapse; degenerate, let oneself go, ruin oneself, run to seed; **be wicked**; disintegrate, fall apart, collapse, fall, totter, droop, stoop, **tumble**; contract, shrink, **become small**; age, **grow old**; fade, wither, wilt, shrivel, perish, crumble, moulder, mildew, grow moss; weather, rust, rot, decay, **decompose**; spoil, stale, lose its taste,

lose its flavour, go flat, go sour, turn; go bad, smell, **stink**; corrupt, putrefy, rankle, fester, suppurate, gangrene, **decompose**; sicken, **be ill**; do worse, make things worse, **aggravate**.

**pervert**, deform, warp, twist, **distort**; abuse, prostitute, **misuse**; deprave, **debauch**; vitiate, corrupt, **make wicked**; lower, degrade, debase, **abase**; **transform**; brainwash.

**impair**, damage, hurt, injure, **harm**; **jumble**; play havoc with, **derange**; dismantle; spoil, maul, mar, botch, **be clumsy**; touch, tinker, meddle with, **meddle**; worsen, deteriorate, exacerbate, embitter, **aggravate**; kill with kindness, **be foolish**; degrade, lower, coarsen; devalue, debase, **cheapen**; blacken, blot, spot, stain, **make ugly**; scar, mark, wrinkle, **blemish**; deface, disfigure, deform, warp, **distort**; corrupt, vitiate (see **pervert**); mutilate, maim, lame, cripple, **disable**; scotch, pinion, cramp, hamper, **hinder**; castrate; expurgate, eviscerate; curtail, dock, **shorten**; cream, skim; adulterate, alloy, **mix**; subvert, shake, sap, mine, undermine, **weaken**; honeycomb, bore, gnaw, fret, erode, corrode, rust, rot, mildew, **decompose**; blight, blast; ravage, waste, scorch, overrun, **lay waste**; wreck, ruin, **destroy**; crumble; fray; exhaust, consume, **waste**; infect, contaminate, poison, ulcerate; taint, canker, foul, pollute, **make unclean**; defile, desecrate, profane.

**wound**, scotch, draw blood, tear, rend, lacerate, mangle, rip, **disunite**; maul, savage, **be violent**; bite, scratch, claw; gash, hack, incise, **cut**; scarify, score, **groove**; nick, **notch**; sting, prick, pink, stab, gore, run through, **pierce**; bruise, contuse, buffet, **strike**; crush, grind; chafe, **rub**; smash, **break**; graze, pepper, wing.

**651 Restoration**

**N.restoration, restitution**; redress, amends, reparation, reparations; finding again, recovery, **taking**; recall, replacement, rescue, salvage, redemption, ransom, salvation, **deliverance**; reformation; **amendment**; reaction; return to normal; reinforcement; **provision.**

**repair**, reparation; rectification; restoration, making like new; mending, darning; clout, patch, darn, reinforcement; new look, face-lift.

**revival**, recovery, **refreshment**; resurgence, recovery, rally, comeback; fresh spurt, new energy; economic recovery, economic miracle, boom; artificial respiration; second youth, Indian summer; face-lift, new look; rebirth, renaissance, new birth; new life, resurrection; resurrection day, **future state**.

**recuperation**, recovery, cure; mending; restoration to health, **remedy**; moderation, **relief**; psychological cure, catharsis.

**mender**, painter, decorator, rectifier; restorer; cobbler; tinker, plumber, handyman; **doctor**; psychiatrist.

**Adj.restored**; like new; born again; reborn; **healthy**; better; back to normal, oneself again; operable; found.

**restorative**, recuperative, medicinal, **remedial.**

**Vb.be restored**, recover, come round, come to, revive, rally; pull through, get well, convalesce, recuperate; **get better**; survive, live through; live again, resurrect, come to life again; reappear, make a comeback; be oneself again; bounce back; return to normal; resume, start again, **begin**; look like new.

**restore**, give back; make amends, **atone**; put back, replace; recall, rehabilitate; reconstitute, reconstruct, reform, **make better**; valet, **clean**; renovate, renew, rebuild, remake, redo; overhaul, service, refit, refurbish; make like new; make whole; reafforest, reclaim; recycle; reinforce, **strengthen**; **replenish**; rally, **bring together**; redeem, ransom, rescue, salvage, **deliver**; release, **liberate.**

**revive**, resuscitate, regenerate, recall to life, resurrect, reanimate; rejuvenate; **refresh.**

**cure**, heal, make well, cure of, break of; nurse, medicate, **doctor**; bandage; nurse through, work a cure, restore to health; (set a bone); close, knit together; right itself, put itself right, work its own cure.

**repair**; amend, emend, right, set to rights, put right, remedy, **rectify**; overhaul, mend, fix; cobble, heel; retread, recover, thatch, **cover; line**; darn, patch; stop, fill (teeth); retouch, revamp; seal, stop a gap, plug a hole, **staunch**; caulk, **close**; splice, bind, tie; piece together, refit, **join**; give a face-lift, refurbish, recondition, renovate, renew, remodel, reform.

**retrieve**, get back, recover, regain, recapture; find again, reclaim, claim back, compensate oneself, **recoup.**

**652 Relapse**

**N.relapse**, lapse; throwback, return, **reversion**; fall; recurrence, fresh outbreak.

**Vb.relapse**, slip back, throw back, return, retrogress, regress; degenerate, **deteriorate**; backslide, lapse; have a relapse, suffer a recurrence.

**653 Remedy**

**N. remedy**, succour, help, **aid**; **moderator**; remedial measure, **amendment**; redress, amends, **restitution**; cure; medicinal value; sovereign remedy, specific, answer, solution; prescription, recipe, formula, nostrum; quack remedy, patent medicine; sovereign remedy, panacea, cure-all; elixir.

**medicine**, pharmacopoeia; vegetable remedy, herb, simple; balm, balsam; medication, medicament, patent medicine, proprietary drug, placebo; pill, tablet, tabloid, capsule, lozenge; draught, potion, elixir; infusion; dose, drench; drops, drip; injection, jab, shot; preparation, mixture, powder, linctus; plaster (see **surgical dressing**); spray, inhaler; medicine chest, medicine bottle.

**prophylactic**, preventive; sanitation, sanitary precaution, quarantine, **hygiene**; prophylaxis; vaccine, TAB; quinine; antiseptic, disinfectant, germicide, insecticide, **poison**; dentifrice, toothpaste, tooth powder, **cleanser**; mouthwash, gargle; fluoride.

**antidote**, quinine; antigen, antibody, antibiotic; sedative; antacid, analgesic, painkiller. See **drug**.

**purgative**, purge, laxative; castor oil; diuretic; emetic; digestive, dill water; douche, enema.

**tonic**, restorative; cordial, tonic water, tonic wine; **stimulant**; caffeine, nicotine, alcohol; spirits; infusion, herb tea; vitamin tablet, iron pill.

**drug**, synthetic drug, antibiotic; penicillin; streptomycin, insulin; hormone, steroid; progesterone; contraceptive pill, **contraception**; analgesic, aspirin, codeine, **anaesthetic**; sedative; barbiturate, **soporific**; narcotic, dope, morphine, opium, cocaine; stimulant; lotus.

**balm**, balsam, oil, emollient, **moderator**; salve, ointment; cream, **cosmetic**; lanolin, liniment, embrocation; lotion, wash; eyewash; placebo.

**surgical dressing**, dressing, lint, gauze; swab; bandage, roller, sling, splint, cast; tourniquet; fingerstall; patch; application, plaster, poultice, compress; tampon, tent, roll; pessary, suppository; traumatic.

**medical art**; therapeutics; medical advice, practice, nature cure; medicine, acupuncture; radiography; diagnosis, prognosis, **pathology**; Christian Science; gynaecology, **obstetrics**; geriatrics, paediatrics; ophthalmology, neurology, dermatology, ear; bacteriology, microbiology, virology; pharmacology, veterinary medicine.

**surgery**, general surgery, plastic surgery, prosthesis; operation, op; bleeding, blood-letting; transplant; mastectomy, vasectomy; drawing, filling; massage, chiropody, pedicure, manicure; electrolysis.

**therapy**, therapeutics, medical care; treatment, nursing, bedside manner; first aid; course, cure; regimen, diet; osteopathy, hormone therapy; chemotherapy; physiotherapy; heat treatment; shock treatment; mental treatment, clinical psychology; child psychology; psychotherapy, psychiatry, psychoanalysis, **psychology**; group therapy, acupuncture; intravenous injection.

**hospital**, infirmary, general hospital, mental hospital, **lunatic asylum**; dispensary, clinic, nursing home, hospice; leper asylum, leper colony; hospital ship, hospital train; stretcher, ambulance; ward, sick bay, sickroom, sickbed; hospital bed, tent, iron lung; respirator, incubator, intensive care unit; x-ray machine, scanner; dressing station; consulting room, surgery, clinic, community health centre; sanatorium, spa; pump room, baths; solarium, sun lamp.

**doctor**, physician; leech, quack, charlatan; veterinary surgeon, vet; herbalist, herb doctor; witchdoctor, medicine man, **sorcerer**; medic, medical student; houseman, intern, registrar; medical practitioner, GP; locum; surgeon; medical officer, sanitary inspector; medical adviser, consultant, specialist; psychiatrist; anaesthetist; midwife; radiotherapist; masseur; optician, oculist; dentist, dental surgeon; medical profession, National Health Service; Red Cross.

**druggist**, apothecary, chemist, pharmacist; pharmacy.

**nurse**, sister, matron; SEN; SRN; special nurse, district nurse, health visitor; nursing auxiliary, ward orderly, dresser, medical attendant, stretcher-bearer; almoner, hospital social worker, **sociology**; lady with a lamp.

Adj.**remedial**, **restorative**; helpful, **beneficial**; therapeutic, medicinal, hygienic, **salubrious**; specific, sovereign; emollient; analgesic, narcotic, anaesthetic, **insensible**; peptic, digestive; emetic, laxative; prophylactic, disinfectant, antiseptic; tonic.

**medical**, pathological; herbal; surgical; traumatic; clinical; operable.

Vb.**remedy**, fix, put right, correct, **restore**; succour, help, **aid**; apply a remedy, treat, heal, work a cure, **cure**; palliate, soothe, **relieve**.

**doctor**, practise, have a practice; treat, prescribe, advise; attend, **minister to**; tend, nurse; give first aid, **revive**; put to bed; medicate, drench, dose, purge; inject, give a jab; dress, bind, swathe, bandage; apply a tourniquet, **staunch**;

poultice, plaster, foment; set; drug, dope; operate, cut open, amputate; bleed; transfuse; massage, rub, manipulate; draw, extract, pull, stop, fill, crown; pedicure, manicure; vaccinate, inoculate; disinfect.

## 654 Bane

N.**bane**, cause of injury, malevolent influence; curse, plague, pest, scourge, ruin, **evil**; malady, **disease**; weakness, bad habit, besetting sin, **vice**; hell, cup, visitation, affliction, **adversity**; woe, funeral, **sorrow**; cross, trial; bore, **tedium**; bugbear; burden, white elephant; stress, strain, perpetual worry, constant anxiety, torment, **worry**; running sore, **ulcer**; acid, gall; emetic; bite, sting, poison dart, fang, briar, nettle, **sharp point**; source of trouble, **pitfall**; viper, adder, serpent, **reptile**; snake; parasite, leech, tapeworm, **insect, creepy-crawly**; mosquito, wasp, **noxious animal**; locust, **destroyer**; holy terror, **tyrant**.

**blight**, rot, mildew, mould, rust, fungus; moth, woodworm, canker, cancer, **decay**; visitation, **plague**; frost, nip, cold; drought.

**poison**; bad food, bad water, pollution; bacteria, salmonella, germ, virus, **infection**; carcinogen; chemical weapon, venom, toxin; deadly poison, germicide, insecticide, pesticide; fungicide, DDT; acid; hemlock, arsenic, strychnine, cyanide; nicotine, **tobacco**; poison gas, mustard gas; choke damp; foul air, miasma, sewer gas; atmospheric pollution, smog; lead pollution; uranium, plutonium; radioactivity, mushroom, fallout, strontium 90, **radiation**; dope, opium, heroin, **drug**; **alcoholism**; lethal dose, overdose.

**poisonous plant**, hemlock, deadly nightshade, henbane.

**poisoning**, homicide; **infection**; botulism; germ warfare, **warfare**.

**Adj. baneful**, pestilent, noisome; virulent, poisonous, venomous, **toxic**; cursed, accursed, **evil**.

## 655 Safety

**N. safety**, security; **multitude**; secure position, permanent post, safe job; social security, welfare state, **sociology**; safe distance, wide berth; all clear, danger past; guarantee, warrant, **certainty**; sense of security, assurance, confidence, **courage**; safety valve, **means of escape**; close shave, narrow escape, **escape**; rescue, **deliverance**.

**protection**, conservation, **preservation**; insurance, surety, **caution**; patronage, auspices, aegis, fatherly eye, **aid**; protectorate, tutelage, custody, **restraint**; safekeeping, keeping, charge, grasp, grip, embrace; ward, **surveillance**; safeguard, precaution, preventive measure, **defence**; sanitary precaution, prophylaxis, quarantine, **hygiene**; segregation; cushion, buffer; screen, cover; umbrella, **shelter**; means of protection, deterrent, **weapon**; safe-conduct, passport, pass, **permit**; escort, convoy, guard, **armed force**; defence, bastion, bulwark, tower of strength; haven, sanctuary, asylum, **refuge**; anchor, **safeguard**; moat, ditch, palisade, stockade, **fence**; shield, breastplate, panoply, armour plate, **armour**.

**protector**, guardian, tutor; guardian angel, patron saint, liege lord, **patron**; preserver, shepherd, bodyguard, lifeguard, strongarm man, bouncer; vigilante; custodian, curator, warden; warder, guard, coastguard; duenna,

governess, nanny, **keeper**; lookout, watch, watchman; firewatcher, fire fighter, fireman; policeman or -woman, police constable, police sergeant, sheriff; copper, cop, **police**; private eye, **detective**; sentry, garrison, security forces; watchdog, guard dog, **dog**; **surveillance**.

**Adj. safe**, without risk; assured, secure, sure, snug; with a whole skin, intact; insured; hygienic, **salubrious**; at anchor; above water; clear; sheltered; held; reliable, **trustworthy**; benign, harmless, **good**.

**invulnerable**, immune, impregnable, sacrosanct; defensible, **strong**, proof, foolproof; weatherproof, waterproof, fireproof; bulletproof; snug, tight, seaworthy, airworthy; armoured.

**tutelary**, guardian, protective; **disinterested**; watchful, **vigilant**; fail-safe; doubly sure; keeping; antiseptic, disinfectant, **salubrious**.

**Vb. be safe**, find safety, come through, **escape**; keep a whole skin, have nine lives; be snug, nestle, stay at home; **lurk**; keep a safe distance, give a wide berth, **avoid**.

**safeguard**, keep safe, guard, protect; spare, **show mercy**; defend; shield; champion; grant asylum, afford sanctuary; **keep**, conserve, **preserve**; treasure, hoard, **store**; **imprison**; ward, mother; nurse, foster, cherish; have charge of, take charge of, **look after**; hide, **conceal**; cushion, cocoon, **support**; insulate, earth; cover, shroud, cloak, shade, **screen**; garage; house, shelter; ensconce, enfold, embrace, **enclose**; make safe, secure, fortify, **strengthen**; fence round, **circumscribe**; arm, armour, shepherd, convoy, escort; flank, support; garrison, mount guard; inoculate, vaccinate; chlorinate, disinfect; warrant, guarantee, **make certain**; keep order, police, patrol.

seek safety, play safe, **be cautious**; lie low, **lurk**; **escape**; **move fast**; live to fight another day, think better of it; shorten sail, take refuge, **seek refuge**.

**Adv.** under shelter; with impunity.

## 656 Danger

**N. danger**, peril; shadow of death; parlous state, forlorn hope, **predicament**; emergency, **crisis**; jeopardy, risk, hazard, ticklish business; black spot, snag, **pitfall**; trap, **ambush**; daring; venture, **undertaking**; slippery slope, road to ruin; sword of Damocles, menace, **threat**; sense of danger, apprehension; rocks ahead, **danger signal**; narrow escape, close shave, near thing, **escape**.

**vulnerability**, danger of; security risk; exposure; instability; easy target, sitting duck; vulnerable point, **weakness**; tender spot; human error.

**Adj. dangerous**, perilous, fraught with danger, treacherous; unfrequented; hazardous, venturesome, dicey, dodgy, chancy, **speculative**; serious, ugly, nasty, critical; at stake; ominous, foreboding; toxic, poisonous; unhealthy, infectious, **insalubrious**; inflammable, explosive.

**unsafe**, slippery, treacherous; insecure, unsound, precarious, dicky; topheavy, **unstable**; shaky, ramshackle, rickety, frail, **dilapidated**; crazy, **weak**; leaky, waterlogged; critical, ticklish.

**vulnerable, liable**; open to, wide open, naked, bare; helpless; unguarded.

**endangered**, facing death; at bay.

**Vb. be in danger, be liable**; play with fire; **be uncertain**; totter, slip, slide, **tumble**; get lost, **stray**.

**face danger**, face death, dice with death; **be courageous**; expose oneself, lay oneself open to; **defy**; face heavy odds; challenge fate, tempt providence, court disaster; **be rash**; venture, dare, risk it, take a chance, **gamble**.

**endanger**, spell danger, face with, imperil, hazard, compromise; risk, stake, venture, **gamble**; threaten danger, loom, forebode, bode ill, menace, **threaten**; run one hard, overtake, **outdo**.

## 657 Refuge. Safeguard

**N. refuge**, sanctuary, asylum, retreat, safe place; traffic island, zebra crossing; last resort, bolthole, foxhole, burrow; trench, dugout, earth, hole, den, lair, covert, nest, lap, hearth, **home**; defensible space, privacy; sanctum, **chamber**; cloister, cell, hermitage, ivory tower, **retreat**; temple, ark, citadel; wall, rampart, bulwark, bastion; stronghold, fastness, **fort**; keep, ward; secret place; dungeon, **prison**; rock, pillar, tower, tower of strength, mainstay, **prop**.

**shelter**, cover, roof; covert, earth, hole; fold; lee; lee wall, windbreak, hedge, **fence**; camp, stockade; shield, wing; fireguard, fender, bumper, mudguard, windscreen, **screen**; umbrella; sun helmet, sunglasses, goggles; protective clothing, overalls; haven, harbour, port; anchorage, quay, jetty, marina, dock, **stable**; **lunatic asylum**; halfway house, sheltered housing; almshouse, charitable institution, hospice; Welfare State.

**safeguard**, means of safety, protection, **safety**; **hindrance**; crush barrier, guardrail, railing; mail, **armour**; arms, deterrent, **weapon**; respirator, gas mask; safety device, safety catch, safety valve, lightning conductor,

fuse, earth; crash helmet; parachute;
safety net; lifeboat, rubber dinghy, life
raft, **raft**; life belt, life jacket, lifeline;
breeches buoy; rope, plank, **means of
escape**; anchor, grapnel, drogue; lead,
brake, **fetter**; bolt, bar, lock, key,
**stopper**; ballast, **offset**; mole, breakwater, sea wall, embankment; lighthouse, lightship, **sailing aid**; jury
mast, **extra**.
Vb. **seek refuge**, take refuge, **seek
safety**; turn to; claim sanctuary, seek
political asylum; make port, reach
safety, reach home, find shelter.

### 658 Pitfall: source of danger
N. **pitfall**, pit, catch; snag, **obstacle**;
booby trap, firetrap, minefield, **trap**;
surprise, **lack of expectation**; **ambush**;
thin ice; quagmire, **marsh**; sandbar,
shoal, shoal water, shallows; reef,
rock; lee shore, steep, chasm, abyss,
crevasse, precipice, **high land**; crosscurrent, undertow, **current**; vortex,
maelstrom, whirlpool, eddy; tidal
wave, flash flood, **wave**; storm, squall,
hurricane, **gale**; volcano, **furnace**;
dynamite, time bomb, powder keg,
**explosive**; **danger**; hotbed, **infection**;
source of trouble, hazard, bane.
**troublemaker**, stirrer, wrecker; **enemy**;
firebrand, **agitator**; ugly customer,
undesirable, delinquent, **ruffian**;
**influence**; yellow peril, Nemesis.

### 659 Warning
N. **warning**, caution; example, lesson,
notice, **information**; word, tip, tip-off,
wink, nudge, **hint**; **publication**; final
warning, final notice, ultimatum,
**demand**; admonition, **reprimand**;
deterrent; protest; warning shot; foreboding, premonition, **prediction**;
voice, voice of conscience, warning
voice, **conscience**; alarm, siren, fogh-

orn, fog signal, alert, red alert, **danger
signal**; stormy petrel, bird of ill omen,
**omen**; gathering cloud, war cloud,
**danger**; symptom, sign; knell; beacon,
light, **signal**, **indicator**; menace,
**threat**.
**warner**, **adviser**; prophet; signaller;
watchman, lookout, watch, **surveillance**; scout, spy; picket, sentry, **protector**; advanced guard, rearguard;
watchdog.
Adj. **cautionary**, warning; **deprecatory**;
exemplary, instructive; prognostic;
ominous; deterrent.
**warned, cautious**; expectant; **prepared**.
Vb. **warn**, caution; give fair warning,
give notice, notify, **inform**; drop a
hint, **hint**; counsel, **advise**; remind,
admonish, **reprove**; spell danger, forewarn, **predict**; forearm, alert, **prepare**;
lour, menace, **threaten**; advise
against, **dissuade**; remonstrate, protest, **deprecate**.
**be warned**, receive notice; beware, take
heed, **be careful**; be taught a lesson.
Int. look out! watch out! cave! mind your
step! look where you are going!

### 660 Danger signal
N. **danger signal**, note of warning, **warning**; murmur, **discontent**; black cap,
evil omen, **omen**; storm cone, gale
warning; warning sound, alarm clock,
alarm bell, burglar alarm, fire alarm,
fire bell, foghorn, fog signal, bell
buoy, motor horn, klaxon, bicycle
bell, police whistle; blast, honk, toot;
alarm, church bell, curfew, siren,
alert, tattoo, beat of drum, **call**; war
cry; fiery cross; warning light, beacon;
red flag, distress signal, SOS, **signal**;
sign of alarm, start, tremor, sweat,
fear.
**false alarm**, cry of 'wolf', scare, hoax;
bugbear, nightmare, bad dream;

blank cartridge; **untruth**; **alarmist**.

**Vb. raise the alarm**, dial 999, alert, arouse, scare, startle, **frighten**; honk, toot; cry blue murder, **proclaim**; give a false alarm, cry wolf, cry too soon; sound a warning, toll, knell.

## 661 Preservation

**N. preservation**, safekeeping, keeping alive; safe conduct, **protection**; saving, salvation, **deliverance**; conservation, conservancy; upkeep, maintenance, support, **provision**; service; insulation; **storage**; reservation, **economy**; self-preservation; game reserve, bird sanctuary, conservation area; taxidermy; cold storage; **hygiene**; preventive medicine, quarantine.

**preserver**, saviour, **deliverance**; amulet, charm, mascot, **talisman**; preservation order; preservative, ice, amber, formaldehyde; camphor, mothball, lavender; spice, pickle, brine, aspic, **condiment**; freezer, **refrigerator**; silo; safety device, seat belt, gas mask, **safeguard**; incubator, respirator, iron lung, life support system.

**Adj. preserving**; preservative, conservative; prophylactic, protective, preventive, hygienic, **salubrious**.

**preserved**, kept, fresh, intact, whole, **perfect**; frozen; potted; **safe**.

**Vb. preserve**, conserve, keep alive, keep fresh, freeze, **refrigerate**, embalm, mummify, stuff; pickle, salt, **season**; souse, marinate; cure, smoke, kipper, dehydrate, sun-dry, **dry**; pot, bottle, tin, can; protect, paint, varnish, whitewash, creosote, waterproof; maintain, service, **repair**; **support**; keep alive, feed, sustain, provision, supply, **provide**; keep safe, garage, **safeguard**; **store**; reserve, save; nurse, tend, **doctor**; cherish, treasure, **look after**; hug, hold, **retain**; keep going,

prolong; save, save alive, rescue, **deliver**.

## 662 Escape

**N. escape**, leak, leakage, loss, **egress**; delivery, rescue, **deliverance**; riddance, **relief**; getaway; flight, flit, French leave; retreat; runaway match; evasion; narrow escape, close shave, close call, narrow squeak, near thing, **danger**; discharge, reprieve, **acquittal**; setting free, **liberation**; impunity; escapism.

**means of escape**, exit, back door, secret passage, **egress**; ladder, fire escape, escape hatch; drawbridge, **bridge**; vent, safety valve, **safeguard**; dodge, device, trick; loophole, escape clause, **qualification**.

**escaper**, runaway; truant; fugitive, refugee; survivor.

**Adj. escaped**, flown; truant, fugitive, runaway; slippery, elusive; free, at large; relieved; exempt.

**Vb. escape**, find or win freedom, **achieve liberty**; make a getaway, break gaol; abscond, jump bail, flit, elope, skip, take French leave; make oneself scarce, beat a hasty retreat, **decamp**; slip through, break loose, get free; **emerge**; secure an acquittal, go scot-free; scrape through, survive, **be exempt**; find relief, **be relieved**; leak. **elude**, evade, welsh, abscond, dodge, **avoid**; lie low, **lurk**; escape notice, be found to be missing, **be absent**.

## 663 Deliverance

**N. deliverance**, delivery, **extraction**; riddance, **relief**; emancipation, **liberation**; rescue; salvage, **restoration**; salvation, redemption; divine function; ransom, **purchase**; release, amnesty; discharge, reprieve, **acquittal**; day of grace, respite, **delay**; truce, standstill, **cessation**; **escape**; dispensation.

**Adj. extricable.**

**Vb. deliver**, save, rescue, throw a lifeline; **extract**; extricate, **unravel**; untie, **disunite**, **disencumber**; **relieve**; release, unlock; emancipate, free, set free, set at large, **liberate**; **acquit**; deliver oneself, **escape**; save oneself; redeem, ransom, **purchase**; salvage, retrieve, recover, bring back, **restore**; spare, excuse, **exempt**.

**Int.** to the rescue! all hands to the pump! help!

## 664 Preparation

**N. preparation**, making ready; clearance; preliminary step, priming; preliminary course, trial run, trial, **experiment**; practice, rehearsal, brief; training, **teaching**; **beginning**; study, prep, homework, **learning**; spadework, **labour**; groundwork, foundation, **basis**; scaffold, scaffolding, **frame**; rough sketch, first draft, outline, blueprint, scheme, **plan**; shadow cabinet, shadow factory; arrangement; **advice**; forethought, **foresight**; bottom drawer, nest egg, **store**.

**fitting out**, logistics, **provision**; appointment, commission, equipment, array, armament; promotion; **debut**.

**maturation**; seasoning; hatching, gestation, incubation, sitting; nursing, nurture; cultivation, tillage, **agriculture**; bloom; fruition.

**preparedness**, readiness, maturity; puberty; fitness, shipshape condition; height of training, pitch of perfection, **perfection**.

**preparer**, coach, pioneer, **precursor**; packer, stevedore, fitter; **provider**; cultivator, planter, **farmer**; brewer, cook, **cookery**.

**Adj. preparatory**; preliminary, preceding; provisional, stopgap; hatching; forthcoming, **impending**; learning, **studious**.

**prepared**, ready, alert, **vigilant**; made ready; all set, ready to go; qualified, practised, at concert pitch, word-perfect; **informed**; tight, snug; armed, fully armed, armed at all points; well-appointed, provided; ready to hand; operational.

**matured**, ripe, mellow, mature; tried, experienced, veteran, **expert**; adult, grown, fledged, **grown-up**; flowering; well-done; wrought; deep-laid.

**ready-made**, ready to use; instant.

**Vb. prepare**, take steps; make ready, bridge, pioneer, **come before**; predispose, incline; **cultivate**; set to work, address oneself to, **begin**; sketch, outline, blueprint, **plan**; plot, concert, prearrange, **predetermine**; forearm, guard against, insure, **seek safety**; anticipate, **expect**.

**make ready**, ready, stow, pack, **store**; commission, tune, adjust, **arrange**; array, **bring together**; set, cock, prime, load; raise steam, crank; equip, crew, man; fit, furnish, dress; arm, provide with arms, provide with teeth, **provide**; improvise; rehearse, drill, groom, exercise, **train**; inure, acclimatize; coach, brief, **inform**.

**mature**, mellow, ripen, bring to fruition, **perfect**; force, invigorate; bring to a head, **climax**; stew, brew, **cook**; hatch, incubate, breed, **breed stock**; grow, farm, **cultivate**; nurse, nurture; elaborate, **carry through**; season, weather, smoke, dry, cure; temper, season, **harden**.

**prepare oneself**, qualify oneself, serve an apprenticeship; study, brief oneself; train, exercise, rehearse, practise, **learn**; shoulder arms; be prepared, stand ready.

Adv. **in preparation**; on the stocks.

## 665 Nonpreparation

N. **nonpreparation**, lack of preparation; potluck; lack of training, want of practice; disqualification; crudity; neglect; rush; **haste**; impromptu, snap answer; surprise, **lack of expectation**.

**undevelopment**; state of nature, native state, virgin soil; raw material, rough diamond; late developer; rough copy; embryo, abortion.

Adj. **unprepared**, backward, behindhand, **late**; makeshift; without preparation, ad lib, impromptu, snap, **spontaneous**; unstudied, **artless**; rash, careless, **negligent**; rush, **hasty**; unguarded, **vulnerable**; caught unawares; shiftless, improvident, thoughtless, happy-go-lucky; scratch; unpractised; fallow, virgin, **unused**.

**immature**, green; callow; adolescent, juvenile, girlish, **young**; undeveloped, half-baked, raw, **imperfect**; backward, **late**; unborn, rudimentary, **beginning**; roughhewn, uncut; before time, premature, abortive; apprentice, undergraduate, **unskilled**; crude, coarse, rude, savage, **artless**; forced, precocious.

**uncooked**, raw, red, rare, underdone; half-baked, cold; undressed; indigestible, inedible, **tough**.

**unequipped**, undressed; **deficient**; unqualified.

Vb. **be unprepared**, lack preparation, **be incomplete**; lie fallow, rust, **deteriorate**; want practice, need training; offer potluck, **improvise**; let tomorrow take care of itself; be premature, **be early**; catch unawares, **surprise**.

Adv. **unreadily**, extempore, off-hand.

## 666 Attempt

N. **attempt**, essay, bid; step, move, gambit, **deed**; endeavour, struggle, strain, effort; tackle, try, some attempt; good try, valiant effort; best effort, best one can do; random effort; determined effort, set, **attack**; trial, probation, **experiment**; go at, shot at, stab at, jab at, crack at, whack at, bash at; first attempt, first go, first shot, first offence, **debut**; final attempt, last bid, last throw; venture, adventure, quest, operation, exercise, **undertaking**; aim, goal, **objective**; high endeavour.

**trier**; fighter, **contender**; idealist, **perfectionist**; activist; undertaker, contractor, entrepreneur, jobber.

Adj. **attempting**, willing; game, **resolute**; searching; tentative; ambitious, venturesome, daring, **enterprising**.

Vb. **attempt**, essay, try; seek to, aim, **intend**; seek, **search**; offer, bid, make an attempt, make shift to, do something about; endeavour, struggle, strive, try hard, **be resolute**; exert oneself; pull hard, strain, sweat, **work**; tackle, have a go, give it a try, give it a whirl, have a shot at, have a crack at, have a stab at, **undertake**; make a go of; take a chance, tempt providence, venture, speculate, **gamble**; test, make trial of, **experiment**; fly a kite, **be tentative**; be ambitious, attempt too much, **fail**.

Int. Here goes!

## 667 Undertaking

N. **undertaking**, job, task, assignment; self-imposed task, labour of love, pilgrimage, **voluntary work**; contract, engagement, obligation, **promise**; operation, exercise; programme, project, design, **plan**; tall order, big undertaking, **hard task**; enterprise; quest, search, adventure, **enquiry**;

venture; occupation, **business**; struggle, effort, campaign, **attempt**.

**Adj. enterprising**, adventurous, venturesome, daring; go-ahead, progressive; alive to opportunity; ambitious; **rash**; responsible.

**Vb. undertake**, apply oneself to; tackle, **attempt**; go about; set forward, set going, **initiate**; proceed to, fall to, set to, buckle to, **begin**; **be courageous**; assume responsibility, take charge of, **manage**; execute; **busy oneself**; assume an obligation, **incur a duty**; engage to, commit oneself, **promise**; get involved, volunteer, **be willing**; **be busy**; show enterprise, pioneer; venture, dare, **face danger**; apprentice oneself, **prepare oneself**.

## 668 Use

**N. use**, disposal, **possession**; employment, application, appliance; exercise, **practice**; resort, recourse; mode of use, treatment, good usage, proper treatment; hard usage, wrong use, **misuse**; effect of use, wear; exhaustion, consumption, **waste**; reuse; benefit, service, **good policy**, utility; office, purpose, point, **function**; long use, wont, **habit**.

**Adj. used**, applied; worn, threadbare, second-hand, dog-eared, well-worn, **dilapidated**; beaten, **known**; hackneyed, stale; practical, utilitarian, **advisable**; makeshift, provisional; subservient, **instrumental**; available, employable, convertible, **useful**; disposable.

**Vb. use**, employ, exercise, practise; apply, exert, bring to bear, administer; give to, consecrate to, dedicate to; assign to, allot (see **dispose of**); make use of, convert, convert to use, **find useful**; reuse, recycle, exploit; milk, drain, **extract**; put to good use, turn to account, use to advantage, make hay with; make play with; make a tool or handle of; take advantage of; put to use, wear, consume, **waste**; handle, thumb, **touch**; tread, follow, beat (a path); work, drive, manipulate, **operate**; wield, ply, brandish; overwork, tax, task, **fatigue**; mould, **form**.

**avail oneself of**, adopt, try; resort to, have recourse to; make do with.

**dispose of**, command; control; allot, assign, **apportion**; spare, requisition; set going, deploy, **motivate**; enjoy, **possess**; consume, expend, absorb, **waste**.

## 669 Nonuse

**N. nonuse**, abeyance, suspension, **inaction**; **absence**; unemployment; forbearance, abstinence; savings, **store**; disuse, superannuation; waiver, surrender; cancellation; write-off.

**Adj. unused**, **absent**; useless; **inexpedient**; reserved; spare, extra; untapped, lying idle or fallow; **new**; left to rot; unnecessary, redundant; free, vacant; unemployed, idle.

**disused**, derelict, cast-off; done with; retired; obsolete, **antiquated**.

**Vb. not use**, abstain, forbear, do without, **avoid**; dispense with, waive, **relinquish**; overlook, disregard, **neglect**; spare, save, reserve, **store**; decline, **reject**.

**stop using**, disuse, **cease**; outgrow; leave to rust, dismantle, **make useless**; have done with, lay aside; discard, dump, ditch, scrap; jettison, throw overboard, **eject**; slough off; relinquish, resign; suspend, withdraw, cancel, **abrogate**; discharge, make redundant, **dismiss**; drop, supersede, replace, **substitute**; be unused, rust, **deteriorate**.

**670 Misuse**

N. **misuse**, abuse, wrong use; maladministration; malpractice; perversion; prostitution; **impiety**; pollution; **waste**; force, **violence**; outrage, injury, evil.

Vb. **misuse**, abuse; put to bad use, misdirect; divert, manipulate, misappropriate, **defraud**; violate, desecrate, **profane**; prostitute, **pervert**; pollute, **make unclean**; do violence to, **force**; strain, **distort**; take advantage of, exploit, **use**; manhandle, knock about, **ill-treat**; maltreat, **oppress**; misgovern, misrule, mishandle, mismanage; overwork, overtax, **fatigue**; work hard, **impair**; squander, **waste**; misapply, use a sledgehammer to crack a nut, **waste effort**.

**671 Action**

N. **action**, doing, performance; steps, move, **policy**; commission; execution, accomplishment; procedure, routine, **practice**; behaviour, **conduct**; movement, play, swing, **motion**; operation, working, evolution, **agency**; force, pressure, **influence**; work, labour; drama, **activity**; occupation, **business**; manufacture, **production**; employment, **use**; effort, endeavour, campaign, crusade, **attempt**; **management**.

**deed**, act, action, exploit, feat, achievement, **prowess**; bad deed, crime, **foul play**; stunt, **ostentation**; gesture, measure, step, move, **policy**; manoeuvre, evolution, **tactics**; stroke, blow, coup; job, task, operation, exercise, **undertaking**; proceeding, deal, doings; work, handiwork, workmanship, **skill**; **masterpiece**; drama, scene; acts, **narrative**.

**doer**, man or woman of action, activist, **busy person**; practical person; hero,

brave person; practitioner, **expert**; stunt man or woman, player, **actor**; performer; criminal; operator, **agent**; contractor, undertaker, entrepreneur; executor, executive, administrator, manager, **director**; hand, workman, operative, **worker**; craftsman, **artisan**; creative worker, **artist**.

Adj. **doing**, acting, red-handed; working, at work, **operative**; industrious, busy, **active**; **habitual**.

Vb. **do**, act, perform; **operate**; **influence**; manipulate, **motivate**; use tactics, twist, turn, manoeuvre, **be cunning**; do something, lift a finger; proceed, proceed with, get going, move, take action, take steps, try, **attempt**; tackle, **undertake**; adopt a measure, enact, legislate, **make legal**; perpetrate, commit, achieve, accomplish, complete, **carry through**; take care of, execute, implement, fulfil; observe; make history, win renown, **have a reputation**; practise, exercise, discharge, prosecute, pursue, wage, ply, employ oneself, **busy oneself**; officiate, **function**; transact, proceed, **do business**; administer, manage, control, **direct**; have to do with, **deal with**; sweat, labour, campaign, **work**; exploit, use; intervene, **aid**; **participate**; **meddle**; conduct oneself, **behave**; play about, lark around, **be absurd**; stunt.

Adv. **in the act**, redhanded; while one is about it.

**672 Inaction**

N. **inaction**, nothing doing, inertia, inability to act; failure to act, neglect; abstention; passive resistance, **defiance**; suspension, abeyance; deadlock, stalemate, **stop**; **insensibility**; passivity, vegetation, doldrums, quiet, calm; **leisure**; rest, **repose**; unemployment; sinecure; Fabian policy, **delay**;

lack of progress; defeatism.

**Adj. nonactive**, inoperative, idle; passive, dull, sluggish, **inert**; **leisurely**; Fabian; **hopeless**; stationary, motionless, immobile, **quiescent**; cold, extinct; without a sign of life, **dead**; unemployed, without employment, **unused**; incapable of action, **impotent**; benumbed, **insensible**; apathetic, phlegmatic, **impassive**; neutral, **indifferent**; **deaf**.

**Vb. not act**, hang fire; refrain, abstain, **avoid**; **watch**; **wait**; procrastinate; let it rip, let things take their course, let well alone; stay neutral, **be indifferent**; do nothing, tolerate, turn a blind eye, **disregard**; sit tight, **be inert**; drift, slide, coast; **despair**; let pass, leave alone, give it a miss, **neglect**; stay still, keep quiet, **be quiescent**; sit back, relax, **repose**; **be useless**; have nothing to do, **have leisure**; pause, desist, **cease**; rust, lie idle, lie fallow; lie dead, **die**.

**Adv. without action**, without movement; nothing doing.

## 673 Activity

**N. activity**, **action**; interest; social activity; **motive**; movement, **sedition**; life, stir, **motion**; alacrity; readiness; expedition, **velocity**; spurt, burst, fit, **spasm**; hurry, flurry, hustle, bustle, frantic haste, **haste**; fuss, bother, ado, to-do, tumult, frenzy, **turmoil**; whirl, scramble, rat race, maelstrom, **vortex**; drama, great doings, much ado, thick of things; plenty to do, **business**; press of business; pressure of work; high street, heavy traffic; press; hum, hive, hive of industry, **workshop**.

**restlessness**, fiddling, aimless activity, **inattention**; fever, fret, **frenzy**; enthusiasm, ardour, fervour, abandon, **warm feeling**; vigour, energy,

enterprise, initiative, push, drive, go, pep; spirit, animation, vitality, **life**; insomnia.

**assiduity**, application, concentration, **attention**; industry, drudgery, **labour**; determination, **resolution**; painstaking.

**overactivity**, excess; displacement activity, **lost labour**; **commotion**; interference; intrigue, **plot**.

**busy person**, zealot, fanatic, **obstinate person**; hard worker, **worker**; factotum, housewife, drudge, dogsbody, fag, slave, Trojan; horse, beaver, ant, bee; eager beaver; busy bee, workhorse; man or woman of action, activist, militant, **doer**; sharp fellow, live wire, dynamo, go-getter, pusher.

**meddler**, stirrer, officious person, spoilsport, busybody, **inquisitive person**; **adviser**; fusspot, nuisance.

**Adj. active**, stirring, **moving**; going, working, incessant; expeditious, **businesslike**; able, able-bodied, **strong**; quick, brisk, nippy, spry, smart, **speedy**; nimble, tripping; energetic, forceful, **vigorous**; up-and-coming, **enterprising**; frisky, coltish, dashing, sprightly, spirited, mettlesome, live, vivacious, **lively**; eager, ardent, **fervent**; fierce, desperate, **resolute**; zealous, prompt, instant, ready, **willing**; awake, alert, watchful, wakeful, **vigilant**; sleepless, restless, feverish, fretful, fidgety, jumpy, fussy, nervy; frantic; **excitable**; involved; aggressive, militant, **warlike**.

**busy**, lively, eventful; stirring, astir; afoot; hard at work, hard at it, fully engaged; at work.

**industrious**, studious, sedulous, assiduous; **laborious**; unflagging, tireless, indefatigable; efficient, workmanlike, **businesslike**.

**meddling**, officious, pushy, intrusive.

**Vb. be active**, show interest, trouble oneself, **participate**; be stirring, stir, move; run riot, **rampage**; rouse oneself; hum, thrive, **prosper**; make progress, **progress**; keep moving; push, shove, thrust, drive, **impel**; be vigorous; rush, surge, **flow**; roar, rage, bluster, **blow**; explode, burst, **be violent**; dash, fly, run, **move fast**; **attempt**; take pains, be attentive; buckle to, **exert oneself**; persist, **persevere**; make short work of; jump to it, show zeal, make things hum, **do**; burn with zeal, **be willing**; anticipate, wake, watch, **be careful**; assert oneself, react, show fight, **defy**; protest, agitate, demonstrate, **deprecate**.

**be busy**, busy oneself; bustle, hurry, scurry, hasten; go all ways at once; **waste effort**; rise early, go to bed late; fuss, fret, fume, **be excitable**; have other things to do, have other fish to fry, **be engaged**; slave, slog, **work**; overwork, overdo it, make work, make heavy weather of, never stop; affect zeal, **be affected**.

**meddle**, interpose, intervene, interfere, be officious; **intrude**; pester, bother, dun, annoy, **trouble**; be bossy, boss, boss one around, **oppress**; tinker, touch, **impair**.

**Adv. actively**; full tilt, whole hog.

**Int.** Wakey wakey! rise and shine! shake a leg! get going!

**674 Inactivity**

**N. inactivity**, inaction; inertia, torpor, lull, suspension, **cessation**; slack period, doldrums, grave, morgue; rust; slump, recession, **decrease**; unemployment, shutdown, absenteeism; **delay**; **leisure**.

**sluggishness**, lethargy, sloth; slow progress; **weakness**; languor, moral

insensibility; stupor, torpor, **insensibility**; apathy; phlegm; **submission**.

**sleepiness, fatigue**; tired eyes; **fantasy**.

**sleep**, slumber, kip; deep sleep; drowse; light sleep, nap, catnap, shut-eye, snooze, doze, siesta, **repose**; winter sleep; coma, trance, hypnosis, **insensibility**; somnambulism; sleepy sickness, **disease**; gate of ivory; Land of Nod; cot, cradle, pillow, bed.

**soporific**, nightcap, sedative, barbiturate; opiate, poppy, opium, morphine, **anaesthetic**; lullaby.

**idler**, drone, slacker, clock-watcher; sleepyhead; **slowcoach**; hobo, bum, tramp, **wanderer**; mendicant, **beggar**; parasite; layabout, good-for-nothing, ne'er-do-well, wastrel; drifter; dummy, passenger, absentee landlord; idle rich; dreamer, sleeper; dormouse, hedgehog; Rip van Winkle.

**Adj. inactive**, motionless, stationary, at a standstill, still, extinct, **quiescent**; inanimate, lifeless, **inert**; torpid, benumbed, unconscious, **insensible**; sluggish, stiff, rusty; listless, lackadaisical, **dejected**; tired, faint, languid; dull, heavy, leaden, stolid, **impassive**; supine, submissive; uninterested; apathetic, **indifferent**; absent; idle, empty, **leisurely**.

**lazy**, slothful, sluggish, work-shy, indolent, idle, bone-idle; **leisurely**; slow; tardy, dilatory, **late**; slack, remiss, careless, **negligent**.

**sleepy**, tired, somnolent, stupid with sleep; drowsy, dozy, groggy; asleep, fast asleep; unconscious, dormant, comatose.

**soporific**, sedative.

**Vb. be inactive**, do nothing, rust, stagnate, vegetate, smoulder, hang fire; delay; take it easy, let things go, **be neglectful**; hang about, **wait**; slouch, lag, loiter, dawdle, dally, **be late**;

stand, sit, lie, lollop, loll, lounge, laze, rest, take it easy, **repose**; slack, skive, shirk, **avoid**; sit around; have nothing to do, loaf, idle; waste time, trifle, dabbie, fiddle-faddle, piddle, potter, putter, **waste effort**; come to a standstill, **decelerate**; dilly-dally, hesitate, **be uncertain**; droop, faint, fail, languish, slacken, **come to rest**; slump, **decrease**; be still, **be quiescent**; discontinue, stop, come to an end, **cease**; strike.

**sleep**, slumber, snooze, nap, catnap; hibernate; sleep well, sleep like a log, sleep like a top, sleep like a little child; dream; snore; go to sleep, fall asleep, take a nap, have a kip; feel sleepy, yawn, nod, doze, drowse; go to bed; roost, perch.

**make inactive**, put to sleep, put to bed; send to sleep, lull, rock, cradle; soothe, **assuage**; deaden, paralyse, dope, drug, **render insensible**; stiffen, cramp, **fetter**; dismantle, **make useless**; **dismiss**.

## 675 Haste

N. **haste**, hurry, scurry, hustle, bustle, flurry, whirl, scramble, **activity**; flap, flutter, fidget, fuss; rush, rush job; feverish haste, race against time; immediacy; push, drive, expedition, **velocity**; acceleration, forced march, dash, **spurt**; inability to wait.

Adj. **hasty**, impetuous, impulsive, **rash**; feverish, impatient, ardent, **fervent**; boisterous, furious, **violent**; precipitate, breathless, breakneck, **speedy**; expeditious, prompt, without delay; making speed; hotfoot, running, racing; unable to wait; hurried, slapdash, cursory, **negligent**; forced, rush; urgent, immediate, **important**.

Vb. **hasten**, expedite; urge, drive, spur, goad, whip, lash, flog, **incite**; rush; be hasty, be precipitate, **be rash**; haste, make haste; post, race, run, **move fast**; overtake, **outstrip**; spurt, dash, make a forced march, **accelerate**; hurry, scurry, hustle, bustle, fret, fume, fidget, **be active**; act without ceremony, brush aside; rush through, dash through, make short work of; work against time or to a deadline; **be late**; make every minute count; make oneself scarce, **decamp**.

Adv. **hastily**, helter-skelter, pell-mell, feverishly, post-haste, apace; with all haste, at short notice; immediately.

Int. hurry up! be quick! buck up! look lively! look sharp! get a move on! get a wiggle on! step on it! quick march! at the double!

## 676 Leisure

N. **leisure**, spare time, convenience; time to kill; sinecure; holiday, break, vacation, leave, furlough; time to spare, ample time; rest, ease, relaxation, **repose**; **resignation**.

Adj. **leisurely**, deliberate, **slow**; at any odd moment; at leisure; at a loose end, at ease; retired.

Vb. **have leisure**, have time enough, have plenty of time, have time to spare; spend, pass; want something to do; take a holiday, **repose**; retire, **resign**; save labour.

## 677 Exertion

N. **exertion**, effort, struggle, **attempt**; strain, stress; tug, pull, stretch, heave, lift, throw; drive, force, pressure, applied energy, **energy**; ergonomics; ado, trouble; muscle, elbow grease; pains, taking pains; overwork; extra work, overtime; battle, campaign, fray.

**exercise**, practice, drill, training, workout, **preparation**; physical education, PE, keeping fit, constitutional; gymnastics, **athletics**; yoga; games, sports, **sport**.

**labour**, industry, work, long haul; spadework, donkeywork; manual labour; housework, daily grind, toil, drudgery, slavery, sweat, fag, grind, strain, treadmill, grindstone; hack work; bull; penal work, hard labour, **penalty**, forced labour, **compulsion**; fatigue, fatigue duty, **duty**; piecework, homework, outwork; task, chore, job, operation, exercise, **deed**; shift, trick, stint, stretch, bout, spell of work, **period**; job of work; working life, working day.

**Adj. labouring**, born to toil; working, hard at it, **busy**, laborious, **industrious**; strenuous, energetic, **active**; painstaking, thorough, **attentive**; taking exercise; athletic.

**laborious**, full of labour; killing; gruelling, punishing; troublesome, weary, wearisome, painful, burdensome; heroic, Herculean; arduous, hard, warm, heavy, uphill, **difficult**; thorough, painstaking; elaborate, artificial; fiddling; **useless**.

**Vb. exert oneself**, apply oneself, make an effort, try, **attempt**; struggle, strain, strive, sweat blood; trouble oneself, bestir oneself; turn every stone, do all one can; strain every nerve, do all one can; strain every nerve, use every muscle, **be active**; **be willing**; drive through, hammer at, slog at, **persevere**; battle, campaign, take action, **do**.

**work**, labour, toil, drudge, fag, grind, slog, sweat; sweat blood; pull, haul, tug, shove, hump, heave; dig, spade, lumber; set about, set to, **begin**; keep at it, plod, **persevere**; work hard, work overtime, moonlight, work double shift, **be busy**; slave, work like a galley slave, work like a horse, work like a Trojan; work oneself to death; overdo it, make work; serve, **minister to**; put to work, overwork, task, tax, **fatigue**.

**Adv. laboriously**.

## 678 Repose

**N. repose**, rest; ease, comfort, **euphoria**; sweet sleep, **sleep**; relaxation, breathing space, breather, **refreshment**; pause, respite, recess, break, **lull**; interval, **interim**; holiday, vacation, leave, furlough, sabbatical year, **leisure**; day of rest, Sabbath, Lord's day.

**Adj. reposeful**, restful; carefree, casual, at ease, **content**; snug, **comfortable**; peaceful, quiet, **tranquil**; sabbatical, holiday, **leisurely**.

**Vb. repose**, rest, take a rest, take it easy, sit back; recline, loll, lounge, laze, sprawl, **be horizontal**; perch, roost; couch, go to bed, go to sleep, **sleep**; relax, unwind, unbend, forget work; breathe, take a breather; **come to rest**; take a holiday, **have leisure**.

**Adv. at rest**.

## 679 Fatigue

**N. fatigue**, languor, lethargy; physical fatigue; mental fatigue; distress; limit of endurance, exhaustion, collapse; strain; hard breathing, **respiration**; faint, swoon, blackout, **insensibility**.

**Adj. fatigued**, tired, **sleepy**; spent, done, fagged; stupid with fatigue, dull, stale; strained; dog-tired, tired to death, ready to drop, dead beat, beat, whacked, knackered, more dead than alive, prostrate; stiff, sore, footsore; haggard, worn, faint, languid; still tired; tired of; jaded.

**panting**, breathless.

**fatiguing**, gruelling, punishing, **labori-**

ous; tiresome, wearisome; wearing, exacting, demanding; irksome, **tedious**.

Vb. **be fatigued**, overdo it; get weary, gasp, pant, puff, blow, grunt, **breathe**; languish, droop, drop, sink, flag, fail, **be weak**; stagger, faint, swoon, feel giddy; yawn, nod, drowse, **sleep**; succumb, drop, collapse; must have a rest; overwork, get stale, need a rest, need a break, need a change, need a holiday.

**fatigue**, tire, wear, exhaust, fag, whack, prostrate; wind; demand too much, task, tax, strain, work, drive, overdrive, flog, overwork, overtax; enervate, drain, distress, harass, irk, jade, **trouble**; tire to death, weary, bore, send to sleep, **be tedious**.

## 680 Refreshment

N. **refreshment**, breather, breath of air, **repose**; break, recess, **lull**; recreation, **restoration**; **revival**; **relief**; **stimulant**; refreshments, **food**; wash.

Adj. **refreshing**, cool, **cold**; bracing, recreational, **restorative**.

**refreshed**

Vb. **refresh**, clean; air, fan, ventilate, **aerate**; shade, cool, **refrigerate**; brace, stimulate, **invigorate**; recruit, recreate, revive, reanimate, recuperate, **restore**; ease, **relieve**; allow rest, give a breather; offer food, **feed**.

**be refreshed**, breathe, draw breath; respire; come to; revive; renew oneself, take a breather; have a change, have a rest, **repose**.

## 681 Agent

N. **agent**, operator, actor, performer, player, practitioner; **doer**; minister, tool, **instrument**; functionary, **officer**, representative, **delegate**; spokesman, **deputy**; proxy, **substitute**; executor,

executive, administrator, dealer; middleman, **merchant**; employer, industrialist, **producer**.

**worker**, **volunteer**; social worker, **philanthropist**; independent worker, freelance, self-employed person; drudge, dogsbody, fag, hack; menial, factotum, domestic servant, **servant**; beast of burden, **slave**; ant, beaver, **busy person**; professional person, business man, business woman, breadwinner, wage slave, employee; brain worker, boffin; clerical worker, girl Friday, man Friday; shop assistant, **seller**; charwoman, dustman, **cleaner**; labourer, farm worker, **farmer**; working man or woman, working girl, workman, hand, operative, factory worker, factory hand; navvy, roadman; plate-layer; docker, stevedore, packer; porter, coolie.

**artisan**, artificer, tradesman, technician; master, **proficient person**; journeyman, apprentice; craftsman or - woman, potter, turner, joiner, carpenter, cooper; wheelwright; shipwright; architect, master mason, mason, bricklayer, plasterer, painter, decorator; forger, smith, blacksmith, goldsmith, silversmith, gunsmith, locksmith; tinker; collier; miner; mechanic, machinist, fitter; engineer; plumber, electrician; weaver, spinner; tailor, cutter, needlewoman; jeweller; glass-blower.

**personnel**, staff, force, company, gang, squad, crew, complement, cadre, **band**; **actor**; mate, colleague, associate, partner, **colleague**; men, payroll; labour, labour pool, labour force, manpower, proletariat.

## 682 Workshop

N. **workshop**, studio; study, library; laboratory, plant, installation; works, factory; workshop, yard; sweatshop; mill, loom; sawmill, paper mill; foundry; steelworks; blast furnace, forge, smithy, **furnace**; power station, gasworks, **energy**; quarry, mine, **store**; colliery, coalmine, pit, coalface; tin mine; mint; arsenal, armoury; dockyard, shipyard; wharf, dock, **stable**; refinery, distillery, brewery; shop, bench, production line; nursery, **farm**; dairy, **stock farm**; kitchen, laundry; office, bureau, business house, firm, company; offices, secretariat, Whitehall; hive of industry, **activity**.

### 683 Conduct

N. **conduct**, behaviour, deportment; bearing, carriage, port; demeanour, attitude, posture, **mien**; aspect, look, **appearance**; tone, tone of voice, delivery, **voice**; motion, action, **gesture**; mode of behaviour, fashion, style; manner, guise, air; poise, dignity, presence; good manners, **courtesy**; bad manners, **discourtesy**; pose, **affectation**; mental attitude, outlook, **opinion**; mood, **feeling**; good behaviour, **virtue**; misconduct; democratic behaviour, common touch; past behaviour, record, history; reward of conduct, deserts; way of life, morals, principles, customs, manners, **habit**; line of action, **policy**; career, course, race, walk, walk of life, **vocation**; observance, routine, **practice**; procedure, process, method, **way**; treatment, direction, **management**; velvet glove; jackboot, iron hand; **deed**; behaviourism.

**tactics**, strategy, campaign, programme, **plan**; line, **policy**; political science, politics, realpolitik; gamesmanship, one-upmanship, **cunning**; **skill**; **advantage**; **delay**; manoeuvre, shift; move, gambit, **deed**; game, **strat-**

**agem**.

Adj. **behaving**; psychological; political, **businesslike**.

Vb. **behave**, act, do; behave well, **be virtuous**; behave badly, misbehave, **be wicked**; deserve well of, deserve ill of; gesture, **gesticulate**; posture, pose, affect, **be affected**; conduct oneself, set an example, lead a good life, **be active**; **participate**; pursue, busy oneself; follow a course; **be free**; employ tactics, manoeuvre, jockey, twist, turn; behave towards, treat.

**deal with**, have to do with, **do**; handle, manipulate, **operate**; conduct, run, **manage**; see to, cope with; transact, enact, execute, carry through; **plan**; work at, work through, **work**; go through, read, **study**.

### 684 Management

N. **management**, conduct, running; agency, **commission**; care, charge, control, **authority**; oversight, **surveillance**; patronage, **protection**; art of management, tact, way with, **skill**; business management, work study, operational research; **policy**; housekeeping, husbandry, economics, political economy; government; regimen, regime, dispensation; regulation, **legislation**; ministry, cabinet, staff work; bureaucracy, civil service; secretariat, government office, **workshop**.

**directorship**, direction, responsibility, control, **command**; dictatorship, leadership; guidance, steerage; pole star, lodestar, **guide**; helm, rudder, wheel, tiller, joystick; needle, compass, binnacle; **sailing aid**; beam, radar, **direction**; remote control.

Adj. **directing**, leading; directional; **authoritative**; **authoritarian**; managerial; executive, administrative;

legislative; high-level, **important**; economic, political; official.

**Vb. manage**, manipulate, manoeuvre, **influence**; **know**; handle, conduct, run; minister, administer, prescribe; supervise, superintend, oversee, **invigilate**; nurse, **look after**; have charge of, **motivate** (see **direct**); keep order, police, regulate; legislate, **make legal**; control, govern, sway, **rule**; know how to manage, have a way with.

**direct**, lead, pioneer, precede, **come before**; boss, dictate, **command**; hold office, hold a responsible position, have responsibility; mastermind, have overall responsibility; **incur a duty**; preside; head, captain, skipper; stroke; pilot, cox, steer, **navigate**; point, **point to**; **indicate**; shepherd, guide, conduct; introduce; escort, **accompany**; channel, funnel; route, train, lead, lead through.

**Adv. in control.**

## 685 Director

**N. director, governor**; cabinet, **council**; board, chair; staff, brass, management; manager; employer, capitalist, boss, **master**; headman, chief, head of state, **superior**; principal, head, rector, moderator, dean, vice-chancellor, chancellor; president, chairman, speaker; premier, prime minister; captain, skipper; stroke, cox, master, **mariner**; steersman, helmsman, **navigator**; pilot, guide; forerunner, **precursor**; drill sergeant; **teacher**; **adviser**; king-maker; **influence**.

**leader**, judge (Old Testament), **governor**; messiah; spearhead, centre forward; shepherd, drover, **herdsman**; pacemaker; toastmaster, MC; high priest; conductor, first violin; drum major; **autocrat**; ringleader, demagogue, **agitator**; captain.

**manager**, responsible person; key person, kingpin, **bigwig**; administrator, executive, executor, **doer**; statesman or -woman, politician; housekeeper, housewife; steward, bailiff, farm manager, reeve; agent, factor, **consignee**; superintendent, inspector, foreman or -woman, gaffer; warden, house master or mistress, matron, nurse, tutor, **protector**; disciplinarian; party manager, whip; custodian, caretaker, curator, librarian, **keeper**; huntsman; circus manager, ringmaster.

**official**, tin god; marshal, steward; shop steward; government servant, **servant**; officer of state, high official, vizier, minister, secretary of state, secretary-general, secretary, bureaucrat, Eurocrat, mandarin, **officer**; judicial officer, magistrate, **position of authority**; commissioner, prefect; consul, proconsul, praetor; first secretary, counsellor, **envoy**; alderman, mayor, **councillor**; functionary, party official, clerk; school prefect, monitor.

## 686 Advice

**N. advice**, counsel; words of wisdom, **wisdom**; therapy; criticism, **estimate**; moral injunction, prescription, **precept**; caution, **warning**; recommendation, proposition, proposal, motion, **supposition**; suggestion, submission; tip, **hint**; guidance, instruction, **information**; charge, **legal trial**; taking counsel, deliberation, huddle, powwow, parley, **conference**; reference, **council**; advice against.

**adviser**, counsellor, consultant, troubleshooter; professional consultant, **expert**; referee, arbiter; advocate, prompter; medical adviser, therapist, **doctor**; legal adviser, counsel, **lawyer**;

guide, mentor, **teacher**; monitor; Nestor, Dutch uncle; oracle, wise man, **sage**; busybody; committee of enquiry, **council**.

**Adj. advising**, advisory; hortative; warning, **cautionary**; didactic; moral.

**Vb. advise**, give advice, counsel, think best, recommend, prescribe, advocate, commend; propose, move, put to, submit, suggest, **propound**; prompt, **hint**; press, urge, exhort, **incite**; advise against, **dissuade**; admonish, **warn**; enjoin, charge, dictate, **command**; **be expedient**.

**consult**, seek advice; hold a public enquiry; take advice, listen to; accept advice, follow advice, advise with, hold a council of war, deliberate, parley, sit round a table, **confer**.

## 687 Council

**N. council**, council board, round table; council chamber, board room; Star Chamber, court, **tribunal**; Privy Council; Curia; vestry; cabinet, panel, quango, think tank, board, Royal Commission; congregation, **assembly**; convocation, **synod**; convention, congress, meeting, summit; durbar, diet; moot; federal council, Security Council; municipal council, soviet; sitting, session, audience, hearing, **conference**.

**parliament**, Upper House, House of Lords, another place'; Lower House, House of Commons; senate; legislative assembly; National Assembly; Supreme Soviet; Congress, Senate; quorum, division.

**councillor**, privy councillor; senator; peer, life peer; Lords Spiritual; representative, deputy, congressman or -woman, member of Parliament, MP, **delegate**; lobby fodder; parliamentarian; municipal councillor, mayor,

alderman, **official**.

**Adj. parliamentary**.

## 688 Precept

**N. precept**, firm advice, **advice**; direction, instruction, injunction, charge, **command**; commission, **mandate**; order, writ, **warrant**; prescription, ordinance, regulation, **decree**; canon, form, norm, formula, rubric; **rule**; principle, rule, moral, **maxim**; recipe, receipt, **remedy**; commandment, statute, act, code, **legislation**; tenet, article, constitution; ticket, party line; canon law, **law**; rule of custom, convention, **practice**; technicality, nice point; precedent, leading case, text, **example**.

**Adj. preceptive**, mandatory, binding; statutory, **legal**; customary, conventional, **usual**.

## 689 Skill

**N. skill**; grace, style; address; ease, **facility**; competence; faculty, capability, capacity, **ability**; all-round capacity; touch, grip, control; mastership, prowess, **goodness**; strong point, forte, major suit; attainment, accomplishment; experience, expertise, professionalism; technology, science, know-how, technique, technical knowledge, **knowledge**; practical ability; art, artistry, delicacy, fine workmanship; finish, execution, **perfection**; craft, **cunning**; worldly wisdom; finesse, tact, discretion, **discrimination**; feat of skill, trick, gimmick, dodge; tightrope walking; **tactics**; skilful use, **use**.

**aptitude**, innate ability; bent, **tendency**; faculty, gift, flair; turn, knack; talent, genius; fitness, qualification.

**masterpiece**, a beauty; magnum opus; workmanlike job, stroke of genius, masterstroke, feat, exploit, hat trick, **deed**; ace, trump, clincher; work of art, curio.

**Adj. skilful**, good, good at, top-flight, first-rate, **excellent**; crack; apt, handy, dexterous, ambidextrous, deft, slick, adroit, agile, nimble, neat; sure-footed; cunning, clever, quick, shrewd, smart, ingenious; politic, **wise**; adaptable, flexible, resourceful, ready; many-sided, versatile; sound, able, competent, efficient; wizard, masterful, masterly, like a master, magisterial, accomplished, finished, **perfect**.

**gifted**.

**expert**, experienced, veteran, tried; practised, **prepared**; finished; proficient, qualified, competent; efficient, professional, businesslike.

**well-made**; deep-laid; finished; happy; artistic, artificial, sophisticated, stylish, **elegant**; cunning; shipshape, workmanlike.

**Vb. be skilful**, be good at, do well, **be good**; shine, excel, **be superior**; show aptitude; know just when to stop; exploit, **use**; take advantage of; get round, **be wise**; exercise discretion, **discriminate**.

**be expert**, turn professional; qualify oneself, **learn**; have experience, be an old hand, know backwards, **know**; play with, demonstrate, stunt.

**Adv. skilfully**, well, with skill, like a master; like a machine; naturally.

## 690 Unskilfulness

**N. unskilfulness**, want of skill; lack of practice; inexperience, **ignorance**; inability; disqualification; **pretension**; booby prize, wooden spoon.

**bungling**, travesty; bungle, botch, dog's breakfast, shambles; poor performance, poor show, bad job, flop, fail-

ure; fumble, muff, fluff, miss, slice, bosh shot, overthrow, misfire, own goal, **mistake**; **inattention**; **misuse**; misrule, maladministration; misconduct, antics; much ado about nothing, **lost labour**.

**Adj. unskilful**; stick-in-the-mud; inept; unable, incapable, **impotent**; incompetent, inefficient, ineffectual; impolitic, stupid, foolish; thoughtless; wild, giddy, happy-go-lucky; feckless, futile; inadequate, **insufficient**.

**unskilled**, raw, green, undeveloped, **immature**; unqualified, inexpert, scratch, ignorant, unversed; ham, lay, amateurish, amateur; unsound, charlatan, quack; specious, pretentious, **affected**.

**clumsy**, awkward, gauche, uncouth, **discourteous**; maladroit; left-handed; ungainly, hulking, gangling; stiff, rusty, **unused**; unaccustomed, unpractised; slapdash, **negligent**; tentative; graceless, **inelegant**; top-heavy, lop-sided, **unequal**; cumbersome, ponderous, ungainly, **unwieldy**; **inexact**.

**bungled**, badly done, faulty, **imperfect**; ill-advised; unhappy, infelicitous; crude, amateurish, home-made, **artless**; slapdash, superficial, perfunctory; half-baked.

**Vb. be unskilful**; tinker; catch a Tartar; mishandle, mismanage, misconduct, misrule, misgovern; misapply, **misuse**; misdirect, **blunder**, forget; ham, overact, underact; go rusty; come a cropper, come unstuck, **fail**; be nervous.

**act foolishly**, make a fool of oneself, **be absurd**; become an object lesson; **lose a chance**, **blunder**; **waste effort**.

**be clumsy**, lumber, bumble, hulk; trip, stumble, blunder; stutter, **stammer**; fumble, grope, flounder, **be tentative**; muff, fluff; pull, slice; overthrow, overshoot, **overstep**; give a catch, give a chance; spill, slop, drop, drop a catch, drop a sitter, **let fall**; catch a crab; bungle, drop a brick, **blunder**; botch, spoil, mar, blot, **impair**; fool with, **meddle**; make a mess of it, make a hash of it, **miscarry**; do a bad job, make a poor fist at, **fail**.

## 691 Proficient person

N. **proficient person**, sound player, expert, adept, dab hand; handyman, **paragon**; Renaissance man; master, graduate; intellectual, mastermind, **sage**; genius, wizard, **prodigy**; magician; maestro, virtuoso; **musician**; first fiddle, champion, black belt, ace; white hope; crack shot, acrobat, gymnast, **athlete**.

**expert**, practitioner, professional, pro, specialist, authority, doyen, professor, **teacher**; pundit, savant, **scholar**; veteran, old hand, old soldier, sea dog; practised hand, practised eye; knowing person, smart customer, cunning fellow; sharp, **trickster**; cosmopolitan, man or woman about town, career woman; tactician, politician; artist, craftsman or -woman; technician, **artisan**; experienced hand, key man or -woman; consultant, **adviser**; boffin; connoisseur, fancier.

## 692 Bungler

N. **bungler**, failure, **loser**; incompetent; muff, butterfingers; lump, lout, clumsy clot, hulk, swab; duffer, stooge, clown, buffoon, booby, clot, clod, stick, oaf, ass, **fool**; slob, sloven, slattern, slut; scribbler, bad hand, bad shot; amateur, novice, greenhorn, colt, raw recruit, **beginner**; quack, **impostor**; landlubber, fair-weather sailor, horse marine; **misfit**.

## 693 Cunning

N. **cunning**, craft, **skill**; lore, **knowledge**; **imagination**; guile, gamesmanship, subtlety; stealth; chicanery, **foul play**; finesse; **deception**; **duplicity**; flattery; disguise; **tactics**; policy, diplomacy, realpolitik; underhand dealing, sharp practice; **influence**; intrigue, **plot**.

**stratagem**, ruse, art, artifice, resource, resort, device, wrinkle, ploy, shift, dodge; machination, game, **plot**; subterfuge; evasion; excuse, **pretext**; white lie; cheat, **deception**; trick; feint, catch, net, web, ambush, Trojan horse, **trap**; ditch, pit, **pitfall**; web of cunning, web of deceit; blind, flag of convenience, **sham**; manoeuvre, move, **tactics**.

**slyboots**, crafty fellow, wily person, serpent, snake, fox; fraud, hypocrite; cheat, **trickster**; glib tongue; tactician.

Adj. **cunning**, learned, knowledgeable, **wise**; crafty, artful, sly, wily, subtle, serpentine, foxy, feline; tricky; secret; Machiavellian; knowing, fly, slick, smart, sophisticated, urbane; canny, pawky, sharp, astute, shrewd, acute; cagey, **reticent**; experienced, **skilful**; resourceful, ingenious; deep-laid; insidious; shifty, slippery, **equivocal**; deceitful; crooked, devious, **dishonest**.

Vb. **be cunning**, try a ruse, finesse, shift, dodge; juggle, manoeuvre, jockey, double-cross, twist, turn, **wriggle**; lie low, **lurk**; intrigue, scheme, play a deep game, spin a web, weave a plot, have an axe to grind, **plot**; contrive, wangle, devise, **plan**; monkey about with, tinker, gerrymander; circumvent, overreach, pull a fast one, trick, cheat, **deceive**; blarney, **flatter**; outsmart, outwit, go one better, know a trick worth two of that, **outdo**;

waylay, undermine, **ambush**.
Adv. **cunningly**.

## 694 Artlessness

N. artlessness, simplicity; inexperience;
candour; truth, **probity**; *ignorance*;
vulgarity, crudity, **bad taste**.

ingenue, ingenuous person; child of
nature, savage; lamb, **innocent**; **ninny**;
greenhorn, novice, **beginner**; rough
diamond, plain man, Philistine;
simple soul, pure heart; provincial,
yokel, rustic, country cousin.

Adj. artless, without art, without artifice; unstudied; **simple**, unvarnished,
**plain**; native, natural, homespun,
homemade; **unskilled**; wild, savage,
primitive, backward, **ignorant**; unsophisticated, ingenuous, childlike,
**innocent**; born yesterday, simple-
minded, callow; guileless, confiding;
unaffected, unreserved, uninhibited,
**spontaneous**; candid, frank, open,
straightforward, **veracious**; single,
true, honest, sincere, **honourable**;
above-board; blunt, outspoken; transparent; prosaic, matter-of-fact, literal,
**accurate**; shy, inarticulate, unassuming, unpretentious, **modest**; Philistine;
tone-deaf, **deaf**; uncouth, **vulgar**; **ill-
bred**.

Vb. be artless, be innocent; eschew artifice; confide; call a spade a spade,
**speak plainly**; **be truthful**.

Adv. **artlessly**, without art, without
affectation; openly, with an open
heart.

## 695 Difficulty

N. difficulty, hardness; nonstarter;
perplexity; complication; inconvenience, embarrassment; drag, friction,
rough ground, hard going, bad patch,
**roughness**; quagmire, slough, **marsh**;
knot, **coil**; problem, crux, hard nut to

crack, poser, teaser, puzzle, headache;
handicap, obstacle, snag, rub, **hindrance**; **hitch**; maze, crooked path,
**convolution**; cul-de-sac, dead end,
impasse, blank wall, **closure**; deadlock, standstill, stoppage, **stop**; stress,
brunt, burden, **fatigue**; trial, ordeal,
temptation, tribulation, **suffering**;
trouble, **adversity**; difficult person,
handful; hot potato.

hard task, test, trial of strength; Herculean task; task, job, hard row to
hoe; handful, tall order, tough assignment, stiff job, hard work, uphill
struggle, **labour**.

predicament, embarrassment, false position, delicate situation; nonplus,
quandary, dilemma, cleft stick; borderline case; catch-22 situation; fix,
jam, hole, scrape, hot water, trouble,
fine kettle of fish, pickle, stew,
imbroglio, mess, muddle; pinch,
strait, straits, pass, slippery slope,
sticky wicket, tight corner, ticklish
situation, hot seat, **danger**; critical
situation, exigency, emergency; **crisis**.

Adj. difficult, hard, tough, formidable;
steep, arduous, uphill; inconvenient,
onerous, burdensome, irksome,
**laborious**; exacting, demanding; big,
insuperable, impracticable, **impossible**; offering a problem, problematic,
more easily said than done; delicate,
ticklish, tricky; awkward, unwieldy,
hard to cope with; intractable, refractory, **disobedient**; stubborn, perverse,
**obstinate**; naughty, **wicked**; clueless,
obscure; knotty, complex, complicated, inextricable, **intricate**; impenetrable, impassable, trackless; thorny,
rugged, craggy, **rough**; sticky, critical.

in difficulties; clueless, **suffering**; hard
pressed, hard put to it; at bay; stuck,

stuck fast, aground.

**Vb. be difficult**, make things difficult; complicate, **bedevil**, inconvenience, bother, irk, plague, lead one a merry dance, **trouble**; set one a problem, pose, perplex, baffle, nonplus, stump, **puzzle**; encumber, clog, hamper, obstruct, **hinder**; make things worse, **aggravate**; lead to an impasse, create deadlock, **make impossible**; go hard with, run one hard, **endanger**.

**be in difficulty**, have a problem; **be tentative**; have more than one can cope with, **be busy**; be at a loss, **be uncertain**; be put to it, be put to trouble, have trouble with; strike a bad patch; cop it, catch a packet, catch a Tartar; have a hard time of it, **have trouble**; suffer; have more than enough; invite difficulty, make a problem of, make heavy weather of, flounder; stick, come unstuck, **miscarry**; swim upstream, struggle, fight, **contend**; have to face it, **face danger**.

**Adv. with difficulty**, with much ado, hardly; uphill; despite; at a pinch.

**696 Facility**

**N. facility**, ease, convenience, comfort; capability, capacity, **possibility**; making easy, **liberation**; free hand, full play, full scope, clean slate, **scope**; facilities, **aid**; leave, **permission**; simplicity; straightforwardness; easy going; fair wind, clear coast, clear road, **opportunity**; straight road, highway, primrose path, **road**; downhill, **descent**.

**easy thing**, a pleasure; soft option, short work, light work, cushy number, sinecure; picnic, doddle, **amusement**; chickenfeed, piece of cake; easy money, fast buck; smooth sailing, easy ride; nothing to it, sitter, easy target, sitting duck; easy meat, soft touch; pushover, walkover, **victory**; cinch, sure thing, dead cert, **certainty**.

**Adj. easy**, facile, cushy; effortless, painless; light, short; **smooth**; **simple**; foolproof; easily done; feasible, **possible**; helpful; downhill, downstream; convenient, **comfortable**; approachable, within reach, **accessible**; open to all, **open**; **intelligible**.

**tractable**, manageable, easy-going, **willing**; submissive; yielding, malleable, ductile, **flexible**; handy, manoeuvrable.

**facilitated**, made easy; light; unfettered, unrestrained; given a chance; at home, quite at home, at ease, **comfortable**.

**Vb. be easy**; be open to all; have a simple answer, **be intelligible**; run well, go like clockwork.

**do easily**; make nothing of, make light of, make short work of; carry all before one, win at a canter, have a walkover, **win**; sail home; be at ease, be at home, take to like a duck to water; take it easy; **submit**; spare effort, save oneself trouble.

**facilitate**, ease, make easy; smooth; grease, oil, **lubricate**; explain, simplify, **interpret**; enable, **empower**; leave it open, allow, **permit**; give a chance to, **make possible**; help, speed, expedite, **aid**; pioneer, blaze a trail, **come before**; give full play to, leave open, leave a loophole, **give scope**.

**disencumber**, free, liberate, **deliver**; clear, weed, **clean**; cut through red tape; disengage, disentangle, extricate, **unravel**; untie, **disunite**; **cut**; ease, lighten, unload, unburden, alleviate, obviate, **relieve**.

**Adv. easily**, readily, like clockwork; swimmingly; without difficulty, just like that; without a hitch, without let or hindrance, freely.

**697 Hindrance**

**N.** hindrance, rub; fixation, hangup, block; blockage, **closure**; blockade, siege, **attack**; control, squeeze, **restraint**; arrest, **detention**; check; drag, friction; interference; sabotage, **opposition**; countermeasure, lockout; defence, **resistance**; disincentive; hostility, **disapprobation**; blacking, boycott; prophylaxis, sanitation, **hygiene**; birth control, **contraception**; ban, embargo, **prohibition**; nuisance value.

obstacle, hindrance, nuisance, drawback, inconvenience, handicap, **difficulty**; bunker, **hazard**; bottleneck, blockage, road block, traffic jam; a hindrance, tie, tether, **bond**; previous engagement; red tape; snag, block, stop, stymie; hurdle, hedge, ditch, moat; jump, barrier, bulkhead, wall, boom, dam, weir, embankment, **safeguard**; bulwark, breastplate, buffer, parapet, portcullis, barbed wire; fence, blockade; curtain, iron curtain, **partition**; stile, gate, turnstile, tollgate; crosswind, headwind, crosscurrent; impasse, deadlock, stalemate, vicious circle, catch-22; cul-de-sac, blind alley, dead end.

hitch, snag, catch, lightning strike, **strike**; repulse, rebuff, **refusal**; spot of trouble; technical hitch, breakdown, failure, engine trouble; puncture, flat; leak, burst pipe; fuse, short circuit; stoppage, holdup, setback, **stop**; something wrong, screw loose.

encumbrance, handicap, drag, clog, shackle, chain, **fetter**; baggage, lumber; cross, millstone, dead weight, **gravity**; pack, burden, load, overload, last straw; onus, incubus, mortgage, **debt**.

hinderer, hindrance; red herring; wet blanket, damper, spoilsport, killjoy; interceptor, fielder; filibuster; interloper; poltergeist, gremlin; **opponent**; rival, competitor, **contender**.

**Adj.** hindering, obstructive; cross, contrary, unfavourable, **adverse**; restrictive; prohibitive, preventive; prophylactic; off-putting; intrusive, obtrusive, **extraneous**; inconvenient, **inexpedient**; hard, rough, **difficult**; onerous, burdensome, **weighty**; tripping; disincentive; defensive.

hindered, waterlogged, cramped, overgrown; held back, stuck, becalmed, **restrained**; single-handed; stranded.

**Vb.** hinder, hamper, obstruct, impede; bother, annoy, inconvenience, **trouble**; embarrass, disconcert, upset, disorder, **derange**; trip; tangle, entangle, enmesh, **ensnare**; come between, intervene, interpose, **meddle**; intercept, undermine, nip, stifle, choke, gag, muzzle, **make mute**; suffocate, repress, **suppress**; quell, kill stone dead, **kill**; hamper, burden, encumber; press, **weigh**; load with, **load**; cramp, handicap, shackle, trammel, **fetter**; restrict, circumscribe, **limit**; check, brake, hold back, **restrain**; set one back, **retard**; lame, cripple, hobble, hamstring, paralyse, **disable**; scotch, wing, **wound**; discountenance, **shame**; intimidate, deter, **frighten**; discourage, dishearten, **dissuade**; mar, spoil, **impair**; damp; snub, rebuff, **refuse**.

obstruct, intervene, interpose, interfere, **meddle**; obtrude, **intrude**; stymie, snooker, **lie between**; buzz, jostle, crowd, squeeze; **follow**; stop, intercept, block, **close**; jam, jam tight, cause a stoppage, bring to a standstill; bandage, bind, **staunch**; dam; divert, **mislead**; parry; barricade, **enclose**;

fence, blockade, **circumscribe**; deny access, **exclude**; prevent, inhibit, ban, bar, **prohibit**.

**be obstructive**, give trouble, **be difficult**; stall; baffle, foil, stymie; counter, **counteract**; check, thwart, frustrate; object, **oppose**; interrupt, interject, heckle, barrack; refuse a hearing, **be loud**; take evasive action, **avoid**; filibuster, **be loquacious**; protract; strike, **halt**; picket, molest; sabotage.

## 698 Aid

**N. aid**, help, helping hand, lift, boost; succour, rescue, **deliverance**; comfort, support, backing; reinforcement; willing help, service, ministry, ministration, **kind act**; interest. good offices; custom, **purchase**; patronage, auspices, countenance, suffrage, favour, **protection**, **influence**; good will, charity, sympathy, **benevolence**; advocacy, championship; good advice, constructive criticism, **advice**; promotion, furtherance, advancement; nursing; first aid, **medical art**; relief, **refreshment**; preferential treatment, favourable conditions, favourable circumstances; fair wind, **propulsion**; facilities, magic carpet, magic wand, **facility**; self-help.

**subvention**, economic aid, monetary help; **gift**; charity, **philanthropy**; social security, benefit, loan, temporary accommodation, **credit**; subsidy, hand-out, bounty, grant, allowance, expense account; stipend, bursary, scholarship, **reward**; supplies, maintenance, support, keep, upkeep, **provision**; manna, **food**.

**aider**, help, assistant, lieutenant, henchman, aide, right-hand man, man Friday, stand-by, support, mainstay; tower of strength, rock, **protector**; district nurse, social worker, counsel-

lor, **adviser**; good neighbour, Good Samaritan; ally; reinforcements, **auxiliary**; **benefactor**; sponsor, **patron**; booster, friendly critic; factor, useful ingredient, **component**; springboard, **instrument**.

**Adj. aiding**, helpful, obliging; kind, well-disposed, well-intentioned; neighbourly, **friendly**; favourable, propitious; of service, of help, **useful**; constructive, well-meant; assistant, auxiliary, subsidiary, ancillary, accessory; contributory; subservient, **serving**; **instrumental**.

**Vb. aid**, help, assist, lend a hand, give a helping hand; give a lift to; spoonfeed; be kind to, do one a good turn; see one through; oblige, accommodate, lend money to, **lend**; facilitate, speed, lend wings to, further, advance, boost, **promote**; abet, instigate, foment, nourish, **induce**; contribute to, be accessory to; lend support to, bolster, **support**; comfort, sustain, hearten, give heart to, encourage, rally, embolden, **give courage**; succour, send help to, relieve, **deliver**; reinforce, fortify, **strengthen**; ease, refresh; **restore**.

**patronize**, favour, be auspicious; sponsor, back, guarantee; recommend; propose, second; countenance, give countenance to, connive at, protect, **safeguard**; join; contribute to, subscribe to, **endorse**; **befriend**; side with, champion, defend, **vote**; give moral support to, intercede; **defray**; entertain, keep, cherish, foster, nurse, mother, **pet**; **purchase**.

**minister to**, help, oblige, **serve**; give first aid to, nurse, **doctor**; squire, valet, mother; be of service to, make oneself useful to, **be useful**; **be willing**; toady, humour, **flatter**; slave, **work**; be assistant to, **be instrumental**.

**Adv. in aid of**; thanks to.

**699 Opposition**

N. **opposition**, antagonism, hostility, **enmity**; conflict, friction, lack of harmony, **dissension**; repugnance, **dislike**; denial; challenge; **defiance**; firm opposition, stand, **resistance**; **revolt**; going against, **disapprobation**; walkout, **dissent**; physical opposition, headwind, crosscurrent, **obstacle**; mutual opposition, tug of war; faction, competition; political opposition, underground, alternative society, **nonconformity**.

**opposites**; **contender**.

Adj. **opposing**; against; hostile, **inimical**; unfavourable, **adverse**; cross; **contrary**; cussed, bloody-minded, **obstinate**; refractory, recalcitrant, **disobedient**; at odds with; militant; facing, face to face, eyeball to eyeball, **frontal**; **opposite**; rival, jealous.

Vb. **oppose**, go against, be contrary; side against, **resist**; **reject**; object, kick, protest, protest against, **deprecate**; **collide**; vote against, **disapprove**; dissociate oneself; contradict, belie, **negate**; counter; work against, **counteract**; thwart, baffle, foil, be **obstructive**; challenge, dare, **defy**; set at naught, **hold cheap**; flout, **disobey**; rebuff, spurn; **refuse**; emulate, rival, match oneself with, compete with, bid against, **contend**; set against.

**withstand**, confront, face, **face danger**; rise against, **revolt**; meet, encounter, **fight**; struggle against, breast, stem; cope with, **be active**; **stand firm**; **resist**.

Adv. **in opposition**, against, versus; despite.

**700 Opponent**

N. **opponent**; adversary, antagonist, foe, **enemy**; assailant; opposite camp; independent party; diehard, irreconcilable; reactionary, counter-revolutionary; dissident, **malcontent**; agitator; rival, competitor, runner-up; fighter; entrant, **contender**; wrangler; common enemy, universal foe, outlaw.

**701 Cooperation**

N. **cooperation**; symbiosis; duet, double harness, tandem; joint effort; team work, working together, concerted effort; relay, relay race, team spirit; lack of friction, agreement, **concord**; party spirit; **inducement**; conspiracy, **plot**; complicity, sympathy; fraternity, solidarity, fellowship, freemasonry, fellow feeling, comradeship; common cause, helping one another; mutual concession, **compromise**; mutual advice, **conference**.

**association**, coming together; **joint possession**; pool, kitty; membership, affiliation; tie-up, **relation**; ecosystem; combination, **union**; solidarity, **whole**; **unity**; fusion, merger; voluntary association, coalition, alliance, league, federation, confederacy; axis, united front, **political party**; an association, fellowship, college, club, fraternity, **community**; set, clique, cell, **party**; trade union, chapel; business association, company, syndicate, combine, consortium, trust, cartel, ring, **corporation**; housing association, economic community, commune, **community**.

Adj. **cooperative**, helpful; married; bipartisan; federal, **corporate**.

Vb. **cooperate**, collaborate, work together; join forces, **participate**; show willing, play ball, reciprocate, respond; lend oneself to, espouse; take part; rally round, **aid**; hang together, stand shoulder to shoulder, sink or swim together; make common cause

with; network, band together, associate, league, ally; coalesce, merge, unite, **be mixed**; combine, make common cause, club together; understand one another, think alike; conspire, **plot**; **consult**; collude, connive; treat with, negotiate, **make terms**.
Adv. **cooperatively**.
Int. All together now!

**702 Auxiliary**
N. **auxiliary**, relay, recruit, fresh troops, reinforcement; second line, paramilitary formation; ally, assistant, helpmate, helping hand; right-hand man, second, tower of strength; adjutant, lieutenant, aide-de-camp; secretary, clerk; midwife; dogsbody, **servant**; server; best man, bridesmaid; **friend**; hanger-on, satellite, henchman, follower, **dependant**; disciple, adherent, **sectarian**; loyalist; stooge, puppet, **instrument**; shadow, familiar; jackal, running dog, creature.
**collaborator**; fellow traveller, fifth column, fifth columnist.
**colleague**, associate, fellow, brother, sister; partner; comrade, companion, playmate; alter ego, second self, faithful companion; mate, chum, pal, buddy, crony, **friend**; helpmate, better half, **spouse**; standby, stalwart; ally; accomplice, accessory.
**patron**, guardian angel, **protector**; well-wisher; champion, advocate, friend at court; supporter, sponsor, backer, guarantor; voter; aficionado, **fan**, **lover**; good friend, Jack at a pinch; rich uncle, **benefactor**; founder; patron of art, **collector**; customer, client.

**703 Party**
N. **party**, movement; group, class, **classification**; confession, com-

munion, denomination, church, **sect**; faction, cabal, cave, splinter group; circle, kitchen cabinet; set, clique; caucus, junta, politburo, committee; club, cell, cadre; ring, closed shop; team, eight, eleven, fifteen; crew, complement, **personnel**; troupe, company, **actor**; gang, knot, bunch, outfit, **band**; horde, **crowd**; side, camp.
**political party**, right, left, centre; Conservative, National Front; Labour; Greens; coalition, popular front, bloc; comrade, Red, commie, Trot; socialist, Fabian; rightist, true blue; leftist; populist, democrat; moderate; party worker, party member, politician; militant, activist, **doer**.
**society**, coalition, combination, combine, **association**; league, alliance, axis; federation, confederacy; economic association, union, EEC, Common Market, free trade area; private society, club, **focus**; secret society, Freemasonry, lodge, cell; friendly society; chapel; group, division, branch, youth movement, Cubs; fellow, associate, member; party member, comrade; corresponding member, affiliate, **component**.
**community**, fellowship, brotherhood, body, congregation, fraternity; guild; race, tribe, clan, sect, **family**; order, **classification**; social class, **social group**; state, **nation**.
**corporation**, body; incorporated society, body corporate, **council**; company, firm, concern; house, establishment, institute; trust, combine, monopoly, cartel, syndicate, conglomerate, **association**; trade association, chamber of commerce, guild.
Adj. **corporate**, incorporate; joint, bonded, federal; allied; social, **sociable**; fraternal, **friendly**; communal.

**sectional**, Masonic, **sectarian**; clannish, exclusive; class-conscious; rightist, true-blue; right of centre, leftist, pink, red; Tory; radical, conservative.

**Vb. join a party**, subscribe; join, become a member; **enter**; enter; belong to, make one of; side with, range oneself with; club together, associate, ally, league; cement a union, merge; found a party.

**Adv. in league**, shoulder to shoulder, back to back; all together.

**704 Dissension**

**N. dissension, dissent; opposition**; disharmony, dissonance, jar, jangle, **discord**; recrimination; odds, friction, tension; **resentment**; hostility, **hatred**; disunity, internal dissension; rift, cleavage, cleavage of opinion, separation; split, faction, **schism**; misunderstanding; breach, rupture, severance of relations; challenge, **defiance**; ultimatum, declaration of war, **war**.

**quarrelsomeness**; warlike behaviour; **defiance**; sharp tongue, **scurrility**; mischief, spite; apple of discord, spirit of mischief; Ate, Mars.

**quarrel**, feud, vendetta, **revenge**; war, **warfare**; strife; conflict, clash, **collision**; legal battle; controversy, dispute, wrangle; paper war, **argument**; wordy warfare, words, stormy exchange, altercation, set-to, abuse, **scurrility**; jar, spat, tiff, squabble, jangle, wrangle, hassle, squall; rumpus, hubbub, racket, row, commotion, scrimmage, fracas, brawl, fisticuffs, **turmoil**; gang warfare, riot, **fight**.

**casus belli**; tender spot, sore point; apple of discord, bone to pick; point at issue.

**quarreller**, wrangler; rival, **contender**;

scold, bitter tongue, **shrew**; aggressor.

**Adj. quarrelling, contrary**; at odds, at loggerheads, **inimical**; schismatic; rebellious, **disobedient**; sore; awkward, cantankerous, **irascible; sullen**; implacable; quarrelsome, bellicose, **warlike**; pugnacious, combative, aggressive, militant; abusive, shrewish, scurrilous; argumentative, contentious.

**Vb. quarrel**, disagree, **dissent**; clash, conflict, **collide**; misunderstand, pull different ways, have a bone to pick, **differ**; recriminate, **retaliate**; part company, split, break with; declare war, **go to war**; go to law, take it to court, **litigate**; dispute; have a feud with; sulk, **be sullen; oppose**.

**make quarrels**, pick a fight, start it; make something of it, challenge, **defy**; irritate, provoke, **enrage**; have a bone to pick, have a crow to pluck; cherish a feud, enjoy a quarrel; embroil, entangle, estrange, set at odds, **excite hate**; create discord, **discord**; sow dissension, make mischief, make trouble; divide, draw apart, disunite, come between, **sunder; aggravate**; set against, match with; incite, **motivate**.

**bicker**, spat, tiff, squabble; nag, jar, spar, spar with; jangle, wrangle, dispute with, **argue**; scold, **cuss**; have words with, row, row with; brawl, **rampage**.

**705 Concord**

**N. concord**, harmony, **melody**; unison, unity, duet, **agreement; consensus**; lack of friction, rapport; solidarity, team spirit; sympathy, fellow feeling, **love**; amity, **friendship**; rapprochement, reunion, reconciliation; good offices; happy family, **peace**; goodwill, honeymoon period.

**Adj. concordant**; eye to eye, unanimous, of one mind, bipartisan; compatible, united, bonded, allied; fraternal, loving, amicable, **friendly**; happy, peaceable, pacific, at peace, **peaceful**.

**Vb. concord; pacify**; agree, **accord**; see eye to eye, play a duet, pull together; reciprocate, respond, run parallel, **concur; be friendly**; remain at peace, **be at peace**.

**706 Defiance**

**N. defiance**, dare, daring, challenge, gauntlet; bold front, brave face, **courage**; war dance, war cry, war whoop, war song, battle cry, **threat**; display, **ostentation**.

**Adj. defiant**, challenging, provocative, bellicose, militant, **warlike**; saucy, **insolent**, rebellious, **disobedient**; greatly daring, **courageous**; stiffnecked, **proud**; reckless, triggerhappy, **rash**.

**Vb. defy**, challenge, **dissent**; oppose; caution, **warn**; demand satisfaction; dare, beard; brave; **face danger**; laugh to scorn, set at naught; **hold cheap**; bid defiance to; show fight, **threaten**; **be proud**; look big, show a bold front; wave a banner, **brandish**; march, demonstrate, stage a sit-in; **be insolent**; shout, **triumph**; crow, bluster, brag, **boast**.

**Adv. defiantly**.

**Int.** do your worst! come on if you dare!

**707 Attack**

**N. attack**, best method of defence; aggression, **injustice**; foul play; assault, grievous bodily harm, **violence**; armed attack, offensive, drive, push, thrust, pincer movement, tac-

tics; run at, dead set at; onslaught, onset, rush, shock, charge; sally, sortie, breakthrough; counterattack; shock tactics, surprise; invasion, incursion, irruption; raid, foray; blitz, air raid, air attack, night attack; storm; boarding; investment, siege, blockade, **surroundings**; challenge, tilt.

**terror tactics**, war of nerves; bloodbath, **slaughter**; **havoc**.

**bombardment**, cannonade, barrage, strafe, blitz; broadside, volley, salvo; fire, gunfire, fusillade, burst of fire; antiaircraft fire, flak.

**lunge**, thrust, pass; cut, stab, jab; bayonet, cold steel; punch, swipe, kick, **knock**.

**attacker**, assailant, aggressor; hawk, militant; spearhead, storm troops, strike force; fighter pilot, air ace, bomber, **armed force**; sharpshooter; raider.

**Adj. attacking**, pugnacious, combative, aggressive, **warlike**; militant, hostile, **inimical**; boarding.

**Vb. attack**; start a fight, declare war, **go to war**; assault, assail, make a dead set at, have at; savage, maul, draw blood, **wound**; let fly at, let one have it; surprise, blitz, overwhelm; invade, encroach; raid, foray, overrun, infest; show fight; counterattack, **retaliate**; thrust, push, impel; erupt, sally, make a sortie, break through, **emerge**; board, lay aboard; storm, carry, capture, **overmaster**; ravage, make havoc, scorch, burn, **lay waste**; harry, drive, beat, corner, bring to bay, **hunt**; challenge, **defy**; oppose; break a lance, **fight**.

**besiege**, lay siege to, invest, surround, blockade, **enclose**; sap, mine, undermine, spring a mine.

**strike at**; lay about one, swipe, flail,

hammer, **strike**, **kick**; go berserk, run amok, **be violent**; have at, have a fling at, fetch a blow, have a cut at; mug; clash, ram, **collide**; make a pass at, lunge; close with, come to close quarters, fight hand to hand; push, butt, thrust, poke at, thrust at; stab, spear, lance, bayonet, run through, **pierce**; strike home, lay low, abase; be **dishonest**.

charge, advance against; rush, mob, **rampage**; make a rush, rush at, run at, dash at, tilt at, ride full tilt at; ram, shock, **collide**.

fire at, shoot at; fire a shot at, take a potshot, pop at, snipe, **shoot**; torpedo, sink; strafe, bombard, blitz, cannonade, shell, fusillade, pepper; bomb, plaster; open fire, let fly, volley; rattle, blast, rake, straddle; take aim, level, **aim**.

lapidate, stone, throw a stone, heave a brick; shy, sling, pelt; hurl at, **propel**.

Adv. aggressively.

## 708 Defence

N. defence, self-defence, **resistance**; art of self-defence, boxing, **pugilism**; judo; counter, parry; posture of defence, guard; defensive alliance, balance of power; safekeeping, **preservation**; **protection**; a defence, rampart, bulwark, screen, buffer, fender, bumper, **safeguard**; deterrent, **weapon**; munitions, **ammunition**.

defences, lines, fieldwork; outwork; earthwork, embankment, mound; mole, boom; wall, barricade, fence, **barrier**; palisade, stockade; moat, ditch; trench, dugout; booby trap, **trap**; barbed wire; spike; Great Wall of China; bunker, **shelter**; barrage, antiaircraft fire, flak; barrage balloon; minefield, mine; smokescreen, screen.

fortification (see fort); bulwark, rampart, wall; parapet, loophole; scarp; curtain, bastion; outwork; buttress.

fort, fortress, stronghold, fastness; citadel, capital, **refuge**; castle, keep, ward, tower, turret, donjon; portcullis, drawbridge; gate, postern, sally port; peel, pillbox; blockhouse, strong point; Roman camp; British camp, **earthwork**.

armour, harness; full armour, panoply; mail, scale armour, armour plate; breastplate; cuirass; hauberk, coat of mail; helmet, helm; visor, beaver; siege cap, steel helmet, tin hat; bearskin, busby; gauntlet; shield, target; protective clothing, riot shield, gas mask, **safeguard**.

defender, champion; patron; loyalist, patriot; bodyguard, lifeguard, Praetorian Guard, **soldier**; watch, sentry; patrol, patrolman; garrison, picket, guard, escort, rearguard; Home Guard, militia, thin red line; fireman, firewatcher; Civil Defence; guardian, warden, **protector**; warder, custodian, **keeper**; **deliverance**.

Adj. defending; defensive, protective, antiaircraft.

defended, armoured; **prepared**; castellated; entrenched; defensible, proof, bulletproof, **invulnerable**.

Vb. defend, guard, protect, keep, watch, ward, **safeguard**; fence, hedge, moat, **circumscribe**; palisade, barricade, **enclose**; block, **obstruct**; cushion, pad, shield, curtain, cover, **screen**; cloak, **conceal**; provide with arms, arm, **make ready**; harness, armour, reinforce, fortify, **strengthen**; stand firm; garrison, man; champion, **vindicate**; rescue, **deliver**.

parry, counter, riposte, fence, fend, hold or keep at bay, keep at arm's length, avoid; turn, avert, **deflect**; play, play with; stall, block, **obstruct**; fight a defensive battle, stalemate; fight back, show fight, give a warm reception to, **resist**; repulse, **repel; withstand**; avail oneself of; **turn back**; survive, scrape through, live to fight another day, **escape**.

Adv. **defensively**, at bay.

## 709 Retaliation

N. **retaliation**, reprisal, **revenge**; requital, recompense, comeuppance, **reward**; desert, deserts; punitive action, retribution, Nemesis, **punishment**; reaction, boomerang, backlash, **recoil**; counter; counterattack, sally, sortie, **attack**; recrimination, riposte, retort, **rejoinder**; a game at which two can play; deterrent.

Adj. **retaliatory**; punitive; reciprocal.

Vb. **retaliate, recoup; punish**; counter, riposte, **parry**; make a requital, be quits, get even with, **avenge**; requite, reward; serve rightly, teach one a lesson; reciprocate; return, retort, cap, answer back, **answer**; recriminate, **accuse**; react, boomerang, **recoil**; kick back, **resist**; hoist one with his own petard.

be rightly served, serve one right; get what was coming to one.

Adv. **en revanche**.

Int. it serves you right! take that! **put that in your pipe and** smoke it! the laugh's on you! now who's laughing!

## 710 Resistance

N. **resistance**, stand, brave front, **opposition**; reluctance; repugnance, **dislike**; demur, **qualification**; protest; passive resistance; rising, insurrection, resistance movement, backlash, **revolt**; self-defence, **defence**; repulsion, repulse, rebuff, bloody nose,

refusal; refusal to work, **strike**.

Adj. **resisting**, standing firm against; reluctant; recalcitrant, **disobedient**; stubborn, **obstinate**; indomitable; tough, proof, bulletproof, waterproof; **repellent**.

Vb. **resist**, offer resistance, give a warm reception, stand against, **withstand**; obstruct, **hinder**; challenge, **defy**; confront, outface, **face danger**; struggle against, contend with, **oppose**; kick, protest, **deprecate**; demur, object, **qualify; cease**; engineer a strike, **halt**; mutiny, rise, **revolt**; make a stand, keep at arm's length, keep at bay, **parry**; make a fight of it, **contend**; **stand firm**; endure, **suffer**; be proof against, repel, rebuff, **refuse**; resist temptation; last, **outlast**.

Int. No surrender!

## 711 Contention

N. **contention**, strife, tussle, conflict, clash, running battle, **dissension**; combat, war, **warfare**; debate, dispute, controversy, polemics, paper warfare, **argument**; altercation, words, **quarrel**; stakes; competition, gamesmanship, rat race; cut-throat competition; sports, athletics, **sport**.

contest, trial, trial of strength, test of endurance, marathon, pentathlon, decathlon, tug-of-war; tussle, struggle, **attempt**; bitter struggle, needle match; equal contest, dingdong fight; close finish, **short distance**; competition, free-for-all; knockout competition, tournament; joust, tilt; prize competition, stakes; match, rally; event, handicap; heat, final, semifinal, quarterfinal, Cup tie; set, game, rubber; sporting event, wager, bet, **sport**; field day, **amusement**; Derby day (see **racing**); athletics, gymnastics; gymkhana, rodeo;

games, Highland Games; Lords, **arena**.

**racing**, speed contest, **speeding**; race, sprint, dash; road race, marathon; slalom, obstacle race; relay race, horse racing, sport of kings; point-to-point, steeplechase, sticks, **leap**; motor race, motor rally, speedway, motocross; cycle race; dog racing; boat race; regatta; racecourse, track, stadium, **arena**.

**pugilism**, noble art of self-defence, boxing, fisticuffs; boxing match, prizefight; mill, spar, clinch, in-fighting; round, bout; **sport**.

**wrestling**, judo, karate; catch, hold; wrestle.

**duel**, affair of honour; single combat, tournament; fencing, swordplay, quarterstaff; bullfight; cockfight; bullring, cockpit, lists; **arena**.

**fight**, hostilities, appeal to arms, **warfare**; battle royal, free fight, free-for-all, roughhouse, horseplay, scuffle, scrum, scrimmage, scramble, dogfight, fracas, uproar, rumpus, **turmoil**; gang warfare, street fight, riot, rumble; brawl, broil, **quarrel**; fisticuffs; affray, set-to, tussle; running fight, close quarters; combat, fray, clash, conflict, **collision**; encounter, dustup, scrap, brush; skirmish; engagement, action, stand-up fight, shoot-out, **battle**; deed of arms, **deed**; campaign, struggle, death struggle; field of battle, battlefield.

**contender**; fighter, gladiator, **combatant**; fencer, swordsman; candidate, entrant; competitor, rival; runner-up, finalist; front runner, favourite, top seed; starter, also-ran; runner, **athlete**.

**Adj. contending**, rival, racing; sporting; running; athletic; contentious, quarrelsome; irritable, **irascible**; aggress-

ive, combative, pugnacious, bellicose, **warlike**; at loggerheads, at odds, at war; keen, cutthroat; hand-to-hand, close, at close quarters; dingdong.

**Vb. contend**, combat, strive, struggle, battle, fight, tussle, wrestle, **attempt**; oppose, **resist**; make a point of, insist; contest, compete, challenge, stake, wager, bet; play, play against, match oneself, vie with, race, run a race; emulate, rival, **be jealous**; **outdo**; enter; tilt with, try a fall, **strike at**; have a hard fight, fight to a finish.

**fight**, have a fight, scuffle, row, scrimmage, scrap, set to, **be violent**; **attack**; lay about one, **strike at**; mix it; box, spar, pummel, jostle, hit, kick, scratch, bite, **strike**; fall foul of, join issue with, **quarrel**; duel; give satisfaction; encounter, have a brush with, skirmish; engage, **give battle**; come to close quarters, close with; fence, fight hand to hand, use cold steel; appeal to arms, **go to war**; combat, campaign, **wage war**; fight hard, **be resolute**.

## 712 Peace

**N. peace**, a quiet life; harmony, **concord**, piping times of peace; peacetime; universal peace; **order**; end of hostilities, **cessation**; truce, armistice, **lull**; **moderation**; cordial relations, **friendship**; pacifism, peace at any price, nonviolence; pipe of peace; league of peace, peace treaty, **treaty**; **amnesty**.

**pacifist**, man or woman of peace, dove; peace party, **moderator**; neutral, civilian, noncombatant; peacemaker, **mediator**.

**Adj. peaceful**, quiet, halcyon, **tranquil**; piping, **palmy**; without war, without bloodshed, bloodless; harmless, **innocent**; easy-going, **amiable**; peaceable, law-abiding, pacific; **pacifist**; unarmed, noncombatant, civilian;

passive, submissive; at peace; neutral; peacetime.

**Vb. be at peace**; be pacific, **be innocent**; avoid bloodshed; **mediate**.

**Adv. peacefully**; without violence.

## 713 War

**N. war**, arms; appeal to arms, undeclared war; paper war, **quarrel**; war of nerves, gunboat diplomacy; police action; real war, internecine war, war of revolution; holy war, crusade, jihad; aggressive war; limited war, major war, total war, atomic war, push-button war; war of attrition; chivalry; martial music, bugle, trumpet; call to arms, bugle call, **call**; battle cry, war whoop, war song, **defiance**; god of war, Mars.

**belligerency**, state of war, state of siege; resort to arms, declaration of hostilities; wartime, wartime conditions, time of war.

**bellicosity**, war fever; love of war, military spirit; militarism; jingoism, chauvinism, **prejudice**.

**art of war**, strategy, **tactics**, **fortification**; **skill**; ballistics; drill, training, **teaching**; logistics, **plan**; military experience, **knowledge**.

**war measures**, war footing, **preparation**; call to arms, clarion call, fiery cross, **call**; war effort, war work, call-up, national service, military duty; blackout.

**warfare**, war, warpath, making war, bloodshed, **violence**; active service; military service, **bombardment**; investment; aerial warfare, economic warfare, blockade, attrition; psychological warfare, propaganda; offensive warfare, **attack**; defensive warfare, **defence**; mobile warfare; campaign, expedition; incursion, invasion, raid; order, word of command, orders,

**command**; password, watchword; battle cry, slogan, **call**; plan of campaign, battle orders, **plan**.

**battle**, battle royal, **fight**; line of battle, array; line, front, battle station; armed conflict, action, scrap, skirmish, brush, collision, clash; offensive, blitz, **attack**; defensive battle, stand, **defence**; engagement, sea fight, dogfight; arena, battlefield, field of battle, theatre of war, area of hostilities.

**Adj. warring**; at war, militant; armed, **prepared**; embattled; engaged, at loggerheads.

**warlike**, bellicose; militant, aggressive, pugnacious, combative; fierce, **cruel**; bloodthirsty; military, paramilitary, martial, veteran; chivalrous; military, naval; operational.

**Vb. go to war**, resort to arms; declare war, open hostilities; appeal to arms, **fight**; take to arms, rise, rebel, **revolt**; call to arms; arm; recruit, conscript; enlist, take a commission.

**wage war**, march to war, war, war against; campaign; shoulder a musket, smell powder; soldier; invade, **attack**; **stand firm**; **defend**; manoeuvre, march; blockade, besiege, invest, **surround**; shed blood, **slaughter**; ravage, burn, scorch, **lay waste**; demolish.

**give battle**, battle, join battle; engage, provoke an engagement; combat, **fight**; take a position, rally, stand, resist; **charge**; open fire, **fire at**; skirmish, brush with, **contend**.

**Adv. at war**.

## 714 Pacification

**N. pacification**; appeasement, **moderation**; reconciliation, rapprochement; accommodation, **agreement**; compromise; good offices; convention, entente, understanding, peace treaty, SALT, **treaty**; suspension of hostilities, truce, armistice, cease-fire, **lull**; forced reconciliation, **compulsion**.

**peace offering, moderator**; appeasement; olive branch, overture, peaceful approach, hand of friendship; flag of truce, white flag, pipe of peace, **peace**; blood money, **restitution**; fair offer, easy terms, **moderation**; amnesty; mercy, **forgiveness**.

**Adj.** pacificatory; **friendly**; happy, content.

**Vb.** pacify, make peace, give peace to; allay, mollify, soothe, **assuage**; heal, **cure**; return a soft answer, coo like a dove, **be friendly**; conciliate, propitiate, **disarm**, reconcile, placate, appease, satisfy, **content**; **bring to rest**; restore harmony; bring to terms, meet halfway, **compromise**; accommodate, **adjust**; bring together, **mediate**; show mercy, **be lenient**; grant a truce, grant an armistice, grant peace, **give terms**; **be at peace**.

**make peace**, cry quits, **cease**; let bygones be bygones, **forget**; come to an understanding, agree to differ; make a truce, suspend hostilities, disarm.

## 715 Mediation

**N.** mediation, good offices; diplomacy; parley, **conference**.

**mediator**, common friend, middleman, matchmaker, go-between, **intermediary**; umpire, referee; representative, attorney, agent, **delegate**; peace party, **moderator**; troubleshooter, ombudsman; marriage guidance counsellor, **adviser**; peacemaker, dove.

**Adj.** mediatory. propitiatory.

**Vb.** mediate, intervene, **meddle**; put oneself between, interpose, **put between**; propitiate; be a go-between; bring together, negotiate; arbitrate, umpire,

judge; **pacify**.

## 716 Submission

**N.** submission; **servitude**; compliance, consent, **assent**; peace at any price, line of least resistance, resignation, fatalism; yielding, white flag, surrender; deference, humble submission, **humility**; act of submission, homage, **loyalty**; kowtow, **obeisance**; quitter; mouse, doormat, **coward**.

**Adj.** submitting, quiet, meek, law-abiding, **peaceful**; submissive, **obedient**; resigned, acquiescent; malleable, **soft**; weak-kneed; supine, prostrate; **humble**.

**Vb.** submit, yield; defer to; bow to, make a virtue of necessity, yield with a good grace, admit defeat; resign oneself, be resigned, **acquiesce**; accept, **assent**; **be indifferent**; withdraw, **turn back**; cease resistance, cry quits, have had enough, surrender; capitulate; yield oneself; renounce authority.

**knuckle under**, succumb, collapse; sag, wilt, faint, drop; be submissive, do homage, **be subject**; eat humble pie, eat dirt, **be humble**; take it, digest, stomach, **suffer**; bend, bow, kneel, kowtow, crouch, cringe, crawl, **stoop**; grovel; **ask mercy**.

## 717 Combatant. Army. Navy. Air Force

**N.** combatant, fighter, **contender**; aggressor, assailant; shock troops; warrior, brave; bodyguard; gunman, strongman man; bully, bravo, rough, rowdy, **ruffian**; swashbuckler; swordsman, fencer, sword, gladiator; **athlete**; toreador, matador, picador; competitor, **contender**; champion, champ; knight, **patron**; wrangler; barrister, advocate.

**pugilist**, pug, boxer, bruiser; flyweight,

bantamweight, featherweight, welter-weight, middleweight, heavyweight; **pugilism**.

**militarist**, militant, warmonger, hawk; Samurai; professional soldier, free-lance, mercenary (see **soldier**), soldier of fortune, adventurer; freebooter, pirate, privateer, buccaneer.

**soldier**, army man; military man, long-term soldier, regular; troops (see **armed force**); conquistador; old sol-dier, veteran; warrior, brave; man-at-arms, centurion; colour escort, colour sergeant, ensign, cornet; sharp-shooter; auxiliary, territorial, Home Guard; yeomanry, yeoman; irregular, irregular troops; raider, freedom fighter; underground fighter; **elite**, **protector** (see **armed force**); volun-teer; pressed man; conscript, recruit, rookie; serviceman, GI, Aussie, sepoy; woman soldier, female war-rior, Amazon; Wren, WRAC.

**soldiery**, cannon fodder; gallant com-pany, merry men, private, private sol-dier, man-at-arms; archer, bowman; lancer; musketeer, rifleman, grena-dier, bombardier, gunner; pioneer, sapper, miner, engineer; signalman; corporal, sergeant, lieutenant, **army officer**.

**army**, host, camp; phalanx, legion; horde, mass, **multitude**; warlike people, martial race; general levy; National Guard, militia; yeomanry; regular army, draft; armed forces, air arm, fleet air arm, fleet.

**armed force**, forces, troops, effectives, men, personnel; armament, armada; ceremonial troops, household troops; Household Cavalry; spearhead, expeditionary force, flying column; parachute troops, paratroops, com-mando, task force; combat troops, field army, line, first echelon; wing,

van, vanguard, rear, rearguard, centre, main body; second echelon, base troops, reinforcements, draft, levy, **auxiliary**; base, staff; detach-ment, picket, party, detail; patrol, night patrol, night watch, sentry, **pro-tector**; garrison, occupation troops, army of occupation.

**formation**, array, line; square, phalanx; legion, cohort, century; column, file, rank; unit, group, detachment, corps, division, brigade, artillery brigade, battery; regiment, squadron, troop; battalion, company, platoon, section, squad, detail, party, **band**.

**infantry**, foot regiment, foot soldier, foot; mountain infantry.

**cavalry**, yeomanry; heavy cavalry, horse, cavalry regiment; horseman, rider; horse artillery; horse soldier, yeoman; trooper; chivalry, knight; man-at-arms, lancer, hussar, dra-goon; armour, armoured car, armoured personnel carrier; tank, Panzer; charger.

**navy**, sea power, admiralty; sail; fleet arm, naval armament, armada; fleet, flotilla, squadron.

**naval man**, naval service, navy, senior service; admiral, Sea Lord, **naval offi-cer**; sailor, **mariner**; able seaman, rating, pressed man; powder monkey; cabin boy; gob, swab; marine, jolly, limey; submariner, **nautical person-nel**; Royal Navy, RN; Wavy Navy.

**warship**, war vessel, war galley, trireme, galleon, **ship**; raider, privateer, pirate ship; armoured vessel, capital ship, battleship; monitor; cruiser, frigate, corvette; mosquito boat, gunboat, motor torpedo boat; destroyer; fire ship; minelayer, minesweeper; sub-marine, U-boat; aircraft carrier, land-ing craft, duck, amphibian; transport, troopship; tender, store ship, flagship, flotilla leader.

**air force**; Royal Air Force Volunteer Reserve; air arm, flying corps, air service, fleet air arm; squadron, flight, group, wing; **aircraft**; battle plane, bomber, fighter, interceptor; flying boat, patrol plane, scout; transport plane; Zeppelin, captive balloon, **airship**; air troops, airborne division; parachute troops; aircraftman, ground staff; fighter pilot, navigator, air crew.

## 718 Arms

**N. arms** (see **weapon**); armament, munitions; arms race; nuclear deterrent; **defence**; arms traffic; ballistics, rocketry, archery.

**arsenal**, armoury, gun room, gun rack, ammunition chest; arms depot, **storage**; magazine, powder barrel, powder keg, powder flask, powder horn; caisson, ammunition box; cartridge belt; quiver; scabbard, sheath, holster, **receptacle**.

**weapon**, arm, deterrent; deadly weapon, armour, plate, mail, **defence**; offensive weapon, **attack**; conventional weapon, **warfare**; secret weapon, death ray, laser; germ warfare, gas, **poison**; natural weapon, teeth, **sharp point**.

**missile weapon**, javelin, harpoon, dart; lasso; boomerang; arrow, shaft, bolt, quarrel; arrowhead, barb; stone, brick, brickbat; shot, ball, bullet, pellet, shell, shrapnel, rocket, bow, longbow, crossbow, catapult, sling; blowpipe; bazooka, cruise missile, ICBM, **missile**.

**club**, mace, **hammer**; ram; bat, staff, stave, stick, switch, quarterstaff; bludgeon, truncheon, cudgel, sandbag, knuckle-duster, cosh, bicycle chain.

**spear**, harpoon, gaff; lance, javelin, pike, assegai; bill, halberd, **sharp point**.

**axe**, battleaxe, tomahawk, hatchet, halberd; bill; poleaxe, chopper, **sharp edge**.

**sidearms**, sword; cold steel, broadsword, claymore, two-edged sword, cutlass, hanger, short sword, swordstick; sabre, scimitar; blade; rapier, tuck; fencing sword, épée, foil; dagger, bayonet, dirk, poniard, dudgeon, stiletto, **sharp point**; machete; knife, **sharp edge**.

**firearm**, small arms, hand gun; flintlock, musket; blunderbuss; rifle; sporting gun, shotgun; bore, calibre; muzzle; trigger, lock; magazine; breech, butt; sight; ramrod.

**pistol**, six-shooter, colt, revolver, repeater, rod, automatic.

**gun**, ordnance, artillery, horse artillery; battery, broadside; artillery park, cannon, bombard, swivel, petard; mortar; piece, field piece, field gun, great gun, cannon royal, heavy metal; howitzer, trench gun; antiaircraft gun, ack-ack, bazooka; assault gun, pom-pom, Maxim, machine gun, flamethrower; caisson; rocket site, silo.

**ammunition**, live shot; round of ammunition, round; shot, buckshot; ball, cannonball, bullet, projectile, **missile**; slug, stone, pellet; shell, shrapnel; flak, ack-ack; wad, cartridge, spent cartridge, dud; cartridge belt, cartridge clip; cartridge case.

**explosive**; powder, gunpowder; saltpetre, high explosive, gun cotton, dynamite, gelignite, TNT; cap, detonator, fuse; priming, charge, warhead.

**bomb**, explosive device; shell, bombshell; grenade, pineapple; megaton bomb, A-bomb, H-bomb; mushroom cloud, fallout; blockbuster; cluster bomb, incendiary bomb, Greek fire;

mine, landmine, limpet; booby trap, **trap**; depth charge, torpedo, tin fish; flying bomb, V-1, V-2; rocket bomb; time bomb, infernal machine.

## 719 Arena
N. arena, field, field of action; ground, terrain; centre, scene, stage, theatre; hustings, platform, floor; amphitheatre, stadium, stand, grandstand; campus, parade ground, forum, **focus**; hippodrome, circus, course, racecourse, turf; track, ring, bullring, ropes; rink, gymnasium, gym; range; playground, beach, lido, pier, fairground, **pleasure ground**; recreation ground, pitch, court, bowling alley, lists; cockpit; bridge table; auction room; examination hall.

battleground, battlefield, field of battle; field of blood; theatre of war, combat zone; front, front line; sector, salient, bulge, pocket; beachhead, bridgehead; **battle**.

## 720 Completion
N. completion, finish, end; terminus, goal; issue, upshot, **event**; result, end product, **effect**; fulfilment, sufficiency; maturity, fruition, readiness, preparedness; culmination, perfection; **attention**; roofing; top, crown, superstructure, **summit**; missing link, **requirement**; last touch, last stroke, clincher; achievement, work done, last straw, **limit**; climax, payoff; resolution, solution, catastrophe, last act, final curtain, **finality**.

effectuation; execution, discharge; performance, **action**; accomplishment, achievement, **success**.
Adj. **completive**, perfective; topmost; conclusive, final, last, **ending**; thorough, thoroughgoing, **resolute**.
completed, full, full-blown, **complete**;

done, highly wrought, elaborate, **perfect**.
Vb. carry through; drive home, clinch, seal; dispose of; complete, consummate, **make complete**; elaborate, **perfect**; ripen, bring to a head, **mature**; get through, get shot of, dispose of, bring to its close, **terminate**; set at rest, **bring to rest**.
carry out, see through, effect, enact, **do**; execute, discharge, implement, effectuate, compass, bring about, accomplish, fulfil, consummate, achieve, **succeed**; make short work of.
climax, cap, crown all, **crown**; reach its peak; come to a crisis; touch bottom; come to its end, come to fruition, **arrive**; have enough of, be through with, **have enough**.

## 721 Noncompletion
N. noncompletion, failure; neglect; deficiency, deficit, **shortfall**; lack, **continuity**; **inattention**; work undone; lack of finality, drawn game; stalemate, deadlock.
Adj. uncompleted, partial, fragmentary, incomplete; undone; half-baked, underdone, **immature**; perfunctory; superficial; left hanging; lacking finish, inchoate, sketchy, **imperfect**; **continuous**.
Vb. not complete, hardly begin, leave undone, leave hanging, **neglect**; skip, scamp, tinker; **wound**; **fail**; defer, postpone.
Adv. on the stocks.

## 722 Success
N. success, glory; success all round, happy outcome, happy ending, favourable issue; success story, progress, steady advance, time well spent, **progression**; fresh advance, breakthrough; run of luck, good fortune;

advantage, lead, first blood, **advantage**; momentary success; exploit, feat, achievement, **deed**; accomplishment, goal; a success, triumph, hit, triumphant success; good hit, good shot, **skill**; lucky stroke, fluke; hat trick, stroke of genius, masterstroke, **masterpiece**; trump, trump card; pass, qualification.

victory, beating, **defeat**; conquest; attack; honours of battle; win; outright win, complete victory, checkmate; narrow win; easy win, runaway victory, love game, walkover, pushover, picnic, **easy thing**; slam, kill, knockout, KO; upper hand, advantage, edge, certain victory, **advantage**; stalemate, **draw**; celebration of victory, triumph, ovation, **celebration**.

victor, winner, champion, medallist, first; conquistador; beater; master, mistress; a success, self-made man or woman, man or woman to watch, rising star, **prosperous person**.

Adj. successful, effective, efficacious, efficient; sovereign, **remedial**; fruitful; happy, lucky; felicitous, masterly; **skilful**; surefire, foolproof; unerring, infallible, surefooted, **certain**; victorious, **excellent**; leading, **superior**; rising, sitting pretty, **prosperous**; triumphant; victorious, glorious.

unbeaten, unbowed, **resolute**; invincible.

Vb. succeed, effect, accomplish, achieve, compass, **carry through**; make a success of, make a go of, make short work of; make good, rise, do well, get promotion, **prosper**; pass, qualify, graduate, give a good account of oneself, **be superior**; advance, break through, make a breakthrough, **progress**; strive to some purpose; have a success, make a hit, make a kill; score a point, arrive, be a success, get

around, click.

be successful, be efficacious, be effective; answer; do oneself proud; compass, manage, **do**; work, act, work like magic, act like a charm, **operate**; take effect, tell, pull its weight, **influence**; bear fruit, **be fruitful**; get it, hit it; be surefooted; be irresistible, **do easily**; be resolute; avoid defeat, **stand firm**.

triumph, celebrate; crow, boast; score; contrive a success, manage, make it, win through; surmount; find a loophole, **escape**; make headway against, **resist**; gain.

overmaster, be superior; master, overcome, overpower, overthrow, overturn, override, **outdo**; prevail, **predominate**; checkmate, trump, ruff; conquer, vanquish, quell, subdue, subject, suppress, crush, **subjugate**; capture, carry, take, storm, **attack**.

defeat (see overmaster); discomfit, dash; repulse, rebuff, **repel**; confound, dismay, **frighten**; best, **be superior**; worst, outplay, outpoint, outflank, outmanoeuvre, outclass, **outdo**; disconcert, trip, **obstruct**; baffle, gravel, nonplus, **puzzle**; defeat easily; beat, lick, thrash, whip, trounce, swamp, overwhelm, crush, drub, trample underfoot; beat hollow, rout, put to flight, scatter, **disperse**; silence, **suppress**; flatten, crush; run hard, corner, check, **endanger**; put an end to, settle, fix, dish, **destroy**; sink, plunge; break, bankrupt, **impoverish**.

win, achieve victory, be victorious; carry all before one, romp home, have a walkover, **do easily**; scrape home, survive; become champion, **be superior**.

Adv. successfully, swimmingly; to some purpose, with good result, with good effect, beyond all expectation; with flying colours.

**723 Failure**

N.failure, lack of success, negative result; misfortune, hindrance; vain attempt, futile effort, lost labour, mess, muddle, bungle; abortion, miscarriage; hopeless failure, damp squib, washout, fiasco, flop; bosh shot, misfire, slip, mistake; dead stop, halt, stop; engine failure, electrical fault, breakdown, hitch; collapse, fall, stumble, trip, descent; weakness; anticlimax; loss.

defeat; nonplus, deadlock, stalemate, stop; lost battle, repulse, rebuff, bloody nose, check, reverse; checkmate, mate, beating, hiding, thrashing; retreat; flight, recession; stampede, panic, fear; rout, landslide; fall, downfall, collapse, wreck, perdition, graveyard, ruin; lost cause; deathblow, quietus; utter defeat, Waterloo; conquest.

loser; also-ran, nonstarter; has-been, extinct volcano; misery, dud, failure, flop, lemon; sacrifice, victim, prey, dupe; born loser; underdog, inferior; dropout, misfit; bankrupt, insolvent.

Adj.unsuccessful, ineffective, pale; inglorious, obscure, empty-handed; unfortunate; vain, negative, fruitless; dud, hanging fire; stillborn, abortive, premature; unplaced, failing; tripping, wandering, uncertain.

defeated, beaten, worsted; inferior; whacked; unplaced; scattered, put to flight; sunk, kaput, brought low, fallen; made a prey.

grounded, stranded; brought low; bankrupt.

Vb.fail; muddle, botch, bungle, blunder; flunk, be found wanting; fail one, disappoint; lose a chance; misdirect, go wide, miss, deviate; draw a blank, return empty-handed, waste effort; lose; overreach oneself, come a crop-

per, fall, collapse, slide, tumble; malfunction, come unstuck; falter, stall, seize; stop, come to a dead stop, come to a dead end; stick, cease; come to a sticky end, deteriorate; run aground, ground, sink, founder; make a loss, crash, bust, break, go bankrupt.

miscarry, be stillborn, abort; misfire, hang fire; fall, crash, tumble; come to naught, come to nothing, be useless; fail to succeed, fall flat, come to grief; burst, bust, explode; flop, prove a fiasco; go wrong, go amiss, go awry, take an ugly turn; make things worse, aggravate; disappoint.

be defeated, lose, suffer defeat, take a beating; just lose, just miss; fall, succumb, be subject; fall a prey to; retreat, lose ground, recede; take to flight; admit defeat, had enough, cry quits, submit; go downhill, deteriorate.

Adv.unsuccessfully.

**724 Trophy**

N.trophy, sign of success; war trophy, spoils, capture, booty; scalp, head; wound; memorial, memento; monument; triumph, ovation, celebration; plum; benefit, benefit match; prize, wooden spoon, reward; sports trophy, cup, pot, plate, shield; award, Golden Rose; laurels, crown, chaplet, garland, wreath, palm, palm of victory; favour, love token, badge; flying colours, ostentation; glory, repute.

decoration, honour, title; honours; citation; rosette, ribbon, sash; athletic honour, blue, oar; medal, gong, star, cross, garter, order; service stripe, VC, Iron Cross; Distinguished Service Cross, Medal of Honour; Legion of Honour, civic crown.

**725 Prosperity**

**N. prosperity**, success; well-being, welfare, weal; boom; roaring trade, favourable trade balance; luxury, Easy Street, **wealth**; golden touch, **plenty**; favour, godsend, **good**; bonanza, luck, break, **chance**; glory, renown, **prestige**.

**palmy days**, heyday, prime; summer, sunshine, fair weather, Indian summer, piping times, **peace**; easy times, clover, velvet, **euphoria**; golden times, Golden Age; expansive times, Elizabethan Age.

**prosperous person**, man or woman of substance, man or woman of property, **rich person**; rising man or woman; child of fortune, lucky fellow, lucky dog; upstart, profiteer; celebrity, hero, **person of repute**; lion, **favourite**.

**Adj. prosperous**; rising, doing well; well set-up, well-to-do, well-off, affluent, comfortable; fortunate, lucky; at ease, **happy**; fat, sleek.

**palmy**, balmy, halcyon, golden, rosy; piping, blessed; providential, favourable, promising, auspicious, propitious, clear, fine, fair, glorious, expansive; agreeable, cosy, **comfortable**.

**Vb. prosper**, thrive, flourish; do well, have a good time of it, **enjoy**; make hay, have it easy, have it made, 'never have had it so good'; grow fat, feed well, **eat**; blossom, bloom, flower, **be fruitful**; win glory, **have a reputation**; boom, drive a roaring trade; profiteer, **gain**; go far, make it, arrive, **succeed**; make money, make a fortune, strike it rich, **get rich**; keep afloat.

**have luck**, have a lucky break, have a run of luck; strike lucky, strike oil, strike a rich vein.

**be auspicious**, promise, promise well, augur well, set fair; favour, prosper,

profit, **benefit**; bless; water; take a good turn, **do good**; glorify, **honour**, **Adv. prosperously**, swimmingly.

**Int.** Good luck! all the best! best of British!

**726 Adversity**

**N. adversity**, adverse circumstances, misfortune, mixed blessing (see **misfortune**); continual struggle, weary way, **difficulty**; hardship, hard life, tough time, **suffering**; pain; bad times, iron age, evil; burden, load, pressure; **event**; worry; misery, dejection; bitter cup, bitter pill; cross, **sorrow**; curse, blight, blast, plague, scourge, visitation, **bane**; cold wind, draught, chill, cold, winter; gloom; ill wind, blow, **opposition**; setback, check, rebuff, reverse, **defeat**; rub, pinch, plight, funeral, **predicament**; poor lookout, trouble ahead; trough, bad patch, rainy day; slump, recession, depression; **threat**; decline, fall, downfall, **ruin**; broken fortune, want, need, distress, extremity, **poverty**.

**misfortune**, bad fortune, bad luck, hard luck; **failure**; evil dispensation, evil star, malign influence; hard case, raw deal, rotten hand; hard lot, hard fate, hard lines; ill hap, mishap, mischance, misadventure, accident, casualty, **chance**; disaster, calamity, catastrophe.

**unlucky person**, poor unfortunate, constant loser, poor risk; star-crossed lover, sport of fortune, plaything of fate, Jonah; down-and-out, **loser**; underdog, **inferior**; new poor, **poor person**; lame dog, lame duck, **weakling**; scapegoat, victim, wretch, **sufferer**; prey, **dupe**.

**Adj. adverse**, hostile, ominous, sinister, inauspicious, unfavourable; bleak, cold, hard; cross, thwart, contrary, untoward; malign; dire, dreadful, ruinous, **destructive**; calamitous; too bad, **bad**.

**unprosperous**, inglorious; unwell; **poor**.

**unfortunate**, ill-fated, star-crossed; fraught, futureless; luckless, hapless, poor, forlorn, miserable, undone, unhappy; stricken, accursed; accident-prone.

**Vb.** **have trouble**; go through it, be hard pressed, fall foul of; strike a bad patch, **suffer**; come to grief, **miscarry**; **be poor**; go downhill, decline, **deteriorate**; sink, **founder**; come to a bad end, **fail**; go hard with, **be difficult**.

**Adv.** in adversity; unfortunately.

## 727 Averageness

**N.** **averageness**, **average**; golden mean, neither too much nor too little; common lot, mixed blessing; average circumstances, a modest competence; plain living, **moderation**; middle class, bourgeoisie; Main Street, suburbia, suburbia; common man, **commoner**.

**Adj.** **middling**, average, mediocre; neither good nor bad, middlebrow; ordinary, commonplace, **median**; common, representative, **typical**; **moderate**, decent, quiet, **modest**; undistinguished, inglorious, nothing to boast of; minor, second-rate, second best, **inferior**; fair, fair to middling; so-so, all right, adequate; tolerable, passable, fifty-fifty, much of a muchness; medium, middle, colourless, grey, **neutral**.

**Vb.** be middling; pass muster, **suffice**; manage well enough, avoid excess, **be halfway**; be imperfect.

## 728 Authority

**N.** **authority**, power; 'they', **master**; Whitehall, **director**; right, prerogative; law, rightful power, lawful authority; legislative assembly, **parliament**; regency, committee, **commission**; office of authority, office, place (see **position of authority**); portfolio, **jurisdiction**; vicarious authority, **influence**; indirect authority, patronage, prestige, credit; leadership, hegemony; supremacy; pride of place, priority, **precedence**; majesty, royalty, crown, **nobility**; dignity; purse strings; sea power, admiralty, trident; acquisition of power, succession, accession; seizure of power.

**governance**, rule, sway, direction, command; control, hold, grip, clutches; domination, whip hand, effective control, reach, long arm; dominion, sovereignty, raj, supremacy; reign, regency, dynasty; foreign rule, empire; imperialism, colonialism, neocolonialism; white supremacy, black power; regime, regiment, regimen; state control, paternalism; bureaucracy, civil service, red tape.

**despotism**, paternalism; tyranny; dictatorship; absolutism, autocracy, absolute monarchy; state socialism, state capitalism; police state, rule of terror, **brute force**.

**government**, direction, **management**; form of government, state system; politics, politicking; constitutional government, rule of law, **anarchy**; theocracy; monarchy; federalism; tribalism, patriarchy; paternalism; squirearchy, aristocracy, meritocracy, oligarchy, minority rule, elitism; triumvirate; rule of wealth, plutocracy; representative government, party system, **political party**, **vote**; democracy; popular will; majority rule, one man one vote; collectivism; communism, Maoism; party rule, Fascism, National Socialism; committee rule; army rule, military government, martial law; mob rule, mob law; syndicalism, socialism; bureaucracy, technocracy; self-government, autonomy, home rule; puppet government, **instrument**; caretaker government, regency, interregnum; sphere of influence, mandate.

**position of authority**, post, place, office, office of power, office of dignity; royalty; regency; emirate, lordship; sultanate; consulate, prefecture; headship, presidency; mastership; government post, Cabinet seat; seat of government, capital, metropolis, palace, White House, Kremlin, Number Ten, Whitehall; secretariat, **workshop**.

**political organization**, body politic; state, commonwealth; country, realm, kingdom, republic, city state, city; temple state; federation, principality, duchy, dukedom; empire, dominion, colony, dependency, protectorate, mandate, **territory**; free world, Third World, **region**; banana republic; buffer state; province, county, **district**; body politic, constitution.

**Adj. authoritative**, competent; magisterial, official; mandatory, binding, compulsory; masterful; commanding, lordly; imperious, bossy; peremptory, arbitrary, absolute, totalitarian, **authoritarian**; powerful, **strong**; leading; preeminent, preponderant, dominant, paramount, **supreme**.

**ruling**, regnant; sovereign; royal, regal, queenly; princely, lordly; imperial; magisterial.

**governmental**, political, constitutional; administrative, official; patriarchal, feudal, democratic, popular, classless, republican; **independent**.

**Vb. rule**, hold sway, reign, reign supreme; govern, control, **command**; manage, hold office, **direct**; have a place, occupy a post, have authority, rule absolutely, **oppress**; dictate; plan; keep order, police.

**take authority**, take office, take command; assume authority, form a government; gain power, take control; seize power, usurp.

**dominate**; preponderate, **predominate**, boss, **command**; overmaster; **influence**; regiment, discipline, drill, drive, **be severe**; dictate, coerce, **compel**; **subjugate**; override, overrule, overawe; **be free**.

**be governed**, have a constitution; owe fealty, owe loyalty, **be subject**.

**Adv. by authority**.

## 729 Laxity: absence of authority

**N. laxity**; **scope**; lack of ceremony; relaxation, **liberation**; **permission**; indulgence, toleration, licence; line of least resistance, **submission**; weak will, feeble grasp, **weakness**; inertia; surrender of control, **resignation**; concession, **compromise**; King Log.

**anarchy**; free-for-all; disorder, chaos, turmoil; licence, indiscipline; anarchism, nihilism; interregnum, power vacuum; misrule; mob law, reign of terror; defiance of authority; deposition.

**Adj. lax**, loose, slack; feeble, soft, **weak**; slipshod, remiss, **negligent**; **indifferent**; informal; happy-go-lucky; permissive, tolerant, easy, gentle, **lenient**; weak-kneed, **irresolute**; lacking authority.

**anarchic**; unbridled; insubordinate, **insolent**, rebellious, **disobedient**; disorderly, unruly, **riotous**; **illegal**; lawless.

**Vb. be lax**; hold a loose rein, give one their head, give rope enough, **give scope**; stretch a point, connive at; tolerate, suffer, **permit**; spoonfeed, indulge, spoil, **be lenient**; **compromise**; relax, **disunite**; lose control, **be impotent**; renounce authority, **relinquish**; abdicate, **resign**; misrule, misgovern, mismanage, reduce to chaos, **derange**.

**please oneself**, let oneself go, indulge oneself, **be intemperate**; be a law unto oneself, defy authority, resist control, **disobey**; act without authority; arrogate, usurp authority, **be undue**.

**unthrone**, unseat, overthrow, force to resign, **depose**; usurp.

## 730 Severity

**N. severity**; pedantry; **hardness**; discipline, firm control, strong hand, tight grasp, **authority**; rod of iron, heavy hand; rigour, extremity; pound of flesh; **restraint**; prudery; visitation, inquisition, harassment; spite, **revenge**; lack of mercy; harsh treatment, cruelty, **inhumanity**; self-denial.

**brute force**, rule of might, gunboat diplomacy, **power**; **compulsion**; **violence**; arbitrary power, absolutism, autocracy, dictatorship, tyranny; Fascism; militarism; martial law, iron rule, iron hand, jackboot, **bludgeon**.

**tyrant**, pedant, stickler; petty tyrant; disciplinarian, martinet, sergeant major; jackboot; hanging judge; heavy father, Dutch uncle; Big Brother, authoritarian, despot, dictator, **autocrat**; boss, commissar; bully, hard master, taskmaster; bloodsucker, publican, predator, harpy; vulture, octopus; ogre, brute, **monster**; King Stork.

**Adj. severe**, austere, Spartan, ascetic; strict, extreme; strait-laced; donnish; hypercritical, **fastidious**; intolerant, censorious; unbending, rigid, **hard**; hard-headed, hard-boiled, flinty, dour; inflexible, obdurate, uncompromising, **obstinate**; inexorable, relentless, merciless, unsparing, implacable, **pitiless**; heavy, stern, stiff; punitive; stringent, Draconian, drastic, savage.

**authoritarian**, masterful, lordly, arrogant, haughty, **insolent**; absolute, unfettered, arbitrary, totalitarian, Fascist; imperative, compulsive; fussy, bossy.

**oppressive**; harsh; exacting, grasping, extortionate, predatory; searching, unsparing; high-handed, overbearing; heavy-handed, rough, bloody, **violent**; brutal, **cruel**.

**Vb. be severe**, be cruel to be kind; exert authority, discipline; deal hardly with; **restrain**; put a stop to, **suppress**; persecute, **pursue**; ill-treat, mishandle, abuse, **misuse**; treat rough, get tough with; visit with, chastise, **punish**; wreak vengeance, **avenge**; **retaliate**; **be illegal**; be extreme; **be pitiless**; **slaughter**.

**oppress**, take liberties, **please oneself**; assume, arrogate, **be undue**; domineer, lord it; overawe, intimidate, **frighten**; bludgeon, **compel**; shove around; bully, bait, harass, plague, annoy, **torment**, persecute, spite, **be malevolent**; break, tame; task, tax, drive, **fatigue**; overtax, exploit, extort, suck, squeeze, grind; trample, tread underfoot, **suppress**; enslave, **subjugate**; ride roughshod, injure, **do wrong**; misgovern, misrule; rule with a rod of iron; whip, scourge, rack, **torture**; shed blood, **murder**; be heavy, burden, crush, **weigh**.

**Adv. severely**.

## 731 Leniency

**N. leniency**; forbearance, soft answer, patience; pardon, **forgiveness**; quarter, mercy, clemency, compassion; pity; humanity, kindness, **benevolence**; favour, sop, concession; indulgence, toleration; sufferance, allowance, leave, **permission**; complaisance; justice with mercy, **moderation**; light rein, light hand, velvet glove; wet, liberal.

**Adj. lenient**, soft, gentle, mild; tolerant; complaisant; easy, easy-going, **lax**; forbearing, longsuffering, **patient**; clement, merciful, **forgiving**; tender; too soft.

**Vb. be lenient**, show consideration, go easy, **moderate**; featherbed, spoonfeed, spoil, indulge, humour, **pet**; gratify, favour, **flatter**; tolerate, allow, connive, **permit**; stretch a point, be lax; concede, **consent**; refrain, forbear, **be patient**; pity, spare, give quarter, **show mercy**; pardon, **forgive**; amnesty, **forget**; relax.

## 732 Command

**N. command**, invitation, summons; commandment, ordinance; injunction; bidding, behest; dictum, say-so; charge, commission, appointment, **mandate**; brief, **information**; directive, order; word of command, word; beck, nod, sign, **gesture**; signal, bugle call, **call**; whip, categorical imperative, dictate, **compulsion**; negative command, taboo, ban, embargo, **prohibition**; countermand.

**decree**, edict, fiat; law, canon, **precept**; bull, papal decree; circular, encyclical; ordinance; decree nisi, decree absolute; decision; act, **legislation**; plebiscite, electoral mandate, **vote**; dictate.

**demand**, claim; requisition, **request**; notice, final demand, ultimatum; blackmail, **threat**; levy, tax demand, **tax**.

**warrant**, commission, written authority; passport, **permit**; writ, summons, subpoena, citation, **legal process**.

**Adj. commanding**, imperative, categorical; mandatory, obligatory, peremptory, compulsive; **authoritative**; decisive, conclusive, final; demanding, insistent, vocal.

**Vb. command**, bid, invite; order, tell, issue a command, give an order, signal, call, nod, beck, motion, sign, **gesticulate**; wink, **hint**; direct, give a directive, instruct, brief; rule, enjoin; give a mandate, charge, **commission**; impose, set a task, make obligatory, **impose a duty**; detail; call together, convene, **bring together**; summon; cite, subpoena, issue a writ, **litigate**; send back, remand; dictate, **compel**; countermand, **abrogate**; lay an embargo, ban, taboo, proscribe, **prohibit**.

**decree**; promulgate, **proclaim**; declare, say, say so, **affirm**; prescribe, ordain, appoint, **predetermine**; enact, make law, legislate, **make legal**; rule, give a ruling, **judge**.

**demand**, require, requisition, **require**; order, indent, **request**; send a final demand, give final notice, present an ultimatum, blackmail, **threaten**; reclaim, **claim**; demand payment, dun, bill, invoice; charge, **price**; exact, levy, **tax**.

**Adv. commandingly**.

## 733 Disobedience

**N. disobedience**, indiscipline; delinquency; refusal to obey orders, **defiance**; disregard of orders; infraction, crime, sin, **guilty act**; passive resistance, **resistance**; opposition; hindrance; **discontent**; mafia.

**revolt**, mutiny; direct action, **strike**; faction, **dissension**; schism; explosive situation; sabotage, **destruction**; disturbance, disorder, riot, gang warfare, tumult, barricades, **turmoil**; rebellion, insurrection, rising, uprising, **outbreak**; putsch; resistance movement, **resistance**; **revolution**; terrorism; civil war, **war**; regicide, **homicide**.

**sedition**; cabal, intrigue, **plot**; terrorism, anarchism, nihilism; treason, lesemajesty, **perfidy**.

**revolter**, awkward person, difficult character, handful, **difficulty**; naughty child, scamp, little monkey, **bad person**; rebel; demonstrator, striker, **opponent**; splinter group, **schismatic**; dissident, **malcontent**; blackleg, scab, **nonconformist**; maverick, lone wolf; traitor, Quisling, fifth columnist; regicide; insurgent; resistance, underground; Black Panther, Black Muslim; Provisional; red, red republican; counter-revolutionary, reactionary, White Russian; mafia, bandit.

**agitator**; demonstrator; tub-thumper, demagogue; firebrand; red, commie; suffragette; ringleader.

**rioter**, rowdy, **ruffian**; wrecker; secret society.

**Adj. disobedient**; naughty, mischievous; awkward, difficult, wayward, restive, impatient of control, vicious, unruly, **violent**; intractable, ungovernable; insubordinate, rebellious, bloodyminded; **contrary**; nonconformist; recusant; recalcitrant; challenging, **defiant**; refractory, perverse, **obstinate**; subversive, revolutionary, reactionary; disloyal; intrusive; wild, feral, savage.

**riotous**; rumbustious, rowdy, unruly, wild, **disorderly**; **lawless**; rebellious.

**Vb. disobey**; be disobedient, misbehave; flout authority; disobey orders, **defy**, **oppose**; commit a crime, be illegal;

violate, infringe, transgress, trespass, **encroach**; turn restive, kick, chafe, fret; bolt, take French leave, be a law unto oneself, **please oneself**.

**revolt**, rebel, mutiny; strike, **cease**; sabotage, **obstruct**; undermine, work underground; secede; betray; agitate, demonstrate, protest, **deprecate**; start a riot, stage a revolt, lead a rebellion, **resist**; rise, renounce allegiance, **achieve liberty**; overthrow, upset.

## 734 Obedience

**N. obedience**, compliance, **observance**; goodness; readiness; **submission**; passivity; morale, discipline, **duty**; deference; **slave**.

**loyalty**, constancy, devotion, fidelity, good faith, **probity**; allegiance, fealty, homage, service, deference, submission; vote of confidence.

**Adj. obedient**, compliant; loyal, faithful, true-blue, steadfast, constant; devoted, dedicated, sworn; offering homage, submissive; law-abiding, **peaceful**; complaisant, amenable, docile; good; filial; ready, **willing**; acquiescent, resigned, passive; meek, biddable, dutiful; manageable, tame; respectful, subservient, obsequious, slavish; **servile**.

**Vb. obey**, comply, do to order, **observe**; come to heel, **conform**; assent, **consent**; listen, hearken, heed, mind, obey orders; observe discipline; hold oneself ready, **be willing**; vote to order; follow, **serve**; be loyal, owe loyalty, bear allegiance, pay homage, **keep faith**; pay tribute, **be subject**; make oneself useful, do Trojan service, **minister to**; yield, defer to, bow, bend, stoop, be submissive, **submit**; grovel, cringe, **be servile**; play second fiddle, **be inferior**.

**Adv. obediently**, to order; yours to command, at your service.

## 735 Compulsion

**N. compulsion**, spur of necessity, **necessity**; law of nature, **law**; act of God; moral compulsion, **conscience**; blackmail, **threat**; negative compulsion, **restraint**; sanction, **penalty**; duress, force, main force, big stick, bludgeon, strong arm, strongarm tactics, **brute force**; pressgang, call-up, draft; extortion, **taking**; slavery, forced labour, labour camp, **servitude**; command performance, **command**.

**Adj. compelling**, compulsive, involuntary, of necessity, inevitable, **necessary**; imperative, peremptory, **commanding**; compulsory, mandatory, binding, **obligatory**; urgent, pressing; overriding; omnipotent, irresistible, **powerful**; forcible, forceful, cogent; high-pressure, sledgehammer, strongarm.

**Vb. compel**, constrain, coerce, **force**; enforce; dictate, necessitate, oblige, bind; order, **command**; impose, **impose a duty**; make one; impress, draft, conscript; drive, dragoon, regiment, discipline; bulldoze, steamroller, railroad, pressgang; bludgeon, **oppress**; requisition, commandeer, extort, exact, **take**; apply pressure, squeeze, **torture**; blackmail, hijack, hold to ransom, **threaten**; be peremptory, insist, make a point of, press, urge; **affirm**; compel to accept, foist; force-feed; hold back, **restrain**.

**Adv. by force**, perforce, of necessity, forcibly; at gunpoint.

## 736 Master

**N. master**, mistress; master or mistress of, captor, possessor; sire, lord, lady, dame; liege, lord, lord paramount, lord's lord, suzerain; protector;

**patron**; seigneur, squire, laird, **aristocrat**; **male**; landlady, **lady**; senator, plutocrat; sir, madam, title; patriarch, **parentage**; senior, head, principal, provost, **superior**; schoolmaster or -mistress, **teacher**; president, speaker, **director**; employer, captain of industry, capitalist, boss, governor, **manager**; leader, lord of creation, **bigwig**; ruling class, ruling party, dominant interest; 'them', Whitehall, Pentagon, **government**; staff, High Command.

**autocrat**, absolute ruler, absolute monarch; despot, tyrant, dictator, Big Brother; tycoon, boss, **bigwig**; petty tyrant, commissar, tin god, **official**.

**sovereign**, suzerain; Majesty, Highness; dynasty, house, royal line, royal blood; royalty, monarch, king, queen, rex, regina; divine king, Pharaoh; emperor, empress; Kaiser; prince, princess, Dauphin, Crown Prince or Princess, Great King, King of Kings, Shah; khan, Great Khan; Celestial Emperor; Mikado; Mogul, Sultan, Sultana; pope, pontiff.

**potentate**, ruler; chief, chieftain, headman; prince; emir, begum; archduke, duke, duchess, Elector; regent, Prince Regent.

**governor**, High Commissioner, Governor-General, Crown Representative, viceroy; proconsul; grand vizier, bey; Prince Bishop; patriarch, archbishop, cardinal; imam, **leader**.

**officer**, functionary, mandarin, nabob, bureaucrat, **official**; civil servant, **servant**; commissar; chief officer, prime minister, grand vizier, vizier, chancellor; constable, marshal, seneschal, warden; mayor, mayoress, alderman, provost, city father, councillor; dignitary, local worthy, **person of repute**; sheriff, bailiff, justice, **judge**; magistrate; president, doge; consul, proconsul, praetor; prefect, district officer; commissioner, revenue officer, collector, headman; mace-bearer, beadle; tipstaff, **law officer**; sexton, verger, **church officer**; courier, **messenger**; party official, whip.

**naval officer,** Sea Lord; admiral, commodore, captain, commander, lieutenant, petty officer, leading seaman, **nautical personnel**.

**army officer,** staff, High Command, staff officer, brass hat; marshal, general, brigadier, colonel, major, captain, lieutenant; ensign, cornet; warrant officer, NCO, sergeant major, sergeant, corporal, lance corporal; adjutant, aide-de-camp, quartermaster, orderly officer; military tribune, legate, centurion; war minister, warlord, commanding officer, commander, commandant; military rank, **degree.**

**air officer,** air marshal, air commodore, group captain, wing commander, squadron leader, flight lieutenant, flying officer, flight sergeant, **air force.**

## 737 Servant

**N. servant, official**; fag, slave; general servant, factotum, **busy person**; humble servant, menial; orderly, attendant; verger, **church officer**; subordinate, underling, **inferior**; assistant, secretary, right-hand man; paid servant, mercenary, hireling, employee, hand; handyman, labourer, **worker**; hack, drudge, dogsbody; farmhand, **farmer**; shepherd, milkmaid, **herdsman**; shop assistant, **seller**; steward, stewardess, cabin boy; waiter, head waiter, barman, pot boy, **tavern**; ostler, groom, stable boy or lad; errand boy, messenger, runner, **courier**; doorman, commissionaire, janitor, **doorkeeper**; porter, **bearer**;

page boy, bellboy; sweeper, **cleaner**; caretaker, housekeeper (see **domestic**); occasional servant, help, daily, char, charwoman; universal aunt; nurse, **keeper**; companion.

**domestic, staff; personnel**; domestic servant, manservant, man, footman, lackey; servant girl, maid, parlour maid, housemaid, chambermaid; domestic drudge, maid of all work, skivvy; kitchen maid, kitchen boy, scullion, housekeeper, butler, cook; steward, chaplain, governess, tutor, nurse, nanny; personal servant, page, squire, valet, batman; gyp, scout; outdoor staff, groom; coachman, chauffeur, **driver.**

**retainer,** follower, following, suite, train, **retinue**; court, courtier; attendant, usher; bodyguard, henchman, squire, page, page of honour, household staff, chamberlain, equerry, steward, bailiff, seneschal; housekeeper; butler; chaplain; lady-in-waiting, companion; governess, nurse, nanny, **keeper.**

**dependant,** client; hanger-on, parasite, satellite, camp follower, creature, jackal, **follower**; stooge, puppet, **instrument**; subordinate, **inferior**; minion, lackey, man, henchman, vassal; pensioner; apprentice, ward, charge, foster child.

**subject,** national, citizen, **native**; liege, vassal; people, citizenry; subject population, dependency, colony, satellite.

**slave,** thrall, slave girl; helot; serf, villein; galley slave, **worker**; temple prostitute; eunuch; chattel, puppet, pawn; machine, robot, **instrument**; captive, **prisoner.**

**Adj. serving**; menial; working; **obedient; subject.**

**Vb. serve,** minister to; accompany; fol-

low, **obey**; tend, squire, valet, dress;
char, oblige; do service, make oneself
useful, **be useful**; **function**.

## 738 Badge of rule

**N. regalia**, royal trappings, emblem of
royalty, crown, orb, sceptre; coronet,
tiara, diadem; rod of empire, sword of
state, **authority**; robe of state, royal
robe; ermine, royal purple; throne,
royal seat, seat of kings; ensign, **flag**;
royal standard, royal arms, **heraldry**;
lion, eagle.

**badge of rule**, emblem of authority,
staff, wand, wand of office, verge, rod,
Black Rod, baton, truncheon, gavel;
signet, seal, ring; sword of state,
sword of justice, mace; pastoral staff;
woolsack, chair, bench; sartorial
insignia, triple crown, mitre; cap of
maintenance, cap of dignity; robe,
mantle, toga.

**badge of rank**, sword, belt, sash, tab,
**badge**; uniform, **livery**; brass, star,
crown; gold braid; chevron, stripe,
anchor, curl; garter, order.

## 739 Freedom

**N. freedom**, liberty, being at large; freedom of action, initiative; free will,
**will**; free thought, free speech; rights,
civil rights; privilege, prerogative;
licence, excess of freedom, indiscipline; free love, **illicit love**; isolationism; emancipation, setting free, **liberation**; franchise, secret ballot, **vote**.

**independence**, freedom of action; freedom of choice, **choice**; floating vote;
freedom of thought, emancipation,
**nonconformity**; individualism, individuality, **speciality**; self-
determination, national status,
**nation**; autonomy, self-government,
**sufficiency**; freehold, **property**; independent means, competence, **wealth**.

scope, play, **range**; swing, rope; field,
room, living space, elbowroom, wide
berth, leeway, margin, clearance,
**room**; latitude, liberty, Liberty Hall;
permissive society; fling, licence,
excess; **opportunity**; facilities, free
hand, blank cheque; free-for-all, free
field, free enterprise, free trade, free
port, free market; open country.

**free person**, freeborn, burgess, citizen,
voter; freedman; free agent, freelance;
independent; neutral, **moderate**; freethinker, liberal; bohemian, **nonconformist**; lone wolf, **solitary**.

**Adj. free**, freeborn; scot-free; at large;
liberated; footloose, go-as-you-please;
exempt, immune; **plain**; broad, broad-
minded, unprejudiced, independent,
**just**; all things to all men, **sociable**;
loose, unbridled, incontinent, wanton,
**impure**; at leisure, retired; at home, at
ease, **leisurely**; free of cost, gratis;
unreserved, **accessible**.

**unconfined**, unfettered, unbridled;
unchecked, unrestrained; uninhibited, informal, casual; free-range,
wandering, random.

**independent**; unilateral, **spontaneous**;
detached, **indifferent**; free to choose,
uncommitted, **neutral**; **unsociable**;
irrepressible; self-sufficient, self-
supporting, self-contained; ungovernable; self-employed, free-lance; unofficial, cowboy, wildcat; single, bachelor.

**unconditional**, without strings; free-for-
all; absolute; open, wide open; arbitrary; freehold.

**Vb. be free**, enjoy liberty; go free, save
oneself, **escape**; take French leave,
**disobey**; be free of, range, have scope,
have play, have a free hand, have
elbowroom; have plenty of rope; feel
at home, make oneself at home; feel
free, be oneself, let oneself go, **repose**;

cut loose, **please oneself**; drift, wander, roam, **stray**; go it alone, stand alone; **will**; have a free mind, be independent; **defy**; be self-sufficient, **suffice**; take liberties, make free with, presume, **be insolent**; dare, venture, make bold to, permit oneself.

give scope, allow initiative, give one his head, allow full play, give free rein to, allow enough rope, **be lax**; give a free hand, **facilitate**; release, set free, enfranchise, **liberate**; let, charter, **permit**; let alone; leave it open.

**Adv. freely**, liberally, at will.

## 740 Subjection

**N. subjection**; subordinate position, inferior rank, inferior status; dependence, tutelage, apron strings, apprenticeship, **learning**; mutual dependence, symbiosis; allegiance, nationality; conquest, colonialism; loss of freedom, **submission**; discipline, **restraint**; yoke, **fetter**.

**service**, employ, employment; tribute; vassalage, **loyalty**; compulsory service, forced labour, **compulsion**.

**servitude**, slavery, bondage, yoke.

**Adj. subjected**; subdued; deprived of freedom, **restrained**; underprivileged; **serving**; downtrodden, underfoot, henpecked; brought to heel; submissive; subservient, slavish, **servile**.

**subject**; satellite; bond, bound, tributary, colonial; liege, vassal, feudal, **obedient**; subordinate, of lower rank, junior, cadet, **inferior**; dependent; subject to, liable to, **liable**; a slave to; voiceless; **servile**; paid.

**Vb. be subject**, pay tribute, **obey**; vote to order; **be inferior**; be a doormat; serve, be a slave; **submit**; pawn, mortgage, **assign**; be a tool, **be instrumental**; cringe, fawn, **be servile**.

**subjugate**, subdue, reduce, subject, over-

master; annex; take captive, **triumph**; take, capture, lead captive, reduce to servitude, enslave; fetter, bind, **imprison**; rob of freedom, disfranchise; treat like dirt, **oppress**; repress, **suppress**; captivate, **impress**; enchant, **bewitch**; dominate, **influence**; discipline, regiment; tame, quell; bring to heel; **dispose of**.

## 741 Liberation

**N. liberation**, setting free, release, discharge, **acquittal**; free expression, catharsis, **feeling**; **separation**; riddance, **relief**; rescue, redemption, salvation, **deliverance**; emancipation; parole, bail; relaxation (of control); absolution, **forgiveness**; deed of release.

**Adj. liberated**; relieved; set free.

**Vb. liberate**, rescue, save, **deliver**; dispense, exempt; pardon, **forgive**; discharge, absolve, **acquit**; make free, emancipate; enfranchise; grant equal rights, end discrimination; release, free, set free, set at liberty; parole, **give terms**; unlock, **open**; loosen, loose, untie, disentangle, extricate, disengage, clear, **unravel**; unstop, uncork; unleash; let loose, leave to wander, turn adrift; charter; give play to, **give scope**; vent, give vent to, **empty**; leave hold, let go; relax, be lax; lift, **relieve**; **abrogate**; disband, send home, **disperse**; unload, **disencumber**.

**achieve liberty**, breathe freely; assert oneself, claim freedom of action; **revolt**; free oneself, shake oneself free; break loose, **escape**.

## 742 Restraint

**N. restraint**, self-control, **temperance**; reserve, repression, **compulsion**; cramp, check, **hindrance**; curb, drag, brake, snaffle, bridle, **fetter**; arrest;

veto, ban, bar, embargo, **prohibition**; legal restraint, **law**; control, discipline, **authority**; **penalty**.

**restriction**, limit; speed limit; curfew; squeeze; duress, pressure, **compulsion**; control; restrictive practices, restraint of trade, exclusive rights, **exclusion**; monopoly, price ring, cartel, closed shop; ring, circle, protection, protectionism, mercantile system, tariff, tariff wall; **economy**; economic pressure, freeze, price control, credit squeeze; blockade.

**detention**, custody, **protection**; arrest; keeping, keep, care, charge, ward; quarantine; remand, refusal of bail; duress; bondage, slavery, **servitude**; burial; confinement; sentence, time, a stretch, porridge; penology.

**Adj. restraining**, restrictive, conditional, with strings; keeping; hidebound; straitlaced, unbending, strict, **severe**; stiff, **rigid**; tight, narrow; close; poky; protective.

**restrained**, **temperate**, reserved, shy; **obedient**; limited, scant, tight; cramped; bound; fogbound, snowbound.

**imprisoned**; landlocked; kept close, incommunicado; **captive**; inside; serving a sentence, doing time, doing porridge.

**Vb. restrain**, hold back, arrest, check, curb, brake, **retard**; cramp, clog, hamper, **hinder**; swathe, bind, **tie**; call a halt, stop, put a stop to, **halt**; inhibit, veto, ban, bar, **prohibit**; bridle, discipline, control, **be severe**; subdue, **subjugate**; restrain oneself; grip, hold, pin, **retain**; fight back; restrict, tighten, limit, keep within bounds, **circumscribe**; assuage, **moderate**; repress, **suppress**; muzzle, gag, silence, **make mute**; censor, **obliterate**; restrict access, **exclude**; restrict supplies, withhold, keep back, stint; restrict consumption, ration, be sparing, retrench; try to stop, resist, **oppose**; police, patrol, keep order.

**arrest**, apprehend, catch, cop, nab, collar, pinch, nick; handcuff, take, make a prisoner, take prisoner, capture, lead captive; kidnap, seize, take hostage; take charge of, hold.

**fetter**, manacle, bind, pinion, handcuff; pillory, tether, picket, **tie**; shackle, trammel, hobble; enchain; chain; make conditions, attach strings.

**imprison**, confine, immure, quarantine, intern; hold, detain, gate; keep close, hold incommunicado; cloister, **seclude**; entomb, bury; cage, kennel, impound, corral, herd, pen, cabin, trap, **enclose**; incarcerate, remand; jug; keep prisoner, refuse bail.

## 743 Prison

**N. prison**; open prison, halfway house; penitentiary, reformatory, Borstal; remand home, sin bin; prison ship; dungeon, black hole, limbo; Tower; Fleet; Sing Sing; criminal lunatic asylum.

**gaol**, jail, clink, jug, can, stir, big house; glasshouse, brig.

**lockup**, nick, police station; roundhouse; cell, Death Row; dungeon cell, dungeon, torture chamber; prison van; dock, bar; pound, pen, cage, coop, kennel; ghetto, reserve; stocks, pillory; lock, padlock, bolt, bar, barred window.

**prison camp**; concentration camp; labour camp; penal settlement or colony, Botany Bay.

**fetter**, shackle, trammel, bond, chain, irons, hobble; manacle, pinion, handcuff, bracelet; straitjacket, corset; muzzle, gag, bit, bridle, snaffle, halter; rein; yoke, collar, harness; curb,

brake, skid, clog, drag, **hindrance**;
lead, tether, rope, leading string,
apron strings, **halter**.

#### 744 Keeper

N. keeper, custodian, curator; record
keeper, **recorder**; charge officer; caretaker, housekeeper; seneschal,
warden; ranger, gamekeeper; guard,
escort, convoy; garrison; watchdog,
sentry, lookout, watchman, watch,
coastguard, lighthouse keeper, **protector**; tutor, duenna, governess,
nurse, nanny, **domestic**; foster parent,
guardian, probation officer, **philanthropist**.
gaoler, jailer, turnkey, warder, prison
guard, prison officer, screw; prison
governor.

#### 745 Prisoner

N. prisoner, captive, capture, prisoner of
war; close prisoner; political prisoner,
prisoner of conscience; detainee, prisoner of state; defendant, accused,
**accused person**; Borstal boy; old lag,
jailbird; gaol inmate, guest of Her
Majesty; convict; lifer, trusty; chain
gang, galley slave, **slave**; hostage, kidnap victim, **security**.
Adj. captive; inside; without bail.

#### 746 Commission: vicarious authority

N. commission, vicarious authority;
committal, delegation; devolution;
deputation, legation, mission,
embassy, **envoy**; regency, **authority**;
representation, proxy; card vote;
agency, trusteeship; **management**;
public service, bureaucracy, **government**.
mandate, trust, charge, **command**; commission, assignment, appointment,
office, task, errand, mission; enterprise, **undertaking**; return, election,

vote; translation, transfer; investment, investiture, installation, induction, ordination, coronation; power of
attorney, written authority, charter,
writ, **warrant**; diploma, **permit**; terms
of reference, **conditions**; responsibility, care, ward, charge.
Adj. commissioned; vicarious, representational.
Vb. commission, empower, charge,
sanction, charter, **permit**; post,
accredit, appoint, collate; assign,
name, nominate; engage, hire, staff,
**employ**; invest, install, ordain;
enthrone, crown, anoint; commit,
leave it to; consign, trust with; delegate, depute, return, elect, give a
mandate, **vote**.
Adv. by proxy.

#### 747 Abrogation

N. abrogation; vacation; cancellation;
recall, repeal; abolition, dissolution;
suspension, disuse, dead letter; undoing, **reversion**; countermand;
reprieve.
deposal, deposition; discharge, sack,
removal; **punishment**; deprivation;
replacement; recall, transfer, relief.
Adj. abrogated, set aside, void; dead;
dormant, **unused**.
Vb. abrogate, annul, cancel; scrub,
**obliterate**; invalidate, abolish, dissolve, nullify, void, vacate; quash, set
aside, reverse, overrule; repeal,
revoke, recall; rescind; undo; countermand; disclaim, disown, deny, **negate**;
repudiate, retract, **recant**; ignore,
**disregard**; call a halt, **restrain**; suspend, discontinue, make a dead letter
of; wish undone, regret; **relinquish**.
depose, unseat; disbar, exclude; dis-
establish; suspend, cashier, **dismiss**;
oust, **eject**; demote, degrade; recall,
relieve, supersede, replace, remove,

transfer.

## 748 Resignation

**N. resignation**; pension, golden handshake, **reward**; waiver, surrender; disclaimer; **leisure**; feeling of resignation, **submission**; quitter; pensioner.

**Adj. resigning**; outgoing, former, retired, one-time.

**Vb. resign**; be relieved, vacate, vacate office; stand aside, leave it to; declare (cricket); scratch, withdraw, surrender, **submit**; quit, chuck it; **assign**; abdicate, abandon, renounce, **relinquish**; retire; decline to stand again, refuse battle; waive, disclaim, abjure, **negate**; retract, **recant**.

## 749 Consignee

**N. consignee**, committee, panel, quango, **council**; counsellor, wise man, working party, **adviser**; stakeholder; nominee, licensee; trustee, executor, **agent**; factor, bailiff, steward, **manager**; caretaker, curator, **keeper**; representative (see **delegate**); legal representative, attorney, counsel, advocate, **law agent**; proxy, **deputy**; middleman, broker, stockbroker, **intermediary**; underwriter, insurer; purser, bursar, **treasurer**; rent collector; secretary of state, **officer**; functionary, **official**.

**delegate**, shop steward; nominee, representative, member; official representative, commissioner; correspondent, **correspondent**; emissary, special messenger, **messenger**; plenipotentiary (see **envoy**); delegation, mission.

**envoy**, emissary, legate, permanent representative, resident, ambassador, High Commissioner; ambassador at large; minister; consul, first secretary, attaché; embassy, legation, mission, consulate, High Commission; plenipotentiary.

## 750 Deputy

**N. deputy**, surrogate, alternate, proxy; scapegoat, substitute, understudy, stand-in; pro-, vice-, viceroy, vice-chancellor; proconsul; vicar; deputy prime minister, **officer**; right-hand man, lieutenant, secretary; alter ego; caretaker government; heir, heir apparent, successor designate, **beneficiary**; mouthpiece, herald, **messenger**; second, advocate, champion, **patron**; agent, factor, attorney, **consignee**.

**Adj. deputizing**; vice-, pro-; plenipotentiary; intermediary.

**Vb. deputize, function**; represent, be executor, **manage**; negotiate, replace, **substitute**.

**Adv. on behalf**, pro.

## 751 Permission

**N. permission**, liberty, **freedom**; leave, sanction, clearance; accordance, grant; licence, warrant; allowance, sufferance, tolerance, toleration, indulgence; passive consent, **consent**; connivance, **aid**; blessing, approval, **approbation**; grace, **benevolence**; concession, dispensation; release, **liberation**.

**permit**, express permission, authority, law, **warrant**; commission, **mandate**; grant, charter, patent, pass, password; passport, visa, safe-conduct; ticket, chit; licence, free hand, blank cheque, **scope**; leave, leave of absence, furlough, holiday; parole, ticket of leave; clearance, all clear, green light, go-ahead.

**Adj. permitting**, permissive, complaisant, tolerant, **lenient**.

**permitted, legal**; patent; open, optional, without strings, **unconditional**; permissible, allowable; printable.

**Vb. permit**, let, **make possible**; give permission, grant leave, grant, accord, vouchsafe, **give**; nod, say yes, **consent**; bless; **offer**; sanction, pass, **approve**; entitle, warrant, patent, patcnt, enable, **empower**; ratify, **make legal**; restore permission; lift, lift a ban, dispense, release, **exempt**; clear, give clearance, **liberate**; concede, allow, **assent**; give one a chance, let one try; favour, privilege, indulge, **facilitate**; leave the way open, open thew door to **open**; foster, encourage; humour, **be patient**; suffer, tolerate, brook, **be lenient**; connive, wink at, **be lax**; allow a free hand, issue a blank cheque; permit oneself, **please oneself**.

ask leave, beg permission, ask if one may; seek a favour, petition, **request**; get leave, have permission; receive a charter.

Adv. **by leave**, with permission, under licence; legally, legitimately.

## 752 Prohibition
N. **prohibition**, injunction; countermand; interference; interdict, veto, ban, embargo; curfew, **restraint**; taboo, Index; **refusal**; **disapprobation**; prohibition of drink, **temperance**; **economy**; repression; abolition, cancellation, suspension; blackout; forbidden fruit, contraband article.

Adj. **prohibiting**, prohibitory, forbidding, prohibitive, excessive, **impossible**; penal, **punitive**; hostile, **inimical**; exclusive, **excluding**.

**prohibited**, forbidden; barred; contraband, illicit, unlawful, **illegal**; taboo, untouchable; **unmentionable**, unprintable.

Vb. **prohibit**, forbid, veto, refuse permission, refuse leave, **refuse**; withdraw permission, cancel leave; countermand, revoke, suspend, **abrogate**;

inhibit, prevent, **hinder**; restrict, stop, **restrain**; ban, interdict, taboo, proscribe, outlaw; black, impose a ban; bar, **exclude**; excommunicate, **eject**; repress, stifle, kill, **suppress**; censor, **obliterate**; **be severe**; **disapprove**; discourage, **dissuade**; clip, narrow, pinch, cramp, **circumscribe**; block; intervene, interpose, interfere.

## 753 Consent
N. **consent**; agreement, **assent**; compliance, **observance**; concession, grant, accord; acceptance, entertainment, allowance, **permission**; sanction; partial consent, **compromise**.

Adj. **consenting**, agreeable, compliant, ready, ready enough, **willing**; yielding.

Vb. **consent**, say yes, nod; give consent, ratify, confirm, **endorse**; sanction, pass, **permit**; **approve**; tolerate, allow, connive, **be lenient**; agree, accede, **assent**; **acquiesce**; come round; force oneself; yield, give way, **submit**; comply, grant a request; grant, accord, concede, vouchsafe, **give**; deign, condescend, **be courteous**; listen, hearken, **hear**; turn a willing ear, go halfway to meet, **be willing**; **content**; accept, jump at; clinch a deal, close with, settle, **make terms**.

## 754 Offer
N. **offer**, proffer; improper offer, bribe, **inducement**; tender, bid, declaration, motion, proposition, proposal; approach, overture, advance, invitation; tentative approach, feeler; present, presentation, offering, gratuity, sacrifice, **gift**; dedication, candidature, application, **request**.

Adj. **offering**, inviting; **shown**; open, available; to let; open to bid.

Vb. **offer**, proffer, make an offer, bid,

tender; present, **give**; dedicate, consecrate; sacrifice to; introduce, broach, move, propose, make a proposition, put forward, suggest, **propound**; approach, approach with, make overtures, make advances; induce, **bribe**; invite, send an invitation, **be hospitable**; hawk, hawk about, **sell**; auction; cater, **provide**; make available, make a present of, **make possible**; pose, confront with.

**offer oneself**, stand, be a candidate, compete, enter, **contend**; volunteer, come forward, **be willing**; apply, **request**.

## 755 Refusal

**N. refusal**; denial, negative answer, nay; uncompromising answer, flat refusal, **defiance**; repulse, rebuff, **repulsion**; denial policy, **resistance**; protest; self-denial; restraint, **temperance**.

**Adj. refusing**, recusant; **deprecatory**; deaf to.

**refused**, inadmissible; **impossible**.

**Vb. refuse**; excuse oneself; disagree, **dissent**; deny, negative, repudiate, disclaim, **negate**; decline, spurn, **reject**; repulse, rebuff, repel; **dismiss**; resist persuasion, be unmoved, **be obstinate**; turn a deaf ear, **be deaf**; hang fire, hang back; have nothing to do with, shy at, jib at, **avoid**; **exclude**; look askance at, dislike, disfavour, discountenance, **disapprove**; refuse permission, **prohibit**; **resist**; oppose, **withstand**; kick, protest, **deprecate**; grudge, begrudge, withhold, **retain**; deny oneself, waive, renounce, **relinquish**; go without, **be ascetic**.

**Adv. denyingly**, with a refusal, without acceptance; never, nothing doing.

## 756 Request

**N. request**, humble petition; negative request; **sale**; strong request, forcible demand, requisition; last demand, ultimatum, **demand**; blackmail, **threat**; claim; consumer demand, **requirement**; postulate, proposition, proposal, motion, suggestion; overture, approach, **offer**; bid, application, suit; petition, memorial, round robin; prayer, appeal, plea (see **entreaty**); pressure, instance, **compulsion**; clamour, cry; invitation, temptation; flag day, bazaar, charity performance; advertising, **advertisement**; small ad; wish, want, **desire**.

**entreaty**; submission; prayer; appeal, apostrophe; solemn entreaty; incantation.

**Adj. requesting**, inviting, mendicant; **offering**; **demanding**; insistent; clamorous, importunate, pressing, urgent, instant.

**supplicatory**.

**Vb. request**, ask, invite, solicit; make overtures, approach, accost, **offer**; woo, **court**; seek, **search**; need, **require**; crave, make a request, prefer an appeal, beg a favour, ask a boon, have a request to make, make bold to ask, **desire**; apply, make application, bid, apply to, appeal to, run to, address oneself to; tout, hawk, solicit orders, **sell**; petition; press a claim, expect, **claim**; **demand**; blackmail, **threaten**; be instant, insist; urge, persuade, **induce**; coax, wheedle, cajole; importune, ply, press, dun, besiege; demand entrance; touch, **borrow**; requisition, **take**; raise money, tax, **levy**; send an ultimatum, **give terms**.

**beg**, cadge, crave, sponge; bum, scrounge; thumb a lift, hitchhike; make a collection, **levy**; **require**.

**entreat**, make entreaty, beg hard; pray,

implore, beseech, appeal, conjure, adjure; invoke; appeal to, **speak to**; pray to, **offer worship**; kneel to; march, **refusal**.

### 757 Deprecation: negative request

**N. deprecation**, negative request, contrary advice; **request**; murmur, cheep, squeak, complaint, **discontent**; exception, demur, protest, **opposition**; reaction, backlash; gesture of protest, **disapprobation**; open letter, round robin; march, **refusal**.

**Adj. deprecatory**; protestant; vocal.

**Vb. deprecate**, advise against, have a better idea, **dissuade**; touch wood, **practise sorcery**; intercede, **mediate**; pray, appeal, **entreat**; **ask mercy**; show embarrassment, **disapprove**; remonstrate, expostulate, **reprove**; jeer, groan, stamp; murmur, beef, complain; object, take exception to; demur, jib, kick, squeak, protest against, cry blue murder, **oppose**; demonstrate; strike, **cease**.

### 758 Petitioner

**N. petitioner**, suppliant; pretender; aspirant, expectant; solicitor; customer; suitor; tout, barker; dun; pressure group, lobby; applicant, candidate, entrant; competitor, runner, **contender**.

**beggar**; mendicant, mendicant friar, fakir; tramp, bum, **wanderer**; parasite, **toady**.

### 759 Promise

**N. promise**, offer; undertaking, commitment; engagement, **marriage**; troth, plight, word, parole, word of honour, sacred pledge, vow, **oath**; declaration; declared intention, **intention**; profession, fair words; assurance, pledge, credit, honour, warrant, warranty,

guarantee, insurance, **security**; voluntary commitment, **compact**; covenant, bond, promise to pay, **debt**; obligation, debt of honour, **duty**; firm date, **undertaking**; party, **signatory**.

**Adj. promissory**, promising.

**promised**; engaged, bespoke, reserved; committed; bound.

**Vb. promise**, say one will **affirm**; proffer, **offer**; make a promise, vow, **swear**; warrant, guarantee, assure, confirm, secure, insure, underwrite, **give security**; pledge, stake; engage, give a firm date, **undertake**; commit oneself, bind oneself, be bound, covenant, **contract**; accept an obligation, accept responsibility, **incur a duty**; promise to pay, incur a debt of honour, **borrow**, bespeak, reserve, **intend**; wed.

**take a pledge**, demand security, **make certain**; adjure, swear, **testify**; make one promise, parole, **believe**; expect, **be certain**.

**Adv. as promised**, duly; truly.

### 760 Compact

**N. compact**, contract, bargain, agreement, mutual undertaking, **undertaking**; debt of honour, **promise**; mutual pledge; engagement, **marriage**; covenant, bond, **security**; league, alliance, cartel; pact, convention, understanding, **agreement**; private understanding, something between them; secret pact, conspiracy, **plot**; conditions; deal, **compromise**; composition, arrangement, settlement; assent, signal, signature; deed of agreement, indenture, **title deed**.

**treaty**, international agreement; peace treaty; convention, concordat, protocol.

**signatory**, subscriber; **witness**; adherent,

party; contractor; **mediator**.

**Adj. contractual**, conventional; bilateral, multilateral; sworn; signed, sealed and delivered.

**Vb. contract**, engage, **undertake**; **promise**; covenant, make a compact, strike a bargain, sign a pact, do a deal, adhere; league, ally; treat, negotiate, **bargain**, **compromise**; stipulate, **give terms**; agree, come to an agreement, arrive at a formula, come to terms, **make terms**; conclude, close, settle; indent, execute, sign, subscribe, ratify, attest, confirm, **endorse**; insure, underwrite, **give security**.

## 761 Conditions

**N. conditions**, making terms, diplomacy, horse-trading, **barter**; formula, terms; final terms, ultimatum, time limit, **threat**; **compulsion**; condition, set of terms, frame of reference; articles, articles of agreement; provision, clause, proviso, strings, reservation, exception, small print, **qualification**; essential clause, **requirement**; rule, **precept**; contractual terms, **treaty**; terms of reference, **mandate**.

**Adj. conditional**; subject to terms, contingent, provisional; guarded, entrenched; binding, **obligatory**.

**Vb. give terms**, propose conditions; condition, bind, attach strings; **demand**; stipulate, **require**, **be severe**; insert a proviso, leave a loophole, **qualify**; add a clause.

**make terms**, negotiate, treat, parley, **confer**; deal with, make overtures, **be tentative**; haggle, **bargain**; proffer, **offer**; yield a point, **compromise**; negotiate a treaty, do a deal, **contract**.

**Adv. on terms**; conditionally, provisionally, subject to, with a reservation; strictly, to the letter; necessarily, sine

qua non; for the last time.

## 762 Security

**N. security**, precaution, **caution**; guarantee, warranty, writ, **warrant**; word of honour, **promise**; patronage, **protection**; surety, bail, caution, parole; pledge, pawn, hostage, stake, stake money, deposit, earnest, token, instalment; token payment, **payment**; indemnity, insurance, **safety**; transfer of security, mortgage, **transfer**; collateral, collateral security, sponsor, underwriter, **patron**.

**title deed**, deed, instrument; unilateral deed, deed poll; bilateral deed, indenture; charter, covenant, bond, **compact**; receipt, IOU, voucher; certificate, marriage lines; seal, stamp, signature, acceptance; valuable security, treasury note, note of hand, bill, treasury bill, bill of exchange; blue chip, gilt-edged security; portfolio, share, debenture; mortgage deed, policy, will, testament, codicil, certificate of probate; archives, **record**.

**Adj. pledged**, pawned, deposited; on lease, on mortgage.

**secured**, insured; gilt-edged.

**Vb. give bail**, go surety, take bail; **take a pledge**.

**give security**, offer collateral, mortgage; pledge, pawn, pop, hock, **borrow**; guarantee, warrant, **make certain**; authenticate, verify, **corroborate**; execute, endorse, seal, stamp, sign, countersign, subscribe, **endorse**; accept, grant a receipt, write an IOU, **receive**; **promise**; secure, indemnify, insure, assure, underwrite, **safeguard**.

## 763 Observance

**N. observance, practice**; full observance, fulfilment, satisfaction, **sufficiency**; adherence to, attention to; performance, discharge, acquittal, **action**; compliance; **conformity**; attachment, fidelity, faith, **loyalty**; sense of responsibility, reliability, **probity**.

**Adj. observant, doing**; watchful, careful of, attentive to, **attentive**; conscientious, diligent, earnest, religious, punctilious; perfectionist, **fastidious**; literal, exact, **accurate**; responsible, reliable, dependable, **trustworthy**; loyal, true, compliant, **obedient**; adherent to; faithful, **honourable**.

**Vb. observe**, heed, respect, regard, have regard to, pay respect to, acknowledge, pay attention to, attend to, be **attentive**; keep, practise, adhere to, cling to, follow, be loyal to, **conform**; comply, **obey**; fulfil, discharge, perform, execute, **do**; satisfy, **suffice**.

**keep faith**, be faithful to, have loyalty; **be honourable**; **pay**; give one his due.

**Adv. with observance**, faithfully; literally, meticulously, according to the spirit of.

## 764 Nonobservance

**N. nonobservance**; inattention; **nonconformity**; anarchism, **anarchy**; shortcoming; protest, disregard, discourtesy, **disrespect**; bad faith, breach of promise, **perfidy**; denial; failure; **penalty**.

**Adj. nonobservant**, lapsed; nonconformist; neglectful, **negligent**; unprofessional; maverick, cowboy; indifferent, informal, **lax**; **disobedient**; unlawful; disloyal; unfaithful.

**Vb. not observe**, abhor, **reject**; discard; set aside, **abrogate**; omit, ignore, skip, **neglect**; disregard, slight; stretch a point, **be lax**; violate, do violence to, trample underfoot, **force**; transgress, **overstep**; **disobey**; desert; fail; break faith, dishonour, **negate**; cancel; be **dishonest**; cut, shirk, dodge, evade, elude, **avoid**; shuffle, quibble, equivocate, **be equivocal**; forfeit, incur a penalty.

## 765 Compromise

**N. compromise**, concession; mutual concession, formula, **compact**; composition, commutation; second best, half a loaf; working arrangement, **way**; **average**; halfway, **middle way**.

**Vb. compromise**, find a formula, find a basis, meet one halfway, **be halfway**; stretch a point, **be lax**; strike an average, go Dutch; compound, commute, **substitute**; arbitrate; **pacify**; make a virtue of necessity.

## 766 Acquisition

**N. acquisition**; collection, **assemblage**; sale; **transfer**; avarice; heap, stack, pile, pool, scoop, jackpot, **accumulation**; finding; finding again, recovery, **restoration**; redemption, **purchase**; appropriation, **taking**; theft; find, windfall, treasure trove; free gift, **gift**; legacy, gratuity, baksheesh, **reward**; benefit match, prize, plum, **trophy**; gravy, **benefit**; easy money, **facility**; pelf, lucre, **money**; plunder, **booty**.

**earnings**, income, wage, salary, screw, pay packet, productivity bonus, **pay**; pay scale, differential; pension, superannuation, 'golden handshake'; emolument, **reward**; allowance, expense account; perquisite, perks; salvage; commission, rake-off, **discount**; return, receipts, proceeds, turnover, takings, revenue, **receipt**; harvest, vintage, crop, aftermath, gleanings; output, produce, **product**.

**gain**, thrift, savings, **economy**; credit side, profit, capital gain, winnings; dividend, share-out; usury, interest, **increment**; lucrative deal; pay increase, rise, raise, **increase**; advantage, benefit; selfish advantage, personal benefit.

**Adj. acquiring**, acquisitive, accumulative; **prosperous**; hoarding, saving.

**gainful**, lucrative, remunerative, **rewarding**; advantageous; fruitful, fertile, **productive**; paying.

**acquired**, had, got; ill-gotten.

**Vb. acquire**, get; earn, gain, obtain, procure, get at; find, strike, come across, **discover**; get hold of, get possession of, annex, **appropriate**; win, capture, catch, land, net, bag, **take**; pick, tot, glean; gather, reap, crop, harvest; draw, tap, milk, mine, **extract**; collect, accumulate, heap, **bring together**; scrape together, collect funds, raise, levy, save, hoard, **store**; buy, preempt, **purchase**; reserve, book, engage, be early; get somehow, beg, borrow or steal; get a living, turn an honest penny, **busy oneself**; get money, draw a salary, draw a pension; have an income, have a turnover, gross, take, **receive**; convert, cash, clear, make; get back, recover, salvage, recycle, regain, redeem, recapture, **retrieve**; take back, resume, reclaim; compensate oneself, **recoup**; break even; attain, reach, catch, incur.

**inherit**, be left, receive a legacy; succeed, succeed to.

**gain**, profit, earn a dividend; make, win; make money, **prosper**; make a fortune, make a killing, turn a pretty penny, **get rich**; scoop, win; sell at a profit.

**be profitable**, profit, repay, be worth-while, **be useful**; pay, pay well; gross, yield, **produce**; pay a dividend, show a profit, **prosper**; accrue.

## 767 Loss

**N. loss**, deprivation, privation; sacrifice, forfeit, lapse, **penalty**; hopeless loss, perdition, **ruin**; setback, check, reverse; loss of profit, overdraft; failure, consumption, **expenditure**; wastage, leakage, **waste**; drain, **decrease**; riddance, **liberation**; **defeat**.

**Adj. losing**, prodigal; deprived; shorn of, bereft, bereaved; minus, without, lacking; quit of; set back, broke, bankrupt, insolvent; **disinterested**.

**lost**, gone; missing, lost, stolen or strayeds **absent**; wanting, lacking, short, **deficient**; irrecoverable, irretrievable, irredeemable; spent; forfeit.

**Vb. lose**; mislay, **misplace**; miss, let slip, **lose a chance**; squander, **waste**; deserve to lose, forfeit, sacrifice; spill, allow to leak; throw good money after bad, sink, **expend**; aggravate; be a loser, **have trouble**; be set back, sell at a loss; be unable to pay, break, go broke, go bankrupt; overdraw, be minus.

**be lost**, be missing, **be absent**; lapse, go to pot; **disappear**; be a good riddance, **relieve**.

## 768 Possession

**N. possession**, rightful possession; hold, grasp, grip; **possessor**; a possession, **property**; tenancy, holding, **estate**; tenure, fee, fief, feud; long possession, prescription; **habit**; exclusive possession, monopoly, corner, ring; preemption; future possession, heritage, reversion; taking possession, appropriation, **taking**.

**Adj. possessing**, holding, propertied,

landed; possessed of; exclusive, possessive.

**possessed**, had; proper, personal, **special**; private; reserved, engaged; inherent.

**Vb.** **possess**, be possessed of, own, have; die possessed of, **bequeath**; hold, grip, **retain**; have absolute disposal of, command, **dispose of**; boast of, **claim**; contain, include, **comprise**; fill, occupy; squat, inhabit; enjoy, **use**; have all to oneself, hog, corner; get, take possession, **take**; recover, **retrieve**; preoccupy, preempt, reserve, book, engage, **be early**; succeed, **inherit**.

**belong**, belong to; go with; be subject to, owe service to, **be subject**.

**Adv.** **possessively**; in one's own right, by right of possession.

### 769 Nonownership

**N.** **nonownership**, vacancy; tenancy; temporary lease; dependence; **poverty**; loss of possession; deprivation, **loss**.

**Adj.** **not owning**, dependent, **subject**; destitute, penniless, **poor**; lacking, minus, without.

**unpossessed**; international, common; vacant, **empty**; derelict.

### 770 Joint Possession

**N.** **joint possession**; joint tenancy; common land, common, global commons; public property, public domain, **property**; joint government; joint stock, common stock, pool, kitty, **store**; socialism, communism, collectivism; collective farm, collective, commune, kibbutz, **farm**.

**participation**, membership, affiliation; co-op., **association**; Dutch treat, bottle party, dividend, share-out; share, lot, whack, **portion**; complicity;

sympathy; fellow feeling, sympathetic strike, joint action.

**participator**, member, partner, co-op., **colleague**; shareholder, stockholder, **possessor**; housing association; sharecropper, **farmer**; socialist; contributor, **patron**.

**Adj.** **sharing**, joint; common, communal, international, global; collective; involved, **corporate**; sympathetic.

**Vb.** **participate**; partake of, take a share, share, go shares, go halves, go fifty-fifty, **apportion**; go Dutch, **defray**.

**communalize**; pool; hold in common.

**Adv.** **in common**, share and share alike; jointly.

### 771 Possessor

**N.** **possessor**, holder; captor; squatter; lodger, occupier, incumbent; trustee; lessee; tenant, householder, franklin, yeoman; vassal, **dependant**; peasant, serf, villein, **farmer**; subtenant.

**owner**, monarch; master, mistress, proprietor; buyer; lord, lord paramount; landed gentry, landed interest; squire, laird, **aristocracy**; man or woman of property, shareholder, stockholder, landlord, landlady; testator.

**beneficiary**; **recipient**; incumbent; expectant, successor, successor apparent; next of kin; heir apparent; crown prince, **sovereign**; joint heir.

### 772 Property

**N.** **property**; possession; stake, venture; personal property, church property; chattel, real property, personal estate, belongings, paraphernalia, effects; baggage; things; cargo, **contents**; goods, wares, stock, stock-in-trade, **merchandise**; plant, furniture.

**estate**; circumstances, what one is worth; resources, **means**; substance, capital, **wealth**; revenue, income, receipt; portfolio; stake, holding, investment; copyright, patent; claim, demand; right, title, interest; living; lease, tenure, freehold, fee, fee simple, fee tail; tenement.

lands, land, acreage, grounds; estate, property, real estate, real property; tenement, holding, tenure, freehold, fief, feud, manor, honour, lordship, domain, demesne; plot, **territory**; farm, ranch, hacienda; common land, common, **joint possession**; dependency, dominion.

dower, dowry, dot, portion, marriage settlement; allotment, allowance, pin money; alimony, birthright; heritage; legacy; heirloom; remainder, reversion; entail.

Adj. proprietary; immovable, real, personal; propertied, landed, feudal, freehold, leasehold; hereditary, heritable; limited.

Vb. dower, endow, possess with, **give**; devise, **bequeath**; grant, allot, **assign**; possess, **commission**; establish, found.

## 773 Retention

N. retention; clinging to; foothold, **support**; bridgehead, beachhead, **advantage**; clutches, grip, gripe, grasp, hold, stranglehold; squeeze; clinch, lock; hug, embrace, clasp, cuddle, **endearment**; keep, ward, **detention**; **refusal**; holding action, pincer movement; plug, stop, **stopper**; ligament, **bond**.

nippers, pincers, tweezers, pliers, wrench, tongs, forceps, vice, clamp, **fastening**; talon, claw, **sharp point**; tentacle, hook, tendril, **feeler**; teeth, **tooth**; paw, hand, **finger**; fist.

Adj. retentive, tenacious, prehensile; vice-like; clinging, adhesive, sticky, gummy, gooey, firm; tight; tight-fisted, **parsimonious**; shut fast, closed.

retained; fast, bound, held; kept; reserved, engaged; kept back; esoteric, incommunicable, **occult**; inalienable.

Vb. retain, hold; grab, buttonhole, hold back, **obstruct**; catch, steady, **support**; hold fast, hold tight, keep a firm hold of; cling to, stick to, adhere; grip, gripe, grasp, clench, clinch, lock; hug, clasp, clutch, embrace; pin, throttle, strangle, **restrain**; detain, **imprison**; contain, **enclose**; keep to oneself, keep back, withhold, **keep secret**; **store**; save, keep, **preserve**; keep back, withhold, **refuse**.

## 774 Nonretention

N. nonretention, parting with, disposal, alienation, **transfer**; **sale**; release, **liberation**; dispensation; dissolution (of a marriage), **divorce**; cancellation; disuse; leak.

derelict; jetsam, **rubbish**; cast-off, slough; waif, stray, orphan, maroon, outcast, pariah.

Adj. not retained; disposed of; left behind; **liberated**; made redundant; derelict; heritable; available.

Vb. not retain, part with, alienate, transfer, **assign**; dispose of, **sell**; be open-handed, **be prodigal**; free, let go, let slip, leave hold of; unlock, **open**; untie, disentangle, **disunite**; forego, dispense with, do without, spare, waive, abandon, cede, yield, **relinquish**; renounce, abjure, **recant**; cancel, revoke, **abrogate**; lift, **liberate**; supersede, replace, **substitute**; disown, disclaim, **negate**; dissolve (a marriage), **divorce**; disinherit, **impoverish**; **marry**; ditch, jettison, throw overboard, **eject**; abandon, maroon; retire; discharge, give notice to quit, **dismiss**; drop, discard; withdraw, resign; estrange; sit loose to, **be indifferent**; leak, **emit**.

## 775 Transfer (of property)

**N. transfer**, transmission, consignment, delivery; settlement; conveyancing, conveyance; assignment; alienation; demise, devise, **gift**; lease, let, rental, hire; **sale**; trade, barter; exchange, **interchange**; changeover; devolution, delegation, **commission**; succession, reversion; pledge, pawn, hostage.

**Adj. transferred**; lent; negotiable; heritable.

**Vb. assign**, convey; grant, **give**; let, rent, hire, **lease**; alienate, **sell**; negotiate, barter, **trade**; **substitute**; exchange, convert, **interchange**; confer, invest with; commit, delegate, **commission**; **marry**; deliver, give delivery, transmit, pass to, **transfer**; pledge, pawn, **lend**; withdraw a gift, give to another; disinherit, **impoverish**; dispossess, expropriate, relieve of.

**bequeath**, will, devise, demise; grant, assign; leave, leave a legacy; make a will, add a codicil; leave a fortune, **be rich**; have something to leave.

**change hands**, pass to another; pass, shift; circulate, **circle**; succeed, inherit, **acquire**.

## 776 Giving

**N. giving**, charity, **philanthropy**; generosity, **liberality**; subscription to; presentation, award, **reward**; delivery, commitment, consignment, conveyance, **transfer**; settlement; grant, accordance; investment, investiture.

**gift**, keepsake, token; present; Christmas box, whip-round, tip, fee, baksheesh, gratuity, drink money, **reward**; token, consideration; bribe, **inducement**; prize, award, presentation, **trophy**; benefit, benefit match,

benefit performance; alms, dole, charity, **philanthropy**; food parcel, free meal; bounty, manna; largesse, hand-out; bonus, bonanza; something extra; perks, expense account; grant, allowance, subsidy, aid; boon, grace, favour, service, labour of love, **voluntary work**; free gift; piece of luck, windfall, **acquisition**; conscience money, **payment**; forced loan, benevolence, tribute, **tax**; legacy, **transfer**.

**offering**, dedication; **piety**; peace offering, collection, sacrifice; Easter offering; subscription, flag day; stake.

**giver**, donor; testator; subscriber, contributor; tributary, **subject**; almoner, blood donor, **benefactor**; distributor of largesse, Lady Bountiful, rich uncle, Father Christmas.

**Adj. giving**, tributary, **subject**; contributory; charitable; generous, bountiful, **liberal**.

**given**, gifted; gratuitous, gratis, free; allowable.

**Vb. give**, bestow, lend, render; afford; provide; vouchsafe, favour with, show favour, grant a boon, **be lenient**; grant, accord, **permit**; gift, donate, make a present of; leave, **bequeath**; endow, enrich; give a prize, present, award, **reward**; confer, vest, invest with; dedicate, consecrate, vow to, **offer**; immolate, sacrifice, **offer worship**; give a present, gratify, tip, consider, remember; **bribe**; bestow alms, give to charity; give freely, lavish, **be liberal**; spare, give free; stand, treat, entertain, **be hospitable**; dispense, allot, **apportion**; contribute, subscribe, pay towards, help, help with money, **aid**; have a whip-round, **participate**; part with, **pay**; share, share with, impart, **communicate**; give one his due; pay tribute; cede, yield, **relinquish**; deliver, **assign**; commit, consign, **commission**; **send**.

## 777 Receiving

**N. receiving**, admittance, **reception**; **acquisition**; acceptance, assumption; succession; collection, receipt of custom; a receipt, windfall, **gift**; toll, tribute, dues, receipts, proceeds, winnings, takings, **earnings**; receiving end.

**recipient**, receiver; trustee, **consignee**; addressee, **correspondent**; buyer; licensee, lessee; heir, successor, **beneficiary**; payee; pensioner; remittance man, **dependant**; winner, scholar; object of charity, **beggar**; **sufferer**.

**receiver**, liquidator, **treasurer**; payee, collector, publican; customs officer; shareholder.

**Adj. receiving**, recipient; receptive; impressionable, **sensitive**; paid; given, favoured.

**Vb. receive**, be given; get, **acquire**; collect, levy, toll, **take**; gross, net, pocket, pouch; accept, **admit**; draw, be paid; have an income, draw a pension; inherit, succeed to; receipt, acknowledge.

**be received**, be drawn; **accrue**; come to hand.

## 778 Apportionment

**N. apportionment**, appointment, assignment, allotment, appropriation; division, partition; shares, deal, dispensation; **limit**; place, seat, station, **degree**; public sector.

**portion**, share, share-out, cut, split; dividend, allotment; lot, contingent; proportion, ratio; quantum, quota; halves, **part**; deal, hand (at cards); dole, mess, modicum, pittance, allowance; ration, ration book, coupon; dose, measure, dollop, whack, helping, slice, **piece**; rake-off, commission,

discount; stake; task, stint, **labour**.

**Vb. apportion**, allot, allocate, appropriate; appoint; assign; assign a part, cast; assign a place, detail, billet; partition, zone; demarcate, **limit**; divide, split, cut; halve, **bisect**; go shares, **participate**; share, distribute, spread around; dispense, administer, serve, deal, **give**; measure, ration, dose; get a share.

**Adv. pro rata**; respectively, each to each, per head.

## 779 Lending

**N. lending**; usury, **credit**; investment; mortgage; advance, loan, accommodation; lease, let, sublet.

**pawnshop**, bank, credit company, finance corporation, building society, International Monetary Fund, World Bank.

**lender**, creditor; harsh creditor; financier, banker; moneylender, usurer, loan shark; pawnbroker, uncle; lessor; backer, angel; tallyman.

**Adj. lending**; extortionate; lent, loaned, on credit

**Vb. lend**, loan; advance, accommodate, allow credit, give one a loan, **credit**; back, finance; invest, sink; **speculate**.

**lease**, let, demise; sublet.

**Adv. on loan**, on credit, on advance; on security.

## 780 Borrowing

**N. borrowing**; loan application; mortgage, **debt**; credit account, credit card; hire purchase, HP, instalment plan; joyride; loan; forced loan, benevolence, **tax**; **deception**.

**Vb. borrow**, touch, **request**; mortgage, pawn, pledge, pop, hock, **give security**; take a loan, exact a benevolence; use a credit card, get credit, get accommodation; **purchase**; promise to pay, raise a loan, float a loan; invite investment; beg, borrow, or steal, **acquire**; cheat, crib, infringe, **copy**.

**hire**, rent, farm, lease, charter.

## 781 Taking

**N. taking**, seizure, capture, rape; taking hold, grasp, apprehension; taking possession, appropriation, assumption; requisition, compulsory purchase, **acquisition**; compulsory saving; taxation, levy, **tax**; taking back, recovery; removal, **displacement**; furtive removal; bodily removal, press gang; raid, spoliation; take, haul, catch, capture, prize, plum, **booty**; receipts, takings, winnings, gleanings, **earnings**.

**expropriation**, forcible seizure, attachment, distress; expulsion; takeover, deprivation; **transfer**; capital levy; extortion; swindle, rip-off.

**rapacity**; thirst, **hunger**; greed, **avarice**; extortion, blackmail.

**taker**, remover; raider; press gang; slaver; captor, **master**; locust, **destroyer**; bloodsucker, leech, parasite, vampire, harpy, vulture, wolf, shark; beast of prey, predator; **receiver**.

**Adj. taking**, grasping, extortionate, rapacious; voracious, ravenous, **hungry**; predatory; acquisitive, possessive.

**Vb. take**, accept, be given, **receive**; take back (see **appropriate**); **admit**; anticipate, **be early**; take hold, clutch, grip, cling, **retain**; seize, snatch, grab, pounce, spring; snatch at, reach, make a long arm; grasp at, clutch at, grab at, make a grab, capture, rape, storm, **overmaster**; conquer, captive, **subjugate**; catch, overtake, intercept, **outstrip**; apprehend, make an arrest,

nab, nobble, collar, **arrest**; make sure of, fasten, pinion, **fetter**; hook, trap, snare, lime, **ensnare**; net, land, bag, pocket, pouch; gross, have a turnover, **acquire**; gather, accumulate, collect, **bring together**; cull, pick, pluck; reap, crop, harvest, glean, **cultivate**; scrounge, tot, ransack, **search**; snaffle; help oneself, **steal**; pick clean, strip, **uncover**; remove, deduct, **subtract**; unload, **displace**; draw, milk, tap, mine, **extract**.

**appropriate**, annex, pirate, **copy**; take possession, assume, **possess**; succeed, **inherit**; **place oneself**; overrun, people, populate, occupy, settle; win, conquer; take back, recover, resume, repossess, recapture, **retrieve**; reclaim, **claim**; commandeer, requisition, **demand**; usurp, arrogate, trespass, squat, **be undue**; make free with; hog; engulf, swallow, **absorb**; devour.

**levy**, raise, extort, exact, **extract**; compel to lend, **borrow**; exact tribute, tax; overtax, suck dry (see **fleece**); exhaust, drain, empty; wring, squeeze, oppress; divert resources.

**take away**, remove, shift, unload, **displace**; **send**; lighten, **disencumber**; abstract, relieve of, **steal**; remove bodily, escort, **accompany**; kidnap, crimp, shanghai, press, impress, abduct, ravish; **decamp**; raid, loot, plunder, **rob**.

**deprive**, bereave, orphan, widow; denude, strip, **uncover**; **depose**; dispossess, usurp; oust, evict, expel, **eject**; expropriate, confiscate, foreclose; disinherit.

**fleece**, pluck, skin, shear, gut; strip, strip bare, **uncover**; swindle, cheat, **deceive**; blackmail, bleed, bleed white, sponge, suck, suck like a leech,

suck dry; soak, sting; **defraud**; devour,
**eat**; bankrupt, leave one without a
penny or cent, **impoverish**.

## 782 Restitution

**N. restitution**, return, reversion; **restoration**; redemption, ransom, rescue,
**deliverance**; recovery; refund; indemnity, damages, **penalty**; amends, reparation.

**Adj. restoring**.

**Vb. restitute**, make restitution, **restore**;
return, render, give back; **pay**; refund,
repay, recoup, reimburse; indemnify,
pay an indemnity, pay damages, compensate; make reparation, make
amends, **atone**; bring back, repatriate;
ransom, redeem, **deliver**; reinstate,
rehabilitate, restore one to favour;
recover, **retrieve**.

## 783 Stealing

**N. stealing**, theft, larceny; robbery; robbery with violence, holdup; rape,
hijack; abstraction, removal, **taking**;
literary theft; joyride; act of theft; job,
fiddle.

**brigandage** banditry, piracy, buccaneering; privateering; raid, foray, **attack**.

**spoliation**, pillage; sack; rapine, **havoc**.

**peculation**, breach of trust; blackmail,
extortion, protection racket; daylight
robbery; rip-off; tax evasion, fraud,
fiddle, swindle; confidence trick, skin
game, **deception**.

**thievishness**, kleptomania; intention to
steal.

**Adj. thieving**; with intent to steal; predatory; **dishonest**.

**Vb. steal**, lift, thieve, pilfer, shoplift,
help oneself; pick locks, blow a safe;
burgle; rob, relieve of; rifle, sack;
swipe, nobble, nick, pinch, pocket,
bone, prig, snaffle, snitch, **take**; forage, scrounge; lift cattle, rustle;

abduct, kidnap, shanghai; abstract,
purloin, filch; crib, copy, infringe
copyright, pirate, **copy**; smuggle, run,
bootleg, poach, hijack.

**defraud**, embezzle, peculate, misappropriate, purloin; fiddle, commit breach
of trust; con, swindle, cheat, diddle,
chisel, **deceive**; rook, pigeon, gull,
dupe; pluck, skin, **fleece**.

**rob**, rob with violence, mug; commit
highway robbery; pirate, buccaneer,
filibuster, maraud, raid; foray, forage,
scrounge; strip, gut, ransack, rifle;
plunder, pillage, loot, sack, ravage,
spoil, **lay waste**; make a prey of,
blackmail; extort, screw, squeeze,
**oppress**.

## 784 Thief

**N. thief**, swell mob, crook; petty thief;
sneaker, sneak thief; pickpocket, dip;
cattle thief, rustler; burglar, housebreaker; poacher, runner; slaver;
fence, receiver of stolen property;
pirate.

**robber**; brigand, bandit, outlaw, Robin
Hood; highwayman; thug, **ruffian**;
gangster, racketeer; gunman; pirate,
buccaneer, corsair, filibuster, privateer; raider, freebooter; wrecker.

**defrauder**; cheat, shark, con man,
**trickster**; forger.

## 785 Booty

**N. booty**, spoil, spoils; spoils of war,
**trophy**; plunder, loot, pillage; prey,
victim, quarry; find, strike, prize, purchase, haul, catch, **gain**; stolen article,
stolen goods, swag; moonshine,
hooch, bootleg, contraband; graft,
blackmail; pork barrel.

## 786 Barter

**N. barter**, exchange, **interchange**;
exchange of goods, truck, truck sys-

tem; traffic, dealing; horse-trading.

**trade**, commercial intercourse; visible trade, foreign trade, protection; free trade, open market, **market**; traffic, slave trade; black market; retail trade, **sale**; capitalism, free enterprise, **scope**; free market economy; mutual profit; dollar diplomacy, **inducement**; commerce, **business**; private enterprise, private sector, venture, **undertaking**; deal, bargain, **compact**; clientele, custom, **purchase**.

**Adj. trading**; commercial, mercantile; wholesale, retail; **speculative**.

**Vb. trade**, exchange, **interchange**; barter, truck; open a trade, merchant, **do business**; handle, fence; **sell**; trade with, finance, back, promote; have an eye to business.

**speculate**, venture, risk, **gamble**; invest; racketeer, profiteer; go bust; operate, bull, bear, stag.

**bargain**, negotiate; haggle, dicker, **make terms**; make a bid, make a takeover bid, preempt; outbid; **offer**; **overrate**; **underestimate**; charge, **give terms**; take; drive a bargain, do a deal, **contract**.

**Adv. in trade**, in business; across the counter.

## 787 Purchase

**N. purchase**; takeover, preemption; redemption, ransom, **deliverance**; hire purchase; **expenditure**; mail order; custom, patronage, consumer demand, **requirement**, inducement; bid, **offer**; first refusal, right of purchase; a purchase, buy, bargain.

**purchaser**, buyer, consignee; buyer of labour, employer; customer, patron, client, clientele, consumer, redeemer; share-buyer, bull, stag.

**Adj. bought**, paid for, redeemed, purchased, bribed.

**buying**, marketing; preemptive, bidding.

**Vb. purchase**, buy, **acquire**; shop, market; **require**; make a good buy; buy outright; **borrow**; **store**; preempt, corner; make a take-over bid; square, suborn, **bribe**; buy back, redeem, ransom, **deliver**; **defray**; **speculate**; buy service, rent, **hire**; bid, **offer**; buy shares, bull, stag.

## 788 Sale

**N. sale**; marketing; disposal; clearance, sell-out; clearance sale, sale of work, bazaar; sale of office; exclusive sale, monopoly, oligopoly, **restraint**; public sale, auction, Dutch auction; good market; sales, boom; bad sales, **adversity**; service, sales talk, pitch, sales patter, spiel; hard sell, **advertisement**; market research, **enquiry**; thing sold, seller, **merchandise**.

**seller**; bear; barrow boy, costermonger, pedlar; shopkeeper, dealer; retailer; sales representative, rep; traveller; agent, tout; shop assistant, shop girl, salesman; clerk, ticket agent; roundsman, milkman.

**Adj. salable**; sold; sought after; available.

**Vb. sell**, make a sale; flog, dispose of; market, vend; bring to market, dump; hawk, peddle, push; tout; **provide**; auction; wholesale; retail; **trade**; sell at a profit, **gain**; sell at a loss, **lose**; undercut, **cheapen**; remainder; **cease**; clear stock, hold a sale; sell again; sell forward.

**be sold**; sell, have a sale, have a market, meet a demand, sell well, boom; be a best-seller; sell badly.

## 789 Merchant

**N. merchant**, merchant prince; livery company, guild, chamber of commerce, concern, firm, **corporation**; business person, man or woman of business; entrepreneur, operator; fence; slaver; wholesale merchant; dealer; middleman, broker, stockbroker; estate agent, financier; banker; money-changer.

**tradespeople**; tradesman, retailer, middleman, tallyman, shopkeeper, **seller**; ironmonger, haberdasher, grocer, provision merchant.

**pedlar**, **seller**; street seller, cheapjack; costermonger, barrow boy.

## 790 Merchandise

N. **merchandise**, article of commerce, line, staple; article, commodity, stock, stock-in-trade, range, repertoire, **store**; freight, cargo, **contents**; stuff, supplies, wares, goods; shop goods; perishable goods, sundries.

## 791 Market

N. **market**, mart; open market, free trade area, Common Market, Comecon; free market, **trade**; black market, underground economy, market cross, forum, **focus**; street market, Petticoat Lane, auction room; fair, motor show; exhibition, exposition, shop window, **exhibit**; corn market, wheat pit, corn exchange; exchange, Change, kerb market, bucket shop; Wall Street; toll booth, custom house.

**emporium**, free port, depot, warehouse, **storage**; wharf, quay; general market, bazaar, arcade, pedestrian precinct.

**shop**, store, emporium, bazaar, boutique, bargain basement, supermarket, hypermarket; concern, firm, establishment, house, corner shop, stall, booth, stand, kiosk, barrow, counter, shop window, window display; premises, place of business, workshop.

## 792 Money

N. **money**, Lsd; pelf, **wealth**; lucre, root of all evil; medium of exchange, cash nexus; currency, sound currency, honest money, legal tender; money of account, sterling, precious metal, gold, silver, ready money, cash, change, **small coin**; pocket money, paltry sum, chickenfeed, peanuts.

**shekels**, brass, tin, dough, lolly, sugar, bread; swag, loot, gravy; soap, palm oil, **incentive**.

**funds**, hot money; liquidity; account; wherewithal, **means**; ready money, finances, exchequer, cash flow, cash supplies, treasure, **provision**; remittance, **payment**; capital; sum of money, amount, figure, sum, quid, smacker; fiver, tenner, pony, monkey, grand; mint of money, pile, packet, **great quantity**; purse, **store**.

**finance**, world of finance; money power, purse strings, almighty dollar; money market, exchange, **market**; exchange rate, parity, par, **equality**; snake; floating pound; rising exchange rate, strong pound; gold standard; green pound; deficit finance, inflation, inflationary spiral; deflation; reflation.

**coinage**, issue; metallic currency, coin, piece; monetary unit, monetary denomination; guinea, sovereign, pound, quid; crown, florin, shilling, bob, sixpence, tanner, penny, copper, halfpenny, farthing; decimal coinage, fifty p, ten p, five p, two p, one p, half p; dollar, buck; half dollar, quarter, dime, nickel, cent; eagle; franc, mark; guilder, krona, krone, lira, peseta, rupee, rand, yen; talent, shekel, ducat, angel, noble, real, piece of eight; change, centime, pfennig, cash, **small coin**; shell money, wampum; numismatics.

**paper money**; wad; note, treasury note, bill, buck; bill of exchange, negotiable instrument; draft, order, check, cheque, letter of credit; note of hand, IOU; coupon, warrant, certificate, bond, **security**.

**false money**, base coin, snide; forgery; dud cheque, **nonpayment**.

**bullion**, bar, ingot, nugget; solid gold, solid silver; precious metal, platinum, gold, silver.

**minter**, mint master; forger; money-changer, **merchant**; cashier, treasurer; financier, capitalist; **rich person**.

**Adj. monetary**; pecuniary, fiscal; sterling, sound, solvent, **rich**; inflationary, deflationary; withdrawn.

**Vb. mint**, coin, stamp; issue, circulate; pass, utter; forge, counterfeit.

**demonetize**, withdraw; clip; devalue, depreciate, inflate, **cheapen**.

**draw money**, cash, cash a cheque, **pay**.

**793 Treasurer**

**N. treasurer**, bursar, purser; cashier, teller, croupier; stakeholder, trustee, steward, **consignee**; liquidator, **receiver**, **accountant**; banker, financier; paymaster, almoner; mint master; bank, **treasury**.

**794 Treasury**

**N. treasury**, treasure house, thesaurus; exchequer, public purse; fund, **store**; custom house; bursary; bank; savings bank, building society; coffer, chest, **box**; treasure chest, depository, **storage**; strongbox, safe, safe deposit, cash box, stocking, mattress; till, cash register, cash desk, slot machine; receipt of custom, box office, gate, turnstile; purse, purse strings, **pocket**; wallet, wad, rouleau, **case**.

**795 Wealth**

**N. wealth**, lucre, pelf, brass, **money**; golden touch; riches, **plenty**; luxury; ease, comfort, easy circumstances; **euphoria**; **credit**; solidity, substance; competence, **sufficiency**; high income, surtax bracket, **receiving**; gain; resources, capital, **means**; bank account; limitless resources, bottomless purse; nest egg, store; tidy sum, power of money, pile, packet, cool million, **great quantity**; fortune; **property**; bonanza, mine, king's ransom; plutocracy, capitalism.

**rich person**, man or woman of means; baron, tycoon, oil magnate, nabob, millionaire, moneymaker, money-spinner, fat cat, capitalist, plutocrat, heir to riches, poor little rich girl, **beneficiary**; jet set; new rich, self-made man, **prosperous person**; plutocracy.

**Adj. rich**, lush, fertile, **prolific**; abundant; luxurious, plush, slap-up; wealthy, opulent, affluent, **prosperous**; well-off, well-to-do, **comfortable**.

**moneyed**, propertied, worth a lot, worth a packet; made of money, rolling, dripping, loaded, stinking rich; flush; solvent, sound, able to pay; all straight.

**Vb. be rich**, turn all to gold; have money, have means, draw a large income; be flush, have credit, command capital, have money to burn; die rich, **bequeath**.

**afford**, be able to pay, be solvent, **have enough**.

**get rich, inherit**; prosper; enrich oneself, make money; make a packet, make a pile, make a bomb, make a fortune, strike it rich, **gain**; seek riches.

**make rich**, enrich, leave one a fortune, **bequeath**; enhance; **augment**;

improve, **make better**.

## 796 Poverty

N. poverty, Lady Poverty; voluntary poverty; Queer Street; loss of fortune, beggary; utter poverty, penury; privation, necessity, need, want, pinch, **requirement**; bare cupboard, empty larder, **scarcity**; famine; light pocket, empty purse, insufficient income, slender means, meagre resources, low water; straits, distress, **suffering**; hand-to-mouth existence, poorness; general poverty, recession, slump, depression; squalor, slum, substandard housing; workhouse, poorhouse.

poor person, broken man or woman, bankrupt, insolvent; hermit, **ascetic**; pauper, indigent, poor beggar, vagrant, tramp, down-and-out, **beggar**; underdog; new poor; **object of scorn**; poor white, white trash; poor relation, **inferior**; Job.

Adj. poor; underprivileged; impecunious, short, short of funds, short of cash; skint, bust, broke, bankrupt, insolvent; broken; deprived; poverty-stricken; needy, indigent, **necessitous**; hungry; straitened, hard put to it; penniless, destitute; without a bean, without a cent, without a sou, without prospects.

beggarly, starveling, shabby, seedy, tattered, threadbare, tatty, **dilapidated**; scruffy, squalid, mean, **dirty**; poverty-stricken.

Vb. be poor, earn little or nothing, scratch a living, scrape an existence; be unable to afford; starve, **be hungry**; want, lack, **require**; become poor, go broke; **deteriorate**; claim supplementary benefit.

impoverish, reduce to poverty, leave destitute, beggar; ruin, **destroy**; rob,

strip, **fleece**; dispossess, disinherit.

## 797 Credit

N. credit, repute, reputation, **prestige**; sound proposition; trust, confidence, reliability, **probity**; limit of credit; line of credit; tick; credit card; credit note; credit balance, **receipt**; account, score, tally, bill; national credit, floating debt, **debt**; loan, mortgage; vote.

creditor, dun; depositor.

Vb. credit, grant a loan, lend; grant, vote; await payment; take credit, open an account, keep an account with, **borrow**.

## 798 Debt

N. debt; obligation, commitment; mortgage, **security**; debit, charge; national debt, promise to pay, debt of honour, **promise**; bad debt, write-off, **loss**; good debt, gain; tally, account; deficit, overdraft, balance to pay, **shortfall**; inability to pay; frozen balance, **nonpayment**; **credit**; overdue payment, arrears, back pay, back rent.

interest, usury, pound of flesh; premium, rate of interest, bank rate.

debtor, loan applicant; bad debtor, insolvent.

Adj. indebted, indebted; liable, committed, responsible, answerable, bound; unable to pay, insolvent.

owed, due, overdue; outstanding; chargeable, payable, returnable, bearing.

Vb. be in debt, owe, have to repay; owe money, pay interest; accept a charge, be liable; get credit, **borrow**; use a credit card, keep an account with; welsh, do a moonlight flit; make oneself responsible, **incur a duty**.

**799 Payment**

**N. payment;** discharge, release, satisfaction, clearance, settlement; **receipt;** cash payment, ready money, **money;** first payment, earnest, earnest money, deposit; instalment, standing order; hire purchase; due payment, subscription, tribute, **tax;** voluntary payment, collection; **offering;** composition; indemnity, **restitution;** remittance, **expenditure.**

**pay,** payoff, pay packet, pay day, wages bill, wages, **salary, earnings;** grant, subsidy; salary, pension, annuity, emolument, fee, garnish, bribe, **reward;** cut, commission, **discount;** something paid, subscription, collection, tribute, **tax;** damages, indemnity, **penalty;** redundancy pay, golden handshake; paymaster, purser, cashier, **treasurer.**

**Adj. paying;** paying in full, paying cash; out of debt, owing nothing.

**Vb. pay,** disburse, expend; contribute, give; barter, **trade;** make payment; come across; pay a high price; pay back, repay, reimburse, compensate; **bribe;** pay wages, remunerate, tip, **reward;** pay cash, honour (a bill); meet, satisfy, redeem, discharge, get a receipt; clear, liquidate, settle, settle an account, **account;** settle a score; **retaliate.**

**defray;** buy a round, stand treat, treat, give; go Dutch, **participate.**

**Adv. cash down;** cash on delivery, C.O. D.; with ready money.

**800 Nonpayment**

**N. nonpayment,** default; stoppage, **penalty;** moratorium, embargo, freeze; refusal to pay, protest, **refusal;** tax evasion; hire purchase; **false money.**

**insolvency,** inability to pay; crash, failure; failure of credit; nothing to pay with, overdraft; **debt.**

**nonpayer;** failure, lame duck; bankrupt, insolvent debtor.

**Adj. nonpaying,** behindhand; unable to pay, insolvent, bankrupt; **indebted; poor.**

**Vb. not pay,** default, embezzle, swindle, **defraud;** get behindhand; stop payment, freeze, block; refuse payment, protest a bill; practise tax evasion, **be dishonest;** divert; dishonour, repudiate; become insolvent, go bankrupt; sink, fail, break, go bust, crash; welsh, **deceive;** abscond, **decamp;** be unable to pay, **be poor; be parsimonious;** cancel a debt, discharge a bankrupt, **abrogate.**

**801 Expenditure**

**N. expenditure, payment;** cost of living; outgoings, overheads, expense account; expense, outlay, investment; fee, tax, **pay.**

**Adj. expending;** generous, **liberal;** extravagant, **prodigal.**

expended, spent, paid.

**Vb. expend,** spend; buy, **purchase;** invest, sink money; afford, stand, disburse, **pay;** give money, donate, **give;** do it proud, be lavish, **be liberal;** fling money around, blow, be prodigal; consume, run through, **waste.**

**802 Receipt**

**N. receipt,** voucher; revenue, royalty; dues; customs, **tax;** turnover, takings, proceeds, returns, receipts, gate money, gate; income, privy purse; emolument, regular income, pay, salary, wages, **earnings; reward;** pension, annuity, tontine; allowance, pocket money, inadequate allowance, pittance; alimony, maintenance; scholarship, **acquisition;** interest, return, rake-off; winnings, capital gain; **gain;**

bonus, premium, **extra**; prize, **trophy**; draw, legacy.

**Adj. received**, paid, acknowledged.

**Vb. acquire**, receive, take.

## 803 Accounts

**N. accounts**, accountancy, commercial arithmetic; book-keeping, entry, audit; account, balance sheet; budget, **provision**; running account, statement of account, statement, bill, invoice, manifest, **list**; account paid, account settled, **payment**; reckoning, computation, score, tally.

**account book**, journal, ledger, register, books, **record**.

**accountant**, cost accountant; cashier, **treasurer**; actuary.

**Adj. accounting**, bookkeeping; reckoning; accountable.

**Vb. account**; budget, cost, value, **estimate**; book, enter, post, debit, credit, **register**; prepare a statement, present an account, charge, bill, invoice; overcharge, surcharge, undercharge, **price**; fiddle, garble, doctor, **defraud**; audit; take stock, inventory, catalogue, **list**.

## 804 Price

**N. price**, rate; piece rate, high rate, ceiling; low rate, floor; price control, fixed price, **restraint**; value, worth, what it will fetch; scarcity value, famine price; price list, tariff; quotation, price charged; amount, figure; ransom, fine, **penalty**; demand, dues, charge; surcharge, supplement, **extra**; overcharge, excessive charge, extortion, ransom; fare, hire, rental, rent, fee, entrance or admission fee; commission, rake-off; salvage; postage; cover charge; bill, invoice, reckoning, shot.

**cost**, damage, **expenditure**; overheads;

wages, wage bill; damages, **penalty**; cost of living, cost of living index.

**tax**, dues; taxation, tax demand, **demand**; rating, **estimate**; rate, levy, toll, duty; charge, forced loan, aid, benevolence, **compulsion**; forced savings; punitive tax, **penalty**; tribute, blackmail, ransom; tithe; national insurance; poll tax, estate duty, death duty; direct taxation, income tax, PAYE, surtax, supertax, company tax, capital levy; indirect taxation, excise, customs, tariff; local tax; purchase tax, VAT; salt tax; feudal tax.

**Adj. priced**, charged, fixed; chargeable, dutiable; paid.

**Vb. price**, cost, assess, value, rate, **estimate**; raise a price, ask a price, charge, require, **demand**; bill, invoice.

**cost**, be worth, fetch; amount to, come to; bear a price.

**tax**, impose a tax; fix a tariff, levy a rate, value; toll, excise, subject to duty, make dutiable; take a toll, **levy**; take a collection, **beg**; fine, **punish**.

## 805 Discount

**N. discount**, reduction, rebate, cut; stoppage; concession, allowance, margin, special price; tare; drawback; cut price, cut rate, special offer, loss leader, **incentive**; bargain price, bargain sale; percentage; commission, rake-off.

**Vb. discount**, deduct, **subtract**; allow a margin, tare; reduce, depreciate, abate, rebate, **abate**; offer a discount, cut, slash, **cheapen**; take a discount.

**Adv. at a discount**, below par.

## 806 Dearness

**N. dearness**; value, high worth; famine price, scarcity value, rarity, dearth, **scarcity**; extortion, rip-off; overcharge, excessive charge, bad value, bad bargain, high price, cost, pretty penny; ruinous charge; cheap money, inflation, inflationary pressure.

**Adj. dear**, expensive; costly; extravagant; exorbitant, excessive, extortionate, preposterous, steep, stiff, skyhigh; prohibitive, more than one can afford; dear at any price, **useless**; rising, inflationary.

**of price**, of value, of worth, **valuable**; priceless, beyond price, invaluable, **useful**; inestimable, worth a king's ransom, worth a fortune; precious, rare, scarce, like gold dust, **infrequent**; at a premium.

**Vb. be dear**, cost a lot, cost a packet, cost a pretty penny, harden; appreciate, escalate, soar, mount, climb; get too dear; prove expensive, cost one dear, cost a fortune.

**overcharge**, sell dear, oversell, ask too much; profiteer, soak, sting, bleed, skin, extort, short-change, hold to ransom, **fleece**; bull, auction, **sell**.

**pay too much**, be stung, be had, be done; pay high, pay dear, buy a white elephant; ruin oneself.

**Adv. dearly**, dear, at a price, at great cost, at huge expense.

## 807 Cheapness

**N. cheapness**; good value, snip, bargain; sale goods, seconds; low price, reasonable charge; cheap rate, excursion fare, **discount**; nominal price, peppercorn rent, easy terms; Dutch auction; fall, slump; deflation, glut, **plenty**.

**no charge**, labour of love, **voluntary work**; free trade, free port; free entry, free admission, free pass, free ticket; free quarters; free board, free service, free delivery.

**Adj. cheap**, inexpensive, moderate, reasonable, fair; cheap to make; sub-standard, shop-soiled; economical, economy, economy size; worth its price; low, going cheap; cut-price; easy to buy; worth nothing, cheap-jack, catchpenny, **useless**.

**uncharged**, gratuitous, complimentary; gratis; free, free of charge; honorary, **voluntary; given**; free.

**Vb. be cheap**, cost little, be economical; cost nothing, be without charge, be free; cheapen, depreciate, decline, sag, fall, drift, slump, plunge, plummet.

**cheapen**, lower, keep cheap, cut, slash; undercharge, underrate, sacrifice, make a present of, **give**; undercut, undersell; dump, unload; glut; **bear**.

**Adv. cheaply**; at cost price, at prime cost, at a discount.

## 808 Liberality

**N. liberality**, munificence, generosity; open heart, open hand, open purse, hospitality, open house; free hand, blank cheque, **scope**; cornucopia, **plenty**; bounty, largesse, **gift**; handsome offer, **offer**; charity, kind act.

**good giver**, liberal donor; Lady Bountiful, Father Christmas, rich uncle, **benefactor**.

**Adj. liberal**, free, free-handed, lavish, prodigal; large-hearted, **disinterested**; bountiful, charitable, hospitable, **sociable**; handsome, generous, splendid, slap-up; lordly, princely, royal, right royal; unsparing, unfailing; abundant, ample, bounteous, profuse, full; **redundant**.

**Vb. be liberal**, lavish, shower largesse, give; overpay, pay well, keep open house, **be hospitable**; do one proud; give a blank cheque, **give scope**; spend freely, **be prodigal**.

**Adv. liberally**, with open hand.

## 809 Economy

**N. economy**, thrift; care; husbandry, good housekeeping; good management, credit squeeze; economy drive; time-saving; saving, sparing; savings, **store**; conservation; **niggard**; good housewife, careful steward.

**Adj. economical**, time-saving; chary of expense, **parsimonious**; thrifty, careful, prudent, canny, frugal, saving, sparing, spare; meagre, Spartan, sparse; marginal, with nothing to spare.

**Vb. economize**, be economical, waste nothing, recycle, reuse; keep within compass; cut back, retrench; pinch, scrape, **be parsimonious**; save, spare, hoard, **store**; plough back, make every penny work, **get rich**.

**Adv. sparingly**, economically, frugally.

## 810 Prodigality

**N. prodigality**, profusion; idle display, idle expenditure, conspicuous consumption, **ostentation**; wasteful expenditure, **waste**; deficit finance; misuse of funds, **misuse**.

**prodigal**, prodigal son, waster, wastrel, profligate, spendthrift.

**Adj. prodigal**, lavish, **liberal**; profuse; extravagant, regardless of cost, wasteful, profligate; uneconomic, spendthrift, improvident, reckless, dissipated.

**Vb. be prodigal**, splash money around; spend money like water; blow everything, squander, **waste**; dissipate, misspend, throw good money after bad; spend more than one has, overdraw; save nothing.

**Adv. prodigally**; like a prodigal, like a spendthrift.

**Int.** hang the expense a short life and a merry one easy come, easy go

## 811 Parsimony

**N. parsimony**; credit squeeze, **economy**; false economy; cheese-paring; grudging hand, closed purse.

**avarice**, cupidity; rapacity, greed, **desire**.

**niggard**, skinflint, screw, scrimp, scraper, tightwad; miser, moneygrubber; squirrel, magpie; churl, codger, curmudgeon; usurer; Scrooge.

**Adj. parsimonious**, careful, **economical**; too careful, frugal to excess; mean, mingy, stingy, near, close, tight; tight-fisted; grudging, churlish, illiberal, ungenerous, uncharitable, empty-handed; chary, sparing, shabby, small-minded.

**avaricious**, grasping, **selfish**; possessive, acquisitive, hoarding, saving; covetous; rapacious, extortionate; mercenary, venal, sordid.

**Vb. be parsimonious**, **retain**; grudge, begrudge, withhold, keep back, **refuse**; stint, skimp, starve, spare, **make insufficient**; scrape, scrimp, pinch; screw, skin a flint, fleece; starve oneself, live like a pauper; hoard wealth, never spend a penny; grudge every farthing, haggle, **bargain**; cadge, beg, borrow, hoard, **be selfish**.

**Adv. parsimoniously**, niggardly, sparingly, on a shoestring.

## 812 Affections

**N. affections**; emotional life; nature, disposition, **character**; spirit, temper, tone, grain, mettle, **temperament**; cast of mind, trait, **state**; personality, psychology, mentality, outlook, **heredity**; being, breast, bosom, heart, soul, core, inmost soul, inner man, **essential part**, **spirit**; attitude, frame of mind, vein, strain, humour, mood;

predilection, turn, bent, bias, **tendency**; passion, **prejudice**; heartstrings, **feeling**; force of character; anthropomorphism, pathetic fallacy.

**Adj. with affections**, affected, cast; instinct with, inborn, inbred, congenital, **genetic**; deep-rooted, **intrinsic**; emotional, demonstrative, **feeling**.

## 813 Feeling

**N. feeling**, experience, emotional life, affect, sensation, sense of, **sense**; emotion, **sentiment**; true feeling, impulse; intuition, instinct; response, reaction, fellow feeling, sympathy; empathy, appreciation, understanding, **knowledge**; impression, deep feeling, deep sense of, **moral sensibility**; religious feeling, **piety**; **benevolence**; **love**; **resentment**; thrill, kick, spasm; shock, turn, **lack of expectation**; pathos, **suffering**; release of feeling; romanticism; manifestation of feeling; expression, play of features, **gesture**; blush, flush; gooseflesh, tremor, quiver, flutter, flurry; stew, ferment, **commotion**; swelling heart; control of feeling, endurance, stiff upper lip, **patience**.

**warm feeling**, glow; full heart, hot head; fervour, ardour, enthusiasm, dash, fire; vigour, zeal, **activity**; mania, **prejudice**; emotion, passion, ecstasy, inspiration, elevation, **excitable state**.

**Adj. feeling**, sensible, sensory, **sentient**; spirited, vivacious, lively, **sensitive**; sensuous, **sensual**; living; bearing, **suffering**; sensitive, vibrant, responsive, involved, sympathetic; tenderhearted; emotional, passionate, full of feeling; unctuous, soulful; intense, tense, **excited**; cordial, hearty; effusive; sentimental, romantic; mawkish, maudlin, treacly, soppy, sloppy.

**impressed**, affected; touched, **excited**; struck, awestruck, struck all of a heap; rapt, ecstatic; lyrical, raving, **excitable**.

**fervent**, fervid, passionate, ardent, tense, intense; eager, breathless; impassioned, vehement, earnest, zealous; exuberant; warm-blooded, impetuous, impatient, **excitable**; warm, fiery, glowing, burning, redhot, flaming, **hot**; hysterical, overwrought, feverish, hectic; strong, furious, **violent**.

**felt**, experienced; heartfelt, cordial, hearty, warm, sincere, **veracious**; deep-seated, profound, **deep**; stirring, heart-warming; emotive, strong, **impressive**; smart, acute, keen, poignant, piercing, trenchant, **sharp**; caustic, burning, **pungent**; penetrating, absorbing; ecstatic; pathetic, affecting.

**Vb. feel**, sense, receive an impression; entertain, take to heart, **be sensitive**; experience, live, live through, taste; bear, endure, undergo, smart, **suffer**; suffer with, share, **participate**; respond, react, tingle, warm to, fire, kindle, catch, be inspired, **be excited**; cause feeling, **impress**.

**show feeling**, demonstrate, **manifest**; enthuse, **be pleased**; get angry; turn colour, look blue, look black; go livid, go purple, **blacken**; look pale, blench, turn pale, go white, **whiten**; colour, blush, flush, glow, mantle, turn red, turn crimson, **redden**; quiver, tremble, wince, flutter, shake, quake; tingle, thrill, vibrate, throb, **oscillate**; palpitate, pant, heave, draw a deep breath, **breathe**; reel, lurch, stagger, stutter, **stammer**.

**Adv. feelingly**, earnestly, heart and soul; with a full heart; heartily, devoutly, sincerely.

**814 Sensibility**

**N. moral sensibility,** soul; thin skin, soft spot, tender spot; sore point, **resentment**; affection; love; spirit, verve, **vigour**, ebullience; **discrimination**; temperament; **sensibility**; touchy person, sensitive plant; bundle of nerves.

**Adj. impressible,** malleable, plastic, **soft**; sensible, aware, conscious of, awake to, alive to, responsive, **sentient**, touched; impressionable, **excitable**; susceptible; romantic, sentimental; soppy, wet; emotional; soft, tender, tender-hearted.

**sensitive**; sore, raw, tender, **sentient**, aesthetic; fastidious, particular; hypersensitive, all feeling, **excitable**; touchy, irritable, impatient, thin-skinned, easily stung, **irascible**.

**lively,** alive, vital, vivacious; skittish, **merry**; irrepressible; mettlesome, spirited, alert, aware, **attentive**; impatient; nervous, highly-strung, overstrung, temperamental; mobile, changeable; impassioned, **fervent**, fanatic; expressive, racy, **forceful**.

**Vb. be sensitive,** have a soft heart, take it to heart, **pity**; tingle.

**Adv. on the raw,** to the quick, where it hurts most.

**815 Insensibility**

**N. moral insensibility;** lack of sensation, stupor, **insensibility**; inertia; lethargy; vegetation; **inattention**; insouciance, detachment, apathy; phlegm, sangfroid; repression, repression of feeling, **patience**; poker face, deadpan expression; thick skin, rhinoceros hide; cold heart, frigidity; **hardness**; lack of feeling, dry eyes, heart of stone, heart of marble, **inhumanity**; **tedium**; **lack of wonder.**

**unfeeling person,** iceberg, icicle, cold fish, cold heart, cold-blooded animal; stoic, ascetic; stock, stone, block, marble.

**Adj. impassive,** unconscious, **insensible**; insensitive; phlegmatic, stolid; wooden; bovine; dull, slow; proof, proof against, ascetic; unconcerned, aloof, distant, detached, **indifferent**; unaffected, calm, **tranquil**; steady, unruffled; imperturbable, without nerves, cool; inscrutable, blank, expressionless, deadpan; unseeing, **blind; deaf**; impersonal, dispassionate, without warmth, reserved, stony, frigid, frozen, icy, cold, cold-blooded, cold-hearted; unfeeling, heartless, soulless, inhuman.

**apathetic;** unmoved; half-hearted, lukewarm, **indifferent**; uninterested; nonchalant, careless, regardless, neglectful, **negligent**; spiritless, lackadaisical; stagnant, **quiescent**; sluggish, supine; passive, **inert**; torpid, numb, benumbed, comatose, **insensible**.

**thick-skinned**; impenetrable, impervious; blind to, deaf to, dead to, closed to; obtuse, insensitive; callous, tough, **hard**; hard-bitten, hard-boiled; shameless, unblushing, amoral.

**Vb. be insensitive, be insensible**; be blind to, **be blind**; lack animation, lack spirit, lack verve; harden oneself, **be pitiless**; **be indifferent**; be a Philistine; **despise**; ignore, **disregard**; be **temperate**; stagnate, vegetate; **be resolute**.

**make insensitive, render insensible**; render callous, steel, toughen, **harden**; sear, **dry**; deafen, **silence; blind; pervert**; blunt, coarsen; satiate, cloy, **sate**; deaden, **blunt**.

**Adv. in cold blood,** with dry eyes, without emotion, with steady pulse; without enthusiasm.

## 816 Excitation

**N. excitation**, rousing; possession, inspiration; calling forth; animation, invitation, appeal, **inducement**; provocation, irritation; impression, image, impact, **influence**; fascination, **sorcery**; rapture, **joy**; emotional appeal, human interest, sentiment, pathos; sensationalism, melodrama; excitement, high pressure, tension, **energy**; state of excitement, ebullience; shock, thrill, **spasm**; stew, ferment, tizzy, flurry, furore, **commotion**; pitch of excitement, fever pitch, orgasm, **frenzy**; climax, **crisis**, excited feeling, passion, emotion, enthusiasm, lyricism, **feeling**; fuss, drama, **excitable state**; temper, fury, rage, **anger**; interest, **curiosity**; **wonder**; awe, **fear**.

**excitant**, tub-thumper, **agitator**; sob sister; headline, **publicity**; fillip, ginger, tonic, **stimulant**; upper, pep pill; sting, prick, goad, spur, whip, lash, **incentive**; fan.

**Adj. excited**, busy, astir, **active**; **bubbly**; tense; feverish, hectic; frantic; glowing, **fervent**; heated, **hot**; red-hot with excitement, violent, **furious**; wild, mad, livid, roaring, **angry**; avid, eager, agog; **feeling**; all of a flutter; restless, restive, overwrought, distraught; beside oneself, hysterical, running amok, a prey to passion; crazy about, **enamoured**; inspired, possessed, impassioned, lyrical, raving, **excitable**.

**exciting**, heady, exhilarating; provocative, piquant, salty, spicy, appetizing; evocative, emotive, suggestive; hair-raising; moving, affecting; heating, kindling, rousing, stirring; cheering, rousing, sensational, dramatic, melodramatic, stunning, mind-blowing; gripping, absorbing.

**impressive**, imposing, grand, stately; regal, royal, queenly, **noble**; awe-inspiring, sublime; picturesque, scenic; striking, dramatic; telling, forceful.

**Vb. excite**, affect, infect, **influence**; **cheer**; touch, move, **sadden**; strike a chord, startle, electrify; raise to fever pitch, **heat**; inflame, kindle, draw a spark, **burn**; sting, pique, irritate, **enrage**; tease, **torment**; **hurt**; **incite**; enthuse, inspire, possess; stir, rouse, arouse, wake, evoke, call forth; thrill, exhilarate, intoxicate; transport, send, **delight**.

**animate**, enliven, quicken; revive, resuscitate, **restore**; inspire; encourage, hearten, **give courage**; give an edge, whet, **sharpen**; urge, nag, spur, goad, lash, **accelerate**; jolt, jog; fillip, give a fillip to, stimulate, ginger, **invigorate**; cherish, foster, foment, **strengthen**; fuel, intensify, fan.

**impress**, leave an impression; project or present an image; interest, hold, grip, absorb; intrigue, rouse curiosity; strike, claim attention, **attract notice**; affect, **influence**; bring home to, drive home; come home to, penetrate, pierce, **be intelligible**; arrest, shake, smite, stun, amaze, astound, stagger, **surprise**; stupefy, petrify, **be wonderful**; dazzle, fill with admiration; inspire with awe, humble; overwhelm; oppress, perturb, disquiet, upset, unsettle, distress, worry, **trouble**.

**be excited**, flare, flame, burn, **be hot**; sizzle, seethe, boil, explode, **effervesce**; thrill to, **feel**; tingle, tremble, **be excitable**; quiver, flutter, palpitate; mantle, flush, **show feeling**; squirm, writhe, **wriggle**; dance, stamp, ramp; jump, **leap**; be unable to sleep.

**Adv. excitedly**; all agog, with beating heart.

**817 Excitability**

N. **excitability**; instability, temperament; hot blood, hot temper; **bias**; headstrong behaviour; **haste**; turbulence; nerves, flap.

**excitable state**, elevation, elation, abandon; thrill, transport, trip, high, ecstasy, inspiration, lyricism, **feeling**; fever, fever of excitement, fret, fume, trepidation, bother, fuss, flurry, whirl; warmth, **heat**; ferment, pother, stew; gust, storm, tempest, **gale**; outburst, outbreak, explosion, scene, **commotion**; brainstorm, hysterics, delirium, fit, agony, **frenzy**; distraction, madness; mania, passion, rage, fury, **violence**; temper, rampage, **anger**.

Adj. **excitable**, raw, **sensitive**; passionate, emotional; susceptible, romantic; suggestible, inflammable, like tinder; unstable, impressionable; variable, temperamental, volatile; fitful, **capricious**; restless, nervy, fidgety, edgy; highly-strung, nervous, skittish, mettlesome, **lively**; irritable, fiery, hottempered, **irascible**; impatient, trigger-happy, **hasty**; impetuous, impulsive, madcap, **rash**; savage, fierce; vehement, boisterous, rumbustious, tempestuous, turbulent, stormy, uproarious, clamorous, **violent**; restive, **riotous**; volcanic, explosive, ready to burst; intolerant, rabid, **furious**; feverish, febrile, frantic, hysterical; tense, electric; inspired, raving, lyrical, **excited**.

Vb. **be excitable**, fret, fume, stamp; shuffle, chafe, fidget; show excitement, show temperament, **show feeling**; tingle with; have nerves, flap; start, jump, **be nervous**; have a temper, **be irascible**; foam, froth, have hysterics, **go mad**; abandon oneself, let oneself go, go wild, run riot, run amok, see red; storm, rush about, rampage; ramp, rage, roar, **be violent**; explode, create, **get angry**; kindle, burn, smoulder, catch fire, **be excited**.

**818 Inexcitability**

N. **inexcitability**, good temper; composure; cool, sangfroid; frigidity, **moral insensibility**; unruffled state, **quietude**; peace of mind, **content**; equanimity, balance, poise, even temper, philosophy, balanced mind, **equilibrium**; self-possession, self-control, **temperance**; repression; detachment; gravity, sobriety; **courtesy**; lack of spirit, lack of mettle; **moderation**.

**patience**, patience of Job; forbearance, endurance, longsuffering; tolerance, toleration; resignation, **submission**.

Adj. **inexcitable**, dispassionate, cold, frigid, heavy, dull, **impassive**; stable; cool, imperturbable, unflappable; steady; moderate, **temperate**; inscrutable, deadpan; deliberate, **slow**; even, level, equable, **uniform**; eventempered, easy-going, sunny; staid, sedate, sober, demure, reserved; grave, **serious**; quiet, **quiescent**; placid, unruffled, calm, serene, **tranquil**; sweet, gentle, mild, meek, innocent; **moderate**; **peaceful**; easy, easygoing, lenient; comfortable, **content**; **indifferent**; acquiescent, resigned, submissive, **obedient**; spiritless, lackadaisical, torpid, passive, **inert**; tame; earthbound, **prosaic**.

**patient**, meek, armed with patience; tolerant, longsuffering, forbearing, stoic, philosophical.

Vb. **keep calm**, be collected; compose oneself, keep cool, keep a cool head; **be insensitive**; relax, take things easy, **repose**; resign oneself, have patience, be resigned, **submit**.

**be patient**, show patience, show

restraint, forbear; stand, tolerate, bear, endure, support, sustain, suffer, abide; resign oneself; brook, take, swallow, digest, stomach, pocket; **forgive**; be tolerant, condone, **be lenient**; turn a blind eye, overlook, be lax; allow, **permit**; ignore provocation, **be at peace**; coexist, **compromise**.

tranquillize, steady, moderate, assuage; calm, rock, lull, **bring to rest**; compose, **pacify**; **relieve**; control, repress, **restrain**.

## 819 Joy

N. joy, **pleasure**; great pleasure, sensation of pleasure, thrill, kick; delight, rapture, exaltation; ecstasy; unholy joy, malice; life of pleasure; honeymoon.

happiness, felicity, good fortune, wellbeing, comfort, ease, **euphoria**; unalloyed delight, rose without a thorn; golden age, age of Aquarius; bliss; cloud nine, nirvana, Paradise, Elysium, Garden of Eden, Arcadia, **fantasy**; happy valley, bower of bliss, home sweet home.

enjoyment, satisfaction, fulfilment, **content**; delectation, relish, zest, gusto; indulgence; full life, hedonism; glee; merry-making, lark, frolic, gambol, **merriment**; fun, treat, excursion, outing, **amusement**; refreshment, good cheer.

Adj. pleased, glad; receiving with open arms; happy, **content**; loving it; **merry**; exalted, overjoyed, **jubilant**; cheering, shouting; ecstatic, raving.

happy, blithe, joyful, joyous, **merry**; radiant, starry-eyed; felicitous, lucky, fortunate, **prosperous**; blessed; at ease, made comfortable, **comfortable**.

Vb. be pleased; feel or experience pleasure, hug oneself, purr, purr with pleasure, **be cheerful**; laugh, smile, **rejoice**; rave, rave about, **show feeling**; solace oneself with, wallow, spoil oneself; **enjoy**; have fun, amuse oneself; gloat; savour, appreciate, relish, **taste**; take a fancy to, like, **love**; think well of, **approve**.

## 820 Suffering

N. suffering, heartache, **melancholy**; nostalgia, **desire**, **discontent**; **fatigue**; nightmare, incubus; affliction, distress, anguish, angst, agony, torture, torment, **pain**; twinge, stab, smart, sting, thorn, **pang**; bitter cup; Passion, Crucifixion, Calvary, martyrdom; rack, **punishment**; purgatory, hell, damnation; **difficulty**; inconvenience, discomfort, malaise; trial, ordeal; shock, blow, visitation, tribulation; **bane**; extremity, **illness**; living death, fate worse than death, **evil**; unhappy times, iron age, **adversity**.

sorrow, grief, gloom, **dejection**; dole, woe, misery, despair; tale of woe, **adversity**; heavy heart, displeasure, **discontent**; chagrin, remorse, **regret**.

worry, discomfort, disquiet, inquietude, fret, dismay, distress; phobia, hangup; anxiety, concern, solicitude, thought, care; responsibility, load, burden; strain, tension; a worry; trouble, evil, bother, irritation, pest, death of, **bane**; **bore**; something to worry about, lookout, funeral; headache, teaser, puzzle, problem.

sufferer, victim, scapegoat, sacrifice; prey, shorn lamb, **dupe**; willing sacrifice, martyr; object of compassion, wretch, misery, patient, **sick person**.

Adj. suffering, ill, sick; bleeding, **pained**; uncomfortable, ill at ease; anxious, unhappy about, apprehensive, **nervous**; sick with worry; longsuffering, downtrodden; made a prey; stricken;

careworn, woeful, woebegone, haggard.

**unhappy**, infelicitous, accursed, **unfortunate**; despairing, **hopeless**; pitiable, poor, miserable; sad, melancholy, despondent, disconsolate; heartbroken, sick at heart; woebegone, **dejected**; weeping, tearful; pained; sorry.

**Vb. suffer**, undergo, endure, go through, experience, **feel**; bear, endure; bear pain, bleed; hurt oneself, be hurt, smart, chafe, ache, **feel pain**; wince, flinch, writhe, squirm, **wriggle**; become a martyr, sacrifice oneself; **stand firm**; have a thin time, go through it, have trouble enough, **have trouble**; trouble oneself, fuss, worry, worry to death, fret; mind, take it badly, take it to heart; sorrow, passion, grieve, weep, sigh, **lament**, pity oneself, be despondent, **be dejected**; have regrets, kick oneself, **regret**.

**821 Pleasurableness**

**N. pleasurableness**, amenity, sunny side, appeal, **attraction**; flattery; charm, fascination, beauty; honeymoon, **joy**; something nice, a delight, a treat, a joy; novelty, pastime, fun, **amusement**; interest, melody, harmony, **music**; spice, zest, relish; dainty, titbit, sweet; balm, **refreshment**; plenty; peace, quietude, leisure; fantasy.

**Adj. pleasurable**, pleasant, nice, good, pleasing, agreeable, grateful; acceptable, welcome; wonderful, marvellous, splendid, **excellent**; painless, **comfortable**; refreshing; peaceful, quiet, **tranquil**; luxurious, voluptuous, **sensuous**; genial, warm, sunny, **cheering**; delightful, delectable, delicious, exquisite, choice; luscious, juicy; delicate, tasty, **savoury**; sugary,

sweet; musical, **melodious**; picturesque, scenic, lovely, **beautiful**; amiable, dear, endearing; attractive, appealing; seductive, inviting; enchanting, ravishing, Siren; haunting, heart-warming, **exciting**; homely, cosy; pastoral; heavenly; beatific, blessed, **happy**.

**Vb. please**, give pleasure, agree with; make things pleasant, **flatter**; lull, soothe, **assuage**; comfort, **cheer**; put at ease, make comfortable, **relieve**; sugar, **sweeten**; stroke, pat, pet, baby, coddle, nurse, **caress**; indulge, **be lax**; charm, interest, **amuse**; rejoice, gladden, make happy; gratify, satisfy, **content**; bless.

**delight**, rejoice, exhilarate, elate, elevate, uplift; thrill, intoxicate, ravish; transport, send, **excite**; flatter; **excite love**; **make appetizing**; refresh; tickle, tickle one to death, titillate, tease; entrance, enrapture; enchant, charm, **bewitch**; impress; allure, seduce, **attract**.

**822 Painfulness**

**N. painfulness**, painful treatment, roughness, harassment; evil; **eyesore**; friction, irritation; **pain**; sore subject, sore point, rub, soft spot, **moral sensibility**; sore, ulcer, bane; shock, **lack of expectation**; disgust, nausea; bitter cup, bitter draught, bitter pill, vinegar; bread of affliction, **adversity**; tribulation, ordeal, cross, **suffering**; trouble, care, **worry**; pathos; sorry sight, sad spectacle, object of pity; heavy news, **sorrow**; hot water, **predicament**.

**annoyance**, death of, pest, curse, plague, bane; embarrassment, **worry**; interference, nuisance; burden, drag; grievance, complaint; hardship, **evil**; last straw, limit; offence, affront, insult, provocation, **indignity**; displeasure, resentment; menace.

**Adj. paining**, sore, tender; dolorous, **painful**; scathing, searing, scalding, burning, sharp, biting, nipping, gnawing; caustic, vitriolic; harsh, hard, rough, cruel, **severe**; gruelling, punishing, searching, exquisite, excruciating, extreme; hurtful, poisonous.

**unpleasant**, disagreeable; uncomfortable, joyless, dreary, dismal, **cheerless**; hideous, **ugly**; thankless; distasteful, **unsavoury**; foul, nasty, beastly, horrible; malodorous, stinking, **fetid**; bitter, sharp, **sour**; invidious, obnoxious, offensive, objectionable, undesirable, odious, hateful, loathsome, nauseous, slimy, revolting, repellent; execrable, accursed.

**annoying**, too bad; troublesome; wearisome, irksome, tiresome, **tedious**; burdensome, onerous, **weighty**; unfortunate, untoward, **adverse**; awkward, impossible; importunate; provoking, maddening; biting.

**distressing**, grievous; moving, affecting; harrowing, heartbreaking, heartrending; pathetic, tragic, sad, woeful, mournful, pitiful, lamentable, **pitiable**; ghastly, grim, dreadful, shocking, appalling.

**intolerable**, insufferable, impossible, insupportable, unbearable, **exorbitant**; past bearing; extreme, enough to make one mad, enough to make a parson swear, enough to provoke a saint.

**Vb. hurt**, injure, **harm**; pain, **give pain**; bite, cut, tear, rend, **wound**; gall, pique, nettle, mortify, **huff**; touch a soft spot, grieve, afflict, distress, **sadden**; corrode, embitter, exacerbate, gnaw, chafe, rankle, fester, **aggravate**; offend, insult, affront.

**torment**, martyr; harrow, rack, **torture**; give one a bad time, maltreat, bait,

bully, rag, persecute, assail, **oppress**; be offensive, snap at, bark at, **be rude**; importune, dun, besiege, **demand**; haunt, obsess; annoy, tease, pester, plague, nag, badger, worry, try, harass, harry, heckle; molest, bother, vex, provoke, ruffle, irritate, needle, sting, chafe, fret, bug, gall, irk, rile, **enrage**.

**trouble**, discomfort, disquiet, disturb, agitate, discompose, disconcert, upset, incommode, **derange**; worry, **embarrass**, **perplex**, **puzzle**; exercise, tire, **fatigue**, weary, bore, **be tedious**; obsess, haunt, bedevil; **depress**; infest, thwart, **obstruct**.

**displease**, **incur blame**; grate, jar, disagree with, give one a pain; disenchant, disillusion, **disappoint**; dissatisfy, **cause discontent**; offend, shock, horrify, disgust, revolt, repel, sicken, nauseate, make one sick, make one vomit, **cause dislike**; appal, **frighten**.

# 823 Content

**N. content**, satisfaction, complacency; self-satisfaction, **vanity**; measure of content, ray of comfort; resignation, **quietude**; ease of mind, nothing left to worry about, **euphoria**; reconciliation; comfort, sitting pretty; **consent**; resignation, **submission**.

**Adj. content**, happy; **peaceful**; cosy, snug, **comfortable**; at ease; **cheerful**; pleased; **disinterested**; without desire, without passion; resigned, acquiescent; fairly content; easily pleased, easygoing, **lenient**; secure, **safe**; thankful, **grateful**.

**contenting**, satisfactory, **sufficient**; tolerable, bearable, passable, acceptable; desirable.

**Vb. be content**, purr, purr with content, **be pleased**; be thankful, **be grateful**; prosper; congratulate oneself, **rejoice**;

be at ease, be at home, sit pat, sit pretty, **enjoy**; **make peace**; take comfort, **be relieved**; rest content; complain of nothing, have nothing to grouse about; acquiesce, **submit**.

content, satisfy, gratify, **please**; meet with approval; make happy; grant a boon, **give**; **sate**; comfort, **cheer**; bring comfort to, speak peace to, **relieve**; be kind to; lull, set at ease, set at rest; propitiate, disarm, reconcile, conciliate, appease, **pacify**.

Adv. **contentedly**, with satisfaction.

## 824 Discontent

N. discontent; displeasure, pain, **disapprobation**; cold comfort; irritation, chagrin, pique, bile, spleen, **resentment**; disquiet, worry; grief, **sorrow**; strain, tension; unrest, **commotion**; nit-picking; ill will, **envy**; competition; grievance, grudge, complaint, **quarrel**; melancholy, ennui, **dejection**; dirty look, grimace, scowl, frown; groan, curse, **malediction**; cheep, squeak, murmur.

malcontent, grouch, Jonah; plaintiff; critic; person with a grievance, angry young man; dissident, dropout; **agitator**; irreconcilable, diehard, **opponent**; hard taskmaster, **tyrant**.

Adj. **discontented**; malcontent, dissident, obstructive; restless, restive, **disobedient**; disgruntled, weary, **unhappy**; sad, unrelieved, disconsolate, **dejected**; grudging, jealous, envious; bitter, **sour**; peevish, testy, cross, **sullen**; grumbling, **deprecatory**; sore; fretful, querulous, petulant; hard to please, hard to satisfy, exacting, **fastidious**; critical, hypercritical, censorious; irreconcilable, hostile, **inimical**.

discontenting, **insufficient**; sickening; **tedious**; obstructive.

Vb. **be discontented**, be critical, crab, carp, find fault, **be fastidious**; lack, miss, feel something is missing, **require**; sneer, groan, jeer, **disapprove**; mind, take offence, take amiss, take ill, take to heart, **resent**; sulk, **be sullen**; look blue, look glum, make a wry face, **be dejected**; moan, mutter, murmur, whine, bleat, beef, protest, complain, object, cry blue murder, **deprecate**; bellyache, grumble, grouse, croak, snap; wail, **lament**; be aggrieved, have a grievance; **oppose**; **revolt**; grudge, **envy**; **quarrel**; make a meal of it; return, **reject**; **regret**.

cause discontent, dissatisfy; **disappoint**; depress; dishearten, discourage, **dissuade**; sour, embitter; upset, chafe, fret, niggle, bite, irritate, **huff**; mortify, **humiliate**; offend, cause resentment, **displease**; shock, **incur blame**; nauseate, sicken, disgust, **cause dislike**; arouse discontent, make trouble, agitate, **revolt**.

## 825 Regret

N. regret; **resentment**; futile regret; soul-searching, remorse, contrition, compunction, regrets; disillusion, **sequel**; nostalgia, **desire**; sense of loss, **demand**; matter of regret, pity of it.

Adj. **regretting**, missing, homesick, wistful; **retrospective**; bitter; irreconcilable, inconsolable, sorry, full of regrets, apologetic, soul-searching, penitent.

**regretted**; regrettable, too bad, a shame.

Vb. **regret**, rue, deplore; never forgive oneself; wish undone, **lament**; hark back, **retrospect**; look back; miss, miss badly, want back; hanker after, be homesick, **desire**; express regrets, feel compunction, feel remorse, be sorry, **be penitent**; **ask mercy**; deplore, deprecate, lament, **disapprove**; **resent**.

## 826 Relief

**N.** relief, rest, **refreshment**; **moderation**; good riddance; **deliverance**; solace, comfort, silver lining, **hope**; feeling better, sigh of relief, **revival**; lullaby, cradle song; salve, **balm**; painkiller, analgesic, **anaesthetic**; sedative, soporific; pillow, **cushion**; ray of sunshine.

**Adj.** relieving, refreshing; analgesic; restorative, **remedial**.

**Vb.** relieve, ease, soften, cushion; relax; temper, **moderate**; lift, raise, lighten, unburden, **disencumber**; spare, **exempt**; save, **deliver**; console, solace, comfort, give hope; encourage, hearten, **cheer**; shade, cool, fan, ventilate; **refresh**; restore, repair, **cure**; bandage, poultice, **doctor**; calm, soothe, nurse, pour balm, pour oil, palliate, mitigate, moderate, alleviate, **assuage**; **smooth**; stroke, pat, **caress**; cradle, lull, put to sleep; **sleep**; **render insensible**; **pity**.

be relieved, relieve oneself, obtain relief; feel relief, draw a long breath, breathe again; console oneself, take comfort, feel better, smile again, **be cheerful**; come to, be oneself again, pull oneself together; rest content, **be content**.

## 827 Aggravation

**N.** aggravation, irritation; **increase**; making worse; complication, **difficulty**.

**Adj.** aggravated; complicated; unrelieved, unmitigated, make worse.

**Vb.** aggravate, intensify, **strengthen**; enhance, heighten, deepen; increase, **augment**; worsen, make worse,

deteriorate; add insult to injury; exacerbate, embitter, further embitter, sour, inflame, **excite**; exasperate, irritate, **enrage**; complicate, make bad worse.

**Adv.** aggravatedly, worse and worse, from bad to worse, out of the frying pan into the fire.

**Int.** so much the worse! tant pis!

## 828 Cheerfulness

**N.** cheerfulness, alacrity; optimism, hope, joy, good humour; vitality, spirits, **life**; light heart, carefree mind, **content**; sparkle, animation, elevation, excitable state; party spirit.

merriment; cheer, high spirits, abandon; gaiety, glee, mirth, hilarity, **laughter**; levity, frivolity, **folly**; merry-making, fun, sport, **amusement**; jubilation, jubilee, **celebration**.

**Adj.** cheerful, cheery, blithe, **happy**, hearty, genial, convivial, **sociable**; sanguine; sunny, bright, radiant; breezy, of good cheer; upbeat, hopeful, resilient, irrepressible; carefree, light-hearted, happy-go-lucky; debonair, bonny, buxom, bouncing; pert, jaunty, perky, chirpy, spry, spirited, sprightly, vivacious, vital, full of pep, **lively**; **willing**.

merry, joyous, joyful; waggish, jocular; gay, light, frivolous; playful, sportive, frisky, frolicsome; arch, sly; merry-making, jovial, jolly, singing; wild, shouting, roaring with laughter, hilarious, uproarious, rip-roaring, rollicking.

jubilant, overjoyed, **pleased**; triumphant, cock-a-hoop; riotous.

cheering, exhilarating, exhilarating, **exciting**; tonic, like a ray of sunshine; balmy, palmy, bracing, **salubrious**.

**Vb.** be cheerful, keep cheerful, **hope**; be **resolute**; take heart, **be relieved**;

brighten, let oneself go, abandon oneself; radiate good humour, smile, beam, sparkle; dance, sing, carol, lilt, chirp, whistle, laugh, **rejoice**; whoop, cheer, **celebrate**; have fun, frisk, frolic, romp, gambol, sport, have a good time, **amuse oneself**; throw a party, make whoopee, **be sociable**.

cheer, gladden, warm, **content**; comfort, console, **relieve**, **please**; inspire, enliven, **animate**; exhilarate, elate, **delight**; encourage, hearten, jolly along, bolster, **give courage**; act like a tonic, **invigorate**.

Adv. cheerfully; airily; allegro.

829 Dejection. Seriousness
N. dejection, low spirits, dumps, doldrums; disillusion; defeatism, pessimism, despair, death wish, suicidal tendency; exhaustion, **fatigue**; heartache, misery, **sorrow**; grey dawn; gloom, dejected look, long face; funereal aspect, downcast countenance, lacklustre eye; cause of dejection, sorry sight, **bore**; care, thought, trouble, **worry**.

melancholy, hypochondria; neurosis; depression, black mood, blues, horrors, sigh; spleen, bile, **discontent**; disgust of life, angst, nostalgia, **suffering**.

seriousness; gravity, solemnity, sobriety; straight face, dead pan; heavy stuff; earnest.

moper, Jonah, **malcontent**; sourpuss, bear with a sore head; damper, wet blanket, killjoy, spoilsport; misery; death's-head.

Adj. dejected, joyless, dreary, cheerless, unhappy, despondent, downbeat, despairing, **hopeless**; beaten, overcome; **nervous**; **suffering**; downcast, downhearted, low; sluggish, listless, spiritless, lackadaisical; lacklustre,

dim; crestfallen, ready to cry; subdued, piano.

melancholic; blue, feeling blue; jaundiced, sour; thoughtful, pensive, full of thought; melancholy, sad; heavy, heavy-hearted, sick at heart, heartsick, **unhappy**; sorry; mournful, doleful, woeful, tearful; cheerless, joyless, dreary; forlorn, miserable, unrelieved, disconsolate; moody, **sullen**; dull, dismal, morose, glum; woebegone; wan, haggard, careworn.

serious, sober, solemn, sedate, stolid, staid, demure, grave, stern, **severe**; sour, dour, Puritan, grim, dark, forbidding, saturnine, **sullen**; inscrutable, deadpan; prim; heavy, dull, solid, **tedious**.

cheerless; unrelieved, dreary, dull, flat, **tedious**; dismal, lugubrious, funereal, dark, forbidding; drab, grey, sombre, overcast, murky; cold.

Vb. be dejected, lose heart, admit defeat, **despair**; succumb; languish, sink, droop, sag, wilt, flag; look downcast, look blue, pull a long face; mope, brood, **think**; lay to heart, sulk, **be sullen**; yearn, long, **desire**; sigh, grieve, groan, **suffer**; weep, **lament**; regret.

be serious, keep a straight face; look grave, look glum; lack sparkle, lack humour, be a bore, **be tedious**; sober, chasten.

sadden, grieve, bring grief, bring sorrow; impress; annoy, pain, **cause discontent**; deny comfort, render disconsolate, drive to despair; crush, overcome, overwhelm, prostrate; orphan, bereave.

depress; dismay, dishearten, discourage, dispirit, unnerve, **frighten**; cast a shadow, **darken**; damp, dampen, be a wet blanket, throw cold water, dissuade; **disappoint**; disgust, **displease**;

strain, weary, **fatigue**; bore, **be tedious**; chasten, sober, **teach**.

## 830 Rejoicing

N. **rejoicing**, manifestation of joy, **festivity**; jubilation, jubilee, triumph, **celebration**; shout, yell, **applause**; cheers, hosanna, **praise**; thanksgiving, **thanks**, psalm, **hymn**; elation, **joy**; **revel**; merrymaking, abandon, **merriment**.

**laughter**; loud laughter, roar of laughter; **ridicule**; laugh, guffaw; chuckle, chortle, gurgle, cackle, crow, coo; giggle, snigger, titter; smile, simper, smirk, grin, twinkle, humour, **wit**; comedy, farce.

**laugher**, giggler, cackler, sniggerer; grinner; mocker, derider; god of ridicule; comic muse.

Adj. **rejoicing**, rollicking, cheering, shouting, **jubilant**; lyrical, ecstatic.

**laughing**; humorous, laughable, risible, derisory, **ridiculous**; comic, comical, funny, **absurd**.

Vb. **rejoice**, be joyful, dance, skip, **leap**; clap, whoop, cheer, **applaud**; shout, yell oneself hoarse, **vociferate**; carol, sing; **praise**; exult, crow, **celebrate**; felicitate, **congratulate**; bless, give thanks, **thank**; abandon oneself, let oneself go, **riot**, **rampage**; make merry, **be cheerful**; have a good time, frolic, frisk, **revel**; have a party, celebrate, **be sociable**; feel pleased, congratulate oneself, gloat, **be pleased**; purr, coo, gurgle.

**laugh**, laugh outright, bubble with laughter; hoot, chuckle, chortle, crow, cackle; giggle, snigger, titter; laugh at, mock, deride, **ridicule**; shake, fall about, roll around, burst with laughter, laugh fit to burst.

**smile**, grin, grimace; smirk, simper; twinkle, beam, flash a smile;

Int. cheers! three cheers! huzza! hurrah! hooray! hosannah! hallelujah! glory be! hail the conquering hero!

## 831 Lamentation

N. **lamentation**, wail, wail of woe, weeping; mourning; black; cypress, willow; crying, greeting, **dejection**; melting mood, **pity**; wet eyes; breakdown, hysterics; cry, tear, teardrop; sob, sigh, groan, moan, whimper, whine, grizzle, bawl, boo-hoo.

**lament**, plaint, complaint, dirge, knell, requiem, threnody, elegy, death song, swansong, funeral oration; keen, wake, **condolence**; howl, shriek, scream, outcry; tale of woe; show of grief, **sham**.

**weeper**; mourner, mute, **funeral**; **malcontent**; dying duck, dying swan.

Adj. **lamenting**, tearful; with moist eyes; ready to cry; mourning, mournful, doleful, lugubrious, **unhappy**; woeful, woebegone, haggard, **dejected**; plaintive; **funereal**; at half-mast; fretful, querulous, with a tale of woe; pathetic, pitiful, lamentable, **pitiable**.

Vb. **lament**, grieve, sorrow, sigh, **suffer**; deplore, regret, **pity**; bemoan; sing a requiem; mourn, wail, keen; express grief; take it badly; complain, beef, bellyache, grouse.

**weep**, weep, greet; be ready to cry; cry, cry like a child, cry like a baby, boo-hoo, bawl; howl, squall, yell, clamour, scream, shriek; sob, sigh, moan, groan, **suffer**; snivel, grizzle, blubber, pule, whine, whimper; get ready to cry, weep without cause.

Adv. tearfully.

## 832 Amusement

N. **amusement**, pleasure, interest, delight; entertainment, dramatic entertainment, happening, **drama**; radio, television; pastime, hobby, labour of love, **voluntary work**; solace, recreation, **refreshment**; relaxation, **repose**; holiday, **leisure**; gala day, **special day**; play, sport, fun, good cheer, **merriment**; occasion, do, show, junket, Gaudy night, **celebration**; outing, excursion, jaunt, pleasure trip; treat, picnic (see *festivity*); garden party, flower show, gymkhana, jamboree, **assembly**; game, game of chance, game of skill; whist drive, bridge party (see *card game*); round games.

**festivity**, visiting, **social round**; fun, **laughter**; social whirl, round of pleasure, round of gaiety; high life, good time; festival, fair, funfair, carnival, fiesta, gala; masque; merrymaking, **merriment**; high day, **special day**; wassail, wake; house-warming, party, **social gathering**; orgy, carouse; bust, binge, blowout; barbecue, bump supper, dinner, banquet, **meal**.

**revel**, rout, rave-up, whoopee, fun, high old time; spree, junket, horseplay; bonfire, pyrotechnics, Fifth of November; play, game, romp, frolic, lark, escapade, antic, prank, rag, trick, **foolery**.

**pleasure ground**, park, chase, grouse moor; green, common; arbour; seaside, lido, bathing beach, holiday camp; playground, recreation ground, links, golf course; rink, tennis court, bowling green, croquet lawn, **arena**; circus, fair, swing, roundabout, merry-go-round, scenic railway, switchback, big wheel, big dipper, tunnel of love, ghost train; dodgems; seesaw, slide, helter-skelter.

**place of amusement**, fairground, funfair, amusement arcade; skittle alley, concert hall, vaudeville, hippodrome; picture house, **cinema**; playhouse, **theatre**; dance floor; dance hall, disco; cabaret, night club, clip joint; bingo hall, casino.

**sport**, outdoor life; sportsmanship, gamesmanship, **skill**; sports; games, gymnastics, **athletics**, leap, **contest**, **racing**, pugilism; outdoor sports, rambling; running; riding, pony-trekking; archery, hunting, shooting and fishing, **chase**; water sports, swimming, bathing; sailing; rock-climbing, mountaineering, **ascent**; **descent**; winter sports, ice hockey; curling; flying, gliding, **aeronautics**; tourism, **land travel**.

**ball game**; King Willow, cricket, baseball, softball, rounders; tennis, ping-pong; badminton; squash; handball, volleyball; fives; netball, basketball; football, soccer, Rugby football; lacrosse, hockey, polo, water polo; croquet, golf, skittles, bowls, curling; marbles; quoits, hoop-la; billiards, snooker, pool; bagatelle, pinball, bar billiards.

**indoor game**; quiz; charades; word game, spelling bee; paper game; darts, dominoes, jigsaw puzzle.

**board game**, chess, draughts, checkers; backgammon; ludo, go.

**children's games**, swinging; leapfrog, hopscotch, **leap**; touch, tag, he, chain he, hide-and-seek.

**card game**, cards, game of cards, rubber of whist, rubber of bridge; whist, auction bridge, nap; écarté, loo, cribbage; quadrille; rummy, canasta, casino, cheat; solo, solitaire, patience; snap, old maid, racing demon; bingo; pontoon, black jack; brag, poker, banker.

**gambling game**, dice; roulette; raffle, tombola, sweepstake, football pool.

**dancing**, dance, ball; masquerade; fancy

dress dance; tea dance, square dance; hop, jam session, disco; **ballet**; choreography.

**dance**, war dance; shuffle; solo dance; clog dance, fan dance; cancan; belly dance; gipsy dance, flamenco; country dance, hay; hornpipe, keel row; folk dance, polonaise, mazurka; jig; fling, reel, Dashing White Sergeant; tarantella, bolero, gavotte, quadrille, minuet; valse, waltz; foxtrot, turkey trot, quickstep; Charleston, black bottom, blues, tango, rumba, samba, conga, conga line, cha-cha; Palais Glide; stomp, bop, jive, rock 'n' roll, twist; snowball; ballerina, **actor**, **entertainer**; **jumper**.

**plaything**, bauble, souvenir, trinket, toy, **bauble**; rattle, Jack-in-the-box, doll; top, yo-yo; marbles; ball, balloon, **sphere**; hoop, tricycle; skateboard; surfboard; popgun, airgun, water pistol; toy soldier, model, model yacht, model aeroplane, clockwork train, model railway; magic lantern, peep show; toy theatre, **exhibit**; puppet show, **image**; pintable; card, cards, pack, stack, deck; domino, tile; draught, counter, chip; chess piece, pawn, knight, bishop, castle or rook, queen, king.

**player**, sportsman or -woman, sporting man or woman; competitor, **contender**; forward, striker, defence, goalkeeper; batsman, fielder, bowler; marksman, archer; chess tiger, chess rabbit; fellow sportsman or -woman, playmate, **colleague**.

**reveller**; drinker, drunk, **drunkard**; eater; **sociable person**; playboy; holidaymaker, tourist, **traveller**; Lord of Misrule, MC, toastmaster.

**Adj.amusing**, entertaining, sportive, full of fun, **merry**; pleasant; laughable, ridiculous, **funny**; recreational,

refreshing; festive, holiday.

**amused, pleased**; festive, sportive, rollicking, playful, waggish, jolly, jovial; horsy, sporty, sporting, **athletic**; at play; easy to please.

**Vb.amuse**, interest, entertain, beguile, divert, tickle, make one laugh; titillate, please, **delight**; recreate, **refresh**; solace, enliven, **cheer**; treat; raise a smile, wake laughter, wow, slay, **be ridiculous**; humour; give a party, be **hospitable**; be a sport, be great fun.

**amuse oneself**, kill time, **have leisure**; play, play at, have fun, enjoy oneself, drown care, **be cheerful**; make holiday, have an outing, have a field day, have a ball; sport; dally, toy, wanton; frisk, frolic, romp, gambol, caper; lark around, skylark, fool about, **be absurd**; jest; play cards, take a hand; game, dice, **gamble**; play games, be devoted to sport; camp, picnic; sail, yacht, fly; hunt, shoot, fish; play golf; ride, trek, hike, ramble; run, race, jump; bathe, swim, dive; skate, ski, toboggan.

**dance**; waltz, foxtrot, Charleston, tango, rumba, jive, stomp, bop, twist, rock 'n' roll; whirl, **rotate**; cavort, caper, jig about; shuffle, hoof, trip, tread a measure, **leap**.

**revel**, make merry, make whoopee, celebrate, **rejoice**; make it a party, have a good time; let oneself go; junket, roister, drown care; feast, banquet, quaff, carouse, wassail; **drink**; **get drunk**; never go home till morning.

**Int.**carpe diem! eat, drink and be merry!

## 833 Tedium

**N.tedium**, ennui, **melancholy**; lack of interest; languor, **fatigue**; too much of a good thing; disgust, nausea, **dislike**; sameness, **repetition**; time to kill.

**bore**: irk, drag, bind, chore; dull work, beaten track, daily round, **habit**; grindstone, treadmill, **labour**; pub bore; drip, wet blanket, killjoy, misery; frump; too much of a good thing.

**Adj. tedious**, devoid of interest; uneventful; slow, leaden, heavy; dry, arid; flat, stale, insipid, **tasteless**; bald, **plain**; humdrum, soulless, suburban, dreary, stuffy, bourgeois, **dull**; stodgy, prosaic, unreadable; prosy, long, long-winded; drowsy, **soporific**; binding, wearisome, tiresome, irksome; wearing, chronic, mortal; repetitious; same, invariable, monotonous, **uniform**; too much; nauseous.

**bored**: stale, weary, jaded, blue, world-weary, weary of life; uninterested, **indifferent**; sick of.

**Vb. be tedious**, pall, lose its novelty, cloy, glut, jade, satiate, **sate**; nauseate, sicken, disgust, **cause dislike**; bore, irk, try, weary, **fatigue**; bore to death, bore stiff; weary to distraction, stay too long; fail to interest, make one yawn, send one to sleep; drag; never end; prove monotonous, repeat oneself; buttonhole, **be diffuse**.

**Adv. boringly**, to death; ad nauseam.

## 834 Wit

**N. wit**, point; ready wit, verbal readiness; **sequel**; salt; sparkle, **intelligence**; humour, wry humour, drollery, pleasantry; **merriment**; trifling, **inattention**; fun, tomfoolery, funny business, **foolery**; comic turn, laugh a minute; broad humour, vulgarity, **bad taste**; farce, knockabout comedy, slapstick, ham, high camp; fancy, **whim**; cartoon, comic strip, caricature; biting wit, cruel humour, satire, sarcasm, **ridicule**; irony, **affectation**; black comedy, gallows humour;

sophistry.

**witticism**, piece of humour, stroke of wit, sally; spoonerism; epigram, conceit; pun; feed line, banter, chaff, badinage; retort, repartee, backchat, **answer**; sarcasm, **satire**; joke, jest, good one; quip, quirk, crank, gag, crack, wisecrack; old joke, stale jest, chestnut; practical joke, hoax; broad jest, dirty joke, story, limerick.

**humorist**, wit; card, character, wag, joker; funny man; teaser; practical joker; comedian, comedienne, comic, **entertainer**; comic writer, **imitator**; raconteur; jester, motley fool, clown, buffoon, stooge, **fool**.

**Adj. witty**, quick; Attic, **elegant**; pointed; brilliant, smart, clever; salty, racy, piquant; fruity; snappy, biting, pungent, keen, sharp; ironic, dry, sly, pawky; facetious, flippant, jocular, waggish; lively, pleasant, gay, **merry**; comic, funny ha-ha, **funny**; comical, humorous, droll; whimsical, **capricious**; playful, sportive, **absurd**.

**Vb. be witty**, scintillate, sparkle, flash; jest, have quip, gag, wisecrack; tell a good story, raise a laugh, **amuse**; pun, equivocate, **be equivocal**; fool, **be absurd**; play with, tease, chaff, rag, banter, twit, make merry with, make fun of, poke fun at, **ridicule**; mock, caricature, burlesque; retort, flash back, come back at, **answer**; have a sense of humour, enjoy a joke.

**Adv. in jest.**

## 835 Dullness

**N. dullness**, dejection; tedium; lack of sparkle, lack of inspiration; lack of humour, inability to see a joke, impenetrable gravity; prose, matter of fact.

**Adj. dull**; straight; deadly dull; stuffy, dreary, deadly; pointless, meaningless, **tedious**; colourless, drab; flat, bland, vapid, insipid, **tasteless**; derivative, superficial; stupid; without laughter, grave, prim, **serious**; graceless, lacking wit, **inelegant**; heavy, ponderous, sluggish, **slow**; stodgy, prosaic, matter-of-fact, pedestrian, unreadable; stale, banal, commonplace, trite, **usual**.

**Vb. be dull**, bore, **be tedious**; prose; never see a joke, not see the point.

## 836 Beauty

**N. beauty**, pulchritude; ripe perfection, **perfection**; grandeur, nobility; splendour, **light**; transfiguration; polish, gloss, ornament; scenic beauty, scenery, view, landscape, **spectacle**; form, fair proportions, regular features, **symmetry**; physical beauty; attraction, charm; appeal, glamour, sex appeal; graces; good looks, handsome features, pretty face; eyes of blue, pearly teeth, trim figure, vital statistics; grace, chic, style, dress sense, **fashion**; delicacy, refinement, **good taste**; appreciation of beauty, aesthetics.

**a beauty**, thing of beauty, work of art; garden, beauty spot; masterpiece; jewel, pearl, treasure, **paragon**; peacock, swan, flower, rosebud, rose, lily; fair one, lady bright; belle, raving beauty, toast, idol, **favourite**; dream girl; beauty queen, Miss World, bathing belle, pin-up girl, cover girl; pin-up, cheesecake; hunk; fine figure of a man or woman; blond(e), brunette, redhead; English rose; dream, vision, poem, picture; angel; stunner, knockout; doll, dolly bird, cookie; glamour puss, glamour girl or boy; heartthrob, dreamboat; vamp, siren, witch; scorcher, lovely, honey, peach, dish; fairy; Grace, Venus; Narcissus.

**Adj. beautiful**, beauteous, of beauty; lovely, fair, bright, radiant; comely, bonny, pretty; sweet, pretty-pretty; nice, good enough to eat; photogenic; handsome, good-looking, wellfavoured; husky; tall, dark and handsome; gracious, stately, statuesque, Junoesque; adorable, divine; lovely to behold; picturesque, scenic; artistic, cunning, curious, quaint; aesthetic, **tasteful**; exquisite, choice, **chosen**; perfect.

**splendid**, sublime, heavenly, superb, fine, **excellent**; grand, **noble**, glorious, ravishing, rich, gorgeous, **florid**; bright, resplendent, radiant, glowing, glossy, magnificent, specious, **showy**; ornate.

**shapely**, regular, classic; buxom, bosomy; clean-limbed, straight, slender, slim, svelte, willowy, **lean**; graceful, elegant, chic; petite, dainty, delicate; **perfect**.

**personable**, prepossessing, agreeable, comfortable, buxom; attractive, dishy, appealing; sexy, cute; enchanting; winsome; clean-cut, wholesome, lusty, blooming, ruddy, **red**; rosy; sightly, becoming, fit to be seen, passable; presentable, proper, decent, neat, natty, tidy, trim; spruce, snappy, dapper, glossy, sleek; smart, stylish, classy, **fashionable**; elegant, dainty, delicate, refined, **tasteful**.

**Vb. be beautiful**, bewitch; beggar all description; be photogenic, photograph well; have good looks, have bright eyes; bloom, glow, dazzle, **shine**; do one credit, win a beauty contest.

**beautify**, trim, improve; brighten, **make bright**; tattoo, **decorate**; set (a jewel); grace, suit, fit, become, go well, flatter; transfigure; give a face-lift; prank, powder, rouge.

## 837 Ugliness

**N. ugliness**; lack of beauty; want of symmetry; lack of form, **deformity**; **blemish**; squalor, filth; plain features, ugly face; a face to stop a clock; wry face, snarl, forbidding countenance, grim look; haggard look; dim eyes, hand of time, **age**.

**eyesore**, blot, botch, patch, **blemish**; aesthetic crime; ugly person, fright, sight, frump; scarecrow, horror, death's-head, gargoyle, grotesque; monster, abortion; harridan, witch; toad, gorilla, baboon, crow; ugly duckling; satyr; Gorgon; Beast.

**Adj. ugly**, lacking beauty; hideous, foul, **unclean**; frightful, shocking, monstrous; repellent, odious, loathsome; beastly, nasty; homely, plain, without any looks; mousy; forbidding, ill-favoured, grim, saturnine, **sullen**.

**unsightly**, worn; unseemly; imperfect; formless, irregular, **amorphous**; grotesque; badly made, disproportionate; misshapen, misbegotten; dumpy, squat; bloated; **colourless**, ghastly, wan, grisly, gruesome.

**graceless**, **inelegant**; squalid, dingy, poky, dreary, drab; lank, dull, mousy; dowdy; garish, gaudy, gross, indelicate, coarse, **vulgar**; rude, crude, rough, rugged, uncouth, **artless**; clumsy, awkward, ungainly, cumbersome, hulking, **unwieldy**.

**Vb. be ugly**, lack beauty, fade, wither, age, **grow old**; look ill, look a wreck, look a mess, look a fright.

**make ugly**; fade, discolour; wither, deteriorate; soil, sully, **make unclean**; spoil, deface, disfigure, mar, blemish, blot; **deform**; pull a face, grimace, **be sullen**; torture, twist, **distort**; mutilate, **impair**.

## 838 Beautification

**N. beautification**; transfiguration, **transformation**; plastic surgery, face-lift, **surgery**; beauty treatment; face mask, face pack, facial; massage, manicure; pedicure, chiropody; sun lamp; toilet, make-up; painting; **ablutions**.

**hairdressing**, scalp massage; shaving, clipping, trimming; cutting, haircut; shave, hair cut, clip, trim, singe; hair style, coiffure, crop, bob, shingle, urchin cut, curling, setting; hairdo, set, wave, perm; curl, coil; bang, fringe, ponytail, chignon, bun; Afro, **hair**; false hair, hairpiece, toupee, switch, **wig**; curling iron, tongs, curl papers; comb, hairpin, hairgrip, slide; hairnet, snood.

**hairwash**, shampoo, rinse, colour tone; bleach, dye, henna, peroxide; hair spray, lacquer, grease; hair-restorer.

**cosmetic**, aid to beauty, patch, beauty spot; make-up, paint, greasepaint, rouge, cream, lanolin, **unguent**; lipstick, lip gloss; nail polish, nail varnish, powder, kohl, mascara, eye shadow, eyeliner; hand lotion, bath oil, bath essence, bubble bath, **cleanser**; antiperspirant, deodorant; scent, perfume, essence, cologne, lavender water, cologne stick; eyebrow pencil; powder puff, compact; vanity case, manicure set, nail file, nail scissors, clippers; shaver, razor, depilatory; toiletries.

**beauty parlour**, beauty salon; boudoir, dressing room, health farm.

**beautician**, beauty specialist; plastic surgeon; make-up artist; barber, hairdresser.

**Adj. beautified**; powdered; bouffant; **beautiful**.

**Vb. primp**; ornament, **decorate**; prank; preen; rouge, paint, shadow, highlight; powder; wear scent; shave; curl, wave; have a hairdo, have a facial, have a manicure, **beautify**.

## 839 Ornamentation

N. **ornamentation**, adornment, garnish; ornate style, **ornament**; baroque; rococo; gilt, **ostentation**; setting, background; silver, china, glass; flower arrangement, wreath, garland, bouquet, nosegay, posy, buttonhole; object d'art, bric-a-brac, curio.

**ornamental art**; architecture, building; painting, statuary, **sculpture**; frieze, dado; capital; pilaster, caryatid, figurehead; boss, cornice, corbel, gargoyle; moulding, beading, fluting; tracery; **facing**; panelling; gilt, gold leaf; lettering, illustration, **art**; batik; **heraldry**; etching, **engraving**; work, handiwork, handicraft, woodwork, fretwork; pokerwork; filigree; carving; intaglio; inlay, inset, mosaic, marquetry; metalwork; setting; cut glass, wrought iron.

**pattern**, motif, print, design, composition, **structure**; detail, geometrical style, rose window, cusp, trefoil; tracery; scrollwork; arabesque; flourish, coil; swag, festoon; weave, diaper, **texture**; paisley, **textile**; chevron, key pattern; check, **chequer**; pinstripe, **stripe**; spot, dot; herringbone, zigzag; watermark, **identification**.

**needlework**, tapestry; cross-stitch, sampler; patchwork; open work, embroidery, smocking; crochet, lace; tatting, knitting, **network**; stitch, purl, plain, stocking stitch, chain stitch, French knot.

**trimming**, piping, valance, border, fringe, frieze, frill, flounce, **edging**; binding; trappings; braid, frog, lapel, star, rosette, cockade, **badge**; bow, **fastening**; pompom; tassel, bead, bugle; ermine, fur, **hair**; feather,

osprey, plume, panache, **plumage**; streamer, ribbon.

**finery**, togs, Sunday best, **clothing**; frippery, chiffon; trinket, gewgaw; tinsel, spangle, sequin, glass, paste, rhinestone, **bauble**.

**jewellery**; diadem, tiara, **regalia**; drop, locket, **hanging object**; crucifix; amulet, charm, **talisman**; rope, string, necklace, choker, chain, **loop**; torque, bracelet, wristlet, bangle; ring, earring, signet ring, **circle**; cameo, brooch, clasp, fibula, badge, crest; stud, pin, collar stud, **fastening**; medal, medallion.

**gem**, jewel; stone, uncut gem; brilliant, sparkler, diamond, rock, ice; solitaire; carbuncle, ruby, pearl, opal; sapphire, turquoise, emerald, beryl, aquamarine; garnet, amethyst, topaz, cornelian, agate, onyx; heliotrope, moonstone, hyacinth; coral, ivory, mother of pearl, jet, amber, jade.

Adj. **ornamental**, decorative, fancy; intricate, elaborate, quaint; picturesque, pretty-pretty; scenic, landscape, topiary; Doric, Ionic, Corinthian, Romanesque; baroque, rococo.

**ornamented**, luxuriant; **ornate**; **variegated**; mosaic, inlaid; overdone, **vulgar**; **florid**; luscious, plush, gilt, gilded, **rich**; gorgeous, garish, flashy, gaudy, meretricious, **showy**.

**bedecked**, wearing, sporting; looking one's best, in one's Sunday best; in one's best, in one's Sunday best; looking one's best, in one's Sunday best; beribboned, festooned.

Vb. **decorate**, adorn, embellish, enhance, enrich; grace, set, **ornament**; paint; **beautify**; garnish, trim, shape; array, deck, bedeck, **dress**; prank, preen; furbish, burnish, **clean**; garland, crown, **honour**; stud, spangle, whitewash, varnish, grain, japan, lacquer, **coat**; enamel, gild, silver; emblazon, illuminate, illustrate, **paint, colour**; border, trim, **hem**; work, embroider, tapestry; pattern, inlay, engrave; encrust, emboss, bead, mould; fret, carve, **groove**, **notch**; wreathe, festoon, trace, scroll, twine.

cultivation, culture; aesthetics, criticism; artistry, flair, **skill**.

**people of taste**; connoisseur, amateur, dilettante; epicure, gourmet, epicure; aesthete, critic; arbiter of taste, **fop**; purist, **obstinate person**; **prude**.

**Adj. tasteful**, gracious; choice, exquisite, **excellent**; simple, **plain**; graceful, Attic, classical, **elegant**; chaste, refined, delicate, **pure**; aesthetic, artistic, **sensitive**; discerning; nice, dainty, finicky, **fastidious**; critical, appreciative, **judicial**; decent, seemly, becoming, **apt**; proper, correct, **fashionable**; **well-bred**.

**Vb. have taste**, **discriminate**; appreciate, value, **judge**; **be fastidious**.

**Adv. tastefully**, properly, agreeably.

## 840 Blemish

**N. blemish**; scar, weal, welt, mark, pockmark; injury, flaw, crack, defect; deformity; stigma, blot, **eyesore**; graffiti; blur, blotch, smudge; smut, patch, smear, stain, tarnish, rust, patina, **dirt**; spot, speck, speckle; freckle, mole, birthmark, strawberry mark; excrescence, pimple, blackhead, carbuncle, wart, **swelling**; acme, eczema, **skin disease**; harelip, cleft palate; cast, squint; cut, scratch, scald, bruise, black eye, cauliflower ear, broken nose, **wound**.

**Adj. blemished**, cracked, **imperfect**, flyblown, **dirty**; shop-soiled; marked; spotted; spotty; knock-kneed, bandy; crooked.

**Vb. blemish**, flaw, crack, injure, damage, **impair**; blot, smudge, stain, smear, sully, soil, **make unclean**; brand, **mark**; scar, pit, pockmark, mar, spoil, **make ugly**; deface, disfigure, **deform**.

## 841 Good Taste

**N. good taste**, taste, restraint, simplicity; best of taste, **goodness**; refinement, delicacy, euphemism, **purity**; fine feeling, nice appreciation, palate, **discrimination**; **etiquette**; tact, consideration, natural courtesy, dignity, manners, breeding, civility, social graces, **courtesy**; propriety, decorum; grace, polish, finish, gracious living;

## 842 Bad Taste

**N. bad taste**, poor taste; bad art, kitsch; international airport plastic; prostitution of talent; yellow press, vulgarism, vandalism; vulgarity; shoddy, frippery, tinsel, glitter, paste, ersatz, **bauble**; lack of feeling; bad joke, untimely jest; frump, dowdy, square.

**ill-breeding**, vulgarity; bad form; bad manners, **discourtesy**; rough behaviour, **disorder**.

**vulgarian**, snob, social climber, cad, bounder; rough diamond; proletarian, **commoner**; Vandal, Philistine; barbarian, savage; punk.

**Adj. vulgar**; **inelegant**; tasteless, gross, crass, coarse; philistine, barbarian, **artless**; commercial; tawdry, cheap, catchpenny, gingerbread, ersatz; flashy, meretricious, **showy**; obtrusive, blatant, loud, gaudy, garish, raffish; shameless, fulsome, excessive; shabby genteel, **affected**; common, low, gutter, sordid, **disreputable**; improper, indelicate, indecorous;

going too far, scandalous, indecent, ribald, obscene, **impure**.

**ill-bred**; non-U, **plebeian**; loud, hearty; insensitive, blunt; impolite, unmannerly, **discourteous**; dowdy, rustic, provincial, countrified, gone native; crude, rude, churlish, uncouth, **ignorant**; unsophisticated, **artless**; barbaric; awkward, gauche, **clumsy**; rowdy, riotous, **disorderly**; superior, **affected**.

**Vb. vulgarize**, cheapen, coarsen, debase, lower; show bad taste.

### 843 Fashion. Etiquette

**N. fashion**, style, mode, cut, **form**; method, **way**; vogue, cult, habit; prevailing taste, current fashion, **modernism**; rage, fad, craze, cry, furore; new look, latest fashion; last word; extreme of fashion, dash, **ostentation**; ton, flair, chic; dress sense, fashion show, mannequin parade, **exhibit**; **affectation**; world of fashion, Vanity Fair, passing show.

**etiquette**, formality; protocol, convention, custom, **practice**; snobbery, done thing, good form; appearances; decorum, propriety, right note, **good taste**; **courtesy**; breeding, polish; ladylike behaviour; manners, best behaviour; grand air, poise, dignity, savvy, **conduct**.

**beau monde**, society; town, best end of town; court, drawing room, salon; top drawer, right people, smart set, upper ten, **nobility**; cream, upper crust, cream of society, **elite**; gilded youth, beautiful people, jet set; fashionable person, glass of fashion; man or woman about town, man or woman of fashion, classy dame; slave to fashion; socialite, playboy, cosmopolitan, **sociable person**.

**fop**, fine gentleman, macaroni, buck,

pearly king; fine lady, belle, pearly queen; debutante; dandy, exquisite, beau; peacock, clothes-horse, fashion plate; coxcomb, puppy; swell, nob, Lady Muck; Corinthian, spark, blood, blade, lad, gay dog; lounge lizard, carpet knight, gallant; ladykiller.

**Adj. fashionable**, modish, stylish; correct; à la mode, chi-chi; exquisite, chic, elegant, well-groomed, **tasteful**; dressy; dashing, snazzy, flashy, **showy**; dandy, smart, classy, swank, swell, swish, posh; new-fangled, **modern**; hip, groovy, trendy, with it; **affected**; conventional, done, **usual**.

**well-bred**, thoroughbred, **noble**; cosmopolitan, sophisticated, urbane; polite, house-trained; U, ladylike, **genteel**; civil, well-spoken, **courteous**; courtly, stately, **formal**; poised, easy, smooth; correct, decorous, proper, decent; considerate, **amiable**; punctilious, **honourable**.

**Vb. be in fashion**, be done, be wont; get with it, **conform**; be sociable; entertain, **be hospitable**; observe decorum; cut a dash, cut a figure, give a lead; look right, pass; have an air, have style; show flair, dress well.

**Adv. fashionably**, in style, à la mode.

### 844 Ridiculousness

**N. ridiculousness**, drollery, wit; **nonconformity**; bathos, anticlimax; **boast**; bombast, **exaggeration**; comic interlude, light relief; light verse, doggerel, limerick, **witticism**; spoonerism, malapropism, bull; comic turn, comedy, farce, burlesque, slapstick, knockabout, **stage play**; paradox, **lack of expectation**.

**Adj. ridiculous**, ludicrous, preposterous, monstrous, grotesque, fantastic, cockeyed, inappropriate, **absurd**; awkward, **clumsy**; silly, **foolish**; derisory; laughable, **risible**; bizarre, rum, quaint, odd, queer, **unusual**; strange, outlandish, **extraneous**; mannered, stilted, **affected**; inflated, extravagant; crazy, crackpot, fanciful, **imaginary**; whimsical, **capricious**.

**funny, abnormal**; comical, droll, humorous, waggish; rich, priceless, sidesplitting, hilarious, a real hoot; light, comic; satirical; burlesque; doggerel; slapstick, knockabout.

**Vb. be ridiculous**, make one laugh, excite laughter, raise a laugh; tickle; entertain, **amuse**; look silly, be a figure of fun, cut a ridiculous figure, be a laughingstock, fool, **be absurd**; descend to pathos; make an exhibition of oneself; poke fun at, make one a laughingstock, **ridicule**.

### 845 Affectation

**N. affectation**, cult, fad, **fashion**; ostentation; assumption of airs, **airs**; striking attitude, high moral tone; pose, public image; mannerism, trick, literary affectation, esoteric vocabulary; euphuism, **ornament**; pout, grimace, **gesture**; coquetry, **caprice**; conceit, **vanity**; euphemism, false shame; irony, backhanded compliment, **ridicule**; **duplicity**.

**pretension**, artifice, sham, humbug, **deception**; shallow profundity; **formality**; pedantry; **prudery**.

**affecter**, humbug, quack, charlatan, **impostor**; **actor**; hypocrite; coquette, flirt; mass of affectation, poser, **vain person**; **humorist**; coxcomb, dandy, fop; purist, pedant; know-all, **wise guy**; prig, puritan, goody-goody, **prude**; bluestocking.

**Adj. affected**, full of affectation, self-conscious; studied, mannered, precious, chichi, **ornate**; artificial,

unnatural, stilted, stiff, starchy, **formal**; prim, mealy-mouthed, sanctimonious, self-righteous, smug, demure; arch, sly, **merry**; coy, cute, twee; **boastful**; shallow, hollow, specious, pretentious, fulsome, stagy, theatrical; camp; striking an attitude, **vain**; **ill-bred**; bogus, **false**; insincere; overdone.

**Vb. be affected**, affect, wear, assume; pretend, feign, make a show of, bluff, **dissemble**; **imitate**; affect zeal, **be busy**; perform, act a part, **act**; overact, ham, **exaggerate**; posture, pose, prance, mince, ponce about; swank, **be vain**; **know**; be elegant; brag, talk big, **boast**; pout, simper, smirk, **smile**; coquette, flirt, languish, **excite love**; **cant**; save appearances.

### 846 Ridicule

**N. ridicule**, mockery, **disrespect**; **laughter**; raillery, ribbing, banter, badinage, chaff; horseplay, practical joke, **foolery**; grin, snigger, laugh, scoff, mock; irony, sarcasm, barbed shaft, backhanded compliment; catcall, hoot, hiss, **censure**; insult, **indignity**; **witticism**.

**satire**, denunciation; parody, burlesque, travesty, caricature, cartoon; skit, spoof, send-up, take-off, **mimicry**; squib, lampoon.

**laughingstock**, object of ridicule, figure of fun, butt, common jest, by-word; sport, game, Aunt Sally; April fool, buffoon, clown, zany, **fool**; stooge, butt, foil, feed, straight man; guy, caricature, travesty, mockery of; eccentric, **crank**; original, card, caution, queer fish, geezer, museum piece, back number, square; fall guy, victim, **loser**.

**Adj. derisive**, flippant; sardonic; quizzical; satirical; ribald, **vulgar**; burlesque.

**Vb. ridicule,** deride, laugh at, grin at, smile at, smirk at; snigger; banter, chaff, rally, twit, rib, tease, roast, rag, poke fun, make merry with, make fun of, make sport of, make a monkey of, kid, fool, make a fool of, make an April fool of; mock, scoff, jeer; turn to a jest, make a joke of, turn to ridicule, **hold cheap;** deflate, make one look silly, humiliate.

**satirize,** lampoon; mock; mimic, **imitate;** parody, travesty, spoof, burlesque, caricature, guy, **misrepresent;** expose, denounce, pillory, **accuse.**

## 847 Hope

**N. hope,** assumption, presumption, **expectation;** sanguine expectation, conviction, **belief;** reliance, trust, confidence, faith, assurance, **certainty;** eager hope, **probability; relief;** safe hope, security, anchor, mainstay, staff, **support;** final hope, last throw; ray of hope, **possibility;** good omen, favourable auspices, promise, fair prospect, **omen;** blue sky, silver lining; optimism, enthusiasm; rosy picture.

**aspiration,** ambition, purpose, **intention;** pious hope, vision, pipe dream; **fantasy;** land of promise, utopia, millennium, **objective.**

**hoper,** aspirant, candidate; hopeful, expectant, heir apparent, **beneficiary;** prisoner of hope; utopian, **visionary.**

**Adj. hoping,** starry-eyed; ambitious, would-be; **imaginative;** hopeful, **expectant;** sanguine, confident, **certain;** airy, uncritical; **jubilant;** reasonably confident.

**promising,** full of promise, favourable, auspicious, propitious, **prosperous;** bright, fair, golden, rosy; hopeful; plausible, likely, **probable;** utopian, **illogical;** visionary, **imaginary.**

**Vb. hope,** trust, confide, have faith; rest assured, feel confident, **believe;** presume, **assume;** speculate, look forward, **expect;** dream of, aspire, promise oneself, soar, aim high, **intend;** have a hope; feel hope, take heart, take hope, **be relieved;** remain hopeful, **stand firm;** hope against hope, keep hope alive, never say die; catch at a straw, **be cheerful; persevere;** be hopeful; flatter oneself, reason boldly, anticipate, **be early;** dream, **imagine.**

**give hope,** encourage, comfort, **cheer;** promise, promise well, bid fair, **be likely;** paint a rosy picture, **predict.**

**Adv. hopefully;** without despair; airily, lightly.

**Int.** nil desperandum! never say die! while there's life, there's hope!

## 848 Hopelessness

**N. hopelessness,** loss of hope, defeatism, dismay, **dejection;** pessimism, despair, last hope gone; resignation, **lack of expectation;** vain hope, **fantasy;** message of despair, wan smile; poor lookout; hopeless case, dead duck; hopeless situation, bad job, bad business, **predicament;** counsel of despair, misery.

**Adj. hopeless,** bereft of hope, without hope, despairing, desperate, suicidal; inconsolable, disconsolate, **dejected;** desolate, forlorn; undone, without resource, **unfortunate.**

**unpromising,** hopeless, without comfort, **cheerless;** desperate; inauspicious, **adverse;** ominous, irremediable; incurable, inoperable; past cure, beyond hope, past recall; incorrigible, irreparable, irrecoverable, irrevocable, irredeemable; irreversible, inevitable; impracticable, **impossible.**

**Vb. despair,** lose heart, lose hope; give way to despair, **be dejected;** submit.

leave no hope, drive to despair, disappoint; be incurable.

## 849 Fear

**N. fear**, dread, awe, **respect**; abject fear; fright, funk, blue funk; terror, state of terror, trepidation, alarm, shock, flutter, flap, flat spin; fit, fit of terror, scare, stampede, panic, **spasm**; flight; horror, cold sweat, blood turning to water; consternation, dismay; defence mechanism, repression, escapism.

**nervousness**, want of courage, lack of confidence; bluster; loss of nerve, mistrust, apprehension, disquiet, solicitude, anxiety, care, **worry**; depression, **dejection**; defeatism, pessimism; trepidation, flutter, tremor; nerves, willies, collywobbles, shivers, jitters, heebie-jeebies; gooseflesh.

**phobia**, claustrophobia, agoraphobia; fear of death; antisemitism, **hatred**; spy mania.

**intimidation**, war of nerves, war cry, fee, faw, fum; **threat**; caution, **warning**; terror, terrorism, reign of terror; sword of Damocles, **punishment**; deterrent, **weapon**; object of terror, goblin, hobgoblin, **demon**; spook, spectre, **ghost**; Gorgon, scarecrow, nightmare; bugbear, ogre, **monster**.

**alarmist**, scaremonger; defeatist, peesimist, doom merchant.

**Adj. fearing**, afraid, frightened, funky; **respectful**; panic-stricken; hysterical; frozen; aghast, awestruck, frightened to death; more frightened than hurt.

**nervous**, defensive, tense, uptight; despairing, **hopeless**; timid, timorous, shy, diffident, self-conscious, **modest**; coy, wary, **cautious**; doubtful, suspicious; windy, **irresolute**; disturbed; apprehensive, uneasy, fearful, anxious, **unhappy**; highly-strung, jumpy, nervy; tremulous, shaky; breathless.

**frightening**, shocking, formidable, redoubtable; hazardous, hairy; tremendous, dreadful, fearsome, **impressive**; grim, grisly, hideous, ghastly, lurid, frightful, revolting, horrible, terrible, awful, appalling, mind-blowing; hair-raising, blood-curdling; weird, eerie, creepy, gruesome, macabre, sinister; portentous, ominous; roaring, **loud**.

**Vb. fear**, funk, be afraid, dread, **respect**; flap; take fright, take alarm; flap, panic, stampede, take to flight, fly; start, jump, flutter; faint, collapse.

**quake**, shake, tremble, quiver, shiver, shudder, stutter, quaver; shake like a jelly, be frightened to death; change colour, blench, pale; wince, flinch, shrink, shy, jib, **avoid**; quail, cower, crouch, skulk, come to heel; stand aghast, freeze, freeze with horror.

**be nervous**, feel shy, **be modest**; suspect, distrust, mistrust, **doubt**; shrink, shy, quail, funk it; be anxious, dread; hesitate, think twice, think better of it, **be cautious**.

**frighten**, fright, grimace; scare, panic, stampede; intimidate, menace, **threaten**; alarm, cry wolf; scare stiff, scare half to death; make one jump, give one a fright, give one a turn, startle, flutter, flurry, **agitate**; start, flush, **hunt**; disquiet, disturb, perturb, haunt; disturb, **trouble**; make nervous, rattle, shake, unnerve; make a coward of; strike with fear, awe, overawe, **impress**; quell, subdue, cow, **overmaster**; amaze, shock, stagger, flabbergast, stun, **surprise**; dismay, confound, abash, disconcert, **derange**; daunt, deter, discourage, **dissuade**; institute a reign of terror, **oppress**; browbeat, bully, **torment**; terrify, horrify, harrow, make aghast, chill, freeze, paralyse, petrify, rivet, turn to stone, **render insensible**; appal.

## 850 Courage

**N. courage**, valour, derring-do; moral courage, **probity**; VC courage, heroism, gallantry, chivalry; self-confidence, self-reliance, ignorance of fear, daring, nerve; defiance of danger, hardihood; spirit, mettle, dash, go, panache; enterprise, **undertaking**; bulldog courage; high morale, fortitude, determination, **resolution**; pluck, spunk, guts, heart, heart of oak, backbone, grit, **stamina**; sham courage, pot valour; desperate courage, courage of despair; brave face, bold front, **defiance**; fresh courage, animation, **inducement**.

**manliness**, manhood, probity; virtue, chivalry; morale, devotion to duty; endurance, stiff upper lip, **resolution**.

**prowess**, derring-do, chivalry, heroism, heroic achievement, gallant act, act of courage; feat, feat of arms, exploit, stroke, **deed**; desperate venture; heroics.

**brave person**, hero, VC; knight; good soldier, stout fellow, brave, warrior, **soldier**; man, man or woman of mettle, man or woman of spirit, plucky fellow, game dog, bulldog; daredevil; bully, bravo, **desperado**; Amazon; gallant knight; gallant company; forlorn hope, **elite**; lion, tiger, bulldog.

**Adj. courageous**, brave, valiant, gallant, heroic; chivalrous; martial, **warlike**; stout, doughty, tall, bonny, manful, tough, red-blooded; militant, bellicose, aggressive; fierce, bloody, savage, **cruel**; bold, **defiant**; dashing, hardy, audacious, daring, venturesome, **rash**; adventurous, enterprising; mettlesome, spirited, lion-hearted; full of courage, full of fight, full of spirit, full of spunk; full of Dutch courage; unbowed, firm, steady, dogged, indomitable, never say die; desperate, determined, **resolute**; of high morale, game, plucky, sporting; unflinching, **willing**.

**unfearing**, intrepid, nerveless, with nerves of steel or of iron; sure of oneself, confident; fearless; undaunted, unabashed, unconcerned.

**Vb. be courageous**, show spirit; fight; venture, adventure, **undertake**; dare, **face danger**; show fight, brave, face, outface, beard, affront, **defy**; confront; **affirm**; show a bold front, **stand firm**, **charge**; laugh at danger, be rash; show prowess, show valour; **keep calm**; endure, **suffer**.

**take courage**, take heart of grace, nerve oneself; show fight, **be resolute**; rally, stand, **stand firm**.

**give courage**, animate, hearten, nerve, make a man of; embolden, encourage, inspire, **incite**; rally, cheer; preserve morale; reassure, give confidence.

**Adv. bravely**, courageously; as bold as brass.

## 851 Cowardice

**N. cowardice**, abject fear, funk, **fear**; craven spirit; want of courage, lack of daring; absence of morale; defeatism; white feather, yellow streak, low morale, faint heart, chicken liver; Dutch courage; discretion, better part of valour; safety first, **caution**.

**coward**, funk, craven; sneak, rat, tell-tale, **informer**; runaway; coward at heart, bully, braggart; baby, **weakling**; quitter; cur, chicken, rabbit, mouse, jellyfish, invertebrate, doormat; **alarmist**.

**Adj. cowardly,** coward, craven; pusil-lanimous, timid, timorous, fearful, unable to say boo to a goose, **nervous;** soft, womanish, babyish, **weak;** spirit-less, without grit, without guts, chicken; sneaking; yellow, abject, base, vile; lacking morale; **hopeless;** prudent, discreet, **cautious;** bashful, shy, coy, **modest;** easily frightened, funky, unstable, infirm of purpose, **irresolute.**

**Vb. be cowardly,** lack courage, **be irresolute; be nervous;** shrink, funk, avoid; hide, slink, skulk, sneak; quail, cower, cringe; show a yellow streak, show fear, turn tail, panic, stampede, scuttle, desert; show discretion, live to fight another day, **be cautious.**

**852 Rashness**

**N. rashness,** lack of caution, **inattention;** neglect; **folly;** lack of consideration, frivolity, levity; indiscipline, temerity, presumption; **haste;** game of chicken; courage of despair, **courage;** needless risk, **danger;** reckless gamble, last throw; reckless expenditure.

**desperado,** daredevil, madcap, hothead; adventurer, plunger; harum-scarum, ne'er-do-well; one who sticks at nothing, gunman; bully, bravo, **ruf-fian.**

**Adj. rash,** ill-advised, harebrained, fool-hardy, wildcat, injudicious, indis-creet, imprudent; careless, slapdash, accident-prone, **negligent;** thought-less, inconsiderate; light, frivolous, airy, breezy, flippant, giddy, harum-scarum, slaphappy, trigger-happy; irresponsible, reckless, regardless, foolhardy, lunatic, wanton, wild, cavalier; bold, daring, audacious, madcap, daredevil, neck or nothing, breakneck, suicidal; overweening, presumptuous, arrogant, **insolent;**

precipitate, hell-bent, desperate, **hasty;** unchecked, headstrong, **wilful; ignorant;** impulsive, impatient, hot-blooded, furious, **excitable;** ven-turesome, **speculative;** adventurous, **enterprising;** improvident, **prodigal.**

**Vb. be rash,** lack caution; expose one-self; charge at, rush at, **hasten;** plunge, gamble; waste; **be prodigal;** play with fire; dice with death, **face danger;** play a desperate game, court disaster, tempt providence; anticipate, aim too high.

**Adv. rashly,** lightly.

**853 Caution**

**N. caution,** care, heed; doubt; instinct of self-preservation; **secrecy;** calcula-tion, careful reckoning, safety first; nothing left to chance, **preparation;** deliberation, mature consideration; sobriety, balance; discretion, worldly wisdom, **wisdom;** insurance, pre-caution, **safeguard;** forethought, **fore-sight;** Fabian policy, **patience;** going slow, one step at a time; **delay.**

**Adj. cautious,** wary, watchful, **attentive; careful;** doubtful, suspicious, **nervous;** insured; guarded, secret, secretive, incommunicative, cagey, **reticent;** experienced, twice shy, **prepared;** cir-cumspect, gingerly, tentative; con-servative, **safe;** responsible, **trust-worthy;** prudent, prudential, discreet, wise; noncommittal, **neutral;** frugal, **economical;** canny; timid; slow, delib-erate, Fabian, **patient;** sober, cool; cold-blooded, calm.

**Vb. be cautious,** beware, take good care, **be careful;** play safe; **be wise;** go slow; conceal; **keep secret;** hide, **lurk;** look, scan; **be tentative;** tread warily, pus-syfoot; look twice, **be mindful;** calcu-late, reckon, **judge;** know when to stop; let well alone, keep aloof, **avoid;**

predict; **look ahead**; **estimate**; assure oneself, make sure, **make certain**; cover oneself, insure, hedge, **seek safety**; leave nothing to chance, **prepare**.

**Adv. cautiously**, with caution, gingerly.

## 854 Desire

**N. desire**, wish, will; summons, call, cry, **command**; dun, **demand**; wanting, want, need, exigency, **requirement**; claim; nostalgia, **regret**; hankering, thinking, daydream, **fantasy**; ambition, aspiration, **hope**; yen, urge, **impulse**; itch; intellectual curiosity, **curiosity**; zeal; passion, ardour, warmth; rage, fury, **frenzy**; monomania, **mania**; appetite, hunger, thirst, hungry look (see **hunger**); cupidity, **avarice**; greed; voracity; lust (see **libido**); inordinate desire.

**hunger**, famine, empty stomach; appetite, thirst; burning thirst, dipsomania, **alcoholism**.

**liking**, fancy, **love**; stomach, appetite, zest; relish, tooth, **taste**; leaning, penchant, propensity, trend, **tendency**; weakness, partiality; affinity, sympathy; mind, **intention**; predilection, favour, **choice**; whim, **caprice**; hobby, craze, fad, mania, **bias**; fascination, allurement, attraction, temptation, seduction, **inducement**.

**libido**, life instinct, sexual urge; sexual desire, passion, rut, heat; lust.

**desired object**, wish, desire, desirable thing, **requirement**; catch, prize, plum, **trophy**; lion, idol, cynosure, **favourite**; forbidden fruit; envy, temptation; magnet, lure, draw, **attraction**; aim, goal, star, ambition, aspiration, dream, **objective**; ideal, **perfection**.

**desirer**; lover; glutton; fancier, amateur, dilettante, **collector**; devotee, idolater;

well-wisher, **patron**; aspirant; pretender; candidate, parasite; ambitious person.

**Adj. desiring**, unable to resist; oversexed, lustful, rutting, must; wanting, **demanding**; missing; inclined, minded; ambitious; would-be, wistful, hankering; demanding more; curious, solicitous, sedulous, anxious; eager, keen, burning, ardent, agog, breathless, impatient; vocal; avid; fond, partial to.

**greedy**, acquisitive, possessive, **selfish**; ambitious, voracious, omnivorous, insatiable; rapacious, grasping; exacting, extortionate.

**hungry**, empty; peckish, ravenous, thirsty, dry.

**desired**; desirable, enviable; acceptable, welcome; appetizing; catchy, attractive, appealing; **voluntary**.

**Vb. desire**, want, miss, **require**; demand; call, summon, **command**; invite, **be hospitable**; wish, pray; wish otherwise, **regret**; covet, **envy**; promise oneself, have a mind to, aim at, have at heart, **intend**; aspire, dream of, dream, daydream, **hope**; want a lot, aim high; expect, **claim**; intercede, invoke; wish ill, **curse**; wish one well; welcome, be glad of, jump at, catch at, grasp at, clutch at, **take**; lean towards, **tend**; favour, prefer, select, **choose**; crave, hanker after; long, yearn, pine, languish; can't wait, must have; like, affect, **love**; take to, warm to, moon after, burn; ogle, make eyes at, solicit, woo, **court**; make a dead set at, run after, chase, **pursue**; lust, lust after, **be impure**; rut.

**be hungry**, hunger, famish, starve, have an empty stomach, be ready to eat a horse; have a good appetite, **eat**; thirst, be dry.

**cause desire**, incline, **motivate**; arouse

desire, **excite love**; stimulate, **excite**; smell good, **make appetizing**; parch, raise a thirst; dangle, tease, titillate, **tempt**; allure, seduce, draw, **attract**; **give hope**.

Adv. **desirously**, with appetite, hungrily, thirstily, greedily.

## 855 Indifference

N. **indifference**; lack of interest, want of zeal; faint praise, two cheers; **lack of wonder**; nothing between them; anorexia; inertia, apathy; insouciance; **inattention**; open mind, equity, **justice**; **middle way**; neutral, **moderate**; **slacker**; wallflower.

Adj. **indifferent**, unconcerned; uninterested; lukewarm, half-hearted; impersonal, phlegmatic, **impassive**; calm, cool, cold; nonchalant, careless, perfunctory, **negligent**; supine, lackadaisical, listless; easy-going, **lax**; unmoved, insensible to; loveless; impartial, inflexible, **just**; noncommittal, moderate, **neutral**; promiscuous; amoral.

**unwanted**; unprovoked; loveless; all one to; insipid, tasteless, **unsavoury**; undesirable.

Vb. **be indifferent**, see nothing wonderful; damn with faint praise; **dislike**; take it or leave it; shrug, dismiss, let go, make light of, **hold cheap**; take neither side, **be neutral**; grow indifferent; fail to move, leave one cold, **make insensitive**.

Int. Never mind! what does it matter! who cares! so what!

## 856 Dislike

N. **dislike**; reluctance; displeasure; **resentment**; **discontent**; dissent; aversion; antipathy, allergy; rooted dislike, distaste, disrelish; repugnance, repulsion, disgust, abomination; hor-

ror, **fear**; **phobia**; prejudice, **bias**; animosity, bad blood, ill feeling, mutual hatred, **hatred**; nausea, turn, vomit; object of dislike, pet aversion, Dr Fell.

Adj. **disliking**; disinclined; squeamish, queasy; averse, hostile, **inimical**; shy; loveless; **indifferent**; sick of.

**disliked**, undesirable; grating, bitter; **repellent**; revolting, abhorrent, loathsome, **hateful**; abominable; nauseous, sickening, fulsome, foul, stinking, **unsavoury**; disagreeable, insufferable, intolerable; loveless; **ugly**.

Vb. **dislike**, disrelish; **reject**; object, **deprecate**; mind, **resent**; take a dislike to; react against, **recoil**; feel sick at, want to heave, **vomit**; shun, **avoid**; look askance at, **disapprove**; sniff at, sneer at, **despise**; make a face, grimace, **be sullen**; be unable to abide, can't stand, detest, loathe, abominate, abhor, **hate**; shudder at, **fear**; wish undone, **regret**.

**cause dislike**, deter, **frighten**; antagonize, **enrage**; set against, set at odds, make bad blood, **excite hate**; satiate, pall, jade, **sate**; disagree with, upset, **disagree**; revolt, repel; offend, grate, jar, **displease**; **torment**; disgust, nauseate, sicken, make one sick; shock, make a scandal, **incur blame**.

Adv. **ad nauseam**.

Int. ugh! horrible! yuk! revolting!

## 857 Fastidiousness

N. **fastidiousness**, nicety, delicacy; **discrimination**; refinement, **good taste**; idealism, artistic conscience, **conscience**; nit-picking, pedantry, hairsplitting; **prudery**.

**perfectionist**, idealist, purist, fusspot, pedant, stickler, hard taskmaster; gourmet, epicure.

Adj. **fastidious**; nice, dainty, delicate;

perspicacious, discerning; particular, demanding, finicky; scrupulous, meticulous, squeamish, **attentive**; punctilious, painstaking, conscientious, critical, hypercritical, fussy, pernickety, hard to please, censorious; donnish, precise, exacting, difficult, severe; prim.

Vb. **be fastidious**; **choose**; refine, **argue**, discriminate; find fault; fuss, say ugh!, feel superior, disdain, **despise**; keep oneself to oneself, **be unsociable**.

## 858 Satiety

N. **satiety**; stuffing, saturation, saturation point; glut, surfeit, too much of a good thing, **tedium**; overdose, excess.

Adj. **sated**, replete; sick of; jaded.

Vb. **sate**, satiate; satisfy, quench, slake; **suffice**; saturate, **fill**; soak, **drench**; stuff, gorge, glut, surfeit, cloy, jade, pall; overdose; sicken, **cause dislike**; spoil, kill with kindness; bore, weary, **be tedious**.

## 859 Wonder

N. **wonder**, state of wonder, wonderment; admiration, hero worship, **love**; awe, fascination; cry of wonder, gasp of admiration, whistle, exclamation, exclamation mark; **silence**; open mouth; shock, surprise, **lack of expectation**; astonishment; stupor; consternation, **fear**.

**thaumaturgy**, magic, **sorcery**; wonderful works; stroke of genius, feat, exploit, **deed**; transformation scene.

**prodigy**, portent, sign, eye-opener, **omen**; something incredible, quite something, phenomenon, miracle, marvel, wonder; drama, sensation; object of wonder or admiration, wonderland, **fantasy**; sight, **spectacle**; infant prodigy, genius, man or woman of genius, **proficient person**; wizard, **sorcerer**; hero, wonder boy, dream girl, bionic man, **paragon**; freak, sport, curiosity, oddity, monster, monstrosity; puzzle.

Adj. **wondering**, awestruck; rapt; pop-eyed, agape; dumb, inarticulate, speechless, breathless, left without words, **silent**; struck all of a heap, thunderstruck; aghast.

**wonderful**, to wonder at, wondrous, marvellous, miraculous, monstrous, prodigious, phenomenal; stupendous, fearful; admirable, exquisite, **excellent**; **best**; striking, awe-inspiring, breathtaking, **impressive**; dramatic, sensational; shocking; rare, exceptional, extraordinary, unprecedented, **unusual**, remarkable, noteworthy; strange, odd, very odd, weird, unaccountable, mysterious, enigmatic; exotic, outlandish, unheard of, **extraneous**; fantastic, **imaginary**; impossible, hardly possible, too good or bad to be true, **improbable**; unbelievable, incredible, inconceivable, indescribable, unutterable, unspeakable, ineffable, **inexpressible**; surprising; mind-blowing, amazing; magic, **magical**.

Vb. **wonder**, marvel, admire, whistle; gasp, gasp with admiration; **love**; stare, goggle at, gawk, gape, look aghast; be awestruck, **fear**; be silent.

**be wonderful**; surpass belief, **cause doubt**; beggar all description, beat everything; spellbind, enchant, **bewitch**; dazzle, strike with admiration, **excite love**; strike dumb, awe, electrify, **impress**; stagger; stun, daze, stupefy, petrify, confound, astound, astonish, amaze, flabbergast, **surprise**; baffle, bewilder, **puzzle**; startle, frighten; shock, **incur blame**.

Adv. **wonderfully**; wondrous strange,

strange to say, wonderful to relate.

Int. Amazing! incredible! I don't believe
it! well I never! blow me down! did
you ever! gosh! wow! how about that!
bless my soul! 'pon my word! goodness gracious! whatever next!

## 860 Lack of wonder

N. **lack of wonder**, lack of astonishment;
composure, **quietude**; cold blood,
**moral insensibility**; lack of imagination; disbelief; matter of course, just
what one thought, nothing to wonder
at.

Adj. **unastonished**; accustomed; calm,
collected; phlegmatic, impassive, **apathetic**; unmoved, **indifferent**; cold-
blooded; blind to, **blind**; **expectant**.

**unastonishing**; customary, common,
ordinary, nothing wonderful, **usual**.

Vb. **not wonder**, see nothing remarkable,
be **insensitive**; **disbelieve**; see
through, **understand**; see it coming,
**expect**; **keep calm**.

Int. no **wonder**; nothing to it; of course;
quite so, naturally.

## 861 Repute

N. **repute**, reputation, report, title to
fame, name, character, **credit**; esteem,
**respect**; opinion, good odour,
favour, popularity, vogue, **fashion**;
acclaim, applause, approval, cachet,
**approbation**.

**prestige**, aura, mystique, magic; glamour, dazzle, lustre, splendour; prowess; glory, honour, kudos, esteem,
estimation, account, worship; face,
caste; degree, rank, ranking, standing,
footing, status, **serial place**; condition, position; precedence; prominence, eminence, **visibility**; distinction, high rank, majesty, **nobility**;
dignity, solemnity, grandeur; name to
conjure with, **influence**; hegemony,

primacy, **authority**; leadership; snob
value.

**famousness**, title to fame, celebrity;
renown, stardom, fame, name, note;
household name; glory, **success**;
notoriety, **disrepute**; **publicity**; posthumous fame, **memory**; undying
name; remembrance.

**honours**, honour, blaze of glory, crown,
halo, nimbus, glory; laurels, wreath,
garland, favour; feather, **trophy**;
order, star, garter, ribbon, medal;
sword, shield, arms, **heraldry**; an honour, distinction, accolade, award,
**reward**; compliment, flattery, incense,
eulogy, **praise**; memorial, statue, bust,
picture, portrait, niche, plaque,
temple, monument; title of honour,
dignity, handle, **title**; patent of nobility, peerage, **nobility**; academic honour, degree, diploma, certificate, **academic title**; source of honour, College
of Arms; honours list, birthday honours, roll of honour, **list**.

**dignification**; coronation, **celebration**;
dedication; promotion, advancement,
**progression**; exaltation, **elevation**;
**restoration**.

**person of repute**, gentle reader; worthy,
sound person, good citizen, loyal subject, pillar, pillar of society; man or
woman of honour, **honourable person**; knight, dame, peer, **person of
rank**; somebody, great man, great
woman, big shot, big noise, big name,
big wheel, VIP, **bigwig**; notable, celebrity, figure, champion; lion, star,
rising star; popular hero; idol, **favourite**; cynosure, model, mirror, **paragon**;
cream, cream of society, **elite**; choice
spirit, leading light, **leader**; grand old
man, **sage**; noble army, great company, bevy, galaxy, constellation,
**band**.

Adj. **reputable**, reputed, of repute, of

good or sound reputation, of credit; **trustworthy**; **honourable**; worthy, creditable, meritorious, prestigious, **excellent**; respectable, well thought of; moral, **virtuous**; popular, modish, **fashionable**.

**worshipful**, reverend, honourable; admirable, **wonderful**; heroic, **courageous**; imposing, august, stately, grand, sublime, **impressive**; lofty, high, **elevated**; mighty, **great**; lordly, princely, queenly, royal, regal, **noble**; glorious, full of honours, titled, time-honoured, ancient, **immemorial**; sacrosanct, sacred, holy.

**noteworthy**, notable, remarkable, extraordinary, **unusual**; fabulous, **wonderful**; of mark, of distinction, distinguished, **important**; conspicuous, prominent, public, **obvious**; eminent, preeminent, **peerless**, foremost, **superior**; ranking, leading, commanding; brilliant, bright, lustrous, **luminous**; illustrious, splendid, glorious.

**renowned**, celebrated, sung; of renown, of glorious name, of fame; famous, historic, illustrious, great, noble, glorious, **excellent**; notorious, **disreputable**; well-known, **known**; of note, noted (see **noteworthy**); resounding; evergreen, imperishable, deathless, immortal, eternal, **perpetual**.

**Vb. have a reputation**, wear a halo; have a good name, have a name to lose; rank, stand high, have status or standing, have a position, enjoy consideration, **command respect**; stand well with, do oneself credit, win honour, win renown, gain prestige, gain recognition, build a reputation, earn a name, acquire a character; be somebody, **prosper**; graduate, **succeed**; cut a figure, cut a dash, cover oneself with glory; rise to fame, flash to stardom;

shine, excel, **be good**; eclipse, overshadow, **be superior**; have precedence, play first fiddle, star, **come before**; have fame, have a great name; make history.

**seek repute**; **be proud**; flaunt, **feel pride**; lord it, queen it, prance, strut; brag, **boast**.

**honour**, revere, regard, **respect**; fear; **worship**; know how to value, appreciate, prize, value, tender, treasure, **love**; show honour, **pay respect**, pay due regard, **show respect**; be polite to, **be courteous**; compliment, **flatter**; grace with, dedicate to, inscribe to; praise, glorify, **acclaim**, **applaud**; deck with laurels, make much of, lionize, chair; credit, **thank**; glorify, commemorate, **remember**; celebrate, renown, **proclaim**; reflect honour, lend distinction or lustre to, do credit to, be a credit to.

**dignify**, glorify, exalt; deify, consecrate, dedicate, **sanctify**; install, enthrone, crown, **commission**; distinguish, **indicate**; advance, upgrade, **promote**; honour, **decorate**; bestow a title, create, elevate, ennoble; dub, knight; give one his or her title, sir, **name**; take a title.

## 862 Disrepute

**N. disrepute**, bad reputation, bad name, bad character, shady reputation, past; **disrespect**; notoriety, infamy, ill repute, ill fame; bad odour, ill favour, disfavour, discredit, black books, bad light, **odium**; dishonour, disgrace, shame (see **slur**); smear campaign; ignominy, loss of honour, loss of reputation; loss of face, loss of rank; comedown.

**slur**, reproach, **censure**; imputation, aspersion, reflection, slander, abuse, **calumny**; slight, insult, **indignity**;

scandal, disgrace, shame, pollution; stain, smear, smudge, **dirt**; stigma, brand, mark, spot, blot, tarnish, taint, **blemish**; dirty linen; bar sinister, badge of infamy, scarlet letter.

**object of scorn**, scandalous person, reproach, byword, contempt, discredit, **bad person**; reject; poor relation, **nonentity**; failure, **loser**.

**Adj. disreputable**, shifty, shady; notorious, of ill fame, nefarious; arrant, **bad**; doubtful, dubious, questionable, objectionable; ribald, improper, indecent, obscene, **impure**; characterless; petty, pitiful; outcast; base, abject, despicable, odious, **hateful**; mean, cheap, low, **vulgar**; shabby, squalid, dirty, scruffy, **unclean**; poor, **dilapidated**.

**discreditable**; ignoble; improper, **inexpedient**; **dishonest**; despicable; shameful, disgraceful, scandalous, shocking, outrageous, unmentionable; too bad.

**degrading**, ignominious, derogatory; beneath one.

**inglorious**, without repute, without prestige, without note; without a name, nameless, **anonymous**; **servile**; **modest**; unknown to fame, unheard of, obscure, **unknown**; unseen, unheard, **invisible**; unsung; **plebeian**; sunk low, shorn of glory.

**Vb. have no repute**, have a past; rank low; play second fiddle, take a back seat, **be inferior**; blush unseen, **be unseen**.

**lose repute**; fall, sink, **descend**; fade, wither; incur discredit, incur dishonour, incur disgrace, achieve notoriety, **incur blame**; disgrace oneself, **fail**; lose prestige, lose face; admit defeat, crawl, crouch; look silly, look foolish, cut a sorry figure, **be absurd**; be brought to book.

**demean oneself**, condescend, stoop,

marry beneath one; make oneself cheap, cheapen oneself; forfeit self-respect.

**shame**, pillory, expose, post; scorn, mock, **ridicule**; snub, **humiliate**; discompose, disconcert, deflate; degrade, downgrade, demote, cashier, disbar, strip, **punish**; blackball, **exclude**; vilify, malign, disparage, **defame**; taint, sully, mar, blacken, tarnish, stain, blot, smear, **make unclean**; debase, defile, desecrate, profane; brand, tar, **mark**; dishonour, disgrace, discredit, give a bad name, be a public scandal, **incur blame**; trample, tread underfoot, outrage, **oppress**; disdain, **despise**; make one blush, **debauch**.

## 863 Nobility

**N. nobility**, distinction, rank, station, order, **degree**; royalty, majesty, prerogative, **authority**; birth; descent, ancestry, line, lineage, pedigree, **genealogy**; noble family, noble house, dynasty, **family**; blood, caste, badge of rank, patent of nobility, coat of arms, crest, **heraldry**.

**aristocracy**, patrician order; nobility; lordship, lords, peerage, House of Lords; dukedom; landed interest, squirearchy; county family, county set, gentry, gentlefolk; great folk; life peerage.

**upper class**, upper ten, upper crust, top layer, top drawer; best people, better sort, chosen few, **elite**; high society, social register, high life, fashionable world; ruling class, **authority**; **rich person**; salaried class.

**aristocrat**, patrician, Olympian; person of high caste, Brahman; thoroughbred; senator, magnate, dignitary; don; gentleman; squire, laird; emperor, king, queen, prince, **sovereign**; nob, swell, **fop**; superior person, bigwig.

**person of rank,** titled person, noble, noble lord or lady, seigneur; lordship; peer, peeress; princess royal, duke, archduke, duchess; marchioness, count, countess; earl, viscount, viscountess, baron, baroness, thane, baronet, knight; bey, begum, emir, khan, **potentate, governor.**

**Adj. noble,** chivalrous; ladylike (see **genteel**); royal, regal, every inch a king or queen; queenly, princely, lordly; ducal; of royal blood, of high birth, of good family; thoroughbred; of rank, titled; haughty, high, exalted, grand, **great.**

**genteel,** patrician; Olympian; superior, high-class, grass roots; U, highly respectable; classy, posh, U, highly respectable; classy, posh, U, of good breeding, **well-bred.**

## 864 Commonalty

**N. commonalty,** commons, third estate, bourgeoisie; citizenry, democracy; silent majority, grass roots; general public; people at large, populace, vulgar herd; mass of society, proletariat; rag.

**rabble,** mob, horde, **crowd;** rout; riffraff, scum, dregs of society, cattle, vermin.

**lower classes,** lower orders, **inferior;** common sort, small fry, humble folk; working class, steerage, steerage class, lower deck; proletariat; slum population; white trash; underworld, low company, low life.

**middle classes,** bourgeoisie; Brown.

**commoner,** bourgeois(e) plebeian; citizen, mere citizen; democrat, republican; proletarian; working man or woman, **worker; native;** little man, common type, **common man;** common person, **inferior;** private; underling, **servant;** upstart, social climber,

Philistine, **vulgarian;** a nobody, **nonentity;** outcaste; Untouchable; villein, serf, **slave.**

**country-dweller,** countryman or - woman, yeoman, rustic, swain, gaffer, peasant, cultivator, **farmer;** boor, churl; yokel, hind, clod, clodhopper; bumpkin, country cousin, provincial, hillbilly; village idiot, **ninny.**

**low fellow,** fellow, cad; **poor person;** guttersnipe, street arab, ragamuffin; down-and-out, tramp, bum, vagabond, **wanderer; beggar;** low type, bully, ugly customer, plug ugly, ruffian, rowdy, rough, **ruffian;** rascal, **knave;** gangster, hood; criminal, delinquent; barbarian, savage, Vandal.

**Adj. plebeian,** common, simple, without rank; ignoble; **middling;** mean, low, low-down, **disreputable;** lowly, base-born, low-born, of low origin, of mean parentage, of mean extraction; servile; humble, of low estate, of humble condition, **inferior;** non-U, proletarian; homely, homespun, **plain;** obscure, **inglorious;** coarse, uncouth, **ill-bred;** cockney, bourgeois, Main Street, suburban, provincial, rustic; **vulgar;** churlish, **ungracious.**

**barbaric,** barbarous, barbarian, wild, savage; without arts, primitive, neolithic, **artless.**

## 865 Title

**N. title,** title to fame, claim; title of honour, courtesy title, handle; honour, distinction, order, **honours;** royal we, editorial we, **formality;** mode of address, Royal Highness, Excellency, Grace, Lordship, Ladyship, noble, my liege, my lord, my lady, dame; Right Honourable; Reverend, Monsignor, His Holiness; padre; your reverence, your honour, your worship;

sire, sir, madam, ma'am, master, mister, mistress, miss, Ms; monsieur, madame, mademoiselle; don, señor, señora, señorita; signora, signorina; Herr, Frau, Fraulein; sahib; comrade.

**academic title,** doctor; doctor of philosophy, PhD; doctor of literature, doctor of divinity; doctor of medicine, MD; doctor of music; bachelor of arts, BA; bachelor of literature; bachelor of science; bachelor of law; bachelor of music; master of arts, MA; master of science, MSc; Professor; reader, lecturer.

## 866 Pride

**N. pride,** proud heart; proper pride, self-esteem; self-respect, self-confidence; conceit, vanity, side, **vanity**; snobbery, **affectation**; false pride, **moral sensibility**; dignity, reputation, **prestige**; hauteur, disdain, **contempt**; overweening pride, hubris; swelling pride, pomp, show, display, **ostentation**; **prejudice**; object of pride, boast, joy, **favourite**; cynosure, pick, flower, **paragon.**

**proud person,** snob; mass of pride, pride incarnate; swank; lord of creation, **bigwig**; fine gentleman, **fop**; turkey cock; **rich person**; class-conscious person, **aristocrat.**

**Adj. proud,** elevated, haughty, lofty, sublime, **high**; **showy**; fine, grand, **fashionable**; grandiose, stately, statuesque, **impressive**; royal, queenly, lordly, **noble**; self-respecting, **courageous**; high-spirited, **lively**; stiff-necked, **obstinate**; mighty, **great**; imperious, commanding, **authoritative**; high-handed; overweening, overbearing, arrogant, **insolent**; brazen, unblushing, unabashed.

**prideful,** full of pride, inflated, swelling,

swollen; stuck-up; upstage, uppish; haughty, disdainful, superior, supercilious, hoity-toity; standoffish, aloof, distant, stiff, starchy, unbending, **ungracious**; feeling pride, proud of; **boastful**; pleased with oneself; cocky, bumptious, **vain**; pretentious, **affected**; pompous, **showy**.

**Vb. be proud,** stand erect, refuse to stoop; give oneself airs, think it beneath one, be too proud to, be too grand to; be stuck-up, swank, swagger, strut; condescend; disdain, **despise**; display hauteur, **be insolent**; lord it, queen it, **oppress**.

**feel pride,** boast of, **boast**; hug oneself, **be pleased**; flatter oneself, think a lot of oneself, **be vain**.

## 867 Humility. Humiliation

**N. humility,** humble spirit; resignation, **submission**; **courtesy**; humble person, mouse, violet.

**humiliation,** letdown, climbdown, comedown, **indignity**; rebuke, reprimand; shame, disgrace, **disrepute**; sense of shame, sense of disgrace, blush, confusion; shamefaced look, hangdog expression; hurt pride, **resentment**.

**Adj. humble,** lowly; meek, submissive, resigned; self-effacing, **disinterested**; **courteous**; harmless, inoffensive, **innocent**; unassuming, unpretentious, without airs, without side, **modest**; mean, low; of lowly birth, **plebeian**.

**humbled,** crestfallen, sheepish, dejected; ashamed, **inglorious**; brought low.

**Vb. be humble,** humble oneself, demean oneself; play second fiddle, **be modest**; be disinterested; condescend, unbend, **be courteous**; stoop, crawl, sing small, eat humble pie; stomach, pocket, **forgive**.

**be humbled,** receive a snub; be ashamed,

be ashamed of oneself, feel shame;
blush, **redden**; feel small.

**humiliate**, humble, chasten, abash, disconcert; lower, deflate; make one feel
small, make one crawl; snub, cut,
crush, squash, **be rude**; slight; mortify, put to shame, **shame**; make a fool
of, make one look silly; **outdo**; daunt,
**frighten**; **overmaster**.

## 868 Vanity

N. **vanity**; vain **pride**, **pride**; conceit,
self-importance, megalomania;
swank, side; assurance, good opinion
of oneself, self-esteem; self-
satisfaction; narcissism, egotism;
exhibitionism, **ostentation**; Vanity
Fair.

**airs**, affectation; swank, ostentation.

**vain person**, Narcissus; self-centred person, coxcomb, **fop**; peacock; know-all,
bighead; Miss Clever; pompous twit,
**insubstantial thing**.

Adj. **vain**, overweening, stuck-up,
proud; egocentric, self-centred, self-
complacent, full of oneself, **selfish**;
smug, pleased with oneself; opinionated, clever clever; bumptious, cocky,
perky, **insolent**; immodest, blatant;
**boastful**; pompous, pretentious, so-
called; **affected**.

Vb. **be vain**; have a high opinion of
oneself; **boast**; admire oneself, plume
oneself, **feel pride**; swank, strut, talk
big, push oneself forward; get above
oneself, give oneself airs, **be
affected**.

**make conceited**, fill with conceit, inflate,
**flatter**.

Adv. **conceitedly**, vainly, swankily.

## 869 Modesty

N. **modesty**, lack of ostentation, retiring
disposition; **prudery**; blush; chastity,

purity; **humility**; unassuming nature;
reserve; modest person, shy thing,
mouse.

Adj. **modest**, without vanity; self-
effacing, unobtrusive, unseen,
unheard, **humble**; quiet, unassuming,
unpretentious; moderate, mediocre;
shy, retiring, timid, diffident, **nervous**; awkward, constrained, inarticulate; bashful, rosy; shamefaced, sheepish; reserved, demure, coy; **affected**;
chaste, **pure**.

Vb. **be modest**, show moderation, ration
oneself, **be temperate**; efface oneself,
yield precedence, **be humble**; play
second fiddle, take a back seat; blush
unseen, **escape notice**; retire, shrink,
hang back, be coy, **avoid**; feel shame,
blush, colour, crimson, mantle, **redden**; **be virtuous**.

Adv. **modestly**; without fuss, without
ceremony, without beat of drum.

## 870 Ostentation. Formality

N. **ostentation**, display, parade, show,
**manifestation**; exhibitionism, **publicity**; splendour; self-importance,
**vanity**; fuss, swagger, pretension, **airs**;
swank, side, strut; bravado, heroics;
**boast**; dramatics, sensationalism,
**exaggeration**; bonhomie; showmanship, effect; solemnity (see **formality**);
grandeur, dignity; rhetoric, flourish;
big drum, **publication**; pageantry,
pomp, circumstance, pride, panache;
flying colours, dash, splash, **finery**;
frippery, glitter, tinsel; idle pomp, idle
show, false glitter, mockery; tomfoolery, **foolery**; travesty, **mimicry**;
exterior, gloss, veneer, polish, varnish; pretence, profession, **pretext**; lip
service, **deception**.

**formality**, state, dignity; royal we,
editorial we, **title**; ceremony, ceremonial, **ritual**; drill; protocol, form,

etiquette; **attention**; routine, **practice**; solemnity, formal occasion, function, red carpet, **celebration**; full dress, regalia, finery, **formal dress**; correct dress, **uniform**.

**pageant**, show, **exhibit**; fete, gala, gala performance, tournament, tattoo; field day, great doings, **celebration**; **spectacle**; set piece, tableau, scene, stage effect, **stage set**; display, stunt; pyrotechnics, carnival, **festivity**, revel; procession, promenade, flypast; turnout, review, parade, array, **assembly**.

**Adj. ostentatious**, showy, pompous; prestige; specious, seeming, hollow, **spurious**; consequential; pretentious, would-be, **affected**; **vain**; inflated, turgid, orotund, windy; grand, highfalutin, splendid, brilliant, magnificent, grandiose, posh; superb, royal, **liberal**; sumptuous, luxurious, costly, expensive, **dear**.

**showy**, flashy, dressy, **fashionable**; colourful, lurid, gaudy, gorgeous, **florid**; tinsel, garish, **vulgar**; flaming, flagrant, blatant, public; brave, dashing, gallant, gay, jaunty, sporty; spectacular, scenic, dramatic, histrionic, theatrical, stagy; sensational, daring.

**formal**, solemn, stately, grand, fine; ceremonious, punctilious, correct, precise, stiff, starchy; of state, public, official; ceremonial, ritual.

**Vb. be ostentatious**, cut a dash, make a splash, make a figure; glitter, dazzle, **shine**; flaunt, sport, **wear**; wave, flourish, **brandish**; trumpet, **proclaim**; **defy**; demonstrate, exhibit, **show**; make a display; stage-manage; polish, veneer, **coat**; shoot a line, **boast**; **attract notice**; put oneself forward, advertise oneself, **be affected**; prance, promenade, swan around; parade, march, march past, fly past; peacock,

strut, swank, **be vain**; make an exhibition of oneself, make people stare.

## 871 Celebration

**N. celebration**, performance, **action**; **remembrance**; observance, **ritual**; ceremony, function, occasion, do; formal occasion, coronation, installation, presentation, **commission**; debut, **beginning**; reception, welcome, **formality**; official reception, **applause**; festive occasion, fete, jubilee, **festivity**; jubilation, cheering, ovation, triumph, salute, salvo, tattoo, roll, fanfare, flying colours; illuminations; firework display; bonfire, **fire**; **trophy**; harvest home, thanksgiving, **thanks**; health, toast.

**special day**, day to remember, great day, **holy day**; Armistice Day, D-Day, Remembrance Sunday; Fourth of July, birthday; wedding anniversary, silver wedding, centenary, bicentenary, **anniversary**.

**Adj. celebratory**, observing; occasional, anniversary, centennial, **seasonal**; festive, jubilant; triumphant.

**Vb. celebrate**, perform, **do**; hallow, keep holy, keep sacred, **sanctify**; commemorate, **remember**, honour, observe, keep, maintain; make it an occasion, make much of, welcome, do one proud, **be hospitable**; do honour to, fete; chair, **elevate**; mob, rush, **rampage**; garland, wreathe, crown, **reward**; lionize, beat a tattoo, fire a salute, fire a salvo; cheer, triumph, **rejoice**; make holiday, **revel**; present, inaugurate, launch, install, **commission**; **begin**.

**toast**, pledge, clink glasses; drink to, drain a bumper, drink a health, **drink**.

**Adv. in honour of**, in memory of, in celebration of, on the occasion of.

## 872 Boasting

**N. boasting**; **ostentation**; swagger, swank, bounce, **vanity**; advertisement, **publicity**; fine talk, **empty talk**, heroics, bravado; chauvinism, jingoism, **bias**; bluster; **threat**.

**boast**, brag; puff, **advertisement**; flourish, bravado, bombast, rant, fustian, tall talk, **exaggeration**; hot air, gas, bunkum, **empty talk**; bluff, bounce, **deception**; presumptuous challenge, **defiance**; big talk, big drum, bluster, idle threat, threat.

**boaster**, braggart; brag, loudmouth; charlatan, pretender, **impostor**; bouncer, **liar**; swank, **vain person**; swashbuckler, Pistol; hot air merchant.

**Adj. boastful**; braggart; **vain**; bellicose, **warlike**; hollow, pretentious, empty, **spurious**; grandiloquent; triumphant, cock-a-hoop.

**Vb. boast**, brag, talk big, shoot a line, bluff, bluster, shout; bid defiance, **defy**; vapour, prate, rant, gas, **mean nothing**; enlarge, magnify, **exaggerate**; trumpet, parade, flaunt, **publish**; puff, **advertise**; sell oneself; flourish, wave, **brandish**; **threaten**; strut, swagger, prance, swank, **be vain**; gloat, hug oneself, **be pleased**; boast of, be proud; **triumph**; exult, **rejoice**.

## 873 Insolence

**N. insolence**, hubris, **pride**; tyranny; bravado, **defiance**; bluster, **threat**; disdain, **contempt**; sneer; **scurrility**; assurance, self-assertion; presumption; hardihood, effrontery; face, front, brazen face.

**sauciness**, disrespect; nerve, gall, brass, cheek, neck; lip, mouth, sauce, V-sign, **gesture**; taunt, personality, insult, affront, **indignity**; throwaway manner, **discourtesy**; defiance,

answer, provocation, backchat, **rejoinder**; raillery, banter, **ridicule**.

**insolent person**, impertinent, cheeky devil; minx, hussy, baggage, madam; whippersnapper, pup, puppy; upstart, tin god, **nonentity**; braggart; **proud person**; bully, hoodlum, swashbuckler, desperado; **ruffian**.

**Adj. insolent**, bellicose, **warlike**; rebellious, **defiant**; scurrilous; lofty, supercilious, disdainful, contemptuous; haughty, snooty, up-stage, **proud**, arrogant, presumptuous; brash, bumptious, bouncing, **vain**; flagrant, blatant; shameless, lost to shame, unblushing, unabashed, brazen; bold, hardy, audacious, **rash**; overweening, overbearing, imperious, magisterial, lordly, arbitrary, high-handed, harsh; **boastful**.

**impertinent**, pert, forward, fresh; impudent, saucy, cheeky, brassy, cool, jaunty, perky, cocky, cocksure, flippant, flip; cavalier, offhand, familiar; breezy, airy; impolite, rude, **discourteous**; defiant, provocative, offensive; personal.

**Vb. be insolent**, get personal, **be rude**; have a nerve, cheek, sauce, give lip, taunt, provoke, **enrage**; retort, answer back, **answer**; get above oneself; presume, arrogate, assume, make bold to, make free with, get fresh; **be proud**; sneer at, **despise**; banter, rally, **ridicule**; express contempt, sniff, snort; **be indifferent**; send to blazes, **defy**; outlook, outface, take a high tone, lord it, queen it; bully, browbeat, treat with a high hand, **oppress**; swank, swagger, swell, look big, **be vain**; brag, talk big, **boast**; be a law unto oneself, **disobey**; defy nemesis, tempt providence.

**Adv. insolently**, impertinently, pertly; outrageously.

**874 Servility**

N. **servility**, abject spirit, lack of self-respect; **submission**; compliance; **humility**; bent back, bow, scrape, duck, bob, **obeisance**; **flattery**; **service**; servile condition, slavery, **servitude**.

**toady**; yes-man, rubber stamp; creep; hypocrite; spaniel, courtier; sycophant, parasite, leech; jackal, hanger-on, gigolo, **dependant**; lackey, **retainer**; born slave, slave; lapdog, poodle; tool, creature, **instrument**.

Adj. **servile**, dependent, **subject**; slavish; mean, abject, base, tame; subservient, submissive; compliant, supple, **obedient**; prostrate, sneaking; creepy, obsequious, unctuous, slimy.

Vb. **be servile**, stoop to anything, **demean oneself**; squirm, roll, sneak, cringe, crouch, creep, crawl, grovel; bow, scrape, bend, bob, duck, kow-tow, make obeisance, kneel, **stoop**; **be humble**; toady to, spaniel, fawn, ingratiate oneself, pay court to, curry favour, **flatter**; squire, attend, **serve**; comply, **obey**; **be instrumental**; whine, wheedle, beg; sponge; **conform**.

Adv. **servilely**, cap in hand.

**875 Friendship**

N. **friendship**, amity, **concord**; friendly relations, relations of friendship, friendly intercourse; companionship, togetherness; fellowship, comradeship, brotherhood, **association**; solidarity, support; acquaintanceship, acquaintance, familiarity, **knowledge**; introduction, recommendation, commendation, overtures, rapprochement, **approach**; reconciliation.

**friendliness**, kindness, **courtesy**; warmth, benevolence; camaraderie, hospitality; greeting, welcome, open arms, handshake, hug, **courteous act**; regard, **respect**; goodwill, fellow feeling, sympathy, response; understanding, same wavelength, entente, honeymoon, **concord**; partiality, **prejudice**; favouritism, **injustice**; support, **aid**.

**friend**, girlfriend, boyfriend; acquaintance, lifelong friend, crony, neighbour, fellow countryman or -woman; cousin, clansman; well-wisher, backer, **patron**; second, **protector**; fellow, sister, brother, partner, associate, **colleague**; ally, **auxiliary**; guest, frequent visitor; young friend, host, **sociable person**; former friend.

**close friend**, soul mate, kindred spirit; best man, bridesmaid; dear friend; intimate, bosom friend, bosom pal; alter ego, other self, shadow; comrade, companion, happy family.

**chum**, crony; pal, mate, cobber, buddy; fellow, comrade, roommate, stable companion, **colleague**; playmate, classmate; pen friend, pen pal.

**xenophile**, Anglophile, **philanthropist**.

Adj. **friendly**, amicable, devoted, **loving**; loyal, faithful, staunch, fast, firm, tried, **trustworthy**; fraternal, sisterly; natural, compatible, congenial, sympathetic, understanding; well-meaning, well-intentioned; hearty, cordial, warm, hospitable, **sociable**; effusive, demonstrative; matey; friendly with, **knowing**; intimate, inseparable, thick.

Vb. **be friends**, have neighbourly relations, hobnob, keep company with, go about together, be inseparable, **be sociable**; have a large acquaintance; embrace, **greet**; welcome, entertain, **be hospitable**; **understand**; like, warm to, become fond of, **love**; mean well.

**befriend**, acknowledge, know; favour, protect; overcome hostility; make welcome; strike an acquaintance, knit friendship; make overtures, **approach**; **court**; take to, warm to, click with; hobnob, make known to each other, introduce, present, commend; renew friendship, **make peace**.

**Adv.** amicably.

**876 Enmity**

**N. enmity**, hostility, antagonism, **opposition**; antipathy, **dislike**; **hatred**; animosity, spite, grudge, ill feeling, ill will, bad blood; **envy**; **ice**; alienation, strain, tension, **dissension**; rancour, **resentment**; **perfidy**; breach, breach of friendship, **quarrel**; hostile act; conflict, hostilities, state of war, **belligerency**; vendetta, feud.

**enemy**; traitor; bad neighbour; antagonist, opposite side, **opponent**; competitor, rival, **contender**; open enemy, foe, hostile force, **combatant**; aggressor; fifth column, Trojan Horse; public enemy, outlaw, pirate; personal enemy, arch enemy; misogynist, **misanthrope**; Anglophobe, **narrow mind**; pet aversion, **hateful object**.

**Adj.** inimical, disaffected; disloyal, unfaithful; aloof, distant, **unsociable**; cool, chilly, frigid, icy, **cold**; incompatible; hostile; irreconcilable; bitter, rancorous; jealous, grudging, **envious**; **malevolent**; at feud, at enmity, at loggerheads; aggressive, militant, at war with; intolerant; venomous, deadly, fell.

**Vb. be inimical**, show hostility; bear ill will, bear malice, **be malevolent**; grudge, **envy**; hound, persecute, **oppress**; chase, **hunt**; battle, **fight**; make war, **wage war**; take offence, take umbrage, **resent**; **quarrel**; be incompatible, conflict, collide, clash, **be contrary**; withstand, **oppose**.

**make enemies**, **be unsociable**; get across,

cause offence, antagonize, irritate, **enrage**; estrange, alienate, make bad blood, set at odds.

**877 Sociality**

**N. sociality**, membership, membership of society, **association**; making one of, being one of; team spirit; fellowship, comradeship, companionship, society; camaraderie; social intercourse, familiarity, togetherness, **friendship**; social circle, **friend**; social ambition; society.

**sociability**, social activity, **conformity**; sociable disposition; social success, popularity; social tact, common touch; social graces, good manners, **courtesy**; **good taste**; ability to mix; readiness to chat; welcome; greeting, glad hand, handshake, embrace, **courteous act**; hospitality, entertaining, open house, Liberty Hall, pot luck, **liberality**; good company, good fellowship, bonhomie; merrymaking; gaiety, **revel**; cheer, **food**; social board, loving cup.

**social gathering**, meeting, **assembly**; reunion, get-together, social; reception, at home; entertainment, **amusement**; singsong, camp fire; party; housewarming, house party, social meal, feast, banquet; communion, love feast, agape, **ritual act**; coffee morning, tea party, bun fight, cocktail party, picnic, barbecue, bottle party, **festivity**; dance, ball, hop, disco.

**social round**, social whirl, season, social entertainment; visiting, calling; stay, visit, call, visiting terms, haunting, **friendship**; engagement; rendezvous, assignation, date, meeting place, club, pub, local, **focus**.

**sociable person**, active member, caller, visitor; convivial person, good fellow; good mixer, good company; social success, catch, lion, **favourite**; jolly person, boon companion, club woman; good neighbour, **friend**; hostess, host, guest; parasite; social butterfly; socialite, ornament of society, social climber.

**Adj. sociable**, gregarious, social, outgoing, fond of company; companionable, affable, chatty, fond of talk; cosy; neighbourly, matey, **friendly**; hospitable, cordial, warm, hearty; convivial, festive, jolly, jovial, **merry**; lively; urbane, **courteous**; easy.

**welcomed**, entertained; welcome; popular, liked.

**Vb. be sociable**, enjoy society, like company, love a party; hobnob, mix with, **be friendly**; mix well, be a good mixer, get around, know how to live, gatecrash; have fun, **amuse oneself**; get together, make it a party, club together, go Dutch, share, go shares, **participate**; take pot luck, **eat**; **drink**; pledge, **toast**; carouse, **revel**; make oneself welcome, make oneself at home; relax, unbend, **repose**; chat to, **converse**; date, make a date; make friendly overtures, **befriend**; introduce oneself; write to, **correspond**.

**visit**, see people, go visiting, sojourn, stay, weekend; call; leave a card.

**be hospitable**, keep open house, **be liberal**; invite, have round, be at home to, receive; welcome, welcome with open arms, hug, embrace, **greet**; preside; do proud, **celebrate**; have company, entertain, **feed**; give a party, **revel**; accept, provide entertainment, **provide**.

**Adv. sociably**.

## 878 Unsociability. Seclusion

**N. unsociability**; autism; refusal to mix, keeping oneself to oneself; home life, domesticity; singleness; **parsimony**; distance, lonely pride, **pride**; cut, cut direct, **discourtesy**; silence, lack of conversation; boycott, **exclusion**; blacklist.

**seclusion**, privacy, private world; island universe, **star**; **quietude**; home life, domesticity; solitude; retreat; confinement; division, **separation**; segregation, quarantine, exile, **exclusion**; reserve, reservation, ghetto, native quarter, harem; gaol, **prison**; godforsaken hole, back of beyond; island, desert, wilderness; hideaway; den, study, sanctum, cloister, cell, hermitage, **retreat**; ivory tower, private quarters, shell; backwater.

**solitary**, unsocial person, iceberg; lonely person, lonely heart; loner, lone wolf, rogue elephant; island; introvert; stay-at-home; troglodyte; recluse, anchorite, hermit; pillar monk; maroon, castaway, **derelict**.

**outcast**, pariah, leper, outsider; outcaste, untouchable; expatriate, alien, **foreigner**; exile, deportee, evacuee, refugee, outlaw, bandit; vagabond, **wanderer**; waif, stray, **derelict**; reject, **rubbish**.

**Adj. unsociable**, unsocial, antisocial, introverted, morose; foreign, **extraneous**; stay-at-home, quiet, domestic; inhospitable, forbidding, hostile; distant, aloof, unbending, stiff; stand-offish, haughty; frosty, icy, cold, **sullen**; close, silent, **taciturn**; cool, impersonal, **indifferent**; solitary, lonely, lone, **alone**; shy, retiring, withdrawn, afraid of company; wild, feral; celibate.

**friendless**, forlorn, desolate; lonely, lonesome, solitary; without company, **alone**; sent to Coventry.

**secluded**, private, latent; quiet, lonely; remote, godforsaken, unfrequented, unseen, **unknown**; desert, desolate, empty.

**Vb. be unsociable**, keep oneself to oneself, shun company, talk to nobody; go it alone, play a lone hand; immure oneself, remain private, stand aloof, *avoid*; stay at home, bury oneself, vegetate, **be quiescent**; retire, make a retreat.

**make unwelcome, disapprove**; repel, keep at arm's length, make one keep his distance; ignore, cut, cut dead, **be rude**; cold-shoulder; rebuff; expel; **eject**; boycott, send to Coventry, blacklist, blackball, **exclude**; refuse to meet, refuse to mix with, have nothing to do with, *avoid*; excommunicate, banish, exile, outlaw, ban, *punish*.

**seclude**, island, isolate, quarantine, segregate; confine, *imprison*.

## 879 Courtesy

**N. courtesy**, chivalry, gallantry; deference, **respect**; consideration, **humility**; civility, manners, good behaviour, good breeding, **good taste**; diplomacy; **formality**; amenity, kindness, **benevolence**; easy temper, good humour, complaisance; common touch, social tact; smooth tongue, *flattery*.

**courteous act**, act of courtesy, polite act, graceful gesture, courtesy, civility, favour, charity, kindness, **kind act**; soft answer; compliment; kind words, **endearment**; introduction, presentation; welcome, reception, invitation; recognition, nod, salutation, salute, greeting, smile, kiss, hug, squeeze, handshake, **respects**; salaam, kowtow, bow, **obeisance**; terms of courtesy, respects, regards, duty, love; farewell, **valediction**.

**Adj. courteous**, chivalrous, generous, noble; courtly, gallant, correct, **formal**; polite, civil, urbane, gentle, ladylike, **well-bred**; gracious, **humble**; respectful; anxious to please, **attentive**; obliging, complaisant, kind; sweet; agreeable, suave, bland, smooth, well-spoken; obsequious, **servile**.

**amiable**, nice, sweet; affable, friendly, **sociable**, considerate, kind; inoffensive, harmless, **innocent**; gentle, easy, mild, lenient; unruffled; good, **obedient**; pacific, peaceable, **peaceful**.

**Vb. be courteous**; show courtesy, treat with deference, **respect**; give one his or her title, call sir, call madam; oblige, **aid**; condescend, **be humble**; notice, **be attentive**; conciliate, speak fair, *pacify*; make oneself agreeable, be all things to all men; return a soft answer, **be patient**; become courteous, express regrets, *atone*.

**pay one's respects**; pay compliments, **flatter**; drink to, pledge, **toast**; homage, kneel, **show respect**; honour, crown, wreathe, garland, chair, **celebrate**.

**greet**, flag, **signal**; accost, **approach**; acknowledge, **notice**; hail, vociferate; nod, wave, smile, blow a kiss; bid good morning, **speak to**; salute, make salutation, uncover; bend, bow, bob, duck, salaam, make obeisance, prostrate oneself, kowtow, stoop; advance to meet, **show respect**; escort, **accompany**; make a salute, present arms, parade, **celebrate**; receive; welcome, welcome home, **be sociable**; welcome with open arms, **be pleased**; embrace, hug, kiss, **caress**; usher, present, introduce, **admit**.

**Adv. courteously**, with respect, with all due deference.

## 880 Discourtesy

**N. discourtesy**, bad manners, failure of courtesy, want of chivalry, lack of manners, scant courtesy; misconduct; want of consideration.

**rudeness**; acerbity, acrimony, asperity; roughness; **inattention**; short answer; sarcasm, **ridicule**; unparliamentary language, rude words, **scurrility**; rebuff, insult, **indignity**; sauce, lip, cheek; shouting; black look, scowl, frown; a discourtesy, piece of bad manners.

**rude person**; savage, barbarian, brute, lout, boor, loudmouth, **insolent person**; curmudgeon, crab, bear; sourpuss, **malcontent**.

**Adj. discourteous**; unceremonious, impolite, rude; unmannerly, uncouth, beastly, savage, barbarian, **ill-bred**; insolent, impudent; cheeky, saucy, pert, forward, **impertinent**; unpleasant, disagreeable; cool, **indifferent**; cavalier, airy, breezy, inconsiderate.

**ungracious**, grim, **serious**; gruff, **sullen**; peevish, testy, **irascible**; difficult, surly, churlish, **unsociable**; grumbling; rough, rugged, harsh, brutal, **severe**; bluff, free, frank, blunt; brusque, short, **concise**; tart, sharp, biting, **pungent**; abusive; offensive; truculent.

**Vb. be rude**, want manners, flout etiquette; **be artless**; display bad manners, show discourtesy, **be insolent**; be beastly to, snub, cold-shoulder, cut, ignore, look right through, cut dead; **eject**; cause offence, **huff**; insult, abuse; take liberties, make free with, make bold; stare, ogle, **gaze**; make one blush, **shame**; shout, interrupt, **get angry**; curse, swear, damn, **cuss**; snarl, growl, frown, scowl, lour, pout, sulk, **be sullen**.

**Adv. impolitely**, discourteously, like a boor.

## 881 Congratulation

**N. congratulation**, compliments; happy returns; salute, toast; welcome, official reception, **celebration**; thanks, **gratitude**.

**Adj. congratulatory**, complimentary; triumphal, welcoming.

**Vb. congratulate**, felicitate, compliment; wish one joy, give one joy, wish many happy returns; sanction a triumph, accord an ovation, give three cheers, clap, **applaud**; fete, mob, rush, lionize, **celebrate**; congratulate oneself, **be pleased**; thank Heaven, **be grateful**.

## 882 Love

**N. love**, affection, friendship, charity; agape, true love, real thing; natural affection; possessive love; conjugal love; sentiment, **feeling**, kindness, **benevolence**; Platonic love, **friendship**; mutual love, mutual affection, mutual attraction, sympathy, fellow feeling, understanding, predilection, **tendency**; preference, **choice**, fancy, **caprice**; attachment, devotion, **loyalty**; courtly love, gallantry; **moral sensibility**; power of love, fascination, **sorcery**; desire; lust, **libido**; regard, **respect**; admiration, **wonder**; dawn of love, crush; madness; worship; romantic love, passion, fire of love, enthusiasm, rapture, ecstasy, transport, **excitable state**; abnormal affection; love psychology; narcissism.

**lovableness**, popularity, gift of pleasing; charm, fascination, appeal; coquetry; sentimental value.

**love affair**; romance; flirtation, amour, entanglement; free love, intrigue, seduction, **illicit love**; something between them; course of love; engagement, **marriage**; broken engagement, broken romance, broken heart.

**love-making**, **endearment**; courtship;

pursuit of love, coquetry; gallantry.

**love-nest,** abode of love, bower, Bower of Bliss; honeymoon cottage, nuptial chamber; harem, seraglio.

**lover,** love, sweetheart; young man, boyfriend; swain, beau, gallant, spark, cavalier, squire, escort, date; steady; suitor, follower, captive, admirer; aficionado, fan, devoted following, fan club; gigolo, lady-killer; paramour; flirt, coquette; vamp.

**loved one,** beloved, love, true love, soul mate, **darling;** intimate, **close friend;** favoured suitor, lucky man, **spouse;** conquest, girlfriend, girl, bird, honey, baby, sweetie; angel, princess; sweetheart, valentine, flame, idol, hero; heartthrob, dream man, dream girl; favourite, mistress, concubine, **kept woman.**

**lovers,** loving couple, love-birds; starcrossed lovers.

**love god,** goddess of love, Venus; Cupid, blind boy.

**love emblem,** turtledove; Cupid-s bow, Cupid's dart golden arrow; bleeding heart, bjroken heart, **love token.**

**Adj. loving,** sisterly; loyal, **disinterested;** making love; affectionate, demonstrative; tender, motherly, conjugal; gallant, romantic, sentimental, lovesick; lovelorn, **dejected;** fond of, fond; possessive, **jealous;** devoted, flirtatious, **capricious;** amatory, amorous, ardent, passionate, **fervent;** lustful.

**enamoured,** inclined to; struck with, caught, hooked; infatuated, besotted, crazy about, **crazy; happy;** ecstatic, **excited.**

**lovable,** congenial, sympathetic; winsome, **amiable;** sweet, divine, adorable; lovely, graceful, good-looking, **beautiful;** attractive, seductive; prepossessing, appealing, engaging, endearing, irresistible; desirable;

enchanting; beloved, dear, darling, pet, fancy, favourite.

**erotic,** aphrodisiac, erogenous; sexy, **impure;** amatory, **excited.**

**Vb. love,** like, care, quite like, be partial to; be fond of; be susceptible, have a heart, bear love towards, hold dear, cherish, cling to, embrace; appreciate, value, prize, treasure, regard, admire, revere, **respect;** adore, worship; burn with love, make love, **unite with;** make much of, spoil, pet, fondle, **caress.**

**be in love,** burn, sweat, faint, **die;** burn with love, glow with ardour, flame with passion, love to distraction, **be insane;** take a fancy to, take a shine to, take to, warm to, dig; **desire;** form an attachment, get infatuated, have it bad; **go mad;** woo, sue, sigh, **court;** chase, **pursue;** honeymoon, **wed.**

**excite love,** arouse desire, **cause desire;** warm, inflame, **heat;** rouse, stir, flutter, enrapture, **excite;** dazzle, charm, enchant, fascinate, **bewitch;** allure, draw, **attract;** make oneself attractive; lure, bait, seduce, **tempt;** flirt, coquette, philander; toy, vamp, **caress;** smile, leer, make eyes, ogle, wink, **court;** attract notice; make a hit, make mad; make a conquest, captivate, **subjugate;** catch, wed; be amiable, make oneself a favourite; steal every heart; curry favour, **flatter.**

**Adv. affectionately,** kindly, madly.

## 883 Hatred

**N. hatred,** hate; revulsion of feeling, disillusion; aversion, antipathy, allergy, nausea, **dislike;** intense dislike, repugnance, abomination; disfavour, displeasure (see **odium**); alienation, **dissension;** hostility, antagonism, **enmity;** animosity, ill feeling, bad blood, acrimony, rancour, **resentment**; malice, ill will, evil eye, spite, grudge; **envy**; wrath, **anger**; hymn of hate, **malediction**; scowl, snap, snarl; phobia, anti-Semitism, racialism, colour prejudice, **prejudice**.

**odium**, disfavour, **disapprobation**; discredit, bad odour, black books, **disrepute**.

**hateful object**; bitter pill; abomination, filth; **enemy**; bugbear, Dr Fell; pest, menace, good riddance, **bane**; rotter, **cad**; heretic, blackleg, scab.

**Adj. hating**, loveless; set against; averse, abhorrent, hostile, **inimical**; envious, malicious, full of malice, malignant; **malevolent**; bitter, rancorous; full of hate, implacable; vindictive; virulent.

**hateful**, odious; invidious, obnoxious; beastly, nasty, horrid; abhorrent, loathsome, abominable; accursed, execrable, **cursed**; offensive, repellent, nauseous, revolting; bitter, sharp, **sour**.

**hated**; loveless; lovelorn.

**Vb. hate**, bear hatred; loathe, abominate, detest, abhor; **avoid**; recoil at, **recoil**; can't bear, can't stand, **dislike**; find loathsome, find obnoxious; refuse, **reject**; spurn, **despise**; execrate, hold accursed, denounce, **curse**; bear malice, **be malevolent**; feel envy, **envy**; bear a grudge, **resent**; scowl, growl, snap, snarl, **be sullen**; insult, **be insolent**; turn to hate.

**excite hate**, grate, jar, **repel**; disgust, nauseate, **cause dislike**; shock, horrify, **incur blame**; antagonize, destroy goodwill, estrange, alienate, sow dissension, create bad blood, end friendship, turn all to hate; poison, embitter, exacerbate, **aggravate**; exasperate, incense, **enrage**.

## 884 Endearment

**N. endearment**, blandishments, compliments, **flattery**; loving words, pet name; affectionate behaviour; osculation; caress, embrace, clasp, hug, cuddle, squeeze, pressure, salute, kiss, smacker; nibble, bite; stroke, tickle, slap, pat, pinch, nip, **touch**; familiarity, advances, pass.

**wooing**; play, lovemaking; wink, glad eye, come hither look, ogle, amorous glance, fond look, sigh; flirtation, coquetry, gallantry, courtship, suit, advances, **love-making**; serenade, love song, love lyric, amorous ditty; love letter; love poem, sonnet; proposal, engagement, **marriage**.

**love token**, favour, ribbon, glove; ring, valentine, love letter; posy; arrow, heart, **love emblem**; tattoo.

**Adj. caressing**, clinging, demonstrative, affectionate, **loving**; soppy; flirtatious.

**Vb. pet**, pamper, spoil, spoonfeed, mother, smother, kill with kindness; cosset, coddle; make much of; treasure, **love**; cherish, foster, **safeguard**; nurse, lap, rock, cradle, baby; sing to; coax, wheedle, **flatter**.

**caress**, love, fondle, dandle; play with, stroke, smooth, pat, paw; kiss; embrace, enfold, lap; clasp, hug, hold one tight, cling, **retain**; squeeze, press, cuddle; snuggle, nestle, nuzzle; nibble; play, romp, wanton, toy, trifle, dally, spark; make love, spoon, pet, neck, snog, smooch; vamp, **excite love**; fawn, rub oneself against; (of a crowd) mob, rush, snatch at.

**court**, make advances; make eyes, ogle, leer, eye, **gaze**; become familiar, get fresh, make a pass; gallivant, philander, flirt, coquette, **excite love**; run after, chase, **pursue**; squire, escort, **accompany**; hang round, **follow**; date, make a date; go steady; sue, woo, pay court to, pay suit to; serenade, caterwaul; sigh, pine, languish, **love**; propose, propose marriage, become engaged, make a match, **wed**.

## 885 Darling. Favourite

N. **darling**, dear, my dear; dear friend; dearest, dear one, only one; love, beloved; heart, sweetheart, fancy, valentine; sweetie, sugar, honey; precious, jewel, treasure; angel, angel child, cherub; poppet, moppet; pet, lamb, chick, chicken, duck.

**favourite**, darling; cosset; jewel; good man, good chap, fine fellow, marvellous woman; brick, sport; first choice, front runner, top seed, only possible choice; boast, pride; national figure, favourite son, Grand Old Man, **person of repute**; idol, hero, golden girl or boy; media personality, star, general favourite, cynosure; pinup girl, **a beauty**; centre of attraction, cynosure, **attraction**; catch, lion.

## 886 Resentment. Anger

N. **resentment**, displeasure, **discontent**; ill humour; rancour; slow burn; umbrage, offence, huff, tiff, pique; bile, spleen, gall; acerbity, acrimony, bitter resentment; hate, **hatred**; animosity, grudge, bone to pick, crow to pluck, **enmity**; spite, **revenge**; malice; hot blood; cause of offence, red rag to a bull, sore point; irritation; provocation, insult, affront, last straw, **indignity**; wrong, injury, **injustice**.

**anger**, irritation; dudgeon, wrath; rage, fury, passion, **excitable state**; temper, tantrum, tizzy, paddy, fume, fret, pet, fit of temper, burst of anger, outburst, explosion, storm, stew, ferment, taking, paroxysm; rampage; shout,

roar; angry look, glare, frown, scowl; growl, snarl, bark, bite, snap, asperity; warmth, heat, high words, **quarrel**; **indignity**; fisticuffs, **fight**.

Adj. **resentful**, stung, miffed; stung, hurt, sore; pained, hurt; warm, indignant; bitter, full of hate, rancorous, virulent; full of spleen, **malevolent**; full of revenge, vindictive; jealous, green with envy, **envious**; grudging.

**angry**, stern, **serious**; impatient, cross, waxy, ratty, wild, mad, livid; irate; stung; hot; angry with, mad at; indignant, beside oneself with rage; shirty; warm, burning; speechless, crying with rage; savage, violent, **furious**; apoplectic, rabid; berserk; roaring; glaring, **sullen**; red with anger, bloodshot, **red**; pale with anger; fierce, **irascible**.

Vb. **resent**, find intolerable, be unable to stomach, **suffer**; feel, mind, feel resentment; take amiss, take ill; take offence, take umbrage, take exception to, **quarrel**; jib, get sore; burn, smoulder, sizzle, simmer; express resentment, **be malevolent**; take to heart, let it rankle, remember an injury, cherish a grudge, bear malice; go green with envy, **envy**.

**get angry**, get cross, get wild, get mad; get sore, go spare; kindle, grow warm, grow heated, colour, redden, flush with anger; take fire, ramp; bridle, bristle; lose patience, forget oneself; throw a tantrum, stamp, shout; let fly, explode; see red, go berserk, go mad, **be excitable**.

**be angry**, interrupt, chafe, fret, fume, fuss, flounce, dance, ramp, stamp, champ; create, perform, make a scene, make a row, **rampage**; turn nasty; rage, rant, roar, bellow, bluster, storm, thunder, fulminate, **be loud**; look like thunder, look black, glare, glower, frown, scowl, growl, snarl, **be sullen**; spit, snap; weep with rage, shake with passion, swell with fury, stamp with rage, dance with fury, **be excited**; let fly, **be violent**.

**huff**, pique, sting, nettle, rankle, smart; wound, **hurt**; antagonize, get across, give umbrage, offend, cause offence, embitter, **excite hate**; **cause dislike**; affront, insult, outrage.

**enrage**, upset, discompose, ruffle, irritate, rile; annoy, vex, pester, bug, bother, **trouble**; do it to annoy, tease, bait, needle, **torment**; bite, fret, nag, gnaw; exasperate; push too far; anger, incense, infuriate, madden, drive mad; goad, sting, taunt, invite a quarrel; make one see red; cause resentment, embitter, poison; exasperate, **aggravate**; embroil, set at loggerheads.

**Adv. angrily**, bitterly; in anger, in fury, in the treat of the moment.

**887 Irascibility**

**N. irascibility**; asperity, gall, bile, vinegar; **moral sensibility**; readiness to take offence; temperament; uncertain temper, hot temper, limited patience; hot blood, inflammable nature; bad temper.

**shrew**, scold, fishwife; termagant, virago, vixen, battleaxe, harridan, fury; Tartar, hornet; bear, **misanthrope**; mad dog; fiery person, redhead.

**Adj. irascible**, impatient, choleric, irritable, peppery, testy, crusty, peevish, crotchety, cranky, cross-grained; prickly, touchy, thin-skinned, **sensitive**; inflammable, like tinder; hot-blooded, fierce, fiery, passionate, **excitable**; quick, warm, hasty, trigger-happy, **rash**; shrewish, vixenish, petulant, cantankerous, querulous;

bitter, **sour**; liverish; scratchy, snappy, snappish, waspish; tart, sharp, short; uptight, edgy; fractious, fretful, moody, temperamental, changeable; gruff, grumpy, ratty, like a bear with a sore head; cross, stroppy, **sullen**.

**Vb. be irascible**, have a temper; snort, bark, snap, bite, **be sullen**; **get angry**.

**888 Sullenness**

**N. sullenness**; ill humour; vinegar; pout, grimace, **discontent**; **discourtesy**; ill temper; spleen, bile, liver; dumps, grouch, temperament; **melancholy**; black look, glare, glower, lour, frown, scowl; snort, growl, snarl, snap, bite.

**Adj. sullen**, forbidding, ugly; saturnine, overcast, cloudy, **dark**; stern, grim, **serious**; cross, **unsociable**; surly, morose, crabbed, crusty, cross-grained, difficult; snappish, shrewish, vixenish, cantankerous, quarrelsome, stroppy; refractory, **disobedient**; grumbling, grumpy; acid, tart, sour; gruff, rough, abrupt, brusque, **discourteous**; temperamental, moody; jaundiced, blue, melancholy; petulant, peevish, shirty, **irascible**; sultry.

**Vb. be sullen**, gloom, glower, glare, lour; look black, scowl, frown; spit; snap, snarl, growl, snort; make a face, grimace, pout, sulk; **be unsociable**; mope, **be dejected**; grouch, grouse, carp, crab, complain, grumble, mutter, smoulder.

**Adv. sullenly**, with a bad grace.

**889 Marriage**

**N. marriage**, matrimony, one flesh; wedlock, wedded state, state of matrimony, wedded bliss; match, union, alliance; conjugal knot, nuptial bond, marriage tie, marriage bed, life together; banns, marriage certificate, marriage lines; marriage god, Hymen.

**type of marriage**, monogamy, bigamy, polygamy, polyandry; second marriage; marriage of convenience; mixed marriage, **mixture**; misalliance; free union, free love; compulsory marriage, forcible wedlock, shotgun wedding.

**wedding**, match, engagement; ring; marriage ceremony; wedding service, nuptial mass, nuptial benediction, **Christian rite**; church wedding, civil marriage, run-away match; solemn wedding, torch of Hymen, nuptial song; wedding day; marriage feast, wedding breakfast, reception; honeymoon; silver wedding, wedding anniversary, **special day**.

**bridal party**, best man, maid or matron of honour, bridesmaid, page; attendant, usher.

**spouse**; marriage partner, man, wife; married couple; bride, young matron; bridegroom, consort, partner, mate, helpmate, better half, affinity; married man, husband, man, old man; henpecked husband; married woman, wedded wife, lady, matron; woman, old dutch, rib, grey mare, Duchess of Fife, joy of my life; squaw; faithful spouse; second husband, second wife, common-law husband or wife.

**polygamist**, Mormon; bigamist.

**matchmaker**, go-between; marriage bureau, personal column; marriage guidance counsellor, **mediator**.

**nubility**, marriageable age; good match, suitable party; welcome suitor, lover.

**Adj. married**; wedded, united, made one; just married, newly-wed.

**marriageable**, nubile, of age, eligible, suitable; engaged, bespoke.

**matrimonial**, marital, connubial; premarital, nuptial; conjugal, matronly.

**Vb. marry**, match, mate; make a match, betroth, espouse; join, couple, splice, hitch.

**wed**, marry, espouse; take a wife, find a husband; **court**; get married, mate with, marry oneself to, unite oneself with, accept a proposal, become **engaged**; say 'I do', be made one, **unite with**; mate, couple; honeymoon; marry well, make a good match; make a bad match, repent at leisure; make a love match; elope; contract marriage, make an honest woman of, go through a form of marriage; marry again; commit bigamy; intermarry.

**Adv. matrimonially**.

## 890 Celibacy

**N. celibacy**, singleness, single state; maidenhood, **purity**.

**celibate**, bachelor; confirmed bachelor; enemy of marriage, misogynist, **misanthrope**; monastic, **monk**; hermit, **solitary**; monastic order, holy orders.

**spinster**, bachelor girl; debutante; maid, maiden; maiden aunt, old maid; **nun**; Amazon.

**Adj. unwedded**; single; free, **independent**; maidenly, virgin, virginal, **pure**; spinster; bachelor; celibate, monastic.

**Vb. live single**; refuse marriage, be free; live like a hermit, **be unsociable**; take orders.

## 891 Divorce. Widowhood

**N. divorce**, dissolution of marriage; divorce decree, decree nisi, decree absolute; separation; consanguinity, affinity; living apart, separate maintenance, alimony; broken marriage, broken engagement; divorce court, divorce case; divorcee, nor wife nor maid; corespondent; single parent.

**widowhood;** widows' weeds **formal dress;** widower, widow, widow woman, relict; dowager, dowager duchess; war widow, grass widower, Merry Widow.

**Adj. divorced,** separated, living apart.

**widowed,** husbandless, wifeless.

**Vb. divorce,** separate, live apart, desert, **relinquish; disunite;** file a divorce suit; get a divorce; put asunder, dissolve marriage, grant a divorce, pronounce a decree absolute.

**be widowed.**

**widow,** bereave, make a widow or widower.

## 892 Benevolence

**N. benevolence,** good will; benignity, kindly disposition, heart of gold; bonhomie; milk of human kindness, goodness of nature, warmth of heart, kindness, charity, **love;** godly love, fraternal feeling, **friendship;** consideration; understanding, concern, fellow feeling, empathy, sympathy, **feeling;** condolence, **pity;** decent feeling, humanity, humanitarianism, **philanthropy;** utilitarianism, **sociology;** hospitality, generosity, magnanimity, **liberality;** tolerance, toleration; mercy, **forgiveness;** God's love, grace of God; blessing, benediction.

**kind act,** kindness, favour, service; good deed, charity, relief, alms; good offices; good turn, helpful act, **aid;** labour of love, **voluntary work.**

**kind person,** Christian; good sort, good neighbour, good Samaritan, wellwisher, **friend; patron;** idealist, do-

gooder, **philanthropist.**

**Adj. benevolent,** well meant, wellintentioned, **friendly;** to oblige; good of one, so good of; sympathetic; kindly disposed, benign, kindly, kind, good, human, decent, Christian; affectionate, **loving;** fatherly, paternal; motherly, maternal; fraternal; sisterly; good-humoured, good-natured, easy, sweet, gentle, **amiable;** merciful, forgiving; tolerant, **lax;** humane, considerate, **lenient;** soft-hearted, tender; pitiful; genial, hospitable, **sociable;** bounteous, bountiful, **liberal;** generous, **disinterested;** beneficent, charitable, humanitarian, doing good; obliging, accommodating, helpful; complaisant, gracious, gallant, chivalrous, **courteous.**

**Vb. be benevolent;** show concern; understand; **forgive;** wish well, bless, bestow a benediction; bear good will, mean well; look with a favourable eye, favour; benefit, **do good;** be a good Samaritan, do a good turn, render a service, oblige, **aid;** reform, **make better.**

**philanthropize,** do good, go about doing good, do good works, have a social conscience, show public spirit, care; get involved, **be active;** reform, improve; visit, be nurse, **minister to;** mother, **pet.**

**Adv. benevolently,** kindly, to oblige.

## 893 Malevolence

**N. malevolence,** ill will, **enmity;** evil intent, bad intention, cloven hoof; spite, gall, despite, malice, malice aforethought; bad blood, hate, **hatred;** venom, **bane;** acrimony, acerbity; rancour, spleen, **resentment;** unholy joy, envy; evil eye, **spell.**

**inhumanity,** lack of humanity, lack of concern; lack of charity; hardness of heart, heart of marble, heart of stone; **hardness**; cruelty, barbarity; ferocity; sadism; vandalism, **destruction**.

**cruel act,** cruel conduct; ill usage, **misuse**; disservice, ill turn; foul play, bloodshed, **violence**; excess; act of inhumanity, inhuman deed, atrocity, outrage; cruelty, torture, barbarity; murder, **homicide**; mass murder, genocide, **slaughter**.

**Adj. malevolent,** meaning harm; ill-natured, churlish, **sullen**; nasty, bloody-minded, bitchy, cussed, **wilful**; malicious, catty; mischievous, baleful, malign, malignant; vicious, venomous, **deadly**; full of spite; jealous, **envious**; disloyal, treacherous; bitter, rancorous, implacable, merciless, **pitiless**; vindictive; hostile, fell, **inimical**; intolerant.

**maleficent,** hurtful; poisonous, venomous, virulent, caustic; working evil, **bad**.

**unkind,** ill-natured, **sullen**; unchristian; cold, hostile, **inimical**; inhospitable, **unsociable**; ungenerous, uncharitable; mean, nasty; rude, harsh, gruff, beastly, **ungracious**; unfeeling, insensible, unmoved, **impassive**; stern, severe; tough, hardboiled, hardbitten, **hard**; inhuman, unnatural.

**cruel,** grim, fell, steely, hard-hearted, callous, cold-blooded; heartless, ruthless, merciless, **pitiless**; bloodthirsty, **murderous**; bloody, **violent**; excessive, extreme; outrageous; feral, tigerish; unnatural, subhuman; brutal, rough, truculent, fierce, ferocious; savage, barbarous, wild; inhuman, fiendish, demoniacal, satanic, hellish, infernal.

**Vb. be malevolent,** bear malice, cherish a grudge, **hate**; show ill will; show envy, **envy**; spite, do one a bad turn; **be pitiless**; gloat; bully, maltreat, ill-

treat; molest, hurt, injure, annoy, **harm**; malign; tease, harry, hound, persecute, torture, **oppress**; raven, **slaughter**; rankle, fester, poison; create havoc, blight, blast, **lay waste**; **bewitch**.

**Adv. malevolently,** with evil intent; spitefully, out of spite.

## 894 Malediction

**N. malediction,** curse; evil eye, **spell**; denunciation, **threat**; onslaught, **attack**; thunder; ban; bell, book and candle.

**scurrility,** vulgarity; bad language; naughty word, expletive, swearword, oath, swear, damn, curse, cuss; invective, vituperation, abuse, mutual abuse, stormy exchange; vain abuse, empty curse, more bark than bite, **threat**; aspersion, reflection, slander, **calumny**; cheek, sauce; epithet, insult, **indignity**; scorn, **contempt**; **reproach**.

**Adj. cursing,** damning; profane, unparliamentary, scurrilous, ribald, **vulgar**; blue; abusive, vitriolic; **cursed**, accursed, execrable; under a spell.

**Vb. curse, bewitch;** wish ill, **be malevolent**; wish one joy of; curse with bell, book and candle; execrate; fulminate, thunder against, **reprove**; denounce, **accuse**; excommunicate, damn, **condemn**; confound, send to blazes; abuse, vituperate, revile, rail, chide, heap abuse, **reprobate**; throw mud.

**cuss,** curse, swear, damn, blast; blaspheme; swear like a trooper, **slang**, abuse, blackguard, **reprobate**; rail at, scold.

**Int. curse!** a curse on! a plaque on! woe to! woe betide! ill betide! confusion seize! confound it! devil take it! blast! damn! dang! darn! drat! hang! the deuce! the dickens!

## 895 Threat

**N.** threat, menace, **malediction**; challenge, dare, **defiance**; blackmail, **demand**; battle cry, war whoop, war of nerves; deterrent, big stick, **weapon**; black cloud, **omen**; secret weapon, **pitfall**; impending danger, sword of Damocles, **danger**; danger signal, fair warning, **warning**; bluster, idle threat, **boast**; bark, growl, snarl.

**Adj.** threatening; defiant; **boastful**; grumbling, **sullen**; portentous, ominous, foreboding; **impending**; ready to spring, **angry**; abusive; deterrent; nasty, unpleasant.

**Vb.** threaten, menace, blackmail, **demand**; hijack, hold to ransom; frighten, deter, intimidate, bully, **frighten**; roar, bellow, **vociferate**; fulminate, thunder, **curse**; bark, talk big, bluster, **boast**; shake, wave, flaunt, **brandish**; make a pass, **defy**; snarl, growl, mutter, **be sullen**; bristle, spit, grow nasty, **get angry**; hold at gunpoint; cover, **aim**; gather, mass, lour, hover; bode ill, presage, disaster, promise trouble, spell danger, **predict**; serve notice, caution, forewarn, **warn**; breathe revenge.

**Adv.** threateningly, menacingly, on pain of death.

## 896 Philanthropy

**N.** philanthropy, humanitarianism, humanity, **benevolence**; humanism, internationalism; altruism; idealism, **virtue**; universal benevolence, utilitarianism; common good, socialism, communism; chivalry; dedication, nonconformist conscience, good works, mission; Holy War, jihad, crusade, campaign, cause, voluntary agency, charitable foundation, charity, **aid**.

sociology, social science, social engineering; poor relief, benefit, dole; Welfare State; community service, social service, social work, good works.

patriotism, public spirit; nationalism, chauvinism, my country right or wrong; Zionism.

philanthropist, benefactor; humanitarian, do-gooder, social worker, **kind person**; community service worker, Peace Corps, volunteer; champion, knight, knight errant; Messiah, **leader**; missionary, person with a mission, dedicated soul; idealist, flower people, **visionary**; utilitarian, Utopian; cosmopolitan, internationalist.

patriot, lover of one's country; nationalist.

**Adj.** philanthropic, humanitarian, humane, human; charitable; enlightened, liberal; cosmopolitan, international; **disinterested**; visionary, dedicated; utilitarian.

patriotic; loyal, true, true-blue.

**Vb.** be charitable.

**Adv.** pro bono publico.

## 897 Misanthropy

**N.** misanthropy, hatred of mankind; inhumanity; egotism.

misanthrope, misogynist; cynic; unsocial animal, **solitary**; bear, **malcontent**.

**Adj.** misanthropic, inhuman, antisocial, **unsociable**.

**Vb.** misanthropize, become a misanthrope, lose faith in human kind.

**Adv.** misanthropically, cynically.

## 898 Benefactor

**N.** benefactor, **philanthropist**; Lady Bountiful, Father Christmas; guard-

ian angel, good genius, **protector**;
founder, supporter, **patron**; **patriot**;
saviour, redeemer, **deliverance**; champion; Good Samaritan, **kind person**;
good neighbour, **friend**; saint, **good person**.

## 899 Evildoer

**N. evildoer**, malefactor; villain, blackguard, bad lot; scamp, monkey, imp of mischief, little devil, holy terror; gossip; traitor; wrecker, Vandal, Hun, iconoclast, **destroyer**; incendiary.

**ruffian**, blackguard, rogue, scoundrel, **knave**; lout, hooligan, hoodlum, **low fellow**; yobbo, punk; bully, terror; rough, tough, rowdy, ugly customer, bruiser; thug; bravo, desperado, assassin, cutthroat, hatchet man, gunman, butcher; genocide; plague, scourge, **bane**; petty tyrant, **tyrant**; brute, beast, savage, barbarian, caveman; cannibal, head-hunter; homicidal maniac, **madman**.

**offender**, black sheep, **bad person**; suspect; culprit, guilty person, lawbreaker; criminal, villain, crook, malefactor, felon; delinquent; recidivist, lag, convict, jailbird; lifer; probationer; mobster, gangster, racketeer; housebreaker, **thief**; forger; bloodsucker; outlaw, public enemy, **enemy**; criminal world, underworld, Mafia.

**hellhag**, fiend; devil incarnate; bitch, virago, **shrew**; fury, harpy, siren; ogre, witch, vampire, werewolf, **monster**.

**noxious animal**, brute, beast, beast of prey, predator; tiger, man-eater, wolf, jackal, fox; kite, vulture, **bird**; snake, serpent, viper, **reptile**; salamander; scorpion, wasp, hornet; pest, locust, **insect**; rat, **bane**; wild cat, mad dog, rogue elephant.

## 900 Pity

**N. pity**; remorse, compunction, **regret**; charity, compassion, humanity, benevolence; soft heart; melting mood, **sorrow**; dejection; sympathy, empathy, understanding, fellow feeling (see **condolence**); self-pity.

**condolence**, sympathetic grief, sympathy, fellow feeling; comfort, **relief**; professional condolence, keen, wake, lament.

**mercy**, quarter, grace; second chance; clemency, forbearance, longsuffering, **forgiveness**; light sentence, **penalty**; acquittal.

**Adj. pitying**, sympathetic, understanding; merciful, clement, full of mercy, **lenient**; melting, tender, tenderhearted, soft, soft-hearted; weak, **lax**; easily touched; disposed to mercy, **forgiving**; humane, charitable; forbearing, **patient**.

**pitiable**, pitiful, piteous, pathetic, heartrending; challenging sympathy.

**Vb. pity**, show compassion, show pity; feel with, **participate**; sorrow, grieve, **lament**; console, comfort, **cheer**; have pity, have compassion, melt, thaw, relent, **forgive**.

**show mercy**, spare, give quarter; commute (a sentence); pardon, amnesty; **forgive**; be slow to anger, forbear; give one a break, give one a second chance, **be lenient**; relent, unbend, show consideration; be cruel to be kind.

**ask mercy**, cry mercy; excite pity, move to compassion, propitiate, disarm, melt, thaw, soften, **pacify**.

**Int.** alas! poor thing! for pity's sake! for mercy's sake! for the love of God! have mercy! have a heart!

## 901 Pitilessness

**N. pitilessness**, lack of pity; rigour; hardness of heart, **inhumanity**; hardness; pound of flesh; short shrift.

**Adj. pitiless**, unfeeling, **impassive**; unmoved; hard-hearted, callous, tough, **hard**; harsh, intolerant, **severe**; brutal, **cruel**; merciless, ruthless, heartless; indisposed to mercy, unrelenting, relentless, inflexible, inexorable, implacable; vindictive.

**Vb. be pitiless**, turn a deaf ear; spare none; be deaf to appeal; persecute, **be severe**; take one's revenge, **avenge**.

**902 Gratitude**

**N. gratitude**, grateful heart, feeling of obligation, grateful acceptance, appreciation.

**thanks**, thankyou; thanksgiving, eucharist, benediction, blessing; **celebration**; grace; thankyou letter; credit, credit title, recognition, full praise; tribute, **praise**; parting present, tip, **reward**; requital, return.

**Adj. grateful**, thankful, appreciative; showing appreciation, blessing; beholden, indebted.

**Vb. be grateful**, have a grateful heart, overflow with gratitude; praise Heaven; feel an obligation, cherish a favour, never forget; receive with open arms.

**thank**, give thanks, praise, bless; acknowledge, credit, **attribute**; appreciate, show appreciation, tip, **reward**; return a favour, requite, repay, repay with interest; return with thanks.

**Adv. gratefully**, with gratitude, with thanks, with interest.

**Int. thanks!** many thanks! much obliged! thank you! thank goodness! thank Heaven! Heaven be praised!

**903 Ingratitude**

**N. ingratitude**, lack of gratitude, lack of appreciation; grudging thanks; obliv-

ion; thankless task, thankless office; thankless person, ungrateful wretch.

**Adj. ungrateful**, discourteous, **forgetful**; incapable of gratitude, **apathetic**.

**unthanked**, thankless, without credit; unrequited.

**Vb. be ungrateful**, show ingratitude; grudge thanks; forget a kindness.

**Int.** thank you for nothing! no thanks to!

**904 Forgiveness**

**N. forgiveness**, pardon, reprieve, amnesty; indemnity, grace, indulgence, **mercy**; cancellation, remission, absolution, **acquittal**; excuse; mutual forgiveness, reconciliation; forgiving nature, **pity**; longsuffering, forbearance, **patience**.

**Adj. forgiving**, merciful; willing to forgive, **lenient**; forbearing, longsuffering, **patient**; reluctant to punish.

**forgiven**, pardonable, venial, excusable.

**Vb. forgive**, pardon, reprieve, amnesty, **forget**; remit, absolve; cancel, **obliterate**; relent, unbend, accept an apology, **be lenient**; be merciful, **show mercy**; bear with, forbear, tolerate, **be patient**; pocket, stomach; forget an injury, ignore a wrong, overlook; connive, wink at, condone, **disregard**; excuse, **justify**; intercede, **mediate**; exculpate, exonerate, **acquit**; be ready to forgive, let bygones be bygones, **be friendly**; restore to favour, **celebrate**.

**beg pardon**, ask mercy; propitiate, placate, **atone**.

**Adv. forgivingly**, without resentment.

**905 Revenge**

**N. revengefulness**; spite; deadly rancour, **resentment**.

**revenge**; vengeance, day of reckoning,

punishment; reprisal, punitive expedition; vendetta, feud, **enmity**.

**avenger**; Nemesis, Eumenides, avenging furies.

**Adj. revengeful**, breathing vengeance; taking vengeance; at feud, **inimical**; implacable, unrelenting, relentless, **pitiless**; vindictive, **malevolent**; rancorous.

**Vb. avenge**, avenge oneself, take vengeance; exact retribution, repay, square an account; get back at, **retaliate**; gloat.

**be revengeful**, **be malevolent**; bear malice, promise vengeance, **hate**; harbour a grudge, have a crow to pluck, **be inimical**; let it rankle, remember an injury, refuse to forget, **resent**.

## 906 Jealousy

**N. jealousy**; jaundiced eye; distrust, mistrust, **doubt**; resentment; **envy**; hate, **hatred**; competition; **love**; eternal triangle, **revenge**; competitor, rival.

**Adj. jealous**, jaundiced, **envious**; possessive, **loving**; suspicious; rival.

**Vb. be jealous**, scent a rival, suspect, mistrust, distrust, **doubt**; view with a jaundiced eye, **envy**; resent competition.

## 907 Envy

**N. envy**, envious eye, **desire**; ill-will, spite, spleen, bile; grudging praise.

**Adj. envious**, green with envy, **jealous**; covetous, longing; grudging.

**Vb. envy**, cast envious looks, resent; covet, crave, lust after, **desire**.

## 908 Right

**N. right**, fitness, what ought to be, what should be; obligation, **duty**; propriety, **etiquette**; **conformity**; **precept**; morality, good morals, **morals**; **virtue**; rectitude, honour, **probity**; deserts;

claim.

**justice**; redress; reform; tardy justice, overdue reform; even-handed justice; retribution, **reward**; **equality**; equity; fair deal, fair treatment, fair play; equal opportunity; good law; Nemesis.

**Adj. right**, rightful, proper; fitting, suitable, **fit**; good, **ethical**; put right; normal, standard, classical.

**just**, upright, righteous, right-minded, **virtuous**; disinterested, unprejudiced, unswerving, **neutral**; detached, impersonal, dispassionate, objective; equal, egalitarian, impartial, evenhanded; fair, square, equitable, reasonable, fair enough; unimpeachable; legitimate, **legal**; sporting, **honourable**; **due**; overdue.

**Vb. be right**, behove, be due; have justice, have good cause.

**be just**, **be honourable**; do justice, hand it to; see justice done, see fair play, **judge**; temper justice with mercy, **show mercy**; right a wrong, redress, remedy, mend, reform, put right, **rectify**; serve one right, **retaliate**; try to be fair; hide nothing.

**Adv. rightly**, with justice; like a judge, equally, without distinction, without fear or favour, fairly, without favouritism.

## 909 Wrong

**N. wrong**, something wrong; something rotten, curse, bane, scandal; disgrace, shame, dishonour, **slur**; **bad taste**; **guilt**; vice, sin; irregularity, crime; misdoing, trespass; misdeed, offence, **guilty act**; a wrong, injustice, mischief, outrage, foul, **foul play**; sense of wrong, complaint, charge; grievance, **resentment**; **bad person**.

**injustice**; miscarriage of justice, wrong verdict; corrupt justice, packed jury, bias; inequity; discrimination, partiality, leaning, favouritism, favour, nepotism; preferential treatment, positive discrimination; party spirit, old school tie, **prejudice**; justice denied; **inequality; foul play.**

**Adj. wrong, bad**; odd, queer, suspect, **abnormal**; unseemly, improper, **vulgar**; wrongheaded, unreasonable, inadmissible; irregular, foul, unwarranted; wrongful, illegitimate, illicit, criminal, **illegal**; culpable, offside, **guilty**; inexcusable, objectionable, reprehensible, scandalous; mischievous; **dishonest**; sinful, vicious, immoral, **wicked.**

**unjust**; uneven, weighted, **unequal**; inequitable; hard, **severe**; foul; discriminatory, one-sided, leaning to one side, partial, prejudiced; **venal**; **illegal.**

**Vb. be wrong**, go wrong, err, **deteriorate.**

**do wrong**, wrong, hurt, injure, do an injury, **harm; be severe**; commit a foul; commit a crime, **be illegal**; transgress, infringe, trespass, **encroach**; wink at, connive at; do less than justice, withhold justice; weight; lean, lean to one side, discriminate against, show partiality, show favouritism, discriminate; favour; go too far; commit, perpetrate.

**Adv. wrongly**; unjustly, illegally; with criminal intent.

## 910 Dueness

**N. dueness**, what is due; responsibility, obligation, **duty**; bare minimum; dues, **payment; debt**; tribute, credit; recognition, **thanks**; qualification, deserts, **right**; claim, title, **right**; birthright; interest, legal right, prescription, ancient lights; human rights, **freedom**; constitutional right, civil rights; privilege; prerogative, privilege; charter, warrant, licence, **permit**; liberty, franchise; bond, security, **title deed**; patent, copyright; recovery of rights, restoration, **restitution; possessor**; heir, **beneficiary**; plaintiff; person with a grievance.

**Adj. due**, payable; coming to one; lawful; constitutional, entrenched, untouchable, unimpeachable, inviolable; confirmed, inalienable; legitimate, rightful, of right, **legal**; heritable, reserved; fit, fitting, **right**; proper, **advisable.**

**deserving**, worthy of, worthy, meritorious.

**Vb. be due**, ought, ought to be, should be, should have been; be due to, have it coming; behove, befit.

**claim**, lay claim to, take possession, **appropriate**; claim unduly, arrogate; **levy**; reclaim, **retrieve**; sue, demand redress, **request**; enforce a claim, exercise a right; establish a right, patent, copyright.

**have a right**, expect, claim; have a claim to, **demonstrate**; justify, substantiate, **vindicate**; get a favourable verdict.

**deserve**, merit, be worthy; earn, have it coming to one, have only oneself to thank.

**grant claims**, give every man his due, **be just**; assign, credit, **attribute**; hand it to, acknowledge, **thank**; allow a claim, warrant, **permit**; admit a right, acknowledge a claim, honour, meet an obligation, honour a bill, **pay**; privilege, give a right, give one a title; allot, prescribe, **apportion**; **make legal**; confirm, **endorse.**

**Adv. duly**, by right, by law, by divine right.

## 911 Undueness

N. **undueness**, lack of expectation; bad taste; demerit, **vice**; ingratitude; absence of right, want of title; gratuity, bonus; too much; **main part**; breach, infraction; impiety.

**arrogation**, assumption, presumption; tyranny; inroad, trespass.

**loss of right**, disqualification; **loss**; deprivation; seizure, robbery; cancellation; waiver.

**usurper, tyrant**; pretender, **impostor**; squatter.

Adj. **undue**; gratuitous; inappropriate, improper, unseemly, **inexpedient**; preposterous, **absurd**.

**unwarranted**; illicit, illegitimate, **illegal**; stolen; excessive, presumptuous, **insolent; wrong**; invalid, weak; forfeit; false, bastard, **spurious**; fictitious, would-be, **affected**.

**unentitled**, without title, uncrowned; unqualified, **without qualifications**, incompetent; underprivileged, without rights; deprived, bereft.

Vb. **be undue**; show bad taste; presume, arrogate, **be insolent**; usurp, borrow, **steal**; trespass, squat, **encroach**; infringe, break, violate, **be illegal**; desecrate, profane.

**disentitle, depose**; disqualify, disfranchise; invalidate, **abrogate**, prohibit; dispossess, expropriate; forfeit, defeat a claim; make illegitimate, **make illegal**; debase, **impair**.

Adv. **unduly**; without desert.

## 912 Duty

N. **duty**, what ought to be done, obligation, onus, responsibility; fealty, allegiance, loyalty; sense of duty; discharge of duty, performance, acquittal, discharge, **observance**; call of duty, bond, tie, engagement, commitment, word, pledge, **promise**; task,

office, charge, **commission**; walk of life, station, profession, **vocation**.

**conscience**, categorical imperative, inner voice, 'still, small voice'.

**code of duty**, code of honour; **precept**.

**morals**, morality, virtue; honour, **probity**; moral principles, ethics, ethical philosophy, moral science, idealism, humanism, utilitarianism, behaviourism, **philosophy**.

Adj. **obliged**; beholden; bound, sworn, committed, engaged; liable, chargeable, answerable, **responsible**, accountable; answerable to God; conscientious; dutiful, **obedient**.

**obligatory**; incumbent; binding, compulsory, mandatory, peremptory, operative; inescapable; strict, unconditional, categorical.

**ethical**, moral, **virtuous**; honest, decent, **honourable**; moralistic, utilitarian.

Vb. **be one's duty**, be incumbent, behove, become, befit, **be due**; belong to, fall to; rest with.

**incur a duty**, accept responsibility, make oneself liable, commit oneself, **promise**; owe it to oneself.

**do one's duty**, obey; discharge, acquit, perform, **do**; **observe**; discharge an obligation, redeem a pledge; honour, meet, **pay**.

**impose a duty**, require, oblige, look to; call to office, offer a post, post, **commission**; assign a duty, saddle with, detail, order, enjoin, decree, **command**; tax, task, **fatigue**; exact, **be severe**; expect it of one, **expect**; bind, condition, **give terms**; take security, **take a pledge**.

Adv. **on duty**; with a clear conscience.

## 913 Undutifulness

N. **undutifulness**, default, want of duty, neglect; **disrespect**; evasion of duty, cop-out; **oblivion**; want of alacrity;

absenteeism, **absence**; **escape**; infraction, breach of orders, indiscipline, mutiny, rebellion; sabotage, **hindrance**; treachery, **perfidy**; **schism**; escapism; truant, absentee; slacker; traitor; rebel; **schismatic**.

**Adj. undutiful**; rebellious, **disobedient**; disloyal, treacherous; irresponsible; truant, absentee, **absent**.

**Vb. fail in duty**, **neglect**; **disregard**; oversleep, **sleep**; default, **disappoint**; mismanage, bungle, **blunder**; forget; shirk, evade, malinger, **avoid**; **be exempt**; play truant, **be absent**; abscond, **escape**; quit, scuttle, scarper, **decamp**; abandon, desert, **relinquish**; break orders, **disobey**; mutiny, rebel, **revolt**; be disloyal, prove treacherous, betray; sabotage, **obstruct**; withdraw, secede.

**914 Nonliability**

**N. nonliability**, dispensation; conscience clause, **qualification**; impunity, privilege, special treatment, benefit of clergy; franchise, charter, liberty, **freedom**; licence, leave, **permission**; **permit**; excuse, **acquittal**; absolution, pardon, amnesty, **forgiveness**; discharge, release, **liberation**; evasion of responsibility, escapism, **resignation**.

**Adj. nonliable**, unaccountable; scot-free; exempt, immune; unaffected; independent, free-born, **free**.

**Vb. exempt**, set apart, set aside; eliminate, **exclude**; excuse, exonerate, exculpate, **acquit**; grant absolution, absolve, pardon, **forgive**; spare, **show mercy**; privilege, charter, permit; dispense, give dispensation, grant impunity, amnesty, **forget**; enfranchise, set at liberty, release, **liberate**; stretch a point, **be lenient**.

**be exempt**, enjoy impunity, **be free**; exempt oneself, excuse oneself, absent oneself, take leave; **transfer**; **escape**.

**915 Respect**

**N. respect**, regard, consideration, esteem, **approbation**; high standing, honour, favour, **repute**; polite regard, attention, **courtesy**; due respect, deference, **humility**; humble service, devotion, **loyalty**; admiration, awe, **wonder**; terror, **fear**; reverence, adoration, **worship**.

**respects**, regards, duty, kind regards, **courteous act**; red carpet, guard of honour, address of welcome, salutation, salaam; nod, bob, duck, bow, scrape, kowtow, **obeisance**; reverence, homage; salute; honours of war.

**Adj. respectful**, **humble**; obsequious, **servile**; submissive; awestruck; polite, **courteous**; ceremonious; prostrate; showing respect, rising, standing, all standing.

**respected**, **reputable**; respectable, reverend, venerable; time-honoured; imposing, **impressive**.

**Vb. respect**, think well of, rank high, esteem, regard, value; admire, **wonder**; defer to, submit; reverence, venerate, exalt, magnify, **honour**; adore, **worship**; revere, **fear**; defer to, **submit**; pay tribute to, **praise**; do homage to, make much of, lionize, **celebrate**.

**show respect**, render honour, pay homage; welcome, hail, salute, present arms, **greet**; cheer, drink to, **toast**; bob, duck, bow, kneel, kowtow, prostrate oneself, **stoop**; observe decorum, stand, rise, uncover; humble oneself, condescend, **be humble**.

**command respect**, awe, overawe, impose, **impress**; enjoy a reputation, rank high, **have a reputation**; compel respect, command admiration, **be wonderful**; dazzle; receive respect, gain honour, gain a reputation.

Adv. **respectfully**, with all respect; saving your grace, saving your presence.

## 916 Disrespect

N. **disrespect**, want of respect, discourtesy; dishonour, disfavour, **disapprobation**; neglect; low esteem, **disrepute**; **scurrility**; scorn, **contempt**; mockery, **ridicule**; impiety.

**indignity**, affront, insult, slight, snub, outrage; V-sign; taunt, jeer, **contempt**; quip, sarcasm, mock, flout, **ridicule**; hiss, hoot, boo, catcall, brickbat, **disapprobation**.

Adj. **disrespectful**, neglectful, **negligent**; insubordinate, **disobedient**; irreverent; **profane**; outspoken, **plain**; rude, impolite, **discourteous**; airy, breezy, offhand, cavalier, familiar, cheeky, saucy, **impertinent**; outrageous, **insolent**; satirical; scurrilous; pejorative; supercilious, disdainful.

**unrespected**, disreputable.

Vb. **not respect**, be unable to respect, **disapprove**; underrate, **underestimate**; have a low opinion of, disdain, scorn, **despise**; denigrate, disparage, **defame**; toss aside, **reject**; show disrespect, lack courtesy, push aside, crowd, jostle, **be rude**; ignore, **disregard**; snub, slight, insult, affront, outrage, **humiliate**; dishonour, disgrace, put to shame, **shame**; trifle with, treat lightly, **hold cheap**; cheapen, lower, degrade; desecrate, profane; abuse, **curse**; taunt, twit, **be insolent**; laugh at, guy, scoff, mock, flout, deride, **ridicule**; jeer, hiss, hoot, heckle, boo, point at, spit at, **reprobate**; mob, hound, chase, **pursue**; pelt, stone, heave a brick.

Adv. **disrespectfully**.

## 917 Contempt

N. **contempt**, scorn, disdain, **pride**; **affectation**; superior airs, smile of contempt, snort, sniff; slight, **indignity**; sneer, dig at; **ridicule**; snub, rebuff, **discourtesy**.

**contemptibility**; byword of reproach, **object of scorn**.

Adj. **despising**, full of contempt, contemptuous, disdainful, snooty; haughty, lofty, airy, supercilious, **proud**; impertinent, **insolent**.

**contemptible**, despicable, beneath contempt; abject, **bad**; petty, paltry, little, mean, **small**; trifling, pitiable, futile.

Vb. **despise**, consider beneath one, **be proud**; disdain, spurn, sniff at, snort at, **reject**; snort; snub, **be rude**; scorn, whistle, hiss, boo, point at, **reprobate**; laugh at, have a dig at, laugh to scorn; scoff, scout, flout, jeer, mock, deride, **ridicule**; **oppress**; disgrace, **shame**.

**hold cheap**, have a low opinion of, ignore, dismiss, discount, **disregard**; belittle, disparage, fail to appreciate, underrate, **underestimate**; decry; think nothing of, think small beer of, laugh at, pooh-pooh; slight, trifle with, treat lightly, treat like dirt, lower, degrade, **humiliate**.

Adv. **contemptuously**, with contempt, with disdain.

**contemptibly**, miserably.

## 918 Approbation

N. **approbation**, approval; satisfaction, **content**; appreciation, recognition, **gratitude**; good opinion, kudos, credit, **prestige**; regard, admiration, esteem, **respect**; good books, good graces, grace, favour, popularity, affection, **love**; adoption, acceptance, welcome, favourable reception, **reception**; sanction, **permission**; nod of approval, blessing; nod, wink, consent, **assent**; countenance, patronage, championship, advocacy, **aid**; friendly notice, favourable review, **estimate**; good word, testimonial, reference, commendation, recommendation.

**praise**, benediction, blessing; compliment, encomium, eulogy, panegyric, adulation, **flattery**; hero worship, **wonder**; faint praise, two cheers; shout of praise, hosanna, alleluia; song of praise; tribute, credit, due credit, **thanks**; complimentary reference, bouquet, accolade, citation, honourable mention, commendation, glowing terms; official biography; puff, blurb, **advertisement**.

**applause**, acclaim, enthusiasm, excitement; warm reception, **celebration**; acclamation, cheering, clap, three cheers; thunderous applause, ovation, encore, curtain call; bouquet.

**commender**; clapper; friendly critic, admirer, fan club; advocate, supporter, **patron**; booster; agent, tout, barker; electioneer, election agent.

**Adj. approving**, content; appreciative, **grateful**; favourable, friendly; complimentary, laudatory, lyrical; lavish, generous; fulsome, uncritical; thunderous, **loud**; ecstatic, **excited**.

**approvable**, admissible, permissible, acceptable, worthwhile, **useful**; meritorious, laudable, estimable, worthy, praiseworthy, creditable, admirable, unimpeachable, beyond all praise, **perfect**; enviable, desirable.

**approved**, tried; blessed; popular, thought well of, **reputable**; favoured, **chosen**.

**Vb. approve**, see nothing wrong with, sound pleased, think highly of, **respect**; like well, **love**; think well of, admire, esteem, value, prize, treasure, cherish, **honour**; appreciate, give credit, salute, hand it to; think good, think perfect; think desirable, **envy**; see to be good, mark with approbation; accept, pass, tick; nod, wink, **assent**; sanction, bless, **permit**; ratify, **endorse**; commend, recommend, advocate, support, back, favour, countenance, give one a reference or a testimonial.

**praise**, compliment, pay compliments, **flatter**; speak well of, speak highly; bless, **thank**; salute, pay tribute to, hand it to; commend, give praise, exalt, extol, glorify, magnify; wax lyrical; **exaggerate**; puff, inflate, overestimate, **overrate**; lionize, trumpet, boost, **advertise**; praise oneself.

**applaud**, receive with applause, welcome, hail, hail with satisfaction; acclaim, receive with acclamation, clap, give a big hand, stamp, whistle; cheer, give three cheers, give three times three; welcome, congratulate, garland, chair, **celebrate**; drink to, **toast**.

**be praised**, get a citation; recommend oneself, seek repute; find favour, win praise, gain credit, **have a reputation**; get a compliment, receive a tribute, get a clap, get a cheer; receive an ovation, **triumph**; deserve praise; pass, do, pass muster.

**Adv. approvingly**, with admiration, with compliments; without demur.

**commendably**, admirably, wonderfully; to satisfaction, to approval.

**Int.** bravo! well done! hear hear! encore! bis! three cheers! hurrah! hosannah!

## 919 Disapprobation

**N. disapprobation**, discontent; return; refusal; disfavour, displeasure, **dislike**; low opinion, **disrespect**; bad books, **disrepute**; niggling; hostility, **enmity**; exception, cavil, **qualifica-**

tion; complaint, clamour, outcry, protest; **anger**; hiss, boo, whistle, catcall, **ridicule**; boycott, bar, ban, **exclusion**; blackball, blacklist, Index.

**censure**, blame; home truth, criticism, stricture; hostile attack, onslaught, **attack**; bad press, critical review; open letter, tirade, diatribe, **opposition**; conviction; **false charge**; slur, slander, innuendo, **calumny**; brand, stigma.

**reproach**; **quarrel**; invective, vituperation, **scurrility**; malediction; aspersion, reflection, **indignity**; taunt, sneer; sarcasm, irony, satire, biting wit, biting tongue, dig, cut, hit, brickbat, **ridicule**; hard words, silent reproach.

**reprimand**; stricture; censure, rebuke, reproof, snub; rocket, raspberry; expression of displeasure, black mark; **punishment**; admonition, rating, roasting, wigging; lecture.

**disapprover**; damper, wet blanket, spoilsport, misery; pussyfoot, puritan, **prude**; **opponent**; critic, knocker; censor; misogynist, **misanthrope**; **malcontent**.

**Adj. disapproving**, unable to approve; sparing of praise, grudging; silent, **taciturn**; unfavourable, hostile, **inimical**; clamorous, **deprecatory**; critical; hypercritical, niggling; caustic, sharp, bitter, venomous, trenchant, mordant; sardonic; censorious; damning.

**disapproved**; found wanting, **insufficient**; fallen foul of; henpecked; **disreputable**.

**blameworthy**, too bad; exceptionable, open to criticism, **bad**; reprehensible, **discreditable**; reprobate, culpable, to blame.

**Vb. disapprove**, fail to appreciate, think little of, take a dim view of; think ill of, **despise**; fail, plough; return, **reject**;

**prohibit**; cancel, **abrogate**; censor, **obliterate**; withhold approval, look grave, **dissent**; disfavour, reprehend, lament, deplore, **regret**; abhor, reprobate, **dislike**; disown, look askance, avoid, ignore; keep at a distance, ban, bar, blacklist, **exclude**; protest, remonstrate, object, take exception to, demur, **deprecate**; discountenance, exclaim, hoot, boo, bay, heckle, hiss, whistle; throw mud; hound, chase, mob, lynch; make a face, spit; look black, **be sullen**; be angry.

**dispraise**, damn with faint praise, damn, **condemn**; fault, niggle, crab, cavil, depreciate, belittle; oppose, tilt at, shoot at, **attack**; let fly, savage, maul, slash, slate, scourge, flay; thunder, fulminate, storm against, **rampage**; cry shame, slang; gird, rail, revile, abuse, execrate, curse; vilify, blacken, **defame**; brand, pillory; expose, denounce, recriminate, **accuse**; sneer, twit, taunt.

**reprove**, reprehend, reproach, rebuke, snub; call to order, caution, **warn**; book, give one a black mark; censure, reprimand, take to task; carpet; remonstrate, expostulate, admonish, castigate, chide, correct; lecture, read one a lecture, give one a wigging, trounce, roast, browbeat, chastise, **punish**.

**blame**, find fault, carp; get at, **bicker**; reprehend, hold to blame, hold responsible; incriminate, complain against, impeach, charge, **accuse**; recriminate, **retaliate**; **condemn**.

**reprobate**, reproach; upbraid, slate, rate, berate, rail, strafe, revile, abuse, blackguard, **curse**; scold, lash.

**incur blame**, catch it; be held responsible; be open to criticism, get a bad name, **lose repute**; stand accused; be an example, be a scandal, shock, revolt, **cause dislike**.

Adv. **disapprovingly**, reluctantly, against one's better judgment, under-protest; reproachfully.

## 920 Flattery

N. **flattery**, blarney, blandishments, sweet talk; flannel, soft soap, salve, incense, adulation; honeyed words, **endearment**; compliment, coquetry; euphemism, hypocrisy, **sham**.

flatterer, coquette; tout, booster; courtier, yes-man; creep, sycophant, parasite, minion, hanger-on, **toady**; fair-weather friend, hypocrite.

Adj. **flattering**, overdone; complimentary, full of compliments; fulsome; sugary, saccharine; mealy-mouthed; bland; smooth, unctuous, slimy, smarmy; obsequious, courtly, **servile**; specious, plausible; false, insincere.

Vb. **flatter**; compliment, **praise**; overdo it; puff, boost, **overrate**; burn incense to, assail with flattery; soft-soap, blarney, flannel; sugar; wheedle, coax, cajole, coo; lull, soothe, beguile, **deceive**; humour, jolly along; make things pleasant, tell people what they want to hear; smooth; make much of, **caress**; fawn, cultivate, court, pay court to; smirk, **smile**; curry favour, toady to, **be servile**; insinuate oneself; flatter oneself, **be vain**.

Adv. **flatteringly**.

## 921 Detraction

N. **detraction**, faint praise, two cheers, understatement; criticism, bad review, bad press, **disapprobation**; onslaught, **attack**; hatchet job; exposure, bad light, **disrepute**; scorn, con-tempt; **maledictation**; abuse, invective, **scurrility**; **untruth**; spite; aspersion, reflection, snide remark (see **calumny**); whisper, innuendo, impu-

tation; smear campaign; brand, stigma; **lack of wonder**.

calumny, slander, libel, false report, **untruth**; smear, dirty word, **slur**; offensive remark, personality, insult, taunt, dig at, brickbat, **indignity**; scoff, sarcasm, **ridicule**; sneer, sniff; caricature; skit, lampoon, squib, **satire**; scandal, scandalous talk, malicious gossip, bad mouth.

detractor, cynic; censor; candid friend, candid critic; critic; knocker; Philistine, **vulgarian**.

defamer, hatchet man; gossip columnist, gutter press; scold, **shrew**; poison pen.

Adj. **detracting**, derogatory, pejorative; contemptuous; scandalous; abusive, scurrilous; shrewish, caustic, bitter, venomous; snide, catty, **malevolent**; candid, **plain**.

Vb. **detract**, depreciate, disparage, sell short; deflate, puncture; **underestimate**; belittle, slight, **hold cheap**; sneer at, sniff at, **despise**; decry, damn with faint praise, fail to appreciate, **disapprove**; find nothing to praise, knock, slam, fault, slash, slate; caricature, guy, **misrepresent**; lampoon; scoff, mock, **ridicule**; whisper, insinuate.

defame, dishonour, damage, compromise, degrade, lower, put to shame, **shame**; give a dog a bad name; denounce, expose, pillory, brand, **accuse**; calumniate, libel, slander, traduce, malign, vilify, denigrate, blacken, tarnish, sully; speak ill of, speak evil, gossip, make scandal, talk about, backbite; discredit, **cause doubt**; smear, smirch, besmirch, spatter, throw mud, fling dirt, **make unclean**; hound, witch-hunt, **hunt**; smell evil, muckrake, **pursue**.

## 922 Vindication

**N. vindication**, restoration, **restitution**; triumph of justice, right triumphant; clearance, **acquittal**; good grounds, just cause, every excuse; self-defence, defence, alibi, plea, excuse, white-wash, gloss, **pretext**; fair excuse, **truth**; partial excuse, **qualification**; reply, **rejoinder**; recrimination; true bill; just punishment, **punishment**.

**vindicator**, advocate, champion; character witness, **witness**, defendant, **accused person**.

**Adj. vindicating**; apologetic.

**vindicable**, defensible, arguable; specious, plausible; allowable; excusable, pardonable, venial; **innocent**; **true**.

**Vb. vindicate**, revenge, **avenge**; do justice to; set right, restore, rehabilitate; maintain, advocate, **argue**; undertake to prove, confirm, make good, prove, **demonstrate**; champion, **defend**; support, offer moral support.

**justify**, warrant, furnish an excuse, give a handle, give one cause; clear, exonerate, exculpate, **acquit**; give colour to, colour, whitewash, varnish, gloss; justify oneself, **plead**; plead ignorance.

**extenuate**, excuse; palliate, mitigate, soften, soft-pedal, slur, gloss, varnish, whitewash; **be lenient**.

## 923 Accusation

**N. accusation**, complaint, charge, home truth; censure, blame, stricture, **reproach**; challenge, **defiance**; recrimination, **rejoinder**; twit, taunt, **indignity**; imputation, information, denunciation; plaint, suit, action; prosecution, citation, summons; true bill; substance of a charge, case, case to answer; particular charge, count, **evidence**.

**false charge**, frame-up; false information, hostile evidence, counterfeit evidence, plant; illegal prosecution, lie, libel, slander, scandal, stigma, **calumny**.

**accuser**, plaintiff; charger; grass, nark, **informer**; common informer; prosecutor; hostile witness, **enemy**.

**accused person**, prisoner; defendant, respondent, corespondent; culprit; suspect, victim of suspicion, marked man; victim.

**Adj. accusing**, accusatory; incriminating, pointing to, condcriminatory; caluminous, defamatory; suspicious.

**accused**, informed against, suspect; charged.

**accusable**; chargeable, liable to prosecution, inexcusable, indefensible; without excuse, without defence, **heinous**; **vulnerable**.

**Vb. accuse**, challenge, **defy**; taunt, twit, **be insolent**; point, point a finger at, reproach, **reprove**; brand, pillory, gibbet, calumniate, **defame**; charge with, hold against, hold responsible, hold to blame, bring home to, **blame**; point at, expose, unmask, **divulge**; denounce, inform against, tell, blab, **inform**; involve, implicate, incriminate; recriminate; make one a scapegoat; accuse oneself, plead guilty, **confess**; involve oneself, lay oneself open.

**indict**, impeach, arraign, inform against, lodge a complaint, lay information against; complain, charge, bring a charge, **litigate**; book, cite, summon, prosecute, sue; bring an action, bring a suit, bring a case; **attack**; lie against, **be false**; frame, fake.

**Adv. accusingly**.

## 924 Probity

**N. probity**, rectitude, goodness, sanctity, **virtue**; **purity**; good character, moral fibre, integrity; high character, nobility; tender conscience; honour, principles, **observance**; reliability, sense of responsibility; candour; good faith, **truth**; fidelity, faith, troth, constancy, **loyalty**; sportsmanship, **justice**, **repute**; chivalry; principle, point of honour, code, code of honour, **right**; court of justice, court of honour.

**honourable person**, man of honour, woman of her word, sound character, trusty soul, **good person**; true lady, perfect gentleman, true knight; fair fighter, fair player, good loser, sportsman, sport, good sport, trump, brick, good sort, true Brit.

**Adj. honourable**, upright, erect, of integrity, of honour, **virtuous**; correct, strict; law-abiding, honest; principled; scrupulous, conscientious, soulsearching; incorruptible; immaculate, **innocent**; stainless, **clean**; noble, highminded, **pure**; ingenuous, guileless, **artless**; good, straight, square, one hundred per cent; fair, equitable, impartial, **just**; sporting; chivalrous, respectable, **reputable**; pious.

**trustworthy**, reliable, dependable, tried, proven; trusty, true-blue, sure, staunch, constant, faithful, loyal, **obedient**; responsible, dutiful; conscientious, religious, scrupulous, meticulous, punctilious, **careful**; candid, frank, open, open-hearted, transparent, ingenuous, without guile, **true**; straightforward, truthful, **veracious**.

**Vb. be honourable**, behave well, behave like a gentleman, **be virtuous**; play fair, shoot straight, **be just**; be a sport, be a brick; fear God, **be pious**; keep faith; hate a lie, **be truthful**; go straight, reform, **get better**.

## 925 Improbity

**N. improbity**; lack of probity, lack of conscience, lack of principle, **inattention**; opportunism; **falsehood**, partiality, **injustice**; corruption, graft, nepotism; disgrace, dishonour, shame, **disrepute**; villainy, roguery; crime, complicity.

**perfidy**, infidelity, **untruth**; bad faith; Judas kiss, **duplicity**; treachery, sellout; treason, **sedition**; fifth column, Trojan horse; breach of faith, broken word, broken faith, broken promise, scrap of paper; cry of treason.

**foul play**, dirty trick; foul, **wrong**; professional foul; trick, shuffle, chicanery; practice; dirty work, job, deal, ramp, racket; fiddle, wangle, hankypanky, monkey business; tax evasion; crime, felony.

**Adj. dishonest**, **wrong**; unprincipled, unscrupulous; shameless, dead to honour, lost to shame; immoral, **wicked**; shaky; supple, flexible; disingenuous, untruthful; two-faced, insincere; tricky, artful, slippery, foxy, **cunning**; shifty, **equivocal**; designing; sneaking, underhand, **latent**; indirect, bent, crooked, devious, oblique, tortuous; insidious, dark, sinister; shady, fishy, suspicious, doubtful, questionable; **spurious**; illicit, **illegal**; foul, **bad**; unclean, **dirty**; mean, shabby, **disreputable**; derogatory; inglorious, ignominious, ignoble.

**rascally**, criminal, **lawless**; picaresque; blackguard; scurvy, arrant, low, lowdown, base, vile; mean, shabby, paltry, pettifogging; abject.

**venal**, hireling, mercenary, **bought**; corrupt.

**perfidious**, treacherous, unfaithful, inconstant, faithless, **false**; disloyal; disloyal, **disobedient**; insidious, dark, Machiavellian; **spurious**.

Vb. **be dishonest**, yield to temptation, be lost to shame; lead a life of crime, **be illegal**; fiddle, wangle, gerrymander, start a racket, racketeer; pcculate, **defraud**; cheat, swindle, **deceive**; betray, play false; play double, double-cross, **dissemble**; fawn, **flatter**; break faith, **be false**; shuffle, dodge, prevaricate, **be equivocal**; **lose repute**; smell fishy.

Adv. **dishonestly**, by fair means or foul, treacherously.

## 926 Disinterestedness

N. **disinterestedness**, **justice**; unselfishness, selflessness, **humility**; self-control, self-denial, self-sacrifice, martyrdom; rising above oneself, heroism, **courage**; elevation of soul idealism, elevation, nobility, magnanimity; chivalry; generosity, liberality, **benevolence**; purity of motive, dedication, labour of love; loyalty, faith, **probity**; **philanthropy**; altruism, consideration, kindness, **courtesy**; compassion, **pity**, charity, **love**.

Adj. **disinterested**, impartial, without self-interest, **just**; **temperate**; incorruptible, honest, **honourable**; self-effacing, modest, **humble**; selfless; devoted, dedicated; loyal, faithful; heroic, **courageous**; thoughtful, considerate, kind, **courteous**; pure; quixotic, high-minded, lofty, elevated, sublime, noble, chivalrous; generous, liberal, unsparing.

Vb. **be disinterested**, sacrifice, sacrifice oneself, put oneself last, take a back seat, **be humble**; rise above oneself; have nothing to gain.

## 927 Selfishness

N. **selfishness**, narcissism, **vanity**; self-pity, self-indulgence, ego trip; self-absorption; egoism, egotism, individualism; self-preservation; axe to grind, personal advantage, selfish benefit; self-seeking, self-interest; I'm all right, Jack; cupboard love; **parsimony**; greed, **avarice**; **injustice**; selfish ambition, power politics.

**egotist**, self-centred person, **vain person**; go-getter, adventurer; money-grubber, miser, **niggard**; hog.

Adj. **selfish**, egocentric, self-centred; personal; self-seeking; **intemperate**; **vain**; with an interest; uncharitable, cold-hearted, **unkind**; mean, petty, paltry; illiberal, ungenerous, **parsimonious**; acquisitive, mercenary; venal, **dishonest**; covetous, **envious**; possessive; **jealous**; designing; mundane, worldly, earthly, worldly-wise.

Vb. **be selfish**, put oneself first, think only of oneself, take care of number one; love oneself, have only oneself to please; hang onto, hog, **retain**; have an axe to grind.

Adv. **selfishly**; on the make; far one's own sake.

## 928 Virtue

N. **virtue**, moral strength, moral tone; goodness, holiness, spirituality, odour of sanctity, **sanctity**; **justice**; rectitude, character, integrity, honour, **probity**; perfect honour; morality, ethics, **morals**; sexual morality, temperance, chastity, **purity**; virtuous conduct, good behaviour, duty done; good conscience, conscious rectitude.

**virtues**; faith, hope, charity; justice, temperance, fortitude; saving quality, saving grace; a virtue, good fault; worth, merit, desert; **perfection**; magnanimity, altruism, idealism; self-control, **temperance**.

Adj. **virtuous**, moral, **ethical**; good, **excellent**; stainless, **pure**, **innocent**;

irreproachable, impeccable, above temptation, **perfect**; holy; principled, right-minded, **right**; righteous, **just**; upright, sterling, honest, **honourable**; dutiful, **obedient**; **disinterested**; generous, well-intentioned; sober, **temperate**; chaste, virginal; proper, exemplary; elevated; meritorious, worthy, praiseworthy.

**Vb. be virtuous, be good**; behave; practise virtue, resist temptation, **be temperate**; rise superior to, have a soul above; go straight, **be honourable**; love good, hate wrong, **be just**; edify, set a good example, **do good**.

**Adv. virtuously**, well, with merit; purely.

## 929 Wickedness

**N. wickedness**, principle of evil; Devil, cloven hoof, Satan; fallen nature; iniquity, sin, **wrong**; **guilt**; **impiety**; ignorance of good; hardness of heart; bad behaviour; loose morals; vice, corruption, depravity; bad character; villainy, roguery, **foul play**; want of principle; crime; **inhumanity**; devil worship; shame, scandal, abomination, enormity, infamy, **disrepute**; delinquency, wrongdoing, wicked ways, career of crime; primrose path, slippery slope; low life, criminal world, underworld; den of vice, sink of iniquity, **sink**.

**vice**, fault, demerit; human weakness, frailty, foible, **weakness**; shortcoming, defect, deficiency, failing, flaw, weak point, weak side; trespass, injury, outrage, enormity, **wrong**; sin, pride, lust, anger, envy, sloth; venial sin, small fault, peccadillo, scrape; **bad taste**; offence, **guilty act**; crime, felony, deadly crime.

**Adj. wicked**, immoral; amoral, **indifferent**; lax, unprincipled, unscrupulous,

**dishonest**; unblushing, callous, shameless, brazen; ungodly, irreligious, profane; evil, **bad**; evil-minded, **malevolent**; **maleficent**; bad, naughty, **disobedient**; weak (see **frail**); sinful, full of sin, **guilty**; graceless, reprobate; hopeless, incorrigible, irredeemable; accursed, godforsaken; hellish, infernal, fiendish, satanic, **diabolic**.

**vicious**; good-for-nothing, ne'er-do-well; hopeless; punk, graceless; miscreant; improper, unseemly, indecent, **vulgar**; without morals, immoral; intemperate; profligate, characterless, lost to virtue, lost to shame, **disreputable**; corrupt, degenerate, sick, rotten; brutal, **cruel**.

**frail**, infirm, feeble, **weak**; human, lax; suggestible, **vulnerable**; fallen, **imperfect**.

**heinous**, heavy, grave, serious, deadly; black, scarlet, abysmal, hellish, infernal; sinful, immoral, **wrong**; criminal, nefarious; monstrous, flagrant, scandalous, shameful, disgraceful, shocking, outrageous, obscene; gross, foul, rank; base, vile, abominable, despicable, **bad**; culpable; reprehensible, indefensible, **unwarranted**; brutal, **cruel**; inexcusable, inexpiable.

**Vb. be wicked**, scoff at virtue; lapse, relapse, backslide; **deteriorate**; do wrong, transgress, misbehave, be naughty; trespass, offend, sin, err, stray, slip, trip, stumble, fall; **be weak**.

**make wicked**, render evil, corrupt, **pervert**; mislead, lead astray, seduce, **tempt**; set a bad example.

**Adv. wickedly**, wrongly, sinfully; viciously, vilely; unforgivably, irredeemably.

## 930 Innocence

**N. innocence**; clear conscience; nothing to declare, nothing to confess; every excuse; **acquittal**; ignorance of evil, **ignorance**; inexperience; purity of heart, state of grace, **virtue**; **purity**; **probity**; **perfection**; golden age.

**innocent**, babe, newborn babe, babe unborn; child; lamb, dove; angel, pure soul; goody-goody; innocent party.

**Adj. innocent**, pure, stainless, spotless, immaculate, **clean**; sinless, unerring, impeccable, **perfect**; green, **ignorant**; guileless, **artless**; well-meaning, well-intentioned, innocuous, harmless, inoffensive, playful, gentle, child-like; goody-goody.

**guiltless**; bloodless; irreproachable, above suspicion; unexceptionable, unimpeachable, with every excuse; pardonable, excusable, venial.

**Vb. be innocent, be honourable; be virtuous**; have every excuse, have a clear conscience, have nothing to be ashamed of, have nothing to confess or declare; **be artless**; stand free of blame, stand above suspicion; acquit oneself.

**Adv. innocently**; with a clear conscience.

## 931 Guilt

**N. guilt**; delinquency; original sin; complicity; burden of guilt; blame, censure, **reproach**; guilt complex; conscious guilt, guilty conscience, guilty behaviour, suspicious conduct, blush, stammer, embarrassment; confession, **disclosure**; twinge of conscience, remorse, shame.

**guilty act**, sin, **vice**; misdeed, wicked deed, misdoing, trespass, offence, crime; misdemeanour, felony; misconduct, malpractice; peccadillo; scrape; lapse, slip, blunder, **mistake**;

fault, failure, dereliction of duty; injustice, injury, **wrong**; enormity, atrocity, outrage, **cruel act**.

**Adj. guilty**; thought guilty, made responsible; responsible, **liable**; at fault, to blame, culpable, chargeable; shameful, reprehensible; without excuse, inexcusable; inexpiable, mortal, deadly, **heinous**; sinful, **wicked**; criminal, **illegal**; **murderous**; red-handed; hangdog, sheepish, shame-faced, ashamed.

**Vb. be guilty**, be at fault; be caught red-handed; plead guilty, **confess**; trespass, transgress, sin, **be wicked**.

**Adv. guiltily**; without excuse; red-handed, in the vary act, flagrante delicto.

## 932 Good Person

**N. good person**, fine human being, sterling character, **honourable person**; pillar of society, model of virtue, perfection, **paragon**; Christian, saint; great saint; angel, **innocent**; heart of gold, **kind person**; good neighbour, Good Samaritan, **benefactor**; idealist, **philanthropist**; **favourite**; hero, **brave person**; goody, good guy, good sort, stout fellow, brick, trump, sport; rough diamond, ugly duckling.

## 933 Bad Person

**N. bad person**, limb of Satan; fallen angel, recidivist, lost sheep, lost soul, one without morals; reprobate, good-for-nothing, ne'er-do-well, black sheep; scallywag, scamp; rake, profligate; wanton, hussy, **loose woman**; wastrel, waster, prodigal son, **prodigal**; scandalous person, reproach, outcast, dregs, riffraff, trash, scum, **object of scorn**; nasty type, ugly customer, undesirable, bad 'un, wrong 'un, thug, bully, **ruffian**; bad lot, bad egg, bad hat, bad character, bad guy, villain; bad influence, bad example; bad child, terror, whelp, monkey, little devil.

**knave**, vagabond, wretch, rascal, rapscallion, **low fellow**; rogue; criminal; thief, pirate, freebooter; villain, blackguard, scoundrel, miscreant; cheat, liar, crook; impostor, twister, **trickster**; sneak, grass, rat, **informer**; renegade; traitor, Quisling, Judas; animal, dog, hound, swine, snake, serpent, viper, reptile, vermin, **noxious animal**.

**cad**, nasty bit of work, scoundrel, blackguard; rotter, blighter, bastard; bounder; jerk, heel, slob, scab, son of a bitch; skunk, dirty dog; pimp, pervert, degenerate; cur, hound, swine, rat, worm; louse, insect, vermin; pig, beast, cat, bitch.

**monster**, horror, unspeakable villain; monster of cruelty, brute, savage; ogre, **tyrant**; Juggernaut; public enemy number one; monster of iniquity or depravity, fiend, demon, ghoul, **devil**; fury; devil incarnate, gorilla, terror, nightmare.

## 934 Penitence
**N. penitence**, contrition, attrition, compunction, remorse, **regret**; humble confession, **disclosure**; confession, Christian rite; **humility**; voice of conscience, **guilt**; white sheet, **penance**; apology; grudging apology.

**penitent**; prodigal son; reformed character.

**Adj. repentant**, contrite, sorry, apologetic, full of regrets; ashamed; weeping; penitent, penitential, penitentiary, doing penance; regenerate, born again.

**Vb. be penitent**, repent, show compunction, feel shame, feel sorry, express

regrets; reproach oneself, go to confession, **confess**; do penance, wear a white sheet, **atone**; lament; scourge oneself; eat humble pie; rue, have regrets, wish undone, **regret**; think again, think better of; **learn**; reform, think better of; **get better**; **recant**.

**Adv. penitently**, like a penitent, in sackcloth and ashes.

**Int.** sorry! mea culpa! repent! for pity!

## 935 Impenitence
**N. impenitence**, lack of contrition; refusal to recant; hardness of heart, **hardness**; despair of, **bad person**.

**Adj. impenitent**, recusant; obdurate, inveterate, stubborn, **obstinate**; without regrets; unrelenting, relentless; without compunction, without a pang, heartless, **cruel**; unmoved; hard, unblushing, brazen; incorrigible, irredeemable, hopeless, lost, **wicked**.

**unrepented**, unregretted, unatoned.

**Vb. be impenitent**, would do it again; refuse to recant, **be obstinate**; **be pitiless**.

**Adv. impenitently**; without compunction.

## 936 Atonement
**N. atonement**, making amends, amends, apology, satisfaction; reparation, indemnity, blood money, conscience money, **restitution**; quits; composition, **compromise**.

**propitiation**, satisfaction, reconciliation; redemption, **divine function**; sacrifice, offering; scapegoat, **substitute**.

**penance**, shrift, confession, sacrament of penance, penitential exercise; purgatory; penitent form, anxious seat, corner, **pillory**; white sheet.

**Adj. atoning**, making amends; apologetic; **offering**; penitential, penitentiary, doing penance, **punitive**.

**Vb. atone**, make amends, make reparation, indemnify, compensate; **beg pardon**; propitiate, conciliate, **pacify**; give satisfaction; sacrifice to, offer sacrifice; expiate; **be disinterested**; reclaim, redeem.

**do penance**; pray, fast, flagellate oneself, suffer purgatory; go to confession, **confess**.

## 937 Temperance

**N. temperance, moderation**; self-denial; self-control, self-discipline, **restraint**; continence, chastity, **purity; sobriety**; forbearance, abstinence, abstention; total abstinence; prohibition; vegetarianism; **economy**; plain living, simple life; frugal diet.

**abstainer, sober person**; pussyfoot; nonsmoker; vegetarian, vegan; dropout; enemy of excess, Spartan, **ascetic**.

**Adj. temperate**, within bounds; measured, **moderate**; plain, Spartan, sparing, **economical**; frugal, **parsimonious**; forbearing, abstemious; dry, teetotal, **sober**; vegan, vegetarian, continent, **restrained**; chaste, **pure; ascetic**.

**Vb. be temperate**, moderate, temper, keep within bounds, observe a limit, avoid excess, know when one has had enough, know when to stop, **be moderate**; keep sober, **be sober**; forbear, refrain, abstain, **avoid**; control oneself, **restrain**; deny oneself, **be ascetic**; go dry; ration oneself, **starve**; diet, **make thin**.

## 938 Intemperance

**N. intemperance**, want of moderation, abandon; excess, luxury; too much; waste, consumer society; want of self-control, indiscipline; indulgence;

addiction, bad habit, **habit**; drug habit; high living; hangover.

**Adj. intemperate**, immoderate, excessive, **redundant**; unmeasured; wasteful, extravagant, profligate, spendthrift, **prodigal**; luxurious, **superfluous**; unrestrained, lacking self-control, **riotous**; incontinent; **drunk**; animal, **sensual**.

**Vb. be intemperate**, plunge, wallow; lack self-control, want discipline, lose control, **be lax**; deny oneself nothing, indulge oneself, **please oneself**; **be prodigal**; run to excess, run riot, exceed, **overstep**; stick at nothing, **waste**; **revel**; drink like a fish, drink to excess, **get drunk**; eat to excess, gorge, pig it, make oneself sick; be incontinent, grow dissipated, **be impure**; addict oneself, become a slave to habit, **be wont**.

**Adv. intemperately**, with abandon; without moderation, without control.

## 939 Sensualism

**N. sensualism**, materialism; sensuality, sexuality; love of pleasure, hedonism, **pleasure**; luxury; full life, life of pleasure, high living; abandon; indulgence; orgy, debauch, **revel**.

**sensualist**, animal, pig, swine, hog; playboy; sybarite, voluptuary; epicure, gourmet, gourmand, **glutton**; hard drinker, **drunkard**; loose liver, profligate, rake; drug addict; degenerate.

**Adj. sensual**, earthy, gross, **material**; carnal, bodily; sexual, venereal, **erotic**; animal, bestial, beastly; voluptuous; luxurious; incontinent, **intemperate**; dissipated, **impure**; riotous, **drunken**.

**Vb. be sensual**, live well, **prosper**; indulge oneself, do oneself proud; run riot, **be intemperate**.

Adv. **sensually.**

**940 Asceticism**
N. **asceticism**; **penance**; ascetic practice, yoga; holy poverty, **poverty**; plain living, simple fare, Spartan fare; fast day, **fast**; self-denial, **temperance**; **economy**; hair shirt.

**ascetic**, spiritual athlete, yogi, fakir, dervish; hermit, anchorite, recluse, **solitary**; Cynic; **penitent**; **sober person**; Puritan; spoilsport, killjoy, pussyfoot.

Adj. **ascetic**; austere, **severe**; Spartan, **temperate**; **sober**; plain, wholesome, **salubrious.**

Vb. **be ascetic**, live like a Spartan; fast, **starve**; live like a hermit, wear a hair shirt; walk through fire.

Adv. **ascetically**, simply, plainly.

**941 Fasting**
N. **fasting**; anorexia, **ill health**; keeping fast, strict fast; spare diet; short commons, **scarcity**; starvation, **hunger.**

**fast**, fast day, Friday, Good Friday, Lent, Ramadan; day of abstinence; hunger strike, **strike.**

Adj. **fasting**; **temperate**; keeping fast, keeping Lent; **lean**; wanting food, **hungry**; sparing, frugal, **economical**; scanty, **scarce**; meagre, thin, poor, Spartan.

Vb. **starve**, famish, **be hungry**; macerate, waste with hunger; have nothing to eat, **be poor**; fast, go without food; keep Lent, keep Ramadan; eat nothing; eat less, diet, reduce, **abate**; make a little go a long way, **be temperate**; keep a poor table, **be parsimonious.**

**942 Gluttony**
N. **gluttony**, greed, voracity; insatiable appetite, **hunger**; good living, indulgence; belly worship, **gastronomy**; bust; blowout, masses of food.

**glutton**; locust, wolf, vulture, cormorant, pig, hog; vampire, blood-sucker; good eater, **eater**; coarse feeder; gourmand, gourmet, epicure.

Adj. **gluttonous**, rapacious; voracious; omnivorous; insatiable, never full, **hungry**; stuffing.

Vb. **gluttonize**; guzzle, bolt, wolf, gobble, devour; fill oneself, gorge, cram, stuff; glut oneself, **eat**; have a good appetite; eat like a trooper, eat like a horse, eat like a pig, make a beast of oneself; make oneself sick; keep a good table.

Adv. **gluttonously**; at a gulp, with one bite.

**943 Sobriety**
N. **sobriety**, **temperance**; state of sobriety, clear head; dry area.

**sober person**, moderate drinker; Band of Hope, temperance society; pussyfoot.

Adj. **sober**, abstemious; **temperate**; teetotal, pussyfoot, dry; clear-headed, with a clear head; unfermented, unalcoholic, soft.

Vb. **be sober**, drink water; never touch drink, **be temperate**; become teetotal; go dry; keep a clear head.

Adv. **soberly**, with sobriety.

**944 Drunkenness. Drug-taking**
N. **drunkenness**; influence of liquor, inspiration; Dutch courage, **courage**; blackout; thick speech, **speech defect**; staggering; drop too much; potation; flowing bowl, booze, liquor, **alcoholic drink**, wine; jag, lush, blind, binge, spree, **revel.**

**crapulence**; hangover, thick head, sick headache.

**alcoholism**, alcoholic addiction, dipso-

mania, **mania**; delirium tremers, D.T.
's, heebiejeebies; red nose.

**drug-taking**, smoking; hard drug, joint,
reefer, roach; shot, fix; narcotic, dope;
nicotine, **tobacco**; cannabis, hemp,
hashish, hash, pot, grass; cocaine,
coke, snow; heroin, horse, smack;
morphine, opium, **drug**; stimulant,
pep pill, speed; LSD, acid, peyote;
drug addiction, drug abuse, drug
dependence, habit; cold turkey; drug
addict, dope fiend, freak; head.

**drunkard**, inebriate, drunk, lush; slave
to drink, alcoholic, pathological
drunk; drinker, boozer, old soak,
souse, sponge; thirsty soul; Baccha-
nal.

**Adj. drunk**, merry, happy, high, elevated, **excited**; mellow, full; **disorderly**.

**tipsy**, squiffy, tight, pissed; stewed;
smashed, sloshed, sozzled, soused,'
plastered; maudlin, tearful; drunken,
muzzy, woozy; dizzy, giddy, staggering.

**dead drunk**, stoned; blind drunk, blind,
blotto; paralytic; gone, shot, stiff.

**crapulous**, with a hangover, with a thick
head; dizzy, giddy, sick.

**drugged**, high, zonked; stoned, **insensible**.

**drunken**, inebriate, intemperate; always
tight, never sober; sodden, vinous,
stinking of liquor; thirsty, bibulous,
fond of a drink; bloodshot, liverish;
given to drink, alcoholic.

**intoxicating**, poisonous; exhilarating,
heady, like wine, **exciting**; stimulant;
opiate, narcotic, psychedelic, mind-
blowing; alcoholic, vinous; hard,
potent, **strong**; neat.

**Vb. be drunk**, have had too much; have
a weak head, succumb, be overcome;
stutter, **stammer**; see double, lurch,
stagger, reel, oscillate.

**get drunk**, have too much, drink deep,
drink hard, drink like a fish, drink to
get tight; crack a bottle, knock back a
few, lush, bib, tipple, fuddle, booze,
guzzle, swig, swill, soak, souse, **drink**;
quaff, carouse, wassail, **revel**.

**drug oneself**, smoke, sniff, snort, inject
oneself, shoot, mainline; take a trip.

**inebriate**, exhilarate, elevate, **excite**;
fuddle, befuddle, stupefy; make
drunk.

## 945 Purity

**N. purity**, perfection; moral purity,
morals, morality, **virtue**; propriety,
delicacy, **good taste**; shame; chastity,
continence, **temperance**; frigidity,
**moral insensibility**; honour, maidenhood, maidenhead.

**prudery**; false shame; gravity; **affectation**; euphemism.

**virgin**, maiden, maid, old maid, spinster,
**celibate**; religious celibate, **monk**,
**nun**; virtuous woman.

**prude**, prig, Victorian, Puritan; guardian of morality, censor, Watch Committee.

**Adj. pure**, perfect; sinless, **innocent**;
maidenly, virgin, virginal; rosy, **modest**; coy, shy; chaste, continent, **temperate**; impregnable, incorruptible,
**honourable**; unfeeling, **impassive**;
frigid, **cold**; immaculate, spotless,
snowy, **white**; good, moral, **virtuous**;
Platonic, elevated; decent, decorous,
delicate, refined, **tasteful**; printable,
quotable, **clean**.

**prudish**, squeamish, Victorian; prim,
**affected**; straitlaced, narrow-minded,
puritan; holy, sanctimonious.

## 946 Impurity

**N. impurity**; **bad taste**; exhibitionism;
loose talk, blue story; smut, dirt, filth,
obscene literature; pornography, soft

porn; blue film, skin flick.

**unchastity;** easy virtue; permissive society; vice, sexual delinquency; lust, **libido;** sexuality; licence, gallantry; seduction.

**illicit love,** forbidden fruit; criminal conversation, unlawful carnal knowledge; incest; perversion, buggery; infidelity; eternal triangle, intrigue, amour, seduction, **love affair;** free love, irregular union, **type of marriage.**

**rape,** indecent assault, grope; gang bang; sex crime, sex murder.

**social evil;** prostitution, indecent exposure; white slave traffic; vice squad.

**brothel;** house of ill fame, house of ill repute.

**Adj. impure,** unclean, nasty, **dirty; insalubrious;** indelicate; vulgar, coarse, gross; ribald, broad, free, loose; strong, racy, bawdy, Rabelaisian; suggestive, provocative, piquant; spicy, juicy, fruity; immoral, equivocal; naughty, wicked, blue; unmentionable, unprintable; smutty, scabrous, stinking, rank, offensive, indecent, obscene, lewd, salacious; prurient, erotic; sexual, sexy, hot.

**unchaste, vicious;** susceptible, **frail;** fallen; of easy virtue, of loose morals, amoral, immoral; incontinent, light, wanton, loose, fast, naughty; wild; immodest, daring; unblushing, shameless, scarlet, meretricious; promiscuous.

**lecherous,** carnal, voluptuous, **sensual;** lustful, prurient; rampant, rutting; hot, randy; oversexed; bestial; lewd, free, loose; dissolute, dissipated, profligate, **vicious.**

**extramarital,** irregular; unlawful; homosexual, Lesbian, **abnormal;** unfaithful.

**Vb. be impure,** be immoral; be unfaithful; be dissipated, **be intemperate;** fornicate, whore, wench; keep a mistress, have a lover; lust, rut, be hot, **desire;** be promiscuous, sleep around; become a prostitute; pimp, procure, keep a brothel.

**debauch,** defile, smirch, **make unclean;** proposition, seduce, lead astray; take advantage of; dishonour, deflower, wreck, ruin, disgrace, **shame;** prostitute, make a whore of; lay, bed, lie with, **unite with;** rape, ravish, violate, molest, abuse, outrage, interfere with, assault.

**Adv. impurely.**

## 947 Libertine

**N. libertine;** gay bachelor; flirt; loose fellow, fast man, gay dog, rip, rake, profligate; lady-killer, gallant, gigolo; false lover, **lover;** corespondent, adulterer; wolf; stud; lecher, flasher, satyr, goat, dirty old man; sex maniac; male prostitute; pervert, **nonconformist.**

**cuckold,** deceived husband, injured husband.

**loose woman,** wanton, easy lay; fast woman, hot stuff; woman of easy virtue; flirt, piece, bit, wench, jade, hussy, minx, miss, sex kitten; baggage, trash, trollop, drab, slut; tart, chippy, scrubber, pick-up; vamp, adventuress, scarlet woman; other woman.

**kept woman,** mistress, paramour, concubine, unofficial wife; bit of fluff, moll.

**prostitute,** pro; white slave, fallen woman; harlot, trollop, whore, strumpet; broad, hooker, scrubber; pick-up, casual conquest; courtesan; temple prostitute, **slave.**

**bawd,** go-between, pimp, ponce, madam; white slaver.

**948 Legality**

**N. legality**, formality, form, formula, rite, due process; form of law; good law; **justice**.

**legislation**; regulation, plebiscite, **vote**; popular decree; law, statute, ordinance, order, **decree**; canon, rule, edict, **precept**.

**law**; body of law, constitution, charter, institution; statute book, legal code; penal code, written law, personal law, international law; law of commerce, commercial law, law of contract, law of crime, criminal law; legal process, **jurisdiction**; writ, summons, lawsuit, **legal trial**.

**jurisprudence**, science of law, legal learning; legal advice.

**Adj. legal**, lawful, **just**, law-abiding, **obedient**; legitimate, competent; permissible, allowable; statutory, constitutional; legislative; made law, ordered; liable or amenable to law.

**Vb. be legal**, legitimate etc. adj.

**make legal**, confirm, ratify, **endorse**; vest, establish; legislate, pass, enact, ordain, enforce, **decree**.

**Adv. legally**, by law, by order.

**949 Illegality**

**N. illegality**, bad law, legal flaw, loophole, irregularity, error of law, wrong verdict; miscarriage of justice, **injustice**; **prohibition**.

**lawbreaking**, breach of law; trespass, offence, civil wrong; malpractice, **foul play**; **guilt**; criminal activity, criminal offence, crime, misdemeanour, felony; wrongdoing, **wrong**; criminology, criminal statistics; criminal.

**lawlessness**; crime wave, **anarchy**; summary justice; kangaroo court, gang rule, mob law, riot, rebellion, **revolt**; arbitrary rule, martial law; jackboot, brute force.

**bastardy**, bar or bend or baton sinister; bastard, illegitimate child, spurious offspring.

**Adj. illegal**, illegitimate, illicit; contraband, hot; incompetent, without authority, informal, unofficial; unlawful, wrongful, **wrong**; irregular, contrary to law; punishable.

**lawbreaking**; **wicked**; **guilty**; criminal; shady, **dishonest**.

**lawless**, without law, chaotic; ungovernable, **riotous**; violent, summary; arbitrary, irresponsible, unaccountable; unofficial, cowboy.

**bastard**, illegitimate, spurious; misbegotten, baseborn; without a father, without a name, without benefit of clergy.

**Vb. be illegal**; be lawless, **do wrong**; encroach, **please oneself**.

**make illegal**, outlaw; **prohibit**; **punish**; suspend, annul, cancel, **abrogate**.

**Adv. illegally**, illicitly, unlawfully, criminally.

**950 Jurisdiction**

**N. jurisdiction**, portfolio, **function**; judicature; competence, legal authority, **authority**; Home Office; local jurisdiction, local authority, corporation, municipality, county council, **council**; **tribunal**; office, bureau, secretariat, **workshop**; legal authority, competence, **mandate**.

**law officer**, legal administrator, Lord Chancellor, Attorney General, Lord Advocate, Solicitor General; Crown Counsel, public prosecutor; legal advocate, district attorney, **judge**; mayor, sheriff, **position of authority**; court officer, tipstaff, bailiff; beadle, mace-bearer, **official**.

**police**; police force; constabulary, military police, police officer, policeman or -woman, constable, copper, cop, patrolman or -woman; police sergeant, police inspector, police superintendent, commissioner of police, chief constable, provost marshal; watch; special patrol group; plainclothes man, **detective**.

**Adj. jurisdictional**, competent; executive, administrative, directive; judiciary, juridical; subject to jurisdiction.

**Vb. hold court**, administer justice, **judge**; **try a case**; take judicial notice.

## 951 Tribunal

**N. tribunal**, seat of justice, woolsack, throne; bar, bar of justice; court of conscience, tribunal of penance, confessional; forum, **council**; public opinion, electorate; bench, board; judicial assembly.

**lawcourt**, court, court of law, court of justice, criminal court, Federal Court, High Court; District Court, County Court; Supreme Court, Court of Appeal; Court of Exchequer, Star Chamber; House of Lords, **parliament**; High Court of Justice, Court of Criminal Appeal; Admiralty Division; Probate Court, Court of Chancery, court of equity; circuit court; assizes; Court of Session, sessions, Central Criminal Court, Old Bailey; court of record, court baron; guild court, hustings; court-martial, drumhead court.

**ecclesiastical court**, Curia; Inquisition, Holy Office.

**courtroom**, court-house; bench, woolsack, jury-box; dock; bar; witness box.

**Adj. judicatory**, judicial

## 952 Judge

**N. judge**, justice, your Lordship; Lord Chancellor, Lord Chief Justice, Lords of Appeal; military judge, Judge Advocate General; chief justice, recorder; sessions judge, district judge, magistrate, coroner; honorary magistrate, JP; bench, judiciary; hanging judge.

**magistracy**, his or her Worship, his or her Honour; arbiter, umpire, referee; assessor, Ombudsman; Recording Angel, **recorder**.

**jury**, twelve just men; grand jury, jury list; juror, juryman or -woman.

## 953 Lawyer

**N. lawyer**, legal practitioner, man or woman of law; common lawyer, barrister, advocate, counsel, junior barrister, stuff gown, junior counsel; senior barrister; silk gown, silk, leading counsel; circuit barrister; **expert**; shyster, crooked lawyer.

**law agent**, attorney, attorney at law; solicitor, legal adviser; legal representative, legal agent, advocate; equity draftsman.

**notary**, notary public; **law officer**.

**jurist**, legal adviser, legal expert, legal light, master of jurisprudence, pundit; student of law, law student.

**bar**, English bar, Inner Temple, profession of law, legal profession; advocacy.

**Adj. jurisprudential**, called to the bar, at the bar; forensic.

**Vb. do law**; take silk; accept a brief, take a case, advocate, plead; practice law.

## 954 Litigation

**N. litigation**, going to law; legal dispute, **quarrel**; issue; lawsuit, suit at law, suit, case, cause, action; prosecution, charge; test case, **experiment**; claim, plea, petition, **request**; affidavit, written statement.

**legal process**, proceedings, legal procedure, course of law, **jurisdiction**; citation, subpoena, summons, search warrant, **warrant**; arrest, apprehension, detention, committal, **restraint**; bail, surety, security, injunction, stay order; writ.

**legal trial**, trial, justice seen to be done; sessions; inquest, inquisition, examination, **enquiry**; hearing, prosecution, defence; hearing of evidence, **evidence**; examination, **testimony**; **reasoning**; **rejoinder**; proof; ruling, finding, decision, verdict; majority verdict, hung jury; favourable verdict, **acquittal**; unfavourable verdict; **punishment**; appeal, retrial; precedent, case law; cause list; case record, dossier, **record**.

**litigant**, party, party to a suit, suitor; plaintiff, defendant, respondent; accused, **accused person**; common informer, **informer**; prosecutor.

**Adj. litigating**, at law with; going to law.

**litigated**; disputable, arguable.

**Vb. litigate**, go to law, institute legal proceedings, start an action, bring a suit, petition, **request**; prepare a case, prepare a brief, brief counsel; file a claim, contest at law, **claim**; take one to court, make one a party, sue, arraign, impeach, accuse, charge, **indict**; cite, summon; prosecute, bring to justice, bring to trial; advocate, plead, call evidence, **argue**.

**try a case**, hear a cause; examine, cross-examine; rule, find, decide, adjudicate, **judge**; pronounce sentence.

**stand trial**, come before; plead guilty; ask to be tried, hear sentence; defend an action.

**Adv. in litigation**, at law, in court, before the judge; subjudice.

## 955 Acquittal

**N. acquittal**, favourable verdict; clearance; absolution, discharge; **liberation**; quietus; reprieve, pardon, **forgiveness**; impunity.

**Adj. acquitted**; clear; immune, exempt; **liberated**.

**Vb. acquit**, prove innocent, justify, whitewash, **vindicate**; clear, absolve, exonerate, exculpate; **exempt**; discharge, let go, **liberate**; reprieve, respite, pardon, **forgive**; quash, allow an appeal, **abrogate**.

## 956 Condemnation

**N. condemnation**, unfavourable verdict, finding of guilty, conviction; damnation, perdition; blacklist, Index; **disapprobation**; **malediction**; doom, sentence, **punishment**; omen; death warrant, execution chamber, Death Row; black cap.

**Adj. condemned**, found guilty, made liable; without a case; lost, burning.

**Vb. condemn**, prove guilty; find liable, find against; find guilty, convict, sentence; sentence to death; **reject**; proscribe, outlaw, bar, **make illegal**; blacklist, **disapprove**; damn, excommunicate, **curse**; convict oneself, **be guilty**; plead guilty, **confess**.

## 957 Reward

**N. reward**, recompense; deserts, **justice**; recognition, thanks, **gratitude**; tribute, proof of regard, **praise**; award, presentation, prize, crown, cup, pot, shield, certificate, medal, **trophy**; honour; birthday honours, **honours**; title; prize money, jackpot; prize fellowship, scholarship, bursary, stipend, exhibition; fee, retainer, payment, emolument, pension, salary, wage, wages, increment, **pay**; productivity bonus, overtime pay, **incentive**; perquisite, perks, expense account; income, turnover, **earnings**; return, profit, **gain**; satisfaction; consideration, **offset**; comeuppance; reparation, **restitution**; bounty, gratuity, golden handshake; commission, rakeoff, kickback; tip, baksheesh, **gift**; **offer**; bait, lure, bribe, **incentive**; hush money, blackmail.

**Adj. rewarding**; generous, open-handed, liberal; remunerative, **gainful**; promising, **offering**.

**Vb. reward**, recompense; award, present, give a prize, offer a reward; bestow a medal, honour with a title, **honour**; acknowledge, pay tribute, thank, **be grateful**; remunerate, **pay**; satisfy, tip, **give**; tip well, **be liberal**; repay, requite, **retaliate**; compensate, indemnify, make reparation; offer a bribe, **bribe**.

**be rewarded**, gain a reward, win a prize, get a medal, receive a title; get paid, draw a salary, earn an income, have a gainful occupation, **acquire**; accept payment, **receive**; take a bribe; **deserve**; reap, reap a profit, **gain**.

**Adv. rewardingly**.

## 958 Punishment

**N. punishment**, sentence; execution of sentence; **reprimand**; discipline; dose, pill, hard lines, trial, visitation, punishing experience, **adversity**; just deserts, meet reward, comeuppance; doom, day of reckoning, divine justice, **justice**; retribution, Nemesis; reckoning, **restitution**; requital, reprisal; **revenge**; penance; self-discipline; hara-kiri, **suicide**; penology.

**corporal punishment**, hiding, beating, thrashing; flogging; slap, smack, rap;

blow, buffet, cuff, clout, stroke, stripe, **knock**; third degree, torture, **pain**.

**capital punishment**, extreme penalty, **death**; death sentence, death warrant; execution, **killing**; hanging, drawing and quartering; strangulation, garrotte; hanging, long drop; crucifixion; burning; massacre, mass murder, mass execution, purge, genocide, **slaughter**; martyrdom; illegal execution, lynch law; judicial murder.

**penalty**, injury, damage, **loss**; task, lines; sentence, penal code, penology; devil to pay; damages, restoration, **restitution**; fine, compulsory payment, **payment**; ransom, **price**; forfeit, deprivation; **detention**; suspension; **restraint**; penal servitude, hard labour, galley service; transportation; expulsion; exile, ban, **exclusion**; reprisal.

**punisher; tyrant**; magistrate, court, law, **judge**; executioner, hangman, Jack Ketch.

**Adj. punitive**, penal; vindictive; **taking**; **painful**.

**punishable**, liable.

**Vb. punish**, visit, afflict, **hurt**; persecute, make an example of, **be severe**; impose; give one a lesson, chasten, discipline, correct, chastise, castigate; reprimand, strafe, rebuke, **reprove**; impose a penalty, sentence, **condemn**; execute justice, execute a sentence, exact a penalty, exact retribution, settle with, **retaliate**; settle, fix, bring to book, give one what was coming to him, revenge oneself, **avenge**; fine, forfeit, confiscate; demote, degrade, downgrade, suspend, **shame**; pillory, masthead; duck, keelhaul; picket, spread-eagle; **imprison**; transport.

**spank**, paddle, slap, smack, slipper, paddle; cuff, clout, drub, trounce, beat, belt, strap, leather, lather, larrup, wallop, welt, tan, cane, birch, switch, whack, dust, **strike**.

flog, whip, horsewhip, thrash, hide, belabour, cudgel, **strike**; scourge; lash, flay; flail, flagellate.

torture; give pain; put one to torture, thumbscrew, rack, mutilate, kneecap; persecute, **torment**.

execute, punish with death, put to death, **kill**; lynch, **murder**; dismember; decimate, crucify, impale; flay, flay alive; stone, stone to death; shoot, fusillade, stand against a wall; burn, burn alive, garrotte, strangle; gibbet; hang; hang, draw and quarter; behead, decapitate, guillotine; electrocute; gas; commit genocide, purge, massacre, **slaughter**.

be punished, suffer punishment, have it coming to one, catch it; regret it; come to execution; swing.

Int. off with his head! à la lanterne!

## 959 Means of Punishment

N. scourge, birch, cat, rope's end; whip, horsewhip, switch; lash, strap, thong, belt; cane; stick, rod, ferule, cudgel, ruler, **club**; rubber hose, bicycle chain, sandbag.

pillory, stocks; corner; chain, irons, **fetter**; prison house, prison, **gaol**.

instrument of torture, rack, thumbscrew, iron boot; Iron Maiden, triangle, wheel, treadmill; torture chamber.

means of execution, scaffold, block, gallows, gibbet; cross; stake; hemlock, **poison**; bullet, wall; axe, guillotine, maiden; halter, rope, noose, drop; garrotte; electric chair, hot seat; death chamber, Death Row.

## 960 Divineness

N. divineness, divinity, deity; divine principle; being of God, divine

essence, perfection; love, Fatherhood; nirvana; impersonal God, world soul; First Cause, **source**; divine nature, God's ways, Providence.

divine attribute, being, existence; perfect being, perfection; **unity**; **infinity**; **presence**; wisdom, knowledge; **power**; eternity, **perpetuity**; **stability**; truth, sanctity, holiness, goodness, justice, mercy; supremacy, sovereignty, majesty, glory, light.

the Deity, God, personal god, Supreme Being; Judge of all men, Maker of all things, Creator, Preserver; Allah; Jehovah, ineffable name, I AM; name of God; our Father; Great Spirit.

Trinity; Holy Trinity; God the Father, God the Son, God the Holy Ghost.

Holy Ghost; Holy Spirit, Spirit of Truth; Dove.

God the Son, Word, Son of God, Word made flesh, Incarnate Son; Messiah, Christ; Lamb of God, Son of Man; Holy Infant, Christ Child; Saviour, Redeemer, Friend; Lord, Master; Bread of Life, True Vine; King of Kings, King of Heaven, King of Glory, Prince of Peace.

divine function, creation, preservation; mercy, compassion, forgiveness; inspiration, comfort, grace, redemption, salvation.

theophany, divine manifestation, descent, descent to earth, incarnation; transfiguration.

theocracy, divine government, divine dispensation, God's law, Kingdom of God; God's ways, providence.

Adj. divine, holy, sacred, sacrosanct, heavenly, celestial; transcendental, sublime, ineffable; religious, spiritual, superhuman, supernatural, transcendent; unearthly; providential.

godlike, divine, superhuman; transcendent; omnipresent, **ubiquitous**;

immeasurable, **infinite**; absolute, living; timeless, eternal, everlasting, immortal, **perpetual**; immutable, changeless, **permanent**; almighty, omnipotent, **powerful**; creative, **dynamic**; prescient, providential; omniscient, **knowing**; merciful, **forgiving**; **loving**; holy; sovereign, **supreme**; **authoritative**; glorious; incarnate.

**deistic**, theistic.

**redemptive**, intercessional, mediatory; messianic.

Adv. **divinely**.

**961 Deities in general**

N. **deity**, god; Olympian, Olympian deity; idol; petty god, lesser deity; demigod, divine hero, divine king; object of worship, fetish, totem, **idol**; pantheon.

**mythic deity**, Pan, Flora; mother earth, earth mother, Great Mother; fertility god; Pluto; sky god, Jupiter; storm god, wind god; sun god; river god, Neptune; Mars; Cupid, Venus; household gods; **fate**.

Adj. **mythological**.

**962 Angel. Saint. Madonna.**

N. **angel**, archangel, heavenly host, choir invisible; heavenly hierarchy; cherub; angel of death; guardian angel.

**saint**, patron saint, saint and martyr, the blessed▪ .▪ .▪; Church Triumphant.

**Madonna**, Our Lady, Mother of God; Queen of Heaven.

Adj. **angelic**; cherubic; saintly, glorified, celestial.

Vb. **angelize**; sanctify.

**963 Devil**

N. **Satan**, fallen angel, Prince of this world; serpent, Adversary, Common Enemy, Enemy of mankind; evil genie; King of Hell; spirit of evil.

**Mephisto**, Mephistopheles, His Satanic Majesty, Old Nick, Old Harry, Old Scratch.

**devil**, fiend; familiar, imp, imp of Satan, **bad person**; **demon**; malevolent spirit; diabolic hierarchy; fallen angel, lost soul, denizen of Hell; cloven hoof.

**diabolism**, **inhumanity**; Satanism; devil worship; witchcraft, black magic, Black Mass, **sorcery**.

**diabolist**, Satanist, devil-worshipper; witch.

Adj. **diabolic**, satanic, fiendish, demoniacal, **malevolent**; infernal, hellish; possessed.

Vb. **diabolize**; possess, bedevil, **bewitch**.

**964 Fairy**

N. **fairy**, fairy world; fairy folk, little people; fairy being; good fairy, **benefactor**; bad fairy, witch; fairy queen; fairy king; Puck; spirit of air; elemental spirit, sylph; genius; fairy ring, fairy lore, folklore.

**elf**, elves, brownie; gnome, dwarf; troll; goblin, flibbertigibbet; imp, sprite, hobgoblin; changeling; leprechaun; poltergeist, gremlin; Puck, Hob.

**ghost**, spirit; visitant, poltergeist; spook, spectre, apparition, phantom, shape, shade, wraith, presence, fetch; **visual fallacy**; control, **spiritualism**; White Lady, Black Shuck.

**demon**, flibbertigibbet, Friar Rush; imp, familiar, familiar spirit, **devil**; banshee; troll, troll woman, ogre, giant; bugbear, **monster**; ghoul, vampire, werewolf; incubus, succubus, nightmare; fury, harpy, Gorgon.

**mythical being**, angel, devil; demon, genie; centaur, satyr, faun; sea nymph, Naiad, water elf; mermaid;

Siren; water spirit, **nymph**; **sorcerer**; Green Man; Yeti, Abominable Snowman, Leviathan, Phoenix.

**Adj.** fairylike, fairy; **lean**; gigantic, **huge**; monstrous, **diabolic**; elvish, impish, Puckish, **maleficent**; magic, **magical**; **imaginary**.

spooky; macabre; weird, uncanny, unearthly, **abnormal**, eerie, supernatural; disembodied, **immaterial**.

**Vb.** haunt, visit, walk; ghost, gibber.

**Adv.** spookishly, spectrally, uncannily; elfishly, puckishly.

## 965 Heaven

**N.** heaven, presence of God, kingdom of heaven, heavenly kingdom, kingdom come; Paradise; eternal home, eternal rest, celestial bliss, blessed state; nirvana; earthly Paradise, Holy City, afterlife, eternal life, eternity, **future state**; resurrection; assumption, translation.

mythic heaven; Elysium, happy hunting grounds; Earthly Paradise, Eden, **fantasy**.

**Adj.** paradisiac; heavenly, celestial, eternal; beatific, blessed, **happy**; Olympian.

## 966 Hell

**N.** hell, lower world, nether regions, underworld; grave, limbo, Hades; purgatory; perdition, inferno, Pandemonium; abyss, bottomless pit; place of torment; everlasting fire.

mythic hell; realm of Pluto, Hades; river of hell; infernal watchdog; infernal judge; nether gods, Pluto.

**Adj.** infernal, bottomless, **deep**; subterranean, **low**; hellish; Stygian; **diabolic**.

## 967 Religion

**N.** religion, religious instinct, **humility**; religious feeling, **piety**; **expectation**; religious quest; natural religion; primitive religion, early faith; nature religion; mysticism; yoga; **philosophy**; **worship**; religious cult, state religion, **cult**.

deism, theism; animism, pantheism, polytheism, monotheism.

**religious faith**, faith, belief; Christianity; Judaism; Islam; Hinduism; Buddhism, Zen; Taoism.

**theology**, study of religion; natural theology, religious knowledge, religious learning, divinity; scholastic theology; tradition, deposit of faith; teaching, doctrine, **definition**, canon; dogma, tenet; articles of faith, credo, **creed**; confession; fundamentalism; higher criticism; comparative religion.

**theologian**; divinity student, divine; doctor; rabbi, scribe, mufti, mullah; scholastic; psalmist; Bible critic.

**religious teacher**, prophet, inspired writer; guru, **sage**; evangelist, apostle, missionary; Messiah, Invisible Imam; founder of Christianity, Christ; Prophet of God; Confucius.

**religionist**; **idolater**; pagan, gentile, **heathen**; adherent, believer; militant, believer, **zealot**; Christian; Jew; Muslim, Moslem; dervish; Hindu; Sikh; Mormon, **sect**; **heretic**.

**Adj.** **religious**, divine, holy, sacred, spiritual; Christian, Moslem, Mosaic; mystic; devout.

**theological** theosophical, scholastic; doctrinal, dogmatic, canonical.

## 968 Irreligion

**N.** **irreligion**; nothing sacred, **impiety**; false religion; disbelief; scepticism, doubt; **philosophy**; lack of faith, infidelity; lapse; apathy.

**antichristianity, opposition**; Satanism; free thinking, free thought, nihilism, **philosophy**; materialism; secularism; **avarice**.

**irreligionist**; dissenter, atheist, **unbeliever**; rationalist, freethinker; agnostic, sceptic.

**heathen**, pagan; infidel; gentile; lapsed Christian.

**Adj. irreligious**, without a god, godless, profane; agnostic, sceptical; ungodly, **wicked**; amoral, morally neutral, **indifferent**; secular, mundane, of this world, worldly, **sensual**; lacking faith, faithless, lapsed; unchristian.

**heathenish**, unholy, **profane**; unchristian; gentile; heathen, pagan, infidel.

**Vb. be irreligious**, lack faith; **disbelieve**; deny God, blaspheme.

**paganize**.

## 969 Revelation

**N. revelation**, apocalypse, **disclosure**; **light**; inspiration, prophecy; intuition, mysticism; direct communication; divine message, God's word, gospel, gospel message; burning bush, epiphany, incarnation, Word made flesh.

**scripture**, word of God, inspired text, sacred writings; Holy Scripture, Holy Writ, Bible; Greek version; canon; Old Testament, Major Prophets; New Testament, Revelation, Apocalypse; Apocrypha; psalter, missal; prayer book, Book of Common Prayer; hymn book, **hymn**; Talmud; Higher Criticism; fundamentalism.

**non-Biblical scripture**, Koran, Hindu scripture; Book of Mormon.

**Adj. revelational**, mystic; inspired; apocalyptic; evangelical.

**scriptural**, sacred, holy; inspired; **authoritative**; Mosaic; gospel, apostolic.

## 970 Orthodoxy

**N. orthodoxy**, correct opinion, right belief; sound theology; religious truth, pure Gospel, **truth**; primitive faith, early Church, Apostolic age; credo, **creed**; catechism, Church Catechism.

**orthodoxism**, strict interpretation; fundamentalism; **conformity**; Christian practice, **observance**; Holy Office, **tribunal**; Inquisition; Index, **disapprobation**; **approbation**.

**Christendom**, Christian world; undivided Church; Christian fellowship; Holy Church, Bride of Christ; Body of Christ, universal Church; Church Militant, visible Church; invisible Church, Church Triumphant.

**Catholicism**, Scarlet Woman; High Church.

**Protestantism**, Calvinism; Methodism, sect.

**Catholic**, Orthodox; Roman Catholic, papist; Old Catholic, Anglican, Episcopalian.

**Protestant**, Anglican, Huguenot; Presbyterian, Baptist, Wesleyan, Quaker, Friend.

**church member**; Christian, disciple of Christ; church people, congregation.

**the orthodox**; evangelical; believer.

**Adj. orthodox**, right-minded, sound, balanced, **judicial**; undivided, **whole**; unswerving, loyal, devout, **obedient**; conventional; precise, strict; intolerant; correct, **accurate**; of faith; authoritative, evangelical, gospel, **genuine**; literal, catholic, universal; held, **credible**; customary, **usual**.

**Roman Catholic**, Catholic, Roman.

**Anglican**, episcopalian; high.

**Protestant**; **sectarian**; Presbyterian, Baptist, Wesleyan, Quaker.

Vb. **be orthodox, believe; conform.**
Adv. **orthodoxly.**

## 971 Heterodoxy

N. **heterodoxy;** erroneous opinion,
wrong belief, false creed, superstition,
**error;** strange doctrine, new teaching;
modernism, Higher Criticism; partial
truth; heresy.
**heresy,** heathen theology, gnosticism.
**heretic.**
Adj. **heterodox, different;** nonconformist; less than orthodox, erroneous,
**mistaken;** unorthodox.
**heretical, heathen.**
Vb. **declare heretical,** anathematize,
**condemn.**
**be heretical,** be unorthodox.
Adv. **heretically,** unorthodoxly.

## 972 Sectarianism

N. **sectarianism,** sectionalism, preju-
**dice; bias;** party spirit; separatism;
nonconformity, **dissent;** Calvinism.
**schism,** division, **quarrel; separation;**
religious schism, Great Schism.
**church party; Catholic; Protestant;**
Broad Church party.
**sect,** division, branch, group, faction,
**party;** order, brotherhood, com-
**munity;** nonconformist sect, chapel;
Salvation Army.
**non-Christian sect;** Hindu sect; Pure
Land sect, **religious faith.**
**sectarian;** follower, adherent, devotee;
Nonconformist; Puritan, Shaker;
Quaker, Friend; Presbyterian, **Protestant;** Mormon; **heretic.**
**schismatic;** rebel; recusant; dissident,
dissenter, nonconformist; wrong
believer, **heretic.**
Adj. **sectarian;** clannish, exclusive, **sectional;** episcopalian, **Anglican;** evangelical, **Protestant;** Puritan, Presbyterian; Pharisaic.

**schismatical,** schismatic; **separate;** nonconformist; recusant; rebellious,
rebel, **disobedient.**
Vb. **sectarianize,** follow a sect, **join a
party.**
**schismatize,** commit schism, separate,
divide, withdraw, secede; **disobey.**

## 973 Piety

N. **piety,** goodness, **virtue;** reverence,
honour, decent respect, **respect;** affection, kind feeling, **benevolence;**
loyalty, conformity, attendance at
worship, **observance;** religion, theism;
religious feeling, pious sentiment; fear
of God, godly fear, **fear; humility;**
pious belief, faith, trust, **belief;** devotion, dedication; enthusiasm, fervour,
zeal, muscular Christianity; inspiration, exaltation; adoration, **worship;**
retreat; mysticism, communion with
God, mystic communion, **religion;
restoration;** act of piety, pious duty,
charity, **philanthropy;** pious fiction,
tract, sermon; Christian behaviour,
Christian life; pilgrimage.
**sanctity,** holiness, goodness, **virtue;**
state of grace, odour of sanctity,
**purity;** holy character; spirituality;
spiritual life; blessed state; enlightenment; rebirth, new birth, **revival;**
adoption, **divine function;** dedication.
**pietism,** show of piety, cant, **sham;** religious mania; tender conscience; **nar-
row mind;** fundamentalism; **hatred;**
prejudice; **philanthropy.**
**pietist,** pious person, real saint, **good
person;** martyr; saint; man or woman
of prayer, mystic; holy man, fakir,
dervish, **ascetic;** hermit, anchorite,
**solitary;** monk, nun, religious, **clergy;**
devotee, dedicated soul; convert, neophyte; believer, **church member;** pilgrim.

**zealot**, fanatic, bigot, iconoclast; Puritan; Pharisee, scribe; **sectarian**; evangelical; missionary, **philanthropist**; militant Christian; **tyrant**.

**Adj. pious**, good, kind, **virtuous**; decent, **respectful**; faithful, true, loyal, devoted, **obedient**; **orthodox**; sincere, **veracious**; pure, otherworldly, spiritual; godly, religious, devout; mystic; holy, sainted; Christian, full of grace.

**pietistic**, ardent, fervent; inspired; austere, **ascetic**; **unsociable**; earnest, pi, self-righteous; precise, Puritan; Pharisaic, **sectarian**; sanctimonious, **affected**; goody-goody, too good to be true, **virtuous**; evangelical.

**sanctified**, made holy, dedicated; reverend, holy, sacred, solemn, sacrosanct; sainted; chosen; **liberated**; regenerate, reborn, born again.

**Vb. be pious**, be holy, wear a halo; mind heavenly things, think of God; fear God, **fear**; have faith, **believe**; **be strong**; humble oneself, **be humble**; go to church, attend divine worship; pray, **worship**; kneel, genuflect, bow, stoop; cross oneself; make offering, sacrifice, **offer**; lend to God, **give**; glorify God, **praise**; **thank**; revere, show reverence, **show respect**; hearken, listen, **obey**; preach at, **teach**; set a good example.

**become pious**, experience religion, get religion, **recant**; reform, repent, receive Christ, **be penitent**; take holy orders, **take orders**; be a pilgrim.

**make pious**, bring religion to, bring to God, convert, **convince**, **admit**; purify, edify, confirm, **strengthen**; inspire, fill with grace, uplift, **make better**; redeem, regenerate, **restore**.

**sanctify**, hallow, make holy, **honour**; consecrate, dedicate, enshrine, dignify; make a saint of, saint, invest with a halo; bless, pronounce a blessing.

## 974 Impiety

**N. impiety**; disregard, **disrespect**; lack of piety, lack of reverence; mockery, **ridicule**; scorn, pride, **contempt**; **malediction**; sacrilege, perversion, abuse, misuse; sin; materialism; **disapprobation**.

**false piety**, **falsehood**; solemn mockery, **sham**; hypocrisy, lip service, **duplicity**; cant, **affectation**.

**impious person**, **malediction**; profane person, gentile, pagan, infidel, unbeliever, **heathen**; idolater; atheist, sceptic; reprobate, **bad person**; recidivist; fallen angel, Wicked One, **Satan**; hypocrite; canter.

**Adj. impious**, ungodly; recusant; godless, **irreligious**; irreligious, irreverent, without reverence; **lawless**; brazen, bold; hard, unmoved, unfeeling, **cruel**; sinful, impure, reprobate, **wicked**; sanctimonious, **affected**.

**profane**, unholy; accursed; infidel, pagan, gentile.

**Vb. be impious**, rebel against God, **be proud**; sin, **be wicked**; swear, blaspheme, **curse**; profane, desecrate, violate, **misuse**; commit sacrilege, defile, sully, **make unclean**; worship false gods, cant, **be affected**; play false, **dissemble**; backslide, **deteriorate**.

## 975 Worship

**N. worship**, honour, reverence, homage, **respect**; holy fear, awe, **fear**; adoration; **humility**; devotion, **piety**; prayer; retreat, quiet time, communion.

**cult**, mystique; type of worship, service, **duty**; service of God, supreme worship; inferior worship; false worship.

act of worship, rite; praise; hymn-singing, psalm-singing, plainsong, vocal music; thanksgiving, blessing, benediction, thanks; offering, sacrifice; self-examination; self-denial, self-discipline; keeping fast; pilgrimage, wandering.

prayers; private devotion, retreat; prayer, bidding prayer; petition, request; suffrage; special prayer, intention; denunciation, threat; malediction; ban; benediction, grace, thanks; collect; Our Father; blessing, rosary; prayer book, missal; call to prayer, call.

hymn, song, psalm, religious song, spiritual; processional hymn, recessional; plainsong, descant, vocal music; anthem, cantata, motet; response; song of praise, Magnificat; Hosanna; Homeric hymn; psalter.

oblation, collection, offering; pew rent; libation, incense, rite; dedication; gratitude; victim, scapegoat, substitute; burnt offering, holocaust; sacrifice, devotion; hecatomb, slaughter; human sacrifice, homicide; self-sacrifice; suttee, suicide.

public worship, common prayer; agape; service, divine service, divine office, mass, matins, evensong, benediction, church service; vocal music; church, piety; assembly; prayer meeting; temple worship, state religion, religion.

worshipper, church member; devotee; admirer; follower, server, servant; idolater; caller; supplicant; man or woman of prayer; mystic, visionary; dervish, prophet, religious teacher; celebrant, clergy; congregation, church member; cantor; psalmist; pilgrim, traveller.

Adj. worshipping; devout, devoted, pious; respectful; fervent; orthodox;

psalm-singing; mystic.

devotional; solemn, sacred, holy; sacramental, mystic; votive, offering.

Vb. worship, honour, revere, venerate, adore, respect; fear; do worship to, pay homage to, acknowledge; pay divine honours to, make a god of one, deify; kneel to, genuflect, humble oneself; bless, give thanks, thank; extol, magnify, glorify, give glory to, praise; hymn, anthem, celebrate, sing; burn incense before; invoke, address, speak to; petition, beseech, intercede, entreat; pray, say a prayer; meditate, contemplate, commune with God, be pious.

offer worship, celebrate, officiate, minister, perform ritual; sacrifice, give; sacrifice to, propitiate, appease, pacify; vow, promise; live a life of praise; dedicate, consecrate, sanctify; enter holy orders, take orders; travel; go to church, go to chapel, go to meeting, be pious; go to service, hear Mass, communicate, take Holy Communion; fast, observe Lent, starve; deny oneself, be ascetic; meditate; chant psalms, carol, sing; praise.

Int. Alleluia! Hallelujah! Hosanna! Glory be to God! Holy, Holy, Holy; Lord have mercy; Lord, bless us! God save!

976 Idolatry

N. idolatry, false worship, superstition, worship; religion; fetishism, anthropomorphism; image worship; idol worship; hocus-pocus, sorcery; cult; sacrifice; sun worship; star worship; fire worship; animal worship; snake worship; devil worship; worship of wealth.

deification; hero worship, respect; king worship, worship.

idol, statue, sculpture; image, cult

image, fetish, totem pole; golden calf,
**deity**; totem; Juggernaut.
**idolater**; pagan, **heathen**.
**Adj. idolatrous**, pagan, heathen; **diabolic**.
**Vb. idolatrize**; deify, **sanctify**; **praise**.
**Adv. idolatrously**.

## 977 Sorcery

**N. sorcery**, magic arts; witchcraft;
magic lore, **knowledge**; magic skill,
**skill**; **magic**; sympathetic magic,
influence; **inducement**; **frenzy**;
superstition; voodoo, hoodoo; **divination**; **rite**; magic rite, incantation;
ghost dance; coven; Hallowe'en.

**spell**, charm, hoodoo, curse; evil eye,
jinx, influence; fascination, **attraction**; obsession, possession; **frenzy**;
incantation, rune; magic sign, pass;
magic word, magic formula, open
sesame, abracadabra; **lack of meaning**; philtre, love potion (see **magic
instrument**).

**talisman**, charm; cross; **safeguard**;
fetish, **idol**; amulet, mascot, lucky
charm; horseshoe, black cat; pentagram; swastika; scarab; emblem, flag,
relic, **refuge**.

**magic instrument**, bell, book and candle;
magic recipe; philtre, potion; wand,
magic ring; magic mirror, magic
sword, flying carpet; wishbone.

**sorcerer**, wise man, seer, soothsayer;
Druid; magus; witchdoctor, medicine
man, **idolater**; illusionist; enchanter,
wizard, warlock; magician; familiar,
imp, evil spirit, **devil**; Pied Piper.

**sorceress**, wise woman, Sibyl; witch,
weird sister; hag; succubus; wicked
fairy, **fairy**.

**Adj. sorcerous**; magician; **wonderful**;
**diabolic**; enchanting; malignant,
**maleficent**; occult, esoteric.

**magical**; otherworldly, supernatural,
uncanny, weird; **magic**.

**bewitched**, enchanted, fey; spellbound;
under the evil eye; cursed.

**Vb. practise sorcery**, cast a nativity,
**divine**; do magic; recite a spell, recite
an incantation; conjure, invoke; raise
spirits; wave a wand; ride a broomstick.

**bewitch**, witch, charm, enchant, fascinate, **attract**; magic; spellbind; hoodoo, voodoo; overlook, blight, blast,
**be malevolent**; curse; taboo, **prohibit**;
walk, ghost, **haunt**.

**Adv. sorcerously**, by means of enchantment.

## 978 Occultism

**N. occultism**, mysticism, **religion**; secret
art, esoteric science, occult lore,
alchemy, astrology, spiritualism,
magic, **sorcery**; **divination**; **prediction**; clairvoyance, second sight,
**vision**; **intuition**; hypnotism; hypnosis, **insensibility**.

**psychics**, psychology; psychic science;
ESP; clairvoyance, second sight, **intuition**; psychokinesis; telepathy; precognition.

**spiritualism**; spirit communication, **sorcery**; **divination**; sitting; spirit manifestation; telekinesis; automatic writing, **writing**; spirit message; control,
**ghost**.

**occultist**, mystic; esoteric; yogi; **sorcerer**; fortune-teller, palmist.

**psychic**, clairvoyant; telepathist; mind
reader; medium; seer, prophet,
**oracle**.

**psychist**, parapsychologist, psychophysicist, psychical researcher.

**Adj. cabbalistic**, esoteric, hermetic,
cryptic, **occult**; dark, mysterious,
**unknown**; mystic, transcendental,
supernatural, **religious**; **spooky**.

psychical, psychic, fey; telepathic, clairvoyant; mind-reading.

paranormal, supernatural, preternatural.

Vb. practise occultism; alchemize, transform; divine; practise spiritualism; have a control; study spiritualism.

## 979 The Church

N. the church, Christendom; theocracy, authority; church government, Vatican, government; hierarchy, order; papacy; presbytery.

ecclesiasticism; benefit of clergy; Holy Office, prohibition.

monasticism; monastic life.

church ministry, call, vocation; mission; cure; spiritual comfort, spiritual leadership, philanthropy; spiritual guidance, confession, absolution, ministration; teaching.

holy orders, orders; apostolic succession, ordination; induction; installation; presentation, appointment, commission; translation, elevation, progression.

church office, management; pontificate, papacy, Holy See, Vatican; primacy; see, bishopric; deanery; incumbency, tenure, possession.

parish, deanery; presbytery; diocese, bishopric, see; province, district.

benefice, incumbency, tenure, living, parsonage, tithe; property; patronage, right of presentation.

synod, convocation, general council, council; episcopal bench; chapter, vestry; kirk session, presbytery, synod, tribunal.

Adj. ecclesiastical; infallible, authoritative; orthodox; apostolic; pontifical, papal, Roman Catholic; patriarchal; episcopal, clerical; episcopalian, presbyterian, sectarian; provincial, parochial.

priestly; spiritual; apostolic, pastoral.

Vb. be ecclesiastical; frock, ordain, order, consecrate, enthrone; cowl, make a monk of; call, confer, nominate, present; prefer, bestow a living, give; translate, transfer; elevate, promote; saint, sanctify; take orders.

Adv. ecclesiastically.

## 980 Clergy

N. clergy, hierarchy; clerical order; secular clergy, regular clergy, religious.

cleric, clerical; priest, deacon; divine; Doctor of Divinity; clergyman, servant of God; reverend, father; padre, sky pilot; beneficiary, parson, rector, incumbent, possessor; nonentity.

pastor, shepherd, minister, parish priest, rector, vicar, perpetual curate; curate; chaplain; penitentiary; spiritual director, spiritual adviser; friar; missionary, philanthropist; evangelist.

ecclesiarch, dignitary, governor; pope, Supreme Pontiff, Holy Father, Vicar of Christ; cardinal; patriarch, primate, archbishop; prelate, bishop; assistant bishop, 'episcopal curate'; Lords Spiritual; archdeacon, deacon; dean, rural dean; canon, canon regular, canon secular; Superior, abbot, abbess; prior, Grand Prior; elder, presbyter, moderator.

monk, monastic, celibate, solitary; hermit, Desert Father, anchorite; Orthodox monk; dervish, fakir, ascetic; brother, regular; superior, abbot, prior; novice, lay brother; friar, religious; fraternity, brotherhood, friary; order, community; Black Monk, Benedictine, Trappist; teaching order.

nun; recluse; religious, bride of Christ; sister, mother; novice; lay sister; Mother Superior, abbess.

church officer, elder, presbyter, deacon, officer; priest, chaplain; minister; lay reader; server, altar boy; chorister, choirboy, cantor, choir; sidesman or -woman; churchwarden; clerk, beadle, verger; sexton.

priest; prophet, oracle; rabbi; imam, mufti; lama, pontiff; Druid; witch doctor.

church title, Holy Father; Eminence; Monsignor; Lordship, Lord Spiritual; Most Reverend; parson, rector, vicar; father, brother; mother, sister.

monastery; friary, priory, abbey; cloister, convent, nunnery; hermitage, retreat; community house, abode; seminary, training school; cell, chamber.

parsonage, presbytery, rectory, vicarage; manse; deanery, abode; Vatican; close, precincts.

Adj. clerical, regular; secular; lay; pastoral; episcopal.

monastic; celibate.

Vb. take orders; become a nun; enter a monastery or a nunnery.

Adv. clerically.

## 981 Laity

N. laity, lay people, people; cure, charge, parish; flock, sheep, fold; brethren, congregation, society, church member; lay brethren, lay community, community.

lay person; lay rector, lay deacon; lay brother, lay sister; novice; lay reader; elder, deacon, church officer; parishioner, church member.

Adj. laical, parochial; lay; secular; temporal, irreligious; profane, unholy.

Vb. laicize, secularize, deconsecrate.

## 982 Ritual

N. ritual, procedure, way of doing things, method, way; due order, order; form, order, liturgy, practice; symbolism, metaphor; ceremonial, ceremony, formality.

ritualism, ceremony.

rite, mode of worship, cult; institution, observance, ritual practice, practice; form, order, ordinance, rubric, formula, precept; ceremony, solemnity, sacrament, mystery, celebration; representation; rite of passage, initiation, baptism, reception.

ministration, performance, action; celebration; sermon, address, teaching; lecture; sacred rhetoric, oratory; pastoral care; pastoral epistle, pastoral letter; confession, shrift, absolution, penance.

Christian rite; sacrament; baptism, reception; First Communion; Holy Communion, Eucharist; penance; absolution, acquittal; Holy Matrimony, marriage; Holy Orders; requiem mass; liturgy, order of service, order of baptism, marriage service, nuptial mass; ordination; ban, bell, book and candle; dedication.

Holy Communion, Eucharist, mass; low mass; public mass, communion; preparation, confession; Preface, Great Amen; kiss of peace.

the sacrament; real presence, transubstantiation, consubstantiation; altar bread; host; reserved sacrament.

church service, office, duty, service, act of worship; liturgy, celebration; matins, prime, none, vespers; morning prayer, matins; evening prayer, evensong, benediction; vigil, midnight mass.

ritual act, symbolism, representation; sprinkling, aspersion; procession, progression; act of worship; obeisance, homage, respects; crossing oneself, gesture; kiss of peace.

ritual object, cross, crucifix; altar,

Lord's table, altar furniture, altar cloth, candle, candlestick; communion wine, communion bread; cup, chalice; cruet; tabernacle; collection plate, salver; incense; holy water; font; wedding garment, wedding ring; relics, sacred relics; shrine, casket, box; Holy Sepulchre, image; rosary; libation dish, patina; prayer wheel; altar of incense; temple veil.

ritualist; celebrant, minister, priest; server.

office-book, ordinal; liturgy; rubric, canon, precept; missal; prayer book, Book of Common Prayer, Alternative Service Book; rosary.

hymnal, hymn book, psalter, book of psalms, hymn.

holy day, feast, feast day, festival, festivity; fast day, fast; high day, day of observance, day of obligation, celebration; sabbath, day of rest, leisure; Lord's Day, Sunday; anniversary; Lady Day; Candlemas; Michaelmas; Advent; Christmas, Yuletide, Noel, Nativity, Epiphany, Twelfth Night; Lent, Ash Wednesday, Good Friday; Holy Week, Passion Week; Easter, Easter Sunday; Ascension Day; Whitsun, Pentecost; Trinity Sunday; Passover; Pentecost; Ramadan.

Adj. ritual, procedural; formal, solemn, ceremonial; processional, recessional; representational, paschal; unleavened; kosher; blessed.

ritualistic, ceremonious, ceremonial.

Vb. perform ritual, say office, celebrate, officiate; lead worship, offer worship; christen, confirm, ordain; minister, give communion; sacrifice, bless, give benediction; ban, ban with bell, book and candle; excommunicate; dedicate, consecrate; purify; burn incense; anoint; confess, absolve, pronounce absolution; take communion; bow, kneel, genuflect, prostrate oneself; sign oneself; take holy water; process; fast, flagellate oneself, do penance.

ritualize, institute a rite; observe, keep, keep holy.

Adv. ritually, ceremonially; symbolically; liturgically.

## 983 Canonicals

N. canonicals, clerical dress, cloth, clerical black, dress; frock, cassock; cloak, gown, cloak; robe, cowl, hood; clerical collar; apron, shovel hat; skullcap; Salvation Army bonnet.

vestments; cassock, surplice; cope, robe; stole, scarf; girdle; mitre, tiara, triple crown, regalia; papal vestment; crook, staff, badge of rank; pectoral, cross; episcopal ring.

Adj. vestmental; canonical, pontifical.

vestured; hooded, monastic; clerical.

## 984 Temple

N. temple, pantheon; shrine; house of God, tabernacle; place of worship, worship; mosque; house of prayer, oratory; sacred edifice, pagoda, ziggurat, edifice; doorway.

holy place, holy ground, sacred precinct; sanctuary; Sanctum, oracle; sacred tomb, sepulchre, Holy Sepulchre; graveyard, God's Acre, cemetery; place of pilgrimage; Holy City; Mecca.

church, God's house; parish church, chapel of ease; cathedral, minster; basilica; abbey; kirk, chapel, tabernacle, temple; meeting house, house of prayer, oratory; synagogue, mosque.

altar, sanctuary; altar stone, altar slab; altar table, altar bread; credence, credence table; ritual object; canopy, altarpiece, triptych, altar screen, reredos; altar cloth, altar frontal; altar rails.

**church utensil**, font; chalice, **ritual object**; pulpit, lectern; bible, prayer book; salver, collection plate; organ, harmonium; bell, carillon, **campanology**.

**church interior**, nave, aisle, apse, transept; chancel, choir, sanctuary; squint; chancel screen, gallery, organ loft; stall; pew, box pew; pulpit; lectern; chapel, confessional; clerestory; calvary, Easter sepulchre; font; sacristy, vestry; crypt, vault; cross, crucifix.

**church exterior**, porch; tympanum, **doorway**; tower, steeple, spire, **high structure**; bell tower, belfry; buttress, **prop**; cloister; presbytery, **council**; churchyard, lychgate; close.

**Adj. churchlike**; Romanesque, Norman, Gothic, Early English, Perpendicular, baroque, Gothic revival.

# A

**abase**
lay waste 160 vb.
abase 306 vb.
pervert 650 vb.
strike at 707 vb.

**abate**
shade off 27 vb.
abate 37 vb.
subtract 39 vb.
decompose 51 vb.
weaken 158 vb.
moderate 172 vb.
make smaller
       193 vb.
shorten 199 vb.
qualify 463 vb.
discount 805 vb.
starve 941 vb.

**ability**
intrinsicality 5 n.
ability 155 n.
influence 173 n.
possibility 464 n.
means 624 n.
utility 635 n.
skill 689 n.

**able, be**
be equal 28 vb.
be able 155 vb.
find means 624 vb.

**ablutions**
water 334 n.
moistening 336 n.
heater 378 n.
ablutions 643 n.
beautification
       838 n.

**abnormal**
nonuniform 17 adj.
abnormal 84 adj.
misplaced 183 adj.
crazy 498 adj.
unexpected
       503 adj.

puzzling 512 adj.
funny 844 adj.
wrong 909 adj.
extramarital
       946 adj.
spooky 964 adj.

**abnormality**
abnormality 84 n.

**abode**
district 179 n.
locality 182 n.
station 182 n.
abode 187 n.
monastery 980 n.
parsonage 980 n.

**abound**
abound 630 vb.
superabound
       632 vb.

**about**
about 33 adv.

**abroad**
abroad 59 adv.

**abrogate**
nullify 2 vb.
disable 156 vb.
weaken 158 vb.
destroy 160 vb.
suppress 160 vb.
counteract 177 vb.
negate 528 vb.
recant 598 vb.
reject 602 vb.
relinquish 616 vb.
make useless
       636 vb.
stop using 669 vb.
command 732 vb.
liberate 741 vb.
abrogate 747 vb.
prohibit 752 vb.
not observe
       764 vb.
not retain 774 vb.
not pay 800 vb.
disentitle 911 vb.
disapprove 919 vb.

make illegal
       949 vb.
acquit 955 vb.

**abrogated**
abrogated 747 adj.

**abrogation**
abrogation 747 n.

**absence**
nonexistence 2 n.
simpleness 44 n.
zero 99 n.
absence 185 n.
farness 194 n.
invisibility 439 n.
unwillingness
       593 n.
avoidance 615 n.
requirement 622 n.
nonuse 669 n.
undutifulness
       913 n.

**absence of**
**intellect**
absence of intellect
       443 n.
absence of thought
       445 n.
unintelligence
       494 n.

**absence of thought**
absence of intellect
       443 n.
absence of thought
       445 n.
inattention 451 n.
intuition 471 n.

**absent**
nonexistent 2 adj.
incomplete 55 adj.
misplaced 183 adj.
absent 185 adj.
disappearing
       441 adj.
unknown 486 adj.
required 622 adj.
unprovided
       631 adj.
unused 669 adj.

inactive 674 adj.
lost 767 adj.
undutiful 913 adj.

**absent, be**
be incomplete
       55 vb.
be excluded 57 vb.
be absent 185 vb.
disappear 441 vb.
run away 615 vb.
relinquish 616 vb.
elude 662 vb.
be lost 767 vb.
fail in duty 913 vb.

**absolute**
absolute 32 adj.

**absorb**
consume 160 vb.
destroy 160 vb.
hold within 219 vb.
draw 283 vb.
absorb 294 vb.
drink 296 vb.
eat 296 vb.
dry 337 vb.
be credulous
       482 vb.
superabound
       632 vb.
appropriate 781 vb.

**abstainer**
abstainer 937 n.

**abstract**
shorten 199 vb.
be concise 564 vb.
abstract 587 n.
select 600 vb.

**abstracted**
thoughtful 444 adj.
abstracted 451 adj.
crazy 498 adj.
forgetful 501 adj.

**abstractedness**
abstractedness
       451 n.

**absurd**
disagreeing 25 adj.
erroneous 490 adj.

**absurd, be**

absurd 492 adj.
foolish 494 adj.
imaginative
   508 adj.
semantic 509 adj.
meaningless
   510 adj.
exaggerated
   541 adj.
useless 636 adj.
laughing 830 adj.
witty 834 adj.
ridiculous 844 adj.
undue 911 adj.

**absurd, be**

rampage 61 n.
be absurd 492 vb.
be foolish 494 vb.
mean nothing
   510 vb.
befool 537 vb.
be capricious
   599 vb.
waste effort
   636 vb.
do 671 vb.
act foolishly
   690 vb.
amuse oneself
   832 vb.
be witty 834 vb.
be ridiculous
   844 vb.
lose repute 862 vb.

**absurdity**

absurdity 492 n.

**abundance**

increase 36 n.
production 159 n.
abundance 166 n.
vegetable life
   361 n.
plenty 630 n.

**academic title**

honours 861 n.
academic title
   865 n.

**academy**

erudition 485 n.
academy 534 n.

**accelerate**

augment 36 vb.
be early 130 vb.
be vigorous 169 vb.
accelerate 272 vb.
impel 274 vb.
promote 280 vb.
hasten 675 vb.
animate 816 vb.

**access**

bond 47 n.
entrance 68 n.
region 179 n.
doorway 258 n.
approach 284 n.
way in 292 n.
outlet 293 n.
passage 300 n.
access 619 n.

**accessible**

near 195 adj.
open 258 adj.
accessible 284 adj.
admitting 294 adj.
communicating
   619 adj.
easy 696 adj.
free 739 adj.

**accompaniment**

relativeness 9 n.
addition 38 n.
speciality 80 n.
accompaniment
   89 n.
synchronism 118 n.
contiguity 197 n.
nondesign 613 n.

**accompany**

accompany 89 vb.
synchronize
   118 vb.
concur 176 vb.
be contiguous
   197 vb.
carry 268 vb.

follow 279 vb.
direct 684 vb.
serve 737 vb.
take away 781 vb.
greet 879 vb.
court 884 vb.

**accompanying**

accompanying
   89 adj.

**accord**

be related 9 vb.
be identical 13 vb.
be uniform 16 vb.
resemble 18 vb.
accord 24 vb.
be equal 28 vb.
combine 50 vb.
be in order 60 vb.
conform 83 vb.
conform 83 vb.
concur 176 vb.
harmonize 405 vb.
assent 483 vb.
mean 509 vb.
be expedient
   637 vb.
concord 705 vb.

**accordingly**

accordingly 8 adv.

**account**

number 86 n.
estimate 475 vb.
register 543 vb.
pay 799 vb.
account 803 vb.

**accountant**

enumerator 86 n.
recorder 544 n.
treasurer 793 n.
accountant 803 n.

**account book**

list 87 n.
record 543 vb.
account book
   803 n.

**account for**

account for 153 vb.

**accounting**

accounting
   803 adj.

**accounts**

accounts 803 n.

**accrue**

be extrinsic 6 vb.
accrue 38 vb.
approach 284 vb.
be received 777 vb.

**accumulation**

great quantity 32 n.
increase 36 n.
medley 43 n.
arrangement 62 n.
accumulation 74 n.
collision 274 n.
collection 627 n.
storage 627 n.
store 627 n.
acquisition 766 n.

**accumulator**

accumulator 74 n.

**accuracy**

accuracy 489 n.

**accurate**

adjusted 24 adj.
definite 80 adj.
attentive 450 adj.
careful 452 adj.
discriminating
   458 adj.
accurate 489 adj.
interpretive
   515 adj.
veracious 535 adj.
perspicuous
   562 adj.
descriptive 585 adj.
artless 694 adj.
observant 763 adj.
orthodox 970 adj.

**accusable**

accusable 923 adj.

**accusation**

accusation 923 n.

**accuse**

attribute 153 vb.

inform 519 vb.
divulge 521 vb.
proclaim 523 vb.
retaliate 709 vb.
satirize 846 vb.
curse 894 vb.
blame 919 vb.
dispraise 919 vb.
defame 921 vb.
accuse 923 vb.

**accused**
accused 923 adj.

**accused person**
list 87 n.
prisoner 745 n.
vindicator 927 n.
accused person
923 n.
litigant 954 n.

**accuser**
accuser 923 n.

**accusing**
accusing 923 adj.

**accusingly**
accusingly 923 adv.

**achieve liberty**
separate 46 vb.
escape 662 vb.
revolt 733 vb.
achieve liberty
741 vb.

**achromatism**
achromatism 421 n.

**acoustics**
acoustics 393 n.
hearing 410 n.
linguist 552 n.

**acquiesce**
acquiesce 483 vb.
submit 716 vb.
consent 753 vb.

**acquire**
bring together
74 vb.
revert 143 vb.
busy oneself
617 vb.
find means 624 vb.

entreat 756 vb.
acquire 766 vb.
change hands
775 vb.
receive 777 vb.
borrow 780 vb.
take 781 vb.
purchase 787 vb.
acquire 802 vb.
be rewarded
957 vb.

**acquired**
acquired 766 adj.

**acquiring**
acquiring 766 adj.

**acquisition**
compensation 31 n.
assemblage 74 n.
reversion 143 n.
transference 267 n.
benefit 610 n.
chase 614 n.
store 627 n.
acquisition 766 n.
gift 776 n.
receiving 777 n.
taking 781 n.
receipt 802 n.

**acquit**
deliver 663 vb.
liberate 741 vb.
forgive 904 vb.
exempt 914 vb.
justify 922 vb.
acquit 955 vb.

**acquittal**
escape 662 n.
deliverance 663 n.
liberation 741 n.
mercy 900 n.
forgiveness 904 n.
nonliability 914 n.
vindication 922 n.
innocence 930 n.
legal trial 954 n.
acquittal 955 n.
Christian rite 982 n.

**acquitted**
acquitted 955 adj.

**across**
obliquely 215 adv.
across 217 adv.

**act**
dissemble 536 vb.
act 589 vb.
be affected 845 vb.

**act foolishly**
act foolishly
690 vb.

**acting**
representation
546 n.
acting 589 n.

**action**
event 149 n.
production 159 n.
agency 168 n.
policy 618 n.
action 671 n.
activity 673 n.
effectuation 720 n.
observance 763 n.
celebration 871 n.
ministration 982 n.

**active**
eventful 149 adj.
stalwart 157 adj.
operative 168 adj.
vigorous 169 adj.
influential 173 adj.
moving 260 adj.
agitated 313 adj.
willing 592 adj.
businesslike
617 adj.
doing 671 adj.
active 673 adj.
labouring 677 adj.
excited 816 adj.

**active, be**
operate 168 vb.
be vigorous 169 vb.
be active 673 vb.
hasten 675 vb.

exert oneself
677 vb.
behave 683 vb.
withstand 699 vb.
philanthropize
892 vb.

**actively**
actively 673 adv.

**activity**
punctuality 130 n.
stimulation 169 n.
vigorousness
169 n.
motion 260 n.
agitation 313 n.
resolution 594 n.
business 617 n.
job 617 n.
instrumentality
623 n.
superfluity 632 n.
action 671 n.
activity 673 n.
haste 675 n.
workshop 682 n.
warm feeling
813 n.

**act of worship**
act of worship
975 n.
church service
982 n.
ritual act 982 n.

**actor**
band 74 n.
substitute 145 n.
cinema 440 n.
interpreter 515 n.
speaker 574 n.
actor 589 n.
doer 671 n.
personnel 681 n.
party 703 n.
dance 832 n.
affecter 845 n.

**actually**
actually 1 adv.
substantially 3 adv.

truly 489 adv.

**adagio**
adagio 407 adv.

**adaptation**
adaptation 24 n.
conformity 83 n.
accuracy 489 n.

**add**
augment 36 vb.
add 38 vb.
affix 45 vb.
join 45 vb.
agglutinate 48 vb.
combine 50 vb.
fill 54 vb.
make complete
54 vb.
put in front 64 vb.
place after 65 vb.
do sums 86 vb.
modify 138 vb.
enlarge 192 vb.
transfer 267 vb.
insert 298 vb.
misinterpret
516 vb.
exaggerate 541 vb.

**addition**
quantity 26 n.
increase 36 n.
increment 36 n.
addition 38 n.
adjunct 40 n.
mixture 43 n.
joining together
45 n.
whole 52 n.
extraneousness
59 n.
sequence 65 n.
numerical result
85 n.
protraction 108 n.
expansion 192 n.
insertion 298 n.
exaggeration
541 n.

**additional**
extrinsic 6 adj.
increasing 36 adj.
additional 38 adj.
complete 54 adj.
sequential 65 adj.
included 78 adj.
inserted 298 adj.
superfluous
632 adj.

**add water**
combine 50 vb.
add water 334 vb.
moisten 336 vb.

**adhesive**
adhesive 47 n.
coherence 48 n.
viscidity 349 n.

**adjunct**
extrinsicality 6 n.
addition 38 n.
adjunct 40 n.
branch 53 n.
part 53 n.
piece 53 n.
component 58 n.
precursor 66 n.
sequel 67 n.
extremity 69 n.
concomitant 89 n.
expansion 192 n.
hanging object
212 n.
interjection 226 n.
equipment 625 n.

**adjust**
adjust 24 vb.
equalize 28 vb.
order 60 vb.
regularize 62 vb.
make conform
83 vb.
time 112 vb.
synchronize
118 vb.
modify 138 vb.
moderate 172 vb.
harmonize 405 vb.

be true 489 vb.
rectify 649 vb.
pacify 714 vb.

**adjusted**
adjusted 24 adj.

**admit**
add 38 vb.
contain 56 vb.
comprise 78 vb.
introduce 226 vb.
open 258 vb.
enter 292 vb.
admit 294 vb.
receive 777 vb.
take 781 vb.
greet 879 vb.
make pious 973 vb.

**admitting**
admitting 294 adj.

**ad nauseam**
ad nauseam
856 adv.

**adult**
adult 129 n.

**adultness**
adultness 129 n.

**advantage**
advantage 34 n.
fair chance 154 n.
power 155 n.
tactics 683 n.
success 722 n.
victory 722 n.
retention 773 n.

**adverse**
inopportune
133 adj.
presageful 506 adj.
evil 611 adj.
inexpedient
638 adj.
harmful 640 adj.
hindering 697 adj.
opposing 699 adj.
adverse 726 adj.
annoying 822 adj.
unpromising
848 adj.

**adversity**
affairs 149 n.
ruin 160 n.
pain 372 n.
evil 611 n.
bane 654 n.
difficulty 695 n.
adversity 726 n.
sale 788 n.
sorrow 820 n.
suffering 820 n.
painfulness 822 n.
punishment 958 n.

**advertise**
predict 506 vb.
communicate
519 vb.
advertise 523 vb.
make important
633 vb.
boast 872 vb.
praise 918 vb.

**advertisement**
exhibit 517 n.
advertisement
523 n.
broadcast 526 n.
writing 581 n.
inducement 607 n.
request 756 n.
sale 788 n.
boast 872 n.
praise 918 n.

**advice**
meditation 444 n.
estimate 475 n.
hint 519 n.
conference 579 n.
inducement 607 n.
preparation 664 n.
advice 686 n.
precept 688 n.
aid 698 n.

**advisable**
circumstantial
8 adj.
fit 24 adj.
opportune 132 adj.

operative **168** adj.
possible **464** adj.
wise **493** adj.
chosen **600** adj.
useful **635** adj.
advisable **637** adj.
used **668** adj.
due **910** adj.

**advise**
propound **507** vb.
hint **519** vb.
incite **607** vb.
warn **659** vb.
advise **686** vb.

**adviser**
estimator **475** n.
sage **495** n.
informant **519** n.
teacher **532** n.
motivator **607** n.
warner **659** n.
meddler **673** n.
director **685** n.
adviser **686** n.
expert **691** n.
aider **698** n.
mediator **715** n.
consignee **749** n.

**advising**
advising **686** adj.

**aerate**
lighten **318** vb.
gasify **331** vb.
aerate **335** vb.
refrigerate **377** vb.
sanitate **647** vb.
refresh **680** vb.

**aeronaut**
aeronaut **266** n.

**aeronautics**
aeronautics **266** n.
aircraft **271** n.
ascent **303** n.
descent **304** n.
plunge **308** n.
sport **832** n.

**afar**
afar **194** adv.

**affairs**
affairs **149** n.

**affectation**
imitation **20** n.
mimicry **20** n.
conformity **83** n.
underestimation **478** n.
sciolism **486** n.
foolery **492** n.
supposition **507** n.
trope **514** n.
sham **537** n.
mental dishonesty **538** n.
neology **555** n.
inelegance **571** n.
conduct **683** n.
wit **834** n.
fashion **843** n.
affectation **845** n.
pride **866** n.
airs **868** n.
contempt **917** n.
prudery **945** n.
false piety **974** n.

**affected**
imitative **20** adj.
depreciating **478** adj.
dabbling **486** adj.
absurd **492** adj.
figurative **514** adj.
hypocritical **536** adj.
untrue **538** adj.
ornate **569** adj.
inelegant **571** adj.
unskilled **690** adj.
ill-bred **842** adj.
vulgar **842** adj.
fashionable **843** adj.
ridiculous **844** adj.
affected **845** adj.
prideful **866** adj.
vain **868** adj.
modest **869** adj.

ostentatious **870** adj.
unwarranted **911** adj.
prudish **945** adj.
pietistic **973** adj.
impious **974** adj.

**affected, be**
imitate **20** vb.
show **517** vb.
cant **536** vb.
be busy **673** vb.
behave **683** vb.
be affected **845** vb.
be vain **868** vb.
be ostentatious **870** vb.
be impious **974** vb.

**affecter**
affecter **845** n.

**affectionately**
affectionately **882** adv.

**affections**
affections **812** n.

**affirm**
attribute **153** vb.
testify **461** vb.
dogmatize **468** vb.
confute **474** vb.
believe **480** vb.
opine **480** vb.
suppose **507** vb.
mean **509** vb.
manifest **517** vb.
be informed **519** vb.
proclaim **523** vb.
affirm **532** vb.
indicate **542** vb.
phrase **558** vb.
speak **574** vb.
plead **609** vb.
decree **732** vb.
compel **735** vb.
promise **759** vb.
be courageous **850** vb.

**affirmation**
affirmation **527** n.

**affirmative**
demonstrating **473** adj.
meaningful **509** adj.
undisguised **517** adj.
informative **519** adj.
affirmative **527** adj.
forceful **566** adj.

**affirmatively**
affirmatively **527** adv.

**affix**
affix **45** vb.

**afford**
have enough **630** vb.
afford **795** vb.

**afloat**
afloat **270** adv.

**after**
after **65** adv.
behind **279** adv.

**again**
twice **91** adv.
again **102** adv.

**against**
against **235** adv.

**age**
age **126** n.
helplessness **156** n.
fold **256** n.
insanity **498** n.
health **645** n.
ugliness **837** n.

**ageing**
ageing **126** adj.

**agency**
agency **168** n.
instrumentality **623** n.
action **671** n.

**agent**
producer **159** n.

machinist 625 n.
doer 671 n.
agent 681 n.
consignee 749 n.

**agglutinate**
agglutinate 48 vb.

**aggravate**
augment 36 vb.
make violent
171 vb.
give pain 372 vb.
exaggerate 541 vb.
deteriorate 650 vb.
impair 650 vb.
be difficult 695 vb.
make quarrels
704 vb.
miscarry 723 vb.
lose 767 vb.
hurt 822 vb.
aggravate 827 vb.
excite hate 883 vb.
enrage 886 vb.

**aggravated**
aggravated
827 adj.

**aggravatedly**
aggravatedly
827 adv.

**aggravation**
aggravation 827 n.

**aggressively**
aggressively
707 adv.

**agitate**
derange 63 vb.
jumble 63 vb.
demolish 160 vb.
force 171 vb.
move 260 vb.
impel 274 vb.
draw 283 vb.
brandish 312 vb.
agitate 313 vb.
blow 347 vb.
cause feeling
369 vb.
distract 451 vb.

gesticulate 542 vb.
frighten 849 vb.

**agitated**
agitated 313 adj.

**agitated, be**
be agitated 313 vb.

**agitation**
agitation 313 n.

**agitator**
revolutionist 144 n.
violent creature
171 n.
incendiarism 376 n.
speaker 574 n.
motivator 607 n.
reformer 649 n.
troublemaker
658 n.
leader 685 n.
agitator 733 n.
excitant 816 n.
malcontent 824 n.

**agrarian**
territorial 339 adj.
agrarian 365 adj.

**agreeing**
agreeing 24 adj.

**agreement**
identity 13 n.
uniformity 16 n.
similarity 18 n.
agreement 24 n.
equality 28 n.
combination 50 n.
conformity 83 n.
concurrence 176 n.
symmetry 240 n.
melody 405 n.
possibility 464 n.
consensus 483 n.
concord 705 n.
pacification 714 n.
compact 760 n.

**agriculture**
assemblage 74 n.
causation 151 n.
production 159 n.
fertilizer 166 n.

tree 361 n.
agriculture 365 n.
maturation 664 n.

**ahead**
before 64 adv.
ahead 278 adv.

**aid**
addition 38 n.
conduce 151 vb.
strengthening
157 n.
agency 168 n.
influence 173 n.
support 213 n.
support 213 vb.
be behind 233 vb.
promote 280 vb.
elevation 305 n.
elevate 305 vb.
make likely 466 vb.
estimate 475 vb.
assent 483 vb.
inducement 607 n.
incite 607 vb.
instrumentality
623 n.
be instrumental
623 vb.
utility 635 n.
be useful 635 vb.
be expedient
637 vb.
remedy 653 n.
remedy 653 vb.
protection 655 n.
do 671 vb.
facility 696 n.
facilitate 696 vb.
aid 698 n.
aid 698 vb.
cooperate 701 vb.
permission 751 n.
give 776 vb.
friendliness 875 n.
be courteous
879 vb.
kind act 892 n.

be benevolent
892 vb.
philanthropy 896 n.
approbation 918 n.

**aider**
aider 698 n.

**aiding**
aiding 698 adj.

**aim**
place 182 vb.
aim 276 n.
aim at 612 vb.
fire at 707 vb.
threaten 895 vb.

**aim at**
aim at 612 vb.
pursue 614 vb.

**air**
rarity 320 n.
gas 331 n.
air 335 n.
ventilation 347 n.
wind 347 n.
salubrity 647 n.

**aircraft**
aircraft 271 n.
ejector 295 n.
air force 717 n.

**air force**
aeronaut 266 n.
aircraft 271 n.
air force 717 n.
air officer 736 n.

**air officer**
aeronaut 266 n.
air officer 736 n.

**air pipe**
orifice 258 n.
respiration 347 n.
ventilation 347 n.
air pipe 348 n.

**airs**
affectation 845 n.
airs 868 n.
ostentation 870 n.

**airship**
sphere 247 n.
airship 271 n.

gas 331 n.
air force 717 n.

**air travel**
stopping place
140 n.
motion 260 n.
air travel 266 n.
aircraft 271 n.
goal 290 n.

**airy**
flying 266 adj.
gaseous 331 adj.
airy 335 adj.

**akin**
relative 9 adj.
akin 11 adj.
similar 18 adj.
included 78 adj.
near 195 adj.
born 355 adj.

**akin, be**
be related 9 vb.
be akin 11 vb.

**alarmist**
false alarm 660 n.
alarmist 849 n.
coward 851 n.

**alcoholic drink**
stimulant 169 n.
alcoholic drink
296 n.
drunkenness 944 n.

**alcoholism**
frenzy 498 n.
poison 654 n.
hunger 854 n.
alcoholism 944 n.

**alfresco out of doors**
alfresco 335 adv.

**alive**
existing 1 adj.
alive 355 adj.

**all**
all 52 n.
completeness 54 n.
everyman 79 n.

**all along**
while 104 adv.
all along 108 adv.
until now 116 adv.

**allocution**
allocution 578 n.

**almost**
almost 33 adv.

**aloft**
aloft 204 adv.
up 303 adv.

**alone**
unrelated 10 adj.
separate 46 adj.
alone 88 adj.
friendless 878 adj.
unsociable 878 adj.

**alphabetically**
alphabetically
553 adv.

**alpine**
alpine 204 adj.

**altar**
stand 213 n.
altar 984 n.

**alterer**
alterer 138 n.

**although**
although 177 adv.

**altimetry**
altimetry 204 n.

**ambush**
latency 518 n.
be stealthy 520 vb.
ambush 522 n.
ambush 522 vb.
trap 537 n.
ensnare 537 vb.
danger 656 n.
pitfall 658 n.
be cunning 693 vb.

**amendment**
compensation 31 n.
interpretation
515 n.
amendment 649 n.
restoration 651 n.
remedy 653 n.

**amiable**
peaceful 712 adj.
well-bred 843 adj.
amiable 879 adj.
lovable 882 adj.
benevolent 892 adj.

**amicably**
amicably 875 adv.

**amiss**
amiss 611 adv.

**ammunition**
box 189 n.
defence 708 n.
ammunition 718 n.

**amnesty**
amnesty 501 n.
obliteration 545 n.
peace 717 n.
peace offering
714 n.
forgiveness 904 n.

**among**
among 43 adv.

**amorphism**
amorphism 239 n.

**amorphous**
nonuniform 17 adj.
incomplete 55 adj.
orderless 61 adj.
amorphous
239 adj.
distorted 241 adj.
fluid 330 adj.
unsightly 837 adj.

**amphibian**
amphibian 360 n.

**amuse**
please 821 vb.
amuse 832 vb.
be witty 834 vb.
be ridiculous
844 vb.

**amused**
amused 832 adj.

**amusement**
pleasure 371 n.
broadcast 526 n.
stage show 589 n.

business 617 n.
trifle 634 n.
easy thing 696 n.
contest 711 n.
enjoyment 819 n.
pleasurableness
821 n.
merriment 828 n.
amusement 832 n.
social gathering
877 n.

**amuse oneself**
rampage 61 vb.
neglect 453 vb.
be absurd 492 vb.
be foolish 494 vb.
be capricious
599 vb.
busy oneself
617 vb.
be pleased 819 vb.
be cheerful 828 vb.
amuse oneself
832 vb.
be sociable 877 vb.

**amusing**
amusing 832 adj.

**anachronism**
anachronism 113 n.
different time
117 n.
untimeliness 133 n.
inexactness 490 n.

**anachronistic**
anachronistic
113 adj.

**anaesthetic**
obstetrics 162 n.
moderator 172 n.
anaesthetic 370 n.
drug 653 n.
soporific 674 n.
relief 826 n.

**analogue**
identity 13 n.
analogue 18 n.
copy 22 n.
compeer 28 n.

adjunct 40 n.
concomitant 89 n.
duality 90 n.
duplication 91 n.
equivocalness
513 n.
actor 589 n.
**analytically**
analytically 51 adv.
**anarchic**
anarchic 729 adj.
**anarchist**
anarchist 61 n.
**anarchy**
disorder 61 n.
government 728 n.
anarchy 729 n.
nonobservance
764 n.
lawlessness 949 n.
**anciently**
anciently 122 adv.
**anemometry**
anemometry 347 n.
**an example, be**
be an example
23 vb.
influence 173 n.
represent 546 vb.
**angel**
angel 962 n.
mythical being
964 n.
**angelic**
angelic 962 adj.
**angelize**
angelize 962 vb.
**anger**
helplessness 156 n.
dissent 484 n.
excitation 816 n.
excitable state
817 n.
hatred 883 n.
anger 891 n.
disapprobation
919 n.

**angle**
angle 242 n.
projection 249 n.
**Anglican**
Anglican 976 adj.
sectarian 978 adj.
**angrily**
angrily 886 adv.
**angry**
furious 176 adj.
frenzied 503 adj.
excited 821 adj.
angry 891 adj.
threatening
900 adj.
**angry, be**
be violent 176 vb.
excrete 302 vb.
be agitated 318 vb.
gaze 438 vb.
gesticulate 547 vb.
be angry 891 vb.
disapprove 924 vb.
**angular**
oblique 220 adj.
crossed 222 adj.
angular 247 adj.
curved 248 adj.
**angular figure**
obliquity 220 n.
angular figure
247 n.
**angularity**
angularity 247 n.
**angular measure**
obliquity 220 n.
angular measure
247 n.
sailing aid 269 n.
measurement
465 n.
**angulated**
angulated 247 adj.
**animal**
fossil 125 n.
young creature
132 n.
animal 365 n.

**animal disease**
animal disease
651 n.
**animal husbandry**
assemblage 74 n.
production 164 n.
propagation 167 n.
grassland 348 n.
animal husbandry
369 n.
agriculture 370 n.
**animality**
animality 365 n.
**animate**
animate 821 vb.
cheer 833 vb.
**anniversary**
date 108 n.
period 110 n.
anniversary 141 n.
special day 876 n.
**anno domini**
anno domini
108 adv.
**annoyance**
annoyance 827 n.
**annoying**
annoying 827 adj.
**anonymous**
one 88 adj.
unknown 491 adj.
concealed 525 adj.
disguised 525 adj.
anonymous
562 adj.
inglorious 867 adj.
**answer**
reversion 148 n.
interchange
151 vb.
reason why 156 n.
effect 157 n.
answer 460 n.
answer 460 vb.
counterevidence
467 n.
argue 475 vb.

confutation 479 n.
interpretation
520 n.
correspond 588 vb.
retaliate 714 n.
witticism 839 n.
be witty 839 vb.
be insolent 878 vb.
**answering**
answering 460 adj.
**anthology**
composition 56 n.
literature 557 n.
reading matter
589 n.
textbook 589 n.
anthology 592 n.
poem 593 n.
choice 605 n.
**anthropology**
zoology 367 n.
anthropology
371 n.
**antichristianity**
antichristianity
973 n.
**anticipation**
anticipation 135 n.
**antidote**
moderator 177 n.
counteraction
182 n.
antidote 658 n.
**antiquarian**
antiquarian 125 n.
collector 492 n.
interpreter 520 n.
chronicler 549 n.
linguist 557 n.
**antiquated**
anachronistic
118 adj.
not contemporary
122 adj.
past 125 adj.
antiquated 127 adj.
useless 641 adj.
disused 674 adj.

**antiquity**
precursor 66 n.
era 106 n.
antiquity 120 n.
archaism 122 n.
oldness 122 n.
unknown thing
    486 n.
monument 543 n.
collection 627 n.

**apart**
apart 46 adv.

**apathetic**
apathetic 815 adj.
unastonished
    860 adj.
ungrateful 903 adj.

**aphoristic**
aphoristic 491 adj.

**apostatize**
apostatize 598 vb.

**apparently**
apparently
    440 adv.

**appear**
be visible 438 vb.
appear 440 vb.
be plain 517 vb.
be disclosed
    521 vb.

**appearance**
modality 7 n.
circumstance 8 n.
similarity 18 n.
beginning 68 n.
data processing
    86 n.
changeable thing
    147 n.
exteriority 218 n.
view 433 n.
visibility 438 n.
appearance 440 n.
probability 466 n.
ideality 508 n.
manifestation
    517 n.
pretext 609 n.

conduct 683 n.

**appearing**
appearing 440 adj.

**applaud**
assent 483 vb.
gesticulate 542 vb.
rejoice 830 vb.
honour 861 vb.
congratulate
    881 vb.
applaud 918 vb.

**applause**
gesture 542 n.
rejoicing 830 n.
celebration 871 n.
applause 918 n.

**apportion**
quantify 26 vb.
sunder 46 vb.
decompose 51 vb.
part 53 vb.
arrange 62 vb.
disperse 75 vb.
bisect 92 vb.
mete out 460 vb.
dispose of 668 vb.
participate 770 vb.
give 776 vb.
apportion 778 vb.
grant claims
    910 vb.

**apportionment**
apportionment
    778 n.

**appraise**
do sums 86 vb.
appraise 460 vb.

**appraiser**
appraiser 460 n.

**approach**
relativeness 9 n.
be related 9 vb.
resemble 18 vb.
beginning 68 n.
entrance 68 n.
futurity 119 n.
be to come 119 vb.
event 149 n.

destiny 150 n.
impend 150 vb.
tend 174 vb.
nearness 195 n.
be near 195 vb.
motion 260 n.
navigate 264 vb.
approach 284 n.
approach 284 vb.
convergence 288 n.
arrival 290 n.
access 619 n.
friendship 875 n.
befriend 875 vb.
greet 879 vb.

**approaching**
approaching
    284 adj.

**approbation**
estimate 475 n.
assent 483 n.
permission 751 n.
repute 861 n.
approbation 918 n.
orthodoxism 970 n.

**appropriate**
dwell 187 vb.
encroach 301 vb.
acquire 766 vb.
appropriate 781 vb.
claim 910 vb.

**approvable**
approvable
    918 adj.

**approve**
choose 600 vb.
select 600 vb.
permit 751 vb.
consent 753 vb.
be pleased 819 vb.
approve 918 vb.

**approved**
approved 918 n.

**approving**
approving 918 adj.

**approvingly**
approvingly
    918 adv.

**apron**
apron 223 n.

**apt**
relevant 9 adj.
apt 24 adj.
special 80 adj.
opportune 132 adj.
plausible 466 adj.
tasteful 841 adj.

**aptitude**
fitness 24 n.
changeableness
    147 n.
ability 155 n.
tendency 174 n.
intelligence 493 n.
learning 531 n.
willingness 592 n.
aptitude 689 n.

**aquatics**
aquatics 264 n.

**arboreal**
arboreal 361 adj.

**arbour**
pavilion 187 n.
arbour 189 n.
cavity 250 n.
screen 416 n.

**arc**
curve 243 n.
arc 245 n.

**archaism**
antiquity 120 n.
archaism 122 n.
old man 128 n.
reversion 143 n.

**arched**
arched 248 adj.

**architectural**
architectural
    187 adj.

**arena**
athletics 157 n.
region 179 n.

**argue**

meeting place 187 n.
horizontality 211 n.
slaughterhouse 357 n.
training school 534 n.
theatre 589 n.
path 619 n.
contest 711 n.
duel 711 n.
racing 711 n.
arena 719 n.
pleasure ground 832 n.

**argue**

disagree 25 vb.
enquire 454 vb.
testify 461 vb.
argue 470 vb.
sophisticate 472 vb.
propound 507 vb.
publish 523 vb.
affirm 527 vb.
confer 579 vb.
dissertate 586 vb.
be irresolute 596 vb.
plead 609 vb.
bicker 704 vb.
be fastidious 857 vb.
vindicate 922 vb.
litigate 954 vb.

**arguing**

arguing 470 adj.

**argument**

disagreement 25 n.
topic 447 n.
question 454 n.
argument 470 n.
supposition 507 n.
conference 579 n.
dissertation 586 n.
quarrel 704 n.
contention 711 n.

**argumentation**

argumentation 470 n.

**aright**

aright 639 adv.

**aristocracy**

superiority 34 n.
social group 366 n.
owner 771 n.
aristocracy 863 n.

**aristocrat**

bigwig 633 n.
master 736 n.
aristocrat 863 n.
proud person 866 n.

**armed force**

band 74 n.
protection 655 n.
attacker 707 n.
armed force 717 n.

**armour**

covering 221 n.
headgear 223 n.
legwear 223 n.
protection 655 n.
safeguard 657 n.
armour 708 n.

**arms**

tool 625 n.
arms 718 n.

**army**

multitude 100 n.
army 717 n.

**army officer**

soldiery 717 n.
army officer 736 n.

**around**

around 225 adv.

**arrange**

adjust 24 vb.
compose 56 vb.
order 60 vb.
arrange 62 vb.
modify 138 vb.
produce 159 vb.
place 182 vb.
be careful 452 vb.

make certain 468 vb.
clean 643 vb.
make better 649 vb.
make ready 664 vb.

**arranged**

arranged 62 adj.

**arrangement**

relation 9 n.
correlation 12 n.
adaptation 24 n.
subdivision 53 n.
composition 56 n.
order 60 n.
arrangement 62 n.
series 71 n.
assemblage 74 n.
classification 77 n.
regularity 81 n.
production 159 n.
location 182 n.
formation 238 n.
amendment 649 n.

**arrest**

arrest 742 vb.
take 781 vb.

**arrival**

beginning 68 n.
aeronautics 266 n.
return 281 n.
approach 284 n.
arrival 290 n.
descent 304 n.

**arrive**

accrue 38 vb.
happen 149 vb.
be present 184 vb.
travel 262 vb.
voyage 264 vb.
approach 284 vb.
arrive 290 vb.
pass 300 vb.
be visible 438 vb.
appear 440 vb.
climax 720 vb.

**arriving**

arriving 290 adj.

**arrogation**

arrogation 911 n.

**arsenal**

accumulation 74 n.
arsenal 710 n.

**art**

composition 56 n.
production 159 n.
form 238 n.
art 546 n.
misrepresentation 547 n.
school of painting 540 n.
ornamental art 839 n.

**art equipment**

pigment 420 n.
art equipment 548 n.

**article**

estimate 475 n.
publicity 523 n.
reading matter 584 n.
article 586 n.

**artisan**

producer 159 n.
clothier 223 n.
artist 551 n.
machinist 625 n.
doer 671 n.
artisan 681 n.
expert 691 n.

**artist**

imitator 20 n.
producer 159 n.
visionary 508 n.
interpreter 515 n.
recorder 544 n.
artist 551 n.
doer 671 n.

**artless**

simple 44 adj.
amorphous 239 adj.
ignorant 486 adj.
foolish 494 adj.

veracious 535 adj.
plain 568 adj.
inelegant 571 adj.
spontaneous
              604 adj.
immature 665 adj.
unprepared
              665 adj.
bungled 690 adj.
artless 694 adj.
graceless 837 adj.
ill-bred 842 adj.
vulgar 842 adj.
barbaric 864 adj.
honourable
              924 adj.
innocent 930 adj.
**artless, be**
be artless 694 vb.
be rude 880 vb.
be innocent
              930 vb.
**artlessly**
artlessly 694 adv.
**artlessness**
artlessness 694 n.
**art of war**
art of war 713 n.
**art style**
art style 548 n.
**art subject**
art subject 548 n.
**as before**
as before 139 adv.
**ascend**
be great 32 vb.
grow 36 vb.
be high 204 vb.
be oblique 215 vb.
be in motion
              260 vb.
fly 266 vb.
emerge 293 vb.
ascend 303 vb.
lift oneself 305 vb.
leap 307 vb.
be light 318 vb.
be visible 438 vb.

get better 649 vb.
**ascending**
ascending 303 adj.
**ascent**
degree 27 n.
increase 36 n.
bond 47 n.
series 71 n.
vertex 208 n.
stand 213 n.
motion 260 n.
progression 280 n.
departure 291 n.
ascent 303 n.
elevation 305 n.
lightness 318 n.
access 619 n.
improvement
              649 n.
sport 832 n.
**ascetic**
philosopher 444 n.
sage 495 n.
severe 730 adj.
poor person 796 n.
abstainer 937 n.
ascetic 940 n.
ascetic 940 adj.
pietist 973 n.
pietistic 973 adj.
monk 980 n.
**ascetically**
ascetically 940 adv.
**ascetic, be**
refuse 755 vb.
be temperate
              937 vb.
be ascetic 940 vb.
offer worship
              975 vb.
**asceticism**
asceticism 940 n.
**ash**
ash 376 n.
coal 380 n.
dirt 644 n.

**ask leave**
ask leave 751 vb.
**ask mercy**
knuckle under
              716 vb.
deprecate 757 vb.
regret 825 vb.
ask mercy 900 vb.
beg pardon 904 vb.
**aspiration**
aspiration 847 n.
**as promised**
as promised
              759 adv.
**assemblage**
joining together
              45 n.
combination 50 n.
composition 56 n.
arrangement 62 n.
assemblage 74 n.
convergence 288 n.
acquisition 766 n.
**assembled**
assembled 74 adj.
**assembly**
union 45 n.
assembly 74 n.
conference 579 n.
council 687 n.
amusement 832 n.
pageant 870 n.
social gathering
              877 n.
public worship
              975 n.
**assent**
agreement 24 n.
accord 24 vb.
concurrence 176 n.
concur 176 vb.
be reasonable
              470 vb.
believe 480 vb.
assent 483 n.
assent 483 vb.
confess 521 vb.
willingness 592 n.

be willing 592 vb.
submission 716 n.
submit 716 vb.
permit 751 vb.
consent 753 n.
consent 753 vb.
compact 760 n.
approbation 918 n.
approve 918 vb.
**assented**
assented 483 adj.
**assenter**
assenter 483 n.
**assenting**
assenting 483 adj.
**assertive**
strong 157 adj.
positive 468 adj.
assertive 527 adj.
**assiduity**
assiduity 673 n.
**assign**
place 182 vb.
transfer 267 vb.
relinquish 616 vb.
be subject 740 vb.
resign 748 vb.
dower 772 vb.
not retain 774 vb.
assign 775 vb.
give 776 vb.
**assimilation**
assimilation 18 n.
**association**
relation 9 n.
mixture 43 n.
union 45 n.
combination 50 n.
group 74 n.
unity 88 n.
accompaniment
              89 n.
concurrence 176 n.
life 355 n.
business 617 n.
association 701 n.
corporation 703 n.
society 703 n.

intelligent 493 adj.
studious 531 adj.
resolute 594 adj.
labouring 677 adj.
observant 763 adj.
lively 814 adj.
cautious 853 adj.
fastidious 857 adj.
courteous 879 adj.

**attentive, be**
specify 80 vb.
hear 410 vb.
gaze 433 vb.
watch 436 vb.
think 444 vb.
be curious 448 vb.
be attentive
450 vb.
be careful 452 vb.
know 485 vb.
foresee 505 vb.
be informed
519 vb.
be active 673 vb.
observe 763 vb.
be courteous
879 vb.

**attic**
attic 189 n.
vertex 208 n.

**attract**
bring together
74 vb.
cause 151 vb.
influence 173 vb.
draw 283 vb.
attract 286 vb.
motivate 607 vb.
delight 821 vb.
cause desire
854 vb.
excite love 882 vb.
bewitch 977 vb.

**attracting**
attracting 286 adj.

**attraction**
relation 9 n.
offset 31 n.

assembly 74 n.
focus 76 n.
energy 155 n.
influence 173 n.
tendency 174 n.
traction 283 n.
attraction 286 n.
inducement 607 n.
pleasurableness
821 n.
desired object
854 n.
favourite 885 n.
spell 977 n.

**attract notice**
influence 173 vb.
be visible 438 vb.
attract notice
450 vb.
be plain 517 vb.
gesticulate 542 vb.
be important
633 vb.
impress 816 vb.
be ostentatious
870 vb.
excite love 882 vb.

**attribute**
attribute 153 vb.
thank 902 vb.
grant claims
910 vb.

**attributed**
attributed 153 adj.

**attribution**
attribution 153 n.

**at war**
at war 713 adv.

**at will**
at will 590 adv.
willingly 592 adv.

**auditory**
auditory 410 adj.

**augment**
shade off 27 vb.
be great 32 vb.
augment 36 vb.
add 38 vb.

do sums 86 vb.
be many 100 vb.
strengthen 157 vb.
be fruitful 166 vb.
enlarge 192 vb.
manifest 517 vb.
store 627 vb.
make rich 795 vb.
aggravate 827 vb.

**auspicate**
auspicate 68 vb.

**auspicious, be**
patronize 698 vb.
be auspicious
725 vb.

**authenticity**
authenticity 489 n.

**author**
substitute 145 n.
producer 159 n.
news reporter
524 n.
literature 552 n.
calligrapher 581 n.
author 584 n.
narrator 585 n.
dissertator 586 n.
prose 588 n.

**authoritarian**
volitional 590 adj.
directing 684 adj.
authoritative
728 adj.
authoritarian
730 adj.

**authoritative**
powerful 155 adj.
influential 173 adj.
directing 684 adj.
authoritative
728 adj.
commanding
732 adj.
proud 866 adj.
godlike 960 adj.
scriptural 969 adj.
ecclesiastical
979 adj.

**authority**
degree 27 n.
greatness 32 n.
superiority 34 n.
precedence 64 n.
power 155 n.
influence 173 n.
judgment 475 n.
bigwig 633 n.
management
684 n.
authority 728 n.
severity 730 n.
regalia 738 n.
restraint 742 n.
commission 746 n.
prestige 861 n.
nobility 863 n.
upper class 863 n.
jurisdiction 950 n.
the church 979 n.

**autocrat**
bigwig 633 n.
leader 685 n.
tyrant 730 n.
autocrat 736 n.

**automobile**
miniature 191 n.
automobile 269 n.

**autumn**
oldness 122 n.
autumn 124 n.

**autumnal**
autumnal 124 adj.

**auxiliary**
inferior 35 n.
extra 40 n.
substitute 145 n.
athlete 157 n.
prop 213 n.
instrument 623 n.
aider 698 n.
auxiliary 702 n.
armed force 717 n.
friend 875 n.

**avail oneself of**
avail oneself of
668 vb.

parry 708 vb.

**avarice**
acquisition 766 n.
rapacity 781 n.
avarice 811 n.
desire 854 n.
selfishness 927 n.
antichristianity
968 n.

**avaricious**
avaricious 811 adj.

**avenge**
retaliate 709 vb.
be severe 730 vb.
be pitiless 901 vb.
avenge 905 vb.
vindicate 922 vb.
punish 958 vb.

**avenger**
avenger 905 n.

**average**
prototype 23 n.
quantity 26 n.
average 30 n.
smallness 33 n.
middle 70 n.
generality 79 n.
statistics 86 n.
middle way 620 n.
imperfection 642 n.
averageness 727 n.
compromise 765 n.

**averageness**
averageness 727 n.

**average out**
average out 30 vb.

**aviational**
aviational 271 adj.

**avoid**
separate 46 vb.
set apart 46 vb.
exclude 57 vb.
vary 147 vb.
be absent 185 vb.
be distant 194 vb.
bring to rest
261 vb.
recoil 275 vb.

deviate 277 vb.
turn back 281 vb.
recede 285 vb.
disregard 453 vb.
answer 455 vb.
be equivocal
513 vb.
be stealthy 520 vb.
be unwilling
593 vb.
be irresolute
596 vb.
avoid 620 vb.
relinquish 616 vb.
circuit 621 vb.
be safe 655 vb.
elude 662 vb.
not use 669 vb.
not act 672 vb.
be inactive 674 vb.
be obstructive
697 vb.
parry 708 vb.
refuse 755 vb.
not observe
764 vb.
quake 849 vb.
be cowardly
851 vb.
be cautious 853 vb.
dislike 856 vb.
be modest 869 vb.
be unsociable
878 vb.
make unwelcome
878 vb.
hate 883 vb.
fail in duty 913 vb.
be temperate
937 vb.

**avoidable**
avoidable 615 adj.

**avoidance**
avoidance 615 n.

**avoider**
avoider 615 n.

**avoiding**
avoiding 615 adj.

**await**
wait 131 vb.
navigate 264 vb.
scan 433 vb.
be uncertain
469 vb.
await 502 vb.

**axe**
sharp edge 251 n.
axe 718 n.

**axiom**
truth 489 n.
axiom 491 n.

**B**

**back**
sequential 65 adj.
ending 69 adj.
back 233 n.

**backwards**
backwards
281 adv.

**bad**
inferior 35 adj.
trivial 634 adj.
profitless 636 adj.
bad 640 adj.
imperfect 642 adj.
deteriorated
650 adj.
adverse 726 adj.
disreputable
862 adj.
maleficent 893 adj.
wrong 909 adj.
contemptible
917 adj.
blameworthy
919 adj.
dishonest 925 adj.
heinous 929 adj.
wicked 929 adj.

**badge**
badge 542 n.

trophy 724 n.
badge of rank
738 n.
trimming 839 n.

**badge of rank**
badge 542 n.
badge of rank
738 n.
vestments 983 n.

**badge of rule**
badge 542 n.
badge of rule
738 n.

**badly**
badly 640 adv.

**badness**
badness 640 n.

**bad person**
changed person
142 n.
revolter 733 n.
object of scorn
862 n.
offender 899 n.
wrong 909 n.
bad person 933 n.
impenitence 935 n.
devil 963 n.
impious person
974 n.

**bad taste**
inaptitude 25 n.
inferiority 35 n.
indiscrimination
459 n.
mistake 490 n.
art 546 n.
inelegance 571 n.
artlessness 694 n.
wit 834 n.
bad taste 842 n.
wrong 909 n.
undueness 911 n.
vice 929 n.
impurity 946 n.

**bag**
bag 189 n.
carrier 268 n.

**ballet**
  composition 56 n.
  ballet 589 n.
  dancing 832 n.
**ball game**
  ball game 832 n.
**balm**
  moderator 172 n.
  lubricant 329 n.
  balm 653 n.
  relief 826 n.
**band**
  band 74 n.
  classification 77 n.
  personnel 681 n.
  party 703 n.
  formation 717 n.
  person of repute
                861 n.
**bane**
  destroyer 163 n.
  influence 173 n.
  resident 186 n.
  killer 357 n.
  evil 611 n.
  badness 640 n.
  infection 646 n.
  plague 646 n.
  insalubrity 648 n.
  bane 654 n.
  pitfall 658 n.
  adversity 726 n.
  suffering 820 n.
  worry 820 n.
  annoyance 822 n.
  painfulness 822 n.
  hateful object
                883 n.
  malevolence 893 n.
  noxious animal
                899 n.
  ruffian 899 n.
**baneful**
  baneful 654 adj.
**bang**
  sound 393 n.
  loudness 395 n.
  be loud 395 vb.

  bang 397 n.
  bang 397 vb.
**bar**
  bar 953 n.
**barbaric**
  barbaric 864 adj.
**bareness**
  bareness 224 n.
**bargain**
  contract 760 vb.
  make terms 761 vb.
  bargain 786 n.
  be parsimonious
                811 vb.
**barrier**
  exclusion 57 n.
  outline 228 n.
  barrier 230 n.
  defences 708 n.
**barter**
  correlation 12 n.
  equivalence 28 n.
  interchange 146 n.
  transference 267 n.
  conditions 761 n.
  transfer 775 n.
  barter 786 n.
**base**
  inferiority 35 n.
  extremity 69 n.
  serial place 73 n.
  source 151 n.
  cellar 189 n.
  layer 202 n.
  lowness 205 n.
  base 209 n.
  basis 213 n.
  interiority 219 n.
  limit 231 n.
**basis**
  prelude 66 n.
  base 209 n.
  basis 213 n.
  preparation 664 n.
**basket**
  basket 189 n.
**bastard**
  bastard 949 adj.

**bastardy**
  bastardy 949 n.
**battle**
  fight 711 n.
  battle 713 n.
  battleground 719 n.
**battleground**
  battleground 719 n.
**bauble**
  bauble 634 n.
  plaything 832 n.
  finery 839 n.
  bad taste 842 n.
**bawd**
  bawd 947 n.
**be**
  be 1 vb.
  be now 116 vb.
  live 355 vb.
  be true 489 vb.
**beachwear**
  beachwear 223 n.
**beam**
  bond 47 n.
  beam 213 n.
  cross 217 n.
  roof 221 n.
  materials 626 n.
**bearer**
  bearer 268 n.
  servant 737 n.
**bearing**
  bearing 268 adj.
**bearings**
  bearings 181 n.
  direction 276 n.
**beast of burden**
  beast of burden
                268 n.
  animal 360 n.
  mammal 360 n.
**beau monde**
  beau monde 843 n.
**beautician**
  friction 328 n.
  cleaner 643 n.
  beautician 838 n.

**beautification**
  beautification
                838 n.
**beautified**
  beautified 838 adj.
**beautiful**
  pleasant 371 adj.
  elegant 570 adj.
  excellent 639 adj.
  pleasurable
                821 adj.
  beautiful 836 adj.
  beautified 838 adj.
  lovable 882 adj.
**beautiful, be**
  be beautiful
                836 vb.
**beautify**
  make better
                649 vb.
  beautify 836 vb.
  primp 838 vb.
  decorate 839 vb.
**beauty**
  symmetry 240 n.
  elegance 570 n.
  pleasurableness
                821 n.
  beauty 836 n.
**beauty, a**
  exceller 639 n.
  a beauty 836 n.
  favourite 885 n.
**beauty parlour**
  beauty parlour
                838 n.
**become**
  become 1 vb.
  evolve 311 vb.
**become pious**
  become pious
                973 vb.
**become small**
  be small 33 vb.
  decrease 37 vb.
  be little 191 vb.
  become small
                193 vb.

be narrow 201 vb.
deteriorate 650 vb.

**bed**
bed 213 n.
resting place
    261 n.

**bedecked**
bedecked 839 adj.

**bedevil**
bedevil 63 vb.
destroy 160 vb.
be unintelligible
    512 vb.
be difficult 695 vb.

**bedim**
bedim 414 vb.

**befool**
befool 537 vb.

**before**
before 64 adv.
before 114 adv.

**before, be**
be 1 vb.
come before 64 vb.
be before 114 vb.

**beforehand**
beforehand
    130 adv.

**befriend**
accord 24 vb.
accompany 89 vb.
patronize 698 vb.
befriend 875 vb.
be sociable 877 vb.

**beg**
beg 756 vb.
tax 804 vb.
be servile 874 vb.

**beggar**
idler 674 n.
beggar 758 n.
recipient 777 n.
poor person 796 n.
low fellow 864 n.

**beggarly**
beggarly 796 adj.

**begin**
become 1 vb.

come before 64 vb.
begin 68 vb.
repeat 102 vb.
time 112 vb.
revert 143 vb.
cause 151 vb.
start out 291 vb.
be born 355 vb.
be visible 438 vb.
appear 440 vb.
be restored 651 vb.
prepare 664 vb.
undertake 667 vb.
work 677 vb.
celebrate 871 vb.

**beginner**
beginning 68 n.
driver 263 n.
incomer 292 n.
testee 456 n.
ignoramus 488 n.
ninny 496 n.
beginner 533 n.
dupe 539 n.
bungler 692 n.
ingenue 694 n.

**beginning**
originality 21 n.
increase 36 n.
unfinished 55 adj.
prelude 66 n.
precursory 66 adj.
beginning 68 n.
beginning 68 adj.
repetition 102 n.
new 121 n.
oldness 122 n.
primal 127 adj.
youth 125 n.
earliness 130 n.
impending 150 adj.
source 151 n.
causal 151 adj.
weak 158 adj.
exiguous 191 adj.
amorphous
    239 adj.
arrival 290 n.

appearance 440 n.
curriculum 529 n.
learning 531 n.
preparation 664 n.
immature 665 adj.
celebration 871 n.

**beg pardon**
beg pardon 904 vb.
atone 936 vb.

**behave**
do 671 vb.
behave 683 vb.

**behaving**
behaving 683 adj.

**behind**
behind 279 adv.

**behind, be**
be behind 233 vb.
follow 279 vb.

**behindhand**
behindhand
    302 adv.

**belief**
possibility 464 n.
probability 466 n.
positiveness 468 n.
belief 480 n.
credulity 482 n.
hope 847 n.
religious faith
    967 n.
piety 973 n.

**believe**
think 444 vb.
assume 466 vb.
be certain 468 vb.
believe 480 vb.
be credulous
    482 vb.
expect 502 vb.
suppose 507 vb.
take a pledge
    759 vb.
hope 847 vb.
be orthodox
    970 vb.
be pious 973 vb.

**believed, be**
be believed 480 vb.

**believing**
believing 480 adj.

**bellicosity**
bellicosity 713 n.

**belligerency**
belligerency 713 n.
enmity 876 n.

**belong**
be intrinsic 5 vb.
belong 768 vb.

**belt**
girdle 47 n.
belt 223 n.
loop 245 n.

**benefactor**
aider 698 n.
patron 702 n.
giver 776 n.
good giver 808 n.
philanthropist
    896 n.
benefactor 898 n.
good person 932 n.
fairy 964 n.

**benefice**
benefice 979 n.

**beneficial**
good 610 adj.
advisable 637 adj.
beneficial 639 adj.
salubrious 647 adj.
remedial 653 adj.

**beneficiary**
survivor 41 n.
successor 67 n.
descendant 165 n.
deputy 750 n.
beneficiary 771 n.
recipient 777 n.
rich person 795 n.
hoper 847 n.
dueness 910 n.

**benefit**
advantage 34 n.
lack of expectation
    503 n.

benefit 610 n.
benefit 610 vb.
good policy 637 n.
do good 639 vb.
be auspicious
                725 vb.
acquisition 766 n.
**benevolence**
carefulness 452 n.
willingness 592 n.
good 610 n.
intention 612 n.
goodness 639 n.
aid 698 n.
leniency 731 n.
permission 751 n.
feeling 813 n.
friendliness 875 n.
courtesy 879 n.
love 882 n.
benevolence 892 n.
philanthropy 896 n.
pity 900 n.
disinterestedness
                926 n.
piety 973 n.
**benevolent**
benevolent 892 adj.
**benevolent, be**
be benevolent
                892 vb.
**benevolently**
benevolently
                892 adv.
**bequeath**
transfer 267 vb.
possess 768 vb.
dower 772 vb.
bequeath 775 vb.
give 776 vb.
be rich 795 vb.
make rich 795 vb.
**besiege**
surround 225 vb.
circumscribe
                227 vb.
close 259 vb.
besiege 707 vb.

**best**
great 32 adj.
crowning 34 adj.
supreme 34 adj.
topmost 208 adj.
best 639 adj.
wonderful 859 adj.
**betimes**
betimes 130 adv.
**between**
between 226 adv.
**bewitch**
convert 142 vb.
engross 444 vb.
motivate 607 vb.
subjugate 740 vb.
delight 821 vb.
be beautiful
                836 vb.
be wonderful
                859 vb.
excite love 882 vb.
be malevolent
                893 vb.
curse 894 vb.
diabolize 963 vb.
bewitch 977 vb.
**bewitched**
bewitched 977 adj.
**beyond**
beyond 34 adv.
beyond 194 adv.
in front 232 adv.
**bias**
inequality 29 n.
influence 173 n.
cause thought
                444 vb.
engross 444 vb.
positiveness 468 n.
intuition 471 n.
bias 476 n.
error 490 n.
eccentricity 498 n.
opinionatedness
                597 n.
caprice 599 n.

motivate 607 vb.
excitability 817 n.
liking 854 n.
dislike 856 n.
boasting 872 n.
injustice 909 n.
sectarianism 972 n.
**biased**
biased 476 adj.
**biased, be**
be biased 476 vb.
**bibliographical**
bibliographical
                584 adj.
**bicker**
disagree 25 vb.
argue 470 vb.
bicker 704 vb.
blame 919 vb.
**bicycle**
bicycle 269 n.
**bifurcate**
bifurcate 92 vb.
**bifurcation**
bifurcation 92 n.
**bigwig**
superior 34 n.
influence 173 n.
person 366 n.
bigwig 633 n.
elite 639 n.
manager 685 n.
autocrat 736 n.
master 736 n.
person of repute
                861 n.
aristocrat 863 n.
proud person
                866 n.
**biography**
record 543 n.
reading matter
                584 n.
biography 585 n.
**biological**
biological 353 adj.
**biology**
heredity 5 n.

conversion 142 n.
propagation 162 n.
physics 314 n.
structure 326 n.
biology 353 n.
zoology 362 n.
**bird**
wanderer 263 n.
diver 308 n.
bird 360 n.
vocalist 408 n.
hunter 614 n.
noxious animal
                899 n.
**bisect**
sunder 46 vb.
bisect 92 vb.
apportion 778 vb.
**bisected**
bisected 92 adj.
**bisection**
bisection 92 n.
**black**
funereal 359 adj.
dark 418 adj.
soft-hued 420 adj.
black 423 adj.
**blacken**
darken 418 vb.
colour 420 vb.
blacken 423 vb.
show feeling
                813 vb.
**blackish**
blackish 423 adj.
**blackness**
blackness 423 n.
**black pigment**
black pigment
                423 n.
cleanser 648 n.
**black thing**
black thing 423 n.
**bladder**
bladder 189 n.
gas 331 n.
**blame**
blame 919 vb.

# blameworthy

accuse 923 vb.
**blameworthy**
blameworthy
919 adj.
**bleacher**
bleacher 421 n.
**blemish**
tincture 43 n.
weakness 158 n.
deformity 241 n.
shortfall 302 n.
maculation 432 n.
mistake 490 n.
identification
542 n.
indication 542 n.
trace 543 n.
defect 642 n.
skin disease 646 n.
wound 650 n.
impair 650 vb.
eyesore 837 n.
ugliness 837 n.
blemish 840 n.
blemish 840 vb.
slur 862 n.
**blemished**
blemished 840 adj.
**blight**
decay 51 n.
insect 360 n.
dilapidation 650 n.
blight 654 n.
**blind**
insensible 370 adj.
screened 416 adj.
screen 416 vb.
blind 434 adj.
blind 434 vb.
dim-sighted
435 adj.
inattentive 451 adj.
distract 451 vb.
indiscriminating
459 adj.
biased 476 adj.
misjudging
476 adj.

ignorant 486 adj.
unwise 494 adj.
deceive 537 vb.
impassive 815 adj.
make insensitive
815 vb.
unastonished
860 adj.
**blind, be**
gaze 433 vb.
be blind 434 vb.
be inattentive
451 vb.
disregard 452 vb.
be biased 476 vb.
not know 486 vb.
not understand
512 vb.
be insensitive
815 vb.
**blindness**
blindness 434 n.
**blood**
haemorrhage
297 n.
blood 330 n.
redness 426 n.
**blood disease**
blood disease
646 n.
**bloodstained**
bloodstained
426 adj.
**blow**
vary 147 vb.
be strong 157 vb.
be violent 171 vb.
enlarge 192 vb.
fell 306 vb.
aerate 335 vb.
blow 347 vb.
sound faint 396 vb.
be active 673 vb.
**blowing**
blowing 347 n.
**blow up**
blow up 347 vb.

**blue**
colour 420 vb.
green 429 adj.
blue 430 adj.
blue 430 n.
purple 431 adj.
**blueness**
blueness 430 n.
**blue pigment**
blue pigment
430 n.
**blunder**
stray 277 vb.
be inattentive
451 vb.
misjudge 476 vb.
blunder 490 n.
not understand
512 vb.
misinterpret
516 vb.
disclose 521 vb.
be ungrammatical
560 vb.
act foolishly
690 vb.
be clumsy 690 vb.
be unskilful 690 vb.
fail 723 vb.
fail in duty 913 vb.
**blunt**
weaken 158 vb.
moderate 172 vb.
blunt 252 vb.
dissuade 608 vb.
make insensitive
815 vb.
**bluntness**
bluntness 252 n.
**blur**
darken 413 vb.
bedim 414 vb.
blur 435 vb.
**board game**
board game 832 n.
**boast**
overestimation
477 n.

exaggerate 541 vb.
defy 706 vb.
triumph 722 vb.
ridiculousness
844 n.
be affected 845 vb.
seek repute 861 vb.
feel pride 866 vb.
be vain 868 vb.
ostentation 870 n.
be ostentatious
870 vb.
boast 872 n.
boast 872 vb.
be insolent 873 vb.
threat 895 n.
threaten 895 vb.
**boaster**
boaster 872 n.
**boastful**
untrue 538 adj.
exaggerated
541 adj.
affected 845 adj.
prideful 866 adj.
vain 868 adj.
boastful 872 adj.
insolent 873 adj.
threatening
895 adj.
**boasting**
boasting 872 n.
**boat**
small house 187 n.
boat 270 n.
**boatman**
boatman 265 n.
**bomb**
nucleonics 155 n.
destroyer 163 n.
fire 374 n.
lighter 380 n.
bomb 718 n.
**bombardment**
havoc 160 n.
propulsion 282 n.
loudness 395 n.

store 627 vb.
restore 651 vb.
make ready 664 vb.
command 732 vb.
acquire 766 vb.
take 781 vb.

**bring to rest**
assuage 172 vb.
place 182 vb.
bring to rest
  261 n.
navigate 264 vb.
pacify 714 vb.
carry through
  720 vb.
tranquillize 818 vb.

**brittle**
small 33 adj.
fragmentary 53 adj.
ephemeral 109 adj.
flimsy 158 adj.
rigid 321 adj.
brittle 325 adj.
powdery 327 adj.
spurious 537 adj.

**brittle, be**
be brittle 325 vb.
variegate 432 vb.

**brittleness**
brittleness 325 n.

**broad**
great 32 adj.
fleshy 190 adj.
large 190 adj.
expanded 192 adj.
broad 200 adj.
tailored 223 adj.

**broad, be**
grow 36 vb.
expand 192 vb.
be broad 200 vb.
overlie 221 vb.

**broadcast**
news 524 n.
broadcast 526 n.
stage play 589 n.

**broadcaster**
broadcaster 526 n.

**broadcasting**
broadcasting
  526 n.

**broadways**
broadways
  200 adv.

**brothel**
brothel 946 n.

**brother or sister
to, be**
be akin 11 vb.

**brown**
whitish 422 adj.
brown 425 adj.
red 426 adj.

**brownness**
brownness 425 n.

**brown pigment**
brown pigment
  425 n.

**brute force**
strength 157 n.
violence 171 n.
despotism 728 n.
brute force 730 n.
compulsion 735 n.
lawlessness 949 n.

**bubble**
stimulation 169 n.
sphere 247 n.
swelling 248 n.
commotion 313 n.
be agitated 313 vb.
effervesce 313 vb.
moisture 336 n.
bubble 350 n.
bubble 350 vb.
pulpiness 351 n.
bauble 634 n.

**bubbly**
gaseous 331 adj.
bubbly 350 adj.
excited 816 adj.

**building material**
edifice 159 n.
housing 187 n.
facing 221 n.
roof 221 n.

building material
  626 n.

**bulk**
piece 53 n.
weakness 158 n.
bulk 190 n.
thickness 200 n.
convexity 248 n.
swelling 248 n.
eating 296 n.
gravity 317 n.

**bullion**
bullion 792 n.

**bunch**
bunch 74 n.

**bungled**
bungled 690 adj.

**bungler**
bungler 692 n.

**bungling**
bungling 690 n.

**buried**
buried 359 adj.

**burn**
destroy 160 vb.
lay waste 160 vb.
kill 357 vb.
inter 359 vb.
be hot 374 vb.
burn 376 vb.
blacken 423 vb.
embrown 425 vb.
waste 629 vb.
excite 816 vb.

**burning**
destruction 160 n.
burning 376 n.

**burst in**
burst in 292 vb.

**bus**
bus 269 n.

**business**
relation 9 n.
affairs 149 n.
production 159 n.
topic 447 n.
predetermination
  603 n.

intention 612 n.
pursuit 614 n.
business 617 n.
policy 618 n.
importance 633 n.
undertaking 667 n.
action 671 n.
activity 673 n.
trade 786 n.

**businesslike**
businesslike
  617 adj.
active 673 adj.
industrious 673 adj.
behaving 683 adj.
expert 689 adj.

**busy**
busy 673 adj.
labouring 677 adj.

**busy, be**
pass time 104 vb.
be engaged
  133 vb.
busy oneself
  617 vb.
undertake 667 vb.
be busy 673 vb.
work 677 vb.
be in difficulty
  695 vb.
be affected 845 vb.

**busy oneself**
pursue 614 vb.
busy oneself
  617 vb.
undertake 667 vb.
do 671 vb.
be busy 673 vb.
behave 683 vb.
acquire 766 vb.

**busy person**
enthusiast 499 n.
volunteer 592 n.
planner 618 n.
doer 671 n.
busy person 673 n.
worker 681 n.
servant 737 n.

**buttocks**
buttocks 233 n.

**buying**
buying 787 adj.

**by authority**
by authority
728 adv.

**by chance**
by chance 154 adv.

**by degrees**
by degrees 27 adv.

**by force**
by force 735 adv.

**by leaps and bounds**
by leaps and bounds 307 adv.

**by leave**
by leave 751 adv.

**by letter**
by letter 583 adv.

**by means of**
by means of
624 adv.

**by name**
by name 556 adv.

**by proxy**
by proxy 746 adv.

**by turns**
by turns 136 adv.

**C**

**cab**
cab 269 n.

**cabbalistic**
cabbalistic 978 adj.

**cabinet**
cabinet 189 n.
shelf 213 n.
stand 213 n.
storage 627 n.

**cable**
cable 47 n.
electronics 155 n.

fibre 203 n.
hanger 212 n.
tool 625 n.

**cad**
nonconformist
84 n.
low fellow 864 n.
hateful object
883 n.
cad 933 n.

**cadaverous**
cadaverous
358 adj.

**caf**
caf 187 n.

**calculation of chance**
calculation of
chance 154 n.

**call**
loudness 395 n.
cry 403 n.
musical note 405 n.
campanology
407 n.
publication 523 n.
call 542 n.
inducement 607 n.
danger signal
660 n.
war 713 n.
warfare 713 n.
war measures
713 n.
command 732 n.
prayers 975 n.

**calligrapher**
calligrapher 581 n.

**calumny**
hint 519 n.
rumour 524 n.
slur 862 n.
scurrility 894 n.
censure 919 n.
calumny 921 n.
false charge 923 n.

**camber**
angularity 242 n.

curve 243 n.
camber 248 n.

**camera**
camera 437 n.
broadcasting
526 n.
photography 546 n.

**campanology**
loudness 395 n.
roll 398 n.
campanology
407 n.
church utensil
984 n.

**campestral**
campestral 343 adj.

**cancer**
cancer 646 n.

**canonicals**
canonicals 983 n.

**canopy**
dwelling 187 n.
pavilion 187 n.
small house 187 n.
canopy 221 n.
screen 416 n.

**cant**
sophisticate
472 vb.
cant 536 vb.
deceive 537 vb.
be affected 845 vb.

**capital punishment**
killing 357 n.
capital punishment
958 n.

**caprice**
nonuniformity 17 n.
multiformity 82 n.
transience 109 n.
fitfulness 137 n.
changeableness
147 n.
inattention 451 n.
unreliability 469 n.
ideality 508 n.
will 590 n.
irresolution 596 n.

tergiversation
598 n.
tergiversator 598 n.
caprice 599 n.
affectation 845 n.
liking 854 n.
love 882 n.

**capricious**
nonuniform 17 adj.
multiform 82 adj.
unconformable
84 adj.
transient 109 adj.
fitful 137 adj.
changeable
138 adj.
changeful 147 adj.
weak 158 adj.
light-minded
451 adj.
unreliable 469 adj.
crazy 498 adj.
unexpected
503 adj.
irresolute 596 adj.
tergiversating
598 adj.
capricious 599 adj.
excitable 817 adj.
witty 834 adj.
ridiculous 844 adj.
loving 882 adj.

**capricious, be**
change 138 vb.
vary 147 vb.
be capricious
599 vb.
improvise 604 vb.

**capriciously**
capriciously
599 adv.

**capsular**
capsular 189 adj.

**captive**
imprisoned
742 adj.
captive 745 adj.

## card game

card game 832 n.

**cardiovascular disease**

cardiovascular disease 646 n.

**careful**

slow 273 adj.
attentive 450 adj.
careful 452 adj.
intelligent 493 adj.
cautious 853 adj.
trustworthy 924 adj.

**careful, be**

be attentive 450 vb.
be careful 452 vb.
expect 502 vb.
be warned 659 vb.
be active 673 vb.
be cautious 853 vb.

**carefully**

carefully 452 adv.

**carefulness**

carefulness 452 n.

**caress**

be near 195 vb.
surround 225 vb.
circumscribe 227 vb.
enclose 230 vb.
strike 274 vb.
approach 284 vb.
rub 328 vb.
touch 373 vb.
gesticulate 542 vb.
please 821 vb.
relieve 826 vb.
greet 879 vb.
excite love 882 vb.
love 882 vb.
caress 884 vb.
flatter 920 vb.

**caressing**

caressing 884 adj.

**carriage**

carriage 269 n.

**carrier**

transferrer 267 n.
carrier 268 n.
courier 524 n.

**carry**

transfer 267 vb.
carry 268 vb.

**carry out**

carry out 720 vb.

**carry through**

make complete 54 vb.
terminate 69 vb.
go on 141 vb.
be vigorous 169 vb.
arrive 290 vb.
be resolute 594 vb.
persevere 595 vb.
be instrumental 623 vb.
perfect 641 vb.
mature 664 vb.
do 671 vb.
carry through 720 vb.
succeed 722 vb.

**cart**

cart 269 n.
follower 279 n.
traction 283 n.

**case**

case 189 n.
treasury 794 n.

**cash down**

cash down 799 adv.

**casual**

extrinsic 6 adj.
irrelevant 10 adj.
accompanying 89 vb.
casual 154 adj.
unintentional 613 adj.

**casus belli**

casus belli 704 n.

**cat**

cat 360 n.

hunter 614 n.

**caterer**

caterer 628 n.

**Catholic**

Catholic 970 n.
church party 972 n.

**Catholicism**

Catholicism 970 n.

**cattle**

beast of burden 268 n.
cattle 360 n.
animal husbandry 364 n.

**cattle pen**

enclosure 230 n.
cattle pen 364 n.

**cauldron**

cauldron 189 n.

**causal**

causal 151 adj.
influential 173 adj.
instrumental 623 adj.

**causally**

causally 151 adv.

**causal means**

causal means 151 n.

**causation**

causation 151 n.

**cause**

relativeness 9 n.
auspicate 68 vb.
specify 80 vb.
accompany 89 vb.
modify 138 vb.
happen 149 vb.
cause 151 n.
cause 151 vb.
producer 159 n.
produce 159 vb.
operate 168 vb.
influence 173 vb.
promote 280 vb.
reasons 470 n.
lurk 518 vb.
will 590 vb.

predetermine 603 vb.
motivator 607 n.
motive 607 n.
induce 607 vb.
instrumentality 623 n.
be instrumental 623 vb.
be instrumental 623 vb.

**caused**

caused 152 adj.

**cause desire**

await 502 vb.
cause desire 854 vb.
excite love 882 vb.

**cause discontent**

disappoint 504 vb.
displease 822 vb.
cause discontent 824 vb.
sadden 829 vb.

**cause dislike**

repel 287 vb.
be unpalatable 386 vb.
dissuade 608 vb.
displease 822 vb.
cause discontent 824 vb.
be tedious 833 vb.
cause dislike 856 vb.
sate 858 vb.
excite hate 883 vb.
huff 886 vb.
incur blame 919 vb.

**cause doubt**

be unlikely 467 vb.
puzzle 469 vb.
cause doubt 481 vb.
be unintelligible 512 vb.
dissuade 608 vb.

be wonderful
          859 vb.
defame 921 vb.
**cause feeling**
cause feeling
          369 vb.
itch 373 n.
**causeless**
causeless 154 adj.
**cause thought**
cause thought
          444 vb.
**caution**
delay 131 n.
slowness 273 n.
attention 450 n.
carefulness 452 n.
foresight 505 n.
unwillingness
          593 n.
irresolution 596 n.
protection 655 n.
security 762 n.
cowardice 851 n.
caution 853 n.
**cautionary**
predicting 506 adj.
informative
          519 adj.
dissuasive 608 adj.
cautionary 659 adj.
advising 686 adj.
**cautious**
late 131 adj.
quiescent 261 adj.
slow 273 adj.
vigilant 452 adj.
doubting 469 adj.
foreseeing 505 adj.
taciturn 577 adj.
unwilling 593 adj.
warned 659 adj.
nervous 849 adj.
cowardly 851 adj.
cautious 853 adj.
**cautious, be**
set off 31 vb.

move slowly
          273 vb.
gaze 433 vb.
be careful 452 vb.
make certain
          468 vb.
be wise 493 vb.
foresee 505 vb.
be irresolute
          596 vb.
seek safety 655 vb.
be nervous 849 vb.
be cowardly
          851 vb.
be cautious 853 vb.
**cautiously**
cautiously 853 adv.
**cavalry**
rider 263 n.
warhorse 268 n.
war chariot 269 n.
cavalry 717 n.
**cavity**
receptacle 189 n.
depth 206 n.
head 208 n.
cavity 250 n.
furrow 257 n.
opening 258 n.
orifice 258 n.
tunnel 258 n.
lowering 306 n.
**cease**
end 69 vb.
time 112 n.
cease 140 vb.
be unproductive
          167 vb.
be quiescent
          261 vb.
depart 291 vb.
be taciturn 577 vb.
relinquish 616 vb.
stop using 669 vb.
not act 672 vb.
be inactive 674 vb.
resist 710 vb.

make peace
          714 vb.
fail 723 vb.
revolt 733 vb.
deprecate 757 vb.
sell 788 vb.
**celebrate**
rampage 61 vb.
remind 500 vb.
make important
          633 vb.
triumph 722 vb.
be cheerful 828 vb.
rejoice 830 vb.
celebrate 871 vb.
be hospitable
          877 vb.
greet 879 vb.
pay one's respects
          879 vb.
congratulate
          881 vb.
forgive 904 vb.
respect 915 vb.
applaud 918 vb.
**celebration**
procession 71 n.
assemblage 74 n.
assembly 74 n.
arrival 290 n.
reception 294 n.
feasting 296 n.
reminder 500 n.
gesture 542 n.
oration 574 n.
victory 722 n.
trophy 724 n.
merriment 828 n.
rejoicing 830 n.
amusement 832 n.
dignification 861 n.
formality 870 n.
pageant 870 n.
celebration 871 n.
congratulation
          881 n.
thanks 902 n.
applause 918 n.

holy day 982 n.
rite 982 n.
**celebratory**
celebratory
          871 adj.
**celestial**
celestial 316 adj.
**celibacy**
celibacy 890 n.
**celibate**
unit 88 n.
celibate 890 adj.
virgin 945 n.
monk 980 n.
**cellar**
cellar 189 n.
depth 206 n.
base 209 n.
hiding-place 522 n.
storage 627 n.
sink 644 n.
**cellular**
cellular 189 adj.
**cemetery**
death 356 n.
cemetery 359 n.
holy place 984 n.
**censure**
list 87 n.
ridicule 846 n.
slur 862 n.
censure 919 n.
**central**
median 30 adj.
middle 70 adj.
interior 219 adj.
central 220 adj.
neutral 620 adj.
undeviating
          620 adj.
important 633 adj.
**centrality**
centrality 220 n.
**centralize**
centralize 220 vb.
**centrally**
centrally 220 adv.

## centre
essential part 5 n.
middle point 30 n.
middle 70 n.
focus 76 n.
centre 220 n.
partition 226 n.
objective 612 n.
chief thing 633 n.

## cereals
cereals 296 n.

## certain
future 119 adj.
unchangeable
    148 adj.
impending 150 adj.
evidential 461 adj.
probable 466 adj.
certain 468 adj.
rational 470 adj.
demonstrated
    473 adj.
believing 480 adj.
known 485 adj.
true 489 adj.
expectant 502 adj.
intelligible 511 adj.
manifest 517 adj.
necessary 591 adj.
successful 722 adj.
hoping 847 adj.

## certain, be
assume 466 vb.
be certain 468 vb.
believe 480 vb.
assent 483 vb.
know 485 vb.
expect 502 vb.
understand 511 vb.
take a pledge
    759 vb.

## certainly
positively 32 adv.
certainly 468 adv.

## certain quantity
certain quantity
    100 n.

## certainty
destiny 150 n.
evidence 461 n.
probability 466 n.
certainty 468 n.
demonstration
    473 n.
discovery 479 n.
belief 480 n.
expectation 502 n.
foresight 505 n.
intelligibility 511 n.
safety 655 n.
easy thing 696 n.
hope 847 n.

## cessation
end 69 n.
finality 69 n.
discontinuity 72 n.
cessation 140 n.
quiescence 261 n.
deliverance 663 n.
inactivity 674 n.
peace 712 n.

## chamber
flat 187 n.
retreat 187 n.
chamber 189 n.
storage 627 n.
refuge 657 n.
monastery 980 n.

## chance
extrinsicality 6 n.
concomitant 89 n.
opportunity 132 n.
changeable thing
    147 n.
event 149 n.
happen 149 vb.
chance 154 n.
chance 154 vb.
probability 466 n.
uncertainty 469 n.
fate 591 n.
gambling 613 n.
nondesign 613 n.
prosperity 725 n.
misfortune 726 n.

## change
difference 15 n.
differ 15 vb.
make unlike 19 vb.
be unequal 29 vb.
fitfulness 137 n.
change 138 n.
change 138 vb.
transition 142 n.
be turned to
    142 vb.
changeableness
    147 n.
vary 147 vb.
motion 260 n.
qualification 463 n.

## changeable
changeable
    138 adj.
converted 142 adj.
changeful 147 adj.

## changeableness
changeableness
    147 n.

## changeable thing
changeable thing
    147 n.
waverer 596 n.
tergiversator 598 n.

## changeably
changeably
    147 adv.

## changed person
changed person
    142 n.

## changeful
changeful 147 adj.

## change hands
change hands
    775 vb.

## changeling. See
## young creature
child 127 n.

## character
character 5 n.
sort 77 n.
speciality 80 n.
form 238 n.

affections 812 n.

## characteristic
characteristic 5 adj.
distinctive 15 adj.
special 80 adj.

## charge
be violent 171 vb.
collide 274 vb.
pursue 614 vb.
charge 707 n.
give battle 713 vb.
be courageous
    850 vb.

## charitable, be
be charitable
    896 vb.

## chase
pedestrianism
    262 n.
following 279 n.
killing 357 n.
cry 403 n.
objective 612 n.
chase 614 n.
sport 832 n.

## chat
rumour 524 n.
chat 579 n.

## chatter
empty talk 510 n.
chatter 576 n.
chat 579 n.

## chatterer
chatterer 576 n.

## cheap
inferior 35 adj.
spurious 537 adj.
trivial 634 adj.
cheap 807 adj.

## cheap, be
be cheap 807 vb.

## cheapen
abate 37 vb.
underestimate
    478 vb.
make useless
    636 vb.
impair 650 vb.

sell 788 vb.
demonetize 792 vb.
discount 805 vb.
cheapen 807 vb.
**cheaply**
cheaply 807 adv.
**cheapness**
cheapness 807 n.
**cheer**
invigorate 169 vb.
excite 816 vb.
please 821 vb.
content 823 vb.
relieve 826 vb.
cheer 828 vb.
amuse 832 vb.
give hope 847 vb.
give courage
850 vb.
pity 900 vb.
**cheerful**
content 823 adj.
cheerful 828 adj.
**cheerful, be**
be pleased 819 vb.
be relieved 826 vb.
be cheerful 828 vb.
rejoice 830 vb.
amuse oneself
832 vb.
hope 847 vb.
**cheerfully**
cheerfully 828 adv.
**cheerfulness**
cheerfulness 828 n.
**cheering**
pleasurable
821 adj.
cheering 828 adj.
**cheerless**
unpleasant 822 adj.
cheerless 829 adj.
unpromising
848 adj.
**chequer**
blackness 423 n.
chequer 432 n.
pattern 839 n.

**chew**
cut 46 vb.
rend 46 vb.
chew 296 vb.
pulverize 327 vb.
**chief part**
main part 32 n.
chief part 52 n.
size 190 n.
**chief thing**
essential part 5 n.
chief part 52 n.
chief thing 633 n.
**child**
child 127 n.
descendant 165 n.
posterity 165 n.
dwarf 191 n.
**children's games**
children's games
832 n.
**chilly**
chilly 375 adj.
**chimney**
chimney 258 n.
air pipe 348 n.
furnace 378 n.
**choice**
superiority 34 n.
separation 46 n.
part 53 n.
precedence 64 n.
opportunity 132 n.
discrimination
458 n.
will 590 n.
willingness 592 n.
choice 600 n.
means 624 n.
chief thing 633 n.
independence
739 n.
liking 854 n.
love 882 n.
**choiceless**
choiceless 601 adj.
**choir**
choir 408 n.

church officer
980 n.
**choose**
will 590 vb.
be willing 592 vb.
choose 600 vb.
desire 854 vb.
be fastidious
857 vb.
**choosing**
choosing 600 adj.
**chosen**
superior 34 adj.
separate 46 adj.
future 119 adj.
fated 591 adj.
voluntary 592 adj.
chosen 600 adj.
excellent 639 adj.
beautiful 836 adj.
approved 918 adj.
**Christendom**
Christendom 970 n.
the church 979 n.
**Christian rite**
immersion 298 n.
moistening 336 n.
nomenclature
556 n.
wedding 889 n.
penitence 934 n.
Christian rite 982 n.
**chromatics**
chromatics 420 n.
**chronicler**
chronicler 544 n.
**chronological**
chronological
112 adj.
**chronologist**
chronologist 112 n.
**chronology**
directory 87 n.
date 104 n.
chronology 112 n.
reference book
584 n.

**chronometry**
chronometry 112 n.
**chum**
male 367 n.
chum 875 n.
**church**
meeting place
187 n.
church 984 n.
**church exterior**
high structure
204 n.
vertex 208 n.
church exterior
984 n.
**church interior**
compartment
189 n.
seat 213 n.
window 258 n.
church interior
984 n.
**churchlike**
churchlike 984 adj.
**church member**
church member
970 n.
pietist 979 n.
worshipper 975 n.
worshipper 975 n.
laity 981 n.
lay person 981 n.
**church ministry**
church ministry
979 n.
**church office**
degree 27 n.
church office
979 n.
**church officer**
officer 736 n.
servant 737 n.
church officer
980 n.
lay person 981 n.
**church party**
church party 972 n.

**church service**
church service
　public worship
　　　　975 n.
　church service
　　　　982 n.

**church, the**
the church 979 n.

**church title**
church title 980 n.

**church utensil**
church utensil
　　　　984 n.

**cinema**
motion 260 n.
spectator 436 n.
optical device
　　　　437 n.
cinema 440 n.
broadcast 526 n.
photography 546 n.
drama 589 n.
stage play 589 n.
theatre 589 n.
place of amusement
　　　　832 n.

**circle**
lamina 202 n.
surround 225 vb.
outline 228 n.
circle 245 n.
go round 245 vb.
traverse 262 vb.
navigate 264 vb.
fly 266 vb.
circle 309 vb.
rotate 310 vb.
circuit 621 vb.
circuit 621 vb.
change hands
　　　　775 vb.
jewellery 839 n.

**circler**
circler 309 n.

**circuit**
run on 71 vb.
deviation 277 n.
circuition 309 n.
circle 309 vb.

route 619 n.
circuit 621 n.
circuit 621 vb.

**circuition**
circuition 309 n.

**circuitous**
circumjacent
　　　　225 adj.
labyrinthine
　　　　246 adj.
deviating 277 adj.
circuitous 309 adj.

**circularity**
circularity 245 n.
rotundity 247 n.

**circumjacent**
circumjacent
　　　　225 adj.

**circumscribe**
set apart 46 vb.
exclude 57 vb.
make smaller
　　　　193 vb.
surround 225 vb.
circumscribe
　　　　227 vb.
outline 228 vb.
enclose 230 vb.
limit 231 vb.
close 259 vb.
approach 284 vb.
converge 288 vb.
insert 298 vb.
circle 309 vb.
safeguard 655 vb.
obstruct 697 vb.
defend 708 vb.
restrain 742 vb.
prohibit 752 vb.

**circumscribed**
circumscribed
　　　　227 adj.

**circumscription**
circumscription
　　　　227 n.

**circumstance**
state 7 n.
circumstance 8 n.

relation 9 n.
degree 27 n.
affairs 149 n.
influence 173 n.
world 316 n.
topic 447 n.
evidence 461 n.

**circumstantial**
circumstantial
　　　　8 adj.
relative 9 adj.

**city**
city 179 n.
housing 187 n.

**civilization**
civilization 649 n.

**claim**
demand 732 vb.
request 756 n.
possess 768 vb.
appropriate 781 vb.
desire 854 vb.
claim 910 vb.
litigate 954 vb.

**class**
eliminate 44 vb.
class 62 vb.
group 74 n.
number with 78 vb.
class 533 n.

**classification**
degree 27 n.
arrangement 62 n.
series 71 n.
classification 77 n.
generality 79 n.
identification
　　　　542 n.
community 703 n.
party 703 n.

**classificatory**
classificatory
　　　　77 adj.

**classroom**
classroom 534 n.
textbook 584 n.

**clean**
unmixed 44 adj.

orderly 60 adj.
unravel 62 vb.
modernized
　　　　121 adj.
new 121 adj.
displace 183 vb.
smooth 253 vb.
empty 295 vb.
rub 328 vb.
aerate 335 vb.
drench 336 vb.
touch 373 vb.
make bright
　　　　412 vb.
white 422 adj.
whiten 427 vb.
plain 568 adj.
clean 643 adj.
clean 643 vb.
salubrious 647 adj.
sanitate 647 vb.
make better
　　　　649 vb.
restore 651 vb.
refresh 680 vb.
disencumber
　　　　696 vb.
decorate 839 vb.
honourable
　　　　924 adj.
innocent 930 adj.
pure 945 adj.

**cleaner**
cleaner 643 n.
worker 681 n.
servant 737 n.

**cleaning cloth**
cleaning cloth
　　　　643 n.

**cleaning utensil**
cleaning utensil
　　　　643 n.

**cleanness**
cleanness 643 n.

**cleanser**
lubricant 329 n.
air 335 n.
fat 352 n.

cleanser 643 n.
prophylactic 653 n.
cosmetic 838 n.
**cleansing**
cleansing 643 n.
cleansing 643 adj.
**clergy**
questioner 454 n.
pietist 973 n.
worshipper 975 n.
clergy 980 n.
**cleric**
cleric 980 n.
**clerical**
ecclesiastical
            979 adj.
clerical 980 adj.
vestured 989 adj.
**clerical dress.**
    **dress**
uniform 223 n.
**clerically**
clerically 980 adv.
**climax**
culminate 34 vb.
augment 36 vb.
be complete 54 vb.
be high 204 vb.
crown 208 vb.
mature 664 vb.
climax 720 n.
**climb**
progress 280 vb.
climb 303 vb.
**climber**
traveller 263 n.
climber 303 n.
**cloak**
wrapping 221 n.
cloak 223 n.
screen 416 n.
disguise 522 n.
canonicals 989 n.
**clock time**
date 104 n.
clock time 112 n.
**close**
join 45 vb.

become small
            193 vb.
make smaller
            193 vb.
close 259 n.
impel 274 vb.
lower 306 vb.
staunch 345 vb.
screen 416 vb.
repair 651 vb.
obstruct 697 vb.
**closed**
contracted 193 adj.
closed 259 adj.
retentive 773 adj.
**close friend**
close friend 875 n.
loved one 882 n.
**closure**
joining together
            45 n.
fastening 47 n.
stop 140 n.
contraction 193 n.
interjection 226 n.
barrier 230 n.
closure 259 n.
difficulty 695 n.
hindrance 697 n.
**clothier**
clothier 223 n.
**clothing**
clothing 223 n.
badge 542 n.
finery 839 n.
**cloud**
accumulation 74 n.
powder 327 n.
gas 331 n.
vaporization 333 n.
water 334 n.
air 335 n.
moisture 336 n.
cloud 350 n.
cloud 350 vb.
dimness 414 n.
opacity 418 n.

**cloudy**
humid 336 adj.
cloudy 350 adj.
dim 414 adj.
semitransparent
            419 adj.
**club**
club 718 n.
scourge 959 n.
**clumsy**
unapt 25 adj.
unequal 29 adj.
unwieldy 190 adj.
slow 273 adj.
rigid 321 adj.
tactual 373 adj.
mistaken 490 adj.
unintelligent
            494 adj.
inexpedient
            638 adj.
bad 640 adj.
clumsy 690 adj.
ill-bred 842 adj.
ridiculous 844 adj.
**clumsy, be**
neglect 453 vb.
blunder 490 vb.
impair 650 vb.
be clumsy 690 vb.
**coal**
coal 380 n.
**coastal**
coastal 339 adj.
**coat**
laminate 202 vb.
coat 221 n.
line 222 vb.
smooth 253 vb.
make opaque
            418 vb.
colour 420 vb.
paint 548 vb.
decorate 839 vb.
be ostentatious
            870 vb.
**code of duty**
code of duty 912 n.

**cognize**
cognize 442 vb.
**cohere**
unite with 45 vb.
cohere 48 vb.
concur 176 vb.
be contiguous
            197 vb.
transfer 267 vb.
be dense 319 vb.
thicken 349 vb.
**coherence**
joining together
            45 n.
union 45 n.
adhesive 47 n.
coherence 48 n.
arrangement 62 n.
unity 88 n.
contiguity 197 n.
density 319 n.
toughness 324 n.
viscidity 349 n.
**cohesive**
cohesive 48 adj.
**cohesively**
cohesively 48 adv.
**coil**
edging 229 n.
coil 246 n.
circuition 309 n.
difficulty 695 n.
hairdressing 838 n.
pattern 839 n.
**coiled**
coiled 246 adj.
**coinage**
small coin 33 n.
coinage 792 n.
**coition**
coition 45 n.
**cold**
wintry 124 adj.
cold 375 adj.
cooled 377 adj.
screened 416 adj.
refreshing 680 adj.
inimical 876 adj.

miniature 191 n.
contraction 193 n.
shortening 199 n.
translation 515 n.
conciseness 564 n.
edition 504 n.
description 585 n.
dissertation 586 n.
compendium
587 n.

**compensate**
correlate 12 vb.
adjust 24 vb.
equalize 28 vb.
compensate 31 vb.
make complete
54 vb.
weigh 317 vb.

**compensation**
compensation 31 n.

**compensatory**
compensatory
31 adj.

**complete**
consummate
32 adj.
whole 52 adj.
complete 54 adj.
revolutionary
144 adj.
destructive 160 adj.
long 198 adj.
symmetrical
240 adj.
sufficient 630 adj.
completed 720 adj.

**complete, be**
be complete 54 vb.
comprise 78 vb.
carry 268 vb.
superabound
632 vb.

**completed**
completed 720 adj.

**completely**
completely 54 adv.

**completeness**
completeness 54 n.

**completion**
completion 720 n.

**completive**
completive 720 adj.

**complex**
complex 61 adj.
crossed 217 adj.
intricate 246 adj.
uncertain 469 adj.
unclear 563 adj.

**complexity**
complexity 61 n.

**component**
intrinsic 5 adj.
adjunct 40 n.
tincture 43 n.
part 53 n.
component 58 n.
included 78 adj.
accompanying
89 adj.
contents 188 n.
element 314 n.
machine 625 n.
aider 698 n.
society 703 n.

**compose**
mix 43 vb.
combine 50 vb.
make complete
54 vb.
compose 56 vb.
arrange 62 vb.
bring together
74 vb.
be included 78 vb.
produce 159 vb.

**compose music**
compose 56 vb.
harmonize 405 vb.
compose music
408 vb.

**composing**
composing 56 adj.

**composition**
joining together
45 n.

compound 50 n.
composition 56 n.
order 60 n.
arrangement 62 n.
accumulation 74 n.
assemblage 74 n.
inclusion 78 n.
product 159 n.
structure 326 n.

**compound**
compound 50 n.

**comprehensive**
comprehensive
52 adj.
inclusive 78 adj.
general 79 adj.

**compression**
compression 193 n.

**compressive**
compressive
193 adj.

**compressor**
ligature 47 n.
compressor 193 n.
stopper 259 n.

**comprise**
join 45 vb.
contain 56 vb.
comprise 78 vb.
be general 79 vb.
hold within 219 vb.
possess 768 vb.

**compromise**
correlation 12 n.
adaptation 24 n.
middle point 30 n.
average out 30 vb.
offset 31 n.
set off 31 vb.
arrangement 62 n.
substitute 145 n.
substitute 145 vb.
interchange
146 n.
moderation 172 n.
be irresolute
596 vb.
way 619 n.

middle way 620 n.
be halfway 620 vb.
cooperation 701 n.
pacification 714 n.
pacify 714 vb.
laxity 729 n.
be lax 729 vb.
consent 753 n.
compact 760 n.
contract 760 n.
make terms 761 vb.
compromise 765 n.
**compromise**
765 vb.
be patient 818 vb.
atonement 936 n.

**compulsion**
uniformity 16 n.
assemblage 74 n.
cause 151 n.
power 155 n.
necessity 591 n.
resolution 594 n.
no choice 601 n.
labour 677 n.
pacification 714 n.
brute force 730 n.
command 732 n.
compulsion 735 n.
service 740 n.
restraint 742 n.
restriction 742 n.
request 756 n.
conditions 761 n.
tax 804 n.

**computerize**
computerize 86 vb.

**computerized**
computerized
86 adj.

**concave**
cellular 189 adj.
low 205 adj.
concave 250 adj.

**concave, be**
be concave 250 vb.

**concavity**
concavity 250 n.

**conceal**
make unlike 19 vb.
imitate 20 vb.
contain 56 vb.
modify 138 vb.
transform 142 vb.
suppress 160 vb.
cover 221 vb.
screen 416 vb.
be unseen 439 vb.
disappear 441 vb.
neglect 453 vb.
mislead 490 vb.
conceal 520 vb.
dissemble 536 vb.
obliterate 545 vb.
store 627 vb.
safeguard 655 vb.
defend 708 vb.
be cautious 853 vb.

**concealed**
concealed 520 adj.

**concealment**
concealment 520 n.

**conceitedly**
conceitedly
    868 adv.

**concerning**
concerning 9 adv.

**concise**
brief 109 adj.
short 199 adj.
aphoristic 491 adj.
concise 564 adj.
taciturn 577 adj.
compendious
    587 adj.
ungracious 880 adj.

**concise, be**
shorten 199 vb.
be concise 564 vb.
be taciturn 577 vb.
abstract 587 vb.

**concisely**
concisely 564 adv.

**conciseness**
conciseness 564 n.

**concomitant**
concomitant 89 n.

**concord**
agreement 24 n.
a mixture 43 n.
combination 50 n.
completeness 54 n.
order 60 n.
consensus 483 n.
cooperation 701 n.
concord 705 n.
concord 705 n.
peace 712 n.
friendliness 875 n.
friendship 875 n.

**concordant**
concordant
    705 adj.

**concur**
accompany 89 vb.
concur 176 vb.
concord 705 vb.

**concurrence**
concurrence 176 n.

**concurrent**
conjunctive 45 adj.
combined 50 adj.
accompanying
    89 adj.
concurrent 176 adj.

**concurrently**
concurrently
    176 adv.

**condemn**
kill 357 vb.
confute 474 vb.
judge 475 vb.
curse 894 vb.
blame 919 vb.
disprise 919 vb.
condemn 956 vb.
punish 958 vb.
declare heretical
    971 vb.

**condemnation**
condemnation
    956 n.

**condemned**
condemned
    956 adj.

**condensation**
increase 36 n.
union 45 n.
coherence 48 n.
contraction 193 n.
centrality 220 n.
condensation
    319 n.
thickening 349 n.
refrigeration 377 n.

**condiment**
tincture 43 n.
food 296 n.
potherb 296 n.
pungency 383 n.
condiment 384 n.
scent 391 n.
preserver 661 n.

**conditional**
qualifying 463 adj.
uncertain 469 adj.
conditional
    761 adj.

**conditionally**
conditionally 7 adv.

**conditions**
arrangement 62 n.
period 106 n.
qualification 463 n.
certainty 468 n.
supposition 507 n.
intention 612 n.
requirement 622 n.
mandate 746 n.
compact 760 n.
conditions 761 n.

**condolence**
lament 831 n.
condolence 900 n.

**conduce**
conduce 151 vb.

**conduct**
gait 260 n.
mien 440 n.
practice 605 n.
action 671 n.
conduct 683 n.
etiquette 843 n.

**conduct. See route**

**conduit**
filament 203 n.
cavity 250 n.
furrow 257 n.
tube 258 n.
way in 292 n.
outlet 293 n.
passage 300 n.
water 334 n.
irrigator 336 n.
current 345 n.
conduit 346 n.
access 619 n.
route 619 n.

**cone**
cone 247 n.
tunnel 258 n.

**confer**
argue 470 vb.
confer 579 vb.
consult 686 vb.
make terms 761 vb.

**conference**
assembly 74 n.
listening 410 n.
enquiry 454 n.
class 533 n.
conference 579 n.
advice 686 n.
council 687 n.
cooperation 701 n.
mediation 715 n.

**confess**
hear 410 vb.
testify 461 vb.
assent 483 vb.
inform 519 vb.
confess 521 vb.
affirm 527 vb.
be truthful 535 vb.
accuse 923 vb.
be guilty 931 vb.
be penitent 934 vb.

be in difficulty
695 vb.
oppose 699 vb.
resist 710 vb.
contend 711 vb.
give battle 713 vb.
offer oneself
754 vb.

**contender**
compeer 28 n.
athlete 157 n.
pedestrian 263 n.
rider 263 n.
incomer 292 n.
respondent 455 n.
testee 456 n.
trier 666 n.
hinderer 697 n.
opposites 699 n.
opponent 700 n.
quarreller 704 n.
contender 711 n.
combatant 717 n.
combatant 717 n.
petitioner 758 n.
player 832 n.
enemy 876 n.

**contending**
contending
711 adj.

**content**
fill 54 vb.
quiescent 261 adj.
euphoria 371 n.
comfortable
371 adj.
sufficiency 630 n.
filled 630 adj.
suffice 630 vb.
reposeful 678 adj.
pacificatory
714 adj.
pacify 714 vb.
consent 753 vb.
inexcitability 818 n.
inexcitable 818 adj.
enjoyment 819 n.
pleased 819 adj.

please 821 vb.
content 823 n.
content 823 adj.
content 823 n.
cheerfulness 828 n.
cheer 828 vb.
approbation 918 n.
approving 918 adj.

**content, be**
be complete 54 vb.
have enough
630 vb.
be content 823 vb.
be relieved 826 vb.

**contentedly**
contentedly
823 adv.

**contenting**
contenting 823 adj.

**contention**
contention 711 n.

**contents**
finite quantity 26 n.
great quantity 32 n.
component 58 n.
bunch 74 n.
contents 188 n.
insides 219 n.
thing transferred
267 n.
property 772 n.
merchandise 790 n.

**contest**
athletics 157 n.
short distance
195 n.
equitation 262 n.
traction 283 n.
arrival 290 n.
contest 711 n.
sport 832 n.

**contiguity**
contiguity 197 n.

**contiguous**
near 195 adj.
contiguous 197 adj.

**contiguous, be**
extend 178 vb.

be near 195 vb.
be contiguous
197 vb.
touch 373 vb.

**contiguously**
contiguously
197 adv.

**continuance**
continuance 141 n.

**continue**
continue 71 vb.
continue 104 vb.
sustain 141 vb.

**continuing**
continuing 104 adj.

**continuity**
uniformity 16 n.
coherence 48 n.
order 60 n.
arrangement 62 n.
sequence 65 n.
continuity 71 n.
accompaniment
89 n.
recurrence 102 n.
perpetuity 110 n.
frequency 134 n.
periodicity 136 n.
continuance 141 n.
production 159 n.
space 178 n.
contiguity 197 n.
motion 260 n.
progression 280 n.
noncompletion
721 n.

**continuous**
increasing 36 adj.
sequential 65 adj.
continuous 71 adj.
perpetual 110 adj.
periodical 136 adj.
unceasing 141 adj.
contiguous 197 adj.
uncompleted
721 adj.

**continuously**
continuously
71 adv.

**contraception**
contraception
167 n.
drug 653 n.
hindrance 697 n.

**contract**
assent 483 vb.
promise 759 vb.
contract 760 vb.
make terms 761 vb.
bargain 786 vb.

**contracted**
contracted 193 adj.

**contraction**
smallness 33 n.
decrease 37 n.
diminution 37 n.
contraction 193 n.
narrowing 201 n.

**contractual**
agreeing 24 adj.
contractual
760 adj.

**contraposition**
contraposition
235 n.

**contrariety**
contrariety 14 n.

**contrarily**
contrarily 14 adv.

**contrary**
unrelated 10 adj.
contrary 14 adj.
different 15 adj.
nonuniform 17 adj.
disagreeing 25 adj.
separate 46 adj.
unconformable
84 adj.
counteracting
177 adj.
inverted 216 adj.
opposite 235 adj.
discordant 406 adj.

**correspond.** See
**inform**
rumour 524 n.

**corroborate**
corroborate 461 vb.
make certain
468 vb.
demonstrate
473 vb.
be true 489 vb.
affirm 527 vb.
swear 527 vb.
give security
762 vb.

**cosmetic**
water 334 n.
unguent 352 n.
scent 391 n.
pigment 420 n.
red pigment 426 n.
balm 653 n.
cosmetic 838 n.

**cosmic**
cosmic 316 adj.

**cosmography**
cosmography
316 n.

**cost**
cost 804 n.
cost 804 vb.

**council**
assembly 74 n.
seniority 126 n.
director 685 n.
advice 686 n.
adviser 686 n.
council 687 n.
corporation 703 n.
consignee 749 n.
jurisdiction 950 n.
tribunal 951 n.
synod 985 n.
church exterior
984 n.

**councillor**
official 685 n.
councillor 687 n.

**counteract**
be contrary 14 vb.
set off 31 vb.
disable 156 vb.
weaken 158 vb.
assuage 172 vb.
influence 173 vb.
counteract 177 vb.
be opposite
235 vb.
recoil 275 vb.
tell against 462 vb.
be obstructive
697 vb.
oppose 699 vb.

**counteracting**
counteracting
177 adj.

**counteraction**
counteraction
177 n.

**counterevidence**
counterevidence
462 n.

**countervailing**
countervailing
462 adj.

**counting
instrument**
counting instrument
86 n.

**country-dweller**
country-dweller
864 n.

**coupling**
coupling 47 n.

**courage**
vigorousness
169 n.
resolution 594 n.
stamina 595 n.
safety 655 n.
defiance 706 n.
courage 850 n.
rashness 852 n.
disinterestedness
926 n.
drunkenness 944 n.

**courageous**
manly 157 adj.
defiant 706 adj.
courageous
850 adj.
worshipful 861 adj.
proud 866 adj.
disinterested
926 adj.

**courageous, be**
face danger
656 vb.
undertake 667 vb.
be courageous
850 vb.

**courier**
rider 263 n.
traveller 263 n.
bearer 268 n.
speeder 272 n.
courier 524 n.
servant 737 n.

**course of time**
time 104 n.
course of time
107 n.
conversion 142 n.
affairs 149 n.
destroyer 163 n.
progression 280 n.

**court**
approach 284 n.
gaze 433 vb.
pursue 614 vb.
request 756 vb.
desire 854 vb.
befriend 875 vb.
be in love 882 vb.
excite love 882 vb.
court 884 vb.
wed 889 vb.

**courteous**
attentive 450 adj.
well-bred 843 adj.
humble 867 adj.
sociable 877 adj.
courteous 879 adj.
benevolent 892 adj.

respectful 915 adj.
disinterested
926 adj.

**courteous act**
arrival 290 n.
valediction 291 n.
obeisance 306 n.
friendliness 875 n.
sociability 877 n.
courteous act
879 n.
respects 915 n.

**courteous, be**
consent 753 vb.
honour 861 vb.
be humble 867 vb.
be courteous
879 vb.

**courteously**
courteously
879 adv.

**courtesy**
obeisance 306 n.
conduct 683 n.
inexcitability 818 n.
good taste 841 n.
etiquette 843 n.
humility 867 n.
friendliness 875 n.
sociability 877 n.
courtesy 879 n.
respect 915 n.
disinterestedness
926 n.

**courtroom**
courtroom 951 n.

**cover**
fill 54 vb.
load 188 vb.
expand 192 vb.
be high 204 vb.
hang 212 vb.
cover 221 vb.
line 222 vb.
dress 223 vb.
close 259 vb.
insert 298 vb.
pass 300 vb.

covered
darken 413 vb.
bedim 414 vb.
screen 416 vb.
conceal 520 vb.
repair 651 vb.

covered
covered 221 adj.

covering
adjunct 40 n.
layer 202 n.
hanging object
212 n.
textile 217 n.
covering 221 n.
stopper 259 n.
disguise 522 n.

coverlet
bed 213 n.
coverlet 221 n.
warm clothes
376 n.
cleaning cloth
643 n.

coward
weakling 158 n.
avoider 615 n.
submission 716 n.
coward 851 n.

cowardice
cowardice 851 n.

cowardly
cowardly 851 adj.

cowardly, be
be cowardly
851 vb.

crackle
crackle 397 vb.

crank
nonconformist
84 n.
nonconformist
84 n.
narrow mind 476 n.
fool 496 n.
crank 499 n.
visionary 508 n.
obstinate person
597 n.

laughingstock
846 n.

crapulence
crapulence 944 n.

crapulous
crapulous 944 adj.

crazy
obsessed 450 adj.
light-minded
451 adj.
misjudging
476 adj.
foolish 494 adj.
unintelligent
494 adj.
crazy 498 adj.
capricious 599 adj.
enamoured
882 adj.

credal
credal 480 adj.

credential
credential 461 n.

credible
plausible 466 adj.
positive 468 adj.
credible 480 adj.
orthodox 970 adj.

credibly
credibly 480 adv.

credit
means 624 n.
subvention 698 n.
lending 779 n.
lend 779 vb.
wealth 795 n.
credit 797 n.
credit 797 vb.
debt 798 n.
repute 861 n.

creditor
creditor 797 n.

credulity
belief 480 n.
credulity 482 n.
deception 537 n.
persuadability
607 n.

credulous
credulous 482 adj.

credulous, be
be credulous
482 vb.

creed
creed 480 n.
theology 967 n.
orthodoxy 970 n.

creepy-crawly
creepy-crawly
360 n.
bane 654 n.

crescendo
crescendo 36 adv.

crinkle
distort 241 vb.
make angular
242 vb.
make curved
243 vb.
crinkle 246 vb.
roughen 254 vb.
fold 256 vb.

crippled
crippled 158 adj.

crisis
juncture 8 n.
crisis 132 n.
reversion 143 n.
event 149 n.
summit 208 n.
limit 231 n.
return 281 n.
needfulness 622 n.
important matter
633 n.
danger 656 n.
predicament 695 n.
excitation 816 n.

cross
joint 45 n.
bifurcation 92 n.
quaternity 95 n.
be oblique 215 vb.
cross 217 n.
cross 217 vb.
angularity 242 n.

vestments 983 n.

crossed
crossed 217 adj.

crossing
mixture 43 n.
joining together
45 n.
joint 45 n.
union 45 n.
arrangement 62 n.
crossing 217 n.
interjacency 226 n.
angularity 242 n.
divergence 289 n.
passage 300 n.
texture 326 n.

crowd
medley 43 n.
all 52 n.
confusion 61 n.
crowd 74 n.
multitude 100 n.
redundance 632 n.
party 703 n.
rabble 864 n.

crown
culminate 34 vb.
crown 208 n.
limit 231 n.
elevate 305 vb.
perfect 641 vb.
climax 720 vb.

crowning
crowning 34 adj.

crucial
crucial 132 adj.

crucible
crucible 142 n.
testing agent
456 n.

cruel
furious 171 adj.
violent 171 adj.
murderous 357 adj.
harmful 640 adj.
warlike 713 adj.
oppressive 730 adj.

courageous
　　　850 adj.
cruel 893 adj.
pitiless 901 adj.
heinous 929 adj.
vicious 929 adj.
impenitent 935 adj.
impious 974 adj.
**cruel act**
violence 171 n.
cruel act 893 n.
guilty act 931 n.
**cry**
feel pain 372 vb.
sound 393 n.
loudness 395 n.
be loud 395 vb.
shrill 402 vb.
cry 403 n.
cry 403 vb.
voice 572 n.
voice 572 vb.
**crying**
loud 395 adj.
crying 403 adj.
**cuckold**
cuckold 947 n.
**culinary**
culinary 296 adj.
**culminate**
culminate 34 vb.
**cult**
practice 605 n.
religion 967 n.
cult 975 n.
rite 982 n.
**cultivate**
augment 36 vb.
cause 151 vb.
produce 159 vb.
generate 162 vb.
make fruitful
　　　166 vb.
invigorate 169 vb.
vegetate 361 vb.
breed stock 364 vb.
cultivate 365 vb.
store 627 vb.

make better
　　　649 vb.
mature 664 vb.
prepare 664 vb.
take 781 vb.
**culture**
culture 485 n.
education 529 n.
civilization 649 n.
**cunning**
superiority 34 n.
sagacity 493 n.
intelligent 493 adj.
wise 493 adj.
duplicity 536 n.
false 536 adj.
deception 537 n.
deceiving 537 adj.
planning 618 adj.
tactics 683 n.
skill 689 n.
cunning 693 n.
cunning 693 adj.
dishonest 925 adj.
**cunning, be**
be wise 493 vb.
deceive 537 vb.
plot 618 vb.
do 671 vb.
be cunning 693 vb.
**cunningly**
cunningly 693 adv.
**cup**
cup 189 n.
cone 247 n.
draught 296 n.
**cure**
strengthen 157 vb.
disaccustom
　　　606 vb.
make better
　　　649 vb.
cure 651 vb.
remedy 653 vb.
pacify 714 vb.
relieve 826 vb.
**curiosity**
curiosity 448 n.

attention 450 n.
enquiry 454 n.
learning 531 n.
excitation 816 n.
desire 854 n.
**curious, be**
scan 433 vb.
be curious 448 vb.
enquire 454 vb.
**current**
high water 204 n.
lowness 205 n.
direction 276 n.
progression 280 n.
return 281 n.
current 345 n.
pitfall 658 n.
**curriculum**
curriculum 529 n.
**curse**
desire 854 vb.
hate 883 vb.
curse 894 vb.
threaten 895 vb.
not respect 916 vb.
dispraise 919 vb.
reprobate 919 vb.
condemn 956 vb.
be impious 974 vb.
bewitch 977 vb.
**cursed**
hateful 883 adj.
cursed 894 adj.
**cursing**
cursing 894 adj.
**curtain**
curtain 416 n.
**curvature**
reversion 143 n.
line 198 n.
deformity 241 n.
angularity 242 n.
curvature 243 n.
convexity 248 n.
concavity 250 n.
deviation 277 n.
**curve**
part 53 n.

prop 213 n.
obliquity 215 n.
curve 243 n.
arc 245 n.
convolution 246 n.
camber 248 n.
**curved**
curved 243 adj.
arched 248 adj.
**curved, be**
be curved 243 vb.
**cushion**
cushion 213 n.
relief 826 n.
**cuss**
bicker 704 vb.
be rude 880 vb.
cuss 894 vb.
**cut**
abate 37 vb.
subtract 39 vb.
cut 46 vb.
make smaller
　　　193 vb.
shorten 199 vb.
form 238 vb.
be sharp 251 vb.
notch 255 vb.
groove 257 vb.
strike 279 vb.
chew 296 vb.
fell 306 vb.
give pain 372 vb.
wound 650 vb.
disencumber
　　　696 vb.
**cylinder**
vat 189 n.
cylinder 247 n.
rotator 310 n.

**D**

**dabbling**
dabbling 486 adj.

**dairy product**
dairy product
296 n.
**damnable**
damnable 640 adj.
**dance**
composition 56 n.
arrangement 62 n.
jumper 307 n.
leap 307 vb.
rotation 310 n.
musical piece
407 n.
ballet 589 n.
dance 832 n.
dance 832 vb.
**dancing**
dancing 832 n.
**danger**
electricity 155 n.
invisibility 439 n.
probability 466 n.
unreliability 469 n.
omen 506 n.
latency 518 n.
gambling 613 n.
danger 656 n.
pitfall 658 n.
warning 659 n.
escape 662 n.
predicament 695 n.
rashness 852 n.
threat 895 n.
**dangerous**
dangerous 656 adj.
**danger signal**
loudness 395 n.
gong 409 n.
signal light 415 n.
prediction 506 n.
signal 542 n.
dissuasion 608 n.
danger 656 n.
warning 659 n.
danger signal
660 n.
**dark**
vespertine 124 adj.

dark 413 adj.
black 423 adj.
latent 518 adj.
unclear 563 adj.
sullen 888 adj.
**dark, be**
be dark 413 vb.
**darken**
darken 413 vb.
bedim 414 vb.
blacken 423 vb.
conceal 520 vb.
depress 829 vb.
**darkling**
darkling 413 adv.
**darkness**
darkness 413 n.
**darling**
loved one 882 n.
darling 885 n.
**data processing**
data processing
86 n.
**date**
date 104 n.
**dated**
dated 104 adj.
**dawn upon**
dawn upon 444 vb.
**dead**
extinct 2 adj.
past 120 adj.
quiescent 261 adj.
dead 356 adj.
buried 359 adj.
colourless 421 adj.
nonactive 672 adj.
**dead drunk**
insensible 370 adj.
dead drunk
944 adj.
**deadly**
destructive 160 adj.
vigorous 169 adj.
deadly 357 adj.
evil 611 n.
harmful 640 adj.
toxic 648 adj.

malevolent 893 adj.
**dead, the**
the dead 356 n.
**deaf**
insensible 370 adj.
deaf 411 adj.
inattentive 451 adj.
indiscriminating
459 adj.
taciturn 577 adj.
nonactive 672 adj.
artless 694 adj.
impassive 815 adj.
**deaf, be**
be deaf 411 vb.
be inattentive
451 vb.
disregard 453 vb.
not know 486 vb.
refuse 755 vb.
**deafen**
deafen 411 vb.
**deafness**
deafness 411 n.
**deal with**
do 671 vb.
deal with 683 vb.
**dear**
destructive 160 adj.
profitless 636 adj.
harmful 640 adj.
dear 806 adj.
ostentatious
870 adj.
**dear, be**
grow 36 vb.
harm 640 vb.
be dear 806 vb.
**dearly**
dearly 806 adv.
**dearness**
dearness 806 n.
**death**
extinction 2 n.
decay 51 n.
transience 109 n.
destroyer 163 n.
quietude 261 n.

death 356 n.
evil 611 n.
capital punishment
958 n.
**death roll**
death roll 356 n.
**debauch**
unite with 45 vb.
force 171 vb.
pervert 650 vb.
shame 867 vb.
debauch 946 vb.
**debt**
requirement 622 n.
encumbrance
697 n.
promise 759 n.
borrowing 780 n.
credit 797 n.
debt 798 n.
insolvency 800 n.
dueness 910 n.
**debtor**
debtor 798 n.
**debut**
debut 68 n.
reception 294 n.
experiment 456 n.
fitting out 664 n.
attempt 666 n.
**decamp**
go away 185 vb.
decamp 291 vb.
emerge 293 vb.
disappear 441 vb.
run away 615 vb.
escape 662 vb.
hasten 675 vb.
take away 781 vb.
not pay 800 vb.
fail in duty 913 vb.
**decay**
extinction 2 n.
decay 51 n.
oldness 122 n.
destroyer 163 n.
death 356 n.
stench 392 n.

dirt 644 n.
ulcer 646 n.
dilapidation 650 n.
blight 654 n.

**decease**
end 69 n.
decease 356 n.
illness 646 n.

**deceive**
make unlike 19 vb.
imitate 20 vb.
modify 138 vb.
substitute 145 vb.
outdo 301 vb.
mislead 490 vb.
keep secret 520 vb.
misteach 530 vb.
dissemble 536 vb.
deceive 537 vb.
represent 546 vb.
relinquish 616 vb.
be cunning 693 vb.
fleece 781 vb.
defraud 783 vb.
not pay 800 vb.
flatter 920 vb.
be dishonest
                925 vb.

**deceiver**
deceiver 540 n.

**deceiving**
deceiving 537 adj.

**decelerate**
decrease 37 vb.
be moderate
                172 vb.
come to rest
                261 vb.
decelerate 273 vb.
be inactive 674 vb.

**deception**
insubstantiality 4 n.
visual fallacy 435 n.
misjudgment
                476 n.
concealment 520 n.
disguise 522 n.
falsehood 536 n.

deception 537 n.
cunning 693 n.
stratagem 693 n.
borrowing 780 n.
peculation 783 n.
pretension 845 n.
ostentation 870 n.
boast 872 n.

**deceptively**
deceptively
                537 adv.

**decipher**
decipher 515 vb.
manifest 517 vb.

**declare heretical**
declare heretical
                971 vb.

**decolorize**
decolorize 421 vb.

**decomposable**
decomposable
                51 adj.

**decompose**
simplify 44 vb.
break 46 vb.
disunite 46 vb.
separate 46 vb.
sunder 46 vb.
decompose 51 vb.
class 62 vb.
be dispersed 75 vb.
disperse 75 vb.
be old 122 vb.
make sterile
                167 vb.
become small
                193 vb.
pulverize 327 vb.
add water 334 vb.
perish 356 vb.
stink 392 vb.
be unclean 644 vb.
deteriorate 650 vb.
deteriorate 650 vb.
impair 650 vb.

**decomposed**
decomposed
                51 adj.

**decomposition**
decomposition
                51 n.

**decorate**
add 38 vb.
transform 142 vb.
coat 221 vb.
variegate 432 vb.
exaggerate 546 vb.
ornament 569 vb.
make better
                649 vb.
beautify 836 vb.
primp 838 vb.
decorate 839 vb.
dignify 861 vb.

**decoration**
decoration 724 n.

**decrease**
finite quantity 26 n.
smallness 33 n.
be small 33 vb.
decrease 37 n.
decrease 37 vb.
subtraction 39 n.
disunion 46 n.
series 71 n.
change 138 vb.
be weak 158 vb.
unproductiveness
                167 n.
be little 191 vb.
become small
                193 vb.
be quiescent
                261 vb.
recede 285 vb.
descent 304 n.
descend 304 vb.
disappear 441 vb.
waste 629 vb.
scarcity 631 n.
deterioration 650 n.
deteriorate 650 vb.
inactivity 677 n.
be inactive 674 vb.
loss 767 n.

**decreasing**
decreasing 37 adj.

**decree**
judgment 475 n.
publication 523 n.
precept 688 n.
decree 732 n.
decree 732 vb.
legislation 948 n.
make legal 948 vb.

**decrement**
decrement 42 n.

**deed**
affairs 149 n.
effect 152 n.
contrivance 618 n.
policy 618 n.
important matter
                633 n.
attempt 666 n.
deed 676 n.
labour 677 n.
conduct 683 n.
tactics 683 n.
masterpiece 689 n.
fight 711 n.
success 722 n.
prowess 850 n.
thaumaturgy 859 n.

**deep**
great 32 adj.
low 205 adj.
deep 206 adj.
oceanic 338 adj.
latent 518 adj.
concealed 520 adj.
unclear 563 adj.
felt 813 adj.
infernal 966 adj.

**deep, be**
be deep 206 vb.
founder 308 vb.

**deeply**
deeply 206 adv.

**defame**
cause doubt
                481 vb.

**defamer**
misinterpret 516 vb.
shame 862 vb.
not respect 916 vb.
dispraise 919 vb.
defame 921 vb.
accuse 923 vb.

**defamer**
defamer 921 n.

**defeat**
be superior 34 vb.
inferiority 35 n.
disperse 75 vb.
stop 140 n.
ruin 160 n.
destroy 160 vb.
propel 282 vb.
outdo 301 vb.
puzzle 469 vb.
confute 474 vb.
rejection 602 n.
victory 722 n.
defeat 722 n.
defeat 723 n.
adversity 726 n.
loss 767 n.

**defeated**
defeated 723 adj.

**defeated, be**
be defeated
723 vb.

**defecation**
defecation 297 n.

**defect**
deficit 55 n.
weakness 158 n.
evil 611 n.
insufficiency 631 n.
defect 642 n.

**defence**
offset 31 n.
exclusion 57 n.
counteraction
177 n.
repulsion 287 n.
avoidance 615 n.
plot 618 n.
protection 655 n.

defence 708 n.
resistance 710 n.
battle 713 n.
warfare 713 n.
arms 718 n.
weapon 718 n.

**defenceless**
defenceless
156 adj.

**defences**
defences 708 n.

**defend**
screen 416 vb.
safeguard 655 vb.
patronize 698 vb.
defend 708 vb.
wage war 713 vb.
vindicate 922 vb.

**defended**
defended 708 adj.

**defender**
defender 708 n.

**defending**
defending 708 adj.

**defensively**
defensively
708 adv.

**defiance**
dissent 484 n.
affirmation 527 n.
negation 528 n.
gesture 542 n.
inaction 672 n.
opposition 699 n.
dissension 704 n.
quarrelsomeness
704 n.
defiance 706 n.
war 713 n.
disobedience
733 n.
refusal 755 n.
courage 850 n.
boast 872 n.
insolence 873 n.
threat 895 n.
accusation 923 n.

**defiant**
disagreeing 25 adj.
unconformable
84 adj.
dissenting 484 adj.
undisguised
517 adj.
assertive 527 adj.
defiant 706 adj.
disobedient
733 adj.
courageous
850 adj.
insolent 873 adj.
threatening
895 adj.

**defiantly**
defiantly 706 adv.

**deficient**
small 33 adj.
inferior 35 adj.
lesser 35 adj.
subtracted 39 adj.
incomplete 55 adj.
deficient 302 adj.
light 318 adj.
unequipped
665 adj.
lost 767 adj.

**deficit**
deficit 55 n.

**definite**
definite 80 adj.
intelligible 511 adj.
manifest 517 adj.
informative
519 adj.
assertive 527 adj.
perspicuous
562 adj.

**deflect**
make oblique
215 vb.
make curved
243 vb.
impel 274 vb.
deflect 277 vb.
repel 287 vb.

mislead 490 vb.
dissuade 608 vb.
parry 708 vb.

**deform**
destroy 160 vb.
deform 239 vb.
distort 241 vb.
make ugly 837 vb.
blemish 840 vb.

**deformed**
deformed 241 adj.

**deformity**
deformity 241 n.
curvature 243 n.
camber 248 n.
ugliness 837 n.

**defraud**
deceive 537 vb.
misuse 670 vb.
fleece 781 vb.
defraud 783 vb.
not pay 800 vb.
account 803 vb.
be dishonest
925 vb.

**defrauder**
defrauder 784 n.

**defray**
patronize 698 vb.
participate 770 vb.
purchase 787 vb.
defray 799 vb.

**defy**
be present 184 vb.
dissent 484 vb.
affirm 527 vb.
negate 528 vb.
be resolute 594 vb.
face danger
656 vb.
be active 673 vb.
oppose 699 vb.
make quarrels
704 vb.
defy 706 vb.
attack 707 vb.
resist 710 vb.
disobey 733 vb.

be free **739** vb.
be courageous
**850** vb.
be ostentatious
**870** vb.
boast **872** vb.
be insolent **873** vb.
threaten **895** vb.
accuse **923** vb.

**degrading**
degrading **862** adj.

**degree**
relativeness **9** n.
degree **27** n.
greatness **32** n.
superiority **34** n.
series **71** n.
serial place **73** n.
classification **77** n.
situation **181** n.
limit **231** n.
importance **633** n.
army officer **736** n.
apportionment
**778** n.
nobility **863** n.

**deification**
deification **976** n.

**deism**
deism **967** n.

**deistic**
deistic **960** adj.

**deity**
deity **961** n.
idol **976** n.

**Deity, the**
the Deity **960** n.

**dejected**
disappointed
**504** adj.
inactive **674** adj.
unhappy **820** adj.
discontented
**824** adj.
dejected **829** adj.
lamenting **831** adj.
hopeless **848** adj.
humbled **867** adj.

loving **882** adj.

**dejected, be**
suffer **820** vb.
be discontented
**824** vb.
be dejected
**829** vb.
despair **848** vb.
be sullen **888** vb.

**dejection**
adversity **726** n.
sorrow **820** n.
discontent **824** n.
dejection **829** n.
lamentation **831** n.
dullness **835** n.
hopelessness
**848** n.
nervousness **849** n.
pity **900** n.

**delay**
interim **104** n.
protraction **108** n.
looking ahead
**119** n.
delay **131** n.
lull **140** n.
slowness **273** n.
negligence **453** n.
unwillingness
**593** n.
deliverance **663** n.
inaction **672** n.
inactivity **674** n.
tactics **683** n.
caution **853** n.

**delegate**
interpreter **515** n.
informant **519** n.
speaker **574** n.
agent **681** n.
councillor **687** n.
mediator **715** n.
delegate **749** n.

**delight**
excite **816** vb.
delight **821** vb.
cheer **828** vb.

amuse **832** vb.

**deliver**
restore **651** vb.
preserve **661** vb.
deliver **663** vb.
disencumber
**696** vb.
aid **698** vb.
defend **708** vb.
liberate **741** vb.
restitute **782** vb.
purchase **787** vb.
relieve **826** vb.

**deliverance**
extraction **299** n.
restoration **651** n.
safety **655** n.
preservation **661** n.
preserver **661** n.
escape **662** n.
deliverance **663** n.
aid **698** n.
defender **708** n.
liberation **741** n.
restitution **782** n.
purchase **787** n.
relief **826** n.
benefactor **898** n.

**demand**
require **622** vb.
warning **659** n.
demand **732** n.
demand **732** vb.
request **756** n.
request **756** vb.
give terms **761** vb.
appropriate **781** vb.
tax **804** n.
price **804** vb.
torment **822** vb.
regret **825** n.
desire **854** n.
threat **895** n.
threaten **895** vb.

**demanding**
incomplete **55** adj.

demanding
**622** adj.
requesting **756** adj.
desiring **854** adj.

**demean oneself**
demean oneself
**862** vb.
be humble **867** vb.
be servile **874** vb.

**demolish**
break **46** vb.
decompose **51** vb.
revolutionize
**144** vb.
weaken **158** vb.
demolish **160** vb.
force **171** vb.
collide **274** vb.
fell **306** vb.
confute **474** vb.
obliterate **545** vb.
wage war **713** vb.

**demon**
badness **640** n.
intimidation **849** n.
devil **963** n.
demon **964** n.

**demonetize**
demonetize **792** vb.

**demonstrate**
attribute **153** vb.
argue **470** vb.
demonstrate
**473** vb.
convince **480** vb.
be true **489** vb.
affirm **527** vb.
be truthful **535** vb.
have a right
**910** vb.
vindicate **922** vb.

**demonstrated**
demonstrated
**473** adj.

**demonstrating**
demonstrating
**473** adj.

**demonstration**
demonstration
473 n.

**dense**
real 1 adj.
substantial 3 adj.
firm 45 adj.
cohesive 48 adj.
complete 54 adj.
assembled 74 adj.
one 88 adj.
multitudinous
100 adj.
unyielding 157 adj.
contracted 193 adj.
thick 200 adj.
formed 238 adj.
closed 259 adj.
weighty 317 adj.
dense 319 adj.
airy 335 adj.
semiliquid 349 adj.

**dense, be**
augment 36 vb.
cohere 48 vb.
become small
193 vb.
make smaller
193 vb.
centralize 220 vb.
be dense 319 vb.
harden 321 vb.
thicken 349 vb.

**density**
permanence 139 n.
stability 148 n.
materiality 314 n.
density 319 n.
opacity 418 n.

**denyingly**
denyingly 755 adv.

**depart**
separate 46 vb.
be excluded 57 vb.
go away 185 vb.
travel 262 vb.
fly 266 vb.
recede 285 vb.

depart 291 vb.
emerge 293 vb.
die 356 vb.
be unwilling
593 vb.
relinquish 616 vb.

**departing**
departing 291 adj.

**departure**
departure 291 n.

**depend**
accompany 89 vb.
depend 152 vb.
be uncertain
469 vb.

**dependant**
inferior 35 n.
successor 67 n.
concomitant 89 n.
follower 279 n.
auxiliary 702 n.
dependant 737 n.
possessor 771 n.
recipient 777 n.
toady 874 n.

**deposal**
deposal 747 n.

**depose**
displace 183 vb.
abase 306 vb.
reject 602 vb.
unthrone 729 vb.
depose 747 vb.
deprive 781 vb.
disentitle 911 vb.

**deprecate**
qualify 463 vb.
dissent 484 vb.
negate 528 vb.
be unwilling
593 vb.
dissuade 608 vb.
warn 659 vb.
be active 673 vb.
oppose 699 vb.
resist 710 vb.
revolt 733 vb.
refuse 755 vb.

deprecate 757 vb.
be discontented
824 vb.
dislike 856 vb.
disapprove 919 vb.

**deprecation**
deprecation 757 n.

**deprecatory**
dissenting 484 adj.
negative 528 adj.
unwilling 593 adj.
dissuasive 608 adj.
cautionary 659 adj.
refusing 755 adj.
deprecatory
757 adj.
discontented
824 adj.
disapproving
919 adj.

**depreciating**
depreciating
478 adj.

**depress**
dissuade 608 vb.
trouble 822 vb.
cause discontent
824 vb.
depress 829 vb.

**deprive**
deprive 781 vb.

**depth**
quantity 26 n.
degree 27 n.
greatness 32 n.
measure 178 n.
space 178 n.
size 190 n.
gap 196 n.
length 198 n.
lowness 205 n.
depth 206 n.
interiority 219 n.
cavity 255 n.
sailing aid 264 n.
meter 460 n.
imperspicuity
563 n.

**deputize**
deputize 750 vb.

**deputizing**
deputizing 750 adj.

**deputy**
inferior 35 n.
substitute 145 n.
intermediary 226 n.
agent 681 n.
consignee 749 n.
deputy 750 n.

**derange**
decompose 51 vb.
be disordered
61 vb.
derange 63 vb.
disperse 75 vb.
enlace 217 vb.
deform 239 vb.
distort 241 vb.
roughen 254 vb.
fold 256 vb.
intrude 292 vb.
agitate 313 vb.
distract 451 vb.
not discriminate
459 vb.
surprise 503 vb.
harm 640 vb.
impair 655 vb.
hinder 697 vb.
be lax 729 vb.
trouble 822 vb.
frighten 849 vb.

**derangement**
derangement 63 n.

**derelict**
leavings 41 n.
survivor 41 n.
derelict 774 n.
outcast 878 n.
solitary 878 n.

**derisive**
derisive 846 adj.

**dermal**
dermal 221 adj.

**descend**
be inferior 35 vb.

decrease 37 vb.

be oblique 215 vb.

be in motion
260 vb.

regress 281 vb.

land 290 vb.

descend 304 vb.

lower 306 vb.

sit down 306 vb.

founder 308 vb.

plunge 308 vb.

weigh 317 vb.

flow 345 vb.

lose repute 862 vb.

**descendant**

descendant 165 n.

**descending**

descending
304 adj.

**descent**

decrease 37 n.

revolution 144 n.

depth 206 n.

incline 215 n.

curvature 243 n.

motion 260 n.

aeronautics 266 n.

descent 304 n.

plunge 308 n.

deterioration 650 n.

facility 696 n.

failure 723 n.

sport 832 n.

**describe**

remind 500 vb.

communicate
519 vb.

record 543 vb.

represent 546 vb.

write 581 vb.

describe 585 vb.

**description**

assimilation 18 n.

mimicry 20 n.

indication 542 n.

representation
546 n.

literature 552 n.

writing 581 n.

reading matter
584 n.

description 585 n.

**descriptive**

descriptive 585 adj.

**desert**

havoc 160 n.

desert 167 n.

space 178 n.

emptiness 185 n.

dryness 337 n.

land 339 n.

plain 343 n.

**deserve**

be good 639 vb.

deserve 910 vb.

be rewarded
957 vb.

**deserving**

deserving 910 adj.

**desiccation**

desiccation 337 n.

**designless**

designless 613 adj.

**desire**

attraction 286 n.

overstepping
301 n.

expectation 502 n.

expect 502 vb.

fantasy 508 n.

will 590 n.

will 590 vb.

be willing 592 vb.

motive 607 n.

intention 612 n.

aim at 612 vb.

require 622 vb.

request 756 n.

request 756 vb.

avarice 811 n.

suffering 820 n.

regret 825 n.

regret 825 vb.

be dejected
829 vb.

desire 854 n.

desire 854 vb.

love 882 n.

be in love 882 vb.

envy 907 n.

envy 907 vb.

be impure 946 vb.

**desired**

desired 854 adj.

**desired object**

desired object
854 n.

**desirer**

desirer 854 n.

**desiring**

desiring 854 adj.

**desirously**

desirously 854 adv.

**despair**

not expect 503 vb.

be disappointed
504 vb.

not act 672 vb.

be dejected
829 vb.

despair 848 vb.

**desperado**

athlete 157 n.

violent creature
171 n.

fool 496 n.

brave person
850 n.

desperado 852 n.

**despise**

underestimate
478 vb.

gesticulate 542 vb.

be insensitive
815 vb.

dislike 856 vb.

be fastidious
857 vb.

shame 862 vb.

be proud 866 vb.

be insolent 873 vb.

hate 881 vb.

not respect 916 vb.

despise 917 vb.

disapprove 919 vb.

detract 921 vb.

**despising**

despising 917 adj.

**despotism**

despotism 728 n.

**dessert**

dessert 296 n.

sweet thing 387 n.

**destiny**

future state 119 n.

futurity 119 n.

destiny 150 n.

cause 151 n.

fate 591 n.

necessity 591 n.

predetermination
603 n.

**destroy**

nullify 2 vb.

abate 37 vb.

disunite 46 vb.

rend 46 vb.

destroy 160 vb.

displace 183 vb.

deform 239 vb.

navigate 264 vb.

eject 295 vb.

extract 299 vb.

kill 357 vb.

slaughter 357 vb.

tell against 462 vb.

ill-treat 640 vb.

impair 650 vb.

defeat 722 vb.

impoverish 796 vb.

**destroyed**

destroyed 160 adj.

**destroyed, be**

be destroyed
160 vb.

**destroyer**

revolutionist 144 n.

destroyer 168 n.

violent creature
171 n.

flattener 211 n.

bane 654 n.

taker 781 n.
evildoer 899 n.
**destruction**
extinction 2 n.
separation 46 n.
decomposition
51 n.
finality 69 n.
destruction 160 n.
outbreak 171 n.
violence 171 n.
counteraction
177 n.
ejection 295 n.
extraction 299 n.
friction 328 n.
killing 357 n.
slaughter 357 n.
waste 629 n.
dilapidation 650 n.
impairment 650 n.
revolt 733 n.
inhumanity 893 n.
**destructive**
revolutionary
144 adj.
destructive 160 adj.
violent 171 adj.
evil 611 adj.
wasteful 629 adj.
harmful 640 adj.
adverse 726 adj.
**destructively**
destructively
160 adv.
**desuetude**
desuetude 606 n.
**detect**
smell 389 vb.
see 433 vb.
detect 479 vb.
be true 489 vb.
understand 511 vb.
disclose 521 vb.
**detective**
spectator 436 n.
inquisitive person
448 n.

detective 454 n.
informer 519 n.
protector 655 n.
police 950 n.
**detector**
detector 479 n.
**detention**
hindrance 697 n.
detention 742 n.
retention 773 n.
penalty 958 n.
**deteriorate**
be inferior 35 vb.
decrease 37 vb.
decompose 51 vb.
be old 122 vb.
be turned to
142 vb.
be weak 158 vb.
be destroyed
160 vb.
be brittle 325 vb.
be unpractised
606 vb.
waste 629 vb.
be ill 646 vb.
deteriorate 650 vb.
relapse 652 vb.
be unprepared
665 vb.
stop using 669 vb.
be defeated
723 vb.
fail 723 vb.
have trouble
726 vb.
be poor 796 vb.
aggravate 827 vb.
make ugly 837 vb.
be wrong 909 vb.
be wicked 929 vb.
be impious 974 vb.
**deteriorated**
deteriorated
650 adj.
**deterioration**
deterioration 650 n.

**detract**
detract 921 vb.
**detracting**
detracting 921 adj.
**detraction**
detraction 921 n.
**detractor**
detractor 921 n.
**deviate**
differ 15 vb.
separate 46 vb.
change 138 vb.
vary 147 vb.
make oblique
215 vb.
flank 234 vb.
make angular
242 vb.
be in motion
260 vb.
navigate 264 vb.
move slowly
273 vb.
deviate 277 vb.
recede 285 vb.
diverge 289 vb.
blow 347 vb.
disregard 453 vb.
be diffuse 565 vb.
avoid 615 vb.
circuit 621 vb.
fail 723 vb.
**deviating**
deviating 277 adj.
**deviation**
irrelevance 10 n.
difference 15 n.
nonuniformity 17 n.
disunion 46 n.
abnormality 84 n.
nonconformity
84 n.
change 138 n.
displacement
183 n.
distance 194 n.
obliquity 215 n.
laterality 234 n.

curvature 243 n.
meandering 246 n.
motion 260 n.
water travel 264 n.
transference 267 n.
deviation 277 n.
divergence 289 n.
traffic control
300 n.
overstepping
301 n.
shortfall 302 n.
descent 304 n.
visual fallacy 435 n.
inattention 451 n.
error 490 n.
tergiversation
598 n.
circuit 621 n.
**devil**
monster 933 n.
devil 963 n.
demon 964 n.
mythical being
964 n.
sorcerer 977 n.
**devotional**
devotional 975 n.
**dextral**
dextral 236 adj.
**dextrality**
dextrality 236 n.
**dextrally**
dextrally 236 adv.
**diabolic**
wicked 929 adj.
diabolic 963 adj.
fairylike 964 adj.
infernal 966 adj.
idolatrous 976 adj.
sorcerous 977 adj.
**diabolism**
diabolism 963 n.
**diabolist**
diabolist 963 n.
**diabolize**
diabolize 963 vb.

**dialect**
speciality 80 n.
unintelligibility
512 n.
language 552 n.
dialect 555 n.
solecism 560 n.
pronunciation
572 n.
speech defect
575 n.

**dialectal**
dialectal 555 adj.

**dictionary**
word list 87 n.
commentary 515 n.
dictionary 554 n.
reference book
584 n.
collection 627 n.

**die**
pass away 2 vb.
end 69 vb.
depart 291 vb.
die 356 vb.
not act 672 vb.
be in love 882 vb.

**dieting**
dieting 296 n.

**differ**
be contrary 14 vb.
differ 15 vb.
be unlike 19 vb.
disagree 25 vb.
be unequal 29 vb.
diverge 289 vb.
quarrel 704 vb.

**difference**
unrelatedness 10 n.
contrariety 14 n.
difference 15 n.
nonuniformity 17 n.
dissimilarity 19 n.
disagreement 25 n.
inequality 29 n.
inequality 29 n.
remainder 41 n.
disunion 46 n.

speciality 80 n.
change 138 n.
divergence 289 n.
variegation 432 n.
discrimination
458 n.

**different**
contrary 14 adj.
different 15 adj.
nonuniform 17 adj.
dissimilar 19 adj.
inimitable 21 adj.
disagreeing 25 adj.
unequal 29 adj.
superior 34 adj.
separate 46 adj.
extraneous 59 adj.
special 80 adj.
multiform 82 adj.
converted 142 adj.
changeful 147 adj.
heterodox 971 adj.

**differentiate**
differentiate 15 vb.
make unlike 19 vb.
set apart 46 vb.
specify 80 vb.
compare 457 vb.
discriminate
458 vb.

**differentiation**
differentiation 15 n.

**differently**
differently 15 adv.

**different time**
different time
117 n.

**difficult**
moot 454 adj.
impracticable
465 adj.
puzzling 512 adj.
unclear 563 adj.
laborious 677 adj.
difficult 695 adj.
hindering 697 adj.

**difficult, be**
be inexpedient
638 vb.
be difficult 695 vb.
be obstructive
697 vb.
have trouble
726 vb.

**difficulty**
complexity 61 n.
enigma 525 n.
imperspicuity
563 n.
difficulty 695 n.
obstacle 697 n.
adversity 726 n.
revolter 733 n.
suffering 820 n.
aggravation 827 n.

**diffuse**
irrelevant 10 adj.
complete 54 adj.
long 198 adj.
veracious 535 adj.
diffuse 565 adj.
inelegant 571 adj.
descriptive 585 adj.
roundabout
621 adj.

**diffuse, be**
be unrelated 10 vb.
specify 80 vb.
repeat oneself
102 vb.
sophisticate
472 vb.
be diffuse 565 vb.
speak 574 vb.
be loquacious
576 vb.
be tedious 833 vb.

**diffusely**
diffusely 565 adv.

**diffuseness**
diffuseness 565 n.

**digestive disorders**
digestive disorders
646 n.

**dignification**
dignification 861 n.

**dignify**
dignify 861 vb.
sanctify 973 vb.

**dilapidated**
decreasing 37 adj.
decomposed
51 adj.
antiquated 122 adj.
flimsy 163 adj.
weakened 163 adj.
destroyed 165 adj.
brittle 330 adj.
dirty 649 adj.
dilapidated
655 adj.
unsafe 661 adj.
used 673 adj.
beggarly 801 adj.
disreputable
867 adj.

**dilapidation**
dilapidation 655 n.

**dilation**
dilation 197 n.

**dim**
insubstantial 4 adj.
vespertine 129 adj.
cloudy 355 adj.
dark 418 adj.
dim 419 adj.
opaque 423 adj.
semitransparent
424 adj.
colourless 426 adj.
blackish 428 adj.
indistinct 444 adj.
dejected 834 adj.

**dim, be**
decrease 37 vb.
cloud 355 vb.
be dark 418 vb.
be dim 419 vb.
lose colour 426 vb.
blur 440 vb.
be unseen 444 vb.
disappear 446 vb.

**diminuendo**
diminuendo 37 adv.

**diminution**
diminution 37 n.

**dimly**
dimly 414 adv.

**dimness**
dimness 414 n.

**dim sight**
eye 433 n.
vision 433 n.
blindness 434 n.
dim sight 435 n.

**dim-sighted**
dim-sighted
435 adj.

**dim-sighted, be**
be dim-sighted
435 vb.

**direct**
come first 34 vb.
make conform
83 vb.
influence 173 vb.
navigate 264 vb.
precede 278 vb.
educate 529 vb.
indicate 542 vb.
do 671 vb.
direct 684 vb.
rule 728 vb.

**directed**
directed 276 adj.

**directing**
directing 684 adj.

**direction**
tendency 174 n.
bearings 181 n.
laterality 234 n.
contraposition
235 n.
itinerary 262 n.
air travel 266 n.
direction 276 n.
directorship 684 n.

**director**
superior 34 n.
guide 515 n.

doer 671 n.
director 685 n.
authority 728 n.
master 736 n.

**directorship**
directorship 684 n.

**directory**
directory 87 n.
chronology 112 n.
guidebook 519 n.
indication 542 n.
reference book
584 n.

**dirt**
leavings 41 n.
covering 221 n.
excrement 297 n.
powder 327 n.
powderiness 327 n.
bubble 350 n.
stench 392 n.
opacity 418 n.
obliteration 545 n.
rubbish 636 n.
dirt 644 n.
blemish 840 n.
slur 862 n.

**dirty**
orderless 61 adj.
travelling 267 adj.
powdery 327 adj.
marshy 342 adj.
bubbly 350 adj.
dim 414 adj.
opaque 418 adj.
black 423 adj.
neglected 453 adj.
negligent 453 adj.
bad 644 adj.
dirty 644 adj.
infectious 648 adj.
beggarly 796 adj.
blemished 840 adj.
dishonest 925 adj.
impure 946 adj.

**dirty person**
slut 61 n.
dirty person 644 n.

**disable**
abate 37 vb.
disable 156 vb.
weaken 158 vb.
suppress 160 vb.
make useless
636 vb.
impair 650 vb.
hinder 697 vb.

**disaccustom**
disaccustom
606 vb.

**disagree**
be contrary 14 vb.
differ 15 vb.
disagree 25 vb.
be unequal 29 vb.
discord 406 vb.
dissent 484 vb.
mean 509 vb.
cause dislike
856 vb.

**disagreeing**
disagreeing 25 adj.

**disagreement**
disagreement 25 n.

**disappear**
pass away 2 vb.
decrease 37 vb.
be transient
109 vb.
cease 140 vb.
be impotent
156 vb.
go away 185 vb.
regress 281 vb.
recede 285 vb.
decamp 291 vb.
be unseen 439 vb.
disappear 441 vb.
be stealthy 520 vb.
obliterate 545 vb.
be lost 767 vb.

**disappearance**
disappearance
441 n.

**disappearing**
disappearing
441 adj.

**disappoint**
fall short 302 vb.
surprise 503 vb.
disappoint 504 vb.
befool 537 vb.
deceive 537 vb.
not suffice 631 vb.
fail 723 vb.
miscarry 723 vb.
displease 822 vb.
cause discontent
824 vb.
depress 829 vb.
leave no hope
848 vb.
fail in duty 913 vb.

**disappointed**
disappointed
504 adj.

**disappointed, be**
be disappointed
504 vb.

**disappointing**
disappointing
504 adj.

**disappointingly**
disappointingly
504 adv.

**disappointment**
disappointment
504 n.

**disapprobation**
cry 403 n.
estimate 475 n.
dissent 484 n.
gesture 542 n.
rejection 602 n.
hindrance 697 n.
opposition 699 n.
prohibition 752 n.
deprecation 757 n.
discontent 824 n.
odium 883 n.
disrespect 916 n.
indignity 916 n.

produce 159 vb.
travel 262 vb.
arrive 290 vb.
cognize 442 vb.
think 444 vb.
discover 479 vb.
believe 480 vb.
manifest 517 vb.
be informed
    519 vb.
disclose 521 vb.
pursue 614 vb.
plan 618 vb.
acquire 766 vb.

**discovering**
discovering
    479 n.

**discovery**
discovery 479 n.

**discreditable**
flagrant 32 adj.
bad 640 adj.
discreditable
    862 adj.
blameworthy
    919 adj.

**discriminate**
differentiate 15 vb.
set apart 46 vb.
specify 80 vb.
compare 457 vb.
discriminate
    458 vb.
know 485 vb.
be wise 493 vb.
name 556 vb.
select 600 vb.
be skilful 689 vb.
have taste 841 vb.
be fastidious
    857 vb.

**discriminating**
discriminating
    458 adj.

**discrimination**
differentiation 15 n.
gastronomy 296 n.
intellect 442 n.

**discrimination**
    458 n.
reasoning 470 n.
judgment 475 n.
sagacity 493 n.
choice 600 n.
skill 689 n.
moral sensibility
    814 n.
good taste 841 n.
fastidiousness
    857 n.

**discursive**
discursive 586 adj.

**disease**
generality 79 n.
helplessness 156 n.
dieting 296 n.
fluid 330 n.
decease 356 n.
insensibility 370 n.
heat 374 n.
insufficiency 631 n.
redundance 632 n.
badness 640 n.
disease 646 n.
dilapidation 650 n.
bane 654 n.
sleep 674 n.

**diseased**
diseased 646 adj.

**disembody**
disembody 315 vb.

**disencumber**
abate 37 vb.
lighten 318 vb.
deliver 663 vb.
disencumber
    696 vb.
liberate 741 vb.
take away 781 vb.
relieve 826 vb.

**disentitle**
disentitle 911 vb.

**disguise**
dissimilarity 19 n.
covering 221 n.
cloak 223 n.

screen 416 n.
disguise 522 n.
mental dishonesty
    538 n.

**disguised**
disguised 520 adj.

**dish**
a mixture 43 n.
sequel 67 n.
dish 296 n.

**dishonest**
unreliable 469 adj.
stealthy 520 adj.
bad 640 adj.
cunning 693 adj.
thieving 783 adj.
discreditable
    862 adj.
wrong 909 adj.
dishonest 925 adj.
selfish 927 adj.
wicked 929 adj.
lawbreaking
    949 adj.

**dishonest, be**
disappoint 504 vb.
be false 536 vb.
deceive 537 vb.
apostatize 598 vb.
strike at 707 vb.
not observe
    764 vb.
not pay 800 vb.
be dishonest
    925 vb.

**dishonestly**
dishonestly
    925 adv.

**disinterested**
substituted
    145 adj.
tutelary 655 adj.
losing 767 adj.
liberal 808 adj.
content 823 adj.
humble 867 adj.
loving 882 adj.
benevolent 892 adj.

philanthropic
    896 adj.
disinterested
    926 adj.
virtuous 928 adj.

**disinterested, be**
be humble 867 vb.
be disinterested
    926 vb.
atone 936 vb.

**disinterestedness**
disinterestedness
    926 n.

**dislike**
difference 15 n.
unwillingness
    593 n.
be unwilling
    593 vb.
opposition 699 n.
resistance 710 n.
tedium 833 n.
be indifferent
    855 vb.
dislike 856 n.
dislike 856 vb.
enmity 876 n.
hatred 883 n.
hate 883 vb.
disapprobation
    919 n.
disapprove 919 vb.

**disliked**
disliked 856 adj.

**disliking**
disliking 856 adj.

**dismiss**
displace 183 vb.
repel 287 vb.
dismiss 295 vb.
stop using 669 vb.
make inactive
    674 vb.
depose 747 vb.
refuse 755 vb.
not retain 774 vb.

**disobedience**
disobedience
733 n.
**disobedient**
revolutionary
144 adj.
violent 171 adj.
negative 528 adj.
unwilling 593 adj.
wilful 597 adj.
difficult 695 adj.
opposing 699 adj.
quarrelling 704 adj.
defiant 706 adj.
resisting 710 adj.
anarchic 729 adj.
disobedient
733 adj.
nonobservant
764 adj.
discontented
824 adj.
sullen 888 adj.
undutiful 913 adj.
disrespectful
916 adj.
perfidious 925 adj.
wicked 929 adj.
schismatical
972 adj.
**disobey**
be contrary 14 vb.
be disordered
61 vb.
negate 528 vb.
oppose 699 vb.
please oneself
729 vb.
disobey 733 vb.
be free 739 vb.
not observe
764 vb.
be insolent 873 vb.
fail in duty 913 vb.
schismatize 972 vb.
**disorder**
unrelatedness 10 n.
nonuniformity 17 n.

disorder 61 n.
derangement 63 n.
discontinuity 72 n.
fitfulness 137 n.
amorphism 239 n.
negligence 453 n.
badness 640 n.
uncleanness 644 n.
ill-breeding 842 n.
**disordered, be**
be disordered
61 vb.
**disorderly**
disorderly 61 adj.
violent 171 adj.
loud 395 adj.
riotous 733 adj.
ill-bred 842 adj.
drunk 944 adj.
**disperse**
decrease 37 vb.
disunite 46 vb.
separate 46 vb.
decompose 51 vb.
be disordered
61 vb.
jumble 63 vb.
disperse 75 vb.
generalize 79 vb.
destroy 160 vb.
displace 183 vb.
lengthen 198 vb.
move 260 vb.
repel 287 vb.
let fall 306 vb.
waste 629 vb.
defeat 722 vb.
liberate 746 vb.
**dispersed, be**
be dispersed 75 vb.
**dispersion**
dispersion 75 n.
**displace**
subtract 39 vb.
exclude 57 vb.
derange 63 vb.
displace 183 vb.
move 260 vb.

transpose 267 vb.
transpose 267 vb.
land 290 vb.
eject 295 vb.
empty 295 vb.
extract 299 vb.
take 781 vb.
take away 781 vb.
**displaced**
displaced 183 adj.
**displacement**
subtraction 39 n.
separation 46 n.
exclusion 57 n.
displacement
183 n.
transference 267 n.
ejection 295 n.
extraction 299 n.
taking 781 n.
**displease**
displease 822 vb.
cause discontent
824 vb.
depress 829 vb.
cause dislike
856 vb.
**dispose of**
dispose of 668 vb.
subjugate 740 vb.
possess 768 vb.
**dispraise**
dispraise 919 vb.
**disregard**
be deaf 411 vb.
be blind 434 vb.
not think 445 vb.
be incurious
449 vb.
disregard 453 vb.
underestimate
478 vb.
not know 486 vb.
conceal 520 vb.
be taciturn 577 vb.
reject 602 vb.
be unimportant
634 vb.

not act 672 vb.
abrogate 747 vb.
be insensitive
815 vb.
forgive 904 vb.
fail in duty 913 vb.
not respect 916 vb.
hold cheap 917 vb.
**disreputable**
not nice 640 adj.
vulgar 842 adj.
renowned 861 adj.
disreputable
862 adj.
plebeian 864 adj.
unrespected
916 adj.
disapproved
919 adj.
dishonest 925 adj.
vicious 929 adj.
**disrepute**
decrease 37 n.
famousness 861 n.
disrepute 862 n.
humiliation 867 n.
odium 883 n.
disrespect 916 n.
disapprobation
919 n.
detraction 921 n.
improbity 925 n.
wickedness 929 n.
**disrespect**
nonobservance
764 n.
ridicule 846 n.
disrepute 862 n.
undutifulness
913 n.
disrespect 916 n.
disapprobation
919 n.
impiety 974 n.
**disrespectful**
disrespectful
916 adj.

# disrespectfully

disrespectfully
916 adv.

dissemble
imitate 20 vb.
mislead 490 vb.
be equivocal
513 vb.
lurk 518 vb.
be stealthy 520 vb.
conceal 520 vb.
dissemble 536 vb.
deceive 537 vb.
be untrue 538 vb.
misname 557 n.
plead 609 vb.
be affected 845 vb.
be dishonest
925 vb.
be impious 974 vb.

dissension
difference 15 n.
disagreement 25 n.
disunion 46 n.
stop 140 n.
argument 470 n.
dissent 484 n.
opposition 699 n.
dissension 704 n.
contention 711 n.
revolt 733 n.
enmity 876 n.
hatred 883 n.

dissent
disagreement 25 n.
disagree 25 vb.
nonconformity
84 n.
argument 470 n.
argue 470 vb.
unbelief 481 n.
disbelieve 481 vb.
dissent 484 n.
dissent 484 vb.
negation 528 n.
negate 528 vb.
unwillingness
593 n.

be unwilling
593 vb.
reject 602 vb.
opposition 699 n.
dissension 704 n.
quarrel 704 vb.
defy 706 vb.
refuse 755 vb.
dislike 856 vb.
disapprove 919 vb.
sectarianism 972 n.

dissentient
dissentient 484 n.

dissenting
dissenting 484 adj.

dissertate
dissertate 586 vb.

dissertation
composition 56 n.
arrangement 62 n.
accumulation 74 n.
commentary 515 n.
diffuseness 565 n.
oration 574 n.
reading matter
584 n.
dissertation 586 n.

dissertator
dissertator 586 n.

dissimilar
different 15 adj.
nonuniform 17 adj.
dissimilar 19 adj.
unequal 29 adj.

dissimilarity
dissimilarity 19 n.

dissimilarly
dissimilarly 19 adv.

dissuade
revert 143 vb.
moderate 172 vb.
cause doubt
481 vb.
dissuade 608 vb.
warn 659 vb.
advise 686 vb.
hinder 697 vb.
prohibit 752 vb.

deprecate 757 vb.
cause discontent
824 vb.
depress 829 vb.
frighten 849 vb.

dissuasion
dissuasion 608 n.

dissuasive
dissuasive 608 adj.

distance
difference 15 n.
futurity 119 n.
range 178 n.
distance 194 n.
length 198 n.
exteriority 218 n.
rear 233 n.
propulsion 282 n.
avoidance 615 n.

distant
dissimilar 19 adj.
extraneous 59 adj.
alone 88 adj.
distant 194 adj.
exterior 218 adj.
invisible 439 adj.

distant, be
be distant 194 vb.
recede 285 vb.
avoid 615 vb.

distinctive
distinctive 15 adj.
separate 46 vb.
discriminating
458 adj.

distort
make unlike 19 vb.
break 46 vb.
modify 138 vb.
transform 142 vb.
force 171 vb.
shorten 199 vb.
make oblique
215 vb.
deform 239 vb.
distort 241 vb.
crinkle 246 vb.
draw 283 vb.

misinterpret
516 vb.
misteach 530 vb.
be false 536 vb.
cxaggerate 541 vb.
misrepresent
547 vb.
impair 650 vb.
pervert 650 vb.
misuse 670 vb.
make ugly 837 vb.

distorted
distorted 241 adj.

distortion
distortion 241 n.

distract
derange 63 vb.
distract 451 vb.

distracted
distracted 451 vb.

distressing
distressing 822 adj.

district
subdivision 53 n.
district 179 n.
place 180 n.
locality 182 n.
abode 187 n.
housing 187 n.
political
organization 728 n.
parish 979 n.

disunion
disunion 46 n.

disunite
disunite 46 vb.
unstick 49 vb.
decompose 51 vb.
part 53 vb.
discontinue 72 vb.
disperse 75 vb.
disable 156 vb.
weaken 158 vb.
demolish 160 vb.
displace 183 vb.
doff 224 vb.
open 258 vb.
soften 322 vb.

make useless
    636 vb.
wound 650 vb.
deliver 663 vb.
disencumber
    696 vb.
be lax 729 vb.
not retain 774 vb.
divorce 891 vb.

**disunited**
disunited 46 adj.

**disused**
disused 669 adj.

**diver**
depth 206 n.
descent 304 n.
diver 308 n.
gravity 317 n.

**diverge**
separate 46 vb.
be dispersed 75 vb.
disperse 75 vb.
bifurcate 92 vb.
make angular
    242 vb.
deviate 277 vb.
diverge 289 vb.

**divergence**
divergence 289 n.

**divergent**
divergent 289 adj.

**dividing line**
dividing line 92 n.

**divination**
equal chance
    154 n.
astronomy 316 n.
divination 506 n.
hermeneutics
    515 n.
nondesign 613 n.
sorcery 977 n.
occultism 978 n.
spiritualism 978 n.

**divine**
divine 506 vb.
divine 960 adj.

practise sorcery
    977 vb.
practise occultism
    978 vb.

**divine attribute**
divine attribute
    960 n.

**divine function**
deliverance 663 n.
propitiation 936 n.
divine function
    960 n.
sanctity 973 n.

**divinely**
divinely 960 adv.

**divineness**
divineness 960 n.

**diviner**
diviner 506 n.

**divorce**
separation 46 n.
unit 88 n.
parentage 164 n.
nonretention 774 n.
not retain 774 vb.
divorce 891 vb.
divorce 891 vb.

**divorced**
divorced 891 adj.

**divulge**
divulge 521 vb.
publish 523 vb.
speak 574 vb.
accuse 923 vb.

**do**
cause 151 vb.
be able 155 vb.
produce 159 vb.
operate 168 vb.
be instrumental
    623 vb.
be useful 635 vb.
do 671 vb.
be active 673 vb.
exert oneself
    677 vb.
behave 683 vb.
deal with 683 vb.

carry out 720 vb.
be successful
    722 vb.
observe 763 vb.
celebrate 871 vb.
do one's duty
    912 vb.

**do before**
do before 114 vb.

**do business**
do business
    617 vb.
do 671 vb.
trade 786 vb.

**doctor**
substitute 145 n.
resident 186 n.
cover 221 vb.
animal husbandry
    364 n.
psychologist 442 n.
insanity 498 n.
mender 651 n.
cure 651 vb.
doctor 653 n.vb.
preserve 661 vb.
adviser 686 n.
minister to 698 vb.
relieve 826 vb.

**doctrinaire**
doctrinaire 468 n.
narrow mind 476 n.
theorist 507 n.

**do easily**
do easily 696 vb.
be successful
    722 vb.
win 722 vb.

**doer**
producer 159 n.
doer 671 n.
busy person 673 n.
agent 681 n.
manager 685 n.
political party
    703 n.

**doff**
decrease 37 vb.

unstick 49 vb.
doff 224 vb.
open 258 vb.
excrete 297 vb.
be plain 517 vb.
disclose 521 vb.
relinquish 616 vb.
stop using 669 vb.

**dog**
dog 360 n.
hunter 614 n.
protector 655 n.

**doggerel**
doggerel 588 n.

**dogmatize**
dogmatize 468 vb.

**do good**
be useful 635 vb.
be expedient
    637 vb.
do good 639 vb.
make better
    649 vb.
be auspicious
    725 vb.
be benevolent
    892 vb.
be virtuous 928 vb.

**doing**
operative 168 adj.
doing 671 adj.
observant 763 adj.

**do law**
do law 953 vb.

**do likewise**
do likewise 20 vb.

**dome**
roof 221 n.
curve 243 n.
cone 247 n.
sphere 247 n.
dome 248 n.

**domestic**
clothier 223 n.
domestic 737 n.
keeper 744 n.

**dominate**
be able 155 vb.

**do one's duty**

prevail 173 vb.
dominate 728 vb.

**do one's duty**
do one's duty
912 vb.

**doorkeeper**
doorway 258 n.
doorkeeper 259 n.
servant 737 n.

**doorway**
entrance 68 n.
lobby 189 n.
threshold 229 n.
front 232 n.
rear 233 n.
doorway 258 n.
stopper 259 n.
way in 292 n.
outlet 293 n.
access 619 n.
church exterior
984 n.
temple 984 n.

**do penance**
do penance 936 vb.

**do sums**
do sums 86 vb.

**double**
dual 90 adj.
dual 90 adj.
double 91 adj.
double 91 vb.
repeat 102 vb.

**doubt**
philosophy 444 n.
dubiety 469 n.
be uncertain
469 vb.
doubt 481 n.vb.
dissent 484 n.
not know 486 vb.
unwillingness
593 n.
be nervous 849 vb.
jealousy 906 n.
be jealous 906 vb.
irreligion 968 n.

**doubtfully**
doubtfully 481 adv.

**doubting**
doubting 469 adj.

**dower**
dower 772 n.
dower 772 n.

**down**
down 304 adv.

**downy**
downy 254 adj.
soft 322 adj.

**do wrong**
be biased 476 vb.
harm 640 vb.
ill-treat 640 vb.
oppress 730 vb.
do wrong 909 vb.
be illegal 949 vb.

**drag on**
drag on 108 vb.

**drain**
gap 196 n.
tunnel 258 n.
lake 341 n.
drain 346 n.
cleanser 643 n.
sink 644 n.

**drama**
composition 56 n.
broadcast 526 n.
literature 552 n.
poem 588 n.
drama 589 n.
amusement 832 n.

**dramatic**
dramatic 589 adj.

**dramatist**
author 584 n.
dramatist 589 n.

**dramatize**
dramatize 589 vb.

**dramaturgy**
dramaturgy 589 n.

**draught**
draught 296 n.
fluid 330 n.
pungency 383 n.

**draught horse**
draught horse
268 n.

**draw**
draw 28 n.
synchronism 118 n.
stop 140 n.
move 260 vb.
navigate 264 vb.
transpose 267 vb.
draw 283 n.
attract 286 vb.
extract 299 vb.
victory 722 n.

**drawing**
dynamic 155 adj.
drawing 283 n.

**draw money**
draw money
792 vb.

**drench**
fill 54 n.
destroy 160 vb.
overlie 221 vb.
flow out 293 vb.
immerse 298 vb.
encroach 301 vb.
soften 322 vb.
drench 336 n.
flow 345 vb.
superabound
632 vb.
clean 643 vb.
sate 858 vb.

**drenched**
drenched 336 adj.

**dress**
dress 223 n.
dress 223 vb.
equipment 625 n.
decorate 839 vb.
canonicals 983 n.

**dressed**
dressed 223 adj.

**dressing**
adjunct 40 n.
dressing 223 n.
appearance 440 n.

**drink**
assuage 172 vb.
empty 295 vb.
drink 296 vb.
have enough
630 vb.
revel 832 vb.
toast 871 vb.
be sociable 877 vb.
get drunk 944 vb.

**drinking**
drinking 296 n.

**driver**
driver 263 n.
carrier 268 n.
speeder 272 n.
passing along
300 n.
domestic 737 n.

**drug**
mouthful 296 n.
anaesthetic 370 n.
pungency 383 n.
drug 653 n.
poison 654 n.
drug-taking 944 n.

**drugged**
drugged 944 adj.

**druggist**
druggist 653 n.

**drug oneself**
drug oneself
944 vb.

**drug-taking**
drug-taking 944 n.

**drum**
drum 409 n.

**drunk**
foolish 494 adj.
intemperate
938 adj.
drunk 944 adj.

**drunkard**
drinking 296 n.
madman 499 n.
reveller 832 n.
sensualist 939 n.
drunkard 944 n.

**drunk, be**
be drunk 944 vb.

**drunken**
disorderly 61 adj.
feeding 296 adj.
sensual 939 adj.
drunken 944 adj.

**drunkenness**
drunkenness 944 n.

**dry**
weak 158 adj.
unproductive
  167 adj.
make smaller
  193 vb.
absorb 294 vb.
powdery 327 adj.
aerate 335 vb.
dry 337 adj.vb.
staunch 345 vb.
hot 374 adj.
burn 376 vb.
heat 376 vb.
sanitate 647 vb.
preserve 661 vb.
make insensitive
  815 vb.

**dry, be**
be dry 337 vb.
be hot 374 vb.

**dryer**
dryer 337 n.

**dryness**
dryness 337 n.

**dual**
dual 90 adj.
double 91 adj.

**duality**
duality 90 n.

**dubiety**
dubiety 469 n.

**due**
advisable 637 adj.
just 908 adj.
due 910 adj.

**due, be**
be right 908 vb.
be due 910 vb.

be one's duty
  912 vb.

**duel**
slaughter 357 n.
duel 711 n.

**dueness**
dueness 910 n.

**duet**
duet 407 n.

**dull**
tedious 833 adj.
dull 835 adj.

**dull, be**
be dull 835 vb.

**dullness**
dullness 835 n.

**duly**
duly 910 adv.

**dunce**
ignoramus 488 n.
dunce 496 n.

**dupe**
weakling 158 n.
credulity 482 n.
ignoramus 488 n.
ninny 496 n.
dupe 539 n.
loser 723 n.
unlucky person
  726 n.
sufferer 820 n.

**duped, be**
be duped 539 vb.

**duplicate**
analogue 18 n.
duplicate 22 n.
duplication 91 n.
reproduction 161 n.
record 543 n.
image 546 n.
representation
  546 n.
script 581 n.

**duplication**
duplication 91 n.

**duplicity**
appearance 440 n.
concealment 520 n.

duplicity 536 n.
deception 537 n.
sham 537 n.
mental dishonesty
  538 n.
cunning 693 n.
affectation 845 n.
perfidy 925 n.
false piety 974 n.

**durability**
durability 108 n.

**duty**
bond 47 n.
liability 175 n.
necessity 591 n.
motive 607 n.
needfulness 622 n.
labour 677 n.
obedience 734 n.
promise 759 n.
right 908 n.
dueness 910 n.
duty 912 n.
cult 975 n.

**dwarf**
small animal 33 n.
dwarf 191 n.

**dwarfish**
dwarfish 191 adj.

**dwell**
stay 139 vb.
be stable 148 vb.
be situated 181 vb.
place oneself
  182 vb.
be present 184 vb.
dwell 187 vb.
live 355 vb.

**dweller**
dweller 186 n.

**dwelling**
dwelling 187 n.
canopy 221 n.
tunnel 258 n.

**dying**
extinct 2 adj.
ephemeral 109 adj.
ageing 126 adj.

dying 356 adj.
sick 646 adj.

**dynamic**
dynamic 155 adj.
operative 168 adj.
vigorous 169 adj.
godlike 960 adj.

**E**

**ear**
ear 410 n.

**earliness**
earliness 130 n.

**early**
instantaneous
  111 adj.
anachronistic
  113 adj.
matinal 123 adj.
early 130 adj.
timely 132 adj.
ill-timed 133 adj.
speedy 272 adj.

**early, be**
be unconformable
  84 vb.
time 112 vb.
misdate 113 vb.
be before 114 vb.
look ahead 119 vb.
be early 130 vb.
precede 278 vb.
arrive 290 vb.
err 490 vb.
foresee 505 vb.
deceive 537 vb.
be unprepared
  665 vb.
acquire 766 vb.
possess 768 vb.
take 781 vb.
hope 847 vb.

**earnings**
increment 36 n.

earnings 766 n.
receiving 777 n.
taking 781 n.
pay 799 n.
receipt 802 n.
reward 957 n.

**earth sciences**
earth sciences
316 n.

**earthwork**
antiquity 120 n.
small hill 204 n.
earthwork 248 n.
tomb 359 n.
signpost 542 n.
monument 543 n.
fort 708 n.

**easily**
easily 696 adv.

**easy**
possible 464 adj.
intelligible 511 adj.
easy 696 adj.

**easy, be**
be easy 696 vb.

**easy thing**
trifle 634 n.
easy thing 696 n.
victory 722 n.

**eat**
abate 37 vb.
absorb 294 vb.
eat 296 vb.
taste 381 vb.
waste 629 n.
have enough
630 vb.
prosper 725 vb.
fleece 781 vb.
be hungry 854 vb.
be sociable 877 vb.
gluttonize 942 vb.

**eater**
eater 296 n.
reveller 832 n.
glutton 942 n.

**eating**
eating 296 n.

**eccentricity**
eccentricity 498 n.

**ecclesiarch**
ecclesiarch 980 n.

**ecclesiastical**
ecclesiastical
979 adj.

**ecclesiastical, be**
be ecclesiastical
979 vb.

**ecclesiastical court**
ecclesiastical court
951 n.

**ecclesiastically**
ecclesiastically
979 adv.

**ecclesiasticism**
ecclesiasticism
979 n.

**economical**
economical
809 adj.
parsimonious
811 adj.
cautious 853 adj.
temperate 937 adj.
fasting 941 adj.

**economize**
economize 809 vb.

**economy**
diminution 37 n.
provision 628 n.
preservation 661 n.
restriction 742 n.
prohibition 752 n.
gain 766 n.
economy 809 n.
parsimony 811 n.
temperance 937 n.
asceticism 940 n.

**eddy**
coil 246 n.
water travel 264 n.
vortex 310 n.
eddy 345 n.
pitfall 658 n.

**edge**
adjunct 40 n.

extremity 69 n.
nearness 195 n.
contiguity 197 n.
roof 221 n.
outline 228 n.
edge 229 n.
limit 231 n.
laterality 234 n.
projection 249 n.
shore 339 n.

**edging**
filament 203 n.
garment 223 n.
edging 229 n.
coil 246 n.
trimming 839 n.

**edible**
edible 298 adj.
soft 322 n.
clean 643 adj.

**edifice**
adjunct 40 n.
composition 56 n.
accumulation 74 n.
edifice 159 n.
house 187 n.
high structure
204 n.
structure 326 n.
temple 984 n.

**edition**
variant 15 n.
duplicate 22 n.
subdivision 53 n.
repetition 102 n.
reproduction 161 n.
miniature 191 n.
letterpress 582 n.
edition 584 n.
amendment 649 n.

**educate**
inform 519 vb.
educate 529 vb.
motivate 607 vb.

**education**
education 529 n.
civilization 649 n.

**educational**
influential 173 adj.
demonstrating
473 adj.
informative
519 adj.
educational
529 adj.
pedagogic 532 adj.
scholastic 534 adj.

**effect**
relativeness 9 n.
remainder 41 n.
sequence 65 n.
sequel 67 n.
end 69 n.
event 149 n.
effect 152 n.
product 159 n.
instrumentality
623 n.
completion 720 n.

**effectuation**
effectuation 720 n.

**effervesce**
be violent 171 vb.
effervesce 313 vb.
bubble 350 vb.
be hot 374 vb.
crackle 397 vb.
hiss 401 vb.
be excited 816 vb.

**egotist**
egotist 927 n.

**egress**
motion 260 n.
wandering 262 n.
departure 291 n.
egress 298 n.
excretion 297 n.
passage 300 n.
gas 331 n.
current 345 n.
escape 662 n.
means of escape
662 n.

**eject**
abate 37 vb.

subtract 39 vb.
eliminate 44 vb.
disunite 46 vb.
exclude 57 vb.
render few 101 vb.
substitute 145 vb.
destroy 160 vb.
displace 183 vb.
externalize 218 vb.
make concave
250 vb.
transpose 267 vb.
impel 274 vb.
propel 282 vb.
eject 295 vb.
extract 299 vb.
reject 602 vb.
clean 643 vb.
stop using 669 vb.
depose 747 vb.
prohibit 752 vb.
not retain 774 vb.
deprive 781 vb.
make unwelcome
878 vb.
be rude 880 vb.

**ejection**
ejection 295 n.

**ejector**
ejector 295 n.

**elapse**
end 69 vb.
continue 104 vb.
elapse 107 vb.

**elapsing**
elapsing 107 adj.

**elastic**
regressive 281 adj.
rare 320 adj.
flexible 322 adj.
soft 322 adj.
elastic 323 adj.

**elastic, be**
soften 322 vb.

**elasticity**
elasticity 323 n.

**elastic - tensile
etc. adj.** bounce,
be
be elastic 323 vb.

**elation. See mania**
psychopathy 498 n.

**electorate**
list 87 n.
estimator 475 n.
electorate 600 n.

**electricity**
electricity 155 n.
radiation 412 n.
metrology 460 n.

**electronics**
electronics 155 n.
microelectronics
191 n.
mechanics 625 n.

**elegance**
elegance 570 n.

**elegant**
apt 24 adj.
elegant 570 adj.
well-made 689 adj.
witty 834 adj.
tasteful 841 adj.

**elegant, be**
be elegant 570 vb.
be affected 845 vb.

**element**
element 314 n.

**elevate**
augment 36 vb.
bring together
74 vb.
cause 151 vb.
strengthen 157 vb.
produce 159 vb.
place 182 vb.
displace 183 vb.
enlarge 192 vb.
make higher
204 vb.
make vertical
210 vb.
support 213 vb.
form 238 vb.

move 260 vb.
impel 274 vb.
promote 280 vb.
draw 283 vb.
elevate 305 vb.
lighten 318 vb.
celebrate 871 vb.

**elevated**
high 204 adj.
elevated 305 adj.
worshipful 861 adj.

**elevation**
increase 36 n.
production 159 n.
progression 280 n.
elevation 305 n.
improvement
649 n.
dignification 861 n.

**elf**
dwarf 191 n.
elf 964 n.

**eliminate**
eliminate 44 vb.
exclude 57 vb.
class 62 vb.
reject 602 vb.
purify 643 vb.

**elimination**
elimination 44 n.

**elite**
superior 34 n.
group 74 n.
chief thing 633 n.
elite 639 n.
soldier 717 n.
beau monde 843 n.
brave person
850 n.
person of repute
861 n.
upper class 863 n.

**eloquence**
eloquence 574 n.

**eloquent**
forceful 566 adj.
rhetorical 569 adj.
eloquent 574 adj.

**elude**
sophisticate
472 vb.
avoid 615 vb.
elude 662 vb.

**embrown**
embrown 425 vb.

**emerge**
result 152 vb.
navigate 264 vb.
recede 285 vb.
land 290 vb.
depart 291 vb.
start out 291 vb.
emerge 293 vb.
pass 300 vb.
flow 345 vb.
be visible 438 vb.
be disclosed
521 vb.
escape 662 vb.
attack 707 vb.

**eminently**
remarkably 32 adv.
eminently 34 adv.

**emit**
flow out 293 vb.
emit 295 vb.
gasify 331 vb.
vaporize 333 vb.
be wet 336 vb.
make flow 345 vb.
be hot 374 vb.
radiate 412 vb.
not retain 774 vb.

**emphasize**
emphasize 527 vb.

**empiricism**
empiricism 456 n.

**employ**
initiate 68 vb.
admit 294 vb.
employ 617 vb.
commission
746 vb.

**emporium**
emporium 791 n.

## empower

computerize 86 vb.
empower 155 vb.
strengthen 157 vb.
make possible
464 vb.
facilitate 696 vb.
permit 751 vb.

## emptiness

emptiness 185 n.

## empty

insubstantial 4 adj.
abate 37 vb.
subtract 39 vb.
lay waste 160 vb.
unproductive
167 adj.
empty 185 adj.
be absent 185 vb.
make smaller
193 vb.
uncover 224 vb.
transpose 267 vb.
empty 295 vb.
extract 299 vb.
let fall 306 vb.
lighten 318 vb.
rare 320 adj.
rarefy 320 vb.
dry 337 vb.
make flow 345 vb.
blow up 347 vb.
unthinking 445 adj.
waste 629 vb.
unprovided
631 adj.
liberate 741 vb.
unpossessed
769 adj.
levy 781 vb.
secluded 878 adj.

## empty talk

insubstantial thing
4 n.
ineffectuality 156 n.
sophistry 472 vb.
overestimation
477 n.

empty talk 510 n.
falsehood 536 n.
fable 538 n.
slang 555 n.
phrase 558 n.
diffuseness 565 n.
magniloquence
569 n.
speech 574 n.
chatter 576 n.
trifle 634 n.
boast 872 n.
boasting 872 vb.

## empurple

empurple 431 vb.

## enamoured

misjudging
476 vb.
foolish 494 adj.
crazy 498 adj.
excited 816 adj.
enamoured
882 adj.

## enclose

affix 45 vb.
tie 45 vb.
set apart 46 vb.
contain 56 vb.
exclude 57 vb.
bring together
74 vb.
comprise 78 vb.
support 213 vb.
hold within 219 vb.
cover 221 vb.
surround 225 vb.
enclose 230 vb.
fold 256 vb.
break in 364 vb.
cultivate 365 vb.
safeguard 655 vb.
obstruct 697 vb.
besiege 707 vb.
defend 708 vb.
imprison 742 vb.
retain 773 vb.

## enclosure

enclosure 230 n.

## encroach

be near 195 vb.
interfere 226 vb.
collide 279 vb.
encroach 301 vb.
attack 707 vb.
disobey 733 vb.
do wrong 909 vb.
be undue 911 vb.

## encumbrance

encumbrance
697 n.

## end

completeness 54 n.
be complete 54 vb.
sequence 65 n.
sequel 67 vb.
end 69 n.
end 69 vb.
elapse 107 vb.
be past 120 vb.
be old 122 vb.
stop 140 vb.
go on 141 vb.
event 149 n.
be destroyed
160 vb.
limit 231 n.
decease 356 n.
intention 612 n.
completion 720 n.

## endanger

endanger 656 vb.
be difficult 695 vb.
defeat 722 vb.

## endangered

endangered
656 adj.

## endearment

correspondence
583 n.
inducement 607 n.
retention 773 n.
courteous act
879 n.
love-making 882 n.
endearment 884 n.
flattery 920 n.

## ending

ending 69 adj.
past 120 adj.
causal 156 adj.
destroyed 160 adj.
completive 720 adj.

## endorse

stabilize 148 vb.
make certain
468 vb.
endorse 483 vb.
sign 542 vb.
patronize 698 vb.
consent 753 vb.
contract 760 vb.
give security
762 vb.
grant claims
910 vb.
approve 918 vb.
make legal 948 vb.

## enemy

troublemaker
658 n.
opponent 700 n.
enemy 876 n.
hateful object
883 n.
offender 899 n.
accuser 923 n.

## energy

quantity 26 n.
causal means
151 n.
energy 155 n.
vigorousness
169 n.
propellant 282 n.
metrology 460 n.
vigour 566 n.
exertion 677 n.
workshop 682 n.
excitation 816 n.

## engaged, be

be engaged
133 vb.
be busy 673 vb.

**engrave**
cut 46 vb.
outline 228 vb.
groove 257 vb.
mark 542 vb.
record 543 vb.
represent 546 vb.
engrave 550 vb.

**engraver**
engraver 551 n.

**engraving**
copy 22 n.
concavity 250 n.
recorder 544 n.
representation
546 n.
picture 548 n.
engraving 550 n.
writing 581 n.
ornamental art
839 n.

**engross**
engross 444 vb.
attract notice
450 vb.
bias 476 vb.

**enigma**
enigma 525 n.

**enjoy**
enjoy 371 vb.
taste 381 vb.
prosper 725 vb.
be pleased 819 vb.
be content 823 vb.

**enjoyment**
enjoyment 819 n.

**enlace**
enlace 217 vb.

**enlarge**
add 38 vb.
enlarge 192 vb.
feed 296 vb.
elevate 305 vb.
blow up 347 vb.
overrate 477 vb.
exaggerate 541 vb.
make important
633 vb.

**enmity**
disagreement 25 n.
opposition 699 n.
enmity 876 n.
hatred 883 n.
resentment 886 n.
malevolence 893 n.
revenge 905 n.
disapprobation
919 n.

**enormous**
enormous 32 adj.
unusual 84 adj.

**enough**
enough 630 adv.

**en passant**
en passant
300 adv.

**enquire**
meditate 444 vb.
be curious 448 vb.
enquire 454 vb.
be tentative
456 vb.
experiment 456 vb.
estimate 475 vb.
not know 486 vb.
be informed
519 vb.
study 531 vb.

**enquirer**
enquirer 454 n.

**enquiring**
enquiring 454 adj.

**enquiry**
attribution 153 n.
inquest 359 n.
listening 410 n.
inspection 433 n.
meditation 444 n.
enquiry 454 n.
experiment 456 n.
comparison 457 n.
certainty 468 n.
argumentation
470 n.
report 519 n.
publicity 523 n.

study 531 n.
dissertation 586 n.
policy 618 n.
undertaking 667 n.
sale 788 n.
legal trial 954 n.

**enrage**
derange 63 vb.
make violent
171 vb.
make mad 498 vb.
make quarrels
704 vb.
excite 816 vb.
torment 822 vb.
aggravate 827 vb.
cause dislike
856 vb.
be insolent 873 vb.
make enemies
876 vb.
excite hate 883 vb.
enrage 886 vb.

**en revanche**
en revanche
709 adv.

**ensnare**
attract 286 vb.
detect 479 vb.
surprise 503 vb.
ambush 522 vb.
ensnare 537 vb.
tempt 607 vb.
hunt 614 vb.
plot 618 vb.
hinder 697 vb.
take 781 vb.

**ensue**
ensue 115 vb.

**enter**
be included 78 vb.
pierce 258 vb.
approach 284 vb.
converge 288 vb.
arrive 290 vb.
start out 291 vb.
enter 292 vb.
pass 300 vb.

flow 345 vb.
be visible 438 vb.
join a party 703 vb.

**enterprising**
attempting 666 adj.
enterprising
667 adj.
active 673 adj.
courageous
850 adj.
rash 852 adj.

**entertainer**
imitator 20 n.
athlete 157 n.
wanderer 263 n.
jumper 307 n.
fool 496 n.
entertainer 589 n.
dance 832 n.
humorist 834 n.

**enthusiast**
enthusiast 499 n.

**entrance**
entrance 68 n.
doorway 258 n.

**entreat**
entreat 756 vb.
deprecate 757 vb.
worship 975 vb.

**entreaty**
report 519 n.
affirmation 527 n.
entreaty 756 n.

**enumerator**
enumerator 86 n.

**envious**
inimical 876 adj.
resentful 886 adj.
malevolent 893 adj.
jealous 906 adj.
envious 907 adj.
selfish 927 adj.

**envoy**
messenger 524 n.
official 685 n.
commission 746 n.
envoy 749 n.

**envy**
discontent 824 n.
be discontented
    824 vb.
desire 854 vb.
enmity 876 n.
be inimical 876 vb.
hatred 883 n.
hate 883 vb.
resent 886 vb.
malevolence 893 n.
be malevolent
    893 vb.
jealousy 906 n.
be jealous 906 vb.
envy 907 n.
envy 907 vb.
approve 918 vb.
**ephemeral**
inferior 35 adj.
ephemeral 109 adj.
substituted
    145 adj.
**epistolary**
epistolary 583 adj.
**epitomizer**
epitomizer 587 n.
**equal**
identical 13 adj.
adjusted 24 adj.
agreeing 24 adj.
equal 28 adj.
joined 45 adj.
numerable 86 adj.
synchronous
    118 adj.
parallel 214 adj.
symmetrical
    240 adj.
interpretive
    515 adj.
sufficient 630 adj.
**equal, be**
be equal 28 vb.
comprise 78 vb.
synchronize
    118 vb.
weigh 317 vb.

be good 639 vb.
**equal chance**
equal chance
    154 n.
nondesign 613 n.
**equality**
relativeness 9 n.
identity 13 n.
similarity 18 n.
equality 28 n.
synchronism 118 n.
stability 148 n.
equal chance
    154 n.
parallelism 214 n.
no choice 601 n.
finance 792 n.
justice 908 n.
**equalization**
equalization 28 n.
**equalize**
equalize 28 vb.
**equally**
correlatively
    12 adv.
equally 28 adv.
**equilibrium**
equilibrium 28 n.
symmetry 240 n.
inexcitability 818 n.
**equine**
equine 268 adj.
**equipment**
equipment 625 n.
**equitation**
equitation 262 n.
**equivalence**
equivalence 28 n.
**equivalent**
correlative 12 adj.
similar 18 adj.
equivalent 28 adj.
compensatory
    31 adj.
substituted
    145 adj.
interchanged
    146 adj.

**equivocal**
similar 18 adj.
unconformable
    84 adj.
double 91 adj.
countervailing
    462 adj.
uncertain 469 adj.
unexpected
    503 adj.
semantic 509 adj.
puzzling 512 adj.
equivocal 513 adj.
false 536 adj.
untrue 538 adj.
unclear 563 adj.
tergiversating
    598 adj.
cunning 693 adj.
dishonest 925 adj.
**equivocal, be**
be contrary 14 vb.
liken 18 vb.
vary 147 vb.
tell against 462 vb.
be uncertain
    469 vb.
sophisticate
    472 vb.
be unintelligible
    512 vb.
be equivocal
    513 vb.
misinterpret
    516 vb.
dissemble 536 vb.
be diffuse 565 vb.
be irresolute
    596 vb.
tergiversate 598 vb.
avoid 615 vb.
not observe
    764 vb.
be witty 834 vb.
be dishonest
    925 vb.

**equivocalness**
equivocalness
    513 n.
**era**
date 104 n.
era 106 n.
chronology 112 n.
antiquity 120 n.
past time 120 n.
oldness 122 n.
literature 552 n.
**erotic**
erotic 882 adj.
sensual 939 adj.
**err**
err 490 vb.
be foolish 494 vb.
misinterpret
    516 vb.
**erroneous**
unreal 2 adj.
irrelevant 10 adj.
impossible 465 adj.
unreliable 469 adj.
illogical 472 adj.
erroneous 490 adj.
absurd 492 adj.
imaginary 508 adj.
**error**
unrelatedness 10 n.
deviation 277 n.
inattention 451 n.
unreliability 469 n.
misjudgment
    476 n.
ignorance 491 n.
sciolism 486 n.
error 490 n.
lack of expectation
    503 n.
fantasy 508 n.
deception 537 n.
inexpedience
    638 n.
defect 642 n.
imperfection 642 n.
heterodoxy 971 n.

demonstrate
473 vb.
assent 483 n.
accuracy 489 n.
supposition 507 n.
mean 509 n.
be intelligible
511 n.
exhibit 517 n.
manifestation
517 n.
manifest 517 vb.
untruth 538 n.
indication 542 n.
indicate 542 vb.
trace 543 n.
accusation 923 n.
legal trial 954 n.

**evidential**
evidential 461 adj.

**evil**
evil 611 n.
evil 611 adj.
nondesign 613 n.
badness 640 n.
harmful 640 adj.
bane 654 n.
baneful 654 adj.
misuse 670 n.
adversity 726 n.
suffering 820 n.
worry 820 n.
annoyance 822 n.
painfulness 822 n.

**evildoer**
evildoer 899 n.

**evolution**
event 149 n.
motion 260 n.
evolution 311 n.

**evolve**
become 1 vb.
unravel 62 vb.
be turned to
142 vb.
result 152 vb.
produce 159 vb.
lengthen 198 vb.

straighten 244 vb.
progress 280 vb.
extract 299 vb.
evolve 311 vb.

**evolving**
evolving 311 adj.

**exaggerate**
augment 36 vb.
enlarge 192 vb.
overstep 301 vb.
overrate 477 vb.
be absurd 492 vb.
imagine 508 vb.
mean nothing
510 vb.
misinterpret
516 vb.
be false 536 vb.
be untrue 538 vb.
exaggerate 541 vb.
misrepresent
547 vb.
act 589 vb.
superabound
632 vb.
make important
633 vb.
be affected 845 vb.
boast 872 vb.
praise 918 vb.

**exaggerated**
exaggerated
541 adj.

**exaggeration**
insubstantial thing
4 n.
greatness 32 n.
increase 36 n.
expansion 192 n.
overstepping
301 n.
overestimation
477 n.
absurdity 492 n.
ideality 508 n.
trope 514 n.
misinterpretation
516 n.

publicity 523 n.
falsehood 536 n.
fable 538 n.
untruth 538 n.
liar 540 n.
exaggeration
541 n.
misrepresentation
547 n.
magniloquence
569 n.
redundance 632 n.
ridiculousness
844 n.
ostentation 870 n.
boast 872 n.

**exam**
exam 454 n.

**example**
relevance 9 n.
analogue 18 n.
duplicate 22 n.
prototype 23 n.
part 53 n.
precursor 66 n.
rule 81 n.
example 83 n.
guide 515 n.
interpretation
515 n.
exhibit 517 n.
precept 688 n.

**excavation**
excavation 250 n.

**excavator**
excavator 250 n.
descent 304 n.

**excellent**
unequal 29 adj.
superior 34 adj.
unusual 84 adj.
chosen 600 adj.
notable 638 adj.
excellent 639 adj.
perfect 641 adj.
skilful 689 adj.
successful 722 adj.

pleasurable
821 adj.
splendid 836 adj.
tasteful 841 adj.
wonderful 859 adj.
renowned 861 adj.
reputable 861 adj.
virtuous 928 adj.

**exceller**
exceller 639 n.

**excitability**
excitability 817 n.

**excitable**
nonuniform 17 adj.
active 673 adj.
fervent 813 adj.
impressed 813 adj.
impressible
814 adj.
sensitive 814 adj.
excited 816 adj.
excitable 817 adj.
rash 852 adj.
irascible 887 adj.

**excitable, be**
be busy 673 vb.
be excited 816 vb.
be excitable
817 vb.
get angry 886 vb.

**excitable state**
violence 171 n.
gesture 542 n.
warm feeling
813 n.
excitation 816 n.
excitable state
817 n.
cheerfulness 828 n.
love 882 n.
anger 886 n.

**excitant**
excitant 816 n.

**excitation**
excitation 816 n.

**excite**
cause 151 vb.
strengthen 157 vb.

invigorate 169 vb.
make violent
171 vb.
make mad 498 vb.
remind 500 vb.
incite 607 vb.
excite 816 vb.
delight 821 vb.
aggravate 827 vb.
cause desire
854 vb.
excite love 882 vb.
inebriate 944 vb.

**excited**
expectant 502 adj.
induced 607 adj.
feeling 813 adj.
impressed 813 adj.
excited 816 adj.
excitable 817 adj.
enamoured
882 adj.
erotic 882 adj.
approving 918 adj.
drunk 944 adj.

**excited, be**
be agitated 313 vb.
enjoy 371 vb.
feel 813 vb.
be excited 816 vb.
be excitable
817 vb.
be angry 886 vb.

**excitedly**
excitedly 816 adv.

**excite hate**
set apart 46 vb.
make quarrels
704 vb.
cause dislike
856 vb.
excite hate 883 vb.
huff 886 vb.

**excite love**
delight 821 vb.
be affected 845 vb.
cause desire
854 vb.

be wonderful
859 vb.
excite love 882 vb.
caress 884 vb.
court 884 vb.

**exciting**
vigorous 169 adj.
striking 369 adj.
eloquent 574 adj.
descriptive 585 adj.
dramatic 589 adj.
inducing 607 adj.
exciting 816 adj.
pleasurable
821 adj.
cheering 828 adj.
intoxicating
944 adj.

**exclude**
abate 37 vb.
subtract 39 vb.
leave over 41 vb.
eliminate 44 vb.
set apart 46 vb.
be incomplete
55 vb.
exclude 57 vb.
cease 140 vb.
transform 142 vb.
eject 295 vb.
screen 416 vb.
disregard 453 vb.
reject 602 vb.
obstruct 697 vb.
restrain 742 vb.
depose 747 vb.
prohibit 752 vb.
refuse 755 vb.
shame 862 vb.
make unwelcome
878 vb.
exempt 914 vb.
disapprove 919 vb.

**excluded**
excluded 57 adj.

**excluded, be**
be excluded 57 vb.

**excluding**
excluding 57 adj.
exterior 218 adj.
prohibiting 752 adj.

**exclusion**
diminution 37 n.
elimination 44 n.
separation 46 n.
exclusion 57 n.
nonconformity
84 n.
strike 140 n.
exteriority 218 n.
partition 226 n.
ejection 295 n.
screen 416 n.
prejudice 476 n.
rejection 602 n.
restriction 742 n.
seclusion 878 n.
unsociability 878 n.
disapprobation
919 n.
penalty 958 n.

**exclusive of**
exclusive of 57 adv.

**excrement**
leavings 41 n.
excrement 297 n.
fluid 330 n.
moisture 336 n.
stench 392 n.
dirt 644 n.

**excrete**
emit 295 vb.
empty 295 vb.
excrete 297 vb.
make flow 345 vb.

**excretion**
excretion 297 n.

**excretory**
excretory 297 adj.

**excusing**
excusing 609 adj.

**execute**
kill 357 vb.
execute 958 vb.

**exemplify**
exemplify 83 vb.
interpret 515 vb.

**exempt**
qualify 463 vb.
deliver 663 vb.
liberate 741 vb.
permit 751 vb.
relieve 826 vb.
exempt 914 vb.
acquit 955 vb.

**exempt, be**
escape 662 vb.
fail in duty 913 vb.
be exempt 914 vb.

**exercise**
athletics 157 n.
teaching 529 n.
hygiene 647 n.
civilization 649 n.
exercise 677 n.

**exertion**
exertion 677 n.

**exert oneself**
be vigorous 169 vb.
be attentive
450 vb.
be careful 452 vb.
search 454 vb.
be resolute 594 vb.
persevere 595 vb.
attempt 666 vb.
be active 673 vb.
exert oneself
677 vb.

**exhibit**
accumulation 74 n.
spectacle 440 n.
exhibit 517 n.
advertisement
523 n.
label 542 n.
collection 627 n.
market 791 n.
plaything 832 n.
fashion 843 n.
pageant 870 n.

**exhibitor**
exhibitor 517 n.

**exhume**
exhume 359 vb.

**exiguous**
exiguous 191 adj.
lean 201 adj.

**existence**
existence 1 n.
cause 151 n.
materiality 314 n.
life 355 n.
appearance 440 n.
truth 489 n.
divine attribute
960 n.

**existing**
existing 1 adj.

**exorbitant**
exorbitant 32 adj.
violent 171 adj.
huge 190 adj.
surpassing 301 adj.
exaggerated
541 adj.
redundant 632 adj.
harmful 640 adj.
intolerable 822 adj.

**expand**
be great 32 vb.
augment 36 vb.
grow 36 vb.
be large 190 vb.
expand 192 vb.
lengthen 198 vb.
be broad 200 vb.
jut 249 vb.
eat 296 vb.

**expanded**
expanded 192 adj.

**expansion**
expansion 192 n.

**expect**
look ahead 119 vb.
assume 466 vb.
expect 502 vb.
foresee 505 vb.
intend 612 vb.

prepare 664 vb.
hope 847 vb.
not wonder 860 vb.
impose a duty
912 vb.

**expectant**
attentive 450 adj.
expectant 502 adj.
foreseeing 505 adj.
warned 659 adj.
hoping 847 adj.
unastonished
860 adj.

**expectantly**
expectantly
502 adv.

**expectation**
futurity 119 n.
looking ahead
119 n.
destiny 150 n.
probability 466 n.
dubiety 469 n.
expectation 502 n.
prediction 506 n.
hope 847 n.
religion 967 n.

**expected**
expected 502 adj.

**expedient, be**
accord 24 vb.
answer 455 vb.
answer 455 n.
suffice 630 vb.
be useful 635 vb.
be expedient
637 vb.
advise 686 vb.

**expediently**
expediently
637 adv.

**expend**
waste 629 vb.
lose 767 vb.
pay 799 vb.
expend 801 vb.

**expended**
expended 801 adj.

**expending**
expending 801 adj.

**expenditure**
waste 629 n.
loss 767 n.
purchase 787 n.
payment 799 n.
expenditure 801 n.
cost 804 n.

**experiment**
modify 138 vb.
calculation of
chance 154 n.
listening 410 n.
be curious 448 vb.
enquiry 454 n.
enquire 454 vb.
456vb.
demonstration
473 n.
discover 479 vb.
gambling 613 n.
gamble 613 vb.
preparation 664 n.
attempt 666 n.
attempt 666 vb.
litigation 954 n.

**experimental**
experimental
456 adj.

**experimentally**
experimentally
456 adv.

**experimenter**
experimenter
456 n.

**expert**
superior 34 n.
old man 128 n.
powerful 155 adj.
mariner 265 n.
seamanlike
265 adj.
instructed 485 adj.
knowing 485 adj.
planner 618 n.
bigwig 633 n.
matured 664 adj.

doer 671 n.
adviser 686 n.
expert 689 adj.
expert 691 n.
lawyer 953 n.

**expert, be**
know 485 vb.
be expert 689 vb.

**explosive**
destroyer 163 n.
propellant 282 n.
ejector 295 n.
fireworks 415 n.
pitfall 658 n.
explosive 718 n.

**expressive**
meaningful
509 adj.
expressive 511 adj.

**expropriation**
expropriation
781 n.

**expulsive**
expulsive 295 adj.

**extempore**
at present 116 adv.
extempore
604 adv.

**extend**
be great 32 vb.
fill 54 vb.
continue 104 vb.
extend 178 vb.
be large 190 vb.
be distant 194 vb.
be contiguous
197 vb.
be long 198 vb.
superabound
632 vb.

**extensive**
extensive 32 adj.
comprehensive
52 adj.
inclusive 78 adj.
universal 79 adj.
spacious 178 adj.

**extenuate**
qualify 463 vb.
plead 609 vb.
extenuate 922 vb.

**exterior**
extrinsic 6 adj.
separate 46 adj.
extraneous 59 adj.
exterior 218 adj.
appearing 440 adj.

**exterior, be**
be exterior 218 vb.

**exteriority**
exteriority 218 n.

**externalize**
externalize 218 vb.

**externally**
externally 218 adv.

**extinct**
extinct 2 adj.
past 120 adj.
disappearing
441 adj.

**extinction**
extinction 2 n.
destruction 160 n.
death 356 n.

**extinguish**
abate 37 vb.
suppress 160 vb.
moderate 172 vb.
extinguish 377 vb.

**extinguisher**
moderator 172 n.
extinguisher 377 n.

**extra**
inequality 29 n.
increment 36 n.
extra 40 n.
component 58 n.
pleonasm 565 n.
superfluity 632 n.
safeguard 657 n.
receipt 802 n.
price 804 n.

**extract**
subtract 39 vb.
produce 159 vb.

displace 183 vb.
uncover 224 vb.
pierce 258 vb.
draw 283 vb.
eject 295 vb.
empty 295 vb.
extract 299 vb.
elevate 305 vb.
manifest 517 vb.
provide 628 vb.
deliver 663 vb.
use 668 vb.
acquire 766 vb.
levy 781 vb.
take 781 vb.

**extracted**
extracted 299 adj.

**extraction**
subtraction 39 n.
displacement
183 n.
transference 267 n.
extraction 299 n.
deliverance 663 n.

**extractor**
extractor 299 n.

**extramarital**
extramarital
946 adj.

**extraneous**
extrinsic 6 adj.
unrelated 10 adj.
disagreeing 25 adj.
additional 38 adj.
separate 46 adj.
nonadhesive
49 adj.
excluded 57 adj.
extraneous 59 adj.
discontinuous
72 adj.
unconformable
84 adj.
unusual 84 adj.
unstable 147 adj.
exterior 218 adj.
interjacent 226 adj.
travelling 262 adj.

hindering 697 adj.
ridiculous 844 adj.
wonderful 859 adj.
unsociable 878 adj.

**extraneousness**
extraneousness
59 n.

**extremely**
extremely 32 adv.
eminently 34 adv.

**extremity**
adjunct 40 n.
remainder 41 n.
completeness 54 n.
extremity 69 n.
vertex 208 n.
edge 229 n.
limit 231 n.
rear 233 n.
goal 290 n.

**extricable**
extricable 663 adj.

**extrinsic**
extrinsic 6 adj.
unrelated 10 adj.
additional 38 adj.
separate 46 adj.
extraneous 59 adj.
exterior 218 adj.

**extrinsicality**
extrinsicality 6 n.

**extrinsically**
extrinsically 6 adv.

**extrinsic, be**
be extrinsic 6 vb.
be exterior 218 vb.

**exude**
exude 293 vb.
emit 295 vb.
excrete 297 vb.
be wet 336 vb.
flow 345 vb.

**eye**
screen 416 n.
eye 433 n.
surveillance 452 n.

**eyeglass**
eyeglass 437 n.

**eyesore**
deformity 241 n.
painfulness 822 n.
eyesore 837 n.
blemish 840 n.

**F**

**fable**
fantasy 508 n.
empty talk 510 n.
fable 538 n.
exaggeration
541 n.
narrative 585 n.

**face**
face 232 n.
form 238 n.
dome 248 n.
protuberance
249 n.
feature 440 n.

**face danger**
be resolute 594 vb.
face danger
656 vb.
undertake 667 vb.
be in difficulty
695 vb.
withstand 699 vb.
defy 706 vb.
resist 710 vb.
be courageous
850 vb.
be rash 852 vb.

**facilitate**
make possible
464 vb.
be intelligible
511 vb.
interpret 515 vb.
tempt 607 vb.
facilitate 696 vb.
give scope 739 vb.
permit 751 vb.

## facilitated

**facilitated**
facilitated 696 adj.

**facility**
possibility 464 n.
intelligibility 511 n.
skill 609 n.
facility 696 n.
aid 698 n.
acquisition 766 n.

**facing**
adhesive 47 n.
facing 221 n.
smoother 253 n.
art equipment
548 n.
building material
626 n.
ornamental art
839 n.

**fail**
be inferior 35 vb.
lose a chance
133 vb.
cease 140 vb.
be impotent
156 vb.
be unproductive
167 vb.
blunder 490 vb.
be disappointed
504 vb.
be useless 636 vb.
attempt 666 vb.
be clumsy 690 vb.
be unskilful 690 vb.
not complete
721 vb.
fail 723 vb.
have trouble
726 vb.
lose repute 862 vb.

**fail in duty**
fail in duty 913 vb.

**failure**
stop 140 n.
helplessness 156 n.
impotence 156 n.
ruin 160 n.

propagation 162 n.
shortfall 302 n.
negligence 453 n.
mistake 490 n.
disappointment
504 n.
lost labour 636 n.
bungling 690 n.
noncompletion
721 n.
failure 723 n.
misfortune 726 n.

**faintly**
faintly 396 adv.

**faintness**
faintness 396 n.

**fair chance**
opportunity 132 n.
fair chance 154 n.
possibility 464 n.

**fairy**
sea nymph 338 n.
fairy 964 n.
sorceress 977 n.

**fairylike**
fairylike 964 adj.

**fake**
make unlike 19 vb.
copy 20 vb.
corroborate 461 vb.
fake 536 vb.
deceive 537 vb.
predetermine
603 vb.
plot 618 vb.
indict 923 vb.

**fall short**
be small 33 vb.
be inferior 35 vb.
be incomplete
55 vb.
be impotent
156 vb.
be short 199 vb.
fall short 302 vb.
be disappointed
504 vb.
disappoint 504 vb.

not suffice 631 vb.
be imperfect
642 vb.

**false**
imitative 20 adj.
unattested 462 adj.
erroneous 490 adj.
false 536 adj.
deceiving 537 adj.
spurious 537 adj.
untrue 538 adj.
affected 845 adj.
perfidious 925 adj.

**false alarm**
insubstantial thing
4 n.
false alarm 660 n.

**false, be**
misteach 530 vb.
be false 536 vb.
be untrue 538 vb.
exaggerate 541 vb.
misrepresent
547 vb.
indict 923 vb.
be dishonest
925 vb.

**false charge**
censure 919 n.
false charge 923 n.

**falsehood**
imitation 20 n.
improbability
467 n.
error 490 n.
ideality 508 n.
empty talk 510 n.
misteaching 530 n.
falsehood 536 n.
deception 537 n.
untruth 538 n.
liar 540 n.
misrepresentation
547 n.
improbity 925 n.
false piety 974 n.

**falsely**
falsely 536 adv.

**false money**
false money 792 n.
nonpayment 800 n.

**false piety**
false piety 974 n.

**family**
family 11 n.
group 74 n.
parentage 164 n.
posterity 165 n.
inhabitants 186 n.
social group 366 n.
community 703 n.
nobility 868 n.

**famousness**
famousness 861 n.

**fantasy**
insubstantial thing
4 n.
rara avis 84 n.
absence 185 n.
visual fallacy 435 n.
appearance 440 n.
misjudgment
476 n.
error 490 n.
fantasy 508 n.
narrative 585 n.
sleepiness 674 n.
happiness 819 n.
pleasurableness
821 n.
aspiration 847 n.
hopelessness
848 n.
desire 854 n.
prodigy 859 n.
mythic heaven
965 n.

**farm**
assemblage 74 n.
place 180 n.
house 187 n.
enclosure 230 n.
soil 339 n.
farm 365 n.
workshop 682 n.

joint possession
770 n.

**farmer**
accumulator 74 n.
producer 159 n.
dweller 186 n.
settler 186 n.
farmer 365 n.
preparer 664 n.
worker 681 n.
servant 737 n.
participator 770 n.
possessor 771 n.
country-dweller
864 n.

**farm tool**
sharp edge 251 n.
conveyor 269 n.
farm tool 365 n.

**farness**
farness 194 n.

**fashion**
generality 79 n.
conformity 83 n.
modernism 121 n.
clothier 223 n.
dressing 223 n.
practice 605 n.
beauty 836 n.
fashion 843 n.
affectation 845 n.
repute 861 n.

**fashionable**
modern 121 n.
usual 605 adj.
personable
836 adj.
tasteful 841 adj.
fashionable
843 adj.
reputable 861 adj.
proud 866 adj.
showy 870 adj.

**fashionably**
fashionably
843 adv.

**fast**
asceticism 940 n.

fast 941 n.
holy day 982 n.

**fastening**
fastening 47 n.
legwear 223 n.
sharp point 251 n.
perforator 258 n.
stopper 259 n.
nippers 773 n.
jewellery 839 n.
trimming 839 n.

**fastidious**
attentive 450 adj.
careful 452 adj.
discriminating
458 adj.
narrow-minded
476 adj.
accurate 489 adj.
capricious 599 adj.
clean 643 adj.
improving 649 adj.
severe 730 adj.
observant 763 adj.
discontented
824 adj.
tasteful 841 adj.
fastidious 857 adj.

**fastidious, be**
be capricious
599 vb.
select 600 vb.
be discontented
824 vb.
have taste 841 vb.
be fastidious
857 vb.

**fastidiousness**
fastidiousness
857 n.

**fasting**
fasting 941 n.
fasting 941 n.

**fat**
cookery 296 n.
fat 352 n.

**fatalist**
fatalist 591 n.

**fate**
finality 69 n.
future state 119 n.
destiny 150 n.
effect 152 n.
chance 154 n.
influence 173 n.
philosophy 444 n.
certainty 468 n.
expectation 502 n.
fate 591 n.
nondesign 613 n.
mythic deity 961 n.

**fated**
impending 150 adj.
certain 468 adj.
fated 591 adj.
predetermined
603 adj.

**fatigue**
helplessness 156 n.
weakness 158 n.
pain 372 n.
imperfection 642 n.
use 668 n.
misuse 670 vb.
sleepiness 674 n.
work 677 n.
fatigue 679 n.
fatigue 679 vb.
difficulty 695 n.
oppress 730 vb.
suffering 820 n.
trouble 822 vb.
dejection 829 n.
depress 829 vb.
tedium 833 n.
be tedious 833 vb.
impose a duty
912 vb.

**fatigued**
fatigued 679 adj.

**fatigued, be**
be fatigued 679 vb.

**fatiguing**
fatiguing 679 adj.

**fatty**
fatty 352 adj.

**favourite**
superior 34 n.
weakling 158 n.
attraction 286 n.
person 366 n.
actor 589 n.
bigwig 633 n.
exceller 639 n.
exceller 639 n.
prosperous person
725 n.
a beauty 836 n.
desired object
854 n.
person of repute
861 n.
pride 866 n.
sociable person
877 n.
favourite 885 n.
good person 932 n.

**favour. See badge**
indication 542 n.

**fear**
expectation 502 n.
expect 502 vb.
motive 607 n.
avoidance 615 n.
danger signal
660 n.
defeat 723 n.
excitation 816 n.
fear 849 n.
fear 849 vb.
cowardice 851 n.
dislike 856 n.
dislike 856 vb.
wonder 859 n.
wonder 859 vb.
honour 861 vb.
respect 915 n.
respect 915 vb.
piety 973 n.
be pious 973 vb.
worship 975 n.
worship 975 vb.

**fearing**
fearing 849 adj.

## feasting
feasting 296 n.

## feature
outline 228 n.
face 232 n.
form 238 n.
feature 440 n.
identification
542 n.

## feeble
repeated 102 adj.
feeble 567 adj.

## feebleness
feebleness 567 n.

## feed
enlarge 192 vb.
feed 296 vb.
vitalize 355 vb.
groom 364 vb.
refresh 680 vb.
be hospitable
877 vb.

## feeding
feeding 296 adj.

## feel
meet with 149 vb.
have feeling
369 vb.
opine 480 vb.
feel 813 vb.
be excited 816 vb.
suffer 820 vb.

## feeler
limb 53 n.
filament 203 n.
protuberance
249 n.
feeler 373 n.
nippers 773 n.

## feeling
crowd 74 n.
sense 369 n.
sentient 369 adj.
intuition 471 n.
opinion 480 n.
knowledge 485 n.
vigour 566 n.

spontaneous
604 adj.
conduct 683 n.
liberation 741 n.
affections 812 n.
with affections
812 adj.
feeling 813 n.
feeling 813 adj.
excitation 816 n.
excited 816 adj.
excitable state
817 n.
love 882 n.
benevolence 892 n.

## feelingly
feelingly 813 adv.

## feel pain
feel pain 372 n.
cry 403 n.
suffer 820 vb.

## feel pride
seek repute 861 vb.
feel pride 866 vb.
be vain 868 vb.

## fell
demolish 160 vb.
flatten 211 vb.
strike 274 vb.
fell 306 vb.

## felt
felt 813 adj.

## female
abnormality 84 n.
adult 129 n.
adultness 129 n.
grown-up 129 adj.
weak 158 adj.
female 368 n.
female 368 adj.

## female animal
female animal
368 n.

## fence
surroundings
225 n.
partition 226 n.

circumscription
227 n.
edge 229 n.
fence 230 n.
stopper 259 n.
screen 416 n.
protection 655 n.
shelter 657 n.

## fertilized
fertilized 162 adj.

## fertilizer
propagation 162 n.
fertilizer 166 n.
agriculture 365 n.

## fervent
forceful 566 adj.
active 673 adj.
hasty 675 adj.
fervent 813 adj.
lively 814 adj.
excited 816 adj.
loving 882 adj.

## festivity
meal 296 n.
rejoicing 830 n.
festivity 832 n.
pageant 870 n.
celebration 871 n.
social gathering
877 n.
holy day 982 n.

## fetid
unsavoury 386 adj.
odorous 389 adj.
fetid 392 n.
unclean 644 adj.
unpleasant 822 adj.

## fetter
tie 45 n.
fastening 47 n.
halter 47 n.
stopper 259 n.
safeguard 657 n.
make inactive
674 vb.
encumbrance
697 n.
hinder 697 vb.

subjection 740 n.
restraint 742 n.
fetter 742 vb.
fetter 743 n.
take 781 vb.
pillory 959 n.

## few
inconsiderable
33 adj.
few 101 adj.
infrequent 135 adj.
scarce 631 adj.

## few, be
decrease 37 vb.
be few 101 vb.

## fewness
fewness 101 n.

## fibre
cable 47 n.
ligature 47 n.
fibre 203 n.
textile 217 n.
textile 217 n.
skin 221 n.
convolution 246 n.
hair 254 n.
texture 326 n.
materials 626 n.

## fibrous
narrow 201 adj.
fibrous 203 adj.

## fiery
violent 171 adj.
fiery 374 adj.
luminous 412 adj.

## fifth and over
fifth and over
96 adj.

## fight
turmoil 61 n.
strike 274 n.
withstand 699 vb.
quarrel 704 n.
attack 707 vb.
fight 711 n.
fight 711 vb.
battle 713 n.
give battle 713 vb.

**go to war** 713 vb.
  be courageous
        850 vb.
  be inimical 876 vb.
  anger 886 vb.
**figurative**
  compared 457 adj.
  semantic 509 adj.
  figurative 514 adj.
  occult 518 adj.
  ornate 569 adj.
  rhetorical 569 adj.
  descriptive 585 adj.
**figure**
  figure 514 vb.
**filament**
  small thing 33 n.
  narrowness 201 n.
  thinness 201 n.
  filament 203 n.
  hair 254 n.
**filial**
  filial 165 adj.
**fill**
  be great 32 vb.
  fill 54 vb.
  bring together
        74 vb.
  be many 100 vb.
  stow 182 vb.
  load 188 vb.
  enlarge 192 vb.
  make smaller
        193 vb.
  overstep 301 vb.
  replenish 628 vb.
  suffice 630 vb.
  superabound
        632 vb.
  sate 858 vb.
**filled**
  filled 630 adj.
**film**
  film 440 n.
  photography 546 n.
**finality**
  completeness 54 n.
  finality 69 n.

**period** 106 n.
**future state** 119 n.
  evening 124 n.
  ruin 160 n.
  decease 356 n.
  completion 720 n.
**finally**
  after 65 adv.
  finally 69 adv.
**finance**
  finance 792 n.
**find means**
  cause 151 vb.
  find means 624 vb.
**find useful**
  find useful 635 vb.
  use 668 vb.
**finery**
  clothing 223 n.
  headgear 223 n.
  loop 245 n.
  plumage 254 n.
  finery 839 n.
  ostentation 870 n.
**finger**
  finger 373 n.
  nippers 773 n.
**finite quantity**
  finite quantity 26 n.
  small quantity 33 n.
  measurement
        460 n.
**fire**
  fire 374 n.
  burning 376 n.
  kindle 376 vb.
  furnace 378 n.
  fire 380 n.
  light 412 n.
  luminary 415 n.
  redness 426 n.
  signal 542 n.
  celebration 871 n.
**firearm**
  propellant 282 n.
  bang 397 n.
  chase 614 n.
  firearm 718 n.

**fire at**
  demolish 160 vb.
  shoot 282 vb.
  fire at 707 vb.
  give battle 713 vb.
**fireworks**
  fireworks 415 n.
**firm**
  firm 45 adj.
  full 54 adj.
  strong 157 adj.
**first**
  first 68 adj.
  fundamental
        151 adj.
**fish**
  fish 360 n.
**fish food**
  fish food 296 n.
  fish 360 n.
**fishing boat**
  fishing boat 270 n.
**fit**
  fit 24 adj.
  advisable 637 adj.
  right 908 adj.
**fitful**
  nonuniform 17 adj.
  discontinuous
        72 adj.
  fitful 137 adj.
  unstable 147 adj.
**fitfully**
  fitfully 137 adv.
**fitfulness**
  fitfulness 137 n.
**fitness**
  relevance 9 n.
  fitness 24 n.
  occasion 132 n.
  ability 155 n.
  tendency 174 n.
**fitting out**
  fitting out 664 n.
**five**
  five 96 n.
**fixed**
  uniform 16 adj.

  equal 28 adj.
  firm 45 adj.
  immemorial
        122 adj.
  unceasing 141 adj.
  fixed 148 adj.
  strong 157 adj.
  located 182 adj.
  deep 206 adj.
  interior 219 adj.
  still 261 adj.
  habitual 605 adj.
**fix the time**
  fix the time 104 vb.
**fixture**
  identity 13 n.
  permanence 139 n.
  fixture 148 n.
**flag**
  cross 217 n.
  shipping 270 n.
  flag 542 n.
  regalia 738 n.
**flagrant**
  flagrant 32 adj.
**flank**
  flank 234 vb.
**flash**
  agitation 313 n.
  fire 374 n.
  flash 412 n.
  glimmer 414 n.
  luminary 415 n.
**flat**
  uniform 16 adj.
  flat 187 n.
  chamber 189 n.
  low 205 adj.
  flat 211 adj.
  smooth 253 adj.
**flatten**
  demolish 160 vb.
  suppress 160 vb.
  make smaller
        193 vb.
  flatten 211 vb.
  straighten 244 vb.
  smooth 253 vb.

**flattener**

strike 274 vb.
fell 306 vb.

**flattener**

flattener 211 n.

**flatter**

repeat 102 vb.
influence 173 vb.
assent 483 vb.
mean nothing
510 vb.
be false 536 vb.
befool 537 vb.
exaggerate 541 vb.
misrepresent
547 vb.
induce 607 vb.
be cunning 693 vb.
minister to 698 vb.
be lenient 731 vb.
delight 821 vb.
please 821 vb.
honour 861 vb.
make conceited
868 vb.
be servile 874 vb.
pay one's respects
879 vb.
excite love 882 vb.
pet 884 vb.
praise 918 vb.
flatter 920 vb.
be dishonest
925 vb.

**flatterer**

flatterer 920 n.

**flattering**

flattering 920 adj.

**flatteringly**

flatteringly
920 adv.

**flattery**

conformity 83 n.
assent 483 n.
empty talk 510 n.
lack of meaning
510 n.
falsehood 536 n.

exaggeration
541 n.
misrepresentation
547 n.
inducement 607 n.
cunning 693 n.
pleasurableness
821 n.
servility 874 n.
courtesy 879 n.
endearment 884 n.
praise 918 n.
flattery 920 n.

**fleece**

fleece 701 vb.
defraud 783 vb.
impoverish 796 vb.
overcharge 806 vb.
be parsimonious
811 vb.

**fleecy**

smooth 253 adj.
fleecy 254 adj.

**fleshy**

fleshy 190 adj.

**flexible**

conformable
83 adj.
flexible 322 adj.
tractable 696 adj.

**flimsy**

insubstantial 4 adj.
flimsy 158 adj.
imperfect 642 adj.

**flog**

strike 274 vb.
flog 958 vb.

**floor-cover**

floor-cover 221 n.

**florid**

florid 420 adj.
variegated 432 adj.
splendid 836 adj.
ornamented
839 adj.
showy 870 adj.

**flourish**

flourish 610 vb.

**flow**

be violent 171 vb.
be in motion
260 vb.
move slowly
273 vb.
burst in 292 vb.
flow out 293 vb.
rotate 310 vb.
liquefy 332 vb.
flow 345 vb.
sound faint 396 vb.
be diffuse 565 vb.
superabound
632 vb.
be active 673 vb.

**flower**

flower 361 n.

**flowing**

furrowed 257 adj.
fluid 330 adj.
flowing 345 adj.
redundant 632 adj.

**flow out**

flow out 293 vb.

**fluctuate**

be unequal 29 vb.
vary 147 vb.
fluctuate 312 vb.
be agitated 313 vb.

**fluctuation**

fluctuation 312 n.

**fluid**

nonadhesive
49 adj.
changeable thing
147 n.
unstable 147 adj.
amorphous
239 adj.
soft 327 adj.
fluid 330 adj.
fluid 330 adj.
liquefied 332 adj.
water 334 n.
watery 334 adj.
moisture 336 n.
humid 336 adj.

flowing 345 adj.

**fluidity**

fluidity 330 n.

**flute**

stridor 402 n.
flute 409 n.

**fly**

ride 262 vb.
fly 266 vb.
decamp 291 vb.
ascend 303 vb.
be light 318 vb.

**flying**

flying 266 adj.
aviational 271 adj.

**focus**

union 45 n.
assemblage 74 n.
focus 76 n.
focus 76 n.
place 180 n.
locality 182 n.
abode 187 n.
meeting place
187 n.
centre 220 n.
convergence 288 n.
objective 612 n.
society 703 n.
arena 719 n.
market 791 n.
social round 877 n.

**fold**

joint 45 n.
derangement 63 n.
jumble 63 vb.
duplication 91 n.
receptacle 189 n.
become small
193 vb.
make smaller
193 vb.
invert 216 vb.
garment 223 n.
enclose 230 vb.
angularity 242 n.
curvature 243 n.

make curved
                    243 vb.
convolution 246 n.
crinkle 246 n.
roughness 254 n.
roughen 254 vb.
notch 255 vb.
fold 256 vb.
fold 256 vb.
groove 257 vb.
rotate 310 vb.
**folded**
folded 256 adj.
**foliage**
branch 53 n.
foliage 361 n.
greenness 429 n.
**follow**
do likewise 20 vb.
be inferior 35 vb.
come after 65 vb.
accompany 89 vb.
ensue 115 vb.
be late 131 vb.
happen 149 vb.
result 152 vb.
be near 195 vb.
be behind 233 vb.
walk 262 vb.
move slowly
                    273 vb.
follow 279 vb.
pursue 614 vb.
obstruct 697 vb.
court 884 vb.
**follower**
imitator 20 n.
retinue 67 n.
concomitant 89 n.
follower 279 n.
dependant 737 n.
**following**
sequence 65 n.
posteriority 115 n.
motion 260 n.
following 279 adj.
following 279 n.
pursuit 614 n.

pursuing 614 adj.
**folly**
insubstantial thing
                    4 n.
ignorance 486 n.
absurdity 492 n.
folly 494 n.
deception 537 n.
merriment 828 n.
rashness 852 n.
**food**
food 296 n.
life 355 n.
materials 626 n.
refreshment 680 n.
subvention 698 n.
sociability 877 n.
**food content**
food content 296 n.
**fool**
misfit 25 n.
ignoramus 488 n.
fool 496 n.
madman 499 n.
entertainer 589 n.
bungler 692 n.
humorist 834 n.
laughingstock
                    846 n.
**foolery**
foolery 492 n.
folly 494 n.
whim 599 n.
revel 832 n.
wit 834 n.
ridicule 846 n.
ostentation 870 n.
**foolish**
ageing 126 adj.
weak 158 adj.
mindless 443 adj.
misjudging
                    476 adj.
credulous 482 adj.
absurd 492 adj.
foolish 494 adj.
crazy 498 adj.
gullible 539 adj.

trivial 634 adj.
ridiculous 844 adj.
**foolish, be**
not discriminate
                    459 vb.
misjudge 476 vb.
be absurd 492 vb.
be foolish 494 vb.
be insane 498 vb.
mean nothing
                    510 vb.
impair 650 vb.
**foot**
foot 209 n.
conveyance 262 n.
finger 373 n.
**footed**
footed 209 adj.
**footwear**
footwear 223 n.
**fop**
people of taste
                    841 n.
fop 843 n.
affecter 845 n.
aristocrat 863 n.
proud person
                    866 n.
vain person 868 n.
**for a long time**
for a long time
                    108 adv.
**force**
derange 63 vb.
be vigorous 169 vb.
force 171 vb.
open 258 vb.
burst in 292 vb.
misuse 670 vb.
compel 735 vb.
not observe
                    764 vb.
**forced, be**
be forced 591 vb.
have no choice
                    601 vb.
**forceful**
keen 169 adj.

assertive 527 adj.
forceful 566 adj.
eloquent 574 adj.
lively 814 adj.
**forcefully**
forcefully 566 adv.
**foregoing**
foregoing 120 adj.
**foreigner**
foreigner 59 n.
dweller 186 n.
native 186 n.
settler 186 n.
wanderer 263 n.
incomer 292 n.
egress 293 n.
outcast 878 n.
**foremost**
foremost 278 adj.
**foresee**
see 433 vb.
assume 466 vb.
be wise 493 vb.
expect 502 vb.
foresee 505 vb.
intend 612 vb.
**foreseeing**
foreseeing 505 adj.
**foresight**
priority 114 n.
anticipation 130 n.
thought 444 n.
carefulness 452 n.
knowledge 485 n.
sagacity 493 n.
foresight 505 n.
prediction 506 n.
policy 618 n.
preparation 664 n.
caution 853 n.
**forestry**
forestry 361 n.
botany 363 n.
agriculture 365 n.
gardener 365 n.
**for ever**
for ever 110 adv.

**forget**

be inattentive
451 vb.
not know 486 vb.
forget 501 vb.
obliterate 545 vb.
relinquish 616 vb.
be unskilful 690 vb.
make peace
714 vb.
be lenient 731 vb.
forgive 904 vb.
fail in duty 913 vb.
exempt 914 vb.

**forgetful**

inattentive 451 adj.
negligent 453 adj.
ignorant 486 adj.
forgetful 501 adj.
ungrateful 903 adj.

**forgive**

abate 37 vb.
put off 131 vb.
disregard 453 vb.
forget 501 vb.
be lenient 731 vb.
liberate 741 vb.
be patient 818 vb.
be humble 867 vb.
be benevolent
892 vb.
pity 900 vb.
show mercy
900 vb.
forgive 904 vb.
exempt 914 vb.
acquit 955 vb.

**forgiven**

forgiven 904 adj.

**forgiveness**

amnesty 501 n.
peace offering
714 n.
leniency 731 n.
liberation 741 n.
benevolence 892 n.
mercy 900 n.
forgiveness 904 n.

nonliability 914 n.
acquittal 955 n.

**forgiving**

forgetful 501 adj.
lenient 731 adj.
benevolent 892 adj.
pitying 900 adj.
forgiving 904 adj.
godlike 960 adj.

**forgivingly**

forgivingly 904 adv.

**forgotten**

forgotten 501 adj.

**forgotten, be**

be forgotten
501 vb.

**form**

modality 7 n.
similarity 18 n.
mould 23 n.
sort 77 n.
make conform
83 vb.
modify 138 vb.
convert 142 vb.
produce 159 vb.
receptacle 189 n.
outline 228 n.
form 238 n.
form 238 vb.
structure 326 n.
appearance 440 n.
feature 440 n.
represent 546 vb.
art style 548 n.
sculpt 549 vb.
plan 618 vb.
way 619 n.
use 668 vb.
fashion 843 n.

**formal**

regulated 83 adj.
slow 273 adj.
inelegant 571 adj.
well-bred 843 adj.
affected 845 adj.
formal 870 adj.
courteous 879 adj.

**formal dress**

formal dress 223 n.
formality 870 n.

**formality**

floor-cover 221 n.
formal dress 223 n.
gait 260 n.
marching 262 n.
etiquette 843 n.
pretension 845 n.
title 865 n.
formality 870 n.
celebration 871 n.
courtesy 879 n.
ritual 982 n.

**formation**

band 74 n.
group 74 n.
production 159 n.
formation 238 n.
art 546 n.
sculpture 549 n.
formation 717 n.

**formative**

such 7 adj.
productive 159 adj.
formative 238 adj.

**formed**

formed 238 adj.

**former**

former 120 adj.

**formerly**

long ago 108 adv.
formerly 120 adv.
anciently 122 adv.

**formication**

formication 373 n.

**fort**

edifice 159 n.
vertex 208 n.
barrier 230 n.
refuge 657 n.
fort 708 n.

**fortification**

basket 189 n.
summit 208 n.
incline 215 n.
projection 249 n.

window 258 n.
fortification 708 n.
art of war 713 n.

**forward**

forward 280 adv.

**fossil**

fossil 120 n.
archaism 122 n.
organism 353 n.
corpse 358 n.

**foul play**

duplicity 530 n.
trap 537 n.
trickery 537 n.
evil 611 n.
contrivance 618 n.
deed 671 n.
cunning 698 n.
attack 707 n.
injustice 909 n.
wrong 909 n.
foul play 925 n.
wickedness 929 n.
lawbreaking 949 n.

**founder**

be deep 206 vb.
descend 304 vb.
founder 308 n.
weigh 317 vb.
perish 356 vb.
fail 723 vb.
have trouble
726 vb.

**four**

four 95 adj.

**fraction**

quantity 26 n.
fraction 98 n.

**fractional**

fractional 98 adj.

**fragmentary**

fragmentary 53 adj.
incomplete 55 adj.
fractional 98 adj.
exiguous 191 adj.
imperfect 642 adj.

**fragrance**

fragrance 391 n.

**fragrant**
pleasant 371 adj.
odorous 389 adj.
fragrant 391 adj.
**fragrant, be**
be fragrant 391 vb.
**frail**
frail 929 adj.
unchaste 946 adj.
**frame**
basket 189 n.
layer 202 n.
base 209 n.
hanger 212 n.
frame 213 n.
structure 326 n.
preparation 664 n.
**free**
original 21 adj.
volitional 590 adj.
free 739 adj.
nonliable 914 adj.
**free, be**
be unconformable
84 vb.
will 590 vb.
behave 683 vb.
dominate 728 vb.
be free 739 vb.
live single 890 vb.
be exempt 914 vb.
**freedom**
unrelatedness 10 n.
originality 21 n.
opportunity 132 n.
freedom 739 n.
permission 751 n.
dueness 910 n.
nonliability 914 n.
**freely**
freely 739 adv.
**free person**
free person 739 n.
**frenzied**
frenzied 498 adj.
**frenzy**
commotion 313 n.
spasm 313 n.

frenzy 498 n.
fantasy 508 n.
lack of meaning
510 n.
illness 646 n.
restlessness 673 n.
excitation 816 n.
excitable state
817 n.
desire 854 n.
spell 977 n.
**frequency**
continuity 71 n.
recurrence 102 n.
frequency 134 n.
**frequent**
many 100 adj.
multitudinous
100 adj.
repeated 102 adj.
frequent 134 adj.
usual 605 adj.
**friction**
diminution 37 n.
subtraction 39 n.
energy 155 n.
slowness 273 n.
collision 274 n.
powderiness 327 n.
friction 328 n.
touch 373 n.
stridor 402 n.
difficulty 695 n.
hindrance 697 n.
**friend**
concomitant 89 n.
auxiliary 702 n.
colleague 702 n.
friend 875 n.
sociable person
877 n.
sociality 877 n.
kind person 892 n.
benefactor 898 n.
**friendless**
separate 46 adj.
alone 88 adj.

defenceless
156 adj.
friendless 878 adj.
**friendliness**
friendliness 875 n.
**friendly**
assenting 483 adj.
aiding 698 adj.
corporate 703 adj.
concordant
705 adj.
pacificatory
714 adj.
friendly 875 adj.
sociable 877 adj.
benevolent 892 adj.
**friendly, be**
combine 50 vb.
assent 483 vb.
concord 705 vb.
pacify 714 vb.
be friendly 875 vb.
be sociable 877 vb.
forgive 904 vb.
**friendship**
relation 9 n.
band 74 n.
accompaniment
89 n.
concord 705 n.
peace 712 n.
friendship 875 n.
sociality 877 n.
social round 877 n.
love 887 n.
benevolence 892 n.
**frighten**
unman 156 vb.
weaken 158 vb.
dismiss 295 vb.
dissuade 608 vb.
raise the alarm
660 vb.
hinder 697 vb.
defeat 722 vb.
oppress 730 vb.
displease 822 vb.
depress 829 vb.

frighten 849 vb.
cause dislike
856 vb.
be wonderful
859 vb.
humiliate 867 vb.
threaten 895 vb.
**frightening**
frightening 849 adj.
**front**
precedence 64 n.
prelude 66 n.
beginning 68 n.
nearness 195 n.
exteriority 218 n.
front 232 n.
preceding 278 n.
**frontal**
preceding 64 adj.
first 68 adj.
near 195 adj.
exterior 218 adj.
frontal 232 adj.
opposite 235 adj.
opposing 699 adj.
**frostily**
frostily 375 adv.
**fruit**
fruit 296 n.
plant 361 n.
**fruitful, be**
grow 36 vb.
be many 100 vb.
reproduce itself
162 vb.
be fruitful 166 vb.
expand 192 vb.
abound 630 vb.
superabound
632 vb.
be useful 635 vb.
get better 649 vb.
be successful
722 vb.
prosper 725 vb.
**fuel**
fossil 120 n.

sources of energy
155 n.
propellant 282 n.
gas 331 n.
oil 352 n.
heater 378 n.
fuel 380 n.
materials 626 n.

**full**
firm 45 adj.
full 54 adj.
assembled 74 adj.
multitudinous
100 adj.
dense 319 adj.
filled 630 adj.
redundant 632 adj.

**fumigator**
fumigator 380 n.

**function**
agency 168 n.
operate 168 vb.
function 617 n.
function 617 vb.
use 668 n.
do 671 vb.
serve 737 vb.
deputize 750 vb.
jurisdiction 950 n.

**fundamental**
intrinsic 5 adj.
beginning 68 adj.
fundamental
151 adj.
generative 162 adj.

**funds**
funds 792 n.

**funeral**
bed 213 n.
funeral 359 n.
weeper 831 n.

**funereal**
funereal 359 adj.
black 423 adj.
lamenting 831 adj.

**funny**
dramatic 589 adj.
amusing 832 adj.

witty 834 adj.
funny 844 adj.

**furious**
destructive 160 adj.
furious 171 adj.
excited 816 adj.
excitable 817 adj.
angry 886 adj.

**furnace**
outbreak 171 n.
chimney 258 n.
ejector 295 n.
cookery 296 n.
gas 331 n.
fire 374 n.
burning 376 n.
furnace 378 n.
pitfall 658 n.
workshop 682 n.

**furrow**
receptacle 189 n.
gap 196 n.
cavity 255 n.
concavity 255 n.
roughness 254 n.
furrow 257 n.
wave 345 n.

**furrowed**
furrowed 257 adj.

**future**
unborn 2 adj.
subsequent
115 adj.
future 119 n.
impending 150 adj.
possible 464 adj.
unknown 486 adj.

**future state**
sequel 67 n.
finality 69 n.
future state 119 n.
destiny 150 n.
reproduction 161 n.
life 355 n.
the dead 356 n.
fantasy 508 n.
revival 651 n.
heaven 965 n.

**futurity**
time 104 n.
posteriority 115 n.
different time
117 n.
futurity 119 n.
destiny 150 n.
possibility 464 n.

**G**

**gain**
increment 36 n.
extra 40 n.
growth 152 n.
product 159 n.
incentive 607 n.
benefit 610 n.
flourish 610 vb.
provision 628 n.
utility 635 n.
find useful 635 vb.
triumph 722 vb.
prosper 725 vb.
gain 766 n.
gain 766 vb.
booty 785 n.
sell 788 vb.
wealth 795 n.
get rich 795 vb.
debt 798 n.
receipt 802 n.
reward 957 n.
be rewarded
957 vb.

**gainful**
profitable 635 adj.
gainful 766 adj.
rewarding 957 adj.

**gait**
gait 260 n.
equitation 262 n.
pedestrianism
262 n.
slowness 273 n.

leap 307 n.

**gale**
turmoil 61 n.
storm 171 n.
storm 171 n.
vortex 310 n.
commotion 313 n.
weather 335 n.
rain 345 n.
gale 347 n.
pitfall 658 n.
excitable state
817 n.

**galley**
galley 270 n.

**gamble**
chance 154 vb.
be tentative
456 vb.
divine 506 vb.
suppose 507 vb.
gamble 613 vb.
endanger 656 vb.
face danger
656 vb.
attempt 666 vb.
speculate 786 vb.
amuse oneself
832 vb.
be rash 852 vb.

**gambler**
gambler 613 n.

**gambling**
gambling 613 n.

**gambling game**
gambling game
832 n.

**gaming-house**
gaming-house
613 n.

**gaol**
gaol 743 n.
pillory 959 n.

**gaoler**
gaoler 744 n.

**gap**
disunion 46 n.
discontinuity 72 n.

weakness **158** n.
emptiness **185** n.
short distance
           **195** n.
gap **196** n.
depth **206** n.
partition **226** n.
valley **250** n.
notch **255** n.
furrow **257** n.
opening **258** n.
defect **642** n.

**garden**
seedbed **151** n.
arbour **189** n.
enclosure **230** n.
flower **361** n.
wood **361** n.
botany **363** n.
garden **365** n.
heater **378** n.
fragrance **391** n.

**gardener**
gardener **365** n.

**garment**
adjunct **40** n.
garment **223** n.

**gas**
fluid **330** n.
gas **331** n.
air **335** n.
fuel **380** n.
stench **392** n.

**gaseous**
gaseous **331** adj.

**gaseousness**
gaseousness **331** n.

**gasify**
gasify **331** vb.
vaporize **333** vb.

**gastronomy**
gastronomy **296** n.
gluttony **942** n.

**gauge**
prototype **23** n.
counting instrument
           **86** n.
altimetry **204** n.

horizontality **211** n.
velocity **272** n.
direction **276** n.
hygrometry **336** n.
testing agent
           **456** n.
gauge **460** n.vb.
estimate **475** n.
indicator **542** n.
recording
instrument **544** n.

**gaze**
gaze **433** vb.
be curious **448** vb.
be attentive
           **450** vb.
gesticulate **542** vb.
be rude **880** vb.
court **884** vb.

**gem**
rock **339** n.
exceller **639** n.
gem **839** n.

**genealogy**
heredity **5** n.
consanguinity **11** n.
series **71** n.
breed **77** n.
list **87** n.
antiquity **120** n.
genealogy **164** n.
nobility **863** n.

**general**
comprehensive
           **52** adj.
inclusive **78** adj.
general **79** adj.
typical **83** adj.
one **88** adj.
spacious **178** adj.
broad **200** adj.
indiscriminate
           **459** adj.
known **485** adj.
inexact **490** adj.
usual **605** adj.

**general, be**
be general **79** vb.

**generality**
average **30** n.
whole **52** n.
completeness **54** n.
inclusion **78** n.
generality **79** n.
conformity **83** n.
social group **366** n.
indiscrimination
           **459** n.
inexactness **490** n.

**generalize**
generalize **79** vb.

**generally**
on an average
           **30** adv.
greatly **32** adv.
generally **79** adv.

**generate**
be akin **11** vb.
mix **43** vb.
unite with **45** vb.
initiate **68** vb.
cause **151** vb.
generate **162** vb.
make fruitful
           **166** vb.
emit **295** vb.
vitalize **355** vb.

**generative**
productive **159** adj.
reproduced
           **161** adj.
generative **162** adj.
prolific **166** adj.
female **368** adj.

**generic**
generic **77** adj.

**genetic**
genetic **5** adj.
reverted **143** adj.
inherited **152** adj.
parental **164** adj.
filial **165** adj.
with affections
           **812** adj.

**genitalia**
genitalia **162** n.

**genteel**
well-bred **843** adj.
genteel **863** adj.

**genuine**
inimitable **21** adj.
certain **468** adj.
genuine **489** adj.
orthodox **970** adj.

**geographic**
geographic
           **316** adj.

**geometry**
geometry **460** n.

**gerontology**
gerontology **126** n.

**gesticulate**
distort **241** vb.
move **260** vb.
hint **519** vb.
gesticulate **542** vb.
be mute **573** vb.
speak **574** vb.
behave **683** vb.
command **732** vb.

**gesture**
mimicry **20** n.
distortion **241** n.
motion **260** n.
knock **274** n.
agitation **313** n.
hint **519** n.
gesture **542** n.
language **552** n.
voicelessness
           **573** n.
speech **574** n.
conduct **683** n.
command **732** n.
feeling **813** n.
affectation **845** n.
sauciness **873** n.
ritual act **982** n.

**get angry**
go mad **498** vb.
show feeling
           **813** n.
be excitable
           **817** vb.

be rude 880 vb.
get angry 886 vb.
be irascible 887 vb.
threaten 895 vb.

**get better**
grow 36 vb.
change 138 vb.
progress 280 vb.
tergiversate 598 vb.
flourish 610 vb.
find useful 635 vb.
get better 649 vb.
be restored 651 vb.
be honourable
931 vb.
be penitent 934 vb.

**get drunk**
be complete 54 vb.
drink 296 vb.
revel 832 vb.
be intemperate
938 vb.
get drunk 944 vb.

**get healthy**
get healthy 645 vb.

**get rich**
flourish 610 vb.
prosper 725 vb.
gain 766 vb.
get rich 795 vb.
economize 809 vb.

**ghost**
immateriality 315 n.
the dead 356 n.
corpse 358 n.
visual fallacy 435 n.
appearance 440 n.
fantasy 508 n.
intimidation 849 n.
ghost 964 n.
spiritualism 978 n.

**giant**
athlete 157 n.
giant 190 n.
tall creature 204 n.

**gift**
extra 40 n.

thing transferred
267 n.
voluntary work
592 n.
incentive 607 n.
benefit 610 n.
subvention 698 n.
offer 754 n.
acquisition 766 n.
transfer 775 n.
gift 776 n.
receiving 777 n.
no charge 807 n.
liberality 808 n.
reward 957 n.

**gifted**
intelligent 493 adj.
gifted 689 adj.

**gild**
colour 420 vb.
gild 428 vb.

**girdle**
girdle 47 n.
compressor 193 n.
strip 203 n.
wrapping 221 n.
belt 223 n.
surroundings
225 n.
loop 245 n.
vestments 983 n.

**give**
attribute 153 vb.
provide 628 vb.
permit 751 vb.
consent 753 vb.
offer 754 vb.
dower 772 vb.
assign 775 vb.
give 776 vb.
apportion 778 vb.
defray 799 vb.
pay 799 vb.
expend 801 vb.
cheapen 807 vb.
be liberal 808 vb.
content 823 vb.
reward 957 vb.

be pious 973 vb.
offer worship
975 vb.
be ecclesiastical
979 vb.

**give bail**
give bail 762 vb.

**give battle**
fight 711 vb.
give battle 713 vb.

**give courage**
strengthen 157 vb.
incite 607 vb.
aid 698 vb.
animate 816 vb.
cheer 828 vb.
give courage
850 vb.

**give hope**
evidence 461 vb.
be likely 466 vb.
predict 506 vb.
give hope 847 vb.
cause desire
854 vb.

**given**
given 776 adj.
uncharged 807 adj.

**give pain**
cause feeling
369 vb.
give pain 372 vb.
touch 373 vb.
hurt 822 vb.
torture 958 vb.

**giver**
giver 776 n.

**give scope**
sustain 141 vb.
facilitate 696 vb.
be lax 729 vb.
give scope 739 vb.
liberate 741 vb.
permit 751 vb.
be liberal 808 vb.

**give security**
promise 759 vb.
contract 760 vb.

give security
762 vb.
borrow 780 vb.

**give terms**
require 622 vb.
pacify 714 vb.
liberate 741 vb.
request 756 vb.
contract 760 vb.
give terms 761 vb.
bargain 786 vb.
impose a duty
917 vb.

**giving**
giving 776 n.adj.

**glimmer**
glimmer 414 n.
hint 519 n.

**glove**
glove 223 n.

**glow**
heavens 316 n.
fire 374 n.
glow 412 vb.
glow-worm 415 n.
redness 426 n.

**glow-worm**
flash 412 n.
glow 412 vb.
glimmer 414 n.
glow-worm 415 n.
visual fallacy 435 n.

**glutton**
destroyer 163 n.
eater 296 n.
sensualist 939 n.
glutton 942 n.

**gluttonize**
gluttonize 942 vb.

**gluttonous**
gluttonous 942 adj.

**gluttonously**
942 adv.

**gluttony**
gluttony 942 n.

**glyptic**
glyptic 549 adj.

reward 957 n.
oblation 975 n.

**grave clothes**
wrapping 221 n.
robe 223 n.
grave clothes
                    359 n.

**gravity**
substantiality 3 n.
quantity 26 n.
inequality 29 n.
energy 155 n.
power 155 n.
bulk 190 n.
size 190 n.
materiality 314 n.
gravity 317 n.
redundance 632 n.
encumbrance
                    697 n.

**graze**
graze 296 vb.

**grease**
lubricate 329 vb.
grease 352 vb.

**great**
great 32 adj.
superior 34 adj.
supreme 34 adj.
increasing 36 adj.
abnormal 84 adj.
many 100 adj.
powerful 155 adj.
strong 157 adj.
influential 173 adj.
large 190 adj.
plenteous 630 adj.
important 633 adj.
worshipful 861 adj.
noble 863 adj.
proud 866 adj.

**great, be**
be great 32 vb.
grow 36 vb.
be many 100 vb.

**greater number**
finite quantity 26 n.
main part 32 n.

advantage 34 n.
chief part 52 n.
part 53 n.
plurality 97 n.
greater number
                    100 n.
power 155 n.

**greatly**
substantially 3 adv.
greatly 32 adv.
on the whole
                    52 adv.
completely 54 adv.
infinitely 103 adv.

**greatness**
greatness 32 n.

**great quantity**
finite quantity 26 n.
great quantity 32 n.
chief part 52 n.
crowd 74 n.
multitude 100 n.
abundance 166 n.
contents 188 n.
bulk 190 n.
plenty 630 n.
redundance 632 n.
funds 792 n.
wealth 795 n.

**greedy**
greedy 854 adj.

**green**
vegetal 361 adj.
green 429 adj.
unhealthy 646 adj.

**greenness**
greenness 429 n.

**green pigment**
green pigment
                    429 n.

**greet**
approach 284 vb.
cry 403 vb.
notice 450 vb.
gesticulate 542 vb.
speak to 578 vb.
be friendly 875 vb.

be hospitable
                    877 vb.
greet 879 vb.
show respect
                    915 vb.

**grey**
colourless 421 adj.
whitish 422 adj.
grey 424 adj.
painted 548 adj.

**greyness**
greyness 424 n.

**groom**
groom 361 vb.

**groove**
cut 46 vb.
make concave
                    250 vb.
fold 256 vb.
groove 257 n.
wound 650 vb.
decorate 839 vb.

**grounded**
grounded 723 adj.

**group**
subdivision 53 n.
group 74 n.
classification 77 n.
self 80 n.
certain quantity
                    100 n.
contemporary
                    118 n.
animal 360 n.
social group 366 n.

**grow**
grow 36 vb.
congregate 74 vb.
come of age
                    129 n.
change 138 vb.
be turned to
                    142 vb.
result 152 vb.
reproduce itself
                    162 vb.
expand 192 vb.
ascend 303 vb.

vegetate 361 vb.

**grown-up**
grown-up 129 adj.
manly 157 adj.
matured 664 adj.

**grow old**
pass time 104 vb.
last 108 vb.
be old 122 vb.
grow old 126 vb.
be weak 158 vb.
deteriorate 650 vb.
be ugly 837 vb.

**growth**
conversion 142 n.
growth 152 n.
product 159 n.
propagation 162 n.
expansion 192 n.
evolution 311 n.

**guide**
magnet 286 n.
guide 515 n.
guidebook 519 n.
teacher 532 n.
directorship 684 n.
director 685 n.

**guidebook**
guidebook 519 n.

**guilt**
intention 612 n.
badness 640 n.
wrong 909 n.
wickedness 929 n.
guilt 931 n.
penitence 934 n.
lawbreaking 949 n.

**guiltily**
guiltily 931 adv.

**guiltless**
guiltless 930 adj.

**guilty**
bad 640 adj.
wrong 909 adj.
wicked 929 adj.
guilty 931 adj.
lawbreaking
                    949 adj.

**guilty act**
overstepping
301 n.
disobedience
733 n.
wrong 909 n.
vice 929 n.
guilty act 931 n.

**guilty, be**
be guilty 931 n.
condemn 956 vb.

**gulf**
entrance 68 n.
gap 196 n.
narrowness 201 n.
curve 243 n.
cavity 250 n.
open space 258 n.
way in 292 n.
gulf 340 n.
access 619 n.

**gullible**
credulous 482 adj.
foolish 494 adj.
gullible 539 adj.

**gun**
gun 718 n.

# H

**habit**
uniformity 16 n.
average 30 n.
order 60 n.
continuity 71 n.
generality 79 n.
regularity 81 n.
recurrence 102 n.
tradition 122 n.
regular return
136 n.
permanence 139 n.
phrase 558 n.
habit 605 n.
use 668 n.

conduct 683 n.
possession 768 n.
bore 833 n.
fashion 843 n.
intemperance
938 n.

**habitual**
orderly 60 adj.
general 79 adj.
immemorial
122 adj.
frequent 134 adj.
habitual 605 adj.
inducing 607 adj.
businesslike
617 adj.
doing 671 adj.

**habitually**
habitually 605 adv.

**habituate**
habituate 605 vb.

**habituated**
habituated 605 adj.

**habituation**
habituation 605 n.

**habitu**
habitu 605 n.

**haemorrhage**
outflow 293 n.
haemorrhage
297 n.

**hair**
sequel 67 n.
filament 203 n.
hanging object
212 n.
weaving 217 n.
wig 223 n.
front 232 n.
laterality 234 n.
loop 245 n.
coil 246 n.
prickle 251 n.
hair 254 n.
softness 322 n.
texture 326 n.
hairdressing 838 n.
trimming 839 n.

**hairdressing**
hairdressing 838 n.

**hairless**
hairless 224 adj.

**hairwash**
hairwash 838 n.

**hairy**
fibrous 203 adj.
sharp 251 adj.
hairy 254 adj.
textural 326 adj.

**half-light**
half-light 414 n.

**halfway, be**
be moderate
172 vb.
lie between 226 vb.
be neutral 601 vb.
be halfway 620 vb.
be middling
727 vb.
compromise
765 vb.

**halt**
terminate 69 vb.
halt 140 vb.
come to rest
261 vb.
be obstructive
697 vb.
resist 710 vb.
restrain 742 vb.

**halter**
halter 47 n.
loop 245 n.
fetter 743 n.

**hammer**
hammer 274 n.
pulverizer 327 n.
tool 625 n.
club 718 n.

**handed**
handed 373 adj.

**handle**
handle 213 n.
tool 625 n.

**hang**
come unstuck
49 vb.
be periodic 136 vb.
vary 147 vb.
be high 204 vb.
hang 212 vb.
be curved 243 vb.
jut 249 vb.
be in motion
260 vb.
fly 266 vb.
descend 304 vb.
oscillate 312 vb.

**hanger**
hanger 212 n.
prop 213 n.
dryer 337 n.
tool 625 n.

**hanging**
nonadhesive
49 adj.
weak 158 adj.
hanging 212 adj.

**hanging object**
extremity 69 n.
hanging object
212 n.
bed 213 n.
covering 221 n.
jewellery 839 n.

**happen**
be 1 vb.
happen 149 vb.
result 152 vb.
chance 154 vb.
be present 184 vb.
appear 440 vb.

**happening**
happening 149 adj.
casual 154 adj.

**happiness**
happiness 819 n.

**happy**
good 610 adj.
prosperous
725 adj.
happy 819 adj.

pleasurable
821 adj.
content 823 adj.
cheerful 828 adj.
enamoured
882 adj.
paradisiac 965 adj.

**hard**
past 120 adj.
strong 157 adj.
hard 321 adj.
resolute 594 adj.
severe 730 adj.
thick-skinned
815 adj.
unkind 893 adj.
pitiless 901 adj.

**harden**
strengthen 157 vb.
be dense 319 vb.
harden 321 vb.
thicken 349 vb.
mature 664 vb.
make insensitive
815 vb.

**hardening**
hardening 321 n.

**hardness**
stability 148 n.
strength 157 n.
covering 221 n.
straightness 244 n.
quiescence 261 n.
density 319 n.
hardness 321 n.
toughness 324 n.
inelegance 571 n.
resolution 594 n.
obstinacy 597 n.
severity 730 n.
moral insensibility
815 n.
inhumanity 893 n.
pitilessness 901 n.
impenitence 935 n.

**hard task**
impossibility 465 n.
undertaking 667 n.

hard task 695 n.

**harm**
be inexpedient
638 vb.
harm 640 vb.
impair 650 vb.
hurt 822 vb.
be malevolent
893 vb.
do wrong 909 vb.

**harmful**
harmful 640 adj.

**harmonic**
harmonic 405 adj.

**harmonious**
harmonious
405 adj.

**harmonize**
harmonize 405 vb.

**harp**
harp 409 n.

**haste**
crowd 74 n.
vigorousness
169 n.
speeding 272 n.
velocity 272 n.
commotion 313 n.
nonpreparation
665 n.
activity 673 n.
haste 675 n.
excitability 817 n.
rashness 852 n.

**hasten**
be early 130 vb.
cause 151 vb.
move 260 vb.
accelerate 272 vb.
move fast 272 vb.
progress 280 vb.
incite 607 vb.
pursue 614 vb.
be busy 673 vb.
hasten 675 vb.
be rash 852 vb.

**hastily**
hastily 675 adv.

**hasty**
brief 109 adj.
furious 171 adj.
speedy 272 adj.
negligent 453 adj.
unwise 494 adj.
unprepared
665 adj.
hasty 675 adj.
excitable 817 adj.
rash 852 adj.

**hate**
dislike 856 vb.
hate 888 vb.
be malevolent
893 vb.
be revengeful
905 vb.

**hated**
hated 888 adj.

**hateful**
not nice 640 adj.
disliked 856 adj.
disreputable
862 adj.
hateful 888 adj.

**hateful object**
enemy 876 n.
hateful object
888 n.

**hating**
hating 888 adj.

**hatred**
contrariety 14 n.
prejudice 476 n.
dissension 704 n.
phobia 849 n.
dislike 856 n.
enmity 876 n.
hatred 888 n.
resentment 886 n.
malevolence 893 n.
jealousy 906 n.
pietism 973 n.

**haunt**
appear 440 vb.
haunt 964 vb.
bewitch 977 vb.

**have a reputation**
be remembered
500 vb.
do 671 vb.
prosper 725 vb.
have a reputation
861 vb.
command respect
915 vb.
be praised 918 vb.

**have a right**
have a right
910 vb.

**have enough**
be complete 54 vb.
have enough
630 vb.
climax 720 vb.
afford 795 vb.

**have feeling**
have feeling
369 vb.

**have leisure**
pass time 104 vb.
not act 672 vb.
have leisure
676 vb.
repose 678 vb.
amuse oneself
832 vb.

**have luck**
have luck 725 vb.

**have no choice**
have no choice
601 vb.

**have no repute**
have no repute
862 vb.

**have no smell**
have no smell
390 vb.

**have rank**
have rank 73 vb.

**have taste**
be elegant 570 vb.
have taste 841 vb.

**have trouble**
feel pain 372 vb.

**heresy**
  unbelief 481 n.
  heresy 971 n.

**heretic**
  nonconformist
                    84 n.
  unbeliever 481 n.
  religionist 967 n.
  heretic 971 n.
  schismatic 972 n.
  sectarian 972 n.

**heretical**
  heretical 971 adj.

**heretical, be**
  be heretical
                    971 vb.

**heretically**
  heretically 971 adv.

**hermeneutics**
  hermeneutics
                    515 n.

**heterodox**
  heterodox 971 adj.

**heterodoxy**
  heterodoxy 971 n.

**hider**
  hider 522 n.

**hiding-place**
  hiding-place 522 n.

**high**
  enormous 32 adj.
  great 32 adj.
  high 204 adj.
  topmost 208 adj.
  vertical 210 adj.
  elevated 305 adj.
  proud 866 adj.

**high, be**
  be superior 34 vb.
  grow 36 vb.
  be large 190 vb.
  be high 204 vb.
  crown 208 vb.
  ascend 303 vb.
  climb 303 vb.

**high land**
  narrowness 201 n.
  high land 204 n.

vertex 208 n.
verticality 210 n.
horizontality 211 n.
prominence 249 n.
roughness 254 n.
ascent 303 n.
elevation 305 n.
land 339 n.
plain 343 n.
pitfall 658 n.

**high structure**
  accumulation 74 n.
  edifice 159 n.
  bulk 195 n.
  high structure
                    204 n.
  vertex 208 n.
  projection 249 n.
  view 433 n.
  church exterior
                    984 n.

**high water**
  high water 204 n.

**hinder**
  add 38 vb.
  derange 63 vb.
  jumble 63 vb.
  halt 145 vb.
  disable 156 vb.
  counteract 177 vb.
  interfere 226 vb.
  retard 273 vb.
  weigh 317 vb.
  be inattentive
                    451 vb.
  disappoint 504 vb.
  avoid 615 vb.
  be useless 636 vb.
  impair 655 vb.
  be difficult 695 vb.
  hinder 697 vb.
  resist 715 vb.
  restrain 742 vb.
  prohibit 752 vb.

**hindered**
  hindered 697 adj.

**hinderer**
  hinderer 697 n.

**hindering**
  hindering 697 adj.

**hindrance**
  inferiority 35 n.
  exclusion 57 n.
  complexity 61 n.
  derangement 63 n.
  protraction 108 n.
  delay 131 n.
  stop 145 n.
  destruction 165 n.
  counteraction
                    177 n.
  interjection 226 n.
  estimate 475 n.
  unwillingness
                    598 n.
  dissuasion 608 n.
  avoidance 615 n.
  safeguard 657 n.
  difficulty 695 n.
  hindrance 697 n.
  failure 723 n.
  disobedience
                    733 n.
  restraint 742 n.
  fetter 743 n.
  undutifulness
                    913 n.

**hint**
  look 433 n.
  gaze 433 vb.
  notice 450 vb.
  evidence 461 n.
  knowledge 485 n.
  sciolism 486 n.
  reminder 505 n.
  remind 505 vb.
  supposition 507 n.
  propound 507 vb.
  latency 518 n.
  imply 518 vb.
  hint 519 n.
  hint 519 vb.
  disclosure 521 n.
  divulge 521 vb.
  gesture 542 n.
  indication 542 n.

indicate 542 vb.
speak low 573 vb.
speak 574 vb.
incite 607 vb.
warning 659 n.
warn 659 vb.
advice 686 n.
advise 686 vb.
command 732 vb.

**hire**
  hire 780 vb.
  purchase 787 vb.

**hiss**
  hiss 401 vb.
  ululate 404 vb.

**hitch**
  disappointment
                    504 n.
  evil 611 n.
  difficulty 695 n.
  hitch 697 n.
  failure 723 n.

**hoarse**
  muted 396 adj.
  nonresonant
                    400 adj.
  hoarse 402 adj.
  vocal 572 adj.
  vocal 572 adj.
  voiceless 573 adj.

**hold cheap**
  be inattentive
                    451 vb.
  disregard 453 vb.
  underestimate
                    478 vb.
  reject 602 vb.
  be unimportant
                    634 vb.
  oppose 699 vb.
  defy 706 vb.
  ridicule 846 vb.
  be indifferent
                    855 vb.
  not respect 916 vb.
  hold cheap 917 vb.
  detract 921 vb.

expansion 192 n.
surroundings
225 n.
road 619 n.
sink 644 n.

**how**
how 619 adv.

**hue**
tincture 43 n.
hue 420 n.

**huff**
hurt 822 vb.
cause discontent
824 vb.
be rude 880 vb.
huff 000 vb.

**huge**
enormous 32 adj.
stalwart 157 adj.
huge 190 adj.
tall 204 adj.
fairylike 964 adj.

**hugeness**
hugeness 190 n.

**human**
human 366 adj.

**humankind**
precursor 66 n.
palaeology 120 n.
parentage 164 n.
life 355 n.
mammal 360 n.
humankind 366 n.

**humble**
depreciating
478 adj.
submitting 716 adj.
humble 867 adj.
modest 869 adj.
courteous 879 adj.
respectful 915 adj.
disinterested
926 adj.

**humble, be**
be unseen 439 vb.
relinquish 616 vb.
knuckle under
716 vb.

be humble 867 vb.
be modest 869 vb.
be servile 874 vb.
be courteous
879 vb.
show respect
915 vb.
be disinterested
926 vb.
be pious 973 vb.

**humbled**
humbled 867 adj.

**humbled, be**
be humbled
867 vb.

**humid**
watery 334 adj.
humid 336 adj.
rainy 345 adj.

**humiliate**
abate 37 vb.
abase 306 vb.
disappoint 504 vb.
be unimportant
634 vb.
cause discontent
824 vb.
ridicule 846 vb.
shame 862 vb.
humiliate 867 vb.
not respect 917 vb.
hold cheap 917 vb.

**humiliation**
humiliation 867 n.

**humility**
inferiority 35 n.
underestimation
478 n.
submission 716 n.
humility 867 n.
modesty 869 n.
servility 874 n.
courtesy 879 n.
respect 915 n.
disinterestedness
926 n.
penitence 934 n.
religion 967 n.

piety 973 n.
worship 975 n.

**humorist**
imitator 20 n.
deceiver 540 n.
dramatist 589 n.
entertainer 589 n.
humorist 834 n.
affecter 845 n.

**hundred**
hundred 96 n.

**hunger**
eating 296 n.
dryness 337 n.
rapacity 781 n.
hunger 854 n.
fasting 941 n.
gluttony 942 n.

**hungry**
dry 337 adj.
taking 781 adj.
hungry 854 adj.
fasting 941 adj.
gluttonous 942 adj.

**hungry, be**
eat 296 vb.
excrete 297 vb.
be unsatisfied
631 vb.
be poor 796 vb.
be hungry 854 vb.
starve 941 vb.

**hunt**
eject 295 vb.
detect 479 vb.
hunt 614 vb.
attack 707 vb.
frighten 849 vb.
be inimical 876 vb.
defame 921 vb.

**hunter**
concomitant 89 n.
rider 263 n.
killer 357 n.
hunter 614 n.

**hurt**
harm 640 vb.
excite 816 vb.

hurt 822 vb.
huff 886 vb.
punish 958 vb.

**hybrid**
hybrid 43 n.
nonconformist
84 n.

**hygiene**
cleansing 643 n.
hygiene 647 n.
prophylactic 653 n.
protection 655 n.
preservation 661 n.
hindrance 697 n.

**hygrometry**
hygrometry 336 n.

**hymn**
vocal music 407 n.
rejoicing 830 n.
scripture 969 n.
hymn 975 n.
hymnal 982 n.

**hymnal**
hymnal 982 n.

**hypocritical**
hypocritical
536 adj.

**I**

**ice**
desert 167 n.
plain 343 n.
ice 375 n.
refrigeration 377 n.
enmity 876 n.

**idea**
product 159 n.
thought 444 n.
idea 446 n.
opinion 480 n.
intelligence 493 n.
supposition 507 n.
ideality 508 n.
image 546 n.

sculpture 549 n.
plaything 832 n.
ritual object 982 n.
**imaginary**
unreal 2 adj.
insubstantial 4 adj.
immaterial 315 adj.
appearing 440 adj.
ideational 446 adj.
impossible 465 adj.
erroneous 490 adj.
supposed 507 adj.
imaginary 508 adj.
descriptive 585 adj.
ridiculous 844 adj.
promising 847 adj.
wonderful 859 adj.
fairylike 964 adj.
**imagination**
originality 21 n.
productiveness
166 n.
vision 433 n.
thought 444 n.
idea 446 n.
imagination 508 n.
metaphor 514 n.
falsehood 536 n.
exaggeration
541 n.
cunning 693 n.
**imaginative**
original 21 adj.
productive 159 adj.
seeing 433 adj.
discriminating
458 adj.
absurd 492 adj.
imaginative
508 adj.
hoping 847 adj.
**imaginatively**
imaginatively
508 adv.
**imagine**
produce 159 vb.
see 433 vb.
cognize 442 vb.

think 444 vb.
be inattentive
451 vb.
suppose 507 vb.
imagine 508 vb.
be false 536 vb.
be untrue 538 vb.
describe 585 vb.
plan 618 vb.
hope 847 vb.
**imitate**
liken 18 vb.
resemble 18 vb.
imitate 20 vb.
conform 83 vb.
show 517 vb.
dissemble 536 vb.
fake 536 vb.
gesticulate 542 vb.
represent 546 vb.
act 589 vb.
be affected 845 vb.
satirize 846 vb.
**imitation**
imitation 20 n.
**imitative**
imitative 20 adj.
**imitatively**
imitatively 20 adv.
**imitator**
imitator 20 n.
conformist 83 n.
deceiver 540 n.
actor 589 n.
humorist 834 n.
**immaterial**
insubstantial 4 adj.
immaterial 315 adj.
rare 320 adj.
mental 442 adj.
psychic 442 adj.
spooky 964 adj.
**immateriality**
immateriality 315 n.
**immature**
unreal 2 adj.
incomplete 55 adj.
beginning 68 adj.

new 121 adj.
young 125 adj.
early 130 adj.
amorphous
239 adj.
sour 388 adj.
unhabituated
606 adj.
imperfect 642 adj.
immature 665 adj.
unskilled 690 adj.
uncompleted
721 adj.
**immemorial**
lasting 108 adj.
perpetual 110 adj.
former 120 adj.
immemorial
122 adj.
permanent 139 adj.
parental 164 adj.
worshipful 861 adj.
**immerse**
immerse 298 vb.
drench 336 vb.
**immersion**
immersion 298 n.
**impair**
abate 37 vb.
subtract 39 vb.
break 46 vb.
derange 63 vb.
modify 138 vb.
disable 156 vb.
weaken 158 vb.
lay waste 160 vb.
influence 173 vb.
deform 239 vb.
distort 241 vb.
infiltrate 292 vb.
encroach 301 vb.
waste 629 vb.
make insufficient
631 vb.
make useless
636 vb.
harm 640 vb.

make unclean
644 vb.
impair 650 vb.
misuse 670 vb.
meddle 673 vb.
be clumsy 690 vb.
hinder 697 vb.
make ugly 837 vb.
blemish 840 vb.
disentitle 911 vb.
**impairment**
impairment 650 n.
**impassive**
inert 170 adj.
still 261 adj.
unfeeling 370 adj.
incurious 449 adj.
inattentive 451 adj.
indiscriminating
459 adj.
unintelligible
512 adj.
nonactive 672 adj.
inactive 674 adj.
impassive 815 adj.
inexcitable 818 adj.
indifferent 855 adj.
unkind 893 adj.
pitiless 901 adj.
pure 945 adj.
**impel**
be vigorous 169 vb.
move 260 vb.
transpose 267 vb.
impel 274 vb.
propel 282 vb.
repel 287 vb.
insert 298 vb.
fell 306 vb.
lower 306 vb.
motivate 607 vb.
be active 673 vb.
attack 707 vb.
**impelling**
impelling 274 adj.
**impend**
impend 150 vb.

**impending**
future 119 adj.
impending 150 adj.
approaching
284 adj.
arriving 290 adj.
probable 466 adj.
expected 502 adj.
preparatory
664 adj.
threatening
895 adj.

**impenitence**
impenitence 935 n.

**impenitent**
obstinate 597 adj.
impenitent 935 adj.

**impenitent, be**
be obstinate
597 vb.
be impenitent
935 vb.

**impenitently**
impenitently
935 adv.

**imperfect**
inferior 35 adj.
fragmentary 53 adj.
incomplete 55 adj.
crippled 158 adj.
deformed 241 adj.
deficient 302 adj.
inelegant 571 adj.
bad 640 adj.
imperfect 642 adj.
immature 665 adj.
bungled 690 adj.
uncompleted
721 adj.
blemished 840 adj.
frail 929 adj.

**imperfect, be**
not suffice 631 vb.
be imperfect
642 vb.
be middling
727 vb.

**imperfection**
imperfection 642 n.

**imperfectly**
imperfectly
642 adv.

**imperspicuity**
imperspicuity
563 n.

**impertinent**
impertinent
873 adj.
discourteous
880 adj.
disrespectful
916 adj.

**impiety**
misuse 670 n.
undueness 911 n.
disrespect 916 n.
wickedness 929 n.
irreligion 968 n.
impiety 974 n.

**impious**
impious 974 adj.

**impious, be**
be impious 974 vb.

**impious person**
impious person
974 n.

**implant**
implant 298 vb.
cultivate 365 vb.

**imply**
be intrinsic 5 vb.
evidence 461 vb.
make likely 466 vb.
mean 509 vb.
imply 518 vb.

**impolitely**
impolitely 880 adv.

**importance**
importance 633 n.

**important**
substantial 3 adj.
relative 9 adj.
great 32 adj.
superior 34 adj.
supreme 34 adj.

crucial 132 adj.
eventful 149 adj.
fundamental
151 adj.
influential 173 adj.
meaningful
509 adj.
important 633 adj.
best 639 adj.
hasty 675 adj.
directing 684 adj.
noteworthy
861 adj.

**important, be**
come first 34 vb.
influence 173 vb.
be important
633 vb.

**importantly**
importantly
633 adv.

**important matter**
reality 1 n.
needfulness 622 n.
important matter
633 n.

**impose a duty**
command 732 vb.
compel 735 vb.
impose a duty
912 vb.

**impossibility**
impossibility 465 n.

**impossible**
unapt 25 adj.
prodigious 32 adj.
excluded 57 adj.
unusual 84 adj.
unthought 445 adj.
impossible 465 adj.
improbable
467 adj.
unbelieved 481 adj.
difficult 695 adj.
prohibiting 752 adj.
refused 755 adj.
unpromising
848 adj.

**impossible, be**
be impossible
465 vb.

**impossibly**
impossibly
465 adv.

**impostor**
imitator 20 n.
substitute 145 n.
sciolist 488 n.
ambush 522 n.
hider 522 n.
sham 537 n.
impostor 540 n.
bungler 692 n.
affecter 845 n.
boaster 872 n.
usurper 911 n.

**impotence**
impotence 156 n.

**impotent**
impotent 156 adj.
crippled 158 adj.
weak 158 adj.
unproductive
167 adj.
unimportant
634 adj.
useless 636 adj.
nonactive 672 adj.
unskilful 690 adj.

**impotent, be**
be impotent
156 vb.
be lax 729 vb.

**impoverish**
abate 37 vb.
defeat 722 vb.
not retain 774 vb.
assign 775 vb.
fleece 781 vb.
impoverish 796 vb.

**impracticable**
closed 259 adj.
impracticable
465 adj.

**impress**
be vigorous 169 vb.

influence 173 vb.
attract 286 vb.
cause feeling
369 vb.
cause thought
444 vb.
attract notice
450 vb.
surprise 503 vb.
motivate 607 vb.
subjugate 740 vb.
feel 813 vb.
impress 816 vb.
delight 821 vb.
sadden 829 vb.
frighten 849 vb.
be wonderful
859 vb.
command respect
915 vb.

**impressed**
impressed 813 adj.
**impressible**
impressible
814 adj.
**impressive**
great 32 adj.
prodigious 32 adj.
influential 173 adj.
striking 369 adj.
forceful 566 adj.
notable 633 adj.
felt 813 adj.
impressive 816 adj.
frightening 849 adj.
wonderful 859 adj.
worshipful 861 adj.
proud 866 adj.
respected 915 adj.
**imprison**
hold within 219 vb.
circumscribe
227 vb.
enclose 230 vb.
close 259 vb.
safeguard 655 vb.
subjugate 740 vb.
imprison 742 vb.

retain 773 vb.
seclude 878 vb.
punish 958 vb.
**imprisoned**
imprisoned
742 adj.
**improbability**
improbability
467 n.
**improbable**
prodigious 32 adj.
unusual 84 adj.
improbable
467 adj.
uncertain 469 adj.
erroneous 490 adj.
unexpected
503 adj.
wonderful 859 adj.
**improbity**
improbity 925 n.
**improved**
improved 649 adj.
**improvement**
improvement
649 n.
**improving**
improving 649 adj.
**improvise**
imagine 508 vb.
represent 546 vb.
orate 574 vb.
improvise 604 vb.
be unprepared
665 vb.
**improviser**
improviser 604 vb.
**impulse**
energy 155 n.
influence 173 n.
spurt 272 n.
impulse 274 n.
propulsion 282 n.
lowering 306 n.
agitation 313 n.
gesture 542 n.
desire 854 n.

**impure**
undisguised
517 adj.
not nice 640 adj.
unclean 644 adj.
free 739 adj.
vulgar 842 adj.
disreputable
862 adj.
erotic 882 adj.
sensual 939 adj.
impure 946 adj.
**impure, be**
desire 854 vb.
be intemperate
938 vb.
be impure 946 vb.
**impurely**
impurely 946 adv.
**impurity**
impurity 946 n.
**inaction**
helplessness 156 n.
inertness 170 n.
nonuse 669 n.
inaction 672 n.
inactivity 674 n.
**inactive**
inactive 674 adj.
**inactive, be**
be inactive 674 vb.
**inactively**
inactively 170 adv.
**inactivity**
inactivity 674 n.
**in addition**
in addition 38 adv.
**in adversity**
in adversity
726 adv.
**inadvertently**
inadvertently
451 adv.
**in aid of**
in aid of 698 adv.
**in and out**
in and out 246 adv.

**inaptitude**
inaptitude 25 n.
impotence 156 n.
inexpedience
638 n.
**in a state of, be**
be in a state of
7 vb.
**inattention**
changeableness
147 n.
changeable thing
147 n.
blindness 434 n.
absence of thought
445 n.
attention 450 n.
inattention 451 n.
negligence 453 n.
mistake 490 n.
folly 494 n.
visionary 508 n.
restlessness 673 n.
bungling 690 n.
noncompletion
721 n.
moral insensibility
815 n.
wit 834 n.
rashness 852 n.
indifference 855 n.
rudeness 880 n.
improbity 925 n.
**inattentive**
inattentive 451 adj.
**inattentive, be**
be inattentive
451 vb.
**in at the death**
in at the death
357 vb.
**inborn capacity or tendency**
heredity 5 n.
**incendiarism**
incendiarism 376 n.
**incentive**
stimulant 169 n.

sharp point **251** n.
impulse **274** n.
incentive **607** n.
shekels **792** n.
discount **805** n.
excitant **816** n.
reward **957** n.
reward **957** n.

**incidentally**
incidentally
**132** adv.

**incite**
make violent
**171** vb.
impel **274** vb.
incite **607** vb.
hasten **675** vb.
advise **686** vb.
excite **816** vb.
give courage
**850** vb.

**incline**
high land **204** n.
lowness **205** n.
incline **215** n.
ascent **303** n.
descent **304** n.

**included**
included **78** adj.

**included, be**
be included **78** vb.

**including**
including **78** adv.

**inclusion**
inclusion **78** n.

**inclusive**
extensive **32** adj.
comprehensive
**52** adj.
complete **54** adj.
composing **56** adj.
inclusive **78** adj.

**in cold blood**
in cold blood
**815** adv.

**incombustibility**
incombustibility
**377** n.

**incombustible**
incombustible
**377** adj.

**incomer**
incomer **292** n.

**in comfort**
in comfort **371** adv.

**incoming**
extraneous **59** adj.
incoming **292** adj.
flowing **345** adj.

**in common**
in common
**770** adv.

**incomplete**
incomplete **55** adj.
amorphous
**239** adj.
deficient **302** adj.
insufficient
**631** adj.
imperfect **642** adj.
uncompleted
**721** adj.

**incomplete, be**
be incomplete
**55** vb.
be unprepared
**665** vb.

**incompletely**
incompletely
**55** adv.

**incompleteness**
incompleteness
**55** n.

**inconsiderable**
inconsiderable
**33** adj.
lesser **35** adj.
little **191** adj.
unimportant
**634** adj.

**in control**
in control **684** adv.

**increase**
finite quantity **26** n.
greatness **32** n.
increase **36** n.

addition **38** n.
adjunct **40** n.
continuity **71** n.
series **71** n.
crowd **74** n.
conversion **142** n.
growth **152** n.
production **159** n.
propagation **162** n.
stimulation **169** n.
expansion **192** n.
ascent **303** n.
redundance **632** n.
improvement
**649** n.
gain **766** n.
aggravation **827** n.

**increasing**
increasing **36** adj.

**incredibly**
incredibly **481** adv.

**increment**
increment **36** n.
remainder **41** n.
accumulation **74** n.
gain **766** n.

**incur a duty**
be liable **175** vb.
busy oneself
**617** vb.
undertake **667** vb.
direct **684** vb.
promise **759** vb.
be in debt **798** vb.
incur a duty
**912** vb.

**incur blame**
be imperfect
**642** vb.
displease **822** vb.
cause discontent
**824** vb.
cause dislike
**856** vb.
be wonderful
**859** vb.
lose repute **862** vb.
shame **862** vb.

excite hate **883** vb.
incur blame
**919** vb.

**incuriosity**
incuriosity **449** n.

**incurious**
incurious **449** adj.

**incurious, be**
be incurious
**449** vb.

**in danger, be**
be in danger
**656** vb.

**in debt, be**
be in debt **798** vb.

**indebted**
indebted **798** adj.
nonpaying **800** adj.

**in deduction**
in deduction
**39** adv.

**in defiance of**
in defiance of
**25** adv.

**independence**
independence
**739** n.

**independent**
unconformable
**84** adj.
governmental
**728** adj.
independent
**739** adj.
unwedded **890** adj.

**indicate**
relate **9** vb.
come before **64** vb.
specify **80** vb.
orientate **276** vb.
point to **276** vb.
attract notice
**450** vb.
evidence **461** vb.
predict **506** vb.
mean **509** vb.
manifest **517** vb.
show **517** vb.

**indicating**

inform 519 vb.
indicate 542 vb.
direct 684 vb.
dignify 861 vb.

**indicating**

indicating 542 adj.

**indication**

indication 542 n.

**indicator**

degree 27 n.
indicator 542 n.
warning 659 n.

**indict**

indict 923 vb.
litigate 954 vb.

**indifference**

indifference 855 n.

**indifferent**

unrelated 10 adj.
inert 170 adj.
moderate 172 adj.
quiescent 261 adj.
incurious 449 adj.
inattentive 451 adj.
negligent 453 adj.
inexpectant
    503 adj.
irresolute 596 adj.
choiceless 601 adj.
neutral 620 adj.
nonactive 672 adj.
inactive 674 adj.
lax 729 adj.
independent
    739 adj.
apathetic 815 adj.
impassive 815 adj.
inexcitable 818 adj.
bored 833 adj.
indifferent 855 adj.
disliking 856 adj.
unastonished
    860 adj.
unsociable 878 adj.
discourteous
    880 adj.
wicked 929 adj.
irreligious 968 adj.

**indifferent, be**

be incurious
    449 vb.
disregard 453 vb.
dissent 489 vb.
not know 491 vb.
negate 528 vb.
be neutral 601 vb.
relinquish 616 vb.
not act 672 vb.
submit 716 vb.
not retain 774 vb.
be insensitive
    815 vb.
be indifferent
    855 vb.
be insolent 873 vb.

**in difficulties**

in difficulties
    695 adj.

**in difficulty, be**

be in difficulty
    695 vb.

**indignity**

annoyance 822 n.
ridicule 846 n.
slur 862 n.
humiliation 867 n.
sauciness 873 n.
rudeness 880 n.
anger 886 n.
resentment 886 n.
scurrility 894 n.
indignity 916 n.
contempt 917 n.
reproach 919 n.
calumny 921 n.
accusation 923 n.

**indiscriminate**

mixed 43 adj.
indiscriminate
    459 adj.
designless 613 adj.

**indiscriminating**

indiscriminating
    459 adj.

**indiscrimination**

indiscrimination
    459 n.

**indissoluble**

indissoluble
    319 adj.

**indistinct**

indistinct 439 adj.

**indivisible**

indivisible 52 adj.

**indoor game**

indoor game 832 n.

**induce**

cause 151 vb.
influence 173 vb.
induce 607 vb.
aid 698 vb.
request 756 vb.

**induced**

induced 607 adj.

**induced, be**

be induced 607 vb.

**inducement**

conversion 142 n.
causation 151 n.
influence 173 n.
attraction 286 n.
inattention 451 n.
inducement 607 n.
cooperation 701 n.
offer 754 n.
gift 776 n.
trade 786 n.
purchase 787 n.
excitation 816 n.
courage 850 n.
liking 854 n.
sorcery 977 n.

**inducing**

inducing 607 adj.

**industrious**

unyielding 157 adj.
vigorous 169 adj.
attentive 450 adj.
careful 452 adj.
studious 531 adj.
persevering
    595 adj.

industrious 673 adj.
labouring 677 adj.

**in earshot**

in earshot 410 adv.

**inebriate**

invigorate 169 vb.
inebriate 944 vb.

**ineffectuality**

ineffectuality 156 n.

**inelegance**

inelegance 571 n.

**inelegant**

unapt 25 adj.
unclear 568 adj.
inelegant 571 adj.
clumsy 690 adj.
dull 835 adj.
graceless 837 adj.
vulgar 842 adj.

**inequality**

unrelatedness 10 n.
difference 15 n.
dissimilarity 19 n.
disagreement 25 n.
inequality 29 n.
superiority 34 n.
changeableness
    147 n.
weakness 158 n.
distortion 241 n.
bias 476 n.
injustice 909 n.

**inert**

weakened 158 adj.
inert 170 adj.
quiescent 261 adj.
latent 523 adj.
irresolute 596 adj.
nonactive 672 adj.
inactive 674 adj.
apathetic 815 adj.
inexcitable 818 adj.

**inert, be**

be inert 170 vb.
be quiescent
    261 vb.
lurk 518 vb.
not act 672 vb.

**inertness**
inertness 170 n.

**inexact**
general 79 adj.
deviating 277 adj.
negligent 453 adj.
indiscriminating
459 adj.
inexact 490 adj.
interpretive
515 adj.
clumsy 690 adj.

**inexactness**
inexactness 490 n.

**in exchange**
in exchange
146 adv.

**inexcitability**
inexcitability 818 n.

**inexcitable**
inexcitable 818 adj.

**inexpectant**
inexpectant
503 adj.

**inexpedience**
inexpedience
638 n.

**inexpedient**
unapt 25 adj.
ill-timed 133 adj.
unwise 494 adj.
rejected 602 adj.
useless 636 adj.
inexpedient
638 adj.
harmful 640 adj.
unused 669 adj.
hindering 697 adj.
discreditable
862 adj.
undue 911 adj.

**inexpedient, be**
be inexpedient
638 vb.

**inexpressible**
unspeakable
32 adj.
unusual 84 adj.

inexpressible
512 adj.
wonderful 859 adj.

**infantine**
infantine 127 adj.

**infantry**
pedestrian 263 n.
infantry 717 n.

**in fashion, be**
be in fashion
843 vb.

**infection**
excretion 297 n.
badness 640 n.
sink 644 n.
uncleanness 644 n.
infection 646 n.
insalubrity 648 n.
impairment 650 n.
poison 654 n.
poisoning 654 n.
pitfall 658 n.

**infectious**
mixed 43 adj.
influential 173 adj.
transferable
267 adj.
unclean 644 adj.
infectious 648 adj.

**inferior**
extrinsic 6 adj.
different 15 adj.
dissimilar 19 adj.
unequal 29 adj.
inconsiderable
33 adj.
inferior 35 n.adj.
low 205 adj.
back 233 adj.
human 366 adj.
insufficient
631 adj.
nonentity 634 n.
unimportant
634 adj.
bad 640 adj.
imperfect 642 adj.
loser 723 n.

defeated 723 adj.
unlucky person
726 n.
middling 727 adj.
dependant 737 n.
servant 737 n.
subject 740 adj.
poor person 796 n.
commoner 864 n.
lower classes
864 n.
plebeian 864 adj.

**inferior, be**
be unlike 19 vb.
be unequal 29 vb.
be inferior 35 vb.
descend 304 vb.
not suffice 631 vb.
obey 734 vb.
be subject 740 vb.
have no repute
862 vb.

**inferiority**
inferiority 35 n.

**infernal**
infernal 966 adj.

**infiltrate**
be mixed 43 vb.
pervade 184 vb.
introduce 226 vb.
infiltrate 292 vb.
infuse 298 vb.
descend 304 vb.
be wet 336 vb.
irrigate 336 vb.

**infinite**
absolute 32 adj.
many 100 adj.
multitudinous
100 adj.
infinite 103 adj.
spacious 178 adj.
huge 190 adj.
godlike 960 adj.

**infinitely**
infinitely 103 adv.

**infinity**
quantity 26 n.

greatness 32 n.
infinity 103 n.
perpetuity 110 n.
space 178 n.
divine attribute
960 n.

**in flight**
in flight 266 adv.

**influence**
relativeness 9 n.
be related 9 vb.
greatness 32 n.
superiority 34 n.
component 58 n.
come before 64 vb.
modify 138 vb.
conversion 142 n.
convert 142 vb.
causation 151 n.
cause 151 n.
cause 151 vb.
effect 152 n.
power 155 n.
agency 168 n.
operate 168 vb.
be vigorous 169 vb.
influence 173 n.
influence 173 vb.
tendency 174 n.
tend 174 vb.
pervade 184 vb.
267 vb.
evidence 461 n.
bias 476 vb.
convince 480 vb.
latency 518 n.
teach 529 vb.
habituate 605 vb.
inducement 607 n.
motivator 607 n.
motivate 607 vb.
plot 618 vb.
instrumentality
623 n.
be instrumental
623 vb.
bigwig 633 n.

be important
633 vb.
improvement
649 n.
make better
649 vb.
troublemaker
658 n.
action 671 n.
do 671 vb.
manage 684 vb.
director 685 n.
cunning 693 n.
aid 698 n.
be successful
722 vb.
authority 728 n.
dominate 728 vb.
subjugate 740 vb.
excitation 816 n.
excite 816 vb.
impress 816 vb.
prestige 861 n.

## influential
influential 173 adj.

## influentially
influentially
173 adv.

## inform
interpret 515 vb.
inform 519 vb.
disclose 521 vb.
divulge 521 vb.
publish 523 vb.
educate 529 vb.
indicate 542 vb.
correspond 583 vb.
warn 659 vb.
make ready 664 vb.
accuse 923 vb.

## informal dress
informal dress
223 n.
uncovering 224 n.

## informant
informant 519 n.

## information
data processing
86 n.
enquiry 454 n.
answer 455 n.
testimony 461 n.
knowledge 485 n.
information 519 n.
message 524 n.
news 524 n.
broadcasting
526 n.
indication 542 n.
interlocution 579 n.
correspondence
583 n.
warning 659 n.
advice 686 n.
command 732 n.

## informative
informative
519 adj.

## informed
instructed 485 adj.
knowing 485 adj.
informed 519 adj.
prepared 664 adj.

## informed, be
hear 410 vb.
discover 479 vb.
believe 480 vb.
know 485 vb.
foresee 505 vb.
understand 511 vb.
be informed
519 vb.

## informer
detective 454 n.
witness 461 n.
informer 519 n.
tergiversator 598 n.
coward 851 n.
accuser 923 n.
knave 933 n.
litigant 954 n.

## infrequency
infrequency 135 n.

## infrequent
discontinuous
72 adj.
unassembled
75 adj.
unusual 84 adj.
few 101 adj.
opportune 132 adj.
infrequent 135 adj.
fitful 137 adj.
improbable
467 adj.
uncertain 469 adj.
scarce 631 adj.
of price 806 adj.

## in front
in front 232 adv.

## in front, be
be in front 232 vb.

## infuse
mix 43 vb.
combine 50 vb.
introduce 226 vb.
infuse 298 vb.
moisten 336 vb.

## ingenue
ingenue 694 n.

## inglorious
inglorious 862 adj.
plebeian 864 adj.
humbled 867 adj.

## ingratitude
oblivion 501 n.
ingratitude 903 n.
undueness 911 n.

## ingress
ingress 292 n.

## inhabitants
inhabitants 186 n.

## inherit
ensue 115 vb.
inherit 766 vb.
possess 768 vb.
appropriate 781 vb.
get rich 795 vb.

## inherited
inherited 152 adj.

## in honour of
in honour of
871 adv.

## inhumanity
violence 171 n.
severity 730 n.
moral insensibility
815 n.
inhumanity 893 n.
pitilessness 901 n.
wickedness 929 n.
diabolism 963 n.

## inimical
disagreeing 25 adj.
separate 46 adj.
counteracting
177 adj.
opposing 699 adj.
quarrelling 704 adj.
attacking 707 adj.
prohibiting 752 adj.
discontented
824 adj.
disliking 856 adj.
inimical 876 adj.
hating 883 adj.
malevolent 893 adj.
unkind 893 adj.
revengeful 905 adj.
disapproving
919 adj.

## inimical, be
counteract 177 vb.
be inimical 876 vb.
be revengeful
905 vb.

## inimitable
dissimilar 19 adj.
inimitable 21 adj.
supreme 34 adj.
special 80 adj.
causal 151 adj.

## initially
initially 68 adv.

## initials
initials 553 n.

## initiate
put in front 64 vb.

fatigue 679 n.
moral insensibility
815 n.
occultism 978 n.

**insensible**
impotent 156 adj.
inert 170 adj.
still 261 adj.
slow 273 adj.
insensible 370 adj.
ignorant 486 adj.
sick 646 adj.
remedial 653 adj.
nonactive 672 adj.
inactive 674 adj.
apathetic 815 adj.
impassive 815 adj.
drugged 944 adj.

**insensible, be**
be impotent
156 vb.
be insensible
370 vb.
be insensitive
815 vb.

**insensitive, be**
be insensible
370 vb.
be incurious
449 vb.
be insensitive
815 vb.
keep calm 818 vb.
not wonder 860 vb.

**inseparably**
inseparably 45 adv.

**insert**
add 38 vb.
mix 43 vb.
affix 45 vb.
join 45 vb.
fill 54 vb.
place 182 vb.
load 188 vb.
hold within 219 vb.
cover 221 vb.
line 222 vb.
introduce 226 vb.

enter 292 vb.
admit 294 vb.
insert 298 vb.

**inserted**
inserted 298 adj.

**insertion**
insertion 298 n.

**inside**
inside 219 adv.

**inside, be**
be inside 219 vb.

**insides**
insides 219 n.

**insipidity**
insipidity 382 n.

**in small compass**
in small compass
191 adv.

**insolence**
insolence 873 n.

**insolent**
defiant 706 adj.
anarchic 729 adj.
authoritarian
730 adj.
rash 852 adj.
proud 866 adj.
vain 868 adj.
insolent 873 adj.
unwarranted
911 adj.
disrespectful
916 adj.
despising 917 adj.

**insolent, be**
defy 706 vb.
be free 739 vb.
be proud 866 vb.
be insolent 873 vb.
be rude 880 vb.
hate 883 vb.
be undue 911 vb.
not respect 916 vb.
accuse 923 vb.

**insolently**
insolently 873 adv.

**insolent person**
insolent person
873 n.
rude person 880 n.

**insolvency**
insolvency 800 n.

**inspection**
inspection 433 n.

**instant**
small quantity 33 n.
date 104 n.
brief span 109 n.
instant 111 n.

**instantaneity**
instantaneity 111 n.

**instantaneous**
instantaneous
111 adj.

**instantaneously**
instantaneously
111 adv.

**instead**
instead 145 adv.

**instructed**
instructed 485 adj.

**instrument**
inferior 35 n.
dupe 539 n.
contrivance 618 n.
instrument 623 n.
means 624 n.
tool 625 n.
nonentity 634 n.
agent 681 n.
aider 698 n.
auxiliary 702 n.
government 728 n.
dependant 737 n.
slave 737 n.
toady 874 n.

**instrumental**
instrumental
623 adj.
mechanical
625 adj.
useful 635 adj.
used 668 adj.
aiding 698 adj.

**instrumental, be**
conduce 151 vb.
be instrumental
623 vb.
minister to 698 vb.
be subject 740 vb.
be servile 874 vb.

**instrumentalist**
instrumentalist
408 n.

**instrumentality**
instrumentality
623 n.

**instrument of
torture**
compressor 193 n.
pain 372 n.
instrument of
torture 959 n.

**insubstantial**
unreal 2 adj.
insubstantial 4 adj.
inconsiderable
33 adj.
incomplete 55 adj.
not one 99 adj.
transient 109 adj.
powerless 156 adj.
flimsy 158 adj.
weak 158 adj.
shallow 207 adj.
immaterial 315 adj.
rare 320 adj.
brittle 325 adj.
airy 335 adj.
shadowy 414 adj.
imaginary 508 adj.
insufficient
631 adj.
trivial 634 adj.
unimportant
634 adj.

**insubstantiality**
insubstantiality 4 n.

**insubstantial thing**
nonexistence 2 n.
insubstantial thing
4 n.

small quantity 33 n.
brief span 109 n.
ineffectuality 156 n.
weak thing 158 n.
lightness 318 n.
transparency
417 n.
sham 537 n.
nonentity 634 n.
vain person 868 n.

**insufficiency**
insufficiency 631 n.

**insufficient**
unequal 29 adj.
small 33 adj.
inferior 35 adj.
fragmentary 53 adj.
incomplete 55 adj.
powerless 156 adj.
unproductive
167 adj.
short 199 adj.
deficient 302 adj.
disappointing
504 adj.
insufficient
631 adj.
inexpedient
638 adj.
imperfect 642 adj.
unskilful 690 adj.
discontenting
824 adj.
disapproved
919 adj.

**insufficiently**
insufficiently
631 adv.

**insular**
insular 344 adj.

**in sum**
in sum 587 adv.

**in suspense**
in suspense
469 adv.

**intact**
intact 52 adj.
complete 54 adj.

perfect 641 adj.
undamaged
641 adj.

**intellect**
intellect 442 n.
thought 444 n.
idea 446 n.
knowledge 485 n.
intelligence 493 n.
intention 612 n.

**intellectual**
philosopher 444 n.
reasoner 470 n.
erudition 485 n.
intellectual 487 n.
sage 495 n.

**intelligence**
head 208 n.
intellect 442 n.
discrimination
458 n.
intelligence 493 n.
wit 834 n.

**intelligent**
intelligent 493 adj.

**intelligibility**
intelligibility 511 n.

**intelligible**
simple 44 adj.
orderly 60 adj.
positive 468 adj.
known 485 adj.
sane 497 adj.
semantic 509 adj.
intelligible 511 adj.
manifest 517 adj.
veracious 535 adj.
perspicuous
562 adj.
easy 696 adj.

**intelligible, be**
be intelligible
511 vb.
interpret 515 vb.
be plain 517 vb.
speak plainly
568 vb.
be easy 696 vb.

impress 816 vb.

**intelligibly**
intelligibly 511 adv.

**intemperance**
intemperance
938 n.

**intemperate**
selfish 927 adj.
intemperate
938 adj.
sensual 939 adj.
drunken 944 adj.

**intemperate, be**
overstep 301 vb.
superabound
632 vb.
please oneself
729 vb.
be intemperate
938 vb.
be sensual 939 vb.
be impure 946 vb.

**intemperately**
intemperately
938 adv.

**intend**
be mindful 450 vb.
expect 502 vb.
will 590 vb.
be willing 592 vb.
be resolute 594 vb.
predetermine
603 vb.
intend 612 vb.
pursue 614 vb.
plan 618 vb.
attempt 666 vb.
promise 759 vb.
hope 847 vb.
desire 854 vb.

**intended**
intended 612 adj.

**intending**
intending 612 adj.

**intention**
destiny 150 n.
expectation 502 n.
will 590 n.

predetermination
603 n.
intention 612 n.
business 617 n.
plan 618 n.
promise 759 n.
aspiration 847 n.
liking 854 n.

**inter**
inter 359 vb.

**interchange**
correlation 12 n.
correlate 12 vb.
equalization 28 n.
equivalence 28 n.
compensation 31 n.
offset 31 n.
union 45 n.
derangement 63 n.
jumble 63 vb.
change 138 n.
modify 138 vb.
substitution 145 n.
substitute 145 vb.
146 vb.
displacement
183 n.
displace 183 vb.
inversion 216 n.
invert 216 vb.
be in motion
260 vb.
move 260 vb.
transference 267 n.
transpose 267 vb.
deflect 277 vb.
transfer 775 vb.
assign 775 vb.
barter 786 n.
trade 786 vb.

**interchanged**
interchanged
146 adj.

**interest**
interest 798 n.

**interfere**
discontinue 72 vb.
interfere 226 vb.

**inutility**
inutility 636 n.

**inversely**
inversely 216 adv.

**inversion**
inversion 216 n.

**invert**
be contrary 14 vb.
bedevil 63 vb.
derange 63 vb.
modify 138 vb.
revert 143 vb.
revolutionize
           144 vb.
demolish 160 vb.
invert 216 vb.
make curved
           243 vb.
navigate 264 vb.
lower 306 vb.

**inverted**
inverted 216 adj.

**inverted, be**
be inverted 216 vb.

**invigilate**
scan 433 vb.
invigilate 452 vb.
manage 684 vb.

**invigorate**
augment 36 vb.
cause 151 vb.
strengthen 157 vb.
operate 168 vb.
invigorate 169 vb.
promote 280 vb.
vitalize 355 vb.
cultivate 365 vb.
cause feeling
           369 vb.
incite 607 vb.
mature 664 vb.
refresh 680 vb.
animate 816 vb.
cheer 828 vb.

**invisibility**
invisibility 439 n.

**invisible**
inconsiderable
           33 adj.
small 33 adj.
minute 191 adj.
distant 194 adj.
shadowy 414 adj.
invisible 439 adj.
disappearing
           441 adj.
neglected 453 adj.
unknown 486 adj.
unintelligible
           512 adj.
latent 518 adj.
inglorious 862 adj.

**invisibly**
invisibly 439 adv.

**involuntary**
involuntary
           591 adj.
unintentional
           613 adj.

**invulnerable**
strong 157 adj.
unyielding 157 adj.
sealed off 259 adj.
certain 468 adj.
salubrious 647 adj.
invulnerable
           655 adj.
defended 708 adj.

**invulnerable. See
fixed**
unchangeable
           148 adj.

**irascibility**
irascibility 887 n.

**irascible**
violent 171 adj.
wilful 597 adj.
capricious 599 adj.
quarrelling 704 adj.
contending
           711 adj.
sensitive 814 adj.
excitable 817 adj.
ungracious 880 adj.

angry 886 adj.
irascible 887 adj.
sullen 888 adj.

**irascible, be**
be excitable
           817 vb.
be irascible 887 vb.

**iridescent**
mixed 43 adj.
changeful 147 adj.
iridescent 432 adj.

**irrelevance**
irrelevance 10 n.

**irrelevant**
irrelevant 10 adj.
unapt 25 adj.
misplaced 183 adj.
deviating 277 adj.
absurd 492 adj.
prolix 565 adj.
unimportant
           634 adj.

**irreligion**
irreligion 968 n.

**irreligionist**
irreligionist 968 n.

**irreligious**
negligent 453 adj.
irreligious 968 adj.
impious 974 adj.
laical 981 adj.

**irreligious, be**
be irreligious
           968 vb.

**irresolute**
changeful 147 adj.
impotent 156 adj.
weak 158 adj.
doubting 469 adj.
irresolute 596 adj.
tergiversating
           598 adj.
choiceless 601 adj.
neutral 620 adj.
lax 729 adj.
nervous 849 adj.
cowardly 851 adj.

**irresolute, be**
conform 83 vb.
vary 147 vb.
be uncertain
           469 vb.
doubt 481 vb.
be irresolute
           596 vb.
tergiversate 598 vb.
be capricious
           599 vb.
be neutral 601 vb.
be cowardly
           851 vb.

**irresolutely**
irresolutely
           596 adv.

**irresolution**
irresolution 596 n.

**irrigate**
irrigate 336 vb.
make flow 345 vb.
cultivate 365 vb.

**irrigator**
irrigator 336 n.

**island**
projection 249 n.
land 339 n.
island 344 n.

**itch**
itch 373 vb.

**itinerary**
itinerary 262 n.
way 619 n.

**J**

**jacket**
wrapping 221 n.
jacket 223 n.

**jealous**
opposing 699 adj.
loving 882 adj.
jealous 906 adj.
envious 907 adj.

selfish 932 adj.

**jealous, be**
contend 711 vb.
be jealous 906 vb.

**jealousy**
jealousy 906 n.

**jerkily**
jerkily 313 adv.

**jersey**
jersey 223 n.

**jewellery**
jewellery 839 n.

**job**
job 617 n.

**join**
accord 24 vb.
add 38 vb.
mix 43 vb.
join 45 vb.
agglutinate 48 vb.
combine 50 vb.
make complete
54 vb.
compose 56 vb.
bring together
74 vb.
produce 159 vb.
make smaller
193 vb.
hang 212 vb.
cross 217 vb.
introduce 226 vb.
close 259 vb.
implant 298 vb.
repair 651 vb.

**join a party**
accrue 38 vb.
unite with 45 vb.
be included 78 vb.
assent 483 vb.
join a party 703 vb.
sectarianize 972 vb.

**joined**
joined 45 adj.

**joining together**
joining together
45 n.

**joint**
joint 45 n.
bond 47 n.
fastening 47 n.
gap 196 n.
pivot 213 n.
angularity 242 n.
projection 249 n.

**joint possession**
store 627 n.
association 701 n.
joint possession
770 n.
lands 772 n.

**journal**
journal 523 n.
book 584 n.
reading matter
584 n.

**joy**
vigorousness
169 n.
pleasure 371 n.
excitation 816 n.
joy 819 n.
pleasurableness
821 n.
cheerfulness 828 n.
rejoicing 830 n.

**jubilant**
pleased 819 adj.
jubilant 828 adj.
rejoicing 830 adj.
hoping 847 adj.

**judge**
cause 151 vb.
notice 450 vb.
answer 455 vb.
discriminate
458 vb.
appraise 460 vb.
make certain
468 vb.
judge 475 vb.
will 590 vb.
choose 600 vb.
mediate 715 vb.
decree 732 vb.

officer 736 n.
have taste 841 vb.
be cautious 853 vb.
be just 908 vb.
law officer 950 n.
hold court 950 vb.
judge 952 n.
try a case 954 vb.
punisher 958 n.

**judgment**
judgment 475 n.

**judiciary**
judiciary 951 adj.

**judicial**
discriminating
458 adj.
judicial 475 adj.
sane 497 adj.
tasteful 841 adj.
orthodox 970 adj.

**jumble**
mix 43 vb.
jumble 63 vb.
impair 650 vb.

**jumper**
jumper 307 n.
dance 832 n.

**juncture**
juncture 8 n.
degree 27 n.
event 149 n.

**junket. See dairy product**
milk 296 n.

**jurisdiction**
authority 728 n.
law 948 n.
jurisdiction 950 n.
legal process
954 n.

**jurisdictional**
jurisdictional
950 adj.

**jurisprudence**
jurisprudence
948 n.

**jurisprudential**
jurisprudential
953 adj.

**jurist**
jurist 953 n.

**jury**
estimator 475 n.
jury 952 n.

**just**
equal 28 adj.
moderate 172 adj.
rational 470 adj.
judicial 475 adj.
wise 493 adj.
choiceless 601 adj.
neutral 620 adj.
free 739 adj.
indifferent 855 adj.
just 908 adj.
honourable
924 adj.
disinterested
926 adj.
virtuous 928 adj.
legal 948 adj.

**just, be**
discriminate
458 vb.
be just 908 vb.
grant claims
910 vb.
be honourable
924 vb.
be virtuous 928 vb.

**justice**
equality 28 n.
judgment 475 n.
no choice 601 n.
indifference 855 n.
justice 908 n.
probity 924 n.
disinterestedness
926 n.
virtue 928 n.
legality 948 n.
reward 957 n.
punishment 958 n.

**justify**
plead 609 vb.
forgive 904 vb.
justify 922 vb.

**jut**
jut 249 vb.

**juxtapose**
connect 45 vb.
bring near 195 vb.
juxtapose 197 vb.
compare 457 vb.

## K

**keen**
keen 169 adj.

**keenness**
keenness 169 n.

**keep calm**
keep calm 818 vb.
be courageous
850 vb.
not wonder 860 vb.

**keeper**
concomitant 89 n.
doorkeeper 259 n.
surveillance 452 n.
collector 487 n.
teacher 532 n.
protector 655 n.
manager 685 n.
defender 708 n.
retainer 737 n.
servant 737 n.
keeper 744 n.
consignee 749 n.

**keep faith**
obey 734 vb.
keep faith 763 vb.

**keep secret**
not know 486 vb.
keep secret 520 vb.
be mute 573 vb.
be taciturn 577 vb.
retain 773 vb.

be cautious 853 vb.

**kept woman**
loved one 882 n.
kept woman 947 n.

**key**
key 405 n.

**kick**
kick 274 vb.
strike at 707 vb.

**kill**
abate 37 vb.
disable 156 vb.
destroy 160 vb.
kill 357 vb.
hinder 697 vb.
execute 958 vb.

**killer**
killer 357 n.

**killing**
death 356 n.
killing 357 n.
capital punishment
958 n.

**kill oneself**
perish 356 vb.
kill oneself 357 vb.

**kind act**
benefit 610 n.
aid 698 n.
liberality 808 n.
courteous act
879 n.
kind act 892 n.

**kindle**
make violent
171 vb.
kindle 376 vb.
fire 380 vb.
make bright
412 vb.

**kind person**
kind person 892 n.
philanthropist
896 n.
benefactor 898 n.
good person 932 n.

**kinsman**
kinsman 11 n.

**knave**
deceiver 540 n.
trickster 540 n.
tergiversator 598 n.
low fellow 864 n.
ruffian 899 n.
knave 933 n.

**knock**
end 69 n.
ruin 160 n.
knock 274 n.
propulsion 282 n.
touch 373 n.
gesture 542 n.
evil 611 n.
lunge 707 n.
corporal
punishment 958 n.

**know**
meet with 149 vb.
have feeling
369 vb.
see 433 vb.
cognize 442 vb.
discriminate
458 vb.
be certain 468 vb.
discover 479 vb.
know 485 vb.
be wise 493 vb.
memorize 500 vb.
remember 505 vb.
understand 511 vb.
be informed
519 vb.
learn 531 vb.
manage 684 vb.
be expert 689 vb.
be affected 845 vb.

**knowing**
sentient 369 adj.
mental 442 adj.
knowing 485 adj.
informed 519 adj.
studious 531 adj.
habituated 605 adj.
friendly 875 adj.
godlike 960 adj.

**knowingly**
knowingly 485 adv.

**knowledge**
certainty 468 n.
knowledge 485 n.
wisdom 493 n.
information 519 n.
publicity 523 n.
means 624 n.
skill 689 n.
cunning 693 n.
art of war 713 n.
feeling 813 n.
friendship 875 n.
divine attribute
960 n.
sorcery 977 n.

**known**
interior 219 adj.
known 485 adj.
remembered
500 adj.
intelligible 516 adj.
published 523 adj.
habitual 605 adj.
usual 605 adj.
used 668 adj.
renowned 861 adj.

**known, be**
be known 485 vb.
be disclosed
521 vb.

**knuckle under**
knuckle under
716 vb.

## L

**label**
adjunct 40 n.
beginning 68 n.
sort 77 n.
list 87 n.
assent 483 n.
exhibit 517 n.

label 542 n.
name 556 n.
edition 584 n.

**laborious**
persevering
595 adj.
industrious 673 adj.
laborious 677 adj.
fatiguing 679 adj.
difficult 695 adj.

**laboriously**
laboriously
677 adv.

**labour**
finite quantity 26 n.
vigorousness
169 n.
job 617 n.
preparation 664 n.
assiduity 673 n.
labour 677 n.
hard task 695 n.
portion 778 n.
bore 833 n.

**labouring**
labouring 677 adj.

**labyrinthine**
labyrinthine
246 adj.

**lack of
expectation**
sequel 67 n.
instantaneity 111 n.
revolution 144 n.
chance 154 n.
agitation 313 n.
improbability
467 n.
unreliability 469 n.
discovery 479 n.
absurdity 492 n.
lack of expectation
503 n.
disappointment
504 n.
pitfall 658 n.
nonpreparation
665 n.

feeling 813 n.
painfulness 822 n.
ridiculousness
844 n.
hopelessness
848 n.
wonder 859 n.
undueness 911 n.

**lack of meaning**
lack of meaning
510 n.
unintelligibility
512 n.
equivocalness
513 n.
spell 977 n.

**lack of wonder**
moral insensibility
815 n.
indifference 855 n.
lack of wonder
860 n.
detraction 921 n.

**lacustrine**
lacustrine 341 adj.

**ladle**
ladle 189 n.
conveyor 269 n.

**lady**
lady 368 n.
master 736 n.

**laical**
laical 981 adj.

**laicize**
laicize 981 vb.

**laity**
laity 981 n.

**lake**
shallowness 207 n.
water 334 n.
lake 341 n.

**lament**
obsequies 359 n.
inter 359 vb.
feel pain 372 vb.
cry 403 vb.
vocal music 407 n.
gesticulate 542 vb.

suffer 820 vb.
be discontented
824 vb.
regret 825 vb.
be dejected
829 vb.
lament 831 vb.
lament 831 n.
condolence 900 n.
pity 900 vb.
be penitent 934 vb.

**lamentation**
lamentation 831 n.

**lamenting**
lamenting 831 adj.

**lamina**
lamina 202 n.

**laminate**
laminate 202 vb.

**lamp**
hanging object
212 n.
gas 331 n.
flash 412 n.
glimmer 414 n.
lamp 415 n.
camera 437 n.
signal 542 n.

**land**
district 179 n.
region 179 n.
basis 218 n.
projection 249 n.
come to rest
261 n.
navigate 264 vb.
fly 266 vb.
approach 284 vb.
land 290 vb.
descend 304 vb.
world 316 n.
land 339 n.

**lands**
lands 772 n.

**land travel**
motion 260 n.
land travel 262 n.
passage 300 n.

curiosity 448 n.
meter 460 n.
sport 832 n.

**language**
speciality 80 n.
language 552 n.
dialect 555 n.
speech 574 n.

**language type**
language type
552 n.

**lapidate**
lapidate 707 vb.

**large**
substantial 3 adj.
great 32 adj.
stalwart 157 adj.
spacious 178 adj.
large 190 adj.

**large, be**
be large 190 vb.
make heavy
317 vb.

**last**
be 1 vb.
continue 104 vb.
last 108 vb.
stay 139 vb.
be obstinate
597 vb.

**lasting**
lasting 108 adj.

**late**
protracted 108 adj.
anachronistic
113 adj.
late 131 adj.
late 131 adv.
ill-timed 133 adj.
slow 273 adj.
neglected 453 adj.
negligent 453 adj.
important 633 adj.
immature 665 adj.
unprepared
665 adj.
lazy 674 adj.

**late, be**
drag on 108 vb.
time 112 vb.
misdate 113 vb.
be late 131 vb.
lose a chance
                        133 vb.
move slowly
                        273 vb.
overstep 301 vb.
fall short 302 vb.
err 490 vb.
be inactive 674 vb.
hasten 675 vb.

**latency**
latency 518 n.

**lateness**
lateness 131 n.

**latent**
private 80 adj.
inert 170 adj.
low 205 adj.
invisible 439 adj.
latent 518 adj.
concealed 520 adj.
deceiving 537 adj.
unclear 563 adj.
avoiding 615 adj.
important 633 adj.
secluded 878 adj.
dishonest 925 adj.

**lateral**
lateral 234 adj.
directed 276 adj.

**laterality**
laterality 234 n.

**latrine**
vessel 189 n.
cleansing 648 n.
latrine 649 n.

**latrine. See
compartment**
chamber 189 n.

**laugh**
be loud 400 vb.
cry 408 vb.
gesticulate 547 vb.
laugh 835 vb.

**laugher**
laugher 835 n.

**laughing**
laughing 835 adj.

**laughingstock**
misfit 25 n.
nonconformist
                        84 n.
fool 501 n.
crank 504 n.
dupe 544 n.
laughingstock
                        851 n.

**laughter**
loudness 400 n.
cry 408 n.
gesture 547 n.
merriment 833 n.
laughter 835 n.
festivity 837 n.
ridicule 851 n.

**law**
rule 81 n.
necessity 596 n.
vocation 622 n.
precept 693 n.
compulsion 740 n.
restraint 747 n.
law 953 n.

**law agent**
consignee 754 n.
law agent 958 n.

**lawbreaking**
lawbreaking 954 n.
lawbreaking
                        954 adj.

**lawcourt**
lawcourt 956 n.

**lawless**
riotous 738 adj.
rascally 930 adj.
lawless 954 adj.
impious 980 adj.

**lawlessness**
lawlessness 954 n.

**law officer**
messenger 529 n.
officer 741 n.

law officer 955 n.
notary 958 n.

**lawyer**
reasoner 475 n.
adviser 691 n.
lawyer 958 n.

**lax**
weak 163 adj.
inert 175 adj.
negligent 458 adj.
irresolute 601 adj.
lax 734 adj.
lenient 736 adj.
nonobservant
                        769 adj.
indifferent 860 adj.
benevolent 897 adj.
pitying 905 adj.
frail 934 adj.

**lax, be**
sustain 146 vb.
disregard 458 vb.
qualify 468 vb.
be lax 734 vb.
be lenient 736 vb.
give scope 744 vb.
liberate 746 vb.
permit 756 vb.
not observe
                        769 vb.
compromise
                        770 vb.
be patient 823 vb.
please 826 vb.
be intemperate
                        943 vb.

**laxity**
laxity 734 n.

**layer**
series 71 n.
compartment
                        189 n.
layer 207 n.
horizontality 216 n.
basis 218 n.
covering 226 n.

**layered**
layered 207 adj.

**lay person**
beginner 538 n.
lay person 986 n.

**lay waste**
lay waste 165 vb.
make sterile
                        172 vb.
be violent 176 vb.
uncover 229 vb.
waste 634 vb.
impair 655 vb.
attack 712 vb.
wage war 718 vb.
rob 788 vb.
be malevolent
                        898 vb.

**lazy**
slow 278 adj.
negligent 458 adj.
profitless 641 adj.
lazy 679 adj.

**leader**
living model 23 n.
superior 34 n.
precursor 66 n.
concomitant 89 n.
navigator 270 n.
motivator 612 n.
leader 690 n.
governor 741 n.
person of repute
                        866 n.
philanthropist
                        901 n.

**lean**
weak 163 adj.
weakly 163 adj.
exiguous 196 n.
long 203 adj.
lean 206 adj.
deformed 246 adj.
legged 267 adj.
underfed 636 adj.
shapely 841 adj.
fasting 946 adj.
fairylike 969 adj.

**leap**
be curved 248 vb.

leaping

gait 260 n.
be in motion
260 vb.
walk 262 vb.
spurt 272 vb.
emerge 293 vb.
overstep 301 vb.
ascent 303 n.
ascend 303 vb.
tumble 304 vb.
leap 307 n.
leap 307 vb.
oscillate 312 vb.
agitation 313 n.
be agitated 313 vb.
flow 345 vb.
ballet 589 n.
pursue 614 vb.
racing 711 n.
be excited 816 vb.
rejoice 830 vb.
children's games
832 n.
sport 832 n.
dance 832 vb.

leaping
leaping 307 adj.

learn
be tentative
456 vb.
know 485 vb.
memorize 500 vb.
understand 511 vb.
be informed
519 vb.
learn 531 vb.
get better 649 vb.
prepare oneself
664 vb.
be expert 689 vb.
be penitent 934 vb.

learner
learner 533 n.

learning
erudition 485 n.
remembrance
500 n.
curriculum 529 n.

learning 531 n.
preparation 664 n.
subjection 740 n.

lease
assign 775 vb.
lease 779 vb.

leaven
cookery 296 n.
lifter 305 n.
leaven 318 n.
bubble 350 n.

leave no hope
leave no hope
848 vb.

leave over
leave over 41 vb.

leavings
leavings 41 n.

lecherous
lecherous 946 adj.

lecture
lecture 529 n.
rostrum 534 n.
oration 574 n.
dissertation 586 n.
inducement 607 n.
ministration 982 n.

left, be
be left 41 vb.
outlast 108 vb.
live 355 vb.
persevere 595 vb.
be superfluous
632 vb.

leg
limb 53 n.
stand 213 n.
leg 262 n.

legal
necessary 591 adj.
preceptive 688 adj.
permitted 751 adj.
just 908 adj.
due 910 adj.
legal 948 adj.

legal, be
be legal 948 vb.

legality
legality 948 n.

legally
legally 948 adv.

legal process
warrant 732 n.
legal process
954 n.

legal trial
listening 410 n.
enquiry 454 n.
experiment 456 n.
advice 686 n.
law 948 n.
legal trial 954 n.

legged
legged 262 adj.

legislation
management
684 n.
precept 688 n.
decree 732 n.
legislation 948 n.

legwear
legwear 223 n.

leisure
interim 104 n.
opportunity 132 n.
lull 140 n.
slowness 273 n.
inaction 672 n.
inactivity 674 n.
leisure 676 n.
repose 678 n.
resignation 748 n.
pleasurableness
821 n.
amusement 832 n.
holy day 982 n.

leisurely
ageing 126 adj.
tranquil 261 adj.
slow 273 adj.
nonactive 672 adj.
inactive 674 adj.
lazy 674 adj.
leisurely 676 adj.
reposeful 678 adj.

free 739 adj.

lend
aid 698 vb.
assign 775 vb.
lend 779 vb.
credit 797 vb.

lender
lender 779 n.

lending
lending 779 n.
lending 779 vb.

length
quantity 26 n.
greatness 32 n.
measure 178 n.
size 190 n.
distance 194 n.
length 198 n.
depth 206 n.

lengthen
augment 36 vb.
continue 71 vb.
spin out 108 vb.
enlarge 192 vb.
lengthen 198 vb.
make thin 201 vb.
be diffuse 565 vb.

lengthening
lengthening 198 n.

leniency
leniency 731 n.

lenient
moderate 172 adj.
lax 729 adj.
lenient 731 adj.
permitting 751 adj.
inexactable 818 adj.
content 823 adj.
amiable 879 adj.
benevolent 892 adj.
pitying 900 adj.
forgiving 904 adj.

lenient, be
be moderate
172 vb.
pacify 714 vb.
be lax 729 vb.
be lenient 731 vb.

permit **751** vb.
consent **753** vb.
give **776** vb.
be patient **818** vb.
show mercy
                **900** vb.
forgive **904** vb.
exempt **914** vb.
extenuate **922** vb.

**lenitive**
lenitive **172** adj.

**less**
less **35** adv.

**lesser**
small **33** adj.
lesser **35** adj.

**let fall**
be deep **206** vb.
move **260** vb.
insert **298** vb.
let fall **306** vb.
make flow **345** vb.
be clumsy **690** vb.

**letter**
list **87** n.
indication **542** n.
letter **553** n.
lettering **581** n.
print-type **582** n.

**lettering**
unintelligibility
                **512** n.
letter **553** n.
lettering **581** n.

**letterpress**
letterpress **582** n.

**levy**
beg **756** vb.
request **756** vb.
levy **781** vb.
tax **804** vb.
claim **910** vb.

**liability**
liability **175** n.

**liable**
tending **174** adj.
liable **175** adj.
probable **466** adj.

vulnerable **656** adj.
subject **740** adj.
guilty **931** adj.

**liable, be**
be liable **175** vb.
be in danger
                **656** vb.

**liar**
liar **540** n.
exaggeration
                **541** n.
boaster **872** n.

**liberal**
plenteous **630** adj.
giving **776** adj.
expending **801** adj.
prodigal **810** adj.
ostentatious
                **870** adj.
benevolent **892** adj.
rewarding **957** adj.

**liberal, be**
superabound
                **632** vb.
give **776** vb.
expend **801** vb.
be liberal **808** vb.
be hospitable
                **877** vb.
reward **957** vb.

**liberality**
giving **776** n.
liberality **808** n.
sociability **877** n.
benevolence **892** n.

**liberally**
liberally **808** adv.

**liberate**
disunite **46** vb.
exclude **57** vb.
revert **143** vb.
extract **299** vb.
restore **651** vb.
deliver **663** vb.
give scope **739** vb.
liberate **741** vb.
permit **751** vb.

not retain **774** vb.
exempt **914** vb.
acquit **955** vb.

**liberated**
disunited **46** adj.
nonadhesive
                **49** adj.
free **739** adj.
liberated **741** adj.
not retained
                **774** adj.
acquitted **955** adj.
sanctified **973** adj.

**liberation**
separation **46** n.
exclusion **57** n.
transference **267** n.
escape **662** n.
deliverance **663** n.
facility **696** n.
laxity **729** n.
freedom **739** n.
liberation **741** n.
permission **751** n.
loss **767** n.
nonretention **774** n.
nonliability **914** n.
acquittal **955** n.

**libertine**
libertine **947** n.

**libido**
libido **854** n.
love **882** n.
unchastity **946** n.

**library**
accumulation **74** n.
erudition **485** n.
library **584** n.

**lie between**
lie between **226** vb.
obstruct **697** vb.

**life**
existence **1** n.
substance **3** n.
vitality **157** n.
blood **330** n.
organism **353** n.
life **355** n.

restlessness **673** n.
cheerfulness **828** n.

**lifelike**
lifelike **18** adj.

**lifter**
lifter **305** n.

**lift oneself**
be high **204** vb.
ascend **303** vb.
lift oneself **305** vb.

**ligature**
ligature **47** n.

**light**
insubstantial **4** adj.
unequal **29** adj.
small **33** adj.
morning **123** n.
weak **158** adj.
ascending **303** adj.
light **318** adj.
rare **320** adj.
bubbly **350** adj.
light **412** n.
glimmer **414** n.
lighting **415** n.
luminary **415** n.
whiteness **422** n.
variegation **432** n.
metrology **460** n.
spurious **537** adj.
trivial **634** adj.
beauty **836** n.
revelation **969** n.

**light, be**
be unequal **29** vb.
be small **33** vb.
decrease **37** vb.
become small
                **193** vb.
fly **266** vb.
be light **318** vb.

**light contrast**
light contrast
                **412** n.

**lighten**
abate **37** vb.
make smaller
                **193** vb.

**litigation**
litigation 954 n.

**little**
small 33 adj.
infantine 127 adj.
weak 158 adj.
little 191 adj.
short 199 adj.
light 318 adj.

**little, be**
be small 33 vb.
be little 191 vb.

**littleness**
littleness 191 n.

**live**
be 1 vb.
pass time 104 vb.
live 355 vb.

**lively**
vigorous 169 adj.
leaping 307 adj.
agitated 313 adj.
alive 355 adj.
forceful 566 adj.
active 673 adj.
lively 814 adj.
excitable 817 adj.
cheerful 828 adj.
proud 866 adj.

**livery**
uniform 223 n.
livery 542 n.
badge of rank
738 n.

**live single**
live single 890 vb.

**living model**
living model 23 n.

**load**
stow 182 vb.
load 188 vb.
transpose 267 vb.
insert 298 vb.
make heavy
317 vb.
be dense 319 vb.
store 627 vb.
hinder 697 vb.

**lobby**
entrance 68 n.
lobby 189 n.
access 619 n.

**locality**
district 179 n.
place 180 n.
locality 182 n.
abode 187 n.
near place 195 n.

**located**
located 182 adj.

**location**
addition 38 n.
arrangement 62 n.
bearings 181 n.
location 182 n.
nearness 195 n.
discovery 479 n.

**lockup**
lockup 743 n.

**locomotive**
locomotive 269 n.
traction 283 n.

**loincloth**
loincloth 223 n.

**long**
great 32 adj.
lasting 108 adj.
long 198 adj.
narrow 201 adj.
prolix 565 adj.

**long ago**
long ago 108 adv.

**long, be**
be long 198 vb.

**long duration**
time 104 n.
period 106 n.
course of time
107 n.
long duration
108 n.
perpetuity 110 n.
age 126 n.
life 355 n.
habit 605 n.

**longitudinal**
longitudinal
198 adj.

**long measure**
long measure
198 n.
measurement
460 n.
metrology 460 n.

**longwise**
longwise 198 adv.

**look**
look 433 n.
attention 450 n.
gesture 542 n.

**look after**
be mindful 450 vb.
look after 452 vb.
safeguard 655 vb.
preserve 661 vb.
manage 684 vb.

**look ahead**
look ahead 119 vb.
foresee 505 vb.
be cautious 853 vb.

**look along**
look along 198 vb.

**look back**
be unconformable
84 vb.
look back 120 vb.
be late 131 vb.
retrospect 500 vb.

**looking ahead**
looking ahead
119 n.

**loop**
halter 47 n.
outline 228 n.
curve 243 n.
loop 245 n.
orifice 258 n.
circuition 309 n.
vortex 310 n.
jewellery 839 n.

**loose woman**
woman 368 n.
bad person 933 n.

**loose woman**
947 n.

**loquacious**
informative
519 adj.
disclosing 521 adj.
diffuse 565 adj.
speaking 574 adj.
loquacious 576 adj.
conversing 579 adj.

**loquacious, be**
mean nothing
510 vb.
inform 519 vb.
publish 523 vb.
be diffuse 565 vb.
speak 574 vb.
be loquacious
576 vb.
converse 579 vb.
be obstructive
697 vb.

**loquaciously**
loquaciously
576 adv.

**loquacity**
loquacity 576 n.

**lorry**
lorry 269 n.

**lose**
decrease 37 vb.
relinquish 616 vb.
fail 723 vb.
lose 767 vb.
sell 788 vb.

**lose a chance**
be late 131 vb.
lose a chance
133 vb.
act foolishly
690 vb.
fail 723 vb.
lose 767 vb.

**lose colour**
change 138 vb.
be dim 414 vb.
lose colour 421 vb.
disappear 441 vb.

**loser**
bungler 692 n.
loser 723 n.
unlucky person
                    726 n.
laughingstock
                    846 n.
object of scorn
                    862 n.

**lose repute**
be inferior 35 vb.
lose repute 862 vb.
incur blame
                    919 vb.
be dishonest
                    925 vb.

**losing**
losing 767 adj.

**loss**
decrease 37 n.
deficit 55 n.
unproductiveness
                    167 n.
absence 185 n.
outflow 293 n.
evil 611 n.
waste 629 n.
inutility 636 n.
impairment 650 n.
failure 723 n.
loss 767 n.
nonownership
                    769 n.
debt 798 n.
loss of right 911 n.
penalty 958 n.

**loss of right**
conversion 142 n.
loss of right 911 n.

**lost**
lost 767 adj.

**lost, be**
be lost 767 vb.

**lost labour**
unproductiveness
                    167 n.
shortfall 302 n.
absurdity 492 n.

folly 494 n.
lost labour 636 n.
overactivity 673 n.
bungling 690 n.
failure 723 n.

**loud**
great 32 adj.
violent 171 adj.
sounding 393 adj.
loud 395 adj.
resonant 399 adj.
strident 402 adj.
ululant 404 adj.
ornate 569 adj.
rhetorical 509 adj.
frightening 849 adj.
approving 918 adj.

**loud, be**
sound 393 vb.
be loud 395 vb.
bang 397 vb.
resound 399 vb.
shrill 402 vb.
vociferate 403 vb.
be heard 410 vb.
deafen 411 vb.
proclaim 523 vb.
emphasize 527 vb.
voice 572 vb.
be obstructive
                    697 vb.
be angry 886 vb.

**loudly**
loudly 395 adv.

**loudness**
loudness 395 n.

**lovable**
lovable 882 adj.

**lovableness**
lovableness 882 n.

**love**
maternity 164 n.
concord 705 n.
feeling 813 n.
moral sensibility
                    814 n.
be pleased 819 vb.
liking 854 n.

desire 854 vb.
wonder 859 n.
wonder 859 vb.
honour 861 vb.
friendship 875 n.
be friendly 875 vb.
love 882 n.
love 882 vb.
court 884 vb.
pet 884 n.
benevolence 892 n.
jealousy 906 n.
approbation 918 n.
approve 918 vb.
disinterestedness
                    926 n.

**love affair**
love affair 882 n.
illicit love 946 n.

**loved one**
loved one 882 n.

**love emblem**
love emblem 882 n.
love token 884 n.

**love god**
love god 882 n.

**love-making**
love-making 882 n.
wooing 884 n.

**love-nest**
love-nest 882 n.

**lover**
concomitant 89 n.
patron 702 n.
desirer 854 n.
lover 882 n.
nubility 889 n.
libertine 947 n.

**lovers**
lovers 882 n.

**love token**
love emblem 882 n.
love token 884 n.

**loving**
friendly 875 adj.
loving 882 adj.
caressing 884 adj.
benevolent 892 adj.

jealous 906 adj.
godlike 960 adj.

**low**
small 33 adj.
short 199 adj.
low 205 adj.
undermost 209 adj.
lowered 306 adj.
infernal 966 adj.

**low, be**
be small 33 vb.
be low 205 vb.
descend 304 vb.

**lower**
abate 37 vb.
suppress 160 vb.
be low 205 vb.
impel 274 vb.
draw 283 vb.
immerse 298 vb.
lower 306 vb.
plunge 308 vb.
weigh 317 vb.
obliterate 545 vb.

**lower classes**
lower classes
                    864 n.

**lowered**
lowered 306 adj.

**lowering**
lowering 306 vb.

**low fellow**
low fellow 864 n.
ruffian 899 n.
knave 933 n.

**lowness**
lowness 205 n.

**loyalty**
submission 716 n.
loyalty 734 n.
service 740 n.
observance 763 n.
love 882 n.
respect 915 n.
probity 924 n.

**lubricant**
smoother 253 n.
lubricant 329 n.

oil 352 n.
silencer 396 n.
**lubricate**
smooth 253 vb.
soften 322 vb.
rub 328 vb.
lubricate 329 vb.
grease 352 vb.
facilitate 696 vb.
**lubricated**
lubricated 329 adj.
**lubrication**
lubrication 329 n.
unctuousness
    352 n.
**lull**
discontinuity 72 n.
interim 104 n.
period 106 n.
delay 131 n.
lull 140 n.
interval 196 n.
quiescence 261 n.
repose 678 n.
refreshment 680 n.
peace 712 n.
pacification 714 n.
**luminary**
luminary 415 n.
**luminescent**
luminescent
    415 adj.
**luminous**
luminous 412 adj.
florid 420 adj.
white 422 adj.
obvious 438 adj.
noteworthy
    861 adj.
**lunatic asylum**
lunatic asylum
    498 n.
hospital 653 n.
shelter 657 n.
**lunge**
lunge 707 n.
**lurk**
be inert 170 vb.

be low 205 vb.
wander 262 vb.
be dark 413 vb.
be dim 414 vb.
be unseen 439 vb.
disappear 441 vb.
escape notice
    451 vb.
lurk 518 vb.
be stealthy 520 vb.
ambush 522 vb.
avoid 615 vb.
be safe 655 vb.
seek safety 655 vb.
elude 662 vb.
be cunning 693 vb.
be cautious 853 vb.

# M

**machine**
component 58 n.
causal means
    151 n.
electronics 155 n.
sources of energy
    155 n.
production 159 n.
instrument 623 n.
instrumentality
    623 n.
means 624 n.
machine 625 n.
**machinist**
machinist 625 n.
**maculation**
maculation 432 n.
**madman**
violent creature
    171 n.
fool 496 n.
madman 499 n.
sick person 646 n.
ruffian 899 n.

**Madonna**
Madonna 962 n.
**magical**
extraneous 59 adj.
instrumental
    623 adj.
wonderful 859 adj.
fairylike 964 adj.
magical 977 adj.
**magic instrument**
magic instrument
    977 n.
**magistracy**
magistracy 952 n.
**magnet**
traction 283 n.
magnet 286 n.
incentive 607 n.
**magniloquence**
magniloquence
    569 n.
**main part**
main part 32 n.
part 53 n.
greater number
    100 n.
redundance 632 n.
chief thing 633 n.
undueness 911 n.
**make angular**
cross 217 vb.
make angular
    242 vb.
make curved
    243 vb.
**make appetizing**
taste 381 vb.
make appetizing
    385 vb.
delight 821 vb.
cause desire
    854 vb.
**make better**
unravel 62 vb.
modify 138 vb.
transform 142 vb.
influence 173 vb.

be attentive
    450 vb.
benefit 610 vb.
do good 639 vb.
purify 643 vb.
make better
    649 vb.
restore 651 vb.
make rich 795 vb.
be benevolent
    892 vb.
make pious 973 vb.
**make bright**
smooth 253 vb.
make bright
    412 vb.
illuminate 415 vb.
be transparent
    417 vb.
clean 643 vb.
beautify 836 vb.
**make certain**
corroborate 461 vb.
testify 461 vb.
make certain
    468 vb.
demonstrate
    473 vb.
discover 479 vb.
endorse 483 vb.
safeguard 655 vb.
take a pledge
    759 vb.
give security
    762 vb.
be cautious 853 vb.
**make complete**
augment 36 vb.
add 38 vb.
make complete
    54 vb.
pervade 184 vb.
crown 208 vb.
carry through
    720 vb.
**make concave**
disable 156 vb.
be deep 206 vb.

make concave
    250 vb.
pierce 258 vb.
transpose 267 vb.
descend 304 vb.
lower 306 vb.
make conceited
    make conceited
    868 vb.
make conform
    make uniform
    16 vb.
make conform
    83 vb.
modify 138 vb.
make curved
    make curved
    243 vb.
make enemies
    make enemies
    876 vb.
make extrinsic
    make extrinsic 6 vb.
externalize 218 vb.
make flow
    liquefy 332 vb.
make flow 345 vb.
purify 643 vb.
make fruitful
    make fruitful
    166 vb.
cultivate 365 vb.
make heavy
    make heavy
    317 vb.
make higher
    augment 36 vb.
make higher
    204 vb.
elevate 305 vb.
make illegal
    disentitle 911 vb.
make illegal
    949 vb.
condemn 956 vb.
make important
    be attentive
    450 vb.

discriminate
    458 vb.
manifest 517 vb.
emphasize 527 vb.
exaggerate 541 vb.
make important
    633 vb.
make impossible
    exclude 57 vb.
make impossible
    465 vb.
negate 528 vb.
be difficult 695 vb.
make inactive
    make inactive
    674 vb.
make insensitive
    make insensitive
    815 vb.
be indifferent
    855 vb.
make insufficient
    shorten 199 vb.
make insufficient
    631 vb.
be parsimonious
    811 vb.
make legal
    do 671 vb.
manage 684 vb.
decree 732 vb.
permit 751 vb.
grant claims
    910 vb.
make legal 948 vb.
make likely
    evidence 461 vb.
make likely 466 vb.
make mad
    derange 63 vb.
make violent
    171 vb.
distract 451 vb.
make mad 498 vb.
excite love 882 vb.
make mute
    abate 37 vb.
silence 394 vb.

make mute 573 vb.
hinder 697 vb.
restrain 742 vb.
make oblique
    make oblique
    215 vb.
deflect 277 vb.
make opaque
    bedim 414 vb.
screen 416 vb.
make opaque
    418 vb.
variegate 432 vb.
make peace
    cease 140 vb.
make peace
    714 vb.
be content 823 vb.
befriend 875 vb.
make pious
    make pious 973 vb.
make possible
    make possible
    464 vb.
facilitate 696 vb.
permit 751 vb.
offer 754 vb.
make quarrels
    make quarrels
    704 vb.
make ready
    time 112 vb.
predestine 150 vb.
dress 223 vb.
start out 291 vb.
find means 624 vb.
provide 628 vb.
make ready 664 vb.
defend 708 vb.
make rich
    make rich 795 vb.
make round
    make curved
    243 vb.
make round
    245 vb.
make sane
    make sane 497 vb.

make smaller
    make smaller
    193 vb.
make sterile
    unman 156 vb.
lay waste 160 vb.
make sterile
    167 vb.
make useless
    636 vb.
make terms
    accord 24 vb.
do business
    617 vb.
cooperate 701 vb.
consent 753 vb.
contract 760 vb.
make terms 761 vb.
bargain 786 vb.
make thin
    abate 37 vb.
make smaller
    193 vb.
lengthen 198 vb.
make thin 201 vb.
laminate 202 vb.
be temperate
    937 vb.
make ugly
    deform 239 vb.
mark 542 vb.
impair 650 vb.
make ugly 837 vb.
blemish 840 vb.
make unclean
    thicken 349 vb.
bedim 414 vb.
decolorize 421 vb.
blacken 423 vb.
variegate 432 vb.
mark 542 vb.
make unclean
    644 vb.
impair 650 vb.
misuse 670 vb.
make ugly 837 vb.
blemish 840 vb.
shame 862 vb.

defame 921 vb.
debauch 946 vb.
be impious 974 vb.
**make uniform**
make uniform
16 vb.
equalize 28 vb.
simplify 44 vb.
join 45 vb.
order 60 vb.
regularize 62 vb.
make conform
83 vb.
gauge 460 vb.
**make unlike**
make unlike 19 vb.
exclude 57 vb.
**make unwelcome**
make unwelcome
878 vb.
**make useless**
disable 156 vb.
make useless
636 vb.
stop using 669 vb.
make inactive
674 vb.
**make vertical**
make vertical
210 vb.
elevate 305 vb.
**make violent**
make violent
171 vb.
**make wicked**
misteach 530 vb.
pervert 650 vb.
make wicked
929 vb.
**malcontent**
dissentient 484 n.
opponent 700 n.
revolter 733 n.
malcontent 824 n.
moper 829 n.
weeper 831 n.
rude person 880 n.
misanthrope 897 n.

disapprover 919 n.
**male**
abnormality 84 n.
adult 129 n.
adultness 129 n.
grown-up 129 adj.
athlete 157 n.
manly 157 adj.
violent creature
171 n.
person 366 n.
male 367 n.
male 367 adj.
master 736 n.
**male animal**
male animal 367 n.
**malediction**
word 554 n.
badness 640 n.
discontent 824 n.
hatred 883 n.
malediction 894 n.
threat 895 n.
reproach 919 n.
detraction 921 n.
condemnation
956 n.
impiety 974 n.
impious person
974 n.
prayers 975 n.
**maleficent**
evil 611 adj.
maleficent 893 adj.
wicked 929 adj.
fairylike 964 adj.
sorcerous 977 adj.
**malevolence**
malevolence 893 n.
**malevolent**
inimical 876 adj.
hating 883 adj.
resentful 886 adj.
malevolent 893 adj.
revengeful 905 adj.
detracting 921 adj.
wicked 929 adj.
diabolic 963 adj.

**malevolent, be**
harm 640 vb.
ill-treat 640 vb.
oppress 730 vb.
be inimical 876 vb.
hate 883 vb.
resent 886 vb.
be malevolent
893 vb.
curse 894 vb.
be revengeful
905 vb.
bewitch 977 vb.
**malevolently**
malevolently
893 adv.
**mammal**
beast of burden
268 n.
mammal 360 n.
hunter 614 n.
**manage**
arrange 62 vb.
look after 452 vb.
motivate 607 vb.
undertake 667 vb.
deal with 683 vb.
manage 684 vb.
deputize 750 vb.
**management**
superiority 34 n.
arrangement 62 n.
agency 168 n.
inspection 433 n.
vocation 617 n.
action 671 n.
conduct 683 n.
management
684 n.
government 728 n.
commission 746 n.
church office
979 n.
**manager**
superior 34 n.
spectator 436 n.
manager 685 n.
master 736 n.

consignee 749 n.
**man and boy**
man and boy
106 adv.
**mandate**
job 617 n.
precept 688 n.
command 732 n.
mandate 746 n.
permit 751 n.
conditions 761 n.
jurisdiction 950 n.
**mania**
attention 450 n.
prejudgment 476 n.
mania 498 n.
desire 854 n.
alcoholism 944 n.
**manifest**
uncovered 224 adj.
open 258 adj.
visible 438 adj.
be visible 438 vb.
appearing 440 adj.
appear 440 vb.
evidence 461 n.
demonstrate
473 vb.
discover 479 vb.
manifest 517 adj.
manifest 517 vb.
disclose 521 vb.
well-known
523 adj.
show feeling
813 vb.
**manifestation**
inspection 433 n.
visibility 438 n.
appearance 440 n.
demonstration
473 n.
discovery 479 n.
manifestation
517 n.
disclosure 521 n.
publicity 523 n.
veracity 535 n.

indication 542 n.
signal 542 n.
representation
546 n.
ostentation 870 n.
**manifestly**
manifestly 517 adv.
**manliness**
manliness 850 n.
**manly**
manly 157 adj.
**man or woman of action**
doer 671 n.
**many**
plural 97 adj.
many 100 adj.
infinite 103 adj.
frequent 134 adj.
redundant 632 adj.
**many, be**
grow 36 vb.
be many 100 vb.
reproduce 161 vb.
reproduce itself
162 vb.
be fruitful 166 vb.
abound 630 vb.
superabound
632 vb.
**map**
arrangement 62 n.
statistics 86 n.
situation 181 n.
distortion 241 n.
itinerary 262 n.
sailing aid 264 n.
world 316 n.
guidebook 519 n.
map 546 n.
plan 618 n.
**marching**
marching 262 n.
**marginal**
marginal 229 adj.
lateral 234 adj.
**marine**
seafaring 264 adj.

seamanlike
265 adj.
**marine life**
marine 270 adj.
marine life 360 n.
**mariner**
traveller 263 n.
water travel 264 n.
mariner 265 n.
circler 309 n.
director 685 n.
naval man 717 n.
**mark**
make uniform
16 vb.
class 62 n.
make conform
83 vb.
limit 231 n.
mark 542 vb.
name 556 vb.
select 600 vb.
intend 612 vb.
blemish 840 vb.
shame 862 vb.
**marked**
marked 542 adj.
**market**
focus 76 n.
meeting place
187 n.
way in 292 n.
exhibit 517 n.
trade 786 n.
market 791 n.
finance 792 n.
**marriage**
misfit 25 n.
mixture 43 n.
coition 45 n.
union 45 n.
interiority 219 n.
promise 759 n.
compact 760 n.
love affair 882 n.
wooing 884 n.
marriage 889 n.
Christian rite 982 n.

**marriageable**
grown-up 129 adj.
marriageable
889 adj.
**married**
joined 45 adj.
married 889 adj.
**marry**
join 45 vb.
not retain 774 vb.
assign 775 vb.
marry 889 vb.
**marsh**
desert 187 n.
lowness 205 n.
horizontality 211 n.
softness 322 n.
moisture 336 n.
lake 341 n.
marsh 342 n.
plain 343 n.
semiliquidity 349 n.
dirt 644 n.
uncleanness 644 n.
pitfall 658 n.
difficulty 695 n.
**marshy**
soft 322 adj.
humid 336 adj.
marshy 342 adj.
semiliquid 349 adj.
pulpy 351 adj.
dirty 644 adj.
insalubrious
648 adj.
**master**
superior 34 n.
director 685 n.
authority 728 n.
master 736 n.
taker 781 n.
**masterpiece**
product 159 n.
exceller 639 n.
perfection 641 n.
deed 671 n.
masterpiece 689 n.
success 722 n.

**matchmaker**
joining together
45 n.
intermediary 226 n.
matchmaker 889 n.
**material**
real 1 adj.
substantial 3 adj.
material 314 adj.
sensuous 371 adj.
tactual 373 adj.
sensual 939 adj.
**materiality**
materiality 314 n.
**materialize**
materialize 314 vb.
**materials**
materials 626 n.
**maternity**
maternity 164 n.
woman 368 n.
**mathematics**
quantity 26 n.
mathematics 86 n.
reasoning 470 n.
**matinal**
matinal 123 adj.
**matrimonial**
matrimonial
889 adj.
**matrimonially**
matrimonially
889 adv.
**matter**
substantiality 3 n.
matter 314 n.
universe 316 n.
solid body 319 n.
**maturation**
maturation 664 n.
**mature**
augment 36 vb.
grow 36 vb.
be complete 54 vb.
be turned to
142 vb.
impend 150 vb.

reproduce itself
162 vb.
soften 322 vb.
perfect 641 vb.
get better 649 vb.
make better
649 vb.
mature 664 vb.
carry through
720 vb.

**matured**
matured 664 adj.

**maw**
maw 189 n.

**maxim**
certainty 468 n.
premise 470 n.
judgment 475 n.
creed 480 n.
maxim 491 n.
lack of meaning
510 n.
affirmation 527 n.
phrase 558 n.
conciseness 564 n.
precept 688 n.

**meal**
meal 296 n.
provision 628 n.
festivity 832 n.

**mean**
specify 80 vb.
mean 509 vb.
be equivocal
513 vb.
imply 518 vb.
indicate 542 vb.
represent 546 vb.
be important
633 vb.

**meander**
meander 246 vb.
deviate 277 vb.
circle 309 vb.
flow 345 vb.

**meandering**
meandering 246 n.

**meaning**
substance 3 n.
relation 9 n.
identity 13 n.
contrariety 14 n.
differentiation 15 n.
accuracy 489 n.
meaning 509 n.
interpretation
515 n.
linguistics 552 n.
etymology 554 n.
word 559 n.
chief thing 638 n.

**meaningful**
evidential 461 adj.
meaningful
509 adj.
intelligible 511 adj.
indicating 542 adj.
important 638 adj.

**meaningless**
insubstantial 4 adj.
absurd 492 adj.
semantic 509 adj.
meaningless
510 adj.
unimportant
634 adj.

**mean nothing**
reason badly
472 vb.
be absurd 492 vb.
be foolish 494 vb.
mean nothing
510 vb.
be unintelligible
512 vb.
be loquacious
576 vb.
boast 872 vb.

**means**
opportunity 132 n.
causal means
151 n.
contrivance 618 n.
instrumentality
623 n.

means 624 n.
materials 626 n.
good policy 637 n.
estate 772 n.
funds 792 n.
wealth 795 n.

**means of escape**
outlet 293 n.
ascent 303 n.
pretext 609 n.
contrivance 618 n.
means 624 n.
safety 655 n.
safeguard 657 n.
means of escape
662 n.

**means of
execution**
killer 357 n.
furnace 378 n.
means of execution
959 n.

**measure**
do sums 86 vb.
measure 178 n.
size 190 n.
navigate 264 vb.
plunge 308 vb.
weigh 317 vb.
metrology 460 n.
measure 460 vb.

**measured**
measured 460 adj.

**measurement**
finite quantity 26 n.
quantity 26 n.
degree 27 n.
arrangement 62 n.
inclusion 78 n.
numeration 86 n.
size 190 n.
long measure
198 n.
depth 206 n.
navigation 264 n.
measurement
460 n.
estimate 475 n.

accuracy 489 n.

**meat**
insides 219 n.
meat 296 n.
corpse 358 n.

**mechanical**
dynamic 155 adj.
instrumental
623 adj.
mechanical
625 adj.

**mechanics**
data processing
86 n.
mechanics 625 n.

**meddle**
be vigorous 169 vb.
counteract 177 vb.
interfere 226 vb.
be curious 448 vb.
busy oneself
617 vb.
impair 650 vb.
do 671 vb.
meddle 673 vb.
be clumsy 690 vb.
hinder 697 vb.
obstruct 697 vb.
mediate 715 vb.

**meddler**
meddler 673 n.

**meddling**
meddling 673 adj.

**median**
median 30 n.
inconsiderable
33 adj.
middle 70 adj.
general 79 adj.
typical 83 adj.
not bad 639 adj.
imperfect 642 adj.
middling 727 adj.

**mediate**
interfere 226 vb.
be instrumental
623 vb.

**mediation**

be at peace
712 vb.
pacify 714 vb.
mediate 715 vb.
deprecate 757 vb.
forgive 904 vb.

**mediation**
mediation 715 n.

**mediator**
moderator 172 n.
intermediary 226 n.
instrument 623 n.
pacifist 712 n.
mediator 715 n.
signatory 760 n.
matchmaker 889 n.

**mediatory,
propotiatory**
mediatory 715 adj.

**medical**
fertilized 162 adj.
medical 653 adj.

**medical art**
medical art 653 n.
aid 698 n.

**medicine**
draught 296 n.
medicine 653 n.

**meditate**
meditate 444 vb.
notice 450 vb.
enquire 454 vb.
estimate 475 vb.
suppose 507 vb.
offer worship
975 vb.

**meditation**
meditation 444 n.

**medley**
nonuniformity 17 n.
medley 43 n.
piece 53 n.
confusion 61 n.
accumulation 74 n.
bunch 74 n.
chequer 432 n.

**meet**
synchronize
118 vb.
meet with 149 vb.
converge 288 vb.
meet 290 vb.

**meeting place**
focus 76 n.
meeting place
187 n.
goal 290 n.

**meet with**
meet with 149 vb.
result 152 vb.
chance 154 vb.
discover 479 vb.

**megaphone**
megaphone 395 n.
hearing aid 410 n.
telecommunication
526 n.

**melancholic**
melancholic
829 adj.

**melancholy**
psychopathy 498 n.
suffering 820 n.
melancholy 829 n.
tedium 833 n.
sullenness 888 n.

**melodious**
pleasant 371 adj.
melodious 405 adj.
musical 407 adj.
musicianly 408 adj.
vocal 572 adj.
pleasurable
821 adj.

**melody**
agreement 24 n.
sound 393 n.
melody 405 n.
music 407 n.
concord 705 n.

**memorize**
memorize 500 vb.

**memory**
thought 444 n.

memory 500 n.
storage 627 n.
famousness 861 n.

**mender**
mender 651 n.

**mental**
immaterial 315 adj.
mental 442 adj.
knowing 485 adj.
diseased 646 adj.

**mental dishonesty**
mental dishonesty
538 n.

**Mephisto**
Mephisto 963 n.

**merchandise**
accumulation 74 n.
product 159 n.
equipment 625 n.
store 627 n.
property 772 n.
sale 788 n.
merchandise 790 n.

**merchant**
intermediary 226 n.
transferrer 267 n.
agent 681 n.
merchant 789 n.
minter 792 n.

**merchant ship**
merchant ship
270 n.

**mercy**
mercy 900 n.
forgiveness 904 n.

**merriment**
enjoyment 819 n.
merriment 828 n.
rejoicing 830 n.
amusement 832 n.
festivity 832 n.
wit 834 n.

**merry**
lively 814 adj.
happy 819 adj.
pleased 819 adj.
merry 828 adj.
amusing 832 adj.

witty 834 adj.
affected 845 adj.
sociable 877 adj.

**message**
information 519 n.
message 524 n.
telecommunication
526 n.
signal 542 n.

**messenger**
precursor 66 n.
omen 506 n.
informant 519 n.
publicizer 523 n.
messenger 524 n.
postal
communications
526 n.
officer 736 n.
delegate 749 n.
deputy 750 n.

**metaphor**
comparison 457 n.
connotation 509 n.
metaphor 514 n.
interpretation
515 n.
latency 518 n.
literature 552 n.
ritual 982 n.

**metaphorically**
metaphorically
514 adv.

**meteor**
meteor 316 n.
luminary 415 n.

**mete out**
mete out 460 vb.

**meter**
altimetry 204 n.
gas 331 n.
meter 460 n.
detector 479 n.

**metrical**
numerable 86 adj.
metrical 460 adj.

**metrology**
metrology 460 n.

**microelectronics**
counting instrument
86 n.
electronics 155 n.
microelectronics
191 n.

**microorganism**
small animal 33 n.
microorganism
191 n.
organism 353 n.
animal 360 n.
plant 361 n.
insalubrity 648 n.

**microscope**
microscope 437 n.

**microscopy**
microscopy 191 n.

**middle**
middle point 30 n.
median 30 adj.
middle 70 n.
middle 70 adj.
focus 76 n.
interim 104 n.
centre 220 n.
central 220 adj.
interjacency 226 n.
intermediary 226 n.
interjacent 226 adj.

**middle age**
middle point 30 n.
middle age 126 n.
adultness 129 n.

**middle classes**
middle classes
864 n.

**middle point**
middle point 30 n.
middle way 620 n.

**middle way**
middle point 30 n.
middle 70 n.
moderation 172 n.
middle way 620 n.
compromise 765 n.
indifference 855 n.

**middling**
median 30 adj.
inconsiderable
33 adj.
typical 83 adj.
middling 727 adj.
plebeian 864 adj.

**middling, be**
be middling
727 vb.

**midnight**
midnight 124 n.
lateness 131 n.
darkness 413 n.

**midstream, be**
be midstream
620 vb.

**midway**
midway 70 adv.

**mien**
form 238 n.
mien 440 n.
gesture 542 n.
conduct 683 n.

**militarist**
militarist 717 n.

**milk**
milk 296 n.

**mimicry**
mimicry 20 n.
disguise 522 n.
acting 589 n.
satire 846 n.
ostentation 870 n.

**mindful, be**
be mindful 450 vb.
remember 500 vb.
be cautious 853 vb.

**mindless**
mindless 443 adj.
unthinking 445 adj.

**mineral**
object 314 n.
mineral 354 n.

**mineralogy**
rock 339 n.
mineralogy 354 n.

**miniature**
small thing 33 n.
miniature 191 n.
record 543 n.

**minister to**
concur 176 vb.
look after 452 vb.
be instrumental
623 vb.
doctor 653 vb.
work 677 vb.
minister to 698 vb.
obey 734 vb.
serve 737 vb.
philanthropize
892 vb.

**ministration**
church ministry
979 n.
ministration 982 n.

**mint**
produce 159 vb.
mint 792 n.

**minter**
minter 792 n.

**minute**
minute 191 n.
indistinct 439 adj.

**minuteness**
minuteness 191 n.

**mirror**
reflection 412 n.
mirror 437 n.

**misanthrope**
enemy 876 n.
shrew 887 n.
celibate 890 n.
misanthrope 897 n.
disapprover 919 n.

**misanthropic**
misanthropic
897 adj.

**misanthropically**
misanthropically
897 adv.

**misanthropize**
misanthropize
897 vb.

**misanthropy**
misanthropy 897 n.

**miscarry**
pass away 2 vb.
reproduce itself
162 vb.
be unproductive
167 vb.
fall short 302 vb.
be clumsy 690 vb.
be in difficulty
695 vb.
miscarry 723 vb.
have trouble
726 vb.

**misdate**
misdate 113 vb.

**misfit**
unrelatedness 10 n.
dissimilarity 19 n.
misfit 25 n.
discontinuity 72 n.
nonconformist
84 n.
displacement
183 n.
bungler 692 n.
loser 723 n.

**misfortune**
untimeliness 133 n.
event 149 n.
chance 154 n.
ruin 160 n.
disappointment
504 n.
evil 611 n.
badness 640 n.
deterioration 650 n.
failure 723 n.
misfortune 726 n.

**misinterpret**
transform 142 vb.
distort 241 vb.
misjudge 476 vb.
blunder 490 vb.
mean nothing
510 vb.

misinterpret
    516 vb.
be false 536 vb.
**misinterpretation**
misinterpretation
    516 n.
**misinterpreted**
misinterpreted
    516 adj.
**misjudge**
mistime 133 vb.
not think 445 vb.
misjudge 476 vb.
underestimate
    478 vb.
not know 486 vb.
blunder 490 vb.
err 490 vb.
be foolish 494 vb.
not understand
    512 vb.
misinterpret
    516 vb.
**misjudging**
misjudging
    476 adj.
**misjudgment**
misjudgment
    476 n.
**mislead**
derange 63 vb.
deflect 282 vb.
blind 434 vb.
puzzle 469 vb.
mislead 490 vb.
misteach 530 vb.
befool 537 vb.
deceive 537 vb.
motivate 607 vb.
obstruct 697 vb.
**mismatch**
mismatch 25 vb.
**misname**
misname 557 vb.
**misnamed**
misnamed 557 adj.
**misnomer**
name 556 n.

misnomer 557 n.
**misplace**
derange 63 vb.
misplace 183 vb.
lose 767 vb.
**misplaced**
misplaced 183 adj.
**misrepresent**
make unlike 19 vb.
distort 241 vb.
sophisticate
    472 vb.
misinterpret
    516 vb.
misteach 530 vb.
be false 536 vb.
misrepresent
    547 vb.
satirize 846 vb.
detract 921 vb.
**misrepresentation**
misrepresentation
    547 n.
**misrepresented**
misrepresented
    547 adj.
**missile**
speeder 272 n.
missile 282 n.
ammunition 718 n.
missile weapon
    718 n.
**missile weapon**
rocket 271 n.
missile 282 n.
propellant 282 n.
missile weapon
    718 n.
**mistake**
mistake 490 n.
absurdity 492 n.
misinterpretation
    516 n.
misteaching 530 n.
solecism 560 n.
bungling 690 n.
failure 723 n.
guilty act 931 n.

**mistaken**
misjudging
    476 adj.
mistaken 490 adj.
unwise 494 adj.
misinterpreted
    516 adj.
misteaching
    530 adj.
heterodox 971 adj.
**misteach**
misteach 530 vb.
**misteaching**
misteaching 530 n.
misteaching
    530 adj.
**mistime**
derange 63 vb.
misdate 113 vb.
mistime 133 vb.
**misuse**
consume 160 vb.
force 171 vb.
sophisticate
    472 vb.
waste 629 vb.
waste 629 n.
ill-treat 640 vb.
impairment 650 n.
pervert 650 vb.
use 668 vb.
misuse 670 n.
misuse 670 vb.
bungling 690 n.
be unskilful 690 vb.
be severe 730 vb.
prodigality 810 n.
cruel act 893 n.
impiety 974 n.
be impious 974 vb.
**mix**
abate 37 vb.
add 38 vb.
mix 43 vb.
join 45 vb.
combine 50 vb.
compose 56 vb.
jumble 63 vb.

modify 138 vb.
weaken 158 vb.
infiltrate 292 vb.
infuse 298 vb.
rotate 310 vb.
agitate 313 vb.
impair 650 vb.
**mixed**
ethnic 11 adj.
different 15 adj.
mixed 43 adj.
combined 50 adj.
component 58 n.
multiform 82 adj.
abnormal 84 adj.
spurious 537 adj.
**mixed, be**
be mixed 43 vb.
be one of 58 vb.
be included 78 vb.
be turned to
    142 vb.
cooperate 701 vb.
**mixture**
mixture 43 n.
union 45 n.
combination 50 n.
composition 56 n.
confusion 61 n.
middle 70 n.
weakness 158 n.
draught 296 n.
liquefaction 332 n.
imperfection 642 n.
impairment 650 n.
type of marriage
    889 n.
**mixture, a**
a mixture 43 n.
compound 50 n.
product 159 n.
dish 296 n.
**mnemonics**
mnemonics 500 n.
**modality**
modality 7 n.
**moderate**
abate 37 vb.

disunite 46 vb.
moderate 172 adj.
moderate 172 vb.
retard 273 vb.
qualify 463 vb.
depreciating
478 adj.
dissuade 608 vb.
avoid 615 vb.
moderate 620 vb.
reformer 649 n.
make better
649 vb.
middling 727 adj.
be lenient 731 vb.
free person 739 n.
restrain 742 vb.
inexitable 818 vb.
relieve 826 vb.
indifference 855 n.
temperate 937 adj.

**moderate, be**
be moderate
172 vb.
be temperate
937 vb.

**moderately**
moderately
172 adv.

**moderation**
average 30 n.
diminution 37 n.
weakness 158 n.
moderation 172 n.
counteraction
177 n.
qualification 463 n.
underestimation
478 n.
avoidance 615 n.
middle way 620 n.
peace 712 n.
pacification 714 n.
peace offering
714 n.
averageness 727 n.
leniency 731 n.
inexitability 818 n.

relief 826 n.
temperance 937 n.

**moderator**
substitute 145 n.
moderator 172 n.
quietude 261 n.
anaesthetic 370 n.
balm 653 n.
remedy 653 n.
pacifist 712 n.
peace offering
714 n.
mediator 715 n.

**modern**
present 116 adj.
synchronous
118 adj.
modern 121 adj.
progressive
280 adj.
fashionable
843 adj.

**modernism**
present time 116 n.
modernism 121 n.
fashion 843 n.

**modernist**
modernist 121 n.

**modernize**
modernize 121 vb.

**modernized**
modernized
121 adj.

**modest**
plain 568 adj.
unwilling 593 adj.
avoiding 615 adj.
artless 694 adj.
middling 727 adj.
nervous 849 adj.
cowardly 851 adj.
inglorious 862 adj.
humble 867 adj.
modest 869 adj.
pure 945 adj.

**modest, be**
be nervous 849 vb.
be humble 867 vb.

**modestly**
modestly 869 adv.

**modesty**
modesty 869 n.

**modify**
mix 43 vb.
modify 138 vb.
transform 142 vb.
influence 173 vb.
qualify 463 vb.

**moisten**
mix 43 vb.
disperse 75 vb.
emit 295 vb.
let fall 306 vb.
add water 334 vb.
moisten 336 vb.
flow 345 vb.
make unclean
644 vb.

**moistening**
moistening 336 n.

**moisture**
moisture 336 n.
rain 345 n.
bubble 350 n.
obfuscation 416 n.

**monastery**
quarters 187 n.
retreat 187 n.
monastery 980 n.

**monastic**
unwedded 890 adj.
monastic 980 adj.
vestured 983 adj.

**monasticism**
monasticism 979 n.

**monetary**
monetary 792 adj.

**money**
quid pro quo 145 n.
incentive 607 n.
means 624 n.
acquisition 766 n.
money 792 n.
wealth 795 n.
payment 799 n.

**moneyed**
moneyed 795 adj.

**monk**
celibate 890 n.
virgin 945 n.
monk 980 n.

**monster**
violent creature
171 n.
tyrant 730 n.
intimidation 849 n.
hellhag 899 n.
monster 933 n.
demon 964 n.

**monument**
antiquity 120 n.
edifice 159 n.
small hill 204 n.
earthwork 248 n.
obsequies 359 n.
tomb 359 n.
reminder 500 n.
monument 543 n.
trophy 724 n.

**moon**
evening 124 n.
moon 316 n.
luminary 415 n.

**moot**
moot 454 adj.
uncertain 469 adj.

**moper**
moper 829 n.

**moral insensibility**
incuriosity 449 n.
indiscrimination
459 n.
sluggishness 674 n.
moral insensibility
815 n.
inexitability 818 n.
lack of wonder
860 n.
purity 945 n.

**morals**
right 908 n.
morals 912 n.
virtue 928 n.

**moral sensibility**
life 355 n.
sensibility 369 n.
discrimination
                458 n.
imagination 508 n.
interpretation
                515 n.
persuadability
                607 n.
feeling 813 n.
moral sensibility
                814 n.
painfulness 822 n.
pride 866 n.
love 882 n.
irascibility 887 n.

**morbidly**
morbidly 646 adv.

**morning**
beginning 68 n.
period 106 n.
morning 123 n.
earliness 130 n.
regular return
                136 n.
ascent 303 n.
light 412 n.

**motion**
degree 27 n.
changeable thing
                147 n.
displacement
                183 n.
motion 260 n.
water travel 264 n.
velocity 272 n.
progression 280 n.
way 619 n.
action 671 n.
activity 673 n.

**motivate**
cause 151 vb.
influence 173 vb.
propound 507 vb.
motivate 607 vb.
be important
                633 vb.

dispose of 668 vb.
do 671 vb.
manage 684 vb.
make quarrels
                704 vb.
cause desire
                854 vb.

**motivator**
motivator 607 n.

**motive**
causation 151 n.
power 155 n.
influence 173 n.
motive 607 n.
plot 618 n.
activity 673 n.

**mottled**
whitish 422 adj.
mottled 432 adj.
marked 542 adj.

**mould**
mould 23 n.

**mouthful**
mouthful 296 n.
savouriness 385 n.

**move**
derange 63 vb.
operate 168 vb.
displace 183 vb.
move 260 vb.
propel 287 vb.
be active 673 vb.

**move fast**
elapse 107 vb.
be transient
                109 vb.
be violent 171 vb.
be in motion
                260 vb.
travel 262 vb.
walk 262 vb.
navigate 264 vb.
move fast 272 vb.
progress 280 vb.
decamp 291 vb.
pass 300 vb.
outdo 301 vb.
run away 615 vb.

seek safety 655 vb.
be active 673 vb.
hasten 675 vb.

**move slowly**
move slowly
                273 vb.

**moving**
dynamic 155 adj.
moving 260 adj.
travelling 262 adj.
flying 266 adj.
progressive
                280 adj.
active 673 adj.

**multiform**
unrelated 10 adj.
different 15 adj.
nonuniform 17 adj.
dissimilar 19 adj.
mixed 43 adj.
multiform 82 adj.
many 100 adj.
changeful 147 adj.
variegated 432 adj.

**multiformity**
multiformity 82 n.

**multitude**
quantity 26 n.
greatness 32 n.
great quantity 32 n.
band 74 n.
crowd 74 n.
plurality 97 n.
multitude 100 n.
abundance 166 n.
safety 655 n.
army 717 n.

**multitudinous**
great 32 adj.
assembled 74 adj.
multitudinous
                100 adj.
frequent 134 adj.
filled 630 adj.

**murder**
destroy 160 vb.
murder 357 vb.
oppress 730 vb.

execute 958 vb.

**murderer**
murderer 357 n.

**murderous**
furious 171 adj.
murderous 357 adj.
cruel 893 adj.
guilty 931 adj.

**music**
combination 50 n.
composition 56 n.
arrangement 62 n.
sound 393 n.
melody 405 n.
music 407 n.
pleasurableness
                821 n.

**musical**
adjusted 24 adj.
musical 407 adj.

**musical, be**
be musical 408 vb.

**musical instrument**
blowing 347 n.
musical instrument
                409 n.

**musical note**
degree 27 n.
series 71 n.
interval 196 n.
ascent 303 n.
roll 398 n.
resonance 399 n.
stridor 402 n.
musical note 405 n.
musical piece
                407 n.

**musical piece**
composition 56 n.
prelude 66 n.
rear 233 n.
melody 405 n.
musical piece
                407 n.
topic 447 n.

**musical skill**
production 159 n.
melody 405 n.

music 407 n.
musical skill 408 n.

**musician**
concomitant 89 n.
producer 159 n.
musician 408 n.
interpreter 515 n.
proficient person
691 n.

**musicianly**
musicianly 408 adj.

**mutatis mutandis**
mutatis mutandis
138 adv.

**mute**
weaken 158 vb.
silencer 396 n.
mute 396 vb.
sound dead 400 vb.
mute 409 n.
make mute 573 vb.

**mute, be**
decrease 37 vb.
cease 140 vb.
be silent 394 vb.
be mute 573 vb.
be taciturn 577 vb.

**muted**
muted 396 adj.

**mythical being**
mythical being
964 n.

**mythic deity**
mythic deity 961 n.

**mythic heaven**
mythic heaven
965 n.

**mythic hell**
mythic hell 966 n.

**mythological**
mythological
961 adj.

**N**

**name**
class 62 vb.
auspicate 68 vb.
specify 80 vb.
word 554 n.
name 556 n.
name 556 vb.
misnomer 557 n.
misname 557 vb.
dignify 861 vb.

**named**
named 556 adj.

**named, be**
be named 556 vb.

**namely**
namely 80 adv.

**naming**
naming 556 adj.

**narrative**
maxim 491 n.
remembrance
500 n.
information 519 n.
report 519 n.
fable 538 n.
record 543 n.
literature 552 n.
narrative 585 n.
dramaturgy 589 n.
dramaturgy 589 n.
deed 671 n.

**narrator**
informant 519 n.
chronicler 544 n.
author 584 n.
narrator 585 n.

**narrow**
small 33 adj.
little 191 adj.
contracted 193 adj.
narrow 201 adj.
fibrous 203 adj.
tall 204 adj.
shallow 207 adj.

restraining 742 adj.

**narrow, be**
decrease 37 vb.
become small
193 vb.
be narrow 201 vb.
converge 288 vb.

**narrowing**
narrowing 201 n.

**narrow mind**
narrow mind 476 n.
ignoramus 488 n.
obstinate person
597 n.
enemy 876 n.
pietism 973 n.

**narrow-minded**
narrow-minded
476 adj.
unwise 494 adj.

**narrowness**
narrowness 201 n.

**nation**
consanguinity 11 n.
native 186 n.
nation 366 n.
community 703 n.
independence
739 n.

**national**
ethnic 11 adj.
national 366 adj.

**native**
earliness 130 n.
native 186 n.
native 186 n.
subject 737 n.
commoner 864 n.

**nautical personnel**
nautical personnel
265 n.
naval man 717 n.
naval officer 736 n.

**naval man**
nautical personnel
265 n.
naval man 717 n.

**naval officer**
nautical personnel
265 n.
naval man 717 n.
naval officer 736 n.

**navigate**
vary 147 vb.
be in motion
260 vb.
navigate 264 vb.
retard 273 vb.
orientate 276 vb.
deflect 277 vb.
draw 283 vb.
approach 284 vb.
start out 291 vb.
pass 300 vb.
direct 684 vb.

**navigation**
navigation 264 n.

**navigator**
navigator 265 n.
director 685 n.

**navy**
shipping 270 n.
navy 717 n.

**nay**
nay 528 adv.

**near**
relative 9 adj.
similar 18 adj.
almost 33 adv.
sequential 65 adj.
future 119 adj.
early 130 adj.
impending 150 adj.
somewhere
180 adv.
near 195 adj.
near 195 adv.
contiguous 197 adj.
circumjacent
225 adj.
sideways 234 adv.
accessible 284 adj.
approaching
284 adj.

**near, be**
come after 65 vb.
be to come 119 vb.
impend 150 vb.
be situated 181 vb.
be near 195 vb.
be contiguous
                197 vb.
fly 266 vb.
approach 284 vb.
pass 300 vb.
be plain 517 vb.
**nearly**
almost 33 adv.
on the whole
                52 adv.
nearly 195 adv.
**nearness**
nearness 195 n.
**near place**
locality 182 n.
near place 195 n.
surroundings
                225 n.
**nebula**
nebula 316 n.
cloud 350 n.
**necessarily**
necessarily
                591 adv.
**necessary**
impending 150 adj.
necessary 591 adj.
choiceless 601 adj.
compelling
                735 adj.
**necessitate**
predestine 150 vb.
make certain
                468 vb.
necessitate 591 vb.
**necessitous**
necessitous
                622 adj.
poor 796 adj.
**necessity**
destiny 150 n.
cause 151 n.

necessity 591 n.
no choice 601 n.
predetermination
                603 n.
requirement 622 n.
inexpedience
                638 n.
compulsion 735 n.
**neckline**
neckline 223 n.
**neckwear**
neckwear 223 n.
**needfulness**
needfulness 622 n.
**needlework**
network 217 n.
formation 238 n.
needlework 839 n.
**negate**
nullify 2 vb.
be contrary 14 vb.
answer 455 vb.
tell against 462 vb.
make impossible
                465 vb.
confute 474 vb.
disbelieve 481 vb.
dissent 484 vb.
affirm 527 vb.
swear 527 vb.
negate 528 vb.
recant 598 vb.
reject 602 vb.
avoid 615 vb.
oppose 699 vb.
abrogate 747 vb.
resign 748 vb.
refuse 755 vb.
not observe
                764 vb.
not retain 774 vb.
**negation**
negation 528 n.
**negative**
contrary 14 adj.
answering 455 adj.
countervailing
                462 adj.

unadmitted
                484 adj.
negative 528 adj.
**negatively**
negatively 2 adv.
**neglect**
be incomplete
                55 vb.
exclude 57 vb.
lose a chance
                133 vb.
be inattentive
                451 vb.
neglect 453 vb.
be unwilling
                593 vb.
avoid 615 vb.
not use 669 vb.
not act 672 vb.
not complete
                721 vb.
not observe
                764 vb.
fail in duty 913 vb.
**neglected**
neglected 453 adj.
**neglectful, be**
be neglectful
                453 vb.
be inactive 674 vb.
**negligence**
negligence 453 n.
**negligent**
inattentive 451 adj.
negligent 453 adj.
forgetful 501 adj.
unwilling 593 adj.
unprepared
                665 adj.
lazy 674 adj.
hasty 675 adj.
clumsy 690 adj.
lax 729 adj.
nonobservant
                764 adj.
apathetic 815 adj.
rash 852 adj.
indifferent 855 adj.

disrespectful
                916 adj.
**negligently**
negligently
                453 adv.
**neither**
neither 601 adv.
**neological**
neological 555 adj.
**neologize**
neologize 555 vb.
**neology**
neology 555 n.
**nervous**
impotent 156 adj.
weak 158 adj.
agitated 313 adj.
distracted 451 adj.
unbelieving
                481 adj.
expectant 502 adj.
irresolute 596 adj.
avoiding 615 adj.
suffering 820 adj.
dejected 829 adj.
nervous 849 adj.
cowardly 851 adj.
cautious 853 adj.
modest 869 adj.
**nervous, be**
be inattentive
                451 vb.
doubt 481 vb.
avoid 615 vb.
be unskilful 690 vb.
be excitable
                817 vb.
be nervous 849 vb.
be cowardly
                851 vb.
**nervous disorders**
nervous disorders
                646 n.
**nervousness**
nervousness 849 n.
**nest**
seedbed 151 n.
nest 187 n.

**network**
correlation 12 n.
ligature 47 n.
complexity 61 n.
receptacle 189 n.
gap 196 n.
filament 203 n.
network 217 n.
canopy 221 n.
enclosure 230 n.
fence 230 n.
formation 238 n.
convolution 246 n.
stripe 432 n.
needlework 839 n.

**neutral**
median 30 adj.
moderate 172 adj.
choiceless 601 adj.
avoiding 615 adj.
neutral 620 adj.
middling 727 adj.
independent
739 adj.
cautious 853 adj.
indifferent 855 adj.
just 908 adj.

**neutral, be**
not discriminate
459 vb.
be neutral 601 vb.
be indifferent
855 vb.

**never**
never 105 adv.

**neverness**
neverness 105 n.

**nevertheless**
nevertheless
463 adv.

**new**
different 15 adj.
dissimilar 19 adj.
original 21 adj.
intact 52 adj.
beginning 68 adj.
first 68 adj.
unusual 84 adj.

lasting 108 adj.
foregoing 120 adj.
past 120 adj.
new 121 adj.
infantine 127 adj.
early 130 adj.
changeable
138 adj.
revolutionary
144 adj.
weak 158 adj.
unknown 486 adj.
unused 669 adj.

**new boy or girl**
beginner 533 n.

**newly**
newly 121 adv.

**newness**
newness 121 n.

**news**
topic 447 n.
disappointment
504 n.
information 519 n.
report 519 n.
publication 523 n.
publicity 523 n.
news 524 n.
broadcast 526 n.
important matter
633 n.

**news reporter**
inquisitive person
448 n.
enquirer 454 n.
informant 519 n.
publicizer 523 n.
news reporter
524 n.
chronicler 544 n.
chatterer 576 n.
interlocutor 579 n.
correspondent
583 n.
author 584 n.

**niggard**
accumulator 74 n.
economy 809 n.

niggard 811 n.
egotist 927 n.

**nightwear**
nightwear 223 n.

**ninny**
ninny 496 n.
dupe 539 n.
ingenue 694 n.
country-dweller
864 n.

**nippers**
fastening 47 n.
foot 209 n.
cross 217 n.
sharp point 251 n.
extractor 299 n.
finger 373 n.
tool 625 n.
nippers 773 n.

**no**
no 484 adv.
nay 528 adv.

**nobility**
greatness 32 n.
superiority 34 n.
group 74 n.
genealogy 164 n.
blood 330 n.
authority 728 n.
beau monde 843 n.
honours 861 n.
prestige 861 n.
nobility 863 n.

**noble**
great 32 adj.
unmixed 44 adj.
impressive 816 adj.
splendid 836 adj.
well-bred 843 adj.
worshipful 861 adj.
noble 863 adj.
proud 866 adj.
courteous 879 adj.

**nobody**
nonexistence 2 n.
insubstantiality 4 n.
nobody 185 n.

**no charge**
no charge 807 n.

**no choice**
no choice 601 n.

**no imitation**
no imitation 21 n.

**nomenclator**
nomenclator 556 n.

**nomenclature**
arrangement 62 n.
identification
542 n.
linguistics 552 n.
etymology 554 n.
nomenclature
556 n.
phrase 558 n.

**nonactive**
nonactive 672 adj.

**nonadhesive**
nonadhesive
49 adj.

**nonage**
nonage 125 n.

**no name**
no name 557 n.

**non-Biblical
scripture**
non-Biblical
scripture 969 n.

**non-Christian sect**
non-Christian sect
972 n.

**noncoherence**
noncoherence 49 n.

**noncompletion**
noncompletion
721 n.

**nonconformist**
variant 15 n.
misfit 25 n.
noncoherence 49 n.
nonconformist
84 n.
exteriority 218 n.
male 367 n.
woman 368 n.
dissentient 484 n.

**now, be**
be 1 vb.
be now 116 vb.

**noxious animal**
creepy-crawly
360 n.
bane 654 n.
noxious animal
899 n.
knave 933 n.

**nubility**
nubility 889 n.

**nucleonics**
nucleonics 155 n.

**nullify**
nullify 2 vb.
not be 4 vb.
abate 37 vb.
destroy 160 vb.

**number**
quantity 26 n.
part 53 n.
specify 80 vb.
number 85 n.
number 86 vb.
list 87 vb.
measure 460 n.

**number with**
add 38 vb.
number with 78 vb.

**numerable**
numerable 86 adj.

**numeration**
numeration 86 n.

**numerical**
numerical 85 adj.

**numerical element**
subtraction 39 n.
numerical element
85 n.
fraction 98 n.
changeable thing
147 n.

**numerical operation**
increase 36 n.
subtraction 39 n.

numerical operation
86 n.

**numerical result**
numerical result
85 n.

**nun**
spinster 890 n.
virgin 945 n.
nun 980 n.

**nurse**
obstetrics 162 n.
nurse 653 n.

**nymph**
vegetable life
361 n.
mythical being
964 n.

# O

**oath**
testimony 461 n.
oath 527 n.
recantation 598 n.
promise 759 n.

**obedience**
obedience 734 n.

**obedient**
orderly 60 adj.
willing 592 adj.
submitting 716 adj.
obedient 734 adj.
serving 737 adj.
subject 740 adj.
restrained 742 adj.
observant 768 adj.
inexcitable 818 adj.
servile 874 adj.
amiable 879 adj.
obliged 912 adj.
trustworthy
924 adj.
virtuous 928 adj.
legal 948 adj.
orthodox 970 adj.

pious 973 adj.

**obediently**
obediently 734 adv.

**obeisance**
curvature 248 n.
obeisance 306 n.
submission 716 n.
servility 874 n.
courteous act
879 n.
respects 915 n.

**obey**
be inferior 35 vb.
conform 83 vb.
acquiesce 483 vb.
be willing 592 vb.
obey 734 vb.
serve 737 vb.
be subject 740 vb.
observe 768 vb.
be servile 874 vb.
do one's duty
912 vb.
be pious 973 vb.

**obfuscation**
obfuscation 416 n.

**object**
substance 3 n.
product 159 n.
object 314 n.

**objective**
extremity 69 n.
focus 76 n.
centre 225 n.
limit 231 n.
goal 295 n.
motive 607 n.
objective 612 n.
chase 614 n.
attempt 666 n.
aspiration 847 n.
desired object
854 n.

**object of scorn**
nonentity 634 n.
poor person 796 n.
object of scorn
862 n.

contemptibility
917 n.
bad person 933 n.

**oblation**
oblation 975 n.

**obligatory**
necessary 591 adj.
compelling
735 adj.
conditional
761 adj.
obligatory 912 adj.

**obliged**
obliged 912 adj.

**oblique**
unequal 29 adj.
unequal 29 adj.
low 205 adj.
oblique 215 adj.
crossed 217 adj.
distorted 241 adj.
angular 242 adj.
curved 248 adj.
directed 276 adj.
deviating 277 adj.
occult 518 adj.

**oblique, be**
be unequal 29 vb.
be oblique 215 vb.
be inverted 216 vb.
cross 217 vb.
be in front 232 vb.
be behind 233 vb.
make angular
242 vb.
navigate 264 vb.
deviate 277 vb.
ascend 303 vb.
tumble 304 vb.
be agitated 313 vb.

**obliquely**
obliquely 215 adv.

**obliquity**
obliquity 215 n.

**obliterate**
nullify 2 vb.
subtract 39 vb.
exclude 57 vb.

depth 206 n.
world 316 n.
water 334 n.
ocean 338 n.

**oceanic**
oceanic 338 adj.

**oceanography**
oceanography
338 n.

**o'clock**
o'clock 112 adv.

**odium**
disrepute 862 n.
odium 883 n.

**odorous**
odorous 389 adj.

**odour**
odour 389 n.
fragrance 391 n.

**odourless**
odourless 390 adj.

**of course**
of course 473 adv.

**offender**
offender 899 n.

**offer**
opportunity 132 n.
approach 284 n.
reception 294 n.
admit 294 vb.
supposition 507 n.
propound 507 vb.
affirm 527 n.
choice 600 n.
incentive 607 n.
bribe 607 vb.
permit 751 vb.
offer 754 n.
offer 754 vb.
request 756 n.
request 756 vb.
promise 759 n.
promise 759 vb.
make terms 761 vb.
give 776 vb.
bargain 786 vb.
purchase 787 n.
purchase 787 vb.

liberality 808 n.
reward 957 n.
be pious 973 vb.

**offering**
voluntary 592 adj.
offering 754 adj.
requesting 756 adj.
offering 776 n.
payment 799 n.
atoning 936 adj.
rewarding 957 adj.
oblation 975 n.
devotional 975 adj.

**offer oneself**
be willing 592 vb.
vote 600 n.
offer oneself
754 vb.

**offer worship**
entreat 756 vb.
give 776 vb.
offer worship
975 n.
perform ritual
982 vb.

**office-book**
office-book 982 n.

**officer**
agent 681 n.
official 685 n.
officer 736 n.
consignee 749 n.
deputy 750 n.
church officer
980 n.

**official**
official 685 n.
councillor 687 n.
autocrat 736 n.
officer 736 n.
servant 737 n.
consignee 749 n.
law officer 950 n.

**offset**
equalization 28 n.
inequality 29 n.
offset 31 n.
extra 40 n.

remainder 41 n.
quid pro quo 145 n.
stabilizer 148 n.
counteraction
177 n.
gravity 317 n.
qualification 463 n.
safeguard 657 n.
reward 957 n.

**of price**
infrequent 135 adj.
valuable 639 adj.
of price 806 adj.

**often**
repeatedly 102 adv.
while 104 adv.
often 134 adv.

**oil**
cookery 296 n.
lubricant 329 n.
oil 352 n.
fuel 380 n.

**old age**
long duration
108 n.
oldness 122 n.
old age 126 n.
weakness 158 n.
folly 494 n.
dilapidation 650 n.

**old, be**
be old 122 vb.
stay 139 vb.
be weak 158 vb.
be unpractised
606 vb.

**old couple**
old couple 128 n.

**olden**
great 32 adj.
periodic 106 adj.
past 120 adj.
olden 122 adj.
architectural
187 adj.

**older**
older 126 adj.

**old man**
old man 128 n.
paternity 164 n.
male 367 n.
fool 496 n.

**oldness**
oldness 122 n.

**old person**
old age 126 n.
old person 128 n.

**old woman**
old woman 128 n.
maternity 164 n.
woman 368 n.

**omen**
precursor 66 n.
foresight 505 n.
omen 506 n.
manifestation
517 n.
messenger 524 n.
indication 542 n.
warning 659 n.
danger signal
660 n.
hope 847 n.
prodigy 859 n.
threat 895 n.
condemnation
956 n.

**omnibus.** See bus
stagecoach 269 n.

**on**
on 305 adv.

**on an average**
on an average
30 adv.

**on behalf**
on behalf 750 adv.

**on duty**
on duty 912 adv.

**one**
identical 13 adj.
inimitable 21 adj.
simple 44 adj.
combined 50 adj.
whole 52 adj.
special 80 adj.

style 561 n.
imperspicuity
                563 n.
ornament 569 n.
ornament 569 vb.
elegance 570 n.
ornamentation
                839 n.
decorate 839 vb.
affectation 845 n.

**ornamental**
ornamental
                839 adj.

**ornamental art**
ornamental art
                839 n.

**ornamentation**
ornamentation
                839 n.

**ornamented**
ornamented
                839 adj.

**ornate**
figurative 514 adj.
diffuse 565 adj.
ornate 569 adj.
ornamented
                839 adj.
affected 845 adj.

**orthodox**
conformable
                83 adj.
regulated 83 adj.
evidential 461 adj.
positive 468 adj.
believing 480 adj.
habitual 605 adj.
orthodox 970 adj.
pious 973 adj.
worshipping
                975 adj.
ecclesiastical
                979 adj.

**orthodox, be**
believe 480 vb.
be orthodox
                970 vb.

**orthodoxism**
orthodoxism 970 n.

**orthodoxly**
orthodoxly
                970 adv.

**orthodox, the**
the orthodox 970 n.

**orthodoxy**
orthodoxy 970 n.

**oscillate**
correlate 12 vb.
be periodic 136 vb.
vary 147 vb.
be weak 158 vb.
walk 202 vb.
voyage 264 vb.
deviate 277 vb.
leap 307 vb.
oscillate 312 vb.
be agitated 313 vb.
roll 398 vb.
be irresolute
                596 vb.
show feeling
                813 vb.
be drunk 944 vb.

**oscillating**
oscillating 312 adj.

**oscillation**
oscillation 312 n.

**ostensible**
ostensible 609 adj.

**ostensibly**
ostensibly 609 adv.

**ostentation**
insubstantial thing
                4 n.
aeronautics 266 n.
spectacle 440 n.
foolery 492 n.
manifestation
                517 n.
publicity 523 n.
duplicity 536 n.
falsehood 536 n.
exaggeration
                541 n.

magniloquence
                569 n.
inelegance 571 n.
deed 671 n.
defiance 706 n.
trophy 724 n.
prodigality 810 n.
ornamentation
                839 n.
fashion 843 n.
affectation 845 n.
pride 866 n.
airs 868 n.
vanity 868 n.
ostentation 870 n.
boasting 872 n.

**ostentatious**
ostentatious
                870 adj.

**ostentatious, be**
be ostentatious
                870 vb.

**outbreak**
revolution 144 n.
havoc 160 n.
outbreak 171 n.
egress 293 n.
voidance 295 n.
revolt 733 n.

**outcast**
nonconformist
                84 n.
ejection 295 n.
outcast 878 n.

**outdo**
be unequal 29 vb.
be superior 34 vb.
be early 130 vb.
be distant 194 vb.
outstrip 272 vb.
outdo 301 vb.
deceive 537 vb.
endanger 656 vb.
be cunning 693 vb.
contend 711 vb.
defeat 722 vb.
overmaster 722 vb.
humiliate 867 vb.

**outflow**
outflow 293 n.

**outgoing**
outgoing 293 adj.
flowing 345 adj.

**outlast**
continue 104 vb.
outlast 108 vb.
be stable 148 vb.
resist 710 vb.

**outlet**
gap 196 n.
orifice 258 n.
outlet 293 n.
drain 346 n.
blowing 347 n.

**outline**
region 179 n.
size 190 n.
distance 194 n.
frame 213 n.
exteriority 218 n.
surroundings
                225 n.
outline 228 n.
outline 228 vb.
edging 229 n.
enclosure 230 n.
limit 231 n.
form 238 n.
circle 245 n.
go round 245 vb.
shore 339 n.
representation
                546 n.
represent 546 vb.
describe 585 vb.
abstract 587 vb.

**outlined**
outlined 228 adj.

**outstrip**
be superior 34 vb.
do before 114 vb.
outstrip 272 vb.
precede 278 vb.
progress 280 vb.
approach 284 vb.
outdo 301 vb.

hasten 675 vb.
take 781 vb.

**overactivity**
overactivity 673 n.

**overcharge**
overcharge 806 vb.

**overcoat**
overcoat 223 n.
warm clothes
376 n.

**overestimation**
overestimation
477 n.

**over five**
over five 96 n.

**overhanging**
overhanging
204 adj.

**overlay**
overlay 221 vb.

**overlie**
overlie 221 vb.

**overlying**
overlying 221 adj.

**overmaster**
be strong 157 vb.
prevail 173 vb.
attack 707 vb.
overmaster 722 vb.
dominate 728 vb.
subjugate 740 vb.
take 781 vb.
frighten 849 vb.
humiliate 867 vb.

**over one hundred**
over one hundred
96 n.

**overrate**
augment 36 vb.
overstep 301 vb.
misjudge 476 vb.
overrate 477 vb.
be credulous
482 vb.
err 490 vb.
misinterpret
516 vb.
advertise 523 vb.

exaggerate 541 vb.
make important
633 vb.
bargain 786 vb.
praise 918 vb.
flatter 920 vb.

**overrated**
overrated 477 adj.

**overstep**
be great 32 vb.
be superior 34 vb.
flank 234 vb.
pass 300 vb.
overstep 301 vb.
exaggerate 541 vb.
superabound
632 vb.
be clumsy 690 vb.
not observe
764 vb.
be intemperate
938 vb.

**overstepping**
overstepping
301 n.

**overturning**
overturning 216 n.

**owed**
owed 798 adj.

**owner**
owner 771 n.

**P**

**pacification**
pacification 714 n.

**pacificatory**
pacificatory
714 adj.

**pacifist**
quietude 261 n.
pacifist 712 n.

**pacify**
assuage 172 vb.
induce 607 vb.

concord 705 vb.
pacify 714 vb.
mediate 715 vb.
compromise
765 vb.
tranquillize 818 vb.
content 823 vb.
be courteous
879 vb.
ask mercy 900 vb.
atone 936 vb.
offer worship
975 vb.

**paganize**
paganize 968 vb.

**pageant**
procession 71 n.
assemblage 74 n.
pageant 870 n.

**pain**
pain 372 n.
cry 403 n.
evil 611 n.
badness 640 n.
illness 646 n.
adversity 726 n.
suffering 820 n.
painfulness 822 n.
corporal
punishment 958 n.

**pained**
pained 372 adj.
suffering 820 adj.

**painful**
sentient 369 adj.
painful 372 adj.
paining 822 adj.
punitive 958 adj.

**painfully**
painfully 32 adv.

**painfulness**
painfulness 822 n.

**paining**
paining 822 adj.

**painkiller. See**
drug
antidote 653 n.

**paint**
compose 56 vb.
colour 420 vb.
represent 546 vb.
paint 548 vb.
decorate 839 vb.

**painted**
painted 548 adj.

**painting**
mimicry 20 n.
composition 56 n.
production 159 n.
colour 420 n.
art 546 n.
representation
546 n.
painting 548 n.

**pair**
combine 50 vb.
pair 90 vb.

**palaeology**
palaeology 120 n.

**palmy**
tranquil 261 adj.
peaceful 712 adj.
palmy 725 adj.

**palmy days**
palmy days 725 n.

**pang**
spasm 313 n.
pang 372 n.
rheumatism 646 n.
suffering 820 n.

**panting**
panting 679 adj.

**paper**
lamina 202 n.
art equipment
548 n.
stationery 581 n.
bookbinding 584 n.
paper 626 n.

**paper money**
paper money
792 n.

**paradisiac**
paradisiac 965 adj.

**paragon**
prototype 23 n.
superior 34 n.
exceller 639 n.
paragon 641 n.
proficient person
691 n.
a beauty 836 n.
prodigy 859 n.
person of repute
861 n.
pride 866 n.
good person 932 n.

**parallel**
relative 9 adj.
parallel 214 adj.
lateral 234 adj.
symmetrical
240 adj.
directed 276 adj.

**parallel, be**
be equal 28 vb.
be parallel 214 vb.

**parallelism**
parallelism 214 n.

**paranormal**
paranormal
978 n.

**parentage**
consanguinity 11 n.
kinsman 11 n.
precursor 66 n.
origin 68 n.
cause 151 n.
source 151 n.
attribution 153 n.
producer 159 n.
propagation 162 n.
parentage 164 n.
master 736 n.

**parental**
parental 164 adj.

**parish**
parish 979 n.

**parliament**
parliament 687 n.
authority 728 n.
lawcourt 951 n.

**parliamentary**
parliamentary
687 adj.

**parry**
deflect 277 vb.
repel 287 vb.
screen 416 vb.
sophisticate
472 vb.
avoid 615 vb.
obstruct 697 vb.
parry 708 vb.
retaliate 709 vb.
resist 710 vb.

**parse**
parse 559 vb.

**parsimonious**
careful 452 adj.
insufficient
631 adj.
retentive 773 adj.
economical
809 adj.
parsimonious
811 adj.
selfish 927 adj.
temperate 937 adj.

**parsimonious, be**
make insufficient
631 vb.
not pay 800 vb.
economize 809 vb.
be parsimonious
811 vb.
starve 941 vb.

**parsimoniously**
parsimoniously
811 adv.

**parsimony**
insufficiency 631 n.
parsimony 811 n.
unsociability 878 n.
selfishness 927 n.

**parsonage**
house 187 n.
parsonage 980 n.

**part**
degree 27 n.

part 53 n.
part 53 n.
incompleteness
55 n.
component 58 n.
bisection 92 n.
fraction 102 n.
trifle 634 n.
portion 778 n.

**partially**
partially 33 adv.

**participate**
be equal 28 vb.
be one of 58 vb.
mete out 460 vb.
be instrumental
623 vb.
do 671 vb.
be active 673 vb.
behave 683 vb.
cooperate 701 vb.
participate 770 vb.
give 776 vb.
apportion 778 vb.
defray 799 vb.
feel 813 vb.
be sociable 877 vb.
pity 900 vb.

**participation**
participation 770 n.

**participator**
participator 770 n.

**particularism**
particularism 80 n.

**particulars**
particulars 80 n.

**partition**
separation 46 n.
middle 70 n.
dividing line 92 n.
gap 196 n.
summit 208 n.
centrality 220 n.
partition 226 n.
barrier 230 n.
limit 231 n.
obstacle 697 n.

**partly**
partly 53 adv.

**part of speech**
adjunct 40 n.
name 556 n.
part of speech
559 n.

**party**
part 53 n.
assemblage 74 n.
prejudice 476 n.
dissent 484 n.
dissentient 484 n.
association 701 n.
party 703 n.
sect 972 n.

**pass**
connect 45 vb.
change 138 vb.
be turned to
142 vb.
cross 217 vb.
be in motion
260 vb.
traverse 262 vb.
navigate 264 vb.
pass 300 vb.
overstep 301 vb.
flow 345 vb.

**passage**
union 45 n.
entrance 68 n.
change 138 n.
transition 142 n.
gap 196 n.
narrowness 201 n.
shallowness 207 n.
open space 258 n.
motion 260 n.
wandering 262 n.
transference 267 n.
passage 300 n.
overstepping
301 n.
access 619 n.
bridge 619 n.

**pass away**
pass away 2 vb.

**pass**
ageing 126 adj.

**passing**
moving 260 adj.
travelling 262 adj.
passing 300 adj.

**passing along**
motion 260 n.
conveyance 262 n.
passing along
300 n.

**pass time**
pass time 104 vb.
elapse 107 vb.

**past**
extinct 2 adj.
past 120 adj.
antiquated 122 adj.
olden 122 adj.
unwonted 606 adj.

**past, be**
come before 64 vb.
elapse 107 vb.
be past 120 vb.
cease 140 vb.
happen 149 vb.

**pastor**
preacher 532 n.
teacher 532 n.
pastor 980 n.

**pastries**
pastries 296 n.

**past time**
precedence 64 n.
time 104 n.
long duration
108 n.
priority 114 n.
different time
117 n.
past time 120 n.
newness 121 n.
possibility 464 n.

**paternity**
old man 128 n.
paternity 164 n.
male 367 n.

**path**
passage 300 n.
path 619 n.

**pathology**
pathology 646 n.
medical art 653 n.

**patience**
leniency 731 n.
feeling 813 n.
moral insensibility
815 n.
patience 818 n.
caution 853 n.
forgiveness 904 n.

**patient**
slow 273 adj.
lenient 731 adj.
patient 818 adj.
cautious 853 adj.
pitying 900 adj.
forgiving 904 adj.

**patient, be**
be lenient 731 vb.
permit 751 vb.
be patient 818 vb.
be courteous
879 vb.
forgive 904 vb.

**patriot**
patriot 896 n.
benefactor 898 n.

**patriotic**
patriotic 896 adj.

**patriotism**
patriotism 896 n.

**patron**
intermediary 226 n.
onlookers 436 n.
witness 461 n.
assenter 483 n.
enthusiast 499 n.
protector 655 n.
aider 698 n.
patron 702 n.
combatant 717 n.
master 736 n.
deputy 750 n.
security 762 n.

participator 770 n.
desirer 854 n.
friend 875 n.
kind person 892 n.
benefactor 898 n.
commender 918 n.

**patronize**
patronize 698 vb.

**pattern**
crossing 217 n.
textile 217 n.
edging 229 n.
curve 243 n.
notch 255 n.
pattern 839 n.

**pause**
be discontinuous
72 vb.
wait 131 vb.
pause 140 vb.
be quiescent
261 vb.
decelerate 273 vb.
arrive 290 vb.

**pavilion**
pavilion 187 n.
arbour 189 n.

**paving**
base 209 n.
basis 213 n.
paving 221 n.
smoothness 253 n.
building material
626 n.

**pawnshop**
pawnshop 779 n.

**pay**
compensate 31 vb.
employ 617 vb.
keep faith 763 vb.
earnings 766 n.
give 776 vb.
restitute 782 vb.
draw money
792 vb.
pay 799 n.
pay 799 vb.
expenditure 801 n.

expend 801 vb.
grant claims
910 vb.
do one's duty
912 vb.
reward 957 n.
reward 957 vb.

**paying**
paying 799 adj.

**payment**
offset 31 n.
part 53 n.
incentive 607 n.
security 762 n.
gift 776 n.
funds 792 n.
payment 799 n.
expenditure 801 n.
accounts 803 n.
tax 804 n.
dueness 910 n.
penalty 958 n.

**pay one's respects**
pay one's respects
879 vb.

**pay too much**
pay too much
806 vb.

**peace**
quietude 261 n.
concord 705 n.
peace 712 n.
peace offering
714 n.
palmy days 725 n.

**peaceful**
inert 170 adj.
moderate 172 adj.
concordant
705 adj.
peaceful 712 adj.
submitting 716 adj.
obedient 734 adj.
inexcitable 818 adj.
content 823 adj.
amiable 879 adj.

**peacefully**
peacefully 712 adv.

## peace offering

**peace offering**
argument 470 n.
peace offering
714 n.

**peculation**
peculation 783 n.

**pedagogic**
pedagogic 532 adj.

**pedestrian**
pedestrian 263 n.
passing along
300 n.

**pedestrianism**
pedestrianism
262 n.

**pedlar**
traveller 263 n.
seller 788 n.
pedlar 789 n.

**penalty**
decrease 37 n.
decrement 42 n.
labour 677 n.
compulsion 735 n.
restraint 742 n.
nonobservance
764 n.
loss 767 n.
restitution 782 n.
pay 799 n.
nonpayment 800 n.
cost 804 n.
price 804 n.
tax 804 n.
mercy 900 n.
penalty 958 n.

**penance**
penitence 934 n.
penance 936 n.
asceticism 940 n.
Christian rite 982 n.

**pendency**
pendency 212 n.

**pending, be**
continue 104 vb.
be pending 131 n.

**penitence**
penitence 934 n.

## penitent

**penitent**
penitent 934 n.
ascetic 940 n.

**penitent, be**
be wise 493 vb.
confess 521 vb.
tergiversate 598 vb.
get better 649 vb.
regret 825 n.
be penitent 934 vb.
become pious
973 vb.

**penitently**
penitently 934 adv.

**people of taste**
sensibility 369 n.
collector 487 n.
enthusiast 499 n.
people of taste
841 n.

**perfect**
consummate
32 adj.
supreme 34 adj.
unmixed 44 adj.
whole 52 adj.
complete 54 adj.
elegant 570 adj.
be elegant 570 vb.
best 639 adj.
excellent 639 adj.
perfect 641 adj.
perfect 641 vb.
clean 643 adj.
preserved 661 adj.
mature 664 adj.
skilful 689 adj.
completed 720 adj.
carry through
720 vb.
beautiful 836 adj.
shapely 836 adj.
approvable
918 adj.
virtuous 928 adj.
innocent 930 adj.
pure 945 adj.

## perfection

**perfection**
prototype 23 n.
superiority 34 n.
completeness 54 n.
summit 208 n.
symmetry 240 n.
goodness 639 n.
perfection 641 n.
preparedness
664 n.
skill 689 n.
completion 720 n.
beauty 836 n.
desired object
854 n.
virtues 928 n.
innocence 930 n.
purity 945 n.
divine attribute
960 n.

**perfectionist**
narrow mind 476 n.
trier 666 n.
perfectionist 857 n.

**perfectly**
perfectly 641 adv.

**perfidious**
perfidious 925 adj.

**perfidy**
latency 518 n.
falsehood 536 n.
deception 542 n.
mental dishonesty
538 n.
untruth 538 n.
tergiversation
598 n.
sedition 733 n.
nonobservance
764 n.
enmity 876 n.
undutifulness
913 n.
perfidy 925 n.

**perforated**
perforated 258 adj.

**perforation**
perforation 258 n.

insertion 298 n.
indication 542 n.
wound 650 n.

**perforator**
perforator 258 n.

**perform ritual**
drench 336 n.
name 556 n.
offer worship
975 vb.
perform ritual
982 vb.

**period**
part 53 n.
time 104 n.
period 106 n.
brief span 109 n.
periodicity 136 n.
regular return
136 n.
limit 231 n.
labour 677 n.

**periodic**
continuous 71 adj.
periodic 106 adj.

**periodical**
discontinuous
72 adj.
regular 81 adj.
repeated 102 adj.
continuing 104 adj.
frequent 134 adj.
periodical 136 adj.
unstable 147 adj.
oscillating 312 adj.

**periodically**
periodically
136 adv.

**periodic, be**
come after 65 vb.
be periodic 136 vb.

**periodicity**
periodicity 136 n.

**perish**
pass away 2 vb.
be destroyed
160 vb.
perish 356 vb.

kill oneself 357 vb.

**permanence**
permanence 139 n.

**permanent**
uniform 16 adj.
perpetual 110 adj.
antiquated 122 adj.
permanent 139 adj.
unchangeable
148 adj.
godlike 960 adj.

**permission**
ability 155 n.
ingress 292 n.
assent 483 n.
facility 696 n.
laxity 729 n.
leniency 731 n.
permission 751 n.
consent 753 n.
nonliability 914 n.
approbation 918 n.

**permit**
stay 139 vb.
opener 258 n.
ingress 292 n.
credential 461 n.
be possible 464 vb.
make possible
464 vb.
assent 483 n.
acquiesce 483 vb.
assent 483 vb.
label 542 n.
instrument 623 n.
protection 655 n.
facilitate 696 vb.
be lax 729 vb.
be lenient 731 vb.
warrant 732 n.
give scope 739 vb.
mandate 746 n.
commission
746 vb.
permit 751 n.
permit 751 vb.
consent 753 vb.
give 776 vb.

be patient 818 vb.
dueness 910 n.
grant claims
910 vb.
nonliability 914 n.
exempt 914 vb.
approve 918 vb.

**permitted**
permitted 751 adj.

**permitting**
permitting 751 adj.

**perpetual**
existing 1 adj.
continuous 71 adj.
infinite 103 adj.
continuing 104 adj.
lasting 108 adj.
perpetual 110 adj.
permanent 139 adj.
unceasing 141 adj.
unchangeable
148 adj.
renowned 861 adj.
godlike 960 adj.

**perpetually**
perpetually
134 adv.

**perpetuate**
perpetuate 110 vb.
sustain 141 vb.
stabilize 148 vb.

**perpetuity**
existence 1 n.
continuity 71 n.
infinity 103 n.
time 104 n.
neverness 105 n.
long duration
108 n.
perpetuity 110 n.
permanence 139 n.
continuance 141 n.
immateriality 315 n.
divine attribute
960 n.

**perseverance**
perseverance
595 n.

**persevere**
continue 71 vb.
stay 139 vb.
go on 141 vb.
stand firm 594 vb.
persevere 595 vb.
be obstinate
597 vb.
pursue 614 vb.
be active 673 vb.
exert oneself
677 vb.
work 677 vb.
hope 847 vb.

**persevering**
persevering
595 adj.

**persistently**
persistently
595 adv.

**person**
self 80 n.
unit 88 n.
object 314 n.
person 366 n.

**personable**
personable
836 adj.

**personnel**
component 58 n.
band 74 n.
list 87 n.
power 155 n.
resident 186 n.
mariner 265 n.
aeronaut 271 n.
person 366 n.
means 624 n.
personnel 681 n.
party 703 n.
domestic 737 n.

**perspicuity**
perspicuity 562 n.

**perspicuous**
perspicuous
562 adj.

**persuadability**
persuadability
607 n.

**pertinently**
pertinently 24 adv.

**pervade**
be 1 vb.
fill 54 vb.
be general 79 vb.
prevail 173 vb.
pervade 184 vb.
lie between 226 vb.
pass 300 vb.

**pervert**
derange 63 vb.
modify 138 vb.
convert 142 vb.
harm 640 vb.
pervert 650 vb.
misuse 675 vb.
make insensitive
815 vb.
make wicked
929 vb.

**pet**
look after 452 vb.
tempt 607 vb.
patronize 698 vb.
be lenient 731 vb.
pet 884 vb.
philanthropize
892 vb.

**petitioner**
petitioner 758 n.

**philanthropic**
philanthropic
896 adj.

**philanthropist**
visionary 508 n.
volunteer 592 n.
reformer 649 n.
worker 686 n.
keeper 744 n.
xenophile 875 n.
kind person 892 n.
philanthropist
896 n.
benefactor 898 n.

pitfall 658 n.
stratagem 693 n.
threat 895 n.

**pitiable**
distressing 822 adj.
lamenting 831 adj.
pitiable 900 adj.

**pitiless**
destructive 160 adj.
resolute 594 adj.
obstinate 597 adj.
severe 730 adj.
cruel 893 adj.
malevolent 893 adj.
pitiless 901 adj.
revengeful 905 adj.

**pitiless, be**
destroy 160 vb.
slaughter 357 vb.
be severe 730 vb.
be insensitive
817 vb.
be malevolent
893 vb.
be pitiless 901 vb.
be impenitent
935 vb.

**pitilessness**
pitilessness 901 n.

**pity**
bond 47 n.
leniency 731 n.
be sensitive
814 vb.
relieve 826 vb.
lamentation 831 n.
lament 831 n.
benevolence 892 n.
pity 900 n.
pity 900 vb.
forgiveness 904 n.
disinterestedness
926 n.

**pitying**
pitying 900 adj.

**pivot**
joint 45 n.
influence 173 n.

pivot 213 n.
centre 220 n.
extractor 299 n.
lifter 305 n.
rotator 310 n.
tool 625 n.
chief thing 633 n.

**place**
arrange 62 vb.
put in front 64 vb.
specify 80 vb.
region 179 n.
place 180 n.
situation 181 n.
locality 182 n.
place 182 vb.
enclosure 230 n.
open space 258 n.
aim 276 vb.
orientate 276 vb.
discover 479 vb.

**place after**
place after 65 vb.

**place of
amusement**
meeting place
187 n.
place of amusement
832 n.

**place oneself**
be in order 60 vb.
have rank 73 vb.
place oneself
182 vb.
dwell 187 vb.
be quiescent
261 vb.
travel 262 vb.
enter 292 vb.
appropriate 781 vb.

**plague**
badness 640 n.
plague 646 n.
blight 654 n.

**plain**
uniform 16 adj.
simple 44 adj.
space 178 n.

lowness 205 n.
horizontality 211 n.
open space 258 n.
land 339 n.
plain 343 n.
soft-hued 420 adj.
meaningful
509 adj.
semantic 509 adj.
intelligible 511 adj.
figurative 514 adj.
undisguised
517 adj.
informative
519 adj.
assertive 527 adj.
veracious 535 adj.
perspicuous
562 adj.
feeble 567 adj.
plain 568 adj.
elegant 570 adj.
inelegant 571 adj.
prosaic 588 adj.
artless 694 adj.
free 739 adj.
tedious 833 adj.
tasteful 841 adj.
plebeian 864 adj.
disrespectful
916 adj.
detracting 921 adj.

**plain, be**
result 152 vb.
be visible 438 vb.
be plain 517 vb.
be disclosed
521 vb.

**plainly**
plainly 568 adv.

**plainness**
plainness 568 n.

**plan**
prototype 23 n.
incompleteness
55 n.
arrangement 62 n.
arrange 62 vb.

statistics 86 n.
cause 151 vb.
production 159 n.
produce 159 vb.
outline 228 n.
think 444 vb.
be wise 493 vb.
foresight 505 n.
foresee 505 vb.
prediction 506 n.
suppose 507 vb.
representation
546 n.
represent 546 vb.
compendium
587 n.
predetermine
603 vb.
intention 612 n.
intend 612 vb.
plan 618 n.
plan 618 vb.
find means 624 vb.
preparation 664 n.
prepare 664 vb.
undertaking 667 n.
tactics 683 n.
deal with 683 vb.
be cunning 693 vb.
art of war 713 n.
warfare 713 n.
desire 854 vb.

**planet**
circler 309 n.
planet 316 n.

**planned**
planned 618 adj.

**planner**
planner 618 n.

**planning**
planning 618 adj.

**plant**
young plant 127 n.
source 151 n.
vessel 189 n.
microorganism
191 n.
filament 203 n.

plate                                                                    132

prop 213 n.
coil 246 n.
vegetable 296 n.
plant 361 n.

**plate**
plate 189 n.
horizontality 211 n.

**plausible**
plausible 466 adj.

**player**
hunter 614 n.
player 832 n.

**playgoer**
playgoer 589 n.

**play music**
shrill 402 vb.
play music 408 vb.

**plaything**
jumper 307 n.
bauble 634 n.
plaything 832 n.

**plead**
plead 609 vb.
avoid 615 vb.
justify 922 vb.

**pleasance**
pleasance 187 n.

**pleasant**
pleasant 371 adj.
sweet 387 adj.
fragrant 391 adj.

**please**
enjoy 371 vb.
please 821 vb.
content 823 vb.
cheer 828 vb.

**pleased**
assenting 483 adj.
pleased 819 adj.
content 823 adj.
jubilant 828 adj.
amused 832 adj.

**pleased, be**
enjoy 371 vb.
gaze 433 vb.
show feeling
                                813 vb.
be pleased 819 vb.

be content 823 vb.
rejoice 830 vb.
feel pride 866 vb.
boast 872 vb.
greet 879 vb.
congratulate
                                881 vb.

**please oneself**
will 590 vb.
be obstinate
                                597 vb.
please oneself
                                729 vb.
oppress 730 vb.
disobey 733 vb.
be free 739 vb.
permit 751 vb.
be intemperate
                                938 vb.
be illegal 949 vb.

**pleasurable**
pleasurable
                                821 adj.

**pleasurableness**
pleasurableness
                                821 n.

**pleasure**
pleasure 371 n.
joy 819 n.
sensualism 939 n.

**pleasure ground**
abode 187 n.
pleasance 187 n.
arena 719 n.
pleasure ground
                                832 n.

**plebeian**
inferior 35 adj.
general 79 adj.
ill-bred 842 adj.
inglorious 862 adj.
plebeian 864 n.
humble 867 adj.

**pledged**
pledged 762 adj.

**plenitude**
plenitude 54 n.

**plenteous**
plenteous 630 adj.

**plenty**
greatness 32 n.
great quantity 32 n.
productiveness
                                166 n.
feasting 296 n.
vegetable life
                                361 n.
store 627 n.
plenty 630 n.
redundance 632 n.
prosperity 725 n.
wealth 795 n.
cheapness 807 n.
liberality 808 n.
pleasurableness
                                821 n.

**pleonasm**
pleonasm 565 n.

**pleonastic**
pleonastic 565 adj.

**plot**
combination 50 n.
combine 50 vb.
concurrence 176 n.
concur 176 vb.
latency 518 n.
secrecy 520 n.
be stealthy 520 vb.
fake 536 vb.
deception 537 n.
deceive 537 vb.
predetermination
                                603 n.
plot 618 n.
plot 618 vb.
overactivity 673 n.
cunning 693 n.
stratagem 693 n.
be cunning 693 vb.
cooperation 701 n.
cooperate 701 vb.
sedition 733 n.
compact 760 vb.

**plumage**
filament 203 n.

skin 221 n.
plumage 254 n.
wing 266 n.
softness 322 n.
trimming 839 n.

**plunge**
be inferior 35 vb.
decrease 37 vb.
be destroyed
                                160 vb.
suppress 160 vb.
motion 260 n.
aquatics 264 n.
navigate 264 vb.
swim 264 vb.
fly 266 vb.
enter 292 vb.
immersion 298 n.
immerse 298 vb.
descent 304 n.
descend 304 vb.
tumble 304 vb.
lowering 306 n.
lower 306 vb.
plunge 308 n.
plunge 308 vb.
be wet 336 vb.
measure 460 vb.
ablutions 643 n.
defeat 722 vb.

**plural**
plural 97 adj.

**plurality**
plurality 97 n.

**pneumatics**
pneumatics 335 n.

**pocket**
pocket 189 n.
garment 223 n.
opening 258 n.
treasury 794 n.

**poem**
subdivision 53 n.
composition 56 n.
literature 552 n.
reading matter
                                584 n.
description 585 n.

**possible**

facility 696 n.
hope 847 n.

**possible**
unreal 2 adj.
future 119 adj.
powerful 155 adj.
liable 175 adj.
accessible 284 adj.
possible 464 adj.
probable 466 adj.
rational 470 adj.
credible 480 adj.
latent 518 adj.
easy 696 adj.

**possible, be**
be possible 464 vb.
be likely 466 vb.

**possibly**
actually 1 adv.
by chance 154 adv.
possibly 464 adv.

**postal
communications**
transferrer 267 n.
courier 524 n.
message 524 n.
postal
communications
526 n.
correspondence
583 n.

**posteriority**
posteriority 115 n.

**posterity**
kinsman 11 n.
survivor 41 n.
sequence 65 n.
successor 67 n.
posteriority 115 n.
futurity 119 n.
effect 152 n.
posterity 165 n.

**post meridiem**
post meridiem
124 adv.

**post-obit**
post-obit 356 adv.

**potentate**
potentate 736 n.
person of rank
863 n.

**potherb**
potherb 296 n.

**pottery**
product 159 n.
receptacle 189 n.
formation 238 n.
brittleness 325 n.
soil 339 n.
pottery 376 n.
sculpture 549 n.
building material
626 n.

**poultry**
meat 296 n.
poultry 360 n.

**poverty**
smallness 33 n.
inferiority 35 n.
decrease 37 n.
piece 53 n.
extremity 69 n.
necessity 591 n.
evil 611 n.
needfulness 622 n.
scarcity 631 n.
uncleanness 644 n.
deterioration 650 n.
dilapidation 650 n.
nonownership
769 n.
poverty 796 n.
asceticism 940 n.

**powder**
small thing 33 n.
leavings 41 n.
remainder 41 n.
powder 327 n.
dirt 644 n.

**powderiness**
powderiness 327 n.

**powdery**
minute 191 adj.
brittle 325 adj.

powdery 327 adj.
dry 337 adj.

**power**
greatness 32 n.
power 155 n.
strength 157 n.
agency 168 n.
instrumentality
623 n.
utility 635 n.
brute force 730 n.
divine attribute
960 n.

**powerful**
great 32 adj.
powerful 155 adj.
strong 157 adj.
169 Adj.
influential 173 adj.
instrumental
623 adj.
useful 635 adj.
compelling
735 adj.
godlike 960 adj.

**powerfully**
powerfully 155 adv.

**powerless**
powerless 156 adj.
weak 158 adj.
inert 170 adj.

**practice**
conformity 83 n.
eating 296 n.
expectation 502 n.
connotation 509 n.
practice 605 n.
business 617 n.
way 619 n.
use 668 n.
action 671 n.
conduct 683 n.
precept 688 n.
observance 763 n.
etiquette 843 n.
formality 870 n.
rite 982 n.
ritual 982 n.

**practise occultism**
practise occultism
978 vb.

**practise sorcery**
deprecate 757 vb.
practise sorcery
977 vb.

**praise**
overrate 477 vb.
description 585 n.
rejoicing 830 n.
rejoice 830 vb.
honours 861 n.
thanks 902 n.
respect 915 vb.
praise 918 n.
praise 918 vb.
flatter 920 vb.
reward 957 n.
be pious 973 vb.
act of worship
975 n.
offer worship
975 vb.
worship 975 vb.
idolatrize 976 vb.

**praised, be**
be praised 918 vb.

**prayers**
prayers 975 n.

**preacher**
preacher 532 n.

**precede**
come before 64 vb.
be before 114 vb.
do before 114 vb.
be in front 232 vb.
walk 262 vb.
precede 278 vb.
motivate 607 vb.

**precedence**
superiority 34 n.
addition 38 n.
precedence 64 n.
priority 114 n.
seniority 126 n.
anticipation 130 n.
front 232 n.

134

preceding 278 n.
importance 633 n.
authority 728 n.

**preceding**
superior 34 adj.
supreme 34 adj.
additional 38 adj.
precedence 64 n.
preceding 64 adj.
precursory 66 adj.
priority 114 n.
prior 114 adj.
foregoing 120 adj.
frontal 232 adj.
motion 260 n.
preceding 278 n.
progression 280 n.
preparatory
        664 adj.

**precept**
prototype 23 n.
rule 81 n.
traffic control
        300 n.
maxim 491 n.
commentary 515 n.
advice 686 n.
precept 688 n.
decree 732 n.
conditions 761 n.
right 908 n.
code of duty 912 n.
legislation 948 n.
office-book 982 n.
rite 982 n.

**preceptive**
preceptive 688 adj.

**precursor**
precedence 64 n.
precursor 66 n.
beginning 68 n.
example 83 n.
priority 114 n.
morning 123 n.
earliness 130 n.
paternity 164 n.
native 186 n.
settler 186 n.

front 232 n.
traveller 263 n.
preceding 278 n.
the dead 356 n.
messenger 524 n.
preacher 532 n.
preparer 664 n.
director 685 n.

**precursory**
precursory 66 adj.

**predestine**
predestine 150 vb.
necessitate 591 vb.
predetermine
        603 vb.
intend 612 vb.

**predetermination**
predetermination
        603 n.

**predetermine**
predestine 150 vb.
prejudge 476 vb.
foresee 505 vb.
predetermine
        603 vb.
motivate 607 vb.
intend 612 vb.
plan 618 vb.
prepare 664 vb.
decree 732 vb.

**predetermined**
predetermined
        603 adj.

**predicament**
circumstance 8 n.
complexity 61 n.
crisis 132 n.
foolery 492 n.
necessity 591 n.
evil 611 n.
danger 656 n.
predicament 695 n.
adversity 726 n.
painfulness 822 n.
hopelessness
        848 n.

**predict**
look ahead 119 vb.

predestine 150 vb.
foresee 505 vb.
predict 506 vb.
be truthful 535 vb.
indicate 542 vb.
warn 659 vb.
give hope 847 vb.
be cautious 853 vb.
threaten 895 vb.

**predicting**
predicting 506 adj.

**prediction**
looking ahead
        119 n.
destiny 150 n.
weather 335 n.
appearance 440 n.
probability 466 n.
expectation 502 n.
foresight 505 n.
prediction 506 n.
policy 618 n.
warning 659 n.
occultism 978 n.

**predominate**
predominate 34 vb.
cause 151 vb.
prevail 173 vb.
weigh 317 vb.
motivate 607 vb.
be important
        633 vb.
overmaster 722 vb.
dominate 728 vb.

**prejudge**
prejudge 476 vb.

**prejudgment**
prejudgment 476 n.

**prejudice**
race 11 n.
exclusion 57 n.
prejudice 476 n.
belief 480 n.
insanity 498 n.
exaggeration
        541 n.
predetermination
        603 n.

bellicosity 713 n.
affections 812 n.
warm feeling
        813 n.
pride 866 n.
friendliness 875 n.
hatred 883 n.
injustice 909 n.
sectarianism 972 n.
pietism 973 n.

**prelude**
prelude 66 n.
beginning 68 n.

**premise**
premise 470 n.
premise 470 n.

**preparation**
arrangement 62 n.
prelude 66 n.
beginning 68 n.
futurity 119 n.
looking ahead
        119 n.
anticipation 130 n.
production 159 n.
thought 444 n.
foresight 505 n.
learning 531 n.
predetermination
        603 n.
provision 628 n.
preparation 664 n.
exercise 677 n.
war measures
        713 n.
caution 853 n.

**preparatory**
precursory 66 adj.
future 119 adj.
impending 150 adj.
businesslike
        617 adj.
preparatory
        664 adj.

**prepare**
arrange 62 vb.
auspicate 68 vb.
begin 68 vb.

**prepared**
be strong 157 vb.
foresee 505 vb.
educate 529 vb.
train 529 vb.
plan 618 vb.
warn 659 vb.
prepare 664 vb.
be cautious 853 vb.

**prepared**
early 130 adj.
impending 150 adj.
tending 174 adj.
on the spot
184 adj.
formed 238 adj.
vigilant 452 adj.
expectant 502 adj.
willing 592 adj.
predetermined
603 adj.
habituated 605 adj.
planned 618 adj.
warned 659 adj.
prepared 664 adj.
expert 689 adj.
defended 708 adj.
warring 713 adj.
cautious 853 adj.

**preparedness**
adultness 129 n.
carefulness 452 n.
preparedness
664 n.
completion 720 n.

**prepare oneself**
look ahead 119 vb.
expect 502 vb.
learn 531 vb.
store 627 vb.
prepare oneself
664 vb.
undertake 667 vb.

**preparer**
preparer 664 n.

**presageful**
presageful 506 adj.

**presence**
existence 1 n.

generality 79 n.
space 178 n.
presence 184 n.
interiority 219 n.
interjacency 226 n.
approach 284 n.
arrival 290 n.
utility 635 n.
divine attribute
960 n.

**present**
existing 1 adj.
present 116 adj.
synchronous
118 adj.
modern 121 adj.

**present, be**
be 1 vb.
accrue 38 vb.
happen 149 vb.
be present 184 vb.
dwell 187 vb.
be near 195 vb.
arrive 290 vb.
watch 436 vb.

**present time**
existence 1 n.
time 104 n.
instantaneity 111 n.
present time 116 n.
synchronism 118 n.
futurity 119 n.
modernism 121 n.
newness 121 n.
presence 184 n.

**preservation**
separation 46 n.
permanence 139 n.
storage 627 n.
protection 655 n.
preservation 661 n.
defence 708 n.

**preserve**
set apart 46 vb.
sustain 141 vb.
drench 336 vb.
dry 337 vb.
season 383 vb.

store 627 vb.
sanitate 647 vb.
safeguard 655 vb.
preserve 661 vb.
retain 773 vb.

**preserved**
preserved 661 adj.

**preserver**
preserver 661 n.

**preserving**
preserving 661 vb.

**press**
press 582 n.

**press, the**
the press 523 n.

**prestige**
greatness 32 n.
superiority 34 n.
influence 173 n.
importance 633 n.
prosperity 725 n.
credit 797 n.
prestige 861 n.
pride 866 n.
approbation 918 n.

**pretension**
duplicity 536 n.
unskilfulness 690 n.
pretension 845 n.

**preterite**
preterite 120 adj.

**pretext**
reason why 151 n.
testimony 461 n.
reasons 470 n.
sophistry 472 n.
mental dishonesty
538 n.
pretext 609 n.
stratagem 693 n.
ostentation 870 n.
vindication 922 n.

**prevail**
predominate 34 vb.
cause 151 vb.
be able 155 vb.
prevail 173 vb.
be wont 605 vb.

motivate 607 vb.

**price**
equivalence 28 n.
statistics 86 n.
list 87 n.
quid pro quo 145 n.
appraise 460 vb.
goodness 639 n.
demand 732 n.
account 803 vb.
price 804 n.
price 804 vb.
penalty 958 n.

**priced**
priced 804 adj.

**prickle**
prickle 251 n.
roughness 254 n.

**pride**
greatness 32 n.
overestimation
477 n.
pride 866 n.
vanity 868 n.
insolence 873 n.
unsociability 878 n.
contempt 917 n.

**prideful**
prideful 866 adj.

**priest**
priest 980 n.
ritualist 982 n.

**priestly**
priestly 979 adj.

**primal**
beginning 68 adj.
secular 106 adj.
past 120 adj.
primal 122 adj.
fundamental
151 adj.

**primp**
primp 838 vb.

**print**
copy 20 vb.
composition 56 n.
compose 56 vb.
reproduction 161 n.

reproduce 161 vb.
form 238 n.
publicity 523 n.
publish 523 vb.
mark 542 vb.
record 543 vb.
printing 550 n.
engrave 550 vb.
writing 581 n.
print 582 n.
print 582 vb.

**printed**
printed 582 adj.

**printer**
engraver 551 n.
printer 582 n.

**printing**
mould 23 n.
photography 546 n.
representation
546 n.
printing 550 n.
print 582 n.

**print-type**
print-type 582 n.

**prior**
existing 1 adj.
original 21 adj.
preceding 64 adj.
dated 104 adj.
prior 114 adj.
former 120 adj.
antiquated 122 adj.
older 126 adj.
early 130 adj.
filial 165 adj.

**priority**
existence 1 n.
originality 21 n.
prototype 23 n.
superiority 34 n.
precedence 64 n.
precursor 66 n.
time 104 n.
priority 114 n.
past time 120 n.
seniority 126 n.
sonship 165 n.

front 232 n.
preceding 278 n.

**prison**
disunion 46 n.
cellar 189 n.
receptacle 189 n.
enclosure 230 n.
refuge 657 n.
prison 743 n.
seclusion 878 n.

**prison camp**
prison camp 743 n.

**prisoner**
interiority 219 n.
slave 737 n.
prisoner 745 n.

**private**
private 80 adj.
unintelligible
512 adj.
occult 518 adj.

**probability**
fair chance 154 n.
liability 175 n.
appearance 440 n.
possibility 464 n.
probability 466 n.
belief 480 n.
truth 489 n.
expectation 502 n.
hope 847 n.

**probable**
future 119 adj.
impending 150 adj.
tending 174 adj.
evidential 461 adj.
possible 464 adj.
probable 466 adj.
credible 480 adj.
true 489 adj.
expected 502 adj.
promising 847 adj.

**probably**
in the future
150 adv.
probably 466 adv.

**probity**
carefulness 452 n.

belief 480 n.
truth 489 n.
veracity 535 n.
artlessness 694 n.
loyalty 734 n.
observance 763 n.
credit 797 n.
courage 850 n.
manliness 850 n.
right 908 n.
morals 912 n.
probity 924 n.
disinterestedness
926 n.
virtue 928 n.
innocence 930 n.

**pro bono publico**
pro bono publico
896 adv.

**procession**
retinue 67 n.
procession 71 n.

**proclaim**
proclaim 523 vb.
affirm 527 vb.
make important
633 vb.
raise the alarm
660 vb.
decree 732 vb.
honour 861 vb.
be ostentatious
870 vb.

**prodigal**
wasteful 629 adj.
plenteous 630 adj.
losing 767 adj.
expending 801 adj.
liberal 808 adj.
prodigal 810 n.
prodigal 810 adj.
rash 852 adj.
bad person 933 n.
intemperate
938 adj.

**prodigal, be**
waste 629 vb.

superabound
632 vb.
not retain 774 vb.
expend 801 vb.
be liberal 808 vb.
be prodigal 810 vb.
be rash 852 vb.
be intemperate
938 vb.

**prodigality**
prodigality 810 n.

**prodigally**
prodigally 810 adv.

**prodigious**
prodigious 32 adj.
huge 190 adj.
super 639 adj.

**prodigy**
superior 34 n.
nonconformity
84 n.
exceller 639 n.
paragon 641 n.
proficient person
691 n.
prodigy 859 n.

**produce**
compose 56 vb.
cause 151 vb.
result 152 vb.
produce 159 vb.
generate 162 vb.
form 238 n.
imagine 508 vb.
manifest 517 vb.
provide 628 vb.
be profitable
766 vb.

**produced**
produced 159 adj.

**producer**
cause 151 n.
producer 159 n.
artist 551 n.
agent 681 n.

**product**
increment 36 n.
remainder 41 n.

tend 174 vb.
promote 280 vb.
elevate 305 vb.
make better
                649 vb.
aid 698 vb.
dignify 861 vb.
be ecclesiastical
                979 vb.

**pronunciation**
linguistics 552 n.
etymology 554 n.
dialect 555 n.
pronunciation
                572 n.
speech 574 n.
speech defect
                575 n.

**prop**
bond 47 n.
stabilizer 148 n.
receptacle 189 n.
hanger 212 n.
prop 213 n.
rear 233 n.
projection 249 n.
leg 262 n.
carrier 268 n.
sail 270 n.
hardness 321 n.
pretext 609 n.
refuge 657 n.
church exterior
                984 n.

**propagation**
propagation 162 n.

**propel**
move 260 vb.
send 267 vb.
impel 274 vb.
strike 274 vb.
propel 282 vb.
eject 295 vb.
eject 295 vb.
elevate 305 vb.
let fall 306 vb.
blow 347 vb.
lapidate 707 vb.

**propellant**
propellant 282 n.

**propeller**
limb 53 n.
propeller 264 n.
aircraft 271 n.
propellant 282 n.

**property**
thing transferred
                267 n.
means 624 n.
equipment 625 n.
store 627 n.
independence
                739 n.
possession 768 n.
joint possession
                770 n.
property 772 n.
wealth 795 n.
benefice 979 n.

**prophylactic**
hygiene 647 n.
prophylactic 653 n.

**propitiation**
propitiation 936 n.

**propound**
propound 507 vb.
affirm 527 vb.
advise 686 vb.
offer 754 vb.

**proprietary**
proprietary 772 adj.

**propulsion**
energy 155 n.
influence 173 n.
impulse 274 n.
propulsion 282 n.
ejection 295 n.
lowering 306 n.
agitation 313 n.
tool 625 n.
aid 698 n.

**propulsive**
propulsive 282 adj.

**pro rata**
pro rata 778 adv.

**prosaic**
plain 568 adj.
prosaic 588 adj.
inexcitable 818 adj.

**prose**
plainness 568 n.
reading matter
                584 n.
prose 588 n.

**prosody**
assimilation 18 n.
recurrence 102 n.
tempo 405 n.
prosody 588 n.

**prospectively**
prospectively
                119 adv.

**prosper**
progress 280 vb.
arrive 290 vb.
enjoy 371 vb.
flourish 610 vb.
do good 639 vb.
get better 649 vb.
be active 673 vb.
succeed 722 vb.
prosper 725 vb.
be profitable
                766 vb.
gain 766 vb.
get rich 795 vb.
be content 823 vb.
have a reputation
                861 vb.
be sensual 939 vb.

**prosperity**
prosperity 725 n.

**prosperous**
opportune 132 adj.
presageful 506 adj.
beneficial 639 adj.
successful 722 adj.
prosperous
                725 adj.
acquiring 766 adj.
rich 795 adj.
happy 819 adj.
promising 847 adj.

**prosperously**
prosperously
                725 adv.

**prosperous person**
progression 280 n.
victor 722 n.
prosperous person
                725 n.
rich person 795 n.

**prostitute**
prostitute 947 n.

**protection**
parentage 164 n.
parentage 164 n.
barrier 230 n.
reception 294 n.
screen 416 n.
surveillance 452 n.
surveillance 452 n.
storage 627 n.
hygiene 647 n.
protection 655 n.
preservation 661 n.
management
                684 n.
aid 698 n.
defence 708 n.
detention 742 n.
security 762 n.

**protector**
concomitant 89 n.
doorkeeper 259 n.
nautical personnel
                265 n.
protector 655 n.
warner 659 n.
manager 685 n.
aider 698 n.
patron 702 n.
defender 708 n.
armed force 717 n.
soldier 717 n.
keeper 744 n.
friend 875 n.
benefactor 898 n.
                970 n.
church party 972 n.
sectarian 972 n.

sectarian 972 adj.

**Protestantism**
Protestantism
970 n.

**prototypal**
prototypal 23 adj.

**prototype**
originality 21 n.
prototype 23 n.
rule 81 n.
example 83 n.
form 238 n.
idea 446 n.
comparison 457 n.
gauge 460 n.
prediction 506 n.
plan 618 n.
paragon 641 n.

**protracted**
protracted 108 adj.

**protraction**
protraction 108 n.

**protuberance**
face 232 n.
angularity 242 n.
protuberance
249 n.
odour 389 n.

**proud**
narrow-minded
476 adj.
defiant 706 adj.
proud 866 adj.
insolent 873 adj.
despising 917 adj.

**proud, be**
walk 262 vb.
defy 706 vb.
seek repute 861 vb.
be proud 866 vb.
boast 872 vb.
be insolent 873 vb.
despise 917 vb.
be impious 974 vb.

**proud person**
proud person
866 n.

insolent person
873 n.

**proved, be**
be proved 473 vb.

**provender**
provender 296 n.

**proverbially**
proverbially
491 adv.

**provide**
fill 54 vb.
support 213 vb.
drink 296 vb.
feed 296 vb.
foresee 505 vb.
find means 624 vb.
store 627 vb.
provide 628 vb.
suffice 630 vb.
preserve 661 vb.
make ready 664 vb.
offer 754 vb.
sell 788 vb.
be hospitable
877 vb.

**provided**
provided 463 adv.

**provider**
provider 628 n.
preparer 664 n.

**provincial**
regional 179 adj.
provincial 187 adj.

**provision**
adjunct 40 n.
extra 40 n.
accumulation 74 n.
contents 188 n.
transference 267 n.
cookery 296 n.
provisions 296 n.
means 624 n.
store 627 n.
provision 628 n.
restoration 651 n.
preservation 661 n.
fitting out 664 n.
subvention 698 n.

funds 792 n.
accounts 803 n.

**provisioning**
provisioning
628 adj.

**provisions**
provisions 296 n.
provision 628 n.

**prow**
prow 232 n.
protuberance
249 n.

**prowess**
deed 671 n.
prowess 850 n.

**prude**
people of taste
841 n.
affecter 845 n.
disapprover 919 n.
prude 945 n.

**prudery**
underestimation
478 n.
severity 730 n.
pretension 845 n.
fastidiousness
857 n.
modesty 869 n.
prudery 945 n.

**prudish**
prudish 945 adj.

**psychic**
psychic 442 adj.
intuitive 471 adj.
psychic 978 n.

**psychical**
psychical 978 adj.

**psychics**
psychics 978 n.

**psychist**
psychist 978 n.

**psychologist**
psychologist 442 n.

**psychology**
psychology 442 n.
insanity 498 n.
therapy 653 n.

psychics 978 n.

**psychopathy**
psychopathy 498 n.

**publication**
hearing aid 410 n.
prediction 506 n.
manifestation
517 n.
disclosure 521 n.
publication 523 n.
broadcast 526 n.
call 542 n.
warning 659 n.
ostentation 870 n.

**publicity**
generality 79 n.
overestimation
477 n.
knowledge 485 n.
manifestation
517 n.
information 519 n.
publicity 523 n.
news 524 n.
broadcasting
526 n.
teaching 529 n.
rostrum 534 n.
exaggeration
541 n.
correspondence
583 n.
excitant 816 n.
famousness 861 n.
ostentation 870 n.
boasting 872 n.

**publicizer**
publicizer 523 n.

**publicly**
publicly 523 adv.

**publish**
attract notice
450 vb.
manifest 517 vb.

**put in front**
mediate 715 vb.

**put in front**
put in front 64 vb.

**put off**
put off 131 vb.

**puzzle**
distract 451 vb.
puzzle 469 vb.
mean nothing
510 vb.
be unintelligible
512 vb.
be difficult 695 vb.
defeat 722 vb.
trouble 822 vb.
be wonderful
859 vb.

**puzzled**
puzzled 512 adj.

**puzzling**
puzzling 512 adj.

**Q**

**quadruple**
augment 36 vb.

**quake**
quake 849 vb.

**qualification**
adjunct 40 n.
change 138 n.
limit 231 n.
counterevidence
462 n.
qualification 463 n.
doubt 481 n.
dissent 484 n.
negation 528 n.
mental dishonesty
538 n.
unwillingness
593 n.
pretext 609 n.
means of escape
662 n.

resistance 710 n.
conditions 761 n.
nonliability 914 n.
disapprobation
919 n.
vindication 922 n.

**qualify**
limit 231 vb.
discriminate
458 vb.
qualify 463 vb.
doubt 481 vb.
dissent 484 vb.
negate 528 vb.
resist 710 vb.
give terms 761 vb.

**qualifying**
qualifying 463 adj.

**quantify**
quantify 26 vb.

**quantitative**
quantitative 26 adj.

**quantity**
quantity 26 n.
degree 27 n.
greatness 32 n.
store 627 n.

**quarrel**
differ 15 vb.
25 vb.
turmoil 61 n.
argument 470 n.
dissent 484 n.
interlocution 579 n.
quarrel 704 n.vb.
contention 711 n.
fight 711 n.
fight 711 n.
war 713 n.
discontent 824 n.
be discontented
824 n.
enmity 876 n.
be inimical 876 vb.
anger 886 n.
resent 886 vb.
reproach 919 n.
litigation 954 n.

schism 972 n.

**quarreller**
quarreller 704 n.

**quarrelling**
quarrelling 704 adj.

**quarrelsomeness**
quarrelsomeness
704 n.

**quarters**
place 180 n.
quarters 187 n.
resting place
261 n.

**quaternity**
quaternity 95 n.

**question**
topic 447 n.
curiosity 448 n.
question 454 n.
empiricism 456 n.
uncertainty 469 n.

**questionable, be**
be questionable
454 vb.

**questioner**
questioner 454 n.

**quid pro quo**
quid pro quo 145 n.

**quiescence**
quiescence 261 n.

**quiescent**
permanent 139 adj.
weak 158 adj.
inert 170 adj.
located 182 adj.
quiescent 261 adj.
insensible 370 adj.
silent 394 adj.
latent 518 adj.
nonactive 672 adj.
inactive 674 adj.
apathetic 815 adj.
inexcitable 818 adj.

**quiescent, be**
be pending 131 vb.
stay 139 vb.
cease 140 vb.
be inert 170 vb.

be moderate
172 vb.
be quiescent
261 vb.
lurk 518 vb.
not act 672 vb.
be inactive 674 vb.
be unsociable
878 vb.

**quietude**
order 60 n.
moderation 172 n.
quietude 261 n.
wind 347 n.
death 356 n.
inexcitability 818 n.
pleasurableness
821 n.
content 823 n.
lack of wonder
860 n.
seclusion 878 n.

**R**

**rabble**
crowd 74 n.
rabble 864 n.

**race**
race 11 n.
breed 77 n.
genealogy 164 n.
posterity 165 n.
humankind 366 n.

**racing**
pedestrianism
262 n.
aquatics 264 n.
speeding 272 n.
gambling 613 n.
chase 614 n.
racing 711 n.
sport 832 n.

**radiate**
emit 295 vb.

think 444 vb.
discriminate
    458 vb.
assume 466 vb.
reason 470 vb.
demonstrate
    473 vb.
judge 475 vb.
suppose 507 vb.
interpret 515 vb.
**reasonable, be**
accord 24 vb.
be certain 468 vb.
be reasonable
    470 vb.
be proved 473 vb.
assent 483 vb.
be wise 493 vb.
be intelligible
    511 vb.
**reasonably**
reasonably
    470 adv.
**reason badly**
reason badly
    472 vb.
misjudge 476 vb.
be credulous
    482 vb.
hope 847 vb.
**reasoner**
reasoner 470 n.
**reasoning**
relevance 9 n.
conformance 24 n.
sequence 65 n.
mathematics 86 n.
intellect 442 n.
philosophy 444 n.
thought 444 n.
discrimination
    458 n.
reasoning 470 n.
demonstration
    473 n.
judgment 475 n.
teaching 529 n.
legal trial 954 n.

**reasons**
reasons 470 n.
**reason why**
reason why 151 n.
attribution 153 n.
motive 607 n.
intention 612 n.
**recant**
revert 143 vb.
opine 480 vb.
disbelieve 481 vb.
negate 528 vb.
recant 598 vb.
reject 602 vb.
abrogate 747 vb.
resign 748 vb.
not retain 774 vb.
be penitent 934 vb.
become pious
    973 vb.
**recantation**
recantation 598 n.
**recede**
decrease 37 vb.
revert 143 vb.
recede 285 vb.
avoid 615 vb.
be defeated
    723 vb.
**receding**
receding 285 adj.
**receipt**
means 624 n.
earnings 766 n.
estate 772 n.
credit 797 n.
payment 799 n.
receipt 802 n.
**receive**
admit 294 vb.
give security
    762 vb.
acquire 766 vb.
receive 777 vb.
take 781 vb.
acquire 802 vb.
be rewarded
    957 vb.

**received**
received 802 adj.
**received, be**
be received 777 vb.
**receiver**
receiver 777 n.
taker 781 n.
treasurer 793 n.
**receiving**
increment 36 n.
    777 adj.
wealth 795 n.
**receptacle**
bunch 74 n.
receptacle 189 n.
handle 218 n.
covering 221 n.
wrapping 221 n.
enclosure 230 n.
storage 627 n.
arsenal 718 n.
**reception**
identity 13 n.
combination 50 n.
inclusion 78 n.
energy 155 n.
transference 267 n.
ingress 292 n.
reception 294 n.
receiving 777 n.
approbation 918 n.
Christian rite 982 n.
rite 982 n.
**recession**
motion 260 n.
regression 281 n.
recession 285 n.
departure 291 n.
eddy 345 n.
defeat 723 n.
**recipient**
recipient 189 adj.
beneficiary 771 n.
recipient 777 n.
**recoil**
correlate 12 vb.
separate 46 vb.
reversion 143 n.

revert 143 vb.
counteraction
    177 vb.
recoil 275 n.vb.
return 281 n.
regress 281 vb.
recession 285 n.
recede 285 vb.
repulsion 287 n.
ascent 303 n.
ascend 303 vb.
elasticity 323 n.
be elastic 323 vb.
tergiversation
    598 n.
avoidance 615 n.
retaliation 709 n.
retaliate 709 vb.
dislike 856 vb.
hate 883 vb.
**recoiling**
recoiling 275 adj.
**record**
copy 22 n.
remainder 41 n.
arrangement 62 n.
class 62 vb.
bunch 74 n.
list 87 n.
chronology 112 n.
time 112 vb.
fossil 120 n.
death roll 356 n.
listening 410 n.
answer 455 n.
evidence 461 n.
testimony 461 n.
information 519 n.
broadcast 526 n.
classroom 534 n.
indicate 542 vb.
record 543 n.vb.
represent 546 vb.
phrase 558 n.
script 581 n.
writing 581 n.
write 581 vb.

reading matter
584 n.
reference book
584 n.
biography 585 n.
description 585 n.
narrative 585 n.
describe 585 vb.
compendium
587 n.
abstract 587 vb.
collection 627 n.
title deed 762 n.
account book
803 n.
legal trial 954 n.
**recorded**
recorded 543 adj.
**recorder**
chronologist 112 n.
recorder 544 n.
calligrapher 581 n.
narrator 585 n.
keeper 744 n.
magistracy 952 n.
**recording**
chronological
112 adj.
recording 543 adj.
**recording
instrument**
hearing aid 410 n.
broadcasting
526 n.
recording
instrument 544 n.
**recoup**
recoup 31 vb.
progress 280 vb.
retrieve 651 vb.
retaliate 709 vb.
acquire 766 vb.
**rectify**
adjust 24 vb.
regularize 62 vb.
modify 138 vb.
plan 618 vb.
perfect 641 vb.

rectify 649 vb.
repair 651 vb.
be just 908 vb.
**recumbency**
recumbency 211 n.
**recuperate**
recuperation
recuperation 651 n.
**recur**
recur 134 vb.
go on 141 vb.
**recurrence**
heredity 5 n.
recurrence 102 n.
periodicity 136 n.
reversion 143 n.
reproduction 161 n.
resonance 399 n.
**red**
fiery 374 adj.
luminous 412 adj.
florid 420 adj.
red 426 adj.
personable
836 adj.
angry 886 adj.
**redden**
colour 420 vb.
redden 426 vb.
show feeling
813 vb.
be humbled
867 vb.
be modest 869 vb.
**redemptive**
redemptive
960 adj.
**redness**
redness 426 n.
**red pigment**
pigment 420 n.
red pigment 426 n.
**redundance**
redundance 632 n.
**redundant**
great 32 adj.
remaining 41 adj.
full 54 adj.
diffuse 565 adj.

plenteous 630 adj.
redundant 632 adj.
liberal 808 adj.
intemperate
938 adj.
**redundantly**
redundantly
632 adv.
**reference book**
directory 87 n.
guidebook 519 n.
reference book
584 n.
**referral**
referral 9 n.
**reflection**
contrariety 14 n.
copy 22 n.
recoil 275 n.
reflection 412 n.
visual fallacy 435 n.
image 546 n.
**reformer**
reformer 649 n.
**reformism**
reformism 649 n.
**refresh**
augment 36 vb.
strengthen 157 vb.
invigorate 169 vb.
refrigerate 377 vb.
make better
649 vb.
revive 651 vb.
refresh 680 vb.
aid 698 vb.
relieve 826 vb.
amuse 832 vb.
**refreshed**
refreshed 680 adj.
**refreshed, be**
be refreshed
680 vb.
**refreshing**
lenitive 172 adj.
pleasant 371 adj.
refreshing 680 adj.
relieving 826 adj.

amusing 832 adj.
**refreshment**
lull 140 n.
strengthening
157 n.
water travel 264 n.
pleasure 371 n.
revival 651 n.
repose 678 n.
refreshment 680 n.
aid 698 n.
pleasurableness
821 n.
relief 826 n.
amusement 832 n.
**refrigerate**
moderate 172 vb.
harden 321 vb.
blow 347 vb.
render insensible
370 vb.
be cold 375 vb.
refrigerate 377 vb.
preserve 661 vb.
refresh 680 vb.
**refrigeration**
refrigeration 377 n.
**refrigerator**
cabinet 189 n.
provisions 296 n.
air 335 n.
ventilation 347 n.
ice 375 n.
refrigeration 377 n.
refrigerator 379 n.
preserver 661 n.
**refuge**
resting place
261 n.
hiding-place 522 n.
protection 655 n.
refuge 657 n.
fort 708 n.
talisman 977 n.
**refusal**
dissent 484 n.
negation 528 n.

**refuse**

| | |
|---|---|
| unwillingness | |
| 593 n. | |
| rejection 602 n. | |
| hitch 697 n. | |
| resistance 710 n. | |
| prohibition 752 n. | |
| refusal 755 n. | |
| deprecation 757 n. | |
| retention 773 n. | |
| nonpayment 800 n. | |
| disapprobation | |
| 919 n. | |

**refuse**

exclude 57 vb.
put off 131 vb.
repel 287 vb.
be deaf 411 vb.
dissent 484 vb.
negate 528 vb.
be unwilling
593 vb.
reject 602 vb.
hinder 697 vb.
oppose 699 vb.
resist 710 vb.
prohibit 752 vb.
refuse 755 vb.
retain 773 vb.
be parsimonious
811 vb.

**refused**
refused 755 adj.

**refusing**
refusing 755 adj.

**regalia**
headgear 223 n.
loop 245 n.
badge 542 n.
regalia 738 n.
jewellery 839 n.
vestments 983 n.

**region**
range 178 n.
space 178 n.
region 179 n.
situation 181 n.
world 316 n.
land 339 n.

political
organization 728 n.

**regional**
regional 179 adj.

**register**
list 87 vb.
register 543 vb.
account 803 vb.

**registration**
gramophone 409 n.
registration 543 n.

**regress**
decrease 37 vb.
repeat oneself
102 vb.
revert 143 vb.
be inverted 216 vb.
navigate 264 vb.
retard 273 vb.
regress 281 vb.
recede 285 vb.
arrive 290 vb.
fall short 302 vb.
descend 304 vb.
flow 345 vb.
deteriorate 650 vb.
relapse 652 vb.

**regression**
regression 281 n.

**regressive**
regressive 281 adj.

**regret**
reversion 143 n.
be impotent
156 vb.
remembrance
500 n.
disappointment
504 n.
be disappointed
504 vb.
be unwilling
593 vb.
abrogate 747 vb.
sorrow 820 n.
suffer 820 vb.
be discontented
824 vb.

regret 825 n.vb.
be dejected
829 vb.
lament 831 vb.
desire 854 n.
desire 854 vb.
dislike 856 vb.
pity 900 n.
disapprove 919 vb.
penitence 934 n.
be penitent 934 vb.

**regretted**
regretted 825 adj.

**regretting**
regretting 825 adj.

**regular**
orderly 60 adj.
arranged 62 adj.
regular 81 adj.
periodical 136 adj.
unceasing 141 adj.
unchangeable
148 adj.
symmetrical
240 adj.
habitual 605 adj.

**regularity**
regularity 81 n.

**regularize**
regularize 62 vb.

**regular return**
recurrence 102 n.
regular return
136 n.

**regulated**
regulated 83 adj.

**reject**
leave over 41 vb.
exclude 57 vb.
repel 287 vb.
eject 295 vb.
dissent 484 vb.
disappoint 504 vb.
negate 528 vb.
vote 600 vb.
reject 602 vb.
be unsatisfied
631 vb.

not use 669 vb.
oppose 699 vb.
refuse 755 vb.
not observe
764 vb.
be discontented
824 vb.
dislike 856 vb.
hate 883 vb.
not respect 916 vb.
despise 917 vb.
disapprove 919 vb.
condemn 956 vb.

**rejected**
rejected 602 adj.

**rejection**
rejection 602 n.

**rejoice**
vociferate 403 vb.
be pleased 819 vb.
be content 823 vb.
be cheerful 828 vb.
rejoice 830 vb.
revel 832 vb.
celebrate 871 vb.
boast 872 vb.

**rejoicing**
rejoicing 830 n.adj.

**rejoinder**
interchange 146 n.
rejoinder 455 n.
negation 528 n.
retaliation 709 n.
sauciness 873 n.
vindication 922 n.
accusation 923 n.
legal trial 954 n.

**relapse**
reversion 143 n.
revert 143 vb.
tergiversation
598 n.
tergiversate 598 vb.
deterioration 650 n.
deteriorate 650 vb.
relapse 652 n.vb.

**relate**
relate 9 vb.

connect 45 vb.
attribute 153 vb.

**related, be**
be related 9 vb.
be akin 11 vb.
be one of 58 vb.
be included 78 vb.
accompany 89 vb.
result 152 vb.
be important
              633 vb.

**relation**
circumstance 8 n.
relation 9 n.
correlation 12 n.
similarity 18 n.
fitness 24 n.
union 45 n.
bond 47 n.
association 701 n.

**relative**
relative 9 adj.
akin 11 vb.
correlative 12 adj.
comparative 27 adj.
included 78 adj.
numerable 86 adj.
attributed 153 adj.

**relatively**
relatively 9 adv.

**relativeness**
relativeness 9 n.

**relevance**
relevance 9 n.

**relevant**
relevant 9 adj.
apt 24 adj.
typical 83 adj.
rational 470 adj.
demonstrating
              473 adj.
important 633 adj.

**relief**
moderation 172 n.
recuperation 651 n.
escape 662 n.
deliverance 663 n.
refreshment 680 n.

liberation 741 n.
relief 826 n.
hope 847 n.
condolence 900 n.

**relieve**
abate 37 vb.
assuage 172 vb.
remedy 653 vb.
deliver 663 vb.
refresh 680 vb.
disencumber
              696 vb.
liberate 741 vb.
be lost 767 vb.
tranquillize 818 vb.
please 821 vb.
content 823 vb.
relieve 826 vb.
cheer 828 vb.

**relieved, be**
escape 662 vb.
be content 823 vb.
be relieved 826 vb.
be cheerful 828 vb.
hope 847 vb.

**relieving**
relieving 826 adj.

**relievo**
relievo 249 n.

**religion**
philosophy 444 n.
news 524 n.
religion 967 n.
piety 973 n.
public worship
              975 n.
idolatry 976 n.
occultism 978 n.

**religionist**
religionist 967 n.

**religious**
immaterial 315 adj.
religious 967 adj.
cabbalistic 978 adj.

**religious faith**
belief 480 n.
religious faith
              967 n.

non-Christian sect
              972 n.

**religious teacher**
sage 495 n.
interpreter 515 n.
religious teacher
              967 n.
worshipper 975 n.

**relinquish**
separate 46 vb.
cease 140 vb.
depart 291 vb.
disregard 453 vb.
dissent 484 vb.
negate 528 vb.
be irresolute
              596 vb.
tergiversate 598 vb.
be neutral 601 vb.
relinquish 616 vb.
not use 669 vb.
be lax 729 vb.
abrogate 747 vb.
resign 748 vb.
refuse 755 vb.
not retain 774 vb.
give 776 vb.
divorce 891 vb.
fail in duty 913 vb.

**relinquished**
relinquished
              616 adj.

**relinquishment**
relinquishment
              616 n.

**remainder**
difference 15 n.
remainder 41 n.
part 53 n.
piece 53 n.
numerical result
              85 n.
fewness 101 n.
antiquity 120 n.
effect 152 n.
superfluity 632 n.

**remaining**
remaining 41 adj.

**remarkable**
remarkable 32 adj.
notable 633 adj.

**remarkably**
remarkably 32 adv.

**remedial**
lenitive 172 adj.
counteracting
              177 adj.
salubrious 647 adj.
restorative 651 adj.
remedial 653 adj.
successful 722 adj.
relieving 826 adj.

**remedy**
a mixture 43 n.
moderator 172 n.
counteract 177 vb.
plant 361 n.
answer 455 n.
contrivance 618 n.
means 624 n.
recuperation 651 n.
remedy 653 n.vb.
precept 688 n.

**remember**
repeat 102 vb.
repeat oneself
              102 vb.
think 444 vb.
be mindful 450 vb.
remember 500 vb.
understand 511 vb.
register 543 vb.
honour 861 vb.
celebrate 871 vb.

**remembered**
remembered
              500 adj.

**remembered, be**
be remembered
              500 vb.

**remembering**
remembering
              500 adj.

**remembrance**
remainder 41 n.
past time 120 n.

reversion 143 n.
remembrance
500 n.
loquacity 576 n.
biography 585 n.
narrative 585 n.
celebration 871 n.

**remind**
remind 500 vb.
hint 519 vb.
warn 659 vb.

**reminder**
reminder 500 n.

**removed**
removed 194 adj.

**rend**
rend 46 vb.

**render few**
abate 37 vb.
render few 101 vb.
weaken 158 vb.
destroy 160 vb.
empty 295 vb.
extract 299 vb.

**render insensible**
assuage 172 vb.
render insensible
370 vb.
make inactive
674 vb.
make insensitive
815 vb.
relieve 826 vb.
frighten 849 vb.

**renowned**
renowned 861 vb.

**reoccur**
reoccur 102 vb.

**repair**
adjunct 40 n.
join 45 vb.
variegate 432 vb.
amendment 649 n.
make better
649 vb.
rectify 654 vb.
repair 656 n.vb.
preserve 661 vb.

**repeat**
be identical 13 vb.
liken 18 vb.
do likewise 20 vb.
accord 24 vb.
augment 36 vb.
conform 83 vb.
number 86 vb.
double 91 vb.
repeat 102 vb.
sustain 141 vb.
reproduce 161 vb.
notice 450 vb.
answer 455 vb.
memorize 500 vb.
remind 500 vb.
mean 509 vb.
be intelligible
511 vb.
advertise 523 vb.
emphasize 527 vb.
describe 585 vb.
habituate 605 vb.

**repeated**
repeated 102 adj.

**repeatedly**
repeatedly 102 adv.

**repeat oneself**
repeat oneself
102 vb.
recur 134 vb.
be diffuse 565 vb.
be tedious 833 vb.

**repel**
influence 173 vb.
repel 287 vb.
dismiss 295 vb.
parry 708 vb.
defeat 722 vb.
refuse 755 vb.
cause dislike
856 vb.
excite hate 883 vb.

**repellent**
repellent 287 adj.
resisting 710 adj.
disliked 856 adj.

**repentant**
repentant 934 adj.

**repetition**
identity 13 n.
uniformity 16 n.
mimicry 20 n.
copy 22 n.
continuity 71 n.
conformity 83 n.
duplication 91 n.
repetition 102 n.
future state 119 n.
frequency 134 n.
continuance 141 n.
reproduction 161 n.
roll 398 n.
answer 455 n.
remembrance
500 n.
affirmation 527 n.
diffuseness 565 n.
vigour 566 n.
perseverance
595 n.
habituation 605 n.
tedium 833 n.

**replace**
replace 182 vb.

**replenish**
drink 296 vb.
store 627 vb.
replenish 628 vb.
suffice 630 vb.
restore 651 vb.

**report**
evidence 461 n.
estimate 475 n.
report 519 n.
broadcast 526 n.
record 543 n.
speech 574 n.
description 585 n.

**reportedly**
reportedly 519 adv.

**repose**
cease 140 vb.
pause 140 vb.
quietude 261 n.

be quiescent
261 vb.
come to rest
261 vb.
sit down 306 vb.
euphoria 371 n.
inaction 672 n.
not act 672 vb.
sleep 674 n.
be inactive 674 vb.
leisure 676 n.
have leisure
676 vb.
repose 678 n.
repose 678 vb.
refreshment 680 n.
be refreshed
680 vb.
be free 739 vb.
keep calm 818 vb.
amusement 832 n.
be sociable 877 vb.

**reposeful**
reposeful 678 adj.

**represent**
make extrinsic 6 vb.
resemble 18 vb.
imitate 20 vb.
outline 228 vb.
form 238 vb.
darken 413 vb.
gauge 460 vb.
evidence 461 vb.
be true 489 vb.
imagine 508 vb.
mean 509 vb.
figure 514 vb.
show 517 vb.
indicate 542 vb.
record 543 vb.
represent 546 vb.
paint 548 vb.
describe 585 vb.
act 589 vb.

**representation**
similarity 18 n.
imitation 20 n.
mimicry 20 n.

copy 22 n.
substitute 145 n.
appearance 440 n.
manifestation
    517 n.
indication 542 n.
record 543 n.
representation
    546 n.
painting 548 n.
picture 548 n.
sculpture 549 n.
description 585 n.
acting 589 n.
drama 589 n.
dramaturgy 589 n.
stage play 589 n.
rite 982 n.
ritual act 982 n.

**represented**
represented
    546 adj.

**representing**
representing
    546 adj.

**reprimand**
warning 659 n.
humiliation 867 n.
reprimand 919 n.
punishment 958 n.

**reproach**
scurrility 894 n.
reproach 919 n.
accusation 923 n.
guilt 931 n.

**reprobate**
name 556 vb.
curse 894 vb.
cuss 894 vb.
not respect 916 vb.
despise 917 vb.
reprobate 919 vb.

**reproduce**
copy 20 vb.
augment 36 vb.
repeat 102 vb.
produce 159 vb.
reproduce 161 vb.

**reproduced**
reproduced
    161 adj.

**reproduce itself**
grow 36 vb.
be mixed 43 vb.
produce 159 vb.
reproduce 161 vb.
reproduce itself
    162 vb.
be fruitful 166 vb.

**reproduction**
imitation 20 n.
copy 22 n.
reproduction 161 n.
propagation 162 n.

**reprove**
dissuade 608 vb.
warn 659 vb.
deprecate 757 vb.
curse 894 vb.
reprove 919 vb.
accuse 923 vb.
punish 958 vb.

**reptile**
serpent 246 n.
reptile 360 n.
bane 654 n.
noxious animal
    899 n.

**repulsion**
energy 155 n.
influence 173 n.
recoil 275 n.
repulsion 287 n.
refusal 755 n.

**reputable**
reputable 861 adj.
respected 915 adj.
approved 918 adj.
honourable
    924 adj.

**repute**
greatness 32 n.
importance 633 n.
trophy 724 n.
repute 861 n.
respect 915 n.

probity 924 n.

**repute, person of**
broadcaster 526 n.
bigwig 633 n.
prosperous person
    725 n.
officer 736 n.
person of repute
    861 n.
favourite 885 n.

**request**
topic 447 n.
enquire 454 vb.
remind 500 vb.
propound 507 vb.
affirm 527 vb.
inducement 607 n.
    622 vb.
demand 732 n.
ask leave 751 vb.
offer 754 vb.
offer oneself
    754 vb.
request 756 n.vb.
deprecation 757 n.
borrow 780 vb.
claim 910 n.
litigation 954 n.
litigate 954 vb.
prayers 975 n.

**requesting**
requesting 756 adj.

**require**
be incomplete
    55 vb.
send 267 vb.
fall short 302 vb.
qualify 463 vb.
necessitate 591 vb.
require 622 vb.
be unsatisfied
    631 vb.
not suffice 631 vb.
demand 732 vb.
beg 756 vb.
request 756 vb.
give terms 761 vb.
purchase 787 vb.

be poor 796 vb.
be discontented
    824 vb.
desire 854 vb.

**required**
required 622 adj.

**requirement**
offset 31 n.
deficit 55 n.
shortfall 302 n.
qualification 463 n.
necessity 591 n.
requirement 622 n.
waste 629 n.
chief thing 633 n.
imperfection 642 n.
completion 720 n.
request 756 n.
conditions 761 n.
purchase 787 n.
poverty 796 n.
desire 854 n.
desired object
    854 n.

**resemble**
correlate 12 vb.
resemble 18 vb.
imitate 20 vb.
accord 24 vb.
be equal 28 vb.
reproduce 161 vb.
taste 381 vb.
appear 440 vb.

**resent**
be discontented
    824 vb.
regret 825 vb.
dislike 856 vb.
be inimical 876 vb.
hate 883 vb.
resent 886 vb.
be revengeful
    905 vb.

**resentful**
resentful 886 adj.

**resentment**
dissension 704 n.
feeling 813 n.

moral sensibility
814 n.
annoyance 822 n.
discontent 824 n.
regret 825 n.
dislike 861 n.
humiliation 867 n.
enmity 876 n.
hatred 883 n.
resentment 886 n.
malevolence 893 n.
revengefulness
905 n.
jealousy 906 n.
wrong 909 n.

**resident**
resident 186 n.

**residing**
residing 187 adj.

**resign**
cease 140 vb.
regress 281 vb.
depart 291 vb.
tergiversate 598 vb.
relinquish 616 vb.
have leisure
676 vb.
be lax 729 vb.
resign 748 vb.
not retain 774 vb.

**resignation**
disunion 46 n.
cessation 140 n.
relinquishment
616 n.
leisure 676 n.
laxity 729 n.
resignation 748 n.
nonliability 914 n.

**resigning**
resigning 748 vb.

**resin**
viscidity 349 n.
resin 352 n.

**resinous**
resinous 352 adj.

**resist**
cease 140 vb.

be violent 171 vb.
oppose 699 vb.
withstand 699 vb.
parry 708 vb.
retaliate 709 vb.
resist 710 vb.
contend 711 vb.
give battle 713 vb.
triumph 722 vb.
revolt 733 vb.
refuse 755 vb.

**resistance**
protraction 108 n.
strike 140 n.
counteraction
177 n.
obstinacy 597 n.
dissuasion 608 n.
hindrance 697 n.
opposition 699 n.
defence 708 n.
resistance 710 n.
disobedience
733 n.
revolt 733 n.
refusal 755 n.

**resisting**
resisting 710 adj.

**resolute**
unchangeable
148 adj.
unyielding 157 adj.
volitional 590 adj.
resolute 594 adj.
persevering
595 adj.
obstinate 597 adj.
intending 612 adj.
attempting 666 adj.
active 673 adj.
completive 720 adj.
unbeaten 722 adj.
courageous
850 adj.

**resolute, be**
gesticulate 542 vb.
will 590 vb.
be resolute 594 vb.

choose 600 vb.
intend 612 vb.
attempt 666 vb.
fight 711 vb.
be successful
722 vb.
be insensitive
815 vb.
be cheerful 828 vb.
take courage
850 vb.

**resolutely**
resolutely 594 adv.

**resolution**
stability 148 n.
vitality 157 n.
vigorousness
169 n.
limit 231 n.
attention 450 n.
gesture 542 n.
will 590 n.
resolution 594 n.
perseverance
595 n.
obstinacy 597 n.
intention 612 n.
assiduity 673 n.
courage 850 n.
manliness 850 n.

**resonance**
resonance 399 n.

**resonant**
sounding 393 adj.
loud 395 adj.
rolling 398 adj.
resonant 399 adj.
melodious 405 adj.
speaking 574 adj.

**resound**
repeat oneself
102 vb.
recoil 275 vb.
rotate 310 vb.
sound 393 vb.
be loud 395 vb.
resound 399 vb.

**respect**
obeisance 306 n.
look after 452 vb.
assent 483 vb.
make important
633 vb.
fear 849 n.vb.
repute 861 n.
honour 861 vb.
friendliness 875 n.
courtesy 879 n.
be courteous
879 vb.
love 882 n.
respect 915 n.vb.
approbation 918 n.
approve 918 vb.
piety 973 n.
worship 975 n.
worship 975 vb.
deification 976 n.

**respected**
respected 915 adj.

**respectful**
fearing 849 adj.
courteous 879 adj.
respectful 915 adj.
pious 973 adj.
worshipping
975 adj.

**respectfully**
respectfully
915 adv.

**respects**
courteous act
879 n.
respects 915 n.
ritual act 982 n.

**respiration**
outlet 293 n.
reception 294 n.
excretion 297 n.
oscillation 312 n.
respiration 347 n.
life 355 n.
loudness 395 n.
cry 403 n.
fatigue 679 n.

**respiratory disease**
respiration 347 n.
respiratory disease
646 n.

**respondent**
exam 454 n.
respondent 455 n.
testee 456 n.
interlocutor 579 n.

**resting place**
resting place
261 n.

**restitute**
restitute 782 vb.

**restitution**
compensation 31 n.
offset 31 n.
reversion 143 n.
restoration 651 n.
remedy 653 n.
peace offering
714 n.
restitution 782 n.
payment 799 n.
dueness 910 n.
vindication 922 n.
atonement 936 n.
reward 957 n.
penalty 958 n.
punishment 958 n.

**restlessness**
restlessness 673 n.

**restoration**
equalization 28 n.
compensation 31 n.
duplication 91 n.
repetition 102 n.
conversion 142 n.
reversion 143 n.
strengthening
157 n.
reproduction 161 n.
improvement
649 n.
restoration 651 n.
deliverance 663 n.
refreshment 680 n.
acquisition 766 n.

restitution 782 n.
dignification 861 n.
piety 973 n.

**restorative**
salubrious 647 adj.
improving 654 adj.
restorative 651 adj.
remedial 653 adj.
refreshing 680 adj.

**restore**
adjust 24 vb.
augment 36 vb.
make complete
54 vb.
double 91 vb.
repeat 102 vb.
modify 138 vb.
transform 142 vb.
revert 143 vb.
reproduce 161 vb.
replace 182 vb.
restore 651 vb.
remedy 653 vb.
deliver 663 vb.
refresh 680 vb.
aid 698 vb.
restitute 782 vb.
animate 816 vb.
make pious 973 vb.

**restored**
restored 651 adj.

**restored, be**
be restored 651 vb.

**restoring**
restoring 782 adj.

**restrain**
abate 37 vb.
exclude 57 vb.
halt 140 vb.
moderate 172 vb.
make smaller
193 vb.
limit 231 vb.
retard 273 vb.
qualify 463 vb.
dissuade 608 vb.
not suffice 631 vb.
hinder 697 vb.

be severe 730 vb.
compel 735 vb.
restrain 742 vb.
abrogate 747 vb.
prohibit 752 vb.
retain 773 vb.
tranquillize 818 vb.
be temperate
937 vb.

**restrained**
small 33 adj.
moderate 172 adj.
circumscribed
227 adj.
quiescent 261 adj.
hindered 697 adj.
subjected 740 adj.
restrained 742 adj.
temperate 937 adj.

**restraining**
restraining 742 adj.

**restraint**
diminution 37 n.
delay 131 n.
cessation 140 n.
helplessness 156 n.
contraception
167 n.
moderation 172 n.
moderator 172 n.
counteraction
177 n.
slowness 273 n.
protection 655 n.
hindrance 697 n.
severity 730 n.
compulsion 735 n.
subjection 740 n.
restraint 742 n.
prohibition 752 n.
sale 788 n.
price 804 n.
temperance 937 n.
legal process
954 n.
penalty 958 n.

**restriction**
restriction 742 n.

**result**
ensue 115 vb.
happen 149 vb.
result 152 vb.

**retain**
join 45 vb.
tie 45 vb.
cohere 48 vb.
prevail 173 vb.
remember 500 vb.
persevere 595 vb.
store 627 vb.
preserve 661 vb.
restrain 742 vb.
refuse 755 vb.
possess 768 vb.
retain 773 vb.
take 781 vb.
be parsimonious
811 vb.
caress 884 vb.
be selfish 927 vb.

**retained**
retained 773 adj.

**retainer**
concomitant 89 n.
bearer 268 n.
retainer 737 n.
toady 874 n.

**retaliate**
correlate 12 vb.
compensate 31 vb.
revert 143 vb.
interchange
146 vb.
recoil 275 vb.
answer 455 vb.
quarrel 704 vb.
attack 707 vb.
retaliate 709 vb.
be severe 730 vb.
pay 799 vb.
avenge 905 vb.
be just 908 vb.
blame 919 vb.
reward 957 vb.
punish 958 vb.

## retaliation

retaliation 709 n.

## retaliatory

retaliatory 709 adj.

## retard

abate 37 vb.
halt 140 vb.
shorten 199 vb.
bring to rest
     261 vb.
retard 273 vb.
hinder 697 vb.
restrain 742 vb.

## retention

retention 773 n.

## retentive

retentive 773 adj.

## reticent

reticent 520 adj.
taciturn 577 adj.
cunning 693 adj.
cautious 853 adj.

## reticular

reticular 217 adj.

## retinue

retinue 67 n.
procession 71 n.
band 74 n.
concomitant 89 n.
rear 233 n.
follower 279 n.
retainer 737 n.

## retreat

retreat 187 n.
chamber 189 n.
hiding-place 522 n.
refuge 657 n.
seclusion 878 n.
monastery 980 n.

## retrieve

recoup 31 vb.
revert 143 vb.
counteract 177 vb.
retrieve 651 vb.
acquire 766 vb.
possess 768 vb.
appropriate 781 vb.
restitute 782 vb.

claim 910 vb.

## retrospect

look back 120 vb.
turn back 281 vb.
retrospect 500 vb.
describe 585 vb.
regret 825 vb.

## retrospective

retrospective
    120 adj.
antiquated 122 adj.
reverted 143 adj.
regressive 281 adj.
ignorant 486 adj.
regretting 825 adj.

## retrospectively

retrospectively
    120 adv.

## return

return 281 n.
arrival 290 n.
departure 291 n.
ingress 292 n.
circuition 309 n.
tergiversation
    598 n.

## revel

eat 296 vb.
foolery 492 n.
rejoicing 830 n.
rejoice 830 vb.
revel 832 n.
pageant 870 n.
celebrate 871 vb.
sociability 877 n.
be hospitable
    877 vb.
be sociable 877 vb.
be intemperate
    938 vb.
sensualism 939 n.
drunkenness 944 n.
get drunk 944 vb.

## revelation

knowledge 485 n.
truth 489 n.
prediction 506 n.

revelation 969 n.

## revelational

revelational
    969 adj.

## reveller

reveller 832 n.

## revenge

compensation 31 n.
quarrel 704 n.
retaliation 709 n.
severity 730 n.
resentment 886 n.
revenge 905 n.
jealousy 906 n.
punishment 958 n.

## revengeful

revengeful 905 adj.

## revengeful, be

be revengeful
    905 vb.

## revengefulness

revengefulness
    905 n.

## reversibly

reversibly 143 adv.

## reversion

start 68 n.
reversion 143 n.
revolution 144 n.
destruction 160 n.
inversion 216 n.
recoil 275 n.
regression 281 n.
return 281 n.
relapse 652 n.
abrogation 747 n.

## revert

revert 143 vb.

## reverted

reverted 143 adj.

## revival

newness 121 n.
reproduction 161 n.
life 355 n.
pungency 383 n.
revival 651 n.
refreshment 680 n.
relief 826 n.

sanctity 973 n.

## revive

convert 142 vb.
strengthen 157 vb.
reproduce 161 vb.
vitalize 355 vb.
get healthy 645 vb.
revive 651 vb.
doctor 653 vb.

## revolt

rampage 61 vb.
revolution 144 n.
be violent 171 vb.
opposition 699 n.
withstand 699 vb.
resistance 710 n.
resist 710 vb.
go to war 713 vb.
revolt 733 n.
revolt 733 vb.
achieve liberty
    741 vb.
be discontented
    824 vb.
cause discontent
    824 vb.
fail in duty 913 vb.
lawlessness 949 n.

## revolter

revolter 733 n.

## revolution

disorder 61 n.
change 138 n.
reversion 143 n.
revolution 144 n.
destruction 160 n.
ruin 160 n.
outbreak 171 n.
overturning 216 n.
lowering 306 n.
obliteration 545 n.
revolt 733 n.

## revolutionary

revolutionary
    144 adj.
destructive 160 adj.
violent 171 adj.

**ritualist**
ritualist 982 n.

**ritualistic**
ritualistic 982 adj.

**ritualize**
ritualize 982 vb.

**ritually**
ritually 982 adv.

**ritual object**
small box 189 n.
cross 217 n.
water 334 n.
ritual object 982 n.
altar 984 n.
church utensil
984 n.

**road**
housing 187 n.
crossing 217 n.
paving 221 n.
limit 231 n.
traffic control
300 n.
road 619 n.
instrument 623 n.
building material
626 n.
facility 696 n.

**rob**
lay waste 160 vb.
take away 781 vb.
rob 783 vb.

**robber**
robber 784 n.

**robe**
robe 223 n.
vestments 983 n.

**rock**
solid body 319 n.
hardness 321 n.
rock 339 n.
mineral 354 n.

**rocket**
aeronautics 266 n.
rocket 271 n.

**roll**
periodicity 136 n.
impulse 274 n.

sound 393 n.
loudness 395 n.
faintness 396 n.
roll 398 n.
roll 398 vb.
resound 399 vb.
play music 408 vb.
call 542 vb.

**rolling**
rolling 398 adj.

**Roman Catholic**
Roman Catholic
970 adj.
ecclesiastical
979 adj.

**roof**
dwelling 187 n.
high structure
204 n.
vertex 208 n.
beam 213 n.
roof 221 n.
dome 248 n.
projection 249 n.
building material
626 n.

**room**
greatness 32 n.
advantage 34 n.
inclusion 78 n.
room 178 n.
emptiness 185 n.
interval 196 n.
storage 627 n.
scope 739 n.

**rostrum**
stand 213 n.
publicity 523 n.
rostrum 534 n.
oratory 574 n.

**rotary**
periodical 136 n.
rotary 310 adj.

**rotate**
be periodic 136 vb.
twine 246 vb.
round 247 vb.
propel 282 vb.

circle 309 vb.
rotate 310 vb.
agitate 313 vb.
be agitated 313 vb.
flow 345 vb.
dance 832 vb.

**rotation**
continuity 71 n.
regular return
136 n.
revolution 144 n.
motion 260 n.
circuition 309 n.
rotation 310 n.
planet 316 n.
ballet 589 n.

**rotator**
rotator 310 n.

**rotund**
round 245 adj.
rotund 247 adj.
convex 248 adj.
tubular 258 adj.

**rotundity**
circularity 245 n.
rotundity 247 n.

**rough**
nonuniform 17 adj.
discontinuous
72 adj.
amorphous
239 adj.
convex 248 adj.
projecting 249 adj.
sharp 251 adj.
rough 254 adj.
textural 326 adj.
flowing 345 adj.
pungent 383 adj.
difficult 695 adj.

**rough, be**
be rough 254 vb.

**roughen**
jut 249 vb.
roughen 254 vb.
notch 255 vb.

**roughness**
nonuniformity 17 n.

inequality 29 n.
discontinuity 72 n.
roughness 254 n.
agitation 313 n.
texture 326 n.
wave 345 n.
difficulty 695 n.

**round**
curved 243 adj.
round 245 adj.
rotund 247 adj.
round 247 vb.

**roundabout**
circuitous 309 adj.
roundabout
621 n.

**round about**
621 adv.

**round and round**
round and round
310 adv.

**route**
water travel 264 n.
air travel 266 n.
direction 276 n.
route 619 n.

**row**
be in motion
260 vb.
row 264 vb.

**rowing boat**
rowing boat 270 n.

**rub**
abate 37 vb.
subtract 39 vb.
uncover 224 vb.
smooth 253 vb.
collide 274 vb.
pulverize 327 vb.
rub 328 vb.
give pain 372 vb.
touch 373 vb.
obliterate 545 vb.
clean 643 vb.
wound 650 vb.

**rubbing**
rubbing 328 adj.

**rubbish**
leavings 41 n.
piece 53 n.
confusion 61 n.
accumulation 74 n.
sham 537 n.
waste 629 n.
rubbish 636 n.
dirt 644 n.
derelict 774 n.
outcast 878 n.

**rude, be**
disregard 453 vb.
reject 602 vb.
torment 822 vb.
humiliate 867 vb.
be insolent 873 vb.
make unwelcome
878 vb.
be rude 880 vb.
not respect 916 vb.
despise 917 vb.

**rudeness**
rudeness 880 n.

**rude person**
rude person 880 n.

**ruffian**
violent creature
171 n.
murderer 357 n.
troublemaker
658 n.
combatant 717 n.
rioter 733 n.
robber 784 n.
desperado 852 n.
low fellow 864 n.
insolent person
873 n.
ruffian 899 n.
bad person 933 n.

**ruin**
decrease 37 n.
remainder 41 n.
ruin 160 n.
descent 304 n.
evil 611 n.
defeat 723 n.

adversity 726 n.
loss 767 n.

**rule**
order 60 vb.
rule 81 n.
policy 618 n.
manage 684 vb.
precept 688 n.
rule 728 vb.

**ruling**
superior 34 adj.
strong 157 adj.
ruling 728 adj.

**rumour**
publication 523 n.
rumour 524 n.
rumour 524 vb.
telecommunication
526 n.
fable 538 n.
chat 579 n.

**rumoured**
rumoured 524 adj.

**run away**
run away 615 vb.

**run on**
run on 71 vb.

S

**sacrament, the**
the sacrament
982 n.

**sadden**
excite 816 vb.
hurt 822 vb.
sadden 829 vb.

**saddle horse**
saddle horse 268 n.

**safe**
covered 221 adj.
certain 468 adj.
safe 655 adj.
preserved 661 adj.
content 823 adj.

cautious 853 adj.

**safe, be**
be safe 655 vb.

**safeguard**
coupling 47 n.
accompany 89 vb.
electricity 155 n.
gap 196 n.
support 213 n.
wrapping 221 n.
coat 226 n.
headgear 223 n.
intermediary 226 n.
sailing aid 264 n.
admit 294 vb.
screen 416 vb.
invigilate 452 vb.
look after 452 vb.
make certain
468 vb.
signpost 542 n.
means 624 n.
protection 655 n.
safeguard 655 vb.
safeguard 657 n.
preserver 661 n.
preserve 661 vb.
means of escape
662 n.
obstacle 697 n.
patronize 698 vb.
armour 708 n.
defence 708 n.
defend 708 vb.
give security
762 vb.
caution 853 n.
pet 884 vb.
talisman 977 n.

**safety**
safety 655 n.
safeguard 657 n.
security 762 n.

**sagacity**
sagacity 493 n.

**sage**
superior 34 n.
old man 128 n.

intellectual 487 n.
sage 495 n.
oracle 506 n.
teacher 532 n.
bigwig 633 n.
adviser 686 n.
proficient person
691 n.
person of repute
861 n.
religious teacher
967 n.

**sail**
propeller 264 n.
sail 270 n.
traction 283 n.

**sailing aid**
sailing aid 264 n.
navigator 265 n.
direction 276 n.
gauge 460 n.
signpost 542 n.
safeguard 657 n.
directorship 684 n.

**sailing ship**
sailing ship 270 n.

**saint**
the dead 356 n.
saint 962 n.

**salable**
salable 788 adj.

**salad days**
salad days 125 n.

**sale**
request 756 n.
acquisition 766 n.
nonretention 774 n.
transfer 775 n.
trade 786 n.
sale 788 n.

**salty**
salty 383 adj.

**salubrious**
nourishing 296 adj.
beneficial 639 adj.
clean 643 adj.
healthy 645 adj.
salubrious 647 adj.

**salubrious, be**
remedial 653 adj.
safe 655 adj.
tutelary 655 adj.
preserving 661 adj.
cheering 828 adj.
ascetic 940 adj.

**salubrious, be**
do good 639 vb.
be salubrious
647 vb.

**salubrity**
salubrity 647 n.

**sanctified**
sanctified 973 adj.

**sanctify**
dignify 861 vb.
celebrate 871 vb.
angelize 962 vb.
sanctify 973 vb.
offer worship
975 vb.
idolatrize 976 vb.
be ecclesiastical
979 vb.

**sanctity**
virtue 928 n.
sanctity 973 n.

**sane**
wise 493 adj.
sane 497 adj.
intelligible 511 adj.

**sane, be**
be sane 497 vb.

**sanely**
sanely 497 adv.

**sanguineous**
sanguineous
330 adj.

**sanitarian**
sanitarian 647 n.

**sanitate**
sanitate 647 vb.

**sanity**
sanity 497 n.

**Satan**
wickedness 929 n.
Satan 963 n.

impious person
974 n.

**sate**
fill 54 vb.
eat 296 vb.
render insensible
370 vb.
suffice 630 vb.
superabound
632 vb.
make insensitive
815 vb.
content 823 vb.
be tedious 833 vb.
cause dislike
856 vb.
sate 858 vb.

**sated**
sated 858 adj.

**satellite**
spaceship 271 n.
satellite 316 n.

**satiety**
satiety 858 n.

**satire**
mimicry 20 n.
trope 514 n.
exaggeration
541 n.
description 585 n.
witticism 834 n.
satire 846 n.
calumny 921 n.

**satirize**
satirize 846 vb.

**sauce**
adjunct 40 n.
stimulant 169 n.
hors-d'oeuvres
296 n.
sauce 384 n.

**sauciness**
sauciness 873 n.

**savouriness**
savouriness 385 n.

**savoury**
edible 296 adj.
fatty 352 adj.

tasty 381 adj.
pungent 383 adj.
savoury 385 adj.
sweet 387 adj.
pleasurable
821 adj.

**scales**
scales 317 n.

**scan**
look along 198 vb.
traverse 262 vb.
scan 433 vb.
watch 436 vb.
be curious 448 vb.
be attentive
450 vb.
enquire 454 vb.
estimate 475 vb.
know 485 vb.
be cautious 853 vb.

**scarce**
few 101 adj.
deficient 302 adj.
scarce 631 adj.
fasting 941 adj.

**scarcity**
decrease 37 n.
fewness 101 n.
production 159 n.
unproductiveness
167 n.
absence 185 n.
scarcity 631 n.
poverty 796 n.
dearness 806 n.
fasting 941 n.

**scent**
scent 391 n.

**schism**
disagreement 25 n.
tergiversation
598 n.
relinquishment
616 n.
dissension 704 n.
revolt 733 n.
undutifulness
913 n.

schism 972 n.

**schismatic**
dissentient 484 n.
tergiversator 598 n.
revolter 733 n.
undutifulness
913 n.

**schismatic**
schismatic 972 n.

**schismatical**
schismatical
972 adj.

**schismatize**
schismatize 972 vb.

**scholar**
antiquarian 120 n.
scholar 487 n.
sage 495 n.
learning 531 n.
learner 533 n.
linguist 552 n.
bookperson 584 n.
expert 691 n.

**scholastic**
scholastic 534 adj.

**school**
edifice 159 n.
curriculum 529 n.
school 534 n.
amendment 649 n.

**school of painting**
art 546 n.
school of painting
548 n.
sculpture 549 n.
artist 551 n.

**science**
physics 314 n.
science 485 n.

**science of forces**
energy 155 n.
science of forces
157 n.

**sciolism**
sciolism 486 n.

**sciolist**
sciolist 488 n.

**scission**
scission 46 n.

**scope**
opportunity 132 n.
influence 173 n.
range 178 n.
ingress 292 n.
facility 696 n.
laxity 729 n.
scope 739 n.
permit 751 n.
trade 786 n.
liberality 808 n.

**scourge**
scourge 959 n.

**screen**
separation 46 n.
canopy 221 n.
shade 221 n.
headgear 223 n.
partition 226 n.
stopper 259 n.
refrigerate 377 n.
darken 413 vb.
screen 416 n.vb.
opacity 418 n.
make opaque
    418 vb.
eye 433 n.
blind 434 vb.
dim sight 435 n.
be unseen 439 vb.
    520vb.
disguise 522 n.
pretext 609 n.
safeguard 655 vb.
shelter 657 n.
defences 708 n.
defend 708 vb.

**screened**
screened 416 adj.

**script**
speech sound
    393 n.
lack of meaning
    510 n.
identification
    542 n.
symbology 542 n.
record 543 n.

phrase 558 n.
script 581 n.

**scriptural**
scriptural 969 adj.

**scripture**
scripture 969 n.

**sculpt**
sculpt 549 vb.

**sculptor**
sculptor 551 n.

**sculpture**
copy 22 n.
composition 56 n.
production 159 n.
high structure
    204 n.
formation 238 n.
relievo 249 n.
art 546 n.
image 546 n.
sculpture 549 n.
ornamental art
    839 n.
idol 976 n.

**scurrility**
slang 555 n.
quarrel 704 n.
quarrelsomeness
    704 n.
insolence 873 n.
rudeness 880 n.
scurrility 894 n.
disrespect 916 n.
reproach 919 n.
detraction 921 n.

**seafaring**
seafaring 264 adj.
marine 270 adj.
oceanic 338 adj.

**sea god**
mariner 265 n.
sea god 338 n.

**sealed off**
sealed off 259 adj.

**seamanlike**
seamanlike
    265 adj.

**sea nymph**
sea nymph 338 n.

**search**
be curious 448 vb.
search 454 n.
search 454 vb.
discovery 479 n.
discover 479 vb.
pursuit 614 n.
pursue 614 vb.
attempt 666 vb.
request 756 vb.
take 781 vb.

**season**
cook 296 vb.
season 383 n.
spice 384 n.
make appetizing
    385 vb.
preserve 661 vb.

**seasonal**
periodic 106 adj.
seasonal 136 adj.
territorial 339 adj.
celebratory
    871 adj.

**seat**
seat 213 n.

**seclude**
set apart 46 vb.
exclude 57 vb.
eject 295 vb.
disappear 441 vb.
conceal 520 vb.
sanitate 647 vb.
imprison 742 vb.
seclude 878 vb.

**secluded**
closed 259 adj.
tranquil 261 adj.
invisible 439 adj.
latent 518 adj.
concealed 520 adj.
secluded 878 adj.

**seclusion**
seclusion 878 n.

**secrecy**
invisibility 439 n.

**secrecy**
secrecy 520 n.
symbology 542 n.
taciturnity 577 n.
caution 853 n.

**secret**
unknown thing
    486 n.
unintelligibility
    512 n.
latency 518 n.
information 519 n.
secrecy 520 n.
secret 525 n.
trap 537 n.
writing 581 n.

**secretly**
secretly 520 adv.

**secret service**
secret service
    454 n.

**sect**
classification 77 n.
party 703 n.
religionist 967 n.
Protestantism
    970 n.
sect 972 n.

**sectarian**
classificatory
    77 adj.
nonconformist
    84 n.
unconformable
    84 adj.
biased 476 adj.
dissentient 484 n.
dissenting 484 adj.
auxiliary 702 n.
sectional 703 adj.
Protestant 970 adj.
sectarian 972 n.
sectarian 972 adj.
zealot 973 n.
pietistic 979 adj.
ecclesiastical
    979 adj.

**sectarianism**
sectarianism 972 n.

**sectarianize**
sectarianize 972 vb.

**sectional**
excluding 57 adj.
biased 476 adj.
sectional 703 adj.
sectarian 972 adj.

**secular**
secular 106 adj.

**secured**
secured 762 adj.

**security**
offset 31 n.
list 87 n.
thing transferred
          267 n.
credential 461 n.
testimony 461 n.
prisoner 745 n.
promise 759 n.
compact 760 n.
security 762 n.
paper money
          792 n.
debt 798 n.

**sedition**
disorder 61 n.
dissent 484 n.
reformism 649 n.
activity 673 n.
sedition 733 n.
perfidy 925 n.

**see**
see 433 vb.
watch 436 vb.
cognize 442 vb.
be mindful 450 vb.
detect 479 vb.
know 485 vb.
be wise 493 vb.
imagine 508 vb.
understand 511 vb.

**seedbed**
origin 68 n.
seedbed 151 n.
abundance 166 n.

**seeing**
seeing 433 adj.

**seek refuge**
dwell 187 vb.
navigate 264 vb.
seek safety 655 vb.
seek refuge 657 vb.

**seek repute**
seek repute 861 vb.
be praised 918 vb.

**seek safety**
gamble 613 vb.
seek safety 655 vb.
seek refuge 657 vb.
prepare 664 vb.
be cautious 853 vb.

**seldom**
seldom 135 adv.

**select**
subtract 39 vb.
set apart 46 vb.
extract 299 vb.
discriminate
          458 vb.
select 600 vb.

**self**
intrinsicality 5 n.
no imitation 21 n.
group 74 n.
set 80 n.
subjectivity 315 n.
spirit 447 n.

**selfish**
unthinking 445 adj.
avaricious 811 adj.
greedy 854 adj.
vain 868 adj.
selfish 927 adj.

**selfish, be**
be parsimonious
          811 vb.
be selfish 927 vb.

**selfishly**
selfishly 927 adv.

**selfishness**
selfishness 927 n.

**sell**
provide 628 vb.
offer 754 vb.
request 756 vb.

not retain 774 vb.
assign 775 vb.
trade 786 vb.
sell 788 vb.
overcharge 806 vb.

**seller**
traveller 263 n.
speaker 574 n.
worker 681 n.
servant 737 n.
seller 788 n.
pedlar 789 n.
tradespeople
          789 n.

**semantic**
semantic 509 adj.

**semiliquid**
semiliquid 349 adj.

**semiliquidity**
semiliquidity 349 n.

**semitransparency**
semitransparency
          419 n.

**semitransparent**
semitransparent
          419 adj.

**send**
disperse 75 vb.
displace 183 vb.
move 260 vb.
send 267 vb.
admit 294 vb.
emit 295 vb.
pass 300 vb.
give 700 vb.
take away 781 vb.

**seniority**
seniority 126 n.

**sense**
sense 369 n.
feeling 813 n.

**sensibility**
weakness 158 n.
liability 175 n.
sensibility 369 n.
moral sensibility
          814 n.

**sensitive**
attentive 450 adj.
receiving 777 adj.
feeling 813 adj.
sensitive 814 adj.
excitable 817 adj.
tasteful 841 adj.
irascible 887 adj.

**sensitive, be**
have feeling
          369 vb.
feel 813 vb.
be sensitive
          814 vb.

**sensual**
material 314 adj.
sensuous 371 adj.
feeling 813 adj.
intemperate
          938 adj.
sensual 939 adj.
lecherous 946 adj.
irreligious 968 adj.

**sensual, be**
be sensual 939 vb.

**sensualism**
sensualism 939 n.

**sensualist**
sensualist 939 n.

**sensually**
sensually 939 adv.

**sensuous**
sensuous 371 adj.
pleasurable
          821 adj.

**sentient**
sentient 369 adj.
feeling 813 adj.
impressible
          814 adj.
sensitive 814 adj.

**separate**
different 15 adj.
separate 46 adj.
separate 46 vb.
nonadhesive
          49 adj.
fragmentary 53 adj.

extraneous 59 adj.
discontinuous
                72 adj.
unassembled
                75 adj.
be dispersed 75 vb.
recede 285 vb.
diverge 289 vb.
cultivate 365 vb.
schismatical
                972 adj.

**separately**
separately 46 adv.

**separation**
unrelatedness 10 n.
separation 46 n.
noncoherence 49 n.
decomposition
                51 n.
derangement 63 n.
discontinuity 72 n.
dispersion 75 n.
unity 88 n.
destruction 160 n.
farness 194 n.
gap 196 n.
partition 226 n.
divergence 289 n.
liberation 741 n.
seclusion 878 n.
schism 972 n.

**sequel**
adjunct 40 n.
remainder 41 n.
sequence 65 n.
sequel 67 n.
end 69 n.
extremity 69 n.
continuity 71 n.
posteriority 115 n.
lateness 131 n.
effect 152 n.
abundance 166 n.
hanging object
                212 n.
rear 233 n.
eddy 345 n.
thought 444 n.

remembrance
                500 n.
tergiversation
                598 n.
amendment 649 n.
regret 825 n.
wit 834 n.

**sequence**
relativeness 9 n.
addition 38 n.
adjunct 40 n.
order 60 n.
sequence 65 n.
continuity 71 n.
posteriority 115 n.
futurity 119 n.
effect 152 n.
near place 195 n.
line 198 n.
following 279 n.
pursuit 614 n.

**sequential**
sequential 65 adj.

**serial place**
circumstance 8 n.
degree 27 n.
average 30 n.
order 60 n.
serial place 73 n.
prestige 861 n.

**series**
increase 36 n.
decrease 37 n.
coherence 48 n.
all 52 n.
arrangement 62 n.
retinue 67 n.
series 71 n.
accumulation 74 n.
group 74 n.
sort 77 n.
continuance 141 n.
following 279 n.

**serious**
wise 493 adj.
forceful 566 adj.
plain 568 adj.
inexcitable 818 adj.

serious 829 adj.
dull 835 adj.
ungracious 880 adj.
angry 886 adj.
sullen 888 adj.

**serious, be**
be truthful 535 vb.
be serious 829 vb.

**seriousness**
seriousness 829 n.

**serpent**
serpent 246 n.

**servant**
inferior 35 n.
mariner 265 n.
aeronaut 266 n.
animal husbandry
                364 n.
spectator 436 n.
instrument 623 n.
nonentity 634 n.
worker 681 n.
official 685 n.
auxiliary 702 n.
officer 736 n.
servant 737 n.
commoner 864 n.
worshipper 975 n.

**serve**
be inferior 35 vb.
follow 279 vb.
busy oneself
                617 vb.
be useful 635 vb.
minister to 698 vb.
obey 734 vb.
serve 737 vb.
be servile 874 vb.

**service**
service 740 n.
servility 874 n.

**servile**
willing 592 adj.
obedient 734 adj.
subject 740 adj.
subjected 740 adj.
inglorious 862 adj.
servile 874 adj.

courteous 879 adj.
respectful 915 adj.
flattering 920 adj.

**servile, be**
obey 734 vb.
be subject 740 vb.
be servile 874 vb.
flatter 920 vb.

**servilely**
servilely 874 adv.

**servility**
servility 874 n.

**serving**
inferior 35 adj.
aiding 698 adj.
serving 737 adj.
subjected 740 adj.

**servitude**
submission 716 n.
compulsion 735 n.
servitude 740 n.
detention 742 n.
servility 874 n.

**set apart**
differentiate 15 vb.
set apart 46 vb.
exclude 57 vb.
be one 88 vb.
space 196 vb.
discriminate
                458 vb.
select 600 vb.

**set off**
set off 31 vb.

**settler**
foreigner 59 n.
settler 186 n.
egress 293 n.

**severable**
severable 46 adj.

**severally**
severally 80 adv.

**severe**
regulated 83 adj.
strong 162 adj.
operative 168 adj.
vigorous 169 adj.

narrow-minded
476 adj.
severe 730 adj.
restraining 742 adj.
paining 822 adj.
serious 829 adj.
fastidious 857 adj.
ungracious 880 adj.
unkind 893 adj.
pitiless 901 adj.
unjust 914 adj.
ascetic 940 adj.

**severe, be**
dominate 728 vb.
be severe 730 vb.
restrain 742 vb.
prohibit 752 vb.
give pain 761 vb.
be pitiless 901 vb.
do wrong 909 adj.
impose a duty
912 vb.
punish 958 vb.

**severely**
severely 730 adv.

**severity**
severity 730 n.

**shade**
shade 221 n.
headgear 223 n.
curtain 416 n.
screen 416 n.

**shade off**
shade off 27 vb.

**shadowy**
amorphous
239 adj.
dark 413 adj.
shadowy 414 adj.
screened 416 adj.
uncertain 469 adj.
imaginary 508 adj.
puzzling 512 adj.

**shallow**
insubstantial 4 adj.
inconsiderable
33 adj.
near 195 adj.

shallow 207 adj.
exterior 218 adj.
inattentive 451 adj.
trivial 634 adj.

**shallowness**
shallowness 207 n.

**sham**
mimicry 20 n.
copy 22 n.
misfit 25 n.
disguise 522 n.
duplicity 536 n.
sham 537 n.
inelegance 571 n.
stratagem 693 n.
lament 831 n.
flattery 920 n.
pietism 979 n.
false piety 974 n.

**shame**
hinder 697 vb.
shame 862 n.
humiliate 867 vb.
be rude 880 vb.
not respect 916 vb.
despise 917 vb.
defame 921 vb.
debauch 946 vb.
punish 958 vb.

**shapely**
symmetrical
240 adj.
shapely 836 adj.

**sharing**
sharing 770 adj.

**sharp**
violent 171 adj.
sharp 251 adj.
hairy 254 adj.
notched 255 adj.
pungent 383 adj.
forceful 566 adj.
felt 813 adj.

**sharp, be**
be sharp 251 vb.

**sharp edge**
sharp edge 251 n.
smoother 253 n.

roughness 254 n.
pulverizer 327 n.
farm tool 365 n.
tool 625 n.
axe 718 n.
sidearms 718 n.

**sharpen**
invigorate 169 vb.
make violent
171 vb.
sharpen 251 vb.
animate 816 vb.

**sharpener**
sharpener 251 n.

**sharpness**
sharpness 251 n.

**sharp point**
fastening 47 n.
extremity 69 n.
angularity 242 n.
protuberance
249 n.
sharp point 251 n.
perforator 258 n.
bane 654 n.
sidearms 718 n.
spear 718 n.
weapon 718 n.
nippers 773 n.

**sheep**
sheep 360 n.

**shekels**
shekels 792 n.

**shelf**
compartment
189 n.
shelf 213 n.

**shelter**
station 182 n.
dwelling 187 n.
retreat 187 n.
stable 187 n.
projection 249 n.
goal 290 n.
screen 416 n.
hiding-place 522 n.
protection 655 n.
shelter 657 n.

defences 708 n.

**shine**
grow 36 vb.
vary 147 vb.
recoil 275 vb.
oscillate 312 vb.
be agitated 313 vb.
shine 412 vb.
illuminate 415 vb.
blur 435 vb.
be visible 438 vb.
be beautiful
836 vb.
be ostentatious
870 vb.

**ship**
layer 202 n.
vertex 208 n.
prow 232 n.
poop 233 n.
water travel 264 n.
transport 267 n.
carrier 268 n.
ship 270 n.
aircraft 271 n.
speeder 272 n.
follower 279 n.
traction 283 n.
warship 717 n.

**shipping**
shipping 270 n.

**shirt**
shirt 223 n.

**shoot**
shoot 282 vb.
fell 306 vb.
kill 357 vb.
fire at 707 vb.

**shooter**
shooter 282 n.

**shop**
shop 791 n.

**shore**
edge 229 n.
limit 231 n.
laterality 234 n.
shore 339 n.

**short**
small 33 adj.
incomplete 55 adj.
brief 109 adj.
dwarfish 191 adj.
short 199 adj.
thick 200 adj.
low 205 adj.
deformed 241 adj.
concise 564 adj.
compendious
587 adj.

**short, be**
be short 199 vb.

**short distance**
draw 28 n.
small quantity 33 n.
short distance
195 n.
interval 196 n.
shortness 199 n.
narrowness 201 n.
straightness 244 n.
contest 711 n.

**shorten**
shade off 27 vb.
abate 37 vb.
subtract 39 vb.
cut 46 vb.
sunder 46 vb.
make smaller
193 vb.
shorten 199 vb.
smooth 253 vb.
cultivate 365 vb.
neglect 453 vb.
be concise 564 vb.
abstract 587 vb.
impair 650 vb.

**shortener**
shortener 199 n.

**shortening**
diminution 37 n.
subtraction 39 n.
decrement 42 n.
scission 46 n.
contraction 193 n.
shortening 199 n.

conciseness 564 n.
compendium
587 n.

**shortfall**
smallness 33 n.
inferiority 35 n.
decrement 42 n.
incompleteness
55 n.
shortfall 302 n.
requirement 622 n.
insufficiency 631 n.
scarcity 631 n.
defect 642 n.
imperfection 642 n.
noncompletion
721 n.
debt 798 n.

**shortly**
shortly 199 adv.

**shortness**
shortness 199 n.

**show**
open 258 vb.
attract notice
450 vb.
detect 479 vb.
interpret 515 vb.
show 517 vb.
be truthful 535 vb.
indicate 542 vb.
dramatize 589 vb.
be ostentatious
870 vb.

**show feeling**
show feeling
813 vb.
be excited 816 vb.
be excitable
817 vb.
be pleased 819 vb.

**show mercy**
be moderate
172 vb.
safeguard 655 vb.
be lenient 731 vb.
show mercy
900 vb.

forgive 904 vb.
be just 908 vb.
exempt 914 vb.

**shown**
obvious 438 adj.
appearing 440 adj.
shown 517 adj.
disclosed 521 adj.
dramatic 589 adj.
offering 754 adj.

**show respect**
stoop 306 vb.
make important
633 vb.
honour 861 vb.
greet 879 vb.
pay one's respects
879 vb.
show respect
915 vb.
be pious 973 vb.

**show style**
phrase 558 vb.
show style 561 vb.
be elegant 570 vb.

**showy**
appearing 440 adj.
manifest 517 adj.
ornate 569 adj.
splendid 836 adj.
ornamented
839 adj.
vulgar 842 adj.
fashionable
843 adj.
prideful 866 adj.
proud 866 adj.
showy 870 adj.

**shrew**
violent creature
171 n.
quarreller 704 n.
shrew 892 n.
hellhag 899 n.
defamer 921 n.

**shrill**
blow 347 vb.
be loud 395 vb.

shrill 402 vb.

**sibilant**
sibilant 401 adj.
vocal 572 adj.

**sibilation**
sibilation 401 n.

**sick**
orderless 61 adj.
lean 201 adj.
dying 356 adj.
frenzied 498 adj.
sick 646 adj.
suffering 820 adj.

**sick person**
list 87 n.
helplessness 156 n.
weakling 158 n.
transferrer 267 n.
sick person 646 n.
sufferer 820 n.

**side arms**
sharp edge 251 n.
sharp point 251 n.
sidearms 718 n.

**sideways**
broadways
200 adv.
sideways 234 adv.

**sign**
endorse 483 vb.
sign 542 vb.
spell 553 vb.
write 581 vb.

**signal**
signal light 415 n.
manifestation
517 n.
communicate
519 vb.
message 524 n.
telecommunication
526 n.
signal 542 n.vb.
warning 659 n.
danger signal
660 n.
greet 879 vb.

navigation 264 n.
propulsion 282 n.
physics 314 n.
touch 378 n.
musical skill 408 n.
knowledge 485 n.
sagacity 493 n.
imagination 508 n.
business 617 n.
contrivance 618 n.
way 619 n.
means 624 n.
goodness 639 n.
deed 671 n.
tactics 683 n.
management 684 n.
skill 689 n.
cunning 693 n.
art of war 713 n.
success 722 n.
sport 832 n.
good taste 841 n.
sorcery 977 n.

**skin**
layer 202 n.
shallowness 207 n.
exteriority 218 n.
interiority 219 n.
skin 221 n.
overcoat 223 n.
hair 254 n.
materials 626 n.

**skin disease**
formication 378 n.
skin disease 646 n.
blemish 840 n.

**skirt**
skirt 223 n.

**slacker**
slowcoach 273 n.
slacker 593 n.
indifference 855 n.

**slang**
unintelligibility 512 n.
slang 555 n.

**slaughter**
destruction 160 n.
demolish 160 vb.
destroy 160 vb.
slaughter 357 n.
slaughter 357 vb.
terror tactics 707 n.
wage war 713 vb.
be severe 730 vb.
cruel act 898 n.
be malevolent 898 vb.
capital punishment 963 n.
execute 963 vb.
oblation 975 n.

**slaughterhouse**
havoc 160 n.
slaughterhouse 357 n.
sink 644 n.

**slave**
inferior 35 n.
thing transferred 267 n.
worker 681 n.
obedience 734 n.
slave 742 n.
prisoner 750 n.
commoner 869 n.
prostitute 952 n.

**sled**
sled 274 n.

**sleep**
evening 124 n.
cease 140 vb.
be inert 175 vb.
quietude 266 n.
be quiescent 266 vb.
insensibility 375 n.
euphoria 376 n.
blindness 439 n.
be inattentive 456 vb.
be neglectful 458 vb.
sleep 679 n.vb.

repose 683 n.vb.
be fatigued 684 vb.
relieve 831 vb.
fail in duty 918 vb.

**sleepiness**
sleepiness 679 n.

**sleepy**
inert 175 adj.
quiescent 266 adj.
abstracted 456 adj.
sleepy 679 adj.
fatigued 684 adj.

**sleeve**
sleeve 228 n.

**sleight**
sleight 542 n.

**slightly**
slightly 33 adv.

**sloping**
sloping 220 adj.

**slow**
protracted 113 adj.
late 136 adj.
inert 175 adj.
slow 278 adj.
flowing 350 adj.
unwilling 598 adj.
lazy 679 adj.
leisurely 681 adj.
inexcitable 823 adj.
dull 840 adj.

**slowcoach**
lateness 136 n.
slowcoach 278 n.
slacker 598 n.
idler 679 n.

**slowly**
slowly 278 adv.

**slowness**
slowness 278 n.

**sluggishness**
sluggishness 679 n.

**slur**
badness 645 n.
slur 867 n.
wrong 914 n.
calumny 926 n.

**slut**
slut 61 n.
negligence 458 n.
dirty person 649 n.
bungler 697 n.

**slyboots**
slyboots 698 n.

**small**
small 33 adj.
fragmentary 53 adj.
fractional 102 adj.
weak 163 adj.
exiguous 196 adj.
little 196 adj.
contracted 198 adj.
insufficient 636 adj.
trivial 639 adj.
contemptible 922 adj.

**small animal**
small animal 33 n.
dwarf 196 n.

**small, be**
be small 33 vb.

**small box**
small box 194 n.

**small coin**
small coin 33 n.
trifle 639 n.
coinage 797 n.
money 797 n.

**small hill**
small hill 209 n.
incline 220 n.
dome 253 n.

**small house**
small house 192 n.

**smallness**
smallness 33 n.

**small quantity**
finite quantity 26 n.
small quantity 33 n.
tincture 43 n.
part 53 n.
piece 53 n.
fraction 102 n.
fewness 105 n.

contents 188 n.
mouthful 296 n.
insufficiency 631 n.
trifle 634 n.

**small thing**
small thing 33 n.
piece 53 n.
minuteness 191 n.
thinness 201 n.
powder 327 n.

**smell**
absorb 294 vb.
emit 295 vb.
smell 389 vb.

**smile**
smile 830 n.
be affected 845 vb.
flatter 920 vb.

**smoke**
smoke 383 vb.

**smooth**
uniform 16 adj.
equal 28 adj.
equalize 28 vb.
nonadhesive
49 adj.
orderly 60 adj.
unravel 62 vb.
regular 81 adj.
make conform
83 vb.
make smaller
193 vb.
flat 211 adj.
flatten 211 vb.
straighten 244 vb.
smooth 253 adj.
smooth 253 vb.
downy 254 adj.
tranquil 261 adj.
soft 322 adj.
textural 326 adj.
rub 328 vb.
rub 328 vb.
touch 373 vb.
deceiving 537 adj.
easy 696 adj.
facilitate 696 vb.

relieve 826 vb.

**smoother**
smoother 253 n.

**smoothness**
smoothness 253 n.

**snaky**
snaky 246 adj.

**snow**
snow 375 n.

**snuff out**
snuff out 413 vb.

**sober**
moderate 172 adj.
temperate 937 adj.
ascetic 940 adj.
sober 943 adj.

**sober, be**
be temperate
937 vb.
be sober 943 vb.

**soberly**
soberly 943 adv.

**sober person**
abstainer 937 n.
ascetic 940 n.
sober person
943 n.

**sobriety**
moderation 172 n.
temperance 937 n.
sobriety 943 n.

**sociability**
sociability 877 n.

**sociable**
accessible 284 adj.
corporate 703 adj.
free 739 adj.
liberal 808 adj.
cheerful 828 adj.
friendly 875 adj.
sociable 877 adj.
amiable 879 adj.
benevolent 892 adj.

**sociable, be**
unite with 45 vb.
meet 290 vb.
be cheerful 828 vb.
rejoice 830 vb.

be in fashion
843 vb.
be friendly 875 vb.
be sociable 877 vb.
greet 879 vb.

**sociable person**
incomer 292 n.
reveller 832 n.
beau monde 843 n.
friend 875 n.
sociable person
877 n.

**sociably**
sociably 877 adv.

**social evil**
social evil 946 n.

**social gathering**
assembly 74 n.
conference 579 n.
festivity 832 n.
social gathering
877 n.

**social group**
social group 366 n.
community 703 n.

**sociality**
sociality 877 n.

**social round**
festivity 832 n.
social round 877 n.

**society**
band 74 n.
group 74 n.
society 703 n.

**sociology**
anthropology
366 n.
vocation 617 n.
reformism 649 n.
nurse 653 n.
safety 660 n.
benevolence 892 n.
sociology 896 n.

**soft**
unstable 147 adj.
weak 158 adj.
lenitive 172 adj.
soft 322 adj.

elastic 323 adj.
marshy 342 adj.
pulpy 351 adj.
comfortable
371 adj.
unsavoury 386 adj.
irresolute 596 adj.
submitting 716 adj.
impressible
814 adj.

**soft drink**
soft drink 296 n.
water 334 n.

**soften**
conform 83 vb.
be weak 158 vb.
weaken 158 vb.
assuage 172 vb.
soften 322 vb.

**soft-hued**
soft-hued 420 adj.

**softness**
softness 322 n.

**soil**
leavings 41 n.
piece 53 n.
shallowness 207 n.
covering 221 n.
soil 339 n.
farm 365 n.
materials 626 n.

**sold, be**
be published
523 vb.
be sold 788 vb.

**soldier**
aeronaut 266 n.
descent 304 n.
defender 708 n.
soldier 717 n.
brave person
850 n.

**soldiery**
soldiery 717 n.

**solecism**
inexactness 490 n.
mistake 490 n.

## sources of energy

sources of energy
155 n.

**sourness**
sourness 388 n.

**sovereign**
sovereign 736 n.
beneficiary 771 n.
aristocrat 863 n.

**space**
quantity 26 n.
greatness 32 n.
grade 73 vb.
inclusion 78 n.
infinity 103 n.
space 178 n.
district 179 n.
size 190 n.
distance 194 n.
space 196 vb.
open space 258 n.
open 258 vb.
air 335 n.
plain 343 n.

**spaced**
spaced 196 adj.

**spaceship**
space travel 266 n.
spaceship 271 n.
follower 279 n.
satellite 316 n.
detector 479 n.

**space travel**
space travel 266 n.

**spacious**
extensive 32 adj.
great 32 adj.
unassembled
75 adj.
spacious 178 adj.
recipient 189 adj.
large 190 adj.
expanded 192 adj.
broad 200 adj.
telluric 316 adj.

**spank**
spank 958 vb.

**sparingly**
sparingly 809 adv.

**spasm**
fitfulness 137 n.
revolution 144 n.
violence 171 n.
impulse 274 n.
spasm 313 n.
pang 372 n.
frenzy 498 n.
gesture 542 n.
illness 646 n.
nervous disorders
646 n.
activity 673 n.
feeling 813 n.
excitation 816 n.
fear 849 n.

**spatial**
spatial 178 adj.

**speak**
cry 403 n.
inform 519 vb.
divulge 521 vb.
publish 523 vb.
affirm 527 vb.
voice 572 vb.
speak 574 vb.
converse 579 vb.

**speaker**
informant 519 n.
preacher 532 n.
phrasemonger
569 n.
speaker 574 n.
actor 589 n.
motivator 607 n.

**speaking**
speaking 574 adj.

**speak low**
sound faint 396 vb.
speak low 573 n.

**speak plainly**
be plain 517 vb.
divulge 521 vb.
affirm 527 vb.
speak plainly
568 vb.

**speak to**
orate 574 vb.
speak to 578 vb.
entreat 756 vb.
greet 879 vb.
worship 975 vb.

**spear**
sharp point 251 n.
spear 718 n.

**special**
characteristic 5 adj.
unrelated 10 adj.
different 15 adj.
nonuniform 17 adj.
original 21 adj.
special 80 adj.
unconformable
84 adj.
unusual 84 adj.
one 88 adj.
semantic 509 adj.
indicating 542 adj.
possessed 768 adj.

**special day**
anniversary 136 n.
important matter
633 n.
amusement 832 n.
festivity 832 n.
special day 871 n.
wedding 889 n.

**speciality**
reality 1 n.
temperament 5 n.
unrelatedness 10 n.
differentiation 15 n.
variant 15 n.
nonuniformity 17 n.
disunion 46 n.
speciality 80 n.
nonconformity
84 n.
unity 88 n.
tendency 174 n.
materiality 314 n.
qualification 463 n.
connotation 509 n.

**be artless 694 vb.**

phrase 558 n.
style 561 n.
independence
739 n.

**specially**
specially 80 adv.

**specify**
differentiate 15 vb.
specify 80 vb.
inform 519 vb.
indicate 547 vb.
name 556 vb.
describe 585 vb.

**spectacle**
spectacle 440 n.
exhibit 517 n.
classroom 534 n.
image 546 n.
stage set 589 n.
stage show 589 n.
beauty 836 n.
prodigy 859 n.
pageant 870 n.

**spectator**
traveller 263 n.
listener 410 n.
spectator 436 n.
inquisitive person
448 n.
witness 461 n.
broadcasting
526 n.
playgoer 589 n.

**speculate**
lend 779 vb.
speculate 786 vb.
purchase 787 vb.

**speculative**
experimental
456 adj.
speculative
613 adj.
dangerous 656 adj.
trading 786 adj.
rash 852 adj.

**speech**
mimicry 20 n.
tradition 122 n.

cry **403** n.
affirmation **527** n.
language **552** n.
voice **572** n.
speech **574** n.
stage play **589** n.
**speech defect**
repetition **102** n.
unintelligibility
    **512** n.
dialect **555** n.
neology **555** n.
solecism **560** n.
inelegance **571** n.
pronunciation
    **572** n.
speech defect
    **575** n.
drunkenness **944** n.
**speech sound**
speech sound
    **393** n.
letter **558** n.
spoken letter
    **553** n.
word **554** n.
voice **572** n.
**speeder**
speeder **272** n.
**speeding**
speeding **272** n.
racing **711** n.
**speedy**
brief **109** adj.
transient **109** adj.
instantaneous
    **111** adj.
speedy **272** adj.
active **673** adj.
hasty **675** adj.
**spell**
spell **553** vb.
incentive **607** n.
instrument **623** n.
malevolence **893** n.
malediction **894** n.
spell **977** n.

**spelling**
spelling **553** n.
**sphere**
part **53** n.
bisection **92** n.
sphere **247** n.
swelling **248** n.
plaything **832** n.
**spice**
spice **384** vb.
**spin out**
spin out **108** vb.
**spinster**
woman **368** n.
spinster **890** n.
**spirit**
insubstantial thing
    **4** n.
essential part **5** n.
self **80** n.
subjectivity **315** n.
life **355** n.
spirit **442** n.
intuition **471** n.
affections **812** n.
**spiritualism**
interpreter **515** n.
ghost **964** n.
spiritualism **978** n.
**splendid**
splendid **836** adj.
**spoken letter**
spoken letter
    **553** n.
**spoliation**
havoc **160** n.
taking **781** n.
spoliation **783** n.
**spontaneity**
spontaneity **604** n.
**spontaneous**
brief **109** adj.
intuitive **471** adj.
involuntary
    **591** adj.
voluntary **592** adj.
spontaneous
    **604** adj.

unintentional
    **613** adj.
unprepared
    **665** adj.
artless **694** adj.
independent
    **739** adj.
**spookishly**
spookishly **964** adv.
**spooky**
insubstantial **4** adj.
spooky **964** adj.
cabbalistic **978** adj.
**sporadically**
sporadically
    **75** adv.
**sport**
athletics **157** n.
aquatics **264** n.
snow **375** n.
chase **614** n.
exercise **677** n.
contention **711** n.
contest **711** n.
pugilism **711** n.
sport **832** n.
**spouse**
concomitant **89** n.
old woman **128** n.
male **367** n.
woman **368** n.
colleague **702** n.
loved one **882** n.
spouse **889** n.
**spring**
spring **123** n.
**spurious**
simulating **18** adj.
substituted
    **145** adj.
erroneous **490** adj.
false **536** adj.
spurious **537** adj.
untrue **538** adj.
ostentatious
    **870** adj.
boastful **872** adj.

unwarranted
    **911** adj.
dishonest **925** adj.
perfidious **925** adj.
**spurt**
increase **36** n.
brief span **109** n.
vigorousness
    **169** n.
spurt **272** n.
progression **280** n.
haste **675** n.
**stability**
uniformity **16** n.
equilibrium **28** n.
durability **108** n.
permanence **139** n.
stability **148** n.
power **155** n.
quiescence **261** n.
resolution **594** n.
obstinacy **597** n.
divine attribute
    **960** n.
**stabilize**
stabilize **148** vb.
**stabilizer**
stabilizer **148** n.
**stable**
stable **187** n.
chamber **189** n.
edge **229** n.
enclosure **230** n.
air travel **266** n.
goal **290** n.
cattle pen **364** n.
storage **627** n.
shelter **657** n.
workshop **682** n.
**stable, be**
stay **139** vb.
be stable **148** vb.
**stagecoach**
stagecoach **269** n.
**stagehand**
stagehand **589** n.
**stage manager**
producer **159** n.

stock farm **364** n.
farm **365** n.
workshop **682** n.

**stoop**
be low **205** vb.
be horizontal
        **211** vb.
be oblique **215** vb.
make curved
        **243** vb.
descend **304** vb.
stoop **306** vb.
knuckle under
        **716** vb.
be servile **874** vb.
greet **879** vb.
show respect
        **915** vb.
be pious **973** vb.

**stop**
equilibrium **28** n.
stop **140** n.
quiescence **261** n.
inaction **672** n.
difficulty **695** n.
hitch **697** n.
defeat **723** n.
failure **723** n.

**stopper**
moderator **172** n.
covering **221** n.
stopper **259** n.
safeguard **657** n.
retention **773** n.

**stopping place**
stopping place
        **140** n.

**stop using**
stop using **669** vb.

**storage**
separation **46** n.
assemblage **74** n.
bunch **74** n.
room **178** n.
location **182** n.
cellar **189** n.
chamber **189** n.
provisions **296** n.

gas **331** n.
lake **341** n.
agriculture **365** n.
farm tool **365** n.
hiding-place **522** n.
storage **627** n.
preservation **661** n.
arsenal **718** n.
emporium **791** n.
treasury **794** n.

**store**
great quantity **32** n.
join **45** vb.
set apart **46** vb.
bring together
        **74** vb.
data processing
        **86** n.
source **151** n.
case **189** n.
receptacle **189** n.
vat **189** n.
excavation **250** n.
emit **295** vb.
water **334** n.
irrigator **336** n.
stream **345** n.
agriculture **365** n.
cultivate **365** vb.
coal **380** n.
mnemonics **505** n.
conceal **525** vb.
dictionary **554** n.
store **627** n.
store **627** vb.
provision **628** n.
provide **628** vb.
plenty **630** n.
redundance **632** n.
safeguard **655** vb.
preserve **661** vb.
preparation **669** n.
make ready **669** vb.
nonuse **669** n.
not use **669** vb.
workshop **682** n.
acquire **766** vb.

joint possession
        **770** n.
retain **773** vb.
purchase **787** vb.
merchandise **790** n.
funds **792** n.
treasury **794** n.
wealth **795** n.
economy **809** n.
economize **809** vb.

**stored**
stored **627** adj.

**storm**
storm **171** n.
commotion **313** n.
powder **327** n.
weather **335** n.
rain **345** n.
gale **347** n.
loudness **395** n.

**stow**
add **38** vb.
fill **54** vb.
stow **182** vb.
load **188** vb.
insert **298** vb.

**straight**
simple **44** adj.
orderly **60** adj.
continuous **71** adj.
symmetrical
        **240** adj.
straight **244** adj.
directed **276** adj.
undeviating
        **620** adj.

**straight, be**
be straight **244** vb.
orientate **276** vb.
steer for **276** vb.

**straighten**
straighten **244** vb.

**straightness**
straightness **244** n.

**straight on**
straight on
        **244** adv.

**stratagem**
trickery **537** n.
pretext **609** n.
contrivance **618** n.
plot **618** n.
tactics **683** n.
stratagem **693** n.

**stratification**
stratification **202** n.

**stray**
be dispersed **75** vb.
wander **262** vb.
stray **277** vb.
recede **285** vb.
be inattentive
        **451** vb.
be uncertain
        **469** vb.
err **490** vb.
be in danger
        **656** vb.
be free **739** vb.

**stream**
great quantity **32** n.
outbreak **171** n.
motion **260** n.
approach **284** vb.
ingress **292** n.
outflow **293** n.
climber **303** n.
water **334** n.
stream **345** n.
plenty **630** n.

**strength**
durability **108** n.
power **155** n.
strength **157** n.
vigorousness
        **169** n.
toughness **324** n.
stamina **595** n.

**strengthen**
augment **36** vb.
accrue **38** vb.
empower **155** vb.
strengthen **157** vb.
invigorate **169** vb.
support **213** vb.

**strengthening**
harden 321 vb.
be tough 324 vb.
corroborate 461 vb.
restore 651 vb.
safeguard 655 vb.
aid 698 vb.
defend 708 vb.
animate 816 vb.
aggravate 827 vb.
make pious 973 vb.

**strengthening**
strengthening
157 n.

**strident**
loud 395 adj.
strident 402 adj.
discordant 406 adj.
vocal 572 adj.

**stridor**
stridor 402 n.

**strike**
affix 45 vb.
strike 140 vb.
disable 156 vb.
demolish 165 vb.
be vigorous 169 vb.
pierce 258 vb.
slowness 273 n.
strike 274 vb.
propel 282 vb.
kill 357 vb.
render insensible
370 vb.
dissent 484 n.
relinquishment
616 n.
ill-treat 640 vb.
wound 650 vb.
hitch 697 vb.
strike at 707 vb.
resistance 710 n.
fight 711 vb.
revolt 733 n.
fast 941 n.
flog 958 vb.
spank 958 vb.

**strike at**
collide 274 vb.

strike at 707 vb.
contend 711 vb.
fight 711 vb.

**striking**
striking 369 adj.

**strip**
strip 203 n.

**stripe**
furrow 257 n.
stripe 432 n.
pattern 839 n.

**stripper**
stripper 224 n.

**strong**
great 32 adj.
unmixed 44 adj.
lasting 108 adj.
powerful 155 adj.
strong 157 adj.
vigorous 169 adj.
violent 171 adj.
large 190 adj.
thick 200 adj.
dense 319 adj.
hard 321 adj.
tough 324 adj.
forceful 566 adj.
invulnerable
655 adj.
active 673 adj.
authoritative
728 adj.
intoxicating
944 adj.

**strong, be**
grow 36 vb.
last 108 vb.
be strong 157 vb.
be vigorous 169 vb.
be pious 973 vb.

**strongly**
strongly 157 adv.

**structural**
structural 326 adj.

**structure**
modality 7 n.
a mixture 43 n.

joining together
45 n.
composition 56 n.
arrangement 62 n.
band 74 n.
production 159 n.
frame 213 n.
pillar 213 n.
outline 228 n.
form 238 n.
matter 314 n.
structure 326 n.
biology 353 n.
zoology 362 n.
building material
626 n.
pattern 839 n.

**student**
student 533 n.

**studentlike**
studentlike 533 adj.

**studious**
thoughtful 444 adj.
inquisitive 448 adj.
attentive 450 adj.
instructed 485 adj.
studious 531 adj.
studentlike 533 adj.
preparatory
664 adj.

**studiously**
studiously 531 adv.

**study**
specify 80 vb.
scan 433 vb.
meditation 444 n.
think 444 vb.
topic 447 n.
curiosity 448 n.
attention 450 n.
be attentive
450 vb.
enquiry 454 n.
enquire 454 vb.
study 531 n.
study 531 vb.
deal with 683 vb.

**style**
meaning 509 n.
style 561 n.
eloquence 574 n.

**stylist**
stylist 570 n.

**stylistic**
stylistic 561 adj.

**subdivision**
subdivision 53 n.

**subject**
inferior 35 adj.
accompanying
89 adj.
caused 152 adj.
liable 175 adj.
fated 591 adj.
subject 737 n.
serving 737 adj.
subject 740 adj.
not owning
769 adj.
giver 776 n.
giving 776 adj.
servile 874 adj.

**subject, be**
depend 152 vb.
be impotent
156 vb.
be liable 175 vb.
be forced 591 vb.
knuckle under
716 vb.
be defeated
723 vb.
be governed
728 vb.
obey 734 vb.
be subject 740 vb.
belong 768 vb.

**subjected**
subjected 740 adj.

**subjection**
subjection 740 n.

**subjectivity**
subjectivity 315 n.

**sub judice**
sub judice 475 adv.

**subjugate**
abate 37 vb.
suppress 160 vb.
overmaster 722 vb.
dominate 728 vb.
oppress 730 vb.
subjugate 740 vb.
restrain 742 vb.
take 781 vb.
excite love 882 vb.

**submission**
conformity 83 n.
concurrence 176 n.
assent 483 n.
flag 542 n.
willingness 592 n.
irresolution 596 n.
sluggishness 674 n.
submission 716 n.
laxity 729 n.
obedience 734 n.
subjection 740 n.
resignation 748 n.
patience 818 n.
content 823 n.
humility 867 n.
servility 874 n.

**submit**
be inferior 35 vb.
conform 83 vb.
be impotent
        156 vb.
acquiesce 483 vb.
be forced 591 vb.
be irresolute
        596 vb.
be induced 607 vb.
relinquish 616 vb.
do easily 701 vb.
submit 716 vb.
be defeated
        723 vb.
obey 734 vb.
be subject 740 vb.
resign 748 vb.
consent 753 vb.
keep calm 818 vb.
be content 823 vb.

despair 848 vb.
respect 915 vb.

**submitting**
submitting 716 adj.

**subsequent**
sequential 65 adj.
dated 104 adj.
subsequent
        115 adj.
future 119 adj.
late 131 adj.

**subsequently**
subsequently
        115 adv.

**substance**
essence 1 n.
substance 3 n.
essential part 5 n.
interiority 219 n.
form 238 n.
materials 626 n.

**substantial**
real 1 adj.
substantial 3 adj.
material 314 adj.
certain 468 adj.
true 489 adj.

**substantiality**
substantiality 3 n.

**substantially**
substantially 3 adv.

**substitute**
analogue 18 n.
offset 31 n.
compensate 31 vb.
inferior 35 n.
come after 65 vb.
successor 67 n.
transience 109 n.
substitute 145 n.
substitute 145 vb.
displace 183 vb.
resident 186 n.
leg 262 n.
ejector 295 n.
eject 295 vb.
actor 589 n.
act 589 vb.

pretext 609 n.
contrivance 618 n.
means 624 n.
imperfection 642 n.
stop using 669 vb.
agent 681 n.
deputize 750 vb.
compromise
        765 n.
not retain 774 vb.
assign 775 vb.
propitiation 936 n.
oblation 975 n.

**substituted**
substituted
        145 adj.

**substitution**
substitution 145 n.

**subtract**
abate 37 vb.
subtract 39 vb.
disunite 46 vb.
do sums 86 vb.
misinterpret
        516 vb.
take 781 vb.
discount 805 vb.

**subtracted**
subtracted 39 adj.

**subtraction**
subtraction 39 n.

**subvention**
subvention 698 n.

**succeed**
happen 149 vb.
cause 151 vb.
flourish 610 vb.
be expedient
        637 vb.
get better 649 vb.
carry out 720 vb.
succeed 722 vb.
prosper 725 vb.
have a reputation
        861 vb.

**success**
superiority 34 n.
sequence 65 n.

progression 280 n.
effectuation 720 n.
success 722 n.
prosperity 725 n.
famousness 861 n.

**successful**
successful 722 adj.

**successful, be**
be successful
        722 vb.

**successfully**
successfully
        722 adv.

**successor**
successor 67 n.
substitute 145 n.
rear 233 n.

**such**
such 7 adj.
circumstantial
        8 adj.

**suddenly**
suddenly 130 adv.

**suffer**
meet with 149 vb.
feel pain 372 vb.
be resolute 594 vb.
stand firm 594 vb.
persevere 595 vb.
be in difficulty
        695 vb.
resist 710 vb.
knuckle under
        716 vb.
have trouble
        726 vb.
feel 813 vb.
suffer 820 vb.
be dejected
        829 vb.
lament 831 vb.
weep 831 vb.
be courageous
        850 vb.
resent 886 vb.

**sufferer**
weakling 158 n.

unlucky person
726 n.
recipient 777 n.
sufferer 820 n.
**suffering**
pain 372 n.
frenzied 498 adj.
perseverance
595 n.
evil 611 n.
badness 640 n.
difficulty 695 n.
in difficulties
695 adj.
adversity 726 n.
poverty 796 n.
feeling 813 n.
feeling 813 adj.
suffering 820 n.
suffering 820 adj.
painfulness 822 n.
melancholy 829 n.
dejected 829 adj.
**suffice**
be equal 28 vb.
fill 54 vb.
conform 83 vb.
be able 155 vb.
support 213 vb.
suffice 630 vb.
be useful 635 vb.
be expedient
637 vb.
be good 639 vb.
be middling
727 vb.
be free 739 vb.
observe 763 vb.
sate 858 vb.
**sufficiency**
completeness 54 n.
plenitude 54 n.
possibility 464 n.
sufficiency 630 n.
redundance 632 n.
utility 635 n.
completion 720 n.

independence
739 n.
observance 763 n.
wealth 795 n.
**sufficient**
complete 54 adj.
powerful 155 adj.
provisioning
628 adj.
sufficient 630 adj.
useful 635 adj.
not bad 639 adj.
contenting 823 adj.
**suicide**
suicide 357 n.
burning 376 n.
punishment 958 n.
oblation 975 n.
**suit**
suit 223 n.
**sullen**
unconformable
84 adj.
unwilling 593 adj.
obstinate 597 adj.
quarrelling 704 adj.
discontented
824 adj.
melancholic
829 adj.
serious 829 adj.
ugly 837 adj.
unsociable 878 adj.
ungracious 880 adj.
angry 886 adj.
irascible 887 adj.
sullen 888 adj.
malevolent 893 adj.
unkind 893 adj.
threatening
895 adj.
**sullen, be**
distort 241 vb.
gesticulate 542 vb.
be unwilling
593 vb.
quarrel 704 vb.

be discontented
824 vb.
be dejected
829 vb.
make ugly 837 vb.
dislike 856 vb.
be rude 880 vb.
hate 883 vb.
be angry 886 vb.
be irascible 887 vb.
be sullen 888 vb.
threaten 895 vb.
disapprove 919 vb.
**sullenly**
sullenly 888 adv.
**sullenness**
sullenness 888 n.
**summer**
summer 123 n.
heat 374 n.
**summery**
summery 123 adj.
**summit**
superiority 34 n.
superiority 34 n.
completeness 54 n.
extremity 69 n.
serial place 73 n.
attic 189 n.
height 204 n.
high land 204 n.
high structure
204 n.
summit 208 n.
limit 231 n.
sharp point 251 n.
ascent 303 n.
perfection 641 n.
completion 720 n.
**sun**
morning 123 n.
sun 316 n.
luminary 415 n.

do sums 86 vb.
bisect 92 vb.
demolish 160 vb.
force 171 vb.
shorten 199 vb.
make quarrels
704 vb.
**super**
super 639 adj.
**superabound**
superabound
632 vb.
**superfluity**
superfluity 632 n.
**superfluous**
additional 38 adj.
exaggerated
541 adj.
pleonastic 565 adj.
wasteful 629 adj.
plenteous 630 adj.
superfluous
632 adj.
useless 636 adj.
intemperate
938 adj.
**superfluous, be**
make complete
54 vb.
be superfluous
632 vb.
be useless 636 vb.
waste effort
636 vb.
**superior**
extrinsic 6 adj.
different 15 adj.
dissimilar 19 adj.
inimitable 21 adj.
unequal 29 adj.
great 32 adj.
superior 34 n.
superior 34 adj.
older 126 adj.
strong 157 adj.
surpassing 301 adj.
necessary 591 adj.
bigwig 633 n.

important **633** adj.
notable **633** adj.
excellent **639** adj.
improved **649** adj.
director **685** n.
successful **722** adj.
master **736** n.
noteworthy
                        **861** adj.
**superior, be**
be extrinsic **6** vb.
be unlike **19** vb.
be unequal **29** vb.
be great **32** vb.
be superior **34** vb.
abate **37** vb.
come before **64** vb.
influence **173** vb.
be high **204** vb.
crown **208** vb.
outstrip **272** vb.
outdo **301** vb.
be good **639** vb.
be skilful **689** vb.
defeat **722** vb.
overmaster **722** vb.
succeed **722** vb.
win **722** vb.
have a reputation
                        **861** vb.
**superiority**
superiority **34** n.
**supine**
impotent **156** adj.
low **205** adj.
supine **211** adj.
inverted **216** adj.
quiescent **261** adj.
lowered **306** vb.
**supplicatory**
supplicatory
                        **756** adj.
**support**
sustain **141** vb.
stabilize **148** vb.
strengthen **157** vb.
operate **168** vb.
moderate **172** vb.

support **213** n.
support **213** vb.
carry **268** vb.
elevate **305** vb.
tool **625** n.
suffice **630** vb.
safeguard **655** vb.
preserve **661** vb.
aid **698** vb.
retention **773** n.
retain **773** vb.
hope **847** n.
**supported, be**
be supported
                        **213** vb.
**supporting**
supporting **213** adj.
**suppose**
put in front **64** vb.
do before **114** vb.
account for **153** vb.
think **444** vb.
assume **466** vb.
premise **470** vb.
estimate **475** vb.
opine **480** vb.
not know **486** vb.
foresee **505** vb.
suppose **507** vb.
**supposed**
prior **114** adj.
attributed **153** adj.
supposed **507** adj.
**supposedly**
supposedly
                        **507** adv.
**supposition**
prelude **66** n.
attribution **153** n.
philosophy **444** n.
idea **446** n.
topic **447** n.
evidence **461** n.
qualification **463** n.
premise **470** n.
opinion **480** n.
supposition **507** n.
affirmation **527** n.

advice **686** n.
**suppositional**
suppositional
                        **507** adj.
**suppress**
suppress **160** vb.
counteract **177** vb.
abase **306** vb.
lower **306** vb.
extinguish **377** vb.
conceal **520** vb.
make mute **573** vb.
hinder **697** vb.
defeat **722** vb.
be severe **730** vb.
oppress **730** vb.
subjugate **740** vb.
restrain **742** vb.
prohibit **752** vb.
**supreme**
great **32** vb.
supreme **34** adj.
first **68** adj.
powerful **155** adj.
influential **173** adj.
topmost **208** adj.
central **220** adj.
important **633** adj.
best **639** adj.
perfect **641** adj.
authoritative
                        **728** adj.
godlike **960** adj.
**surgery**
scission **46** n.
psychology **442** n.
surgery **653** n.
beautification
                        **838** n.
**surgical dressing**
compressor **193** n.
covering **221** n.
wrapping **221** n.
surgical dressing
                        **653** n.
**surpassing**
surpassing **301** adj.

**surprise**
cause feeling
                        **369** vb.
be neglectful
                        **453** vb.
cause doubt
                        **481** vb.
surprise **503** vb.
disappoint **504** vb.
be unprepared
                        **665** vb.
impress **816** vb.
frighten **849** vb.
be wonderful
                        **859** vb.
**surround**
be exterior **218** vb.
surround **225** vb.
circumscribe
                        **227** vb.
outline **228** vb.
go round **245** vb.
circuit **621** vb.
wage war **713** vb.
**surroundings**
circumstance **8** n.
entrance **68** n.
nearness **195** n.
exteriority **218** n.
surroundings
                        **225** n.
attack **707** n.
**surveillance**
attention **450** n.
surveillance **452** n.
protection **655** n.
protector **655** n.
warner **659** n.
management
                        **684** n.
**surveyor**
enumerator **86** n.
surveyor **460** n.
**survivor**
survivor **41** n.
successor **67** n.
**sustain**
sustain **141** vb.

**tall**
  large **190 adj.**
  long **198 adj.**
  tall **204 adj.**
  legged **262 adj.**
**tall creature**
  giant **190 n.**
  tall creature **204 n.**
**tamed**
  tamed **364 adj.**
**tapering**
  tapering **251 adj.**
**tardily**
  tardily **131 adv.**
**taste**
  tincture **43 n.**
  absorb **294 vb.**
  eat **296 vb.**
  pleasure **371 n.**
  enjoy **371 vb.**
  taste **381 n.**
  taste **381 vb.**
  make appetizing
        **385 vb.**
  experiment **456 vb.**
  discrimination
        **458 n.**
  be pleased **819 vb.**
  liking **854 n.**
**tasteful**
  agreeing **24 adj.**
  elegant **570 adj.**
  beautiful **836 adj.**
  personable
        **836 adj.**
  tasteful **841 adj.**
  fashionable
        **843 adj.**
  pure **945 adj.**
**tastefully**
  tastefully **841 adv.**
**tasteless**
  unmixed **44 adj.**
  weak **158 adj.**
  still **261 adj.**
  tasteless **382 adj.**
  unsavoury **386 adj.**
  feeble **567 adj.**

  deteriorated
        **650 adj.**
  tedious **833 adj.**
  dull **835 adj.**
**tasty**
  edible **296 adj.**
  pleasant **371 adj.**
  tasty **381 adj.**
  pungent **383 adj.**
  savoury **385 adj.**
**tavern**
  focus **76 n.**
  tavern **187 n.**
  chamber **189 n.**
  servant **737 n.**
**tax**
  decrement **42 n.**
  exclusion **57 n.**
  demand **732 n.**
  demand **732 vb.**
  gift **776 n.**
  borrowing **780 n.**
  taking **781 n.**
  levy **781 vb.**
  pay **799 vb.**
  payment **799 n.**
  receipt **802 n.**
  tax **804 n.**
  tax **804 vb.**
**teach**
  convert **142 vb.**
  admit **294 vb.**
  break in **364 vb.**
  argue **470 vb.**
  judge **475 vb.**
  convince **480 vb.**
  show **517 vb.**
  inform **519 vb.**
  publish **523 vb.**
  teach **529 vb.**
  orate **574 vb.**
  habituate **605 vb.**
  depress **829 vb.**
  be pious **973 vb.**
**teacher**
  scholar **487 n.**
  sage **495 n.**
  interpreter **515 n.**

  lecture **529 n.**
  teacher **532 n.**
  director **685 n.**
  adviser **686 n.**
  expert **691 n.**
  master **736 n.**
**teaching**
  mimicry **20 n.**
  conversion **142 n.**
  visibility **438 n.**
  argument **470 n.**
  culture **485 n.**
  metaphor **514 n.**
  information **519 n.**
  teaching **529 n.**
  class **533 n.**
  habituation **605 n.**
  vocation **617 n.**
  preparation **664 n.**
  art of war **713 n.**
  church ministry
        **979 n.**
  ministration **982 n.**
**tearfully**
  tearfully **831 adv.**
**tedious**
  identical **13 adj.**
  repeated **102 adj.**
  long **198 adj.**
  prolix **565 adj.**
  feeble **567 adj.**
  plain **568 adj.**
  redundant **632 adj.**
  fatiguing **679 adj.**
  annoying **822 adj.**
  discontenting
        **824 adj.**
  cheerless **829 adj.**
  serious **829 adj.**
  tedious **833 adj.**
  dull **835 adj.**
**tedious, be**
  be diffuse **565 vb.**
  be loquacious
        **576 vb.**
  fatigue **679 vb.**
  trouble **822 vb.**
  be serious **829 vb.**

  depress **829 vb.**
  be tedious **833 vb.**
  be dull **835 vb.**
  sate **858 vb.**
**tedium**
  recurrence **102 n.**
  repetition **102 n.**
  diffuseness **565 n.**
  bane **659 n.**
  moral insensibility
        **815 n.**
  tedium **833 n.**
  dullness **835 n.**
  satiety **858 n.**
**telecommunication**
  electronics **155 n.**
  reception **294 n.**
  ejector **295 n.**
  sound **393 n.**
  hearing aid **410 n.**
  publication **523 n.**
  message **524 n.**
  telecommunication
        **526 n.**
  signal **542 n.**
  recording
    instrument **544 n.**
**telescope**
  astronomy **316 n.**
  telescope **437 n.**
  detector **479 n.**
**tell against**
  tell against **462 vb.**
**telluric**
  telluric **316 adj.**
**temperament**
  temperament **5 n.**
  state **7 n.**
  composition **56 n.**
  tendency **174 n.**
  habit **605 n.**
  affections **812 n.**
**temperance**
  moderation **172 n.**
  will **590 n.**
  avoidance **615 n.**
  restraint **742 n.**
  prohibition **752 n.**

**temperate**
refusal 755 n.
inexcitability 818 n.
virtues 928 n.
temperance 937 n.
asceticism 940 n.
sobriety 943 n.
purity 945 n.

**temperate**
moderate 172 adj.
feeding 296 adj.
resolute 594 adj.
restrained 742 adj.
inexcitable 818 adj.
disinterested
　　926 adj.
virtuous 928 adj.
temperate 937 adj.
ascetic 940 adj.
fasting 941 adj.
sober 943 adj.
pure 945 adj.

**temperate, be**
be moderate
　　172 vb.
avoid 615 vb.
be insensitive
　　815 vb.
be modest 869 vb.
be virtuous 928 vb.
be temperate
　　937 vb.
starve 941 vb.
be sober 943 vb.

**temple**
edifice 159 n.
house 187 n.
high structure
　　204 n.
temple 984 n.

**tempo**
tempo 405 n.

**tempt**
attract 286 vb.
attract notice
　　450 vb.
distract 451 vb.
ensnare 537 vb.
tempt 607 vb.

cause desire
　　854 vb.
excite love 882 vb.
make wicked
　　929 vb.

**tend**
go on 141 vb.
conduce 151 vb.
tend 174 vb.
point to 276 vb.
approach 284 vb.
be likely 466 vb.
choose 600 vb.
be useful 635 vb.
desire 854 vb.

**tendency**
temperament 5 n.
modality 7 n.
continuity 71 n.
continuance 141 n.
ability 155 n.
tendency 174 n.
liability 175 n.
direction 276 n.
probability 466 n.
bias 476 n.
willingness 592 n.
choice 600 n.
habit 605 n.
intention 612 n.
aptitude 689 n.
affections 812 n.
liking 854 n.
love 882 n.

**tending**
tending 174 adj.

**tentative, be**
move slowly
　　273 vb.
touch 373 vb.
be blind 434 vb.
be careful 452 vb.
enquire 454 vb.
search 454 vb.
be tentative
　　456 vb.
be uncertain
　　469 vb.

not know 486 vb.
attempt 666 vb.
be clumsy 690 vb.
be in difficulty
　　695 vb.
make terms 761 vb.
be cautious 853 vb.

**tergiversate**
tergiversate 598 vb.

**tergiversating**
tergiversating
　　598 adj.

**tergiversation**
tergiversation
　　598 n.

**tergiversator**
tergiversator 598 n.

**terminate**
make complete
　　54 vb.
terminate 69 vb.
time 112 vb.
cease 140 vb.
destroy 160 vb.
be resolute 594 vb.
carry through
　　720 vb.

**territorial**
territorial 339 adj.

**territory**
territory 179 n.
enclosure 230 n.
air travel 266 n.
political
　　organization 728 n.
lands 772 n.

**terror tactics**
terror tactics 707 n.

**testee**
testee 456 n.

**testify**
testify 461 n.
affirm 527 vb.
swear 527 vb.
take a pledge
　　759 vb.

**testimony**
testimony 461 n.

certainty 468 n.
affirmation 527 n.
oath 527 n.
legal trial 954 n.

**testing agent**
testing agent
　　456 n.

**textbook**
cookery 296 n.
curriculum 529 n.
classroom 534 n.
literature 552 n.
textbook 584 n.
anthology 587 n.

**textile**
piece 53 n.
product 159 n.
fibre 203 n.
textile 217 n.
roughness 254 n.
texture 326 n.
materials 626 n.
pattern 839 n.

**textural**
textural 326 adj.

**texture**
fibre 203 n.
texture 326 n.
pattern 839 n.

**thank**
rejoice 830 vb.
honour 861 vb.
thank 902 vb.
grant claims
　　910 vb.
praise 918 vb.
be pious 973 vb.
worship 975 vb.

**thanks**
rejoicing 830 n.
celebration 871 n.
thanks 902 n.
dueness 910 n.
praise 918 n.
act of worship
　　975 n.
prayers 975 n.

**thaumaturgy**
thaumaturgy 859 n.

**theatre**
compartment 189 n.
seat 213 n.
view 433 n.
cinema 440 n.
theatre 589 n.
place of amusement 832 n.

**theocracy**
theocracy 960 n.

**theologian**
theologian 967 n.

**theological**
theosophical
theological 967 adj.

**theology**
creed 480 n.
theology 967 n.

**theophany**
theophany 960 n.

**theorist**
theorist 507 n.

**therapy**
assembly 74 n.
gerontology 126 n.
dieting 296 n.
water 334 n.
psychology 442 n.
insanity 498 n.
representation 546 n.
pathology 646 n.
hygiene 647 n.
therapy 653 n.
advice 686 n.

**thermometry**
thermometry 374 n.

**thick**
fleshy 190 adj.
short 199 adj.
thick 200 adj.
fibrous 203 adj.

**thicken**
thicken 349 vb.

**thickening**
thickening 349 n.

**thickness**
thickness 200 n.

**thick-skinned**
thick-skinned 815 adj.

**thief**
incomer 292 n.
thief 784 n.
offender 899 n.

**thieving**
thieving 783 adj.

**thievishness**
thievishness 783 n.

**thing transferred**
thing transferred 267 n.

**think**
cognize 442 vb.
think 444 vb.
be attentive 450 vb.
reason 470 vb.
imagine 508 vb.
be dejected 829 vb.

**thinness**
thinness 201 n.

**thoroughbred**
thoroughbred 268 n.
speeder 272 n.

**thought**
production 159 n.
intellect 442 n.
thought 444 n.
idea 446 n.
attention 450 n.
wisdom 493 n.
supposition 507 n.

**thoughtful**
thoughtful 444 adj.
ideational 446 adj.
attentive 450 adj.
wise 493 adj.

**threat**
destiny 150 n.
limit 231 n.
incentive 607 n.
intention 612 n.
danger 656 n.
warning 659 n.
defiance 706 n.
adversity 726 n.
demand 732 n.
compulsion 735 n.
request 756 n.
conditions 761 n.
intimidation 849 n.
boast 872 n.
boasting 872 n.
insolence 873 n.
malediction 894 n.
scurrility 894 n.
threat 895 n.
prayers 975 n.

**threaten**
impend 150 vb.
predict 506 vb.
dissuade 608 vb.
intend 612 vb.
endanger 656 vb.
warn 659 vb.
defy 706 vb.
demand 732 vb.
compel 735 vb.
request 756 vb.
frighten 849 vb.
boast 872 vb.
threaten 895 vb.

**threatening**
threatening 895 adj.

**threateningly**
threateningly 895 adv.

**three**
three 93 n.
three 93 adj.

**threshold**
threshold 229 n.

**through**
through 623 adv.

**throughout**
throughout 54 adv.

while 104 adv.
widely 178 adv.
aloft 204 adv.

**thrower**
thrower 282 n.

**thus**
thus 8 adv.

**thus far**
thus far 231 adv.

**tie**
relate 9 vb.
add 38 vb.
tie 45 vb.
bring together 74 vb.
stabilize 148 vb.
produce 159 vb.
place 182 vb.
wear 223 vb.
repair 651 vb.
fetter 742 vb.
restrain 742 vb.

**tied**
tied 45 adj.

**tighten**
tighten 45 vb.
fill 54 vb.
strengthen 157 vb.
make smaller 193 vb.
support 213 vb.
close 259 vb.
harden 321 vb.

**time**
time 104 n.
fix the time 104 vb.
course of time 107 n.
chronometry 112 n.
time 112 n.
space 178 n.
measure 460 vb.

**timekeeper**
timekeeper 112 n.

**timely**
apt 24 adj.
chronological 112 adj.

extraction 299 n.

**trade**
correlate 12 vb.
union 45 n.
interchange
146 n.
transference 267 n.
ingress 292 n.
vocation 617 n.
do business
617 vb.
provide 628 vb.
assign 775 vb.
trade 786 n.
trade 786 vb.
sell 788 vb.
market 791 n.
pay 804 vb.

**tradespeople**
tradespeople
789 n.

**trading**
trading 786 adj.

**tradition**
tradition 122 n.

**traffic control**
timekeeper 112 n.
crossing 217 n.
traffic control
300 n.
indicator 542 n.
access 619 n.
road 619 n.
route 619 n.

**train**
produce 159 vb.
train 269 n.
experiment 456 vb.
train 529 vb.
habituate 605 vb.
railway 619 n.
make ready 664 vb.

**trainer**
trainer 532 n.

**training school**
training school
534 n.
monastery 980 n.

**tram**
tram 269 n.

**tranquil**
moderate 172 adj.
tranquil 261 adj.
comfortable
371 adj.
reposeful 678 adj.
peaceful 712 adj.
impassive 815 adj.
inexcitable 818 adj.
pleasurable
821 adj.

**tranquillize**
tranquillize 818 vb.

**transfer**
add 38 vb.
subtract 39 vb.
disunite 46 vb.
sequence 65 n.
displace 183 vb.
move 260 vb.
transference 267 n.
transfer 267 vb.
carry 268 vb.
following 284 n.
admit 294 vb.
eject 295 vb.
pass 300 vb.
relinquishment
616 n.
depose 747 vb.
security 762 n.
acquisition 766 n.
nonretention 774 n.
transfer 775 vb.
assign 775 vb.
gift 776 n.
giving 776 n.
expropriation
781 n.
be exempt 914 vb.
be ecclesiastical
979 vb.

**transferable**
transferable
267 adj.

**transference**
transference 267 n.

**transferred**
transferred 775 adj.

**transferrer**
transferrer 267 n.

**transform**
transform 142 vb.
revolutionize
144 vb.
influence 173 n.
make better
649 vb.
pervert 650 vb.
practise occultism
978 vb.

**transformation**
nonconformist
84 n.
transformation
138 n.
conversion 142 n.
transference 267 n.
improvement
649 n.
beautification
838 n.

**transience**
transience 109 n.

**transient**
circumstantial
8 adj.
inconsiderable
33 adj.
elapsing 107 adj.
transient 109 adj.
unstable 147 adj.
short 199 adj.
dying 356 adj.
disappearing
441 adj.
uncertain 469 adj.

**transient, be**
be transient
109 vb.
pass 300 vb.
disappear 441 vb.

**transiently**
transiently 109 adv.

**transition**
transition 142 n.
passage 300 n.

**translate**
transform 142 vb.
transpose 267 vb.
be deaf 411 vb.
translate 515 vb.
phrase 558 vb.

**translation**
copy 22 n.
transference 267 n.
translation 515 n.
spelling 553 n.
phrase 558 n.

**transparency**
thinness 201 n.
covering 221 n.
window 258 n.
transparency
417 n.
optical device
437 n.
perspicuity 562 n.
materials 626 n.

**transparent**
insubstantial 4 adj.
narrow 201 adj.
undimmed 412 adj.
transparent
417 adj.
intelligible 511 adj.
disclosing 521 adj.
perspicuous
562 adj.

**transparent, be**
be transparent
417 vb.
be visible 438 vb.
be disclosed
521 vb.
disclose 521 vb.

**transport**
motion 260 n.
air travel 266 n.
transport 267 n.

passage 300 n.
**transpose**
jumble 63 vb.
modify 138 vb.
interchange
                146 vb.
replace 182 vb.
transpose 267 vb.
empty 295 vb.
infuse 298 vb.
make flow 345 vb.
**trap**
adhesive 47 n.
enclosure 230 n.
velocity 272 n.
ambush 522 n.
trap 537 n.
incentive 607 n.
chase 614 n.
pitfall 658 n.
stratagem 693 n.
defences 708 n.
bomb 718 n.
**travel**
travel 262 vb.
emerge 293 vb.
offer worship
                975 vb.
**traveller**
foreigner 59 n.
precursor 66 n.
traveller 263 n.
aeronaut 266 n.
thing transferred
                267 n.
spectator 436 n.
enquirer 454 n.
detector 479 n.
reveller 832 n.
worshipper 975 n.
**travelling**
travelling 262 adj.
**traverse**
traverse 262 vb.
voyage 264 vb.
**treasurer**
accumulator 74 n.
provider 628 n.

consignee 749 n.
receiver 777 n.
minter 792 n.
treasurer 793 n.
pay 799 vb.
accountant 803 n.
**treasury**
accumulation 74 n.
box 189 n.
storage 627 n.
treasurer 793 n.
treasury 794 n.
**treaty**
conference 579 n.
peace 712 n.
pacification 714 n.
treaty 760 n.
conditions 761 n.
**treble**
augment 36 vb.
treble 94 adj.
treble 94 vb.
**trebly**
trebly 94 adv.
**tree**
nest 187 n.
tall creature 204 n.
tree 361 n.
**triality**
triality 93 n.
**tribunal**
certainty 468 n.
council 687 n.
jurisdiction 950 n.
tribunal 951 n.
orthodoxism 970 n.
synod 979 n.
**trickery**
trickery 537 n.
**trickster**
trickster 540 n.
avoider 615 n.
expert 691 n.
slyboots 693 n.
defrauder 784 n.
knave 933 n.
**trier**
trier 666 n.

**trifle**
insubstantial thing
                4 n.
small quantity 33 n.
minuteness 191 n.
shallowness 207 n.
trifle 634 n.
**trimming**
hanging object
                212 n.
edging 229 n.
trimming 839 n.
**Trinity**
Trinity 960 n.
**triplication**
triplication 94 n.
**triumph**
defy 706 vb.
triumph 722 vb.
subjugate 740 vb.
boast 872 vb.
be praised 918 vb.
**trivial**
trivial 634 adj.
**trope**
trope 514 n.
**trophy**
badge 542 n.
monument 543 n.
objective 612 n.
elite 639 n.
trophy 724 n.
acquisition 766 n.
gift 776 n.
booty 785 n.
receipt 802 n.
desired object
                854 n.
honours 861 n.
celebration 871 n.
reward 957 n.
**tropical disease**
tropical disease
                646 n.
**trouble**
recur 134 vb.
agitate 313 vb.
give pain 372 vb.

be inexpedient
                638 vb.
harm 640 vb.
meddle 673 vb.
fatigue 679 vb.
be difficult 695 vb.
hinder 697 vb.
impress 816 vb.
trouble 822 vb.
frighten 849 vb.
enrage 886 vb.
**troublemaker**
troublemaker
                658 n.
**trousers**
trousers 223 n.
**true**
real 1 adj.
evidential 461 adj.
plausible 466 adj.
certain 468 adj.
true 489 adj.
veracious 535 adj.
vindicable 922 adj.
trustworthy
                924 adj.
**true, be**
be 1 vb.
be 1 vb.
be proved 473 vb.
be true 489 vb.
be truthful 535 vb.
**truly**
actually 1 adv.
imitatively 20 adv.
positively 32 adv.
truly 494 adv.
truthfully 535 adv.
**trustworthy**
certain 468 adj.
genuine 489 adj.
wise 493 adj.
veracious 535 adj.
safe 655 adj.
observant 763 adj.
cautious 853 adj.
reputable 861 adj.
friendly 875 adj.

trustworthy
    924 adj.

**truth**
reality 1 n.
power 155 n.
certainty 468 n.
demonstration
    473 n.
truth 489 n.
information 519 n.
disclosure 521 n.
veracity 535 n.
vindication 922 n.
probity 924 n.
orthodoxy 970 n.

**truthful, be**
be true 489 vb.
confess 521 vb.
be truthful 535 vb.
be artless 694 vb.
be honourable
    924 vb.

**truthfully**
truthfully 535 adv.

**try a case**
enquire 454 vb.
hold court 950 vb.
try a case 954 vb.

**tube**
cylinder 247 n.
cavity 250 n.
tube 258 n.
conduit 346 n.

**tubular**
tubular 258 adj.

**tumble**
come unstuck
    49 vb.
be weak 158 vb.
be destroyed
    160 vb.
be inverted 216 vb.
fly 266 vb.
collide 274 vb.
enter 292 vb.
tumble 309 vb.
be brittle 325 vb.
deteriorate 650 vb.

be in danger
    656 vb.
fail 723 vb.
miscarry 723 vb.

**tune**
musical note 405 n.
tune 407 n.

**tunnel**
excavation 250 n.
tunnel 258 n.
bridge 619 n.

**turmoil**
turmoil 61 n.
havoc 160 n.
violence 171 n.
knock 274 n.
commotion 313 n.
loudness 395 n.
discord 406 n.
activity 673 n.
quarrel 704 n.
fight 711 n.
anarchy 729 n.
revolt 733 n.

**turn back**
be inverted 216 vb.
turn round 277 vb.
turn back 281 vb.
recede 285 vb.
depart 291 vb.
pass 300 vb.
circle 309 vb.
tergiversate 598 vb.
parry 708 vb.
submit 716 vb.

**turned to, be**
be turned to
    142 vb.

**turn round**
navigate 264 vb.
turn round 277 vb.
tergiversate 598 vb.
run away 615 vb.

**tutelary**
tutelary 655 adj.

**twenty and over**
twenty and over
    96 n.

twice
twice 91 adv.

**twine**
distort 241 vb.
be curved 243 vb.
make curved
    243 vb.
twine 246 vb.
rotate 310 vb.
decorate 839 vb.

**type of marriage**
type of marriage
    889 n.
illicit love 946 n.

**type size**
type size 582 n.

**typical**
uniform 16 adj.
general 79 adj.
regular 81 adj.
typical 83 adj.
usual 605 adj.
middling 727 adj.

**tyrant**
violent creature
    171 n.
bane 654 n.
tyrant 730 n.
malcontent 824 n.
ruffian 899 n.
usurper 911 n.
monster 933 n.
punisher 958 n.
zealot 973 n.

# U

**ubiquitous**
existing 1 adj.
comprehensive
    52 adj.
general 79 adj.
universal 79 adj.
influential 173 adj.
ubiquitous 184 adj.

godlike 960 adj.

**ugliness**
ugliness 837 n.

**ugly**
inelegant 571 adj.
unpleasant 822 adj.
ugly 837 adj.
disliked 856 adj.

**ugly, be**
be ugly 837 vb.

**ulcer**
ulcer 646 n.
wound 650 n.
bane 654 n.

**ululant**
ululant 404 adj.

**ululate**
ululate 404 vb.

**ululation**
ululation 404 n.

**unadmitted**
unadmitted
    484 adj.

**unanimously**
unanimously
    483 adv.

**unapt**
unapt 25 adj.

**unassembled**
unassembled
    75 adj.

**unastonished**
unastonished
    860 adj.

**unastonishing**
unastonishing
    860 adj.

**unattested**
unattested 462 adj.

**unbeaten**
unbeaten 722 adj.

**unbelief**
unbelief 481 n.

**unbelieved**
unbelieved 481 adj.

**unbeliever**
unbeliever 481 n.
irreligionist 968 n.

promise **759** n.
compact **760** n.
trade **786** n.
courage **850** n.
**under the sun**
under the sun
**316** adv.
**undervalued**
undervalued
**478** adj.
**under way**
under way **264** adv.
**underwear**
compressor **193** n.
hanger **212** n.
prop **213** n.
underwear **223** n.
**undevelopment**
undevelopment
**665** n.
**undeviating**
undeviating
**620** adj.
**undimmed**
undimmed **412** adj.
**undisguised**
undisguised
**517** adj.
**undisputed**
undisputed
**468** adj.
**undue**
inexpedient
**638** adj.
undue **911** adj.
**undue, be**
please oneself
**729** vb.
oppress **730** vb.
appropriate **781** vb.
be undue **911** vb.
**undueness**
undueness **911** n.
**undulatory**
undulatory **246** adj.
**unduly**
unduly **911** adv.

**undutiful**
undutiful **913** adj.
**undutifulness**
undutifulness
**913** n.
**unentitled**
unentitled **911** adj.
**unequal**
unrelated **10** adj.
different **15** adj.
nonuniform **17** adj.
dissimilar **19** adj.
unequal **29** adj.
numerable **86** adj.
fitful **137** adj.
weighty **317** adj.
clumsy **690** adj.
unjust **909** adj.
**unequal, be**
be unequal **29** vb.
predominate **34** vb.
**unequipped**
unequipped
**665** adj.
**unevenly**
unevenly **29** adv.
**unexpected**
unexpected
**503** adj.
**unexpectedly**
unexpectedly
**503** adv.
**unfearing**
unfearing **850** adj.
**unfeeling**
unfeeling **370** adj.
**unfeeling person**
unfeeling person
**815** n.
**unfinished**
unfinished **55** adj.
**unfortunate**
evil **611** adj.
unsuccessful
**723** adj.
unfortunate
**726** adj.
unhappy **820** adj.

hopeless **848** adj.
**ungracious**
concise **564** adj.
plebeian **864** adj.
prideful **866** adj.
ungracious **880** adj.
unkind **893** adj.
**ungrammatical**
ungrammatical
**560** adj.
**ungrammatical, be**
be ungrammatical
**560** vb.
**ungrateful**
forgetful **501** adj.
ungrateful **903** adj.
**ungrateful, be**
be ungrateful
**903** vb.
**unguent**
lubricant **329** n.
unguent **352** n.
cosmetic **838** n.
**unhabituated**
unhabituated
**606** adj.
**unhappy**
unhappy **820** adj.
discontented
**824** adj.
melancholic
**829** adj.
lamenting **831** adj.
nervous **849** adj.
**unhealthy**
weakly **158** adj.
colourless **421** adj.
imperfect **642** adj.
unhealthy **646** adj.
**uniform**
identical **13** adj.
uniformity **16** n.
uniform **16** adj.
similar **18** adj.
agreeing **24** adj.
equal **28** adj.
simple **44** adj.
cohesive **48** adj.

indivisible **52** adj.
orderly **60** adj.
continuous **71** adj.
regular **81** adj.
one **88** adj.
repeated **102** adj.
unchangeable
**148** adj.
uniform **223** n.
symmetrical
**240** adj.
smooth **253** adj.
tranquil **261** adj.
coloured **420** adj.
indiscriminate
**459** adj.
accurate **489** adj.
livery **542** n.
inexcitable **818** adj.
tedious **833** adj.
formality **870** n.
**uniform, be**
be uniform **16** vb.
repeat oneself
**102** vb.
**uniformist**
uniformist **16** n.
**uniformity**
uniformity **16** n.
**uniformly**
uniformly **16** adv.
**unimportance**
unimportance
**634** n.
**unimportant**
unimportant
**634** adj.
**unimportant, be**
be unimportant
**634** vb.
**uninstructed**
uninstructed
**486** adj.
**unintelligence**
unintelligence
**494** n.

**unintelligent**
unintelligent
494 adj.
**unintelligibility**
unintelligibility
512 n.
**unintelligible**
unintelligible
512 adj.
**unintelligible, be**
be unintelligible
512 vb.
**unintentional**
unintentional
613 adj.
**union**
addition 38 n.
mixture 43 n.
union 45 n.
coherence 48 n.
combination 50 n.
accompaniment
89 n.
concurrence 176 n.
contiguity 197 n.
interjacency 226 n.
convergence 288 n.
association 701 n.
**unit**
whole 52 n.
component 58 n.
unit 88 n.
**unite with**
unite with 45 vb.
generate 162 vb.
love 882 vb.
wed 889 vb.
debauch 946 vb.
**unity**
identity 13 n.
originality 21 n.
simpleness 44 n.
coherence 48 n.
combination 50 n.
whole 52 n.
completeness 54 n.
speciality 80 n.
unity 88 n.

association 701 n.
divine attribute
960 n.
**universal**
comprehensive
52 adj.
unassembled
75 adj.
universal 79 adj.
ubiquitous 184 adj.
usual 605 adj.
**universe**
substantiality 3 n.
whole 52 n.
arrangement 62 n.
generality 79 n.
universe 316 n.
**unjust**
unjust 909 adj.
**unkind**
harmful 640 adj.
unkind 893 adj.
selfish 927 adj.
**unknown**
unconformable
84 adj.
unusual 84 adj.
new 121 adj.
unknown 486 adj.
unintelligible
512 adj.
latent 518 adj.
disguised 520 adj.
inglorious 862 adj.
secluded 878 adj.
cabbalistic 978 adj.
**unknown thing**
unknown thing
486 n.
secret 525 n.
**unlike**
be unlike 19 vb.
**unlikely, be**
chance 154 vb.
be unlikely 467 vb.
cause doubt
481 vb.
not expect 503 vb.

be untrue 538 vb.
**unlit**
unlit 413 adj.
**unlucky person**
unlucky person
726 n.
**unman**
unman 156 vb.
**unmeant**
unmeant 510 adj.
**unmixed**
unmixed 44 adj.
**unpalatable, be**
be unpalatable
386 vb.
**unpleasant**
painful 372 adj.
unsavoury 386 adj.
fetid 392 adj.
unpleasant 822 adj.
**unpossessed**
unpossessed
769 adj.
**unpractised, be**
be unpractised
606 vb.
**unprepared**
unprepared
665 adj.
**unprepared, be**
be unprepared
665 vb.
**unproductive**
unproductive
167 adj.
**unproductive, be**
be unproductive
167 vb.
**unproductiveness**
unproductiveness
167 n.
**unpromising**
unpromising
848 adj.
**unprosperous**
unprosperous
726 adj.

**unprovided**
unprovided
631 adj.
**unravel**
simplify 44 vb.
disunite 46 vb.
unravel 62 vb.
straighten 244 vb.
smooth 253 vb.
evolve 311 vb.
deliver 663 vb.
disencumber
696 vb.
liberate 741 vb.
**unreadily**
unreadily 665 adv.
**unreal**
unreal 2 adj.
erroneous 490 adj.
supposed 507 adj.
**unrelated**
unrelated 10 adj.
**unrelated, be**
be unrelated 10 vb.
**unrelatedly**
unrelatedly 10 adv.
**unrelatedness**
unrelatedness 10 n.
**unreliability**
unreliability 469 n.
**unreliable**
unreliable 469 adj.
**unrepented**
unrepented
935 adj.
**unrespected**
unrespected
916 adj.
**unsafe**
unsafe 656 adj.
**unsatisfied, be**
be unsatisfied
631 adj.
**unsavouriness**
unsavouriness
386 n.
**unsavoury**
tasteless 382 adj.

**urban**
  urban 187 adj.
**urbanize**
  urbanize 187 vb.
**use**
  profit by 132 vb.
  agency 168 n.
  operate 168 vb.
  require 622 vb.
  utility 635 n.
  find useful 635 vb.
  make better
                    649 vb.
  use 668 n.
  use 668 vb.
  misuse 670 vb.
  action 671 n.
  do 671 vb.
  skill 689 n.
  be skilful 689 vb.
  possess 768 vb.
**used**
  weakened 158 adj.
  operative 168 adj.
  used 668 adj.
**useful**
  operative 168 adj.
  instrumental
                    623 adj.
  important 633 adj.
  useful 635 adj.
  advisable 637 adj.
  beneficial 639 adj.
  used 668 adj.
  aiding 698 adj.
  of price 806 adj.
  approvable
                    918 adj.
**useful, be**
  benefit 610 vb.
  be instrumental
                    623 vb.
  be useful 635 vb.
  be expedient
                    637 vb.
  minister to 698 vb.
  serve 737 vb.

  be profitable
                    766 vb.
**usefully**
  usefully 635 adv.
**useless**
  incomplete 55 adj.
  orderless 61 adj.
  powerless 156 adj.
  flimsy 158 adj.
  absurd 492 adj.
  spurious 537 adj.
  superfluous
                    632 adj.
  trivial 634 adj.
  useless 636 adj.
  inexpedient
                    638 adj.
  bad 640 adj.
  deteriorated
                    650 adj.
  dilapidated
                    650 adj.
  unused 669 adj.
  laborious 677 adj.
  dear 806 adj.
  cheap 807 adj.
**useless, be**
  be impotent
                    156 vb.
  be superfluous
                    632 vb.
  be useless 636 vb.
  be inexpedient
                    638 vb.
  harm 640 vb.
  not act 672 vb.
  miscarry 723 vb.
**uselessly**
  uselessly 636 adv.
**usual**
  imitative 20 adj.
  regular 81 adj.
  typical 83 adj.
  known 485 adj.
  aphoristic 491 adj.
  plain 568 adj.
  usual 605 adj.
  trivial 634 adj.

  preceptive 688 adj.
  dull 835 adj.
  fashionable
                    843 adj.
  unastonishing
                    860 adj.
  orthodox 970 adj.
**usurper**
  usurper 911 n.
**utility**
  benefit 610 n.
  instrumentality
                    623 n.
  importance 633 n.
  utility 635 n.
  good policy 637 n.
  use 668 n.

**V**

**vain**
  affected 845 adj.
  prideful 866 adj.
  vain 868 adj.
  ostentatious
                    870 adj.
  boastful 872 adj.
  insolent 873 adj.
  selfish 927 adj.
**vain, be**
  be affected 845 vb.
  feel pride 866 vb.
  be vain 868 vb.
  be ostentatious
                    870 vb.
  boast 872 vb.
  be insolent 873 vb.
  flatter 920 vb.
**vain person**
  · insubstantial thing
                    4 n.
  wiseacre 495 n.
  exhibitor 517 n.
  affecter 845 n.
  vain person 868 n.

  boaster 872 n.
  egotist 927 n.
**valediction**
  valediction 291 n.
  courteous act
                    879 n.
**valley**
  gap 196 n.
  narrowness 201 n.
  high land 204 n.
  lowness 205 n.
  depth 206 n.
  valley 250 n.
  furrow 257 n.
  plain 343 n.
  conduit 346 n.
**valuable**
  great 32 adj.
  good 610 adj.
  important 633 adj.
  profitable 635 adj.
  valuable 639 adj.
  of price 806 adj.
**vanity**
  folly 494 n.
  content 823 n.
  affectation 845 n.
  pride 866 n.
  vanity 868 n.
  ostentation 870 n.
  boasting 872 n.
  selfishness 927 n.
**vaporific**
  vaporific 333 adj.
**vaporization**
  vaporization 333 n.
**vaporize**
  vaporize 333 vb.
**vaporizer**
  vaporizer 333 n.
**variant**
  variant 15 n.
  speciality 80 n.
  abnormality 84 n.
**variegate**
  variegate 432 vb.
**variegated**
  unequal 29 adj.

**mixed 43 adj.**
discontinuous
72 adj.
multiform 82 adj.
changeable
138 adj.
crossed 217 adj.
coloured 420 adj.
variegated 432 adj.
ornamented
839 adj.

**variegation**
variegation 432 n.

**vary**
change 138 vb.
vary 147 vb.
tergiversate 598 vb.
be capricious
599 vb.

**vat**
vat 189 n.

**vegetable**
vegetable 296 n.
plant 361 n.

**vegetable life**
life 355 n.
vegetable life
361 n.
fuel 380 n.
absence of intellect
443 n.

**vegetal**
vegetal 361 adj.

**vegetate**
vegetate 361 vb.

**vehicle**
retinue 67 n.
conveyance 262 n.
transport 267 n.
carrier 268 n.
vehicle 269 n.

**vehicle. See flat**
small house 187 n.

**vehicular**
vehicular 269 adj.

**velocity**
motion 260 n.
aeronautics 266 n.

velocity 272 n.
meter 460 n.
activity 673 n.
haste 675 n.

**venal**
unjust 909 adj.
venal 925 adj.

**venereal disease**
venereal disease
646 n.

**ventilation**
ventilation 347 n.

**veracious**
simple 44 adj.
certain 468 adj.
true 489 adj.
undisguised
517 adj.
veracious 535 adj.
plain 568 adj.
artless 694 adj.
felt 813 adj.
trustworthy
924 adj.
pious 973 adj.

**veracity**
veracity 535 n.

**verbal**
verbal 554 adj.

**verbally**
verbally 554 adv.

**vernal**
new 121 adj.
vernal 123 adj.
young 125 adj.

**verse form**
form 238 n.
verse form 588 n.

**vertex**
vertex 208 n.
roof 221 n.
sharp point 251 n.

**vertical**
vertical 210 adj.
sloping 215 adj.
straight 244 adj.
ascending 303 adj.
elevated 305 adj.

**vertical, be**
be vertical 210 vb.
ascend 303 vb.
elevate 305 vb.
lift oneself 305 vb.

**verticality**
verticality 210 n.

**vertically**
vertically 210 adv.

**vespertine**
vespertine 124 adj.

**vessel**
vessel 189 n.
cavity 250 n.
water 334 n.
pottery 376 n.
metrology 460 n.
sink 644 n.

**vestmental**
vestmental 983 adj.

**vestments**
vestments 983 n.

**vestured**
vestured 983 adj.

**via**
via 619 adv.

**vice**
bane 654 n.
undueness 911 n.
vice 929 n.
guilty act 931 n.

**vicious**
evil 611 adj.
deteriorated
650 adj.
vicious 929 adj.
lecherous 946 adj.
unchaste 946 adj.

**victor**
superior 34 n.
exceller 639 n.
victor 722 n.

**victory**
superiority 34 n.
easy thing 696 n.
victory 722 n.

**view**
whole 52 n.

range 178 n.
high structure
204 n.
open space 258 n.
convergence 288 n.
view 433 n.
visibility 438 n.
appearance 440 n.
spectacle 440 n.
opinion 480 n.
exhibit 517 n.
manifestation
517 n.
art subject 548 n.

**vigilant**
attentive 450 adj.
vigilant 452 adj.
expectant 502 adj.
persevering
595 adj.
tutelary 655 adj.
prepared 664 adj.
active 673 adj.

**vigorous**
great 32 adj.
dynamic 155 adj.
stalwart 157 adj.
operative 168 adj.
vigorous 169 adj.
violent 171 adj.
speedy 272 adj.
forceful 566 adj.
resolute 594 adj.
healthy 645 adj.
active 673 adj.

**vigorous, be**
be vigorous 169 vb.
be active 673 vb.

**vigorously**
vigorously 169 adv.

**vigorousness**
vigorousness
169 n.

**vigour**
vigorousness
169 n.
affirmation 527 n.
style 561 n.

deception 537 n.

incentive 607 n.

ghost 964 n.

**vitality**

vitality 157 n.

vigorousness

169 n.

blood 330 n.

health 645 n.

**vitalize**

vitalize 355 vb.

**vocal**

sounding 393 adj.

literal 553 adj.

vocal 572 adj.

speaking 574 adj.

**vocalist**

vocalist 408 n.

entertainer 589 n.

**vocal music**

repetition 102 n.

cry 403 n.

vocal music 407 n.

voice 572 n.

poem 588 n.

stage play 589 n.

act of worship

975 n.

hymn 975 n.

public worship

975 n.

**vocation**

motive 607 n.

vocation 617 n.

conduct 683 n.

duty 912 n.

church ministry

979 n.

**vocative**

vocative 578 adj.

**vociferate**

vociferate 403 vb.

rejoice 830 vb.

greet 879 vb.

threaten 895 vb.

**voice**

sound 393 n.

speech sound

393 n.

sound 393 vb.

cry 403 n.

spoken letter

553 n.

neologize 555 vb.

voice 572 n.

voice 572 vb.

speech 574 n.

speak 574 vb.

conduct 683 n.

**voiceless**

silent 394 adj.

voiceless 573 adj.

stammering

575 adj.

taciturn 577 adj.

**voicelessly**

voicelessly

573 adv.

**voicelessness**

voicelessness

573 n.

**voidance**

voidance 295 n.

**volitional**

volitional 590 adj.

**voluntary**

volitional 590 adj.

voluntary 592 adj.

spontaneous

604 adj.

uncharged 807 adj.

desired 854 adj.

**voluntary work**

will 590 n.

voluntary work

592 n.

vocation 617 n.

undertaking 667 n.

gift 776 n.

no charge 807 n.

amusement 832 n.

kind act 892 n.

**volunteer**

volunteer 592 n.

worker 681 n.

philanthropist

896 n.

**vomit**

vomit 295 vb.

be ill 646 vb.

dislike 856 vb.

**vomiting**

vomiting 295 adj.

**vortex**

coil 246 n.

vortex 310 n.

commotion 313 n.

eddy 345 n.

gale 347 n.

activity 673 n.

**vote**

statistics 86 n.

substitution 145 n.

enquiry 454 n.

experiment 456 n.

judgment 475 n.

judge 475 vb.

affirmation 527 n.

vote 600 n.

vote 600 vb.

patronize 698 vb.

government 728 n.

decree 732 n.

freedom 739 n.

mandate 746 n.

commission

746 n.

legislation 948 n.

**voyage**

voyage 264 vb.

**vulgar**

inferior 35 adj.

indiscriminating

459 adj.

feeble 567 adj.

inelegant 571 adj.

unwonted 606 adj.

artless 694 adj.

graceless 837 adj.

ornamented

839 adj.

vulgar 842 adj.

derisive 846 adj.

disreputable

862 adj.

plebeian 864 adj.

showy 870 adj.

cursing 894 adj.

wrong 909 adj.

vicious 929 adj.

**vulgarian**

upstart 121 n.

ignoramus 488 n.

vulgarian 842 n.

commoner 864 n.

detractor 921 n.

**vulgarize**

vulgarize 842 vb.

**vulnerability**

vulnerability 656 n.

**vulnerable**

defenceless

156 adj.

liable 175 adj.

probable 466 adj.

imperfect 642 adj.

vulnerable 656 adj.

unprepared

665 adj.

accusable 923 adj.

frail 929 adj.

**W**

**wage war**

fight 711 vb.

wage war 713 vb.

be inimical 876 vb.

**wait**

pass time 104 vb.

wait 131 vb.

pause 140 vb.

be in motion

260 vb.

be quiescent

261 vb.

await 502 vb.

**walk**

be irresolute
596 vb.
not act 672 vb.
be inactive 674 vb.

**walk**
be in motion
260 vb.
walk 262 vb.
move slowly
273 vb.
emerge 293 vb.

**wander**
be dispersed 75 vb.
be in motion
260 vb.
wander 262 vb.
stray 277 vb.

**wanderer**
foreigner 59 n.
nonconformist
84 n.
displacement
183 n.
wanderer 263 n.
rotator 310 n.
idler 674 n.
beggar 758 n.
low fellow 864 n.
outcast 878 n.

**wandering**
wandering 262 n.
deviation 277 n.
act of worship
975 n.

**war**
disagreement 25 n.
destroyer 163 n.
vocation 617 n.
dissension 704 n.
war 713 n.
revolt 733 n.

**war chariot**
war chariot 269 n.

**warfare**
slaughter 357 n.
poisoning 654 n.
quarrel 704 n.
contention 711 n.

fight 711 n.
warfare 713 n.
weapon 718 n.

**warhorse**
warhorse 268 n.

**warlike**
powerful 155 adj.
violent 171 adj.
active 673 adj.
quarrelling 704 adj.
defiant 706 adj.
attacking 707 adj.
contending
711 adj.
warlike 713 adj.
courageous
850 adj.
boastful 872 adj.
insolent 873 adj.

**warm**
summery 123 adj.
warm 374 adj.

**warm clothes**
warm clothes
376 n.

**war measures**
war measures
713 n.

**warm feeling**
restlessness 673 n.
warm feeling
813 n.

**warn**
foresee 505 vb.
predict 506 vb.
hint 519 vb.
signal 542 vb.
dissuade 608 vb.
warn 659 vb.
advise 686 vb.
defy 706 vb.
threaten 895 vb.
reprove 919 vb.

**warned**
warned 659 adj.

**warned, be**
be warned 659 vb.

**warner**
warner 659 n.

**warning**
precursor 66 n.
omen 506 n.
hint 519 n.
dissuasion 608 n.
warning 659 n.
danger signal
660 n.
advice 686 n.
intimidation 849 n.
threat 895 n.

**warrant**
precept 688 n.
warrant 732 n.
mandate 746 n.
permit 751 n.
security 762 n.
legal process
954 n.

**warring**
warring 713 adj.

**warship**
sailing ship 270 n.
ship 270 n.
warship 717 n.

**waste**
decrease 37 n.
abate 37 vb.
decrement 42 n.
dispersion 75 n.
disperse 75 vb.
disable 156 vb.
consume 160 vb.
destroy 160 vb.
destroy 160 vb.
lay waste 160 vb.
desert 167 n.
make sterile
167 vb.
outflow 293 n.
reception 294 n.
require 622 vb.
waste 629 n.
waste 629 vb.
make insufficient
631 vb.

redundance 632 n.
deterioration 650 n.
impair 650 vb.
use 668 n.
dispose of 668 vb.
use 668 vb.
misuse 670 n.
misuse 670 vb.
loss 767 n.
lose 767 vb.
expend 801 vb.
prodigality 810 n.
be prodigal 810 vb.
be rash 852 vb.
be intemperate
938 vb.

**wasted**
wasted 629 adj.

**waste effort**
fall short 302 vb.
attempt the
impossible 465 vb.
be foolish 494 vb.
waste 629 vb.
be superfluous
632 vb.
waste effort
636 vb.
misuse 670 vb.
be busy 673 vb.
be inactive 674 vb.
act foolishly
690 vb.
fail 723 vb.

**wasteful**
destructive 160 adj.
wasteful 629 adj.
superfluous
632 adj.

**watch**
be impotent
156 vb.
be present 184 vb.
see 433 vb.
watch 436 vb.
acquiesce 483 vb.
not act 672 vb.

**water**
fluid 330 n.
fluidity 330 n.
water 334 n.
lake 341 n.

**waterfall**
sources of energy
155 n.
high water 204 n.
outflow 293 n.
descent 304 n.
moistening 336 n.
waterfall 345 n.
conduit 346 n.

**water travel**
motion 260 n.
water travel 264 n.

**watery**
fluid 330 adj.
watery 334 adj.
humid 336 adj.

**wave**
increase 36 n.
periodicity 136 n.
outbreak 171 n.
high water 204 n.
shallowness 207 n.
convolution 246 n.
swelling 248 n.
roughness 254 n.
furrow 257 n.
oscillation 312 n.
commotion 313 n.
water 334 n.
ocean 338 n.
wave 345 n.
pitfall 658 n.

**waverer**
waverer 596 n.

**way**
itinerary 262 n.
policy 618 n.
way 619 n.
means 624 n.
conduct 683 n.
compromise 765 n.
fashion 843 n.
ritual 982 n.

**way in**
way in 292 n.

**weak**
small 33 adj.
inferior 35 adj.
ephemeral 109 adj.
impotent 156 adj.
powerless 156 adj.
weak 158 adj.
inert 170 adj.
moderate 172 adj.
little 191 adj.
narrow 201 adj.
brittle 325 adj.
watery 334 adj.
irresolute 596 adj.
unhealthy 646 adj.
unsafe 656 adj.
lax 729 adj.
cowardly 851 adj.
frail 929 adj.

**weak, be**
be impotent
156 vb.
be weak 158 vb.
be imperfect
642 vb.
be ill 646 vb.
be fatigued 679 vb.
be wicked 929 vb.

**weaken**
abate 37 vb.
mix 43 vb.
modify 138 vb.
disable 156 vb.
unman 156 vb.
weaken 158 vb.
demolish 160 vb.
moderate 172 vb.
rarefy 320 vb.
add water 334 vb.
qualify 463 vb.
impair 650 vb.

**weakened**
weakened 158 adj.

**weakling**
helplessness 156 n.
weakling 158 n.

**male** 367 n.
**ninny** 496 n.
**sick person** 646 n.
**unlucky person**
726 n.
**coward** 851 n.

**weakly**
weakly 158 adj.

**weakness**
decrease 37 n.
transience 109 n.
old age 126 n.
impotence 156 n.
weakness 158 n.
brittleness 325 n.
female 368 n.
feebleness 567 n.
irresolution 596 n.
defect 642 n.
ill health 646 n.
illness 646 n.
impairment 650 n.
vulnerability 656 n.
sluggishness 674 n.
failure 723 n.
laxity 729 n.
vice 929 n.

**weak thing**
insubstantial thing
4 n.
weak thing 158 n.
brittleness 325 n.

**wealth**
euphoria 371 n.
good 610 n.
means 624 n.
plenty 630 n.
prosperity 725 n.
independence
739 n.
estate 772 n.
money 792 n.
wealth 795 n.

**weapon**
destroyer 163 n.
perforator 258 n.
hammer 274 n.
protection 655 n.

safeguard 657 n.
defence 708 n.
weapon 718 n.
intimidation 849 n.
threat 895 n.

**wear**
wear 223 vb.
show 517 vb.
be ostentatious
870 vb.

**weather**
lowering 306 n.
weather 335 n.
indicator 542 n.

**weave**
mix 43 vb.
tie 45 vb.
combine 50 vb.
compose 56 vb.
produce 159 vb.
weave 217 vb.

**weaving**
weaving 217 n.

**wed**
be akin 11 vb.
unite with 45 vb.
combine 50 vb.
choose 600 vb.
promise 759 vb.
be in love 882 vb.
excite love 882 vb.
court 884 vb.
wed 889 vb.

**wedding**
wedding 889 n.

**weep**
cry 403 vb.
weep 831 vb.

**weeper**
weeper 831 n.

**weigh**
be unequal 29 vb.
grow 36 vb.
load 188 vb.
descend 304 vb.
lower 306 vb.
founder 308 vb.
weigh 317 vb.

cheerful 828 adj.
courageous
850 adj.
**willing, be**
will 590 vb.
be willing 592 vb.
undertake 667 vb.
be active 673 vb.
exert oneself
677 vb.
minister to 698 vb.
obey 734 vb.
consent 753 vb.
offer oneself
754 vb.
**willingly**
willingly 592 adv.
**willingness**
willingness 592 n.
**win**
do easily 696 vb.
win 722 vb.
**wind**
roughness 254 n.
propellant 282 n.
descent 304 n.
gas 331 n.
gaseousness 331 n.
air 335 n.
wind 347 n.
**window**
window 258 n.
air pipe 348 n.
view 433 n.
**windy**
unstable 147 adj.
violent 171 adj.
airy 335 adj.
windy 347 adj.
**wine**
wine 296 n.
drunkenness 944 n.
**wing**
limb 53 n.
plumage 254 n.
wing 266 n.
aircraft 271 n.

**winter**
winter 124 n.
**wintriness**
wintriness 375 n.
**wintry**
wintry 124 adj.
**wisdom**
thought 444 n.
judgment 475 n.
knowledge 485 n.
wisdom 493 n.
policy 618 n.
advice 691 n.
caution 853 n.
**wise**
judicial 475 adj.
knowing 485 adj.
aphoristic 491 adj.
wise 493 adj.
foreseeing 505 adj.
advisable 637 adj.
improved 649 adj.
skilful 689 adj.
cunning 693 adj.
cautious 853 adj.
**wiseacre**
wiseacre 495 n.
**wise, be**
see 433 vb.
cognize 442 vb.
know 485 vb.
be wise 493 vb.
foresee 505 vb.
understand 511 vb.
plan 618 vb.
be skilful 689 vb.
be cautious 853 vb.
**wise guy**
affecter 845 n.
**wit**
laughter 830 n.
wit 834 n.
ridiculousness
844 n.
**with**
with 89 adv.
synchronously
118 adv.

**with affections**
with affections
812 adj.
**with difficulty**
with difficulty
695 adv.
**with observance**
with observance
763 adv.
**without**
without 185 adv.
**without action**
without action
672 adv.
**withstand**
withstand 699 vb.
parry 708 vb.
resist 710 vb.
refuse 755 vb.
**witness**
witness 461 n.
reminder 505 n.
informant 519 n.
signatory 760 n.
vindicator 922 n.
**witticism**
confutation 474 n.
maxim 491 n.
absurdity 492 n.
equivocalness
513 n.
trickery 537 n.
neology 555 n.
conciseness 569 n.
witticism 834 n.
ridiculousness
844 n.
ridicule 846 n.
**witty**
witty 834 adj.
**witty, be**
be witty 834 vb.
**woman**
athlete 157 n.
person 366 n.
woman 368 n.
**womankind**
womankind 368 n.

**wonder**
lack of expectation
503 n.
excitation 816 n.
wonder 859 n.
wonder 859 n.
love 882 n.
respect 915 n.
respect 915 n.
praise 918 n.
**wonderful**
prodigious 32 adj.
unusual 84 adj.
impossible 465 adj.
unbelieved 481 adj.
unexpected
503 adj.
wonderful 859 adj.
noteworthy
861 adj.
worshipful 861 adj.
sorcerous 977 adj.
**wonderful, be**
surprise 503 vb.
impress 816 vb.
be wonderful
859 vb.
command respect
915 vb.
**wonderfully**
wonderfully
859 adv.
**wondering**
wondering 859 adj.
**wont, be**
be uniform 16 vb.
be in order 60 vb.
be general 79 vb.
conform 83 vb.
repeat oneself
102 vb.
be periodic 136 vb.
learn 531 vb.
be obstinate
597 vb.
be wont 605 vb.
be in fashion
843 vb.

**wood**
be intemperate
938 vb.

**wood**
bunch 74 n.
interiority 219 n.
roughness 254 n.
hardness 321 n.
wood 361 n.
garden 365 n.
materials 626 n.

**wooden**
wooden 361 adj.

**wooing**
wooing 884 n.

**word**
identity 13 n.
substitute 145 n.
speech sound
393 n.
word 554 n.
neology 555 n.
speech 574 n.

**word list**
word list 87 n.

**work**
persevere 595 vb.
attempt 666 vb.
do 671 vb.
be busy 673 vb.
work 677 n.
deal with 683 vb.
minister to 698 vb.

**worker**
producer 159 n.
stamina 595 n.
doer 671 n.
busy person 673 n.
worker 681 n.
servant 737 n.
slave 737 n.
commoner 864 n.

**workshop**
crucible 142 n.
production 159 n.
chamber 189 n.
gas 331 n.
equipment 625 n.
activity 673 n.

workshop 682 n.
management
684 n.
position of authority
728 n.
shop 791 n.
jurisdiction 950 n.

**world**
materiality 314 n.
world 316 n.
land 339 n.
truth 489 n.

**worry**
agitation 313 n.
carefulness 452 n.
expectation 502 n.
evil 611 n.
bane 654 n.
adversity 726 n.
worry 820 n.
annoyance 822 n.
painfulness 822 n.
discontent 824 n.
dejection 829 n.
nervousness 849 n.

**worship**
progression 280 n.
fire 374 n.
call 542 n.
honour 861 vb.
respect 915 n.
respect 915 vb.
religion 967 n.
piety 973 n.
be pious 973 vb.
worship 975 n.
worship 975 vb.
deification 976 n.
idolatry 976 n.
temple 984 n.

**worshipful**
worshipful 861 adj.

**worshipper**
worshipper 975 n.

**worshipping**
worshipping
975 adj.

**wound**
cut 46 vb.
weaken 158 vb.
be violent 171 vb.
groove 257 vb.
pierce 263 vb.
strike 274 vb.
rub 328 vb.
pain 372 n.
ill-treat 640 vb.
ulcer 646 n.
wound 650 n.
wound 650 vb.
hinder 697 vb.
attack 707 vb.
not complete
721 vb.
trophy 724 n.
hurt 822 vb.
blemish 840 n.

**wrapping**
receptacle 189 n.
wrapping 221 n.
lining 222 n.
enclosure 230 n.
bookbinding 584 n.

**wrestling**
wrestling 711 n.

**wriggle**
vary 147 vb.
distort 241 vb.
wriggle 246 vb.
be in motion
260 vb.
leap 307 vb.
be agitated 313 vb.
be cunning 693 vb.
be excited 816 vb.
suffer 820 vb.

**write**
compose 56 vb.
mark 547 vb.
record 548 vb.
spell 558 vb.
write 581 vb.

**write prose**
write prose 586 vb.

**writing**
composition 56 n.
production 159 n.
representation
546 n.
letter 558 n.
writing 581 n.
print 582 n.
reading matter
584 n.
spiritualism 978 n.

**written**
informative
519 adj.
recorded 548 adj.
literal 558 adj.
written 581 adj.

**wrong**
evil 611 adj.
inexpedience
638 n.
inexpedient
638 adj.
bad 640 adj.
wrong 909 n.adj.
unwarranted
911 adj.
foul play 925 n.
dishonest 925 adj.
vice 929 n.
wickedness 929 n.
heinous 929 adj.
guilty act 931 n.
lawbreaking 949 n.
illegal 949 adj.

**wrong, be**
be wrong 909 vb.

**wrongly**
wrongly 909 adv.

**X**

**xenophile**
xenophile 875 n.

**Y**

**yellow**
colourless 421 adj.
yellow 428 adj.
unhealthy 646 adj.

**Yellowness**
Yellowness 428 n.

**yellow pigment**
yellow pigment
428 n.

**young**
subsequent
115 adj.
new 121 adj.
vernal 123 adj.
young 125 adj.
infantine 127 adj.
grown-up 129 adj.
strong 157 adj.
studentlike 533 adj.
immature 665 adj.

**young creature**
certain quantity
100 n.
young creature
127 n.
source 151 n.
weakling 158 n.
product 159 n.
posterity 165 n.
animal 360 n.
bird 360 n.

**young plant**
young plant 127 n.
descendant 165 n.
plant 361 n.

**young. See flimsy**
weak 158 adj.

**youngster**
youth 125 n.
youngster 127 n.
male 367 n.
woman 368 n.

**youth**
beginning 68 n.

newness 121 n.
youth 125 n.
youngster 127 n.
helplessness 156 n.
posterity 165 n.

**Z**

**zealot**
religionist 967 n.
zealot 973 n.

**zero**
nonexistence 2 n.
insubstantiality 4 n.
quantity 26 n.
smallness 33 n.
zero 99 n.

**zodiac**
zodiac 316 n.

**zoo**
medley 43 n.
accumulation 74 n.
zoo 364 n.
collection 627 n.

**zoological**
zoological 362 adj.

**zoologist**
zoologist 362 n.

**zoology**
zoology 362 n.